D1312784

A HISTORY OF

LONDON

STEPHEN INWOOD

MACMILLAN

First published 1998 by Macmillan

an imprint of Macmillan Publishers Ltd
25 Eccleston Place, London SW1W 9NF
and Basingstoke

Associated companies throughout the world

ISBN 0 333 67153 8

Copyright © Stephen Inwood 1998

The right of Stephen Inwood to be identified as the
author of this work has been asserted by him in accordance
with the Copyright, Designs and Patents Act 1988.

All rights reserved. No part of this publication may be
reproduced, stored in or introduced into a retrieval system, or
transmitted, in any form, or by any means (electronic, mechanical,
photocopying, recording or otherwise) without the prior written
permission of the publisher. Any person who does any unauthorized
act in relation to this publication may be liable to criminal
prosecution and civil claims for damages.

9 8 7 6 5 4 3 2 1

A CIP catalogue record for this book is available from
the British Library.

Typeset by SetSystems Ltd, Saffron Walden, Essex
Printed and bound in Great Britain by
Mackays of Chatham plc, Chatham, Kent

For Anne-Marie

I do not at all like that city. All sorts of men crowd together there from every country under the heavens. Each race brings its own vices and its own customs to the city. No one lives in it without falling into some sort of crimes.... Whatever evil or malicious thing that can be found in any part of the world, you will find in that one city.

– The *Chronicle* of Richard of Devizes, *c.* 1190.

It is difficult to speak adequately or justly of London. It is not a pleasant place; it is not agreeable, or cheerful, or easy, or exempt from reproach. It is only magnificent. You can draw up a tremendous list of reasons why it should be insupportable. The fogs, the smoke, the dirt, the darkness, the wet, the distances, the ugliness, the brutal size of the place, the horrible numerosity of society, the manner in which this senseless bigness is fatal to amenity, to convenience, to conversation, to good manners – all this and much more you may expatiate upon.... But these are occasional moods; and for one who takes it as I take it, London is on the whole the most possible form of life. I take it as an artist and as a bachelor; as one who has the passion of observation and whose business is the study of human life. It is the biggest aggregation of human life – the most complete compendium of the world. The human race is better represented there than anywhere else, and if you learn to know your London you learn a great many things.

– Henry James, *Notebooks*

Contents

List of Illustrations

SECTION ONE

1. A third-century Roman ship.

2. The Roman Wall at Cooper's Row.

3. Westminster Abbey in the Bayeux Tapestry.

4. William I's first writ to London.

5. London in 1252.

6. A thirteenth-century baker.

7. Sir Richard Whittington on his deathbed.

8. London Bridge, *c.* 1550.

9. Billingsgate dock and market in 1598.

10. Twelve sixteenth-century craftsmen.

11. The Red Bull playhouse.

12. London Bridge in 1616.

13. The Tower of London in 1616.

14. A Cheapside procession in 1638.

15. New Palace Yard in 1647.

16. The Royal Exchange, *c.* 1647.

17. Covent Garden Piazza, *c.* 1647.

18. Christopher Wren's City steeples.

19. Wren's Monument to the Great Fire, *c.* 1680.

65. 1 Canada Square, Canary Wharf.

66. A view of the City of London in March 1998.

ACKNOWLEDGEMENTS

I am grateful to the following organizations and individuals for permission to publish pictures in their possession:

Guildhall Library, Corporation of London, for numbers 14, 23, 24, 32, 34, 40, 45, 52 and 60.

The Corporation of London Record Office for numbers 4 and 6.

The London Metropolitan Archives for number 61.

Nicola Ritchie, photographer, for numbers 2 and 62–6.

Picture number 7 is reproduced courtesy of the Mercers' Company.

The City of London Police for number 59.

Numbers 45, 48–50 and 53–4 are from *Pictorial London*.
Numbers 46–7 and 51 are from *Living London*.
Numbers 1 and 54–58 are from *Wonderful London*.
Numbers 37 and 41–2 are from *Old and New London*.

The rest of the pictures are from private collections.

COVER PICTURES

Front cover photograph by Alfred G. Buckham, *The Heart of the Empire*.
Back cover photograph by Noel Griggs, *Battersea Power Station*.
Both courtesy of the Royal Photographic Society, Bath.

Acknowledgements

In general I have worked on this book alone, helped by the writings of other historians rather than personal contact with them. In many ways I was guided, as the social investigator Charles Booth was in the 1890s, by 'the root idea . . . that every fact I needed was known to some one, and that the information had simply to be collected and put together'. My debt to the countless historians who have written on the history of London will be plain from my references and bibliography. But there are several people to whom I feel particularly grateful. Dr Roy Porter gave me very valuable advice, and helped smooth the path to publication. The expert and generous criticism of Dr Caroline Barron saved me from several errors and misjudgements in chapters three and four. Dr John Ritchie advised me on local authority housing policy and the Docklands Development Corporation. Nicola Ritchie walked around London with me and took photographs of its modern buildings. John Williamson, Thames Valley University's cartographer, kindly drew the maps of Roman, medieval and modern London. I am grateful to John Murray (Publishers) Ltd, for allowing me to reproduce two verses from John Betjeman's poem 'Middlesex' from his *Collected Poems*.

The encouragement and advice of my friends, colleagues and former colleagues at Thames Valley University, Professor John Armstrong, Barry Davis, Marsha Howard, Dr Curt Noel, Dr Nicholas Reeves, Lesley Stevenson and Dr Philip Woods, helped me understand unfamiliar issues and generally kept me going. My fellow historians at Thames Valley University also helped me to find time in our busy teaching schedules to work on the book. I am grateful to my mother, Jessie Inwood, my late father, William Inwood, and his boyhood friend, John Postance (who died while this book was being prepared for publication), for remembering for me their lives in London in the 1930s and 1940s. The conspiracy among my friends to ask, whenever we met, 'How is the book going?' made it impossible to abandon the project once I had begun it. Kate and Jurgen Fricke, Sheila and Geoff Moss, Annie and Neil Dawson, Mary and David Spicer, Ann Lalic and

Peter Gordon, John Moores and Jonathan and Sue Pettinger Moores were especially supportive. I received valuable help from Patrick Frazer, Michael Alcock, Birgit Moores and my brother Michael Inwood, and from Simon Winder of Macmillan Press. Without the help of the librarians at Thames Valley University, Richmond and Ealing Public Libraries and the Guildhall Library my research would have been impossible. John Fisher, of the Guildhall Library's picture collection, was particularly friendly and helpful. At Macmillan, Mary Mount, Nicholas Blake and especially Tanya Stobbs patiently guided me through the unfamiliar process of turning a floppy disk into a book, and prodded me, in the friendliest fashion, when I worked too slowly. Macmillan's sharp-eyed copy editor, Helen Dore, corrected many mistakes in the manuscript, and Isobel McLean produced a comprehensive index. I am very grateful to Macmillan General Books for encouraging me to write this book as I wanted to, and not imposing a word limit which would have prevented me doing justice to London's overwhelmingly interesting and varied history.

Finally, and most of all, I must thank my family for tolerating the intrusion of this book into our lives for the past nine years. My older sons, Thomas and Joseph, can hardly remember a time when I was not writing it, and my youngest, Benjamin, has shared me with it since the day he was born. All this time my wife, Anne-Marie, who has a demanding career of her own, took on more than her share of household and family duties (without complaining once) in order to give me time to research and write. Because of this, and because she makes the world a nicer place to live in, I dedicate this book to her.

STEPHEN INWOOD,
Richmond, April 1998

Foreword

THERE HAVE BEEN MANY LONDONS, as Stephen Inwood notes in his spirited and swarming book: West End and East End, north and south of the river, literary London, architectural London, society London, London posh and poor. Every historian has his own take on this unique city, and Inwood is no exception. His attention is firmly on London's inhabitants. It is the citizens who have successively made and remade this great city who are his heroes – not just princes, patricians and politicians but Londoners at large, of all classes, creeds, races and trades throughout the whole of its history.

It is no accident that the story of London begins with 'foreigners'. There was no settlement at all on the banks of the Thames before the arrival of the Romans. Londoners owe their city, so to speak, to the Italians, and its whole development, as meticulously evoked here, is a tale of the successive migration of wave upon wave of outsiders who have made their mark upon London, given it their own distinctive flavour, while at the same time becoming assimilated into the metropolitan melting-pot.

After the Romans left, Angles and Saxons invaded, but in time the Anglo-Saxon invaders turned native, and it was they who then defended the re-emerged city against the Viking marauders. The Normans in due course planted the Tower, the new walls, a new St Paul's Cathedral, and developed the precinct in the west: Westminster.

During the High Middle Ages communities of traders and merchants – Jews, Lombards and other Italians, and the Germans of the Baltic Hanseatic League – made their contribution to the city. At a later stage religious refugees flooded in – weavers from the Low Countries in the sixteenth century, Huguenots from France – bringing their own particular faiths, languages and cultures, as well as craft skills and financial acumen. In the second half of the nineteenth century the East End experienced Jewish immigration from Central and Eastern Europe, and since the Second World War there has been Commonwealth immigration on a large scale as well as an influx of peoples from all other nations of Europe, Africa, Asia and the

Americas, making London today one of the world's most cosmopolitan cities, a great experiment in a polyglot and multi-racial society.

And that is to mention only 'foreign' immigrants. At least from medieval times, the metropolis has been a magnet for incomers from Britain itself – from the Home Counties, the South-West, East Anglia, and not least from Wales, Scotland and Ireland. Around 1700, it has been estimated, fewer than half the city's inhabitants were actually Londoners born and bred.

It has not only been the masses who have migrated – the navvies, porters and domestic servants. London's great achievers have mainly come from outside. In art, as Inwood shows, Stuart patronage drew Peter Lely from Utrecht and Godfrey Kneller from Lübeck, while under the Hanoverians, Allan Ramsay came from Edinburgh, John Opie from Cornwall, Sir Thomas Lawrence from Bath, and Joshua Reynolds from Devon.

Inwood burrows into every aspect of the lives of the Londoners, their appearance, their domestic life, their housing – which from early times meant that problem so familiar today, overcrowding. In 1333 Andrew Aubrey and his wife Joan complained that their neighbours had removed a party wall opening on to their privy, 'so that the extremities of those sitting upon the seats can be seen, a thing which is abominable and altogether intolerable'.

In particular, Inwood examines what held them all together. In the Middle Ages it was in large measure religious institutions which provided the cement and the focus of the daily round. A high percentage of the land and property lay in ecclesiastical hands; everywhere there were not just churches but religious hospitals, schools and almshouses. That ecclesiastical dominance came to an end with the Dissolution of the Monasteries in the Henrican and Edwardian Reformation. But it did not put a stop to religious ties, for the parish system remained strong. And London's local government, with its intricate networks of wards, and its aldermen and Lord Mayor at the Guildhall, helped bond outsiders and insiders, migrants and natives born. Above all, occupations created a sense of community, as is evident from street names like Cock, Duck, Cow and Chicken Lanes, or Poultry, Bladder Street and the notorious Pudding Lane (where puddings, or entrails, were sold). The City companies organizing such trades created a sense of identity and encouraged the dream that you too might, like Dick Whittington, come to London, make your fortune and become Lord Mayor.

Later on, in the eighteenth and nineteenth centuries, once religion was no longer so important in everyday life and most workers had ceased to be integrated into the guilds, it was the opportunities afforded by a busy commercial city full of amusements and entertainments that fostered Londoners' sense of pride at living in a vast and vibrant metropolis.

London was always a city of contrasts. Historians have debated how far it was at odds with itself – the rich versus the poor, the West End versus the East End. On the whole Inwood judges that although there certainly were such polarities, London was a *successful* city because it had a capacity to transcend such divisions – to bring people together more than it put them asunder. Examining the theatre in the age of Shakespeare, on Bankside and also in Shoreditch just north of the City walls, he shows that the playhouses were attended by both the élite and the groundlings, the fashionable and mere City apprentices. Plays were oriented for everybody. That also applies to the theatre in the Georgian era. The huge new auditoriums of Drury Lane and Covent Garden certainly had their blue-blooded patrons but they drew in sober citizens – and the artisans who cheered and jeered in the gods.

That tradition of integration, that shared culture of Londoners, is something Inwood regards as remaining powerful even in the twentieth century. A new dance – the 'Lambeth Walk' – was introduced as a cockney routine in the 1920s. It then was regularized at the Locarno dance hall so that everybody could do the easy steps: 'Everything free and easy, do as you darn well pleasey'. Soon, Inwood writes, 'its success in "Mayfair ballrooms, suburban dance halls, cockney parties and village hops" suggests that the nostalgic fiction of the cheerful, resilient, easy-going cockney had taken root not only in fashionable circles (where knowledge of the London poor had always been second-hand at best) but in working-class London itself'. Without sentimentality or nostalgia, Inwood shows how London has radiated an atmosphere so pervasive and persuasive that it has created a strong sense of local loyalty: once in London, people want to be and do as the Londoners themselves.

This provides a possible key to the puzzle which raises itself time and again in this book and which confronts everybody interested in London's past, present and future. Over the centuries the fear has often been expressed that London was somehow going to explode or implode: it couldn't thrive, it couldn't survive, it was becoming too big, too diverse, quite ungovernable. The great nineteenth-century radical journalist William Cobbett called London 'the great wen'.

Particularly in the eighteenth and nineteenth centuries, there was the notion that the mob would take over. Indeed, with the Gordon Riots of 1780, radical activity in the age of the French Revolution, the Chartist rallies of the 1840s and the new trade unionism of the 1880s – grounded not in the industrial North but in London's docks – this was a justifiable fear. Was not Karl Marx beavering away in the British Museum writing *Das Kapital*? In a later age, the race riots that flared in Notting Hill in the 1950s rekindled such anxieties.

And yet Inwood's long look at London's history suggests that, on the whole, the fears of authorities and pessimists – or indeed the dreams of revolutionaries – have rarely been borne out. Over the centuries London has been a quite astonishingly stable city. When other European towns were going up in flames during the sixteenth-century Reformation, London by and large evolved peacefully from Catholicism to Protestantism. In the seventeenth-century Civil War, London remained a stronghold of order, beyond the gunfire and the slaughter. In more recent times, while other European cities were being taken over by communist putsches or fascist coups, London remained remarkably free of civil bloodshed.

This stability, this success – this apathy, some might say – cannot be credited to the efficiency of London's government. For, as Inwood highlights, one of the great oddities of London has been the utter inadequacy of its frameworks of government. In a series of lucid analyses of the medieval City, of the eighteenth-century oligarchy, of the nineteenth-century Metropolitan Board of Works, the London County Council, and its successor, the fleeting and ill-fated Greater London Council, Inwood shows that London never has been governed by a body comprehensive, integrative, and capable of dealing with London's problems as a whole – crime, policing, housing, education, health, transport, and so forth. London has routinely been a mosaic of clashing and conflicting parish-pump authorities – or no authorities at all. Be they the eighteenth-century Corporation or the GLC, these have often come into conflict with central government, sometimes with disastrous consequences. Back in the twelfth century, Inwood points out, William Fitzstephen, one of London's first chroniclers, opined that London was a great city so long as it was under a great governor.

Well, London has rarely had such a governor. Nevertheless, London has been a great city. How? This paradox is explained in large measure in terms of the astonishing success of the capital's economy. With great clarity and conviction Inwood shows how from the Middle Ages London successively became a centre of manufactures, one of the great financial capitals in the eighteenth and nineteenth centuries, the world's greatest port with the triumph of the British Empire, the nucleus of technical and professional expertise, a fashion centre, and so forth. All such activities provided enterprise, employment, and an attractive location for foreign dealers, traders and capital. London's economic success bred success. The metropolis demanded more workers, those workers found work. They didn't all think that London's streets were paved with gold, but they knew that – unlike many other places – they would find work and food. What struck the hungry and penniless Kentish hero of the fifteenth-century ballad *London Lickpenny* as he wandered through London's streets, Inwood tells us, was the feast of food on display: strawberries, cherries, peas, 'rybbes of befe, both fat and fine', hot sheep's feet, cod, mackerel, pepper, saffron and cloves.

And so London grew and grew more successful and wealthy. Although there always was a *lumpen proletariat* and an underworld, although nineteenth-century reformers and evangelists fretted about outcast London, there never was the likelihood that Londoners *en masse* would starve to death or, out of sheer hunger and unemployment, raze the city to the ground.

Interweaving separate themes with enviable skill, Inwood demonstrates how London's economic success and its cultural attractiveness helped it overcome a succession of catastrophes, from the plague of 1665 and the Great Fire (1666) through to the Blitz. London's confidence shone through in expressions of London pride – be it the Great Exhibition of 1851 or its repeat run a century later in the Festival of Britain. It was that great political philosopher, Edmund Burke, who said that an institution without the means of reformation is one without the means of preservation. The history of London bears Burke out. Constant change has kept London stable. It is a story of continual 're-invention'. Quite rightly, in his last chapters Inwood explores the latest transformations taking place since the 1960s: the decline of old industries, of traditional working-class localities, the decline in total population – and yet regeneration with new waves of immigrants, with the rebirth of the City as a global financial centre in the age of electronic communications, with the rebuilding of Dockland.

The success of such changes still hangs in the balance, and London's future, perhaps more than ever, nowadays depends upon a balance of forces which is global, not merely national. London is certainly not *nowadays* in charge of its own destiny, if it ever has been. But what permeates this book is a sense of the sheer enduring attractiveness of London as a place to live and thrive. At the end of the eighteenth century the born-and-bred cockney Charles Lamb allowed his friend William Wordsworth all his mountains so long as he could thrive among the hurray of Holborn.

Throughout this book we are presented with a remarkable variety of peoples and communities who found that London was the stage upon which to lead their lives and focus their hopes. All this is chronicled with sureness of touch. It has been said that 'God is in the details', and that is certainly true of this book which powerfully conveys the sights, sounds and smells of a city where, as Thomas Dekker, writing in 1606, noted, 'in every street, carts and coaches make such a thundering as if the world ran upon wheels: at every corner, men, women, and children meet in such shoals, that posts are set up of purpose to strengthen the houses, lest with jostling one another they should shoulder them down. Besides, hammers are beating in one place, tubs hooping in another, pots clinking in a third, water tankards running at tilt in a fourth.' Deeply researched, drawing on a multitude of sources, bringing individuals to life through unfamiliar anecdotes, exploring the whole metropolis from Croydon to Cricklewood, from dockers to duchesses, Stephen Inwood shows how the history of London is truly the history of Londoners.

ROY PORTER

Preface

Remark each anxious toil, each eager strife,
And watch the busy scenes of crowded life.
– Samuel Johnson, *The Vanity of Human Wishes* (1749)

WHEN I WAS A BOY, living in the pleasant suburb of West Dulwich, London seemed a remote and fascinating place. I watched my father setting off each night in his black London cab (its licence number is for ever engraved on my mind) to cruise the streets of the West End looking for fares. I was fascinated by the exotic places announced on the front of the big red buses: Chalk Farm, Crystal Palace, Shepherd's Bush, Elephant and Castle, Turnham Green, Earl's Court, Peckham Rye, the Angel Islington. When in the end I went to some of these places, thanks to London Transport's old Red Rover tickets, they were a sad disappointment. There was no palace, no farm, no shepherd, no elephant, no angel, just streets of shops and houses that were, to me, uninteresting and repetitive. London, I found, is not a city that can easily be enjoyed in ignorance. Now, through teaching and walking and writing the history of London, I have recaptured my old sense of wonder at the immensity, the complexity and the deep-rootedness of this ugly and beautiful place. Through this book, I hope to transmit to others some of the pleasures of understanding a great city through its history.

Author's Note

I have followed the convention that 'the City' (with a capital letter) refers to the administrative district within and near the ancient walls, and to its government, while 'the city' means the London urban area in general.

For those who have forgotten, a pound until 1968 was divided into twenty shillings, or 20s, each of which was worth 12 pence, or 12d. A modern penny is equivalent to 2.4 old pence. I have used the currency units which were appropriate to the period under discussion.

Introduction

THE HISTORY OF LONDON, or, at least, *this* history of London, does not
have one overarching theme, unless that theme is the immense variety of
the millions of lives that have been lived there, or the multitude of parts
the city has played in the 2,000 years of its existence. We may think of
London as a seat of government, an imperial capital, the home of a vast population, a great international port, a manufacturing town, a huge shopping
centre, a generator of wealth, a concentration of poverty, a den of crime
and vice, a breeding-ground for disease, an artistic and literary inspiration,
a global financier, or a collection of villages, and be right in every case. To
some, it has seemed to be a city of unmatched beauty and infinite
friendship, to others, a vision of hell or a bottomless well of loneliness. To
emphasize one or two of these identities at the expense of the others would
be to misrepresent and diminish the history of the city, and even to focus
on the contrast between one extreme and the other is to ignore the lives of
the middling sort of Londoners, the millions who occupied the spacious
territory between Grosvenor Square and Thieving Lane.

Although this book attempts to bring out the uniqueness and variety of
London's history, it also tries to make sense of it. London's complex
development does not conform to a preconceived pattern of urban growth.
The city developed in its own peculiar way, as other great cities have, often
ignoring the rules laid down for it by geographers and urban studies
departments. Nevertheless it is essential, if the history of London is to
amount to more than an accumulation of incidents and anecdotes, a story
of 'one damned thing after another', to look for some general truths, to
find some threads that unite apparently disconnected events, and to
distinguish the normal from the exceptional in the history of the city. A
few of these unifying themes will be identified in this introduction.

To start with, London has always been a city that relied on migrants,
from other parts of England, from Ireland or further afield, to maintain
its economic, cultural and demographic vigour. It was founded in an almost deserted spot by foreign conquerors, and its population has been

replenished by invaders – with swords or suitcases – ever since. Until this century London was an exceptionally unhealthy place, and without a steady flow of newcomers, who had heard more about its money supply than its water supply, its population would have been in almost constant decline, at least up to the 1790s. London's wealth and economic success have usually depended on immigrants, too. In the Middle Ages, London owed its trading and financial supremacy to the capital, connections and commercial skills of Jews, Flemings, Germans, Frenchmen and Italians, and its crafts and guilds were replenished by newcomers from East Anglia and the Midlands. In the late seventeenth and eighteenth centuries London's industrial and commercial life was enriched by Huguenot and Jewish refugees, and in the nineteenth the triumph of London as an international financial centre was made possible by the arrival of European banking families in the City. In our own time Commonwealth immigration renewed London's economic and demographic vigour when the tide was starting to flow strongly against it. Londoners have nearly always resented these new arrivals, and misunderstood their role in the success of the city. Xenophobia and the search for exotic scapegoats for indigenous problems are the threads that link the murderous attacks on Jews in the 1260s and Flemings in 1381, to Evil May Day in 1517, the Popish Plot of 1679, the Gordon Riots of 1780, and the Notting Hill Riots of 1958.

London's purpose as a city, the reason for its existence and its great success over the centuries, has never been straightforward. From its very beginning, in the first century, it has played many parts. Londinium was a military stronghold, a centre of government, a trading and industrial town, a place of recreation and luxury. Over the course of time London lost some of these functions and gained others, but it has almost always been a city of many dimensions, able because of this to maintain its wealth and importance when other cities (Winchester, Boston, Bath or Whitehaven, for instance) have lost their role and declined. In the Middle Ages, the coalescence of Westminster, the national centre of government, courtly life and aristocratic culture, with the City of London, the country's main concentration of population and trading activity, created a double-headed town whose wealth, influence and magnetism began to dominate English life, as it has done ever since. This combination of functions gave London a flexibility and durability that enabled it to retain its central position in national life for 1,000 years, a continuity of political and economic leadership which no other European capital can match. And between the 1960s and 1990s, when two of London's most important traditional roles, as a port and manufacturing city, were lost, its other functions rescued it from collapse, though not from decline. It retains its historic functions as a service town, a financial centre, the home of government and the professions, and a centre of leisure, shopping and tourism.

London has often been regarded as nothing more than a great consumer, a city in which spending, rather than making, was the essential activity. This has never been completely true. For most of its history London was a manufacturing city, and for several centuries it has been the greatest manufacturing centre in the country. It has, to a large degree, fed, furnished, clothed and housed its own people. It has also been the great centre of service industries, the professions, entertainment and public administration. Studies based on nineteenth- and twentieth-century statistics suggest that Londoners were more likely to work for their livings than people in other parts of England. Still, it is important to recognize and understand London's importance as a consumer, too. Its own industry, and much of its trade, depended on the city's huge demand for food, clothes and other consumer goods, and the farmers of the South-Eastern counties and the miners of Tyneside have served London's needs for centuries. To many contemporaries, and some historians, this made London a parasite, a vast and greedy mouth sucking the goodness out of the national body and never contributing its share to the common fund. We see things differently now. Production is useless without distribution and consumption, and great markets stimulate the introduction of new ways of producing things. London's role in developing the arts of marketing, retailing, advertising, display and fashion is one of her most important contributions to the growth of the modern commercial and industrial economy. And heavy or factory-based industry, which has never been especially strong in London, is no longer regarded as the ultimate achievement of modern economic development. London's long history as a centre of services (professional, financial, cultural, distributive and domestic) and of consumer goods places it in the main stream of western economic development, not in a backwater.[1]

Londoners have always been great consumers of entertainment. For most of its history London had a social and political élite whose members (either London-based or in town for the 'season') had little to do but enjoy themselves, and this group provided the most profitable and accessible market for a storyteller, painter or musician in search of wealth or advancement. Thus London and Westminster have been a potent force in the development of élite culture in England, from the days when Chaucer, Gower and Froissart found favour at the Court of Richard II, to those when Purcell, Wren, Dryden, Hobbes, Newton and the members of the Royal Society enjoyed the patronage of Charles II. London's second strength as a cultural centre, as a wider commercial market for music, pictures, plays, books and newspapers, increasingly asserted itself from the sixteenth century onwards. The histories of printing, theatre, commercial concerts, newspapers, pictures and the novel, certainly from the sixteenth century to the nineteenth, are all intimately associated with the tastes and spending power of Londoners. The same is true of the music hall, the exhibition, the museum and the pleasure garden. So to watch Londoners at leisure is also to observe the growth of élite, commercial and popular culture in England.

For a city that is the home of national government, London has often been a surprisingly poorly governed place. One of the reasons for this has been its tendency to outgrow its own political institutions. Within its ancient walls, London has had a strong and effective government, based on a constitution that developed between the tenth and fourteenth centuries. But from the early Middle Ages London spread outside its walls, into areas over which the mayor and aldermen had no authority. This led to a fragmentation of administrative responsibility which has affected London ever since. From the Middle Ages to the mid-nineteenth century most of London beyond the walls was governed by a motley assortment of manorial courts, parish vestries or county JPs, most of which had neither the will nor the ability to cope with the problems of a growing suburban population. In the nineteenth century London acquired a few authorities (the Metropolitan Police, the Metropolitan Board of Works, the London School Board, the London County Council) which treated some of the problems of the city as a whole. But even these had fragmented and incomplete responsibilities, and all but the first covered an area which London had already outgrown. Only between 1965 and 1986 did London have an administration, the Greater London Council, which covered most of its built-up area. But the GLC, like the Metropolitan Board of Works, lacked the range of powers needed by a true urban government, and never managed, in its short life, to overcome the political and administrative fragmentation that has characterized London's government since at least the sixteenth century.

There is no particular reason to see London's lack of a unified government before the nineteenth century as a great disadvantage to the majority of its inhabitants. Government was not, as a rule, conducted for the benefit of the majority, and Londoners in the lightly governed suburbs would have more chance to live, work, play and worship as they pleased than those living in the City. One of the pleasures of studying the history of London is to watch its rulers and the central government trying to grapple with the maladies that afflicted large towns. The same problems recurred in one form or another over the centuries: swindlers and streetwalkers, drunken brawls, neighbourly disputes, industrial noise and stench, polluted water, unauthorized buildings, food shortages, raging epidemics, mob disorder and the homeless poor, with their 'filthy and nasty savours'. What made London's problems special was the monstrous size of the city. Medieval London's population was modest enough, though it was large by English standards. But in the sixteenth century it rose (it is thought) from about 50,000 to 250,000, and by 1800, with almost a million people, London was easily the biggest city in Europe. So in the eighteenth century, and still more in the nineteenth, when London's population grew seven-fold, those with responsibility for governing London (mainly national politicians) had to deal with urban problems on a massive scale. They did so, at least until the middle of the nineteenth century, with an utterly inadequate understanding of the problems they faced, and with an extreme reluctance to develop the administrative and legal structures that were eventually deployed to solve them. It would not be too much to say that in many respects the development of the modern interventionist state in the nineteenth and early twentieth centuries was driven by the urgent need to respond to the social and environmental problems of the world's first giant city. Developments in public health, water supply, policing, municipal housing, transport management and the 'welfare' approach to poverty were all shaped by perceptions of the size of these problems in London, and the impossibility of leaving their solution to private initiative.

For most of its history London has grown in an unplanned way. The Romans probably built a planned city, but even here there were signs of unplanned ribbon development along the main roads out of town. Alfred and his successors imposed a simple grid system on Anglo-Saxon London's streets. But after that planning was rare, and spontaneous growth, moulded by geography, landownership and transport lines, determined the shape and appearance of London. It grew, in spite of official regrets, along its transport routes and into the surrounding countryside, spreading (to use a few contemporary images) like a 'polypus', a stain, a fungus, a mighty carbuncle, a marching giant, a facial blemish (Cobbett's 'great wen'). A few men (Inigo Jones, Christopher Wren, John Nash, Patrick Abercrombie) tried to impose a pattern on London's sprawl, but the scraps of planned city which they managed to achieve only serve to emphasize the improvisation or chaos of all the rest. No Haussmann, no Mussolini or Ceauşescu ever reconstructed London to his taste, and although this made London a messy and confusing city, with few grand effects or noble vistas, it also made it a supremely interesting one. This was Samuel Johnson's advice to James Boswell, a newcomer to London, in 1763: 'Sir, if you wish to have a just notion of the magnitude of this city, you must not be satisfied with seeing its great streets and squares, but must survey the innumerable little lanes and courts. It is not in the showy evolutions of buildings, but in the multiplicity of human habitations which are crowded together, that the wonderful immensity of London consists.'

London lost much from this lack of overall control, too. Throughout its history, and even in recent times, landowners and builders have been given a free hand to construct and destroy much as they liked. Medieval castles and palaces, ancient monasteries, Tudor houses, Wren churches, Hanoverian terraces, Victorian offices and stations, have all in their turn fallen under the sledgehammer and the bulldozer, making way for the new roads and buildings constantly needed by a land-hungry and prosperous city. To most Londoners today, and to many in earlier generations, this repeated destruction is a matter of deep regret. Others would answer that London's continued prosperity has always depended on adapting its physical structure to the needs of the day. It is easier, no doubt, to preserve a stagnant or declining city, a Shrewsbury or a Chester, than one which has hardly ever stopped growing or making money. Sentiment, antiquity and beauty have never been a defence against the demands of profit or commercial efficiency in London.

London's importance in the country's national life made it a prize to be fought for, and an ally to be wooed. Anyone who wanted to seize or retain power in England had to win London's support or break open its gates: Boudicca, Theodosius, Alfred the Great, Canute, William of Normandy, Simon de Montfort, Wat Tyler, Jack Cade, Henry Bolingbroke, Edward IV, Henry VII, the Earl of Essex, Charles I, Oliver Cromwell and Adolf Hitler all regarded London as the prize they had to win, or the nut they had to crack. This made London an unwilling battleground during much of its medieval history, but also gave it useful bargaining power, and a mighty sense of its own significance when it helped to tip the balance between two rivals for power.

For centuries, governments have feared the size and power of London, and tried to develop policies to minimize the city's threat to authority and order. Therefore central government has taken an interest in London's policing and food supply, and in the regulation of its spiritual and recreational life. It has also tried, from time to time, to stop London getting any bigger. The new towns and population dispersal policies of the 1940s and 1950s were part of a tradition that stretched back to Elizabeth I's proclamations against new building over 400 years ago. One of the things governments have always feared is London's ability to muster a huge mob, and threaten the citadels of power in Westminster or the City. The volatility of the London crowd, its ability to absorb new and dangerous ideas, its readiness to follow a charismatic popular leader, have terrified monarchs from the Empress Matilda to Charles I, and politicians from Pitt the Younger to David Lloyd George. In its own way, Margaret Thatcher's hostility to Ken Livingstone and the GLC was a part of this long tradition. Inevitably, the moments when these fears were most acute feature more prominently in this book than more placid times. This should not obscure the important fact that London's apparent power to disrupt and overthrow was very rarely mobilized, and that an underlying stability, a habit of quiescence or uncoordinated local activity, is probably more important in London's history than a revolutionary or rebellious tradition. London's revolutionary power was often feared, sometimes deliberately exaggerated, but seldom experienced. The theme of political stability and social harmony, a paradox in a city often noted for the great gulf between its rich and poor citizens, is an important, if sometimes understated, one in London's history.

In examining these issues, it is often difficult to avoid crossing the line between London's history and England's. The two are so closely intertwined that to separate them is sometimes virtually impossible, in economic, social and cultural affairs as well as political ones. London has been the home of national government, and the city in which many of England's most important political struggles have been fought, for close on 1,000 years. Plainly, it would be a mistake to treat all these national events as part of the city's history, simply because they happened there. My intention has always been to clarify the ways in which national events affected the development of London, how London's activities influenced England, or the ways in which London's experiences either reflected or diverged from those of other cities, or the country as a whole. To deal with London's affairs only when they were different from those of the rest of the country would have produced a very peculiar account of its history. On the other hand, to deal with developments in London as if they were happening there and nowhere else would put the book in the position of the London local newspaper whose post-Christmas front page led with the headline 'Queen Broadcasts to People of St Pancras'.

Like a biography, the study of a single city has to focus on its subject without exaggerating its uniqueness or overemphasizing its importance in the wider process of national or international historical development. London's history has been unique, but it has also shared many of the problems and experiences of other great cities, and been affected by the circumstances and developments which have shaped the history of England, or urban England, in general. To maintain both these arguments, that London's history is special, but also that it has much in common with that of other cities and other parts of England, is not always easy to do, and to constantly reiterate that what was happening in London was also happening elsewhere would have become tedious. A study of a single city is bound to emphasize the special influence and importance of its subject, and at least when that city is London this emphasis is not often misplaced. It is for the reader to bear in mind that in many ways London was simply a big city, and that the experiences of its inhabitants had much in common with those of other men and women in other great cities at a similar stage of their development. Londoners were not the only citizens to struggle for self-government, to see their gates forced open by ambitious aristocrats and angry peasants, to build up and tear down monasteries and palaces, to watch their city burn to the ground, to flee from the plague, to spend their leisure hours in coffee houses, pubs and pleasure gardens, to poison their own water supply, to work in sweatshops and department stores, to suffer air raids, or to move into tower blocks. A city's similarity to others, as much as its uniqueness, gives its history a value and an importance beyond the parochial. What happened to Londoners happened to others too, and sometimes in devising ways of coping with the problems of urban growth they beat a path for other cities to follow.

There are so many different Londons that a single book is bound to ignore or undervalue many of them. George Sims's lively multi-authored survey of *Living London* at the time of Queen Victoria's death had chapters on dozens of different 'Londons'. Many of these are given short shrift in this book: Dancing London, Cat and Dog London, Gardening London, Dissenting London, French London, Equine London, Cricket London, Telephone London, Uniformed London, Cycling London, Ballooning London and Lunatic London all receive less than their due, if they are mentioned at all. I have found myself drawn instead towards Loafing London, Evicted London, Kerbstone London, Hospital London, Newspaper London, Criminal London, Afflicted London, Money London, Water London, Hooligan London, Servant London, Bar and Saloon London, Music Hall London, and a few Londons that Sims did not think of. There has been a tendency, I am sure, to spend more time on the sick, the disgruntled, the hungry and the disreputable Londoner at the expense of the comfortable and contented. This emphasis may reflect my personal priorities, or my judgement about what historians have come to regard as most significant about London's past. Others could place their emphasis elsewhere (except perhaps on ballooning), and claim equal validity for their choice. I can only repeat what H. J. Dyos said in 1971: 'I am encouraged by the fact that the place was so vast that almost anything one can say about it is bound to be true.'[2]

Dr Johnson, towards the end of his life, urged James Boswell to 'explore Wapping'. Boswell did so, but found the experience a disappointment, perhaps (he said) because of 'that uniformity which has in modern times, in a great degree, spread through every part of the metropolis'. This presents an even greater problem in the London of our day, but it still remains true, as Johnson said, that 'men of curious enquiry might see in it such modes of life as very few could ever imagine'.[3] You can still walk the streets that Boswell and Dickens walked, and even, if you look carefully, see some of the buildings that they saw. The tendency of each new generation of Londoners to rebuild the town to suit their own tastes and needs is so strong that in many parts of the city (including the City itself) looking for remnants of old London is like searching for survivors after an earthquake. It is also just as rewarding when you find them. Luckily, the slate is never wiped completely clean. London has preserved some of the greatest monuments of its ancient and more recent past, probably some of the most impressive to be found in any European city: the Tower of London, Westminster Hall (now scandalously closed to the general public), Westminster Abbey, St Bartholomew-the-Great, the Temple Church, St Helen's, Lambeth Palace, the Guildhall (but why is the wonderful crypt never open?), Southwark Cathedral, St James's Palace, the Banqueting House, Middle Temple Hall, Kensington Palace, St Paul's Cathedral, St Stephen Walbrook, the Chelsea Royal Hospital, the Greenwich Royal Naval College, Lincoln's Inn, the streets of Mayfair, Regent's Park, the Natural History Museum, St Pancras Station. The 'showy evolutions of buildings' have generally survived better than the 'innumerable little lanes and courts', but these can be found, too, if you look around the City, Clerkenwell, Covent Garden, Spitalfields, Shoreditch, Finsbury, Southwark, Soho, St James's, Chelsea, Hampstead, and many other parts of this battered but not yet obliterated city.

You can also see London's past through a thousand pairs of eyes. London's powerful attraction as the centre of printing, publishing, theatre, and the courtly and commercial consumption of entertainment of all kinds drew to it almost every significant figure in the history of English letters. Many of the most famous and characteristic Londoners, including Shakespeare, Marlowe, Dryden, Swift, Addison, Fielding, Smollett, Dr Johnson, Carlyle, Dickens, Shaw and Wells (from Bromley), were cultural migrants. But it is also true that London produced as rich a crop of native-born writers as any city in the past 1,000 years. Chaucer, Thomas More, Spenser, Ben Jonson, Middleton, Dekker, Bacon, Donne, Milton, Pepys, Vanbrugh, Defoe, Blake, Pope, Byron, Keats, Bentham, Gibbon, Fanny Burney, Lamb, Macaulay, Disraeli, Mayhew, John Stuart Mill, William Morris, Christina Rossetti, Browning, Trollope, Waugh, Wodehouse and Betjeman were all born Londoners. Thanks to these native and adopted citizens, there is hardly a place on earth that has been described, praised, analysed or reviled more often or more skilfully than London. Its ugliest blemishes, its most secret pleasures, its darkest streets, are all within our reach, on the library shelf. And the impression that emerges from these writings more strongly than anything else is of a city of unsurpassed vitality and variety, a place which offered 'all that life can afford' to those who were not too timid, lazy or impoverished to enjoy it. Charles Lamb, in his letter to William Wordsworth refusing an invitation to visit the Lake District, expresses the joy of living in London as well as anyone:

> I don't much care if I never see another mountain in my life. I have passed all my days in London, until I have formed as many and intense local attachments as any of you mountaineers can have done with dead nature. The lighted shops of the Strand and Fleet Street: the innumerable trades, tradesmen and customers: coaches, waggons, playhouses: all the bustle and wickedness round about Covent Garden: the very women of the Town: the watchmen, drunken scenes, rattles – life awake, if you awake, at all hours of the night: the impossibility of being dull in Fleet Street: the crowds, the very dirt and mud, the sun shining upon houses and pavements: the print-shops, the old book-stalls, parsons cheapening books: coffee-houses, steams of soups from kitchens: the pantomimes – London itself a pantomime and a masquerade: all these things work themselves into my mind, and feed me without the power of satiating me. The wonder of these sights impels me into night walks about her crowded streets, and I often shed tears in the motley Strand from fulness of joy at so much life.[4]

PART ONE

THE FIRST
THOUSAND YEARS,
AD 43–1066

Chapter 1

Londinium

WRITING THE HISTORY of Roman and Saxon London presents special difficulties. Written evidence, which is overwhelmingly extensive for London's recent history, is almost entirely absent for its first 1,000 years. For the pre-Roman and Roman period (up to AD 410), there are a few paragraphs in the works of Caesar and Tacitus, some scraps of writing on tombstones and wooden tablets, a third-century account of the first-century invasion by Cassius Dio, contemporary descriptions of isolated events by Eumenius and Ammianus Marcellinus, and seven mentions in geographical or administrative lists. All this amounts to under four pages of modern text.[1] There are no maps of London until the sixteenth century, no pictures of much value until the fifteenth century, and no sustained descriptive accounts until Fitzstephen's in 1173. Our knowledge has come chiefly from archaeologists, who began to take a scholarly interest in London's Roman past in the early nineteenth century. Recently, archaeologists have seized chance opportunities offered by wartime bombing and postwar redevelopment to discover what they could of London's past before the deep foundations of new buildings destroyed the evidence for good. The most important work was done by Professor Grimes in the postwar years (1946–62), and by the Museum of London's Department of Urban Archaeology, which was set up in 1973 to rescue the last remnants of ancient London from the office building boom of the 1960s and 1970s. By 1973 well over half of the City's archaeological deposits had already been destroyed or badly damaged by roads, underground railways and offices, and only 118 of the City's 677 acres were apparently intact. But hasty excavations on patches of land awaiting redevelopment have provided some of the broad outlines of London's history in the Roman and Saxon millennium. A detailed chronology will never be possible, but at least some mysteries are being cleared up, and some speculations being proved or disproved, by new discoveries.[2]

Before the Romans

Enough evidence has been discovered, for instance, to establish that London was a Roman new town, not a Romanized version of an ancient British settlement. Medieval chroniclers liked to trace London's foundation, like that of Rome, back to Homeric heroes. Geoffrey of Monmouth, writing in the early twelfth century, had Brutus, great-grandson of Aeneas, arriving in Britain (then called Albion) about 1,000 years before Christ, finding it 'uninhabited except for a few giants', and building a new Troy, Troia Nova, on the banks of the Thames. The name 'Londinium' was said by Geoffrey of Monmouth to derive from King Lud, the ruler of 'Lud's Town' just before Julius Caesar's invasion of Britain in 55 BC. John Stow, the late sixteenth-century historian of London, had the wit to discount these tales as a pardonable attempt to ennoble the city by giving it a spurious antiquity and 'by interlacing divine matters with human'.[3] It was clear to Stow that when Caesar arrived there was no substantial British settlement where the City of London now stands.

Modern archaeologists have found evidence of pre-Roman settlement and trade in the Greater London area, but without the heavy concentration of finds discovered in such places as Colchester, St Albans and Canterbury. The first known inhabitants of the Greater London area were the late Ice Age (about 8000 BC) hunters whose flint tools and reindeer bones were found in Uxbridge in the 1980s. It is clear that in the Bronze Age (about 2200–700 BC) settlers were attracted by the fertility and convenience of the Thames valley, and remnants of an eighth- or ninth-century BC trading and manufacturing centre were found at Egham in the 1970s. A prehistoric village found at Heathrow seems to have been occupied in the Bronze and Iron Ages. Recently, pottery found in the City, Southwark and Westminster suggest Bronze Age settlements nearer to London's centre.[4] For the Iron Age (about 700 BC–AD 43), coin finds indicate a late Iron Age riverside population between Kingston and Barnes, a possible settlement in West London around 100 BC, and a few buildings, perhaps a farmstead, in Southwark, at the time of the Roman occupation. In 1983 a waterlogged wooden platform, the foundations of a riverside village on Thorney Island, near the ancient Westminster ford, was found deep in the mud near Richmond Terrace, off Whitehall. Plentiful finds of military equipment, including the British Museum's magnificent Battersea shield, in the Thames upstream of the modern City, testify to a continuing tradition of offerings to river gods or, others say, carelessness.[5]

The fact that the Romans took the name of their settlement from the Celtic name *Londinion*, which was probably derived from the personal name *Londinos* (from the word *lond*, 'wild'), does not indicate (as some Victorian historians took it to do) that they were taking over an existing Celtic town. In fact, as Mortimer Wheeler pointed out in 1928, the Romans often preferred native names, 'even for frontier-posts planted by them on previously uninhabited sites', and they often preferred unsettled sites to settled ones for their administrative centres.[6] It may seem strange that a spot so suited to settlement should have been generally ignored until the Roman invasions. But the land near the City is marshy and liable to flooding, the heavy clay soils were hard for early farmers to work, and the wide tidal river was not fordable below Westminster. For people more interested in security from attack than in trade or administration, exposed riverbanks are not attractive places to settle, and the Thames in the immediately pre-Roman period probably acted as a barrier to divide kingdoms, not a trade route to unite them. London, as we shall see, thrives best in times of peace, commercial prosperity and centralized government.

The Belgae, invaders from north-eastern Gaul who controlled southern Britain from about 100 BC until AD 43, were not a primitive people. They fought with chariots, they minted gold and bronze coins, and made and traded pottery and other manufactures.[7] In the century after Caesar's invasion one Belgic tribe, the Catuvellauni, became dominant over the other southern tribes, and occupied urban strongholds at Camulodunum (Colchester) and Verulamium (near St Albans). The Belgae traded with Roman Gaul, exporting corn, cattle, hides, metals, dogs and slaves in return for luxury goods. Although the Catuvellauni were strong, they presented no threat to the Roman Empire, and the decision to revive the plan of conquest abandoned by Caesar was taken on political, not military, grounds. The scholarly and unimpressive Emperor Claudius, and the Roman nobility, needed a quick and easy military victory to enhance their prestige, and Britain, the prize which even Caesar had not won, offered the opportunity they wanted.

THE FOUNDING OF LONDINIUM

The Roman invasion force of perhaps 40,000 men landed unopposed at Richborough, in eastern Kent, and somewhere else on the south coast (maybe near Chichester) in AD 43, and won a major battle against the Catuvellauni on the Medway. According to Cassius Dio, who wrote nearly

200 years later, probably from lost contemporary accounts, Aulus Plautius led his forces towards the Thames, crossed it by swimming or perhaps a makeshift bridge, and attacked and chased off the native forces. The invaders then encamped to await the Emperor Claudius with his elephants and the Praetorian Guard.[8] Recent archaeological evidence, and the pattern of the first Roman roads, suggest that this camp was not on the site of the future Londinium, but upstream, nearer the site of modern Westminster. Although most Roman roads through the London area were constructed to reach the Thames at the site of the Roman bridge within the city, two of the earliest ones do not do so. Watling Street, the vital strategic route from Richborough to the Thames and on to Verulamium, seems to have been constructed in the early 40s to reach the river at Westminster, the lowest fordable point. Its northward turn through Southwark towards London Bridge was probably added a few years later. Another early road, linking Camulodunum to Silchester through Staines, and following modern Holborn and Oxford Street, by-passed the Londinium site altogether, which suggests that it was built before the town had been founded.[9] In these early years the Romans needed a safe crossing at Westminster, but not a town on the Thames. After the rapid defeat of the Catuvellauni, and the establishment of the Roman headquarters at Camulodunum, the immediate task was to impose military control of southern Britain and the Midlands. Once this was achieved, by about AD 47, the Romans could turn their attention to the building of new towns to consolidate their conquest. 'The Roman empire was an urban empire. Where Rome found no cities it was obliged to create them, and where cities could not survive then neither could Rome.'[10]

At some time after the invasion, around AD 50, the Governor of Britain (probably Ostorius Scapula, AD 47–52) decided to establish a permanent political and trading town on the north bank of the Thames, where two flat-topped gravel hills (now Ludgate Hill and Cornhill) rose 15 metres above the marshes, and where the wide and meandering river (over half a mile across at high tide) was just narrow enough to bridge, yet still deep enough here, almost at its tidal limit, to handle maritime vessels.[11] So perfectly did the topography of the spot suit the requirements of bridge-builders that all the subsequent bridges, Roman, medieval, and modern, have been built within a few metres of the first, with its southern end on a firm sandy island between the creeks and mudflats of Southwark, and its northern end near Fish Street Hill, where a massive Roman timber pier-base was found in 1981. The bridge on this site was the only bridge over the Thames in London until 1750, and the easternmost one until 1894.

Although the chosen site had other advantages, including a good water supply, its ability to command the land, river and sea communications of southern Britain from the lowest bridgeable point on the Thames has been the key to London's commercial and administrative predominance for almost 2,000 years. Once the first bridge was built Londinium became the inevitable focal point for the network of metalled roads constructed to link the Kentish and south coast ports with the main Roman towns north of the Thames, Camulodunum (Colchester), Verulamium (St Albans) and Lindum (Lincoln). This road network, with London at its hub, remained the basis of southern England's land transport system until the eighteenth century. It is not clear that the Romans built Londinium as a commercial centre, but in this favoured position London was almost bound to become, in the words of the eighth-century historian Bede, 'a trading centre for many nations who visit it by land and sea'.

BOUDICCA'S REVOLT

London's early success is known to us because of its first great disaster, its destruction by fire in AD 60. A layer of reddish fire debris nearly a half metre thick identifies Londinium as it was when Boudicca, Queen of the Iceni, whose Norfolk kingdom was about to be taken under direct Roman rule, burned it (along with Camulodunum and Verulamium) to the ground. The main area of settlement was on the eastern gravel hill (Cornhill), at the northern end of the bridge. Here there was an open gravelled area, perhaps a market-place, bordered by large wooden buildings of uncertain purpose, and a grain store. Two roads running parallel to the river, and now under Lombard Street and Fenchurch Street and Cannon Street and Eastcheap as they pass the bridge, had already been constructed, and scorched drainage pipes, iron rings for wooden water mains and Samian pottery from southern Gaul suggest the existence of a prosperous and well-planned trading community. The size of this earliest Londinium is not known, but there were certainly wooden buildings and wattle and daub huts, perhaps for industrial use, on the east and west fringes of the modern City at Aldgate and Newgate Street. These, Dominic Perring suggests, were much more likely to have been 'ribbon development' along the main roads to Colchester and Silchester than a part of the central built-up area, which probably did not extend beyond Cornhill.[12]

For once, reliable written evidence allows us to confirm the archaeological record. The great Roman historian Tacitus had a particular interest in this remote outpost of the Empire, because his father-in-law Agricola was in Britain in AD 60, 69, and (as Governor) 77–83. In his *Annals*, written in the early second century, Tacitus provides a graphic and authoritative account of Boudicca's disastrous rebellion. He gives us an insight into the reasons for British hostility to their new masters: rapacious taxation, brutality towards native rulers, the theft of British land and houses by ex-soldiers settling at Camulodunum, and the imposition of an alien religion of emperor-worship. In short, the Romans had failed to win the trust and cooperation of the local ruling class. The rebels, drawing support from all over the province, had several early successes. Camulodunum and its settlers were destroyed, and so was most of the Legion sent from Lindum (Lincoln) to relieve it. Suetonius, the Governor, was in Anglesey, but managed to get his troops to London before Boudicca and her much larger force arrived there. Tacitus' account is the first written reference to London:

> This town did not rank as a Roman settlement [*colonia*], but was an important centre for business-men and merchandise [*copia negotiatorum et commeatuum maxime celebre*]. At first, he hesitated whether to stand and fight there. Eventually, his numerical inferiority – and the price only too clearly paid by the divisional commander's rashness – decided him to sacrifice the single city of Londinium to save the province as a whole. Unmoved by lamentations and appeals, Suetonius gave the signal for departure. The inhabitants were allowed to accompany him. But those who stayed because they were women, or old, or attached to the place, were slaughtered by the enemy. Verulamium suffered the same fate.
>
> The natives enjoyed plundering and thought of nothing else. By-passing forts and garrisons, they made for where loot was richest and protection weakest. Roman and provincial deaths at the places mentioned are estimated at 70,000. For the British did not take or sell prisoners, or practise other war-time exchanges. They could not wait to cut throats, hang, burn, and crucify – as though avenging, in advance, the retribution that was on its way.[13]

Suetonius had a more professional, though much smaller, force, and greater tactical expertise, and the rebellion ended in catastrophic defeat for Boudicca somewhere in the Midlands. Tacitus' brief description of London as a busy trading centre, not yet called a *colonia*, raises the question of what its status in the Empire was. The two titles bestowed by the Romans on their most successful and independent cities were *colonia* (a newly established settlement of military veterans) and *municipium* (a chartered town, usually of native origin), and Tacitus' words suggest that London was at least near to deserving one of them. There is no doubt that in the fifty years following the fire it was chosen as the new administrative capital of Britain. Although we do not know for certain when this happened, its commercial prosperity, its central location and its unrivalled accessibility made it the obvious choice to replace Camulodunum when a new provincial procurator, Julius Classicianus, arrived to take charge of Britain's financial administration after the rebellion. The discovery in 1852 and 1935 of two sections of Classicianus' tombstone re-used as building blocks in the later Roman fortifications established that his headquarters had indeed been somewhere in London.

Agricola's governorship (AD 77–83), one of the few that we know about in any detail (thanks to Tacitus), saw the pursuit in Britain of Emperor Vespasian's policy of urban renewal, administrative reform, and the assimilation of native peoples. Tacitus' account of his father-in-law's policy serves as a description of the imperial strategy pursued throughout the Flavian and Antonine period (AD 69–180):

> To induce a people, hitherto scattered, uncivilized and therefore prone to fight, to grow pleasurably inured to peace and ease, Agricola gave private encouragement and official assistance to the building of temples, public squares and private mansions. He praised the keen and scolded the slack, and competition to gain honour from him was as effective as compulsion. Furthermore he trained the sons of chiefs in the liberal arts. . . . The result was that in place of distaste for the Latin language came a passion to command it. In the same way, our national dress came into favour and the toga was everywhere to be seen. And so the Britons were gradually led on to the amenities that make vice agreeable – arcades, baths and sumptuous banquets. They spoke of such novelties as 'civilization', when really they were only features of enslavement.[14]

The Romans established their control over newly conquered territories by a combination of enticement, assimilation and sound administration. By the development of cities they displayed the superior advantages of Roman civilization, drew native rulers into the Roman way of life, created centres of administration and taxation, and gave Roman settlers opportunities to profit from trade and public office. The London of the late first century was designed to play a leading role in this seductive imperialism. Rebuilding immediately after the fire seems to have been unimpressive and slow, but between about AD 80 and 120 (under the Flavian Emperors Domitian and Trajan) a new London, with public buildings fit for a great provincial capital, was constructed.

THE DISCOVERY OF FLAVIAN LONDON

Many of the main features of Flavian London have been discovered, one by one, since the Second World War. Of the major buildings, only the city walls and the basilica, or town hall, were known about before 1945. Some of the basilica's vast walls were observed and drawn by Henry Hodge in 1880, when the Leadenhall Market buildings on Cornhill were being rebuilt. The significance of his drawings was realized in the 1920s, and since then fairly comprehensive information about the basilica and the great forum immediately to its south has been assembled from several excavations.[15] In 1985–6 the eastern end of the basilica was exposed by the demolition of Leadenhall Court. A modest basilica and forum had been built on this site about a decade after Boudicca's rebellion, but the size of the second basilica and forum, probably constructed in the early years of the second century, indicate the high status London had achieved by this time. The basilica, 167 metres long, surpassed any rivals in Britain and Gaul, perhaps any outside of Rome itself, and the whole forum complex, about 167 metres square, was exceptionally large by provincial standards.[16]

Little is known about how London was governed from the basilica, except what can be inferred from knowledge of better-documented provincial cities. The city would have been run by two senior and two junior magistrates and a town council of 100 men of substantial property elected by free-born male citizens in an annual assembly. The magistrates and their officials were responsible for policing, justice and public order, the collection and administration of city and provincial revenues, the upkeep of public buildings, water supply and drainage, roads, baths, temples, theatres and quays. Licensing tradesmen, controlling markets, appointing public contractors, and ensuring a steady supply of reasonably priced basic foodstuffs (especially corn) were all part of a city government's usual duties. These urban oligarchs, drawn increasingly from Romanized British landlords, were expected to fund many civic works and public entertainments from their own pockets – a high price to pay for the pleasures and prestige of city life.[17]

The first major discovery after the devastation of the City in the Second World War came in 1949, when William Grimes of the London Museum found a huge 12-acre fort in the north-west corner of the City wall, in the area called Cripplegate.[18] The fort, whose ragstone walls can still be seen in Noble Street, near the Museum of London, was built in the late first or early second century, perhaps under Emperor Trajan (98–117) or in time for Emperor Hadrian's visit in 122. Dating is determined, as usual in Roman sites, by the finding of datable coins, tiles and (especially) pottery fragments in or under the walls, and by examining the relationship between the feature in question and others of known date. This was not a defensive fort, built in the aftermath of the Boudiccan revolt, but a military depot accommodating well over 1,000 troops, made up of the Governor's personal guard (usually 1,000 men), soldiers with policing or administrative duties in London, and men in transit to other stations. The presence of perhaps 1,500 soldiers, receiving regular wages in good imperial coin, must have been a healthy stimulus to London's trades, services and manufactures. Since London was not a legionary centre (these were at York, Caerleon and Chester) the construction of this unusually large fort strongly suggests that the town had been chosen as the permanent headquarters of the provincial government of Britain.

By 1960 a few archaeologists, led by the Guildhall Museum's Peter Marsden and with hardly any public funding, were on the trail of the Governor's palace. Discoveries of mosaic floors, columns and massive walls in the seventeenth and nineteenth centuries led them to investigate the area east of Cannon Street Station, where office developments in 1960 and 1964 were about to obliterate all remaining Roman structures. Hasty excavations uncovered large formal gardens, an ornamental pool, the walls and foundations of a great hall and an extensive series of smaller rooms, running for about 130 metres along the riverside and covering about 5 acres. Its size and various remnants of official activity suggest that this was the Governor's palace, the administrative centre of the province of Britain. Although much of it has now been destroyed by development, the west wing is probably still safe under Cannon Street Station. It is possible (as Dominic Perring argues) that this was not one building, but several, including perhaps a temple and baths. In either case, this ostentatious development dates from around 100, and is thus a part of the grand reconstruction of London that took place in the years AD 80–120.[19]

The Governorship was a prestigious appointment, and was usually held by distinguished men of senatorial rank, at least until the division of the province early in the third century. After Agricola (77–83) most Governors are known to us only by name (if at all), but this indicates our lack of written sources, not the insignificance of the office. As the Emperor's representative, the Governor was the military commander of the province, as well as its chief justice and administrator. Financial administration was the separate responsibility of the provincial procurator. The Governorship lost much of its power and prestige in the administrative reforms of the third and fourth centuries.

LIFE AND WORK

Although hardly any contemporary written material on London's economic or social life exists from this period, a certain amount can be learnt from archaeological discoveries and from what is known of urban life elsewhere in the Empire. These sources do not help us to solve the fundamental problem of estimating London's population. Since the 1920s estimates of the total population of Roman Britain have risen from 500,000 to around 5 million, but this is largely because of the discovery of new settlements by aerial photography, motorway building, and so on. Estimates of London's population are not quite so upwardly mobile. Calculations based on the third-century walled area of 330 acres can lead to rather high results. This same walled area could accommodate, in the early seventeenth century, over 120,000 people, and John Morris argues from this, and from comparison with imperial Rome, that Roman London held about 100,000 people.[20] But it is not at all certain that the walls were constructed to include only the built-up area, despite their high cost to the city in men and materials. In the west the walls seem to have enclosed several acres of uninhabited or derelict land, in order to achieve the defensive advantage of commanding the higher ground before the sharp slope into the Fleet valley. Although remnants of Roman occupation have been found scattered all over the walled area (and more are found every year) the evidence does not suggest continuous occupation of all sites for three or four centuries, and there are many indications of agricultural land use within the walls after about 200. In the second century, though, it seems that London filled most of its walled area, and even spilled beyond it to the north and south. The central area, Dominic Perring argues, bears the marks of a crowded city, in which land was at a premium. Other evidence – the size of its forum and public buildings, its substantial military, official and mercantile communities, the remarks of Tacitus – suggests that Roman London's population at its peak (around AD 150) was large. But there are many things we cannot know about Roman London, and its population is one of them.[21]

The wealthy (especially wealthy men) always leave a clearer mark on the historical record than the poor, and such information as we have about Roman Londoners mainly illuminates the lives of the rich. There are many remnants in London of the domestic and public comforts which the well-off expected to enjoy in any great imperial city. Stone houses (built from Kentish ragstone), tiled roofs, mosaic floors, painted plaster walls, private bath-houses, jewellery, expensive imported tableware, represent the material luxuries that Tacitus knew would persuade native landlords to accept the advantages of Roman citizenship. Citizens expected (and paid for) good public facilities too, and one of these, the large public bath-house at the junction of Upper Thames Street and Huggin Hill, was discovered and excavated by Peter Marsden in 1964, just as it was about to be destroyed. These baths, perhaps built around AD 100 and extended twenty years later, offered the usual steam room, warm room, cold room and cold plunge, and served the combined purposes of hygiene, exercise, relaxation and (until Hadrian insisted on segregated buildings) sex. Another place of relaxation and enjoyment, the amphitheatre, the scene of beast and gladiator shows, and other officially or privately sponsored entertainments, was at last discovered in 1987–8, under the Guildhall and its yard, just south-east of the fort. It seems to have been built around AD 120, perhaps to replace another on its site. The fact that it is the biggest yet found in Britain (an ellipse of 130 by 110 metres outside, and 70 by 50 metres within) is further evidence that London's population was particularly large.[22]

Although the wealthy enjoyed such imported luxuries as fine glazed pottery from central and southern Gaul, Italian wine and glassware and Spanish olive oil, much of their expenditure would have provided work for the freemen, freedmen and slaves who made up the bulk of London's population. We know of these people less through their houses and possessions (although their mean wattle and daub dwellings have been found at Newgate and elsewhere) than through the products and tools of their trades. Naturally there was always work for labourers and craftsmen in the building trades: mosaicists, plasterers, painters, stonemasons, carpenters and tilers. It was probably a tile-maker who sent this enigmatic message through the centuries, scratched in Latin (London's only written language) on a tile: 'Austalis has been going off by himself every day for thirteen days.' The demand for their labour would have been augmented by the frequent rebuilding of London, especially after the Boudiccan fire of AD 60 and the Hadrianic fire which destroyed over 100 acres (probably accidentally) around AD 125. About AD 200, building the massive 2-mile wall must have employed thousands of men, to dig the defensive ditch 2 metres deep, and transport, shape, lift and lay the 85,000 tons of ragstone to a height of over 6 metres.[23]

Direct evidence for the variety of crafts and trades in early Roman London comes mainly from the bed of the Walbrook, the wide stream that divided the two hills of the city. All sorts of tools connected with building crafts have been found in the first- and second-century deposits: chisels for wood and stone, saws, bits, gouges, picks, rules, dividers and trowels. There are tools indicating dockwork and farming, too: crane-hooks, dockers'-hooks, chains, a jemmy, ploughshares and hoes. Middle-class occupations are represented by surgeons' scalpels and spatulas, and hundreds of styli, the writing implements of Roman clerks and calligraphers. It may well be that these tools were produced by the iron and bronze workers whose workshops have been found over the river in Southwark and on the western edge of the city under the demolished General Post Office on Newgate Street. Potters, goldsmiths, forgers, flour-millers and enamellers were all at work in Roman London, and remnants of shoemaking and leatherwork, including tanning tanks and a skin pegged and stretched ready for cutting, have been found in the Walbrook valley.[24] This diversity of crafts and trades reflects the durability of particular materials (stone, wood, bronze, gold, iron, glass, leather) in certain conditions, and the rapid response of archaeologists as sites have become available. The evidence suggests that London craftsmen worked to satisfy local needs, especially for pots, basic foods and leatherware, but cannot be taken to imply that London was a great manufacturing centre serving the province or the empire. We must be careful not to be led by our knowledge of London's later economic greatness into making false assumptions about its early history.

A TRADING CENTRE

This is one of the lessons brought home by Gustav Milne's book on *The Port of Roman London*, which summarizes the findings of the rescue excavations on the waterfront near Billingsgate and London Bridge between 1979 and 1982. It is easy to assume that Roman London was a great international port, drawing its wealth and importance from trade just as it did in more recent centuries. Milne, writing with some authority, doubts that this was the case.[25] He and his collaborators argued that the Thames was a tidal river without a deep-water port, and was therefore unable to handle larger seagoing trading vessels or the ships of the Roman fleet, the

Classis Britannica. The ports that handled the main flow of imperial trade and military supplies would have changed over time, depending on the location of the army, threats from marauders, and perhaps silting, but there is no evidence from riverside excavations that London was one of them. The vessels that traded in the Thames were, in all probability, small sailing ships and flat-bottomed barges like the ones found during the building of County Hall in 1910 and at Blackfriars in 1962. The modest size and area of the warehousing discovered on the Roman riverfront, and the fact that none of the seventy Roman Londoners known to us from inscriptions is identified as a merchant, leads Milne to conclude that London was a significant port, serving a substantial Thames valley hinterland and a cosmopolitan colonial population greedy for Roman home comforts, but not a great imperial trading centre. It existed primarily as an administrative centre, served, as other towns were, by a harbour. Milne's argument is not absolutely conclusive, since it relies partly on the lack of evidence so far for a major trading role, and since it is possible for a great port to thrive, as eighteenth-century London did, with inadequate docking facilities, especially if its road and river network for onward distribution is good. But it reminds us not to jump (in either direction) to conclusions which the evidence does not justify.[26]

The riverside excavations, which took place near Thames Street, about a 100 metres north of the river today, uncovered a series of well-constructed terraces, supported by strong masonry walls and great oak timbers, almost perfectly preserved in the waterlogged earth. Among them, near Fish Street Hill and about 30 metres east of the present London Bridge, was found a strong wooden pier base that probably supported a wooden bridge over the Thames. The late first-century quayside, dated by pottery, coins and dendrochronology (tree-ring dating) to between AD 70 and 100, advanced from the natural riverbank by about 10 metres, and further constructions around AD 125, 150 and 230 added another 40 metres of reclaimed land, stretching perhaps 600 metres along the river. On these flat terraces, safe from tidal flooding, were the warehouses which stored amphorae (tall two-handled vessels) containing Spanish and North African olive oil, Mediterranean and Rhineland wine, grape syrup or fish sauce, and also the pottery lamps, figurines, kitchenware and tableware imported from Italy and Gaul to satisfy the London market. The quays, terraces and warehouses appear to have been planned and financed by the town council, reflecting the same vigorous and confident spirit that prompted the building of the forum and basilica around the same time.

Although London was involved in trade with every part of the Roman

Empire, some of its most important requirements were locally produced. Salt, important for preserving as well as flavouring, came from the Thames estuary, and oysters, which the Romans regarded as a British delicacy, were collected off the north Kent coast. London iron and leather working were based on local supplies of raw material. Above all, London needed reliable supplies of reasonably priced grain. This has been recognized throughout London's history as the essential underpinning of her social stability. In Roman times, and for many centuries afterwards, grain and other farm produce could easily be brought from Kent, Essex, Surrey and the Thames valley by river or road.

London was the meeting place of six major roads to important provincial cities, each passing through roadside villages which offered a change of horses to imperial messengers, and perhaps a market-place for local farmers. North of the Thames, Watling Street headed north-west for Brockley Hill (as the present Edgware Road does) and on to St Albans; Ermine Street (today's Kingsland Road) went directly north via Enfield to York; the Colchester Road went north-east, crossing the river Lea at Old Ford; and the Silchester Road (now Oxford Street and Bayswater Road) passed through Brentford and Staines on its way west. South of the Thames, twisting to avoid the Southwark marshes, and supported on timber rafts where avoidance was impossible, Watling Street headed towards Richborough and Dover, with its first posting-station at Crayford, and Stane Street went south-west through Ewell to Chichester. Both these roads had minor branch roads towards Sussex and the important iron industry of the Weald.[27]

LONDINIUM IN DECLINE

This picture of a powerful and prosperous city, the administrative and perhaps commercial capital of Britain, a centre of luxury and ostentatious public works at the hub of the provincial communications network, is well established by archaeological evidence from the first and early second centuries. What happened to London between the mid-second century and the end of Roman rule in 410 is much less certain. It is no longer generally accepted that London prospered as a centre of trade and population throughout the Roman period, only to be abandoned and ruined when Roman protection was removed in 410. There was almost certainly substantial economic and demographic decline well before this date, although John Morris's *Londinium*, written in the early 1970s, argues that

London thrived until around 350. The archaeologists' view, expressed by Peter Marsden, Ralph Merrifield and Dominic Perring, is that London's heyday as a great centre of population and commerce did not last much beyond the Hadrianic fire of about AD 125, and that from 150 onwards it survived mainly as a centre of government and officialdom, without strong economic roots. They suggest that a steep decline between 150 and 220 was partially arrested by the officially inspired reconstruction of London's public buildings after about 220, which helped to sustain the city's wealth and imperial reputation (but not its population) until the late fourth century.[28]

The evidence for London's loss of population comes from three sites in Southwark and three in the western half of the city (Milk Street, Watling Court and Newgate Street), which were abandoned by their occupants in the later second century and not reoccupied until late Roman or late Saxon times. In all of them a thick layer of dark earth was deposited, probably with the deliberate intention of establishing farms or gardens. Horticulture within a city was not unusual and does not mean that town life was collapsing, but it does suggest demographic decline. This evidence is reinforced by the demolition of the Huggin Hill baths before 200, and the striking scarcity of Roman material (coins, pottery and tools) in wells, streams and rubbish pits from the late second century onwards. A falling population might also explain the decline in imports of glass and pottery in the late second century, but other factors, such as the rise of native British production and the disruption of trade by piracy and imperial civil war, could have caused this.

Various explanations have been advanced for London's sudden decline in the second century, including the impact of barbarian raids and the effects of a disastrous plague. It is more likely that London, along with other towns that had developed rapidly in the expansionist phase of the Roman Empire, was undermined by changes in the pattern of imperial trade. When the Empire stabilized in the second century the need for military supplies and the flow of captured riches (slaves, for instance) diminished, and imperial settlers began to live on the products of the local countryside, rather than Italian imports. Trade by-passed towns and shopkeepers abandoned their shops, while the rural economy, measured by the size and number of villas, prospered. London retained its administrative functions and a limited number of economic ones, but not enough to sustain its previous population. If we can estimate the number of Londoners from the amount of rubbish they threw away, then London's population between 150 and 400 was less than half that of AD 50–150. 'The order of change suggested by the evidence is simply staggering; it is difficult to escape the conclusion that a large part of the city, perhaps as much as two-thirds, had somehow vanished.'[29]

Perhaps Roman London's most prosperous years were over by 200, but it was still a city of great political and strategic importance. Sculpted blocks used as building material in the fourth-century riverside wall (found in 1975) show that a monumental arch, 8 metres high, was erected in about 200, and that two derelict temples were rebuilt a few decades afterwards. Merrifield suggests the possibility that the arch was part of a grand rebuilding of the derelict south-western corner of the city as a religious and recreational quarter, perhaps during the long visit of Emperor Septimus Severus in 208. At about the same time, London's strategic importance was reaffirmed and reinforced by the building of the defensive wall around the town, either by Severus or by Albinus, the rival he defeated and killed in 197. This great wall, which marked the limits of London well into the Middle Ages and survived largely intact until the eighteenth century, is easily the most impressive remnant of Roman London visible today. Although the original purpose of the wall was almost certainly defensive, it is not clear which particular attacker was feared. The northern border, where there were frequent Scots raids and rebellions, was too far away to be a danger, and the great barbarian breakthrough of the mid-third century, in which over fifty unwalled Gaulish towns were overrun, could not be foreseen. So it is most likely that the wall was built in the course of the imperial power struggle between Emperor Severus and Clodius Albinus, the ambitious Governor of Britain, in the 190s, or as a mark of Severus' renewed interest in his remote province after his victory in 197. Rebuilding of the Cannon Street palace and the Thames quayside, and the building or reoccupation of many masonry houses (about forty have been found) indicate that there was a general revival in London's fortunes in the early third century, though its new role might have been more social and political than commercial.[30]

The discovery by Professor Grimes in 1954 of a mid-third-century temple dedicated to the eastern god Mithras casts a little light on the social and cultural lives of the soldiers and bureaucrats who dominated London at this time. Mithraism was a masculine mystery cult whose emphasis on exclusiveness, secrecy, loyalty, and strange rituals in animal costumes had a particular appeal to men of this class. In the fourth century the temple was attacked, and the cult's treasures, including heads of Mithras, Minerva and Serapis, were hidden under the floor, where they were found 1,600 years later. They are now displayed in the Museum of London. A second eastern cult, of wider and more enduring appeal, was probably also winning support in late third-century London, despite occasional persecution. Early in the fourth century, under the pro-Christian Emperor Constantine (306–337), Christianity became the favoured imperial religion, and in 314 we find Restitutus, Bishop of London, at the Council of Arles with bishops from York and Lincoln. No Roman Christian churches have yet been found in London, and this is a reminder that non-discovery and non-existence are by no means the same thing.[31]

IMPERIAL DISINTEGRATION

Early in the third century, probably under Emperor Caracalla (211–217), London's administrative role was diminished by the division of Britain into two provinces, with capitals and governors in York (*Britannia Inferior*) and probably London (*Britannia Superior*). From 238 until 284, until the great reforming emperor Diocletian (284–305) restored order and unity, the Roman Empire was in chaos, with thirty-six emperors in forty-six years, and the Franks and the Alamanni, powerful barbarian peoples, making destructive attacks deep into the imperial heartlands of Gaul and Northern Italy. From 260 to 274 Britain was part of a breakaway 'Empire of the Gauls', and again from 287 to 296 she was ruled independently by the self-proclaimed Emperor Carausius and then by his assassin Allectus. Britain seems to have been relatively prosperous in these unsettled years, and London, though temporarily cut off from its wider imperial connections, benefited from being the centre of Carausius' smaller empire, and was the home for the first time of official coin production. Carausius was murdered by a colleague, Allectus, in 293, and three years later a second Roman invasion of Britain took place. Constantius Chlorus, a Caesar (junior emperor) under Emperor Diocletian, landed in force and pursued, defeated and killed Allectus. A band of Frankish mercenaries broke away from the defeated army, and were in the process of plundering London when they were caught and slaughtered by Constantius' troops in the city itself. A fine commemorative gold medallion, found near Arras in 1922, shows Constantius arriving in triumph in London, welcomed as 'the restorer of eternal light' by a kneeling personification of the city.[32]

Although London was restored to its place in the Roman administrative and commercial network in 296, its status was never again quite what it had been in the boom years of the early second century. Early in the fourth century, probably after Diocletian's abdication in 305, military administration in

Britain was removed to a new military commander, and civil government was divided between the governors of four new provinces. The four provinces were grouped into one diocese, headed by a *vicarius* who was almost certainly based in London. The *vicarius* was not answerable directly to the Emperor in Rome, as earlier governors had been, but to an imperial deputy, the Praetorian Prefect, usually resident in Trier, in eastern Gaul. For the rest of the fourth century it was unusual for the Governor or the *vicarius* in London to have direct access to the Emperor in Rome or the new eastern capital, Constantinople.

In spite of this, the financial and bureaucratic burdens of imperial rule were much greater in the fourth century than they had been before. Faced by barbarian threats on all sides in the late third century, Diocletian had abandoned the traditional small-army policy of his predecessors and greatly increased, perhaps doubled, the size of the imperial forces. This, alongside the duplication of imperial courts and provincial administrations resulting from the reforms of Diocletian and Constantine the Great, and Constantine's vast building programmes in Rome and Constantinople, imposed huge tax burdens on the provinces. Britain was prosperous in the early fourth century, and was regarded as an important source of wealth and supplies for the imperial armies. London, according to a late fourth-century list of official posts, the *Notitia Dignitatum*, was the location of Britain's imperial treasury, the collection point for the diocesan revenue, and the centre of a growing bureaucracy. It is puzzling that the archaeological record suggests that it was a shrinking and increasingly derelict city, a town of blocked drains, dismantled or abandoned buildings, declining trade and industry and diminishing population. Perhaps the urban upper classes, demoralized by their loss of wealth and power under Diocletian and Constantine, were unwilling to spend their money on grand public buildings and good municipal services, or their time on burdensome civic duties.[33]

After Constantine's death in 337, the problems of London became increasingly entwined with the intense difficulties experienced by the Empire as a whole, and the history of the city cannot sensibly be discussed in isolation from the broader imperial context. London was an imperial capital, and its economy and culture could only thrive within the imperial system. As this system began to disintegrate in the Western Empire later in the fourth century, London's chances of prosperous survival dwindled. Two destructive forces were at work upon the Empire. One was the growing power of the barbarians, whose attacks from the east and the north were gaining in strength, coordination and intelligence. The other was the tendency of the Empire to waste its forces in civil wars between rival emperors, often representing different imperial armies. Britain was the home base, and the unwilling financier, of several of these contestants. Constantine II, Constantine the Great's son, launched his disastrous attack on Italy from Britain in 340, and Magnentius, the Western Emperor, drew on British support in his unsuccessful attempt to win the whole Empire in 353. His death led to severe reprisals in Britain, with many executions, arrests and property seizures, and the suicide of the *vicarius*. In 383 Magnus Maximus led an army revolt in Britain, gained control of the Western Empire, and was finally defeated and killed by Theodosius the Great in 388. On two further occasions Britain was cut off from the Empire beyond Gaul by the rebellions of imperial pretenders: Eugenius in 392–394, and Constantine III in 407–409. After the latter, Roman authority in Britain was never re-established. Not only were these rebellions costly in men, money and provisions, but their cumulative effect was probably to persuade many people that Britain no longer had much to gain from the imperial connection.

BARBARIANS AT THE GATES

What made these conflicts more disastrous than those of the third century was the greater readiness and ability of barbarian peoples to take advantage of them. London had been bothered by threats to its shipping from Saxon pirates from early in the third century, when a fort was built at Reculver, on the north Kent coast, to protect the Thames estuary. Eight more forts were built later in the third century along the East Anglian and south-eastern coast, which became known, because of the threat it faced, as the Saxon Shore. And there had been the unpleasant affair of the Frankish mercenaries in 296. Generally, though, London and southern Britain escaped the dangers and destruction suffered in more exposed parts of the Empire. Then, in 367, there was an apparently coordinated attack by the Scots, Picts, Attacotti and Irish in the north and west, and the Franks and Saxons on the Channel coast of either Gaul or Britain. Although one of Britain's senior military commanders were killed and the other ambushed, and the countryside around London was pillaged, the city seems to have escaped serious injury. It was rescued in 367 by an expeditionary force led by Theodosius (father of Theodosius the Great), who made London the centre of his successful campaign to recover and refortify the diocese, and initiated Roman Britain's last long period of stability and prosperity. At around this time, and perhaps to mark its rescue, London was renamed Augusta. This was an honorary or official title, and never displaced the traditional name.[34]

Theodosius' restoration programme probably gave London one of its last major Roman constructions, a riverside defensive wall joining the two ends of the landward wall from (in modern terms) Blackfriars to the Tower. This riverside wall was mentioned by William Fitzstephen in 1173, but its existence was not finally demonstrated until excavations in 1974–6. The wall was made of ragstone (supplemented by reused monumental masonry blocks) with a rough stone and concrete filling, resting in places on a raft of oak piles and chalk. Since the quayside was thus cut off from the warehouses and the town, the wall tends to confirm London's decline as a trading centre. By this time, in any case, barbarian incursions along the Rhine had greatly reduced the value of the Thames–Rhine route as a supply line for the continental armies. Nevertheless, London was still a place worth defending, and its vulnerable south-eastern corner was further strengthened by bastions along the land wall, from which a small force firing iron-tipped bolts from catapults could repel a large army of barbarians, who did not have siege skills.

The last decades of the fourth century were dominated by the largely successful efforts of Theodosius the Great (379–395) to hold back the Goths (driven westwards by the advance of the Huns) on the Danube and to recover the Western Empire from military usurpers. After his death, things fell apart. The main immediate threat to the Empire was from the Visigoths, led by Alaric, who were in Illyricum (roughly, modern Yugoslavia) and northern Italy at the beginning of the fifth century, seeking employment rather than war. It had become common practice in the fourth century to employ free barbarian troops under their own commanders attached to the imperial armies, and Alaric was a powerful and unpredictable employee. Preoccupied with this problem, Stilicho, the miltary commander who dominated the Western Empire under Emperor Honorius (395–423), also faced two challenges in the west. In 406 the army in Britain, which had possibly not been paid for some years, mutinied, and invaded Gaul and Spain under the usurper Constantine III between 407 and 409. Meanwhile, early in 407, an army of Germans (Vandals, Alans and Suebi) crossed the Rhine into Gaul. In 409 Constantine lost control of his army, and found himself trapped in his imperial city, Arles, by an alliance of rebel troops and Germans. Gaul and Spain were looted, and Britain, invaded by Saxons and left defenceless by Constantine III, could expect the same treatment.

What could the British do? Constantine's officials and soldiers (if any were left in the diocese) were an expensive irrelevance, and Constantine was in Arles, unable to pay them or send help against the Saxons. According to the Byzantine historian Zosimus, writing around 500 (and summarizing earlier sources), the British 'revolted from Roman rule and lived by themselves, no longer obeying Roman laws. The Britons took up arms and, fighting for themselves, freed the cities from the barbarian pressure.' With the expulsion or murder of Constantine's officials the Roman administration of Britain came to an end, and with it London's role as capital of the diocese. Rome was sacked in 410 by Alaric and his Visigoths, angry at the Senate's refusal to pay them, and the Emperor Honorius, who was apparently asked to send help to Britain, was in no position to do so.[35] If Romano-British civilization was to survive the Saxon onslaught in the fifth century, it would have to do so without Roman military support.

What was happening to London in these final imperial decades is by no means certain, although recent excavations have provided some interesting clues. West of the Walbrook there is hardly any sign of late fourth-century occupation, and significant evidence of dereliction and agricultural activity in the ubiquitous 'dark earth' deposits. But in the east, especially in the corner now occupied by the Tower of London, clear evidence of administrative and domestic life at the end of the fourth century and beyond has been found. In 1976–7 excavations within the Tower of London uncovered a well-built Roman defensive wall, dated by coins to after 400, which was apparently intended to strengthen the existing riverside defences of the south-east of the city. In this same area several discoveries of gold coins and silver ingots dating from the late fourth or early fifth centuries suggest that Roman officials in London were still receiving imperial funds for the wages of Roman troops or (more likely) barbarian mercenaries. In his riverside excavations, Gustav Milne has discovered some quite lavish rebuilding after 370, and signs of prosperous domestic occupation at least up to 400.[36] And nearby, in Lower Thames Street, a large private bath-house, perhaps attached to an inn, was still in use after 395, and probably up to 420 or 430, when its tiled roof collapsed and layers of silt began to cover the site. This is taken by archaeologists to represent Roman London's fate in miniature – no fire or destruction, but abandonment, natural decay, and very few signs of reoccupation until the mid-seventh century.

Chapter 2

Anglo-Saxon London

SAXONS IN THE WEST END

Already diminished in area and population, London must have suffered further loss of wealth and function after the ending of Roman administration in 410. Its place in the imperial bureaucratic and commercial network was gone. The money-based economy did not operate in Britain between about 420 and the seventh century, and although rural production could still prosper through barter, urban merchants, craftsmen and officials depended upon the free circulation of coinage for their livelihoods. Only London's position on the road system, and the defensive strength of its mighty walls, allowed it to retain some importance in the fifth century. The Roman roads outside London continued to be used, and travellers on them still had to pass through the gates in London's wall. Within the town, the fact that the Roman street plan seems to have been ignored, and was replaced with a later Saxon one which only follows the older streets when they are the shortest route between the gates, suggests a clear break in occupation in the fifth and sixth centuries. The almost total absence of early Saxon pottery, glass or burials within the city walls appears to confirm this. The same is true of the riverside settlement in Southwark, which appears, from the lack of archaeological finds, to have been deserted between about 400 and 850.[1]

The struggle between the British and the settlers or invaders from North Germany known collectively as the Anglo-Saxons lasted for at least a century. Saxon soldiers first settled in Britain not as invaders, but as mercenaries employed in the late Roman and the post-Roman period as defenders against barbarian attack. According to Gildas, the British priest whose polemical history of *The Ruin and Conquest of Britain*, written before 550, is one of the best sources for the fifth century, this policy led to disaster around 450. The British leader Vortigern (the name means high king in Celtic) is said to have imported Saxon mercenaries as a defence against Pictish raiders, local rivals, or perhaps even the Romans (who were still in Gaul). Several sources (the *Gallic Chronicle* of 452, Gildas, and Bede's *Ecclesiastical History of the English People*) tell us that there was a Saxon revolt in the middle of the fifth century, and an unanswered British appeal for help to Aetius, the last effective Roman ruler in Gaul. The *Anglo-Saxon Chronicle*, first written in the late ninth century, but using a variety of older sources, has this well-known entry for the year 457: 'In this year Hengest and Aesc fought against the Britons at a place called Crecganford (Crayford?) and there slew 4,000 men; and the Britons then forsook Kent and fled to London in great terror.' Whether they found there a surviving British settlement or just the protection of deserted walls it is impossible to say.[2]

Although the British won a famous (but mysterious) victory at Mount Badon around 500, Saxon control spread from the South-East along the south coast, up the Thames valley, into the Midlands and East Anglia by about 550. The London region must have been engulfed in this advance, but the City has yielded hardly any trace of Saxon occupation before about 750. Professor Grimes, who led the excavation of bombed areas between 1947 and 1962, reported 'the absence of structural, or indeed any other, evidence for the occupation of London in the early part of the Saxon period', and believed that this was 'not due to the later destruction of the levels in which they would have occurred'. Intensive excavation by the Museum of London team in the 1970s and 1980s yielded very little evidence of Anglo-Saxon building in the City before about 850.[3]

Yet Bede, writing (in 730) of Augustine's attempt to establish Mellitus as Bishop of London in 604, called London the capital of the East Saxons, 'a trading centre for many nations who visit it by land and sea'.[4] Was there an early Saxon London or not? Archaeological and documentary sources seemed to be in irreconcilable conflict. This conflict now seems to have been resolved. Mortimer Wheeler, working on London in the 1920s, noticed that Saxon finds were more common west of the Roman walls than within the City, and suggested that there might have been a settlement there. Since 1985 excavations in Covent Garden have confirmed that there was indeed a large Saxon settlement along the Thames, perhaps 200 acres in area, between Whitehall and the marshy Fleet valley. On the Jubilee Hall site in Covent Garden in 1985 the Museum of London's archaeologists found remains of rectangular buildings supported by wooden posts sunk into the ground, a hearth, rubbish pits and wells, loom weights, slag from iron and bronze furnaces, animal bones, oyster shells and eighth-century pottery imported from northern France. This busy seventh- and eighth-century settlement, set outside the walls which Saxons did not need and perhaps did not like, was probably the *Lundenwic* of Bede's account. It is also believed that memories of the Saxon old town, the old wic, gave its name to the area, and thus the road, called the Aldwych.[5]

TRADE AND CHRISTIANITY

In Gaul, the shared acceptance of Christianity established some continuity between Roman society and the Frankish and Visigothic kingdoms established in the later fifth century. In Britain, where the conquerors were pagan, the social and cultural transition must have been much more abrupt, although the career of Gildas, a north British cleric writing in Wales around 550, is a reminder that Christianity and Latin learning still survived in the north and west. The reconversion of southern Britain was begun in 597 by Pope Gregory the Great, who sent Augustine to build upon the goodwill of Ethelbert of Kent, the chief king, or Bretwalda, of England. London's claim to be Augustine's archiepiscopal see was overridden by the political advantages of choosing Ethelbert's capital, Canterbury, but London was chosen, along with York and Rochester, as one of the first episcopal sees.

Abbot Mellitus' establishment as Bishop of London in 604, and the building of the first cathedral of St Paul at the western end of the walled city do not mark the re-emergence of London as a Christian town within the Roman fold. On Ethelred's death in 616 Mellitus was driven out of London by the pagan King of Essex, and Christianity was not re-established there until Theodore of Tarsus, Archbishop of Canterbury from 668 to 690, installed St Eorconweald as bishop around 675. Although Eorconweald founded abbeys near London (at Barking and Chertsey), evidence for Christian activity in seventh-century London is very thin. St Bride's, in Fleet Street, has the remains of Saxon churches in its crypt, but Grimes, who excavated them in the 1950s, could not confirm (or deny) that they are pre-eleventh century. It is true that St Bride was a sixth-century Irish saint, but a dedication to a saint of recent and local origin was unusual before the tenth century. The Saxon arch of All Hallows-by-the-Tower, exposed by wartime bombing, has a better claim to be regarded, on stylistic grounds, as late seventh or early eighth century.[6] Nevertheless, London was a major Christian city by the eighth century, the centre of a diocese covering Essex, Middlesex and parts of Hertfordshire, and the place from which St Boniface embarked on his great missions to convert the Germans. With the rising influence of the Church, two Roman skills unknown to the early Saxon settlers (but of the utmost importance to historians) made their reappearance: writing, and building in stone.

Bede's description of London in 730 as 'an emporium for many nations' is confirmed by a range of seventh- and eighth-century evidence. Its name at this time, *Lundenwic*, ends in the Anglo-Saxon word for a trading town, *wic*.[7] A charter of Frithuwold, sub-King of Surrey, granting land near the river in 672–4, refers to 'the port of London, where ships come to land', and Bede himself mentions a slave trader from Frisia (the area round the Rhine estuaries) in London in 679. Three major eighth-century European trading towns, Dorstadt, Domburg and Quentovic, were conveniently placed for trade with the Thames estuary. At the same time, there is a reference in a Kentish law-code to a hall in London where Kentish merchants and their clients had to register their transactions with the king's reeve. Where there is trade there will be taxation, and three charters of Ethelbald, King of Mercia (the Midlands kingdom), issued between 733 and 745 granted customs-free access to London for the ships of two bishops and an abbess.[8] As trade and taxation returned, so did the use of coinage. A few gold coins minted in London from about 640 (sometimes marked *Londuniu*) have been found, mostly in Kent and Essex, and the fairly widespread circulation of silver or silver and copper coins (*sceattas*) in the eighth century, minted in London and elsewhere, suggests the beginnings of a money economy. In the early ninth century, London was producing Mercian pennies and receiving coins through trade or taxation from Kent and East Anglia.[9] The essential components of an urban economy were slowly being reassembled.

Bede refers to London as the capital of Essex, but it was a border town over which three more powerful Anglo-Saxon kingdoms, Kent, Wessex and Mercia, exerted some control from time to time. The evidence of coin production, church appointments and royal charters shows that for 200 years, from around 670 until the Viking occupation in 870, London's overlord was usually the great Midlands kingdom of Mercia. Especially under Offa (757–796), Mercia was a significant power, involved in commerce and diplomacy with Charlemagne's empire, and London was its most convenient port for European trade. Traditionally, it was believed that Offa had a palace in London, of which the church of St Alban, Wood Street, was the royal chapel. This is not impossible. The Saxon church could have been eighth century (though there is no evidence that it was), and it lies on the main road through the old Roman fort, which (if it still survived) would have been a fine location for a palace. We are talking, in any case, not of a permanent headquarters but of a temporary residence, a place for the royal household to stay while Offa held court, received gifts, settled disputes, issued charters and hunted. No doubt Offa was an illiterate and ruthless man, but his introduction of regular coinage, his encouragement of trade with the Franks and his establishment of one supreme political authority over most of England, created the circumstances in which London's natural advantages could bring it prosperity again.

The London of Alfred the Great

After Offa's death in 796 supremacy in the Thames valley, and control of London, was disputed between Mercia and Wessex. Their rivalry was ended, though, by the arrival of a common enemy in the mid-ninth century. Coastal attacks by Danish raiders began in the 830s, and soon threatened the whole east and south coast. London was raided in 841 and 851, and it may have been in response to these raids that Londoners moved from their vulnerable Strand settlement into the comparative safety of the walled city. Perhaps, Martha Carlin has argued, the Mercians rebuilt the bridge on its old Roman foundations at around this time, as a defensive barrier against the Danish fleet. If so, the strategy was unsuccessful, since London was occupied in the winter of 871–2 (and probably until 886) by the Danish Great Army, which advanced from Reading under Ivar the Boneless.[10] By this time the Danish army had gained control of Northumberland and East Anglia, killing their kings, and by 873 Burgred of Mercia had fled to Rome, preferring his kingdom's dismemberment to his own. The Danes, though not their Great Army, probably remained in London for the next fifteen years. The following decades were decisive ones in the history of London and England. In 871 Ethelred of Wessex, the only English king to have had recent military success against the Danes, died, leaving the kingdom to his brother Alfred. By 878 Alfred had been forced to retreat to the Isle of Athelney, in the Somerset marshes, but in May 878 he gathered his forces and inflicted a decisive defeat on what was left of the Danish army (many Danes having already settled in the conquered kingdoms) at Edington, near Chippenham. The record for the next few years is unclear, but we are told (by the Anglo-Saxon Chronicle and Asser's *Life* of Alfred) that Alfred advanced eastwards, and in 886, 'after the burning of towns and the slaughter of peoples', 'Alfred occupied London, and all the English people submitted to him, except those who were in captivity to the Danes; and he entrusted the city to ealdorman Ethelred to rule'.[11] We have to remember that the authors of these accounts were

Alfred's followers, determined to magnify their leader's part in the defeat of the Danes. Perhaps Ethelred, who was ealdorman of Mercia as well as being Alfred's son-in-law, played a bigger part in the reoccupation of London than the sources admit, and thus earned the right to rule it as part of Mercia after 886. Control of London did not pass to Alfred's son, Edward the Elder, on Alfred's death in 899, but only when Ethelred died in 911. It may not be true that Alfred's occupation of London was followed by his recognition as king of England, but it is striking that the chronicler should have regarded the capture of London, a small and doubtless battered settlement with an ancient name and reputation, as an appropriate occasion for the unification of the kingdom.[12]

The well-told story of Alfred's heroic success in saving Anglo-Saxon society and culture from being overwhelmed by Danish influence, and in making possible the reconquest and unification of England by his son and grandsons by 955, may have led to exaggerated praise of his other achievements. But he seems truly to have possessed, alongside all his military, intellectual and political talents, unusual gifts as a town planner. By 886 Alfred and his allies controlled about half of England, south-west of a line drawn roughly from London to the Mersey. In order to strengthen his kingdom against future Danish attacks Alfred initiated a policy of building a network of fortified towns, or burhs, located on important lines of communication, and intended to be centres of trade, civilization and administration, as well as refuges for English villagers in the nearby countryside. A document known as the *Burghal Hidage* lists the burhs established by Alfred of Wessex. They include Roman walled towns such as Winchester, Exeter and Chichester, newly planned and fortified towns such as Cricklade and Wallingford, and London's southern bridgehead, South-wark, or *Suthringa geweorche* ('the defensive work of the men of Surrey'). This is the first appearance of Southwark, by this or any other name, in an historical document.[13] London itself is not mentioned, perhaps because it was not in Wessex, but it is very likely that Ethelred, Alfred or his son Edward the Elder (King of Wessex, 899–924) made major changes to the defences, street plan and trading facilities of London, restoring and repopulating the town.

London was a frontier town, only 4 miles west of the river Lea, where Danish territory began. If they had not done so when the Danish raids started, it made sense now for Londoners to move back inside the Roman walls. From the late ninth century the bulk of Saxon finds come from within the walled area, and London is increasingly referred to as *Lunden-burh* (meaning a fortified town) rather than *Lundenwic* (a port or market).

Perhaps the old walls were an adequate defence for London as they stood, or perhaps Alfred or his successors repaired them.[14] The purpose of the *Burghal Hidage* was to specify the number of men needed to garrison the walls and earthworks of the burhs, and to allocate these duties to the inhabitants of particular pieces of land (hides) nearby. It is possible that something like this was organized in or around London, and that this formed the basis of the later system of 24 wards, which existed in London by the early twelfth century.

In his other burhs Alfred established new streets on a simple grid or 'fishbone' pattern, and it is likely that some of London's new Saxon streets date from Alfred and Ethelred's time, when it seems that the ruined Roman city was reoccupied after being virtually deserted for three centuries. The Saxons would have found a few main thoroughfares linking the main city gates and (if it existed) the bridge, still running fairly close to the old Roman roads, but rarely along them. As in other reoccupied Roman towns the survival of the walls and gates dictated that the new main roads would echo the old ones, even if there was no continuity of memory or occupation. The Strand, Fleet Street and Ludgate Hill, together constituting the Saxon Akemannstreet, entered the west of the city through Ludgate, and probably continued past St Paul's, roughly along the present Cannon Street and Eastcheap, leaving the city by a south-eastern gate. Where this street passed near St Paul's it was probably joined by two others, one going north to Aldersgate, where St Martin-le-Grand now runs, and another going east and forking to Aldgate and Bishopsgate, along the modern Lombard Street and Fenchurch Street, and Threadneedle Street and Bishopsgate respectively. The streets most likely to date from Alfred's time are Fish Street Hill, Botolph Lane, Gracechurch Street, and Philpot Lane, running north and south from Eastcheap, the wide market street of Alfred's town. Bread Street, Garlick Hill and Bow Lane, running from Cheapside down to the river, could also date from Alfred's reign, but they are more likely to be a part of the early tenth century expansion of London.[15]

In the decades following the Anglo-Saxon seizure of London the trading quays along the Thames were rebuilt. Two land grants issued by Alfred to his supporters, the Bishop of Worcester and the Archbishop of Canterbury, in 889 and 898 refer to trading rights on the Thames, and indicate the existence of a small landing-place, or hithe, known then as Ethelred's hithe and now as Queenhithe. The land in question contained the remains of the Roman baths at Huggin Hill. Archaeological evidence from another site, New Fresh Wharf, just east of London Bridge, indicates that quayside construction took place there in the tenth century. There was a timber landing-stage and fourteen rows of wooden stakes, either a defensive stockade or supports for a jetty, and a rubble, clay and timber embankment, projecting 20 metres southwards from the Roman riverside wall, and extending 19 metres or more towards Billingsgate, where a wharf is known to have existed before 1016. The whole construction is remarkably flimsy and crude compared to the massive Roman timberwork it was replacing. The timbers have not proved easy to date accurately, and there is no reason to allocate these quays to Alfred and Ethelred's time. It is fair to say, though, that Alfred's policy of urban renewal and encouragement of trade started a process of construction, settlement and commercial expansion which made London a busy port and market town by the eleventh century.[16]

A Trading City

In the late Saxon period, between Alfred's reign and 1066, London developed from a riverside village into a well-populated town of some economic and political significance. Wooden quays had been built along much of the riverfront, at Queenhithe, Billingsgate and Dowgate, near the mouth of the Walbrook (and modern Cannon Street Station). There was an extensive network of small gravelled streets, especially near the Thames and in the western half of the city. The remains of about forty late Saxon wooden houses, mostly with cellars or sunken floors, some with central stone hearths and earth latrines, have been excavated along several of these streets, particularly Milk Street, Bow Lane and Ironmonger Lane, all off Cheapside, and Pudding Lane, Fish Street Hill and Botolph Lane, off Eastcheap. Cheapside (Westcheap) and Eastcheap had become the main market streets of the two halves of the city (*ceap* is the Anglo-Saxon word for a market), distributing merchandise from local and international trade.

Londoners' trades, crafts and more durable possessions are illustrated by a scattering of artifacts discovered in their houses, rubbish pits, cess-pits and wells: crude pottery cooking pots, beakers and lamps from the Thames valley (known as shelly ware, because of shell fragments in the clay), woollen cloth and a little silk, simple leather shoes, pewter jewellery, loom weights, quernstones (for grinding flour) from the Rhineland, and the remains of fish, livestock and fruit.[17] And a few Londoners, at least, made their mark in a wider European sphere. There were probably London merchants in tenth-century Italy, exchanging the cargoes of woollens, tin and slaves they had brought down the Rhine for bullion, silk and spices, and London's wealth was known, in the vaguest of terms, as far away as Isfahan.[18]

One extraordinary document gives us an insight into the organization and variety of London's trade at the end of the Anglo-Saxon period. This is the royal ordinance issued by Ethelred II ('the Unready', 978–1016) or perhaps Cnut (or Canute, 1016–1035) to regulate trade and fix tolls in London. The ordinance shows that Billingsgate (mentioned for the first time in this document) was used by merchants from northern France (Normandy, Ponthieu, the Île de France and the town of Rouen), Flanders, and the towns of Huy and Liège on the river Meuse. Commodities on which a toll was due, either in money or a proportion of the cargo, included wine and blubber-fish (both from Rouen), planks, cloth, wool and local farm produce. T. H. Lloyd, the leading historian of the wool trade, suggests that this very early reference to English wool exports may be a mistranscription, with *lanam* (wool) being mistakenly written in place of *lardam* (bacon). Subjects of the German Emperor were given special privileges:

> Besides wool [or bacon] which has been unloaded and melted fat they were also permitted to buy three live pigs for their ships. But they were not allowed any right of pre-emption over the burgesses, and [they had] to pay their toll and at Christmas two lengths of grey cloth and one length of brown and 10 lbs of pepper and five pairs of gloves and two saddle-kegs of vinegar, and the same at Easter.

Farmers selling their produce in London's markets were also subject to royal exactions: 'From hampers with hens, one hen as toll, and from one hamper of eggs, five eggs as toll, if they come to the market. Women who deal in dairy produce pay one penny two weeks before Christmas and another penny a week before Christmas.'[19]

Several pieces of evidence, including this ordinance, confirm that there was a bridge across the Thames again by Ethelred's time. The location of the early Anglo-Saxon trading town to the west of the walled city suggests that the Roman bridge had been breached or destroyed, but perhaps enough of it had survived to provided a basis upon which the Anglo-Saxons, with their limited skills, could build. It is fairly likely that a bridge existed, or was rebuilt, in Alfred's reign, linking his two burhs of London and Southwark, and a charter of Edgar's reign (959–975) tells us that a widow accused of witchcraft was thrown off the bridge and drowned for pin-sticking.[20]

LAW AND ORDER

The written evidence available to historians generally reflects the preoccupations of the literate élite: the Church, warfare and administration. The lives of the poor and middling are rarely mentioned unless for some reason they become involved in these grander concerns, perhaps as taxpayers or wrongdoers. Of the many legal documents surviving from Anglo-Saxon England one, apparently an agreement between King Athelstan (924–939) and the bishops, reeves (royal officials) and nobles of London, sheds light on the particular problems of life in tenth-century London. It describes the organization by these leading citizens of a 'peace guild' (or frith gild) to enforce the king's laws in and around London, and to do so at a profit. The members of the guild were grouped into tens, and the tens into hundreds, with one overall leader and ten senior members (one from each group) to enforce their duties and administer their funds. Their main concern was theft of cattle and other goods, and their remedy was the pursuit, capture, trial and execution of the thief, using overwhelming force if his kindred tried to protect him. If the thief were taken, his property would be used to compensate the victim for his loss, and then divided between the thief's wife (if she were innocent), the king and the guild. Owners of slaves were to pay into a fund to give half a pound compensation to those who lost slaves by theft or escape, and recaptured slaves were to be stoned to death or hanged. Slaves, who were an accepted form of property until after the Norman Conquest, would have been captives in war, or brought by Viking traders from the Baltic, or perhaps people enslaved as a punishment. Whether this guild was a case of municipal self-help, or (more likely) a response to King Athelstan's demand for action against crime, it is an early example of wealthy Londoners' perennial concern for the safety of their property.[21] It is an example too of the emergence of social groupings other than the kindred group as urban society and its problems became more complex. The peace guild was based upon social duty and common interest, and involved feasting, drinking and prayer for members' souls, as well as cooperative law enforcement. In this mixture of business, pleasure and religion it was a precursor of the craft and trade guilds that began to appear in the twelfth century.

The impression should not be given that law in London was only enforced by self-appointed groups of vigilantes. Anglo-Saxon London had an open-air court of great antiquity and authority, the folkmoot, an assembly of all citizens on the high ground north-east of St Paul's, which had responsibility for order, and sole authority for proclaiming outlaws. Most of what we know of the folkmoot comes from the twelfth and thirteenth centuries, when its meetings were thrice-yearly and its duties had become formalized and limited to acknowledging the new sheriff and guarding the city from fire and crime. By this time, in an obscure process beginning in the tenth or eleventh century, the folkmoot had lost most of its power to another more convenient and less democratic institution. This was a court of Danish origin, or at least with a Danish name, the husting (house thing, or indoor assembly), which first appears in a reliable document in 1032, during Cnut's reign. It has been suggested that an indoor court limited to London's leading men, and meeting regularly under the presidency of the king's reeve, must already have existed to deal with the day-to-day business of the town, and that 'husting' was a new name rather than a new court.[22] The name stuck, and by the twelfth century the Court of Husting had regular Monday sittings in the Guildhall, dealing with disputes over debt, trade, measurement and land. It had become London's shire court, presided over by the king's official, the portreeve or, as he came to be known in the eleventh century, the shire reeve or sheriff.[23]

The authority of the law did not apply equally to every part of the town. There were areas of special immunity, where the personal authority of a lord or Churchman carried more weight than the City courts. Great men with estates in London were sometimes granted judicial rights over an enclosure (haga, or haw) around their property, or within a burh. Street names ending in -bury, as in Lothbury, Aldermanbury and Bucklersbury, and the City ward of Bassishaw, indicate the locations of some of these privileged estates. The most important and long-lasting rights of private jurisdiction were known as sokes. These involved the possession of legal powers by a noble or an institution over a group of tenants, either within a particular district or scattered, exercised through a private court. If the soke covered a distinct plot of land, the area would be immune from city jurisdiction. Where these rights were in private hands, they seem to have become insignificant, but not non-existent, by the thirteenth century. The private jurisdictions of the Church, though, were more durable, and were the subject of disputes between the City and the clergy throughout the Middle Ages.[24]

One identifiable and important Anglo-Saxon soke belonged to a group known as the *cnihtengild*, an association of Englishmen whose status is now unclear, though the word *cniht* later became knight, and their role was probably military. The *cnihts* were granted 'jurisdiction (sake and soke) over their men within the city and without' by Edward the Confessor around 1043, and the charter was reaffirmed twice before 1107. Although their rights were not confined to a specific area, it is clear from later documents that their authority covered a large district inside the main eastern gate, Aldgate, and a huge area called the Portsoken, running outside the eastern side of wall down to the river. Whoever the *cnihts* were, the *cnihtengild* was obviously a powerful group, and it seems likely that its privileges depended upon an obligation to defend the vulnerable eastern side of the city. In 1120 or 1121, perhaps because its services were no longer needed, the guild was dissolved, and all its property, powers and immunities were granted to the Priory of Holy Trinity, founded by Henry I's wife Matilda in 1107. With these powers over the land and soke of the guild, the prior of Holy Trinity became one of the aldermen of the City, and remained so until Henry VIII's destruction of the Priory in 1531.[25]

THE VIKINGS RETURN

In 980, after nearly a century of relative peace, England began to suffer a new wave of Scandinavian raids. London was attacked in 994 by a combined Danish and Norwegian fleet of ninety-four ships, and put up so stout a resistance, according to the *Anglo-Saxon Chronicle*, that the Vikings were driven off, and 'suffered more harm and injury than they ever thought any citizen would do to them'. Sporadic Viking attacks continued throughout Ethelred's reign (978–1016), and twice, in 1009 and 1013, London's defences held firm. This is a testimony to the effectiveness of the Roman fortifications, and indicates that London was large enough now to provide a powerful garrison, which was reinforced in 1013 by Ethelred's personal army.

In the last three years of the struggle between the Anglo-Saxons, led by Ethelred and his son Edmund ('Ironside'), and the Danish army of Swein and (from 1014) Cnut, control of London became the decisive issue. London's submission to Swein in 1014 drove Ethelred to Normandy, and when Ethelred returned later that year, on the death of Swein, his first action (if we believe Snorri Sturleson's early thirteenth-century saga) was to recapture London from the Danes. Since the Danes had fortified Southwark and the bridge, Ethelred and his ally, the saintly King Olaf of Norway, decided to tie ropes from their ships to the posts supporting the bridge, and pulled it into the river, together with the Danish army. In 1015 Cnut returned, and was soon in control of most of England, while Ethelred and Edmund were holding London and the south-east. When Ethelred died in April 1016, and Edmund left his London base to recapture Wessex,

Cnut laid siege to the city. This was not an easy task. To cut off London's supplies from upriver, Cnut's men had to dig an artificial channel around the Southwark end of the bridge, and drag some of their ships through it. The Danes then built earthworks around the outside of the city wall, from which they were briefly dislodged by Edmund's relieving army. Eventually, Cnut abandoned the siege, and launched a land and river attack on London. This also failed, and Cnut's force withdrew, chased by Edmund, who eventually caught up with them and was decisively beaten by them at Ashingdon, in Essex. Edmund died in November 1016, and the kingdom fell to Cnut.[26]

One of the clear realities, through all these twists and turns, was the national importance of London. This was partly due to London's prestige, its great defensive strength in a key strategic position controlling the Thames valley, and its large and influential population. Furthermore, the city was an important economic and financial centre, England's biggest centre of coin production, its largest international port, and the main contributor to royal finances. King Athelstan's laws of between 926 and 930 established eight official moneyers in London, compared to seven in Canterbury and six in Winchester, and it appears that about a quarter of England's coinage was produced in London.[27] The Danish need to pay their mercenaries, and the English need to buy off Danish raiders in cash, made London a place of key importance for both sides. It appears that Cnut made London his military headquarters between 1016 and 1036, and London was the focal point of the struggle between Edward the Confessor and Godwin, the powerful Earl of Wessex, from 1051 to 1053.

It was during these conflicts that the citizens of London began to develop the claim that they had the right to elect the king of England. They chose Edmund Ironside in 1016, elected Edward the Confessor by popular acclaim in 1042, and 'offered' the crown to William of Normandy in 1066. In so far as these acclamations were something more than recognitions of the inevitable, they may well reflect the influence of the military or naval forces stationed in London, rather than that of the citizens, but the memory of these moments of power provided the basis for a tradition which was revived on several occasions in the Middle Ages.[28]

DANISH LONDON

Although the Vikings often lived up to their bloody popular image, there is no evidence that London suffered great physical damage at their hands.

Some historians believe that the Danish impact on English towns was 'stimulating and constructive'.[29] They argue that Danish control, especially under Cnut and his sons Harold (1035–40) and Harthacnut (1040–42), enabled London to become part of the great Viking trading network, encompassing Russia, Greenland, Lappland, and Byzantium (reached overland through Russia), and dealing in furs, slaves and walrus ivory. The evidence for this (as for so many other things in the Anglo-Saxon period) is not very substantial, and there is no reason to believe that Scandinavian trade supplanted London's important links with the German, Flemish and French merchants mentioned in Ethelred's code. On the other hand, Danish demands for cash tribute from London were only too substantial. London had to pay £10,500 of the £83,000 England paid to Cnut in 1018, on top of equally vast exactions six years earlier. This may be impressive proof of London's prosperity, and it shows why both sides thought London was worth fighting for, but the 1018 payment, which was nearly twenty times the normal annual taxation of twelfth-century London, must have had a very depressing effect on the city's economy. Some of the money, at least, might have gone back into circulation in London, because Cnut used it to pay the wages of the large mercenary fleet he kept stationed near the city, perhaps to guarantee London's loyalty.[30] But this enormous drain on London's bullion, along with heavy Norman taxation forty years later, helps to explain the disappearance of London merchants from Italy and Byzantium until the later twelfth century.[31]

The Vikings, once feared as pagans, seem to have been active participants in the creation of London's impressive collection of small parish churches, which was mainly the work of the eleventh and twelfth centuries. By the year 1000 there were probably only three or four churches within the city walls, and possibly two or three in the old Saxon town to the west: certainly St Paul's, All Hallows-by-the-Tower and St Andrew Holborn, and perhaps St Alban Wood Street, St Mary-le-Bow, St Peter Cornhill and, to the west, St Bride's in Fleet Street. Yet in the 1170s William Fitzstephen claimed that there were 126 parish churches and thirteen conventual churches in London and its suburbs. Of these, the majority were probably founded before 1100, or even before 1066, not as a Norman imposition, but in a late rush of Danish and Anglo-Saxon piety.[32] Some church names give a clear indication of their origin, if not their date. The five churches in the City, and one in Southwark, dedicated to St Olaf (or St Olave), the Norwegian king who helped Ethelred in 1014, are all Danish foundations of some time after 1030, when Olaf died. St Bride's and St Clement Danes are also probably Danish foundations. Pamela Nightingale has put forward the interesting idea that these eight churches, far from being a gesture of integration or reconciliation, were Danish garrison churches, all strongly built and strategically located, a part of Cnut's iron grip on his prize conquest. The four City churches of St Botolph, the early English patron saint of travellers, were surely placed at London's gates by English benefactors. Since there were plenty of rich English Londoners after 1066 these foundations are not necessarily pre-Conquest.[33]

The proliferation of churches in eleventh- and twelfth-century London cannot be used as an index of population growth. Churches were not built to meet the growing needs of the worshipping community, but rather as a reflection of the piety and vanity of wealthy patrons. Individual landlords, clergymen, or groups of townsmen united by neighbourhood, common origin or occupation, paid for the building of small churches, and maintained them as their own property, on their own land. Many of them carried the patron's name alongside the saint's: St Mary Woolnoth, St Martin Orgar, St Nicholas Acon (Haakon), St Nicholas Aldred, and so on. Their initial purpose was to provide a place of worship for their owners, and to win them earthly and heavenly credit, but most of them became places of local worship within the parish framework, which developed in the eleventh and twelfth centuries into the shape it retained until 1907. London was so full of parish churches by the late twelfth century that hardly any more needed to be built within the walls in subsequent centuries, despite very great population growth. In the century after about 1050 private owners gave up ownership of their churches to cathedrals or monastic communities, partly to ensure their long-term survival, partly yielding to a more assertive and powerful Church hierarchy. One of the main beneficiaries of this process was Canterbury Cathedral, which is recorded in a document of 1100 as the owner of eight and a half London churches, six of them given by their priests, and the others by their lay owners, Brihtmaer, Gumbert and Aelfwine.[34]

THE CONFESSOR AND HIS MAUSOLEUM

Whether we see it as beneficial or (more convincingly) depredatory, Danish rule in London only lasted twenty-six years. On the death of his two sons Cnut's line ended, and Ethelred's exiled son, Edward ('the Confessor'), returned to reign as the penultimate English king. In view of London's later development as a city with two centres, royal in the west and commercial in the east, Edward's most important action as far as London was concerned was his decision to pay for the rebuilding of a monastic church on Thorney Island, where the branches of the Tyburn flow into the Thames at Westminster, near the old Roman ford. This decision started the growth of a centre of royal and political power at Westminster which in the long run contributed enormously to London's prosperity and importance, and created a dramatic tension between east and west which runs through London's medieval and modern history. The early history of the Westminster religious community is obscured by the fact that the twelfth-century Abbey became a factory of lies and forged charters, but it is quite likely that Offa of Mercia founded a small church there in the 780s, and there is convincing evidence of a well-endowed monastic community around 960. Since Cnut's son and successor Harold Harefoot had been buried there in 1040 the existing church could not have been in too neglected a condition, and it is even suggested that Cnut or his son might have already moved the royal residence from within the City to Westminster before Edward's succession.[35]

It is not known why Edward the Confessor wanted a mausoleum in Westminster, instead of choosing, as Cnut had done, to be buried with Alfred and the Wessex kings at Winchester. He was in pious rivalry with his wife Edith, who rebuilt a nunnery at Wilton, and perhaps, as Frank Barlow says, 'he was asserting his independence and pleasing himself'. Whatever his motivation, he was prepared to spend on it 'a tenth of his entire substance in gold, silver, cattle and all other possessions'.[36] Several of his successors, including William I, Stephen, Henry I and Henry II, chose to be buried in abbeys they had founded or refounded. Edward wanted to live at Westminster as well as die there, not as a saintly recluse, but as a practical monarch who needed to maintain control over a rich and powerful town, yet avoid the pressures and dangers of living within its walls. All Edward's successors followed him in choosing Westminster, rather than the City, as their main London home, and it may be that the abandoned royal palace within the City, which is traditionally believed to have been inside the Roman fort in the north-western corner of the walls, was taken over by the new monastery of St Martin-le-Grand in the 1060s.[37]

Edward had lived in exile in France for twenty-five years, at a time when the Romanesque style was becoming popular among church builders there, and his new abbey brought the fashion across the Channel. It was 'the first in England', wrote William of Malmesbury in the twelfth century, 'erected in the fashion which all now follow at great expense'. He may have been influenced also by Robert of Jumièges, Bishop of London from 1044 to 1051, whose abbey at Jumièges in Normandy is regarded as the model for Edward's church. Westminster Abbey was almost completely demolished when Henry III rebuilt it between 1240 and 1272, but we know roughly what it looked like from a contemporary description and from a stylized representation of it in the Bayeux Tapestry. It was a large and well-proportioned cruciform building, constructed sturdily in dressed stone, with a long nave with six double bays, a lofty lantern tower over the crossing, and double arcading all around the nave. The crossing, a contemporary wrote, 'rises simply at first from a low and sturdy arch, then swells with many a winding staircase ingeniously ascending and finally as a plain wall reaches the wooden roof which is covered with lead'.[38] So the 'Norman' style of building came to England before – but only just before – the Normans themselves arrived.

PART TWO

MEDIEVAL LONDON, 1066–1520

Chapter 3

Power and Conflict

THE CONQUEST

By the time Westminster Abbey was consecrated on 28 December 1065 Edward the Confessor was already close to death, too ill to attend the ceremony. He died in his palace at Westminster a week later, having entrusted the kingdom to Harold, Earl of Wessex. Harold chose to be crowned in the Abbey, beginning a tradition that has lasted for 900 years. The new King, who had spent twenty years working for this prize, enjoyed it for less than ten months before losing his life on a battlefield near Hastings. After destroying the English army, William of Normandy recognized that the submission of London was necessary before he could claim the kingdom. This submission was not a foregone conclusion. London was a well-fortified city, garrisoned, according to the contemporary account of William of Poitiers, by 'a numerous and formidable force', so large that the town could hardly hold it. In the words of the twelfth-century *Song of the Battle of Hastings*: 'London is a great city, overflowing with froward inhabitants and richer in treasure than the rest of the kingdom. Protected on the left side by its walls, on the right side by the river, it neither fears enemies nor dreads being taken by storm.'[1]

After a month spent securing the South-East, William tried a direct advance on London through Southwark and over the bridge. This failed, and William decided instead to isolate London by devastating Southwark and most of the surrounding countryside, as far west as Wallingford. The circumstances in which the political and Church leaders gathered in London surrendered to William are described in different ways by contemporary chroniclers. William of Jumièges claims that the Normans had to fight a bloody battle against 'a large company of rebels' in the 'central square of the city', but William of Poitiers, 'Florence of Worcester' and other writers agree that the Saxon bishops and earls, along with the leading citizens of London, surrendered peacefully to William at Berkhamsted, nearly 30 miles north-west of the city. As the *Anglo-Saxon Chronicle* puts it:

'They submitted out of necessity after most damage had been done – and it was a great piece of folly that they had not done it earlier.'[2] William was crowned in Westminster Abbey on Christmas Day 1066, and in return issued a writ (which still survives) greeting the bishop, portreeve and burgesses of London, and confirming rights of inheritance:

> I give you to know that I will that you be worthy of all the laws you were worthy of in the time of King Edward. And I will that every child shall be his father's heir after his father's day. And I will not suffer any man to do you wrong. God preserve you.

An unfortunate incident marred the Coronation Day. The noise of the citizens acclaiming William as king was taken by his guards as the sound of rebellion, and 'without reason they started to set fire to the city'.[3]

Although the Norman Conquest is usually taken to be one of the few decisive turning-points in English history, so much so that lists of monarchs often omit the Anglo-Saxon kings, it does not mark a fresh start in London's development. Most of the familiar features of early medieval London were already in place before 1066. The commercial economy had been re-established, and London was already England's leading city in terms of wealth, population and national and international trade, including trade with Normandy. The streets had taken on much of their medieval pattern, and the great expansion of church-building was already well advanced. The guilds and fraternities of medieval London were anticipated in the *cnihtengild* and frith gild. In the government of the town, both the sheriff and the court of Husting made an easy transition from the Saxon to the Norman period, and the next major change, the creation of the mayor, did not happen for over a century. The subdivision of the city into twenty-four wards was probably already taking place, although they are not listed until 1127, and the emergence of the aldermen as leaders of the wards and members of the City's governing council had its origins in the Husting and its ancestors, although they do not appear in the written record as leaders of wards until 1111.[4] London's administrative and ecclesiastical subdivisions were not completely formed by 1066, but the arrival of the Normans was not a turning-point in their development. This continuity of development despite the great upheaval of the Conquest was not confined to London. According to Susan Reynolds, 'It is difficult to see any significant change in English urban institutions which can be attributed to the Conquest.'[5]

William I's most enduring impact on London's topography came from his need to build strongholds, as William of Poitiers tells us, 'against the fickleness of the vast and fierce populace'. By the end of William's reign in

1087, London was guarded in the west by Baynard's Castle and Montfichet Tower, both located within the walls, south of Ludgate and south-west of St Paul's, and in the south-east by the White Tower, making London safe from future Danish attacks. Montfichet, the least important of the three, was destroyed in 1276 to provide land and stone for the new house and church of the Blackfriars. Baynard's Castle was demolished for the same reason, but it was rebuilt a little to the east of Blackfriars, resting on the Roman riverside wall. Its remains were discovered in 1972, but then destroyed in subsequent redevelopment. The Church provided safer tenants, as far as Edward I was concerned, than the aristocracy.[6] The White Tower probably began as a wooden fort on an earth mound, but after 1078 it was rebuilt in Caen limestone by Bishop Gundulf of Rochester, the architect of Rochester Castle. It still remains, a massive reminder of Norman military dominance, as the keep of the present Tower of London, surrounded by outer walls built in the thirteenth century by Henry III and Edward I.

LONDON AND THE CROWN

The custodians of Baynard's Castle, Montfichet and the Tower were important feudal magnates, men of great influence in the early medieval city. In the twelfth century the lords of Baynard's Castle successfully claimed control over all fishing in the rivers from the castle west to Staines, and were apparently regarded as the leaders of the London militia in time of war. The castellan of the Tower of London could dominate London on the King's behalf or, occasionally, his own. Although not much is known about the relations between London and the first three Norman kings, there is no doubt that while the three castles were held by loyal men the monarch had the upper hand. Even when London was hostile, beleaguered kings could take refuge in the Tower, and hold out there till their fortunes improved. In a period of weak kingship the power of a rogue castellan, such as the mighty Geoffrey de Mandeville, custodian of the Tower during the civil war between King Stephen and the Empress Matilda in the early 1140s, could gravely threaten London's rights and prosperity, as well as the king's. The intermediaries between the City and the Norman kings were the sheriffs, usually two at a time, who were responsible for collecting London's taxes and delivering a fixed annual sum, or farm, to the royal Exchequer. Until 1130 and probably for most of the twelfth century these were royal appointees, perhaps chosen because of their landholdings or other interests in London, and for their ability to establish a smooth working relationship between the king and one of his main sources of financial support.[7]

During the twelfth century London, or rather London's ruling élite of aldermen, began to achieve a degree of self-government, especially the right to choose their own sheriff. Concessions could be won in times of crisis from weak kings, who would trade their direct control over London for money and political support. This is what Stephen seems to have done in 1135, at the beginning of his twelve-year struggle for control of England against Henry I's daughter Matilda. It is not certain exactly what Stephen promised in 1135, but in 1141, when he was Matilda's captive and desperately needed support, he recognized London as a commune, a self-governing urban confederation with the right to choose its own officials and collect its own taxes. The existence of independent towns such as those of Northern France or Northern Italy was unacceptable to Norman and Angevin kings, and although the commune was recognized briefly in 1141 and a little more permanently in 1191 it generally remained an ideal that was unattainable, except in a diluted form. There is no reason to suppose, though, that Londoners welcomed weak kingship because of the liberties it enabled them to take. A trading city needs peace and security above all, and it may be that London was only forced to seek greater powers when the king was too weak to protect its interests, or to defend it against an overmighty constable of the Tower. A strong and undisputed ruler such as Henry I (1100–1135), Henry II (1154–89), or Edward I (1272–1307) would want much closer control over his chief city, and would have ample means with which to achieve it.[8]

When royal power hung in the balance, as in Stephen's reign, and during John's struggles with William Longchamp in 1191 and with the barons in 1215–16, London's men, money and strategic position could help tilt the scales. In return for the recognition of commune status and other concessions, and spurred on by the Empress Matilda's high-handed treatment when she held the City in 1141, London contributed greatly to Stephen's survival as King. In 1141, with Stephen in captivity and Matilda on the point of being crowned in Westminster, the Londoners responded to the arrival of Stephen's queen (also called Matilda) with an army outside the City by rising *en masse* to attack the Empress and her supporters during her pre-coronation feast, forcing them to flee while 'a mob of citizens, great beyond expression or calculation, entered their abandoned lodgings' and plundered them. As well as preventing Matilda from gaining legitimacy through a coronation, London provided men for the siege of Winchester, which led to Stephen's release, and probably kept the King supplied with money throughout the civil war.[9]

THE LIBERTIES OF LONDON

Since the struggle for a degree of independence from direct royal control and feudal restrictions is such an important theme in the history of twelfth- and thirteenth-century London, it is necessary to establish what the leading citizens wanted, apart from the vague 'commune' aspiration. The famous charter granted to London by Henry I between 1130 and 1133 is our best guide here. The terms of this charter are surprisingly generous ones to have been conceded by a strong king, and this, along with the fact that the original of the document does not exist (although charters were usually lovingly preserved), has led to serious doubts about its authenticity. It may instead have been granted by Stephen in 1141, or just be a forgery intended to strengthen London's claims to privileges later in the century.[10]

Genuine or not, the charter gives us a very full picture of the rights and powers that leading Londoners aspired to in these years. These included, above all, the right to choose their own sheriff and their own justice, and to administer their financial and judicial affairs without outside interference and in their own courts. 'No one else shall be justice over these men of London.' The tax farm should be fixed at £300, rather than over £500. Londoners should be allowed to trade free of all tolls and taxes all over England, and they should be given powers to reclaim all debts owing to them. Various troublesome traditional burdens were to be removed: Danegeld, murder-fine (a communal fine for an unsolved murder), excessive fines of over £5, the billeting of the royal household in London, trial by combat, and penalties for technical errors in the hustings and folkmoot procedure. Churches, barons and citizens should continue to enjoy the revenues from their sokes, and citizens should retain their hunting rights in Middlesex, Surrey and the Chilterns.[11] This last privilege was important in a society where illicit hunting in royal forests could be punished by the loss of '*oculos et testiculos*'.

Even a strong king might accept some of these claims, since London's prosperity provided income for the Crown. Henry II recognized many of the liberties listed in Henry I's charter, but he removed the two most important ones, London's right to appoint its own sheriff and justice. The implication of the 1155 document is that these rights had not existed in Henry I's day. Furthermore Henry, who had no intention of pandering to

London's pretensions to independence, raised the tax farm to over £500.[12] Londoners had to wait for Henry II's death in 1189, and the succession in turn of his two sons, Richard I (1189–99) and John (1199–1216), for the achievement of their programme of civic rights. While Richard was in Palestine in 1190–92 John and Richard's Chancellor and Constable of the Tower, Longchamp, struggled for control of the kingdom. Longchamp had Richard's authority, but he was unpopular in London. In October 1191 John advanced on the City in force, and Longchamp took refuge in the Tower, while citizens watched to prevent his escape. Meanwhile the leading citizens agreed with John's friends in London, led by Richard fitz Reiner, that they would open the gates to John, and help him gain control of the kingdom, in return for his recognition of the commune. On 8 October, the day after his entry into the city, John held an historic gathering of nobles, bishops and citizens, in which he granted London commune status, in return for recognition as Richard's heir presumptive. This was something, a hostile chronicler recorded, 'which neither King Richard nor his predecessor and father, Henry, would have allowed to be done for a million silver marks. How many evils arise from the conspiracy may be gathered from its very definition, which is this: a commune is the tumult of the people, the terror of the realm, and the tepidity of the priesthood.' In practice, John had accepted London's right to organize itself roughly as Rouen, Soissons and Liège had already done, with a civic leader called a mayor, and a ruling group of *échevins*, or skivins, who were perhaps only aldermen with a new French name. In return Londoners besieged Longchamp in the Tower, forced him into surrender and exile, and allowed John to take control of the kingdom.[13]

What happened to the commune for the rest of Richard's and John's reigns is not known in detail, except that Henry fitz Ailwin, a member of one of the old English families still powerful in Norman London, held the mayoralty continuously until his death in 1212, and the skivins disappeared, to be replaced by the long-established leaders of the twenty-four wards, the aldermen. London remained aloof from John's rebellion against the King in 1194, and in return for this and a gift of 1,500 marks (£1,000) Richard renewed Henry II's charter, and tacitly accepted the commune. On his accession in 1199 John also allowed the commune to stand, without formally acknowledging it, and accepted the important principle that London should appoint its own sheriffs, in return for 3,000 marks. It was not until May 1215, when he was embroiled in the baronial troubles that were soon to produce Magna Carta, that John granted London a new charter, introducing the principle of an annually elected mayor, 'who shall be faithful to us, discreet and fit to govern the City'. This crucial concession won the majority of citizens to John's side, but a smaller faction opened the gates to the barons on 17 May, enabling them to use the City as their headquarters in their negotiations with the King over the following month. London did not gain much from its enforced alliance with the victorious barons. True, its 'ancient liberties and free customs' were confirmed in the final agreement at Runnymede in June 1215, but what it really wanted was freedom from arbitrary royal taxation, 'tallages and aids', all reference to which was omitted from the revised version of Magna Carta issued in 1216.[14]

MAYOR AND ALDERMEN

The framework of London's constitution that emerged from John's reign retained its shape for the rest of the Middle Ages, although its rulers were not drawn throughout from the same social groups. The sheriffs, rulers of London until 1190, were from now onwards elected members of the City oligarchy, still intermediaries between king and City, with the burdensome task of collecting the tax farm, but increasingly subordinate to the mayor. Sheriffs were still leading citizens, the 'eyes of the mayor', and part of the group from whom future mayors would usually be drawn. The sheriff's court lost its old importance, and handled mainly cases of trespass and debt, while important cases went before the Husting, where the mayor now presided with sheriffs and aldermen in attendance, or (increasingly) the mayor's court, which from the early thirteenth century onwards took on the work which the weekly Husting could not manage.[15]

The mayor was the City's chief magistrate and legislator, at the same time the effective leader of London's government and the embodiment of its corporate identity in rituals and pageantry, which became more ostentatious as time went on. In spite of these almost royal trappings no mayor after fitz Ailwin served for life, although from 1214 to 1337, when a few powerful families dominated city politics, fourteen mayors held the office for between three and eight years each. After this, mayors usually served for one or two years, though Sir Nicholas Brembre served five times between 1376 and 1386, and Richard Whittington was mayor in 1397, 1406 and 1419, the last medieval mayor to serve more than two terms. The mayor was elected from among the aldermen each October by a gathering of the commonalty, those who had gained, by apprenticeship, inheritance or purchase, the right to call themselves citizens or freemen of London.

Exactly who was entitled to attend this gathering was a matter of controversy. On rare and radical occasions a large proportion of London's several thousand freemen crowded into the Guildhall to elect a popular figure of their choice. Sometimes the attempt succeeded, as with the election of Thomas fitz Thomas in the 1260s, but more often, as in the repeated failure to elect a tailor, Ralph Holland, in 1439–44, it did not. These occasions were usually followed by a decree announcing that 'to prevent tumults' the election of mayors and sheriffs should be confined, 'as of old accustomed', to men individually summoned to attend, 'the more discreet and powerful citizens', *'probi homines'*, 'good men', 'wealthier and wiser men', and so on. In short, the electorate was packed with voters who could be relied upon to approve one of the senior men that the aldermen themselves had in mind.[16] This was not sham democracy, but a reflection of the belief that the decisions of the leading men of the community would inspire approval and consensus among lesser citizens. 'Sufficient and discreet citizens' of the wards might also find themselves called to consult with the mayor and aldermen on matters of importance to the City, in a gathering that was later to be known as the Common Council. Such meetings were summoned several times in the 1280s and 1290s, and perhaps represented an older tradition of selective consultation. The early fourteenth-century City records make it plain that by that time the citizens called to the Guildhall for consultation were elected, generally by their wards and occasionally (as in 1312 and 1351) by their crafts.[17] Those below the level of citizenship – apprentices, labourers, women and the destitute – were not asked their opinion and were not expected to offer it.

The courts and electoral assemblies of the City were always held in a great hall known as the Guildhall, standing roughly on the site it still occupies, near the south-east corner of the Roman fort and on the site of the ancient amphitheatre. The origins of the Guildhall are uncertain. There is a possible reference to a Guildhall in a charter of 1127, and archaeologists have discovered foundations dating from about that time. Although Fitzstephen does not mention it in 1170, Gerald of Wales, writing about twenty years later, talks about a hall for public meetings which was also a well-known drinking house.[18] The Guildhall was used for courts and assemblies in the thirteenth century, and was probably rebuilt between 1270 and 1290, with a stone undercroft which survives as the western part of the crypt of the present Guildhall. It is hard to believe that the early Guildhall was 'an olde and lytell cotage', but by 1411 it was considered too unimpressive to match the swelling importance of the city's rulers and the dignity of civic ceremony, and a new building was begun under the supervision of the master mason John Croxton. Croxton's Guildhall, which took nearly thirty years to complete, still survives, although the roof, the front, the windows, and many internal details have been altered and restored after fire and bombing.[19]

In normal circumstances thirteenth- and fourteenth-century London was ruled by a wealthy élite, a group of twenty-four aldermen (twenty-five after 1394), the leaders of the City wards. In the thirteenth century aldermen generally went through a process of election by the *probi homines*, or 'respectable men', of their ward, with the mayor and aldermen having a final veto over the choice. Once elected, they held office for life, unless the king removed them, despite short-lived attempts in 1319 and 1376 to introduce annual elections. In practice these elections involved very little freedom of choice, and many alderman seem to have held office almost by proprietary or hereditary right. The prior of Holy Trinity Priory was always the alderman of Portsoken, the large ward east of the city wall, and until the later Middle Ages many other wards were probably dominated by the families who held (or had once held) rights of private jurisdiction, or sokes, over them. Stow's *Survey of London* gives an account of the purchase in 1281 of the aldermanry of Farringdon ward from Thomas de Aderne by Ralph le Fevre. The ward passed to his son, Nicholas de Farndon (four times mayor of London), who bequeathed it in 1334 to John de Pulteney (also four times mayor).[20]

Aldermen had enormous power at both ward and City level. The mayor was chosen from their number, and sitting with the mayor in the Husting they were the effective governors and justices of the City. Those who insulted them were humiliated by public penance, and traditionally anyone who struck an alderman could lose his hand. Until the fourteenth century most wards were known by the name of their alderman (in the judicial hearings of 1276 only Portsoken and Cheap wards were not), and within the ward the alderman maintained order, organized defence and military service, and presided over the ward courts, the wardmotes, which heard local cases and ran the daily administration of their district. Their rewards came in the form of power, prestige, income from various fees and fines, and the ability to shape city policy to harmonize with their social and economic interests.[21]

THE RULING ÉLITE

Thirteenth-century aldermen came from the richest sections of London society, and drew their wealth from three main sources: land, royal patronage and commerce. They all owned property acquired by inheritance, marriage or purchase: sokes, shops, tenements, selds (large indoor bazaars), warehouses, quays, urban mansions and rural manors, often spread over many parishes and several counties. Most members of London's élite were also enriched by royal employment or contracts. Almost half the aldermen and sheriffs of the period 1200–1340 whose interests have been identified held posts in the Exchequer or the Wardrobe, or as royal suppliers or contractors, or in some other branch of royal service. Even those without a Court appointment were more than likely to be involved in satisfying the royal household's growing appetite for wine, cloth, furs and provisions. A third of the aldermen of 1200–63 identified by Gwyn Williams were involved in supplying the Court with wine.[22]

Although rich Londoners were involved in trade, before the fourteenth century they were not as a rule full-time merchants, and certainly not specialist traders in one commodity. For the efficient use of shipping, and to maintain the supply of money they needed for the conduct of their trade, importers needed to be exporters too. For instance grocers, importers and distributors of spices, wax, dyes, fruit and alum, were also exporters of wool and woollen cloth. The interests of most trading fraternities were equally complex, and it is a mistake to think of them as being concerned only with the commodity which gave their association its name. The ruling families of the early and mid-thirteenth century, the Basings, Bukerels, Blunds, Viels, Rokesleys and Gisors, generally traded wholesale in wine, wool and cloth. The pattern changed a little in the upheavals of Edward I's reign (1272–1307), and in the fourteenth century dealers in fur, leather, fish, corn and groceries joined the vintners and the now dominant wool and cloth traders in the court of aldermen. As the prosperity of different trades rose and fell, and as Londoners won or lost control of trade in particular commodities, so dominance within the élite passed from one mercantile interest to another. But from the fourteenth century to the eighteenth wealthy merchants maintained their predominance in city government, broken only in a few exceptional years.

London merchants were usually participants in commercial enterprises which foreign merchants, Flemish, Gascon, Picard, Italian and German, controlled, and the ambivalent relationship between citizens and aliens is a theme that runs right through the history of medieval London. The relationship was not always hostile. Londoners needed the commodities brought by aliens, and cherished the right to distribute alien imports in London and the provinces. When aliens gained control of England's wool or cloth exports, as their wealth and royal favour often allowed them to do, London merchants petitioned and protested, but the greatest threat to London's prosperity came when aliens took their trade elsewhere, to the provincial fairs or a rival port, perhaps Boston, Hull or Southampton. It was vital to London that it should remain the main conduit through which English imports and exports flowed, and the alien presence, irritating as it sometimes became, was a crucial part of this. The guarantee of a right of travel and trade for alien merchants in England, 'free from all evil tolls', and a promise of fair treatment for enemy aliens in wartime, was included in Magna Carta probably at the request of Londoners.[23]

De Montfort and the Common Citizens

Although the ruling élite did not exclude outsiders, and indeed constantly refilled its death-depleted ranks with rising Londoners and successful provincial immigrants, it did its best to ensure that lesser citizens (and of course all non-citizens) were excluded from the effective conduct of civic affairs. Occasionally this exclusion broke down, and a surge of popular feeling, aroused by a national crisis, a scandal over corrupt tax collection, or the resentment felt by craftsmen against their mercantile masters, propelled a popular mayor into office. There is a good example of this in the early 1260s, when Henry III's power was challenged by Simon de Montfort's baronial revolt. Heavy taxation, royal favouritism towards alien merchants (especially the Cahorsins, from Henry's lands in south-western France), the King's repeated interventions in London's government, and his very damaging establishment in 1245 of two new annual fairs in Westminster, had impoverished and infuriated London's traders and craftsmen.[24] Popular support for de Montfort exploded into violence on the streets of London in June 1263, and in July Henry's queen, Eleanor, was pelted and abused by the London mob as she tried to get from the Tower to Windsor. The aldermen were desperate that the City should not commit itself irreversibly to one side in a conflict whose outcome was unpredictable, but when the Mayor, Thomas fitz Thomas, put himself at the head of the popular movement, aldermanic authority crumbled. One of the aldermen, Arnold fitz Thedmar, later wrote an aggrieved account of fitz Thomas's excursion into popular democracy:

> This mayor ... had so pampered the City populace, that, styling themselves the "Commons of the City", they had obtained the first voice in the City. For the Mayor, in doing all that he had to do, acted and determined through them, and would say to them, – "Is it your will that so it shall be?" and then, if they answered "Ya, Ya", so it was done. And on the other hand, the aldermen or chief citizens were little or not at all consulted on such matter; but were in fact just as though they had not existed.[25]

In the civil war of 1263–5, the support of London's common citizens gave de Montfort a refuge and a stronghold. They saved him from destruction in December 1263 by opening the City gates to his army when it was trapped in Southwark, with royal armies advancing from Croydon and Merton. London provided the bulk of de Montfort's infantry in the capture of Rochester in April 1264, and the majority of his casualties in his victory over the King at Lewes in May.[26]

In the disorderly events of 1263–5 we can see some of the ambitions and resentments of lesser citizens coming to the surface. Acting through the resuscitated popular Folkmoot, not the élite-dominated Husting, the citizens pulled down houses and enclosures built by aldermen on public streets and land, and asserted the right of craftsmen to organize and control their trades under the protection of civic ordinances. There was an uglier side to popular self-indulgence. There were ferocious attacks on the Jews, leaving about 500 dead, and French and Italian merchants had to take shelter alongside them in the Tower. These policies, which were recorded with outrage by fitz Thedmar, ended in 1265 with the defeat of de Montfort at Evesham, and the return of Henry III to punish Londoners, regardless of the positions they had adopted individually, for their communal disloyalty.[27] Sixty leading Londoners, including many royalists, were dispossessed (though some recovered their property later), a massive fine of 20,000 marks (£13,333) was imposed on the town, and its liberties were suspended for two years. These penalties were long remembered as the cost of deviating from the principle which guided so many of London's political interventions from the days of Cnut to those of Henry VIII: always to choose the winning side.

THE IMPACT OF EDWARD I

Prince Edward, who had been closely involved with the control and punishment of London in the 1260s, became King in 1272. Edward I's policy towards London is a reminder that all its charters meant as little in the face of a king determined to bend the City to his will as they did when a great baronial army was at the gates, with friends inside to open them. London's closeness to Westminster, which gave the town great influence when the monarch was weak, made it all the more vulnerable to royal control when the king's power revived. The conqueror of Wales and the Hammer of the Scots was not one to allow London's civic liberties, some of them of questionable validity, to impede the exercise of his royal prerogative. Edward was not motivated by particular hostility towards London, but by a determination to crack down on disorder, corruption and lawlessness throughout the realm by introducing a comprehensive reform of policing, justice and central government. London, whatever its pretensions to self-government, could not be exempted from these changes, and its rebellion against Edward's father showed that it was in dire need of them. To strengthen his control over the City, Edward pursued his father's rebuilding and reinforcement of the Tower, completing his work on the Inner Wall and adding a new Outer Wall. At about the same time he destroyed what was left of Baynard and Montfichet Castles, which were as likely to be used by rebels as by loyal men, and handed their sites to trusted religious orders.[28]

At first Edward acted indirectly, pushing a mayor of his choice, Henry le Waleys, into a campaign between 1281 and 1284 against curfew-breakers, criminals, dishonest tradesmen, and all those unruly elements that had made London ungovernable in the 1260s. Edward's direct intervention was prompted by an ugly outbreak of disorder and feuding, culminating in the lynching in July 1284 of a leading goldsmith, Laurence Duket, in St Mary-le-Bow church, by the henchmen of Alderman Ralph Crepyn, Common Clerk of the City. A year later, following a riot in Newgate gaol, Edward established a judicial commission to investigate disorder in London, and when the mayor and aldermen protested the King replaced them with a royal warden, Ralph of Sandwich. New ordinances were issued in 1285, introducing firmer policing and tougher punishments, bringing the court of Husting into line with national common law principles, and injecting more professionalism into City administration. Most devastating of all, they gave alien merchants full trading rights in London and swept aside the valuable commercial and retailing privileges enjoyed by London citizens. In 1289, as a final humiliation, the royal Treasurer was installed in the Guildhall to administer the City's finances.[29]

Edward I's reforms created a more complex, bureaucratic, expensive and well-documented system of government for London, and integrated the City into a national system of justice and administration. London's three most important paid officials, the Common Clerk, the Recorder and the Common Sergeant, date from Edward I's reign, and so do the Tun (a new prison on Cornhill) and the Stocks, a new food market. The reforms also initiated the accumulation of legal and administrative records, the letter books and court rolls, which have so enriched the study of medieval London.[30] Gwyn Williams, in his influential and complex account of London's economic and political development in the thirteenth and fourteeth centuries, claimed that Edward I's reign 'was a watershed in the history of London', in which the political power so long monopolized by a closed circle of patrician families was opened up to the very social groups which had given their support to de Montfort in the 1260s, the craftsmen and the lesser trades. By breaking the continuity of control enjoyed until the 1280s by a privileged élite, he argues, Edward I's direct rule enabled rising mercantile interests, fishmongers, skinners, Baltic traders and corn-mongers, to break into the aldermanic circle. London's mayor and charter were restored in 1298, but the ruling oligarchy of interconnected families was broken, and London's administrative and political climate was changed for good.[31]

Pamela Nightingale, in her recent study of the grocers, or pepperers, one of the mercantile groups which Williams included in London's ruling 'patriciate', rejects this interpretation of the events of Edward I's reign. The thirteenth-century pepperers were not a 'dynastic' group of intermarried families, nor were they especially prosperous or well organized. High mortality rates made it very unlikely that London's dominant families would last long enough to be regarded as 'dynasties', though a few managed to stay at the top of civic life for several generations.[32] Along with other London merchants, the pepperers endured a long period of recession in the first seventy years of the thirteenth century, while great provincial fairs and the east coast ports took the lion's share of the wool trade. Flemish merchants, who derived ample supplies of bullion from their cloth trade with Germany, were able to sell their cloth and buy their supplies of English wool in provincial fairs, by-passing London in favour of the more convenient and freer east coast ports, Boston and Lynn. Neither the wool nor the wealth it generated passed through London, and without wool,

London pepperers had nothing to exchange for the spices, wax, silk and other valuables they had once brought back from Genoa and Northern Spain,¹ and England's spice trade fell into the hands of Italians, Cahorsins (from southern France) and Spaniards.[33]

The Wool Trade and the Staple

Flemish control of the provincial wool trade, which depressed the whole of London's overseas commerce in the thirteenth century, came to an abrupt end in 1270, when all Flemish merchants in England were arrested as a result of a dispute between England and Flanders. By the time the dispute was settled in 1287 the Flemings had lost their position in the English wool trade to Italian and Hanseatic (North German) merchants, who were happy to wait in the capital while London merchants toured the provincial fairs buying the wool that would eventually be exported to pay for Baltic and Mediterranean imports. The tendency of Italian and Hanseatic merchants to operate through London was partly a matter of custom, but largely sprang from the fact that they could get the best price for their imports in London, not at the provincial fairs. Edward I's wars, which made the longer east coast sea routes more dangerous, also promoted the concentration on London. After eighty years in the doldrums, the pepperers' fortunes revived in the 1270s and 1280s as they toured the provincial fairs, selling wax, almonds, sugar and spices and buying up wool for their Italian and Hansard partners. In the 1280s, when Edward I's export tax on wool gives us the first good statistics on the trade, London exported about 7,000 sacks of wool a year, a little behind Boston (9,600 sacks), but well ahead of Hull, Southampton and Lynn. By 1297 London's wool exports (at nearly 9,000 sacks) were 50 per cent higher than Boston's, and about a third of the English total. Londoners and London-based aliens continued to dominate the wool trade in the early fourteenth century, handling about 40 per cent of exports to Boston's 20 per cent.[34] It made sense now for large Italian galleys to navigate the difficult Gibraltar route loaded with alum, spices and luxury cloth for London, since they could return with cargoes of English wool for the growing Florentine cloth industry. After a century on the sidelines, while provincial fairs, east coast ports and Flemish merchants had taken the bulk of the vital wool trade, London was back in the centre of the picture.[35]

As London's economy started to take off, migrants flocked to the city, especially from East Anglia, the South-East and the East Midlands, either to buy their citizenship, take up an apprenticeship, or labour for a wage. Stimulated by the revival of commerce, the crafts and trades that fed, shod, furnished and clothed London's thriving population expanded too, either in the City itself or illicitly on its outskirts. It was this growth in population and economic activity that created the disorder that led Edward I to take direct control of the City in 1285. Fearing the threat of unbridled competition from migrants or the alien merchants favoured by Edward I, the more organized crafts and trades appealed for the ratification of rules that excluded outsiders, and pressed for representation on the Court of Aldermen to give their crafts greater protection. Some crafts – fishmongers, skinners, ropers, cornmongers, ironmongers – achieved this representation in the late thirteenth century, and the rivalry between craft and mercantile guilds injected a new element of contention into aldermanic elections in the years ahead. In 1298, in return for their newly won status, the Mayor (Henry le Waleys again) made the craft and trade guilds responsible for enrolling and policing the men of their mistery or trade.[36]

Edward I needed a large and steady supply of loans and taxes to finance his campaigns in France, Wales and Scotland, and to secure this supply he initiated several innovative policies which had profound effects on London's long-term economic development. Edward had acquired since the 1260s an understanding of international trade and ways in which it could be regulated and taxed, and in 1275 he introduced England's first regular national customs duties (on exports of wool, wool fells and leather). Other kings had readily fleeced the wool merchants when they needed money, but none had done so as systematically as Edward, who introduced a structure for organizing and exploiting English trade which lasted for 300 years. Other goods were taxed, but wool, the greatest trading commodity, was hit the hardest, with an export duty of half a mark (6s 8d) a sack. The long-term effect of this and subsequent export taxes was to give English cloth producers (who got their wool untaxed) a price advantage over their great Flemish rivals, and to enable them, during the course of the fourteenth century, to develop a product which could match or beat Flemish cloth in European markets. In the mid-fourteenth century, while wool exports declined, the domestic cloth industry flourished, and woollen cloth became England's main manufactured product and London's chief export for the next four centuries.[37]

Collecting these taxes was not easy, and to make payment more certain and trade safer Edward I initiated the policy of encouraging wool merchants to concentrate their transactions in one or more specified towns, known as staples (from the old French word *estaple*, an emporium or mart). The obvious place for these staples was in the Low Countries, the destination of most English wool exports, and in the 1290s Edward introduced voluntary staples in various convenient towns, including Dordrecht, Brabant, Malines and Antwerp. The staple policy was formalized by Edward II, who established a compulsory staple at St Omer in 1313. This forced alien exporters (especially those from the Low Countries) to make an inconvenient detour, and gave an advantage to London merchants, who administered the staple in their own interest. Military and political considerations forced the government to move the staple from time to time, and Antwerp, Bruges and Middelburg were chosen at various times in the fourteenth century. Different London merchants preferred different staples, depending on which was the best centre for the purchase of the goods they imported: St Omer for wine, Bruges for spices and Italian goods, Antwerp for Baltic supplies.[38] Finally Calais, which was captured in 1347, was fixed upon as the best choice, and it remained the one staple (with occasional breaks) from 1363 until its loss to the French in 1558.

These arrangements seem obscure and complex now, but to London merchants they might mean the difference between prosperity and hardship. Commercial policies, rather than the abstract constitutional principles so emphasized by Victorian historians, probably shaped London merchants' attitudes towards royal government. The staple policy especially favoured London merchants, because the inconvenience of shipping wool to an intermediate port discouraged alien exporters, and London was better placed than the other main wool-exporting towns, particularly Boston, for trade with Flanders. London's advantages were greatest in times of war, when its merchants could organize protective convoys, and its shorter sea route was the safest available. The men who controlled London's wool exports to the staple, the staplers, became a dominant force in London's political and economic life, though their supremacy faded as the wool trade declined in the later Middle Ages. From time to time, the continental staple was abandoned in favour of a group of home staples, through which all wool exports had to pass. This drew alien merchants to England, and gave landlords a better price for their wool, but it tended to harm the trade of English merchants, by allowing aliens to export directly from England to their destination ports. Londoners had some consolation, because London was usually one of the few major ports chosen as a staple, and thus wool exports and imported goods were still channelled through the capital. They were therefore generally happy with a home staple policy. All these benefits were diminished or destroyed, though, when the king sold exemptions to Italian or alien merchants, or granted them free or exclusive trading rights, as he sometimes did. By doing this a king could unite the bulk of London's merchants and lesser traders against him (except for those whose interests were tied up with royal service or consumption), but he might be prepared to take this risk in time of war, when the government needed Italian loans and taxes, and perhaps the naval assistance of Genoese shipping.[39]

ALIENS AND THE CROWN

London's prime importance to medieval kings was as a source of loans, taxes and gifts. Ever since the reign of William I English kings had relied on alien financiers for the loans they always needed. Jews, who settled in London and several provincial towns after 1066, were the main source of loans until the middle of the thirteenth century, by which time they had been so impoverished by royal taxation and extortion, and penalized by anti-usury laws, that they had lost their usefulness. A series of very heavy royal levies between 1241 and 1255 devastated Jewish finances, and forced Jewish creditors to sell their debts to non-Jews at cut prices. In addition, the crusading spirit induced Henry III to introduce harsh anti-Jewish laws in 1253, and public fury over a trumped-up ritual murder case in York in 1255 provided a pretext for murderous attacks on London Jews in the 1260s. Simon de Montfort, later mythologized as a champion of English liberty, inspired the worst massacre in 1264. Edward I expelled the Jews from England in 1290, and their stone houses and synagogues, concentrated in the area near Cheapside still known as Old Jewry, were taken over by Christians. Only those who had been converted to Christianity were allowed to stay, lodged in a House of Converts in Chancery Lane, built for them by Henry III in 1232. There is no evidence of a last rush of converts, although conversion was made more attractive in the 1280s, when converts were allowed to retain a life interest in half their property, rather than surrendering it all to the Crown, as they had previously done.[40]

To replace the Jews, Edward I turned to alien, especially Italian, merchants, whose ample capital (derived from trade, banking and collecting papal taxes in England), and their dependence on Crown protection, made them ideal royal financiers. The biggest Italian merchant families, the Riccardi, Frescobaldi, Bardi and Peruzzi, were immensely wealthy, far richer than London's richest traders. They had excellent trading connections with English monasteries, which were major wool producers, and with the Italian cloth industry, and most of England's wool exports were in their hands. Their ample supplies of bullion and Mediterranean luxuries gave them a clear advantage over native London traders. Alien merchants were almost as unpopular in London as the Jews were, but royal policy was generally to favour any group rich enough to pay for the King's protection. Edward I used his period of direct rule over London (1285–98) to assert the rights of alien merchants and to protect them against the sharp practices and false weights of Londoners. In return for paying extra import and export duties, alien merchants, whether Italian, French, Flemish or German, were given full rights of trade, travel and residence in England, free of all local tolls and restrictions, and guaranteed a fair hearing of their commercial and criminal cases in special piepowder courts (for itinerant merchants with *pie poudrous*, or dusty feet). These rules were imposed on London by Edward I in 1285, and on England in the *Carta Mercatoria* of 1303.[41] Such privileges were galling to London merchants and retailers, and they struggled, with occasional success, to have them revoked. But the growth of alien trade which the *Carta Mercatoria* created was an immense stimulus to the London economy. The customs records suggest that in the period 1303–11, when aliens were favoured, London's share of national trade was high, and in 1311–22, when alien privileges were removed, London's trade slumped. In the 1350s and 1360s, when Londoners' trading privileges were suspended and aliens had freedom of the City's trade, London's share of England's alien trade rose to about 70 per cent, and the City (if not its citizens) was at the centre of the national trading network.[42]

Edward I was replaced by his inadequate son, Edward II, and his Gascon favourite, Piers Gaveston, in 1307. London soon became involved in the fierce struggle between the King and a group of barons known as the Ordainers, who bid for London's favour by announcing the abolition of the *Carta Mercatoria* and its alien privileges in 1311. Hostility to aliens and other outsiders drew the wider body of citizens into the dispute, and the Mayor, John de Gisors, warned alien merchants not to stay in London more than forty days. The suspension of the *Carta Mercatoria*, along with the establishment of the St Omer Staple two years later, gave native Londoners a greater share of the wool trade, but the next few years were overshadowed by Edward II's terrible defeat at Bannockburn and the great famine of 1315–18, when rain and disease destroyed crops and herds, and London wheat prices doubled. Hardship and commercial crisis created popular discontent, and a group of mercers, led by the demagogue William de Hackford and supported by the King's new favourite, Hugh le Despenser, were able to exploit the anti-alien mood and win leadership of the City in 1319. The outcome of this popular movement was a new charter, which the King accepted in June 1319.[43]

The constitutional significance of this charter, so strongly emphasized in traditional histories of London, is now disputed.[44] Many of its strongest clauses were directed, in a fairly traditional way, against alien merchants and the privileges they had been granted by Edward I and his son. But there were constitutional changes too, albeit ones which had rather limited practical effects: mayors were to hold office for one year only, aldermen were to be elected annually and not to sit for two consecutive years, and the commonalty (the assembly of common citizens) was to elect and control paid City officials, and share custody of the common seal of the City. One clause marked a real advance in the power and privileges of the crafts: 'No man of English birth and especially no English merchant, who followed any specific mistery or craft, was to be admitted to the freedom of the City except on the security of six reputable men of that mistery or craft.' This was an important breakthrough for the craft guilds, since from this constitutional base each craft or mistery (the word derives from the old French *mestier*, meaning a calling or trade) was able to gain control over admittance to its particular branch of trade or manufacture in the century ahead. As a French chronicler wrote of 1319: 'At this time many of the people of the trades of London were arrayed in livery, and a good time was about to begin.'[45]

This was not strictly true. In 1322, after the defeat of the Ordainers, the King placed London under the control of Hugh le Despenser, whose task was to extract money from the City to fund the war against Robert the Bruce. Despenser's oppressive and rapacious rule, and his restoration of the *Carta Mercatoria* to win favour with alien financiers, antagonized London opinion at all social levels, to such a degree that when Queen Isabella and her lover, Mortimer, landed in England in September 1326 the furious hostility of the London crowd to Edward and his friends played a key role in their triumph. In October the King fled the City and Londoners rose in support of Isabella, whose letters calling for their help were posted all over the town. Nobody associated with royal government was safe from the mob. The leader of the Gascon merchants was murdered, and Edward's Treasurer, Bishop Stapledon of Exeter, was beheaded with a butcher's knife in Cheapside. His head was sent to the Queen, and his naked body was dragged through the streets. Throughout the crisis, the collusion of the city élite and the menace of the London mob were vital to Mortimer's success. When some of the Members of Parliament who were assembled in Westminster to depose the King in 1327 hesitated, Mortimer used the threatening presence of the London mob in Westminster Hall to stiffen their resolve. London's reward for at last choosing the winning side was a reduction in its rate of taxation, control over Southwark, and a new charter guaranteeing the City's constitution, reducing the tax farm to £300, restoring the restrictions on alien merchants, and settling several long-running issues in London's favour.[46]

PAYING FOR THE HUNDRED YEARS' WAR

After the enormous changes of Edward I's reign, and the conflicts of Edward II's, the long reign of Edward III (1327–77) gave London a period of relative political stability. The charters of 1319 and 1327, and Edward III's success as a monarch, calmed the tensions between citizens and aldermen, and City and king, which had dominated the preceding century. London remained an oligarchy, governed by aldermen from a few mercantile guilds, especially the fishmongers, grocers, drapers, vintners, mercers, skinners and goldsmiths, whose relative importance rose or fell as their trades prospered or declined. The power granted to common citizens in 1319 to control the common seal and elect paid City officials did not amount to much in practice, but their control over citizenship and craft membership were real enough, and ensured generally harmonious relations between élite and commonalty until the 1370s. Two great problems confronted Londoners in the mid-fourteenth century. One was the arrival of a monstrous disease, the Black Death, which carried off about a third of London's population in 1348–9, and then came back for more. The second was the money-raising policy of a powerful and irresistible king, who had no hesitation in placing the demands of war finance above the trading interests of his kingdom's greatest city.

To pay for his struggle for France and Flanders in the early years of the Hundred Years' War (1337–1453), Edward III needed to exploit and control the wool trade. He did this by following the staple policy of his predecessors, but he also tried the expedient of replacing a single overseas staple (Bruges or Calais) with fifteen home staples, of which the most important was London. Each variation in the staple system found some friends in London, but Edward III's practice of selling exemption licences to Italians in the 1360s did not. London's special privileges were not Edward's concern. In 1351, in response to the wage and price inflation following the Black Death, Edward's Parliament stripped London of its precious franchise, and allowed alien and provincial merchants to compete freely with Londoners in the wholesale and retail trades of the City. At a stroke, the bulk of London's trade was handed over to Italian and Hanseatic merchants. Nothing could have outraged London's merchant and craft fraternities more than this, except perhaps the restoration of the *Carta Mercatoria* two years later. These two measures gave Italian and Hanseatic merchants a free run in London for the next twenty years, and, though London's trade grew enormously, aliens took the lion's share of it. Crafts and trades formalized their associations in an attempt to keep interlopers out, and the City repeatedly petitioned the King for the restoration of its privileges in the 1350s and 1360s. Even the grocers, who were doing well out of the growing trade in dyes, spices and Italian goods, felt the pinch when Italian spicers established a community in Bucklersbury in the 1360s, to conduct their own business in London. Londoners might splutter, but a king of Edward III's stature had little to fear from their discontents, and he needed Italian money and Genoese naval support. In 1365 he started selling licences to Italian merchants, allowing them to avoid Calais and trade direct with Italy, and in 1369 he forced the City to release and protect a notorious Italian swindler and smuggler, Nicholas Sardouche, who had been imprisoned in 1368. Sardouche was knifed and killed by mercers in 1370.[47]

So long as the king had undisputed authority, there was not much Londoners could do about the level of royal demands. Edward III did not follow his three predecessors in suspending London's government or imposing his own direct rule on the City, but his mastery was clear enough. London was a part of the royal demesne lands, owing obedience directly to the king, and bound to pay him whatever he asked. The City argued in 1255 that they should pay only voluntary aids to Henry III, but there was no precedent for this, and he continued to raise compulsory dues, or tallages, as he needed them. Tallage declined in importance in the early fourteenth century, and was abolished in 1340, but by this time two new sources of revenue, the wool customs (begun by Edward I), and the Parliamentary subsidy (usually a tenth of the movable wealth of boroughs and royal demesne lands, a fifteenth elsewhere), had been introduced.[48] As royal expenditure grew, especially during the Hundred Years' War, so did the demands upon London's mercantile community for subsidies, customs and loans. When the king was popular, strong and successful overseas, large sums of money could be extracted without creating serious conflict, even when individual lenders were ruined. Thus Edward III was able to call upon the City for money throughout his reign, and Henry V, using a combination of sound finance, pageantry and well-publicized military success, was able to coax large amounts of money from London to finance his campaigns of 1415–22. But London merchants had a strong interest in the preservation of England's French possessions, especially Calais, and when they were in danger in the 1430s and 1440s the money kept on flowing.[49]

JOHN DE NORTHAMPTON AND THE PEASANTS' REVOLT

In the early 1370s the ageing King's personal authority declined, and a combination of plague, taxation, the wartime dislocation of trade and anti-Italian feeling increased the support for radical opponents of royal policy, especially William Essex and the draper John de Northampton. These two, with ten others, were briefly imprisoned after street disorders in May 1371. In 1372 the naval disaster of La Rochelle highlighted the vulnerability of London's overseas trade. Three years later John de Northampton, despite his record of street violence, was elected to the Court of Aldermen, evidence that he had support in the City élite. In 1376 the 'Good' Parliament condemned corrupt and incompetent government and impeached (among others) three London aldermen who were loyal to the King. This marked the end of the senile King's effective rule, and his son, John of Gaunt, moved to regain London's support. He bought off the leading London wool merchants, the staplers, by restoring the Calais Staple, and seems to have formed an alliance or understanding with John de Northampton, who was now a power in the City, thanks in part to his popular following. The mayor and aldermen, mostly leading staplers, feared that Gaunt would exploit the division between themselves and John de Northampton to seize control of London, and therefore reached a compromise with Northampton. They agreed to his demand that the Common Council should be elected by misteries rather than wards, and would be consulted by the Court of Aldermen twice a quarter, and whenever laws affecting the Commonalty were passed. This made the Common Council a regular part of London's constitution, and earned John de Northampton a reputation among later historians as an early democrat. He was certainly a demagogue, ready to appeal to the lesser citizens' hostility towards the merchant élite and the high prices charged by the victualling interests, but his personal motives have always been ambiguous. It seems likely that his true aims were self-advancement and the promotion of the interests of one section of the mercantile élite, the rising clothing interest (mostly drapers, mercers and goldsmiths), against another, the dominant wool exporters of the staple (mostly grocers and fishmongers). Still, the shift from a ward to a craft electorate clearly had radical implications. While the

Common Council was elected by the crafts, the City's common clerk wrote in 1419, 'Tumults increased among the people, and the great were held in contempt by the small.'[50] Gaunt, on the other hand, was certainly no friend of the City's liberties (though he temporarily restored its franchise in December 1376), and his insistence on the resignation and annual re-election of the Court of Aldermen was intended to get his own men into power, not to democratize the City constitution. Gaunt had few friends in London, and when rumours spread in 1377 that he meant to take London under royal control, Northampton's popularity could not prevent a mob from attacking Gaunt's Savoy Palace and forcing the Duke to flee to Kennington.

Whatever Northampton's relationship with Gaunt was, it was not enough to save London from the latter's retribution when Edward III died in 1377, and the eleven-year-old Richard II (Edward III's grandson) came to the throne. The Gloucester Parliament of 1377 withdrew London's franchise again, and granted Italian merchants the right to avoid Calais and trade directly between Southampton and Genoa. This was the gravest possible threat to London's commercial supremacy, and the City was prepared to pay dearly, in loans to the Crown, to persuade the government to reconsider its policy. But the Genoese, with the profits from their new Southampton trade, could pay more. Gaunt's pro-Italian policy, the heavy cost to Londoners of his futile military escapades, and his utter failure to protect London's trade against French naval supremacy, meant that many leading merchants had a certain sympathy, at least in its early stages, for the Peasants' Revolt, the great rebellion against the government and its unpopular poll tax that broke out in June 1381. The chronicler Froissart believed that Londoners coordinated or incited the risings in Kent and Essex, and even if this is untrue it is certainly the case that the Mayor, William Walworth, could have done more to secure the City against the rebels when their approach was known.[51]

If John de Northampton was a radical leader, a defender of the common people against a rapacious mercantile élite, then London's experience in the Peasants' Revolt is hard to explain. When the rebels crossed the bridge and entered London, they were joined by large numbers of Londoners, from vagrants to master craftsmen. If class war was in the air, this should have been the signal for a popular assault on aldermen, victuallers and wealthy merchants. Instead, while Wat Tyler's rebels (reputedly over 100,000 of them) plundered Lambeth Palace and the Temple Church, broke open the Marshalsea, Fleet and Newgate Prisons, and dragged Archbishop Sudbury of Canterbury (the Chancellor) and

Robert Hales, the Prior of the Hospital of St John Clerkenwell (the King's Treasurer), from the Tower to be executed, Londoners marched down Fleet Street to the Savoy Palace, the magnificent home of Northampton's patron, John of Gaunt, and destroyed it by fire. The Londoners who were beheaded by the mob were not grocers, fishmongers or aldermen, but lawyers, Flemish merchants (whose headless bodies were said to have been piled forty high), and men connected with tax collection and law enforcement, such as Richard Lyons (who was a notoriously corrupt royal tax collector and courtier as well as an alderman and vintner) and Roger Legett. The few merchants who died were the victims of private grudges rather than concerted action. After three days of mayhem, the London rebellion ended on 15 June, when the young Richard II met the rebels at Smithfield, and William Walworth earned a knighthood by pulling Wat Tyler from his horse and mortally wounding him. Walworth at once raised the City militia, and on St John's Fields, Clerkenwell, the rebels were surrounded 'like sheep in a pen'.[52]

Four months later Northampton, who had kept clear of the troubles, was elected Mayor, presumably through the influence of Gaunt, or through the desire of the London élite to propitiate Gaunt and regain London's trade from Southampton. As Mayor, Northampton acted as Gaunt's agent, first trying to extract loans to fund the Duke's Castilian adventure, and when that failed, attacking and breaking the power of the hitherto dominant staplers, who had refused to lend money to Gaunt. He did this by exploiting popular resentment against the powerful fishmongers (who held a quarter of the seats on the Court of Aldermen) at a time of high food prices. In the Parliament of 1382 Northampton won a restoration of London's franchise and liberties, but not the trading privileges of the victuallers (grocers, fishmongers, and so on), who included the leading exporters of wool to the staple. This broke the fortunes of the fishmongers, who were already suffering from French command of the eastern coastal waters, but not of the prosperous and politically experienced grocers, led by the redoubtable Nicholas Brembre. Meanwhile, Richard II was growing up and Gaunt's influence was waning. In the mayoral election of October 1383 Northampton was beaten by Brembre, who had won the King's favour through loans and his loyalty during the Peasants' Revolt. Northampton did not accept defeat quietly. In February 1384 he led about 500 of his followers (mostly mercers and drapers) to the Fleet Bridge, apparently in the hope of reinforcements from Gaunt. Gaunt's men did not appear, and Brembre, strengthened by the support of the citizens and the King, arrested Northampton and removed him to prison in Dorset and a royal trial at

Reading. Probably because of Gaunt's influence, Northampton escaped a painful execution, and was released three years later. Meanwhile, Brembre changed the rules governing the election of the mayor and sheriffs, so that the electorate included 'the more sufficient men of the city' as well as common councillors. Under the new rules he was elected for another term in October 1384, despite the spirited and unruly opposition of tailors, goldsmiths and other discontented craftsmen, Northampton's old supporters.[53]

The only significant constitutional legacy of Northampton's challenge to the staplers was the enhancement of the role of the Common Council. From 1376 there was a clear distinction between the older and larger body of citizens, the 'immense commonalty', summoned at election times, and the smaller body of around 100 leading citizens, the Common Council, elected by the wards, which met at least once a quarter to discuss legislation, examine City accounts, and comment on matters of importance to the City. The powers of the Common Council, especially its right to inspect the City's finances, gave freemen a significant role in the government of later medieval London. But the other reforms of 1376, that the Council should be elected by misteries rather than wards (to ensure that a wider range of crafts would be represented), that aldermen should be elected annually, and that the mayor and aldermen should be chosen by the Common Council, were all reversed in or soon after 1384. From 1384 the aldermen reasserted their control over mayoral elections, and from 1394 aldermen were again elected for life.[54]

In the fifteenth century the election of the mayor (always an ex-sheriff) fell increasingly under the control of the leaders of the main merchant guilds, which had gained royal charters recognizing them as self-governing corporations, and entitling their leading members to wear a distinctive uniform, or livery. Twelve Livery Companies, mostly trading rather than craft associations, achieved supremacy over the rest, and effectively chose and provided the mayor and aldermen of London from the fifteenth century onwards. In order of precedence and (roughly) power, these were the mercers, grocers, drapers, fishmongers, goldsmiths, skinners, tailors, haberdashers, ironmongers, salters, vintners and shearmen. Mercers, grocers and drapers provided sixty-one of the eighty-eight fifteenth-century mayors, and 105 of the 173 aldermen. No mayors, and only three aldermen, came from outside of the top ten companies.[55]

LONDON AND RICHARD II

Brembre retained the mayoralty until 1386, but he did not enjoy the fruits of his victory for long. He advanced loans to Richard II, and became one of the King's unpopular inner circle, against which an overwhelming coalition of five leading magnates, known as the Lords Appellant, was formed in 1387. Londoners in general did not share Brembre's loyalty to the headstrong and inadequate King, and as Richard II's unpopularity and isolation grew, so did Brembre's. Misled perhaps by Brembre's support or by the welcome the City gave him when he entered it on 10 November 1387, Richard relied on London's help against the Appellants. But when he summoned his two leading opponents, Gloucester and Arundel, to meet him at Westminster in November 1387, crowds of Londoners rushed to join the Appellants' army at Waltham Cross, and the King felt obliged to promise a Parliament at which his five hated favourites could be tried. When Richard appealed for the City's military support on 30 November, its leaders told him that Londoners were untrained in warlike skills, but when the Appellants' army arrived at Clerkenwell after Christmas they were welcomed with ceremony and friendship, and five hundred men were allowed to enter London, to confront Richard in his refuge in the Tower and force him to submit to their control. Showing unusual courage and loyalty to the King, Brembre (the only one of the five endangered royal servants who had not fled) was tried for his life before the Merciless Parliament in February 1388, and the evidence of the mayor and aldermen was decisive in establishing his guilt. On the day of his conviction, 20 February, he was dragged to Tyburn on a hurdle and hanged, drawn and quartered as a traitor.[56]

By 1392 Richard had recovered his authority, and was in a position to humble London as he had been humbled five years before. The King's motives in moving against London in May and June 1392 are not completely clear. He claimed, as Edward I had done, that London's lawlessness and 'lack of good ruling' made royal intervention necessary, but his need for money, and the fact that individual and corporate loans from London had completely dried up since Brembre's execution, were more important considerations. Richard believed that London's refusal of loans was a gesture of defiance, prompted by the removal of their liberties by the Parliament of 1389. It may be, though, that London merchants had no money to lend. In 1388 the Genoese made Southampton their North European headquarters, and their trade in cloth, woad, alum and dyes began to by-pass London. The decline of the Bohemian mines and an acute shortage of silver coin created a long depression in the 1390s, and London merchants found it increasingly difficult to raise or advance credit, or to find capital for trading ventures. Bankruptcies among leading grocers were common around 1390, and plague, riots and food shortages in 1389–91 added to the atmosphere of crisis. To make matters worse, Italian merchants had plenty of bullion from new mines in Serbia and Bosnia, and in a free market Florentines and Venetians were able to dominate the London cloth and spice trades.[57]

The first step in Richard's systematic humiliation of London was the removal in May 1392 of the royal Exchequer, Chancery and Common Pleas to York, followed by a summons to fifty leading citizens to appear before the King and Council in Nottingham, where London's liberties and privileges were revoked. The mayor and sheriffs were dismissed and imprisoned, and replaced by a royal warden and two new sheriffs. Many prominent Londoners were forced to answer for the recent misgovernment of the City before a royal tribunal, and the City's income was taken under royal control. Finally, in July 1392, London was ordered to pay a huge corporate fine of £100,000, almost the equivalent of the Crown's annual income. By staging a lavish reception for the King and Queen, with the water conduits flowing with wine, and loading Richard with precious gifts, the City was able to win pardons for its dignitaries, have its fine cut (perhaps to £10,000), and gain the temporary return of its liberties. In October 1392 a new mayor was elected and government offices began to return from York. Over the next few years the King made concessions on alien trade and restored the lifetime election of aldermen, but London remained under his control and heavy taxes were levied. As late as 1397 the King imposed his own choice, Richard Whittington, as mayor, and only then returned London's liberties in full in exchange for a gift of 10,000 marks. The quarrel with Richard II, which cost London about £30,000 in fines, loans and gifts, demonstrated the city's vulnerability to the power of the Crown, and exemplified the high-handedness which soon destroyed the King.[58]

The London élite feared Richard (as he meant them to), and caution was their watchword. London played no active part in the invasion of England by Gaunt's son, Henry Bolingbroke, in July 1399, and only committed itself to Henry's side when Richard was beaten and captured in August. A delegation of leading citizens let Henry know that he would be well received in London, and he was able to call upon Londoners to legitimize his seizure of the throne by acclaiming his succession in a great assembly in Westminster Hall. This was a re-enactment of the part played by Londoners when Edward II was deposed in 1327, and it recalled the claims of the citizenry to have elected Cnut and Edward the Confessor. The claim was false, but London's support was always an asset, and its hostility could be dangerous. The appearance of popular support which a cheering crowd of Londoners could provide was a convenient buttress for a doubtful claimant, and a king who could not arouse the enthusiasm of the capital when he was challenged by a rival was vulnerable, as Edward II, Richard II and Henry VI all discovered. London's goodwill, on the other hand, could be of real value to a king in danger. When Bolingbroke (as Henry IV) faced an immediate challenge from a rebellion of Richard's former dukes in January 1400, Londoners helped him to raise an army of 20,000 and defeat the rebels.[59]

LONDON AND HENRY V

The fall of Richard II brought political peace, but not commercial prosperity, to London. The Anglo-French war and a bitter dispute with the Hanseatic League interrupted London's trade, and merchants put aside their differences over the staple and wool or cloth exports to make common cause against the alien.[60] Even in difficult times, individual merchants could prosper. Richard II's closest ally in the City, Richard Whittington, was not damaged by the King's fall. He became one of Henry IV's most important creditors, was one of the three London merchants appointed to Henry's council in 1399, served on many royal legal commissions, and was elected mayor again in 1406 and 1419. Between 1400 and 1413 he made loans totalling at least £24,000 to Henry IV, who was always impoverished and rarely repaid in cash, and then a further £7,500 to Henry V. Most of these loans were repaid, as royal loans usually were, by having specific Exchequer revenues (perhaps the Southampton wool subsidy or the Norfolk fifteenth) 'assigned' to them, but to recover others Whittington had to collect the London wool subsidy and take some of the debt from it, and export wool free of royal dues. Perhaps he recovered more than the sum he had originally loaned, and thus earned interest on his investments, but it is just as likely that his reward was power, a measure of influence with the King, rather than profit. The fact that Whittington was able to leave over £5,000 in cash to found a college, almshouses and the Greyfriars and Guildhall libraries, and to rebuild Newgate Prison, owes more to the fact that he died a childless widower without the merchant's usual interest in establishing a country estate, than to the profits of usury.[61]

By the time of Henry IV's death in 1413 London was in a sad state. Plague, alien competition and a shortage of good coin depressed trade, population and guild membership, and the demand for shops in Cheapside was sluggish.[62] Yet even in such times the reign of Henry V (1413–22) showed how an intelligent and effective king could tap London's resources to fund an active and successful foreign policy. Victories in France offered emotional satisfaction, appeared to protect London's trading interests, and yielded booty and ransoms which helped offset the heavy costs of war. Henry made sure that his campaigns would win the maximum political and financial support in London by explaining his aims in person to the mayor and aldermen in March 1415, and sending them a full account of his capture of Harfleur six months later. Londoners loaned 10,000 marks in 1415, and contributed generously to Parliamentary subsidies, in the knowledge that their money was being well spent. News of Agincourt was greeted with an immense procession from London to Westminster in October, and Henry was received in London with triumphant pageantry a month later. As he went through the city, Henry was greeted by giant effigies, mock castles and elaborate tableaux. The tower of one of the Cheapside water conduits was surrounded by niches, 'and in each niche was a beautiful young girl, in the posture of a statue; and in their hands were golden cups from which they very lightly puffed gold leaf upon the King's head as he rode by'.[63]

When Harfleur was besieged in May 1416, royal proclamations in English called on citizens to speed to its relief 'with corne, brede, mele, or floure, wyne, ale, or biere, fysshe, flesshe, or any other viteille, clothe, lynnen, wollene, or eny merchaundise, shetys, breches, doublettys, hosene, schone, or eny other manere ware of armure, artilrye, or of othere stuffe'. Again, in 1418, at the siege of Rouen, Henry called on Londoners to send small ships with food and drink 'for the refresshing of us and our said hoost'.[64] The shipments were sent, ensuring that those outside Rouen ate well, while those within starved. There had rarely been such whole-hearted support in London for a royal military policy. London's reactions to the successes of Edward I and Edward III were soured by resentment at the way they were paid for, but Henry V's victories were won without sacrificing good government and sound finance, and without bullying Londoners for loans which would never be repaid. In fact, as Caroline Barron's work on

London's royal loans demonstrates, Henry V's victories cost London much less than Henry VI's defeats.[65]

THE COLLAPSE OF ROYAL AUTHORITY

After Henry V's death in 1422 (a tragedy commemorated for many years by the London misteries) the Crown passed to his infant son, Henry VI, and power to the late King's brothers, the Dukes of Bedford and Gloucester. Gloucester (who ruled England as Protector while Bedford controlled the French territories) soon found his position challenged by his uncle, Henry Beaufort, Bishop of Winchester, a man of great experience and wealth. From 1413 to 1444 Beaufort was the mainstay of the Crown's finances, making loans in those years totalling over £200,000, outstripping London's contribution. The conflict between these two men almost led to open warfare on the streets of London in October 1425, when Beaufort's army, assembled in the Bishop's Southwark estates, faced a large crowd of Londoners, supporting Gloucester, on the northern bank of the Thames. Only the intervention of the Archbishop of Canterbury prevented the confrontation from turning into a battle on London Bridge.

Henry VI's reign was dominated by the loss of all the King's French lands (except Calais) by 1453, and by the collapse of royal authority in England thereafter, owing partly to failure overseas, and largely to the feeble-mindedness of a King whose second childhood, it has been said, followed immediately upon his first. For commercial and sentimental reasons Londoners wanted the French lands retained, and they invested heavily in their defence, both on an individual and corporate basis. Between 1427 and 1454 London and Londoners (including merchants of the Calais Staple) lent an average of about £6,000 a year to Henry VI, even though his ability to repay seemed to be getting steadily weaker. Another of Henry's desperate devices to raise cash in the 1430s, his sale of perpetual monopolies on important London commercial posts (wine-gauger, cloth-packer, wine-drawer, Port of London garbeller), caused serious inconvenience to city merchants until they were revoked by Edward IV in 1478.

London's allegiances in the aristocratic conflicts of the 1450s and 1460s, the so-called Wars of the Roses, were not clear-cut. The aims of the mercantile élite were to maintain in power a King who owed them so much money, but also to keep in touch with the King's opponents, and to make sure that the city was protected against the armed forces of either side.

Popular opinion blamed the Lancastrians, and especially the small clique of nobles and officials that surrounded the King, for England's humiliation in France and for the economic recession of the 1440s, and sympathized with Henry's main critic and rival, Richard, Duke of York, who was portrayed in Yorkist propaganda as an efficient soldier and administrator who had done well in France in the 1430s and 1440s. This pro-Yorkist sympathy played an important part in determining the outcome of the conflict between Lancaster and York.[66]

London's political divisions reflected the conflict between craftsmen and merchants that had surfaced repeatedly during the previous 200 years. In 1383 the mercantile élite had defeated John of Northampton, but the supremacy of a few rich companies was not accepted without question, as the well-documented dispute between the artisan tailors and the mercantile drapers in the 1430s and 1440s shows. The tailors, who had aspirations to move into the more profitable and prestigious wholesale cloth trade, came into conflict with the drapers in 1439 over the question of which company had the right to inspect and approve the quality of cloth on sale in London. The Master of the tailors' company, Alderman Ralph Holland, was a man with a long-standing radical reputation, who had been briefly imprisoned in 1426. His selection as one of the two mayoral candidates in 1439 and 1440 shows that the voice of the common citizen still counted for something in the electoral process. Holland's rejection by the Court of Aldermen for the third time in 1441 (in favour of Robert Clopton, a draper) tested the tailors' patience too far, and a riot broke out in the Guildhall. The response of the City authorities was to imprison the rioters, revoke the tailors' controversial powers of search, and obtain a royal writ limiting the vote in future mayoral elections to named and summoned individuals. This was a vital issue, and before the election of October 1443 artisans from several companies, including brewers, saddlers, tailors and skinners, met secretly to plan an armed rising to challenge the royal writ and restore the rights of craftsmen that were guaranteed (so they believed) by the Great Charter of 1319. One tailor even dared to propose the revolutionary principle that a charter with Parliamentary endorsement should carry more weight than a royal writ. The conspiracy was exposed, Holland was removed from the aldermanry, and the public mood was calmed by concessions in the new charter of 1444. Nevertheless, the episode is a reminder that John Lilburne, John Wilkes and William Lovett, London radicals of later centuries, were inheritors of an anti-oligarchic tradition with an obscure but ancient pedigree.[67]

As warfare drew to a close in France, recrimination began in England.

In June 1450 a popular uprising took place in Kent in protest against local oppression and misgovernment, and a large army marched to Blackheath, under the leadership of Jack Cade. Once outside London, the rebels produced a manifesto calculated to win support among the citizens, attacking the household clique whose selfishness and incompetence had led the King into defeat and penury. These arguments struck a sympathetic chord in London and in the armies of aristocratic retainers which were gathered to help Henry defeat the rebellion. On 18 June the approach of Henry's army from Clerkenwell forced the rebels to disperse, but within a week the King had withdrawn to Kenilworth, panicked by signs of discontent within his own army and capital, and ignoring the mayor's urgent appeal for him to stay and protect the town. Cade's Kentish army, reinforced from Essex, occupied Southwark by 2 July, and entered London the following day, after threatening to set fire to the bridge. Once inside the town, the rebel force, perhaps 25,000 strong, began looting the richer houses, while the leaders 'tried' and executed about twenty royal servants, and a few other unpopular characters. The looting and violence pushed the Common Council and the Tower garrison into action, and on the night of 5–6 July a force of Londoners 'laid hands when it was night on those who were dispersed about the City and beat then and drove them out of the city and shut the gates'. The rebels, encamped in Southwark, made an assault on the bridge, but after a battle in which over 200 died Cade's men were offered a royal pardon and dispersed. Cade was soon caught and killed, and his body brought to London for dismemberment.[68]

Disaffection in London, which had been evident well before Cade's rebellion, continued after it, fuelled by the arrival of soldiers from the English armies defeated in France. In November 1450 a more dangerous element was added by the arrival of aristocratic armies accompanying their lords to the opening of Parliament. The presence of these private armies at times of conflict was always a serious threat to peace and order in the city, 'for the good people stood in dread and doubt, for the variance between the lords'.[69] Many of these armed retainers and ex-soldiers joined the mob that looted the house of the Duke of Somerset, the defeated English commander in Normandy, and forced him to flee for his life to the Tower on 1 December. But London's allegiance to the King had not completely evaporated, and in February 1452, when York marched on the capital to replace Somerset as the King's chief minister, the City, obedient to the King's request, closed its gates to the Duke's army, and instead gave free passage to Henry's force, enabling him to bring York to heel.

SUPPORTING THE YORKISTS

From March to December 1454, during Henry's temporary mental break-down, York ruled as Protector, and in May 1455 the power struggle entered a bloodier phase when the Yorkists defeated and killed Somerset at St Albans. It was not until February 1456 that Henry, with the help of his determined wife, Margaret, was able to regain control of his government. Within six months, though, he had to abandon London and move his administration to the Midlands. The King was motivated, it seems, by a sense of London's hostility to him, and he was intimidated by the disorder which broke out in late April 1456 against Italian merchants and, by implication, the royal policy which gave them preferential trading rights. Although the riots were easily put down by the City authorities, and seem to have caused little damage, they encouraged Henry to move his Court to Coventry for a year in 1456, once again abandoning his duty to keep order in London. The Italians also decided London was too dangerous a place to live, and moved out to Southampton and Winchester.[70]

In March 1458, Henry made a last effort to reconcile the warring aristocratic families, who were gathered in London with large retinues for a great council, by bringing them together in a 'love day', a symbolic procession to St Paul's followed by a solemn ceremony of friendship. But the fundamental problem, Henry VI's personal inadequacy, was unchanged, and in September 1459 hostilities broke out again. As the conflict reached its climax in 1460, London's support for the Yorkist side emerged as a decisive factor. Popular anti-Lancastrianism, stimulated by Yorkist propaganda and Henry's manifest failings, was reinforced by anger in the merchant community at the King's granting of preferential export licences to royal favourites and Italians and his repeated abandonment of the capital in times of danger. So on 2 July 1460 the Yorkist army, invading from its base in Calais, was allowed, after some hesitation, to enter London, and the Yorkists were given the propaganda advantage of a civic reception in St Paul's. At this point the civic authorities threw their influence and money behind the Yorkist cause. By 16 July Henry was a captive in London, and within a few days his allies in the Tower had been captured and killed.[71]

By contrast, when the Lancastrians had in two successive victories killed Richard of York in December 1460 and defeated his leading ally, Warwick, in St Albans in February 1461, rescuing the King at the same time, the royal army was refused entry into London. The aldermen were prepared to negotiate and send supplies, but the citizenry slammed the gates, opening them instead to York's son, Edward, Earl of March, who was given a hero's welcome on 27 February. This was London's most decisive intervention in the conflict, and one that arose from the initiative of common citizens, briefly overruling the compliant pragmatism of the City élite. Once again the tradition that a usurper's claim to the throne could be legitimized by popular acclamation was called upon, and the citizens of London, gathered first in St Paul's, then in Westminster, hailed Edward IV as King on 4 March 1461. Edward raised money in London for a very large army, and won a conclusive victory at Towton at the end of March. Henry, captured again in 1465, spent five years in the Tower.[72]

After 1461 London's role was more passive and pragmatic, seeking to run with the tide of events, rather than alter its flow. When Warwick, preferring a French alliance to a Burgundian one, broke with Edward in July 1469 and invaded from Calais, London opened its gates to him. When Warwick brought the bewildered Henry out of the Tower and restored him to the throne in October 1470 Londoners were unimpressed, but compliant. In April 1471 Edward's recapture of London was unopposed, and he was able to emerge from it to defeat and kill Warwick at Barnet on 13 April, and to crush Queen Margaret's Lancastrian army at Tewkesbury on 4 May. Only Thomas Neville, the Bastard of Fauconberg, was not made welcome, when he tried to enter the City with an unruly army of Kentishmen in King Henry's name on 14 May 1471. When his 3,000 Kentish seamen attacked the gates of Bishopsgate and Aldgate, the citizens 'sallied out of the gates and made a stout resistance and put them to flight'.[73] King Edward, now the undisputed master of England, re-entered the capital a week later, and had Henry VI, 'this goostly and vertuous prince', killed in the Tower.[74] When Edward died in 1483 the citizen assembly in the Guildhall almost withheld the traditional acclamation from his brother Richard when he claimed the throne, but at last mustered some half-hearted applause, 'more for fear than for love'. And when Henry Tudor claimed the crown on the strength of his victory over Richard III at Bosworth in August 1485 he was greeted at Shoreditch by trumpeters, loyal verses, a splendid deputation and a gift of 1,000 marks.[75]

THE GROWTH OF WESTMINSTER

An account of London's part in national politics is likely to concentrate too much on conflict and bloodshed. In general, London's rulers were unwilling participants in aristocratic quarrels, and did their best to minimize the damage these conflicts might do to the City's economic and social life. If London's prosperity owed anything to political developments, it was not to these bloody battles for power, but the gradual transformation of the little settlement of Westminster into a centre of royal administration from the thirteenth century onwards. In the long run, London's unique position in national life emerged from the fusion of these two towns, London and Westminster, into one great centre of commerce and government.

Medieval Westminster was a small town about 2 miles upriver from London, and joined to the City by a line of noble and clerical mansions strung out along Fleet Street and the Strand. In 1086 the manor had only twenty-five substantial houses, and a scattering of small farms, but by 1300, after a period of rapid growth, its population may have been approaching 3,000. After 1300, and especially after 1348, disease cut the population back from its unknown peak to a figure of around 2,000 in 1400. There were further severe population losses in the fifteenth century, but after 1470 there seems to have been a recovery, taking the population back towards 3,000 by the 1520s. These trends probably mirrored demographic trends in London itself.[76]

Royal efforts to make Westminster a commercial centre in its own right were not particularly successful. In the 1350s Westminster was one of the ten English staple towns with a monopoly of the wool trade, and the road from London became broken and muddy from the coming and going of carts and horses, until the home staple policy was abandoned in favour of the Calais Staple in 1363. Westminster did, though, have its great annual fair each October, the survivor of the two fairs established by Henry III in 1245. Even this fell under the control of London cloth and fur dealers, and faded into insignificance during the fourteenth century, just as most of the other great fairs in England and Europe did.[77] Westminster thrived, instead, as a local supplier of local needs. By the fifteenth century it had at least sixty alehouses, and the precincts of the Abbey were full of shopkeepers and craftsmen, enjoying the freedom from City taxes, guild restrictions and environmental rules which came with Westminster's sanctuary status. There was also a busy colony of Flemish and German tailors, cobblers, hatters, metalworkers and spectacle-makers in Westminster, and at least fifty London dealers in gold, cloth, clothes, groceries and other high-value goods had branch offices in the suburb.[78] And there were the inevitable prostitutes: a mid-thirteenth-century traveller listed the whores of Charing among the sights of London, alongside the relics of Westminster and the churchyard of St Paul's.

The craftsmen, retailers, builders, innkeepers, entertainers, gamblers and prostitutes of Westminster made their livings from the expenditure of the inhabitants and entourages of two great institutions, the Abbey and the royal household. The Abbey, with its sixty or so monks, was the landlord of a growing proportion of Westminster (two-thirds by 1400), and a major local employer, especially when it was being rebuilt in the 1350s and 1360s.

THE CAPITAL OF ENGLAND

The progressive expansion in both size and political and administrative importance of Westminster Palace was the major driving force behind the growth of the town. William I's coronation in 1066, and the building of Westminster Hall, perhaps the biggest hall in Europe at the time, by William II in 1097–9, confirmed the palace as one of the centres of Norman kingship. William I held great councils in Westminster in 1076 and 1084, and held court there each Whitsuntide when he was in England. Since Norman kings were always on the move in England or France, taking their household with them, it would be wrong to think of Westminster as the capital of England. What could not be carried with the king's mobile household, especially the main royal treasury and financial records, was stored at Winchester, not Westminster, and kings had smaller local treasuries distributed in castles all around the country. But by 1200 it had become clear that the most convenient place to store the bulk of the royal treasure was in Westminster, which thus became the home of the Exchequer, the place where royal revenues were collected and stored until they were needed elsewhere.[79]

The concentration of government in Westminster was associated with a growing emphasis on Westminster Abbey as a centre of royal ceremonial in the thirteenth century. Although the Norman and Angevin kings were crowned in Westminster Abbey, no English kings (and only one queen) were buried there between 1066 and 1272. But Henry III (1216–72) developed a passion for the cult of Edward the Confessor, who represented, in Henry's mind, the legitimacy of the Norman-Angevin line and the virtues of peaceful kingship. Between 1245 and 1269 Henry III spent a fortune (perhaps £50,000) creating a lavish shrine for the saint (the Confessor was canonized in 1161) and demolishing and rebuilding the Abbey in a style grand enough to equal Louis IX's impressive new Gothic cathedral in Reims. It is very possible that the Abbey's master mason in the early stages of the work, Henry of Reyns, had learned his craft at Reims, but whether or not this is the case the architectural influences on the second Abbey, like those on the first, were very strongly French. By the time of Henry's death the Lady Chapel, the chapter-house, the cloister, the chancel, the transepts and the eastern end of the nave were finished, and the Confessor had been transferred to his new shrine. Henry's three successors were not very interested in the Confessor's cult (though they bore his name and were buried in his Abbey), and it was left to Richard II and his great master mason, Henry Yevele, to resume the construction of the nave in 1375. Another century of inactivity followed Richard II's fall in 1399, and the nave was only completed in 1503–6, at the same time as Henry III's Lady Chapel was being replaced with Henry VII's chapel, the one we see today. The Abbey's intimate association with English kingship saved it from destruction in the 1540s, and its western end was finally finished by Hawksmoor and John James in 1745, 500 years after Henry III's foundation stone was laid.[80]

Using the deeds and accounts of the Abbey, Gervase Rosser has traced the gradual growth of a colony of royal officials in Westminster from the 1150s onwards. Richard fitz Neal and William of Ely, royal treasurers from 1165 to 1215, had a house in Westminster, which passed in 1222–4 to Hubert de Burgh, the justiciar, the official who wielded royal authority when the king was abroad. This house, on the riverfront 500 metres north of Westminster Hall, passed to the Archbishop of York in 1241, and remained his residence, York Place, until the fall of Cardinal Wolsey in 1529. At about the same time as fitz Neal moved to Westminster, the Mauduit family, hereditary royal chamberlains of the Exchequer, did the same, buying up property west of the Abbey.[81]

As royal administration became more bureaucratic, and the scope of royal justice grew with the reforms of Henry I and Henry II, it became increasingly inconvenient for the whole machinery of government to follow the king around England and France, or up to the Scots and Welsh borders. Westminster, close to but not controlled by London, was the natural home for those parts of royal administration which detached themselves from the mobile household. Under Henry II in the 1170s and 1180s the 'chief court' (*capitalis curia*) in Westminster Hall became the headquarters of a great new system of royal justice, a place where judges could always be found to hear citizens' complaints, where the weightiest decisions were taken, and where the accumulation of custom, judgement and precedent known as common law was developed.[82] In Magna Carta in 1215 it was agreed that lawsuits heard before the royal justices in the Court of Common Pleas should 'not follow the king, but be held in one fixed place'. This place was Westminster. Under Henry III Westminster became the frequent resting-place of the household, and the King's government made use of Abbey premises and employed its monks as administrators. Simon de Montfort's representative Parliament was held there in 1265, and Edward I, who called about fifty Parliaments of one sort or another between 1275 and 1307, generally chose to hold them in a convenient room in the Palace or Abbey at Westminster. Under Edward III the high cost of the wars in France gave Parliament much greater control over taxation, and all but one of the thirty-two Parliaments called between 1338 and 1377 were held in Westminster. The full assembly sat in the Painted Chamber of the Palace, and the Commons used the chapter-house of the Abbey until about 1380, and the Abbey refectory thereafter.[83]

Although some aspects of government were becoming more detached from the king's person, they had to remain in contact with the king. Thus, when war took Edward I and his two successors frequently to Scotland between 1298 and 1338 not only did the itinerant departments of state go with them, but the Exchequer and Common Pleas migrated to York for a total of fifteen years, leaving the tradesmen of Westminster to bemoan the loss of their customers. But in 1338 the outbreak of the Hundred Years' War with France forced Edward III to move his Exchequer back to Westminster, where 'it might be nearer to him in the parts beyond the sea', and within twenty years its supremacy over the other main financial departments, the Chamber and the king's Wardrobe, had been established. The sixty or so employees of the two departments of the Exchequer, the exchequers of account and receipt, worked in two chambers off Westminster Hall.[84]

By the later fourteenth century Westminster Hall was bursting with activity. Parliaments were held there, and so were the great royal feasts at Christmas and other times. Stow tells us that Richard II, who restored and enlarged the Hall in 1397–8, adding its stupendous hammerbeam roof, 'kept a most royal Christmas there, with daily justings and runnings at tilt', in 1398. Within a year he was deposed by a Parliament sitting in the same Hall, and his successor was celebrating his coronation there. When the feasting was over Westminster Hall resumed its second major function, as the centre of royal justice and the 'cradle of the Common Law'.[85] Near the main entrance, the Court of Common Pleas dealt with cases of trespass and other civil disputes according to the increasingly complicated and time-consuming provisions of common law, while at the far end the King's Bench heard serious criminal cases, and poached business from its rival. Conflict between these two superior courts over the extent of their jurisdiction went on until the nineteenth century. In another part of the great Hall sat the Court of Chancery, presided over by the Chancellor, the king's secretary and adviser, the keeper of the Great Seal. The Chancery had been an itinerant department, and still sometimes travelled with the king, but the growth of its judicial functions in the fourteenth century, preparing and issuing writs and other legal documents, hearing petitions to the king's council and dispensing justice according to a new and flexible code of equity, eventually made it immobile. The immense volume of surviving paperwork (or parchment-work) generated by the Chancery, King's Bench and Common Pleas testifies to the huge amount of business they conducted. Westminster Hall remained the headquarters of royal justice until the opening of the new Law Courts in the Strand in 1882.[86]

Although in the long term the establishment of Parliament and the main government departments at Westminster was of great significance to London, the immediate impact was limited, since Parliaments did not last very long (usually under a month), nor were they called as regularly in the fifteenth century as they had been in the fourteenth. The number of men employed in the Westminster-based offices, the Exchequer, the Privy Seal, the King's Bench, Chancery, and Common Pleas was very small by later standards, about 250 under Edward III, and hardly more than 200, it has been estimated, in the late fifteenth century.[87]

THE ROYAL COURT AT WESTMINSTER

To be called the capital of England, Westminster had to capture the royal household, the royal council and the king himself, who was the real centre of power in England until the late seventeenth century. Twelfth- and thirteenth-century kings spent much of their time on the move, campaigning in Wales, Scotland or France, or trying to hold their far-flung empire together. Some small departments had a permanent London base in Edward I's day, but the most important part of the king's government, the royal household and its spending department, the Wardrobe, followed the king on his travels. The royal mews at Charing organized royal hunting activities, and the Great Wardrobe in the Tower and its storehouse at Blackfriars (not to be confused with the much more important Wardrobe department of the household) bought and stored the household's supply of cloth, furs and spices.[88] In the fourteenth century kings gradually abandoned the nomadic life, and began to spend more time in Westminster and their other Thames valley palaces, Sheen, Eltham and Windsor. After the campaigns of the 1330s, Edward III's itineraries were generally confined to south-eastern England, and in the 1360s the need to consult his councillors, meet foreign envoys and hold Parliaments kept him within a day's journey of Westminster. Meetings of Edward III's permanent administrative council, the body of leading magnates and royal officials that heard difficult cases and took responsibility for much of the daily business of government, generally took place in London, often in Westminster Palace or the Tower, and sometimes in a church or monastic house in the City itself. In the early 1340s the council began using the 'new chamber' in Westminster which later, as 'Star Chamber' (*camera stellata*), became its regular home. The court of Star Chamber was abolished in 1641, and the buildings were used as a storehouse for the Exchequer's wooden tallies, which in turn helped cause the fire which destroyed the Star Chamber building and most of the rest of Westminster Palace in 1834.[89]

In the reign of Richard II (1377–99) an elaborate and expensive courtly life developed, migrating between the royal palaces around London. Court patronage, together with the influence of London's increasingly literate merchant class, helped to make London for the first time a literary centre of international renown in the decades around 1400. Thomas Usk, Thomas Hoccleve, John Lydgate, John Gower and Geoffrey Chaucer wrote for a courtly and civic audience, and between them give us an excellent picture of the society and tastes of medieval London.[90] Court life became more permanently settled in the London area after the death in 1422 of Henry V, the last true warrior-king, and the accession of the exceedingly unwarlike Henry VI.

It is not easy to assess the population of the late medieval Court. The paid members of the royal household numbered around 400 under Edward III, and rose to over 875 (half of them Esquires of the Household or Yeomen of Chamber) by 1448. Henry VI's queen had another 300 servants of her own, until drastic reductions in both these households were imposed by a Great Council of nobles in 1454. Edward IV (1461–83) kept his household smaller, perhaps 600 in all including kitchen staff, clerks, grooms, musicians and pages, as well as the knights and esquires who attended the King.[91]

The nobles, gentlemen, clerics, careerists and petitioners who were drawn to the Court by ambition, duty, curiosity, the hope of power, protection, favour or reward, or the need to defend their family's interests and estates, are much harder to number, but perhaps of greater importance to London's development. The 'pull' of London was noticed in 1170 by Fitzstephen, who claimed that 'almost all the bishops, abbots and magnates of England' had houses in London, where 'they live, and spend largely, when they are summoned to great councils by the king or by their metropolitan, or drawn thither by their private affairs'. In later centuries, many of these great men had their own palaces or town houses in London, either within the City walls (especially in the south-western corner) or in the western suburbs. In all, there were forty-five inns or mansions in London belonging to ecclesiastical lords in 1500, and about thirty owned by noblemen. Most of London's ecclesiastical mansions were established in the twelfth and thirteenth centuries, while the lay ones were built or bought a little later, mostly after 1300, when political and legal matters drew the nobility to the City. The appeal of the western districts to men of fashion and ambition was already strong. Few mansions were built in the eastern half of the City, and none in the eastern or north-eastern suburbs, but there were many stretching westward along the Thames, Fleet Street and the Strand, several in Westminster, and a dozen (mostly ecclesiastical) in Southwark. The Abbots of Cirencester, Faversham and Tewkesbury, the Bishops of St David's, Salisbury, Exeter, Chester, Bath, Worcester, Carlisle, Durham and Lincoln all had their inns along or near the banks of the Thames until they were destroyed or fell into the hands of favoured courtiers in the sixteenth century.[92]

A few of these mansions survived in a ruinous condition into the eighteenth or nineteenth centuries, long enough for artists to record their final battered appearance, but today only a wall of Winchester Palace in Southwark and the chapel (now St Etheldreda's Church) and undercroft of Ely Place in Holborn remain. Even in their heyday many of these mansions must have appeared modest from the outside, since parts of their street frontages were rented to shopkeepers. The greatest of the lay mansions was John of Gaunt's Savoy Palace, occupied and fortified by successive Earls and Dukes of Lancaster (the richest of London's titled families) from 1270 to 1381, when it was attacked and rendered unusable in the Peasants' Revolt. It was rebuilt as a hospital for the poor in the early sixteenth century, and later it was used as a military hospital and a barracks, until the site was cleared for the approach to Waterloo Bridge in 1816. By the fifteenth century the number of great houses had grown considerably. In Henry VI's reign the list of residents of noble mansions in London resembles a Shakespearean cast-list: the Dukes of Gloucester, York, Norfolk and Exeter, the Earls of Warwick, Ormond, Westmoreland and Northumberland, and Lords Scrope, Bardolf and Lovel. Fifteenth-century England's best-known lesser landed family, the Pastons, did not have a London house, and had to rent rooms in a commercial inn, of which there had been several in London since the fourteenth century.[93] They are no doubt typical of many landowners who had to come to London in order to fight local property disputes in the royal courts and, if they could, penetrate the royal household.

Ecclesiastical and lay lords had houses in London for a variety of reasons. For some, the purpose might have been social, to have a place to entertain and be entertained, and to meet others of the same social standing. A more important aim would be to accommodate a large household when its head was called to Westminster to advise or serve the king, or had business to conduct in the City. Justifying his purchase of an estate in Southwark in the middle of the twelfth century, Henry of Blois, Bishop of Winchester, mentioned the 'many inconveniences and losses that I and my predecessors have sustained through the lack of a house of our own to use when called to London on royal or other business'. Others were motivated by economic considerations. Heads of noble and religious houses needed a place from which to organize the purchase of supplies for their households, and perhaps to arrange the sale of the produce (especially wool) of their estates. These economic activities were of great interest to London merchants and shopkeepers. The spending power of the aristocracy was much larger, in total, than that of the Crown, and the more of their cloth, crockery, books, wine, spices, saddlery, jewellery, furs, meat and other luxuries they bought in London, the better for the town's prosperity. Great households had their storehouses, or wardrobes, in the City, often near the markets of Cheap, just as the king and his family did. This was why the calling of Parliaments in the provinces (as kings did when they were displeased with London) was such a blow to the city, and why London's rulers tried so hard to make amends to noble households that had been attacked or offended by unruly citizens.[94]

The power of the royal Court to attract men of wealth and ambition from across the kingdom redoubled the economic and demographic impact upon London of Westminster's rise as a royal suburb. In time, the magnetic attraction of Westminster would become an enormous driving-force in London's growth and prosperity, bringing about the rise of the West End in the seventeenth and eighteenth centuries. In fact, the process was already beginning, with the spread of great mansions along Fleet Street and the Strand, and the growth of a modest legal enclave from Gray's Inn to the Temple. London, of course, was not simply a passive beneficiary of Westminster's growth. London's power, wealth, beauty and cultural diversity, and its ability to satisfy royal and aristocratic appetites, acted as a powerful magnet, drawing the Court and administration towards the city. William Dunbar, who came to London with a Scottish embassy in 1501, diplomatically celebrated the city's enticing qualities:

> Gem of all joy, jasper of jocunditie,
> Most mighty carbuncle of virtue and valour;
> Strong Troy in vigour and in strenuity,
> Of royal cities rose and giraflower,
> Empress of towns, exalt in honour;
> In beauty bearing the throne imperial,
> Sweet paradise precelling in pleasure.
> London, thou art the flower of cities all. . . .
>
> Strong be thy walles that about thee stands,
> Wise be thy people that within thee dwells,
> Fresh is thy river with his lusty strands,
> Blythe be thy churches, well sounding be thy bells,
> Rich be thy merchants that in substance excels,
> Fair be their wives, right lovesome, white and small,
> Clear be thy virgins, lusty under kells:
> London, thou art the flower of cities all.

Chapter 4

Economy and Society

LONDON'S EXCELLENT POSITION on the tidal reaches of the Thames, its large population (estimated at anything between 40,000 and 100,000 on the eve of the Black Death in 1348), the skill and capital of its merchants and alien residents, and the stimulus of royal and aristocratic demand, made it England's most important trading town by far, prosperous even when other towns struggled in the later Middle Ages. Its trading wealth enriched its ruling class, and made the town an immensely desirable ally for medieval kings and their challengers.

THE LONDON MARKET-PLACE

The range of imports and exports handled on London's quays and wharves, stretching from London Bridge to the Tower, and in the markets, shops and warehouses of the City, was impressive. What struck the hungry and penniless Kentish hero of the fifteenth-century ballad *London Lickpenny* as he wandered through the streets of London was the variety of food on offer: strawberries, cherries, peas, 'rybbes of befe, both fat and fine', hot sheep's feet, cod, mackerel, pepper, saffron and cloves. There were great profits to be made in buying and selling victuals, particularly grain, fish, spices and wine, and victualling guilds (pepperers or grocers, vintners, fishmongers and cornmongers) were among the City's strongest political groups. By medieval standards, London was a large and affluent market for food and drink, and its constant demand must have been important to those areas within easy reach of the city by sea, river and road, especially East Anglia, the South-East, the Thames valley and Gascony. Londoners were active in the east coast herring trade, mainly in Yarmouth, and London merchants bought stocks of grain in such regional distribution centres as Henley and Faversham. The prosperity of several nearby market towns, such as St Albans, Brentford, Kingston and Barking, probably depended on supplying London with agricultural produce. The regulation of the distribution, pricing and quality of these food supplies was one of the most sensitive and difficult tasks of the City administration.[1]

Unable to afford the fruit, fish, beef and pies that he was offered, London Lickpenny had to go hungry. But a sympathetic taverner gave him a pint of wine, perhaps claret from Gascony, or cheaper wine from the Rhineland. From 1152, when Henry II married Eleanor of Aquitaine, to the disastrous defeats of 1453, Gascony was English territory, and the Bordeaux region was the main source of English wine. London merchants dominated the trade for most of the thirteenth century, often exporting English or Baltic grain to Gascony in return. Under Edward I's open trade policy in the 1290s Gascon merchants won control of the trade, and Londoners only regained their position when their legal advantages over aliens were restored in 1327. Within ten years of this the start of the Hundred Years' War disrupted production, devastated vineyards and brought pirates on to the sea routes, bringing the best years of the wine trade to a close. Gascon exports fell from their 1305–9 peak of over 100,000 tuns a year to under 10,000 tuns by 1380, and did not reach their old levels again until the 1480s. The wine trade, which had been one of the most important commercial interests of the twelfth- and thirteenth-century élite, played a more modest part in the political and economic structure of later medieval London.[2]

Ever since the Viking settlements the Baltic trade had been important to London, and in the thirteenth and fourteenth centuries Baltic commodities such as timber, furs, fish, tar, pitch, timber, iron, naval supplies, potash, grain, honey and wax, became a major element in the city's commerce. Merchants specializing in Baltic produce, skinners (furs and hides), corders (rope, canvas and pitch), ironmongers and cornmongers, were prominent among those who pushed their way into citizenship and power in the late thirteenth and early fourteenth centuries. Like much of London's trade, the Baltic trade was controlled by alien merchants, with Londoners playing a subordinate role. German merchants, either from Cologne, or from the so-called Hanseatic ports on the north German coast, Lübeck, Hamburg, Danzig, and many others, were the masters of north European trade, and London was a major western outpost in a trading system which stretched eastwards to Novgorod. The Hanseatic merchants, known as Easterlings, established a community in London which became one of the most powerful forces in the City's commercial life in the later Middle Ages.

Medieval monarchs did more than their share to rid the Russian forests of squirrels and sable, by buying their pelts in vast numbers. A single robe for Henry IV used the skins of 12,000 squirrels and eighty ermine, and Edward III's household used 79,220 trimmed minever (squirrel) skins in 1344–5, a year in which furs took up 42 per cent of the Great Wardrobe's budget. To put these royal sales into perspective, Richard II's average annual purchase of over 108,000 squirrel and 1,634 ermine skins between 1392 and 1394 was the equivalent of a third of the 325,000 furs imported into London in March–November 1390.[3] The King and his entourage set standards of fashion which merchants, craftsmen and lesser Londoners struggled to imitate, probably encouraged rather than deterred by the sumptuary legislation of 1337 and 1363, which restricted expensive imported furs to people of high rank, and confined the lesser sort to rabbit, fox, lamb and cat. 'Common lewd women', a proclamation of 1350 complained, paraded in London 'in the manner and dress of good and noble dames', and should henceforward wear clothes that were untrimmed and unlined, 'so that all folks ... may have knowledge of what rank they are'.[4]

THE TRADE IN WOOL AND CLOTH

Cloth was the stock-in-trade of several of the leading London guilds, the mercers, drapers, tailors, and haberdashers, and was by far the most important commodity in London's later medieval overseas trade. Until the fourteenth century much of the woollen cloth sold in London was made in Flanders from exported English wool. Flanders was northern Europe's outstanding industrial area in the early Middle Ages, and sold its woollen cloth throughout Europe and in the East. England produced Europe's finest wool, and although some of it was used by the home cloth industry a vast amount was bought, from the middle of the twelfth century, by Flemish merchants for processing in Ypres, Ghent, Douai, St Omer, Arras or Bruges.[5] At first, the Flemings, who may have had their own trading association, or Hanse, in London, were the leading alien cloth importers and wool exporters. In the 1260s and 1270s disputes between England and Flanders damaged the position of Flemish merchants in London, and Italian merchants and bankers, who penetrated the English economy as collectors of papal taxes and as royal financiers, displaced them as the dominant force in wool and cloth, trading with Florence as well as Flanders. With the rise of the English cloth industry after about 1350, imports of

Flemish cloth declined. Drapers, who shared the trade in imported Flemish cloth with alien merchants, were one of the most powerful mercantile groups in thirteenth-century London.

The best wool was produced in Lincolnshire, and for most of the thirteenth century Boston, rather than London, was the leading wool exporting port. Furthermore, most of London's share of the trade was in the hands of Flemish, French, German or Italian merchants. In the years 1271–4, ninety-six native London merchants held licences to export wool, and of these a dozen or so seem to have been dealers on quite a large scale.[6] London's share of the national wool trade grew to about 35 or 40 per cent in the last decades of the thirteenth century, and the fourteenth-century royal policy of concentrating exports in a single staple town across the Channel helped native Londoners to wrest a substantial share of the trade from alien merchants. It is possible that by the 1330s Londoners handled almost half London's wool exports, but the available evidence does not allow precise estimates to be made. The London families who exported significant amounts of wool (drapers, grocers, vintners and fishmongers, mostly) were among London's political leaders in the fourteenth century. Wool exports began their long decline in the 1360s, as supplies were diverted from the Flemish to the English woollen industry, but they remained important throughout the fifteenth century, and the Calais staple's monopoly ensured that London merchants would control the bulk of them.[7]

By adding a third to the export price of raw wool, royal taxation gave a decisive advantage to the English cloth industry, and by the 1420s cloth exports had overtaken wool in value, and were on their way to a pre-eminence in English trade which lasted until the rise of the cotton industry in the late eighteenth century. English cloth exports rose from 5,000 to almost 40,000 cloths a year between 1350 and 1400, and were over four times that figure (around 160,000 cloths a year) by the 1490s. They rose even more rapidly after the trade treaty with the Netherlands, the *Magnus Intercursus*, was signed in 1495. Two of the three main cloth-producing regions, the West Country and East Anglia, were within London's reach, and London-based merchants, with their capital, numbers, international experience and political influence, were able to seize the bulk of this trade, doubling their exports and increasing their national share from about 66 per cent to about 85 per cent between 1500 and 1550. In 1500, this trade was shared equally between native merchants and alien (mostly Italian and Hanseatic) ones. The centre of the cloth trade was Blackwell (originally Bakewell) Hall, a large building next to the Guildhall, acquired by the City in 1396. Only here could country clothiers display and sell their cloth to London merchants, and the market, which took place from Thursday to Saturday morning, was controlled and regulated by the mayor. From here, by 1500, nearly all the cloth went to Antwerp, which had overtaken Bruges as the centre of north European trade in the later fifteenth century. Most of it went by sea direct from London, but a small proportion (perhaps 15 per cent) was sent by cart or packhorse to Southampton, where it was loaded on to Venetian galleys. When this arrangement ended in the 1530s Southampton's economy went into a severe decline.[8]

As cloth surpassed wool in export value, the protected wool staplers were overtaken in importance by the unregulated cloth exporters, dealing mostly with the great trading towns of the Low Countries. These free traders, most of them mercers, banded together in groups for mutual protection and support, under the name of merchant adventurers. Groups trading with Prussia and Scandinavia won royal recognition as companies around 1400, but when English merchants were driven out of the Baltic trade in the fifteenth century they were eclipsed by the company established in 1407 to trade with the Netherlands, which became known simply as the Merchant Adventurers of England. Common interests and difficulties, whether in the form of taxation, relations with English or foreign rulers, or dangers at sea, increasingly drew the separate bands of London adventurers together, and they were recognized as a Fellowship, under the control of a governor (always a mercer) and two lieutenants, in 1486. The Fellowship made and enforced trading rules, chartered fleets to take their cloth to the quarterly marts, organized armed convoys when the seas were unsafe, and coordinated their policies with Henry VII. London's wealth and power, together with the King's desire for a unified trading organization, enabled the Fellowship to bring Adventurers from Norwich, York and other towns under its control, and by the 1520s the Governor and General Court of the Adventurers, sitting in the London Mercers' Hall, was regulating and organizing the entire national cloth trade with the Netherlands.[9]

THE WEALTH OF LONDON

The enormous distance that opened up in the later Middle Ages between London's wealth and that of other towns (which helps explain the emphasis which rival factions placed upon possessing the capital) rested on London's trading success, especially in the cloth trade. London's share of England's overseas trade, which had been about a third in the fourteenth century, rose rapidly after 1400, to perhaps two-thirds by 1500 and 85 per cent by 1540.[10] While many provincial towns suffered economic decline in the fifteenth century, among them York, Lynn, Nottingham, Leicester, Yarmouth, and the Lincolnshire wool trading towns (Boston, Beverley and Lincoln), others, including London, Bristol, Norwich, Exeter and Coventry, prospered. This was a regional trend, with the southern and south-western towns increasing their share of the wool and cloth trades at the expense of the north and north-east. The divergence in prosperity between the north and south is demonstrated by a comparison of the assessed wealth of the counties of England for the lay subsidies of 1334 and 1515. While national wealth had tripled, the assessed wealth per acre of London and Middlesex in 1515 was more than twelve times greater than it had been in 1334, and that of Lincolnshire and Yorkshire had only risen by about 50 per cent. The City of London's wealth had risen almost fifteen-fold in 180 years, and was ten times greater than that of the richest provincial town, Norwich. London's tax contribution in 1543 was as large as that of all other English towns combined.[11] Declining towns blamed their misfortunes on London, and to some extent they were right. London's superior geographical position, its excellent credit facilities and its ability to influence commercial policy helped it to draw trade away from York, Hull, Boston, Lynn and Bristol, and its rise as England's centre of government contributed to the decline of Winchester.[12]

The lavish expenditure of the king and his Court played a major part in the business of successful London merchants throughout the Middle Ages. Perhaps the survival of the king's account books gives royal supplies a greater prominence than they deserve, but winning orders from the king's household, whether they were for fish, wine, groceries, cloth, fur, saddlery, spices or wax, was the fastest way into the medieval mercantile élite. This was as true of the Gisors, Basings, Bukerels, Rokesles and Cornhills in the thirteenth century, as it was of Richard Whittington, supplier of fine cloths to Richard II and Henry IV between the 1380s and the 1410s. Dealers in everyday necessities, such as the ironmonger Gilbert Maghfeld, whose ledgers for 1390–95 survive, did not depend so heavily on royal purchases, but vintners, mercers and skinners did very well from courtly extravagance.[13]

ALIEN TRADERS

London owed much of its commercial success to the presence there of prosperous and economically sophisticated alien communities. The aliens of fifteenth-century London, mostly Flemings and other Lowlanders, Germans and Italians, with a few Icelanders, Jews and Portuguese, made up 2–4 per cent of the population, with a high concentration in Southwark. Over 2,000 alien men were assessed for the alien poll tax in London and the suburbs (including Westminster and Southwark) in 1445–6, but it is likely that 1,000 or more Flemings were excluded from this total. The great majority of aliens, perhaps 90 per cent, were Flemings, Hollanders or Germans, known collectively as the Doche. Many of these were craftsmen, important in clock-making, goldsmithing, leather, brewing and tailoring, and later in printing. Sylvia Thrupp has argued that aliens were fairly well integrated into London society, but evidence from Southwark in 1440 and 1551 suggests that aliens chose their employers and their marriage partners from their own people, and mostly lived near each other in the eastern parish of St Olave. There is no sign, though, that they avoided English churches or holding local offices, and some of the most common Flemish occupations – brewer, alehouse-keeper and (it was said) prostitute – would have brought them into close contact with native Londoners. There was still an anti-alien tradition in fifteenth-century London, but it was not as brutal as it had once been. The outbreaks of anti-Flemish violence in 1425 and 1436, which were sparked off by events in France, were brief and fairly easily suppressed, and during Cade's control of London there was no repetition of the horrifying butchery of aliens that had taken place in 1381. The worst attack on Flemings in late medieval London was committed in 1470 by Warwick's army of Kentishmen, who plundered Flemish beer-houses and 'sparid noo Flemyngys that cam in theyr daunger'. Peaceful coexistence was more common (but less noticed) than conflict, and brutality was on the wane.[14]

The two main alien merchant communities, the Italians and the Germans of Lübeck, Hamburg, Danzig and the other Hanseatic towns, were in a more privileged and isolated position. The Hansards dominated London's trade in Baltic and Slavonic goods, hides, furs, linen, timber, iron, ashes, fish, tar, pitch, wax, honey and grain, and handled about a fifth of English broadcloth exports. In 1267 north German merchants were granted rights of trade and association similar to those already possessed by Cologne merchants, and from 1281 all German merchants shared one guildhall in

Upper Thames Street. From within this fortified enclave, known as the Steelyard, a small group of Hanseatic merchants (only twenty of them in 1370) were able to trade with the benefit of the generous tax and customs concessions granted by Edward I's *Carta Mercatoria* of 1303, safe from the assaults of jealous Londoners. In 1494, for instance, a mob attacked the Steelyard, but 'the Easterlyngys had soo strongly shorid and fortyfyed' their enclosure that they were able to hold off their attackers until the mayor came and dispersed them. The Hansards' bargaining skills and their ability to offer generous payments to the Crown no doubt played an important part in winning trading concessions for their community. Among other privileges, the Hanse elected an alderman, maintained the gate at Bishopsgate, and paid a lower duty on cloth exports than Londoners paid. No other alien group was as successful as the Hansards in establishing and protecting their position in medieval London.[15]

From the late fourteenth century English merchants pressed for reciprocal trading rights in the Baltic, and the government acted on their behalf without long-term success. A series of indecisive conflicts culminated in the seizure of Hanseatic possessions in London by Edward IV in 1468, a five-year naval war, and the expulsion of English merchants from the Baltic. After this Edward IV, who had been helped by the Hanse in his struggle with Henry VI in 1470, restored their property and privileges, which they retained (with a few interruptions) until 1597. The privileges of Hanseatic merchants were resented, but they ensured that their trade in linen, wax and Baltic goods was channelled through London, rather than Ipswich or another east coast port, helping London to avoid the general trade depression of the mid-fifteenth century. Londoners' penetration of the Baltic trade was delayed until the sixteenth century. The Hanse's great days were over by that time, but German merchants continued to occupy the Steelyard, which was rebuilt after the Great Fire, until 1852.[16]

The most important group of alien merchants in London, the Italians, never succeeded in winning the communal privileges won by the Hansards. Perhaps this was because they lacked national unity as a group (though the same could be said of German merchants), or because they operated as competing companies, gaining strength from their ties with the Crown, not with each other.[17] In the fifteenth century they fell foul of the belief that a nation should accumulate as much gold and silver as possible. *The Libelle of English Policye*, a patriotic bullionist poem written around 1436 to urge the government to 'cheryshe marchandyse' and to use seapower to control trade in the Channel, including the trade of the Low Countries, was especially critical of Italians. They drained gold and silver from England by importing useless luxuries, it argued, buying English wool cheaply on credit, and using the profits to bribe the government and lend at high interest to native merchants:

> And thus they wolde, if ye will so beleve,
> Wypen our nose with our owne sleve.[18]

A small group of about seventy Italian merchants, mostly resident in London, handled about a quarter of England's overseas trade and dominated its banking system, using financial techniques and capital not available to native merchants. Attempts to control them by legislation were thwarted by their value to the Crown as a source of loans and customs revenues, which they paid at more than twice the native rate. As usurers and luxury importers, and without the walls of a fortified enclosure to protect them, the Italians were an easy target for riotous apprentices. Anti-Italian riots, sparked off by street brawls and sexual rivalry, and probably encouraged by certain London mercers and staplers, continued intermittently from April 1456 to 1458, causing the Italians such distress that they tried to move their headquarters to Southampton. This was a real threat to London's commercial primacy. When Genoese and Florentine trade had moved to Southampton between the 1420s and 1450s London's trade in cloth, and in the dyes, soap and alum the Italians supplied for the English cloth industry, was badly hit.[19]

Andreas Franciscus, visiting London as part of an Italian delegation in 1497, found the town an uncomfortable place for a foreigner. Londoners, tall, well-exercised, overfed and under-educated, put him in constant fear of violence:

> Londoners have such fierce tempers and wicked dispositions that they not only despise the way in which Italians live, but actually pursue them with uncontrolled hatred. . . . At Bruges, we could do as we liked by day as well as by night. But here they look askance at us by day, and at night sometimes drive us off with kicks and blows of the truncheon.[20]

The Italians were victims of ill-informed xenophobia. In reality, they were net importers of bullion into England, their imports, mostly spices, woad, alum and silk, were not all useless luxuries, and they provided capital and shipping which London merchants could not supply. When the Italians' control of Mediterranean trade declined in the later fifteenth century, Dutch and Spanish traders, rather than Londoners, took their place.[21]

THE RISE OF GUILDS

Those who controlled the wholesale trade of London, and dominated its political life, were a small élite of a few hundred men. Below them were craftsmen and retailers, the majority of citizens, and below them again were their apprentices, labourers and the poor, the bulk of London's population. 'By far the greater part of the people of your city live by their merchandise and by the workmanship of their hands,' the King was told in 1321.[22]

Craftsmen do not figure in accounts of London's political history until the popular mayoralties of Thomas fitz Thomas in 1261–5 and of Walter Hervey in 1271–3, but it is possible to trace their earlier development through the fraternities or guilds some of them formed in the twelfth and thirteenth centuries. The two earliest London trades to form an organization which received official recognition were the weavers, who were granted charters by Henry I before 1130 and by Henry II between 1154 and 1162, and the bakers, who had arranged to pay their taxes in a lump sum to the Exchequer in 1155. Many, perhaps most, guilds were associations with no economic purpose. In 1180 a list of fines for unlicensed guilds records eighteen London guild fraternities, of which only four seem to be related to trades: goldsmiths, pepperers, clothworkers and butchers. Of the rest, five were apparently devoted to building London's stone bridge (which was built between 1176 and about 1209), two perhaps had a religious purpose, and the rest were named after their leading member. Throughout the Middle Ages there were many guilds serving religious, social and neighbourly purposes, and even craft and trade guilds had spiritual, festive and charitable functions which were by no means subordinate to their economic ones.[23]

It is quite possible that most of the guilds mentioned in the twelfth-century records did not last very long, but in the thirteenth century evidence of permanent craft organization is easier to find. The fishmongers, gathered in their riverside parishes, acted collectively to deal with royal taxation and settle internal disputes, probably from 1220 or earlier. Goldsmiths, who had important duties in matters of royal finance and checking the quality of coinage, certainly had an organization in the 1270s, and perhaps several decades earlier. We find the lorimers (makers of bridles, bits, spurs and stirrups), joiners, girdlers, cordwainers and wool-packers winning recognition for their ordinances in the reforming days of 1261–4 and 1272–3, when craftsmen enjoyed a moment of political power, and losing it again in the reaction of 1274. Skinners and tailors were each involved in collective property transactions in the 1270s, and both had formed fraternities by 1300. Elspeth Veale argues persuasively that Edward I's reign (1272–1307) was a decisive period in the formalization of craft and trade associations. This was partly because population growth and immigration made it harder for crafts to maintain the informal local understandings they had previously relied on, and mainly because the King's favours towards alien merchants forced Londoners to demand explicit recognition of what they had once taken for granted. For example, the London vintners were forced to insist on their monopoly over wine retailing, and to assert their control over the measurement and quality of wine, by the intrusion of Edward's favoured Gascons into their domestic trade, and the pepperers united to defend their London market against Picard interlopers. Perhaps the same fears prompted the mercers to introduce formal guild arrangements around 1300, electing a master, registering apprentices and controlling entry into their trade. The recognition of craft organizations continued under Edward II, and by the first years of Edward III's reign (1327–77) the main crafts were established as a fully accepted part of London's economic life. Four craft fraternities, the goldsmiths, girdlers, skinners and tailors, received royal charters in 1327, giving them control over their craft in London and, to some extent, throughout the kingdom. In 1328 twenty-five crafts were listed as having the right to elect their own officers, and by the end of the century at least forty more had received civic recognition.[24]

The guilds which won the greatest political and economic power were organizations of dealers and wholesalers, men with capital and entrepreneurial ability, rather than simple manufacturers and retailers. This hierarchical pattern of crafts began to emerge in the thirteenth century, as economic activity became more complex and large-scale. Thus the bakers fell under the control of wholesale grain dealers, the weavers became pieceworkers for rich cloth merchants (burellers), the blade-makers and sheathers were employed by the cutlers, the coppersmiths were in the grip of the girdlers, the fullers were mastered by the entrepreneurial dyers, and the painters, joiners and lorimers, who between them produced saddles, were controlled by the saddlers who marketed their finished product. During the political and economic upheavals of the late thirteenth century it was not so difficult, or revolutionary, for the leaders of the entrepreneurial trades, the skinners, fishmongers and grocers, to join well-established wool, cloth and wine merchants in the aldermanic class. The fishmongers, with their control over one of the mainstays of the medieval diet, their plentiful shipping, and their trading interests in wine, grain, wool and Baltic produce, rose from the status of outsiders and rebels in 1263 and 1272 to be the most powerful interest group in the fourteenth-century élite.[25]

In the fourteenth century the strongest guilds began to display their wealth and power by building or acquiring impressive mansions, or halls, to accommodate their feasts and meetings. The Goldsmiths (1339) and Merchant Taylors (1347) were first, and the Skinners, Cordwainers and Saddlers followed at the end of the century. Smaller guilds used taverns or hired halls for the night, but between 1400 and 1530 a further forty guilds managed to acquire halls of their own. Almost every one of these halls was destroyed in the Great Fire of 1666 and most were ruined again in the Second World War. Only the fifteenth-century courtroom of the Vintners' Hall, and the kitchen, hall and crypt of the Merchant Taylors, survived both disasters.[26]

GUILD REGULATIONS

The craft ordinances of the fourteenth century provide an insight into the aims of the guilds at that time, and into the organization of London's medieval economy. The rules, drawn up by the misteries, approved by the mayor and aldermen, and enforced by about six wardens who were leading men in the craft, always excluded non-citizens (known as foreigns) from the exercise of the craft or retailing its products. They stipulated a minimum seven-year apprenticeship for those wishing to enter the craft as citizens, and imposed discipline on rebellious apprentices and labourers by forbidding their employment by other members of the craft without their previous master's permission. Usually, work on Sundays and major feast days and at night was forbidden, sometimes with the explanation that nightwork produced bad-quality goods and disturbed the neighbourhood. All crafts tried to maintain the quality of their goods by specifying particular materials, techniques and levels of workmanship. The heaumers (makers of helmets), farriers and barber-surgeons emphasized the danger to the public from bad workmanship, while others, such as the pepperers, potters, pewterers, armourers and cutlers, claimed to be defending consumers against fraud. Some trades, the girdlers and braelers (makers of braces), forbade the employment of women other than the master's wife and daughters.[27]

Perhaps there was altruism in these rules, but the common purpose was to restrict the number of masters and retailers, control the lives of apprentices and labourers, prevent competition by controlling materials and working hours, limit the influx of products from outside London by making sure they met quality standards and were retailed by craft members, exclude interlopers, and facilitate illicit price-fixing. Craft ordinances could also be useful in settling disputes between crafts by establishing a demarcation line between their work (bowyers and fletchers, for example) or recognizing the supremacy of one craft over another. Disputes between crafts could lead to murderous battles, and resolving them, 'nurturing love among all manner of folks', was always an aim of good civic government.[28]

THE LOCALIZATION OF CRAFTS

The task of enforcing guild rules was made easier by the localization of most trades and crafts within the City. The pelterers' ordinances of 1365 explicitly confined pelterers (skin-dealers) to Walbrook and Cornhill wards, and Budge Row, 'so the overseers of the trade may be able to oversee them'.[29] As in other medieval cities, people of particular callings lived and worked near each other, fostering companionship and mutual support, as well as facilitating guild control, and helping to protect those whose work was noisy, smoky or smelly from neighbours' complaints. In the 1170s, as William Fitzstephen tells us, 'those engaged in business of various kinds, sellers of merchandise, hirers of labour, are distributed every morning into their several localities according to their trade'.[30] For instance London's longest street, Thames Street, was the main location for cookshops where travellers could eat by day or night. Local concentrations of crafts and trades are confirmed by the tax records of 1292 and 1319. The riverside wards, Tower, Billingsgate, Bridge, Dowgate, Queenhithe and Castle Baynard, were inhabited particularly by fishmongers, woolmongers and cornmongers, with vintners and taverners predominant in Vintry Ward. Mercers were concentrated in Broad Street, Bassishaw and Cheap, and metalworkers in Coleman Street and Cheap Ward. Two suburban areas, the extramural part of Cripplegate and Farringdon Without, specialized in tanning and leatherwork. There were concentrations of skinners in Walbrook, pepperers in Cordwainer, goldsmiths in Aldersgate, and fripperers, or small dealers, in Cornhill Ward.[31]

Many City street names indicate the location of trades and crafts, but since these often date from before or soon after the Conquest, and were in written use by the thirteenth century, the information they contain generally relates to the early Middle Ages. Throughout the Middle Ages Cheap (which was called Cheapside only from the sixteenth century) was

London's main market, and the old English streets and lanes running off and near it still bear names indicating the goods that were made and sold in them. Honey Lane and Milk, Bread and Wood Streets probably denote eleventh-century markets, and the workshops of twelfth- or thirteenth-century craftsmen gave names to Cordwainer, Silver, Lime, Cannon (Candlewick) and Roper Streets, and a long list of early lanes: Ironmonger, Soper, Spurrier, Lad (ladles), Distaff, Needlers, Mede, Limeburner and Hosier Lanes are all recorded by around 1300.

The keeping of livestock is well represented in the early street names in Farringdon Without, around Smithfield, where on Fridays, Fitzstephen tells us, countrymen stood selling their 'implements of husbandry, swine with long flanks, cows with full udders, oxen of immense size, and woolly sheep'. The living animals reared and sold in Cock, Duck, Cow and Chicken Lanes were taken for slaughter at the western end of Newgate Street, known as the Shambles or the Fleshshambles, and reappeared on the stalls in Poultry, Newgate Market, Bladder Street, and Pudding Lane (where puddings, or entrails, were sold). The persistence of farming activity and animal rearing even in the heart of medieval London is denoted by many street names: two Huggin Lanes, where hogs were raised, Addle Street, where dung littered the path, Oat Lane, Goose Lane, and Seething Lane, where corn was threshed.[32]

Newgate and Cheap remained the main market streets for meat, poultry and other provisions, and food was also sold from stalls in Cornhill, Gracechurch Street and Eastcheap. By the thirteenth century London had several markets that specialized in particular commodities. For grain, the most important commodity of all, Londoners could go to Billingsgate and Queenhithe, ancient landing places for corn, salt and other provisions, or to the markets in Newgate and Gracechurch Street. Billingsgate's transformation into a specialist fish market was not completed until 1698, but there were fish markets in Old Fish Street and New Fish Street (now Fish Street Hill), near the bridge. Two new covered markets were provided by the City authorities, the Stocks Market at the east end of Poultry (on the site of the present Mansion House) in 1283, and Leadenhall, a privately owned market half-way along Cornhill, which was bought in 1411 and rebuilt in the 1440s.[33] It was hoped that the building of the Stocks market would stop butchers, poulterers and fishmongers blocking Cheap with their wares, and that Leadenhall would take 'foreign' fishmongers, and victuallers of all sorts, off the cluttered streets. Leadenhall was also a City granary, and became an important market for wool, leather and cloth.[34] But the provision of covered markets could not keep pace with the growth of trade, and Stow recorded around 1600 that 'Country People which brought provisions to the City, were forced to stand with their stalls in the open street, to the damage of their goods, and Danger of their persons, by the Coaches, Carts, Horses, and Cattle that pass through.' Street markets, especially evening ones, presented problems of disorder, cheating, evasion of guild controls, and obstruction. It was in Cornhill, which was known as a market for old clothes and furniture, that London Lickpenny saw for sale the hood that had been snatched from him in Westminster. Even the long-established market for garden produce at the south-east corner of St Paul's Churchyard was found to be a nuisance to priests and worshippers, because of 'the scurrility, clamour, and nuisance of the gardeners and their servants, there selling pulse, cherries, vegetables and other wares', and was moved south towards Blackfriars in 1345.[35]

Retailing was not always done in the open air. A recent survey of medieval Cheapside property shows that the street was lined with little shops, even in the early thirteenth century. As the population grew, the demand for prime locations on Cheap led to the subdivision of the already small plots, so that the average shop in the 1320s was probably about 7 feet wide and 12 feet deep. Customers, it seems, would usually have been served on the street, as they are today from the City's sweet and newspaper kiosks, by the man or (very often) the woman within. In many cases, a wooden shutter would be lowered every morning, opening the shop's front window and providing a projecting counter at the same time. Some shops on Cheap, especially those built in front of St Mary-le-Bow in the 1270s, were stone-built, but most were substantial wooden lean-tos, which could be quite easily amalgamated or subdivided as rents or trading conditions changed. With the fall in population after the 1330s rents fell, shops grew in size, and some previously valuable plots were deserted. It took until about 1600 for rents on Cheapside to recover to their 1300 level, and the tiny thirteenth-century shops never returned. Down alleys off the main streets, where property was cheaper, there were larger stone-walled covered bazaars, known as selds, in which a number of traders (maybe fifteen or twenty) rented a plot, each standing beside a cupboard, chest or table full of merchandise. In Derek Keene's view Cheapside, London's busiest shopping street but by no means its only one, had around 400 shops and 4,000 trading plots, employing enough people 'to populate a market town of considerable size'.[36]

Apart from the provisions trades of Cheap, and the activities inevitably associated with the river, most of the crafts and trades of London changed their locations at some time in the Middle Ages. Soper Lane (now part of

Queen Street), was successively the home of soapmakers, pepperers, curriers, cordwainers and pie-sellers between the thirteenth and sixteenth centuries. The Cheapside survey shows that in 1300 St Lawrence Lane, off Cheap, was occupied by at least nineteen traders in leather and skins. By 1400 there were only three leather businesses left in the area. A large colony of mercers and silkwomen disappeared from Soper Lane over the same period, and in Bow Lane drapers took the place of shoemakers and hosiers.[37]

Stow, writing around 1600, gives us many examples of traders who had changed their location, 'as they have found their best advantage'. The goldsmiths had moved from Gutheron's Lane to Cheap, the grocers and pepperers from Soper Lane to Bucklersbury, the drapers from Lombard Street to Candlewick Street, the ironmongers from Ironmonger Lane to Thames Street (which had lost its cookshops), the hosiers from Hosier Lane to Cordwainer Street (which the shoemakers and leather-dressers had deserted) and Birchin Lane (once the home of barbers). The poulters had recently moved from Poultry into Gracechurch Street, the bowyers of Bowyers Row had scattered, the paternoster (or rosary) makers had moved from Paternoster Row to St Paul's Churchyard, and the patten-makers of St Margaret Pattens Lane were 'cleane worne out'.[38]

Craft rules were intended, above all, to preserve the advantages of established craftsmen and traders, the freemen of London, from the intrusions of 'foreigns', people without citizenship living either within or outside the City walls. These people, the unenfranchised, certainly constituted the majority, perhaps around three-quarters, of medieval London's adult population. They were mostly free men and women, since serfs who had escaped to London from rural bondage became free after a year's residence in the City, but they were unlikely, unless they were apprentices, ever to become guildsmen, and thus freemen or citizens of London. Although it was generally true that foreigns were people of low social and economic status – apprentices, journeymen, labourers, street sellers, servants, suburban tradesmen, the destitute, criminals, and so on – they also included many craftsmen and traders in areas of work which had not been organized into guilds. A list of 111 London crafts compiled in 1422 by the clerk of the brewers mentions many occupations which were free of formal guild restrictions: corsours (horse-dealers), marbelers, bookbinders, jewellers, organ-makers, feathermongers, piemakers, basket-makers, mirrorers, quilters, parchmyners (makers of parchment), and many others. Some of these were skilled crafts, in which artificial restrictions on new entrants were unnecessary.[39] In 1309 one of London's richest merchants, the skinner

Robert Persone, was a non-freeman, preferring the concrete advantages of exemption from civic duties and taxes to the intangible benefits of citizenship.

THE BLACK DEATH AND LONDON'S POPULATION

We cannot know with any accuracy how many people lived in medieval London. The city was not included in the Domesday survey of 1086, which forms the basis of most calculations of the population of eleventh-century England, and the lists of between 1,636 and 1,820 taxpayers in the lay subsidy rolls of 1292, 1319 and 1332 do not include non-citizens (foreigns), citizens with moveable property worth under 6s 8d or 10s, women (except for a few well-off widows), clergymen, or those who had simply managed to evade payment. In some wards, such as Lime Street, with its eleven taxpayers spread over almost three parishes, and Portsoken, with twenty-three taxpayers in 1332, the 'dark figure' of the poor, the 'foreign', and the dishonest is obviously so large as to reduce even the most learned calculations to guesswork. Thus Ekwall, working on the subsidy rolls, finds it 'difficult to believe' that London's population in 1300 was much less than 40,000, a figure accepted by Gwyn Williams and Susan Reynolds. There is ample room for disagreement, with Professor Russell suggesting 60,000 for 1340, and Derek Keene outbidding them all with a suggestion of 100,000. His estimate of 25,000 for 1100 is also well above the more commonly suggested figure of about 18,000.[40] Growth at this pace would have relied heavily on immigration, and Ekwall's studies of London surnames, which often indicated birthplace or occupation, show that there was indeed a substantial influx of tradesmen and artisans from the Home Counties, especially Essex and Hertfordshire, and of merchants from the East Midlands. The latter probably explains the fact that London's dialect, predominantly East Saxon until around 1300, was mainly East Midlands thereafter.[41]

All population estimates have to try to calculate the enormous impact on London of the Black Death, by any standards one of the most significant and disastrous events in London's (and England's) history. Bubonic plague is carried in the blood of black rats, and transmitted to humans by the bite of the rat flea. It had been spreading from Asia across southern Europe since 1346, and spread from Dorset through southern England after August 1348, reaching London in the winter of 1348–9. It remained in the city for a year. Its effects on a community without hygienic or medical defences, and lacking acquired resistance to the plague bacillus, were horrendous. Those who caught the disease suffered large swellings in their armpits and groin, extensive internal bleeding (which produced the black blotches typical of the plague), the onset (not surprisingly) of depression and despair, and probable death within five days. Pneumonic plague, which seems to have been present too, keeping the epidemic going through the winter and into the spring, attacked the lungs, and killed more swiftly. The pestilence (as it was called) spread most quickly, and hung on longest, in crowded poorer areas, where people were malnourished, and could not afford to escape.

In the absence of parish registers or other reliable sources, estimates of the proportion of the population of Europe, England or London that died in this first plague depend upon patches of information from particular communities (especially Church ones), contemporary observers, and indirect economic evidence, such as changes in wages and rents. At one extreme a chronicler, Galfridi le Baker, thought only one in ten English people survived, and at the other the epidemiologist J. F. D. Shrewsbury believed that only one in twenty died. Both of these are probably wide of the mark. Church and manorial records in England suggest a national death rate of between 30 and 40 per cent in 1348–9, and London, like other big cities, may have suffered more than its fair share of deaths. About a third of the grocers' fraternity died, but some guilds escaped less lightly. The hatters lost all six of their wardens, the cutlers all eight of theirs. Westminster Abbey lost twenty-six monks and an abbot (half the community), St James's Hospital lost most of its brethren, and 100 Greyfriars died. The enormous increase in the number of wills enrolled in the court of Husting, from about twenty in a normal year to over 370 in 1348–9, indicates the scale of plague mortality among people with property. Contemporary figures have to be treated with caution. Two new suburban plague cemeteries were created, and in one of these, on the future Charterhouse site, 50,000 victims (probably more than the total population of London) were said to have been buried. Recent excavations suggest that the number buried in the West Smithfield and Tower cemeteries together was only a quarter of this figure.[42]

The plague had abated by December 1349, but London's sufferings were not over. Severe outbreaks of pestilence returned in 1361–2, this time especially killing children, who had not acquired resistance in 1348–9, again in 1368–9, and repeatedly thereafter. Between 1407 and 1479 the plague visited London eleven times (six of them in the 1420s and 1430s), and although it appeared less frequently after 1480 its shadow was not lifted until after the last terrible outbreak of 1665. It is impossible to disentangle the demographic effects of the plague from that of the many other epidemic and endemic diseases that afflicted London (and the rest of the country) throughout the fourteenth and fifteenth centuries. These were centuries of tuberculosis, typhus, influenza, leprosy, dysentery, smallpox, diptheria and measles, 'fevers and fluxes, coughs, heart disease, cramps, toothaches, catarrhs and cataracts, scabs, boils, tumours, burning agues, frenzies and foul evils'.[43]

The effect of the first plague on London's population was dramatic enough to create a labour shortage and large wage increases, and the cumulative effect of later plagues and other diseases must have cut the population back severely. If London's population before the plague was around 45,000, a fairly conventional estimate, and its loss in 1348–9 was a third, around the possible national average, then a post-plague total of about 30,000 would not be unlikely, and accords with the fact that 23,000 Londoners (excluding only aliens, tax-evaders, clergy and children under fourteen) paid the poll tax in 1377. But the conventional wisdom also assumes that there was little or no population growth between 1350 and 1500, and that London's population in 1500 was at least 50,000, perhaps 70,000, giving us a sum that does not add up. Either London's pre-plague population was higher, or London escaped lightly from the plague, or there was real urban and suburban growth, with migration outrunning the high mortality rate, between 1350 and 1500.[44]

Derek Keene has argued, perhaps on rather slender evidence, that conventional assumptions may be completely wrong. His work on the Cheapside area, which shows intense demand for commercial property around 1300, much slacker demand from 1348 to around 1530, and a return to pre-plague levels by 1600, has led him to suggest that London's population in 1300 may have been near 100,000, making it almost as large as Paris, and that it fell during the hungry and diseased years of the early fourteenth century and in the Black Death to 50,000, where it remained until the great population boom of the later sixteenth century. The paucity of hard evidence, especially on the number of labourers and non-citizens, who were no more likely to rent a shop on Cheapside than they were to pay a Parliamentary subsidy or appear on a guild register, should lead us to keep an open mind. And a recent study of London's grain supply (also involving Derek Keene) concludes that the higher estimates of London's population in 1300 'should perhaps be moderated a little', and that 'England in 1300 is unlikely to have sustained a population of as many as 5 millions and a capital city in excess of 80,000 inhabitants'.[45]

LABOURING PEOPLE

The lives of the poor and powerless are not entirely hidden from us. We hear of unfortunate lepers cast out from churches and taverns, forced to beg with their bodies entirely cloaked, and eventually driven out of the City in 1276, to live perhaps in a suburban leper hospital. There were ten of these hospitals near London by 1500, when leprosy had begun to decline and disappear.[46] We hear also about the street-sellers, the hucksters and burlesters, who sold their cheese, fish, vegetables or hats in London, despite the complaints of the guildsmen whose business they were taking away. Guild records and regulations tell us something about apprentices, who might serve from seven to fourteen years, kept but not paid by their master. Although this was a traineeship for which the boy's parent had paid a fee of up to £10, it did not always end in admission to a guild as a citizen and craftsman. Perhaps more than half the apprentices in two well-studied crafts, the grocers and skinners, never became freemen, but instead died, wandered off, or drifted down into unskilled labour because they could not pay the citizenship fee. Among skinners, Elspeth Veale suggests, it may be that boys taken from poorer families for a low fee were taken on as cheap labour, not potential masters.[47]

Many crafts relied on a pool of unskilled labourers, working alone on piecework, 'in chambers secretly in alleys and upon stairs and houses in corners', or employed in a workshop alongside one or two others. The 'putting out' system, in which workers in their own homes produced goods for a master who sold them as his own, was commonplace in medieval London.[48] It is unusual to hear of a master in medieval London employing more than fifteen or sixteen men, though large building works must have involved more men than this. We hear most about workmen when they tried to improve their conditions by joint action with others of their trade, as their masters had done. In 1350, when their bargaining position was strengthened by the labour shortage brought about by the Black Death, builders' labourers, carters, glovers' workmen, shearmen (who sheared the nap from woollen cloth), farriers and domestic servants were accused of taking 'immeasurably more than they were wont to take before the time of the pestilence'. City regulations were issued threatening to imprison craftsmen and labourers who refused traditional daily wage rates: between 4d and 6d for masons, carpenters, plasterers and tilers, and 3d or 3½d for their labourers. At this rate a labourer would have been able to buy with his daily wage twelve cheap loaves, 3 gallons of ale, a gallon of cheap wine, or half a pair of shoes, at prices prevailing in London up to 1350.[49]

Nationally, labourers' wages rose rapidly in the 1350s and 1360s, despite the Statute of Labourers of 1351, which tried to hold them down. In Westminster building labourers' wages doubled by the 1360s, and it is hard to see how the London authorities, for all the threats of imprisonment and the guild agreements to stick to the old rates, could have resisted the general trend. Several crafts passed rules against enticing workers from one master to another, and labourers were occasionally arrested and fined for taking excessive wages, but the guilds were probably fighting a losing battle against economic realities. Westminster builders' wages fell back a little in the later fourteenth century, but then rose rapidly in the 1430s, and remained at twice their pre-1348 level for most of the fifteenth century. Thorold Rogers, the late Victorian master of this subject, regarded the fifteenth century as 'the golden age of the English labourer', and modern research has not overturned this picture. 'At no time were wages, relatively speaking, so high, and at no time was food so cheap.' In London labourers' wages were 25 or 30 per cent higher than in the rest of England, although this would have been offset in part by higher prices. According to the household accounts of the Bishop of Bath and Wells in 1338, the prices of such basic goods as candles, oats and pigs were about 50 per cent higher in London than in Somerset. Some imported luxuries were cheaper in London, but this did not help the poor.[50]

No doubt it is true that labourers' families on typical rates of pay could afford nothing but the poorest standards of food, heating and lighting in their single tenement rooms, and that their chattels, to judge from most court and coroners' reports, were valueless. Nevertheless, wages tended to rise faster than prices, creating a long-term increase in real wages which probably left labourers better off in 1500 than they had ever been before, or were to be again until the nineteenth century. The 'alliances, confederacies, or conspiracies' of London journeyman shearers, weavers, cordwainers, saddlers and tailors, imitating the fraternities of their masters with suits of livery, patron saints and church affiliations to provide 'a certain feigned odour of sanctity' to their illicit associations, suggest a new sense of bargaining power among working men in the later fourteenth century. Its basis, though, was a labour scarcity produced by recurrent plagues and a high death rate.[51]

'Bruisers and Nightwalkers'

There is a temptation to represent the 'foreigns' of medieval London as an assortment of thieves, beggars, prostitutes and cheats, the misfits who are always turning up in the City records, usually on their way to prison or the pillory. Such people, though surely a small proportion of the non-citizen population, attract our attention because they are colourful and comparatively well recorded, and because they have been a source of constant irritation to London's rulers for at least 800 years. Any busy town will have its share of brawls, thefts and murders, and there is no reason to suppose that London's crime problem was unusually severe. Sudden increases in the number of wrongdoers appearing in the mayor's court probably tell us more about the zeal of the mayor than about real fluctuations in crime levels. A vigorous mayor, or one driven by fear of royal displeasure or intervention, merely trawled deeper into London's underworld, and thus leaves us a fuller account of the creatures dwelling there. The austere Richer de Refham, who was under pressure from Edward II to act against robbers, murderers and procuresses, brought to trial a succession of common offenders in 1311. Elmer de Multone, a 'bruiser and nightwalker', 'wont to entice strangers and persons unknown to a tavern, and there deceive them by using fake dice', would have been equally at home in Elizabethan or Victorian London. So would Margaret de Huntyngdone, a 'common strumpet' committed to the Tun, a prison for petty offenders in Cornhill, for harbouring men of bad repute, or Richard de Pelham, imprisoned in 1311 for defrauding strangers and being a 'rorer', a disturber of the peace. The association between crime, prostitution, late-night taverns, gambling, and taking advantage of strangers is familiar in almost any century in London's history.[52]

While the mayor, sheriffs and aldermen heard most cases of robbery and assault, cases of murder and manslaughter were tried by itinerant royal justices, usually sitting in the Tower. The records of these Eyres, as the sittings were called, along with the records of the coroners' courts, tell us something about those Londoners who died by malice or misfortune, rather than natural causes. The worst incidents occurred when civic authority was weak, as in the 1260s and the 1320s, when there was horrifying mob violence against Jews, aliens and royal officials. Street battles between men of rival crafts could also lead to bloodshed on a grand scale. The goldsmiths' and parmenters' fight with the tailors and cordwainers in 1267, and the battle of skinners and fishmongers in 1340, were two of the worst of these.

Individual killings were more likely to occur as a result of angry arguments, usually over women or property, than as premeditated murders. The problem of spontaneous violence was exacerbated by drinking, the lack of medical care, and the ready availability of knives and sticks of many kinds. Carving knives, Irish knives, whittling knives, double-edged knives (poniards), broad knives (bidaus), misericordes (for dispatching horses), would be ready to hand, and the better-equipped brawler might even have a battle-axe: pole-axes, halberds, belts, and gisarms were all used in London fights. Working sticks could kill, and coroners' courts heard of balstaffs, cudgels, faggot sticks, distaffs, bedstaffs, billets and crutches being used as murder weapons.[53]

Keeping the Peace

Medieval London was protected from crime by an assortment of preventive, policing and penal policies. It was exempt, by the terms of Henry II's charter, from two Norman innovations, the murder fine and trial by battle, but not from the older system of frankpledge, which obliged each ward to eject any non-freeholder who attempted to stay in the ward more than three days without finding three sureties for his good behaviour. Staying in London more than three days without sureties was a felony, and a ward harbouring such a man, especially if he had committed a crime, was liable to a heavy fine when the royal justices arrived with the itinerant Assizes. The ward was therefore responsible for its own policing and for its own wrongdoers, and the city as a whole could be punished, as it was by Edward I, if law enforcement fell below an acceptable standard. It was in their own interests, then, for Londoners to join the hue and cry when a felony had been committed, and this ancient system of communal pursuit was still operating as late as the eighteenth century.

According to Stow, an 8 o'clock curfew was introduced by William I, but was ineffectively enforced after 1100. Between 1281 and 1284 the Mayor, Henry le Waleys, launched a campaign against lawlessness, supported by Edward I, which included the revival of an effective curfew, with a new prison, the Cornhill Tun, for curfew breakers, or nightwalkers. In 1282 he ordered the registration of all ward residents, all hostel guests, and all members of trades, and a nightly curfew to be rung from St Martin-le-Grand and all parish churches. All the City taverns and gates were to be closed, and crossing the river by bridge or boat by night was forbidden. Six competent men were to police each ward by night, and each gate was to be guarded by two skilful sergeants. A further proclamation in 1329 said that only reputable citizens or their servants, 'for reasonable cause and with light' were to be out after curfew, and that all taverns, where wrongdoers 'seek refuge, and watch the time for their misdoing', should close by night. Whether London's unpaid watchmen were really able to clear the dark streets of nightwalkers, rorers, strumpets and vagrants is a matter for conjecture.[54]

Petty offenders were fined or imprisoned, or subjected to the public humiliation of the pillory, or a shameful procession through the streets, perhaps dragged on a hurdle, or carried on horseback facing the tail and wearing a fool's cap, sometimes accompanied by a band of musicians. Public ridicule was used especially for cheats, scolds, bawds and dishonest tradesmen. A baker pilloried with rotten or underweight dough round his neck, a taverner forced to drink his own sour wine, or a butcher decorated with his putrid meat, was a warning to customers and to other tradesmen. Murderers and thieves, especially those caught red-handed, could be hanged, unless they could find refuge in one of London's 120 or more churches or monastic precincts. Here the felon could claim sanctuary for forty days, a right that was rarely violated, and would be given a choice between surrendering for trial or forfeiting his possessions, making for the nearest port (usually Dover or Southampton) and abjuring the realm for ever. Felons (especially those with local sympathizers) often escaped from unguarded churches by night, and from the fourteenth century they could find permanent refuge in one of the two large monastic sanctuaries, Westminster or St Martin-le-Grand. These both contained ample accommodation for debtors, thieves, murderers and even heretics, and the monasteries welcomed the rents their tenants paid. These two unpoliced havens, one of them within the City walls, made a mockery of London's law enforcement. 'What a rabble of thieves, murderers, and malicious heinous traitors, and that in two places specially: The one at the elbow of the City, the other in the very bowels,' Sir Thomas More complained early in the sixteenth century. '. . . Thieves bring thither their stolen goods, and there live thereon. There devise they new robberies; nightly they steal out; they rob and reve and plunder and kill . . .' As a royal servant More took a dim view of the right of sanctuary, but it could also play a civilizing role by protecting suspects from instant revenge, giving time for tempers to cool and the true facts of a case (for instance, an accidental killing) to emerge. The antiquity and social value of sanctuary enabled it to survive, in a limited form, beyond the destruction of the monasteries in the 1530s. Sanctuary for criminals continued until 1623, and for civil offenders (especially debtors) until legislation of 1697 and 1723. Among the London sanctuaries abolished in these two Acts were the Minories, Whitefriars, Salisbury Court, Mitre Court, Baldwin's Gardens, the Savoy, the Clink, the Mint and Stepney. A few of these, especially Whitefriars (Alsatia), between Fleet Street and the Thames, were still notorious criminal neighbourhoods in the early nineteenth century.[55]

Murders and all unnatural deaths were first examined by the city's coroner, a royal appointee who was also the king's chamberlain or butler. The coroners' rolls give a hint of the dangers of daily life in a medieval town. Drowning, either in the Thames while swimming or after falling from the bridge, or in a well or a latrine, was a common mishap. In 1275 a water-carrier was drowned when his boat slipped from under him as he tried to place his water pail on the riverbank. Drunkenness and darkness were a dangerous combination, especially when there were rough steps to descend, or candles to be balanced next to dry straw beds. Children were vulnerable to animals, too, and we hear of them being crushed by carts, trampled by horses, and mauled by pigs. Falling walls and solars (overhanging upper storeys) were an occasional danger, and in 1271 the collapse of the bell-tower of St Mary-le-Bow killed thirteen people. Worse still was the crushing to death in 1322 of fifty poor men and women as they waited outside Blackfriars Monastery for alms from a fishmonger's will.[56]

FIRES AND NUISANCES

William Fitzstephen's remarkable description of London written in the 1170s as a prologue to his life of Thomas Becket mentions 'the immoderate drinking of fools and the frequent fires' as London's only inconveniences, and it is likely that fire, rather than crime, was the greater danger to life and property in the early medieval city. There were disastrous fires in 1077, 1087 (in which St Paul's and 'the largest and fairest part of the whole city' was destroyed), 1092, 1100, 1133 and 1136. In 1212 people crowded on the new stone bridge to watch a fire in Southwark, and when the bridge itself caught fire at its northern end a great many (Stow's *Survey* asks us to believe over 3,000) were burned or drowned as they tried to escape on to overcrowded ships.[57] Alderman Arnold fitz Thedmar, writing in the 1270s, adds a little detail to Fitzstephen's comment on fires:

> It should be remembered that in ancient times the greater part of the
> city was built of wood, and the houses covered with straw and stubble,

and the like. Hence it happened that when a single house had caught fire, the greater part of the City was destroyed through such conflagration; a thing that took place in the first year of the reign of King Stephen. . . . After this, many of the citizens, to the best of their ability to avoid such a peril, built stone houses upon their foundations, covered with thick tiles, and protected against the fury of the flames.[58]

Since this protected other properties by stopping the spread of fire, a City ordinance of 1189 (or soon after), the Assize of Buildings, encouraged the building of stout stone party walls by establishing rules of shared construction and ownership between neighbours, and ordering that if only one neighbour could afford to build, the other should provide the 3 feet of land. The Assize also covered such contentious matters as the drainage of rainwater, the size and location of sewage pits, the obstruction of views, and permission for new buildings.[59] Further rules insisted that reed or rush roofs should be plastered over, and that wooden houses creating a fire hazard in Cheapside should be removed. These rules, Stow believed, made fires less common thereafter.

Life in a crowded community offered ample opportunities for conflict and dispute, and it was the business of the civic administration to see that these were settled without violence. Disputes between owners of adjoining properties could be adjudicated by the mayor and aldermen, applying the rules contained in the Assize of Buildings and the Assize of Nuisance. The fourteenth-century records of these hearings offer an amusing insight into the problems of everyday life in medieval London. The use and upkeep of party walls, blocked and overflowing gutters, cesspits too close to a neighbour's land, noisy tenants, loss of light, and dangerous or overhanging structures, were regular sources of conflict. The invasion of privacy, often seen as a modern obsession, was also a problem in crowded medieval streets, where broken walls led to trampled gardens, stolen fruit, dumped rubbish, and 'private business' exposed to public inspection. Sometimes malice was involved: in 1333 Andrew Aubrey and his wife Joan complained that their neighbours (Joan and William) had removed a party wall opening on to their privy, 'so that the extremities of those sitting upon the seats can be seen, a thing which is abominable and altogether intolerable'. Joan and William complained, in reply, that Andrew and his wife had drilled a hole in their cellar ceiling from the room above.

In a community of craftsmen and tradesmen, in which houses and workshops were side by side, industrial nuisances were a frequent problem. In 1378 Thomas Yonge complained that his neighbours, who were armourers, had built a forge in the close, or back-yard, of their tenement, and that the blows of their sledgehammers were shaking his walls, disturbing his sleep, spoiling the wine and ale in his cellar and reducing the rental value of his property. The armourers (who lost the case) argued in reply that 'good and honest men of any craft, viz. goldsmiths, pewterers, goldbeaters, grocers, pelters, marshals, and armourers are at liberty to carry on their trade anywhere in the City, adapting their premises as is most convenient for their work'.[60] Perhaps the most offensive trade of all was butchery, with its noise, stench, refuse and filthy water, but not until 1361 was there any effort to remove butchers from residential areas. Until 1843 the road in which the Butchers' Hall was situated, next to the Newgate Shambles, was called Stinking Lane.

Many disputes, of course, involved the community as a whole. Broken paving, dangerous chimneys, foul privies and other public nuisances were usually dealt with in local courts, or wardmotes, but occasionally the citizens brought a complaint of nuisance through the Common Sergeant, particularly over private buildings that encroached on streets or other common property (purprestures) or low overhanging upper floors. Street obstructions were a serious problem, often the target for riotous mobs, and in the royal judicial hearings of 1276 over 100 Londoners were fined (6s 8d for Christians, £5 for Jews) for building them.[61]

FOOD AND WATER

The control of weights and measures, and of food standards and prices, was a duty taken very seriously by the mayor and aldermen. To some extent this was a defence of the interests and reputation of the powerful victualling crafts, and a way of harassing 'foreign' (non-citizen) food-sellers, but the public interest and public order were considerations where basic foodstuffs were concerned. There was a natural conflict of interest between the food wholesalers and retailers, who wished to use their guild powers, especially after 1300, to exclude out-of-town retailers from London's streets and markets, and the employers and consumers in the non-victualling crafts and among the 'foreign' population, who wished to buy from the cheapest source. Most victualling crafts were too weak to win the exclusion of 'foreign folks' from selling in the town. Non-citizens were allowed to sell leather and metalwares, meat, hay, poultry, fish, fruit and vegetables, butter and cheese in specified markets (often Leadenhall), usually only in the morning, and were generally compelled to sell off all their produce before the market closed. There was particular concern over illicit evening markets ('evechepynges'), the car-boot sales of their day, in which, it was claimed, 'foreigns' would sell stolen or faulty goods under cover of darkness, and which attracted 'cutpurses and other evildoers', and women practising 'the sin of harlotry'. The Soper Lane evechepynge was closed down in 1297, and that in West Chepe and Cornhill was restricted in 1393.[62]

Only one group of food dealers, the fishmongers, had the wealth and political weight to achieve, by royal charter in 1364, the exclusion of 'foreign' sellers from the London market. Fish was a vital part of the diet of the poor, and before 1364 'foreigns' had been allowed to sell herrings, saltfish, stockfish and salmon from their boats at Billingsgate and in other riverside streets, as well as carrying it through the city 'for sale to divers working men'. After 1364 the high price of fish became a popular grievance which the populist John de Northampton exploited as mayor in 1381, by introducing measures to break the fishmongers' monopoly by giving outsiders absolute freedom to trade. Only when he went on to attack the power of the grocers and vintners was he defeated and ruined in 1383. Despite his defeat, 'foreign' fishmongers were never again shut out of the London market, except for a brief period in 1399.[63]

Severe shortages of basic foods, or rapid price rises, bringing with them the danger of social and political unrest, were generally averted by London's power to attract produce from a wide and fertile agricultural region, and by civic supervision of the pricing of important foodstuffs such as bread, poultry, meat, fish, wine and beer. Only in years of European famine, such as 1315–17, did Londoners have to start eating their dogs. The belief that London was full of food was no doubt a more important attraction for rural migrants than the idea that it was 'paved with gold'. Dealers who tried to raise the price of basic foods by forestalling (intercepting goods before they reached the market, and then reselling them), engrossing (buying a large supply of a commodity to drive up its price) or regrating (buying in one market and reselling in another), were treated as criminals. In 1363 and 1364 William Cokke and John Attewode were pilloried for trying 'by secret words whispering' to enhance the price of wheat by 2d a bushel, 'in order to create dearness thereby... to the distress of the common people'. In general, the City's regulations penalized middlemen (or women) who bought and resold simply to make a profit, but encouraged those who resold for the convenience of the common people. Trading rules issued in July 1384, after the fall of John de Northampton, ordered burlesters and hucksters (generally female street-sellers) not to stand in one place selling the oysters, mussels and fresh or salt fish they had bought in the market, but to 'pass along the streets and lanes of the city to sell it to the commons'. Similar rules were in force as late as 1588.[64]

In Fitzstephen's day, the City authorities did not have to worry about water supply. The water from Holywell, Clerkenwell and St Clement's Well, just north of the walls, was, he boasted, 'sweet, wholesome and clear', and in addition to other suburban springs there were, Stow tells us, wells in 'every street and lane of the city'. The Thames and its tributaries, the Walbrook and the Fleet (also known as the Hole Bourne or Turnmill Brook), were probably still fit to drink. By the thirteenth century these local supplies had become inadequate or polluted, and the citizens, following the example of monastic houses, 'were forced to seek sweet waters abroad ... for the poor to drink, and for the rich to dress their meat'. After 1236 fresh water was carried in lead pipes from Tyburn Springs (roughly where Bond Street Station stands today) down to the hamlet of Charing, along Fleet Street and over the Fleet Bridge, climbing Ludgate Hill (by gravitational pressure) to a public conduit in Cheapside. This conduit, administered by a local warden, supplied water free to all comers, and for a fee for those who wanted a private supply. Illegal 'tapping-in' inevitably took place, and a culprit caught in 1478 was paraded through the streets with a miniature conduit leaking on his head. In the fifteenth century the system was extended, partly from private bequests, with new conduits in Fleet Street, Cornhill, Gracechurch Street and elsewhere, and new supplies in Islington, and in the 1540s water was brought from springs in Hampstead, Muswell Hill, Hackney and Marylebone.[65] Water supply provided further grounds for dispute between citizens and victuallers. In the 1330s and 1340s there were complaints to the Husting that brewers were using the Cheapside conduit for making ale, and fishmongers were washing their fish in it. The butchers, again, were the worst offenders. They were allowed to take the entrails of animals slaughtered in the Newgate Shambles to Butchers' Bridge, a jetty overhanging the Fleet, and to clean or dump them in the river.

THE FLEET VALLEY

The Fleet was at the western boundary of the City, but by the twelfth century there was already suburban settlement along its banks. On its west bank, the church of St Andrew Holborn was described as 'old' in 951, and St Bride's was probably pre-Norman. By the thirteenth and fourteenth centuries their congregations would have included the tanners, tilers and cutlers who lived and worked near the river. The king's Fleet Prison was built on the east bank before 1155, and in the thirteenth century large monastic houses were constructed near the river's mouth, Blackfriars to the east, Whitefriars to the west. West of the Whitefriars, about a quarter of a mile from the Fleet, the crusading order of Knights Templar built their house and round Temple (which still survives) in 1185. After the destruction of the Templars in 1312 their property passed to the Knights Hospitallers, the Order of St John, who also had their own Priory about half a mile up the Fleet valley. By 1290, these local residents were beginning to complain about the stench of sewerage, rubbish and butchers' waste in the Fleet, which overpowered even the smell of the Whitefriars' incense. The problem was not really solved by the removal of slaughtering to Knightsbridge and Stratford, 3 miles from the city, in 1361, and the appointment of seven Fleet Bridge wardens in 1367. The pollution and obstruction of the Fleet, reducing its navigability and dirtying the Thames, was a constant problem for the City authorities until it was covered over as a sewer in the 1760s, just as the even filthier Walbrook had been 300 years ealier.[66]

The area round the Fleet valley, from Smithfield west to Holborn, and south past Fleet Street to the river, was medieval London's largest and most heavily populated suburb. Several wards straddled the City walls, but only in Farringdon Ward did the extramural population become so great that the ward had to be split (in 1394) into two, one 'Within' and the other 'Without' the wall. Farringdon Without was a huge ward, almost half the size of the walled city, and far less densely populated than the intramural wards. In 1319 the area had 104 subsidy-payers (citizens with movables worth over 6s 8d) compared with the seventy-two of the average ward. The City's jurisdiction ended at Temple Bar, just past Chancery Lane, where the ward ended. Beyond the bar, buildings stretched westwards along the Strand, and where the river turned south at the village of Charing, the ribbon of development turned too, following King Street (roughly the present Whitehall) until it joined up with the royal and ecclesiastical settlement which had grown up around Westminster Abbey.

THE LEGAL QUARTER

Apart from the usual suburban mixture of craftsmen, foreigns and religious houses, Farringdon Without was notable for its communities of lawyers and their students, who began to settle in the thinly occupied land along the western boundary of the ward, from north of Holborn, down Chancery Lane and Fetter Lane, to the Temple and the Thames, in the fourteenth century. Lawyers, attracted by the growing business of the royal courts in Westminster and in the City courts, found shelter and companionship by jointly renting accommodation and offices on the fringes of the City, within easy reach of Westminster, and near Chancellor's Lane (Chancery Lane), where the clerks of the Chancery, one of the key administrative departments of medieval government, were concentrated. Their landlords were church-men and religious houses (the Knights of St John, the Bishop of Chichester, the Dean of Lincoln), or noble landowners.

Gradually, in the fifteenth century, the communities developed a collegiate atmosphere, taking in students, keeping formal records, and eventually, from 1492 onwards, building their own halls, chapels, and living quarters. Like students elsewhere, they did not always live in harmony with their neighbours, and in the 1450s a series of unpleasant disputes culmi-nated, in April 1459, in an armed battle which left several people injured or dead. By 1470 Sir John Fortescue could describe the four major Inns of Court (Gray's and Lincoln's Inns, and the Inner and Middle Temple) and the ten Inns of Chancery (which prepared students for entry to the four dominant Inns) as 'the academy of the laws of England'. The area, he wrote, was away from the City 'where the tumult of the crowd could disturb the students' quiet, but it is a little isolated in a suburb of the city and nearer to the aforesaid courts, so that the students are able to attend them daily at pleasure without the inconvenience of fatigue'. Most law students were of noble families, and learned singing, dancing, and 'all games proper for nobles', as well as the elements of law. The Inns of Court were not large institutions, having only about sixty resident members each. It was the boom in legal business, along with population growth and the rising demand for education from landed families, which quadrupled their intake in the sixteenth century and filled the great Tudor halls which survive today.[67]

NORTHERN AND EASTERN SUBURBS

The area of heavy suburban development in 1270 extended around the north-western corner of the walled City, where the wards of Aldersgate and Cripplegate spread outside the walls, continuing along the streets of Smithfield and out to Clerkenwell, and along Grub Street and Whitecross Street, in the area now occupied by the Barbican development. East of the present Moorgate, as the mid-sixteenth-century maps show, the northern wall of the city was bordered by open fields, and things had not changed very much since Fitzstephen heard the pleasing clack of mills on streams north of the city in the 1170s. Moorfields (where Finsbury Circus is today), where the ancient walls impeded the flow of the Walbrook, was an uninhabitable marsh. In 1415 a new gate, Moorgate, was created, to allow Londoners to walk by causeways out to the hamlets of Isledon (Islington) and Hoxton, and in the sixteenth century the fens were drained so effectively that cloth could be laid on the ground to dry. Moorfields remained open land until the eighteenth century.

East of Moorfields, the road stretching north from Bishopsgate, passing the village of Shoreditch on its way to Lincoln, had a few houses, but the land on either side was undeveloped. This open land continued round most of the eastern edge of the City until the later sixteenth century. Portsoken Ward, which had passed from the *cnihtengild* to Holy Trinity Priory in 1121–2, and which covered the area immediately east of the wall, had only forty-four citizens able to pay the lay subsidy of 1319, and only twenty-three in 1332, although there were also untaxed 'foreigns' and members of religious orders living in the area. There was a scattering of houses along Houndsditch, running parallel to the wall, in Aldgate, and in the area just west of the Tower, but the rest of the future East End was countryside, or religious estates.

The four parishes east of London (Whitechapel, Stepney, Hackney and Bromley) were important sources of food for the medieval city. London butchers fattened their cattle on the marshy pastures of Poplar and Bethnal Green, and the millers of the Lea valley and the bakers of Stratford, to the irritation of City bakers, were major suppliers of bread to London. The industrialization of the eastern suburbs was already beginning, too. There were fulling mills along the Lea, cleaning and thickening woollen cloth, lime-burners in Limehouse, brick- and tile-makers in Whitechapel, and bell-founders on Houndsditch. Most important for London's future, the Thames from the Tower east to Blackwall was becoming, by 1500, a centre of ship repair and provisioning, and occasional shipbuilding, serving merchant shipping and the royal fleet. In the sixteenth century, Wapping, Ratcliff and Blackwall became major centres of shipbuilding and repair, and the embarcation point for some of the great Tudor voyages of discovery.[68]

Stow, writing in 1603, speaks of Hog Lane (Petticoat Lane, or Middlesex Street), Whitechapel, Houndsditch and Minories as roads which had been transformed in his lifetime from country lanes, with a few scattered tenements between the fields, into busy city streets. He remembered fetching milk from the farm of the nuns of the Minories, not 200 yards east of the City wall, and the time, 'within these forty years', when Hog Lane

> had on both sides fayre hedgerowes of Elme trees, with Bridges and easie stiles to passe over into the pleasant fieldes, very commodious for Citizens therein to walke, shoote, and otherwise to recreate and refresh their dulled spirites in the sweete and wholesome ayre, which is nowe within a few yeares made a continuall building throughout, of Garden houses and small Cottages.[69]

ACROSS THE RIVER

South of the Thames, Southwark was London's bridgehead, gateway, and defence against attack. Its growth was retarded by flooding, which resulted from subsidence, from the westward movement of the tidal limit, and from the building-up of the opposite bank of the river for the convenience of London's trade. Southwark was also liable to be devastated by invaders or Kentish rebels frustrated by their failure to penetrate London's defences. After the Conquest Southwark remained a small trading and fishing settlement, yielding the king an annual revenue of £16 in trade tolls. By 1327, when Southwark got its first royal charter, its annual tax farm was only £10, compared to London's £300. The taxable area was small, extending about 500 yards along the riverfront, and 100 yards southwards from the bridge. This was the borough proper, the 'Guildable Manor' controlled by the Earls of Surrey and the king's bailiff. The king's authority in Southwark was also represented (from about 1370 until the mid-nineteenth century) by the two royal prisons on Borough High Street, the Marshalsea and King's Bench. Beyond this, the four outlying manors of Southwark were owned and administered by ecclesiastical and monastic land-lords. Thirteen abbots, priors and bishops had their town houses, or inns, in Southwark, within easy reach of London and Westminster. East of the bridge and the High Street there was the manor of the Archbishop of Canterbury, acquired in 1131, about sixty years before he gained control of the manor of Lambeth, about a mile to the west. The Cluniac order, whose eleventh-century Bermondsey Priory was on high ground half a mile south-east of the bridge, was given the land west of the bridge, extending along the whole of the riverfront opposite the City of London, by Henry I between 1103 and 1113. The westernmost part of their estate, Paris Garden, was rented to the Templars in the 1160s and then passed to the Knights of St John, the Hospitallers. The land nearer the bridge (known later, for obscure reasons, as the Clink) was rented to the Bishop of Winchester, who built his great inn, Winchester House, on it in 1109. On this land Bishop Beaufort assembled the army which almost came to blows with the citizens of London in 1425. The name of the bishop's prison, the Clink, was applied in popular usage to small prisons in general from the eighteenth century. The house decayed in the seventeenth century, but one wall of the great hall still stands, a little to the west of the church of St Mary Overie, which was from 1106 the church of an Augustinian (or Austin) Priory. The church was rebuilt in the new Gothic style after a fire in 1212, and survives now as Southwark Cathedral, a reminder of the great power wielded by abbots, bishops and priors in medieval Southwark.[70]

Church control did not mean that Southwark enjoyed a notably Christian way of life. For most of the fifteenth century, and perhaps earlier, Paris Garden was a sanctuary for London's thieves and scoundrels, and within the Liberty, or private jurisdiction, of the Bishop of Winchester, which covered much of the riverfront west of the bridge, moral and legal controls were lax. The south bank of the river was notorious from the twelfth to the seventeenth century (when Covent Garden stole its reputation) as a centre of prostitution. Seven Bankside 'stewmongers' paid the poll tax in 1381, and all of them seem to have been making a very good living. The activities of the Southwark brothels, or stews, were regulated by ordinances issued in the fifteenth century by the Bishop of Winchester, controlling rents and opening days, banning enticement and the sale of food and drink, forbidding the employment of diseased, married or unwilling women, and insisting that a prostitute who took money from a customer should 'ly still with him' all night long. Henry VIII brought this early experiment in state-regulated prostitution to an end by ordering the closure of the Southwark stews in 1546. This was by no means the first attempt to eradicate brothels, and there is no evidence that it was any more successful than such prohibitions usually are. Prostitutes driven from Southwark simply reappeared in Shoreditch, St Katharine's or Holborn. There was also prostitution in the City, with its four Love Lanes, three Maiden Lanes, and one (now renamed) Gropecuntelane, and the City authorities never managed, although they tried, to restrict prostitution to Southwark and Smithfield.[71]

Southwark's harbouring of refugees from City justice gave London a pretext for petitioning the king for control over the borough in 1326. Since it was only one of many bolt-holes, the more powerful motive must have been to gain control of Southwark's unregulated crafts and trades, and end their evasion of London's guild and retail rules. By 1300 London had won control of the whole length of the bridge, and in 1276–8 it stopped the market there. But there was still a market in Southwark, where corn, poultry and cattle could be bought up and resold in London at inflated prices, and 'foreign' craftsmen could undercut their London competitors. Edward III's generous London charter of 1327, which allowed the mayor and aldermen to appoint Southwark's tax collector, the bailiff, began the gradual assertion of the City's control over the south bank. The City repeatedly petitioned the king for extensions to its authority in Southwark, but not until 1444 did London get the economic and judicial powers it wanted, and these only covered the small Guildable Manor, not the much larger areas remaining under Church control. Only in 1550, after Henry VIII had obtained, by seizure or exchange, most of the Church estates on the south bank, was the City able to buy from the Crown (for £980) control of almost all the lands of Southwark, which thus became the twenty-sixth and last City ward, Bridge Ward Without.[72]

COMMON PLEASURES

London was spreading to the south and west, and it was a large city by contemporary standards, but it retained a strongly rural flavour throughout and beyond the Middle Ages. Many of the medieval Londoners' recreations were country games, dependent on the survival of open spaces to the north and east of the walls. William Fitzstephen's description of London in the 1170s offers us a glimpse of the lives of children and adolescents, taking fighting cocks to school on Carnival day, and then going out to play ball in the suburban fields. These fields were Londoners' main playgrounds, the scene of mock mounted combats on Sundays in Lent, and of 'archery, running, jumping, wrestling, slinging the stone, hurling the javelin beyond a mark and fighting with sword and buckler' in the summer. On winter holy days bears, bulls and boars were baited and killed, and if the great marsh of Moorfields, just north of the walls, was frozen over, 'swarms of young men issue forth to play games on the ice', risking their limbs in an age when fractures could cripple or kill.

> Some, gaining speed as they run, with feet set well apart, slide sideways over a vast expanse of ice. . . . Others, more skilled at winter sports, put on their feet the shinbones of animals, binding them firmly round

their ankles, and, holding poles shod with iron in their hands, which they strike from time to time against the ice, they are propelled swift as a bird in flight or a bolt shot from an engine of war.[73]

Most of the games Fitzstephen mentions have a military flavour, with youths learning to tilt at each other on horseback, on ice, or on small boats in the middle of the Thames, or watching races between chargers at the weekly horse market at Smithfield, 'smooth both in fact and in name', north-west of the walls. The recreations of young women, other than dancing, are not mentioned. Hunting, the only sport guaranteed by the early charters, took place with hawks, falcons and hounds in the woodlands of Middlesex, Hertfordshire, the Chilterns and northern Kent.

Drinking was the universal social activity, and taverns, selling Gascon and Rhenish wine and locally brewed ale, were the essential centres of refreshment and recreation for the less well-off, whose own rooms offered few comforts. A census of London brewers counted 269 in 1420, including twenty women, and records for 1309 show that there were 354 taverns in the City, as well as those across the river in Southwark, a well-known centre of brewing and innkeeping. London's drinking places ranged from large and well-respected inns offering accommodation and good food to London's many visitors, and decent taverns selling wine as well as beer, to little alehouses and dingy cellars giving shelter to nightwalkers, prostitutes and swindlers.[74]

In the 1380s Southwark High Street was lined with about twenty-five inns and drink-sellers for travellers and locals, and one of these, the Tabard Inn, Chaucer's 'gentil hostelrye', serves as an example of the better sort of establishment, with its spacious rooms and stables, its gated courtyard, its 'vitaille at the beste', and its gracious and judicious host:

> A large man he was with eyen stepe [bright eyes] –
> A fairer burgeys was ther noon in Chepe –
> Boold of his speche, and wys, and wel ytaught,
> And of manhod hym lakked right naught.[75]

For the disreputable alehouse, we can turn to the coroners' rolls and court records, with their reports of drunken brawls and wrestling contests that went too far, of loaded dice and uneven chequer (or queck) boards, and curfew-breaking. In William Langland's *Piers the Plowman*, written in the late fourteenth century, Glutton drinks in such a place, alongside Tim the tinker, Clement the cobbler, Davy the ditcher, Hick the hackneyman, and an assortment of prostitutes, scavengers, rat-catchers, fiddlers and old-clothes men, a cross-section of London's low-life. While his companions bartered for each others' clothes, Glutton 'yglubbed a galon and a gille' of ale, with comical and unsavoury consequences. But as the author of *London Lickpenny* knew, London was a town where pleasure, like everything else, cost money, and in harder times even Glutton might have to tighten his belt. It was Stow's opinion that the 'immoderate drinking of fools' which Fitzstephen had criticized had by 1600 'mightily encreased, though greatlie qualified among the poorer sort, not of any holie abstinencie, but of meere necessitie'.[76]

Lack of time, as well as lack of money, restricted the recreations of labourers and apprentices. The normal working day seems to have run from 6 a.m. to 9 p.m., and since taverns were fined for staying open after curfew at 9 p.m., there was little chance for legitimate drinking or outdoor recreation except on Sundays and holy days, which the ordinances of many crafts kept free of work. Apprentices, always under their master's eye, were particularly restricted. They were forbidden to gamble, to waste their master's time in taverns or sexual relationships, or to play any of the popular tavern games, chess, dice, tables (backgammon), or queck (a gambling game in which pebbles were rolled on to a chequered board).[77] The conflict between the interests of the master and the revelry of his apprentice is the theme of the cook's unfinished tale in *Canterbury Tales*, in which 'Perkyn Revelour', Chaucer's riotous apprentice, enjoys London's social opportunities to the full:

> At every bridale [wedding party] wolde he synge and hoppe;
> He loved bet the taverne than the shoppe.
> For whan ther any ridyng [procession] was in Chepe,
> Out of the shoppe thider wolde he lepe –
> Til that he hadde al the sighte yseyn,
> And daunced wel, he wolde nat come ayeyn –
> And gadered hym a meynee [company] of his sort
> To hoppe and synge and maken swich disport;
> And ther they setten stevene [made an appointment] for to meete,
> To playen at the dys in swich a streete.[78]

THE FESTIVE YEAR

London's working year was punctuated by a variety of festivals and ceremonies, either civic, royal, spiritual or commercial. Christmas was both a popular and religious festival, celebrated with masques and mumming, the raising of a great tree in Cornhill, and evergreen decorations in churches, houses and streets. Although popular festivals were potentially unruly, they were generally sponsored and encouraged by the guilds and civic leaders. Most great households, Stow tells us, employed Lords of Misrule to organize Christmas entertainments, and May Day celebrations, with their games, dances, street bonfires and relaxation of social controls, had full official support. Throughout the summer, festival days were celebrated with bonfires and street decorations, and wealthier citizens provided outdoor feasts at which their neighbours could sit 'and bee merrie with them in great familiaritie'. Guilds associated with a particular saint organized processions and festivities on their saint's day, and won prestige for the splendour of their shows. One of the most lavish of these was the Corpus Christi procession of the skinners, whose leading members belonged to the Fraternity of Corpus Christi. Above all, there was the Midsummer watch, in which every guild and every ward took part in a massive armed procession through the City, traditionally to keep order while Londoners celebrated all night with bonfires, pageants, and dancing, assisted by musicians, giants, morris men and (it was claimed in 1569) 'vagabonds, rogues, pickpurses, querellers, whorehunters and drunkerds'. Fire, rather than riot, was the great danger on these occasions.[79]

Regular annual festivals were supplemented by occasional celebrations of royal births and marriages, coronations, and military victories. Good relations between London and the king were vital to both sides, and when the monarch was weak or despised a lavish display of royal pomp or civic loyalty was an important propaganda weapon, creating at least an illusion of royal majesty and popular support. Thus Edward II, Richard II, and Henry VI, probably the least successful of medieval kings, all received the most lavish and costly entertainments. At the birth of Edward II's son in 1312 the mayor and citizens went in a torchlit procession through the city, carolling and dancing as they went, and the conduit in Cheap ran with wine for all. In August 1392, when his relations with London were at their worst, Richard II was given an extravagant entertainment by the City, and Henry VI's public image was repeatedly enhanced by government-financed celebrations for his coronation in 1429, his return from France in 1432, and his marriage in 1445.[80] Whatever their motives, these great occasions added to London's attractiveness as a place to live in or visit.

The advantages of these festivities in fostering social and political harmony and releasing tensions outweighed the threat they posed to law and order. From time to time the authorities tried to suppress Christmas rowdiness, as in 1334, when people were forbidden to go 'disguised with false faces, or in any other manner, to the houses of the good folks of the city, for playing at dice there', and there were occasional bans on football and other rough games. But it was not until the sixteenth century, when population growth and religious divisions created more fundamental concerns over public order, that popular sports and festivals were strongly attacked. After 'Evil' May Day 1517, when young Londoners, true to their medieval traditions, attacked alien craftsmen and merchants for their supposed takeover of London's industries, the maypole outside St Andrew Undershaft was pulled down, and the festival declined. Another pole was erected in the Strand a few decades later, though, and remained there until 1717. The Midsummer watch was suspended on Henry VIII's orders in 1539, and was never successfully revived. But popular culture is not easy to eradicate, and the battle between the desire for order and the need for fun would continue for many centuries.[81]

Many medieval pastimes were still familiar to John Stow, perhaps in a more commercialized form, in the sixteenth century. Cocks still fought in special pits while men of all classes gambled on the result, and the 'meaner sort' played ball in streets and fields. Other sports, especially such martial ones as jousting, wrestling, mock river battles, and riding at the quintain, a shield on a swinging horizontal bar, were dead or dying in Stow's youth. Longbow practice, which in the Middle Ages was regarded as a patriotic duty, was still common in 1500, but by Stow's time it was 'cleane left off and forsaken'. Because of the closing of common fields 'our Archers for want of roome to shoote abroad, creepe into bowling Allies, and ordinarie dicing houses, nearer home, where they have roome enough to hazard their money at unlawful games: and there I leave them to take their pleasures'. Hawking and hunting were still popular among those with time and money, but ice slides were now 'children's play' and maidens were no longer allowed to 'daunce for garlandes hanged thwart the streetes, which open pastimes in my youth, being now suppressed, worser practises within doors are to be feared'. These 'worser practises', enjoyable as their discovery would be, are usually hidden from our view.[82]

The development of a domestic culture, involving perhaps reading, music, games, or eating and drinking with friends and family, was only possible for those with comfortable accommodation, something which poorer Londoners did not have until recent times. Only better-off citizens, especially the merchant community, had space in which to enjoy their domestic life indoors. Most of the great medieval stone mansions belonged to nobles or churchmen, but a few merchants were wealthy enough to build on a grand scale, as John Gisors did in Basing Lane in the thirteenth century, and Sir John Pulteney in Pountney Lane in the fourteenth. The hall of one of these great mercantile mansions, Sir John Crosby's house in Bishopsgate (built in 1466), was moved to Chelsea in 1907, and still survives. But Crosby was a knight and a favoured royal servant, and the size of his palatial home should not lead us to imagine that all London merchants lived in such splendour. The typical merchant's house had a cellar, a ground floor occupied by a shop and storage space, a spacious hall (or dining room) and perhaps a kitchen and parlour (a small reception room), on the first floor, and a large family bedroom and a servants' chamber at the top. By 1400 some merchants preferred the privacy of three or four bedrooms, but the single family bedroom remained common. The hall, heated by wood or coal fires, lit by candles and natural light from windows which, by about 1300, might have been glazed, and furnished with simple wooden furniture, cushions and tapestries, was the main centre of domestic life.[83]

LITERACY AND EDUCATION

To judge from the rarity of substantial book collections in their wills and inventories, London merchants may not have been great book-buyers, although they were generally literate in English, and perhaps in Latin. A list of male witnesses before a diocesan court about 1470 records forty-eight men as literate (perhaps in Latin), and sixty-eight as not. Some crafts were better-educated than others. Drapers, grocers, mercers, merchants, pewterers and shearmen mostly passed the clerk's test, as did half the tailors and barber-surgeons, while bakers, brewers, joiners, labourers and smiths failed it.[84] Yet there was a healthy market for books in London and Westminster, so much so that monastic scribes, even when they adopted a faster cursive script and began using paper instead of parchment after 1300, were not able to satisfy it. Commercial book production in specialized book shops developed in the fourteenth and fifteenth centuries, and in 1403 we find the text-letter writers, illuminators, bookbinders and booksellers of London applying for and receiving their craft ordinances.[85] Some mass-produced books were fairly cheap, but for those unable to buy there were libraries in some London churches and (if you could gain access) in monasteries. After 1423 John Carpenter, London's scholarly Common Clerk, used a bequest in Sir Richard Whittington's will to establish London's first public library, for citizens as well as the clergy, next to the Guildhall. It was plundered and destroyed by Protector Somerset in 1549. John Shirley, an early fifteenth-century London publisher and bookseller, also ran a lending library, and his manuscripts bore a bookplate with this request:

> When you this book have read and followed plain
> To Johan Shirley give it back again.[86]

Perhaps the Court aristocracy, rather than London merchants, were the best book-buyers, and certainly it was to them that Chaucer, Hoccleve and Lydgate looked for patronage and support. It was also in Westminster, rather than the City, that William Caxton established the first English printing press in 1476, hoping to appeal to a courtly clientele, and win some Abbey business, too. Over the next fifteen years Caxton printed about eighty different works, most of them calculated to appeal to the aristocratic customers who were most likely to pass his shop: courtly poetry, French romances, books of manners and history, and religious works. The gulf between courtly and mercantile taste was not unbridgeable, though: Caxton was himself a mercer and Merchant Adventurer, and had been the leader of the English community in Bruges, and Thomas Hoccleve dedicated poems to citizens as well as courtiers. Occasionally, Caxton published works at the request of 'a singuler frende and gossib' of his in the City, and there was obviously a London demand for printed books as well as a Westminster one.[87]

Caxton's assistant and successor, Wynken de Worde, who took over the press in 1491, was more interested in the London market, and in 1500 moved his shop to St Paul's Churchyard, and his press to Fleet Street, 'at the sign of the Sun', where other printers and booksellers were already established. By the time Wynken de Worde died in 1535, having published almost 800 books, Fleet Street was the national centre of printing, and remained so until the 1980s. The availability of cheap printed books had incalculable consequences for the intellectual and religious life of London, as Bishop Tunstall, the leader of the fight against Protestant heresy in the City in the 1520s, recognized: 'We must root out printing or printing will root out us.'[88]

The intellectual life of medieval London was dominated by the Church. Elementary schooling, where it was provided, was often in the hands of parish priests, and secondary schools, or grammar schools, were all Church-run, and taught little but Latin. Fitzstephen mentions three principal twelfth-century grammar schools, which were attached (though he does not say so) to St Paul's, St Martin-le-Grand and Holy Trinity Priory, and there were also schools at St Mary-le-Bow and in Westminster Abbey, and perhaps elsewhere. One of the chief purposes of these schools was to train boys to sing and read in church services, but what the boys learned would have had secular benefits, too. From time to time new grammar schools were opened in defiance of the Bishop of London and the Chancellor of St Paul's, the licensing authorities, and there seems to have been a rash of new schools, challenging the Church monopoly, in the 1390s. In the fifteenth century the variety of schools available to Londoners grew wider. At least five new 'song schools' (attached to churches) were founded, and there seems to have been a proliferation of little elementary schools run by priests, scriveners or 'dames'. Cornhill became something of a centre of private-enterprise grammar schooling in the early fifteenth century, and business, according to a petition of 1447, was brisk: 'There is great numbers of learners and few teachers, and all the learners are compelled to go to the same few teachers, and to no other, the masters wax rich in money, and the learners poor in cunning.'[89]

The rising demand for education for the sons and apprentices of merchants and craftsmen in the fifteenth century reflected the growing need for literacy in business and other careers (especially the law), and perhaps a desire to break free from the intellectual tutelage of the Church. In the later fourteenth century English, rather than French or Latin, was increasingly used in posters, proclamations, wills, letters, guild rules and other documents, and illiteracy began to be a social and commercial handicap. Old and new forms of education flourished side by side. In Stow's later years most of the Church schools were 'sore decayed', but he remembered, in his youth, seeing the pupils of the rival schools arguing over the principles of Latin grammar in public debate at St Bartholomew's, just as Fitzstephen had seen them 400 years earlier, scoring points by scholarship or sarcasm, 'nipping and quipping their fellowes'. Some doubted the educational value of Latin disputation. Whe John Colet refounded St Paul's School in 1509 his Statutes anounced that the boys would 'use no cockfighting, nor riding about of victory, nor disputing at St Bartholomew's, which is but foolish babbling and loss of time'. The finest of the newer schools, and the great rival of St Paul's, was the free school of St Anthony's Hospital, in Threadneedle Street, which educated Sir Thomas More and Archbishop Whitgift.[90]

CHURCH AND CHARITY

The practical influence of the Church spread far beyond the field of learning and scholarship. The main London hospitals (places of asylum and protective hospitality, rather than medical treatment) were administered by religious communities, although they were generally founded and sustained by the gifts of rich Londoners, courtiers or the Crown. Queen Matilda, Henry I's wife, was the first of these patrons, founding a leper hospital at St Giles-in-the-Fields, Holborn. About fifteen years later, in 1123, Rahere, a courtier or courtly cleric, established the Priory and Hospital of St Bartholomew, alongside Smithfield horse market. This was the first of London's general hospitals, and it was followed before the end of the twelfth century by St Thomas's Hospital, in Southwark, and the Priory of St Mary Spital-without-Bishopsgate, founded by a rich citizen, Walter Brown. St Mary Spital, which had 180 beds in the mid-fourteenth century, was London's largest hospital, and one of the biggest in England. Other hospitals specialized in particular groups: St Katharine's-by-the-Tower (founded by Stephen's wife Matilda in the 1140s) cared for old men and women; St James's, Westminster, sheltered lepers (or 'leprouse virgines', according to Stow); St Mary Bethlehem, outside Bishopsgate (founded in 1247 by Simon fitz Mary, one of the leading aldermen of the 1230s and 1240s), specialized from the 1370s onwards in the care and restraint of the insane; the Priory of Elsing Spital, Cripplegate (founded in 1329 by William Elsing, a mercer) had beds for 100 blind men; and St Augustine Papey, on the wall near Aldgate (founded in 1442) housed old and disabled priests. Pregnant women found shelter in St Mary Spital, and St Thomas's and St Bartholomew's had a special responsibility for women who were pregnant but unmarried. With very few exceptions, late fifteenth-century London's twenty-one hospitals and almshouses did not provide professional medical care. A recent study found that the only reference to expert medical care in any English hospital before 1500 was in the will of a London mercer in 1475, which left £25 to provide a single surgeon for all London's hospitals and prisons. Early in the next century the Savoy Hospital (founded and richly endowed for 100 old men by Henry VII) and St Mary Bethlehem had professional physicians.[91]

It was customary for rich citizens to leave a third of their wealth to charitable or religious causes. A study of 700 wills between 1401 and 1530 suggests that prisoners benefited from a quarter of wills, young girls from around 10 per cent, and hospitals from 14 to 24 per cent. Only 3.5 per cent of wills left money for education, but the poor, debtors and the insane were common beneficiaries, and money was sometimes left for such civic improvements as road, wall and bridge repair, water supply, markets, and almshouses.[92] One driving force behind all this generosity was the belief in purgatory, which became widespread in the thirteenth century. Since the common purpose of these bequests was to speed the dead man's soul through purgatory into heaven, it was usual to leave property to those professionally qualified in spiritual matters. Thus the parish clergy were remembered in 41 per cent of fifteenth-century London wills, friars in 35 per cent, monks in 15 per cent, and nuns in 11 per cent. By this process the Church gradually gained possession of a very large proportion of the land in and around London, and it was to prevent land falling into the unbreakable grip of the 'dead hand' of the Church that statutes of Mortmain were enacted in 1279 and afterwards. But Londoners could buy licences exempting their gifts from these acts, and the process of accumulation continued until the Reformation.

The best way to shorten your stay in purgatory, in the view of later medieval Londoners, was to endow a chantry chapel, where a chaplain would sing daily masses for his benefactor's soul for a number of years, or even in perpetuity. Those unable to afford a chantry might pay instead for an obit, an annual service for the founder's soul. Chantries gave light work and an easy living to a great number of clergymen: almost every church had at least one chantry chaplain, and in 1379 there were in London 497 chaplains, most of them supported by chantries. Temporary chantry endowments were very common in the fourteenth century, and even in the later fifteenth century, after a period of decline, chantries were included in 40 per cent of wills. Over 400 permanent chantries were created between 1300 and 1548, and although there was a good deal of rationalization of chantry work by the establishment of chantry colleges in the fifteenth century, a survey in 1546 found that there were still 317 chantry priests in London. To modern minds this may seem a misguided use of funds, but a study of a well-endowed fifteenth-century London parish, St Mary-at-Hill (in Billingsgate), suggests that the income from its seven perpetual chantries helped to produce a well-administered and socially active church community and perhaps contributed to the growth of neighbourly involvement in parish life.[93]

Worldly and spiritual life were inextricably mixed. Guilds were as much religious associations as they were social or economic ones, and most of them had their origin as fraternities of citizens attached to a parish church, which perhaps gradually became dominated by men of the main local craft. In this church, the men of the mistery would hold their saint's-day service, attend funerals and masses for members who had died, and perhaps maintain a chantry priest. The religious connection also enabled craft associations to enforce secrecy and obedience before civic recognition was won in the fourteenth century. The saddlers were associated with St

Martin-le-Grand, the skinners with St John Walbrook, the grocers with St Antonin in Watling Street, the painters with St Giles Cripplegate, the brewers with All Hallows London Wall, the carpenters with St Thomas Acon, the drapers with St Mary-le-Bow, St Mary Abchurch and St Michael Cornhill, the pouchmakers with St Paul's, and so on.

Many local fraternities never developed an economic purpose, but simply supported and attended a parish church, paid for its lighting and repair, and sometimes supported a chantry priest. Parish fraternities united people of all social levels (except those too poor to pay their dues), women on almost equal terms with men, in communal devotion and mutual support. Members received money (perhaps informally) when they were in trouble, help in resolving their disputes, moral guidance while they were alive, and burial and masses when they were dead. Many fraternities became important neighbourhood organizations, with their own feasts and saint's-day processions, a common livery, and even (in five cases) fraternity halls. Only seven London fraternities left records, but evidence from wills suggests that none existed before the 1330s, that about eighty were formed between 1349 and 1400, and another forty-five during the next century. Perhaps fear of death from the plague and anonymous burial in an unhallowed grave explains this wave of communal piety, but it is also likely (as Caroline Barron argues) that the relative prosperity created by the Black Death enabled tradesmen and artisans (the bulk of fraternity membership) to use their combined wealth to mimic the individual practices of richer Londoners, who had been endowing personal chantries since about 1300. Parish fraternities remained popular right up to the Reformation: thirty were founded after 1500, and in the 1520s and 1530s almost a quarter of Londoners whose wills were enrolled in the Commissary Court left money to their fraternities.[94]

The establishment of large numbers of small churches in the eleventh and twelfth centuries, mostly through the private investment of rich and noble families, meant that there was hardly any need for new foundations after about 1200. Fitzstephen, in 1173, could already count 126 parish churches, as well as thirteen attached to religious communities. The work of the later Middle Ages was to maintain, enlarge, enrich and rebuild the existing ample stock. More than fifty parish churches were enlarged or rebuilt between 1300 and 1448, especially in the plague years after 1348. If Fitzstephen's count is right, a few parish churches had disappeared by 1500, when there were only 114, and of these almost all were consumed in the Great Fire of 1666. A handful of medieval parish churches survive in London today: St Olave Hart Street and St Andrew Undershaft, rebuilt in 1450 and the 1520s respectively, are examples of the many churches that were enriched and enlarged by bequests, gifts of land and plate, and new belfries, chapels, aisles and porches, and St Ethelburga, squashed into its tiny plot on Bishopsgate, perhaps best represented the cramped and humble medieval parish church, until it was destroyed by an IRA bomb in 1993.

At the other extreme there was the great cathedral of St Paul's. The Anglo-Saxon church burned down in 1087, and the Norman and Gothic Cathedral that replaced it in the twelfth and thirteenth centuries was a huge and impressive structure, a few feet longer but much higher than the present cathedral. Its slender spire, rising 489 feet above Ludgate Hill (85 feet higher than Salisbury's), was damaged by lightning in 1447, and destroyed by lightning or fire in 1561. The Cathedral was important in civic ceremonial and its physical presence dominated the city (as we can see from sixteenth-century panoramas), but the part it played in medieval London's spiritual life was less impressive. Inside the Cathedral, scriveners drafted commercial documents, lawyers met their clients, tradesmen sold their wares, and Londoners took short cuts from Carter Lane to Paternoster Row, and used the building as a public meeting place. Even worse, Bishop Braybrooke complained in 1385, they played ball in the nave and shot birds in the churchyard. As for the thirty canons and many chantry priests of the cathedral, fourteenth-century Londoners seemed to agree with Chaucer that they had chosen the path of the mercenary, not the shepherd.[95]

MONASTIC ORDERS

The mixture of piety, anxiety, competition and ostentation that inspired the generosity of Crown, courtiers and citizens led also to the establishment and enrichment of an impressive collection of religious communities in medieval London. The Crown, with its control of land all around the City, was the most important benefactor, and most early foundations were under royal patronage. Apart from the canons of St Paul's and the Abbey in Westminster, the oldest of these was the College of St Martin-le-Grand, which was established by a royal chaplain, Ingelric, just before 1066, probably on the site of the Anglo-Saxon royal palace abandoned when the Confessor moved to Westminster. By William's charter of 1068, the College was freed from 'every yoke of royal service' and from the control of the Church hierarchy, and many later charters show that it enjoyed special royal favour. Since the Dean of the College was usually the leading royal minister, and its canons were often Chancery clerks, it is reasonable to regard St Martin-le-Grand as 'a college of civil servants', a 3-acre royal enclave within the city walls.[96]

There was still open space inside the twelfth-century city, and in 1107 Henry I's queen, Matilda, founded the Augustinian Priory of Holy Trinity within Aldgate, which was granted by royal charter in 1121 control over the gate of Aldgate, and all the lands east of the walls, stretching from Aldgate down to the Thames. Within a century there were religious communities all around the walls of London. On the river just east of the Tower was the Hospital of St Katharine (founded by Stephen's Queen in the 1140s), and in Shoreditch, north of Bishopsgate, was the priory of St John the Baptist, or Holywell priory (an Augustinian nunnery founded before 1158), and the Priory of St Mary Spital (1197). In the north-west were Rahere's Augustinian priory and hospital of St Bartholomew (1123), the Benedictine nunnery of St Mary Clerkenwell, and the knightly Hospital of St John of Jerusalem, both of these founded by a Suffolk landlord, Jordan of Bricett, around 1130. To the west were the inns, palaces and spacious gardens of bishops and abbots along Holborn, Fleet Street and the Strand, usually covering over half an acre, and often much more, and the great estates of Westminster Abbey. South of the Thames, there were the priories of Bermondsey (1082) and St Mary Overy Southwark (1106), and the whole riverbank as far as Lambeth was in the hands of the Church.[97]

In the thirteenth century friars, with their reputation for poverty, piety and spiritual and welfare work, attracted royal and citizen support. The Dominicans, or Blackfriars, were the first to get a London house, initially on Holborn (about 1221), then moving to land between Ludgate and the Thames in 1274, the site of the old Baynard's and Montfichet Castles, where the wall was moved westward to accommodate them. The Dominicans repaid the generous patronage of Edward I by providing the King and his successors with a well-defended enclave within the City, a place where Parliament, Chancery or the King's Council could sometimes meet, and where royal guests could be lodged. In 1225 the Franciscans, or Greyfriars, were given a large estate by a rich ex-sheriff, in a rather undesirable area north of the Newgate Shambles, and in 1241 the Carmelites, or Whitefriars, were given a large plot west of the walls, completing the ecclesiastical acquisition of all the land between Fleet Street and the Thames. The Austin, or Augustine, friars were granted a large area in the north of the City, just west of Broad Street, in 1253, and the Crutched, or Cross, friars were given about 2 acres north-west of the Tower in 1298. Although friars were often mocked for their moral shortcomings they became increasingly popular among London's propertied classes, and about 35 per cent of wills between 1376 and 1531 contained bequests to them.[98]

Nunneries had a special social role as refuges or depositories for the unmarried daughters of wealthy citizens, and there were several of them in and near the City. Apart from those in Holywell and Clerkenwell, there was St Helen's Priory (founded before 1216), which owned much of the area near Bishopsgate, within the City walls, and the Minoresses of St Clare (1293), occupying 5 acres east of the wall, near the Minories.

The great age of new monastic foundations in London was over by 1300. Of the seventeen significant foundations between 1300 and 1530, six were hospitals or almshouses and nine were colleges of priests. Of the other two, one was St Mary Graces (1349), a Cistercian abbey east of the Tower, and the other was the Charterhouse, founded in 1371 by Sir Walter de Manny, one of Edward III's best military commanders, on 13 acres north of Smithfield. The Carthusians offered an example of scholarship and self-denial which the other late medieval religious houses were rarely able to emulate and, when the time came, put up the most principled and saintly resistance to Henry VIII's policies in the 1530s. To judge from the rate of bequests, respect for some of London's thirty-nine religious houses, mainly those of friars and Carthusians, was still strong in the 1520s, though not, as it turned out, strong enough to save them.[99]

THE WORLDLY CHURCH AND ITS CRITICS

Inevitably, the Church was a worldly force as well as a spiritual one. It was easily the largest landowner in London and its suburbs, and bequests and investments meant that its holdings of ordinary residential and commercial property were constantly growing. In 1312 the mayor and aldermen complained that monasteries and other religious landlords, owning a third of the city's rental income, paid nothing towards its walls and defences. But by the Reformation, if all Church and monastic property is included, Marjorie Honeybourne believes that it 'would be a much nearer estimate to say that two-thirds of London was in the hands of religious persons'. Derek Keene's detailed study of about 9 acres around Cheapside seems to support this guess, since he found that between them parish churches and (especially) religious houses owned over 60 per cent of this valuable district by 1530.[100] Church landlords also appear in a high proportion of fourteenth-century Assize of Nuisance cases. So when the monasteries were dissolved in 1539 the impact on property ownership must have been enormous, not just on the suburban fringes, where religious estates abounded, but 'in every alley of the City'.[101]

The constant enrichment of the Church by gifts and bequests, the language of letters and wills, the enormous emphasis placed on the sacraments, the magical power of the mass, the endowment of chantries and obits, show that religious belief and observance permeated almost every aspect of London life. When priests were criticized, it was not because their services were not valued, but the reverse. How could a sinful, ignorant, lazy, worldly or (worst of all) absent clergyman intercede effectively for the souls of his parishioners? Drunken, greedy, criminal, lecherous and lazy churchmen appear often in the works of Chaucer and Langland, and turned up occasionally (but not so often) in the City courts, which had jurisdiction over them. The trial of one or two fornicators each year, out of over 700 London clergy, was not a bad record, but, as Thomas More pointed out, it gave ammunition to the Church's enemies: 'But let a lewde frere be taken wyth a wench, we wyll geste and rayle uppon the hole order all the yere after, and saye lo what sample they gyve us.' Pluralism was a more serious problem. By Henry VIII's reign, a third of London parish priests held more than one living (although London livings were rich enough to make this unnecessary), and in 1522 a quarter of parishes were left in the care of curates or assistant clergy, who generally lacked the education and intellect needed for their work.[102]

Doubts about the moral conduct of the clergy were important, because the clergy set standards for others to follow, and the Church laid down the city's moral code and, along with the City courts, enforced it. At the end of the fifteenth century an average of nine people a week were cited before the London Commissary Court (the bishop's court), half of them for adultery and sexual offences, and the rest for such offences as slander, blasphemy, missing church services, and breach of faith. The guilty usually had to do penance by walking before the cross in the Sunday procession, barefoot, dressed in a sheet, and holding a candle. The Church's authority was not always accepted. Barbers and other fifteenth-century craftsmen kept their shops open on Sundays in defiance of repeated instructions to close, and some cordwainers, when ordered by a papal bull in 1468 to stop Sunday trading and to stop making shoes with long pointed toes, 'said that the pope's curse was not worth a fly'.[103]

Mockery and defiance could lead to a more general denunciation of the Church. When John Wyclif attacked the wealth of the monasteries and questioned papal and ecclesiastical authority in the 1370s and 1380s, he struck a vein of anti-clericalism in London. Despite their hatred for his patron, John of Gaunt, the London crowd supported Wyclif when he was questioned by the bishops at Lambeth in 1378, and interrupted the Blackfriars synod (the 'Earthquake Council') discussing his doctrines in 1382. Inspired by Wyclif and the popular mayor, John de Northampton, a chronicler tells us, 'the Londoners began to grow insolent beyond measure. . . . They said that they not only abominated the negligence of curates but detested their avarice. For, desiring money, they omitted the penalties prescribed by law, and took bribes, to allow those guilty of fornication and incest to live at ease in their crimes.'[104] But London was not a major centre of the Lollard heresy (as Wyclif's enemies called it), and it was not subjected to a disciplinary visitation, as Oxford and Leicester were. In January 1414 Sir John Oldcastle, a hero of Henry IV's French campaigns, tried to start a Lollard insurrection with London as its headquarters, but hardly any Londoners joined the rising, which was easily suppressed.[105]

Lollards were present in unknown numbers in London throughout the fifteenth century, a secret fellowship reading aloud in each others' houses from their precious and illegal English bibles, and occasionally brought to light by an arrest, a recantation, or a burning at Smithfield or St Giles'. Anticipating Luther, they denied transubstantiation, purgatory, exorcism and other 'necromancy', and rejected the worship of images, crosses and saints, confession, pilgrimage, chantries and monastic celibacy, all of which were deeply valued by Londoners in general. Even in the 1520s, when imported Lutheran writings and Tyndale's translation of the New Testament were stirring up fresh interest in Lollard ideas, heretics were a despised minority in London. Those who avoided death by abjuring their beliefs (as many did) and wearing the sign of heresy, the faggot, on their clothes, found themselves ostracized, unable to do business or find work.[106] But their time was about to come, and with their triumph, it might be said, medieval London came to an end.

PART THREE

LONDON FROM
THE REFORMATION TO
THE GREAT PLAGUE,
1520–1665

Chapter 5

Reformation, Population
and the Plague

THE HERETICAL TRADITION

On 2 December 1514, Richard Hunne, a respectable merchant tailor and citizen of London, was found hanging, probably murdered, in a cell in the Lollards' Tower, the Bishop of London's prison next to St Paul's. Hunne had been involved in a long legal dispute with the rector of Whitechapel over mortuary fees for his infant son, and he had Lollard sympathies and an anti-clerical disposition. His death, and the burning of his body as a heretic's (which meant that his family was left penniless), became a *cause célèbre* which crystallized long-standing anti-church feelings in London, and set people 'raging against the clergy'. A coroner's jury found that Hunne had been killed by the Bishop's gaolers, and Richard Fitzjames, the Bishop of London, believed that no jury could be found in the city to acquit his clerk of the murder.[1] There was something more than the old hostility towards overfed or lecherous clerics at work here. The Lollard heresy was still very much alive in the early sixteenth century, and there was a steady stream of prosecutions in the London diocesan courts (forty in 1510, thirty-seven in 1517). There were even doubts within the Church hierarchy itself. In 1511 John Colet, Dean of St Paul's and founder of St Paul's School, preached a much-publicized sermon in which he advocated a reformation of the Church, and denounced the carnal corruption of priests: 'They give themselves to feasts and banqueting; they spend themselves in vain babbling; they give themselves to sports and plays; they apply themselves to hunting and hawking; they drown themselves in the delights of this world.'[2] In the years following the Hunne case, anti-clerical feelings were intensified by the career of Thomas Wolsey, Cardinal, Archbishop of York, and Lord Chancellor from 1515 to 1529, who personified all the vices Colet had condemned – pride, wealth, ambition, temporal power and worldly morality – in their most extreme form.

The alternatives to a traditional Church-dominated society were much more obvious in the sixteenth century than they had been before. The rise of the Inns of Court as almost a third university provided the basis for a more secular culture in sixteenth-century London, and challenged the Church's monopoly of intellectual life. The growth of printing and bookselling created a flow of Lutheran and reformist ideas from the continent which successive Bishops of London could not stem, and gave English opponents of the Church a chance to spread their views. The most effective critics of the Church in the 1520s were two London lawyers, Christopher St German and Simon Fish. St German argued for the supremacy of common and statute law over canon law, and gave academic support to the progressive subjugation of the Church to the will of the state. Fish took a more popular approach, and mocked the clergy for taking bread from the mouths of the sick and needy, hiding the truths of religion, selling prayers for money, perverting justice, seducing women and growing fat on the labour of others. Writings like this reflected and reinforced a strand of anti-clerical, if not heretical, opinion in London, and helped create an important basis of popular support for Henry VIII's attack on the Church in the 1530s. They did not have a clear run, of course. During the chancellorship of Sir Thomas More, from 1529 to 1532, book agents were sent to the Tower (where some of them died) or imprisoned in More's house in Chelsea, heretical books were burned, and so, if they refused to recant, were their readers.[3]

ROYAL SUPREMACY

While More's persecution was creating Protestant martyrs, political events at Court were giving heretics friends in high places. Henry VIII's obsessive desire for a divorce from Catherine, to enable him to marry Anne Boleyn, and the impossibility of persuading the Pope, who was under the control of Catherine's nephew, the Emperor Charles V, to grant him one, began to open the King's mind in 1530 to thoughts of a break with Rome. Reformers with anti-papal and anti-clerical views, especially the London-educated lawyer Thomas Cromwell, gained influence at Court, while conservatives began to seem more of a danger to royal policy than heretics were. Recognizing that the battle was being lost, More resigned the chancellorship in May 1532. Cromwell and Anne Boleyn, now dominant at court, had friends in the very communities of Lollards, printers and book-runners that More had been trying to extirpate, and Protestant ideas began to gain a hold which would not easily be broken. In a trading town with strong links with northern Germany, the flow of Lutheran ideas was almost unstoppable.

In March 1533 the passage of the Act in Restraint of Appeals to Rome formally ended the subordination of the English Church to the papacy, and in November 1534 the Act of Supremacy declared that the King was supreme head of the Church. The views of Londoners, except the most indiscreet or courageous ones, on these events are not easy to discover. The King's marriage to Anne Boleyn in January 1533 was not popular, but citizens had pressing reasons for keeping their opinions to themselves. London women caught speaking in favour of the divorced Catherine in 1533 were stripped, beaten, nailed by their ears to the Cheapside fountain, the Standard, and expelled from the city. When citizens and clergy were required to swear loyalty to Anne in April 1534, only More, Bishop Fisher of Rochester, and a single London priest refused. More and Fisher were executed in the summer of 1535. All the aldermen, whatever their private views, took the oath, and so did Stokesley, the Bishop of London, until then the scourge of heretics in London.[4]

In the fundamentals of Catholic faith, though, citizens appear to have remained fairly conservative throughout Henry's reign, just as the King did. The great majority of London wills analysed by Susan Brigden indicate traditional beliefs in the Virgin, Purgatory and prayers for the dead, while only a minority (6 per cent in the 1530s, 13 per cent in the 1540s) were written in Protestant terms. But the fashion for endowing chantries was declining steeply, and had been since the early fifteenth century, when a half of all wills had contained chantry endowments. By the 1520s only 9 per cent did so, and in the 1530s, only 2 per cent.[5]

The most forthright denial of Henry's supremacy came from London's least worldly inhabitants, the monks of the Charterhouse. In May 1535 three Carthusian priors, including John Houghton of London, were executed at Tyburn before a vast crowd for denying royal supremacy, and in June three more London Carthusians followed them. Finally, after two years of browbeating and persuasion, ten Carthusians who still refused to submit were taken to Newgate in May 1537 and left there to starve. Other religious houses chose an easier path, and submitted to the new order.[6]

A New Religion

Compliance saved monks' skins, but not their communities. The vast wealth of the monastic houses, and their vulnerability to attack in the reforming and anti-clerical atmosphere of the 1530s, made them an irresistible target for an impecunious King and his Protestant minister. The possibility of taking over a large community and selling off its land without arousing a public outcry was already clear. In 1532 the Prior of Holy Trinity Aldgate, one of the noblest and oldest of all London's religious houses, had been forced by heavy debts to surrender the priory to Henry VIII, along with property in sixty London parishes worth £300 a year. It was acquired by the Lord Chancellor, Lord Audley, who demolished it and sold off its ancient stones as building material. Between 1536 and 1540 Cromwell set about discrediting the monasteries and seizing their assets. By 1540 the whole monastic structure, which had taken 500 years to create, had been swept away. In London there was little open resistance to the Dissolution. In the attack on smaller houses in 1536, only one London house, Elsing Spital, was destroyed, and Londoners did not rise in sympathy with the conservative Pilgrimage of Grace that year, although it was feared that they would. Before the final Act of Dissolution in 1539, many houses had already surrendered, their members perhaps persuaded by the lure of pensions, parish livings, and even bishoprics. In October 1538 St Thomas Acon surrendered, followed the next month by the five friaries, and the nuns of St Clare and St Helen's. Nuns (without job prospects) and friars (without pensions) had the most to lose from the Dissolution. The rest followed within a year or two of the Act of 1539.

Most Londoners, naturally, wanted a quiet life and, not wishing to burn for their faith, were ready to drift with the prevailing wind. The wind, though, was exceptionally changeable in the middle decades of the century. In the 1530s Cromwell, who was a moderate reformer, licensed Coverdale's translation of the Bible and made sure a copy was in every church, prevented the aldermen from electing an anti-Protestant mayor, and encouraged the removal of sacred images from city churches. Only Anabaptists and other religious and social radicals, abhorrent to the King and to the well-off in general, were really unsafe. London's large alien communities were breeding grounds of Anabaptism, and in 1535 ten Dutch Anabaptists were burned.[7]

In June 1540 Thomas Cromwell's execution removed the Protestants' main protection, and the scope of persecution widened, with the mayor and aldermen joining Bishops Gardiner of Winchester and Bonner of London in the hunt for heretics. Within days of Cromwell's death three leading Protestant preachers, Robert Barnes, Thomas Garret and William Jerome, were burned at Smithfield. The attack on the dealers in heretical books around St Paul's was resumed in 1542, and an underground network of Protestant printers was exposed. Dr Edward Crome, Vicar of St Mary Aldermary, the leading voice of Protestantism in the 1540s, was arrested in 1546 along with many associates, and was forced to make a public recantation at St Paul's Cross. The last major attack on heresy (until Mary's reign) was the arrest, torture and burning (at Smithfield) in 1546 of Anne Askew, a well-connected Lincolnshire Protestant who had been spreading the gospel among London's apprentices and labourers since 1544.[8]

Despite all this, there were substantial numbers of Protestants in London in the 1540s, and it was said that it was difficult to find juries ready to convict people charged with heresy. The new religion thrived in pockets, in secret conventicles, and in the congregations of reforming clergymen. Susan Brigden has traced over fifty Protestant clergy in London in the 1540s, usually reflecting the views of the clerical or lay patron of the living they held. The congregations of St Bride's, St Vedast, All Hallows Honey Lane, St Mary-at-Hill, and several others, had rectors who ignored orthodox ceremonies, perhaps abandoned confession, holy water and priestly vestments, and preached radical doctrines, while others in churches nearby were still worshipping in the old way.[9]

After Henry's death in 1547, and the accession of the young and Protestant Edward VI, power fell into the hands of ambitious nobles who had done well from the Dissolution, and whose interests, if not their beliefs, led them to favour the new faith. So once again the wind changed, turning persecutors into victims, and overlords into underdogs. Bishop Bonner, after temporizing for two years, lost his diocese and spent four uncomfortable years in the Marshalsea Prison. Catholic priests fled to the continent (one of them taking John Houghton's arm with him) while London became a refuge for European Anabaptists and radical sects. Now Catholic works had to be smuggled into England, while London's printing presses, more active than ever, turned out Protestant tracts, many of them mocking or denouncing the mass, at the rate of about 100 a year. The veneration of images was abolished, and City churches rapidly lost the stock of treasures they had accumulated over the centuries. Beads, crosses, pictures, candlesticks, chalices, wall-paintings, coloured glass, statues, holy relics, were hidden or destroyed, and by the end of 1550 only one London church, St Nicholas Cole Abbey, still retained an altar. Latin service books were removed from churches, and replaced by reformed Prayer Books, a compromise one in 1549 and a fully Protestant one in 1552.[10]

THE USES OF MONASTIC LAND

The Reformation, and especially the Dissolution of the Monasteries, changed the face of London. Twenty-three major religious houses, all occupying large sites in or near the City, were taken over by the Crown and, in most cases, sold off between 1543 and 1547, when Henry VIII desperately needed money to finance his wars against France and Scotland. The grip of the church's 'dead hand' was broken, too, on great numbers of city shops and tenements, which monasteries had accumulated as gifts over the centuries. Some religious houses, such as St Mary Spital and St Mary Clerkenwell, owned property in more than sixty parishes, and well over 100 English monasteries had property in London. All this land came on to the market at a time when London's population was starting to grow at a rapid rate after two centuries of stagnation, and the uses to which it was put give an excellent impression of how the city was changing in the mid-sixteenth century.

Some of the monastic lands fell into the hands of aristocrats, or those about to be ennobled. The Duke of Norfolk, not inhibited by his Catholicism, inherited Thomas Audley's new mansion on the site of Holy Trinity Priory, and called it Duke's Place. Lord Lumley had a mansion where Crutched Friars had been. The Lord Treasurer, Sir William Paulet (soon to become the Marquess of Winchester), sold off the stone, monuments and lead of Austin Friars, and built himself a town house, preserving the nave of the old church as a chapel for the Dutch Protestant community. The Charterhouse, the only London monastic estate to survive in anything like its medieval form into the twentieth century, passed first to Sir Edward North, then to the Duke of Northumberland, and then (in 1565) to the Duke of Norfolk. In 1614 it became a school and a home for poor gentlemen, and it retains the second of these functions to this day.

The inns of abbots and priors which occupied much of Fleet Street, the Strand and Holborn were all confiscated, and several bishops' inns, though not seized, were forcibly exchanged for other properties. Several abbots' inns were converted into large inns for travellers: the abbots of Glastonbury, Lewes, Malmesbury, Peterborough and Cirencester saw their town houses become the Dolphin, Walnut Tree, Castle, Bell and Popingay Inns. Some inns made ideal mansions for aristocrats, rich aldermen and Court favourites under Edward VI and Elizabeth. Somerset House replaced the Bishop of Worcester's Inn on the river, the Bishop of Bath's Inn became Arundel House, the Bishop of Carlyle's Inn became Bedford House, and Salisbury Inn went to Thomas Sackville, the first Earl of Dorset. The Bishop of Exeter's house was rebuilt in 1563 as Leicester or Essex House, and Norwich Place passed to a series of royal favourites before falling into the hands of the Duke of Buckingham in the 1620s. Its river gate, known as the York Watergate, is still there today, next to Charing Cross Station. The biggest prize of all went to the King, who ejected the Archbishop of York (Wolsey's position until 1529) from York Place, and turned it into his own Palace of Whitehall, with a new cockpit, tiltyard and tennis court. It remained the main royal residence in London until 1698, when all of it, except James I's Banqueting House, was burned to the ground.

Many estates were cleared and used for housing, either (as in White-friars, St Mary Spital and Holywell Priory) 'lodgings for Noble men and others', or (near St Bartholomew-the-Great) 'tenements for brokers, tiplers, and such like'. Two livery companies gained new halls, the leathersellers in St Helen's and the mercers in St Thomas Acon. Other estates were turned to commercial use, as storehouses, workshops, carpenters' yards or places of entertainment. By 1600 there was a wine tavern at St Martin-le-Grand, a tennis court at Crutched Friars, and bowling alleys in the grounds of St Clare's Minories. Crutched Friars was also the site of a glass-making workshop, St Clare's, near the Tower, became an armoury, and St Mary Graces was demolished to make way for a naval stores and ship's biscuit factory.[11]

The transition from the sacred to the profane is best represented by the building of theatres in Blackfriars, which became in the 1550s the home of the Queen's Revels and the Blackfriars Playhouse, and in Holywell Priory, where 'two houses for the shewe of Activities, Comedies, tragedies and histories', the Curtain and the Theatre, were built in 1576–7. The fact that old monastic areas retained their immunity from City jurisdiction, taxation and trade regulations made them ideal sites for theatres, industry or crime. The City remained surrounded by 'Liberties' whose inhabitants it could not control: Blackfriars, Whitefriars (notorious for crime), Great and Little Bartholomew's, Coldharbour, Charterhouse, Clerkenwell, the Temple, the Minories, the Savoy, Bankside (where theatres joined the brothels and bear-pits), Bishopsgate, and others. The first five of these exemptions were much restricted in 1608, but others lasted in a modified form for centuries: St Martin's until 1815, and St Katharine's until 1825.[12]

Except where they served an important parochial or social function, the city appears to have accepted the destruction of the monasteries without much complaint, and citizens were happy to join in the dismemberment of institutions whose spiritual vigour had already faded. But in the scramble for profit, the demands of charity and worship were not quite forgotten. Fifteen monastic churches were saved, either as chapels for new hospitals and colleges, or as parish churches for existing parishes, or parishes newly created on monastic sites. Four still surviving monastic churches, St Mary Overy, St Bartholomew-the-Less, the choir of St Bartholomew-the-Great, and the nuns' half of St Helen's (which was joined to the existing parish church), became parish churches, as did St John's Clerkenwell, St Katherine Creechurch (which had been attached to Holy Trinity Aldgate) and St Alphege (the chapel of Elsing Spital), of which fragments can still be seen.

Much of the city's educational system, and almost all of its provision of care for the old, sick, helpless and insane, had depended on religious communities, and the mayor and aldermen were not happy to see this work destroyed. A letter to the King from the Mayor, Sir Richard Gresham, in 1538, and a petition from the Court of Aldermen in 1539, pointed out the damage caused to the City by the loss of monastic hospitals and churches: 'the poor, sick, blind, aged and impotent persons ... lying in the street, offending every clean person passing by with their filthy and nasty savours', and worshippers 'put out of their pews, and the church pestered with people'. There was an unseemly wrangle in 1540, with the Common Council bidding 1,000 marks for the four main friaries, and Henry calling them 'pinchpence' for offering so little for such valuable estates. Better buyers were found for Whitefriars, Blackfriars and Austin Friars, but Greyfriars was eventually granted to the city in 1546, along with St Bartholomew's Hospital and Bethlem Hospital (which had never been closed). Under Edward VI, the City obtained and reopened St Thomas's Hospital, for the poor and infirm, and Henry VIII's rambling Bridewell Palace, alongside the polluted Fleet, as a workhouse for the poor and idle, the destitute and prostitute. The City founded Christ's Hospital for 'poor fatherless children' within Greyfriars, and the Hospital of St Katharine survived, protected by its ancient connection with English queens, to care for the old and sick. Thus a rudimentary system of care and shelter was salvaged from the wreck of the monastic hospitals, though one barely adequate for the growing needs of Elizabethan London.[13]

A POPULATION BOOM

The establishment of new hospitals and the freeing of monastic land was timely, since London in the 1530s was entering a period of very rapid population growth, which transformed it in the space of 150 years from a middle-ranking European town of about 50,000 or 60,000 people, smaller than Paris, Rome, Naples, Venice, Antwerp and several others, into a monster of over 500,000, the greatest city in Christendom. Although the broad dimensions of this growth are fairly clear, its precise scale and timing are still the subject of a debate which may never be resolved. Until the nineteenth century, all population figures rest upon estimates based on unreliable data. Tax records may help, but involve estimates of the non-taxed population and household size. Occasional official or unofficial population surveys are useful, but they generally omitted the 'floating population' and outlying areas, and used unsound or unknown enumeration techniques. Parish registers, recording baptisms, marriages and burials, were kept by parish clergy (on government orders) from 1538, and survive for several London parishes. These are of enormous importance in pre-nineteenth-century population study, but they can only yield population figures if assumptions are made about birth and death rates, and about the relative populations of registered and unregistered parishes, and if allowances are made for under-registration, especially of 'chrisoms' (babies who died before christening) and non-Anglicans who disapproved of infant baptism (a large group after 1642).

London has a further useful source of information in the Bills of Mortality, weekly and annual records of the numbers of deaths and christenings in the London area, compiled by the parish sextons, especially in plague years, probably since 1519. Each sexton was assisted by two 'searchers', often old women without medical knowledge, whose diagnoses may not have been reliable, but whose enumeration was probably accurate enough. But none of these annual totals survives from before 1563, and until 1579 the Bills only cover plague years, when the death rate was abnormally high and the christening rate unusually low. In these years population calculations arrived at by multiplying the number of deaths or christenings by an assumed normal death or christening rate would be very misleading. The area covered by the Bills changed over time, as different parishes were recognized as being part of the settled urban district, and as the London authorities recognized the value of having information from outlying townships in time of plague. At first, only the ninety-seven parishes within (or straddling) the walls were included, but by the 1590s the Bills covered sixteen extramural parishes wholly or partly within the City's jurisdiction, both north and south of the river, an area about six times as large as the walled City. From 1603, the Bills included ten 'out-parishes' on the edge of the town, increasing the area covered by about 130 per cent, and after 1636 they included Westminster and six 'distant' parishes, Stepney, Hackney, Islington, Rotherhithe, Newington and Lambeth. This group of 130 parishes, large parts of which remained rural until the nineteenth century, covered an area over ten times as large as the 113 parishes included in the 1590s.[14] It is clearly important, when examining London's population, to remember which of these 'Londons' we are talking about.

By calculating the number of christenings in London in plague-free years between 1565 and 1665, and relating these to the birth rate which contemporary statisticians believed to prevail in seventeenth-century London (between 30 and 35 births per 1,000 people), Ian Sutherland has produced plausible figures for London's population in these years. If the birth rate was in the middle of Sutherland's range (32.5 per 1,000), then the population of the inner 113 parishes was 85,000 in 1565, 155,000 in 1605, and 206,000 in 1625. If we take the larger area of 123 parishes, the population was 200,000 in 1605, 260,000 in 1625, 313,000 in 1650, and 460,000 in 1665. The biggest London, of 130 parishes, was 370,000 in 1650, and 550,000 in 1665. After 1642, the christening figures become a more inaccurate record of the birth rate, but by combining the burial figures with the likely death rate in non-plague years, the population estimates can be extended to give totals of between 245,000 and 280,000 for the 113 parishes, 440,000 to 500,000 for the 123 parishes, and 560,000 to 640,000 for the 130 parishes in the late 1690s. It is obvious from these figures that London had undergone an enormous transformation in these years, and that the bulk of its growth, especially later in the period, was due to the intensification of settlement in the ten 'out-parishes' and the seven 'distant' parishes, which held, by the 1690s, the majority of Londoners.[15]

The figures calculated by Finlay and Shearer from the parish registers of three City and twelve suburban parishes emphasize even more strongly the shifting balance of population, from roughly a quarter suburban to three-quarters suburban between 1560 and 1680. According to their figures (which have not been uncritically accepted) the population of the eastern suburban parishes rose fourteen-fold in these years, from 10,000 to 140,000, while that of the western and northern suburban parishes each rose from about 5,000 each to over 60,000. The four parishes of Southwark, according to Boulton's figures, grew more slowly, from about 10,000 to 32,000 over the same period, but if we add the more distant parishes of Bermondsey, Lambeth and Newington the population of the southern suburbs would be nearer 50,000 in 1680. We are no longer dealing with the rustic and sparsely populated suburbs that Stow remembered from his childhood, but with new urban areas that stood comparison with England's largest provincial towns. In 1603 the four parishes of Southwark, with an estimated population of 19,000, had 4,000 more inhabitants than Norwich, the biggest provincial town.[16]

Although all these figures involve a good deal of intelligent guesswork, there is general agreement that the population of London and the suburbs connected to it rose from about 50,000 or 60,000 in 1520, to 200,000 by 1600, 400,000 by 1650, and over 500,000 by 1700. London's population grew roughly twice as fast as that of the country as a whole. The population of England was probably about 2.3 million in 1520, rising to 3 million in 1550, about 4 million in 1600, and a little over 5 million in 1700. Thus London's share of the national total doubled in each century, from about 2.5 per cent in 1520 to almost 5 per cent in 1600, and over 10 per cent in 1700.[17] It was in these centuries, to use a contemporary image, that England's head really began to swell.

ALIENS AND MIGRANTS

Unlike the rest of the kingdom, London did not enjoy a 'natural' population growth in the sixteenth and seventeenth centuries. On the contrary, baptism and burial records show that without migrants London's population would have fallen in every quarter-century from 1550 to 1800. London's high mortality rate was enough to diminish significantly England's overall population growth between 1625 and 1775, and actually to pull the national population down between 1650 and 1700.[18] Well-informed contemporaries such as John Graunt, the seventeenth-century London haberdasher whose work on the Bills of Mortality makes him the father of modern demography, recognized this dependence on migration: 'London is supplied with people from out of the country, whereby not only to repair the overplus difference of burials ... but likewise to increase its inhabitants.'[19] Graunt also noticed that this 'overplus' was significant only in plague years: in other years (before 1642) burials and baptisms were roughly in balance. London's total natural decrease has been calculated at about 575,000 between 1550 and 1700, and to replace this loss and to increase London's population by about 450,000 between 1520 and 1665, net migration into the capital must have run at an average of almost 6,000 a year. The total inward and outward flow of migrants was of course much greater than this.[20]

The most distinctive migrant group, alien settlers from France and the Low Countries, formed a substantial minority of London's inhabitants. Persecution and religious conflict in France and the Spanish Netherlands produced a flow of Protestant refugees from the 1560s onwards, though the alien population of London and the suburbs does not seem to have risen dramatically between 1567, when it was 4,700 (almost 5 per cent of London's population) and 1593, when it was 5,450 (under 4 per cent).[21] Aliens had an impact on London life which was disproportionate to their numbers, both because of their contribution to industrial and commercial activity, and because of the hostility they suffered from apprentices, craftsmen, merchants and all those in search of scapegoats.

Broadly speaking, London attracted two types of English migrant. There were those drawn to London, as ambitious young men and women had been for centuries, in hope of betterment through employment, apprenticeship, higher wages or successful marriage. One ambitious six-teenth-century migrant summarized these attractions thus: 'In London we find rich wives, spruce mistresses, pleasant houses, good diet, rare wines, neat servants, fashionable furniture, pleasures and profits the best of all sort.' The lure of London was especially strong in the North, and strangely weak in the South-West. Of the 1,055 men who became London freemen between December 1551 and October 1553, 390 (37 per cent) came from London and the South-East, 340 (32.2 per cent) from East Anglia and the Midlands (as far north as the Humber), 259 (24.5 per cent) from Yorkshire and the North, but only 20 (under 2 per cent) from the South-West. Although London never lost its power to attract the long-distance migrant, by the end of the seventeenth century the distances travelled by the average immigrant apprentice were much shorter, and most of them came from the southern counties and south Midlands, with few from the North and almost none from Devon and Cornwall.[22]

Then there were 'subsistence' migrants, forced to leave their homes in desperate search for food, work or somewhere to live. These impoverished migrants were especially common at times of rapid rural population growth (as the years 1520–1650 were) when agriculture was unable to absorb the growing workforce, and in years of dearth. Population growth was the fundamental problem. It produced a land shortage which reduced the size of rural smallholdings and created a five-fold rise in food prices. This roughly halved real wages in the sixteenth century, and made it difficult for adolescents to find places as living-in servants, workers or apprentices, or to make their livings as independent labourers. Repeated slumps in the cloth industry and frequent harvest failures compounded the problem. Young men and women, squeezed out of their home towns or villages by a combination of these circumstances, set off for areas where farm labour was needed, where wages were higher, where food supplies were surer, or where opportunities for urban work were said to be greater. Many of these migrants moved locally, but there was a steady drift from the upland pastures of the North and West to the more arable Midlands and South, and several of the most well-trodden migrant routes ended in London and the South-East.

'CATERPILLARS OF THE COMMONWEALTH'

London, John Howes wrote in 1587, was the refuge for all those 'caterpillars of the commonwealth' who could not make an honest living elsewhere. 'All serving men whose Lords and Maisters are dead resort to London to provide them Maisters. All maisterless men whose maisters have cast them offe for somme offence or other comme to London to seke service ... lustie roges and common beggers, whose profession is neyther to be a souldier nor a servingman, hearinge of the greate lyberalletie of London cometh hither to seke reliefe.' But London, he emphasized, 'can not releve Englande'.[23]

Contemporaries made a distinction between migrants and vagrants. Migrants were moving from one place of settlement to another, while vagrants had become rootless and nomadic, tramping from place to place, supporting themselves by begging, casual labour, and (so it was generally believed) crime. In most cases vagrants were simply failed migrants, unable to find a new place of settlement, who had taken on the characteristics of paupers and vagabonds, and found themselves whipped, branded, pilloried, gaoled, or even hanged, as vagrants, rogues or 'sturdy beggars'. Poor migrants who arrived in London looking for a job, a home, and a place in society, often found that the capital's expanding economy had no honest work to offer them, and they became urban or suburban vagrants, living in the slums of Stepney or Southwark, and surviving (if they did survive) by begging, scavenging and stealing. Others succumbed to malnutrition, exposure or disease, and joined the many nameless vagrants listed in parish registers as having 'died in the street'.[24]

Vagrants, especially those crowded into London's slums, were feared and misunderstood by those in authority in sixteenth- and seventeenth-century England. They were seen as 'masterless men', misfits in a hierarchical society, people who wilfully avoided honest labour in favour of a life of crime, cheating, fornication and rebellion. This stereotype was refined and reinforced by Elizabethan writers who arranged the crimes and friendships of vagrants into a complex and colourful subculture of professional cheats and criminals, an underworld with its own hierarchy and secret language, or cant, and schools for the transmission of specialized criminal skills. Robert Greene, in a series of pamphlets published in the 1590s, set out to warn Londoners and visitors to the city of the tricks and plots that awaited them: 'for not only simple swains, whose wits is in their hands, but young gentlemen and merchants, are all caught like conies in the hay, and so led like lambs to their confusion'. No doubt Greene's world of cony-catchers (swindlers), priggers (horse-stealers), card and dice sharps, nips (cut-purses), foists (pickpockets), lifts, markers and santers (the three members of a professional thieving team), and curbers (who hooked clothes from open windows), really existed in Southwark, Stepney and St Giles', but his writings romanticized and obscured the dismal realities of life in the poorer suburbs of Elizabethan London.[25]

There was enough truth in the picture presented by Greene and others to give it plausibility. Occasionally, especially in the 1590s, London was bothered by gangs of discharged soldiers who had turned to crime, and there were plenty of inns and 'harbouring houses' where cutpurses and prostitutes met and drank together, either as friends or (the authorities believed) members of a gang. In 1585 William Fleetwood, the Recorder of London, reported to Lord Burghley, the Lord Treasurer, that he had discovered near Billingsgate 'a schole howse sett up to learne younge boyes to cutt purses', where a successful pupil could qualify as 'a Publique Foyster' or 'a judiciall Nypper' by taking coins from a purse without ringing a bell attached to it. The names of forty-five cutpurses and eighteen 'Harboringe Howses for Maisterless Men' were enclosed with the letter. Similar stories were familiar to readers of *Oliver Twist* 250 years later, and were again taken to represent everyday life in the London slums.[26]

COPING WITH GROWTH

The rise of population, especially in the poorer suburbs, presented London's rulers with problems of public order, public health and social welfare on an unprecedented scale. Alongside the rise of begging and crime, the city had to cope with horrifying medical problems, demands for poor relief which could no longer be left to the Church, and the dangerous issue of the supply and distribution of food. National legislation sometimes provided a framework for civic action, but it was often inappropriate to the unique and urgent problems of the capital. A survey in 1552, initiated by Bishop Ridley and the Lord Mayor, Sir Richard Dabbes, found that within the City wards there were 2,100 people in need of relief, including 300 orphans, 600 sick or aged, 350 'poore men overburdened with theire children', 650 'decayed householders' and 200 idle vagabonds.[27]

London's first response to the problem was based on the five ex-monastic hospitals, Bethlem, Bridewell, St Thomas's, St Bartholomew's, and Christ's, each with its own special function. St Bartholomew's had begun to take in diseased beggars in 1547, and in 1552 260 of the aged and lame were given shelter in St Thomas's, and 380 abandoned children found refuge in Christ's Hospital. The Bridewell, which opened in 1553, represented a radical departure from the medieval charitable tradition, and tried to solve the problem of idleness, the progenitor, as the authorities saw it, of beggary and crime, by setting the idle to work 'in making of feather-bed ticks, wool-cards, drawing of wire, spinning, carding, knitting, and winding of silk, and other profitable devices'.[28] Before long the Bridewell had become little more than a prison for vagrants, prostitutes and petty thieves, more likely to corrupt than reform. The Bridewell Court Books suggest a sharp rise in the number of 'offenders' dealt with each year, from 445 in 1560–61 to 1639 in 1624–5, but the figures are incomplete and the trend may not be accurate. About half of these were accused of nothing but vagrancy or idleness, and the great majority, it seems, were teenage boys, who were (Howes complained) 'packte up and punnyshed alyke in Brydewell with rogues, beggers, strompets and pylfering theves'. A few unlucky ones were forced into the army or navy or shipped off (mainly between 1618 and 1622) to Virginia, but an increasing number were simply discharged with or without punishment. Although hundreds of paupers passed through Bridewell's doors each year, it rarely held more than 150, a tiny proportion of London's workless class.[29] It was a model which was copied, though, in many provincial towns, and 'bridewells' remained a part of the penal system well into the nineteenth century.

Punishment, rather than rescue or reform, was the prevailing policy towards 'masterless men' in Elizabethan London. In 1582 the Queen, taking the air near Islington, found her coach surrounded by 'rogues', and this prompted William Fleetwood to order a search of the City, Westminster and Southwark for vagrants. Hundreds were arrested and punished in the Bridewell, before being sent back to their counties of origin. Hardly any of them, Fleetwood reported to Lord Burghley, were Londoners, and most were newly arrived from the countryside. 'The chieff nurserie of all these evell people is the Savoye, and the brick kilnes near Islyngton.' The Savoy Hospital had been re-endowed by Queen Mary in 1556 as a shelter for the poor, and was used as a nightly refuge by the homeless. In the seventeenth century it was used mainly for wounded soldiers, but it retained the right to give sanctuary to some offenders until 1697.

The civic hospitals could not handle London's problems of destitution and ill-health by themselves. Their capacity was smaller than that of the dissolved monastic hospitals, and their income from royal endowments and civic tolls was not enough to meet their rising costs. To some extent the gap was filled by private charitable bequests, a tradition which the Reformation had not broken. The city poor still received their little doles at the funerals of the well-off, and were still sometimes trampled in the crush. Charitable giving increased in mid-century, reflecting the rise in population and prices, the decline of purely religious bequests, and the vacuum left by the destruction of the monasteries. Over 60 per cent of a sample of the wills of well-off citizens between 1570 and 1573 left money to the poor, either in hospital (23 per cent), in prison (18 per cent) or living in the City parishes (44.5 per cent). By the mid-1590s the total amount bequeathed to the poor in cash and endowments had risen in real terms by over 50 per cent, although the rise in population and destitution by this time meant that the money had to be spread even more thinly than ever. Children, the old and the sick were seen as the most deserving recipients, and the able-bodied poor, especially recent arrivals in the parish, were regarded with the utmost suspicion. Migrant lodgers, or 'inmates', were being sought and expelled from many parishes by the 1590s.[30]

The charitable impulse was assisted by official action. In 1552 money was collected in churches, inns, guilds, and from householders to support the hospitals and provide weekly pensions for 600 poor families, and a statute of 1563 made contributions compulsory, and appointed the governors of Christ's Hospital to administer the fund. In the 1590s about a fifth of the £11,723 spent annually by the hospitals, the parishes or the livery companies on the relief of the poor came from the parish poor rate. Without money from the poor rates Christ's Hospital, the largest and perhaps most effective of the five city hospitals, could not have done its work. The economic and public order problems of the 1590s proved that these sums were inadequate, especially in the poorer riverside and extramural parishes, and in 1598 a system of household rating, administered by JPs, churchwardens and overseers of the poor, was created, and remained the basis of parish poor relief until 1834.[31]

These parochial arrangements did little to help the poorer suburban parishes, where the need for relief was greatest, but where a large proportion of householders were too poor to pay rates and taxes. In Southwark, where only two-thirds of householders were ratepayers, and over a tenth of households (especially female-led ones) were on parish relief in 1622, parish pensioners received around ninepence a week, around a half of what a careful single person could live on. To supplement their incomes, poor women might take in lodgers, keep poultry or hogs, act as wet-nurses or foster-parents for parish orphans, or earn money by washing, baking, sewing or spinning. When all else failed, Southwark, like the rest of London, had plenty of pawnshops, where small and expensive loans could be raised on the security of clothes, household linen or rings.[32]

The problem of unemployment, especially amongst the young, attracted plenty of comment but little new action in the later sixteenth century. Homeless and abandoned children were a particular concern. In 1587, John Howes wrote, 'manye lytle prettie children, boyes and gyrles, doe wander up and downe in the stretes, loyter in Powles [St Paul's], and lye under hedges and stalles in the nights'.[33] In the 1640s several Puritan writers suggested schemes which would set the young poor to work and study, giving them training and 'reformation' rather than punishment. One of these schemes was put into practice in 1649, when the Long Parliament set up the Corporation of the Poor, and provided it with two confiscated royalist properties, Heydon House and the Royal Wardrobe, to use as workhouses for the unemployed and as day schools for young paupers. Thus were 100 or more young scholars, as one of their school songs put it, 'from Dunghill to King's Palace transferred'. Educating around 100 children and providing a workhouse for about 1,000 adults was costly, and a variety of municipal labour schemes offered by the Common Council foundered on the opposition of the workers whose jobs were being transferred. Finally, the Corporation lost its two properties when Charles II returned in 1660, and the children were taken in by Christ's Hospital. The workhouse idea, with its combination of training, punishment and the possibility of profits, was an attractive one, and became an important part of London's policy towards the poor after 1720.[34]

'LORD HAVE MERCY ON US'

Rising population in the City and its suburbs intensified the danger of epidemic and endemic disease. In addition to the existing medieval infections, sixteenth-century Londoners now had to face the dangers of sweating sickness, which arrived in London in 1485, killing two mayors, four aldermen, and 'a wonderful number' of people. There were four further epidemics of the 'English Sweat' (in 1508, 1517, 1528 and 1551), all of them brief but lethal, before its unexplained disappearance in 1551. The very serious epidemic of 1557–9, which was thought to be sweating sickness, was probably some sort of influenza. Another shocking and destructive disease arrived (or appeared to arrive) in the 1490s, when a European pandemic of syphilis, or French pox, began. Syphilis shares several of the symptoms of leprosy, including sores and loss of voice and hair, and it is possible that the two diseases had been confused in the Middle Ages, but its virulence and incidence were apparently much greater in the early sixteenth century than ever before. Responding to the crisis, the government tried to suppress the Bankside brothels in 1535 and 1547, but they continued to thrive in all the extramural areas. Ian Archer's bawdy-house distribution map, based on the records of the Bridewell and other courts in the 1570s, shows the heaviest concentrations in Clerkenwell, Smithfield, Shoreditch and Aldgate, and about twenty inside the City walls. Quacks and barber-surgeons did well from the disease, although they had no effective cure to offer, and the 'pox' became an attractive subject for moral propagandists, whether they were attacking the licentiousness of monks, the Court, vagabonds or of London in general. Syphilis came to symbolize the dangers and disorders of London life, the downfall that awaited the unwary libertine.[35]

Even in a good year London was an unhealthy place, with its high levels of tuberculosis, typhus, smallpox, scurvy, measles, influenza and infant mortality, but the disease that created the greatest fear and despair among Londoners was undoubtedly the plague. Plague had declined in rural areas, but in London it was almost constantly present, flaring up into disastrous epidemics on many occasions during the sixteenth century. There was a serious outbreak in 1499–1500, in which 20,000 were reported (implausibly) to have died, and a long succession of plague years between 1511 and 1518, which terrified Erasmus and kept the royal Court away from Westminster. In the 1530s and 1540s there were probably seven or more epidemic years, and the relatively plague-free 1550s were followed by an outbreak in 1563 which killed a higher proportion of Londoners than any subsequent epidemic. From 1563 to 1665 there were nine years in which plague reached epidemic levels: 1563, 1578, 1582, 1593, 1603, 1609, 1625, 1636 and 1665. In four of these, 1578, 1582, 1609 and 1636, mortality was double its usual annual level, and in 1593 deaths were four times greater than usual. In 1665, the year of the so-called Great Plague, there were over 97,000 recorded burials in the London area (including distant parishes), perhaps a fifth of the whole population, and five times the usual number. But the plagues of 1603 and 1625 were at least as severe as this, relative to London's population, and in 1563 there were 20,372 recorded burials, almost eight times the normal level, out of a population of about 85,000.[36]

The geographical distribution of plague mortality changed in the final century of the disease. In 1563, when rich and poor lived in the same inner-city parishes, death rates in the City centre were high, and the suburbs, where the effects of poverty were mitigated by lower population density, escaped more lightly. By 1603 the intensive settlement of suburban fields and monastic land, mainly by the poor, leaving richer Londoners within the walls (especially in the more central parishes), was creating a different pattern of mortality. Plague deaths were highest in the eastern, northern and southern suburbs, lowest in the City centre, and mixed in the west, where there were both rich and poor districts. Parishes near or beyond the walls and the river possessed all the conditions that encouraged rats, fleas and the plague bacillus to thrive. The population was crowded into courts, alleys and tenements, and there was a constant influx of foreign and provincial migrants. Poor washing facilities, lack of spare clothing, inadequate diet, and a plentiful supply of rats, attracted by grain stores, markets and rubbish, and living in the thatch and plaster of houses, made the poor suburban and riverside population particularly vulnerable.

In all the major seventeenth-century epidemics, suburban mortality rates were greater than those in the wealthy City-centre parishes, and in 1665 they were more than twice as high. In that year the disease began in the north-western suburbs in April, and spread eastwards through rat-infested alleys towards Whitechapel and Stepney, rather than along the main roads into the City, as it would have done if human contagion had carried it. In the last week in June there were only four deaths recorded in the City, and Samuel Pepys did not feel compelled to move his wife out to Woolwich until July, or to go himself until early August. The growing contrast between suburban and inner-city mortality rates may be due, also, to the increasing tendency of the well-off to flee to the countryside during epidemics, a practice which the poor were unable to mimic. So the parishes with the least wealth and the most inadequate administrative structures had the biggest problems to deal with, and often it was as much as they could do to get the dead, without identity or ceremony, into the ground. How the parish of Stepney managed to dispose of 600 bodies a week in the late summer of 1665 is hard to imagine.[37]

In every epidemic a nucleus of about ten experienced aldermen remained in London with the Lord Mayor to administer the City. Their success in controlling the spread of the disease was limited, though, by their ignorance of its causes, their unwillingness to raise adequate tax income, and their inability to impose their policies (when they had any) on wards, parishes, liberties, suburbs and Londoners in general. The initiative for effective control on the best continental lines came from central government, rather than the City rulers. In 1518 Wolsey, concerned about the danger to the Court, introduced Parisian precautions, including marking infected houses and making the sick carry white sticks. He also established the College of Physicians and introduced, in 1519, the London Bills of Mortality, which gave advance warnings of epidemics and, as time went on, helped create a much fuller understanding of the social and seasonal incidence of the plague.

Over the next sixty years, the mayor and aldermen were pushed by the Privy Council into accepting that the plague was spread by contagion rather than foul gases (miasma) rising from putrefying refuse, and towards implementing the government's favoured policy of isolating the sick in their homes or, preferably, in suburban pesthouses. The policy was so expensive and difficult to enforce in a large and complex city that even in 1563–4 it was not introduced until the epidemic was almost over. In the 1570s and 1580s Lord Burghley and the Privy Council repeatedly urged the mayor and aldermen to employ a team of doctors, to hire enough officers to enforce household segregation for the sick and supply the isolated houses with food, to build pesthouses, to prevent vagrancy and new building, to publish a list of infected inns, and raise extra taxes to deal with the plague. The City preferred to rely on individual charity, and to allow infected households to send one member out for food. In 1583 the City accepted a book of plague orders which included the closure of playhouses, controls on funerals, street-cleaning and the expulsion of vagrants. But London's first pesthouse was not built until the 1590s, physicians (two of them) were not employed until 1625, and household isolation was not enforced (and paid for by a new City tax) until 1636. It may be that the increasing concentration of the plague in poorer neighbourhoods made a policy that punished the families of the sick by banishing or imprisoning them, cutting them off from friends and clergy, and probably leaving them to die, more acceptable to the City élite. It made it easier, too, for commentators to blame the misfortunes of victims on their own moral and hygienic errors.[38]

There was a new initiative, and a new *Book of Orders*, from Charles I's Privy Council in 1630, along with some interesting recommendations from Sir Theodore de Mayerne, the King's French physician. He suggested pesthouses, true (forty-day) quarantine, and a board of health with authority over the whole of London. He also mentioned 'rats, mice, weasels and such vermin' as plague carriers, but no one took up the idea.[39] Drawing up Books of Orders was one thing, but enforcing them was quite another. The worst problem, the City rulers claimed again in 1625, was 'in the skirts of the City, where the parishes spread into other Counties, and the multitude of inmates was without measure', and where the City's policies of street-cleaning and the marking and isolation of infected houses could not be imposed.

Much of the work of inspecting suspected victims, locking and watching infected houses and distributing money to the needy, was left to the parishes, some of which coped better than others. The rules they were trying to implement had little public support, and without adequate policing the system was bound to break down, especially in severe epidemics. In 1665 watchmen helped the sick break the padlocks off their locked houses, and a crowd tried to close up the Lord Mayor's house. Infected people often defied quarantine restrictions, sitting out of doors, begging, leaning out of their windows, and breaking out of their houses, sometimes with the help of friends. Visiting the sick, helping friends, and attending the funerals of neighbours and fellow-craftsmen were ancient social obligations, not to be abandoned even in such fearful times. 'For if we break these bonds,' a minister said in 1603, 'I see not how human societies may continue.'[40]

THE LAST PLAGUE

Samuel Pepys, whose work in the Navy Office kept him in London, Woolwich or Greenwich during the epidemic of May–December 1665, left an excellent account of the problems of imposing a strict policy of plague limitation on a fearful but independent-spirited people with limited parish resources. The ban on funeral processions was impossible to enforce: 'but

Lord, to consider the madness of the people of the town, who will (because they are forbid) come in Crowds along with the dead Corps to see them buried'. By August, most of those accustomed to exerting authority in the city had fled: 'But now, how few people I see, and those walking like people that had taken leave of the world.' At the Royal Exchange, there was 'not a man or merchant of any fashion, but plain men all'. In September, when people were dying at a rate of over 8,000 a week, quarantine had been abandoned: 'there being now no observation of shutting up of houses infected, that to be sure we do converse and meet with people that have the plague upon them'. By mid-October the plague was abating, but the people were demoralized: 'But Lord, how empty the streets are, and melancholy, so many poor sick people in the streets, full of sores, and so many sad stories overheard as I walk, everybody talking of this dead, and that man sick, so many in this place, and so many in that.' In December the town began to fill again, and Pepys's wife returned from Woolwich: 'to our great joy, the town fills apace, and shops begin to be open again. Pray God continue the plague's decrease – for that keeps the Court away from the place of business, and so all goes to wrack as to public matters, they at this distance not thinking of it.' Finally, in January 1666, when plague deaths were down to about seventy a week, a few aristocrats began to return, to the delight of those whose livelihoods depended upon them:

> But Lord, what staring to see a nobleman's coach come to town, and porters everywhere bow to us, and such begging of beggars. And a delightful thing it is to see the town full of people again, as now it is, and shops begin to open, though in many places, seven or eight together, and more, all shut; but yet the town is full compared with what it used to be – I mean the City end, for Covent Guarden and Westminster are yet very empty of people, no Court nor gentry being there.[41]

The plague lingered in London and elsewhere into the 1670s, but after that it disappeared almost entirely from England. There is still argument over why this happened. Since the disease disappeared from the whole of Europe, local explanations such as the cleansing effects of the Great Fire of 1666 (which in any case missed the worst suburban areas) have no value. The constant flow of migrants from plague-free areas into London and other cities makes it unlikely that populations acquired immunity to the disease, and the arrival of the brown rat, *Rattus Norvegicus*, to displace the more dangerous black rat, *Rattus rattus*, did not happen until the eighteenth century. The acquisition of immunity by the rats themselves, advanced as a possible explanation by Andrew Appleby, seems more likely to explain the twenty-year gaps between epidemics of the disease than its lasting disappearance.[42]

Perhaps, as Paul Slack believes, the measures developed so haltingly since about 1500 to impede the spread of plague, especially the quarantining of ships from infected areas, really worked in the end. The Privy Council and the City rulers had quarantined a ship from Lisbon in 1580, and tried to stop infection spreading from Hamburg and Amsterdam by stopping ships in the Thames in 1663–4.[43] Trade with the Low Countries was so great that once the plague reached Amsterdam London could not escape it. But Amsterdam was plague-free after 1670, and intercepting ships from infected Mediterranean and Levantine ports was a simpler task, and one that was taken very seriously after 1665. In 1720–22 there was plague in Marseilles (because a ship had not been quarantined), and two suspected ships from Cyprus were burned in the Thames. By the time quarantine was relaxed in 1825 changes in the rat population and the urban environment, and perhaps in the fleas and the bacteria, made a new epidemic unlikely. So the Great Plague of 1665, although nobody knew it at the time, brought to an end three centuries of unusual danger and suffering for Londoners. None of the remaining epidemic diseases, or those yet to arrive, could match the plague in its devastating impact.[44]

Chapter 6

Stability, Prosperity and Growth

IF SOCIAL CONDITIONS were so bad, if London's population was running out of control and its streets were full of masterless men, why did large-scale disorder not break out more often than it did? What hidden strengths in London's social or administrative structure, what reserves of orderliness or forbearance among its people, kept London stable in these impoverished years? Popular rebellions were feared, and food shortage and high prices were believed to be their most likely cause, but they rarely happened. Youngsters, and apprentices in their twenties, were the most rebellious group, chafing under the economic and sexual frustrations of apprentice-ship, impatient with the authority of older men, attracted to radical religious doctrines, and prone to express their feelings in gang violence. They were keen to defend their opportunities for sport and play against encroachments. In 1514, they marched out into the suburban common fields, which had recently been enclosed by farmers, and, crying 'Shovels and spades', uprooted the hedges and filled in the ditches, reclaiming the land for their traditional games.

A LOYAL CITY

The worst outbreak of youthful violence, and probably the worst of all London riots in the sixteenth century, the Evil May Day riot against aliens in 1517, was a tame affair by earlier or later standards. Aroused by some inflammatory preaching from a priest in Spitalfields, 1,000 disorderly young men (mostly apprentices) defied the curfew during the night of 30 April, and ran wild around Cheapside for four hours the following day, ignoring the appeals of Thomas More and looting shops and houses in St Martin's and Cornhill. But nobody was killed, and the whole incident was over by mid-afternoon, thanks to the arrival of the Duke of Norfolk with 2,000 soldiers. By executing about fifteen rioters, and freeing another 300 or so after a great show of contrition and forgiveness in Westminster Hall, Henry

VIII showed that he was not prepared to tolerate anti-alien disorders in future. Anti-alien feeling remained strong in London, especially when there were shortages of food or work to blame them for, but rioting did not recur. Evil May Day was remembered as a shocking example of youthful turbulence for many years, and although there were further disturbances in the sixteenth century, often connected with Shrove Tuesday football matches, none of them was serious enough to overshadow it in the mythology of riot.[1]

A London uprising in sympathy with a powerful provincial challenge to the Crown was most to be feared, but in the sixteenth century it did not happen. Sir Thomas Wyatt's Kentish rising against Queen Mary's proposed Spanish marriage in January 1554 came closest to pulling it off. Real wages were nearly at their lowest, the Spanish match was 'much misliked' in London, and youngsters had already snowballed the King of Spain's retinue. A force of 500 Londoners, the Whitecoats, were sent out to Gravesend to resist Wyatt, but instead they joined him, telling him that 'London longed sore for their coming'. Wyatt's men were well received, and well behaved, in Southwark, but in the City Mary appealed to the citizens to arm themselves in her defence, and aldermen were told to keep 'a vigilant eye' on their wards. Journeymen, apprentices and the young were not to be trusted, but the livery companies sent their own members to hold London Bridge against the rebels, forcing Wyatt to take the long route into the City through Kingston, 15 miles upstream. His approach to the City through St James's and Charing Cross was almost unopposed, and along Fleet Street the citizens watched him uneasily. But at the last minute Ludgate was locked against him, and Wyatt, 'seeing he could not come in, and belike being deceived of the aid which he hoped out of the city', turned back to defeat and capture at Temple Bar.[2]

The ingredients which had nourished discontent and rebellion in the medieval city were rarely present in the sixteenth century. Except for the crisis of Edward VI's reign the monarchy was strong, and the Tudors, especially Elizabeth, handled the city intelligently. Elizabeth's demands for City appointments for her courtiers were modest compared to those of Henry VII and Henry VIII, and so were her taxes. Lord Burghley, her chief minister from 1558 to 1598, maintained excellent relationships with City officials and respected the City's privileges and interests. The Privy Council worked closely with the mayor and aldermen to protect London's food supplies and trading rights, maintain order, control the plague and restrict suburban growth. Elizabeth's reward, in February 1601, was the ignominious failure of the Earl of Essex's attempt to raise the City against her. He hoped to raise a citizen army by offering 'an all-hail and a kiss to the City', but Londoners were not tempted to join him as he paraded along Cheapside, and his ambitions were crushed against the locked doors of Ludgate, just as Wyatt's had been.[3]

STABILITY IN ADVERSITY

In the past few years several historians have considered the question of the apparent harmony of social, political and ideological relationships in Elizabethan London, and their accounts differ in emphasis and detail rather than fundamentals.[4] First of all, the mercantile élite which ruled the City was united, or able to conceal its divisions from those it ruled. London's rulers were not split between different courtly factions, and they shared a common allegiance to the Protestant Reformation. There was rivalry between different trading companies, but overlapping membership and a shared concern to defend London's privileges against provincial ports enabled the élite to avoid damaging internal conflicts. However rich London's rulers were, they had risen through the livery companies, and understood the society they were governing. They had not bought or inherited their offices, or received them as gifts from the Crown. This, a City officer argued, was 'an incouragement to the one to governe well, a provocation to the other to obey well, the band of love & societie knitting both together, banishing discord, the poison of all commen weales'. Despite their shortcomings, the social policies pursued by this élite towards the poor, sick and hungry did enough to avert famine and revolt.[5]

The economic problems faced by London in the later sixteenth century were unprecedented in their scale and intensity. London's population was not only far larger than ever before, but far poorer. Although London wage rates were about 30 per cent higher than those in the rest of southern England, prices were higher too, and price inflation since 1510 had been very damaging to the living standards of the labouring poor. Figures drawn mainly from Oxford and southern England indicate that the price of food and other essentials rose by about 250 per cent between 1500 and the 1580s, almost twice as fast as wage rates, thus cutting the real wages of labourers by 40 per cent. In the 1590s a series of bad harvests increased living costs further (to about five times their 1500 level), and depressed real wages (in 1597) to 29 per cent of their average level in the 1490s, making this the poorest year in English history for the labouring family. This was a far cry from the 'Elizabethan Golden Age'. Real wages recovered to about 40 per cent of their 1490s level by 1600, and then remained fairly stable at this level for thirty years.

London retail price and wage figures, collected from livery company accounts by Steve Rappaport, slightly modify this picture. There was fairly steady food price inflation throughout the century, with very rapid increases in the period of currency debasement, 1544–51, and in the harvest collapse of 1593–7. A healthy demand for labour, it seems, kept real wages at about 80 per cent of their 1500 value until the 1580s, except for a brief fall during the period of debased currency in the early 1550s. But in the disastrous 1590s overpopulation and harvest failure brought real wages down again, and in 1597 they were about 60 per cent of their 1500 level. This 40 per cent fall is much less than that suggested by earlier accounts, but it was still very severe, and it is not surprising that 1595 is one of the few years in which Tudor London came near to deserving the reputation for rowdiness and riot that generations of historians have given it.[6]

Feeding a Hungry City

London's vast population had to be fed. This was a matter for national government as well as City aldermen, since a breakdown in food supplies might lead to dangerous unrest. London had the wealth, power and continental trading connections to ensure steady supplies in all but the worst of times. F. J. Fisher explained London's relationship with Britain's food producers in an article written sixty years ago. As London's demand grew, her supplies were drawn from more distant parts of the British Isles, but her most important suppliers continued to be Kent, the Home Counties, East Anglia and the Thames valley. Corn, the most essential commodity, came mostly from northern Kent, London's regular granary, and also from Essex and Norfolk. The upper Thames was an important supply route, channelling the corn of Berkshire, Oxfordshire and Buckinghamshire through Reading, Oxford, Kingston and Henley down to Queenhithe, 'the verie chiefe and principall water-gate of this citie'. Malt and barley for London's large brewing industry came from Kent, Norfolk and the Home Counties, while oats came mainly from Essex and Kent, and hops from Kent, Surrey and Suffolk.

While grain generally came by water, either down the coast or along the Thames or the Lea, cattle were driven on foot from the pastures of Wales and northern England, and fattened in Lincolnshire, East Anglia or the South. Sheep came from the Chilterns and Northamptonshire, pigs were bred and fattened in Suffolk and all around London, and poultry and rabbits were bought in the Home Counties. Cheese and salted butter were shipped down the east coast from Essex and Suffolk, and from as far as Yorkshire and Northumberland. It would be wrong to suggest that farming in these distant counties was dominated by the London market, but in particular districts, especially the Thames valley, the South-East, and parts of the east coast, the London connection produced more specialized, intensive and commercial agriculture.[7]

This effect is best illustrated by the growth of market gardening in the environs of London after about 1580. By the early seventeenth century Londoners, who had traditionally bought their fruit and vegetables from France or the Low Countries, were getting their apples, cherries, pears, hops, cabbages, cauliflowers, peas, parsnips, turnips and carrots from the orchards and gardens of Kent, Surrey, Middlesex, Essex and Hertfordshire. So great was the demand, and so valuable the produce, that gardeners in Stepney, Bermondsey, Battersea, Kensington, Fulham, Chelsea and Lambeth could live well on 3 acres, enriched with manure from the city streets. In 1605 the suburban gardeners won their royal charter as the London Gardeners' Company, and within fifty years they claimed to be employing 1,900 labourers and apprentices. Not only fruit and vegetables, but milk, butter, eggs, poultry, bacon, 'Roses, Raspesses, strawberries, gooseberries, herbes for foode and phisick', flowed into the city from these suburban gardens. In Middlesex, it was written in 1618, men 'wholly dedicate themselves to the manuringe of their lande', and their wives 'twice or thrice a weeke conveyeth to London mylke, butter, cheese, apples, peares, frumentye, hens, chyckens, egges, baken, and a thousand other country drugges, which good huswifes can frame and find to gett a pennye. And this yeldeth them a lardge comfort and releefe.'

These country wives sound like the women who sold their eggs and dairy produce at Billingsgate in Ethelred's reign, and they were still subject to many of the restrictions imposed on 'foreign' hucksters and basket-women in the Middle Ages. But an expanding market and a spreading city encouraged the profiteering, manipulation and illicit trading that the medieval rules (revised and refined in the sixteenth century) had been designed to prevent, and professional informers made a living by reporting these abuses to the Exchequer. One of these informers, Hugh Alley, produced a pamphlet in 1598 (recently published as *Hugh Alley's Caveat*) which gives a fascinating account of how London's markets worked, and what they looked like. Alley's protests led to the establishment in 1600 of a new group of four market overseers (including Alley) to turn the rising tide of free enterprise, but in a city of 200,000 people their task was as hopeless as Canute's. Inevitably, supplying London was now a far more complicated affair than it had ever been before, and the city's food passed through many hands before it reached the customer's mouth. Grain was bought by provincial dealers, milled or malted in Enfield, Hertford, Luton, St Albans, or one of a dozen milling towns, and sold to city bakers or brewers. Meat went from pasture farmer to grazier, from grazier to suburban butcher, before being sold in Leadenhall or Cheapside. Enterprising London retailers increasingly penetrated this chain of middlemen, travelling into the Midlands to buy cattle, to Kent for grain and hops, into East Anglia for cheese and fish, and stealing the business, it was loudly complained, of country dealers. Often these rural deals and partnerships were based on family and friendship ties which migrant Londoners still had in their native counties.[8]

These impressive supplies did not save London from price rises and food shortages. Some goods remained cheap, among them fish, ale and firewood, but meat, poultry and egg prices all quintupled in the sixteenth century, and flour prices rose dangerously when harvests failed. London could call upon grain supplies from the North-East and the South-West, and from overseas, but flour still rose by over 80 per cent in 1527 and 1573, and by a total of 290 per cent from 1593 to 1597. Even at such a time, Londoners did not starve, but several years of malnutrition weakened their resistance to disease, and by 1597 death rates were high, though not approaching the rates experienced in plague years.[9]

The City's responses to the problems of the 1590s included a drive against vagrants and unruly crowds, a search for alternative sources of supply, the opening of new markets and the distribution of grain from emergency stores. A new Southwark grain market was built in the 1570s and a market near Bishopsgate, for malt and yarn, was opened in 1599.[10] The establishment of emergency grain stores had been a fairly common act of death-bed charity, and Stow mentions such 'common garners' at Leadenhall and in the Bridge-house, at the Southwark end of the bridge, where there were also ten ovens for baking bread 'when neede should require'. In the 1520s the City authorities began importing corn to maintain these emergency stores, asking the companies to foot the bill, and in the 1570s the duty of stocking the Bridge-house and Bridewell granaries was given directly to the livery companies, who performed the task with variable efficiency. In 1574 the Lord Mayor, responding to questions from the Privy Council after a very bad year, said that the City had 2,000 quarters of corn in its Bridge-house store (well under half its capacity), and another 6,000 quarters in the hands of ninety-eight white and brown bakers and ninety-one brewers. Since the city's weekly consumption in 1574 was over 4,000 quarters (half of it used in brewing) these stores did not represent a very wide safety margin. Luckily, 1574 and the rest of the decade were years of plenty.

The real test of London's emergency plans came in the 1590s. On 12 and 13 June 1595, crowds of apprentices seized fish and butter, paying for it what they considered a 'fair', not market, price. Two days later there was a riot outside the Lord Mayor's house, and a crowd of over 1,000 apprentices pulled down the pillories in Cheapside. In July the Crown responded to the threat of unrest by appointing a provost marshal for the City, with martial law powers to arrest and even execute anyone found disturbing the peace, and early in 1596 the City employed two more marshals, with twelve assistants, to keep order on both sides of the river. Vagrants, always the scapegoats in any period of disorder, were rounded up and sent to the Bridewell, or displayed in public cages.[11] At the same time, measures were taken to safeguard London's supplies of basic foods. By September 1595, with two years of dearth still to come, the City's stores were empty, and the aldermen made arrangements to import wheat and rye from the Baltic, and asked the Lord High Admiral to send them corn captured from the Spanish. From 1594, the City organized the sale of 10,000 quarters of grain annually at a little below market prices, and in 1596 4,000 loaves were distributed weekly to the poorest families. These were inadequate amounts, but they demonstrated concern, and perhaps helped prevent the food riots of 1595 from turning into something more dangerous. In 1630, the worst year of dearth in the early seventeenth century, the store was down to 1,500 quarters in October, and two years later several company wardens were sent to Newgate for failing to contribute to the common store. In 1631, to assist planning for future emergencies, the Privy Council ordered the Court of Aldermen to assess the population of the City and Liberties, and their grain consumption. The City's response was that there were 130,280 Londoners, consuming each month a minimum of 5,000 quarters of wheat, figures which seem much too low.[12]

A COMMUNITY OF CITIZENS

Of course London was full of tensions and disputes, between neighbours, between citizens and aliens or 'foreigns' (those without citizenship), between livery companies competing for the same work, between craftsmen and wholesalers (often within the same company), between apprentices, journeymen and masters, but most of these could be resolved without violence. The ward, the parish, the livery company, the Court of Aldermen, and even Parliament, Star Chamber or the Privy Council, offered citizens ways of pursuing their grievances by litigation, arbitration or legislation, instead of riot. Thus companies lobbied for tougher laws against alien and non-citizen craftsmen and retailers, used paid informers to catch them out, and took them to court (not always successfully), but there were no more anti-alien riots.

An important point to emerge from recent research on Elizabethan London is that the number of Londoners who were unfree, and unable to participate in the privileges and duties of citizenship, was much smaller than was previously assumed. In appealing to the freemen of London against Wyatt in 1554 Mary was not calling upon a small and vulnerable élite, but a large proportion of men over twenty-seven (the average age of admission to citizenship) in the City and the wards under its control. In 1531 an Act of Parliament restricted guild fees for enrolling new apprentices to 2s 6d, and for admitting them to the guild at the end of their training to 3s 4d, and this seems to have greatly increased the proportion of Londoners who became guildsmen, and thus freemen. It has been calculated by Steve Rappaport that at least 70 per cent of men joining London's adult (over twenty-seven-year-old) labour force in 1552–3 were admitted as freemen, having gone through about eight years of apprenticeship. Using different sources, Valerie Pearl estimates that three-quarters of adult male house-holders in the City and Liberties, or about half of those in the City and out-parishes, were citizens in the middle of the seventeenth century.[13] So almost three-quarters of the dominant section of City society, men past their mid-twenties, were actively involved in the complex and ancient network of wards, precincts (ward subdivisions), parishes and livery companies (or guilds) that governed and defended London.

Yet sixteenth- and seventeenth-century London was still an oligarchy, ruled by twenty-six aldermen and a Lord Mayor, as the mayor was usually called from the 1540s. The more 'democratic' elements in its constitution, the Common Council and Congregation, had very limited powers. The Common Council was the City's legislative body, elected by freemen in the wards, and convened and dismissed at the will of the Lord Mayor, usually about five times a year. In theory the Common Council had wide powers, but in practice its approval of City laws, taxes and expenditure was a formality, its elections and sittings were dominated by aldermen, and the bulk of City legislation came directly from the Lord Mayor and aldermen. Aldermen often coopted a few senior Common Councilmen on to import- ant financial and administrative committees, by-passing the full Council of 212. The Congregation, or Common Hall, was an electoral body consisting of all the liverymen of the City (perhaps 4,000 men in 1641), and any others who could crowd unobserved into the Guildhall. Its right to elect the Lord Mayor, a sheriff, the City chamberlain, two bridgemasters, two auditors of accounts, and two of the City's four Members of Parliament, was circumscribed by rules and traditions which meant that in effect men approved or nominated by the Court of Aldermen were always chosen. In general, this aldermanic control was facilitated by the fact that the members of all these groups belonged to a broad élite, sharing common views on matters of City and national government. Only when this consensus broke down, as it did in 1640, did the Council and Congregation try to assert their independence.[14]

Although the ruling élite was narrow, poorer freemen were not excluded from the running of their city. Most of the real administration of the City, policing, cleaning, poor relief, taxation, was performed at ward, parish and guild level, and involved a high degree of citizen partici- pation. Wards were run on a participative rather than democratic basis. Each ward had between 100 and 300 elected officials: 'prickers, benchers, blackbookmen, fewellers, scribes within and scribes without, a halter-cutter, introducers, upperspeakers and underspeakers, butlers, porters', inquest- men, scavengers, constables, watchmen, a beadle, jurymen and Common Councilmen. Freemen and ratepayers, who elected most of these officials, were more than likely to have to take on these jobs, especially the less desirable ones, from time to time. They were also answerable to the jurisdiction of the ward court, the December wardmote inquest, for immorality or bad behaviour. The key figure in the ward was the alderman's deputy, who would be resident (unlike the alderman) in his ward, and was slowly taking over the wardmote inquest's jurisdiction in matters of vagrancy, delinquency, illegitimacy and dispute resolution. As long as citizens felt that this system of communal self-government and mutual support protected their interests, the chances of social stability were high.[15]

It is likely that citizens felt a greater loyalty to their parish than to their ward. The parish exerted a spiritual as well as an administrative power over its members, and it called them together weekly, rather than annually. How regularly and how enthusiastically parishioners went to Sunday services, especially in the larger parishes where controls were weaker and churches were overcrowded, it is hard to establish, but Protestantism thrived in

London, and there is little evidence that the Church was held in contempt. The worldly affairs of the 109 parishes were administered by vestries, which collected and dispensed poor relief (which still came as much from private charity as from the poor rates) and exercised the moral control over the poor that usually went with it. Since vestries also nominated candidates for many ward offices, it was significant that more and more of them were becoming 'select' vestries, limited to around twenty ex-officials, in these years. By 1635, over half the City parishes were run by these small élites, and the stability of their communities depended on the degree to which the vestries put their ideals of neighbourliness and paternalism into practice.[16]

THE POWER OF GUILDS

London society was clearly very unequal in terms of wealth, status and power, but it offered its male inhabitants reasonable opportunities of advancement and success. High levels of mortality and emigration, economic growth, small production units and the traditional progression from apprentice to citizen and householder offered by the companies, ensured that most of those who came to seek their fortunes were able, if they stayed and survived, to become citizens, run their own shop, and participate fully in ward and parish life, even if the ambitions which Dick Whittington's story had inspired in them were unattainable. City companies recruited their apprentices from all over the country and all social groups, especially the sons of ordinary farmers. About 60 per cent of apprentices died, or returned home, before their seven years were up, but about 40 per cent went on to become journeymen, and about three-quarters of these became householders in their late twenties or early thirties, and were thus entitled to run a business on their own account. Above the level of householder the upward path became narrower, especially for men of humble origin. About a quarter of householders, mostly the ones with the best connections and the best health, became liverymen, and in time members of the Court of Assistants, the privileged élite of the livery companies.[17]

Especially in the largest companies (the merchant tailors and drapers with over 2,000 members, the grocers and clothworkers with over 1,000), the chances of ordinary artisans, the yeomen, achieving high status were slim, and it was important for the cohesion of the company that ritual and policy should engender a sense of participation and common interest. In the smaller and less prestigious companies, such as the plumbers, founders or plasterers, there was real conviviality and a common pursuit of craft goals. But the bigger companies were run by mercantile élites which had little enthusiasm for sharing their feasts and funerals with artisans, or for enforcing craft regulations on engrossing, forestalling, and apprenticeship numbers, which were intended to protect small producers and traders against large ones. But conflicts with common enemies (aliens, foreigns and other companies), the élite's occasional responsiveness to artisan demands, and the charity and poor relief they controlled, helped to keep the spirit of fellowship and mutual benefit alive, and when disputes did break out between craftsmen and wholesalers they were usually contained within the company, rather than sparking off city-wide conflicts.[18]

In many companies, the members were not united by a shared interest in a particular trade or craft. By 1600, the greatest trading guilds, the mercers, grocers, skinners, drapers, haberdashers, merchant tailors and the rest, were dominated by merchants whose main interest was in the cloth trade. Ambitious merchants joined a livery company to become freemen of the City, and for the status and social benefits of membership, rather than out of an interest in groceries, skins or haberdashery. Perhaps, on the return journey from Antwerp, their ships would carry imports appropriate to their company, but decreasingly so. This process had been very rapid in the Skinners' Company, where the disappearance of fur traders from the upper ranks of the company took place between 1520 and 1550, after which date the mercantile leaders of the skinners were 'indistinguishable from other London merchants in the variety and scope of their interests'.[19] In the mid-1570s, members of the merchant tailors were making shoes, cutlery, candles, and dealing in skins, bread, cheese and wine. Even the clothworkers fell under the control of cloth exporters, whose views on exporting unfinished cloth were the opposite of those of the craftsmen. Although the smaller craft companies continued to represent the interests of their crafts, the great trading companies, especially the leading twelve, increasingly lost touch with the trades whose names they carried, and retained only their non-economic functions. They offered a route to civic power and prestige, provided pageantry, feasts, charity and municipal administration, and built and maintained magnificent halls, but they were no longer the simple craft or trade associations they appeared to be. Their flexibility, though, enabled Londoners to respond rapidly to changes in demand, and allowed companies to survive long after their original trades had disappeared.[20]

The companies of Tudor London were involved in almost every aspect of City life. Most of their religious activities, the obits and chantries, the masses for the dead and the saint's day processions, were abandoned in the Reformation, but their charitable endowments, funeral feasts, care for the welfare of guild members, and lavish displays of pageantry continued undiminished. The companies were intimately involved in the government of the City. The Court of Aldermen, whose members were drawn from the twelve great companies, relied on the companies to maintain the City's emergency grain stores, to assess and collect taxes, to provide loans for the Crown, to control prices and markets, to provide armed men to police London on days when trouble was expected, and to raise armies for the Crown at times of rebellion, war, or visits from foreign monarchs. London's famous Trained Bands, the citizen militia assembled when the city was in danger from riot or invasion, were raised and armed by the livery companies.[21]

As associations for economic regulation, however, the guilds faced serious problems. City companies still had all their medieval powers to control their trade or craft, regulate apprenticeship, maintain the quality of goods, oversee the conduct of members and settle disputes between them, and many took these duties very seriously. Whether they were ever able to enforce these controls, even in the later Middle Ages, is another question. One long-standing weakness in their control was the 'custom of London', which allowed a freeman to practise any trade, regardless of which guild he belonged to and to which craft he had been apprenticed. This allowed freemen to change their jobs and take advantage of the opportunities offered by economic change, and it also meant (especially after about 1570) that a decreasing proportion of craftsmen belonged to guilds which would really regulate their work. Companies challenged the 'custom' from time to time, but they were strongly resisted by other companies, who found the flexibility offered by the tradition too valuable to be abandoned. The case of John Tolley, whose right to practise as an upholsterer after apprentice-ship as a wool-packer was challenged in court in 1615, confirmed that the ancient custom still survived. Its value, the court concluded, was greatest where a freeman became too feeble to continue a physically demanding craft, and needed a trade 'more befitting his crazy body'.[22]

Suburban growth was an equally serious challenge to guild control. Although charters granted after the 1550s gave companies rights of regulation covering the suburbs, the practical problems of maintaining control over a town that was growing in area, population and economic activity at such a pace were insurmountable. The suburban areas where company control was weakest were the very areas where craft and manufacturing grew fastest in the sixteenth and seventeenth centuries. This was partly because dirty and distasteful trades had been excluded from the City, partly because such trades as shipbuilding and clothwork needed space, and because land and labour were cheaper in the suburbs, and partly because manufacturers wanted to avoid the quality controls and apprenticeship rules of the guilds. The clearest indication that the guilds were losing their grip on the London economy is the decline in the proportion of apprentices in the population, from around 15 per cent (about 30,000) in 1600 to under 5 per cent (about 25,000) in 1700.[23] Evidence from individual parishes suggests that this decline was already far advanced by 1600, and that the neglect of apprenticeship in the suburbs was mainly to blame.

THE PATTERN OF WORK

Research by A. L. Beier on parish burial registers, which recorded occupations, even those of female and adolescent employees, gives the best picture of the distribution of manufacturing and other work throughout the London area. The registers show an economy of enormous diversity, with hundreds of crafts and trades, and with manufacturing employment increasingly outstripping commercial and service occupations. London was not really the ever-open throat, the parasitic city of consumers, that it was often taken for, but England's greatest manufacturing city. From 1540 to 1700, the years covered by Beier's analysis, about 23 per cent of the London and suburban workforce were involved in the cloth or clothing industries, as weavers, tailors, hosiers, haberdashers, cappers, or one of twenty other trades. About 9 per cent were leatherworkers, either skinners or tanners, or in the heavy leather crafts (shoemakers, saddlers and cobblers), and the light leather crafts (glovers and pursers). Another nine per cent worked in metals, as armourers, smiths, cutlers, locksmiths, coppersmiths, braziers and wiredrawers, or as jewellers, goldsmiths and silversmiths, and 7 or 8 per cent worked in the building trades. All these proportions held fairly steady until 1700, but the victualling trades (bakers, brewers, butchers, costermongers, millers, fishmongers, oystermen, tapsters, and so on) were growing fast, from about 9 per cent before 1600 to 16 per cent by 1700. It is hard to separate producers from dealers, and many of these tradesmen were both, but it seems that about 60 per cent of London's workforce was involved in production. Merchants, who were concentrated in the City, made up nearly 13 per cent of the working population before 1600, but had declined to only 7 per cent a century later, when the suburbs outweighed the centre. Transport workers (watermen, sailors, porters, ostlers, coachmen and shipwrights) were around 7 per cent, and professionals and officials were in relative decline, from 9 per cent to 4.5 per cent. Their numbers would have been much higher, though, if Beier's sample had included the western suburbs or Westminster, where royal officials, lawyers, gentlemen, and professionals were heavily concentrated.[24]

Whether we look at employment patterns, taxation figures, mortality rates or contemporary descriptions, it is clear that by the seventeenth century there were several different Londons. First, and still most important, there was the City within the walls, with its dense and mixed population, characterized by large dwellings and a high proportion of taxpayers. Wealth was concentrated mainly in the centre of the City, away from the walls and the western riverfront. A declining proportion of the City workforce, around 40 per cent, were craftsmen and producers, while about 20 per cent were merchants. Then there were the poorer suburbs to the north, south and east, where population was more scattered, but growing rapidly, and where houses were small and cheap, non-taxpayers were in a majority, and plague mortality was high. Here, probably 85 per cent of the workforce were involved in manufacture or transport, with only a small proportion of merchants or professionals, and guild control was weak. Finally, there were the western suburbs and Westminster, which contained several areas of poverty, but also rich districts with large houses and high rents, occupied by courtiers, lawyers and landed families on a seasonal visit to the capital.

The Growth of the Eastern Suburbs

The distinction between the wealthy western suburbs and the poorer eastern ones was already obvious to John Stow in 1600, and became even clearer over the following half-century. The riverside road running east from the Tower to Ratcliff had lately become, Stow said, 'a continuall streete, or filthy straight passage, with Alleyes of small tenements or cottages builded, inhabited by saylors and victualers', and east of Aldgate the common fields had been 'incroched upon by building of filthy Cottages', a blemish on the city. The early developments were near the City wall, in Whitechapel, East Smithfield, St Katharine's and the Minories. Many of the houses here were shacks built almost overnight for sub-letting, most of them in tiny alleys off the main streets. Proximity to the river and the City wall made rents high, but most of the households here were too poor to pay the Hearth Tax of 1664. Brick-making, leatherwork, brewing and metalwork were significant industries in this area, and in Whitechapel the production of cannons and guns was taking over from bell-founding, which had declined after the Reformation. Growth in the eastern suburbs was not entirely unplanned. In the 1630s and 1640s, when the riverside hamlets of Wapping, Shadwell and Ratcliff were developed, creating a 2-mile built-up area from the Tower to Limehouse, landlords insisted on a more orderly layout of regular streets, although they did not control the design of individual buildings. Spitalfields, developed between 1660 and 1680, was laid out on a grid pattern, with few alleys and courtyards. These later suburbs were generally less crowded, and over half their householders were taxpayers in 1664.

The riverside hamlets east of the City already had a shipbuilding and maritime tradition. There were wharves at Ratcliff and Wapping in the fourteenth century, and Henry VIII made regular use of the shipwrights, victuallers and smiths of Blackwall and Poplar for the repair, supply and refitting of ships such as the *Mary Rose* and the *Henry Grace Dieu*. In Elizabeth's reign, Willoughby's expedition to Russia, Frobisher's to the north-west passage, and Raleigh's to Guinea all set sail from east London. The maritime villages of Wapping, Shadwell, Ratcliff, Limehouse and Poplar grew rapidly between 1600 and 1650, when the rise of trade with the Middle and Far East created a demand for bigger ships. In 1664 these five areas contained 7,847 households, over half the population of east London, the majority of them making their livings from the river, as mariners, shipbuilders and watermen. North of the Ratcliff Highway and east of Spitalfields and Whitechapel, the parish of Stepney was still largely rural, and remained so until the early nineteenth century. Bow, Stepney, Stratford and Bethnal Green were villages, whose inhabitants were kept busy farming, milling, weaving and baking for London and the sea-going population.[25]

In the City and the western suburbs rich and poor lived close together, but by 1650 East London had already acquired the largely working-class complexion that it has had ever since. Titled residents were almost unknown in the eastern suburbs, and well-off householders were scarce. Houses in East London were mostly one- or two-storeyed, with narrow frontages of 12–15 feet, and a timber and board construction which was not meant to last long. Daily life was commonly lived in one all-purpose downstairs room, and there might be one or two bedrooms, with extra beds squeezed in where they would fit. This was a cramped and rather gloomy existence, but perhaps more comfortable than that of many East

Enders in the 1890s. Sub-letting of single rooms, cellars, and out-houses to lodgers or 'inmates' might have made conditions worse than the records suggest. In 1665 the Middlesex Justices complained of the overcrowding caused by the 'harbouring and placing of inmates and undersitters in houses and cellars', the subdivision of tenements, and the 'pestering and filling the same with inmates and poor indigent and idle and loose persons'.[26]

Wealth and Power in Southwark

London's most ancient suburb, and still one of its most important, was Southwark. The City had exercised much-disputed jurisdiction over the Guildable Manor, the small area near London Bridge, since 1327, and by Edward VI's Charter of 1550 a payment of £627 gave it control over two much larger manors, Great Liberty Manor, which included the riverfront three-quarters of a mile eastwards from the bridge and a narrow area running for a mile along the Old Kent Road, and King's Manor, which extended over a mile south-west from the bridge, almost as far as Lambeth Palace. The riverside liberties of the Clink and Paris Gardens, stretching west from the bridge for three-quarters of a mile, were not under City jurisdiction.[27]

Each of these areas had distinctive economic and social characteristics. Paris Gardens and the Clink were fairly poor communities, in which 40 per cent of the workforce were watermen, carrying Londoners to and from the brothels, bear-gardens and playhouses of the Bankside. East of the bridge, the parish of St Olave's had a maritime and shipbuilding community, and was a major centre of woollen cloth production. Leatherwork, dyeing, brewing and soap-boiling were also significant industries in Southwark. Between St Olave's and the Clink was the Guildable Manor, a trading and business area centred on the Borough High Street, one of the main highways into London. There was a food market in the High Street four days a week, and the street was lined with prosperous shops, mostly butchers and grocers, a few shoemakers, saddlers, joiners, tailors and chandlers, and several large inns, of which one, the George, partly survives. The alleys and yards to either side of the High Street housed a poorer population of labourers, widows, retailers and craftsmen, families involved in one of over 100 local trades.

Thanks to the researches of Jeremy Boulton, a great deal is known about the economic and social organization of this little part of central

Southwark, the Boroughside, in the seventeenth century. His findings help us to understand how Southwark (and perhaps other London suburbs) managed to avoid falling into chaos in these years, in spite of plague, population growth, poverty and inadequate administration. London's rapid growth did not create a monster city devoid of authority, friendship, mutual obligations, shared beliefs, and all those neighbourly connections that hold a community together. Instead, London was divided into communities small enough to allow business, administrative and social relationships to be conducted on a face-to-face basis, as they had always been. Although Southwark's population tripled between 1550 and 1630, and although the Boroughside was on a great highway, it was not populated primarily by a 'floating' population of servants, migrants and lodgers, temporary residents unlikely to put down roots in the neighbourhood. The parish kept a list of all householders, and these show a more stable population than might have been expected. Of those listed in 1609, for instance, nearly a half were still in the same houses after five years, and 29 per cent remained after ten. Over a third of those who had gone had died, and many of the rest moved within the Boroughside, because of changes in their financial or family circumstances. Studies of other parts of London between the 1550s and the 1640s confirm that there was a solid core of 'persistent' residents, giving stability and continuity to otherwise fluid populations.[28]

Many of the residents of the Boroughside, like those of the City parishes, were attached to their neighbourhood by ties of business, friendship and family, and by participation in the Church or local government. Over 80 per cent of Boroughsiders found their marriage partners from within the parish, and most of them chose neighbours to witness and oversee the execution of their wills, and to stand surety for them when the manorial court demanded it. The average size of households (including servants and apprentices) in the Boroughside in 1631 was 3.8, since there were many poor widows (but few widowers) living alone, infant and child mortality was high, and children rarely stayed at home beyond the age of sixteen. The cohabiting 'extended family' beloved by sentimentalists turns out to be a myth in Southwark, as it was elsewhere. But about a fifth of Boroughside families had relatives in the district, and kinship ties within the neighbourhood were important, especially to new immigrants and those impoverished by old age.[29]

Wealth and power was unequally distributed in the Boroughside, as in the rest of London. The well-off innkeepers, grocers, goldsmiths and professionals of the High Street wielded power as vestrymen, constables, churchwardens and overseers of the poor over the widowed, the old, the unskilled and the unlucky of the back-alleys. But Boulton's work confirms what an anonymous writer said of Londoners in the 1580s, that 'the greatest part of them be neyther too rich nor too poore, but doe live in the mediocritie'. Almost 70 per cent of Boroughsiders were not assessed for poor rates in 1622, but many of these were far from being paupers. Only a quarter of those who died in 1622 had paupers' funerals, and only 11.4 per cent of households received any poor relief in that year. There was, then, a solid middling group, perhaps a half of all Boroughside householders, who neither paid into the parish poor fund, nor relied upon its support. Rappaport reached the same conclusion in the City: 10 per cent dependent on poor relief, 25 per cent rich enough to contribute towards royal subsidies, and a 'middling' majority, the bedrock of London's social and political stability.[30]

In 1662 John Graunt contrasted the sound administration of the City with the chaos of the out-parishes, where 'many of the poorer parishioners through neglect do perish and many vicious persons get liberty to live as they please, for want of some heedful eye to overlook them'.[31] The opinion of such an astute observer is not to be dismissed, and it rings true of early seventeenth-century Shadwell, which seems to have been rather ignored by the parish vestry and manorial court of Stepney, which had nominal jurisdiction over it. Only after the 1660s, when a wealthy London speculator, Thomas Neale, took control of the hamlet, did Shadwell at last gain its own parish church and local market.[32] Graunt's criticisms apply, also, to those areas claiming exemption from local courts, the notorious 'liberties' of which Southwark had more than its share. Apart from the Clink and Paris Gardens, there were two large areas at the southern end of the Borough High Street, the King's Bench and the Mint, where rogues, prostitutes, debtors and even Catholics could seek refuge from the courts.

Southwark, though, was not a raw suburb, but an ancient and important community, which two authorities, the City of London and the Lord Lieutenant of Surrey, competed to control. Southwark was a City ward (Bridge Ward Without), with its own (unelected) alderman, and the mayor and aldermen of the City appointed the steward, who was responsible for holding Southwark's manorial courts, and the bailiff, who ran the Borough's financial affairs. The City's interest in the administration of Southwark does not seem to have been very great. Southwark's aldermen rarely stayed long, and from the 1630s their duties (settling disputes, keeping the peace, making sure the streets were lit and cleaned) were taken over by the Surrey magistrates. After 1618 the Southwark bailiff was freed from direct City control, and in return for paying the City an annual rent (of between £30 and £130) he was left to draw an income from fair and market dues, court fines and fees, prisoners' fees, royalties on waifs and strays and felons' goods, and so on. From this income, which the bailiff guarded jealously from the incursions of the Surrey magistrates, a variety of judicial and ceremonial expenses had to be met, and the borough gaol, the Compter, had to be maintained. This system, with all its potential for extortion and mismanagement, lasted until 1757.[33]

These conflicts and confusions do not mean that the inhabitants of Southwark lived in a state of administrative anarchy. Particularly in Boroughside, the manorial court exercised a close control over the market and over local traders. Butchers found using defective scales or fouling the streets with blood and offal, bakers and innkeepers who overcharged for bread and ale, and traders who broke the rules of fair trading by engrossing or forestalling, would all appear before a jury of local people in the manorial courts, although there is no reason to believe they changed their ways. The parish vestry of St Saviour's, which included the Boroughside, the Clink and Paris Garden, was even more active. Six churchwardens assessed and collected poor rates, and distributed relief, while parish 'searchers' diminished the burden on the rates by finding and ejecting lodgers and 'inmates' who seemed to be potential paupers. Parish officials spied out innkeepers and victuallers who traded during church services, and saw that they appeared before the Bishop of Winchester's court. Almost all the householders of early seventeenth-century Boroughside were involved with parochial or manorial administration in one way or another, as jurors, officials, pensioners, offenders or ratepayers.[34]

The parish of St Saviour's, with over 5,000 householders in the 1630s, could not expect the high level of participation possible in a small City parish, but it did not abandon the task of caring for its parishioners' souls. Like some other London parishes, it used a system of tokens, costing communicants 3d each, to be delivered to each household, and to be presented at the church when Holy Communion was taken. Until the Civil War, two professional parish clerks kept full and up-to-date lists of all the householders and communicants in the parish, so that sacramental tokens could be delivered, and attendance at Holy Communion could be staggered and monitored. Although Southwark was regarded as a stronghold of radical Protestantism, it appears that 90 per cent of householders in St Saviour's attended Holy Communion annually in the 1630s. Only after 1640 did the unifying force of common religious observance, symbolized by the almost universal acceptance of baptism, Holy Communion and the ritual of 'churching' women after childbirth, break down.[35]

SUBURBAN GOVERNMENT

The question of suburban government was a troublesome and important one, both for the City and the Privy Council. The enforcement of City policy in almost every field – apprenticeship rules, building regulations, control of playhouses and brothels, plague precautions, the pursuit of criminals and vagrants – was vitiated by its lack of authority over the liberties, suburbs and out-parishes. The suburbs, it was claimed in 1592, were 'in many places no other but dark dens for adulterers, thieves, murderers and every mischief worker', and by 1603 it was clear that they were the main breeding-grounds of the plague. The City gained limited law enforcement powers over several liberties (Blackfriars, Whitefriars, Little and Great St Bartholomew's, Coldharbour and Duke's Place) in its charter of 1608, but it refused to take responsibility for the administration of the whole suburban area. In 1633, responding to City complaints about excessive suburban building development, and suburban craftsmen enjoying 'without charge, equal benefit with the freemen and citizens of London', the Privy Council proposed 'to enlarge the government of the cittie on everie side as far as anie contiguous buildings extend, together with the number of wardes and Aldermen to make the government uniforme'. Why the City rulers rejected this chance to extend their empire over the whole of London is unclear, but Valerie Pearl suggests that the élite feared that they would lose their dominant position in an expanded urban government.[36]

In 1636 the Privy Council decided to solve the suburban problem without City cooperation, and created a new suburban Corporation to control the trades, crafts and apprentices of all the suburbs up to 3 miles from the City. This new body was not to have wide governmental duties, but it encroached on the suburban powers of the City livery companies, its authority extended to the liberties within the City boundaries, and its large organization (four wardens, forty assistants, two chamberlains and a governor) made it a potential rival to the City itself. Like so many of Charles I's impressive schemes, the enterprise degenerated into a money-making venture, admitting unqualified freemen for a fine of 20s (payable to the King), and it was abandoned at some time during the political crisis of 1640–41.[37]

CONTROLLING LONDON'S GROWTH

The difficulty of governing London's sprawling suburbs through an assortment of wards, parishes, manorial courts and county magistrates is
illustrated by the failure of the City and Crown to enforce their building
regulations. By about 1580, the City and the Court had become concerned
about the effect of London's growth on the problems of food supply, public
order and the plague, and began to unite in a common determination to
put a stop to new housing development. In 1580, responding to pressure
from the mayor, Elizabeth issued the first royal proclamation forbidding
the building of houses or tenements within 3 miles of the City gates where
none had stood before, or the subdivision of existing houses to take more
tenants. The reasons given in the proclamation, and in the ones that
followed it, were that a city of such a size could not be 'well governed by
ordinarie justice', or be 'provided of sustenation of victual, foode, and
other necessaries for man's life, upon reasonable prices, without which no
citie can long continue'. Its growth, moreover, might lead to the decay of
other towns.[38] During the 1580s the City authorities were pressed by the
Privy Council to enforce the proclamation, but did little. In 1593 an Act of
Parliament repeated and widened the regulations, but five years after this
the Council was still reprimanding the City and the Middlesex magistrates
for their 'slacke and negligent oversight', and warning them to be on their
guard against prefabricated buildings erected overnight by those that 'doe
cause the frame to be made in other places and suddenly sett upp the
same'.[39] The aldermen and magistrates had powerful weapons against illicit
developers, including fines, demolition, imprisonment, and a summons to
appear before the court of Star Chamber, but they could not achieve the
general enforcement of the policy. In June 1602, following a second royal
proclamation, there was a new effort to enforce the rules, which failed to
impress the newsmonger John Chamberlain: 'this week they have begun
almost in every parish to light on the unluckiest, here and there one, which
God knows is far from removing the mischief'.[40]

The policy did not die with the Queen in 1603. James I issued a further
nine proclamations between 1603 and 1625, laying stronger emphasis on
sheds, cellars and subdivided houses, where 'the worst sort' found their
lodgings, and extending the radius of the prohibited area in 1615 to 7
miles. In 1615 an extremely powerful Commission, containing all the
leaders of City and national government, was set up to see that the policy
was carried out, and examples were made of many individuals, especially

poor and uninfluential ones. But each successive proclamation was a confession of the failure of its predecessors. The impact of the policy seems to have been unimpressive, even in the district surrounding Whitehall Palace, where the Crown's desire to keep plague at bay must have been most acute. Most of the land between the river and St James's Park, 23 acres in all, was occupied by Whitehall Palace, but south of the Palace and around the Abbey building was going on rapidly, much of it in squalid backstreets where labourers and servants inhabited sheds, cellars and small multi-occupied houses. Despite the presence of Whitehall Palace, Westminster seems to have contained a fairly small titled population, and an unusually large number of taverns. The prospect of crumbs from the Court, and the traditional sanctuary rules, attracted a population of prostitutes, thieves, 'rascals and idle persons', who no doubt spent some of their time in the House of Correction built in Tothill Fields, south of the Abbey, in 1623.[41]

James was often ready to suspend the rules for the benefit of his favourite courtiers. Between 1603 and 1610 the Earl of Salisbury was allowed to build smart houses on public land near St Martin's Lane, to extend his palace on the Strand, and to build next to it, in the grounds of Durham House, the New Exchange. This was a large stone-fronted building which was rented out to a multitude of small traders, and became a popular shopping centre until it was demolished in 1737. James flattered himself, in 1615, that he would be able to say that 'we found our Citie and suburbs of London of stickes, and left them of bricke, being a material farre more durable, safe from fire and beautiful and magnificent'. To achieve this he tried to impose rules on those who were licensed to build, specifying the thickness of walls and the height of storeys, forbidding projecting windows, and insisting on brick frontages in the main streets.[42]

But both James I and Charles I were always looking for extra-parliamentary revenue, and the temptation to accept fines for illicit development, rather than insisting on demolition, was irresistible. Their willingness to sell exemptions to their own building rules led to a divergence between Crown and City policy, and was one of Parliament's many complaints against Charles I in the Grand Remonstrance of 1641. In 1632 a petition to the Privy Council complained of 'newly erected tenements in Westminster, the Strand, Covent Garden, Holborn, St Giles's, Wapping, Ratcliff, Limehouse, Southwark, and other places', attracting swarms of beggars, inflating food prices, polluting the Thames, and increasing the risk of plague. And in 1638 the City provided the Building Commissioners with a list of 1,361 suburban houses which had been built illicitly. Almost half of these, 618, were in the west (especially Drury Lane and Long Acre), 404 were in the north (Clerkenwell, Holborn, St Giles Cripplegate, and Bishopsgate), 282 in the east (mainly in Wapping), and only fifty-seven in Southwark.[43]

INIGO JONES AND THE WEST END

Although these figures understate the pace of building in the early seventeenth century, they clearly indicate the predominance of westward development in these years. In 1600 (and even in 1625) the area west of Lincoln's Inn, and between the Strand and Holborn, was undeveloped apart from some aristocratic building along Drury Lane. The churches of St Giles and St Martin's really were 'in the Fields' in Stow's day. By the 1640s the whole district had become a fashionable suburb, the beginning of the West End. Queen Street and Long Acre, running east to west across the area, were lined with brick houses in the 1630s, and there were narrow alleys leading off the main thoroughfare. St Martin's Lane, running north from Charing Cross, had been transformed from a country lane into a smart street in the 1630s, and the Earl of Leicester had begun building in the fields which still bear his name. William Newton, one of the leading developers of Queen Street, was also largely responsible for the building of houses around Lincoln's Inn Fields, against stiff local and City opposition, but with royal approval, in the late 1630s.

Charles I exacted an aesthetic, as well as a financial, price from those seeking licences to build. One of the conditions of royal support was the acceptance by Newton of the Italian style of building favoured by the Court and by Inigo Jones, Surveyor-General of the King's Works and the architect of the Banqueting House and the Queen's House in Greenwich. The houses round Lincoln's Inn (of which one, number 59–60, survives) had red brick facades, Ionic pilasters, and roof-level balustrades, classical features revived in Italy by Palladio, and introduced into England by Jones. Thus the King and his great Court architect used the building regulations to graft fashionable Italian style on to 'a city of gables, mullioned windows, carved barge-boards, corner-posts, and brackets', just as Jones had grafted a classical portico on to the west front of old St Paul's Cathedral.[44]

Inigo Jones's influence was even greater in the other major scheme of the 1630s, the development of the Covent Garden estate in the grounds of the Earl of Bedford's house on the Strand. Bedford paid £4,000 for the building licence and in fines, and probably employed Jones as his architect, and between them they produced London's first square, or piazza, modelled by Jones on those he had admired in Livorno and Paris. The Piazza had well-proportioned terraces of stuccoed, arcaded and pilastered houses on its east and north sides, Bedford House to the south, and Inigo Jones's great Tuscan church of St Paul's, 'the noblest barn in Europe', to the west. The only part of this ambitious scheme to survive today is the church, which was carefully rebuilt after a fire in 1795. Both Newton and Bedford did well from their concessions to courtly 'good taste', and their developments became favourite addresses for the aristocratic and landed families who liked to spend the winter and spring months in London. Even though fashion moved further west later in the century, the model of graceful and exclusive aristocratic living established at Lincoln's Inn Fields and Covent Garden in the 1630s continued to influence the development of the West End over the next 200 years.

Merchant Adventurers

At the centre of this spreading metropolis was the City of London, and at the centre of the City, dominating its political and economic life, was its merchant élite. In the sixteenth century, the wealth of the City élite, and the prosperity of London as a trading town, depended to an extraordinary degree on the export of one commodity to one great market. Woollen cloth was the only English product which was in great demand in Europe, and the bulk of it was exported from London to Antwerp. Accurate statistics cannot be given, because of the inadequacy of the customs records, and the possibility of smuggling from other ports, but London's share of English cloth exports rose from roughly 65 per cent in 1500 to over 80 per cent (perhaps even 90 per cent) in the late 1540s, when the cloth trade, and London's share of it, both reached their peak.

London's trading position was greatly strengthened by the rise of Antwerp as the supreme centre of north European trade between 1480 and the 1560s. Beginning as a convenient entrepôt for trade from the Baltic, the Rhineland and the Netherlands, Antwerp became the main outlet for German, Silesian and Bohemian goods, and the northern base for the worldwide trade of Italian and Portuguese merchants. It was thus not only the best place for the English to sell their cloth, but an unrivalled source of imports for the domestic market. The *Magnus Intercursus*, an Anglo-Netherlands trade treaty of 1495, gave English merchants the right to trade fairly freely in Antwerp. Improvements in shipping, navigation and pilotage made it easier for larger vessels to negotiate the Thames in the early sixteenth century, and since the Thames estuary stands immediately opposite the Scheldt, Antwerp's unique commercial ascendancy was bound to give London great advantages over other English ports. Bristol, Exeter and Southampton all lost trade to London after about 1500, and only Ipswich, which also had good communications with Antwerp, held its share. Southampton was especially badly hit from the 1530s onwards when Italian and London cloth merchants ceased to use it as an out-port, though its long decline may have had as much to do with the problems of the Wiltshire cloth industry as with the influence of London.[45]

English cloth exports in the early sixteenth century were shared fairly evenly between the association of English traders known as the Company of the Merchant Adventurers and alien merchants, mainly Italians and Hanseatics. The cloth was shipped from London twice a year, for the Antwerp fair in May and the declining Barrow fair in November, and the quantity exported annually rose from under 50,000 shortcloths in 1500 to over 100,000 in the 1540s, and a peak of 132,000 cloths in 1550. Two main types of cloth were exported, West Country and East Anglian broadcloths for northern Europe, and cheaper and narrower kerseys for the south. Broadcloths were mostly exported undyed and unfinished, making them particularly welcome in Antwerp, where many artisans made their livings from finishing English cloth. In London, where clothworkers were keen to capture this finishing work for themselves, the Merchant Adventurers had to struggle to preserve their right to export unfinished cloth. The merchants claimed that London clothworkers finished cloth so poorly that the job had to be done again in Antwerp, and a practical trial in the 1560s supported their argument, but the issue remained unresolved. Ever since 1377, statutes had restricted the export of unfinished cloths, but the Crown was prepared, for a price, to grant licences exempting the Merchant Adventurers from the law.[46]

The Merchant Adventurers were not, strictly speaking, a London company. Their membership was national, and their headquarters, where their interests were represented by the Governor, Treasurer, and Secretary of the Company, were in Antwerp. In practice the Company was controlled by a group of rich Londoners, no more than fifty in all, who owned the bulk of the cloth shipped to Antwerp each spring, and held the majority of company offices. From time to time, this London élite faced complaints from lesser London and provincial cloth merchants against their oligarchic power, but since London merchants, particularly Merchant Adventurers, were the Crown's main source of loans and credit, they could usually rely on royal support in these disputes. The London Adventurers were allowed to tighten their control of the company in the 1550s, when the cloth trade was in recession. When cloth producers complained, as they did in 1550, that the Adventurers used their control of the Blackwell Hall market to keep prices low, the Lord Mayor and his colleagues argued that excess supply, slack demand in Antwerp, and poor quality ('the naughtinesse of the making') were to blame. Through their hold on England's most profitable export trade, the Merchant Adventurers had unprecedented power in the City and its major livery companies. Almost every mayor between 1550 and 1580 was a Merchant Adventurer, and they dominated the Court of Aldermen.[47]

The complaints of provincial traders against the Merchant Adventurers focused attention on the impact of London's trading success on provincial ports. London's near-monopoly of cloth exports was among several reasons given for the decay of trade in Hull in the mid-sixteenth century (probably the 1550s, when trade was depressed):

> Item, by meanes of the sayd Companies (the Government whereof is rewlled onely in the Citie of london) all the whole trade of merchandize is in a maner brought to the Citie of london; whereby all the welthye chapmen and the best clothyers are drawen to london, and other portes have in a maner no trafficque, but falleth to a great decay, the smart where we feele in our port of Kingston upon hull.[48]

There was some truth in this, but London would always be an easy scapegoat for towns facing complex economic problems.

NEW TRADING PATTERNS

By the 1560s, the problems of the out-ports (especially Hull's) were about to be eased a little by the decline of Antwerp and the rise of new markets which would not suit London or the Adventurers quite so well. The first cracks in the London–Antwerp relationship appeared in the 1550s, when market saturation and the recovery in the value of sterling brought London shortcloth exports down from over 130,000 to about 95,000 cloths a year. The Merchant Adventurers responded to the depression by trying to restrict the number of merchants involved in the cloth trade. In 1555 they increased their entry fines for new members from ten to a 100 marks, and persuaded the Crown to restrict the trading privileges of the Hansards, who were unfairly blamed for the Antwerp glut. The Hanseatic League retaliated against English traders in the Baltic, but they never regained the share of English trade they had enjoyed in the 1540s.[49] In the 1560s London's relationship with Antwerp was finally destroyed by political disputes between Elizabeth I and the Spanish rulers of the Netherlands. Trade was interrupted in 1563–4, when the English moved to Emden, and again in 1569, when they transferred to Hamburg. In the 1570s the Spanish–Dutch conflict, and the sack of Antwerp in 1576, ended any hopes that the old Antwerp-centred system would ever be restored.

The fall of Antwerp was especially harmful to the Italian trading community in London. The great Italian firms had headquarters in Antwerp and controlled much of the business there. The goods they brought overland from Italy and other parts of the Mediterranean, silks, velvets, oriental drugs, spices and dyes, gave Antwerp much of its attraction as a market-place. These Florentine, Genoese and Venetian firms had London agents, who in the 1540s had handled about a third of London's cloth exports and an even larger share of its imports. The Italians had already been damaged by the reimposition of disadvantageous customs duties in 1546, and by a succession of restrictive trade regulations introduced in the 1550s in response to pressure from the Merchant Adventurers, but it was the severing of English trade with Antwerp in 1569, and the upheavals of the 1570s, that really brought Italian dominance of English trade to an end.[50]

A key figure in the commercial policies of the 1550s and 1560s was Sir Thomas Gresham (1519–79), mercer and Merchant Adventurer, probably the richest commoner in England, and the crown's financial agent in Antwerp. As financial adviser to Edward VI, Mary and Elizabeth, Gresham devised a plan to revive the exchange value of sterling after the disastrous debasement of 1543–51 by restricting the flow of English currency into Antwerp.[51] Gresham's name is remembered today for its doubtful associa- tion with Gresham's 'law' ('bad money drives out good'), but his lasting contributions to London's history are the two great institutions founded with his enormous fortune. The first of these was the Royal Exchange, which was built in imitation of the Antwerp bourse in 1566–7. This had been a favourite project of the Gresham family since the 1530s. Why should London merchants 'be contented to stand and walk in the rain, more like pedlars than merchants', when those of Pisa, Venice, Florence, Genoa, Valencia and Barcelona had enjoyed the comfort and dignity of a covered hall since the fourteenth century, those of Bruges, Antwerp, Lyons and Toulouse since the fifteenth century, and Amsterdam since 1530? The Royal Exchange became the centre of the City's business life, and its shop-lined courtyard was a popular social and recreational centre. The uses of the 'Change' altered over time. In the eighteenth century it was let to insurers, bankers and the East India Company, but only since 1921 has it lost its original function as a meeting-place for City merchants and brokers. Gresham's building was destroyed in 1666, and the present Exchange, still topped by a grasshopper, the Gresham family's emblem, was built after another fire in 1838.[52]

Gresham left the Royal Exchange to the City and the Mercers' Company, on condition that they devoted some of its profits to pay for seven lecturers in divinity, astronomy, music, geometry, law, physic and rhetoric to teach at his mansion in Broad Street, which was to be called Gresham College. By this bequest, Gresham intended to put learning at the service of industry and commerce. In contrast to Oxford and Cambridge, its lecturers were appointed by merchants rather than clerics, and their lectures were free, often in English, and open to all. Unlike university scholars, Gresham lecturers readily embraced and popularized mathematics and new scientific ideas, and emphasized their practical applications, rather than discoursing obscurely on the works of the ancients. While Oxford men repeated the ideas of Aristotle and Galen, the early Gresham lecturers (from 1597) seized upon the work of Napier, Mercator and Giordano Bruno, and made sure (as Gresham had intended them to) that London's navigators, barber-surgeons and businessmen understood the practical value of the latest scientific thinking. At least in mathematics and astronomy, Gresham College established a tradition of research and teaching which has remained unbroken, for it was a group of 'Greshamists', meeting in rooms in the College in 1645, that began the scientific association which in 1660 became the Royal Society of London.[53]

TRADING COMPANIES

London's navigators needed the practical scientific advice on offer at Gresham College, because after 1569 merchants had to seek out in distant countries the customers and suppliers they had met until then in nearby Antwerp. Trade with Germany and central Europe, which consumed most of England's woollen cloth and supplied in return linen and canvas (about a sixth of London's imports), fustian (a cloth of cotton and flax), metals and metalwares, was re-established at Hamburg, and in the 1590s Amsterdam emerged as the new Dutch entrepôt, though without Antwerp's old mastery of European trade. But in the search for more exotic imports

Londoners, who had lost the habit of sending ships even into the Mediterranean early in the century, were now forced to establish direct trading links with the Baltic, Southern Europe, the Middle East, Russia, Africa, the Far East and North America.

Trade on these longer routes was costly, speculative and unsafe, and ships faced dangers from European and North African pirates, enemy shipping, unfriendly local rulers and bad weather. Merchants with interests in a particular area therefore sought safety and capital by joining together in a joint stock company, which could raise capital from landowners and other non-mercantile investors, or in a looser federation known as a 'regulated company', on the lines of the Merchant Adventurers. This policy had the added benefit, for leading London merchants and their friends in government, of controlling entry into these trades, and thus preventing a recurrence of the market saturation of the 1550s. The first of these new joint stock companies, the Muscovy Company, was incorporated in 1555 after Chancellor and Willoughby, searching for a north-east passage to the Orient, made contact with Tsar Ivan the Terrible. The Turkey Company (1581), the Venice Company (1583), the Levant Company (a merger of the Turkey and Venice Companies in 1592), the East India Company (1600) and the Virginia Company (1609) followed, as London's worldwide trading network grew.

The companies were open to provincial merchants, but their ruling oligarchies were Londoners, and London merchants were still at an advantage in these costly and complicated routes. Provincial merchants and producers saw one trading area after another falling into London's grip, and they struggled hard, under the banner of free trade, to reverse the trend. In the Parliament of 1604, there was a concerted provincial assault on the privileges and exclusiveness of the major London-based companies, especially the Merchant Adventurers and the Muscovy and Levant companies, the three whose monopolies seemed to be least justified by the nature of their trade, and most harmful to provincial ports. The East India Company was not attacked, because its monopoly seemed necessary, nor was the Eastland Company, a regulated company founded in 1579 to control the trade with the Baltic (and overlapping in membership and trading interests with the Merchant Adventurers), since a majority of its members came from east coast ports. The main achievement of the agitation was to stop Iberian trade, which was reviving after the war with Spain, falling under the control of a London-based company. London's share of England's overseas trade, in so far as it can be calculated, was down to about 75 per cent by 1600.[54]

1. The remains of a third-century Roman merchant ship, discovered near Westminster Bridge in 1910, when the foundations for County Hall were being excavated. Now in the Museum of London.

2. The Roman and Medieval Wall as it stands today, at Cooper's Row, near the Tower of London.

3. The burial of Edward the Confessor in Westminster Abbey, depicted in the late eleventh-century Bayeux Tapestry. The fact that the Abbey had just been built is indicated by the man fixing a weather vane to the roof.

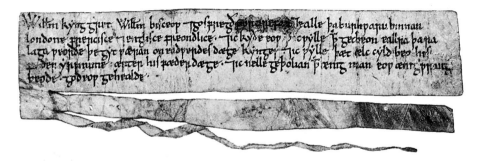

4. 'I will not suffer any man to do you wrong.' William the Conqueror's first writ to London (see page 54).

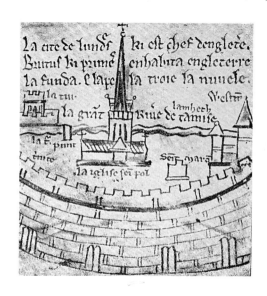

5. The earliest surviving view of London, from an itinerary compiled by Matthew Paris, 1252. It shows the wall and, from left to right, Westminster Abbey, St Paul's, and the Tower.

6. A baker at work, from a
thirteenth-century manuscript.

7. Richard Whittington, mercer
and three times mayor of London, on
his deathbed in 1423. A drawing from
the 1442 copy of the Whittington
Ordinances, pen and paint on vellum.

8. London Bridge and the City waterfront, seen from the Southwark side.
The church in the foreground is St Olave's, Tooley Street. From Wynegaerde's
pen-and-ink panorama, c. 1550

9. The port and market of Billingsgate handled fruit, grain, salt and other commodities, as well as fish. Drawn by a market overseer, Hugh Alley, in 1598.

10. Twelve sixteenth-century craftsmen at work.

11. The Red Bull playhouse, in St John Street, Clerkenwell, in the early seventeenth century. Falstaff, a simpleton and a French dancing master are on stage, and the audience are all around them (see page 210).

12. London Bridge and the City skyline in 1616, from Nicholas Visscher's panoramic view, seen from the south bank. Notice the traitors' heads on display above the southern gate, and the nineteen wooden piers ('starlings') that supported the twelfth-century bridge.

13. The Tower of London, Tower Hill and shipping on the Thames, from Visscher's panoramic view of 1616.

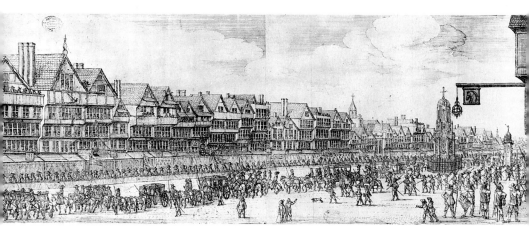

14. Charles I's mother-in-law, Marie de Medici, making her way along Cheapside,
the City's great processional street, in 1638.

15. New Palace Yard, seen from the Thames in 1647, drawn by Wenceslaus Hollar.
Westminster Hall is on the left, with the Abbey in the background, the Great Conduit
(1444) in the centre and the fourteenth-century Clock Tower (roughly on the site
of Big Ben) on the right.

16. A morning scene, before the start of business, in the courtyard of Thomas Gresham's Royal Exchange, about 1647. Etching by Hollar.

17. Afternoon in the Covent Garden Piazza *c*.1647, about ten years after St Paul's Church and the houses around the square were completed. Etching by Hollar.

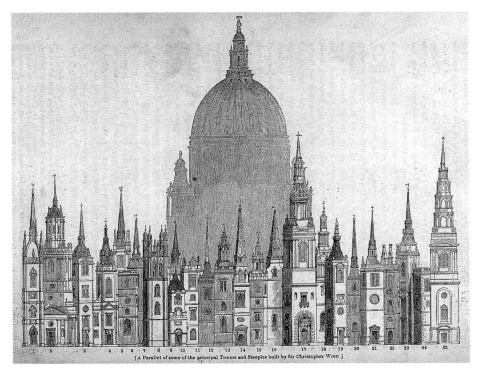

[A Parallel of some of the principal Towers and Steeples built by Sir Christopher Wren.]

18. The towers and steeples of some of Christopher Wren's City churches drawn to scale against St Paul's for Charles Knight's *London* (1841–4). Only 14 of these 25 churches are still standing, along with 2 of which only the towers remain.

19. Wren's Monument to the Great Fire, the tallest free-standing stone column in the world, was completed in 1677. The column is 202 feet tall and stands 202 feet to the west of the spot in Pudding Lane where the fire began. A 1680s engraving by Johannes de Ram.

The range of goods entering early seventeenth-century London was impressive. The Merchant Adventurers pursued their old trade in cloth and mixed imports in north-west Europe. The Levant Company made large profits by importing currants, pepper, spices, wines, silk and raw cotton from the Ottoman Empire, and exporting finished woollen cloth. The East India Company brought pepper and spices from the East Indies and indigo and calico from India, but had little success in selling thick English cloth in return. The Muscovy (or Russia) Company, whose fifteen directors and two agents wielded, it was complained in 1604, 'a Monopoly in a Monopoly', exported finished cloth, and imported furs, wax, oil, timber and ropes.[55] The Eastland Company, struggling against superior Dutch competition, exchanged finished cloth for linen, grain, naval stores and precious metals in the Baltic. Wine imports from France and Spain rose five-fold between 1563 and 1620, and as a proportion of London imports increased from 11 per cent to 17.5 per cent. The most important commodities in the Atlantic trade were fish and furs, and two exotic products of the Spanish and Portuguese colonies, tobacco and sugar. By the 1640s English colonists in Virginia and the West Indies had captured the tobacco trade, and were sending 1,800,000 lb a year to London, where around 330 independent merchants were involved in the trade. The English and Dutch challenge in the sugar trade came a little later, and it was largely a Portuguese monopoly until the 1640s.[56]

DISTANT MARKETS

Between the 1560s and the 1640s, then, London was transformed from Antwerp's satellite into a major international port with trading connections stretching from the East Indies to the New World. The ports of north-west Europe, which supplied about 80 per cent of London's imports in the 1550s and two-thirds in 1602, only supplied 35 per cent in 1635, while the share of southern Europe and the Levant (the east Mediterranean) had risen between 1604 (when the war with Spain ended) and 1635 from 18 to 44 per cent. Imports from the Far East and America, which were to dominate London's overseas trade in the eighteenth century, were respectively 11 per cent and 5 per cent of her imports in 1634, and re-exports of these non-European goods were becoming an important part of the capital's trade. By becoming such a great importer of luxury goods – silks, calicoes, sugar, tobacco, spices, fruit and wine – and distributing them throughout the country by ship, barge, cart and packhorse, London, F. J. Fisher has suggested, helped turn the English into a nation of spenders and consumers, and (because you have to earn before you can spend) helped 'to reduce that leisure preference that is so serious an obstacle to economic expansion in simple economies'. London, in other words, helped to commercialize England.[57]

The shift in London's trade from nearby to distant destinations had important effects on the shipbuilders of East London. In the 1560s, the Merchant Adventurers used about thirty ships, totalling perhaps 1,500 tons, in their Antwerp trade, and no merchant ships of over 100 tons were built on the Thames. Between 1591 and 1618, though, 317 such ships, totalling over 90,000 tons, were built in East London, especially in the East India Company yards in Deptford and Blackwall. The first East India Company ship completed at Deptford, the *Trade's Increase*, was almost 1,000 tons, and sank off Java on its maiden voyage. East Indiamen thereafter were usually under 500 tons, and the first to exceed 1,000 tons, the *Ceres*, was not launched until 1787.[58]

Distant markets were also warmer ones, where it was difficult to sell the heavy broadcloths that were the mainstay of London's northern trade. In India, it was reported, great men only bought English cloth for their elephants and horses. One answer to this problem was to trade in foreign produce, either re-exported through London or taken directly from one overseas port to another. Thus London merchants traded Baltic and Russian goods and Newfoundland cod direct with Spain and the Mediterranean, sold East Indian, American and Mediterranean goods to northern Europe, and were involved in the regional trade of the Baltic, the Mediterranean, the Far East and the Caribbean. The other solution was to produce a type of cloth more suited to the Mediterranean market. These lighter and less hard-wearing cloths, the so-called 'new draperies', were produced mainly in East Anglia, from coarse, long-fibred wool. With these cheap, colourful and varied fabrics London merchants were able to exploit the Spanish market after the peace of 1604, and undercut their Italian rivals in Turkey. By 1640, the 'new draperies' made up three-quarters of London's non-broadcloth exports.[59]

While independent merchants and the Levant and East India companies prospered, the Merchant Adventurers suffered a political and commercial decline. Between 1614 and 1616, they were damaged by an opportunistic attempt by a syndicate made up of their trading rivals (especially members of the Eastland Company), led by Alderman Cockayne, to take over their trading monopoly. The Cockayne project was a fiasco, and collapsed after two years (mainly because individual Adventurers would not support it), but it cost the Adventurers £80,000 in bribes and payments to James I to regain their charter, and their trade never recovered its old prosperity. European demand was depressed by continental currency manipulations in the early 1620s and by the Thirty Years' War from 1618 to 1648, continental (especially Dutch) cloth producers were taking a greater share of the trade, and the new draperies were penetrating traditional broadcloth markets. Broadcloth exports from London in the 1620s and 1630s were about 10 per cent below their 1598–1604 average, and between 1606 and 1640 the number of Merchant Adventurers and the volume of their exports were halved.[60]

Falling cloth exports meant destitution and disorder in the countryside, and in 1622 the Crown yielded to provincial pressure and opened the cloth trade to free competition. The Adventurers regained their monopoly in 1634, but their commercial decline brought political decline, and the new generation of aldermen in the 1620s and 1630s had made their fortunes in the Russia, Spanish, East India and (especially) Levant Companies, not in the broadcloth trade. Of aldermen elected between 1600 and 1625, half were overseas traders, and almost half of these were primarily involved in the Merchant Adventurers' trade. By 1640, almost half the aldermen were members of the Levant and East India interest, and the few Merchant Adventurers who were aldermen were heavily involved in the Eastern trades too. The age of the long-distance merchant had arrived.[61]

Chapter 7

The Pleasures of London

It was a commonplace in the early seventeenth century that London was too big for its own and England's good. The metaphor of bodily dispropor-tion, the swollen head on the feeble body, was a popular one: 'It is no good state for a body to have a fat head, thin guts, and lean members,' as Sir Thomas Roe put it in 1640. This, Sir William Davenant said, was 'the common and received notion', and one shared by monarchs, who feared the social and political consequences of unbridled urbanization. For Thomas Dekker, writing in 1606, the town had already acquired the unpleasant environmental qualities familiar to modern Londoners: polluted air and water, traffic congestion, industrial noise.

> In every street, carts and coaches make such a thundering as if the world ran upon wheels: at every corner, men, women, and children meet in such shoals, that posts are set up of purpose to strengthen the houses, lest with jostling one another they should shoulder them down. Besides, hammers are beating in one place, tubs hooping in another, pots clinking in a third, water tankards running at tilt in a fourth.[1]

But London's vices were also its virtues. Its busy streets, its ostentation and immorality, its boundless opportunities for profit and loss, gave it an excitement and attractiveness which no other English city could rival. To sing London's praises was as conventional among poets as it was to praise the wisdom of a monarch or beauty of a lover, so William Dunbar's claim in 1501 that London was 'the flower of cities all', 'sovereign of cities, seemliest in sight, of high renown, riches and royalty', may not tell us what the city was really like. But the many pictures of London produced between 1500 and 1666 confirm that it was indeed a grand and impressive city. The fine panoramic view from the Southwark side (as most subsequent views were) drawn by the Flemish artist Anthonis van den Wyngaerde in the

1550s, the earliest surviving realistic picture of London, shows the full sweep of the town from Westminster Abbey to Greenwich Palace, with the mass of city rooftops dominated by the lofty Gothic spire of St Paul's Cathedral, and interspersed with the towers of over 100 medieval churches. Later long views, especially the famous and much-reproduced 1616 view by Claes Visscher of Amsterdam, and the Bohemian Wenceslaus Hollar's more accurate etching of 1647, depict a city spreading into its suburban fields, but with its major features mostly unchanged, and its houses, despite James I's 'sticks into bricks' ambition, still in the medieval timber and plaster style. Hardly any of these houses survive today, although many did into the nineteenth century, but Staple Inn (Holborn), the gatehouses of St-Bartholomew-the-Great (Smithfield) and the Inner Temple (Strand), and the façade of Sir Paul Pindar's house in the Victoria and Albert Museum give a hint of what a London street must have looked like before the Great Fire.[2]

The mapping of London also began in the mid-sixteenth century. The earliest known map, a pictorial bird's-eye view produced around 1559, only survives in two engraved copper plates, one showing Bishopsgate and Moorfields (this is now in the Museum of London), the other the eastern half of the city from Bow Church almost to the Tower. This map was probably the basis of the well-known map of London published by Braun and Hogenberg in Cologne in 1572, and the large woodcut map attributed to Ralph Agas that appeared around 1633, but the borrowings of sixteenth-century artists and cartographers from each other have not been fully unravelled.[3]

Foreign visitors were united in admiring London's wealth and size, and all regarded its twelfth-century bridge, supporting and supported (financially speaking) by a street of fine large houses, and with its display of traitors' heads on the Southwark gateway, as one of Europe's finest sights. The Venetian merchant Alessandro Magno, who spent six weeks in London in 1562, was impressed by the beauty of the Thames, with its swans and pleasure-boats, and by the fine gardens, and surprised by the pitiful condition of St Paul's, with its statues broken and its tower recently destroyed by lightning. He regarded London as a city of pleasure and freedom, a prodigious consumer of meat, fish and oysters (eaten raw with barley bread), washed down with beer that was 'healthy but sickening to taste' and 'cloudy like horse's urine'. Alessandro had mixed feelings about Southwark's bloodsports, particularly the baiting of bears, which was 'not very pleasant to watch', and like other visitors he commented on the freedom of women, and the easy relations between the sexes:

The Englishwomen have great freedom to go out of the house without menfolk; ... Many of these women serve in the shops. Many of the young women gather outside Moorgate to play with young lads, even though they do not know them. Often, during these games, the women are thrown to the ground by the young men who only allow them to get up after they have kissed them. They kiss each other a lot. If a stranger enters a house and does not first of all kiss the mistress on the lips, they think him badly brought up.... In the same way at dances, men hold women in their arms and hug them very tightly, and for each dance they kiss them in a very lustful way.[4]

However much this horrified the moralists who loved to denounce London's sinful ways ('O London, London! Repent, repent!') it was an added attraction for country gentlemen. Furthermore, even after the loss of its monasteries London was a beautiful city, with some fine wide streets, well-stocked shops and markets, 120 churches, an impressive (if battered) cathedral, a magnificent Guildhall and Royal Exchange, and an abundance of royal palaces and noble mansions.

NOBLE CONSUMERS

It is not surprising, then, that the new houses of Lincoln's Inn Fields, Covent Garden and Great Queen Street were taken by landowners who wanted a comfortable base from which to enjoy London's rich cultural, social and political life, and to escape from the tedium of rural and provincial society in the winter. This tendency to spend part of the October to June period in the capital, creating the beginnings of the London 'season', is fairly clear by James I's reign. In resolving 'to spend the greatest part of the rest of my lyf for the winter and spring quarter abowt london' in 1605, John Wynn of Gwydir was taking part in a fashionable seasonal migration which was widely noticed and often regretted at the time. James I criticized those 'swarms of gentry who, through the instigation of their wives and to new-model and fashion their daughters (who, if they are unmarried, marred their reputations, and if married, lost them) did neglect their country hospitality and cumber the city, a general nuisance to the kingdom'. From time to time, especially when Charles I was trying to live without Parliamentary taxation in the 1630s, landowners were ordered back to their estates, where their judicial, military and social duties lay, and in 1632 thirty-seven noblemen (a quarter of the peerage), 147 baronets and knights (about a sixth of the national total) and 130 gentlemen appeared before the court of Star Chamber for defying such an order. Gentlemen, the Lord Keeper complained in 1632, 'go from ordinaries to dicing-houses, and from thence to play-houses. Their wives dress themselves in the morning, visit in the afternoon and perhaps make a journey to Hyde Park, and so home again.' Before this clearance, it is estimated that over 100 peers owned or leased homes in London.[5]

Several factors intensified this demand in the seventeenth century. Many landowners had already enjoyed their first taste of city delights as students, either at a London school, or more likely at the Inns of Court, whose annual admissions rose from around 150 in the 1560s to a peak of about 280 in the 1610s and 1630s. These students, who were nearly all from landed families, might well find the study of the common law tedious and difficult, but there was no obligation upon them to pursue it, and many chose instead to 'turne themselves to the delights of youth', of which London offered an inexhaustible supply.[6] Road improvements, and the introduction of the coach (apparently from Holland in 1564), gave gentlemen a speedier and safer journey into town, and enabled them to bring their families and belongings with them. The *Carriers Cosmography* of 1637 listed over 200 carriers and wagoners who regularly brought people and goods to London. The concentration in London of the best professional advice, whether legal, financial, medical or aesthetic, the ever-expanding importance of Westminster as a source of power, jobs and favours, the rising influence of the capital over national tastes and fashions, all combined to draw to London landed families who in the days of horse travel would have been content with the entertainments and social opportunities on offer in their own counties.[7]

The supply of goods and services which had attracted landowners to London in the first place responded to the influx of wealthy customers by expanding still further. Professional men, from doctors, lawyers and architects to playwrights, dancing masters and astrologers, could make a better living in London than anywhere else. The three best-known astrologers of the early and mid-seventeenth century, Simon Forman, John Booker and William Lilly, all came to London to make their careers, and their notebooks, listing thousands of cases, give an insight into the range of problems a successful London consultant would be called upon to deal with. Housewives who had lost their washing or their husbands, employers looking for escaped servants, shipowners worried about missing ships or unsure whether to insure vessels still at sea, wives wanting to know when their husbands would die, and servants, students, lovers, parents, businessmen and politicians with problems of all kinds turned to astrologers for advice. Female servants were the astrologers' most frequent customers, but the gentry consulted them too, and paid more for their advice.[8]

The seasonal demand of hundreds of landed families for transport, accommodation, servants, entertainment, food, clothes, and luxury goods, helped stimulate economic growth in London and occupy its rising population for at least part of the year. The drivers of hackney coaches, who first plied for hire along the Strand around 1625, the carriers of sedan chairs, the Thames watermen, the multitudes of domestic servants, workers in inns and cookshops, the makers of leatherware, watches, silk and glassware, depended on the winter influx of rich customers. Fashion, the perfect device for parting the rich from their money, flourished in London. Elizabeth and her successors, by their own example and by their liking for well-dressed courtiers, set its pace. Between 1608 and 1613 James I bought about 180 suits and almost 2,000 pairs of gloves, and in one year Charles I bought 513 pairs of boots, shoes or slippers. In the same year, 1627, the Duke of Buckingham spent £3,000 on clothes. Moralists might rail against 'the fantastical folly of our nation', the rage for farthingales, codpieces and galligaskins, but aristocratic vanity and fashion-consciousness helped employ, in the clothing trades, almost a quarter of London's workforce.[9]

It was in the sixteenth and early seventeenth centuries, in the words of the leading historian of shopping, that 'retailing began to come of age and to take seriously the business of wooing the customer'.[10] The rapid increase in population, the growing number of rich and spendthrift seasonal visitors, the rise of the West End and the increasing range of consumer goods led to an expansion in the size and number of shops, and created new shopping areas in the Strand and Fleet Street. After a slow start, the 160 little lock-up shops in the Royal Exchange were let at over 50 shillings a year in the 1570s, and in 1609 the Earl of Salisbury's New Exchange took the principle of the shopping precinct into the Strand. From Elizabeth's reign onwards, comments on the growth of conspicuous expenditure, on the lure of fashion and display, and on servants imitating the apparel of their employers, are common among contemporary observers and modern historians. The anonymous 'Apology' printed at the end of Stow's Survey, and written around 1580, praised the value of retailing, the 'handmaid to merchandise, dispersing by piecemeal that which the merchant brings in gross', and regarded shopping as an important element in London's economic and social life.[11]

THE RISE OF THE PLAYHOUSE

Courtiers and West End gentlemen, along with law students from the Inns of Court, played a part, perhaps a decisive part, in making London a great centre of commercial theatre between the 1570s and 1642. Hitherto, itinerant actors had performed to crowds in market-places or inn yards, or to private aristocratic audiences in noble halls, but no single centre had been large or rich enough to sustain a permanent group of players, performing regularly in a purpose-built theatre. London, with its unique combination of courtly patronage, wealthy men and women of leisure, well-heeled citizens, and vast numbers of students, apprentices, artisans and labourers in search of entertainment, presented opportunities for profit which attracted impresarios, actors and writers from all over England.

Some City inns with galleried courtyards, notably the Bel Savage, near Ludgate, showed plays in the 1570s, but to exploit the new market acting companies had to free themselves from the control of innkeepers by building their own theatres. Probably the first man to do this was the joiner James Burbage, one of the greatest theatrical entrepreneurs, who built a wooden playhouse in 1576 in Finsbury Fields, just to the west of Shoreditch High Street. Burbage's playhouse, which he called 'The Theatre', made rich profits despite the construction of a rival theatre, the Curtain, almost alongside it in 1577. Further playhouses in a similar style, with three levels of galleries surrounding an unroofed yard containing a raised stage and a standing area, were built over the next thirty years, all of them on suburban sites outside the hostile control of the City. Philip Henslowe, Burbage's main rival, built the Rose on Bankside in 1587, and the Fortune, about a third of a mile north of Cripplegate (a few minutes' walk from the present Barbican Arts Centre), in 1600. James Burbage's last enterprise, the Blackfriars Theatre, a covered playhouse for winter performances, was opened within the old Blackfriars monastery in 1597, the year of his death. Two years later the Finsbury Fields lease expired, so Burbage's sons Cuthbert and Richard dismantled the Theatre, rebuilt it in the Clink liberty of Southwark, and renamed it the Globe. There was now an oversupply of playhouses, especially on Bankside. Francis Langley's Swan only showed plays between 1596 and 1601, and the Rose was demolished in 1606. Henslowe and Edward Alleyn (his son-in-law and leading actor) re-established themselves in the Clink in 1614 by building the Hope, a combined bear-garden and theatre, but it concentrated on animal-baiting after 1616, and the Fortune remained their main open playhouse.

Players were vulnerable to the vagrancy laws, and needed noble or royal patrons to shield them and to find them engagements at Court. In the 1570s and 1580s the Queen and many of her leading courtiers dabbled in theatrical patronage, and in the 1590s two dominant companies emerged, the Lord Chamberlain's Men (with Burbage, Shakespeare, and Will Kempe, the famous comic actor) and the Admiral's Men (with Henslowe and Alleyn). After 1603, James I's enthusiastic patronage gave the acting companies a period of unprecedented security and prosperity, and players were able to perform in smaller and more comfortable 'private' playhouses on the western edge of the City, where well-off playgoers could be charged at least sixpence for their seats. The fashionable 'hall' playhouses were the Blackfriars, which the King's Men (Shakespeare's company) occupied from 1609 to 1642, the Cockpit, Drury Lane, occupied by Christopher Beeston's Queen's Company from 1616, and the Salisbury Court, built in Whitefriars (behind St Bride's Church) in 1629. These existed alongside the 'public' amphitheatres, the Globe (the King's Company's summer quarters), the Fortune, and the Red Bull, in Clerkenwell. Each theatre had its special qualities. The Red Bull was known for its warlike, over-acted and out-dated plays and its unsophisticated audience, while the Blackfriars and Globe staged the work of the greatest Jacobean dramatists, Shakespeare, Ben Jonson, Francis Beaumont, John Fletcher, George Chapman, Thomas Middleton and Philip Massinger.

Permanent companies performing to regular playgoers could no longer repeat a few well-known stories, but needed a constant supply of new plays. These were provided by Christopher Marlowe, John Lyly, Thomas Kyd and George Peele in the 1580s, with Ben Jonson, Shakespeare and Thomas Dekker joining them in the 1590s. One of the leading impresarios, Philip Henslowe (whose diary is the best source for the business side of theatrical management), handled over 300 plays between 1592 and 1600, when a repertory was being created almost from scratch.[12] Among the twenty-five or so poets who wrote for the theatre between 1580 and 1642, Shakespeare, who wrote thirty-seven plays mostly for the Chamberlain's and King's Companies between 1590 and 1613, was a sluggard next to Thomas Heywood, who claimed authorship of 220 plays, and Thomas Dekker, who wrote or co-wrote thirty-two plays between 1598 and 1600, at a wage of around 12s a week. Once a stock of plays had been created, the volume of new writing diminished, and playgoers could be treated to a mixture of old and new works.

Privileged Playgoers or 'Penny Stinkards'?

All these men, from Shakespeare to the lowest hacks, had to please the London audience if they wished to earn a good living. But there has been much argument over who made up this audience, whose tastes, it might be said, helped bring about the flowering of English drama. Were Shakespeare, Marlowe, Jonson, Massinger and the rest addressing the 'little cockney family', the common men and women of London, as Alfred Harbage argued in the 1940s, or were they writing for the 'privileged playgoer', the aristocrats, gentlemen and law students of the West End, as Ann Cook maintains? Are we dealing with popular or élite culture?[13] Cook argues that London's 'privileged' population, perhaps 37,000 in 1603, was large enough to make up the bulk of the average daily audience of around 5,000, if (as the sources suggest) many of them were habitual playgoers. Unlike apprentices, shopkeepers and labourers, gentlemen and students were free between 2 and 5 o'clock, when plays were performed. They also had the money to spend on tickets, fares and fruit (to eat or to throw). Even the cheapest standing places in the pit of the Globe or the Rose cost a penny, a fifth of a labourer's daily wage in the impoverished 1590s, and the great majority of the 9–10,000 seats available in the 1610s cost 2d, 3d or more. The masses, Cook concludes, 'simply did not follow a pattern of existence that fostered playgoing, except on rare occasions'. Regulations enacted by the Common Council in 1538 insisted that journeymen should work from 6 a.m. to 6 p.m. in winter, with a total of ninety minutes' breaks for breakfast, dinner, and an afternoon drink, for 7d, and two hours longer for an extra penny in summer. Anyone keeping to these hours could not be a regular playgoer.[14]

On the other hand, London's 'unprivileged' population was very large, and included many self-employed tradesmen who would have had no difficulty in finding 2d or 3d for a gallery seat in the Globe or the Fortune. The old assumption that well-off 'seasonal' residents predominated at the Blackfriars and the Cockpit, the successors to the noble halls, while native Londoners, the middling as well as the poor, patronized the cheaper suburban amphitheatres, with their much larger capacity (3,000 instead of between 500 and 900), harder seats, and open roofs, is supported by a great deal of contemporary comment. In July 1597 the mayor and aldermen wrote to the Privy Council, requesting the closure of the Theatre, Curtain and Bankside playhouses, as sources of moral corruption, bodily infection and social insubordination:

Among other inconveniences it is not the least that they give opportunity to the refuse sort of evil-disposed and ungodly people that
are within and about this city to assemble themselves.... divers
apprentices and other servants... have confessed to us that the said
stage-plays were the very places of their rendezvous, appointed by
them to meet with such other as were to join with them in their
designs and mutinous attempts.... They are the ordinary places for
vagrant persons, masterless men, thieves, horse-stealers, whore-
mongers, cozeners, coney-catchers, contrivers of treason and other
idle and dangerous persons to meet together.... They maintain
idleness in such persons who have no vocation, and draw apprentices
and other servants from their ordinary work...[15]

Even if we dismiss this as an attempt by the City to discredit playhouses
by denigrating their audiences, or authority's typical panic reaction to new
forms of entertainment, many less prejudiced observers confirm that the
public theatres attracted the poor as well as the better-off. At the Curtain
in 1613 an Italian diplomat found himself among a 'gang of porters and
carters', and in 1624 John Chamberlain reported that *Gondomar* had been
seen 'by all sorts of people old and younge, rich and poore, masters and
servants, papists and puritans'. Playwrights themselves accepted that they
were writing, in part, for 'a dull Audience of Stinkards sitting in the Penny
Galleries', and that their applause might come from the 'Brawny hands' of
a 'Greasie-apron audience'.[16] Thomas Dekker, who wrote plays by the
dozen for the Rose, Fortune, Cockpit and Red Bull, regarded 'your gallant,
your courtier and your captain' as his best paymasters, but knew that
audience approval, 'the breath of the great beast', depended equally on the
'groundling and gallery-commoner': 'your stinkard has the selfsame liberty
to be there in his tobacco-fumes, which your sweet courtier hath: and that
your carman and tinker claim as strong a voice in their suffrage, and sit to
give judgement on the play's life and death, as well as the proudest Momus
among the tribe of critic'.[17] The 'penny Stinkard' appears so often in
Dekker's analysis of his audience that it is impossible to dismiss him as a
Puritan invention. To avoid them, John Marston said, you had to go to the
boys' productions at St Paul's: 'I saw the children of Powles last night....
I' faith I like the Audience that frequenteth there with much applause: A
man shall not be choakte with the stench of Garlicke, not be pasted to the
barmy Jacket of a Beer-brewer....'[18]

THE PURITAN SUPPRESSION

It was well known that playgoers of all social levels often had things other than the drama on their minds. 'In our assemblies at plays in London', the playwright Stephen Gosson remarked in 1579,

> you shall see such heaving, and shoving, such itching and shouldering to sit by women: such care for their garments, that they be not trod on: such eyes to their laps, that no chips light in them: such pillows to their backs, that they take no hurt: such masking in their ears, I know not what: such giving them pippins to pass the time: such playing at foot-saunt without cards: such tickling, such toying, such smiling, such winking, and such manning them home, when the sports are ended.[19]

It was notorious that prostitutes, whose brothels were conveniently nearby, went to the theatre to find customers, and that young gentlemen went to be seen and admired. At the Blackfriars and the Cockpit, gallants paid extra to sit on stage, where they could lead the hissing or applause, befriend poets and actors, and show off their best features to the crowd. Ben Jonson had the measure of these ostentatious playgoers:

> Today I go to the Black-fryers Play-house,
> Sit i'the view, salute all my acquaintance,
> Rise up between the Acts, let fall my cloake,
> Publish a handsome man, and a rich suite.[20]

Most of this came to an end in September 1642, when the Long Parliament decreed that 'Whereas public sports do not well agree with public calamities, ... public stage-plays shall cease and be forborne'. The ban was not completely effective. Short plays or 'drolleries', sometimes based on Shakespearean scenes, continued to be performed on the street, in inns and at fairs, and there were illicit plays in the Fortune, Cockpit, Salisbury Court and the Red Bull in the 1640s. The last three of these were reopened for two or three years in 1660, but Restoration drama, provided by the King's Company in Drury Lane and the Duke's Company in Lincoln's Inn Fields, was almost exclusively for a fashionable audience, and rich and poor no longer shared a common theatrical experience after 1660. Samuel Pepys, a keen playgoer since his boyhood, commented on the contrast between Restoration and pre-Civil War theatres in 1667: 'Now, all things civil, no rudeness anywhere; then, as in a bear-garden. Then, two or three fiddlers; now, nine or ten of the best. Then, nothing but rushes upon the ground and everything else mean; and now, all otherwise.'[21] Then, he might have added, Marlowe, Jonson and Shakespeare; now, Dryden, Etherege and Shadwell.

THE ATTRACTIONS OF THE COURT

Landlords came to London for power as well as pleasure. Above all, they were drawn by the presence of the royal Court, and their desire or obligation to attend the monarch there. The Tudors had fifty or more residences, mostly in the South-East, and spent time in some of them on their summer progresses, or when there was plague in London. But as a rule the monarch was to be found in one of the palaces in or near London, perhaps at Hampton Court, Greenwich, Richmond, Windsor, Eltham, Nonsuch or Whitehall. Whitehall Palace, which Henry VIII seized from Wolsey in 1529, became the chief royal residence, replacing Westminster Palace, which was afterwards used for ceremonial purposes. Henry added two impressive gatehouses (the Holbein Gate and the Whitehall Gate) to Wolsey's York Place, and built a tiltyard, a tennis court and a cockpit on new land west of the Palace. Still further west he built a small private palace, St James's Palace, on the site of a leper hospital for young women. Elizabeth, who loved to tour the country (though she never went further north than Stafford), returned to London each autumn, to spend Christmas at Whitehall, and made it the centre of court life. Whitehall Palace remained a rambling assortment of generally undistinguished buildings until James I commissioned Inigo Jones to replace Elizabeth's 'old, rotten, slight' Banqueting House with a new one more in keeping with his dignity. This was burnt down in 1619, and its replacement (also by Jones) still remains, the only part of Whitehall Palace, apart from 'Henry VIII's wine cellar', to survive a fire in 1698.

At its peak in the 1540s, before Elizabeth's economy drive, the Court employed about 200 gentlemen, or at least half the English peerage and a fifth of the greater gentry. Under a centralized monarchy, landlords could not expect advancement without royal patronage. Men were held at Court by pleasure or duty, the hope of favour or the fear of disfavour, the expectation of titles, gifts, offices, pensions, monopolies or estates, the wish to reduce their tax assessments, or the desire to win local power as Lord Lieutenant or Justice of the Peace. A man with no friends at Court, said Lord Burghley, was 'like a hop without a pole, ... a football for every insulting companion to spurn at'. Moreover, young aristocrats probably found Court life attractive, with its tournaments, gambling, sports and fancy dress balls, and its opportunities for romantic dalliance and youthful hooliganism. And those who spent too much on dice, entertainment or self-adornment were trapped at Court by debts which they could never repay.[22]

England was not a highly militarized or bureaucratic country, and dignified profitable employment was only available for a minority of the peers and gentry who haunted the Court, hoping to find incomes to cover the expenditure on houses, entertainment, servants and clothes which their status, and Court life, committed them to. But the Crown needed to retain peers and great landlords at Court, to enhance royal prestige and to minimize the danger of local rebellions, and monarchs could use land, annuities, pensions, titles and other favours to bind these men to Westminster. The generosity of the Crown and the nature of the benefits on offer varied over time. The plunder of monastic land meant rich pickings for Henry's courtiers in the 1540s and early 1550s, but in her old age Elizabeth increasingly restricted the flow of gifts and titles. After about 1590, many courtiers turned instead to taking bribes in return for using their influence over legal or political decisions, and by the reign of James I, and especially in the 1620s, the corruption of the Court was notorious.

Under Elizabeth and the Stuarts, courtiers were rewarded with grants giving them lucrative control over parts of the economy which were nominally under state regulation. The cloth trade, the Levant trade in currants and silks, the Mediterranean sweet wine trade, and virtually all luxury import trades, paid a proportion of their profits to the Earls of Leicester, Essex, or Salisbury, or other Elizabethan or Jacobean favourites. Regulations devised to protect home industries or maintain quality standards were perverted to provide courtiers with easy incomes in the form of 'monopolies' over particular products, enabling them to sell licences and exemptions to genuine producers. After 1603 the Elizabethan trickle of gifts, pensions and titles became a Jacobean flood, mostly running into the pockets of the Duke of Buckingham and the Scots, and Charles I's policy of retrenchment in the 1630s came too late to rescue royal finances or the Crown's reputation, but in time to alienate many disappointed peers from the royalist cause. Although many other issues were involved, the growing contempt and hostility which country gentlemen, yeomen, Londoners, taxpayers, consumers, voters and Parliamentarians felt towards the corruption, parasitism, extravagance and moral decay of the Court at Whitehall was a vital component of the developing conflict which led to the Civil War.[23]

Chapter 8

London in the Civil War,
1640–1660

THE DEPLETION OF ROYAL WEALTH by inflation and the costs of patronage and the Court, Parliament's reluctance to vote tax revenue when it saw money being squandered and misused, and the anger caused by the methods employed by James to enrich his favourites, gave Charles I a difficult inheritance in 1625. But Charles's own policies between 1625 and 1642 turned difficulty into disaster. Chief among these policies was Charles's pursuit, through Archbishop Laud, of an aggressively anti-Calvinist religious policy, emphasizing the altar above the pulpit, and sacraments above preaching and predestination, and threatening a restoration of the Catholic doctrines and rituals which already infected the royal Court. Moderate Calvinists (believers, with reservations, in the predestined salvation of the 'elect'), who had dominated the Anglican Church since the 1580s, were thus driven into political opposition. The bitterness and suspicion created by this policy made it more difficult for Charles to solve his financial problems, which were the result of the erosion of the real value of royal landed income by a century of inflation, and his involvement in a costly, unsuccessful and unpopular war against France and Spain in the 1620s.

Elizabeth had solved her financial problems by extreme parsimony and good relations with Parliament; James I tackled his by keeping his foreign policy cheap, by employing a brilliant London merchant, Lionel Cranfield, to reduce corruption and balance the budget, and by trying to remove customs duties from Parliamentary control. Charles, after the failure of his early attempts to persuade Parliament to grant him the money he needed, determined to raise revenue on his own authority, and to rule alone, free from the attacks on his policies that always accompanied parliamentary subsidies. Between 1629 and 1640, the so-called Eleven Years' Tyranny, Charles cut his costs by making peace with France and Spain, and improved his finances by increasing his customs revenue, raising 'forced loans', imposing extra duties on certain goods ('Impositions'), turning Ship Money, an emergency levy to fight piracy, into a regular direct tax, and reviving various defunct feudal dues. These methods redoubled the national opposition to Charles, and made it inevitable that, should Parliament ever be recalled, its hostility towards the Crown would be intense. The outbreak of war with the Scots in 1639, and the Scottish occupation of northern England in 1640, forced Charles to turn to Parliament for financial support, and to pay the price Parliament demanded, the abandonment of the measures and ministers that had sustained him since 1629.

LONDON AND THE CONSTITUTIONAL CRISIS

These conflicts were national ones, and the parliamentary opposition expressed the views of country gentlemen and landlords from all over England towards Laudianism, non-Parliamentary rule, and arbitrary taxation. But the attitudes and actions of Londoners played a vital part in the way events unfolded between 1640 and 1642, and in determining the outcome of the Civil War that broke out in the summer of 1642. Looking back on these events in the 1670s, Clarendon, the royalist historian and propagandist, saw London as 'the sink of all the ill humour of the kingdom', the enemy whose 'unruly and mutinous spirit' brought Charles I down.[1] Londoners were capable of giving a violent dimension to political conflicts, they readily turned national political figures into popular heroes or villains, they were numerous enough to defy an army, and they were twenty minutes' march from Westminster. The stoning to death of Buckingham's unpopular astrologer, John Lambe, in 1626, showed what a crowd of angry apprentices could do.[2] However shallow their understanding of the constitutional issues (and we should not dismiss them as an 'ignorant multitude'), Londoners' beliefs and actions could shape history. Londoners, of course, were not one group but many, as divided in their attitudes to kingship, Parliament, Puritanism, the social order and taxation as the rest of England was. Yet London did, in the end, commit itself to the Parliamentary cause, and we need to understand how this came about.

The simple view of London's nineteenth-century historians, that the City, as a bastion of freedom, naturally took the Parliamentary side, was discredited by Valerie Pearl in 1961. London's ruling élite, she argued, had such close ties with government, based on centuries of financial and political interdependence, that its support for the Crown, whatever its unpopularity elsewhere, was almost guaranteed. The Crown protected aldermen from those who challenged their oligarchic power, and bolstered their prestige with honours and favours. The Privy Council helped the City's rulers find grain when normal supplies had failed. The great trading companies (which dominated the Court of Aldermen) relied on the Crown for their charters, monopolies and export licences, and for defence against the attacks of provincial ports and Parliament. In 1621, for instance, James I stifled a House of Commons attack on the Merchant Adventurers with the warning: 'Meddle not with those things that belong to me and the state.' In return, the City helped the Crown to administer shipping and supplies in wartime, provided the government with around a tenth of its troops, and rendered countless services in matters of trade and finance, and in diplomatic relations with distant foreign powers. The City's leading law officer, the Recorder, was nearly always chosen by the monarch, and he usually progressed into high government office, perhaps as Solicitor-General, Chief Justice, Lord Chancellor or Speaker of the House of Commons. By maintaining order and sound government in London, the mayor and aldermen rendered vital service to the stability of the realm, and they expected (and got) royal support for their power and privileges in return. Above all, the City supported the Crown with loans, either raised by the Court of Aldermen (like the £120,000 lent to Elizabeth between 1575 and 1598) or from individual merchants. As long as security was given, usually in the form of Crown lands or anticipated revenues, and interest was paid, the City would meet royal needs for ready cash.[3]

The community of interests between the City oligarchy and the Crown was so strong that even the insults and extortions of Charles I could not break their alliance. Within three years of his accession in 1625, the City authorities had raised £180,000 in loans for Charles, strengthening his hand against Parliament in 1628. After 1629, in his efforts to raise revenue without Parliament, Charles pressed the municipal authorities even harder. Between 1629 and 1637, the King bombarded the City with threats and legal actions against its charters and estates, especially its Irish lands and Crown land held as security for the loans of 1627–8. The City rulers defended their interests, but they were keen to compromise, and in 1637 paid £12,000 for a new charter (confirming old privileges), and accepted the loss of Irish estates worth over £100,000. Ship Money, the most unpopular of Charles' exactions, fell heavily on London merchants, but it was not resisted (after an initial protest) by the City authorities, who used house to house visitations and property seizures to collect the tax between 1635 and 1640. Only in 1639, when the King tried to raise a loan of

£100,000 without adequate security, did the majority of aldermen refuse to cooperate.[4]

It is worth remembering that the King's power over London and its rulers was enormous, and the compliance of the Lord Mayor and aldermen with royal policies was a matter of realism as much as enthusiasm. It would be misleading simply to identify the Court of Aldermen and the Common Council with the royalist party in London. Some of the King's richest and most effective London supporters, such men as the customs farmers Sir Paul Pindar and Sir Nicholas Crispe, held no municipal office. Some aldermen were devout Puritans and opponents of Laudian reforms (for instance, Sir James Cambell and Sir Nicholas Rainton, Lord Mayors in 1629–30 and 1632–3), and others (notably Isaac Penington and Sir Thomas Soames, two of the City MPs) emerged in 1640 as leading opponents of the King. But most senior aldermen, and all four Lord Mayors from 1638 to 1642, were firm royalists, and were almost bound by their great wealth, their leading positions in privileged trading companies, and their oligarchic power in the City's constitution, to find the growth of a popular radical movement in London in the 1630s threatening and repugnant. Whatever their personal views, the aldermen and Common Councilmen were in a difficult position. If they gave expression to the grievances of their citizens, they faced damage to their own careers and the City's privileges from a hostile monarch. If they ignored or suppressed them (the course they chose), then citizens would find their leaders elsewhere, and the oligarchy itself would become one of their targets.

THE STRENGTH OF PURITANISM

Discontent in London took several forms, but its common themes were religious radicalism, Puritanism and anti-Catholicism. The Puritans, the keepers of the Protestant conscience within the Anglican Church, felt the greatest hostility to Archbishop Laud's attempt to reassert the primacy of ritual and hierarchy, and return to what in their view were Catholic practices. Although two-thirds of London parish livings were in the control of the Church or the Crown, in about a dozen the vestry chose the minister, and as a result there were well-established Puritan congregations in St Anne's Blackfriars, St Stephen's Coleman Street (an old Lollard stronghold) and All Hallows Bread Street, as well as suburban ones in Hackney and Rotherhithe. Puritans were hungry for good sermons and lectures, and in the late 1620s 107 of the 129 London parishes had lecturers, partly financed by a group of clergy and wealthy City merchants known as the Feoffees for Impropriations.[5] St Antholin's in Watling Street, the intellectual centre of London Puritanism, had provided daily lectures since 1559. Puritan ministers were a powerful political force, drawing together Londoners of different social groups, alerting them to the danger of a Catholic revival, and giving 'middling people', shopkeepers, craftsmen, and apprentices, the confidence to assert their own opinions against those of people they had been accustomed to obey.

The Puritans could look both up and down the social scale for support. The merchant community was by no means solidly royalist in the late 1630s. Even the Merchant Adventurers and the Levant and East India Companies, with their royal charters and monopoly privileges, had been angered by Charles's policies in the 1630s, especially his interventions on behalf of royal favourites and his attempts to extract excessive customs payments. Parliament saw the possibility of winning their support, and the general attacks on monopoly companies which had taken place in the sessions of 1621 and 1624 were replaced in 1640–41 by attacks on notorious individual monopolists, customs farmers, and concessionaires. So, thanks to Charles's folly, substantial minorities among the chartered companies eventually gave their support to Parliament. As might be expected, though, the fullest support for the anti-royalist cause came from merchants who traded independently of royal charters and monopolies in the unprotected North American and West Indies markets.[6] These North American merchants also had personal connections with City and parliamentary Puritans through their membership of two trading and colonizing companies which organized the emigration and settlement of Puritans in America, the Massachusetts Bay Company and the Providence Island Company.

The support for Puritanism within London's population as a whole probably had more to do with the prevailing mood of anti-popery than with an appreciation of the finer points of Calvinist theology. Anti-Catholicism thrived on memories of the Mary Tudor's persecutions, which were constantly refreshed by readings from England's second most printed book, Foxe's *Actes and Monuments*, the '*Book of Martyrs*'. The widespread fear of Catholic conspiracies was reinforced by the discovery of a plot, conceived by Robert Catesby but named in popular memory after Guy Fawkes, to blow up the King and both Houses of Parliament (and 'blow the Scots back to Scotland') in November 1605. Hatred of Catholicism was redoubled by fear and contempt for the Irish, and hostility to the great Catholic powers, France and Spain, whose ambitions (it was believed) had endangered England over the past century, and whose influence was known to be strong at the Caroline Court. There was a general belief that Catholicism was an idolatrous, superstitious, priest-ridden perversion of true Christianity, that it still had a strong and secret hold on the clergy, the nobility and the Court, and that it would use sedition, conspiracy and foreign or Irish troops to regain control of England. The way in which Charles's religious policies terrified the godly, and prepared their minds for rebellion, can be seen in the diary of Nehemiah Wallington, the Puritan turner of St Leonard's Eastcheap. The 1630s, for Wallington, were a time in which 'prelates and papists' tried to introduce 'popery little by little to the overturning of the gospel'. In his mind the Irish Catholic rebellion that started in October 1641 was yet another proof that papists were plotting 'to bring their damnable superstition and idolatry amongst us'. These were not mere constitutional questions, but the struggle of God against Antichrist.[7]

THE COMPOSITION OF THE CROWD

From 1640 popular unrest in London began to force the pace of events in the Guildhall and in Westminster itself. Archbishop Laud, who was the royal servant most closely associated in the public mind with Charles's policies, was the favourite target. On 11 May 1640, when the Short Parliament had been dissolved after only three weeks, a crowd of City apprentices, suburban leatherworkers and watermen, 'a rabble of mean, unknown, dissolute persons',[8] assembled in St George's Fields, Southwark, and marched on Lambeth Palace hoping to find Laud, 'the Fox', who had gone to earth in Whitehall. For taking part in this riot, John Archer, a Southwark glover, became the last man in England to be tortured on the rack before his execution. The motives of the crowd were more than simply religious. The attack on Laud and the bishops represented, for some, a general rejection of authority and hierarchy, and suggested that there might be dangerous times ahead for the City and company élites, and for the social structure itself. One of the instigators of the demonstration was John Lilburne, lately an apprentice in the London cloth trade, now in prison for circulating seditious pamphlets, and soon to be leader of the radical Leveller movement.[9]

There were ideas at work in London that went far beyond the arguments against royal absolutism that were familiar to opposition MPs. The rapid growth of London over the previous century, and the high level of religious and political awareness of its inhabitants, made the metropolitan crowd a formidable but dangerous weapon. Could it be controlled by the Puritan ministers and Members of Parliament who hoped to use its power against Charles and his government? Would it stop when its work on their behalf was completed? Was it wise to stir up unpredictable social forces, however good the cause might be? Over the next two years doubts such as these drew a growing number of 'moderate' opponents of the King into the royalist camp, helping to give Charles a fighting chance of victory in the Civil War. In this way, the London 'mob' played an important part in shaping the parties that faced each other in 1642.

Popular opposition to the Crown was not confined to street demonstrations. Common Hall was not subject to aldermanic veto (as Common Council was), and its electoral proceedings were loose enough to allow a fairly high degree of popular participation. In the elections of September 1640, which aroused public excitement across the country, Common Hall defied the wishes of the King and the aldermen, and elected four popular Puritan burgesses to represent the City in the Long Parliament. One of the four, Alderman Isaac Penington, was a leading London Puritan, and became a major force in the Parliamentary cause. Common Hall's surprising rejection of the City Recorder, whom Charles intended to be Speaker of the Commons, was a severe blow to the King, Clarendon believed, 'and infinitely disordered his service beyond a capacity of reparation'.[10] The City MPs, and the four Puritan MPs for Southwark and Westminster, acted as intermediaries between London radicals and the Long Parliament, and Captain John Venn, elected for the City in 1641, had particularly close links with the popular movement. These men could represent the views of Londoners in the House of Commons, and try to ensure that the crowd arrived in Westminster to intimidate, encourage or protect Parliament at the appropriate moment.

The crowd, though, had its own motives, beliefs and leaders, and royalist claims that it was manipulated by the Parliamentary opposition or stirred up by rabble-rousers were never very convincing. There were radical preachers, pamphleteers and politicians in London, but loyalist messages were promoted equally strongly. Traditional festivals and processions reinforced civic pride and subordination, royal coronations, funerals and visits were marked with lavish ceremonial, most parishes had loyal and conformist clergy, and plays were censored (not always effectively) by the Master of the Revels. If these powerful forces could not win the battle for the public mind, it may be because their message was unwelcome.

Londoners, unlike people elsewhere in England, could choose between different religious and political ideas. They could hear lecturers and preachers of various persuasions, and even attend the meetings of illicit sects in private houses. Above all, many of them could read. The work of David Cressy, based on a range of signed documents, including national loyalty oaths administered by the clergy on Parliament's behalf in the 1640s and the depositions of witnesses in Church courts, suggests that literacy in London, especially in the City, was exceptionally high. In four City parishes, only 22 per cent of men taking the Protestation of loyalty to the Protestant religion in 1641 were unable to write their names, compared to a national figure of 70 per cent. Illiterate gentlemen, still common in the north, were a rarity in the London Church courts, and among London and Middlesex tradesmen and craftsmen illiteracy was around 28 per cent between 1580 and 1700, compared to about 45 per cent in Exeter and Norwich, and much higher rural levels. Of 167 apprentices and servants who appeared as witnesses before Church courts in these years, only 48 (28 per cent) were unable to sign their depositions. London women, who shared the almost complete illiteracy of women in the rest of England until mid-century, moved well ahead of the national average after 1660, achieving a literacy rate of about 50 per cent by 1700. In these years, Cressy believes, there must have been 'an educational revolution' for women in the capital. Literacy could be put to good use in the 1640s. London was the national centre of printing, and in the revolutionary decades pamphlets and newspapers poured off the presses in vast numbers. The Thomason collection contains about 15,000 pamphlets and 7,000 news-sheets published in London between 1640 and 1663.[11]

Royalists naturally represented the London crowd as composed of men of the lowest social and moral stature, whose actions, stirred up and directed by Parliamentary leaders and City MPs, gave no additional validity to the opposition cause, but instead discredited it. To them, they were 'the scum of all the profanest rout, the vilest of all men, the outcast of the people', 'mechanic citizens, and apprentices', 'mean and unruly people of the suburbs', 'Brownists, Anabaptists, and other sectaries', whose guiding intelligence came from Venn, Penington, and the opposition leaders in the House of Commons. Their sympathizers emphasized, on the other hand, the religious sincerity of the crowds, and the presence among them of 'aldermen, aldermen's deputies, merchants, Common Council-men, subsidy-men, and citizens of London, of rank and quality'. Both sides were right, because there were, in Brian Manning's words, 'two levels of agitation' in London, one among men of substance (but not the highest power) in the City, and another among religious radicals, apprentices, journeymen and the poor, mainly in the suburbs, and led by men such as Lilburne.[12]

All observers agree that apprentices played a leading part in the demonstrations and petitions of 1640–42. Although they were a declining proportion of the capital's population in the seventeenth century, there were still about 30,000 London apprentices in the 1640s, enough to make up a formidable crowd. Apprentices were young (in their late teens and twenties) rather than 'mean'. Many came from landed or mercantile families where political interests were nothing new, and most were migrants who had broken away from conservative village communities, and were thus open to new ideas and attachments. Although their lives were closely controlled by apprenticeship rules, many apprentices might have discovered a freer and more heroic ideal of life from the plays, books and ballads written about and for them. The story of Dick Whittington, recounted in a ballad and a play in or before 1605, is the best-known of these, but Thomas Dekker's play about Simon Eyre (who was Mayor in 1445), *The Shoemaker's Holiday* (1599), and Richard Johnson's *Nine Worthies of London* (1592) both tell similar stories of young men rising from obscurity to fame. Those who preferred to see the apprentice as a super-hero, performing feats of strength and daring against the infidel, would enjoy Heywood's *The Four Prentices of London*, first performed at the Fortune or Red Bull around 1600, or the songs and stories about Aurelius, the Valiant London Prentice, and his exploits in Turkey.[13] Whether or not these stories inspired them with a sense of their power and importance, apprentices quite often joined together in riotous activity, especially in their Shrove Tuesday attacks on brothels or (in 1617) the Blackfriars playhouse, and it is not surprising to see their sense of unity and power turned against more significant targets in the 1640s.

DANGEROUS FORCES

Petitions, signed by many but presented by a respectable few, were the usual way of applying public pressure on Parliament. In December 1640 a long and well-reasoned petition, signed by around 15,000 Londoners and calling for the abolition of the episcopacy and 'Root and Branch' reform of the Church, was presented to the House of Commons by Penington, backed up by a crowd of over 1,000. Clarendon claimed that the signatures were gathered for a modest petition which, by 'strange uningenuity and mountebankry', was replaced with a more extreme one before being presented.[14] The debate on the petition in February 1641 focused on the desirability of involving the 'multitude' in affairs of state, an issue which became, for many MPs, more important than questions of episcopacy and royal power.

Desirable or not, the London crowd was a force that could not be ignored. In March 1641, the Earl of Strafford, Charles's energetic chief adviser, the architect (with Laud) of the King's most hated policies, was on trial for treason in the House of Lords, and seemed likely to be acquitted. In April the House of Commons began instead to consider a Bill of Attainder, which could condemn Strafford without a trial. On 21 April, when the Commons were to vote on the Bill, a petition said to be signed by 20,000 people, demanding Strafford's execution, was brought to the Commons by a crowd of 10,000. The Bill was passed by a majority of 145, but nearly 200 MPs stayed away, perhaps afraid to have their names displayed in the City as friends of Strafford. The Lords' discussions early in May were equally overshadowed by the presence of a huge mob on 2 and 3 May (Wallington, who was one of the crowd, thought 15,000 were there), and it is likely that their passage of the Bill of Attainder on 8 May was influenced by fear of disorder if Strafford escaped. Many of his friends thought it wise to keep away from Westminster until the Bill was passed. The King's decision to accept the Bill, in Clarendon's view, came after his advisers (and Strafford himself) persuaded him that it was the only way to save himself and his family from the mob in Whitehall, and 'to allay that frantic rage and combination in the people'.[15]

Strafford's execution ('His head is off! His head is off!') bought Charles some time, but radical forces were not dormant in the summer of 1641. A trade depression and an outbreak of plague maintained a mood of crisis in the city. Laud was in the Tower, and the London pulpits and printing presses were freed from his persecution and censorship. Radical news-sheets were displayed and read out in taverns and shops, dozens of sectarian groups which had worshipped in secret now came into the open and began winning converts among the artisans, and there were violent attacks on altar rails and on over-elaborate services in London churches. Separatism carried a social as well as a religious message. Separatist preachers were craftsmen and 'mechanic fellows': John Greene the hatmaker, John Spencer the coachman, Praise-God Barebone the Fleet Street leather-seller. When working men, and even working women, preached the gospel, anything could happen: 'These things, if they be not looked into, will bring us in time to community of wives, community of goods, and destruction of all.'[16]

The question of whether Parliament should seek the alliance of these dangerous forces in its struggle against the King came to a head in November 1641. On the 11th, news arrived in London of a Catholic rebellion in Ireland, in which, it was wildly reported, many thousands of English Protestants had been raped, murdered or brutally assaulted. The loss of Ireland was confidently predicted, and rumours of a new Popish Plot to murder opposition MPs and take over the country spread through the town. In this excited atmosphere the House of Commons debated the Grand Remonstrance, a moderate statement of Parliament's case against the King, addressed not to Charles but to the people at large. This decision to 'remonstrate downward, tell stories to the people', was too much for many MPs to take, and the Remonstrance passed by only eleven votes. Many of the ablest future royalists, including Edward Hyde (the future Earl of Clarendon) made their final break with Parliament during these debates. Better a foolish but chastened king than a world turned upside down. Charles could feel the shift in his favour, and it was announced that on 25 November he would pass through the City on his way to Westminster. This, his advisers believed, would consolidate his growing support in the City, and dislodge John Pym, the opposition leader in the Commons, as the City's favourite. The City's welcome was so lavish, the Guildhall banquet so splendid, the claret in the Cheapside conduits so plentiful and the Mayor and Recorder's protestations of loyalty so effusive, that Charles was convinced, he said, that 'all these former tumults and disorders have only risen from the meaner sort of people', while the 'better and main part of the City have ever been loyal and affectionate to my person and government'. A week later a deputation of aldermen assured the King of the City's loyalty, and went away with seven knighthoods. The King's friends might well believe that sectarian excesses had drawn London, that vital ally, into the royal camp.[17]

THE KING LOSES HIS CAPITAL

Winning the élite was no longer enough. They could not control the suburbs, and even in the City the authority of the Lord Mayor and the royalist aldermen was in tatters by December 1641. They were unable to stop the gathering of signatures for two giant petitions, one from about 15,000 men of substance, demanding the removal of bishops from the House of Lords, and the other from 30,000 young men and apprentices, calling for the abolition of episcopacy altogether. On 21 December, ward elections gave the Puritans greater strength, probably a majority, on the Common Council, and brought Parliament's supporters closer to full control of the City. Two days later Charles appointed a loyal but disreputable soldier, Colonel Lunsford, as Lieutenant of the Tower, apparently with the intention of seizing military control of London as a prelude to moving by force against his remaining Parliamentary opponents. If this was Charles's plan, everything depended on staging a rapid coup before the London crowd realized what was happening.

But Lunsford was a notorious thug, and Londoners were feverishly sensitive (especially since the Irish rebellion) to rumours of army coups and Catholic plots. There was an immediate petition against Lunsford, and on Christmas Eve the Commons demanded his removal before blood was shed. On 26 December Gurney, the Lord Mayor, warned the King that the apprentices were out of his control, and Lunsford was dismissed. But there were still soldiers in London, waiting to be paid after the Scottish war, and the fear of a coup remained. From 27 to 29 December 1641, the 'December days', there were huge crowds of citizens and apprentices in Westminster, jostling the bishops and calling for their expulsion from the Lords, and guarding Parliament against the expected royal attack. On 27 December, there was a fight between Lunsford's officers and a group of citizens and sailors with stones and cudgels, and news of the fight brought the apprentices to Westminster in force. Charles issued a proclamation against 'riotous and tumultuous assemblies' and told the Lord Mayor to order the Trained Bands to shoot to kill, but the next day the crowds were back in even larger numbers (10,000, it was said), threatening to enter or attack Westminster Abbey. A group of well-armed gentlemen drove them back, fatally wounding Sir Richard Wiseman, one of the leaders of the crowd. It is said that in these clashes the terms 'Cavalier' and 'Roundhead' first came into use. The House of Commons was divided in its attitude to the mob. Half viewed their intimidation with fear and outrage, but the rest regarded the crowd as their only protection against the royal soldiers, and were unwilling to offend them or send them away. It would be unwise, an opposition MP diarist noted, 'to discontent the citizens of London, our surest friends, when so many designs and plots were daily consulted of against our safety'. Through John Venn, the City MP, the opposition leaders were able to exercise a restraining influence over the apprentices, who clearly had leaders and minds of their own, and on 30 December, by imprisoning twelve bishops, they managed to satisfy and disperse the crowds.[18]

The opposition's argument was that Parliament had more to fear from the armed force that Charles was assembling at Whitehall than from the London mob. In addition to Lunsford and 120 officers, the King was attended by an impressive collection of armed gentlemen, and had been promised the support of 500 law students from the Inns of Court. Whether Charles could expect effective help from his friends in the City was more open to question. During the 'December days' the Trained Bands had failed to respond to the Lord Mayor's summons, and his orders for a continual watch and ward were generally ignored. Many of the middling sort, on whom the running of the City depended, were on the side of the apprentices, and had probably been with them in Westminster. Craftsmen, shopkeepers and many merchants were now hostile to the Court, and had closed up their shops and armed themselves against a royalist attack.

On 3 January 1642 Charles made his decisive move, and charged Lord Mandeville and five opposition leaders in the House of Commons, Pym, Hampden, Holles, Haselrig and Strode, with high treason. The next day, when Charles came to the Commons with 300 or 400 armed men to 'pull those rogues out by the ears', the six escaped by barge to the City, and took shelter in the Puritan stronghold of Coleman Street, Penington's parish. The six were followed by the whole House of Commons, which moved its sittings to the safety of the Guildhall for a week. The alliance of London and Parliament was complete. At the same time the Common Council, now in opposition hands and working with the City MPs, elected a Committee of Safety to take charge of the City's defence, by-passing the Court of Aldermen. On 5 January, Charles addressed the mayor, aldermen and Common Council in the Guildhall, asking 'their loving assistance' in bringing the six to trial. But Charles discovered that day, if he did not know it already, that power in the City was no longer in the hands of the men who had feasted him in November.

As Charles left the Guildhall large hostile crowds, chanting 'The Privileges of Parliament!', surrounded him 'in a most undutiful manner, pressing upon, looking into, and laying hold on his coach', and leaving him in no doubt as to the attitudes of shopkeepers and 'the ruder sort' towards him. The King returned safe, but upset, to Whitehall, but the Lord Mayor and the Recorder were not so lucky. Near Ludgate, Gurney was pulled from his horse, and the citizens' wives 'fell upon the Lord Mayor, and pulled his chain from his neck, and called him a traitor to the City, and to the liberties of it, and had like to have torn him and the Recorder to pieces'.[19] London was a far more formidable city than it had been when Edward I or Richard II had brought it to heel, and it is hard to see how Charles could have mastered it now. That night, false rumours of a royal attack spread through the town and within an hour there was a fully equipped citizen army on the streets, the gates and portcullises were shut, chains were drawn across the roads, and women had built barricades and boiled cauldrons of water.[20]

After his humiliation on 5 January, 'the worst day in London ... that ever he had', Charles was sure that he and especially his wife were no longer safe in Whitehall, and on 10 January he left for Hampton Court and Windsor, abandoning the capital to his opponents. The following day, the five MPs returned in a triumphant procession to Westminster, and 5,000 men of Buckinghamshire marched into London in support of Parliament, the first of many county demonstrations to arrive over the next six weeks. Charles' decision to give up London is commonly regarded as a key moment in the slide into civil war and royal defeat.[21] The power of royal supporters in the City was destroyed in January and February 1642, as the Common Council and the Committee of Safety, working closely with Pym and Parliament, took control of the town. The Committee of Safety took over the Trained Bands from the mayor, and gave command to Philip Skippon, a reliable Puritan and, as it turned out, a first-rate officer. In February a petition signed by Gurney, thirteen aldermen and over 300 of London's richest men against the Committee of Safety's control of the Trained Bands was rejected by Parliament, and in March the Common Council successfully asserted its right to meet and make decisions without the approval of the mayor and aldermen, overturning the traditional aldermanic veto. Sympathy for the Crown and desire for a compromise settlement remained strong among the City élite, but hopes of such a compromise faded in the spring of 1642. Gurney was impeached, deposed, stripped of his property and sent to the Tower in July–August 1642, and on 22 August, three days after Isaac Penington was chosen to replace Gurney as Lord Mayor, Charles raised his standard at Nottingham and the Civil War began.

LONDONERS AT WAR

London's men and money played a vital part in Parliament's survival in the first year of the war, when the chances of royal victory were strongest. The Earl of Essex's army, which fought the drawn battle of Edgehill in October 1642, was composed mainly of 10,000 London volunteers, and Parliament's money, in the early months of the war, came from City loans. There was a municipal loan of £100,000 in September 1642, and a steady flow of smaller contributions. Urged by Puritan preachers, citizens came 'thronging in with their plate and rings; not sparing their very thimbles and bodkins'.[22] From November 1642 Parliament introduced a weekly assessment, first in London, then throughout the areas under its control. This, along with a new excise tax and sales of royal lands, made Parliament less dependent on City loans after 1642. The taxation of London was organized by committees in the Haberdashers' and Weavers' Halls and collected by hundreds of exceedingly unpopular assessors and collectors. War taxes, more than anything else, eroded Londoners' enthusiasm for the war.[23]

In general, the local militias, untrained, undisciplined and unwilling to leave their counties, were a failure in the war. London's Trained Bands, though, were of a different calibre. They were not hardened soldiers, but they had drilled in the Artillery Ground in Bishopsgate, and had been enlarged and reorganized by Skippon into nine well-commanded regiments, over 10,000 men in all. 'They were the reserve on which the Parliament relied in every emergency,' said C. H. Firth. 'Without their aid, Essex could not have relieved Gloucester, nor could Waller have repulsed Hopton's invasion of Sussex.'[24]

Their first major engagement came on 13 November 1642. After Edgehill Charles might have raced to London, with the chance of ending the war at a stroke. Instead, he made his way slowly south, via Oxford and Reading, reaching and sacking Brentford, to the west of London, on 12 November. By this time, Essex's army had returned to London, and Skippon was ready with the Trained Bands. On 13 November at Turnham Green, 7 miles west of the City, the 24,000-strong citizen army blocked the way, and forced Charles to withdraw to Oxford without a fight. Frightened by this advance, and by the sack of Brentford, Londoners turned out in huge numbers between October 1642 and summer 1643 to fortify the town, each parish and every trade supplying its contingent of unpaid labourers in an impressive display of communal solidarity. Each day 20,000 Londoners marched out with shovels and banners, tailors and watermen alongside gentlemen vintners and lawyers. Women, 'from ladies down to oyster wenches, Labour'd like pioneers in trenches', Samuel Butler mocked in *Hudibras.* It was a golden rule, now as in the days of Henry VI, that London should not become a battleground. By mid-1643, 18 miles of trenches and earth ramparts 18 feet high, linking twenty-four large wooden forts, encircled almost the whole built-up area, from Knightsbridge to Wapping, and Shoreditch to Newington.[25]

In the summer of 1643 royal forces advancing on the capital from the South-West besieged Gloucester. The Trained Bands marched out under the Earl of Essex, forced Charles to lift the siege, and then acquitted themselves well at Newbury on 20 September against the royal army that attempted to impede their return to London. Even Clarendon, the royalist historian, admired the soldierly conduct of the London Trained Bands at the Battle of Newbury:

> The London train-bands, and auxiliary regiments, ... behaved them-
> selves to wonder, and were in truth the preservation of that army that
> day; for they stood as a bulwark and rampire to defend the rest, and,
> when their wings of horse were scattered and dispersed, kept their
> ground so steadily that, though Prince Rupert himself led up the
> choice horse to charge, and endured their storm of small shot, he
> could make no impression upon their stand of pikes, but was forced
> to wheel about.

Their march back to London after raising the siege he 'reckoned amongst the most soldierly actions of this unhappy war'.[26]

London's commitment to the war effort was far from whole-hearted. In December and January 1642–3 several thousand Londoners, tired of war taxation and the interruption of business, petitioned for peace, and in May 1643 a royalist plot with substantial support was discovered. On 9 August 1643 a mob of women, demanding peace, stoned soldiers outside Parliament. Mobs of equal or larger size could be found to put the opposite viewpoint, and in any case the peace movement foundered on the King's refusal to compromise. Londoners were shopkeepers, not warriors, and the Parliamentary commanders found it increasingly difficult to keep citizen soldiers in the field for extended campaigns. In November 1643 Waller, the City commander, was forced to abandon an attack on Basing House, south of Reading, by the desertion of the Trained Bands, who marched off with shouts of 'Home! Home!' In July 1644, after two more campaigns in which the London troops had let him down, Waller advised Parliament to raise a standing army of professional soldiers in place of the unreliable and mutinous City Brigade, with whom it was 'impossible to do anything of importance'. 'I am confident', he added on 8 July, 'that above 2,000 Londoners ran away from their colours.'[27]

Second Thoughts

By late July 1645, thanks to the new national professional force, the New Model Army, the Civil War was as good as won. In May 1646 Charles surrendered to the Scots army, who handed him over to Parliament in February 1647. What should happen to him after his defeat was unclear. The generally desired outcome, that he should be restored to the throne with reduced powers, was placed out of reach by the King's refusal to accept the consequences of his defeat, or to negotiate honestly. Londoners were divided, as they had been throughout the war, between outright royalists, moderates or Presbyterians who desired a compromise which would leave the constitution and social structure largely unchanged, and the more radical Independents, who wanted a clear military victory followed by religious toleration and social reform.

The Presbyterians could rely upon an impressive degree of popular and propertied support to make their case. There was still affection for the monarchy, or dislike of the alternative to it, in the capital. The 'middling sort of men' who took control of London from the élite at the start of the war, men 'that never lived beyond view of the smoke of their own Chimnies', soon grew impatient with the war taxes they had to pay to upstart Parliamentary officials from Haberdashers' Hall, and they feared the prospect of a city run by radical sects, or plundered by the New Model Army, more than they feared the return of a chastened king. In September 1646 a royalist, Sir John Gayre, was elected Lord Mayor. From the middle of 1646 the Presbyterians, with a majority on Common Council, drew closer to the London royalists, and to a strong House of Commons group, led by Denzil Holles, that wanted a compromise peace. From May 1646 they petitioned Parliament repeatedly to end the war and introduce a Scottish-style Presbyterian system of Church organization (run by themselves as elders), and by the end of the year the Commons had been intimidated by mob pressure into cooperating with them.

In the spring and summer of 1647 Holles and the City Presbyterians and royalists set about bringing the Trained Bands under their control, and strengthening them to face the New Model Army, which was marching south towards London with the captive King. Then, as the army approached, the Presbyterians' well-laid plans fell apart. Timidity, fear of defeat and pillage, and distaste for the idea of a counter-revolutionary coup which might restore Charles and the royalists to absolute power, led most members of the remodelled Trained Bands to ignore the call to arms, and persuaded Parliament to open negotiations with the New Model Army. Holles and the City Presbyterians were not finished yet. On 26 July 1647, three days after Parliament had passed a Militia Act to restore control of the Trained Bands to the Independents, a great crowd of citizens, apprentices and watermen, organized and led by Holles and the Common Council, burst into the Commons, held Speaker Lenthall in his chair, and forced MPs to repeal the Militia Act and invite the King to London. But terrorizing the Commons was one thing, and facing the New Model Army was another. When its first detachments arrived from Kent on 2 August, the City's commander in Southwark yielded the bridge, and the following day Fairfax entered London without resistance. Cromwell took control of the City, and Holles and the Presbyterian leaders were impeached or driven into flight. Once again, as on so many other occasions, London tradesmen showed greater attachment to survival, order, property, and freedom from plunder and bloodshed, than to the abstract principles others expected them to die for.[28]

LEVELLERS

The citizens' longing for a return to the old paths was reinforced by their fear that political revolution would open the way to those who wanted to overturn property and hierarchy along with monarchy. London, along with the army, was a centre of the popular radical movements fostered by the intellectual freedom of the 1640s, which had great hopes that a new world, either spiritual or social, would emerge from the wreck of the old. Although many of the radical religious sects that troubled propertied and conformist Englishmen in the 1640s and 1650s originated outside London, most of them, Quakers, Baptists, Ranters and the rest, had strong support in the capital. The Fifth Monarchy Men, who believed that the earthly rule of Christ and his saints was about to begin, were predominantly a London movement, with twenty-nine of their seventy-two known groups located there between 1650 and the 1680s. In 1661 a London cooper, Thomas Venner, led a Fifth Monarchist rising in London, and lost his head for it. And Gerrard Winstanley, a failed London clothier and the founder of the Diggers, chose St George's Hill, 16 miles south-west of London, for his brief experiment in common property-ownership in 1649–50.[29]

The movement which seemed most threatening in the late 1640s was the one called (by its opponents) the Levellers. The Levellers' political aims were quasi-democratic, and their social views were egalitarian ('none comes into this world with a saddle on his back, neither any booted and spurred to ride him') rather than socialist. Faster legal procedures, fairer punishment, prison reform, the closure of debtors' prisons, the payment of army wage arrears, religious toleration, the abolition of tithes and monopolies, democratic elections for City and livery company offices, and a sovereign

House of Commons elected annually on a wide male franchise were among their regular demands.

The movement was powerful in the late 1640s because of its popularity in the army, and its power was broken when Cromwell crushed the Leveller mutiny at Burford in May 1649. But it was very much a London movement, a refinement of the ideas and antagonisms that had motivated the crowds of apprentices and craftsmen in December 1641. The main Leveller leaders, John Lilburne, William Walwyn and Richard Overton, were all Londoners (though not London-born), and the movement can be said to have begun when the three of them started working together in London in 1645. Their pamphlets (often written in Newgate or the Tower) came by the hundred from secret London presses, their programmes were designed to appeal particularly to City craftsmen and tradesmen (rather than to unfree labourers), and their mass petitions relied heavily on metropolitan signing-power. In 1647 Leveller leaders met regularly in the Whalebone Tavern, behind the Royal Exchange, and tried to turn their popular following in London into an organized political force. There was a committee of active men in every City ward and suburban parish, they explained to Kentish supporters, 'to read the Petition at meetings for that purpose, and to take Subscriptions, and to move as many as can possibly, to goe in person when the day of delivering it shall be appointed'.[30] Some indication of the extent of London's support for the Levellers comes from the great crowds of mourners wearing the Leveller sea-green colours at the funeral processions of Thomas Rainsborough and Robert Lockyer (an executed mutineer) in November 1648 and April 1649, and the bonfires and church bells when a jury at the Guildhall found Lilburne not guilty of treason in October 1649. Once the army was in Cromwell's hands, though, this support counted for little, and Walwyn and Overton (but not Lilburne) gave up the struggle after 1649.

'CRUEL NECESSITY'

Fear of radicalism, along with impatience at high taxation and the interruption of trade, encouraged a strong mood of royalism and war-weariness in the capital in the late 1640s. In the spring of 1648 most of the counties round London petitioned for a treaty with the King and an end to military rule. On 4 May a crowd of Essex petitioners were cheered through London on their way to Westminster Hall, where several of them were killed in a confrontation with troops. All through the Second Civil War of

May–August 1648, when royalist risings in Wales, Kent and Essex, and a Scots invasion were crushed by the New Model Army, London's governors and leading citizens petitioned for the King to be brought from captivity on the Isle of Wight to London 'in honour, freedom and safety'.[31] Much as the restoration of a contrite and trustworthy Charles I appealed to Cromwell, Henry Ireton and other army leaders, they gradually realized that such a man did not exist, and that the only sure way to consolidate the gains made in the war was for the King to be put on trial. At the beginning of December 1648 the army marched on London from the west, with the intention of bringing Londoners to heel and (more importantly) purging the Commons of its royalist majority. On 6 December and the following days about half of the House of Commons was removed (the famous 'Pride's Purge'), leaving just a Rump, and the City was intimidated by armed occupation. The now-compliant Parliament enacted ordinances excluding those who had wanted compromise with the King from the Common Council elections of 21 December, ensuring that the new Council would be dominated by radicals or 'saints', men of the 'middling sort' who had wholeheartedly supported the war.[32]

The military occupation of London and Westminster was followed rapidly by the trial and execution of the King. Charles's execution, on 30 January 1649, was not the popular affair that Strafford's had been. It took place alongside the Banqueting House in Whitehall, rather than at Tower Hill, to avoid a procession through the City and to give ample room for troops to control the crowd. Charles spoke nobly, but inaudibly, from the scaffold, and as the axe fell, one eye-witness recalled, 'there was such a dismal groan among the thousands of people that were within sight of it (as it were WITH ONE CONSENT) as he had never heard before'.[33]

After the execution, most of what followed in London was anti-climax. There was no social or political revolution, despite the victory of the 'saints' in the Common Council elections, and their ejection of the Presbyterian mayor and aldermen. In 1650 the radicals on the Common Council tried to increase the power of journeymen and small masters over the livery companies, but the Rump stifled the campaign. Failing here, the radicals tried to break the hold of the livery companies over Common Hall, the body which chose the mayor, by widening its electorate to include all householders. Once again conservative forces in the City and the Rump thwarted them. By this time Cromwell was already moving towards a more conservative position, and in December 1652, after various changes in the electoral rules, a much less radical Common Council was elected, and the traditional authority of the Lord Mayor was restored. The London radicals enjoyed a last moment of power in the so-called Barebones Parliament of July–December 1653, a nominated assembly which contained a high proportion of metropolitan Baptists, including the eponymous Praise-God Barebone. Their plans for the abolition of tithes and the simplification and acceleration of the legal process were interrupted, however, by Cromwell's dissolution of the Parliament in December. After the failure of Barebones and Cromwell's appointment as Lord Protector in December 1653, all prospect of radical revolution was gone, and the City fell into the hands of its old rulers once more.[34]

CROMWELLIAN LONDON

After all the upheavals of the 1640s, life and government in Cromwellian London did not differ dramatically from that of pre-Civil War days. The image of a society tyrannized by sanctimonious kill-joys stems from the Puritans' attack on playhouses and bear-pits, and their suppression of what, in their view, were the pagan festivals of May Day and Christmas. Puritans were not teetotallers, and the most popular pastime at all social levels, drinking in taverns and alehouses, went on as usual, as the early pages of Samuel Pepys's diary show. London gained a new and important social institution in 1652 when a Greek, Pasqua Rosee, opened the City's first coffee house in St Michael's Alley, near the Royal Exchange. Coffee drinking caught on at once, especially among the better-off, and by 1662 there were eighty-two coffee-rooms in the City, and many more in the suburbs. Cocoa or chocolate houses arrived in London in the 1650s, too. It was not Cromwell, but the fun-loving Charles II, who tried (in 1676) to force coffee houses to close.

Music and opera flourished in London under Cromwell's patronage. *The Siege of Rhodes*, the first true English opera, was performed in London in 1656, and others followed, using women for the first time on the stage. There was music and dancing at Cromwell's Court, the municipal street musicians known as the Waits continued their performances, and public dancing was still popular. There were many musical clubs in London taverns in the 1650s, and those, like Samuel Pepys, who were keen on group singing or playing could buy songs, catches, madrigals and instruction manuals from England's first specialist music shop, which was opened by John Playford, 'the father of English music publishing', near the Temple in 1652.[35]

The royalist John Evelyn did not find Puritan London an unentertaining city. In September 1657 he saw a rope-dancer and a bearded lady, and the following May he 'went to see a coach-race in Hyde Park, and collationed in Spring Garden'. Spring Gardens, near Charing Cross, and Mulberry Gardens were London's two pleasure gardens, 'the usual rendezvous for ladies and gallants'. After a brief closure in the mid-1650s Spring Gardens, which had been public since the 1630s, resumed their usual functions: 'For it is usual here to find some of the young company till midnight,' it was written in 1659, 'and the thickets of the garden seem to be contrived to all advantages of gallantry.' Any 'gallants' who pressed their advantage too far had to remember that the 1650 Adultery Act made adultery between a man and a married woman a capital offence, but might be reassured by the knowledge that the terms of the Act made guilt extremely difficult to prove, rendering the law almost unenforceable. Within the City the efforts of the wardmote to control moral and religious conduct 'diminished most noticeably in the 1650s', and never recovered. In this respect, the Puritan decade was a time of change, but change towards, rather than away from, greater individual freedom.[36]

In matters of religion, Cromwellian London was, on the whole, as tolerant as Stuart London had been. Presbyterianism, which abolished bishops but preserved the parish structure and the social hierarchy, had a strong appeal to the City élite, and in the years 1645–7 there was a concerted effort to drive radical Independent ministers out of their livings. This attempt to impose a uniform Presbyterian system on London was thwarted by the intervention of the New Model Army in 1647–8, and thereafter, while many of the richer City parishes remained Presbyterian, Independent ministers and lecturers resumed their work in about twenty parishes. The laws against Catholics and Anglicans were not rigorously enforced, and a huge number of Protestant sects were allowed to worship freely unless, like the Quakers, they disrupted social order or the worship of others. The Anglican John Evelyn was horrified to find London pulpits occupied by 'blasphemous and ignorant mechanics', but he had no difficulty in finding preaching more to his taste, except on Christmas Day, when services were not allowed. The ending of episcopal patronage gave some parishes the power to elect their own ministers (often after a trial sermon and negotiations over pay and conditions), and at least nine City parishes used this freedom of choice to elect Anglican ministers or lecturers in the 1650s.[37] A mark of Cromwell's personal tolerance was his decision in December 1655, against opposition from merchants, lawyers and some of his own councillors, to allow Jews to live and worship in England, ending their 365-year banishment. The Jews built their first synagogue in

Creechurch Lane in 1657, and another in 1701, the Spanish and Portuguese Synagogue in Bevis Marks, which still survives.

The Protectorate rested on Cromwell's unique ability to command the support of army and Parliament, and his death in September 1658 made the return of Charles II almost inevitable. By December 1659, according to two contemporary witnesses, London was nearing anarchy: 'The City lies under the highest discontents that ever I knew it. Shops are shut up, trade gone, fears and jealousies multiply.' 'We are here in great disorder, and expect to be in blood every hour.' The recipient of this second letter, General Monck, commander of the English army in Scotland, marched on London in February 1660, and took control of the City and Westminster. In the capital, Monck found a population in which latent royalism, disillusion with the Protectorate, dislike of the Puritan sects and hostility to the cost and oppression of the army were bubbling rapidly to the surface. In December 1659 troops had fired on a great crowd of apprentices presenting a petition for a free Parliament to the Common Council, leaving six or seven dead. Hatred of the army did not always mean a wish to see monarchy restored, but opinion seems to have been flowing in that direction.[38]

The republican Rump Parliament tried to save itself by setting Monck against the City (the army's paymaster), but Monck evaded this trap, and instead made common cause with the Lord Mayor and Common Council against the Rump, and restored to their places the MPs who had been ejected for their royalism in December 1648. The restored Long Parliament in turn dissolved itself, and in May 1660 a new Parliament agreed on terms for Charles II's return to England as King. The bonfires and the roasting of rumps of meat when the Rump fell, and the festivities when Charles arrived in London on 29 May seem to indicate a complete reversal of the attitudes that had terrified Charles I in 1642, but it is difficult to distinguish genuine popular feelings from the civic pageantry and public rejoicing that were conventional and expedient whenever power changed hands. No doubt there were many who would have agreed with Thomas Blacklocke, who foolishly told customers in the Red Lyon Inn, Southwark, that the King should be brought back in a wheelbarrow, with 'his Breach . . . stuck full of Nettles', but most of them had the sense to keep quiet. Londoners were not submissive or chastened. They had grown accustomed to developing and asserting their political and religious views, and when the restored monarchy fell short of their expectations, as it was bound to do, they would not be slow to show their displeasure. The new King, like the old Protector, understood the fickleness of public adulation.[39]

PART FOUR

LONDON, 1660–1815

Chapter 9

Fire, Rebuilding and Suburban Growth

THE GREAT FIRE OF 1666

In May 1660 Charles II took possession of a capital that was still, except in some of its western suburbs, medieval in its layout and construction. Most of its streets were narrow, and made narrower still by the practice of building upper storeys that projected over the roadway. There were very few wide City streets (Cornhill, Fenchurch Street and especially Cheapside were among them), and large open spaces within the walls, except near the Tower, had mostly disappeared since the Dissolution. In a city of timber-framed buildings with thin lath and plaster walls and often with straw on their floors, crowded so closely together, it was likely that the disastrous fire that astrologers and preachers had often predicted would sooner or later take place.

There were dozens of ways for a fire to start in a pre-industrial town. Houses and workshops were lit by candles or rushlights, and heated by open coal or wood fires, which were also used for cooking. Friction matches were not invented until the 1820s, and since tinder boxes took several minutes to create a flame, buckets of hot coals were often taken from one room or house to another to light a fire. Many urban crafts used fires or furnaces, usually in workshops in ordinary city houses. Bakers, brewers, dyers, soap-boilers, cooks, smiths, metalworkers, brick-makers and launderers were all dangerous trades in a wooden city. An oil shop caused the fire that devastated Southwark High Street in 1676, and a careless washerwoman started the blaze that destroyed Whitehall Palace in 1698. The blame for the Great Fire of 1666 falls upon a baker, Thomas Farryner, who thus became (for those who see history in terms of individual contributions) one of the three or four most influential men in the history of London.[1]

The Great Fire began at the end of a hot dry summer, about an hour after midnight on Sunday, 2 September, in Pudding Lane, just east of

London Bridge. There was a strong wind from the east, and within a few hours the fire had consumed the wood-and-pitch houses of Pudding Lane, burned the Star Inn on Fish Street Hill (at the end of London Bridge), and gained a hold in Thames Street, 'the lodge of all combustibles, oil, hemp, flax, pitch, tar, cordage, hops, wines, brandies and other materials favourable to fire, all heavy goods being warehoused there near the waterside, and all the wharfs for coal, timber, wood etc being in line consumed by it'. If arsonists had plotted the destruction of the City, wrote Edward Waterhouse, they could not have chosen a better spot, 'where narrow streets, old buildings all of timber, all contiguous to each other, all stuffed with aliment for the fire, all in the very heart of the trade and wealth of the City'.[2]

By Sunday morning it was clear that the whole city was in danger. Samuel Pepys watched the fire raging along the riverfront, 'nobody to my sight endeavouring to quench it, but to remove their goods and leave all to the fire', and went to Whitehall to urge the King to order the pulling down of houses to stop the fire spreading. This was the approved policy, but it was not so easy to achieve. Householders who were not in immediate danger resisted it, and the demolished houses could still transmit the fire if they were not cleared away properly. Demolition by gunpowder was suggested by seamen from the dockyards, but this was considered too drastic and costly a remedy. Furthermore, the fire was advancing on such a wide front, and in so many directions, that blocking its path in one or two streets was not enough. Pepys met the Lord Mayor, Sir Thomas Bludworth, in Cannon Street on Sunday and found him 'like a man spent, with a handkercher about his neck. To the King's message, he cried like a fainting woman, "Lord, what can I do? I am spent! People will not obey me. I have been pulling down houses. But the fire overtakes us faster than we can do it."' Bludworth was later widely criticized for his ineffectiveness in the early stages of the fire, for failing to take it seriously when it first broke out, and refusing to demolish houses without the owners' consent. His cheerful prediction that 'a woman might piss it out', must rank as one of history's most unfortunate misjudgements. By Sunday evening, Pepys could see from the Bankside 'one entire arch of fire from this to the other side of the bridge, and in a bow up the hill, for an arch of above a mile long'.[3]

Most of the devices that parish constables and beadles were meant to take to fires – leather buckets, ladders, ropes, fire-hooks – were of little use in such a blaze, and hand-squirts and manually operated water-pumping machines made little impression, and were often lost in the fire. Blazing buildings were too hot to approach, and the fire dried out the houses it was about to consume. Most citizens recognized that flight was the best policy, and on Monday the streets were full of carts piled high with furniture and merchandise, and casks of wine and oil being trundled towards the City gates, and the river was thick with heavily laden barges. Panic and desperation seem to have been widespread. 'From the beginning, I know not by what despondency, or fate,' John Evelyn wrote on 3 September, 'they hardly stirred to quench it; so that there was nothing heard or seen but crying out and lamentation, and running about like distracted creatures.' One of those 'distracted creatures', Lady Hobart, wrote in great distress to her husband that day:

> I am all most out of my wits, we have packed up all our goods & cannot get a cart for money, they give 5 & 10 pound for carts. I have sent for carts to my Lady Glaskock if I can get them, but I fear I shall los all I have and must run away. O pray for us now the crys macks me I know not what to say, O pety me. I will breck open the closet and look to all your things as well as I can, I hop if it come to us it will be Thursday but it runs fearsly, O i shall los all i have . . .[4]

On Monday the fire crossed Cornhill, helped by the timbers of demolished houses left lying in the street, and quickly ran westwards down it to consume the Royal Exchange, racing along its galleries and bringing its statues crashing down. At this point, the Puritan Thomas Vincent tells us, the fire from Cornhill met others from the east and south, and burst into Cheapside 'with such a dazzling light and burning heat and roaring noise by the fall of so many houses together that was very amazing'.[5] Now the western half of the City was defenceless. On Tuesday, the worst day of the fire, St Paul's caught fire, the flames reaching it from the houses near its new portico, and spreading up the wooden scaffolding that had been placed round it during recent renovation work. When great lumps of stone and burning timber fell into St Faith's Chapel, the entire stock of books stored there by London stationers was lost. The heat and noise was overwhelming: 'the stones of St Paul's flew like grenados, the melting lead running down the streets in a stream, and the very pavements glowing with fiery redness', Evelyn wrote on Tuesday. That night, Thomas Vincent saw the great Guildhall glowing like 'a bright shining coal as if it had been a palace of gold or a great building of burnished brass'. But the medieval masonry withstood the fire, and the City records remained safe in the crypt.

Organized and determined fire-fighting could be effective where other circumstances were favourable. On Tuesday Pepys, having buried his papers, his wine and a parmesan cheese, organized the naval dockyard workers to save the Navy Office (near the Tower) by blowing up the surrounding buildings, and the Tower was saved in the same way. An alderman with 'a hatful of money' bought enough labour to stop the fire spreading past Leadenhall, whose thick stone walls helped check the blaze. The saving of this north-eastern corner of the City was only possible, though, because it was up-wind of the main fire.

In the west the King and his brother, the Duke of York, took charge of fire-fighting on Monday, but the magic of monarchy had no apparent effect while the wind was strong. On Tuesday the fire crossed the river Fleet, and was burning along Fleet Street as far as the Temple, and efforts were concentrated on saving Whitehall by creating a fire-break at Somerset House. According to John Evelyn, it was only on Wednesday, when the fire was threatening Whitehall, that it was at last agreed to follow naval advice, and use gunpowder to create gaps wide enough to stop the flames. More significantly, the east wind dropped late on Tuesday night, enabling Londoners, assisted by seamen and gentlemen of the court, and inspired by the much-praised efforts of the King and the Duke, to bring the fire under control at the Temple Church, Fetter Lane, Holborn Bridge and Smithfield on Wednesday. The Lord Mayor and his men had a harder time at Cripplegate, where a south wind was still helping the fire, but even here they were successful. By Thursday the fire was under control, and on Friday John Evelyn was able to walk through the ruins of the wider streets, though the heat 'continued so intense, that my hair was almost singed, and my feet unsufferably surbated'. Visiting the fields of Highgate and Islington, Evelyn guessed there were '200,000 people of all ranks and degrees dispersed, and lying along by their heaps of what they could save from the fire, deploring their loss'.[6]

The fire destroyed property, rather than life. In view of the speed and extent of the physical destruction, the loss of life in the fire was strangely small. Only nine deaths were recorded, although others probably went unnoticed. In contrast, the total value of real and movable property lost was estimated later to have been £10,000,000. Of 448 acres within the City walls, 373 acres had been burned, along with 63 acres of the old western suburbs, as far as Fetter Lane. The burnt area was devastated but not, as we can see from Hollar's etching of London after the fire, levelled to the ground. St Paul's and most of the burnt-out churches were still standing, but too ruinous, in most cases, to be repaired. A few apparently post-fire churches, though, have medieval walls, and many, including St Mary-at-Hill, St Mary-le-Bow, St Mary Abchurch and St Bride's, were rebuilt on their old foundations or crypts. The Guildhall was gutted, but its walls were sound, and it was repaired. In all, eighty-seven parish churches, forty-four Company halls, about 13,200 houses, and many public buildings, including Christ's Hospital, Bridewell, Newgate Prison, the Custom House, Blackwell Hall (and the cloth within), the Royal Exchange, Baynard's Castle and the three western City gates were lost. Twenty-two churches were left, either in the east or north-east of the City, or beyond the walls to the north-west, and of these eleven have survived the efforts of rebuilders, developers and bombers, and are with us today. Among the finest of these are St Bartholomew-the-Great, St Helen Bishopsgate, St Olave Hart Street, St Katharine Creechurch (a Laudian foundation) and the Temple. Another, St Ethelburga's, was destroyed by an IRA bomb while this book was being written.

REBUILDING THE CITY

After the Great Fire, the government's first priority was to prevent disorder, help the homeless and get business and government moving again. Tents and huts were erected in the suburban fields, and emergency provisions and storage were provided, but many of the homeless preferred to build sheds on the ruins of their burnt houses. Within four days, according to Clarendon (who, as chief minister at the time, presents the arrangements in a very favourable light), the fields were clear: 'all found shelter in so short a time, either in those parts which remained of the city and in the suburbs, or in the neighbour villages'. More disinterested accounts suggest that many spent the cold winter of 1666–7 in makeshift shelters on Moorfields. Street clearing was left at first to individual property owners, but it took £100 from the King's pocket to get the work done in November.[7]

The rebuilding of London offered a unique opportunity to fit the City for its role as the centre of a large metropolis, to solve the problems of traffic congestion, overcrowding, inconvenient food markets, inadequate riverside facilities and fire danger which had grown worse as the population grew. At first, it was felt that the best way to achieve this would be to adopt one of the grandiose plans put forward within days of the Great Fire by Christopher Wren, John Evelyn, Robert Hooke and others for a completely redesigned city of wide boulevards and grand piazzas, a city fit for a great European monarch. By mid-September, though, the King, Parliament and the City had agreed that the practical and financial difficulties involved in adopting a plan which ignored all existing property rights, however attractive it might seem on paper, were insuperable. The City, burdened with many of the costs of running a large town, but drawing its revenues only from the small central area within and near the walls, was in an extremely poor financial state in 1666. Its annual expenditure, at £25,000, was almost twice its income of under £14,000, and its debts stood at £279,000, and were rising rapidly. Most of the City's income came from property which was now in ashes, and from citizens who were scattered, perhaps ruined by their own losses, and unlikely ever to return if they were not allowed to rebuild their houses quickly. The King's finances were little better, and Parliament was unwilling to pay London's bills. The City did not even have the £100,000 it needed to rebuild its own public buildings, let alone the vast sums it would be forced to pay in compensation to landlords if it implemented Wren's or Evelyn's design.[8]

On all sides there was a sense of urgency. Charles needed the flow of Customs and Excise revenue from London's trade, on which his credit and his government was based. The City needed to restore its business as soon as possible if it hoped to regain its old ascendancy over the suburbs and the provinces, and private citizens needed homes and incomes, and a rapid return to the status quo. But it was also clear from the royal proclamation of 13 September that the King would not allow individual householders to build themselves another tinder-box city of wooden houses and narrow alleys. Houses would be of brick or stone (as they already were in the new western suburbs), main streets would be wide enough to stop a fire, there would be a broad quay along the Thames, and private builders could start their work only when detailed rebuilding rules had been agreed.

In early October, the job of deciding how to rebuild the city was delegated to six extremely well-chosen men, the Commissioners for Rebuilding. Three were royal nominees: Christopher Wren, a Professor of Astronomy and amateur architect; Hugh May, a royal official with architectural experience; and Roger Pratt, a practising architect. Three were chosen by the City: Robert Hooke, curator of experiments at the Royal Society and Professor of Geometry at Gresham College; and two men with vital local knowledge, Edward Jerman and Peter Mills, the City Surveyor. Their suggestions, along with ideas contributed by the King and the City, became the basis of the first Rebuilding Act, which Parliament passed, after much delay, on 8 February 1667. This established road widths, building standards and procedures for resolving disputes, and allowed reconstruction to begin at last.

In general, the Act achieved its four goals of speed, simplicity, economy and improvement. By establishing three standard house designs, with specified storey heights and wall thicknesses, the Act helped to produce a high standard of building, and it also simplified contracts, reduced disagreements between neighbours, and enabled individual landlords or tenants to rebuild as soon as they could afford to, leaving projecting bricks (toothing) to form a bond with houses built later on. Contracts often referred to buildings 'of the first sort' (cellar, two storeys and a garret) on by-lanes, 'of the second sort' (with an extra storey) on 'streets and lanes of note', and 'of the third sort' (four storeys and a garret) on principal streets. Those building mansions 'of the fourth sort' had more freedom, but they, like all the rest, could only build in brick or stone, without projecting jetties or windows, with drainpipes rather than spouting gutters, and to a maximum of four storeys. Party walls, drainage, and windows, which had been perennial sources of litigation and unneighbourly dispute since the Middle Ages, were all covered carefully by the Act, to minimize friction and delay. The 1667 Acts fell short of the dramatic redesign of the City envisaged at first by Wren and Hooke, but in their clarity, good sense and simplicity they provided a model which other English towns that experienced disastrous fires in the decades ahead were often happy to follow.[9]

Disputes were bound to occur, and a Fire Court chaired by eminent royal judges was created to offer settlements which were free, fair, fast and final. The obligation to rebuild was placed on leaseholding tenants, and difficult disagreements often arose between them and their landlords over the extent to which tenants should be compensated for their spending by a lengthening of their lease. Some tenants could not afford to rebuild within the three years and nine months specified by the 1667 Act, and these had to be compensated for the loss of their lease, while the right to rebuild was sold to someone able to undertake it. Many City properties presented even more complex problems, especially when there were charitable beneficiaries of the rental income, when houses were divided between several owners, where deeds were burned, where owners could not be found, or had died in the recent plague, or where the dimensions of the previous building were unclear. Many such cases were settled by the wards, which still operated in the ruins, or by the Court of Aldermen, but disputes between the City and individuals who had built into the line of a new street (perhaps moving the marker stakes by night) or who demanded more compensation for loss of land to street-widening than the City was prepared to give, went to the Fire Court.[10]

The work of administering the Act (and a second Act passed in 1670) fell to the mayor and aldermen, whose activity in these years was prodigious. In addition to ensuring, through their surveyors ('discreet and intelligent persons . . . knowledgeable in the art of building'), that sites were measured and building regulations obeyed, they had to plan and implement the widening of the streets and the creation of new markets, pay compensation to those who lost land thereby, rebuild all the City's public buildings, and undertake major works on the river Fleet and the new Thames quay. All this was done on the tightest of budgets. The Act of 1667 granted the City the yield of a tax of a shilling a ton for ten years on all coal imported into London, to be spent on compensating landowners, rebuilding prisons, and completing the work on the Fleet and the Thames quay. Coal was a good commodity to tax, used by all and hard to smuggle, but the yield was too low and the use to which it could be put too restricted. In 1670 the tax was tripled, and extended for another ten years. Of each 3s, though, only half went to the City, and the rest to the rebuilding of the City churches and St Paul's. This gave the City an extra annual income averaging £18,000 in the 1670s and £23,000 in the 1680s, but it would still have been driven into bankruptcy if it had not defied the Act and used its share of the tax as a general building fund.[11]

Rebuilding the City of London was an enormous enterprise, and called for labour and building materials on a vast scale. To ensure a good supply of moderately priced labour, the 1667 Act offered the freedom of the City for seven years (which could be extended for life) to all those who worked on the rebuilding. Although the craft companies tried to defend their privileges against this intrusion the clause had the effect, along with London's attractive wage differential, of drawing ample labour to the capital, and preventing local workmen from enriching themselves during the years of rebuilding. The City had powers to control prices and wages, but they did not need to use them. Baltic timber was plentiful, and brickmaking, a traditional London industry, expanded rapidly in Moorfields, Islington and St Giles-in-the-Fields. The most serious difficulty (aside from lack of money) was a shortage of stone, which forced the City, the Companies and the Church to spread their rebuilding over ten years or more.

Money, materials and a mercantile sense of priorities determined the order in which the new City was built. Of the public buildings, work started at once on Newgate Prison and Sessions House and the ruinous but reparable Guildhall, which were nearly finished by 1671, along with the Wood Street and Poultry Compters, Blackwell Hall, Wren's Custom House and the Royal Exchange, grander and more prominently placed than before. Work on Bridewell and Christ's Hospital took rather longer, and the Monument, a huge commemorative pillar of Portland stone, was finished in 1677. Its inscription (partly removed in 1831) confirmed the common belief that Catholic plotters had started the fire, and richly deserved this rebuke in Alexander Pope's *Moral Essays*, written in 1732:

> Where London's column, pointing at the skies
> Like a tall bully, lifts the head and lies.

The work of the house-builders, simplified by the 1667 Act and the Fire Court, went on rapidly. Of the 8,000 houses eventually built in place of the 13,200 lost, half were finished by the end of 1669, and nearly all by late 1672. Not one of these City houses of 1667–72 survived the Second World War, but houses of a similar type are plentiful in other parts of London, and it is clear that the general effect was harmonious and orderly, without excessive standardization. Each house, the developer Nicholas Barbon remarked, displayed the skills of the craftsman who had built it: 'Some being set out with fine brick-work rubbed and gaged, were the Issue of a master bricklayer. If stone coyned, jamb'd, and fascia'd, of a stone mason. If full of windoe . . ., a Glazier's; if full of Balcone and balustrading, a Carpenter.'[12]

Most of the City companies were in their new halls by 1672 or soon after. For many of them the loss of their halls, added to the serious financial problems they already shared with the City, was a severe blow, yet most had managed to raise enough money through mortgages, sales of plate or appeals to members, to begin building fairly quickly, and only three of the forty-four lost halls were not rebuilt. Most of the rebuilt halls that survived into the twentieth century were destroyed in the Second World War, but those of the apothecaries, the innholders, the skinners, the stationers, the vintners and the tallow chandlers are at least partly seventeenth-century, and the Merchant Taylors' Hall has substantial medieval remnants, too.

The rebuilding of the parish churches came last of all, delayed by problems with money and materials, and by disagreements over which fifty-one churches (the figure specified in the 1671 Act) should be rebuilt, and which thirty-six should not. The design of all the new churches and St Paul's was in the hands of Christopher Wren, and this became his major contribution to the rebuilding, and his legacy to the post-Great Fire and modern City. Since Wren had to design fifty-one parish churches, his great virtue was his enormous sense of variety, his ability to draw upon a range of European examples and adapt their ideas to the peculiar circumstances and sites of the City. His own preference was for galleried and centrally planned churches, in which 'all who are present can both hear and see', but he did not try to impose one standard church design on the City or on those who assisted him. For £265,000, about 36 per cent of the coal tax, the City gained a rich variety of new churches, some on the traditional Gothic nave and aisle plan (St Bride's), some in the form of a Greek cross (St Anne and St Agnes, St Martin Ludgate), some in the Dutch style (St Benet's), surmounted by a range of towers, domes, lanterns, pinnacles, cupolas, and spires in almost every available style. So, instead of the uniformity that one supervising architect might have created, London was given a skyline as diverse and interesting as the one destroyed in the fire.

Only twenty-four of Wren's City churches survived the Second World War, many of them greatly altered internally, either by Victorian Gothic enthusiasts or post-war rebuilding. To get an impression of the variety and beauty of Wren's work for the City, one should visit St James Garlickhithe, St Margaret Lothbury, St Martin Ludgate, St Mary Abchurch, St Mary-at-Hill, St Peter Cornhill and St Stephen Walbrook. And, of course, the new St Paul's Cathedral, which Wren saw through from its foundation in 1675 to its completion in 1710, bowing to conservative clerical opinion by giving it a traditional long nave and chancel, but out-manoeuvring his critics to top it with a great Renaissance dome, which dominated the City skyline until the post-war office-building boom.

Some aspects of the rebuilding plans were never successfully completed. The projected opening of a half mile of the river Fleet to commercial shipping by widening it to 40 feet and lining it with wharves and store-houses, was dogged by the impossibility of controlling the flow of rubbish, sewage, mud and floodwater into it from the City and the northern suburbs. Wren completed the scheme in 1674, at a cost of £50,000, but few ships used the canal, and the wharves were used more as a roadway, a workshop and a dump than for unloading cargo. The canal north of the Fleet Bridge (now Ludgate Circus) was covered over in 1733, and the rest disappeared in 1766, when Farringdon Street and New Bridge Street, the approach to the new Blackfriars Bridge, were built. The attempt to beautify and improve the north bank of the Thames by extending the existing open quay between the Tower and London Bridge westwards to the Temple was recognized as a failure in the 1670s. The City had no money to spend on the scheme, and the traders in foodstuffs who still used Queenhithe and the area west of the bridge needed sheds and storage, not the fine open quaysides that appealed to the King and his court. It was a legacy of this failed scheme that most of the riverfront from London Bridge to Queen-hithe was still clear of buildings as late as 1832.[13]

The new City was not spacious. Only two new roads were built (King

Street and Queen Street, running from the Guildhall to Thames Street) and the major thoroughfares were only widened to 35 or 40 feet, narrow enough to ensure that traffic congestion would persist. Houses 'of the first sort' were built in their old cramped frontages on the existing medieval alleys, many of which were not widened even to the modest fourteen feet laid down as a minimum in 1667. Thus, in John Summerson's words, 'the special character of the City as a medieval growth crystallized in Stuart and Georgian brick' was created.[14] One irritating medieval feature was removed. As London's population expanded, the growth of street-selling, especially by butchers in Newgate, Leadenhall and the Stocks (where Cornhill joins Poultry), and traders of all kinds in Cheapside, caused serious congestion, which various attempts at regulation and relocation had not solved. Now, at the King's suggestion, the markets were removed from the main streets into new market-places: the Shambles from Newgate to Newgate Square, Cheapside Market to Honey Lane, the Stocks market to the nearby site of St Mary Woolchurch, and the Leadenhall Street market into the enlarged Leadenhall.[15]

However quickly the City was rebuilt, a permanent loss of population could not be averted. The fire merely accelerated a drift to the suburbs (especially in the west) which the City authorities had shown themselves powerless to prevent for the past eighty years. The poor could not afford the higher rents of the new brick houses, and had established themselves in cheaper southern or eastern neighbourhoods. Tradesmen had discovered that business was better, taxes were lower, and communal duties were less onerous around Covent Garden or the Strand, and many had bought new leases there. A census in 1673 showed that 3,423 of the new City houses were unoccupied, and spurred the City into trying to drum its freemen back into their old places, and offering citizenship on easy terms to provincial craftsmen.[16]

THE REVIVAL OF WESTMINSTER

While the City struggled to regain its population and economic pre-eminence, Westminster flourished. The restoration of the monarchy and the resumption of courtly life in 1660 brought the familiar crowds of courtiers, aristocrats and ambitious gentlemen flocking back to London. The attractions which drew provincial landowners to the Tudor capital exerted an even stronger appeal in the century after 1660. London was once more the centre of Court life, fashion, entertainment, shopping, and ostentation. For the more serious-minded, it was also the home of government, patronage, Parliament, literature, the law, and business. Daniel Defoe, writing in the 1720s, argued (a little unconvincingly) that 'one of the principal causes of the prodigious conflux of the nobility and gentry from all parts of England to London, more than ever was known in former years', was their desire to deal in government and trading company stocks.[17] From 1689, Parliament sat every year, usually from November to May, bringing most of England's 160 peers and around 500 gentlemen to town, and political duties were mingled with the social pleasures of the winter season.

The London season, which was in its infancy in 1600, reached maturity in the eighteenth century, and participation in its rituals became almost inescapable for those of high social standing. The dullness of the summer months, when 'people of quality' were in Bath or Tunbridge, or on their country estates, was often remarked upon by full-time Londoners. On 8 October 1710, Jonathan Swift lamented the lack of dinner invitations, and the dullness of his favourite coffee house. 'I hope it will mend in winter; but now they are all out of town at elections, or not come from their country houses.' And Horace Walpole found the town deserted in August: 'there is not a coach to be seen, the streets are new paving, and the houses new painting, just as it always is at this season'.[18] Between November and April, though, London's receptions, routs, levées, masquerades, balls, dinner parties, clubs, coffee houses, pleasure gardens, theatres, shops and shows offered a life of variety and excitement which no provincial town, not even Bath, could match.

Before the Civil War it was common for visiting landowners to live within the City, but the combined effect of the war, the plague and the fire made this much rarer after the 1660s. City men themselves did not often move to the West End, but the overflow of City tradesmen and artisans into Lincoln's Inn Fields, Covent Garden and the Strand reduced the prestige of these districts, and encouraged titled families to move to Soho, St James's and Mayfair in search of more exclusive and congenial society. The Strand lost its old aristocratic magic. The Savoy was now a refuge for the disreputable, a hospital and workshops, and Durham House, which was used as a barracks during the Civil War, was mostly demolished in 1660. Four Strand palaces (Essex, Arundel, York and Burghley) were demolished for redevelopment in the 1670s, leaving only Somerset House (the home of Stuart queens until the 1690s) and Northumberland House, where the Percy family stayed on until 1874, as reminders of the old aristocratic suburb, defying the commercialization of the area around Charing Cross.

A few aristocratic families, particularly those whose fortunes had been augmented by the development of their West End estates, built themselves town mansions on a grand scale. Burlington House, Marlborough House, Spencer House and Dover House are good surviving examples of the twenty or so that existed in the eighteenth century. In general, the modern aristocrat no longer wanted a vast palace for his London *pied-à-terre*, unless he intended to entertain on a very grand scale. A spacious terraced house with modern sanitation (spring water piped into the house, and a drain running down to the river) and a view on to a well-kept private square suited his needs. Often this was a matter of economy, but many who lived in leased terraced houses could have afforded better. Horace Walpole commented in 1743 that the nobility had 'contracted themselves to live in coops of a dining room, a dark back room with one eye in a corner, and a closet. Think what London would be, if the chief houses were in it, as in the cities of other countries, instead of dispersed like great plums in a great pudding of country.' The country mansion was the focus of the nobleman's loyalty and expenditure, while his London house could be abandoned, demolished, or sublet when another part of town became more fashionable.[19] The migration of the Russells, Earls of Bedford, from their palace on the Strand, first (in 1586) to a mansion in Covent Garden (Bedford House, demolished in 1706), then in 1700 to another in Bloomsbury Square (Bedford House, demolished in 1800) illustrates this process, though the Bedfords moved northwards on their own estates, rather than westwards, and lived in grander houses than most.

ARISTOCRATIC DEVELOPERS

The City authorities were almost alone now in resisting the inevitable expansion of the town. Charles II continued to issue occasional prohibitions on new buildings, and Parliament discussed the problem, but nothing effective was done to enforce the old policy. Even before the plague and the Great Fire precipitated a flight from the City, two important building schemes were under way in the west of London, establishing the principles of business and planning which were to dominate West End development for over 150 years. North-east of Lincoln's Inn Fields, the Earl of Southampton had been waiting to develop his Bloomsbury estate since the 1630s, and laid out a square in front of his new mansion in the 1650s. In 1661 he sold forty-two-year leases on plots around Southampton (later Bloomsbury) Square to men undertaking to build good brick houses, which would in due course revert to the Earl's family. Later leases were generally sixty or ninety-nine years, but this basic principle, which gave landowners immediate cash, a steady income from ground rents, and a more valuable property in the long run, guided most future estate developments. The outcome (as Evelyn put it in 1664) was 'a little town', not just a residential square for aristocrats and gentlemen, but also meaner streets for the shopkeepers and tradesmen who served them.[20]

Southampton's rival as a developer was Henry Jermyn, the Earl of St Albans, a loyal companion to Charles II in his exile. In 1662 the King granted him a lease (converted to a freehold in 1665) on the 45-acre field to the north of St James's Palace, the King's favourite London residence. Taking advantage of the rising aristocratic demand for West End properties, Jermyn leased or sold twenty-two plots to friends or speculative builders, who created London's most desirable residential development, St James's Square. Around it, in the rectangle formed by Piccadilly, St James's Street (newly paved in 1660), the Haymarket and Pall Mall, were streets designed for a complete community, from the aristocrats and courtiers of Charles Street, King Street and Jermyn Street, to the tradesmen and shopkeepers of Rose and Crown Yard and St James's Market. The area even had its own Wren church, big enough to hold 2,000 fashionable worshippers. The idea of the square as the central feature of a smart residential development, which Jermyn borrowed from Inigo Jones (who had imported it from Italy), was adopted by all the later developers of London's West End, and by many provincial cities, too.

The brakes were off, demand was high, and landowners with estates near the Palace, and courtiers granted land by the King, were not slow to follow Jermyn's example. To gain building licences from the King, landlords had to win the approval of Surveyor-General Wren, but good-quality houses and convenient thoroughfares were usually acceptable. Fine houses were built along Pall Mall in the 1660s and 1670s, and the streets west of St James's Street were developed in the 1680s, mostly by Henry Bennet, Earl of Arlington. In 1664 the King granted 29 acres on the north side of Piccadilly to the Earl of Clarendon, another loyal exile, who sold large plots to Lord Berkeley, Sir William Pulteney and the Earl of Burlington. Four great mansions were built on the plots. Clarendon built himself a magnificent palace, which passed to the Duke of Albemarle (Monck's son), and was sold, as Evelyn put it, to 'certain rich bankers and mechanics', who demolished it in 1683 to make room for a 'new town'. Evelyn watched with distaste as a 'little army of artificers' cleared the ground for Bond Street and Albemarle Street, which were completed by 1700. Pulteney's mansion later became a fashionable hotel, Berkeley House burned down in 1733, and Burlington House alone survives, much remodelled, as part of the Royal Academy. Part of the grounds of Berkeley House were developed as Stratton Street and Berkeley Street in the 1680s. East of St James's, the Earl of Leicester began turning the fields in front of his mansion into a handsome and fashionable square in the 1670s, and the Soho pastureland north of this, as far as the Tyburn Road (later Oxford Street), was developed in the 1670s and 1680s by James Long, Sir William Pulteney, the Earl of St Albans and the Duke of Monmouth, Charles II's illegitimate son. Soho Square and Golden Square were the focal points of this smart new neighbourhood.

Courtly politicians such as St Albans and Arlington could win land from the King, gain building licences, reap handsome profits, and have their names remembered in streets and squares, but they relied upon the entrepreneurial skills and the risk-taking of speculative builders. Some of these were men of position: Sir Thomas Clarges and Sir Thomas Bond, each with a street off Piccadilly to his name; Colonel Panton, who built Coventry Street, Rupert Street, Panton Street, Whitcomb Street and Oxendon Street between Haymarket and Leicester Fields in the 1670s; Gregory King, herald and statistician (of whom we hear more later), builder of King's Square (Soho Square) in the 1680s; and Thomas Neale, Master of the Mint, developer of the seven streets radiating from Seven Dials, north of Covent Garden, in the 1690s. But the greatest of them, one of the key figures in the formation of the West End, was Nicholas Barbon, son of Praise-God Barebone, the Anabaptist parliamentarian.

The Strand palaces, with their huge gardens running down to the river, were obvious targets for the developer. In the 1670s Barbon bought Essex House, demolished most of it, and built Essex Street and Devereux Court, which Strype, in 1720, found 'well inhabited by gentry' and by public houses and coffee houses for the lawyers of the Temple. Next door to Essex House was Arundel House, once the inn of the Bishop of Bath and Wells and the home of Protector Somerset in the 1540s. It was replaced (not by Barbon) with Arundel, Norfolk, Howard and Surrey Streets in the 1670s. York House, the home of George Villiers, Duke of Buckingham, was sold for redevelopment in 1672, and Barbon built the new streets, called, to popular amusement, George Street, Villiers Street, Duke Street, Of Alley and Buckingham Street. Barbon's greatest scheme, though, was the development of a large area north of High Holborn, between Gray's Inn Fields and Red Lion Square, in the 1680s and 1690s. Most of the area between High Holborn and Great Ormond Street, including Red Lion Square, Lamb's Conduit Street and Bedford Row, was Barbon's work.[21]

In some ways Barbon was the archetype of the modern property developer. He built on a large scale, well or poorly as the occasion demanded, used standardized designs and fittings, always kept a close eye on the market, destroyed ancient mansions and playgrounds without remorse, bullied or bluffed those whose property stood in his way, sweet-talked or evaded his clients and creditors, and died with his debts unpaid. Alert to every chance of a profit, he branched out (unsuccessfully) into banking, and pioneered the fire insurance business in the 1670s and 1680s. In a society where others were still talking about London's growth in terms of the ideal head size, Barbon was a rational defender of the modern speculative builder: 'The natural increase of mankind is the cause of the increase of the City, and there are no more houses built each year than are necessary for the growth of the inhabitants.' Builders only build 'because there are Tenants for the houses when built, and a continuance every year to build more'. Moreover, the building trade was a great employer of labourers and craftsmen, and 'those that make the materials for Building, such as Bricks, Lyme, Tyle, etc., imploy many more and with those that furnish the Houses, such as Upholsterers, Pewterers, etc., they are almost Innumerable'.[22]

Barbon did not have a great deal of capital, and (like the landlords) he tried to avoid committing his own money to his projects. Whenever he could, he sold off leases to individual builders, who hoped to recover their building costs by selling their houses before they were completed, and before substantial payments on the lease fell due. This precarious system became normal in the eighteenth century. A master-builder (perhaps a bricklayer or carpenter) took on the task of building a house, and sub-contracted the work he could not do himself to other craftsmen (glaziers, tilers, plumbers, painters, plasterers, and so on), keeping cash payments to a minimum until a buyer was found. If the system worked, the master-builder might make a fortune; if not, he might end his days in the Marshalsea Prison. In more prestigious schemes, the builder might be working under the instructions of an architect (perhaps no more than an ambitious craftsman), but it was cheaper to draw inspiration from one of the multitude of builders' pattern-books published in London after 1715. It was through the pattern-book, more than through the work of individual architects, that the restrained classical Palladian style dominated the design of the West End house between 1720 and 1760.[23]

London Spreading

Throughout the late seventeenth and the eighteenth century the demand for London housing continued to grow, and landlords, architects, master-builders and craftsmen continued to satisfy it. The painstaking and beautiful maps produced by John Ogilby and William Morgan in 1676, by the Huguenot John Rocque in the 1740s, and by Richard Horwood between 1799 and 1813 tell the story of London's growth. Although expansion was most spectacular in the west, there was extensive development to the north and east of the City, and south of the Thames. In the east, most of the land between Cable Street–Back Lane and the Thames was built over between 1660 and 1700, and so were Goodman's Fields, between Mansell Street and Back Church Lane. North of Whitechapel Street, the suburb of Spitalfields was growing rapidly, helped by the arrival of French Protestant refugees in the 1680s and 1690s. The 5-acre Artillery Ground was sold for development in 1683, and the new Spitalfields Market was chartered in 1682. The 1769 edition of John Rocque's map shows the further growth of Spitalfields as a prosperous silk-weaving community, and modest growth further east, in the suburban villages of Mile End, Stepney and Bethnal Green. But the 1813 edition of Horwood's map shows streets of new terraced houses spreading north from Cable Street (Back Lane) to Commercial Road (White Horse Lane), which was constructed in 1800, and on up to Whitechapel Street. Stepney, Mile End and Bethnal Green, though still surrounded by fields, were distinctly urban communities by 1813, and the roads linking them with the City and with each other (Whitechapel Street, Bethnal Green Road, Dog Row, Globe Lane) were lined with long ribbons of terraced housing. Maps can be misleading, since they do not show density of occupation, and none between 1676 and 1799 showed individual houses. Bethnal Green, which on Rocque's map appears to be a small village, was estimated in 1743 to have 15,000 inhabitants, and in the census of 1801 its population was recorded at over 22,000, as big as that of Oxford and Cambridge combined. Stepney's population in 1801, including Spitalfields and the riverside towns of Wapping and Shadwell, was 113,281, larger than that of any town in the British Isles except Dublin (170,000), the City of London (128,129) and Westminster (160,759).[24]

South of the Thames, development was stimulated a little by the replacement of the ancient Lambeth ferry by Westminster Bridge in 1750, but the road from the bridge to Southwark ran across the marshy land of St George's Fields, and did not attract much settlement at first. Blackfriars

Bridge, opened in 1769, had a much greater impact, allowing overspill from the overcrowded Fleet Street area into cheaper but still convenient suburban housing on the site of the old Paris Garden. In 1813 there was heavy settlement along the Westminster Bridge Road and along the river between Lambeth Palace and Vauxhall Gardens (on Kennington Lane), although much of north Lambeth (where Waterloo Station stands) was marshy, and was still occupied by market gardens and tenter grounds, where newly made cloth was stretched out to dry. Lambeth's population in 1801 (not all of it urban) was almost 28,000. The area round Great Surrey Street (now Blackfriars Road), running south from Blackfriars Bridge, was densely inhabited by 1813, and where this road met those from Westminster and London Bridges there was a new suburban centre, extending from what had been St George's Fields south to the heavily populated villages of Newington, Walworth and Kennington. The population of Southwark, including this southern sprawl, was 62,669 in 1801, and that of the south-eastern riverside communities, Bermondsey and Redriff (Rotherhithe) was 46,281. If we include Camberwell, where good water, good air and good turnpike roads were already beginning to turn a farming community into a suburb, then 144,000 people, about a sixth of London's population, lived in these southern suburbs in 1801.[25]

There had been suburban expansion to the north of the City since the Middle Ages, and between 1660 and 1760 the town edged a little nearer to Sadler's Wells, Finsbury Fields and Hoxton. London grew, it was often said, like a 'polypus', ignoring the open fields, but spreading along the new and well-maintained turnpike roads, which gave good access to the centre by wagon or coach. By 1813 there were thick ribbons of terraced housing along the main northbound roads, tying the old settlements of Islington and Hoxton and the new ones of Pentonville and Somers Town to the urban sprawl. Much of Moorfields, which Londoners had taken up their shovels and spades to save from enclosure in 1514, fell to the developer in 1777, when Finsbury Square and its surrounding streets were laid out, but Bunhill Fields and the Finsbury Artillery Ground were left undeveloped, and remain so today.

THE WEST END

The building of West London proceeded with more speed and planning than that in other quarters of the town, because demand for housing was richer and more buoyant, investment was easier to attract and landed estates were larger. The process that started before 1700 continued, with aristocratic estates rather than the Crown now providing the land. In 1700 the area north of Piccadilly was mostly open fields west of Great Swallow Street (now Regent Street), except for a small part of Mayfair, and little had been built north of Tyburn Road (Oxford Street) and Great Russell Street. The wars of 1689–1713 depressed the building industry by increasing interest rates and creating a shortage of Baltic fir, the timber favoured by London builders, but between 1713 and the 1730s there was a rush to develop the valuable estates north and south of the Tyburn Road. The Earl of Scarborough's loyally named Hanover Square and George Street (1717–19) were bordered in the 1720s by the Earl of Burlington's Savile Row and Burlington Street to the south, and the City of London's Brook and New Bond Streets to the west. Then in the 1730s and 1740s the Duke of Devonshire outdid them all with Berkeley Square, which at once became one of the best addresses in town.

The greatest landowner in the area north of Piccadilly was Sir Richard Grosvenor, whose father, Sir Thomas, had inherited about 100 acres in the corner formed by Tyburn Road and Park Lane through his marriage in 1677 to Mary Davies, a City heiress. The full story of the development of the Grosvenor estate between 1720 and the 1780s is told in volume 39 of the *Survey of London*. Grosvenor employed Thomas Barlow, a carpenter and master-builder, to plan the layout of the estate, and to make building agreements with contractors, or 'undertakers'. Undertakers received leases on one or more building plots (usually between sixty and ninety-nine years) in return for ground rent and a promise to build on each plot 'a good and substantial brick dwelling house', following the line of neighbouring houses. Uniformity of size and style was not demanded. They then built the houses themselves, or sub-let smaller plots to other builders, in return for a ground rent. The builders raised mortgages to finance their work, either from the Grosvenor family or from local gentlemen, tradesmen, widows or spinsters, and also saved money by bartering their own craftsmanship for that of other builders. To avoid bankruptcy, a common hazard in the building trade, the builders had to sell their houses as soon as possible, preferably before they were finished. By these means, the estate was developed rapidly until 1740 (when the huge centrepiece of the estate, Grosvenor Square, and the biggest streets were complete), very slowly from 1740 to 1755, and steadily for the next twenty years. By the 1780s about 1,375 houses, two chapels, a workhouse and many stables and workshops had been built, and the Grosvenor family's income from ground rents was well over £3,000 a year, about ten times the land's original agricultural rental.[26]

Since the great attraction of the West End was its closeness to Westminster and the Court at St James's, the estates north of the Tyburn Road were less likely to succeed than those in Mayfair and Soho. Much of this land had been bought in 1708 by Henry Cavendish, Duke of Newcastle, and in 1717 Edward Harley, Earl of Oxford, Newcastle's son-in-law, began to build a new residential district on this estate, with Cavendish Square at its centre. But the scheme faltered for lack of investors in the 1720s, and a great mansion projected for the square's north side was left uncompleted. In their rush for profit, builders and landlords had run ahead of demand. 'Here it is', James Ralph wrote in 1734, 'the modern plague of building was first stayed.' As with other plagues, the respite was temporary, and the 1769 edition of Rocque's map shows the square and its surrounding streets almost complete.[27]

By this time the demand for high-quality housing had caught up with and overtaken the supply, and other developments north of Tyburn Road (by then renamed Oxford Street, after its owner and its destination) were beginning. East of Cavendish Square building on the Portland and Berners estates stretched almost to Tottenham Court Road. Henry Portman, whose family had owned the western half of Marylebone since 1553, started to develop Portman Square and its nearby streets in the 1760s, and Manchester Square filled the gap between the Portman and Harley-Cavendish estates in 1776. As usual, the noble developer had his own mansion on the square, and the Duke of Manchester's house, now the home of the Wallace Collection, is one of the few West End mansions that can easily be visited.

In 1756–7 the New Road (now the Marylebone, Euston, Pentonville and City Roads) was built, to link the villages of Paddington and Islington and by-pass the built-up area. This, incidentally, was another aristocratic initiative, pushed through Parliament by the Duke of Grafton, against the opposition of the Duke of Bedford. In 1769 Rocque's map shows the New Road was still separated from London by the open spaces of Lamb's Conduit and White Conduit Fields. Eighty acres of Lamb's Conduit Fields, between Tottenham Court Road and Southampton Row, from Holborn to the New Road, belonged to the Russells, Dukes of Bedford, who also owned Covent Garden. In the 1770s the Bedfords resumed the development of the Bloomsbury area that had been started in the 1660s, and the result, Bedford Square, is the only Georgian square which survives undamaged today. Progress north of this was slow, but it accelerated after 1800, when Russell Square (1800–14) was built. The eastern half of Lamb's Conduit Fields, between Woburn Place and Gray's Inn Road, belonging to Thomas Coram's Foundling Hospital, was also developed from the 1790s, and Horwood's map shows most of the estate built up to the New Road (Euston Road) by 1813. The driving force here was James Burton, a builder who played a key part in the growth of Regency London, from Bloomsbury to Regent Street and St John's Wood. Only White Conduit Fields, owned by the New River Company, between Gray's Inn and St John's Roads, remained undeveloped in 1813.

There is little sign here of the wartime collapse in public and private building emphasized by Sir John Summerson. The northward growth of Bloomsbury, the extension of the Portman and Portland estates (between Edgware Road and Cleveland Street) up to the New Road, the creation of Fitzrovia (around Fitzroy Square) and Euston Square by the Dukes of Grafton (the Fitroys of Euston Hall), the beginning of Camden Town by Lord Camden and of Canonbury (beyond Islington) by Jacob Leroux, all belong to the war years (1793–1815). Growth in the east, stimulated by the building of the Docks and the Commercial Road, was even faster. Since London's population grew by about 25 per cent between 1801 and 1815, this expansion is hardly surprising. In the public sphere, work on the Waterloo, Vauxhall and Southwark Bridges, the enormously costly Millbank Penitentiary, Sir John Soane's Bank of England and the London, West India, East India, Surrey and Commercial Docks all began before the end of the war.[28]

Legal and aesthetic factors played their part, alongside fashion, economics and demography, in shaping the development of the later eighteenth-century West End. The Building Act of 1774 summarized and strengthened the regulations that had been enacted after the Great Fire, and made sure that houses of the four sorts, or 'rates', would be built to decent and uniform structural standards. The same Act imposed tighter restrictions on the use of decorative or protruding woodwork, and thus revived the fortunes of a Lambeth factory which had perfected the production of a type of decorative artificial stoneware known as Coade Stone. The influence of the 1774 Act sometimes produced long terraces of dignified monotony (take a walk along Gower Street), but changes in architectural style, especially in the freer use of stone or stucco embellishments, counteracted its effects. In the 1760s and 1770s formal Palladian models were displaced by the more imaginative ideas popularized by two Scottish architects, William Chambers and Robert Adam. Chambers's great work was Somerset House, the government's new office building on the Thames, which was built between 1776 and 1780 on the site of Protector Somerset's grand but unwanted Renaissance palace. Three of London's most prestigious learned societies, the Royal Academy, the Royal Society and the Society of

Antiquaries, took over the north wing of the new building, and the rest was used by the Navy Office, the Stamp Office, and various other government departments.[29]

Adam was more innovative and influential, especially in the design of high-class domestic architecture. Adam's highly visible Adelphi Terrace, and the great houses he built for the Duke of Buckingham (Chandos House) and the Countess of Home (Home House in Portman Square) in the early 1770s set a new fashion in decorative stone and plaster work, and by the end of the century hundreds of West End gentlemen and tradesmen were living in houses that were built and furnished in the 'Adam' style. The greatest enterprise of Robert Adam and his brothers James and William, the Adelphi (Greek for 'brothers'), was financed in a peculiarly eighteenth-century way. In 1768 the brothers leased a site between the Thames and the Strand, levelled the sloping riverbank by constructing brick arches (some of which can still be seen in Lower Robert Street) and built a magnificent Royal Terrace with five fine streets around it. But the houses did not sell, the Ordnance Department decided the brick vaults were too damp for storage, and the scheme had to rescued from bankruptcy by a giant lottery. In 1774 at Jonathan's Coffee House (the Stock Exchange in embryo) gamblers bought 4,370 tickets at £50 each, hoping to win one of 108 empty houses in the Adelphi. The Adelphi prospered, and in the nineteenth century the splendour of its houses and the misery of the beggars and criminals who made their homes in the vaults beneath them provided one of London's more poignant contrasts. The demolition of the Royal Terrace in 1936 was a milestone in the uglification of London, but there is enough left in the side streets of the Adelphi to make it (as Dr Johnson might have said) 'worth seeing, but not worth *going* to see'.[30]

ALL CLASSES OF MEN

It was a commonplace that London was a socially segregated city, with different quarters reserved for people of different income and occupation. Joseph Addison, writing in the *Spectator* in 1712, spoke of London as 'an Aggregate of various Nations distinguished from each other by their respective Customs, Manners, amd Interests ... the Inhabitants of St James's ... are a distinct people from those of Cheapside, who are likewise removed from those of the Temple on the one side, and those of Smithfield on the other by several Climates and Degrees in their way of Thinking and Conversing together'.[31] This remark is often repeated but it is not really true, at least not in the geographical sense. Residents of the landed class, even with their servants and families, could not have made up more than a small percentage of the 225,000 inhabitants of Westminster and St Marylebone in 1801. In a by-election in 1749 Westminster had 9,465 voters, more than any other constituency. The list of voters included people of 395 different occupations, including 846 victuallers, 491 tailors, 379 carpenters, 300 peruke makers, 285 shoemakers, 271 butchers, 269 chandlers, 183 bakers, 141 distillers, 88 chairmen (carriers of sedan chairs), 83 labourers, and 41 watermen. Many of these unfashionable residents were concentrated in more commercial parts of the old West End, the Strand, Covent Garden, and Soho. But there were concentrations of cheesemongers and cabinet-makers in St James's, clockmakers and poulterers in St George's Hanover Square, watermen and labourers in the area round Westminster Abbey, which contained several streets of the lowest reputation.[32] By moving west and north the landed élite hoped to separate themselves from City tradesmen, but their dependence on labourers, servants, washerwomen, retailers, craftsmen and professionals was enormous, and even in the smartest areas the developers recognized this by building for all classes. In fashionable developments, wrote John Gwynn, the influential mid-century writer and builder, 'it will be found Necessary to allot smaller Places contiguous, for the Habitations of the useful and laborious People, whose dependence upon their Superiors requires such a Distribution'. This could be done, the architect Samuel Cockerell added in 1790, 'without the lower Classes interfering with and diminishing the Character of those above them'.[33]

There were those, of course, whose livelihoods depended on 'interfering with' those above them, and there were neighbourhoods in the West End that seemed to have been colonized by beggars, prostitutes and thieves. The notorious district of St Giles', only two hundred yards south of fashionable Bedford Square, had been the setting for Hogarth's *Gin Lane* in 1750, and many streets in the Covent Garden area had evil reputations by the middle of the century. Some of the alleys at the eastern end of St James's, near the Haymarket, were unsavoury places. Even some new developments could quickly become slums if the timing, location or quality of the building was wrong. This is what happened to Somers Town, which was begun in the 1780s.

The success of West End estates depended on their attractiveness to landed and aristocratic residents. The squares in particular were intended for occupants of the highest class, and it was a mark of the decline of Soho and Golden Squares that they could muster only four peers between them in the 1740s. The parish of Soho's decline continued for the rest of the century: between 1740 and 1791 its tally of titled ratepayers fell from about twenty to seven.[34] All but three of the 23 householders of St James's Square were aristocrats in the 1720s, and Hanover Square's 24 householders in 1725 included three Dukes, eight lords, four titled men and women, and a general. The Grosvenor estate in 1751 was home to almost a quarter of the House of Lords, and in 1790 the Square, still 'the very focus of feudal grandeur, elegance, and fashion', had three dukes, six earls, a viscount, and 21 other titled people among its 47 householders.[35] Later in the century the fashionable new districts to the north of Oxford Street, especially Cavendish Square, Portman Square, Harley Street and Portland Place, put up a spirited challenge to Mayfair, but Grosvenor Square managed to hold its own.

THE MIDDLE CLASS

Particular streets and squares might be 'exclusive', but no London neighbourhood was without its share of middle-class residents. The tax assessments of 1798, on the 30 per cent of London householders with incomes of over £60 per annum, appear to show that people of middling and high income were distributed fairly evenly across the capital, with a predominance of high taxpayers in the City and the West End (including Covent Garden) and low taxpayers in the southern and eastern suburbs, where the rich were very thin on the ground, but where there were plenty of manufacturers and tradesmen. Middling taxpayers, many of them shopkeepers, earning around £80 per annum, made up around 10 per cent of the population in all London parishes, from the side roads of Marylebone and Hanover Square to the main streets of Shoreditch and Bermondsey. Even an area as fashionable as the Grosvenor estate contained an impressively mixed community. In Grosvenor Square and the four main streets off it 117 of the 277 original householders (42 per cent) had peerages or other titles, but only a street away from the Square we are back in the humdrum world of chandlers, victuallers, milliners, innkeepers, builders and coachmen. In 1749 the voting population of Mount Street, North and South Audley Streets, Davies Street, and the poorer streets just south of the Tyburn Road, consisted of 205 tradesmen, 41 gentlemen, and a few servants and professional men.[36]

Informed guesses, guided by voting lists, London business directories (of which many were published in the eighteenth century), tax assessments, information on particular occupations, and comparison with other cities, suggest that London's middle classes, including businessmen, merchants, tradesmen, manufacturers, shopkeepers, and those in the 'arts' and 'professions', made up between a fifth and a quarter of its population. Peter Earle estimates that there were 20,000 or 25,000 middling households in early eighteenth-century London (between 19 and 24 per cent of households), Rudé puts the figure at 30,000 (only about 14 per cent) in 1800, and Schwarz suggests 28,000 (between 16 and 21 per cent, on his reckoning) for 1798, or 36,000 if the income barrier is lowered from £80 to £60 a year, to include well-paid artisans and some skilled workers. The rest of the population, apart from around 3 per cent in the landed class, were workers and their families, either self-employed producer-retailers or skilled artisans, the working-class élite, or labourers. As Schwarz concludes, 'two-thirds of the working population and half of the entire adult male population were unskilled or semi-skilled'.[37]

The commercial, financial and manufacturing sections of middle-class London will be examined later, but London was also the centre of the professions, and lawyers, clergymen, teachers, government officials and medical men abounded there. Peter Earle, drawing his information from Gregory King's analysis of English society in the 1680s and Geoffrey Holmes's work on the professions, estimates that London in 1730 had around 5,000 lawyers, 1,000 clergymen, 2,500 teachers and 1,000 physicians, surgeons and apothecaries. Excluding those who received only a workman's wage (especially charity school teachers), professional men and their families made up about a third of Earle's London middle class. The law was the most lucrative and attractive profession, and London remained the centre of training and practice, despite the abolition of the prerogative courts (Star Chamber and Requests) in 1640–2. Although the plum legal posts and the highest courts were in London the centralization of the English legal system must not be exaggerated. The number of students taken by the Inns of Court did not continue its rapid seventeenth-century growth, and England's several hundred local courts handled much more business than the central courts at Westminster did. The 3,834 attorneys listed as entitled to practise in the Westminster Courts of King's Bench and Common Pleas would not all have been London-based, and it had long been the practice to allow equity cases, technically reserved for the court of Chancery, to be heard by local commissions. Much of this work 'in the great provincial ant-heap of the law' was handled by solicitors, a new breed of lawyers without training in one of the London Inns. Since there was such an abundance of work for provincial lawyers, who proliferated in every sizeable town, Peter Earle's guess that half England's lawyers lived in London need not be accepted without question. Still, the legal profession, with its army of clerks, under-clerks and apprentices, constituted a numerous and wealthy section of the London middle class.[38]

London's concentration of people and (especially) wealth also attracted large numbers of medical practitioners, from high-status physicians, descending through surgeons and apothecaries to quacks. Barbers had pulled teeth and performed minor surgery, and apothecaries had made and sold drugs and medicines, since the Middle Ages, but they were only craftsmen, trained by apprenticeship, and in the sixteenth century the university-educated physicians, their superiors in rank if not ability, won ascendancy over them. The Royal College of Physicians (founded in 1518) was given the right in 1551 to license all practitioners within a 7-mile radius of London, and used its monopoly to repress new medical ideas and methods (including the advances of Paracelsus) and to hold back the growth of the cheaper medical crafts. Their control was not absolute: of the roughly 500 men practising medicine in London in 1600, about half were unlicensed 'irregulars'. After about 1690 the College's licensing system broke down in the face of the refusal of many London doctors to apply for licences and pay the fees. There were 136 College-approved practitioners in 1695, but only seventy-eight in 1719, while the physicians' main rivals, the apothecaries, went from strength to strength. In the plague of 1665 most apothecaries remained in London with their poor patients, while most physicians fled with their rich ones, and in 1704 the Society of Apothecaries successfully challenged the College of Physicians' licensing powers in the House of Lords. Apothecaries far outnumbered physicians: there were at least 337 in London and the out-parishes in 1695 (each with an assistant or two), and in 1704 it was complained that in London there was 'no alley or passage without the painted pot' of an apothecary's shop.[39]

Surgeons, meanwhile, were gaining confidence and reputation from their work during the wars of 1690–1713, and practical experience from dissecting the corpses of felons hanged at Tyburn, a practice introduced in 1540 and augmented by the Murder Act of 1752. Anatomical teaching, especially in William Hunter's private academy and in the London hospitals, steadily refined the surgeon's art, but the lack of anaesthetics and of antiseptic methods delayed decisive progress until the next century. Speed, rather than cleanliness, was the surgeon's main accomplishment: a good surgeon could amputate a limb or remove a gallstone in five or ten minutes, keeping the patient's agony to a minimum. Most victims of surgery did not live to tell the tale, but the patient's experience is powerfully expressed in the diary of Fanny Burney, who suffered a mastectomy in Paris in 1811.

Surgeons were much in demand for their skill in treating venereal disease with compounds of mercury. When James Boswell caught gonorrhoea for the third (and by no means the last) time in 1763, after a night of 'luscious fatigues' with a Covent Garden actress, Louisa Lewis, he turned to his friend, the surgeon Andrew Douglas, rather than a cheap but unreliable quack. High medical fees, his disgust with Louisa, and a period of enforced celibacy, rather than a fear that he would not be cured, were his main concerns. After this, Boswell bought a supply of condoms, and generally had intercourse 'in armour', which gave him only 'dull satisfaction'.[40]

Successful professional men stood on the borderline between the gentry and the trading classes. A London surgeon with a good reputation and the right social connections could earn a large fortune, particularly from treating venereal disease. Top apothecaries, too, might earn £2,000 a year if they had a working relationship with a successful physician, and the richest physicians accumulated fortunes which put them on a level with the wealthiest lawyers and merchants, and with well-off country gentlemen. Sir Hans Sloane, physician to George II and president of the Royal College, died in 1753 (aged ninety-three) leaving a world-famous collection of incalculable value which became the nucleus of the British Museum's collection, and a very large estate in Chelsea. This was developed in the 1770s as Hans Town, including Sloane Street, Hans Place, Cadogan Place and Sloane Square. Good investments in land, stocks or patents could multiply a doctor's professional earnings, as they did in the case of Sloane and the great Dr John Radcliffe, who left £140,000 in 1714, much of it for a library and hospital in Oxford. The desire of wealthy doctors, lawyers and other professionals for fashionable houses helped to fill the best West End streets and squares. Sloane and Radcliffe both lived on Bloomsbury Square, along with several prominent lawyers; Leicester Square attracted physicians, painters and intellectuals (John Hunter, William Hogarth, Joshua Reynolds, Isaac Newton); Bedford and Russell Squares were popular with lawyers, and Cavendish Square housed George Romney and several other fashionable painters.[41]

So London's westward expansion served the needs of a much wider social group than the aristocrats whose names are immortalized in the streets and squares of the West End. There was accommodation in Westminster and Marylebone for a new 'urban gentry' of merchants, doctors, lawyers and other professionals, as well as the tradesmen, artisans, servants, chairmen, portraitists and dancing masters who served their needs. The effect of their demand for housing was to create a pace of urban development which Horace Walpole, from his country retreat in Strawberry

Hill, viewed with amazement and foreboding. In July 1776, two weeks after the American Declaration of Independence heralded (as he thought) the end of the British Empire, he wrote to his friend Sir Horace Mann:

> As its present progress is chiefly north, and Southwark marches south, the metropolis promises to be as broad as long. Rows of houses shoot out every way like a polypus; and so great is the rage of building everywhere, that, if I stay here a fortnight, without going to town, I look about to see if no new house is built since I went last. America and France must tell us how long this exuberance of opulence is to last! The East Indies, I believe, will not contribute to it much longer. Babylon and Memphis and Rome, probably, stared at their own downfall.... This little island will be ridiculously proud some ages hence of its former brave days, and swear its capital was once as big again as Paris, or – what is to be the name of the city that will then give laws to Europe – perhaps New York or Philadelphia.[42]

Chapter 10

Population and Health

A Devourer of People

It may be pleasant to dwell on the comfortable and cultured lives of the upper classes, but we must remember the advice of Dr Johnson: 'Sir, if you wish to have a just notion of the magnitude of this city, you must not be satisfied with seeing its great streets and squares, but must survey the innumerable little lanes and courts. It is not in the showy evolutions of buildings, but in the multiplicity of human habitations which are crowded together, that the wonderful immensity of London consists.'[1] Even the briefest survey reveals a contrast as stark as that between the creamy stucco facade of a Nash terrace and the cheap brickwork behind it.

London was still a devourer of people, a drain into which a fair proportion of England's growing rural population flowed and disappeared. Although observers still complained that the capital was like a swelling head on a shrunken body, they did so because they lacked accurate demographic information. In spite of a constant and heavy flow of migrants, London's population grew at the same rate as that of England and Wales as a whole, and remained at around 11 per cent of the national total between the 1690s and 1801. In contrast to this, between 1520 and 1690 its population had risen ten-fold, while England's had only doubled, and London's share of the national total had risen from 2 to 11 per cent. The population of London in the 1690s has been calculated in a variety of ways. Gregory King, engraver, genealogist, 'curious computer' and pioneer of social statistics, worked from birth, burial and marriage statistics collected for tax purposes under the Marriage Duty Act of 1694, a summary of the Hearth Tax returns of 1690, his own knowledge of London and some intelligent guesswork to achieve an estimate of the population of London and England. His method, in brief, was to multiply the number of houses (derived, with adjustments, from the Hearth Tax) by the average household size (derived from the Marriage Duty assessments) to arrive at a population figure of 80,190 for the City within the Walls, and 530,000 for the whole of

London (the area covered by the Bills of Mortality), in a national population of 5,500,000. In the 1930s Jones and Judges used the Marriage Duty records to confirm a City population of around 80,000, probably a little down on its peak before 1665–6. King also used the Bills of Mortality to establish the number of London burials, multiplying them by a figure derived from the assumed London death rate to calculate a London population of a little over 500,000. In other hands, estimates based on the Bills of Mortality have produced an all-London figure of between 560,000 and 640,000, based on assumed annual burial rates of between 37.3 and 34.2 per 1,000 inhabitants.[2] The work of the Cambridge Group for the History of Population and Social Structure, which gathered new information from 404 parish registers, does not alter the picture, since none of the sample parishes were London ones. E. A. Wrigley's estimates of London's population between 1650 and 1800 have won general acceptance because they are a sensible compromise between the best previous calculations, not because they stem from new work by the Cambridge Group. Wrigley's figures are as follows:

1650	400,000
1700	575,000
1750	675,000
1800	900,000[3]

Because its population was so mobile, and because levels of religious nonconformity were so high, reducing the value of Anglican parish registers as a source, calculating London's population presents special problems. Wrigley and Schofield, in their authoritative survey of England's population history, say that the

> trend of events in London in the later years of the eighteenth century is especially difficult to establish with confidence. Public and nonconformist burial grounds developed earlier in London than elsewhere and some of them were large. Anglican coverage of baptisms was also affected by the number and size of the nonconformist congregations, many of which maintained separate baptism registers.[4]

J. T. Krause points out that the registers were particularly accurate between 1695 and 1705 (because of the Marriage Duty Act) and that 'the system virtually collapsed between the 1790s and 1820' when Methodism boomed, and the Anglican church lost control of the rapidly expanding population. So comparing the 1700 and 1800 registers is particularly risky.[5] In her *London Life in the Eighteenth Century*, still, after seventy years, the best social history of Hanoverian London, Dorothy George ignored these difficulties and assumed that registered baptisms in 1700 'bore the same relation to the total population as they did in 1801', and thus worked back from the known 1801 population to arrive at a figure for 1700 of 674,500, about 100,000 above what is now regarded as a reasonable estimate. Comparing this with a 1750 figure of 676,750 led her to conclude that London's population had remained static over the half-century, and fallen between 1720 and 1750. In fact, population calculations based on her baptism figures show a strange undulating pattern: a 7 per cent fall in the 1700s, a 22 per cent rise in the 1710s, static 1720s, a 10 per cent fall between 1730 and 1750, static 1750s, a 15 per cent rise in the 1760s, a slight fall in the 1770s, a 19 per cent rise in the 1780s, and a 5 per cent fall in the 1790s. Dorothy George's population figures, too confidently based on inadequate parish registration, colour her account of social conditions in early eighteenth-century London, and set the tone of her book. The first half of the century, in her account, was a time of almost unparalleled demographic disaster, in which the beneficial impact of lower food prices and dispersal of population into the suburbs was more than counteracted by 'an enormous consumption of very cheap, fiery and adulterated spirits'. The second half, in contrast, experienced a marked 'advance in health, cleanliness, order, sobriety and education'. There is some statistical support for this contrast between the first and second halves of the century, but it is not quite as strong as Dr George (and the many who have accepted her figures) believed it to be.[6]

Since we do not know how many people lived in London, nor how many died there, in the eighteenth century, we cannot be sure what its annual mortality rate was. Nevertheless, it is clear that London's death rates were extremely high in the century, particularly in its second quarter. Wrigley and Schofield's calculation of London burials suggests that London had an annual mortality rate of between 40 and 45 per 1,000 between 1700 and 1725, and between 45 and 50 per 1,000 between 1725 and 1750, compared with a national rate of about 28 per 1,000. The London rate fell to under 40 per 1,000 between 1750 and 1775, and to a little over 30 per 1,000 in the period 1775–1800, drawing closer to the national rate, which had fallen to about 25 per 1,000.[7]

This high death rate gave London a demographic history that set it apart from the rest of the country. In every decade except (perhaps) the 1790s London had a large excess of burials over baptisms. The gap was not quite as wide as Dr George thought, because burials were registered more efficiently than baptisms, nor did it diminish dramatically after 1750. If

Wrigley and Schofield's figures are correct, baptisms in every decade from the 1690s to the 1770s were between about 75 and 83 per cent of burials, with one exceptionally unhealthy decade, the 1740s, in which the figure fell to 64 per cent, even lower than the 1670s and 1680s (both about 68 per cent). Improvement came in the 1780s (90 per cent) and the 1790s (96.5 per cent). John Landers, who has written extensively on London mortality, agrees that the striking period of improvement was not in the 1750s and 1760s, but in the last quarter of the century.[8] From 1800 London at last went into demographic surplus after at least 250 years of deficit. London's contribution to the early stages of England's demographic revolution (which took the population of England and Wales from about 6 million in 1741 to 12 million in 1821) was strongly negative until about 1780, weakly negative until 1800, and positive (but not significant) up to 1825. Between 1650 and 1775, London 'lost' about 900,000 people (the total surplus of burials over baptisms in Wrigley and Schofield's figures), almost a half of the number 'gained' by the rest of the country. But in 1800–25, the city 'gained' about 88,000, while the rest of England gained 2,470,000. London's 'natural' population thus shadowed England's, falling in the eighteenth century, when England's growth was modest, and beginning to rise after 1800, when England's population started to grow at well over 10 per cent a decade.[9]

NEW ARRIVALS

Since there were about 6,000 more burials than baptisms a year in eighteenth-century London, while its actual population rose on average by about 3,250, it must have received over 9,000 migrants a year to bridge the difference between the two figures. As London also lost large numbers of emigrants – transported convicts, soldiers and sailors who died away from home, and people who decided (or were forced) to return to the countryside – the actual migrant figure must have been a good deal higher than 9,000 a year.[10] The migrants who sustained London's population growth mostly came, as they had always done, from the countryside and provincial towns of England. There are no accurate figures, but Peter Earle's analysis of 4,115 witnesses (1,994 men and 2,121 women) before Church courts between 1660 and 1725 is very useful. In this sample, about 58 per cent of Londoners aged fifteen to twenty-four were migrants, and over 80 per cent of those over forty-five, with an average of 71.5 per cent over all age groups. This suggests that many migrants came to London for good, not for a few years of apprenticeship or money-making, and that they outlived native Londoners. Roughly speaking, about a third of migrants came from nearby counties (60 miles or less), and 30 per cent had travelled from more distant counties (125 miles or more). The proportion coming from Scotland or Ireland was about 10 per cent, and rising.[11] Dr Bland's record of patients treated in the Westminster General Dispensary between 1774 and 1781 suggests a similar picture. Of 3,236 married people he saw, about a quarter said they were London-born, 58 per cent were English or Welsh migrants, 6 per cent were Scots, over 8 per cent were Irish, and under 2 per cent were from elsewhere.[12] By the 1780s London probably had an Irish population of over 20,000, mostly living, as poorer migrants generally did, in St Giles' and the riverside parishes east of the Tower.[13]

It was commonly, and probably correctly, believed that most migrants were young men and women without strong ties of marriage, work or property in their home counties, the sort of people who had always been drawn by the high wages, job opportunities and social and cultural attractions of London. Some saw the city as a refuge from starvation, disgrace or arrest, and others were driven, like Mary Young, by 'an itching desire to see London'.[14] Arthur Young, writing in 1771, believed that improved coach services and turnpike roads had accelerated the migrant flow, 'rendering the going up and down so easy that the numbers who have seen London are increased tenfold and of course ten times the boasts are sounded in the ears of country fools, to induce them to quit their healthy clean fields for a region of dirt, stink and noise. And the number of young women that fly thither is almost incredible.'[15] Many new arrivals would have contacts in London who might find them work or lodgings. Earle tells us that of the ninety-one families living in the small Shropshire town of Myddle in 1672, fifteen had members resident in London. Strong country girls were much in demand as domestic servants, but Hogarth warned (in *A Harlot's Progress*) that prostitution was their more likely career. No doubt he exaggerated (how well would *A Servant's Progress* have sold?), but Boswell's *Journal* shows that the dangers were real enough.

Non-English migrants were not so numerous, but they played an influential part in London's economic and social life. Huguenots, French Protestants deprived of their religious rights by Louis XIV in 1685, arrived in large numbers in the 1680s. By 1688 a London relief committee claimed to have assisted 13,500 of them, but since many Huguenots came with capital, and since the flow continued well after 1688, the numbers arriving in London could easily have been more than twice that figure. The Soho community in Westminster was served by fourteen Huguenot churches, and there was an even larger French settlement in Spitalfields. Their contribution to the diversification of London industry and technology over the next century was considerable. The making of guns, watches, clocks, precious metalwares, glass, lenses, paper, tapestry, printed calico, wigs, fans and shoes benefited from Huguenot skills, and they created the Wandsworth felt hat industry. In Spitalfields and Bethnal Green the silk industry, which had existed on a fairly modest scale since the later Middle Ages, was transformed into a major producer by the arrival of French weavers.[16]

London's Jewish population grew from a few hundred in the 1660s to around 8,000 in 1750, and perhaps 15,000 or 20,000 (Patrick Colquhoun's estimate) in 1800. The early settlers were Sephardic Jews from Spain and Portugal, some of them well-off members of the City's financial class, others craftsmen in engraving, watch-making and glass-cutting, others poor pedlars and dealers. Italian Jews, including the Montefiore brothers and Benjamin d'Israeli, grandfather of the future Prime Minister, arrived in the early eighteenth century, and several thousand Ashkenazi Jews took refuge in London from persecution and political disruption in Central and Eastern Europe. The Jews arriving from Bohemia in the 1740s and Poland in the 1770s were desperate, poor, and unwelcome even to the richer Sephardic Jews upon whose charity they depended. Religious observance and racial prejudice excluded them from most of London's more prosperous trades, and they seem to have made their livings in a few small crafts and in old clothes dealing. The popular stereotype of the criminal central European Jew was well-established by the end of the century. Archenholtz, in 1780, described them as living 'by cheating and nocturnal rapine', and in 1800 the influential magistrate Patrick Colquhoun blamed their poverty for driving Jewish pedlars into 'the most complicated arts of fraud and deception'.[17]

Anyone familiar with Hogarth's pictures will know that black slaves were common in eighteenth-century London. Their presence was nothing new. The first group of five West African slaves had been brought to London as early as 1555, and in 1596 and 1601 Elizabeth I unsuccessfully ordered the expulsion of 'the great numbers of negars and Blackamoores which ... are crept into this realm'. From the 1650s there developed a triangular trade between English ports (mainly London, Bristol and Liverpool), West Africa and the West Indies, in which English manufactures were traded for African slaves, who were exchanged for American tobacco and West Indian sugar (commodities themselves produced by the labour of slaves) for the English market. Merchants, naval officers and officials commonly brought young black slaves with them to London, and well-dressed black slave-servants (often given classical names such as Zeno or Pompey) became a fashionable addition to the households of aristocrats and high-class prostitutes. In the 1680s advertisements for the recapture of runaway slaves, who usually had their name and that of their owner engraved on a metal collar, were often placed in the *London Gazette*. Escaped or liberated slaves, or blacks who had arrived in London as sailors, were absorbed into the city's poorer population, as beggars, labourers, riverside workers, entertainers, seamstresses or prostitutes. Marriages between black men and white women were not uncommon, and were regarded with predictable disapproval: 'The lower classes of women in England are remarkably fond of the blacks, for reasons too brutal to mention.'[18] The member of London's free black community best known to us is Samuel Johnson's valet and friend, Francis Barber, but we should remember the writer Ignatius Sancho, the violin virtuoso George Bridge-tower, and the anti-slavery campaigners Ottobah Cugoano and Olaudah Equiano.

The long dispute over the legality of slavery in England, and particularly over the right of slave owners to recapture escaped slaves and ship them to the West Indies, was largely settled in favour of freedom by Lord Chief Justice Mansfield's famous judgment in 1772, and although slaves continued to be sold and recaptured in London thereafter, most English slaves had freed themselves by the 1790s. It is impossible to establish how many blacks lived in late eighteenth-century London, since contemporary estimates were nearly always made by writers whose intention was to stimulate fears about the black presence. The figure of 20,000 London blacks was often repeated in the 1760s, and in the Mansfield case a national figure of about 15,000 slaves (excluding free blacks) was accepted. In the 1780s numbers were augmented by the arrival of blacks who had fought on the British side in the American War of Independence, and by Lascars, Indian sailors left in London by the East India Company. Still, under 1,000 blacks received money from a relief committee set up in London in 1786, and only 350 could be bribed or bullied into joining the disastrous 'resettlement' convoy to Sierra Leone in 1787. Shyllon guesses that the British black population never exceeded 10,000 before 1800, and it seems unlikely that over half of this total lived in London.[19]

'Gin Mania'

The reasons for London's very high death rate have been debated ever since the days of Graunt, Petty and King. Gregory King, who calculated that London needed 2,000 immigrants a year to hold its population steady, and 5,000 to maintain its rate of growth, blamed the deficit on coal smoke, which 'does impede the fecundity of teeming Women, and ... suffocates and destroys a Multitude of Infants'. London marriages, though plentiful, produced fewer children, he believed, because of high levels of adultery, intemperance and business pressure, and the age difference between husbands and wives. The doctor and medical writer Thomas Short blamed 'a close, sultry Atmosphere, not ventilated, but loaded with excrementitious and animal Effluvia', together with irregular eating and sleeping, and the 'effeminate, slothful, luxurious spending of our Days'.[20] The commonly accepted modern view was put forward by Dorothy George in 1925. Epidemics, bad sanitation and occasional food shortages played their part, she argued, but none of these factors was especially severe in the period 1720–50, when death rates were highest. 'The only explanation seems to be that usually given by contemporaries – the orgy of spirit-drinking which was at its worst between 1720 and 1751, due to the very cheap and very intoxicating liquors, which were retailed indiscriminately and in the most brutalizing and demoralizing conditions.'[21]

There had certainly been a growing popular taste for spirits for a century or so, and the heavy duties imposed on French brandy in the 1690s, along with the ending of the distilling monopoly in 1689 and the doubling of duties on beer between 1688 and 1710, had given gin a competitive advantage over its rivals. Gin was cheap, tasty, intoxicating and readily available, and its sellers thrived. William Maitland, the historian of London, reckoned that there were 8,659 brandy-shops in London in 1737, compared to about 6,000 alehouses, with a heavy concentration in the poorer suburbs of the East End and Southwark, where there was one gin-shop for every seven or eight houses. Nearly half of these were small general stores run by chandlers, who had a reputation as gin-sellers, and a quarter were run by women, who had been gradually pushed out of their strong position in the victualling and alehouse trades since the sixteenth century. Gin-sellers also operated (in the words of the Middlesex magistrates in 1726) 'in the streets and highways, some on bulks set up for that purpose, and others in wheelbarrows, and many more who sell privately in garrets, sellars, backrooms and other places'.[22]

In 1735 a powerful campaign against gin-selling began in London, led by a group of Middlesex magistrates who were members of the Society for Promoting Christian Knowledge and prominent in several moral reform projects, including a scheme to resettle London debtors in Georgia. This group had the support of the Master of the Rolls and the Prime Minister, Sir Robert Walpole, who saw the advantage of winning favour with the Dissenters by moving against gin. With the help of landed MPs, who regarded distilling as damaging to the grain interest (because it depressed the brewing trade), a draconian Gin Act was passed in 1736, giving magistrates and excise men the power to prosecute unlicensed sellers. Such was the resistance to the Act from respectable householders, Tory newspapers and some parish vestries (who had not called for legislation), as well as the poor, that the Act was suspended in 1739 and repealed in 1743. Only in 1751, after a further campaign, this time using the persuasive skills of William Hogarth, was a more modest and effective Gin Act passed. This act, which is said to have reduced national gin consumption from 8 million to about 2 million gallons a year, is regarded by Dr George as ' a turning-point in the social history of London'.

Dorothy George's account of the 'gin mania' of the 1720s–40s is drawn from the pamphlets and reports issued by the Middlesex magistrates and their allies in 1726, 1735–6 and 1751. The Middlesex justices laid almost every contemporary evil at the door of gin-drinking: laziness, poverty, 'all the vice and debauchery among the inferior sort of people', crime, violence and vulnerability to infections. Worst of all, 'mothers habituate themselves to these distilled liquors, whose children are born weak and sickly, and often look shrivel'd and old as though they had numbered many years'. Children abandoned to parish care, infant mortality, young people set on the road to prostitution and crime, all came from 'this certain destroyer', gin. The horrors depicted in Hogarth's *Gin Lane*, a picture produced at the height of the anti-gin campaign in 1751, told (George says) the 'essential truth' about St Giles', where one house in four was a gin shop. London was the centre of gin production and consumption, and its appalling mortality record, Dr George concludes, must be attributed to this fact. Thus the partisan arguments of a group of evangelical magistrates have passed into the historical record, and are repeated by T. S. Ashton, Phyllis Deane and George Rudé. Only Peter Clark has subjected their claims to detailed critical analysis.[23]

The Mortality Rate

The tendency to hold the poor responsible for their own misfortunes, and to blame one distasteful activity (usually drinking to excess) for all society's ills, is common among the well-off, and the 'gin mania', like other such 'moral panics', has to be treated with caution. No doubt cheap and nasty spirits contributed to child and adult mortality, but they are not likely to have played as large a part as the other medical and environmental evils that existed in eighteenth-century London, most of which the reforming Middlesex magistrates had no interest in exposing. The greatest dangers for Londoners were infectious diseases and the circumstances that allowed them to spread. We have an enduring picture of Hogarth's *Gin Lane* drunkard, dropping her baby down a flight of steps, but the real threats to infants, the group with by far the highest mortality rate, were a range of infantile diseases, fostered by malnutrition, maternal ignorance and ill-health, bad water, dirty food, poor hygiene and overcrowding.

To judge from the Bills of Mortality, nearly 40 per cent of deaths in London between 1700 and 1750, and about a third thereafter, were due to deaths among children under two years old. Of every 1,000 children born in early eighteenth-century London, over 350, perhaps 400, would be dead within two years, and fully half of all London burials throughout the century were of children. These heavy losses were not confined to the poor and gin-sodden. In healthy Putney, Edward Gibbon lost all six of his brothers and sisters in infancy. More accurate records kept by the relatively prosperous and sober Quaker community suggest that infant mortality was even higher than the Bills of Mortality imply. Quakers lost a third of their children in their first year of life, nearly a half before they were two, and about two-thirds before their fifth birthday, between 1700 and 1775. Significant improvement came only between 1775 and 1800, when 23 per cent of Quaker children died in their first year, and 47 per cent before they were five. It would be hard to argue that this improvement took place because of the rising price of gin, and Landers, who gathered these figures, was more inclined to attribute the improvement to a possible increase in the practice of breast-feeding, with its well-known benefits to health.[24]

The causes of this enormous infant death rate, and its late eighteenth-century decline, are uncertain. The 'searchers', whose diagnoses are recorded in the Bills of Mortality, blamed about 12 per cent of infant deaths on 'teething', and around 75 per cent on 'convulsions'. This was a popular catch-all diagnosis which could cover the early stages of smallpox, and perhaps other childhood diseases, including measles, scarlet fever, diphtheria and whooping cough, as well as the symptoms of gastritis or infantile diarrhoea. Infants were especially vulnerable to gastric disorders, and it is significant that the old description of these disorders, 'griping of the guts', fell into disuse as the word 'convulsions' became more popular. Smallpox, one of the great eighteenth-century killers, was mainly a disease of infants and children, and most adult Londoners, unless they were migrants, had already had the disease. Well over 50 per cent of Quakers who died of smallpox between 1650 and 1800 were under five, and the disease did not often cause death among the over-thirties.[25]

The plague was gone for good, but other infectious diseases seem to have increased in intensity in the early eighteenth century, particularly smallpox, typhus and tuberculosis ('consumption'), which probably accounted between them for about 60 per cent of non-infant deaths in London. London was unique among English towns in its size and density of population and the severity of its sanitary and housing problems, and it is not surprising that the impact of these infections was greater there than elsewhere in the country. Diseases which affected other communities as occasional unwelcome visitors were permanent residents in the capital. Typhus appears, as 'fever' or 'spotted fever', in every year's Bills of Mortality, constituting about 15 per cent of London's recorded deaths from 1700 to 1775, and 11.5 per cent from 1775 to 1800, and smallpox was ever-present, causing about 8 per cent of recorded deaths. Tuberculosis held steady as other diseases declined later in the century, so its share of recorded deaths rose from about 14 per cent in 1700–1750 to nearly 25 per cent between 1775 and 1800. Because its worst diseases were endemic rather than epidemic London mortality was less volatile than England's as a whole, but from time to time a particularly strong outbreak of one disease or another pushed mortality to unusual heights: typhus in 1694 and 1741, smallpox in 1740, 1763 and 1772, infant diseases in 1740 and tuberculosis in 1800. Three of London's ten worst years fell in the 1740s. Most of these years of high mortality were also times of very high bread prices, though occasionally (as in 1709–10) there might be bread shortages without a rise in smallpox or fever deaths. There was also a seasonal pattern of death: respiratory tuberculosis, influenza and typhus in the winter months, when thick, dirty and lousy clothes were worn day and night, dysentery and diarrhoea in the summer, when flies transmitted bacteria from filth to food, and water was at its most foul. From the 1690s, the summer diseases, especially dysentery and infant diarrhoea, tended to decline, while the winter ones rose.[26]

Environmental and economic factors, rather than gin, were at the root of these diseases. Droplet infections such as tuberculosis, influenza, measles, scarlet fever and diphtheria, and contagions such as smallpox, spread easily in London's crowded streets and houses, and there was always a high chance of coming into contact with a sufferer. The habit of feeding babies with inappropriate solid and liquid foods must have sent thousands of infants to their graves. A doctor wrote in 1773: 'they are fed on meat before they have got their teeth, ... biscuits not fermented, or buttered rolls, or tough muffins floated in oiled butter, or calves-feet jellies, or strong broths ... or are totally neglected'.[27] It is very likely that water, which carried dysentery and typhoid, or milk, which could transmit dysentery, diphtheria and tuberculosis, killed more Londoners than the demon gin. Such sanitary horrors as crowded cellars and lodging-houses, overflowing graveyards and cesspits and stinking water supplies were more fully publicized by the reforming Victorians than by the more apathetic Georgians, but these problems were as bad, probably worse, in the eighteenth century.

DRINKING WATER

Water quality varied, depending on the source of the supply and, to some extent, the wealth of the recipient. The old system of free public conduits had fallen out of use by 1750, and Londoners who could afford the annual fee had their basement cisterns filled by one of several commercial companies. The majority, of course, relied on public standpipes carrying very intermittent commercial supplies, or water from a well or spring, and perhaps on rainwater, the Thames, or street water-sellers. A pumped supply from the Thames, powered by a great waterwheel at the northern end of London Bridge (driven by the rapid flow of the river as it squeezed through the narrow arches), had been provided by the London Bridge Waterworks since 1582, and this supply was gradually increased by the construction of extra wheels under more arches, including one on the Southwark side in 1767. By 1822, when the planned rebuilding of the bridge led to the transfer of the Company's business to the New River Company, it was supplying 4 million gallons a day to 10,000 customers.

Sir Hugh Myddleton's New River Company (1606–1902), the most successful and long-lived of all London's water companies, drew water from springs in Chadwell and Amwell in Hertfordshire, and from the river Lea. The supply was carried 39 miles in an open channel to reservoirs at

New River Head, Clerkenwell (south of Pentonville Road), and from there
the sluggish and murky water was transmitted in leaky wooden pipes to the
company's paying customers in London. The company installed a steam
pump in 1768. Most of the other companies used the Thames. In East
London, the Shadwell Waterworks Company (1669–1807) supplied its
customers (8,000 houses in 1807) with water pumped from the Thames, by
horse-power until 1750 and steam-power thereafter, and in the west the
York Buildings Waterworks (1675–1818), near the Strand, pumped Thames
water (by steam between 1712 and 1731) to 2,500 houses. The West End
also received supplies from the Hampstead Water Company (founded in
1692), which drew its water from Hampstead Ponds, and the Chelsea
Waterworks Company (1723–1902), which used horse, steam and river
power to pump Thames water to reservoirs in Hyde, Green and St James's
Parks, and thence to Westminster and the new West End estates. West
Enders therefore drank the Thames before it had received the filth and
sewage of the city, while East Enders enjoyed a richer brew. Some of south
London's growing population was supplied from the Thames by the
Southwark Water Company (1760–1845) and the Lambeth Water Works
Company (1785–1902). The creation of five new companies between 1805
and 1811 threatened the profits of the water companies, until they reached
mutual agreements in 1815–17.[28]

If the companies took an interest in new technology, it was in steam
pumps to enable them to reach higher districts and the upstairs water
closets of fashionable houses, and iron mains (first used by the Chelsea
company in 1746) to reduce the leakage from elm pipes. There was no
attempt to filter the water or protect it from pollution until the Chelsea
company introduced slow sand filtration in 1829, after strong public
criticism of the state of London's water. No doubt the foul supplies
described in the 1820s were worse than those of the eighteenth century,
because of the rapid growth of population and (after 1778) the installation
of water closets in richer houses. But even before this the Thames received
all the discharges of the river Fleet, that 'nauceious and abominable sink of
nastiness', and of the laystalls (dumps for dung and refuse) at the river's
edge. London had a complex and unplanned network of sewers, which had
grown piecemeal as new districts were inhabited, but these were meant to
carry surface water rather than sewage, which accumulated in cesspools
until the night soil men cleared it out. In practice, the inert and corrupt
Commissioners of Sewers who had administered the drainage of the
London area since the sixteenth century did little to protect or improve the
system, and public complaints suggest that the drains carried sewage and

the refuse of pigsties and slaughterhouses, as well as rainwater. Perhaps it was a blessing that some of these sewers were so wide and undulating that their contents never reached the Thames.[29]

Opinions differed on whether it was safe to drink London's water. Jonathan Swift gives us this memorable picture of the liquid that flowed into the Thames, via the Fleet, after a City shower in 1710:

> Now from all parts the swelling Kennels flow,
> And bear their Trophies with them as they go:
> Filth of all Hues and Odours seem to tell
> What street they sail'd from, by their Sight and Smell.
> They, as each Torrent drives, with rapid Force
> From Smithfield or St Pulchre's shape their Course,
> And in huge Confluent join at Snow-Hill Ridge,
> Fall from the Conduit prone to Holborn-Bridge.
> Sweepings from Butchers Stalls, Dung, Guts, and Blood,
> Drown'd Puppies, stinking Sprats, all drench'd in Mud,
> Dead Cats and Turnip-Tops come tumbling down the Flood.[30]

Not surprisingly, Swift drank wine, because 'water is so dangerous'. On the other hand the *New View of London*, in 1708, praised London's 'clean, wholesome' supply, as did a House of Commons committee in 1820, pronouncing it 'very superior to that enjoyed in every other city in Europe' only twelve years before London's first cholera outbreak. César de Saussure, a visitor from Lausanne in 1725–30, was impressed with the abundance and quality of the supply, and the use to which it was put:

> The amount of water English people employ is inconceivable, especially for the cleansing of their houses.... All furniture, and especially all kitchen utensils, are kept with the greatest cleanliness ... Would you believe it, though water is to be had in abundance in London, and of fairly good quality, absolutely none is drunk? The lower classes, even the paupers, do not know what it is to quench their thirst with water.[31]

The novelist Tobias Smollett expressed a more jaundiced view in 1771, through the eyes of the London-hating Matthew Bramble:

> If I would drink water, I must quaff the mawkish contents of an open aqueduct, exposed to all manner of defilement, or swallow that which comes from the River Thames, impregnated with all the filth of London and Westminster. Human excrement is the least offensive part of the concrete, which is composed of all the drugs, minerals, and

poisons used in mechanics and manufacture, enriched with the putrefying carcases of beasts and men, and mixed with the scourings of all the wash-tubs, kennels, and common sewers within the bills of mortality.[32]

This, from a surgeon with over twenty years' experience of London, says enough to explain why so many, especially the young, died of intestinal infections in eighteenth-century London.

SLUM LIVING

Housing conditions in the poorer parts of eighteenth-century London could probably match the worst dwellings found by Edwin Chadwick in the 1840s or Charles Booth in the 1890s. Jerry-built and patched-up houses, sub-divided tenements let to families unable to afford a proper rent, common lodging-houses which fostered crime and disease, stinking alleys and courtyards, wet, airless and fully occupied cellars, sheds and hovels thrown up on waste ground, were all plentiful in Georgian London. Timber and daub houses run up in a hurry to evade the seventeenth-century building regulations were still common in the inner suburbs, and new houses built on short-lease land were made with bricks so poor, and walls and timbers so thin, that it was not unusual for them to collapse before they were occupied. 'Here falling houses thunder on your head, And here a female atheist talks you dead,' Samuel Johnson wrote, *On Taking Leave of London*. Peter Earle's selection from the dwellings mentioned by Church court witnesses captures the variety of London lodgings: 'In a bedchamber and a dining room ... in a garret ... in part of a cellar ... in one room in Shoe lane which I furnish myself ... in chambers ... in an almshouse ... in an alehouse ... in one of the parish rooms ... in a bagnio in Brownlow Street ... in the Palace of St James ... in a sort of ragg shed ... on the pipes that belong to the Water-house at the Bridge'.

Most contemporary descriptions of working-class housing emphasized its potential for lawlessness and vice. Henry Fielding, explaining the *Causes of the Late Increase of Robbers* in 1751, blamed 'the immense number of lanes, alleys, courts and bye-places', which seemed to have been 'intended for the very purpose of concealment.... Upon such a view the whole appears as a vast wood or forest in which the thief may harbour with as great security as wild beasts do in the deserts of Arabia and Africa.' Writing in 1753, Saunders Welch, High Constable of Holborn, regarded the common lodging-houses of St Giles', Saffron Hill and Shoreditch as a particular danger: 'There have within a few years arisen in the outskirts of this town a kind of traffic in old ruinous houses which the occupiers fill up with straw and flock beds, which they nightly let out for twopence for a single person or threepence for a couple. . . . the houses are open all night to receive rogues and plunder.' The medical and human costs of slum living were less often noticed, but Dr Willan, physician to the London Public Dispensary from 1783 to 1803, writing in 1801, makes them clear:

> It will scarcely appear credible, though it is precisely true, that persons of the lowest class do not put clean sheets on their beds three times a year. . . . that from three to eight individuals of different ages often sleep in the same bed; there being in general but one room and one bed for each family. . . . The room occupied is either a damp cellar, almost inaccessible to the light, and admitting of no change of air; or a garret with a low roof and small windows, the passage to which is close, kept dark, and filled not only with bad air, but with putrid excremental effluvia from a vault at the bottom of the staircase. Washing of linen, or some other disagreeable business, is carried on, while infants are left dozing and children more advanced kept at play whole days on the tainted bed: some unsavoury victuals are from time to time cooked. . . . The above account is not exaggerated.

In these conditions typhus, tuberculosis, measles, smallpox and all the diseases of infancy would flourish. Five districts, Dr Willan said, were notorious for their wretchedness: St Giles' (the Irish ghetto), parts of Rotherhithe and Upper Westminster, East Smithfield, and the area north-east of the City, stretching from Gray's Inn Road to Bunhill Fields.[33]

Improvement

Francis Place, the radical tailor, made the point when reformers were 'discovering' these urban horrors in the 1820s and 1830s that the London of his own youth in the 1780s had been much worse: 'Notwithstanding the vice, the misery and disease which still abounds in London, its general prevalence has been greatly diminished.' In his youth, well-off women 'wore petticoats of camblet, lined with dyed linen, stuffed with wool and horsehair and quilted, . . . day by day till they were rotten', but now even the poorest wore 'washing clothes' of cheap cotton, and bodies, clothes and dwellings were cleaner.

The children of tradesmen ... keeping good houses in the Strand for instance ... all of them when I was a boy had lice in their hair. The children I examined today do not seem to be at all troubled with these vermin.... Multitudes now wear shoes and stockings ... who within my recollection never wore any ... I did not see one child with a scald head, nor one with bandy legs called cheese-cutters, that is with the shin bone bowed out. The number of children who had 'cheese-cutters' was formerly so great that if an estimate were now made it would not be believed.[34]

The question of living standards in these years is controversial, but Place is a good witness, and the fall in the mortality rate from around 1780 supports his claims.

Various changes might have brought about this improvement. Changes in the virulence of particular diseases, especially diarrhoea and dysentery, might have helped. Environmental improvements and reforms, and changes in medical practices, might have had a part to play, especially in reducing infant mortality, smallpox and typhus. If there had been a rise in real wages, bringing better nutrition, housing and clothing, this would have had beneficial effects on health. Calculating trends in real wages demands information on retail prices, rents, patterns of consumption, employment levels, non-money income and total family earnings which is not yet available. Probably the main determinant of living standards in a pre-industrial economy in which bread is the staple food, where wages are set by tradition and the workers' bargaining power is weak, is the price of grain, especially wheat. Wheat prices fluctuated from year to year, causing acute short-term hardship and outbreaks of smallpox and fever. To take an extreme example, they tripled between 1707 and 1709 (the worst year between 1661 and 1795), almost doubling the price of a 4-pound loaf. But in general wheat and bread prices in the London area remained fairly low and steady between 1700 and 1763, in contrast to the high prices that prevailed in much of the period from 1630 to 1699. From the 1760s, despite higher agricultural output, rising national population began to eat away the grain surplus, pushing wheat and bread prices upwards. In the years of the Revolutionary and Napoleonic Wars (1793–1802, 1803–15) wartime inflation, population growth and the dislocation of trade exaggerated this upward trend, taking the price of a 4-pound loaf in London to around 1s 3d in 1800–01 and 1810–13, over three times its usual price between 1700 and 1763. Since wage rates did not usually change with prices, wage-earners enjoyed a plateau of prosperity from about 1720 to 1755, and suffered a steady decline in real wages between 1760 and 1793. Wartime inflation at last broke the fixed wage rate for building craftsmen and labourers (and comparable workers in other sectors), but their wage rises between 1793 and 1812 (of around 75 per cent) did not keep up with rising prices, and real wages, which had already fallen by about a third since the 1750s, fell by a further 10 or 15 per cent in the worst years of the war. Only after 1814, when falling prices did not take money wages down with them at the same pace, did Londoners enjoy a gradual return to the living standards of 1720–55. There is much uncertainty in these arguments, but if they are generally correct then the fall in mortality between 1750 and 1815 cannot be attributed to rising real wages or cheaper food. Housing and hygiene seem to have been more important than nutrition as determinants of mortality in eighteenth-century London.[35]

Since it is likely that the high death rate of Londoners reflects the appalling environmental conditions of a huge city lacking effective sanitary administration, it is possible that public and private action to provide essential civic amenities (street-cleaning, sewers, simple medical provision) paid off in improved public health after the 1780s. Of all eighteenth-century medical practices, only smallpox inoculation had undoubted value as a saver of life. The Greek practice of injecting lymph from a mild smallpox victim into a healthy patient was introduced into England from Turkey in rather a primitive form in 1714 by Dr John Woodward and popularized by Lady Mary Wortley Montagu during the London epidemic of 1721. The technique was discredited by a few well-reported deaths in the mid-1720s, but a safer method (using a shallow scratch) was reintroduced from Carolina in 1743, and in the late 1740s London doctors began inoculating well-off patients on a fairly large scale. Mass inoculation on the scale achieved in some rural areas was impossible in London, but at least the flow of rural migrants would have been less smallpox-prone than before. There was a free Inoculation Hospital, but its activities were on a small scale at first, and it excluded the under-sevens, the most vulnerable group. By the late 1760s, though, it was inoculating over 1,000 people a year, and in the 1770s there were efforts to inoculate infants in their homes. Dispensaries and the Foundling Hospital were also active inoculators, and later in the century Daniel Sutton, the most active of England's greatest family of inoculators, offered his services to 'artificers, handicraftsmen, servants, labourers, etc.' in London, as did many of his imitators, and inoculation became much more widespread. Since recorded smallpox deaths accounted for over a tenth of all London deaths in the 1770s, and the true rate, especially among babies (with their mysterious 'convulsions') and pregnant women, might have been twice as high, the spread of inoculation (after a slow start) could have been responsible for part of London's mortality improvement after 1780. The increasingly unreliable Bills of Mortality show a modest decline in annual smallpox deaths from the 1760s, and a steep fall in the early nineteenth century, when Jenner's safer cowpox vaccination (first publicized in 1798) was widely available.[36]

In other respects the significant medical advance for eighteenth-century Londoners was in the availability of treatment, rather than its effectiveness. Dispensaries or outpatient clinics, which offered free or cheap medicine, inoculation, advice and midwifery to the poor, were probably more relevant to the lives of common people than hospitals or commercial doctors. In the 1690s London physicians had briefly opened dispensaries to damage the business of their rivals, the apothecaries, but the first permanent dispensary, 'for the Relief of the Infant Poor', was established in Red Lion Square in 1769. There were at least sixteen in London by 1790 and thirty by 1840, but since by this date they had around 100,000 patients, under 5 per cent of London's population, their effectiveness in propagating habits of hygiene, especially among the 'undeserving', whom they often turned away, may be doubted.[37]

Successes in minor surgery, inoculation, and the treatment of malaria, gout and venereal disease, limited as they were, impressed rich Londoners enough to persuade them to endow five new general hospitals between 1720 and 1750. One of these, Guy's (1724), was financed by the bequest of a Lombard Street bookseller, Thomas Guy, who had made a fortune in South Sea Company stock. But dying bequests of this sort, which had been the mainstay of London's charities for centuries, were becoming unfashionable (since they deprived a donor's heirs at no personal cost to himself), and the other four, the Westminster (1720), St George's (1733), the London (1740) and the Middlesex (1745), were funded by the subscriptions of groups of wealthy (and living) citizens, united into a sort of charitable joint stock company. In addition, the three older hospitals, St Bartholomew's, St Thomas's and Bethlem, were rebuilt, and a succession of specialist institutions was founded: Thomas Coram's Foundling Hospital (1739) for abandoned children, the Lock Hospital (1746) for venereal diseases, St Luke's (1751) for the insane, and several lying-in hospitals, beginning in 1739 with a small maternity hospital in Jermyn Street, and continuing with at least six more by 1765. It may well be, as McKeown and Brown argued in an influential article in 1955, that ignorance and dirt, leading to high rates of puerperal fever, made these early maternity hospitals worse than useless, but they offered rest and food, and there were some advances in cleanliness and ventilation. There was also a flourishing organization, the Lying-In Charity (founded in 1757), which trained midwives and provided home deliveries for married women at a tenth of the cost of a hospital delivery. This was conducting almost 5,000 home deliveries a year in the 1770s, almost a third of all recorded births. Seemingly small improvements can make a big difference in the delicate business of childbirth, and for these or other reasons recorded maternal mortality was halved during the eighteenth century.[38] It may also be that midwives communicated the growing medical belief in breast-feeding to illiterate mothers, thus helping to bring about a significant decline in infant mortality after 1780.

CHILDHOOD AND CHARITY

Once an infant had survived the dangers of birth, it faced the perils of childhood. All children were at risk, but none so much as the children of the poor and the unmarried. Single servant girls might kill their illegitimate infants, out of shame rather than poverty, but there is no way of knowing how commonly this took place. Twenty-three women, mostly unmarried servants, were indicted for infanticide in Southwark between 1660 and 1800, but others would have escaped detection. 'Common Whores, whom all the World knows to be such, hardly ever destroy their Children,' Bernard de Mandeville believed, '.... not because they are less Cruel or more Virtuous, but because they have lost their Modesty.'[39] Many more illegitimate or unwanted infants were left on the streets, or handed over to the parish authorities, who in turn passed them on to 'nurses', whose evil reputation as baby-killers seems to be justified, or placed them in crowded and underfunded parish workhouses, to be cared for by female paupers. A Parliamentary committee of 1767 reported that only seven in 100 work-house infants survived for three years. Survivors were eventually appren-ticed (until twenty-four for boys, twenty-one for girls), usually to poor masters in unskilled trades, who used the children as unpaid labourers rather than trainees. Workhouse 'apprentices' swept London's chimneys, hawked milk and fruit round its streets, and laboured unpaid in the worst branches of tailoring, shoemaking, stocking-making, baking, river work and domestic service. These were often overcrowded and declining trades, but later in the century industrialization offered new outlets, and London pauper children were packed off to work in the cotton-spinning mills of Lancashire and Cheshire. Between 1802 and 1811, 2,026 parish children were 'apprenticed' into the textile trades of the Midlands and North, while

3,789 were found work in London or at sea. A law of 1816 prevented the parishes (in theory) from sending their children more than 40 miles from London.[40]

In the 1740s and 1750s, when concern over depopulation and the waste of life in London was strong, organizations which saved unwanted and abandoned children from starvation or vice had a special appeal to charitable donors. The Foundling Hospital received well over £100,000 between 1739 and 1756, and was able to buy a large estate in Bloomsbury, which it developed in the 1790s when donations were scarce. Of the 1,384 children it took in by 1756, 724 (52 per cent) died, a far better record than that of the parish authorities and their murderous 'nurses', whose failures in child care had prompted Thomas Coram's endeavours. The number of mothers and children needing shelter was enormous, and in 1756 Coram was voted £100,000 by Parliament on condition that he opened the Foundling Hospital to all comers. Within four years nearly 15,000 children had been taken in (not all from London), but conditions deteriorated, two-thirds of the intake died, and Parliament abandoned the scheme. The Foundling reverted to its selective policy, favouring sailors' and soldiers' orphans, and the survival rate doubled in ten years. But its reputation and its income were damaged by the experiment in open access, and in 1786 its intake was restricted to ten children a year.[41]

Perhaps the most creative and effective philanthropist in mid-century London was Jonas Hanway (1712–86), traveller, Russia trader and pioneer of the umbrella. In his writings and campaigns, Hanway exposed a wide range of London's social evils, especially involving the young: parish infants and their nurses, the climbing-boys employed by London chimney sweeps (whose hardships were reiterated in Kingsley's *Water Babies* in 1863), blacks left to beg in London after discharge from the army in 1783, and girls lured into prostitution. Saving young girls from vice was given a high priority among London philanthropists, and two institutions, the Lambeth Asylum for Orphaned Girls and Hanway's Magdalen House for penitent prostitutes (both near St George's Circus, Southwark), were founded in 1758–9 to tackle the problem. With Hanway's excellent business contacts, especially in the Russia Company, the Magdalen raised over £24,000, and admitted (without necessarily reforming) over 1,000 women in its first ten years. The Lock Hospital (built behind the gardens of the future Buckingham Palace in 1746), which dealt with venereal disease, the occupational hazard of prostitution, attracted much less support, and spent much of the century in debt. Hanway's most successful charity was the Marine Society (1756), a humane alternative to the press gang, whose aim, to take boys off the streets of London and find them places on naval and merchant ships, attracted enormous support from practical and patriotic men in the City. Well into the nineteenth century the Marine Society was thought to offer the best solution to London's growing problem of homeless and criminal boys. It was this problem of policing and moral regeneration, rather than the preservation of life, which seemed to attract philanthropists towards the end of the eighteenth century, when shortage of people was no longer regarded as a problem.[42]

Chapter 11

An Urban Culture

Despite all that has been said about the squalor of its streets and the unruliness of its people, eighteenth-century London was a beautiful and fascinating city, which attracted artists and tourists from all over Europe. Dutch and Flemish painters, in particular, appreciated the grandeur and variety of London's post-Great Fire skyline and the liveliness of its fairs and markets, and the great Canaletto, who lived in London from 1746 to 1756, painted a series of about forty pictures which presented the city as an urban paradise, the aesthetic equal and the cultural superior of Rome and Venice. Canaletto celebrated the achievements of Sir Christopher Wren, the beauty of the Thames, which, with its wherries and state barges, looked oddly like Venice's Grand Canal, and London's most impressive new public construction, Westminster Bridge, which he painted or drew about twenty times. For those Londoners not rich enough to commission a work by the Venetian master there was always Samuel Scott, 'the English Canaletto', whose talents could even lend enchantment to the mouth of the stinking Fleet.

It was not the beauty of London, of course, that drew artists, musicians and writers to it, but the money they could make there. Dr Johnson's assertion that 'No man but a blockhead ever wrote, except for money' could well be applied to all the creative professions of eighteenth-century London. It was the city's unique combination of courtly and aristocratic patronage with a large and growing commercial market for books, periodicals, prints, paintings, plays and concerts, rather than its wealth of native talent, that made London's musical, artistic and literary life so rich and varied. It may be, as William Empson says, that 'the arts are produced by overcrowding', but rich crowds seem to produce, or attract, more art than poor ones.

The relative weight of patronage and commerce in stimulating the arts changed over the century, and varied from one art form to another.

Writers, for instance, were more able to benefit from the mass market than painters and sculptors, whose work generally needed an individual wealthy buyer. In London, the wealthiest buyer was the royal Court. Stuart patronage drew Peter Lely (1618–80) from Utrecht, Godfrey Kneller (1646–1723) from Lübeck and Michael Dahl (1656–1743) from Stockholm. Under the Hanoverians a succession of British and continental painters made a living from courtly commissions: Sir James Thornhill (1675–1734), whose work adorns the dome of St Paul's Cathedral and Greenwich Hospital, was Court painter to George I, and Philip Mercier, who came from Hanover in 1716, found work at the Court of Frederick, Prince of Wales. George III and his Court generally patronized British artists: Allan Ramsay from Edinburgh, John Opie, the 'Cornish Wonder', and Sir Thomas Lawrence, from Bath. For those who could not get Court commissions, there were in London plenty of aristocrats and gentlemen whose hunger for pictures of themselves, their wives, their children, their horses and their possessions could keep a much wider community of artists in employment. The most successful society painters in London in the 1760s had arrived in the town in their twenties or early thirties: Joshua Reynolds from Devon, George Romney from Kendal, George Stubbs from York, Angelica Kauffmann from Switzerland, Johann Zoffany from Germany and Benjamin West from Pennsylvania. Some, including Ramsay and Thomas Gainsborough, resisted the lure until their forties, and a few (notably Joseph Wright of Derby) ignored it altogether.

There was artistic life beyond the Court. In 1711 Kneller, the dominant figure of his day, brought about twenty artists together to form England's first academy of art, in a house in Great Queen Street. When artistic disagreements broke the academy up after about ten years Thornhill, who had replaced Kneller as governor, opened his own school in Covent Garden. A rival school in St Martin's Lane was more successful than Thornhill's, perhaps because it offered 'drawing from the Naked', but it had to close when its treasurer stole its funds. After Thornhill's death in 1734 his son-in-law, William Hogarth, started a new academy, also in St Martin's Lane, which became the centre of London's community of painters for the next thirty years. In the 1750s several members of Hogarth's academy began to campaign for a national academy under royal patronage, and this plan eventually succeeded in 1768, when George III granted a charter to the Royal Academy of Arts. The new Academy took its members and fittings from St Martin's Lane, and under the skilful management of Joshua Reynolds and Sir William Chambers it established itself as London's leading exhibition centre and art school. The Academy was shown every favour, moving to successively more commodious and impressive buildings as its power grew. In its fine rooms in the new Somerset House its annual exhibitions were an impressive and popular sight in the 1780s, with 700 pictures packed frame to frame. Its later moves to the National Gallery in Trafalgar Square and to Burlington House took place in 1837 and 1868.[1]

Reynolds, painting aristocrats at 30 guineas a foot, made the biggest fortune, but London offered enterprising painters other ways of making a living. The American John Copley, who arrived in London in 1776, borrowed an idea from Mrs Salmon's waxworks, and charged visitors a shilling to see his popular historical paintings. William Hogarth, the most impressive and original of all the artists working in eighteenth-century London, rarely won fashionable commissions. Instead, he painted smaller family groups, or 'conversation pieces', for well-off clients, and from the 1730s he began to exploit the wider middle-class market by producing prints of lively London scenes, which sold at between 6d and 10s 6d each. Like his contemporary and admirer, Henry Fielding, Hogarth depicted the moral and physical chaos of London life, the decadence of its social and political élite, the corruption of its young men and women, the brutality and ignorance of its lower classes, and the appalling consequences of dishonesty, greed, cruelty, drunkenness and mercenary marriage. Hogarth's moral purpose was sincere, but he no doubt saw the commercial advantages of pleasing two audiences, those who abhorred the evils of the age, and those who wanted to look at pictures of them. Whatever we think of Hogarth's moral prescriptions, there is no doubt that his 'modern moral subjects', *A Harlot's Progress, A Rake's Progress, Four Times of the Day, Marriage à la Mode, Industry and Idleness* and *The Four Stages of Cruelty* present an account of the unpleasant realities of city life which no other eighteenth-century writer or artist could surpass.

WRITING FOR PROFIT

Traditionally, aristocratic and courtly patronage had supported writers, too. This was declining in the eighteenth century, but not yet dead: Addison, Pope, Swift, Gay, Johnson and Goldsmith all enjoyed a degree of noble or royal assistance. Johnson's mighty denunciation of patrons in general, and Lord Chesterfield in particular, in 1754, shows that the breed was not extinct: 'Is not a Patron, my Lord, one who looks with unconcern on a man struggling for life in the water, and, when he has reached ground, encumbers him with help?'[2] As patronage faltered, the London public offered an alternative means of survival. The London theatres had provided hard-working professional writers with a reasonable income since the sixteenth century, and continued to do so after 1660, as the careers of Dryden, Congreve, Gay, Fielding and Sheridan testify. Aphra Behn (1640–89), said to be the first English woman to earn her living as an author, did so mainly by writing for the London stage.

But London's large literate public, both resident and seasonal, and its growing number of publishers, bookshops, libraries, newspapers and periodicals, opened the way after 1700 for the rise of professional writers whose works were read, rather than performed. Writing, as Defoe put it in 1725, had become 'a very considerable branch of English Commerce.... The Booksellers are the Master Manufacturers or Employers. The several Writers, Authors, Copyers, Sub-writers, and all other Operators with pen and Ink are the workmen employed by the said Master Manufacturers.' London was clearly the centre of this new industry. By 1705 there were about 150 bookshops in London, and only another 300 shops selling books, along with other stock, in the rest of England.[3] Until 1695, when the Licensing Act lapsed, printing was confined to London, York, Oxford and Cambridge. Although the book trade was thrown open to all towns in 1695, a close-knit group of London booksellers and copyright owners, men such as Jacob Tonson, who published Dryden, Congreve, Pope, Addison and Steele, and claimed copyright on *Paradise Lost* and the works of Shakespeare, Andrew Millar (publisher of Johnson, Hume and Fielding), Robert Dodsley (publisher of Johnson, Goldsmith and the *Annual Register*), Barnaby Lintot (publisher of Pope, Gay and Farquhar) and the Longman and Rivington families, continued to dominate national book production and distribution. Until 1774 this small circle (or 'conger') of London booksellers claimed perpetual copyright on most English and classical texts, and provincial dealers relied on the goodwill of London publishers or agents for their books.[4]

Although publishers, rather than writers, made the biggest fortunes, an author with business acumen could win worthwhile rewards. One of the first writers to turn London's rising demand into personal profit was Alexander Pope, whose almost £9,000 payment for translating the *Iliad* and the *Odyssey* made him financially independent, and paid for a house and 5 acres of land in Twickenham in 1719. The method Pope used to make his fortune was to collect advance payments, or promises to pay, from subscribers whose names would be listed in the finished book. This form of collective patronage financed the publication of over 2,000 works during the century.[5]

Professional writers had to turn their hands to whatever the market demanded. A literary form which was perfectly suited to the needs of the busy Londoner was the periodical essay, which was introduced by Steele in the *Tatler* in 1709, and taken up by almost every important London writer (particularly Johnson, Smollett and Goldsmith) during the rest of the century. The elegant and sharp-witted essays of Joseph Addison and Richard Steele in the *Tatler*, the *Spectator*, and the *Guardian* between 1709 and 1714, caught the mood of educated middle-class Londoners perfectly, and seem to have been especially popular with women readers, who were excluded from so many other leisure pursuits. Addison aimed to bring 'philosophy out of closets and libraries, schools and colleges, to dwell in clubs and assemblies, at tea-tables and coffee-houses', and did more than anyone else to create (and transmit to us) the coffee-house culture of eighteenth-century London.

The periodical and newspaper industry that developed in London after 1700 created work for a small army of professional writers, some of them men of great ability, others little more than hacks. The outstanding professional writer of his generation was Daniel Defoe, who made his unsteady living by turning out a prodigious quantity of journalism, political pamphlets, travel books, commercial manuals, 'true adventures' and fiction. From 1704 to 1713 he single-handedly produced a thrice-weekly magazine, the *Review*, which aimed to attract less sophisticated readers, and 'wheedle them in ... to the knowledge of the world'. Defoe's lodgings in Ropemaker Alley, west of Moorfields, were next to Grub Street, whose name became a metaphor for the whole world of underpaid journalism and pamphleteering. The area was obliterated in the Second World War, and is now covered by the Barbican development. Others had to follow Defoe in making a living from journalism: Samuel Johnson, until his royal pension in 1762, Tobias Smollett, despite the success of his *Complete History of England* in 1757, and Oliver Goldsmith, until his triumph with *She Stoops to Conquer* a year before his death in 1774.

Books were expensive, and could only reach a mass market in serial form, or in cheap pirated copies, but demand was strong enough to create bestsellers of a wide variety of works: sermons, histories, political and literary satires in verse or prose, translations of the classics, travel books, pastoral verse, literary criticism and dictionaries could all find an audience. Perhaps the most important product of this commercialization of literature was the growing popularity of long works of prose fiction, or novels. The development and perfection of the English novel between 1715 and 1750 was largely the achievement of four professional writers, all Londoners by birth or adoption, starting with Defoe's *Robinson Crusoe, Moll Flanders* and *Colonel Jack*, progressing through Samuel Richardson's *Pamela* and *Clarissa*, and culminating in Henry Fielding's *Joseph Andrews* and *Tom Jones* and Tobias Smollett's *Humphrey Clinker* and *Roderick Random*. These men were writing for profit, and they knew at first hand the tastes and interests of the middle-class London public whose spending power they hoped to exploit. Defoe had been a hosier in Cornhill, and had failed in a variety of businesses, Richardson was a prosperous printer and publisher in Salisbury Court, Fielding was a playwright, theatre manager, lawyer and magistrate, and Smollett was a surgeon and Grub Street hack.[6]

Most of England's professional writers, even those who preferred a rustic existence, spent at least a part of their working lives in London. London gave them contact with readers, subscribers, patrons, editors, booksellers and fellow-writers, as well as an inexhaustible supply of subject matter. How could a writer mock the follies of the political or literary world, unless he lived in London? How else could he catch the spirit of coffee-house society, expose the entertaining vices of the urban underworld, or denounce the falsity and unpleasantness of city life? Even William Blake, who attacked the cruelty and oppression of the city with unparalleled ferocity in his poem *London*, felt obliged to live there for all but three of his seventy years. In those sixty-seven years in London, his eccentric genius brought him little public success, but no repression. His three years in Sussex ended in his arrest and trial for treason.[7]

The arrival of painters and writers from all over England and Europe is a reminder that the common image of London as the nation's dominant cultural force, 'the central point where arts originate, and from whence they ramify' (as someone said in 1801), needs a little modification. It is certainly true that provincial fashions in dress, architecture, urban design, news-gathering, music, retailing and many other things often took their lead from London, and that the upper and middle classes in smaller towns were eager to copy London tastes in everything from churches to underwear. But many of these tastes had not really originated in London. London, as Peter Borsay says, was a cultural entrepôt, absorbing the latest fashions in music, painting, architecture, food and clothing from Italy, France, Germany and the rest of Britain, and then passing them on again, with their status enhanced by their success in the capital. Although London's dominance was impressive, the tide of tastes and ideas ran in two directions: into London with migrants and visiting artists and writers, and out again through pattern books, newspapers and people who had visited or worked in London, perhaps as craftsmen or architects.[8]

THE FULL FLOW OF TALK

London was the great market-place for ideas and conversation, as it was for more tangible merchandise. 'Whoever has once experienced the full flow of London talk,' said Dr Johnson, 'when he retires to country friendships and rural sports, must either be content to turn baby again and play with the rattle, or he will pine away like a great fish in a little pond, and die for want of his usual food.'[9] Boswell tells us why Johnson journeyed painfully from Lichfield to die in London in 1784: 'such was his love of London, so high a relish had he of its magnificent extent, and variety of intellectual entertainment, that he languished when absent from it, his mind having become quite luxurious from the long habit of enjoying the metropolis.... such conversation as London affords, could be found nowhere else.'[10]

Johnson's friends were judged by their conversational skills: Burke's conversation was 'very superior indeed', Mrs Montagu's came in 'a constant stream', and Goldsmith 'talked always at random'. So important a part did conversation play in the intellectual life of London that clubs were formed to encourage it. An early example is the scientific club begun in the 1640s, given royal patronage by Charles II in 1663, and known thereafter as the Royal Society. In Gresham College, where the Royal Society had most of its meetings until 1710, Samuel Pepys, John Evelyn, John Dryden and other gentlemen of intellectual curiosity, could learn from some of the greatest scientists of the age, among them Robert Boyle, Robert Hooke, Edmund Halley, Christopher Wren and Isaac Newton. In the Kit-Cat Club, formed around 1700, Congreve, Vanbrugh, Steele and Addison mixed with Whig politicians under the secretaryship of the powerful publisher, Jacob Tonson. The Scriblerus Club (Pope, Swift, Arbuthnot and Gay) was the Tories' equivalent, but it only lasted for a few months in 1714. Dr Johnson's own club, known later as the Literary Club, first met in 1764, at the Turk's Head tavern, Gerrard Street. Its early members, including Goldsmith, Joshua Reynolds and Edmund Burke, were joined later by Garrick, Boswell, Adam Smith, Sheridan, Gibbon, Charles James Fox, Joseph Banks, and an assortment of writers, aristocrats and bishops. Even simpler folk liked to talk, and London, it has been estimated, had about 2,000 clubs in the early eighteenth century, including, the *Spectator* said in 1711, 'Street-Clubs, in which the chief inhabitants of the street converse together every night'.[11]

The intellectual society of eighteenth-century London was dominated by men, but it was not exclusively masculine. In the 1720s and 1730s Lady

Mary Wortley Montagu, poet, letter-writer, and pioneer of smallpox inoculation, was a powerful force in London society, and from 1750 to after 1800 a group of society hostesses known as the Blue Stockings, led by Elizabeth Vesey, Frances Boscawen and Elizabeth Montagu, organized conversational parties for men and women of intellect and wit. Regular attenders included Dr Johnson and his circle, the popular poet and essayist Hester Chapone, the novelist and diarist Fanny Burney, the linguist and Greek translator Elizabeth Carter, and Hannah More, the playwright, novelist and prolific producer of evangelical tracts. The Blue Stocking ladies had no Boswell to record their wit, but the conversation in their salons was, if we can accept Dr Johnson's judgement, of the highest quality.

Salon ladies might discuss the latest French ideas, but the most potent stimulus to conversation was the immensity and vitality of London itself. The dense crowds that filled its public places, and its vast and confusing network of streets, lanes and squares, attracted, amazed and befuddled the visitor, and emphasized the insignificance of lesser towns. Refugees from rural tedium and small-town parochialism who yearned to see 'the full tide of human existence' could stand at Charing Cross and watch it flooding past. There were no doubt some who, like Smollett's town-hating Matthew Bramble, regarded London as a 'great reservoir of folly, knavery, and sophistication' 'where every corner teems with fresh objects of detestation and disgust', but most visitors found something to suit their tastes. The essayist Charles Lamb tried to explain to his country-loving friends the pleasures of living in this wicked, filthy and overcrowded city in a letter to The Reflector in 1810:

> This passion for crowds is nowhere feasted so full as in London. The man must have a rare recipe for melancholy, who can be dull in Fleet Street. I am naturally inclined to hypochondria, but in London it vanishes, like all other ills. Often, when I have felt a weariness or distaste at home, have I rushed out into her crowded Strand, and fed my humour, till tears have wetted my cheek for inutterable sympathies with the multitudinous moving picture, which never fails to present at all hours, like the scenes of a shifting pantomime.
>
> The very deformities of London, which give distaste to others, from habit do not displease me. The endless succession of shops where Fancy mis-called Folly is supplied with perpetual gauds and toys, excite in me no puritanical aversion.... I love the smoke of London, because it has been the medium most familiar to my vision. I see grand principles of honour at work in the dirty ring which encompas-

ses two combatants with fists, and principles of no less eternal justice in the detection of a pick-pocket. . . .

Where has spleen her food but in London? Humour, Interest, Curiosity, suck at her measureless breasts without a possibility of being satiated.[12]

Boswell in London

London, as James Boswell remarked, was a different place to different people:

A politician thinks of it merely as the seat of government in its different departments; a grazier, as a vast market for cattle; a mercantile man, as a place where a prodigious deal of business is done upon 'Change; a dramatick enthusiast, as the grand scene of theatrical entertainments; a man of pleasure, as an assemblage of taverns, and the great emporium for ladies of easy virtue. But the intellectual man is struck with it, as comprehending the whole of human life in all its variety, the contemplation of which is inexhaustible.[13]

Nobody expresses the intense excitement of escaping from small-town life into the hurly-burly of London better than Boswell, who arrived in London (on his second visit) from Presbyterian Edinburgh in November 1762, at the age of twenty-two. His *Journal* for 1762–3, written in weekly instalments for his friend John Johnston, is a record of the activities of a young man greedy for all the social, cultural and sexual pleasures on offer in Europe's biggest city. In London Boswell found variety, unpredictability, entertainment, company and (when he needed it) anonymity:

London is undoubtedly a place where men and manners can be seen to the greatest advantage. The liberty and whim that reigns there occasions a variety of perfect and curious characters. Then the immense crowd and hurry and bustle of business and diversion, the great number of public places of entertainment, the noble churches and superb buildings of different kinds, agitate, amuse, and elevate the mind. Besides, the satisfaction of pursuing whatever plan is most agreeable, without being known or looked at, is very great. Here a young man of curiosity and observation may have a sufficient fund of present entertainment, and may lay up ideas to employ his mind in age.

Boswell was a man of modest income and noble ambition, of low inclinations and high aspirations. His *Journal* shows us London life at its highest and its lowest, from the splendours of a rout at the Duchess of Northumberland's mansion at Charing Cross to the misery of the impoverished and dejected prostitutes he met in the Strand and St James's Park. It was one of Boswell's great pleasures to saunter around the streets of the town, along Holborn or the Strand, into the Temple ('a pleasant academical retreat') or Covent Garden, or through the City, flattering himself with comparisons with Londoners of earlier generations: 'I patrolled up and down Fleet Street, thinking on London, the seat of Parliament and the seat of pleasure, and seeming to myself as one of the wits in King Charles the Second's time.' On 19 January 1763 Boswell and two friends walked the whole length of the town, from Hyde Park Corner to an inn just beyond the Whitechapel turnpike, where they 'drank some warm white wine with aromatic spices, pepper, and cinnamon'. There were days of perfect conviviality: on 19 March 1763 Boswell breakfasted with his friend Dempster, had coffee at Child's coffee house in St Paul's Churchyard, sauntered to the Exchange and the Guildhall, dined at Dolly's Beefsteak House, listened to the choir in St Paul's, walked through the Temple and Holborn, took tea at Dempster's, and went to a grand rout at Northumberland House.[14]

A Variety of Pleasures

Like other Londoners in all ages, Boswell made most of his own entertainment, reading, flirting, singing, eating, drinking, talking, walking, and watching the world go by. But he also had at his disposal a range of commercialized and organized recreations that was growing with every decade. Some of these were relatively new: daily newspapers and magazines, circulating libraries and well-stocked bookshops, public concert halls, race meetings and professional boxing matches. Others had been available since Pepys's day, or before: taverns, brothels, fairs, coffee houses, pleasure gardens and theatres. London had been a pleasure town for centuries, and although it enjoyed a growth in its commercial leisure facilities (or an 'urban cultural renaissance') in the eighteenth century it was not, as some provincial towns were, starting from scratch.[15]

With a population so vast, so varied, so hungry for diversion and excitement, and so ready to pay for it, it is no wonder that London offered every conceivable entertainment, every marketable pleasure. Freaks and curiosities of every kind were on commercial display, from hermaphrodites and dwarfs to operatic cats and acrobatic monkeys. When the real thing was not available, waxworks would do almost as well. Mrs Salmon's Fleet Street exhibition of historical tableaux and horrific scenes in wax opened in 1711 and prospered for over a century, until it was outdone by Madame Tussaud's new display in Baker Street, which opened in 1835. A display of rather greater importance could be seen after 1759 in Montagu House, Bloomsbury, the first home, and the present site, of the British Museum. The Museum was created by Act of Parliament in 1753 to preserve three great London collections, the Cottonian Library, the Harleian Manuscripts and the antiquarian and natural history collection of Sir Hans Sloane, who died in 1753. Montagu House was bought and converted for under £25,000, the proceeds of a lottery, and 'studious and curious persons' were admitted, under the most restrictive and time-consuming conditions, at the rate of ten an hour. Opening hours were short (usually six hours a day) and weekend closure, along with careful vetting of applicants, excluded the lower classes. Visitors were hurried through the vast and poorly organized collection in less than an hour, and most were left, like William Hutton, with a sense of disappointment. 'I considered myself in the midst of a rich entertainment, consisting of ten thousand rarities, but, like Tantalus, I could not taste one.' In 1810 freer entry was granted to 'any person of a decent appearance', but even in 1836 it was Museum policy to exclude 'sailors from the dock yards and girls whom they might bring with them'.[16]

Perhaps sailors did not feel their exclusion too keenly. They were welcome, at least, in London's many brothels and bagnios, which promised the satisfaction of all male (and some female) sexual desires, despite the efforts of morality campaigners and magistrates. Brothel-keepers, notably Mrs Goadby of Berwick Street, Mother Needham of St James's, and Molly King and Mother Douglas of Covent Garden, were familiar figures in contemporary novels and prints, enticing innocent country girls into their employment. Sex tourists in London's main bagnio district could even buy a guide-book, Harris's *List of Covent Garden Ladies*, to help them find a prostitute to suit their taste and income.[17]

ON THE STAGE

As in Shakespeare's day, there was a close affinity between brothels and theatres, which shared the same neighbourhoods, the same customers and sometimes the same employees. The growth of the theatre was inhibited between the 1660s and the 1843 by the government's restrictive licensing policy, which was motivated by political rather than moral fears. In 1660 Charles II granted royal warrants to two theatrical entrepreneurs, Thomas Killigrew and Sir William Davenant. These two monopolists ran troupes known respectively as the King's Company and the Duke of York's Company, the former in the Theatre Royal, which moved from Bridges Street to Drury Lane in 1674, and the latter in the Lincoln's Inn Fields Theatre and (from 1671) the Dorset Garden Theatre, off Fleet Street. The two companies merged in 1682 and London was left with a single monopoly theatre, the Theatre Royal, Drury Lane (built by Wren in 1672–4), until William Congreve and others reopened the Lincoln's Inn Fields Theatre in 1695. This was rebuilt in 1714 by John Rich, who moved the company in 1732 to the new Covent Garden Theatre, Bow Street, just around the corner from the Theatre Royal. These two 'patent theatres' were the dominant theatres in eighteenth-century London, and they responded to increasing public demand for drama by enlarging their auditoriums in the 1790s to hold over 3,000 people each. The patent theatres of the 1790s were so huge that only the most stentorian performers of the day, notably Sarah Siddons and her brothers, John and Charles Kemble, could dominate them.[18] Both theatres were burned to the ground in 1808–9 and rebuilt, a little smaller, shortly afterwards.

These two theatres were the only ones licensed for dramatic performances in London, but others circumvented the legislation in the 1720s and 1730s, giving Londoners a choice of four or five playhouses. In Goodman's Fields, Whitechapel, there were two theatres in the 1730s, one specializing in circus acts, but the other staging serious plays. The other main rivals of the patent theatres were in the Haymarket, where Vanbrugh's grandiose and ill-planned King's Opera House (1705) staged lavish Italian operas in the 1720s and 1730s, and the 'Little Theatre', built in 1720, specialized in farces and satires (many by Henry Fielding) ridiculing Robert Walpole and his administration. Walpole tried to use the 1714 Vagrancy Act against unlicensed players, but a prosecution failed in 1733, and so in 1737 government control was strengthened by the passing of the Licensing Act, which made unlicensed theatres liable to closure, and gave the Lord Chamberlain the censorship powers he retained until 1968.

The 1737 Act brought the unlicensed theatres to heel, and shaped the development of drama in London for a century. The Goodman's Fields Theatre had its last great success in 1741, when David Garrick, the greatest actor of the century, had his first triumph in Richard III, but it was closed down soon afterwards. The Little Theatre in the Haymarket was more successful. Under the clever management of Samuel Foote, a famous and cruel mimic, it eventually won a licence in 1766 to run a summer season between May and September, when the main theatres were closed. A year earlier, a new brick theatre replaced the wooden building at Sadler's Wells, which had been offering its customers a mixture of tumbling, rope-dancing, music and drama since the 1690s.[19] Around the end of the century entrepreneurs realized that there was money to be made by offering London's million inhabitants musical and dramatic entertainments that were not covered by the 1737 Act. In the 1790s Philip Astley's equestrian circus in Lambeth, the Royal Amphitheatre, started presenting melodrama and comedy, and in 1806 this great showman also built the Olympic Pavilion off the Strand. In 1809 the Royal Circus on Blackfriars Road was converted into a theatre, the Surrey, by Robert Elliston, one of the great actor-managers of his day. Elliston also made a success of Astley's struggling Olympic when he took it over in 1813. In these years musical theatre was concentrated increasingly along the Strand. As well as the Olympic, the Strand had the Lyceum (1809), one of the greatest Victorian theatres, and the Adelphi (founded in 1806 as the Sans Pareil), the most important of the 'minor' theatres.[20]

In the summer indoor theatre was supplemented by the theatrical booths of the London fairs: the May Fair near Piccadilly, the Southwark Fair in September (both closed in the 1760s) and the great Bartholomew Fair held at Smithfield for the two weeks following 24 August. The actors and writers of Drury Lane were not too proud to earn their summer livings among the acrobats, wire-walkers, trained monkeys, contortionists, puppeteers and pickpockets of Bartholomew Fair, and even the renowned Colley Cibber, poet laureate, manager of the Drury Lane in the 1710s and 1720s, and the victim of Alexander Pope's most withering satire, acted in the Smithfield booths.[21]

The gulf between the 'popular culture' of Smithfield and Southwark and the 'élite culture' of Covent Garden and the Haymarket was not very great. The fairground booths drew their actors from the royal theatres, and the theatre managers constantly searched for new ways to please the crowd. In the battle for audiences the two main theatres used everything from Shakespearean revivals (where Garrick excelled) to ballad operas, wire-walkers, wild animals and performing dogs. The *Spectator* made fun in 1711 of the tendency of opera impresarios to fill their productions with popular entertainments drawn from all corners of the town: in one 'there was a Rary-Show; in another, a Ladder-dance; and in others a Posture-Man, a moving Picture, with many Curiosities of the like Nature'.[22] As a theatrical entrepreneur no one excelled John Rich, manager of the theatres at Lincoln's Inn Fields and Covent Garden from 1714 to 1761. Rich saw the commercial possibilities of adapting and embellishing the Italian pantomime for the London stage, and his success forced the Drury Lane (under the management of Cibber and Garrick) and the Smithfield showmen to follow suit. Rich made the 'afterpiece', the short farce or pantomime that usually followed the main play, a regular feature of London theatre. The policy of selling half-price tickets to those who came to see the afterpiece was so popular with poorer playgoers that when David Garrick and John Beard tried to abolish the concession at Drury Lane and Covent Garden in 1763 the two theatres were almost torn apart by rioters. It was Rich, too, who took the opportunity offered by the declining popularity of the Italian operas of Handel and others to challenge them with an English language ballad opera without the tiresome whine of overpaid Italian castrati. The enormous success of Gay's *Beggar's Opera* in 1728 (a triumph that made 'Gay rich and Rich gay') established the ballad opera as a regular feature of London theatre for the rest of the century. Moreover, it was Rich's Covent Garden Theatre that staged the great oratorios (*Messiah, Belshazzar, Judas Maccabeus,* and several others) that Handel produced in London in the 1740s.[23]

The transformation of London's musical life after about 1670 provides a convincing example of the 'commercialization of culture' described by J. H. Plumb. Pepys's diary gives a picture of a rich musical life in the 1660s, but one focused on the Court, the Church and the private home, not on the concert hall. Commercial public concerts did not exist in Europe until 1672, when John Banister, after his dismissal as Charles II's bandleader, began a series of afternoon concerts in his house in Whitefriars, open to all who paid the shilling entrance fee. When these ended in 1678, 'the musical small-coal man', Thomas Britton, a Clerkenwell coal-hawker and self-taught musician, began organizing weekly subscription concerts in the loft over his coal-house, and continued to do so until his death in 1714. For 10s a year, subscribers could hear the great Dr Pepusch on the virginal, John Banister on the violin or the young Handel on a five-stop organ. Britton is an odd example of the way in which people of talent could break through the social barriers that divided rich and poor in London. He continued to sell coal in the streets, but after work he sometimes joined the Duke of Devonshire and a clutch of earls (including Robert Harley, Earl of Oxford) in book-buying expeditions round the streets of London.[24] By the time of Britton's death, public concerts were commonplace in London, especially around Covent Garden. Hickford's Room, in Brewer Street, the

Academy of Ancient Music (meeting in the Crown and Anchor Tavern, in the Strand), and the Castle Tavern, Paternoster Row, offered the most popular concerts until 1775, when they were eclipsed by the opening of the Hanover Square Rooms. London's wealth and size ensured that its citizens would hear the best (or almost the best) that the Continent had to offer. Among European cities, only Vienna had more resident Italian composers than London between 1675 and 1750. With Italian and English operas, musical interludes and accompaniments during most plays, orchestras in the better pleasure gardens, and Handel's prodigious output, Londoners could enjoy a rich musical life.[25]

'A Monstrous Ant-hill'

Theatre and concert impresarios such as Rich, Garrick, Handel, Foote and Heidegger (manager of the Haymarket Opera House from 1713 to the 1740s) had to compete not only with each other, but with the many diversions and entertainments on offer throughout the town. For Ned Ward, the 'London Spy', the streets themselves were a living theatre, where 'the whims and frolics of staggering bravadoes and strolling strumpets', brawling watermen, ballad-singers, street dancers, fruit, nut or pudding sellers, card sharps, overdressed City beaux parading along Cheapside, and the City Trained Bands (now more ludicrous than heroic) offered constant amusement. Almost a century later, the young William Wordsworth was drawn to London by childhood dreams of bishops and kings, of Westminster, St Paul's and the Guildhall, of 'the River proudly bridged', of the lamps and domes of Vauxhall and Ranelagh, and of neighbours who lived as strangers. His childish expectations were not met, but he found instead a 'monstrous ant-hill on the plain', and a city as enthralling, in its way, as anything he could have imagined. In many respects, what struck him as he paced London's 'endless streets' was what had impressed Ward, Boswell, and dozens of other visitors before him:

> . . . the quick dance
> Of colours, lights, and forms; the deafening din;
> The comers and the goers face to face,
> Face after face; the string of dazzling wares,
> Shop after shop, with symbols, blazoned names, . . .

> . . . A raree-show is here,
> With children gathered round; another street

> Presents a company of dancing dogs,
> Or dromedary, with an antic pair
> Of monkeys on his back; a minstrel band
> Of Savoyards;. . . .

The notorious May Fair was long gone when Wordsworth came to town, but at Smithfield the Bartholomew Fair showmen were drawing the crowds more or less as they had done for centuries:

> . . . What a shock
> For eyes and ears! What anarchy and din,
> Barbarian and infernal, – a phantasma,
> Monstrous in colour, motion, shape, sight, sound! . . .
> . . . All moveables of wonder, from all parts,
> Are here – Albinos, painted Indians, Dwarfs,
> The Horse of knowledge, and the learned Pig,
> The Stone-eater, the man that swallows fire,
> Giants, Ventriloquists, the Invisible Girl,
> The Bust that speaks and moves its goggling eyes,
> The Wax-work, Clock-work, all the marvellous craft
> Of modern Merlins, Wild Beasts, Puppet-shows,
> All out-o'-the-way, far-fetched, perverted things . . .[26]

Fairs were a nuisance, especially on the crowded streets of Southwark or the developing aristocratic quarter of Mayfair, and the steady decline of their trading functions had made them vulnerable to the more censorious attitudes towards popular pastimes current in the eighteenth century. The Southwark Fair, one of England's greatest fairs, was suppressed in 1763, and the May Fair, having survived its temporary abolition in 1709, was closed down in 1764. Fairs that did not impede the property developer lasted much longer. The Charlton Horn Fair, a celebration of cuckoldry with ancient but obscure origins, survived until 1872 in spite of Defoe's call for its suppression: 'The mob indeed at that time take all kinds of liberties, and the women are especially impudent for that day; as if it was a day that justify'd the giving themselves a loose to all manner of indecency and immodesty, without any reproach.'[27]

THE PLEASURES OF SUFFERING

According to John Strype, whose edition of Stow's *Survey of London* appeared in 1720, the most popular London diversions were 'football, wrestling, cudgels, ninepins, shovelboard, cricket, stowball, ringing of bells, quoits, pitching the bar, bull and bear baitings, throwing at cocks and ... lying at alehouses'. Twenty years later, Maitland added 'sailing, rowing, swimming and fishing in the River Thames, horse and foot races, leaping, archery, bowling in alleys, and skittles, tennice, chess, and draughts; and in the winter scating, sliding, and shooting'. This is a pattern of leisure very similar to that described by William Fitzstephen in 1170, with its emphasis still on ball games, athletic contests, animal fights, human combat and river sports. Even Sir John Fielding's magisterial call in 1758 for action against 'Diversions calculated to slacken the Industry of the useful Hands', particularly such alehouse games as 'Cards, Dice, Draughts, Shuffle-boards, Missisippi Tables, Billiards, and covered Skittle-Grounds', had its antecedents in medieval complaints about idle apprentices.[28]

Animals were still the focus of many London pastimes. The popularity of performing animals – dancing bears, horses and dogs, drum-playing hares, acrobatic monkeys – was very long-standing, and the newer vogue for 'learned' animals, mainly pigs, was a variation on a traditional theme. The taste for animal displays, especially equestrian ones, was exploited commercially by Philip Astley, who set up England's first modern circus near Westminster Bridge in 1769. The ancient interest in wild or exotic animals was also readily satisfied in eighteenth-century London, either in fairground booths, private displays in taverns, or at the royal menagerie in the Tower. Tigers, Ned Ward said in 1700, were 'now so common they are scarce worth mentioning'. Animals also helped satisfy the Londoners' enduring taste for violence. At Hockley-in-the-Hole and Saffron Hill (both in Clerkenwell), and Tothill Fields, Westminster (south of Horseferry Road), bulls and (less often) bears were baited by fighting dogs, as they had been for at least 500 years. The old sport of cock-fighting was still popular with all classes. At a cock-fight in Shoe Lane in 1663, Pepys found 'a strange variety of people', from MPs to apprentices. Boswell watched cocks fighting at the Royal Cockpit, St James's Park, and although he felt 'sorry for the poor cocks' he managed to stay for five hours. By 1800 most people of refinement had lost their taste for these rough sports, and the way was open for legislation against them. Cockpits were banned in London in 1833, and the long struggle to suppress dog-fighting, duck-hunting and bull-baiting had achieved a fair degree of success by the same time. Bear-baiting continued at Tothill Fields, it was said, until 1793, and bull-baiting until around 1820. In compensation for the loss of these ancient pleasures Londoners could go to horse races at Epsom, where the Oaks and the Derby were first run in 1779 and 1780.[29]

For those who preferred to watch human suffering, London still offered ample opportunities. Until 1770 Bethlehem Royal Hospital (Bedlam), the palatial lunatic asylum on Moorfields, was open to the public as a sort of human zoo, where visitors could pay a few pence to bait the chained inmates. Visits were restricted to ticket-holders in 1770, and when a new Bethlem was built in St George's Fields in 1815 the entertainment was abandoned altogether. Prize-fights, male, female or mixed, with swords, cudgels or fists, could be seen at Hockley, in fairground booths, and in commercial amphitheatres, of which Figg's and Broughton's, in Oxford Street, were the best known. Commercial sword-fights seem to have been staged affairs, but the boxing matches were real enough, and participants could be severely injured. Boxing became a little more 'scientific' in the 1780s, when the great champion Daniel Mendoza of Whitechapel set up a boxing school. Mendoza and many of his pupils were Jewish, and because of the spread of boxing among them, Francis Place believed, it 'was no longer safe to insult a Jew unless he was an old man and alone'. Mendoza's contests were sometimes enormously long: at Croydon in 1792 he won in the twenty-third round, and at Bromley in 1806 it took him fifty-three rounds to beat Henry Lee. His last serious fight took place in 1820, when he was fifty-six years old.[30]

Punishment was still regarded as a public spectacle, as it had been for centuries. Petty criminals were often pilloried or whipped in public, and executions at Tyburn (until 1783) and Newgate thereafter were treated as a public holiday. For multiple hangings, or when the criminal was notorious, there might be crowds of 30,000 or more (80,000 was the record), hoping to witness a particularly theatrical or drunken performance, to hear a dramatic declaration of guilt or innocence from the condemned, or to applaud a courageous farewell. Among those who watched the two-hour procession from Newgate to Tyburn, or gathered around the gallows, cheering or groaning as if they were at a pantomime, there were no doubt many who came to mourn the passing of a friend or relative, and many who viewed the spectacle, as Boswell did, with 'a very great melancholy'. Before 1752, it was not unusual for friends of the hanged to fight with troops to save the corpse from the surgeon's dissecting table. On average, around thirty-five criminals were hanged each year in London and Middlesex between 1750 and 1800, and twice in the 1780s there were almost 100. In the early nineteenth century the authorities began to fear the disorderly consequences of using punishment as a spectator sport, and executions, along with whippings and the pillory, became much less common. Public whippings and hangings took place occasionally until the

1860s, but the ancient pleasure of pelting pilloried criminals with fruit, mud, dead cats or (for sex offenders and informers) stones was lost in 1816.[31]

ALEHOUSES AND COFFEE HOUSES

The cockpit, the bear garden and the gallows suggest that eighteenth-century London was still, in some respects, a medieval town. A more pleasant reminder of the continuity of London's recreational history was the survival of the drinking-house. These were of three main types. At the top of the hierarchy were inns, of which there were about 200 in the 1730s. Inns, with their narrow facades and large courtyards, provided lodging and refreshment for the well-off, warehousing and marketing facilities for merchants, and stabling and repairs for wagons and stagecoaches. The greatest coaching inns were on the main routes out of town: passengers going to the East Midlands or Yorkshire waited at the inns of Aldersgate, those for the South-East went to the George, the Talbot, or one of the other inns in the Borough High Street, those for Essex went to the Aldgate inns, and so on. These were the transport centres of pre-railway London, and it was the coming of the railway stations in the 1830s and 1840s that killed them off.[32] Taverns shared most of the social functions of inns, offering the better-off private rooms in which to drink wine, eat, gamble, do business, and meet their friends. There were nearly 500 taverns in London in the 1730s, weathering the challenge of the coffee houses with some success. Pepys, for instance, often met colleagues, tradesmen or friends in taverns, and in the 1760s Samuel Johnson and James Boswell met and dined regularly in the Mitre Tavern, Fleet Street, where they first planned their trip to the Hebrides. A tavern, Dr Johnson told Boswell, offered more ease and carefree enjoyment than a private house:

> no man, but a very impudent dog indeed, can as freely command what is in another man's house, as if it were his own. Whereas, at a tavern, there is a general freedom from anxiety. You are sure of a welcome; and the more noise you make, the more trouble you give, the more good things you call for, the welcomer you are.... No, Sir, there is nothing which has yet been contrived by man, by which so much happiness is produced as by a good tavern or inn.[33]

For the common man there were alehouses on every street, perhaps 6,000 of them in the 1730s. Ale and beer were an immensely important part of the Londoner's diet, and alehouses supplied them in great variety. There were flavoured ales (sugar, spices, cherries, wormwood, or a newly killed cock were popular flavourings), and a growing selection of London and provincial brews. As possible sources of disorder and social protest, alehouses were licensed and supervised by the magistrates, but as certain sources of excise revenue, they were shielded from the attacks of more extreme moral reformers. Alehouses were generally becoming more respectable and offering a wider range of useful services. As well as cheap food and beer, they often provided lodgings, tobacco, credit, newspapers, employment information, and meeting places for trades, societies and clubs. There were still alehouses that catered for criminals and prostitutes, but most alehouse keepers tried to keep on good terms with magistrates and brewers, and even aspired to join the urban élite themselves. Ned Ward mocked their pretensions in 1700: 'His wife must now be called Madam, his sons, young masters, and his daughters, misses, and he that salutes the old lickspiggot with any other title than that of Mr Churchwarden, runs the hazard of the forfeiture of his good looks, friendship and conversation.' At the same time, the spread of spirit houses (over 8,000 of them in 1739) and cheap doss-houses diverted the fire of morality crusaders towards more subversive targets. Thus, in Hogarth's *Beer Street*, the alehouse appears as a haven of healthy refreshment and conviviality, the essential social institution of happy working-class life.[34]

In expanding and improving the services they offered, taverns and alehouses were responding to the challenge of new competitors in the field of public refreshment. For cheap and simple eating, London had chophouses, cookshops and beefsteak-houses. In the 1760s James Boswell was fond of Clifton's chop-house, near the Temple, and Dolly's steak-house in Paternoster Row: 'You come in there to a warm, comfortable, large room, where a number of people are sitting at table. You take whatever place you find empty; call for what you like, which you get well and cleverly dressed. You may either chat or not as you like. Nobody minds you, and you pay very reasonably.'[35]

More serious rivals to the tavern as a social centre were the coffee and chocolate houses. Coffee rooms spread rapidly after the Restoration. The first, Pasqua Rosee's Head, was established in 1652 in St Michael's Alley, off Cornhill, where the Jamaica Wine House now stands. By 1663, when licensing was introduced, there were eighty-two in the City, and by 1739, according to Maitland, there were 551 in the whole of London. The success of coffee and chocolate houses reflected the popularity of the products they offered – Turkish coffee, West Indian sugar and cocoa, Chinese tea, Virginian tobacco, and newspapers – and also their ability to satisfy a wide range of interests, from the salacious to the scholastic. Their variety impressed César de Saussure in 1726: 'Some coffee-houses are a resort for learned scholars and for wits; others are the resort of dandies or of politicians, or again of professional newsmongers; and many others are temples of Venus. . . . they pass for being chocolate houses, and you are waited on by beautiful, neat, well-dressed, and amiable, but very dangerous nymphs.'[36]

Coffee houses quickly became important centres for the transmission of news and information, and customers chose the house that suited their particular needs. In Charles II's reign radical newsletters circulated in coffee houses, which were regarded as centres of anti-Stuart conspiracy. In the 1690s members of the rising financial world of insurance, stock and commodity dealing and shipping services used the coffee houses around the Royal Exchange for office space, contacts and information, and continued to do so well into the nineteenth century. Coffee houses acted as postal centres, lost property offices, business addresses, doctors' consulting rooms, matrimonial agencies, masonic lodges, auction rooms, gambling dens, and meeting places for criminals, politicians, scientists, clergymen and intellectuals. Each house reflected the character of its neighbourhood. In Pall Mall and St James's Street, there were aristocratic houses that specialized in politics and high risk gambling: the St James's Coffee House for Whigs, the Cocoa Tree for Tories, and White's Chocolate House for those who were ready to stake their fortunes on the throw of a dice. Around Covent Garden, coffee houses attracted actors, writers, 'wits' and prostitutes. From the 1670s until 1700 Will's Coffee House, the meeting place of John Dryden and his circle, had the highest reputation for witty conversation, though Ned Ward, when he visited it, 'found much company, and but little talk'. It was supplanted in the 1710s by Button's Coffee House (also in Russell Street), which had the patronage of Joseph Addison, Richard Steele, and Jonathan Swift. Presumably, the more learned discussions of Isaac Newton, Edmund Halley, Hans Sloane and other members of the Royal Society who met at the Grecian Coffee House in Devereux Court attracted fewer eavesdroppers. By the 1750s the Bedford Coffee House, in the Piazza, the meeting place of Henry Fielding, David Garrick, Samuel Foote, Oliver Goldsmith and other members of London's theatrical élite, was in the ascendant. Boswell preferred the more sober atmosphere of Child's, in St Paul's Churchyard, which had been mentioned in the first issue of Addison's *Spectator* in 1711: 'I think myself like him, and am serenely happy there. There is something to me very agreeable in having my time laid out in some method, such as every Saturday going to Child's.'[37]

Boswell arrived in London as the golden age of coffee-house society was coming to an end. Many of the more specialized houses were becoming private subscription clubs, in which coffee-drinking was overshadowed by the real business of the members. White's, the Cocoa Tree and the St James's all became private clubs in the 1740s, and the other famous gaming clubs of St James's Street, Almack's, Brooks' and Boodle's, were private from the start. The establishment of Lloyd's insurance society in 1771, and of the Stock Exchange in 1773, reduced the importance of Lloyd's and Jonathan's Coffee Houses, but the mercantile coffee houses around Exchange Alley were not quite finished. The Baltic Coffee House in Threadneedle Street did not become a members' club (and later the Baltic Exchange) until 1823, Garraway's survived as a coffee and auction house until 1872, and the Jerusalem Coffee House retained its East India Company business until 1889. Coffee-drinking became far more common when the coffee tax was cut in 1808 and 1825, and perhaps because of this the coffee shops of Victorian London, of which there were 1,000 or more, never achieved the intellectual or social distinction of Will's, Button's and the Cocoa Tree.[38]

HIGH SOCIETY

What people in London, as elsewhere, needed most of all were places to meet each other. For men (but not women) of the lower and middle classes there were alehouses, taverns and coffee houses, and for the gentry and aristocracy, whose prime purpose in coming to London was to meet people of their own sort, a wide range of institutions and rituals developed. First in importance were their own houses, where breakfast, tea and dinner parties, and the grander routs and levées, allowed the rich to meet without popular intrusions. Exclusive political, social and gaming clubs performed a similar function. For those wishing to meet a wider circle, and perhaps strike up new friendships, subscription balls in commercial assembly rooms offered useful opportunities. Masked balls, or masquerades, were popular with those who wanted to overstep the bounds of respectable etiquette, to see and not be seen. Until the 1740s there were regular masquerades at Heidegger's Haymarket Opera House, and in the 1760s Mrs Cornelys' assemblies in Carlisle House, Soho Square, offered the most fashionable opportunities for aristocratic misbehaviour. In 1772 Mrs Cornelys was ruined by scandal and by competition from two rival assembly rooms, Almack's, off St James's Street, and the Pantheon in Oxford Street. She returned to obscurity and died in the Fleet Debtors' Prison in 1797. Her victorious competitors, meanwhile, established themselves as places at which every member of London's social élite had to be seen. Perhaps, Dr Johnson conceded, there was not half a guinea's worth of pleasure in seeing the Pantheon, 'but there is half a guinea's worth of inferiority to other people in not having seen it'. The Pantheon, the 'winter Ranelagh', never recovered its exclusive appeal after a great fire in 1792, by which time the masquerade, with its casual approach to social and sexual barriers, had gone out of fashion. Good management enabled Almack's Assembly Rooms to keep their grip on the fickle world of high fashion until at least the 1830s. William Almack, founder also of Brooks' and Boodle's Clubs, was an entrepreneur whose success rested on exploiting exclusiveness as a marketing device. A group of six or seven titled 'lady patronesses' controlled ticket sales to Almack's, and admission became a clear sign of social success. The appeal of Almack's assemblies, like that of his West End clubs, depended as much on who was kept out as on who was let in.[39]

Of all the public meeting places available to London's leisured élite, none were more important to them than the pleasure gardens of Ranelagh and Vauxhall. Even before the Civil War, there had been fashionable gardens in which people of 'quality' could promenade, picnic and talk together. Spring Gardens, at Charing Cross, had been the 'usual rendezvous for ladies and gallants' from the 1590s to 1660, but thereafter it was supplanted by the New Spring Gardens, or Vauxhall Gardens, in Lambeth. The importance of Vauxhall Gardens in London's social life, and especially in the lives of respectable women, who were out of place in taverns, clubs and coffee houses, is plain from the frequency with which they are mentioned in contemporary letters, memoirs and novels. In 1667 Samuel Pepys found it 'mighty divertising' 'to hear the nightingales and other birds, and here fiddles and there a harp, and here a jew's trump, and here laughing, and there fine people walking' at 'Foxall'. In 1711 Jonathan Swift went to hear the nightingales, and in 1712 Addison's Sir Roger de Coverley viewed Vauxhall's fragrant and shady bowers as 'a kind of Mahometan paradise'. In their early days the Gardens were free and not very fashionable, but they were firmly established on the aristocratic social scene by Jonathan Tyers and his son, who between them managed and owned Vauxhall from 1728 to 1792. Tyers excluded the poor by charging a modest shilling entry fee, and built pavilions, music and supper rooms, and picturesque ruins and cascades. He lit the grounds with 1,000 glass lamps, and wooed high society from May to September with nightly musical entertainments. His famous ridottos, musical assemblies in the Italian style, at a guinea a ticket, were enormously popular with the élite, and the more socially mixed nature of the regular crowds does not seem to have alienated the well-off. Dr Johnson was friendly with the younger Tyers, and Boswell regarded Vauxhall, with its 'mixture of curious shew,– gay exhibition,– music, vocal and instrumental, not too refined for the general ear' as being 'peculiarly adapted to the taste of the English nation'.[40]

There was clearly a great demand for the easy-going but respectable social intercourse offered by commercial pleasure gardens, despite the fact that they did not offer the exclusiveness one might expect the well-off to demand. In 1742 a syndicate with a capital of £36,000 opened Ranelagh Gardens, next to the Chelsea Hospital. Within a few months Ranelagh's twice-weekly ridottos were attracting King George II and the highest aristocracy. Horace Walpole was an early enthusiast: 'There is a vast amphitheatre, finely gilt, painted and illuminated, into which everybody that loves eating, drinking, staring, or crowding, is admitted for twelve-pence', he told Sir Horace Mann in 1742. And in 1744: 'Ranelagh has totally beaten Vauxhall. Nobody goes anywhere else – everybody goes there.... The company is universal: there is from his Grace the Duke of Grafton down to children out of the Foundling Hospital – from my Lady Townshend to the kitten.' Ranelagh was more expensive to enter than Vauxhall, its crowds were less rowdy, its season was longer, and its great Rotunda, in which people of fashion promenaded while the leading musicians of the day (including the young Mozart in 1764) played, was one of the wonders of the town. Like Vauxhall's, its purpose was partly sexual. Edward Gibbon regarded Ranelagh as 'the most convenient place for courtships of every kind – the best market we have in England'. Perhaps this helps explain the decline of pleasure gardens when high society became more sexually and socially fastidious. Until the end of the century Ranelagh held its popularity, attracting great crowds by road and river with firework displays, masquerades and balloon ascents. Then, in 1803, the Rotunda was closed and in 1805 the vast building, almost the size of the Albert Hall, was demolished. Vauxhall lasted until 1859, though its last decades were marked by a succession of temporary closures.

There were about sixty less fashionable pleasure gardens and tea gardens all around eighteenth-century London, especially in Chelsea, Lambeth, Clerkenwell and Islington. A few, including Marylebone Gardens (west of Upper Wimpole Street) and Cuper's Gardens (near the present

National Theatre), approached Ranelagh and Vauxhall in their musical entertainments and aristocratic appeal. Most relied upon middling and working families, who would walk to the edge of town, especially on a Sunday, for fresh air, tea, beer, swimming, fishing, courting, bowling and cheap entertainment. Some prospered on the strength of the apparently curative effects of their spring waters. Several of these, including Finch's Grotto Gardens, the Restoration Spring Gardens and Lambeth Wells, were in or near St George's Fields in Lambeth, but most were along the banks of the Fleet and the New rivers in the northern fields of Tottenham Court, Pancras, Islington, and White Conduit, within easy reach of the city crowds, where the iron-rich water tasted convincingly medicinal. Within the area enclosed by the New Road there were the Adam and Eve Tea Garden, Bowling Green House, Bagnigge Wells, Islington Spa, London Spa, Mulberry Gardens and Sadler's Wells, and beyond the New Road were Hampstead Wells, Kilburn Wells, Pancras Wells, White Conduit House and Highbury Barn. Some of these failed or were closed down when their clientele became too disreputable, some were overtaken by suburban development, and others survived as places of popular entertainment into the Victorian era. This was not, of course, a suburban paradise. Brick kilns, night-soil pits and dust heaps blemished the landscape, and citizens had vagrants, footpads and hogs for company on their Sunday walks along the Fleet. For true rusticity, Londoners had to follow the Fleet beyond Pancras Wells and the popular resort of Kentish Town up to its source in the hills of Hampstead and Highgate. But this was a long climb, and the merchants, professionals, writers and artists who had retreated to Hampstead were not often bothered by London's rougher crowds.[41]

The most important gardens of all still survive. St James's Park was transformed from a marshy field to a royal deer chase by Henry VIII, and into a formal garden for the Court by James I. Charles II had the Park extended and landscaped, and allowed the public into most of it. By the eighteenth century the right of public access was too well entrenched to be withdrawn, and on Sundays the Park was crowded. On summer evenings and winter afternoons the Mall, on the northern edge of the Park, was the favourite promenade of well-dressed Londoners, and at night, when the gates were locked, the grounds were patrolled by prostitutes and (as we learn from Boswell) their customers. Green Park was smaller and less fashionable, but Hyde Park, on the edge of the Hanoverian West End, was an important centre of aristocratic courtship, display and social mixing, as well as popular recreation. It was seized as a royal hunting ground by Henry VIII, opened to the public by Charles I, sold for £17,000 by

Parliament in 1652, and restored to royal ownership and free public use in 1660. Within the Park there was the Ring, a fenced area encircled by two concentric carriage tracks, around which families of 'quality', from Charles II downwards, paraded in their carriages in the early evening, half in one direction, half in the other. The Ring ceased to be London's promenade in the 1730s, when the rich moved their carriages to Rotten Row (the King's Road, or Route du Roi), the well-lit road connecting Hyde Park with Kensington Gardens. Although precise arrangements changed, Hyde Park remained a centre of London's fashionable promenade, the equivalent of the Champs-Elysées or Madrid's Pasea del Prado, until fairly recent times. In 1898, Baedeker's *Guide* described the 'unbroken files of elegant equipages and high-bred horses in handsome trappings, moving continually to and fro, presided over by sleek coachmen and powdered lacqueys', to be seen in South Carriage Drive between 5 and 7 o'clock each evening.[42]

So Londoners could be entertained by the finest musicians – Handel, Mozart, Haydn – or gawp at freaks, lunatics and tormented animals. They could watch David Garrick and Sarah Siddons at Drury Lane, or corpses swinging on the Tyburn gallows. From the low delights of the cockpit and the brothel to the higher pleasures of the Royal Academy and the British Museum there was in London, as Dr Johnson told Boswell, 'all that life can afford'.

Chapter 12

Making a Living

LONDON'S WEALTH came from many sources, but its life-blood was trade, especially overseas trade. As far as can be judged from the import and export statistics, London's trading pre-eminence within England was as great in 1700 as it had been a century earlier. In the early seventeenth century, London handled around 70 per cent (by value) of English foreign trade, and in 1700 its share was around 76 per cent, with an even bigger share of imports and re-exported colonial goods.[1] Over the following century (mainly after 1740) London's predominance slowly diminished, as the west coast ports, especially Whitehaven and Liverpool, took a larger share of the booming Atlantic trade, and exports of northern industrial goods, mainly cotton, became more important. But in 1770 London still handled almost 69 per cent of England's overseas trade, whose value had risen by around 130 per cent over the period. Its share in 1790 had fallen to about 63 per cent, but the value of London's overseas trade was £23 million, compared to £9.9 million in 1700.[2] London's enormous consumption of imported food and raw materials, its monopoly of the rich East India trade, its convenient position for the re-export of colonial goods to Europe and at the hub of England's internal distribution system, and its unrivalled credit, banking, exchange and insurance services for merchants all guaranteed it a strong position, whatever happened to patterns of world trade.

THE COMMODITIES OF TRADE

London merchants dominated English trade with every part of the world, except Ireland, where merchants found the short crossing to the western ports easier and safer, especially in wartime. Throughout the period 1700–70 the Port of London handled over 80 per cent of England's trade with the Mediterranean and its imports from western Europe, and about three-quarters of colonial trade. Its share of the Baltic trade and west

European imports was a little less, but it was usually over 65 per cent until the 1740s, and about 60 per cent thereafter.[3]

Many of the goods passing through the Port of London in 1700 would have been familiar to a medieval merchant. Londoners handled two-thirds of England's woollen exports, and these, at £2 million, were almost 73 per cent of the value of London's home-produced export trade. These woollens were no longer the unfinished broadcloths of old, but finished cloths, either heavy broadcloths for northern Europe and Turkey or thinner and narrower says, serges, stuffs and perpetuannas for the south. There had been significant diversification since 1640, when woollens had been almost 90 per cent of London exports: by 1700 there were substantial exports of grain, silk, metalwares and other manufactures, foodstuffs, lead and tin. Europe and the Mediterranean were still London's (and England's) main export markets. About half of London's imports (by value) were traditional goods from familiar places: north European linen, flax, hemp, timber and iron, and Mediterranean silk (raw, thrown and woven), wine, brandy, fruit and oil. What had changed the picture was the rapid growth since 1660 of colonial trade with the North American and West Indian plantations, which sent molasses and sugar (London's second most valuable import in 1700, after linen), tobacco and dyes, and the East India Company's imports of calico, silk and pepper. London's exports to the colonies were mainly cloth and manufactures.[4]

In the 1640s the Dutch had taken over much of the colonial trade, but the Navigation Acts of 1651 and 1660 and the Staple Act of 1663, along with the English capture of New Amsterdam (New York) excluded them, and gave British merchants a near monopoly of commerce with British territories in the West Indies and North America. By the terms of these Acts Dutch ships and other third parties were excluded from England's import trade with the Baltic and Mediterranean, all major colonial exports (sugar, tobacco, dyestuffs and cotton) had to go in English or colonial ships to English ports, and European exports to English colonies had to go via England. Thanks partly to the enforcement of this legislation, over a third of London's exports in the early eighteenth century were re-exports of colonial and Asian goods, and the long-standing dependence of London merchants on Dutch middlemen and ports was broken. The value of London's imports, exports and re-exports doubled between the 1660s and 1700.[5]

After the rapid increase of London's trade, especially with America, Turkey, the West Indies and Norway, between 1660 and 1689, the next sixty years were a time of slower growth. Three decades of war held back commercial growth, especially in the important Anglo-French trade, but there were other factors, too. French West Indian competition ousted English sugar from European markets, the Levant trade declined, Glasgow took the tobacco trade, Liverpool and Bristol captured much of the slave trade when the Royal Africa Company lost its monopoly in 1698, Indian calico was hindered by European protective legislation and linen imports were static. The value of London's trade rose by only around 43 per cent between 1700 and 1750. New growth came after the peace of 1748, with the development of new re-export trades in Carolina rice, China tea and West Indies coffee, and the boom in American and Indian demand for English manufactures. Above all, imports of West Indies sugar, to sweeten the tea and coffee, almost doubled in volume and value between 1740 and 1770, making it by far the most significant of London's imports.

TRADING CLUBS AND COMPANIES

The regulated companies, the privileged associations of independent and competing merchants that had helped maintain London's commercial supremacy before 1640, were in decline by 1700. The dangerous trading conditions that had justified their existence were passing, and they no longer enjoyed the government's protection when vigorous independent merchants challenged their monopolies. The enfeebled Merchant Adventurers lost their last privileges in 1689 and the Eastland Company faded away after losing its Baltic monopoly in 1673. The Levant Company did rather better, although its apparent monopoly of the Ottoman trade was often attacked. By the time Parliament forced the Company to open its membership to all comers in 1753 its great days were over. Apart from a little fruit, coffee, cotton and drugs, the Ottoman Empire had hardly anything to offer the English market but silk, and wanted nothing in return but broadcloth. As supplies of better French broadcloth and cheaper Bengal and Chinese silk grew in the early eighteenth century, England's Levant trade withered. Levant Company silk imports halved between 1720 and 1760, and its broadcloth exports fell by about 80 per cent. Until the 1760s, the dwindling group of active Levant merchants (about 150 in 1675, and forty-two in 1731) were still a significant part of London's mercantile élite. They were mostly rich men, not so much because the trade was unusually lucrative, but because the long delay between investment and return excluded those without capital of £10,000 or so. Out of sixty-one Levant merchants in London in 1740, nineteen were also directors of the Bank of

England, the South Sea Company, or one of the two biggest insurance companies.[6]

Joint stock companies (companies which sold shares to anyone who wished to invest in their enterprises) had mixed fortunes. The oldest of them, the Muscovy Company, managed to survive the loss of its special privileges (and lasted into this century), and the Hudson's Bay Company (1670) pursued its dangerous trade in Canadian furs without English competition until 1763, but the Royal Africa Company, created in 1671, faded after losing its monopoly of the slave trade in 1698. The strongest of the old joint stock companies was the East India Company, which had a monopoly on English trade with India and the Far East. By the 1680s the Company was a political and territorial power in India, as well as a commercial one, and a major financial and political force in the City, too. In 1698, after the flight of James II, the Company's enemies took advantage of its closeness to the fallen King to create a New East India Company. Ten years later the two companies amalgamated as the United East India Company to face the rising challenge of the French Company, and eventually achieved commercial and political dominance in India in the Seven Years' War (1756–63) and the following decades. The Company's trade, mostly imports of pepper, China tea, drugs, spices, saltpetre, silks and calicoes, all came through London, and made up around 15 per cent of the value of the capital's import trade in 1700. Although these were light, high-value commodities, East India Company ships, which had to be able to defend themselves, were the largest ships in the English merchant fleet. The cargo of a fully laden East Indiaman could be worth a fortune, though few were as valuable as that of the *Berkeley Castle*, which sailed from Madras in 1681 with a load worth £80,000.[7]

Although London lost its pre-eminence as a slave trading port to Liverpool, dealing in slaves and in the products of slave labour remained one of the chief sources of wealth for London's mercantile élite. The credit with which West Indies planters bought their slaves came from London banking houses, including Barclays and Barings, and from the Bank of England itself. Many Bank of England directors, deputy governors and governors had slave and sugar interests, and together with the London-based plantation owners and the West Indies merchants and political agents they constituted a formidable force in London and national politics. They had no chartered company to represent their interests, but at first met informally in the Jamaica Coffee House in St Michael's Alley, near the Royal Exchange. A succession of increasingly formal organizations was set up to regulate and defend the trade: a Planters' Club in the 1740s, the

Society of West India Merchants in the 1760s, and the West India Committee in the 1780s. Through these associations and a strong parliamentary group the West India interest was able to exert remarkable influence over British commercial and foreign policy, taking a leading part in the campaign to force Walpole into a Spanish war in 1739, helping to shape the Peace of Paris in 1763, and forcing the City to accept the construction of the West India Docks in the 1790s. William Beckford, the organizer of the Elder Pitt's support in the City in the 1760s, was the greatest Jamaica sugar-planter. But the West India interest's last great battle, to save the slave trade from abolition, ended in defeat in 1807.[8]

Although the upper ranks of City society contained a fair number of manufacturers, wholesalers, financiers and rich professionals, overseas merchants probably outnumbered any other wealthy group. Peter Earle's analysis of a sample of 295 well-off citizens who died between 1665 and 1720 identified sixty-one who left a fortune of over £5,000. Of these, thirty-one were overseas merchants, while only one was a banker, ten were manufacturers, eight were haberdashers or drapers, and eleven were traders in other goods.[9] No firm distinction can be drawn between trade and finance, of course. Leading merchants were often directors of one or more of London's major monied companies, and such giants as Sir Gilbert Heathcote (Lord Mayor, 1710–11), Sir Theodore Janssen and Sir Peter Delmé had very big feet in both worlds. The most powerful trading company, the East India Company, was also a great finance house, and the South Sea Company, despite its mercantile title, was almost entirely concerned with finance after 1720.

A CROWDED RIVER

Light and valuable cargoes, particularly silk (between £2,000 and £4,000 a ton in 1754) and other cloth, offered the greatest profits, but heavy and bulky cargoes contributed more to the work of the river and the port. East India imports in 1752–4 needed only about 8,000 tons of shipping a year, compared to North America's 88,000 tons (for pitch, tar, tobacco, rice and timber), 47,000 tons for West Indies sugar, and 263,000 tons for Norwegian wood. Of the 3,500 barges and small craft that cluttered the Thames in the 1790s, 1,700 were employed in the coal and timber trades, and the coastal coal trade to London, which increased from around 400,000 tons in 1700 to almost a million tons by 1800, outweighed all London's import trade. It was the growth of spruce and fir imports from Norway and the Baltic, iron from Sweden, sugar and tobacco from the colonies, and, above all, coal from Newcastle and Sunderland, that filled the Thames with ships and its quays and docks with warehousemen, dockers, watermen, labourers, porters, packers, seamen, shipbuilders, victuallers, repairers, coal-heavers and lightermen. In Ralph Davis's estimation, these port and river trades employed a quarter of London's workforce in the eighteenth century.[10]

As the volume of trade grew, especially in the second half of the century, overcrowding on the Thames became an increasingly serious problem, creating costly delays and heavy losses from pilferage, rats and bad weather. Some congestion was inevitable, especially when the summer fleets from the West Indies coincided with the coal fleets and ships bringing corn and provisions to the capital, but it was made immeasurably worse by the rule obliging ships with cargoes on which import duty was charged to unload on a 500-yard stretch of 'legal quays' between London Bridge and the Tower. The seventeen legal quays established by Elizabeth in 1558 were increased to twenty in 1665, and there were 1,200 yards of 'sufferance wharves' on the south bank and east of the Tower for lightly taxed cargoes. But these facilities were inadequate for a port a third of London's size, and the queue of ships waiting to unload stretched past Wapping and Shadwell to Limehouse Reach, almost blocking the main channel. Most ships were moored in midstream and had to be unloaded and loaded by lighters, a cumbersome process which added to the congestion. To Defoe in the 1720s, the sight of 2,000 seagoing vessels between London Bridge and Limehouse was a source of pride and pleasure, but not to the merchants whose goods were waiting to be unloaded. There were complaints about these delays throughout the eighteenth century, and there was a commission in 1765, but the City Corporation, port officials, watermen and the owners of the legal quays resisted any change until the 1790s, when they were at last forced to give way.

In 1793 the West Indies merchants, whose bulky and valuable cargoes of sugar, rum, coffee and dye-woods suffered most from delays and losses, threatened to take their trade elsewhere unless something was done to ease the overcrowding. In alliance with City insurance companies, they proposed an obvious solution, the creation of wet docks in the low-lying river bends east of the Tower. There were already two wet docks, the Howland Dock (or Greenland Dock), built in 1700 in Limehouse Reach, and the East India Company's even older Blackwall Dock, near the river Lea, but these were shipyards, not licensed for unloading dutiable cargo. What the West Indies and other merchants wanted were secure walled docks, large enough to accommodate their ships and cargoes in the peak summer season, and as close to the City as possible. Between 1796 and 1799 their battle with the City Corporation was fought out in a House of Commons Committee, whose decisions helped to ensure London's future as a great port, and to create the nineteenth-century East End. In the ten years following the Committee's last report in 1799 there was a dock-building boom, costing over £7 million, which satisfied the pent-up needs of the previous century and equipped London to deal with the demands of the century ahead.

The first docks to be sanctioned and built (between 1800 and 1802) were the 54-acre West India Docks on the marshy and almost uninhabited bend in the river known as the Isle of Dogs, about 2 miles east of the Tower. These set the pattern for the docks that followed. The West India Docks were a private venture, financed by the West India Dock Company, whose shareholders hoped for (and received) handsome dividends from the docks' twenty-one-year monopoly of the West Indies' import and export trade. The two docks (one for imports, one for exports) were surrounded by huge bonded warehouses, mostly built by George Gilt and the canal engineer William Jessop. The whole 240-acre area was enclosed within high walls and dock gates, and policed by the Company's own guards, to eliminate the pilfering and theft that the magistrate Patrick Colquhoun had publicized (and no doubt exaggerated) in 1797. The more westerly site originally favoured by the West Indies merchants, Wapping, was allocated to the dock and bonded warehouses of the London Dock Company, which was given a twenty-one-year monopoly on all cargoes of rice, wine, tobacco and brandy from Europe and North America. The London Dock (1800–1805) was half the size of the West India Dock, but cost three times as much (over £3 million), because the land between the Ratcliff Highway and the Thames was inhabited, and heavy compensation had to be paid. The docks, walls, wine vaults and warehouses (demolished in the 1970s) were the work of Daniel Alexander (who later built Dartmoor and Maidstone Prisons) and John Rennie, later the architect of London, Waterloo and Southwark Bridges. Wapping had its own police office, the headquarters of the efficient Thames police force created by Colquhoun.[11]

The East India Company had no urgent need for new docks and warehouses. Its trade was not bulky, and it already had its Blackwall Dock, and its magnificent (and still surviving) warehouses in Cutler Street, near Hounsditch. But they opened their own walled and policed docks at Blackwall in 1806, and joined the West India Dock Company in financing the privately built Commercial Road, which linked both dock systems with the companies' warehouses and sugar refineries in Whitechapel. The bulkiest of all London's import trades, the Baltic, Canadian and Norwegian timber trade, was accommodated in a sprawling system of interconnecting docks on the south side of the Thames in the Rotherhithe bend. The first of these, the Grand Surrey Basin, opened in 1807, and the Greenland Dock (the old Howland Dock) and the East Country Dock followed a little later. Two major companies, the Grand Surrey and the Commercial Dock Companies, competed in this south bank dock system until their amalgamation in 1864.[12]

The Chain of Supply

International merchants were at the top of London's commercial world, but the system which they dominated depended upon the work of a far greater number of lesser traders, warehousemen, wholesalers, retailers, refiners, processors, drovers, travelling salesmen, factors, middlemen and dealers of all sorts. For example, the great cargoes of sugar that arrived in London each summer were handled by sugar factors, who earned their commission from the planters or merchants by selling the sugar to wholesale or retail grocers, or to sugar bakers, who refined it before selling it on to grocers. A smaller proportion might be sold to speculators (hoping that war, harvest failure or shipwreck would raise prices) or to merchants who re-exported sugar to Ireland.[13] The very costly raw silk brought back by the Levant Company from Turkey (where it had been bartered for English broadcloths) passed to silk dealers who employed women to spin it into yarn, which they sold to London and provincial weavers. Imported linen and calico was sold to drapers, who perhaps had it printed or finished before selling it to London or provincial retailers or travelling salesmen, and imported tobacco went to wholesalers, who passed it on to retail tobacconists such as Fribourg and Treyer, whose shop in the Haymarket survived until 1981.

Exporters, too, were at the end of a long and sophisticated distribution chain. Defoe, in his account of the Leeds market in the 1720s, explained how London dealers bought Yorkshire cloth to sell it to London factors and warehouse-keepers, who sold it to wholesalers and shopkeepers, or to merchants in the American, Levant or Baltic trade. Levant merchants needed Gloucestershire or Yorkshire broadcloth, known in the Levant as *londra* and *mezzo-londrine*, to exchange for Persian and Syrian silk in Aleppo. They bought it not from the clothiers themselves, but from a few rich and powerful Blackwell Hall factors, who had control, at least in the first half of the eighteenth century, of the export trade in woollen cloth, easily London's most valuable export. A lazy Levant trader could leave the whole of his business in the hands of factors. Blackwell Hall factors would provide the cloth, and have it dyed, finished, packed and baled ready for shipping to Aleppo, Stamboul or Smyrna in ships provided (until 1744) by the Levant Company. Then it was up to the factor resident in Turkey, usually a young Englishman trying to make enough money to return to London and enter the Levant trade on his own account, to strike the best bargain and ship the silk back to London.[14] Almost every other commodity, whether for export or domestic consumption, went through a similar chain on its way from the producer to the consumer. Cargoes of coal were sold to London brokers, or 'crimps', who sold it to industrial users or retailers and hawkers. London corn factors bought corn direct from farmers, and resold it in London to speculators, large bakers and mealmen, millers and maltsters. London's supply of cheese, which was available in growing variety in the eighteenth century, was controlled by a club of about twenty-five wholesalers, whose factors bought almost all the produce of Cheshire (by far the largest English supplier), and who monopolized the transport routes from Chester, Liverpool and Ipswich, forcing London's 300 or so lesser cheesemongers to submit to their control and accept their prices.[15]

THE ARTS OF RETAILING

When imported or home-produced goods finally reached the London consumer, they did so through the long-established combination of street markets, peddlars, hawkers, and retail shops. There is much talk of a 'consumer revolution' in eighteenth-century England[16] but in London conspicuous consumption and impulse buying were long-established, and the arts of enticement and advertising were at least as old as the cries of medieval street traders. The permanent shop, rain-proof and relatively secure, usually in the front room of a merchant or craftsman's house, had been a familiar feature of the urban scene since the Middle Ages. Derek Keene's survey of Cheapside counted around 400 tiny shops in that busy street in 1300, and identified a trend towards fewer and larger shops over the next 200 years. In Elizabeth's reign goldsmiths and silk mercers mon-opolized Cheapside, but by the 1630s they had been joined by an assortment of stationers, girdlers, milliners and druggists.[17] Beyond Cheapside, there were thriving new shopping centres in the Royal Exchange, and in the Earl of Salisbury's retailing enterprise in the Strand, the New Exchange.

After the Restoration the craftsman–shopkeeper still survived, especially in the selling of guns, clocks, spectacles, and other costly products, but the simple retailer, selling imported or locally made goods, was the more common figure. Retailers were well aware, as they always had been, that by inducement and encouragement customers could be persuaded to spend more than they otherwise would have done. Shopkeepers in Cheapside, it was said, did more business if their wives were handsome, and in the New Exchange, according to Ned Ward, the 'London Spy' of the 1690s, young men were enticed into buying gloves and trinkets by the charms of the women who served in the shops. It was common for widows or daughters to inherit the business of a shopkeeper who died without sons, and in the Strand in 1750 nearly 7 per cent of shops were run by women.

The most prominent shop advertisements were the heavy wooden or copper shop signs, or elaborate painted models representing the merchandise on offer, which swung menacingly over pedestrians' heads until they were removed by order of the City authorities in 1762. During the eighteenth century it became common for shopkeepers to issue handbills or trade cards to publicize their services, and surviving collections of these bills illustrate the growing range of goods available to the London shopper. Every imaginable product, from such ancient luxuries as asses' milk and fireworks to the newer delights of milk chocolates, thief-proof coffins and sprung rumps (or bustles) could be found in London shops. Newspaper advertising was less commonly used in the early eighteenth century. This was certainly a great age of advertising and 'puffing', and the Press depended heavily on advertising revenue, but most of this came from private announcements, and advertisements for books, quack medicines, auctions and plays. After around 1750 retailers made more use of the Press, and furniture, tablewares and ready-made clothes joined Ching's Patent Worm Lozenges and Dr Forthergill's Female Pills in the newspaper columns.[18]

The greatest changes in retailing in the eighteenth century were in shop design and display, in the number and wealth of customers, and in the range of goods on offer. Daniel Defoe complained about the trend towards costly shop fitments and displays in 1713:

> It is a modern custom and wholly unknown to our ancestors to have tradesmen lay out two-thirds of their fortune in fitting up their shops. By fitting them up, I do not mean furnishing their shops with wares

and goods to sell; but in painting and gilding, fine shelves, shutters, boxes, glass doors, sashes and the like, in which, they tell us now, ''tis a small matter to lay out two or three hundred pounds'.[19]

Although the secret of plate-glass manufacture was introduced into England in the 1770s, most shopkeepers still used small panes of crown glass (or bottle glass), which obscured the view of the goods within. The fine shop windows in Oxford Street so admired by Sophie de la Roche, a German visitor to London in 1786, were made up of many small panes, not large sheets: 'Behind the great glass windows absolutely everything one can think of is neatly, attractively displayed, in such abundance of choice as to make one greedy. . . . There is a cunning device for showing women's materials. They hang down in folds behind the fine, high windows so that the effect of this or that material, as it would be in a woman's dress, can be studied.' Such advanced techniques might be expected of drapers, who were in the vanguard of the consumer revolution, but even fruiterers piled their 'pineapples, figs, grapes, oranges and all manner of fruits' in showy pyramids behind 'handsome glass windows'.[20] Even the best shops were small, with frontages of about 15 feet. The hatter James Lock (1765), and the wine merchant Berry Brothers and Rudd, both in St James's Street, and the rather later shops in Goodwin's Court (between St Martin's Lane and Bedfordbury) give an impression of what Georgian shops looked like.

Oxford Street's supremacy as a shopping street had not yet arrived in the 1780s, despite Sophie's enthusiasm. The capital's smartest and busiest retailing streets were still in the City and the older western suburbs. The walk from Charing Cross to Whitechapel, Dr Johnson told Oliver Goldsmith in 1773, would take you 'through, I suppose, the greatest series of shops in the world'. Pierre Grosley, in 1765, was most impressed by Cheapside, Fleet Street and the Strand, where the shops were 'brilliant and gay, as well on account of the things sold in them, as the exact order in which they are kept; so they make a most splendid show, greatly superior to anything of the kind in Paris'. For elegance and 'grand company', he said, nothing could beat the shops in the passages off Fleet Street and the Strand, where the 'stuffs exposed to sale, fine furniture and things of taste, or the girls belonging to them, would be motives sufficient to determine those that walk, to make that their way in preference to any other'.[21] Walking further west, the affluent mid-century shopper would find fashionable retailers all along Charing Cross, Pall Mall, St James's Street and the Haymarket, where hay was still sold in an open market until 1830, but more mundane dealers in Piccadilly and Swallow Street. Butchers, greengrocers and other food-sellers could be found in the off-street buildings of Hungerford, St James's, Oxford, Bloomsbury and Covent Garden Markets.

CONSPICUOUS CONSUMPTION

As a retail market, London played a vital part in the transformation of English manufacturing that began in the later eighteenth century. In 1765 Josiah Wedgwood decided to open a London showroom to win the aristocratic London market and stimulate sales of his high-quality Staffordshire pottery. He first opened a shop in Grosvenor Square, and then another in Great Newport Street, Soho, and exhibition rooms in nearby Greek Street. Pall Mall, which Wedgwood rejected as 'too accessible to the common Folk', was chosen by Matthew Boulton as a base from which to capture the vital London market for his Birmingham wares: buttons, buckles, saucepans, candlesticks, cruets, snuff-boxes and so on. The stimulus to industrial entrepreneurship came from many sources, and there were rich overseas and provincial markets too, but London's huge and consumerist population, easily reached by road, canal or coastal ship, provided an incentive to industrialization possessed by no other European country in the late eighteenth century.[22]

For some commodities, particularly food, coal and beer, London's sheer size acted as a powerful stimulant to new production techniques: agricultural enclosure and new crop rotations, steam pumps and railways in the Tyneside mines, mass-produced London porter. But London's special appeal to producers lay in its large population of rich and extravagant consumers, the 'legislators of taste', many of whom had come to the capital specifically to dress themselves, their wives and even their servants in the latest fashions, and to equip their country houses with the best cutlery, china and furnishings. Moreover, the consumerism of the well-to-do infected the rest of London society. In London, Defoe claimed in the 1720s, 'the poorest citizens live like the rich, the rich like the gentry, the gentry like the nobility, and the nobility strive to outshine one another'. Servants mimicked the fashions of their employers, spreading them down the social scale, and the aristocratic taste for new products – tea, cotton, metalwares, pottery, furniture, handbags, cutlery – helped to launch them into the London and provincial markets, both of which took their lead from the West End. Even overseas markets, especially in America, were influenced by London. Thus social emulation, stimulated by the 'flourishing pride' of Londoners, helped to turn a preference for leisure into a preference for goods, drove people of all classes (except the poorest) into satisfying their desires rather than their needs, and helped create the consumer demand which was, in Harold Perkin's words, 'the ultimate economic key to the Industrial Revolution'.[23] This is why Wedgwood, the supreme entrepreneur, made such efforts to win the West End, and why Boulton held his great London sales at Easter, 'to ensure that those up for the season (and their retinue of servants) carried back to the provinces exciting news of the new fashions'.[24]

No goods were more important in fashionable London retailing than textiles and clothing, and none were of greater significance to the industrializing north. The accelerating pace of change in London fashions, with new colours and cuts every season, made it imperative for the great industrial cotton spinners to have reliable and sharp-eyed agents in the capital. The letters sent to Samuel Oldknow, the great Stockport cotton producer, by his London agent illustrate the link between London fashions and the industrial revolution in Lancashire: 'We want as many spotted muslins as you can make, the finer the better.... You must give a look to invention – industry you have in abundance. We expect to hear from you as often as possible and as the Sun shines let us make Hay.' And later on: 'The Buff stripes are liked best but still do not pursue it – turn the loom to something else. They are not fine enough for people of fashion, for which they are only calculated for.... Try your skill at Table Linen.... Arkwright must lower his Twist and he must spin finer; tell him the reputation of our Country against Scotland is at stake.'[25] In 1786 almost the entire output of Oldknow's Stockport and Marple cotton mills was handled by two London warehousemen, and without their skills, and the retailing success of the London stores that sold the finished product to London customers, the efforts of the Cheshire spinners might have been wasted.[26]

LONDON AND THE INDUSTRIAL REVOLUTION

While the economies of Lancashire, Derbyshire and the West Riding were beginning to be transformed by industrialization at the end of the eighteenth century, London, along with many other old towns (York, Exeter, Norwich, Bristol, and so on), seems to have been by-passed by industrial change. No cotton mills, no ironworks, no smoking factory chimneys, disturbed its pattern of traditional workshop and craft industries in the decades around 1800. Land and labour were not cheap in London, there was not much water-power, and there were no local sources of coal and iron, the essential industrial raw materials. Although the power of the livery companies was fading rapidly in the eighteenth century, and had never been strong in the suburbs, manufacturers did not have the complete freedom of action that they enjoyed in such unchartered towns as Manchester and Birmingham.

The controversy over London's contribution to England's economic growth is both a contemporary and a modern one. Many contemporaries regarded London as a parasite, a devourer of England's wealth and people, a centre of luxury and ostentation, a swollen head or spleen sucking strength from an enfeebled body. In 1725 Defoe answered this common complaint by arguing that 'all collected bodies of people are a particular assistance to trade: and, therefore, to have one great and capital city in a kingdom, is of much greater advantage to it than if the same number of people dwelt in several places'. 'As every part of the kingdom sends up hither the best of her produce, so they carry back a return of wealth; the money flows from the city to the remotest parts, and furnishes them again to increase that produce, to improve the lands, pay rent to their landlords, taxes to their governors, and supply their families with necessaries; and this is Trade.' If it were not for London, he said, 'the land must lie waste and uncultivated, the cattle run wild'. 'London circulates all, exports all, and at last pays for all'.[27] Fifty years later, Adam Smith made much the same point in Book Three of the The Wealth of Nations.

Modern historians are divided, too. To Fernand Braudel, London, like Paris, was 'a luxury that others had to pay for', 'an example of deep-seated disequilibrium, asymmetrical growth, and irrational and unproductive investment on a nation-wide scale'. London and other capital cities 'would be present at the forthcoming industrial revolution in the role of spectators'.[28] Others, particularly E. A. Wrigley and Martin Daunton, have pointed out that without spectators the show would not be performed, and without customers industrialization would not have taken place. Even London's destruction of human life, Wrigley argues, helped reduce England's population growth to a rate which favoured industrial expansion. In a conservative and underproductive economy a centre of luxury and consumption might be a source of poverty and hunger, but in an adaptable and inventive society, where producers were able to react creatively to growing demand, London's size and wealth helped to stimulate economic modernization.[29] London's own influence since the sixteenth century, as a consumer, a manufacturer, and a centre of trade, finance and fashion, had helped to create a commercialized and market-oriented nation in which industrialization was more likely to occur.

London had far more to do with the Lancashire cotton industry than might appear to be the case. It was the port of entry for most raw cotton imports until about 1795, and its merchants dominated the market in cotton cloth up to 1815. London bills of exchange were the main means of payment for Lancashire cotton dealers, and London merchant banks were a major source of credit for northern industrialists and exporters, even after the centre of the cotton trade had moved to Manchester. London's contribution to the modernization of cotton technology was substantial, too. In the words of S. D. Chapman, whose arguments are used here, London was 'a nursery for techniques brought from the Continent or from India until they were ready for transplanting to the provinces, where there was less competition for land, labour and capital'.[30] Dutch looms, fustian and calico printing and the stocking knitting frame were all adopted by seventeenth-century London manufacturers before they spread to the north, and the water-powered Derby silk-throwing mill, which became the prototype for the early Lancashire cotton mills, was established by two London silk merchants, Thomas and John Lombe, in 1719. The importance of London wholesalers and capitalists to the hosiery firms of Nottingham and Derbyshire was even greater. Most firms had London bases, and some were effectively run from Wood Street, the centre of the City's textile warehousing.[31]

Only the narrowest definition of the Industrial Revolution, focusing entirely on steam power and factory production, could exclude London's manufacturers from a part in it, and that definition would exclude other workshop towns, notably Birmingham and Sheffield, too. The idea that London was a non-participant in Britain's economic growth, or that it was a pre-industrial backwater left behind by the modernization of the northern towns, rests on a false picture of what was happening to the British economy between, say, 1780 and 1850. London was England's – and the western world's – greatest manufacturing town in the eighteenth and nineteenth centuries, and its reliance on skill, the division of labour, muscle-power, and cheap sweated work was typical of the pattern of most British industries, except cotton-spinning, as late as 1850.[32]

WEAVING AND STITCHING

London's outstanding characteristic as a manufacturing centre was the enormous variety of crafts and trades it contained. A few major industries, particularly textiles and clothing, building, metalwares and leather, were very large employers, with perhaps 100,000 workers between them in the 1720s, but the bulk of the labour force worked in smaller crafts. Robert Campbell's *London Tradesman*, published in 1747, listed over 200 distinct manufacturing occupations, though many of these were subdivisions of larger trades. London manufacturers produced a wide range of goods, mostly (but not exclusively) for the local market. They were leading national producers of paint, varnish, printer's ink and glue; of snuff, bread, beer, spirits and vinegar; of ships, sails and rope; of carriages, furniture and musical instruments; of silk, printed calico, clothes, stays, stockings, hats, shoes and leather goods; of watches, jewellery, precious and base metal-wares, and surgical, optical and nautical instruments; and of tools, swords, cutlery, guns and heavy artillery. In 1700, twenty-four of England's ninety or so glass-houses were in London (mostly in Whitechapel and on the south bank) and almost a third of England's candles were London-made. About two-thirds of Britain's sugar refineries were in London, as well as the majority of its printers and publishers and its largest concentration of soap-makers and tobacco refiners.[33]

The various branches of the clothing and textile trades, taken together, were probably London's biggest manufacturing employer in the eighteenth century. Every type of cloth was produced in London, though not always on a very large scale. There were spinners and weavers of woollens and worsteds, linen weavers, lace-makers, tassel-makers, fancy embroiderers, livery lace weavers, ribbon and tape weavers, and stocking weavers. Many of these, especially the ribbon and stocking weavers, were seeing their wages depressed by cheap provincial competition, and stocking manufacture was migrating to Nottingham and Leicester. London was also gradually losing its dominance of the calico-printing industry, which employed around 700 workers in 1721. The greatest London textile industry by far was the Spitalfields and East London silk industry, which involved (in Peter Earle's estimation) up to 40,000 or 50,000 masters, throwsters (spinners), weavers, knitters and dyers, many of them Huguenots, in the early eighteenth century.[34] There had been silk ribbon weavers in London for centuries, but Huguenot settlement in Spitalfields after 1685 expanded the industry, especially in the weaving of wider cloths, and made London one of the greatest silk-weaving centres of Europe.

The silk industry was subject to extreme fluctuations in demand and raw material supply, and was vulnerable to provincial and overseas competition. Imports of Indian calico were seen as a grave threat until they were prohibited in 1720, and there were constant complaints about the oversupply of labour, particularly cheap Irish, female and child labour. Vulnerability and weight of numbers made silk weavers outstandingly militant, especially in the 1760s. Yielding to riots, Parliament passed the Spitalfields Acts in 1773, restricting entry to the trade and controlling wage levels in London. This had the effect of accelerating the growth of cheaper and more efficient silk production (often financed by London entrepreneurs) outside London, particularly in Macclesfield, Manchester, Coventry and rural Essex. Silk weaving continued to provide a precarious and intermittent living for thousands of hard-pressed men, women and children, Irish and native-born, in East London until the disastrous impact of competition from provincial power looms in the 1840s. In 1824 there were still an estimated 50,000 silk weavers, mostly sweated labourers, in London. Other branches of the industry did not last so long. Spitalfields silk stocking knitting, which probably involved 2,500 knitting frames in 1730, declined rapidly thereafter, and silk throwing was destroyed by competition from provincial silk-spinning mills between 1750 and 1800.[35]

The social structure of London, Campbell argued in 1747, rested on the skills of tailors and other fashion workers: 'There are Numbers of Beings in and about this Metropolis who have no other identical Existence than what the Taylor, Milliner, and Perriwig-Maker bestow upon them: Strip them of these Distinctions, and they are quite a different Species of Beings.' This was one of London's largest and oldest trades. According to the master tailors' petition of 1721, there were over 7,000 journeymen tailors on strike in London in that year, and if we add the less well-organized branches of the industry, especially those dominated by women, the figure would be much higher. Peter Earle's analysis of 1,436 female witnesses before London Church courts between 1695 and 1725 suggests that 19 per cent of working women (and 13 per cent of all London women) made a living from making or mending clothes. Gregory King estimated that there were 300,000 females in London in 1695, about 180,000 of them being permanent residents of working age (over sixteen). So if King's figures and Earle's are not too misleading, there were about 23,400 women in the clothing and mending trades around 1700. It is likely that the many women who listed their employment as 'needlework', 'plainwork', 'mantua-maker', 'milliner', 'stay-maker' or 'slop-work' suffered the same low wages, long hours and irregular income as Victorian sweated workers. The ready-made garment industry, with its heavy reliance on low-paid home work, was already well established in London in the 1720s, alongside the fashionable bespoke trade of the West End. Even in the West End trade, little of the customers' money found its way into the purses of the ordinary seamstresses and milliners. In Robert Campbell's view, the tedium and hardship of earning 5 or 6s a week in millinery or mantua-work was almost sure to lead young women into immorality, and he cautioned parents against it. As for the male workers, Campbell did not fear for their virginity, but regarded their economic position as unenviable: 'They are as numerous as Locusts, are out of Business about three or four Months in the Year, and generally as poor as Rats.'[36]

The leather and fur industry, probably England's second most valuable industry in 1770 (and third in 1800), was a traditional London trade, especially in Southwark and Bermondsey, where dressers, cutters, boot- and shoemakers, hatters, glovers, harness-makers and saddlers pursued their crafts well away from richer residential areas. This was one of the industries (along with hosiery, silk spinning, metalwares, hatting and calico printing) in which employment was leaking away to low-wage areas in the provinces. Even before 1750 London shopkeepers were employing shoe-makers in Northampton and elsewhere, and the process which eventually ruined many London industries had begun.[37] But there were still many thousands of small masters and their wives, apprentices and journeymen, stitching shoes from ready-cut leather in cramped garrets, defying the efforts of the Cordwainers' Company (representing the richer manufactur-ers) to drive them out of business. Successful entrepreneurs might employ dozens of domestic workers: one in 1738 claimed a workforce of 162.[38] Making hats, mostly from Canadian beaver fur, was another South London speciality. This was one of several industries (glass, silk, paper, tapestry, calico printing and precision instruments were others) which benefited from the arrival of skilled Huguenot immigrants after 1685. London dominated English (and even European) hatting in the early eighteenth century, though growth must have been impeded by the workers' extreme hostility to unapprenticed labourers. One such man was beaten to death by Southwark hatters in 1742.[39]

METAL AND WOOD

If, as Adam Smith argued in *The Wealth of Nations* (1776), the division of labour was the key to manufacturing efficiency, then Clerkenwell, just to the north of the City, was at the centre of the new industrial economy. By the minute subdivision of their craft into over 100 specialized processes, the watchmakers of Clerkenwell, St Luke and Shoreditch had made themselves the world's leaders in output and quality, beating their rivals in Paris and Geneva. London's technical and commercial primacy was established in the late seventeenth century by such masters as Thomas Tompion and Daniel Quare, inventor of the repeater watch, and maintained by the great eighteenth-century watchmakers, George Graham, John Ellicott and Thomas Mudge, inventor of the perpetual calendar watch. In 1796, just before Pitt's watch tax brought a temporary depression to the industry, London was producing around 180,000 silver and 6,000 gold watches, and exporting up to half of them. The London workforce, mostly specialists making wheels, pinions, springs, hands, dials, chains, keys, and many other tiny parts in their own houses, numbered at least 8,000, and there were others in Lancashire, all working for masters who assembled, signed and sold the finished product.[40]

The range and quantity of metal goods produced in these parishes was enormous. Clerkenwell was a great centre for the production of jewellery, gold and silver wares, pewter and brass, and precision instruments of all kinds. All the instruments of surgery were made there: 'Knives, Lancets, Trepans, Bistoras, Scissars, Cupping-Cases, Spatulas', and so forth. The mathematician, the scholar and the navigator needed the instrument-maker's skills: 'He makes Globes, Orrerys, Scales, Quadrants, Sectors, Sun-Dials of all sorts and dimensions, Air-Pumps, ... Telescopes, Microscopes of different Structures, Spectacles, and all other Instruments invented for the Help or Preservation of the Sight.' Later in the century, London led the world in the production of accurate and practical marine chronometers. Simpler work might be farmed out to workers in rural Lancashire, and Birmingham and Sheffield could produce cheaper and better gun components, cutlery and scissors, but Clerkenwell was still supreme in the making of higher-value goods. This was an industry in which the skills of London craftsmen benefited from their association with the scholarship of London scientists. The fertile genius of Robert Hooke, Fellow of the Royal Society and Professor of Geometry at Gresham College, Bishopsgate Street (his home from 1665 to 1703), provided London watch- and instrument-makers with enough technical advances to inspire them for generations. Hooke guided Tompion's work on the use of spiral springs to regulate the balance of watches, and made pioneering advances in the construction of barometers, odometers, quadrants, weather clocks, telescopes, hearing aids, anemometers and watchmaking machinery.[41]

It would be wrong to assume that London's metal trades were passive and conservative in the face of the rise of provincial industrialization later in the eighteenth century. London metalworkers and engineers ranked alongside those of Birmingham in their inventiveness: John Pickering's hammer and die method of producing brasswares from sheet metal, Joseph Bramah's hydraulic press, ever-sharp pencil, suction beer-engine, rotary wood-planing machine and precision 'unpickable' locks, Henry Maudslay's screw-cutting lathe and machine tools, were all developed in London. Two of the three greatest centres of engineering in England, the Woolwich Arsenal and Maudslay, Sons and Field, were in London. Bramah, eighteenth-century London's most successful and inventive engineer, found Maudslay working in the Woolwich Arsenal in 1789, and nine years later, only two years after the opening of Watt's new Soho Foundry in Birmingham, Maudslay established his own engineering works, which was moved, as it grew, from premises near Oxford Street to Westminster Bridge Road, in Lambeth.

Maudslay was the greatest pioneer of precision engineering, insisting on absolute accuracy in screw threads (produced on his own screw-cutting lathe), plane surfaces and measurement. His bench micrometer, accurate to a ten-thousandth of an inch, revolutionized engineering accuracy, and established methods which have only been superseded in recent times. He was able to develop the skills of workers from existing London industries, particularly watchmaking, coach-building and cabinet-making, Bramah's original trade. Maudslay was also the leading innovator in mass-production with machine tools. Between 1802 and 1807, in collaboration with Sir Samuel Bentham, the inventive brother of the philosopher Jeremy Bentham, and the French refugee Marc Brunel, Maudslay developed a series of forty-three machines which would produce 130,000 pulley-blocks a year for the Royal Navy, using ten unskilled men to replace the work of 100 skilled craftsmen. Maudslay's workshop produced many of the most outstanding Victorian mechanical engineers: James Clement (pioneer of planing machines for metal), Richard Roberts (inventor of the self-acting spinning mule), Sir Joseph Whitworth (the great Manchester machine-tool-maker, the first to work to accuracies of a millionth of an inch), and James Nasmyth (inventor of the magnificent steam-hammer shown at the

Great Exhibition in 1851). Most of Maudslay's pupils took their skills to the Manchester textile industry, but enough stayed in London to maintain Lambeth's position as a centre of engineering.[42]

Workers in wood probably outnumbered workers in metal. Thousands were employed in the furniture and coach-building trades, which were concentrated in the area round Covent Garden. London offered a mass market together with a large middle-class demand for quality furniture and an unparalleled number of aristocratic and royal clients. This expanding market, along with the arrival of Huguenot and Dutch craftsmen in the 1680s, with their new techniques of joinery, upholstery, marquetry and veneer, and the availability of large quantities of American and West Indian walnut, rosewood, deal, satinwood and, above all, mahogany allowed London to become Europe's leading furniture producer and a major exporter. The trade was in the hands of hundreds of upholsterers and cabinet-makers, who organized the labour of a wide range of specialists, working at home or in workshops: joiners, chair and bed-post carvers, looking-glass grinders and framers, castor- and spring-makers, needle-women, and so on. Thomas Chippendale of St Martin's Lane, whose reputation was established by the publication of his catalogue in 1754, is the most famous name, but the largest manufacturer was George Seddon and Son, whose 2-acre site in Aldersgate Street stocked £120,000 worth of furniture, carpets, timber, linen, glass and upholstery in 1789, and employed 3–400 craftsmen and apprentices.[43] Coach-makers, too, had to bring together the skills of many specialists: carvers, joiners, brass-founders, harness-makers, wheelwrights, tyre-smiths, glaziers and painters. They also needed good financial reserves to cope with slow-paying aristocratic customers: 'They deal with none but Nobility and Quality, and according to their Mode must trust a long Time, and sometimes may happen never to be paid.'[44]

London still held its lead as a shipbuilding centre, despite damaging competition from America and from Newcastle and Whitby. In the 1720s, Defoe estimated that there were thirty-three shipbuilding yards and twenty-two repair yards, stretching like 'one great arsenal' from London Bridge to Blackwall, and in the two years 1790–91, when accurate statistics begin, London yards built 119 ships, over 16,000 tons in all, nearly 16 per cent of the tonnage built in England in those years. London yards specialized in strong and well-armed vessels: ships for the Levant and West India trade, fighting ships at Henry VIII's royal dockyards at Deptford and Woolwich (each employing around 900 men in the 1770s), and East Indiamen at the large Blackwall yard. Subsidiary shipping trades clustered around the yards:

blockmakers, sailmakers, chandlers, coopers, instrument-makers, anchor-smiths, ropemakers and makers of slops, or sailors' clothing.[45]

FOOD AND DRINK

The manufacture and sale of food and drink was one of London's largest employment sectors. The Westminster poll book of 1749, listing 9,465 voters according to their 395 occupations, records that 1,441 (15 per cent) were victuallers, butchers, bakers and distillers. Except in times of severe shortage, bakers gave Londoners the white bread they demanded, often using alum to achieve the desired effect with inferior flour. Accusations of more serious frauds, involving chalk and ground bones, were less plausible, but there is little doubt that the widespread adulteration of many foods exposed by Frederick Accum in 1820 was already taking place in London in the late eighteenth century, when guild and legislative controls were weakening. Accum found ground peas and beans in bread, sulphuric acid and other 'flavour enhancers' in beer, dried hedgerow leaves in tea, and many other more or less harmful deceptions.[46] Baking remained a small-scale craft until the development of the steam oven in the late nineteenth century, but flour-milling made an important step towards industrial production. The Albion Steam Flour Mill, built by James Rennie in 1785–8, used two of Watt's 50-horsepower steam engines to drive eighty millstones and to power its cranes, hoists, sifters and dressers. The mill, which employed seventy-five men and a capital of £106,000, was burned down in 1791, perhaps by the millers whose livelihoods it threatened.[47]

In the other major grain-based industry, brewing, there was a true industrial revolution in the eighteenth century. The great size of the London market had encouraged the growth of specialist wholesale brewers, the 'Common Brewers', before 1600. In eighteenth-century London vic-tualling brewers, who brewed for retail in their own inns, were increasingly rare, although they were common elsewhere. The economies of scale available to well-capitalized brewers were not technologically advanced, but they were effective, none the less. First, they adopted a new type of strong, heavy beer known as porter (invented by Ralph Harwood in 1722), whose dark colour and bitter flavour came from the use of well-roasted malt. Then they constructed large and efficient brewhouses, in which intelligent design and huge cisterns (holding up to 500,000 gallons) reduced labour costs. In the 1780s the use of thermometers and saccharometers (which measured the fermentable matter in a quantity of malt or barley) enabled big brewers to produce their beer to an exactly calculated strength, and thus to manipulate quality, price and profit as they chose. Finally, in the 1790s the main brewers installed steam engines, which took over all the work of grinding, pumping, lifting, mashing and stirring previously done by men and horses. Mechanization and efficiency did not mean loss of quality. The most successful brewers paid meticulous attention to the price and quality of the malt or barley they bought, and beat their competitors by offering stronger, cheaper and better porter to London innkeepers.

Brewing on such a large scale, and survival through years of high grain prices, demanded very heavy investment, and it became increasingly difficult for new firms to enter the field. By 1800 about a dozen major brewers, mostly with backing from City commercial or banking interests, had gained three-quarters of the London strong beer market. The largest firm in 1810, producing 235,000 barrels a year, was the Anchor Brewery in Southwark, which a group linked to a network of Quaker bankers, the Barclays, Gurneys, Lloyds and Bevans, had bought from Dr Johnson's friends, the Thrales, in 1781. The great London brewers, Samuel Whitbread, Richard Meux, Sir Benjamin Truman, John Perkins (of the Thrale/Barclay brewery) and Sampson Hanbury, were true pioneers of industrial mass production, or, as one of them said in 1830, 'the power-loom weavers of brewing'. They were also men of great social and political weight, serving as aldermen, JPs, sheriffs, MPs (especially for Southwark) and sometimes Lord Mayor.[48]

WORKING WOMEN

There were women workers in many of the industries described above, but the heaviest concentrations appear to have been in the textile and clothing trades. The best analysis of women's work in eighteenth-century London comes from Peter Earle's study of 1,436 female witnesses who appeared before London Church courts between 1695 and 1725. In this sample, 54 per cent of women supported themselves entirely by paid work, 16 per cent had a job and some other means of support, and only 30 per cent (mostly wives) had no paid employment. Spinsters and widows were most likely to work for a living (under 20 per cent had no paid work), whilst only 31 per cent of wives, mainly those with lower-status husbands, supported them-selves entirely by paid work. Family work was not as common as might be supposed, although some of it went unrecorded. Of 396 working wives, only forty-six worked with their husbands (mostly selling food or drink), and only a handful of widows carried on their husbands' trades. In general, women seemed to be confined already to the low-paid 'woman's work' familiar from the mid-nineteenth-century censuses: domestic service (25 per cent), making or mending clothes (19 per cent), nursing and midwifery (12 per cent), cleaning and laundry work (10 per cent), victualling (9 per cent), shopkeeping (8 per cent), hawking (6 per cent) and textiles (almost 5 per cent). Dorothy George's sample of eighty-six women from the Old Bailey Sessions Papers, 1728–1800, confirms the importance of shopkeeping, hawking, street-selling and the clothing industry for working women, and the rarity of husbands and wives sharing the same work. There were women in middle-class employments, as schoolteachers, innkeepers or manufacturers, but for the great majority work was unskilled, underpaid and unremitting. As working women aged, there was no retirement to look forward to, but a descent into harder and lower-paid jobs, cleaning, nursing, washing or selling in the street.[49]

For younger women, domestic service was the greatest employer. The ready availability of domestic work, paying (in 1750) around £5 a year, plus food, clothes and lodging, made London especially attractive to female migrants. In Earle's sample of 1,004 working women, 64 per cent of those under twenty-five were servants, and 30 per cent of those aged twenty-five to thirty-four. This was not a career, but an apprenticeship for married life. The average time spent in one job (in Earle's City sample) was about a year, and few women stayed in service beyond the age of thirty-five, and hardly any beyond forty-five. How many servants there were in London is uncertain, especially because the word was used to describe all living-in employees, whether their work was domestic or not. Jonas Hanway believed that one in thirteen of London's population in 1767 (50,000 of 650,000) were servants, and a modern estimate suggests around 10 per cent. Peter Earle's work on London Church court records between 1695 and 1725 suggests that a quarter of London's working women (and 17.5 per cent of all London women) were servants, which would indicate a female servant population of around 32,000 in those years. At the same time, there were probably about 8,000 male servants, mainly employed in larger households as footmen, butlers, valets and kitchen staff, or as grooms, coachmen or postillions for London's 2,500 private coaches. In 1780 London employers paid tax on a total of 11,822 male servants.[50]

The majority of female servants worked as 'maids-of-all-work' in small households, either alone or with one other. The best West End houses might have had fifteen or twenty servants, or even more, but Earle's analysis of 176 City families with servants shows that almost 57 per cent had only one servant, and under 11 per cent had over three. D. A. Kent makes the point that even bricklayers and milk-sellers had servants, though they may have been living-in labourers rather than domestics. In his St Martin-in-the-Fields sample, under 4 per cent of servants had aristocratic employers, and only 10 per cent professional ones. The rest worked for artisans, craftsmen, publicans, tradesmen and shopkeepers, and enjoyed, Kent concludes, a life which compared fairly well with that of London or rural labourers in terms of food, lodging, security and disposable income. Their work was heavy, and their status and income were low, but this was the lot of almost all women (as well as most men) of the labouring class. Servants might supplement their wages by taking tips, selling cast-off clothes and waste food, and pilfering, but like other workers they found their right to perquisites constantly undermined by the growing body of embezzlement law in the eighteenth century. Those who took too much were running a grave risk. Of sixty-five servants hanged at Tyburn between 1703 and 1772, twenty were women, and twenty-one were found guilty of robbing their masters.[51] Some employers took a more benign interest in their servants. William Hogarth painted a portrait of the six servants, perhaps a house-keeper, two housemaids, a coachman, a valet and a boy, who lived with him and his family in his house in Leicester Square, and the proud employer of an athletic footman named an inn after him in Charles Street, off Berkeley Square – 'I Am the Only Running Footman'.

THE BEGINNING OF BANKING

In the seventeenth and eighteenth centuries, London's position as a financial centre underwent a transformation which established it as the world's leading money market. Ever since the Middle Ages London's commercial wealth had made it an important centre of capital, finance and investment, and a vital source of royal borrowing. The system of credit had traditionally been in the hands of those with surplus cash, perhaps goldsmiths, courtiers, tax farmers or successful English or alien merchants. In the sixteenth and seventeenth centuries some of these men, particularly goldsmiths, jewellers and scriveners, became part-time bankers, holding deposits on behalf of others, making loans, paying and receiving interest, buying and selling Exchequer tallies (notched sticks indicating a government debt), and discounting (buying at a cut price, before payment on them was due) bills of exchange, promissory notes and other forms of paper currency. The banking activities of scriveners developed from their work in drawing up legal documents, arranging mortgages, handling property transactions, and putting borrowers in touch with lenders. Goldsmiths had secure premises and high reputations, and were increasingly used as individuals with whom money and valuables could be safely deposited. Charles I's raid on the Mint in 1640 made the attractions of depositing money with a trustworthy private banker even greater. The issue of banknotes as receipts for deposits, the use of written orders, or cheques, to transfer money from one account to another, and the lending out of depositors' money at a higher rate of interest, all developed in the seventeenth century. By preventing hoarding and making money available to merchants and manufacturers, bankers encouraged trade and stimulated economic growth.

The demand for banking services was not limited to that of the Crown and the merchant community. Wealthy visitors to London needed money for shopping, gambling, renting and furnishing their houses, paying servants or tradesmen, or marrying their daughters. Some simply carried gold and silver coin from their country estates, and suffered fewer losses than all the stories of highwaymen on the main roads would lead us to expect. Some managed to make an arrangement with a local tradesman, usually a butcher or grazier, who earned money in London (especially at Smithfield) and needed to transfer it to his country home. A simple exchange of money and receipts between the landlord or his estate manager and the tradesman, perhaps with a small fee for the latter, gave both parties money where they wanted it, and avoided risky cash movements. Using this system of 'returns' Lord Fitzwilliam was able to transfer around half of the income from his Northamptonshire estates to London between 1686 and 1700, and the Verneys a more modest 30 per cent of their Buckinghamshire rents. Others, and a growing number, relied on the system of promissory notes, cheques and paper money developed by goldsmiths, scriveners and merchants in the seventeenth century.[52]

Some of these part-time bankers gradually shed their non-banking activities and emerged, by 1700 or thereabouts, as the founders of the first English banking houses. Sir Francis Child (1642–1713), goldsmith, pawnbroker, alderman and Lord Mayor (1698–9), is said to have concentrated exclusively on banking after 1690 (though he was still an active jeweller and goldsmith in the 1680s), and Sir Richard Hoare's banking business had dropped its goldsmith activities by the time of his death in 1718. These two businesses still survive, but most of the forty-four London goldsmith–bankers known to have existed in 1677 did not make it through the storms and bankruptcies of the next fifty years into the calmer waters of the later eighteenth century, and their activities are harder to reconstruct. By the 1720s there were thirteen firms, mostly in the Strand–Fleet Street area, specializing in aristocratic business, including Childs, Hoares, Coutts and Goslings. Herries Bank, in St James's Street, took its service to the mobile aristocrat a step further, and issued traveller's cheques for the Grand Tour.[53]

The greatest single client of London bankers was, of course, the monarch. In the 1570s Elizabeth turned away from Antwerp, and towards London, for her loans, and simplified the system by abolishing the laws against usury in 1571. The growth of government financial needs in the seventeenth century, especially during the Civil War, forced the Crown to ask the City Corporation to raise short-term loans on its behalf on an ever-larger scale: £70,000 in 1608, £100,000 in 1610 and 1617, £120,000 in 1627–8, over £1 million between 1660 and 1680, and £592,000 in 1689–93. Those with political obligations to the Crown, particularly customs farmers, royal officials, monopolists and chartered companies, found it difficult to refuse requests for loans. The East India Company advanced £290,000 in cash and goods between 1669 and 1678, and royal debts to Sir Stephen Fox, paymaster of the Forces from 1661 to 1676, reached £445,000.

The emergence of a group of royal bankers in mid-seventeenth-century London is described in Clarendon's *Life*:

> The bankers did not consist of above the number of five or six men, some whereof were aldermen, and had been Lord Mayors of London. . . . They were a tribe that had risen and grown up in Cromwell's time, and never heard of before the late troubles, till when the whole trade of money had passed through the hands of the scriveners: they were for the most part goldsmiths, men known to be so rich, and of so good reputation, that all the money of the kingdom would be trusted or deposited in their hands.

Charles 'always treated those men very graciously, as his very good servants, and all his ministers looked upon them as very honest and valuable men'. When the King needed money quickly, the bankers were called before him, and each offered to lend what he could, at a rate of interest to be settled by the Crown. They had borrowed at 6 per cent, and expected 8 or 10 per cent to compensate them for the risk involved in lending to a borrower who was above the law. The bankers were offered the security of various branches of the royal revenue, but in the last resort they relied upon the King's honour, and might pay a heavy price for doing so. The political unpopularity of this group of bankers, who were widely believed to be profiting from the government's difficulties in the Dutch war, made it possible for Charles, owing them well over £1 million, to suspend capital repayments in 1672. This so-called 'Stop of the Exchequer' ruined five leading City bankers, and fatally wounded the two biggest, Sir Robert Viner and Edward Backwell, although its impact was not severe enough to halt the growth of private banking in London.[54]

THE NATIONAL DEBT

The betrayal of 1672 made it clear that some sort of central bank, guaranteed by Parliament rather than the King, was needed to give investors confidence in lending to the Crown. Then the 1688 revolution transformed the relationship between Crown and people, and the war of 1689–97 redoubled the government's need for long-term loans. In the early 1690s there was a speculative boom in which more than 100 joint-stock companies (five times the number existing in 1690) were floated, most of them in an unseaworthy condition: water companies, treasure-hunting ventures, manufacturing enterprises, and so on. Among these new speculations were a variety of schemes for meeting the government's need for loans. In 1693 investors were asked to buy shares in a state tontine, which would pay gradually increasing annuities as the original subscribers died off, or (for those who preferred a faster return) to buy interest-bearing tickets for a £1 million state lottery. Holders of these annuities and lottery tickets were also invited to exchange them for stock in a new bank, the Million Bank, which lasted until 1796. A scheme of more lasting significance was put forward in 1694 by William Paterson, a Scottish adventurer acting as spokesman for a powerful City group. This was the idea (borrowed from the Bank of Amsterdam and the banks of the Italian city states) of a joint stock company authorized by charter to raise £1,200,000 by public subscription to cover the debts left by Charles II, to buy up other government debts, to issue bank notes, deal in bullion and bills of exchange, and provide the government with indefinite credit in return for regular interest payments, set at first at 8 per cent. The credit of a parliamentary monarch like William III was far stronger than Charles II's, and the Bank of England's first £1,200,000 capital was raised in twelve days. Of the 1,268 initial subscribers, 1,111 (87.6 per cent) lived in or near London, and most were merchants or financiers. A substantial number of investors were courtiers and politicians, almost 10 per cent were Huguenots, and 12 per cent were women.[55]

From these small beginnings the national debt grew until it dominated the government's annual expenditure and the City's financial world. It stood at £14 million in 1700, £35 million in 1713, and around £50 million from 1720 to 1742. A substantial body of writers and politicians regarded the debt as a great evil, but their efforts to liquidate it were never successful, and each war sent it to new heights: £76 million in 1748, £132 million in 1763, £214 million in 1782 and £745 million in 1815. The bulk of this sum (at least between 1720 and 1780) was virtually permanent funded debt, much of it held by the three main monied companies, the Bank of England, the East India Company, and the South Sea Company. The last of these was founded by the Tory government in 1711 in the hope that it would take over the debt from the Whig-controlled Bank and East India Company.

The Londoners who made up the great majority of leading stockholders in these three companies were the 'monied élite' of the eighteenth-century City. The 168 holders of more than £10,000 worth of Bank of England or East India Company stock in 1723–4 included thirty-seven foreigners (mostly Dutch) and eleven other non-Londoners, and a selection of lawyers, physicians, brewers, goldsmith bankers, widows, peers and government officials. The great majority of leading stockholders were London merchants, among them Sir Peter Delmé, Sir Dennis Dutry, Sir Gilbert Heathcote and Abraham Craiesteyn. Jewish stockholders, who were often singled out for abuse by critics of the world of finance, numbered only six in 1723–4, though some of them (Anthony da Costa, Francis Pereira) were among the City's richest merchants. The greatest Jewish financier of the century, Samson Gideon, was at the start of his spectacular climb to wealth and gentility in 1723, but in the 1740s and 1750s he made £350,000 as the government's chief loan agent and banker. Several thousand Londoners held small or middling stakes in the loans floated by the government from time to time, and their wealth, drawn from trade, craft or the professions, was vital to the government's financial strategy. Londoners made up the majority of the Bank of England's 2–3,000 voting proprietors (those with stock of £500 or more), though a large minority (perhaps a quarter) were Dutch, and a fair number came from the Home Counties. The stability of the system depended on the money and skill of around 100 City merchants and financiers, especially the governors and senior directors of the three great companies. This small community of plutocrats was wooed and protected by Robert Walpole, but heartily detested by such men as Sir John Barnard, the City's MP from 1722 to 1761 and the champion of its lesser merchants and tradesmen against the monied élite. For much of the century there was a fundamental division between the usually anti-government traders and craftsmen, entrenched in the Common Council and Common

Hall, and the rich City élite, many of them aldermen, whose investments bound them to the Whig administration in mutual dependence.[56]

THE BANK OF ENGLAND AND THE EAST INDIA COMPANY

The relationship between the Treasury and the Bank of England became increasingly intimate. Between 1695 and 1724, when the Bank, still a speculative venture, had to weather a succession of political and financial crises, it had a firm ally in William Lowndes, Secretary of the Treasury. In 1708 Lowndes ensured that the Bank's new charter strengthened its monopoly of joint stock banking, and gave it a formal veto over the issue of Exchequer Bills, which the Bank was obliged to cash on demand. In March 1710 the Bank was saved from the Sacheverell mob by Horse Guards sent from St James's. The Bank organized the state's loans, lotteries and tontines, financed its wars, and steadied the financial system in the chaos of the South Sea Bubble crisis of 1720. Under pressure from Walpole, the directors even helped to save the rival company from extinction by taking up £4 million of South Sea stock after the crisis. Under Walpole's ministry (1721–42) the personal and political connection between the Court of Directors and the government became closer still, and the Bank became an integral part of the administration of national finances. By the time the Bank's charter was renewed for the third time in 1764, most government departments held accounts in Threadneedle Street (where the Bank had built new premises in 1734), the Bank regularly advanced money on the security of anticipated land tax and malt tax receipts, and the Bank's government business, mainly in the form of Exchequer Bills and a long-term official debt of over £11 million, produced 80 per cent of its profits. When the Charter was renewed in 1781 Lord North could rightly argue that the Bank of England had become, 'from long habit and usage of many years ... a part of the constitution', doing the money business of the government 'with much greater advantage to the public, than when it had formerly been done at the Exchequer'. This quasi-constitutional relationship was symbolized by the permanent military guard provided by the government for the Bank after the attack on it by the Gordon Rioters in 1780.[57]

The strength of the Bank was tested by periodic panics and international financial crises, mostly connected with major wars. It rode the Jacobite panic of 1745 fairly easily, and withstood the pressures of the Seven Years' War (1756–63). In 1772 an international crisis was partly triggered by problems in the East India Company, which found itself unable to repay its normal £300,000 loan to the Bank because the Bengal famine and rising defence costs had reduced its annual profits by over £500,000. The Bank was able to supply the Treasury with £1.4 million to relieve the Company, and the smooth relationship between the Bank and the Company resumed its previous course. The crises of the 1760s and 1770s demonstrated the superiority of London to Amsterdam as a financial centre. In 1763 unwise speculation in unsecured war loans ruined several Amsterdam financiers, and stability was restored by loans from the Bank of England. In the crisis of 1772–3 a succession of bankruptcies among Dutch financiers who had speculated unwisely in East India Company stock brought business in Amsterdam to a standstill, until the Bank of England acted to restore confidence. In both cases the London system, in which respectable banks were not too closely enmeshed with Change Alley speculators, and in which the Bank of England exercised an overall control, was shown to be safer than the decentralized and uncontrolled Amsterdam system, in which inexperienced speculators could endanger the whole credit structure. Amsterdam's supremacy was finally destroyed by the war of 1780–3, when the Dutch, abandoning their long-standing neutrality and their most important financial partner, threw in their lot with America and France. The outcome was disastrous. Dutch trade was strangled by a British naval blockade, and in 1781 the Bank of Amsterdam failed. Amsterdam never recovered its position at the centre of world trade and finance, which was seized by London. If there were any further doubts about Amsterdam's demise and London's ascendancy, they were ended by the French occupation of Amsterdam in 1795. Two years after this, in 1797, fears that the French were about to invade Britain forced the Bank of England to suspend gold payments for the first time in over a century. They were not resumed until 1821.[58]

Since its foundation, the accumulation and circulation of gold and silver bullion had been one of the Bank's main duties. Large quantities of bullion passed through London in the eighteenth century because of England's favourable trade balance with Portugal, which paid for its imports in Brazilian gold, and through the rising trade in contraband silver from Spanish America. The Bank held large reserves in its Bullion Room, generally covering over a third of its liabilities, and much of the gold was minted into guineas in the Tower of London and went into circulation. By the end of the century London had supplanted Amsterdam as Europe's premier bullion market.[59]

The Bank of England was primarily a bank of government and

commerce. In its first century it opened no branch offices in London or elsewhere, it did not welcome provincial business or any business which could not be conducted in person, and its private mortgage and loan business soon dwindled away. It issued few banknotes worth under £20 (a labourer's annual wage) until the 1790s, and most of its notes circulated among London's wealthy élite. It was not yet the 'bankers' bank', since no country banks, and only a minority of London banks, held accounts with it. But the Bank handled most ministerial and revenue business, and the East India and the South Sea Companies had regular overdrafts of around £300,000 and £40,000 respectively. Clapham's analysis of the Bank's 1,340 clients on 1 January 1800 shows how important the Bank had become to London's merchants and manufacturers. The biggest groups of creditors were overseas merchants, especially those trading with the West Indies and Ireland, linen drapers and Manchester warehousemen, tea and sugar dealers, Blackwell woollen factors and Spitalfields silk manufacturers. Below these came corn factors, ironmongers, coal merchants, hatters, hosiers, booksellers, and a host of dealers and shopkeepers representing over fifty London trades. The Bank truly was, as it was often called, the Bank of London.[60]

The Bank of England's charter prevented the establishment of other joint-stock banks in England until 1826, and in London until 1833. But partnership banks thrived, serving the commercial or West End market, and dealing in Exchequer Bills, Navy Bills, departmental issues, government bonds and annuities, East India, Bank and South Sea stock, and all the other securities that fuelled the London money market. In addition to their discounting and mortgage business, the private banks also issued banknotes on a small scale. Banking partnerships came and went, but the comers slightly outnumbered the goers, and the total rose from around 24 in 1725 to 36 in 1765, 52 in 1786 and 69 in 1803. About half of these were City banks concentrated in and near Lombard Street, specializing in the needs of merchants, manufacturers and financiers, as well as government securities. Later in the century, most of these City banks also acted as agents for country banks, honouring their bills, cashing their notes, and buying securities on their behalf. At the same time, the City banks were moving towards a system in which they would be able to conduct transactions with each other without sending clerks from street to street carrying cash and bills. Thirty-one City banks established the London Clearing House in 1773, and most opened accounts at the Bank of England, which thus began to assume its nineteenth-century position as the bankers' bank.[61]

The constitution of the East India Company was like that of the Bank of England: those with at least £500 stock elected a Court of twenty-four directors from those with at least £2,000 stock, who in turn chose a Chairman and Deputy. Like the Bank, the Company emerged from the instability of the 1700s and 1710s to form, under Walpole, part of the solid triumvirate of financial companies that stabilized and supported the Whig regime. The Company raised much of its capital by issuing India Bonds to a total value, after 1744, of £6 million. These bonds, yielding between 3 and 5 per cent, were among the most popular investments in eighteenth-century London, and long-term East India stock was one of the few stocks (along with Bank and South Sea stock and government securities) traded on the stock market. From the 1760s, East India stock was the world's leading speculative stock, and its sudden fall helped trigger the European financial crisis of 1772. After the 1690s, the government no longer needed to extort loans from the East India Company, but the success of Treasury loans rested on the readiness of a select group of rich City financiers to underwrite them, and as a rule the leaders of the East India Company, along with those of the Bank and the South Sea Company, headed the list of subscribers.[62]

Until the 1760s the Company was run independently and ably by its Court of Directors, but in 1763 the importance of the Company as a source of revenue and credit led the government to intervene directly in the power struggle between Robert Clive, the Company's great soldier, and Laurence Sulivan, its able Chairman. Thereafter, the government's need for revenue, the growing imperial importance of India, increasing public disquiet over the Company's methods, and the crisis in the Company's finances exposed in 1772 ensured that ministerial intervention in East India Company affairs would continue. Lord North's 1773 Regulating Act began the slow transfer of authority from the Company to the Crown, a process not completed until 1858.[63]

ON 'CHANGE ALLEY

Dealing in company stocks and government debt was not new in the City, and the stock of the East India Company and other joint-stock trading companies had been bought and sold since their foundation. But the speculative boom of the early 1690s, which saw the establishment of the Bank of England and the creation of government securities and annuities of a much greater value than before, created stock-dealing on a new scale. The £4.25 million raised in new company flotations, the £1 million raised by the government in a tontine and annuities in 1693, the £1 million raised through lottery tickets and the £1.2 million Bank of England stock issued in 1694, between them provided enough stock to sustain a specialized market in shares and securities. The rules and techniques of stockbroking (buying and selling stocks on behalf of clients) were copied from those prevailing in the Amsterdam Bourse, Europe's leading securities market. In the company boom of 1694 John Houghton published a guide to share dealing which listed almost sixty companies, and gave an account of how shares were traded:

> The manner of managing the trade is this; the Monied Man goes among the Brokers (which are chiefly upon the Exchange, and at Jonathans' Coffee House), sometimes at Garroways and at some other Coffee Houses, and asks how Stocks go? and upon information bids the Broker buy or sell so many Shares of such and such Stocks if he can at such and such Prices: Then he tries what he can do among those that have Stock, or power to sell them; and if he can, makes a Bargain.[64]

Stockbrokers were unpopular almost from the moment of their birth. The first stock-market bubble burst in 1696, and in a wave of recrimination legislation was passed in 1697 which limited the number of brokers to 100, and imposed a code of conduct which forbade collusion, dealing in futures, and brokers dealing on their own account, a practice known as jobbing. At around the same time, brokers were excluded (or perhaps removed themselves) from the Royal Exchange, where merchants of higher repute had transacted business since the 1560s, and congregated in the coffee houses of Exchange Alley, particularly Garraway's and Jonathan's, the direct ancestor of the modern Stock Exchange. The 1697 Act lapsed in 1707, and the brokers and jobbers of 'Change Alley were able to practise their 'pernicious Art' without further restraint until a new and even more spectacular boom and crash in 1720.

The South Sea Company, unlike the East India Company, was not a true trading company. It had been set up in 1711 by Harley and various London merchants who were excluded from the privileged circle of Bank of England directorships, in order to rival and perhaps destroy the Bank as the linchpin of government finance. In 1718, inspired by John Law's success in monopolizing public credit in France, the South Sea Company's directors offered to take over about £30 million of the national debt on better terms than those offered by the Bank. The Bank counter-bid, but the South Sea Company's new offer was accepted in April 1720, and the

Company began persuading holders of annuities and other government debts to convert into South Sea stock. The popular delusion that trade with the Spanish American colonies, in which the South Sea Company alone among English merchants had a share, would be fabulously profitable, reinforced by bribes to prominent politicians and courtiers, special 'offers' to investors, and dishonest dealings in their own stock by the Company's directors, drove the value of South Sea stock up from £100 to over £1,000 between April and June 1720. This was the famous South Sea Bubble. Profits, and the expectation of profits, sent investors and speculators wild, and attracted money into a mass of other new company promotions, most of them emanating from the taverns and coffee houses between Cornhill and Lombard Street. Around 190 schemes were floated between September 1719 and August 1720, most of them involving insurance, fishing, foreign trade, land development or manufacture, and a few of them merely intended to separate fools from their money as quickly as possible. To halt this proliferation, and to prevent the diversion of funds from the South Sea Company, the government brought forward a bill (which became law, the so-called Bubble Act, on 9 June 1720) that declared illegal all companies formed without a charter, and all dealing in their shares. It was not until late August, though, that the threat of this Act, along with the collapse of Law's French schemes, a drying-up of money, and profit-taking by the wise or lucky, pricked the Bubble. With its own bankers, the Sword Blade Bank, sliding into bankruptcy, the South Sea Company ran out of stratagems to inflate the value of its stock, and its price fell by 75 per cent in September 1720, taking other stocks, and the fortunes of hundreds of City men, landlords, MPs, courtiers and gamblers with it.

After the Bubble, the fashion for buying the stock of newly floated companies did not recover, partly because the Bubble Act made it more difficult, and mainly because the public lost its taste for high-risk investments. Investors were happy to take their 3 or 4 per cent from the government's fixed-interest securities, known as the Funds or, after the consolidation of the national debt in 1751, as Consols. For the rest of the century businesses drew their capital from partnerships or bank loans, and stockbrokers and jobbers made their livings from dealing in the stock of the few remaining joint-stock companies (the Bank of England, the East India, South Sea, Hudson's Bay and New River companies, and the London Assurance and Royal Exchange Assurance), in lottery tickets and in the many new loan stocks issued by the government.

The business of stock-dealing or jobbing acquired its own set of rules and techniques, mostly copied from Amsterdam, in the early eighteenth century. Well before 1720, it was common for dealers to gamble on trends in stock prices by making speculative time bargains. 'Bulls' and 'Bears' gambled respectively on the rise or fall of share prices, hoping for a profit when the day of reckoning, the quarterly Rescounter Day, came along. The whole business, which was laid bare in Thomas Mortimer's *Every Man His Own Broker* in 1761, was viewed with the deepest hostility by outsiders, and legislation in 1734 (Barnard's Act) and 1746 attempted to eradicate its shadier practices, without much success. Brokers and jobbers (women as well as men) continued to crowd into the offices of the Bank of England and the South Sea Company, which issued the most important market stocks, and the East India Company, whose volatile stocks attracted more specialist dealers, including the great Samson Gideon. Even a severe fire on 25 March 1748, which destroyed the whole Exchange Alley area, including Jonathan's Coffee House, could not stop the rise of the stockbroker. New Jonathan's was quickly rebuilt, and remained the centre of stock-dealing until 1773, when its members clubbed together to build a larger home behind the Royal Exchange, which they decided to call the Stock Exchange. Business continued to grow, and in 1801 550 dealers, wishing to exclude amateurs and interlopers, moved to a private subscription club in Capel Court, on a site which the Stock Exchange continued to occupy until the 1990s. By the time of this move, stockbrokers had shaken off the gambling image, and were able to present themselves as reputable professional men, an essential part of the vast system of public credit that underpinned the British war effort against the French.[65]

SPREADING THE RISK

While stock-dealing developed on the basis of Londoners' love of a gamble, insurance, a business of equal importance to the City's future, grew from their desire to avoid unnecessary risks. Fire and losses at sea, two of the greatest threats to fortune, could be insured against in the late seventeenth century. The Great Fire of 1666 popularized fire insurance, and in 1680 the property developer Nicholas Barbon took advantage of public demand by setting up a Fire Office to insure London houses. Two others, the Friendly Society (1684) and the Hand-in-Hand (1696), followed, and a third, the Sun Fire Office (1710), extended its cover to goods, and included properties outside London. By 1710, around 25,000 Londoners were insured against fire. The speculative mania of 1719–20 produced the next leap forward, when two new joint-stock insurance companies, the London Assurance and the Royal Exchange Assurance, managed to survive the general collapse and establish themselves as major players in the insurance business. Two companies, the Sun and the Royal Exchange, dominated fire insurance without serious competition until 1782, when the Phoenix was founded. Just after 1800, there was a rapid expansion in the number of companies, and the dominance of these three was broken. Insurance was a risky business, and the calculation of premiums was not a well-developed science, so the companies tried to reduce their losses by employing Thames watermen as part-time firemen, ready to extinguish fires in houses bearing the company badge. These were small operations. In 1790 the Sun, the biggest company, had only six fire-engines and two barges to protect its £35 million-worth of insured London property, and the combined patrol assembled by the Sun, Phoenix and Royal Exchange (the three 'Great Offices') in 1791 had only thirty members. In 1832 the main companies, led by the Sun, formed a larger force, the London Fire Engine Establishment, which served London for the next thirty-three years. London was not the tinder-box it had been before 1666, but many of the eighteenth century's worst fires were in the capital. There were serious fires in Wapping in 1716 and 1725, in Exchange Alley in 1748, in the Gordon Riots in 1780, at Albion Mills in 1791, and on the Ratcliff Highway in 1794.[66]

If householders and businessmen feared fire, merchants and shipowners had even more to fear from storm, shipwreck, piracy, mutiny or enemy action. Risks could be reduced by shared ownership and a convoy system, but at least since the sixteenth century some London merchants had insured their cargoes, and occasionally their ships, with Italian or Dutch underwriters. By the later seventeenth century it was possible to buy insurance in London from individual brokers or underwriters, who could be contacted in the Royal Exchange or in one of the taverns specializing in maritime business. In 1692, just as the war against France was increasing the demand for marine insurance, Edward Lloyd's Coffee House moved from Tower Street to Lombard Street, and took over the shipping business previously concentrated in the Ship and Castle Tavern in Cornhill. Lloyd employed runners to bring the latest shipping news, and for a short time, in 1696–7, he produced a news-sheet, *Lloyd's News*. For almost 100 years, Lloyd's remained the best place for a ship's master to make contacts, whether he wanted a cargo, passengers or insurance. The position of the Lloyd's underwriters was threatened in 1720 by the creation of the Royal Exchange and London Assurance Companies, which were granted charters which excluded other companies and partnerships (but not individuals) from marine insurance. As it turned out, these two companies concentrated on fire and life insurance, and their corporate monopolies effectively protected individual underwriters from the competition of other more vigorous companies or partnerships until 1824. By preventing underwriters from acting in partnership or in companies, the charters of 1720 forced them to find information and mutual support by gathering informally in a convenient centre. Sitting all day in Lloyd's Coffee House, individual underwriters were able to share their risks, find business, and gather the shipping information they needed if they were to make sound decisions. By this means, Lloyd's underwriters knew more about the safety of individual ships than the shipowners themselves, and were thus able to spot the best risks. From 1734 they had a regular shipping list, *Lloyd's List*, and from the 1760s a full *Register of Shipping* was issued by the more prominent underwriters.

Some of the uncertainties arising from the small-scale nature of Lloyd's operations were mitigated by the rise of insurance brokers (usually successful underwriters), who took and often held premiums, gave credit to merchants, and guaranteed the soundness of the insurer and underwriter to each other. This system of personal connection, shared risks and specialized information enabled Lloyd's underwriters, who were not men of great wealth, to cover bigger risks and more hazardous routes than their rivals in the two big companies. Their business grew as English trade expanded, and as the habit of insurance became more widespread among the merchant community. In 1769 a large group of underwriters and brokers, mainly the younger ones, decided that the atmosphere of a public coffee house was unsuitable for their growing business, and broke away to establish a members-only club, New Lloyd's Coffee House in Pope's Head Alley. Two years later they moved into the Royal Exchange, where they remained, with a short break, until 1928. The organization was managed by a committee, but it remained (until the crisis of the 1990s) an association of individuals, each responsible for the risks he had insured.[67]

Men of Fortune

The 300 or 400 men who controlled the mercantile and financial worlds of eighteenth-century London became extremely wealthy. Fortunes of over £50,000 were fairly common, and some left over £100,000. At the very top, such men as Sir Peter Delmé, Samson Gideon and Sir Gilbert Heathcote were worth between a quarter and a half million pounds each, almost on a par with the richest aristocrats. What did they do with their money, and what ambitions drove them on? One common assumption was (and is) that most rich Londoners hoped to use their fortunes to escape from city life, to buy a country estate, and to enter or return to the landed class. Several historians have studied this mercantile 'flight to the land', to see how widespread it was. The Stones' study of the landed élite between 1540 and 1880 concludes that mobility between the élite and the classes below it was 'far less than might have been expected', and that professional men and government officials, rather than merchants, were most likely to join the landed gentry. Of those merchants who bought country seats, many were 'transients who left no permanent imprint on county society'. The opportunities for translating City wealth into land which were offered by the dissolution of the monasteries in the sixteenth century did not come again, and in the eighteenth century mobility was at its lowest point.[68] Two other traditional bridges between land and business, intermarriage and the entry of the younger sons of landlords into trade, are also regarded by the Stones as rather less important than had hitherto been believed. Very few 'esquires', and hardly any aristocrats, sent their sons into trade, and those apprentices whose fathers called themselves 'gentleman' probably came from urban 'pseudo-gentry' stock. Landowners, especially those embarrassed by debts, were prepared to restore their family fortunes by marrying the daughters of London businessmen, but even in Hertfordshire, just beyond London's northern suburbs, only 18 per cent of landlords born between 1650 and 1750 had wives from business families, and this proportion halved over the next century.[69]

Several historians have approached the question of the intermingling of City and landed families from the London perspective. To go back a little, R. G. Lang's study of 140 aldermen between 1600 and 1624 concluded that only between 16 and 25 per cent of the group had landed origins (generally from the lower end of the gentry), and that although most had invested in rural property, very few did so with the intention of retiring to it. Only eighteen of the 140 seem to have withdrawn from the city into rural retirement, and most, however wealthy, 'were deeply bound to the city ... by their business affairs, by civic office, by their circles of city friends, and most of all by the respect, prestige, and honour that attended success in the city and which could not be translated, like so much capital, to another social milieu'.[70] By the years 1694–1714 London's business élite had grown in size and complexity, now including East India and South Sea Company and Bank of England directors, as well as overseas and domestic merchants, bankers and manufacturers. Many of its richest members had decided to avoid the burdens of citizenship and not to seek office as aldermen. Henry Horwitz's study of 62 aldermen and 66 members of the wider City élite in these years shows that half were sons of Londoners, and only 15 per cent were sons of gentry. Most of them married within the London business community, and only 14 married into the landed class. But with their children the story was different. Nearly half the merchants' daughters in Horwitz's sample married into the gentry, and 39 per cent of their eldest sons became landlords. By the 1740s and 1750s, according to a study of seventy-four aldermen, marriages between the City élite and the landed class had become even more common, perhaps as a result of social mingling in parliament or in the London season. Over two-thirds of daughters of London alderman marrying in these years married landed gentlemen, and about 40 per cent of City businessmen who married chose landlords' daughters as their wives. But these aldermen were still strongly committed to civic life, and displayed many of the characteristics of a permanent civic élite. Nearly half of them (46 per cent) were the sons of City businessmen, and their own sons, in turn, were likely to follow them into banking or trade. Only a handful bought estates of over three hundred acres, and their country villas were nearly always within commuting distance of the City. City life gave them everything they wanted: wealth, power, a share in the rich social life of the season, and opportunities to mix and marry with the gentry.[71]

A picture emerges of a self-confident and largely self-perpetuating urban élite, still showing some inclination to turn urban success into landed prestige and security, but generally preferring the profits and pleasures of city life to a future as second-rate country gentlemen. Land, in any case, was not quite the investment it used to be. The financial revolution of the 1690s meant that the merchant élite could invest in government bonds or company stocks at 5 or 6 per cent, or London leases, yielding around 10 per cent, as opposed to landed estates, which yielded, after taxes and repairs, under 3 per cent, and live more comfortable and interesting lives as urban gentlemen. Peter Earle's analysis of the investments of London businessmen dying between 1665 and 1720 shows that although a quarter owned some land only eight owned a country estate worth over £5,000, although over seventy could have afforded one. Most citizen landowners had property in London or the suburbs, and some had a few farms in the Home Counties. Much of the rural land they owned, moreover, had been acquired through marriage or inheritance, and did not imply a desire for rustic retirement. On the other hand, those who had already retreated to the countryside and died there would not be in Earle's sample.[72]

Only a small proportion of rich Londoners bought country estates, but as Earle's sample includes only about one in fifty or sixty of London's middle class, their impact on the counties around the capital could still be impressive. Since sixteen of Earle's 375 owned a suburban 'villa', it may be that over 800 well-off Londoners had a rustic retreat in Essex, Surrey, Kent, Hertfordshire or Middlesex. In the 1720s Defoe commented on the number of estates in Essex and Surrey that had been bought by City merchants, building themselves country houses that almost equalled the noble mansions he saw at Richmond, Twickenham and Fulham. Some City merchants even joined the summer exodus from London to country houses and fashionable watering-places. Peckham, Carshalton, Clapham, Streatham, and Tooting, Defoe said, were studded with citizens' summer houses, 'wither they retire from the hurries of business, and from getting money, to draw their breath in a clear air, and to divert themselves and families in the hot weather', before returning 'to smoke and dirt, sin and seacoal' in the winter. Epsom was the City businessman's spa, and Defoe found them there looking 'as if they had left all their London thoughts behind them'. Some of them, it is true, had to ride daily into the City, leaving their families to enjoy the waters. These men were not joining the landed gentry, but trying (like West End aristocrats) to get the best of both worlds.[73]

Chapter 13

The Art of Government

THE GOVERNMENT of eighteenth-century London is a subject of bewildering complexity. No single authority wielded power over the metropolitan area, and the central government between 1688 and 1834 seemed to be almost indifferent to local administration, however scandalous its failings. There was no uniform pattern. In the City and the districts under its control the wardmotes, the Common Council and the Lord Mayor and aldermen still exercised their ancient powers. Westminster, not being a chartered town, had no mayor and aldermen, but Lord Burghley had given it a unified local government authority, the Court of Burgesses, in 1585. Twelve burgesses, one for each ward, were given responsibility for street maintenance, law enforcement, the control of nuisances, alehouses and tenements, and other local duties. What happened to the burgesses in the seventeenth century is obscure, but in the eighteenth century their powers were whittled away, and the responsibility for local affairs fell into the hands of the parish vestries, justices of the peace and improvement commissioners, giving Westminster a patchwork of authorities much the same as that covering the rest of suburban London.[1]

PARISH DUTIES

Parliament enacted laws by the handful, defining and augmenting the powers of parish vestries and other local agencies, but these were local Acts, reflecting parochial initiative rather than government policy, and their general effect was to make metropolitan administration even more complicated and fragmented. Alongside the parishes, Parliament, responding to local pressures, created special statutory agencies with powers to raise rates, taxes or tolls to carry out specific local tasks. The most famous and numerous of these were the turnpike trusts, which took over most of London's major highways in the eighteenth century, turning them into toll roads and relieving parishioners of the labour and expense of maintaining them. In addition, Parliament created about 100 bodies of commissioners in London, mostly after 1748, with the power to levy local rates to pay for a public service or civic improvement, usually lighting, cleaning, draining, paving, or watching the streets. Sometimes the commissioners were the parish vestrymen themselves, and the improvement act simply augmented parochial powers. In other cases, Parliament created a separate statutory body, unelected and self-renewing, perhaps by-passing a notoriously incompetent parish vestry. Commissions varied in the extent of the area they covered and the duties they performed. Some, like the Westminster Paving Commissioners, covered several parishes, while others, like the commissioners for St James's Square, Golden Square or Lincoln's Inn Fields, were responsible for just a few streets.[2]

Despite the rise of improvement commissions, the main burden of local administration outside the City rested on the parish vestries, which were freer from central control between 1688 and 1835 than at any time before or since. Some of these were old parishes: St Marylebone, St Pancras, Cripplegate and Shoreditch (all in the north), Stepney and Whitechapel in the east, St Andrew Holborn and the five Westminster parishes (St Clement Danes, St Mary-le-Strand, St Martin-in-the-Fields, St George-in-the-Fields and St Margaret's) in the west, and the southern parishes of Bermondsey, Lambeth, Newington, Rotherhithe, St Saviour, St George, St Olave and St Thomas. Between 1660 and 1743 population growth led to the division of some of these vast and overpopulated parishes and the creation of seventeen new ones. Westminster gained six new parishes (Covent Garden, Soho, St James's, St George's Hanover Square, St John's and St George's Blooms-bury), and from 1720 to 1743 Stepney lost most of its huge area to five new parishes (Stratford-le-Bow, Spitalfields, St-George-in-the-East, Limehouse and Bethnal Green).

The need for more churches, rather than administrative efficiency, was the usual reason for dividing parishes. Eleven of the new parishes were established as a result of the Church Building Act of 1711. This provided £350,000 for building fifty new churches to strengthen the hold of Anglicanism on the capital at a time when High Church Tories feared the power of Dissenters (Presbyterians, Baptists, and so on). Rather than build fifty modest churches, the Church Building Commissioners spent the money on a dozen grand designs by the most fashionable architects, among them Nicholas Hawksmoor (St Anne Limehouse, Christ Church Spital-fields, and four others), Thomas Archer (St John's, Smith Square), and John James (St George's, Hanover Square). After this the passion for church-building faded away, and the next burst of activity did not come until 1818, when Parliament voted the Church of England £1 million to fight the challenge of Methodism and apathy. In the growing suburbs, population ran well ahead of church accommodation. In 1810 the very rich parish of St Marylebone still had only one Anglican church for its population of 70,000, although the wealthy could rent a pew in one of eight private commercial chapels owned by local landlords.[3]

OPEN AND SELECT VESTRIES

Parochial government, which affected the lives of Londoners far more than central government did, came in many different forms. In outlying rural districts such as Chelsea and Kensington all local ratepayers were allowed to participate in the vestry meetings that set the poor rate and the church rate, and appointed the unpaid officials who did the essential work of the parish. As parish populations grew, these open vestry meetings became more unwieldy and incapable of reaching decisions. Some, such as Woolwich and Greenwich, responded by moving to a system of elected vestries, where the parishioners retained ultimate authority but handed over executive power to a smaller group. In Hackney, a small executive vestry coexisted with open parish meetings which set rates and appointed officials. Other open vestries found themselves overwhelmed by population growth, and saw their parish meetings change from cosy gatherings of local farmers to huge mass meetings in the space of two or three decades. This is what happened to St Pancras, whose population rose from 600 in 1776 to 31,779 in 1801. As a result parish administration slid into chaos, perhaps exaggerated by the propertied group that wanted to take power into its own hands. In Bethnal Green, the huge open vestry became the power base for fifty years (from 1787 to around 1840) of a corrupt and tyrannous demagogue, Joseph Merceron. Even in Chelsea the open vestry system did not prevent the village from being plundered by incompetent and corrupt parish officers, who saw their offices simply as a source of profit.[4]

Wealthy parishioners had been unhappy with the turbulent and over-democratic nature of open vestries for centuries, and had used their parliamentary and ecclesiastical influence to replace them with close or 'select' vestries, in which anything from a dozen to 100 leading ratepayers and office-holders ran the parish, replenishing their numbers by cooption and extinguishing all remnants of democratic control. At least fifty, about a quarter of London's parishes, were 'select' at some time between 1689 and 1835. Several vestries, including Stepney, Hackney and about twenty

City parishes, had their membership restricted by the Bishop of London in the early seventeenth century, to avoid 'tumult' and 'confusion', and others had been captured in a coup by a vestry élite, as St Martin-in-the-Fields was in the 1550s. In the eighteenth century new select vestries were created by Acts of Parliament, especially the 1711 Church Building Act. In St Marylebone a number of aristocrats who were developing parts of the parish into a fashionable suburb were determined to wrest control of the vestry from the tradesmen who had run it, not incompetently, hitherto. The two sides struggled for about three years, but in eighteenth-century Parliaments property always counted more than numbers, and in 1768 a select vestry of 103 of the wealthiest men of the parish was established.[5]

A few select vestries, particularly St George's Hanover Square and St Marylebone, provided honest and efficient government, policing, lighting, draining and paving their parishes to a high standard, maintaining their churches, relieving the needy, even caring for the sick and insane. After 1776 St Marylebone was one of the few parishes to have its own infirmary, as well as workhouse accommodation for 1,000 parish paupers. But in general the record of closed vestries, in the view of the Webbs, was no better than that of the despised open vestries. Most select vestries, they conclude, 'sank to the lowest depths of venality and peculation, accompanied not infrequently by positive cruelty and oppression'. 'In the majority of these parishes the close body fell into the hands of the small shopkeepers and builders, to whom the opportunities for eating, drinking and making excursions at the public expense, and the larger gains of extending their little businesses by parish work, offered an irresistible temptation.' The secrecy of parish accounts made it impossible to see where all the money was going, and it was easy to blame rate increases on the greed and fecundity of the parish poor, but it was widely known that parish funds helped fill the bellies and pockets of vestrymen. The system of cooption, Defoe wrote in 1714, ensured a cosy continuity, as 'rogue succeeds rogue, and the same scene of villainy is still carried on'. 'These Select Vestries,' the *Sunday Times* wrote in 1828, 'are a focus of jobbing: the draper supplies the blankets and linen; the carpenter finds the church pews constantly out of repair; the painter's brushes are never dry; the plumber is always busy with his solder; and thus the public money is plundered and consumed.' Parliamentary sympathy generally sheltered select vestries from reformers in the eighteenth century, and only in the 1820s, when the oligarchic spirit began to give way to reforming radicalism, was there a successful movement to reintroduce democratic elements into the closed parishes, culminating in Hobhouse's Act in 1831.[6]

THE ART OF WALKING

Local government in London, as in the rest of England, relied on the unpaid work of local people, each performing tasks appropriate to their social status. In 1700 the work of the parish was done by unpaid officers, mostly of the trading class: churchwardens, overseers of the poor, surveyors of the highways and constables. These men were meant to collect the poor rate and distribute it to the needy, maintain the highways and see to it that parishioners did their six days' unpaid 'statute' labour on the roads or paid the wages of a substitute, collect the church rate and keep the parish church in good repair, keep the peace, see to it that householders' obligations to light and clean the streets were observed, and build and run any institutions (mainly watch-houses and workhouses) they thought the parish needed. During the eighteenth century, as parish populations grew and these tasks became heavier, most parishes moved towards a rate-based system, converting the duty to serve into the duty to pay, and spending the money raised on professional (or, at least, paid) officials. Camberwell appointed a paid vestry clerk in the 1690s, and by 1816 almost all London parishes had done the same. By 1756 there were 180 professional beadles in London north of the Thames, helping the unpaid constables and overseers in their expanding duties. Local acts usually gave parishes the power to collect rates for services which had previously been provided by householders. Most Westminster parishes gained the power to collect a watch rate to pay nightwatchmen between 1734 and 1736, the City and Spitalfields were empowered to collect a lamp rate in the 1730s, and St Marylebone's local act in 1756 gave the vestry the right to raise watch, lamp and highway rates and pay watchmen or contractors to take over traditional parish duties.[7]

Of all these duties, one of the most important was paving. Georgian Londoners were preoccupied with the dangers and inconveniences of walking the streets of the town. The unpaved streets, the open drains or 'kennels', the heavy traffic of coaches, carts and sedan chairs, the ruts and puddles filled with foul liquid, the open cellar flaps, swinging shop signs and piles of refuse and dung, the lurking footpads and prostitutes, could turn a walk through London into an adventure, especially in the dark of a moonless night. John Oldham listed the familiar complaints in his *Reasons for not Living in London*, written in the 1670s:

> While tides of followers behind you throng,
> And, pressing on your heels, shove you along;

> One with a board, or rafter, hits your head,
> Another with his elbow bores your side;. . . .
> If what I've said can't from the town affright,
> Consider other dangers of the night:
> When brickbats are from upper stories thrown,
> And empty chamber-pots come pouring down. . . .
> Nor is this all which you have cause to fear;
> Oft we encounter midnight padders [footpads] here . . .

In 1716 John Gay gave some advice to those who wished to 'walk clean by Day, and safe by Night' in his *Trivia, or the Art of Walking the Streets of London*. The walker, equipped with shoes with 'firm, well-hammer'd Soles', a strong cane and quick wits, had to guard against several hazards. First there was the crush of pedestrians, which would drive him into the roadway, where wagons and coaches would run him down. Then there were the muddy and uneven paths, often paved with round and wobbling pebbles, and obstructed by stalls, cellars and signs, bringing twisted ankles, wet feet and ruined clothes:

> Should thy Shoe wrench aside, down, down you fall,
> And overturn the scolding Huckster's Stall,
> The scolding Huckster shall not o'er thee moan,
> But Pence exact for Nuts and Pears o'erthrown

By day, cheats, wig-snatchers and pickpockets plunder the pedestrian:

> Where's now thy Watch, with all its Trinkets, flown?
> And thy late Snuff-Box is no more thy own

And by night every danger is magnified by the darkness, especially along back-streets and in Lincoln's Inn Fields, lit only by the 'Link-Boy's smoaky Light':

> Though thou art tempted by the Link-Man's Call,
> Yet trust him not along the lonely Wall;
> In the Mid-way he'll quench the flaming Brand,
> And share the Booty with the pilf'ring Band.

Near Covent Garden and Drury Lane the walker should resist the harlot's lure:

> 'Tis she who nightly strowls with saunt'ring Pace,
> No stubborn Stays her yielding Shape embrace;. . . .

> With flatt'ring Sounds she sooths the cred'lous Ear,
> My noble Captain! Charmer! Love! my Dear!

Otherwise, money and (worse still) health might be lost:

> Then shall thy Wife thy loathsome Kiss disdain,
> And wholesome Neighbours from thy Mug refrain

These were the routine complaints of Londoners since the Middle Ages, and Gay, Swift and Pope liked to exaggerate the ugly blemishes on a city which in other lines they idealized as 'Augusta', the modern Rome. But many of their criticisms were justified, and were repeated by more prosaic commentators throughout the century. Perhaps, as Bernard de Mandeville argued in 1714, filth was inseparable from prosperity:

> For if we mind the materials of all sorts that must supply such an infinite number of trades and handicrafts . . . the multitudes of horses and other cattle that are always daubing the streets, the carts, coaches and more heavy carriages that are perpetually wearing and breaking the pavement of them, and above all the numberless swarm of people that are constantly harassing and trampling through every part of them . . . it is impossible London should be more cleanly before it is less flourishing.

But the problem was made worse by the growth of London well beyond the relatively efficient control of the City authorities, who had always struggled to keep their streets clean and unobstructed, along with the impact of iron-bound coach and wagon wheels on poorly made roads, and the damage done by water companies in laying their elm pipes, whose leakiness added to the mess.

Merchants, shopkeepers, professionals and landed gentlemen had achieved higher standards of comfort and cleanliness in their domestic lives, and expected similar improvements in their public environment. Gentlemen and their families came to London for its elegance and high fashion, to enjoy the contrast between urban and rural life, not to wade through mud and dung and arrive at their clubs and parties looking like country bumpkins. Perhaps it is not surprising, then, that street conditions, rather than sanitation or slum housing, should have been the main focus of the public drive for urban improvement in the eighteenth century.[8]

PAVING AND LIGHTING THE STREETS

Ever since the Middle Ages, City of London householders had been obliged to light, clean and repair the streets outside their houses, and in the sixteenth century the obligation to pave was extended to residents of the Strand, Fleet Street, Holborn, Aldgate High Street and Gray's Inn Road. From time to time the duration and amount of street-lighting was varied, but the principle of individual responsibility was maintained. In the fifteenth and sixteenth centuries, candle-lanterns were displayed from All Hallows to Candlemas (31 October–2 February), from dusk to 9 o'clock curfew. From 1599 the season was extended to include all of October and February, and in 1662 it was prolonged to Lady Day (25 March). Throughout the summer, after curfew, and on moonlit nights no lights were displayed. As night-life increased after the Restoration, with taverns, coffee houses, eating-houses and hackney carriages all doing business well after 9 o'clock, the demand for more effective and extensive street-lighting grew. In the 1680s several improved street lights had been developed, combining oil lamps, lenses and reflectors to provide a more powerful, economical and directed beam. Groups of householders combined to hire lighting contractors to take over their responsibilities, and in 1694 the City authorities gave the Convex Lights Company a monopoly of such deals within the City for an annual fee of £600. From 1694 the City was lit from 6 o'clock to midnight for 117 nights a year. This first step towards communal lighting was followed in 1736 by an Act which allowed the City to raise a special lighting rate to pay for all-year, all-night lighting by private companies under contract to individual wards. This gave the City around 4,000 hours of lighting a year, compared to 300 or 400 before 1694, and 750 from 1694 to 1736. For the first time, householders could not escape the lamp rate by setting up a lamp of their own. Street-lighting was recognized as an effective deterrent to crime, and several suburban parishes obtained local Acts of Parliament to raise a compulsory lamp rate as the City had done: Christchurch Spitalfields in 1738, Shoreditch in 1749, Bethnal Green in 1751. Most of Westminster was dark until 1762, and St Marylebone, north of Oxford Street, did not get a fully effective Act until 1770, but from the middle of the century the lamplighter, with his ladder on his shoulder, was a familiar figure on London's streets.[9]

London, which had been regarded as one of Europe's darkest capitals, now gained a reputation as its most well-lit. De Saussure, in 1725, reported that 'most of the streets are wonderfully well lighted' by the new globular lanterns, and in 1785 William Hutton enthused: 'Not a corner of this prodigious city is unlighted. . . . but this innumerable multitude of lamps affords only a small quantity of light, compared to the shops. By these the whole city enjoys a nocturnal illumination; the prospects are preserved, and mischief prevented.' All these perceptions depended on what the observer was used to, and it was still dark enough in May 1763 for James Boswell to 'engage' a 'jolly young damsel' on Westminster Bridge without fearing discovery: 'The whim of doing it there with the Thames rolling below us amused me very much.' Until the introduction of gas lamps in the decades after 1807 (when Pall Mall was gaslit) street lamps were 'little brightish dots, indicative of light but yielding, in fact, very little'. Their narrow beams hardly reached beyond the pavement's edge, and poorer streets were left in the dark.[10]

In street-paving, as in lighting, the City led the way. By insisting that householders employed the City's own paviors it had achieved uniformly surfaced roads and flat flagged pavements in the seventeenth century, while Westminster had uneven and pot-holed streets, and treacherous footpaths separated from the roads by rows of posts. In the 1750s Jonas Hanway could 'hardly find five square yards of true even pavement' in Westminster. In 1762 these conditions prompted the appointment of a House of Commons Committee to examine the paving and lighting of the whole of West London, which recommended 'that the paving, cleansing, repairing and lighting, as well as removing nuisances, and making the town more ornamental and commodious should be put under the management of Commissioners'.[11] This was not the first time that Parliament had set up a group of trustees or commissioners empowered to levy local rates, raise loans, and take over the responsibilities of householders and parish vestries. St James's Square was given trustees in 1725, and about twenty other towns had them before 1760. But the creation of the Westminster Paving Commissioners established this as a common solution to the problem of urban street maintenance, and by 1835 about 300 bodies of Improvement Commissioners, 100 of them in London, had been created. Some of these bodies were elected, but most, and nearly all the London ones, were cliques of lifetime nominees and coopted members, answerable to no one. In time, their duties sometimes expanded to include traffic control, nuisance removal and policing, as well as lighting, paving and street-cleaning.

As a result of the Westminster Paving Act of 1762, householders were relieved of their paving, lighting and cleaning duties in return for an annual rate, levied only when their own street was improved. Between 1762 and about 1780 the Commissioners completed an enormous task, replacing the uneven pebble footpaths on the better streets with raised pavements made from flat slabs of Aberdeen granite, and giving roads side gutters in place of central drains. This allowed the growing volume of passenger and goods traffic to flow more freely, and separated pedestrians from vehicles. By the 1780s Westminster's streets were winning praise from foreign visitors, and the City, which did not use Aberdeen granite till about 1800, was compared unfavourably with the West End. If we end the story there, it appears to be a tale of improvement triumphing over chaos, but, as the Webbs make clear, in the 1780s and 1790s the parish vestries and many smaller neighbourhoods won their own local Acts, reclaiming street maintenance powers from the Westminster Paving Commissioners. Some of these, particularly St Marylebone, did the job well, but most (notoriously St Pancras) did not, and by 1815 the growth of traffic and the excavations of water and gas companies had reduced the system to a condition reminiscent of its state in 1762. Outside the City, London's streets were in the hands of a huge number of uncoordinated authorities: about 100 groups of commissioners, about fifty turnpike trusts (responsible for some main roads), and the parish vestries. An attempt in 1817 to create a unified authority was defeated by the pressure of the vestries, and the system escaped effective reform until 1855.[12]

When the Improvement Commissioners and parish vestries took on the duty of paving the roads, they also took over the householder's responsibility to keep them clean. This was an increasingly difficult and important task. There was too much rubbish now for it to be dumped in the river, and those remote fields to which 'dirty trades' had been exiled in the Middle Ages were now parts of the suburban sprawl. Elegant Londoners regarded the traditional method of sewage disposal, throwing it out of the window, with growing distaste. In the City, which had faced these problems for centuries, satisfactory communal solutions had been devised. In return for a customary fee, householders and tradesmen could leave their rubbish out at night, when it would be collected in covered carts by 'Rakers,' who collected 'all the dung, soil, filth, seacoal, ashes and other dirt' from the houses, streets, back-alleys and laystalls, and got rid of it where they could. In Westminster, where the pressure of population growth was greater, conditions were far worse, and the attempt to copy the City's system in legislation of 1662 and 1691 was not a success. Rakers were employed, but they ignored many streets, and used open carts. 'The Rakers,' Hanway complained in 1754, 'not only drop near a quarter of their dirt, and render a whole street, perhaps already cleansed, in many spots very filthy, but it subjects every coach and every passenger, of what quality whatsoever, to be overwhelmed with whole cakes of dirt at every accidental jolt of the cart; of which many have had a most filthy experience.'[13]

Towards the end of the century the multitude of paving authorities (the vestries and local Commissioners) took over street-cleaning, and employed scavenging contractors chosen, it appears, more for cheapness than efficiency. What saved London's rubbish disposal system from complete failure was the growth towards 1800 of a strong commercial demand for urban refuse. Not only did canals and the growth of agriculture raise the market price of human and animal manure, but the suburban brick-making industry began to consume large quantities of London 'dust' (coal-ashes, cinders, and so on). St Margaret's Westminster paid its scavenging contractor £150 in 1799, but charged him £150 in 1801, and £625 in 1825. Marylebone, always a well-run parish, charged its contractors £1050 in 1796 and £2350 in 1803, and got a better service, too. These were the days of the 'Golden Dustman' of Dickens's *Our Mutual Friend*, when mountains of household dust and ashes were worth a fortune. By the late 1830s, though, when the cholera panic had made street-cleaning a matter of public health as well as comfort and convenience, the price of rubbish had collapsed, and local authorities had to think again about the cost of removing it, and the cost of leaving it where it was.[14]

A Dangerous City?

Alongside their environmental duties, the parish vestries were responsible for maintaining law and order. The reader of descriptions of London's street life, from *London Lickpenny* to John Gay's *Trivia*, or of the dozens of manuals of warning and advice that were published from the sixteenth century onwards, must assume that it was unusual to walk the length of the Strand or Cheapside without losing a purse or handkerchief, or being thrown to the ground by ruffians. Many contemporaries also regarded London as a very criminal place, especially in peacetime, when the population of young and disreputable men was not thinned by military recruitment and the press gang. All the eighteenth-century 'crime waves' in London, whether measured in the number of prosecutions and executions or the level of press and public concern, came in peacetime, and especially at the end of wars, when unemployed and violent ex-soldiers and sailors armed with cutlasses and pistols turned to crime for a living. There was a period of panic and high prosecution levels after 1713, and others in the mid-1720s, 1738, 1748–56, after 1763, after 1782 and after 1815.[15] Following the peace of Aix-la-Chapelle in 1748 prosecuted crime, crime reports in newspapers and monthly magazines, and public anxiety all increased, and in 1751 a House of Commons committee produced several ideas for improving policing and toughening the deterrent effect of punishment. This was the year, too, in which Henry Fielding, the novelist and Bow Street magistrate, published his famous *Inquiry into the Causes of the Late Increase of Robbers*.

Two pieces of legislation came out of this period of concern: the 1752 Disorderly Houses Act, which was intended to increase controls on places of entertainment and encourage the prosecution of brothels (and introduced a government subsidy for private prosecutors in deserving cases), and the 1752 Murder Act, which aimed to intensify the deterrent effect of hanging by declaring that the bodies of hanged murderers should be delivered to surgeons for dissection or hanged in chains on a public gibbet. This was not the first or last time that concern over crime levels in London prompted legislation which shaped the national penal or policing system. The 1718 Transportation Act, which made transportation to America or the West Indies the most common punishment for serious crime, emerged from a London panic, and the establishment of a new penal colony in Botany Bay in New South Wales in 1786 resulted from a City protest over a crime wave arising (it was thought) from demobilization and the ending of transportation to America. The moral reform crusades of the 1690s and the 1780s–90s, both of which left their mark on national legislation and culture, sprang largely from fears about moral breakdown in the metropolis. And when the penal tide began to turn after 1800 it was the evidence of the bankers and traders of London and Westminster that did most to persuade the Select Committee of 1819 that law enforcement would be improved by the abolition of capital punishment for non-violent crimes where hanging appeared to deter the public from bringing prosecutions.[16]

The image of London as a 'sink of iniquity', a 'thieves' kitchen', is so powerful that it is not easy to see through it to the reality beneath. Londoners were sure that they lived in a dangerous town, but perhaps they were more influenced by the unprecedented publicity given to crimes, trials and executions in Press reports, magistrates' and victims' advertisements and handbills offering rewards, and the mass of factual and fictional accounts of low life, than by first-hand experience. According to William Maitland, the most authoritative contemporary historian of eighteenth-century London, the famous Mohocks, young men who were said to have run riot in 1712, slitting noses, cutting off ears, and rolling people downhill in barrels, were just a newspaper invention. 'This Rumour gaining universal

Credit, struck such a Terror among the Credulous and Timorous that at the Approach of Night many durst not stir abroad, for Fear of being Mohock'd ... it does not appear that ever any person was detected of any of the said Crimes.'[17]

When James Boswell visited a cockpit in 1762, he wore his oldest clothes, left behind his watch, purse and pocket-book, and armed himself with an oaken stick. But Boswell suffered no robberies or thefts in 1762–3, any more than Pepys had done in the 1660s, although neither of them avoided the worst parts of town. Well-publicized muggings and assaults, reported in the *Gentleman's Magazine* or the daily Press, helped give contemporaries (and historians) the impression that crime was an everyday experience. London was a great and growing city, and even if its crime rate had been falling there were bound to be enough incidents to fill many newspaper columns. Horace Walpole's comments on the danger of the London streets are fairly typical: in 1750 he told Sir Horace Mann that in London 'one is forced to travel, even at noon, as if one were going to battle', and in 1782 he reported that 'we are in a state of war at home that is shocking. I mean, from the enormous profusion of housebreakers, highwaymen, and footpads.' Foreign visitors, whose appearance and ignorance of the town made them easy targets, reinforced London's criminal reputation. César de Saussure reported in 1726 that footpads armed with pistols, and pickpockets of 'extraordinary dexterity' were common in the town, and that his snuff box had been stolen in a crowded alley.[18]

It is extremely difficult to know whether these accounts reflect a heightened awareness of crime or a real increase in the problem of theft and assault. Statistics of indictments are of limited value in demonstrating long-term trends (and of hardly any value in assessing absolute levels of crime), since they reflect the effectiveness of policing and the willingness of victims to bring prosecutions, as much as changing crime levels. Short-term fluctuations suggest that high bread prices and postwar demobilization increased levels of prosecution (and probably levels of crime), and long-term trends suggest that life and property were safer in the eighteenth century than they had been a century earlier. J. M. Beattie, whose work on Southwark is one of the best studies we have of London crime between 1660 and 1800, concludes that the rate of murder convictions in Southwark fell by about five-sixths between 1660 and 1800, and that among most social groups there was a rise in civility, and a growing disinclination towards violence: 'Men and women seem to have become more controlled, less likely to strike out when annoyed or challenged, less likely to settle an argument or assert their will by recourse to a knife or their fists, a pistol, or a sword.' One contemporary observer, at least, concurs with Beattie's impression. Pierre Jean Grosley, whose visit to London in 1765 produced a popular guide-book, did his best to test London's reputation as a crime-infested city. He twice fell asleep in public, exposing his pockets to thieves, and he wandered carelessly in crowded streets and low districts. Despite all this he lost nothing, and though he saw plenty of quarrels settled by fist fights, he was surprised to find that London, although it was policed only by unarmed old men, was much less violent than other European cities.

> London is the only great city in Europe where neither murders nor assassinations happen. This I found by experience, as far as it was possible for me to find it. Returning from the play-house late at night, I chose, in preference to great streets, narrow passages, very indifferently lighted.... I had in this respect as full and satisfactory information as I desired. Even in the most violent disturbances, when I was in the midst of the mob, I have seen them threaten weakly, plunder some houses obnoxious to them, throw a few stones, and, though surrounded by troops, remain in a kind of awe, as well as the soldiers, through mutual fear of the effusion of blood. In a word, the people of London, though haughty and ungovernable, are in themselves good-natured and humane: this holds even amongst those of lowest rank.... If, notwithstanding the great care of the coachmen and carmen to avoid them, there arises some confusion and perplexity, their readiness to turn aside, to retire, to open, to lend each other a hand, if there be occasion, prevents this confusion from degenerating into one of those bloody affrays which so often happen at Paris.... I have seen four hundred coaches together at Ranelagh, which placed themselves in a file, passed each other, and were always ready at the first word, without either guards or directors to keep them to order. At public festivals, and all ceremonies which attract a crowd, let it be ever so great, children and persons low in stature, are seen to meet with tender treatment.[19]

Londoners in search of scenes of violence were most likely to find them at Tyburn (near Marble Arch) or, after 1783, outside Newgate Prison, where London's public hangman did his work. The miserable sight of men and (less often) women choking at the end of a rope became increasingly familiar in the later Hanoverian period, when London was, without question, the execution capital of Europe. Between 1701 and 1750 281 people were hanged in London (not counting Southwark), but the number rose enormously thereafter, especially in the 1760s (246 hangings) and the 1780s (501). Hangings diminished during the French wars (374 between

1791 and 1815), but revived with a vengeance between 1816 and 1820, when 140 people were hanged. The slaughter only ended when the Whigs came to power, full of reforming zeal and progressive middle-class ideals, in the 1830s. The majority of the 2,000 and more who died on the London gallows between 1700 and 1830 were burglars, thieves, robbers or forgers, though a fair number (perhaps a quarter) had been convicted of murder or rape. Nearly all of them (90 per cent in the 1780s) were under twenty-one.[20]

AMATEURS AND PROFESSIONALS

When every allowance has been made for sensationalism and panic, it is still likely that London experienced higher levels of crime than the rest of the country. It contained a vast population of young men and women, many of them impoverished and unable to find steady work. Its great concentration of houses, shops, warehouses, ships, taverns and well-off pedestrians offered endless temptations to opportunist thieves as well as professionals, and its many narrow alleys and unpoliced slum districts made escape and concealment easy. In small communities the enjoyment or disposal of stolen goods (unless they could be eaten quickly) was dangerous, but in London a newly acquired coat would not be noticed, and there were plenty of pawnbrokers, marine stores, second-hand dealers, publicans and professional receivers who would buy anything from candle and soap scraps to watches and jewellery. Although we must not forget the sense of community that even large suburbs could develop (as Jeremy Boulton's work on Southwark emphasizes) the fact that the poorer parts of London offered anonymity and opportunities for wrongdoing was already apparent to Adam Smith in the 1770s: 'In London a man is sunk in obscurity and darkness. . . . His conduct is attended to by nobody, and he is therefore very likely to neglect it himself, and to abandon himself to every low sort of profligacy and vice.' The parental and neighbourly controls that kept village boys out of mischief had less restraining effect among young migrants in Southwark or Stepney. Even in the West End, as James Boswell discovered, London offered 'the satisfaction of pursuing whatever plan is most agreeable, without being known or looked at', though he used this freedom for sexual rather than criminal purposes.[21]

Crime in London differed in some respects from the rural crime that prevailed in the rest of England. London thieves were more likely to steal clothes (their favourite target), household goods, metalwares, money and valuables than their country counterparts, and less likely to take food.[22] Women formed a much higher percentage of prosecuted criminals in London than in rural counties, perhaps because they led more independent lives than in the country, and faced the problems of supporting themselves through low-paid and irregular work in an overcrowded job market. A few women criminals gained notoriety in eighteenth-century London, distinguishing themselves from the general run of thieves and prostitutes by their skill or ambition. Mary Young specialized (until she was hanged in 1741) in picking pockets and purses in church, while false hands remained on her lap, and Moll King, who used the same technique in the 1720s, perhaps inspired Defoe's *Moll Flanders*. The vast majority of crime was petty and unprofitable, and only makes sense in the context of the poverty that was the common lot in eighteenth-century London.

The exploits of a few desperadoes, whose careers were seized upon and glamorized by pamphleteers and writers of 'confessions', have inevitably overshadowed the lives of common thieves. Dick Turpin, who emerged from the unpleasant group of robbers and rapists known as the Gregory Gang in 1735, became one of England's most famous men on the strength of eighteen months' highway robbery in Putney and Epping Forest. Highwaymen like Turpin and James Maclean (hanged in 1750) gained a reputation for courtesy and gentility, partly because the fact that they were on horseback (which in itself elevated them above the skulking footpad) enabled them to escape without first disabling their victims, and even to exchange pleasantries with them. Highwaymen preyed on the carriages and stagecoaches that had to cross the open commons and heaths on the outskirts of London. By sometimes showing favour to women and the poor, they gained themselves a largely undeserved 'Robin Hood' image.[23]

A feature of London crime that worried contemporaries was its high level of organization. Criminals in London were not lonely or isolated figures. Friendly taverns and lodging-houses ('flash-houses') gave them shelter, companionship and a base in which to plan their raids and sell their goods to receivers. Although the notorious Whitefriars (or Alsatia) sanctuary had lost its privileges in 1697 after a riotous battle with the Temple lawyers, and the last remaining sanctuary, the Southwark Mint (abolished in 1723), no longer sheltered felons, there were districts of dense courts and alleys all over London where thieves and prostitutes could live and work in relative safety. The size and importance of criminal gangs were clearly exaggerated by law and order propagandists like Henry Fielding, and by all those who made a living from sensationalizing crime, but such gangs did exist, and their activities gave London crime a special menace.

John Hawkins's gang, a group of about six men, specialized in robbing coaches on the roads in and out of London, and even within the town, in the early 1720s, until they were destroyed by a combination of betrayal by one of their members (a common danger for gangs) and the efforts of Jonathan Wild. There were also several loosely organized gangs of footpads in London around 1720, including James Shaw's gang of thirteen or more, and James Carrick's gang of about fifteen, both of which were betrayed and destroyed by Wild between 1721 and 1723.[24]

Jonathan Wild, the supreme criminal organizer of eighteenth-century London, the model for Peachum in John Gay's *Beggar's Opera*, realized that as much money could be made by catching thieves and returning stolen goods as from the simpler craft of stealing. This was especially so in the panic of 1720–21, when the government (apparently on Wild's advice) offered a bounty of £100 (in addition to the usual £40 reward) for the conviction of street robbers in London. Wild, calling himself the 'Thief-Taker General', worked on both sides of the law at the same time. He ran a 'Lost Property Office' in the Old Bailey, along the road from Newgate Prison and the Old Bailey Sessions House, London's main criminal court. From here he contacted the victims of theft (either in person or through newspaper advertisements), and received rewards for arranging the return of their goods (which he was careful not to handle himself). Within a few months of beginning these activities in 1714, Wild was using his knowledge of London's thieves and burglars to make arrests, persuade gang members to give evidence against their colleagues, and pocket the rewards. The destruction of the 'Whitehall Gang', who burgled the Banqueting House in 1714, was Wild's first success. Wild used his power as a 'thief-taker' to gain ascendancy over London's professional criminals, informing against those groups or individuals who would not submit to his authority or tried to sell their stolen goods elsewhere. Wild used the press to establish a reputation as an intrepid law-enforcer, and claimed to have sent sixty-seven criminals to the gallows, and eight to the penal colonies, in his career. The 1718 Transportation Act contained a clause which made taking rewards for returning stolen property without giving evidence against the thief a felony, but it was not until 1725 that the City Recorder moved against Wild, who was tried at the Old Bailey and executed (along with twelve others) at Tyburn in May.[25]

Until the rewards system was replaced by the granting of costs by Bennet's Act in 1818, bounty hunters, some of them as unscrupulous as Wild, continued to thrive in London. Some, like Stephen Macdaniel in the 1750s, framed the innocent and naive, while others, like Ralph Mitchell (also in the 1750s) and William Payne, who brought sixty-nine prosecutions between 1768 and 1771, were genuine private detectives. Well into the next century the capture of major criminals in Westminster and the City was in the hands of virtually freelance thief-hunters, who usually retired with large fortunes.

Keeping Watch

What enabled Wild and others like him to thrive was the failure of London's policing system to meet the challenge of urban growth. London's law enforcement depended on unpaid communal service, supplemented after the Restoration by a large number of paid watchmen. In the City, which was comparatively well policed, the ancient obligation on each ward to provide men to guard the walls by night had become a duty to watch the streets, and all householders were bound to take their turn on the nightly watch. The man responsible for organizing the watch in each precinct (the small areas into which wards were subdivided) was the unpaid part-time constable. As far back as the sixteenth century busy householders had been paying others to walk the streets on their behalf, and a crude system of professional policing had developed, relying on the cheap labour of (it was generally said) old, dishonest and simple-minded men. The system was reformed in 1663, when the number of constables on duty each night was reduced from around 240 (one per precinct) to twenty-six (one per ward), and a body of paid nightwatchmen (on paper nearly 1,000, but in practice around half that number) was established in the City.

In the rest of London the ancient system of parochial watch was also being supplemented by arrangements a little more suited to urban circumstances. In Westminster the Court of Burgesses presided over a system similar to the City one, with householders generally paying others to perform their duties as watchmen and constables. Like the City beadles, the burgesses acted as conduits for this money, and a good deal of it found its way into their own pockets. From the 1730s parishes began to introduce a more effective system, in which communal duties were replaced by a rate-funded body of paid nightwatchmen. The well-off and well-run parish of St George's Hanover Square was the first to move to this new system (in 1734), and the City (in 1737) and most metropolitan parishes followed suit within a few years. The effectiveness of London's policing depended largely on how well these men did their job. If, as most contemporary witnesses maintained, they were drunken and cowardly buffoons, 'fuddling in the watch-house or sleeping in their stands', then London's criminals had little to fear. But the Old Bailey and Southwark court records suggest that they were sometimes active men, questioning suspects, chasing off muggers and working together to make arrests. The effectiveness of the nightwatch depended very much on the willingness of individual parishes to spend money on it, hiring young ex-soldiers (as Marylebone, St James's and St George's Hanover Square did) rather than old paupers. The general impression is of uneven but real improvement in street patrols by the end of the century.[26]

MAGISTRATES AND POLICEMEN

London faced a further problem in the quality of its magistrates, whose combination of policing and judicial powers made them key figures in law enforcement. The growth of criminal business in London placed impossible burdens on unpaid part-time Justices of the Peace, and well before 1700 gentlemen magistrates in the Middlesex parishes (north of the river, excluding the City) were giving way to 'Blue Apron Men', tradesmen and craftsmen who hoped to make a living from fines and fees, if not plain corruption. Corruption was certainly not confined to 'men of mean degree' in eighteenth-century public life, but the 'trading justices', fostering crime and prostitution, taking protection money from brothels, selling licences and warrants, using constables to sweep the streets for petty offenders who could be profitably bailed, became stock figures in the novels of Fielding and Smollett (Justices Thrasher, Squeezum, Gobble and Buzzard), and may almost have deserved Edmund Burke's furious attack in 1780, after the Gordon Riots: 'The Justices of Middlesex were generally the scum of the earth – carpenters, brickmakers and shoemakers; some of them were notoriously men of such infamous characters that they were unworthy of any employ whatever, and others so ignorant that they could scarcely write their own names.'[27]

The fact that most Middlesex justices made a living from their work did not always prevent them from doing it well. Thomas De Veil, whose offices in Leicester Fields, Soho and finally Bow Street, Covent Garden, between 1729 and 1746, gave him responsibility for some of London's most difficult areas, seems to have combined profiteering and sexual profligacy with effective law-enforcement. De Veil's particular contribution was to turn part of his house in Bow Street into a public office, where cases would be heard openly, and the public were encouraged to take part as witnesses and observers. De Veil's successors at Bow Street, Henry Fielding (1748–54) and his half-brother Sir John Fielding (1750–80), built on De Veil's work, making their court in Bow Street into a 'police office' in which open pre-trial hearings weeded out malicious and frivolous charges, and to which victims of crime could bring their complaints to be investigated. Henry Fielding used his skills as a publicist to urge the public to join the fight against crime as witnesses or prosecutors, using the press, pamphlets, and his own bi-weekly paper, the *Covent Garden Journal*, to heighten public awareness. In 1772 Sir John Fielding launched a General Preventative Plan which extended this scheme to cover the whole country, placing Bow Street at the centre of a national network of criminal information. Fielding published a bulletin called the *Weekly Pursuit*, which communicated descriptions of stolen goods and suspected thieves to magistrates all over England, to enable them to arrest thieves who were being sought in other areas. This imaginative and successful scheme won government funding, and the *Pursuit* became the *Hue and Cry*, and after 1829 the *Police Gazette*. The Fieldings gained a reputation for fair and efficient justice, and under their control the Bow Street Magistrates' Court became the driving force for police reform in the metropolis and beyond.[28]

Henry Fielding's attempt to create a force of professional 'thief-takers' who would be motivated by public spirit rather than profit was not such an immediate success. Six ex-constables were recruited in 1750, under the command of the redoubtable Saunders Welch, High Constable of Holborn, to operate out of Bow Street. The government was persuaded to provide an annual subsidy of £200 in 1753, and two years later salaries were paid secretly to John Fielding and Saunders Welch. The Bow Street patrol had some impressive successes, notably the raid on Black Boy Alley in 1754, but its existence was spasmodic and it was not expanded. A mounted patrol of eight armed men, intended to protect the main roads as far out as Ealing, Clapham, Greenwich and Highgate, was abandoned after a year for lack of funding in 1764, and at the time of his death in 1780 John Fielding still had a force of only six men, two of them mounted. For all their propaganda efforts, the Fieldings never succeeded in destroying the belief, shared by politicians, parliamentarians and the public, that policing, even in London, was best left to the parishes, that a centrally controlled professional police force would endanger individual liberties and lead to 'French-style' absolutism, and that the threat of hanging or transportation was the best defence against crime. The fact that this belief survived so long (up to and beyond 1829) may suggest that the everyday experience of crime was not as appalling as the Fieldings and other publicists claimed.

Even in 1785, when the Gordon Riots of 1780 and the ending of transportation to America had heightened fears of disorder in London, William Pitt's Bill to create a single professional police force and a body of stipendiary magistrates for the whole metropolis was submerged by an avalanche of opposition, and had to be withdrawn. The political error of trying to include the City in the metropolitan system (an error not repeated by Peel in 1829) was partly to blame for Pitt's defeat, but there was widespread resistance from those who valued the gentleman magistracy and all those who, like the *Daily Universal Register* (later *The Times*), 'would rather lose their money to an English thief, than their liberty to a Lieutenant de Police'.[29] Pitt achieved some of his aims in the more modest Middlesex Justices' Act of 1792, which created seven new Police Offices, roughly on the Bow Street model, each with three salaried magistrates and up to six paid policemen, with a new power to arrest 'ill-disposed and suspected Persons'. There were two courts in Westminster (Queen Square and Marlborough Street), two in east London (Shadwell and Lambeth Street), one in Southwark (Union Hall), one in Hatton Garden and one in Shoreditch (Worship Street). At the same time the armed Bow Street patrol was increased to seventy men. The whole system was under Home Office control, and after about 1810 most of the stipendiary magistrates were qualified barristers. There were parallel improvements in the City, though here the patrol was much smaller – only twenty-four men in 1824.[30]

This was a major advance in the provision of relatively honest, open and accessible justice for Londoners, but only a timid step towards a professional police force for a city of almost a million people. In 1796 Patrick Colquhoun, one of the new magistrates, published a *Treatise on the Police of the Metropolis* which argued that the problem of crime in London was far more serious than had previously been realized, and that 115,000 Londoners lived wholly or partly from crime. Public attention was always focused on burglars, thieves, pickpockets and robbers, he argued, but this small group of about 2,000 professionals was responsible for less than an eighth of the £2 million-worth of property lost in London each year. About a third of this loss came from petty thefts by servants, apprentices, porters and other amateurs, another third from theft from quays and dockyards, and the rest, he believed, through forgery and coining. There was a trend throughout the century towards defining the taking of traditional perquisites (scraps of food from kitchens, pieces of cloth and metal from workshops, small quantities of sugar, coffee, tea, tobacco and metal from ships' cargoes) by working men and women as embezzlement or theft, and Colquhoun's calculations rest heavily on this broader definition of workplace crime. Servants and riverside labourers regarded these 'perks' as part of their payment for the job, and continued to do so well into the nineteenth century. Some of Colquhoun's other definitions are questionable, too. His assertion that London had 60,000 prostitutes (one to every four or five men), a figure that was repeated uncritically for the next sixty years, included in that category all unmarried women living with men.[31]

The Home Office's response to Colquhoun's highly influential work was to establish in 1800 a new Thames Police Office at Wapping, with a force of river police large enough to deal with crime along the Thames. Other forces soon followed, all attached to the Bow Street Office. In 1805 a Horse Patrol of sixty men, mostly ex-cavalrymen, was created to rid the main roads out of London of highwaymen. Squeezed by suburban growth and effective policing, this romantic (or romanticized) breed became extinct around 1831, when the last mounted highway robbery was recorded. After 1815, when returning soldiers created another 'crime wave', the Bow Street foot patrols in central London (except the City) were increased to around 100 men, and the gap between this force and the Horse Patrol was filled by a Dismounted Patrol of 100 men, England's first uniformed policemen, who guarded the suburban districts around 5 or 6 miles from the centre. Crime at night was the constant fear, and it was not till 1822 that the first day patrol was established, and even then it consisted of only twenty-seven men. By the 1820s, then, London was quite a heavily policed city, with around 450 professional officers under the magistrates' (and thus the Home Office's) control, and about 4,000 City or parochial watchmen. How effective these men could be, most of them lacking training, motivation and leadership, and confined within parish boundaries, was a question which the Parliamentary Committees of the 1810s and 1820s would attempt to answer.

Chapter 14

Politics and Public Order

THE HEARTY WELCOME given by Londoners to Charles II in 1660 did not mean that the City was abandoning its traditional suspicion of royal authority or its opposition to overmighty government. Echoes of the 'December Days' of 1641 sounded out over the next 150 years, triggered by a great variety of grievances, but motivated by the same general hostility to the Court and its agents that had sent Strafford and Laud to the block. Other characteristics of the politics of 1640–42 were repeated, too: the conflict between the loyalist City élite, with its Court contacts and government contracts, generally controlling the Court of Aldermen and the mayoralty, and the middling and lesser merchants and craftsmen, dominant in Common Council and Common Hall, and struggling to assert the authority of these more representative institutions over the oligarchic power of the aldermen; and the powerful and ambiguous role of the crowd, sometimes manipulated by opposition groups within the City, sometimes breaking free of political control and pursuing causes of its own.

THE CHANGING CROWD

As the events of 1640–42 made clear, London's huge population of young apprentices, journeymen and labourers enabled it to produce formidable and dangerous crowds at times of political, religious or economic tension. The complete breakdown in the political consensus that made the riots of 1640–41 so devastating was not repeated after 1660, but many of the factors that had contributed to the pre-Civil War crisis still operated in the calmer post-Restoration world. Religious bigotry, directed mainly against Catholics, could still bring thousands on to the streets, especially at times of unemployment and trade depression. Opposition groups in the City were still ready to use the London crowd against the government, though they were more aware now of the dangers of doing so. And working people, who were extremely vulnerable to tax changes and to fluctuations in wages and prices, but lacked the vote and found long strikes difficult to sustain, still saw demonstrations and violence as the most effective way of imposing their will on rulers and employers. In most London riots religious and constitutional rhetoric, élite manipulation, economic tensions, traditions of pageantry and 'Misrule' and youthful 'high spirits' were intertwined.

Since the crowd is a powerful player in the politics of late Stuart and Hanoverian London, it would be wise to clarify its identity. There is a temptation to talk of the London crowd, or 'mob', as it was usually called after the 1690s, as a single entity, a monster with many heads but a single brain. Its frequent changes of outlook between 1660 and 1800, from anti-royalist to royalist and back again, from anti-Catholic to anti-Dissenter, from anti-Stuart to anti-Hanoverian, from Whig to Tory, from radical to conservative, thus appear to be the oscillations of an immature and fickle mind. Of course, as Tim Harris points out, 'a crowd is a collection of individuals, and every time a new crowd appears, the individuals are regrouped.... each crowd is different from the last'.[1] London was large enough for many crowds to exist within it, some pursuing strictly economic goals, others motivated by xenophobia or religious bigotry; some royalist, others hostile to the Court; some seeking political change, others clinging to the old order. There were City crowds and suburban ones, 'respectable' crowds of craftsmen and tradesmen, whose opinions might influence Common Hall and the Common Council, and 'rough' crowds of unenfranchised coal-heavers and sailors, more concerned about food, wages, taxes and work than the finer points of the constitution.

LONDON AND CHARLES II

There was distrust between Charles II and the City from the start. The City sent four independent-minded MPs to the Cavalier Parliament in 1661, and the King (remembering the role of the trained bands in his father's fall) placed the City militia under the command of royal appointees, and threatened to alter the City's constitution if loyal men were not elected to Common Council. The harassment or persecution of religious Dissenters (especially Quakers and Baptists) in the 1660s (and again in the 1680s) under the legislation known collectively as the Clarendon Code, alienated many who had supported the Restoration. Anti-popery was reawakened by suspicion of the Court, where the King's mother, wife, brother and mistresses were Catholics, and by the growing dislike of the atmosphere of debauchery and frivolity that surrounded the King. The word in London in

1662 was that 'the Bishops get all, the Courtiers spend all, the Citizens pay for all, the King neglects all, and the Divills take all'. This growing disillusionment exploded on 23–24 March 1668, when crowds of young men, mostly apprentices and sailors, attacked and demolished bawdy houses in Poplar, Shoreditch, Holborn and Moorfields. Brothels, especially those that gave bad value, were traditional targets, but some of the crowds marched behind banners of leveller green, and there was talk of pulling down 'the great bawdy house at Whitehall'. The King saw political significance in the riots, and indicted their leaders for treason.[2]

Perhaps the Court treated the 1668 Bawdy House Riots with more seriousness than they deserved, but in the mid-1670s an openly anti-Court atmosphere developed in the capital, fuelled by Charles's growing closeness to Louis XIV and the marriage of James (the King's brother and heir) to a Catholic princess, bringing the prospect of a popish dynasty. Republican pamphlets and verses began to circulate in radical coffee houses, and there were November pope-burning processions from 1673 onwards, some of them said (implausibly) to involve between a quarter and a half of the population of London. Public anxiety was already high in August 1678, when Titus Oates 'revealed' a Popish Plot to murder Charles, to set fire to London, and to place James on the throne. Over the next four years opposition politicians, mostly Dissenters and their sympathizers, exploited this anxiety to create a movement to exclude James from the succession, using ballads, pamphlets, processions and newspapers to rally public opinion, especially in London, to the 'exclusionist' cause. Around 70 per cent of male Londoners were literate in the 1670s, and even the illiterate could hear newspapers read in coffee houses, join in anti-papist ballads and processions, or enjoy exclusionist plays and woodcuts. Popular support in London was vital to the exclusionist cause, and in the Parliamentary elections of March and September 1679, in which the opposition (known as 'Whigs') won clear majorities, the City liverymen in Common Hall chose four exclusionist MPs. Two of the City MPs, Thomas Pilkington and Sir Thomas Player, were leading figures in the first Exclusion Parliament in 1679. In Westminster the enormous electorate returned Sir William Waller, an anti-Catholic fanatic.

The Earl of Shaftesbury, the Whig leader, tried to build upon his popular support by pamphleteering and mass petitioning after Parliament was prorogued in June 1679, and although the Court party (now known as the Tories) fought back with their own loyal clubs and meetings, with warnings of republicanism and anarchy, and their own anti-Whig scare story (the 'Meal-tub Plot'), London opinion was generally with the opposition, at least until the Popish Plot panic faded in 1680–1. On 17 November 1679 the Whigs and Dissenters of the Green Ribbon Club organized an enormous procession and pope-burning to celebrate Queen Elizabeth I's official birthday, and vast crowds lit hundreds of bonfires to welcome Monmouth (Charles's illegitimate son and an alternative heir to the throne) a fortnight later. At the same time signatures for mass petitions were collected in taverns and by doorstep canvassers in the City, Westminster and Southwark. If the Whigs wanted a national movement to force Charles to call Parliament, it was vital that 'London should lead the dance'. This combination of genuine popular feeling and cynical crowd manipulation by opposition politicians became very familiar over the 100 years.[3]

Charles appears to have lost the contest for votes and popular support in London in 1679–81, but unlike his father he had nerve, political skill, intelligence, and control of the City militia. By calling the third Exclusion Parliament at Oxford in March 1681, he robbed the Whigs of the support of the London mob, and by negotiating secret French subsidies he could afford to dissolve Parliament after a few days. Cut off from their London supporters, there was nothing the Whigs could do about the dissolution, and without further elections their popular following did not count for much. In any case, public feeling had begun to swing back to Charles, and even to James, in 1681 and 1682, with loyal demonstrations and Tory successes in the Common Council elections of December 1681 and 1682.[4]

The Whigs still had enough support in London, especially in Common Hall and from the Lord Mayor and sheriffs, to defend Shaftesbury against royal retribution. When the King tried to use the courts to destroy Shaftesbury in November 1681 the Lord Mayor and the sheriffs made sure that his case would come first before a Whig grand jury, which threw his indictment out and discredited the prosecution witnesses. To Charles, who knew the capital's part in his father's destruction, and its dangerous ability to give a lead to the nation, it now seemed imperative that London's opposition should be broken. Although strenuous efforts were made to rally loyal feeling in the City, it was difficult for the Tories to win control of Common Council, the elected legislative assembly, or Common Hall, the mass meeting of liverymen which chose the City's four MPs and shared in the choice of the sheriffs and the Lord Mayor. But the Court of Aldermen had a Tory majority, and the man next in line for the mayoralty, and chosen in 1681, was a 'flexible and faint-hearted' ex-dissenter, Sir John Moore, who could be persuaded to support the King. Moore was able to spearhead Charles's campaign to win control of other vital City offices in 1681–2. Using the Lord Mayor's authority, the militia, ballot-rigging, and selective challenges to the right of dissenters to vote in Common Hall, Tory sheriffs and a royalist successor to Moore were chosen, and Whig control of the upper reaches of the City constitution was broken. Tory sheriffs meant a Tory jury, and Shaftesbury, realizing that the game was up, fled to Holland in 1682. Some other City Whigs, including Thomas Pilkington, the City MP, and Sir Samuel Bernardiston, foreman of Shaftesbury's grand jury, were imprisoned. After this, the crisis was over. There were no more crowd disturbances after 1682, even during Monmouth's rebellion in 1685, and the government was able to prosecute about 4,000 dissenters between 1682 and 1686 without opposition. Only in 1686, when James II had alienated the Anglican majority, did crowd trouble begin again. In June 1683, after a long legal wrangle, the City's charter was declared forfeit and replaced by a constitution in which London's government was in the hands of the Lord Mayor and aldermen, all royal appointees, and the Common Council played no part. The 'democratic' constitution of London, which had been such a danger to Charles and his father, was destroyed.[5]

WHIG AND TORY, COURT AND COUNTRY

Charles II's achievement in mastering London was thrown away by his brother James II, whose policies between 1685 and 1688 (an unpalatable mixture of Catholicism, absolutism and incompetence) drove almost the whole political nation into opposition. In October 1688, when William of Orange's invasion was imminent and James's position was crumbling, London's charter was hurriedly restored, along with other unconvincing last-minute concessions. James's eventual flight from London on 11 December 1688 (and again, after his temporary recapture, ten days later) created fears of anarchy and mayhem in the capital, which encouraged Whigs and Tories to work for a rapid compromise and the restoration of stable government under William. Perhaps because of the efforts of a group of peers and bishops, who set up an emergency government in the Guildhall when James fled, the expected unrest in the capital did not amount to much, apart from a fierce but brief outburst of anti-Catholic rioting on the nights of 11 and 12 December. Later in December, while William and the peers were making plans for a Convention Parliament, Common Council elections were held and the aldermen displaced in 1683 were restored.

In the fifteen years after the 1688 Revolution there were confusing realignments in political loyalties within the City. For a while, the wealthy exclusionist aldermen reinstated in December pursued a policy of radical reform in City and national politics. They proposed a radical revision of the City's constitution, giving Common Hall, the City's most democratic assembly, full power to elect the Lord Mayor and both sheriffs, and the freemen of the wardmote the right to choose their own alderman, regardless of whether he possessed the usual £10,000 estate. The authority of the Lord Mayor and aldermen to summon, control or veto the Common Council was to be removed, and Common Council was to be the City's supreme legislative assembly. But rich Whig aldermen were not natural democrats, and the radical attitudes they had developed in the heat of their conflict with Charles and James II soon faded. In May 1690 the new Tory-dominated Parliament rejected the revised City constitution, and in June Tories won a majority on the Common Council. Faced with a hostile Common Council, the Whig aldermen lost interest in their earlier proposals, and, as the old exclusionists died off, members of the City's political and business élite found themselves drawn into the profitable world of government war finance that developed in the 1690s. By subscribing to the Bank of England in 1694 and the New East India Company in 1698, the Whig City élite resumed their old friendship with the Court, and by 1695, when the aldermen clashed with the liverymen over the extent of the legislative and elective powers of Common Hall, their transition from radicalism to oligarchy was complete. As Whigs shifted their position from opposition to establishment they lost the electoral support of citizens in the poorer wards near the river and near and beyond the walls, and retained only the rich inner-City wards, while poorer and more radical voters drifted over to the Tories, who had adopted, by 1710 or thereabouts, most of the radical and oppositionist policies which the Whigs had abandoned in the 1690s.[6]

Londoners' fundamental attachment to the rights of freemen and liverymen in wardmotes and Common Hall, as opposed to the power of the élite in the Guildhall or Whitehall, remained unchanged, but their party affiliations (when they had them) were altered, as was their perspective on the Revolution of 1688. They were also drawn towards Toryism by a romantic nostalgia for the half-remembered days of Charles II, whose kingly virtues seemed enormous compared with those of most of his successors. So by 1709 the Tories outnumbered Whigs on the Common Council, drawing their votes from the tradesmen and craftsmen of the outer wards.[7] This change of view became abundantly clear in March 1710, when London experienced one of its worst riots of the eighteenth century. On 5 November 1709 the High Anglican Tory clergyman, Dr Henry Sacheverell, gave a sermon in St Paul's Cathedral attacking Dissenters and their friends in Church and State, and implicitly denouncing the 1688 Revolution. Defying the Court of Aldermen, Sacheverell (who loved to play to the crowd) published this sermon and sold it in vast numbers, so that when he was tried for seditious libel in Westminster Hall in February and March 1710 the significance of his stand was clear to thousands of Londoners. On 1 March, the third day of the trial, popular support for Dr Sacheverell, stirred up by High Church clergy and apparently coordinated by Tory gentlemen, broke into open rioting.

These were not wild riots provoked by economic hardship, but planned and disciplined attacks on well-chosen targets. Six important Dissenting meeting-houses west of the City were destroyed, and their furnishings burned in great bonfires well away from other properties. When groups of rioters were overtaken by troops in the early hours of 2 March, they were on their way to attack the houses of leading Whigs and Low Churchmen, and the epitome of the new Whig war finance, the Bank of England, which had its headquarters in Grocers' Hall. Purely economic targets, such as grain warehouses or workshops, were ignored. Geoffrey Holmes has discovered clear evidence of well-off management and leadership in the Sacheverell riots. Of the ninety-one rioters whose jobs or status are known, only four were apparently illiterate or unemployed, thirty were apprentices or domestic servants, twenty-six were self-employed tradesmen or crafts- men, about ten were professional men, and ten or more were gentlemen. This establishes the Sacheverell riots as 'the most respectable urban disorder of the century'. The discipline and equipment of the demolition squads, the evidence of well-dressed men disguised in great-coats directing oper- ations, the excellent information which guided the crowd from target to target, make it clear that this was a political riot, planned and organized by London Tories. Nevertheless, the willing participation of at least 5,000 Londoners (about 1 per cent of the population) indicates a fairly wide- spread hostility towards Dissenters, including Huguenots and Protestant refugees recently arrived from the Palatinate, as well as native non- conformists. The Sacheverell crowds were also expressing weariness after seventeen years of continental war, dislike of the growing clique of City financiers (many of them of immigrant descent) with a vested interest in prolonging the fighting, and hostility to the Whig oligarchy which had gained power, locally and nationally, as a result of the 1688 Revolution.[8]

The Tory government of 1710–14 and the Peace of Utrecht (1713) satisfied Londoners, but the accession of George I in August 1714 and the fall and trial of the Tory ministers revived popular hostility to the Whigs. By May 1715 anti-Hanoverian and anti-Whig demonstrations were commonplace, especially on Stuart anniversaries (Charles II's restoration, Oak Apple Day, Queen Anne's Coronation Day, the birthday of James the 'Old Pretender', and so on). Apart from straightforward military suppression (which was made easier by the Riot Act of August 1715) the government's favourite tactic was to appeal to popular anti-popery. During and after the half-baked Jacobite uprising of late 1715 there was a succession of anti-Catholic pageants, pope-burning parades and victory ceremonies, staged by City and Westminster Whigs in the hope of undermining pro-Stuart sentiment in the capital. To supplement this propaganda effort, gangs of loyalist toughs from Whig taverns known as 'Mug-houses' were organized to attack Tory crowds. A series of battles between 'Mug' and 'Jack' (Jacobite) gangs, and Tory attacks on 'Mug-houses', culminated in July 1716 in a mob attack on Read's Mug-house in Salisbury Court (next to St Bride's, Fleet Street), after which five rioters were hanged, the first London victims of the new Riot Act.[9]

The persistence of popular Toryism in London, surviving even the mighty appeal of anti-popery, is very striking. Doubtless there was a degree of crowd manipulation, though not on the scale of 1710, and the High Church clergy, including Dr Sacheverell, were still very active, particularly in some of the most anti-government parishes. But anti-Whiggery was clearly well rooted in popular feeling by 1715, and remained so for the rest of the century, nourished by a set of interlinked hostilities: to the House of Hanover, to long continental wars, to the Low Church and Dissent (especially in its moral reform guise), to political management and corruption (intensified by the introduction of seven-year Parliaments in 1716), to the extension and misuse of executive power, and to the City monied interest.

Sentimental attachment to the charismatic Stuart dynasty was apparently still strong in London in 1715 and 1716, to judge from the sympathetic welcome given to the Jacobite rebels when they arrived in the capital for trial and execution, and from the pro-Stuart slogans chanted by the crowds on Oak-Apple Day (29 May) 1715. Governments continued to fear a resurgence of London Jacobitism for the next thirty years, but affection for the Stuarts seems to have faded away fairly quickly after 1716. The great army stationed in Hyde Park in 1722, when Bishop Atterbury's planned Catholic uprising was exposed, turned out to be unnecessary, and at the time of Charles Stuart's invasion in 1745, most of the ninety-seven Londoners tried in the government's panicky reaction to signs of Jacobitism were either tipsy artisans making ill-judged anti-Hanoverian remarks in taverns, or Irish Catholics from the slums and back-streets of Southwark,

St Giles', Marylebone, Holborn and the East End. Jacobitism seems to have vanished from the mainstream of London popular feeling in the 1720s and 1730s, to be replaced by a sturdy libertarianism which damned the Stuarts and the Hanoverians alike.[10]

NEWSMONGERS

The political attitudes of Londoners were shaped and informed by a growing flow of fact and opinion. To reinforce the pamphlets, ballads and broadsides that had kept them abreast of political events for a century or more, Londoners now had an enormous supply of daily, thrice-weekly and weekly newspapers. In the fifteen years after the abolition of licensing in 1695 around twenty newspapers appeared in London, beginning with the *Post Boy* and the *Post Man*, and England's first regular daily paper, the *Daily Courant* (1702). Taxation replaced censorship as the government's favoured method of impeding the flow of political information to the lower classes. Most newspapers managed to find ways of avoiding the stamp duty introduced in 1712, but Walpole's 1725 Stamp Act forced them to double their prices to 1d or 2d, and by 1776 the normal price had been pushed up to 3d (half the price of a 4-pound loaf). There were many unstamped farthing dailies and thrice-weeklies in the late 1730s, but the hawkers selling them were driven off the streets in 1743.

High prices restricted the sales of most newspapers to 3–4,000 copies each, including their increasingly important provincial sales. These were the circulations achieved by the *Post Man* and *Post Boy*, by Addison and Steele's daily *Spectator* (1711–12), and the half-dozen evening papers that appeared between 1730 and 1750. By 1730 there were around six morning dailies, selling under 10,000 copies between them, but circulations rose to 2–3,000 each in and after the 1740s. Circulations of 10,000 or more were achieved by the very successful *Gentleman's Magazine*, and by the anti-Walpole *Craftsman* in the early 1730s.

The readership and influence of the London papers were far greater than their low sales figures suggest. Better road transport and an improving postal service gave the London Press a growing national role in the eighteenth century, and in London contemporaries estimated that each copy of a daily paper was read by twenty people, with double that number for weeklies. The 'Mercuries' who sold London's newspapers (mostly hawkers and pamphlet shops) were willing to hire as well as sell, and working men could club together to buy a paper. Most of all, the coffee houses, of which there were about 560 in 1739, swelled the numbers of newspaper readers. 'What attracts enormously in these coffee-houses,' César de Saussure wrote in 1726, 'are the gazettes and other public papers. All Englishmen are great newsmongers. Workmen habitually begin the day by going to coffee-rooms in order to read the latest news. I have often seen shoeblacks and other persons of that class club together to purchase a farthing paper. Nothing is more entertaining than hearing men of this class discussing politics and topics of interest concerning royalty.' Even allowing for some exaggeration, it is hard to imagine a plainer description of a politically aware population.[11]

A Tradition of Opposition

The persistent opposition of the City's middling and lesser inhabitants, those who dominated Common Council, Common Hall, and the streets, was one of Sir Robert Walpole's greatest difficulties in the 1720s and 1730s, and helped to destroy his administration in 1742. The City electorate, the 8,500 liverymen who sat in Common Hall, had more than doubled between 1660 and 1722, and its four MPs, led from 1722 to 1761 by the popular and authoritative alderman Sir John Barnard, lent weight to the opposition. London's power did not rest in its direct parliamentary representation, though. With over a tenth of England's population, but only ten of the 489 English MPs (four for the City, and two each for Westminster, Southwark and Middlesex), London was the most under-represented place in the country. Of course, many MPs for other constituencies were Londoners (over fifty), and all MPs were part-time London residents. But London could influence and lead national opinion, it could give opposition politicians the 'outdoor' support they needed, and it could put direct pressure on Westminster by mass petitions and street demonstrations. The Court of Aldermen, with its natural affinity for authority, remained loyal to the government, but the wards and the Common Council had drifted steadily to the Tories since 1710, and Common Council legislation of 1711, 1712 and 1714 had forced the Court of Aldermen to accept directly elected ward nominees as new aldermen, rather than choosing from a list of four. The ward nominees, the Court complained in 1719, might be 'no ways fit for their Company or for the Magistracy of the City'.

The obvious course, as far as Walpole was concerned, was to follow the example set by Charles II in 1683, and revise the City's constitution to concentrate power in the hands of the government's rich allies among the monied élite, Bank of England, East India Company and South Sea Company directors, government fundholders and contractors, and the leaders of the richer livery companies, and to exclude as many poorer citizens as possible from legitimate politics. This was his aim in the 1725 City Elections Act, which shifted power decisively from the Common Council to the Court of Aldermen. Walpole (and some recent historians) might present this as a necessary reform, to bring order to chaotic and poorly supervised Common Hall elections, and restore the ancient and recently eroded powers of aldermen. But Walpole was not noted for his concern over electoral irregularities, and City elections, unlike those in Westminster and elsewhere, were not marred by excessive violence, bribery or impersonation. The ministry's plain intention (George I was told) was to 'secure the government of that important place entirely in the hands of those who are zealous for your Majesty's interests' by removing 3,000 poorer freemen from the ward electorate, and restoring the Court of Aldermen's veto over Common Council legislation and petitions.[12]

The 1725 Act did not stifle the government's opponents for long. By 1733 the opposition was in control of the City again, and Walpole's stock was as low as ever. The City's large, experienced and well-informed electorate was not amenable to the system of political corruption and patronage which served the government so well in the rest of the country. Its voters (and even its non-voters) had political opinions of their own, and knew how to express them in elections, petitions and street demonstrations, with or without the approval of the Court of Aldermen. Walpole tried to counter the influence of the popular anti-ministerial journals, the *Craftsman* and *Mist's Weekly Journal*, and the ruthless attacks of the cartoonists and balladeers, by buying and subsidizing pro-government newspapers, among them the *Daily Courant*, the *Free Briton* and the *London Journal*. Yet in the crisis over Walpole's new excise taxes in 1733, when the capital was subjected to a barrage of free ministerial newspapers, handbills, ballads and pamphlets, London's hostility to the Excise Bill proved to be unshakeable, and the City's vigorous opposition to a measure which (as they saw it) would erode individual privacy and penalize City traders played a leading part in forcing Walpole to withdraw it. On 11 April 1733, on leaving the Commons after abandoning the Bill, Walpole had to scurry from coffee house to coffee house to escape a beating from a London mob, and that night the triumphant crowd burned effigies of the chief minister and the Queen. Yet to speak of the London mob 'bellowing its mindless hatred' after heavy drinking sessions in opposition taverns, as J. H. Plumb does, is to forget that Walpole's men were as generous with their drinks and as well served by hacks and propagandists as the opposition were. The difference between them was that one side was playing to the fixed, but not mindless, principles of many Londoners, and the other was not.[13]

In the last few years of his ministry, Walpole's support in the City was so weak that even his stronghold, the Court of Aldermen, was lost. As in 1733, the opposition to him between 1738 and 1742 united trading interests and popular feeling. In March 1738 two City MPs, Micajah Perry and Sir John Barnard, presented a petition from London's Atlantic merchants to the Commons, urging the government to defend British trading interests against Spanish privateers. The other major ports followed London's lead. Exaggerated stories of the torture and mutilation of British seamen (including the famous loss of Robert Jenkins's ear) helped to whip up popular hostility to the old Spanish enemy, and Walpole's conciliatory foreign policy was presented as a betrayal of national interests. From 1739, Walpole's position in the City crumbled. His favoured candidate for Lord Mayor was rejected by Common Hall in September 1739, despite being the most senior contestant, and in Common Council elections over the next two years even the wealthy central wards near the Royal Exchange fell to the opposition. In October 1739 Walpole went reluctantly to war with Spain, but even this won him no credit in the City, which instead lionized Admiral Vernon, captor of Porto Bello. In the general election of 1741 government candidates were humiliated, and in 1742 the opposition won control of the Court of Aldermen for the first time since the 1680s. Through its petitions and its instructions to City MPs, the Common Council gave a lead to other boroughs and counties, reinforcing the influence of the nationally distributed London press, and making the City a rallying point for Tory opinion across the country. It is hard to know how much this influenced the national result of the 1741 election, which destroyed Walpole's Commons majority and led to his resignation, but it is clear that support 'out of doors', and especially in London, was commonly regarded as an essential part of a successful opposition's armoury.

Although London's hatred had been focused for twenty years on Robert Walpole, the City's anti-government stance was too deeply rooted to be ended by a change of Prime Minister. William Pulteney, who had used London's support to gain power in 1742, was almost bound to betray all the City's hopes for reform when he was in Walpole's place, and he duly did so. Even in the Jacobite invasion crisis of 1745, when the Catholic threat increased support for the ministry among City moderates, a majority of Common Councillors refused to support a loyalist declaration. After the crisis, though, government propagandists (including Henry Fielding) used the Jacobite smear against radical oppositionists, and Common Hall elected loyalist or Whig MPs in the 1747 general election. Their hostility to the government might have been temporarily softened, too, by the removal of the aldermanic veto on Common Council decisions in 1746.[14]

The only real break in the City's opposition tradition came in 1756–61, during the wartime ministry of William Pitt, who managed the unique trick of retaining while in office the loyalty of those who had supported him in opposition. Pitt's appeal to Londoners came from the fact that he was an outsider, never a Court favourite, and that he pursued, with spectacular success, a colonial war policy which satisfied London jingoism and City trading interests. Pitt's strength in the City was increased by his close alliance with Alderman William Beckford, City MP and sheriff, and Lord Mayor in 1762 and 1769, a dominant figure in City politics. Pitt's dismissal in October 1761, his replacement by the royal favourite Bute, and the Peace of Paris in February 1763, which seemed to the City (though not to others) to sacrifice national trading interests, led to a resumption of hostilities between London and the administration.

A part of London in which the government could generally expect to win elections was Westminster, where Court patronage and aristocratic influence in the four fashionable West End parishes (St Margaret's Westminster, St John's Westminster, St George's Hanover Square, St James's Piccadilly) outweighed the votes of the independent-minded tradesmen and shopkeepers, mostly outfitters and victuallers, of the commercial parishes nearer the City (St Anne's Soho, St Paul's Covent Garden, St Martin-in-the-Fields, and St Clement Danes). Here, as Nicholas Rogers puts it, the 'pressures of Court and aristocratic authority, the peculiarities of Westminster's luxury economy, helped to perpetuate a system of social stratification where deference and dependency held sway, and emasculated the emergence of class interests in a truly articulated form'. Even in Westminster the enormous power of the government and its aristocratic allies as employers and landlords, and as customers of the area's many luxury tradesmen, did not guarantee success when the administration was unpopular. In 1741 the voters of Soho, Covent Garden and the Strand came within an ace of electing the opposition hero Admiral Vernon, and might have done so if the High Bailiff had not closed the poll after a mob, with its usual supply of dead cats and dogs, had surrounded the Covent Garden hustings for five days. The election of 1749 was even more disorderly, with the poorer electors agitated by the recent execution of the Strand wigmaker, Bosavern Penlez, for his part in a Bawdy House Riot, and by the arrival of a French acting troupe with foreign plays for the well-to-

20. The great Frost Fair of December 1683 to February 1684, seen from the Temple stairs. This fair, which is described in John Evelyn's diary, brightened an otherwise hungry and disease-ridden winter.

21. The new West End around 1707. A Prospect of St James' Palace and Park, and the fashionable suburb developing to the north and east of the Palace. Drawn by Leendert Knyff and engraved by Johannes Kip.

22. The Custom House and quayside in Lower Thames Street, the focal point of London's trade. It was rebuilt by Thomas Ripley after Wren's building was damaged in an accidental explosion in 1714. Engraving by William Henry Toms.

23. London firefighters in the 1720s. The water-pumping machine had to be filled by hand.

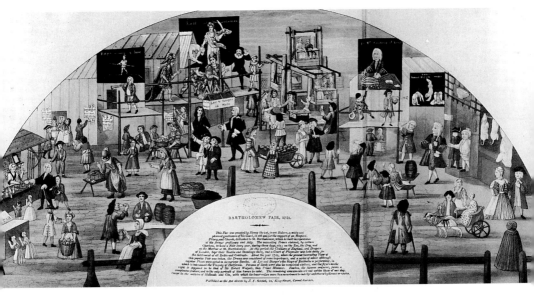

24. 'All moveables of wonder, from all parts, are here'. Fruit and gin sellers, acrobats, rope dancing, melodrama, Faux the conjuror, a dogcart, and even a primitive Ferris wheel in Bartholomew Fair in (roughly) its six hundredth year. A fan design of 1721.

25. Lawyers, litigants, booksellers and haberdashers in Westminster Hall, 1745. The Courts of King's Bench and Chancery are at the far end (left and right), and Common Pleas is in the right foreground. The drawing is by Hubert Gravelot.

26. 'The most convenient place for courtships of every kind': a Costume Ball in Ranelagh Gardens, Chelsea. The Gardens and the Rotunda were nine years old when this engraving (attributed to Remigius Parr) was published in 1751 (see page 314).

27. The Royal Cockpit, near St James' Park. This print, by William Hogarth, was published in 1757, five years before Boswell's visit, described on page 307.

28 & 29. Thomas Rowlandson and Augustus Charles Pugin jointly produced
the aquatints to illustrate Rudolph Ackermann's *Microcosm of London* (1809).
Rowlandson drew the figures, Pugin the buildings. These two examples show Bow
Street Police Court, the headquarters of policing and justice in Westminster, and the
Charing Cross pillory, where petty offenders were pelted with fruit (or worse).
The pillory was abolished in 1816.

30. Leather and hide dealers in Leadenhall Market, the City's general provisions market since the fifteenth century. Rowlandson and Pugin, *Microcosm of London* (1809).

31. Sampling the merchandise at the London Corn Exchange, Mark Lane. Aquatint by Rowlandson and Pugin for the *Microcosm of London* (1809).

32. George Cruikshank's thoughts on John Gay's theme (see pages 363–4), *The Art of Walking the Streets of London*. The dangers illustrated include umbrellas, street-corner collisions, pedestrians who take up the whole pavement, outlandish fashions, people blocking the path, mud, bookworms and attacks on nightwatchmen. Etchings published in 1818, adapted from earlier drawings by George Woodward.

33. Old London Bridge lost its famous houses in the 1750s, and by 1820 it was unstable, as well as inconvenient to shipping. Rennie's granite replacement was built between 1824 and 1831, and the old bridge was demolished a year later. Edward William Cooke's drawing shows work in progress in August 1830.

34. Working men on the march. Thousands of trade unionists rallied on Copenhagen Fields, Islington, on 21 April 1834 to petition Parliament for the release of five Dorchester labourers, the 'Tolpuddle Martyrs'. W. Summers.

35. The Houses of Parliament (the Palace of Westminster) on fire on Thursday 16 October 1834, watched by an appreciative crowd. Only Westminster Hall and the Jewel Tower were saved.

do. To counter popular hostility, the Court party, led by the Duke of Bedford, produced and distributed 227,500 letters and broadsheets to put its case. The government won the election by about 150 votes in a poll of over 9,000, but it was becoming clear that victory in Westminster, with England's biggest borough electorate, would depend in future on more than arm-twisting and 'treating'. This, like the City's, was an electorate that would have to be persuaded.[15]

THE INDUSTRIAL CROWD

It would be misleading to present London crowds as nothing more than occasional participants in conflicts between government and opposition politicians. They had interests and values of their own. Apprentices and young men and women gathered in response to familiar rallying cries – 'Prentices and clubs!', 'Shovels and spades!' – to punish those who had transgressed communal moral standards, threatened their economic or social interests, or offended their religious or patriotic prejudices. Through the tradition of 'Hue and Cry' crowds were encouraged to give chase to miscreants on the run from the local constable, and the pillory relied for its effect upon lusty public participation. Often, a crowd would pursue and punish wrongdoers on its own initiative, without waiting for a cry of 'Stop Thief!' Pickpockets would be drenched under a pump, dishonest shops and brothels ransacked or destroyed, strike-breakers, informers and cheats beaten up or worse. Constables might look to the public for help, but an unpopular officer could become a target himself, and crowds would sometimes 'rescue' a local figure from arrest, even (as happened in the Bawdy House Riots of 1668) breaking open the prisons where their fellow-rioters were held. With the decline of the Church courts after 1660, crowds often took over the task of enforcing the moral code, especially against promiscuous women and pregnant servants, the commonest victims of public abuse and assault. Women took a prominent part in these moral riots and in attacks on cheating shopkeepers. Of the hundreds of cases of riot that came before the Middlesex Quarter Sessions between 1660 and 1721, the great majority were petty local incidents like this, without conventional political significance.[16]

It has often been observed that riots could be a form of 'collective bargaining' between labourers and masters. Although there were various laws against unions or combinations of workmen, primitive unions existed in London and elsewhere in the eighteenth century. The London journeymen feltmakers 'conspired and combined together' in 1696 to raise their piece-rates for making hats, and their organization had a spasmodic existence throughout the next century. As the workforce in particular trades grew, workmen were able to use the institutions in which their masters liked them to wait for work or wages to organize on their own behalf. In 1721 the London master tailors complained that over 7,000 journeymen tailors, collecting names and money in the public houses where employers usually recruited and paid them, had 'lately entered into a combination to raise their wages, and leave off working an hour sooner than they were used to do'. They were demanding 12s 9d a week, 2s above their normal rates, and leaving work, if they came at all, at eight instead of nine, 'their usual hour, time out of mind'. 'Very great numbers of them go loitering about the town, and seduce and corrupt all they can meet', offering, the master tailors claimed, a 'very ill example to journeymen in all other trades; as is sufficiently seen in the Journeymen Curriers, Smiths, Farriers, Sail-makers, Coachmakers, and artificers in divers other arts and misteries, who have actually entered into confederacies of the like nature; and the Journeymen Carpenters, Bricklayers and Joiners have taken steps for that purpose, and only wait to see the event of others'. Parliament quickly made tailors' unions illegal in the London area, but their organization continued, fighting industrial disputes in 1744, 1752, 1764 and 1768, and gradually pushing up their rates of pay. The public houses which employers used as 'houses of call', convenient centres for recruiting temporary workers, became local union bases, sending delegates to a committee which initiated and organized strikes and fixed target rates of pay. The magistrate Sir John Fielding believed there were forty of these local 'box clubs' in 1756, run by a 'Grand Committee for Management of the Town', and Francis Place, writing in 1824 (the year that combinations became legal), described the tailors' organization as 'a perfect and perpetual combination, ... all but a military system', centred on 'upwards of twenty regular or "Flint" houses of call'.[17]

Of the 120 industrial disputes known to have occurred in London between 1717 and 1800, many involved a degree of violence. Working men had a tradition of violent action, and their legal and financial position made prolonged strikes difficult to win, unless trade was unusually brisk. As Adam Smith pointed out, combinations of employers were far more likely to hold out for weeks or months than their men were, and non-union labour was not hard to find. Swift raids on workshops or warehouses, the destruction of looms and other machines, and assaults on strike-breaking labourers, were easy and popular alternatives. In 1710, for instance, the

London framework knitters smashed more than 100 stocking-knitting frames to force their masters not to employ too many apprentices. Journeymen were especially hostile to the use of imported labour to break strikes or bring down wages, and there were some bloody conflicts between Londoners and immigrant workers. In July 1736 there were riots in Shoreditch, Whitechapel and Spitalfields against the employment of cheap Irish workers as demolition men and silk weavers. Large mobs, reportedly 2–3,000 strong, destroyed Irish public houses and lodgings in Brick Lane, Goodman's Fields and Rosemary Lane, wounding several Irishmen. A detachment of guards was called out from the Tower, and the crowd melted away 'as if a Hole had been dug in the Bottom of the Street, and they had all dropped into it at once'. The nine men arrested were given one or two years' imprisonment, a more severe punishment than the fines commonly inflicted on rioters, but mild compared with the hanging they might have suffered. Rioting resumed in September, and again in 1737, but this time the provocation was the new Gin Act, and the targets were the informers the government relied upon for its enforcement.[18]

The riots of 1736 were not the first occasion on which the silk weavers of Spitalfields and the surrounding area had used collective violence to protect their livelihoods. Silk weavers were exceptionally vulnerable to fluctuations in fashion, trade and seasonal demand, to competition from French and Italian producers and cheap Indian calico, from migrant and female labour, and from labour-saving machinery. Master weavers might prosper, as their fine terraced houses in Spitalfields still testify, but for the many thousand journeymen weavers, and for the many women and children employed as weavers, silk winders and throwsters, this was an overstocked, underpaid and precarious trade. Silk winders and throwsters were among the earliest groups to face competition from factory-based mechanical production (from Lombe's Derby mill in 1719 and others after 1750), and all silk workers were acutely aware of the threat of imports and mechanization. The weavers responded by forming well-organized combinations to maintain wage rates and delay mechanization, and using street violence to push the government to pass protective legislation. Riots in 1675 destroyed new labour-saving Dutch looms, and in 1697 weavers twice mobbed the Commons in support of a bill to limit the East India Company's silk imports. A greater threat came from calico, plain cotton imported from India and printed in London. Between June 1719 and July 1720 Spitalfields silk weavers attacked and abused women wearing calico, tearing the clothes from their backs, and abusing them as 'calico madams'. One woman was assaulted by a crowd of weavers, who 'tore, cut, pulled off her gown and petticoat by violence, threatened her with vile language, and left her naked in the fields'. A group that tried to march to Lewisham to destroy the calico printing presses was stopped by troops, who shot one of them dead. The passing of an Act in 1720 banning the wearing of calico stopped the riots, without solving the long-term problems of the London silk industry.[19]

THE TROUBLED 1760s

The silk weavers were on the streets again in the 1760s, a decade in which rising wheat and bread prices helped to bring many of London's economic and political tensions to a head. London did not suffer from food shortages, nor from the food riots that were commonplace over much of eighteenth-century England, but rising prices led to wage demands and industrial conflict, some of it extremely bloody. The ending of wartime protectionism in 1763, and the continued spread of engine-looms, depressed the silk industry. In 1763 the weavers rioted for higher wages and smashed engine-looms, and in 1765 8,000 of them marched on Parliament, destroyed the Duke of Bedford's coach, and won a ban on foreign silk imports. In 1768 low wages and high prices brought matters to a crisis. The silk weavers, organized into secret societies to escape conviction for conspiracy or combination, launched attacks on engine-looms and their operatives, and tried to intimidate masters into raising wage rates and subscribing to workers' funds. Early in 1769, 1,500 weavers attacked the large weaving workshop of Lewis Chauvet, and damaged seventy-six looms. In September 1769 the government, following the advice of Sir John Fielding, decided to use troops to bring the weavers to heel. Late that month troops were stationed in Spitalfields, and two weavers were killed when soldiers raided the Dolphin Tavern, one of the weavers' strongholds. In a typical and successful attempt to terrorize the weavers into submission, two of their leaders were hanged in Bethnal Green in December 1769. In 1773 the Spitalfields Act introduced magisterial wage control and a consultation procedure to settle disputes, and peace (but not prosperity) returned to the silk industry.

The government had more than silk weavers to worry about. After the freezing winter of 1767–8, which damaged river trades and brought an unusually large number of rural migrants into the city, industrial unrest became more generalized. Coal-heavers, seamen, hatters, tailors, glass-grinders, coopers, sawyers and watermen were all in dispute in 1768–9.

Some of the ugliest incidents involved the Wapping and Shadwell coal-heavers, around 670 men, mostly Irish, who unloaded the Newcastle colliers when they arrived in London. Like the silk weavers, the coal-heavers were concentrated in a small area, and their shared sense of communal solidarity enabled them to form effective secret organizations and act as a united force. Traditionally, these men had been organized and usually cheated by publicans known as 'undertakers', who took a substantial proportion of the heavers' wages in payment for drink, lodging and shovel hire. An Act of 1758 tried to end this oppression by establishing a new scheme run by William Beckford, Alderman for Billingsgate, providing the coal-heavers with sickness and other benefits in return for 10 per cent of their wages. By 1768 the new scheme was discredited, the undertakers had regained much of their control, and heavers' high wages were being cut by the spread of a new unloading system, replacing shovels with baskets and pulleys, which could be operated by fresh unskilled labour. With the help of a Tower Hamlets magistrate, Ralph Hodgson, the coal-heavers formed a new organization, the Bucks, and went on strike. When the old undertakers began to recruit unskilled labourers to unload the ships, the coal-heavers, with the support of an Irish terrorist gang called the Whiteboys, attacked their public houses. In one of the worst incidents, the Roundabout Tavern, Shadwell, was besieged throughout the night of 20–21 April 1768. Three coal-heavers and the undertaker's sister died in the attack, and in July seven coal-heavers were hanged for their part in it. Efforts to agree new rates failed, and the strike continued through the spring. The sailors and labourers hired by the undertakers to unload the ships were repeatedly attacked (and in one case murdered) by the coal-heavers in May and June, but eventually Guardsmen were stationed along the riverside, and the strikers were forced to return to work at their old rates of pay.[20]

'WILKES AND LIBERTY!'

May 1768, a month of unusually high bread prices, was a time of widespread economic and political tension in London. As well as the coal-heavers' and silk weavers' disputes, a sailors' strike had brought trade on the Thames to a halt, 2,000 watermen demonstrated outside the Mansion House, and the hatters were in the middle of a violent strike. At the same time, the most effective demagogue of the century, John Wilkes, was at the peak of his public influence. Londoners often made popular heroes of anti-government figures, as they did with Sacheverell and Admiral Vernon.

Wilkes was unique, though, in his ability to combine a rakish and irreverent appeal to the crowd's traditions of disorder and misrule with the exploitation of issues of real constitutional significance, among them freedom from arbitrary arrest, the rights of voters to elect their own MPs, the reporting of parliamentary debates and the extension of the franchise. Wilkes was an opportunist and a man of dubious moral standards (two very useful political qualities), but he can be seen as the midwife of the campaign for radical constitutional reform which dominated popular politics for the next 100 years.[21]

Wilkes first came to prominence in 1763, when the fall of Pitt and the Peace of Paris had created a mood of discontent in the City. His libellous attack on Lord Bute (in Number 45 of the *North Briton*), and his successful challenge to the government's right to arrest unnamed writers and publishers under a so-called 'General Warrant', made Wilkes a popular hero in 1763, when the slogan 'Wilkes and Liberty' was first heard on the streets of London. Between 1763 and 1768 Wilkes was in France, avoiding prosecution for publishing an extraordinarily obscene poem, *An Essay on Woman*, but on his return to London in February 1768, a cold and hungry month, he moved quickly to take advantage of the political and economic unrest that already existed in the capital. His defiant exploits of 1763 were still remembered, and Wilkes had no difficulty in attracting popular support. But popularity did not win elections, and Wilkes failed in his attempt to become a City MP in March 1768. Still, Wilkes had followers among ordinary tradesmen and craftsmen, the 'forty shilling freeholders' who made up the majority of the electorate of the county constituency of Middlesex, which included the poorer urban parishes surrounding the City and Westminster north of the Thames. The Middlesex election of 28 March 1768 was a fairly riotous affair, though no worse than many disputed elections were. Crowds of weavers in Piccadilly and on the roads to Brentford stopped all those who were not wearing a blue cockade for Wilkes, and scratched 'Wilkes and Liberty' or 'Number 45' on every coach. Mobs broke all the windows in the Mansion House, and for two nights crowds gathered in the West End to force the rich to light their lamps for Wilkes.

Wilkes's victory, won on the strength of his libertarian reputation and his support among the middling sort, might have given him the status and security from his creditors that he needed, and ended his career as a popular hero, if the government had not made the mistake of arresting him for seditious and obscene libel in April 1768. To defy the government and be sent to gaol for it was the surest way into Londoners' hearts. On 27

April, when his trial began at Westminster Hall, crowds rescued him and dragged his coach through the City, and on 10 May, the day Parliament opened, around 20,000 of his supporters gathered on St George's Fields, Lambeth, outside the King's Bench Prison, where he was held. Troops were called in to disperse the crowd, and about ten Wilkites were killed in what became known as the massacre of St George's Fields. Imprisonment was not a political handicap to Wilkes, since he was a poor public speaker, and such a difficult character that his influential City allies found it easier to support him in his absence. On the other hand, he was a master of written controversy, and issued a stream of handbills, pamphlets and open letters, all reprinted in the London and provincial Press, to keep himself in the public eye and to identify himself with the popular catch-all cry for 'Liberty'. He did not, though, try to establish a connection between his plight and those of the coal-heavers, silk weavers and other striking groups, and the industrial and political movements remained separate. The Press was a growing force in the 1760s. Individual circulations were no greater than they had been in the 1730s, but the total number of dailies, thrice-weeklies, weeklies and monthlies (most of them duplicating each other's material) was higher, and so was their aggregate readership.[22]

Wilkes may have been a licentious scoundrel, committed to nothing but his own advancement, but he found himself at the centre of a fundamental transition in London's political outlook. Up to the 1750s, the City had thrown its weight behind opposition politicians, and echoed their complaints about corruption, patronage and placemen. From the 1760s, City politicians and politically conscious Londoners were against the political system itself, rather than simply against each successive government. This ideological change was not the work of Wilkes, but of such men as William Beckford, James Townshend, Richard Oliver, John Sawbridge, and Sir Joseph Mawbey (all of them wealthy MPs), Sergeant John Glynn, lawyer and MP for Middlesex, and the militant Brentford clergyman John Horne. These were not 'Wilkites', but radicals who hoped to exploit Wilkes's charismatic appeal to the suburban masses to advance their own campaign for limited parliamentary reform.

A key figure in this group was Alderman William Beckford, City MP and ally of William Pitt, an enormously rich Jamaica sugar planter whose combination of slave-owning and campaigning for parliamentary reform recalls Samuel Johnson's jibe against the American revolutionaries, that 'we hear the loudest yelps for liberty among the drivers of negroes'. Beckford's speeches in the Commons in 1761 had shown the way, with their call for the abolition of 'little, pitiful boroughs', adequate representation for

London, and an oath against electoral bribery. Beckford was not a democrat. His maxim was that 'power should follow property', not numbers, and that due recognition should be given to 'the middling people of England, the manufacturer, the yeoman, the merchant, the country gentleman, they who bear all the heat of the day'. Parson Horne (later Horne Tooke) had more democratic views, and through his ideas and his long career he linked the timid middle-class reformism of the Wilkites with the more whole-hearted radicalism of Thomas Hardy and the London Corresponding Society in the 1790s. In February 1769 these men (though not Beckford) formed the Society for the Supporters of the Bill of Rights, with the aim of paying Wilkes's debts and pressing for the abolition of corrupt and underpopulated constituencies, for a fair allocation of parliamentary seats to large population centres, and for the secret ballot. Wilkes was not keen to see his personal cult obscured by wider issues, but he was in prison and could do little to stop it. As far as his City friends were concerned, Wilkes was best behind bars. Within months of his release in April 1770 he had fallen out with nearly all of them. But by that time the identification of Wilkism with radicalism was complete, and Wilkes had to make the best of it.[23]

The decision of the House of Commons to expel Wilkes from his Middlesex seat in February 1769 gave the new radical movement an excellent start. Wilkes was elected and expelled three more times, in February, March and April, when Henry Luttrell, the Court candidate, was given the seat. Every stage of this fiasco was accompanied by rioting by the labourers, craftsmen and small tradesmen who were Wilkes's most active supporters. Here was a great issue: if Parliament could choose its own members, what powers were left to the voters? The City radicals saw this as the basis for a nationwide campaign, and they used their influence as property owners and MPs in various parts of the country to start a petitioning movement for reform. In fact, the social basis for radicalism did not yet exist in the provinces, 'Wilkes and Liberty' counted for little, and the metropolitan example did as much to alienate the country gentry as to win them over. About twenty-five petitions were presented (signed by over 50,000 voters), but the movement fizzled out, leaving London alone to keep the radical cause alive.[24]

Until the rise of the Yorkshire Association in 1779 radicalism was a metropolitan phenomenon, with provincial outposts only where City men had Parliamentary seats. Only London had what it took to mount an independent and sustained radical campaign – freedom from aristocratic patronage and control, a vast and articulate middle class, a high level of literacy and political knowledge among its working people, powerful representative institutions through which popular issues could be raised and developed, an ancient tradition of asserting the wishes of its citizens in national affairs, and the ability to threaten Parliament by bringing enormous crowds into Westminster. The new unity of purpose between the City and suburbs made the capital an even more formidable force. A fresh and important issue was added to the radical repertoire in 1771, when the House of Commons tried to stop London newspapers printing its debates by sending a messenger to arrest a City printer. The messenger was himself arrested and brought before three City radicals, Brass Crosby (the Lord Mayor), and Aldermen Oliver and Wilkes, and charged with assault. Crosby and Oliver were called before the Commons, which was surrounded by a crowd of around 50,000, and both were sent to the Tower for a few weeks. But the law against Parliamentary reporting was allowed to lapse, and the political education of Londoners, and of newspaper readers everywhere, took another step forward.

In the City, the death of Beckford in 1770, a few weeks after making the brave or impudent speech to George III which is commemorated on his statue in the Guildhall, cleared the way for Wilkes's climb to the top of the tree. His ambition to become Lord Mayor was blocked in 1772 and 1773 by the opposition of his ex-allies, Townshend and Sawbridge, but he succeeded at last in 1774, the year he finally took his seat for Middlesex. During his mayoralty Wilkes tried to keep the radical pot on the boil by giving the City's support to the American colonists as they approached open revolt against the crown. Americans took much comfort from this, but the issue was not one of central importance to Londoners (least of all Wilkes), and opinion within the City, especially in Common Council, was divided. Once war broke out in 1776 London opinion appears to have rallied behind the government, and Wilkes's radical career faded away. He remained an MP until 1790, and enjoyed the comfortable office of City Chamberlain from 1779 to 1797.[25]

GORDON AND BIGOTRY

The extent of the political education Londoners had received from the Wilkes affair, and the depth of their attachment to the idea of liberty, whose name they were so ready to shout, was called into question in 1780. The Gordon Riots of June that year, London's biggest and most destructive civil disorder of this or of any subsequent century, had many of the characteristics of a traditional religious riot – bigotry, outside manipulation and violence. The Catholic Relief Act of 1778, which was intended to remove some of the penal laws against Catholics, was unpopular with the City Common Council and the wider London public, and a young MP on the make, Lord George Gordon, saw the chance to advance his career on a wave of popular support. On 2 June Gordon assembled a great crowd of perhaps 60,000 on St George's Fields, intending that they should accompany him to Westminster to present a massive petition, as crowds had done for a century and more. Inflamed by Gordon's harangue, the crowd broke into four sections and marched by different routes to Parliament, picking up support as they went. The crowd spent the afternoon and evening terrorizing members of the Houses of Lords and Commons, their fury topped up by Gordon's frequent reappearances. That night crowds burned the Sardinian embassy to the ground, and ransacked the Bavarian one. Saturday was a rest day, but on Sunday and Monday Catholic chapels were looted, and Irish districts invaded, while the Lord Mayor pursued a policy of benign non-intervention. From Tuesday onwards the targets became more worrying to the authorities. On Tuesday, 6 June, Parliament and Lambeth Palace were threatened, the Bow Street police office and Newgate Prison (where rioters were held) were destroyed, the house of Lord Mansfield, the Lord Chief Justice, was ransacked, and Clerkenwell Bridewell and New Prison were opened. Gordon had no control over the mob, and small detachments of troops and constables were intimidated. On Wednesday Catholic shops, taverns and houses all over London were destroyed, the homes of rich supporters of the Act were demolished, the Bank of England was attacked, the Fleet and King's Bench Prisons opened and burned (freeing about 1,600 debtors), and the Catholic Thomas Langdale's gin distillery was set on fire, taking with it about twenty houses and several looters. This parish, St Andrew Holborn, was the one in which the greatest damage was done. Now the City began to regret its earlier tolerance, and the government finally took action to suppress the riot. The City Militia and the Honourable Artillery Company went into action, Wilkes and his fellow Common Councillors took up arms to defend the Bank, Jeremy Bentham joined the Lincoln's Inn militia, and about 10,000 troops were brought into the capital on Wednesday and Thursday with orders to fire on the crowd. This they did, and by the Thursday night, when the riots were over, at least 285 rioters were dead or dying. A further 450 rioters were arrested and twenty-five were hanged, but Gordon, who had apparently not intended things to get out of hand, was acquitted of high treason. He was imprisoned for libel in 1788, and died in Newgate in 1793.

Although the Gordon Rioters have never had much sympathy from historians, the assumption that they were mostly criminals, vagrants or unemployed was long ago dispelled by George Rudé, whose analysis of the 160 who went for trial shows that 70 per cent were journeymen, apprentices, labourers and servants, and the rest mostly small employers. These were not ignorant and disreputable ruffians, but social groups with a long and impressive tradition of political involvement, not entirely dependent on monied leadership for their sense of direction. Moreover, their actions were not quite as wild and bigoted as first impressions suggest. The crowd controlled London, often unopposed, for five days, but not one of the city's 14,000 Catholics was killed, and only sixty Catholic houses were damaged. In the poorer Irish areas, Wapping, St George-in-the-East and St Giles', only nine houses were damaged or destroyed. There was no wild orgy of looting and destruction. The crowds made for well-selected targets, with cries of 'Newgate a-hoy!' and 'Hyde's house a-hoy!'. Among these were Catholic chapels and schools, places connected with drinking and law enforcement, including eight prisons and around twenty crimping houses (for holding pressed sailors) and spunging houses (for debtors), several large workshops, and the houses of rich Catholics, judges, and those associated with the Catholic Relief Act. To some participants, the destruction or breaking open of all the main City and suburban prisons, and many minor gaols, was a noble action, a more concrete contribution to 'liberty' than anything Wilkes had devised. William Blake, who had just completed his apprenticeship as an engraver, joined in the attack on Newgate and saw the burning of this, London's Bastille, as a real and symbolic act of liberation. Horace Walpole, who watched and recorded the whole affair, noticed a strange 'mixture of rage and consideration' in the riots. The mob took furniture into the streets to burn it safely in small fires, and allowed fire engines to save the houses next to the ones they wished to destroy. There is a sense of carefully controlled power here which is reminiscent of the 'respectable' Sacheverell riots of 1710. In 1780, sadly, the army did not show the restraint it had shown seventy years before.[26]

THE MATURITY OF RADICALISM

Soon after the Gordon Riots radical artisans and small employers lost the alliance and leadership of the City rulers. Radicals won nine of the twelve London and Southwark seats in September 1780, and Charles James Fox, the leading radical Parliamentarian of the 1780s and 1790s, took his

Westminster seat for the first time. But the City élite fell out with Fox when, in his disastrous coalition government of 1783–4, he attacked the chartered rights of the East India Company, and thus threatened, in the City's view, London's own chartered liberties. Fox's rival and the King's choice as Prime Minister, the Younger Pitt, favoured moderate reform, and most of the City's radical élite, including Alderman Wilkes, gave him their support in the general election of 1784, helping his supporters to win ten of the twelve London seats. Even when his early radicalism changed into oppressive conservatism in the 1790s, Pitt retained the allegiance of the City élite, and held it until his death in 1806. The shock of the Gordon Riots and of the French Revolution and the bloody events that followed it, created a more conservative mood among aldermen and Common Councillors. Fifteen of the twenty Lord Mayors and most new aldermen between 1789 and 1808 were Pittites, or (an old label with a new meaning) Tories. Fox just managed to hold on in Westminster, where the violent and extremely hard-fought elections of 1784 and 1788 epitomized the bitter struggle for popular support between the Foxite and Pittite camps.

Although radicalism had lost its appeal for the London wealthy, its ideas were still attractive to, and understood by, a substantial section of London's vast and politically awakened population. The new radical programme, shaped in the 1770s by the American Revolution and the writings of Major Cartwright, in the 1780s by the Society for Constitutional Information and the ideas of the French Revolution, and in the early 1790s by Thomas Paine's *Rights of Man*, now contained all the policies adopted by the Chartists sixty years later – universal manhood suffrage, equal constituencies, secret ballots, annual Parliaments, and MPs who were paid and needed no property qualification. Moreover, the 'middling and lesser men' who really wanted these things were beginning to work for them independently, without waiting for aristocratic or mercantile leadership. This is why the nine 'well-meaning, sober and industrious men' who met in the Bell Tavern in Exeter Street, off the Strand, to establish the London Corresponding Society (LCS) in January 1792 have a special place in the history of popular politics. Their secretary and treasurer was Thomas Hardy, a Piccadilly bootmaker.

London was not the only centre of artisan radicalism in the early 1790s. The enormous influence of Thomas Paine's *Rights of Man* spread to every corner of the kingdom in 1792–3, and many growing industrial towns (Sheffield, Manchester, Derby, Coventry, Stockport) had their own Corresponding Societies. At this time of rising prices the LCS struck a vein of popular support which amazed its founders and horrified the government.

By the end of 1792 about 1,000 artisans, tradesmen and workmen, each paying a penny a week, were attending LCS meetings in taverns all over London, especially in Spitalfields. The LCS had its well-off members, including its chairman Maurice Margarot, its leading spokesman Joseph Gerrald (both lawyers), and John Thelwall, an attorney's clerk and writer, but there is no doubt that the bulk of its 5,000 or more members were drawn from the artisans and tradesmen whose role until the 1790s had been limited to giving noisy support to richer leaders. In 1793 and 1794 Thelwall's popular lectures, cheap editions of Paine's *Rights of Man*, and the publications of radical booksellers like Thomas Spence, of High Holborn, spread the message of liberty and equality to many thousands of Londoners.[27]

These were not aristocratic party games, but a real threat to the rule of property, and Pitt's government, knowing from events in France what such ideas could lead to, harried the radicals from the start. LCS meetings were reported on by spies and broken up by the attacks of government-organized 'loyalist associations', and the two best LCS spokesmen, Gerrald and Margarot, were sentenced to fourteen years' transportation by tame Scottish juries in 1794. In May 1794, after a mass LCS rally in Chalk Farm, Pitt, who may really have believed that the Corresponding Societies threatened 'to overturn government, law, property, security, religion, order, and every thing valuable in this country', had twelve LCS leaders, among them Hardy, Thelwall and Horne Tooke, arrested and charged with high treason. The three were successfully defended by the great Foxite advocate Thomas Erskine (who had defended Gordon in 1781) and their acquittals in November and December 1794, and the release of the rest, created immense popular excitement in London. Pitt's repression shook the LCS, and drove Hardy into retirement, but the Society recovered in 1795, when the average price of a 4-pound loaf reached 9½d in London, over 30 per cent higher than in any year since 1709. At LCS rallies in St George's Fields and Copenhagen Fields, Islington, in June and October peaceful crowds of perhaps 100,000 heard rational arguments for universal male suffrage. Pitt responded by criminalizing political lectures and unlicensed meetings of over fifty people, and making it an offence to bring the Crown or constitution into contempt.

These so-called 'Two Acts' were aimed directly at LCS tactics, and destroyed the society as a law-abiding mass movement. In 1799 the LCS itself was prohibited, and its leaders were forced to choose between the relative safety of writing and education (the path followed by Francis Place and John Thelwall) or a dangerous underground life of plots and 'secret' meetings, harried by spies, loyalist mobs and the Bow Street officers. About fifty of those who dared to remain in the LCS after 1796 were arrested early in 1798, and held without trial until 1801 or 1802, many of them in Cold Bath Fields Prison. As E. P. Thompson has shown, there was a small radical underground movement through the years of repression, but Pitt's legislation against newspapers, meetings, lectures and combinations, together with the strong appeal of patriotism in wartime, effectively stifled the great public movement that had been developing in the early 1790s.

The only legitimate path that had not been blocked was the electoral one. There was support for reform among the liverymen of Common Hall, who managed to get their reformist MP, Harvey Combe, chosen as Lord Mayor in 1799. Thomas Hardy, the founder of the LCS, was one of a group which formed the Society of the Independent Livery of London in 1800. But support for Pitt was still strong in the City, and the radicals had better hopes among the voters of Westminster and Middlesex. The rich and eccentric radical Sir Francis Burdett, who had attacked the conditions in which radicals were held in Cold Bath Fields Prison, won a Middlesex seat by a single vote in a lively campaign in 1802, though his election was annulled and he failed to win the seat in 1804 and 1806. In Westminster, whose 12,000 voters included many radical tradesmen, traditional aristocratic electioneering methods, combined with the desperation of its poorer inhabitants, could still win the day. These were the scenes witnessed by Francis Place, now a tailor at 16 Charing Cross Road, at the by-election caused by Fox's death in 1806:

> I saw the servants of the Duke of Northumberland, in their showy dress liveries, throwing lumps of bread and cheese among the dense crowd of vagabonds they had collected together. To see these vagabonds catching the lumps, shouting, swearing, fighting and blackguarding in every possible way, women as well as men, all the vile wretches from the courts and alleys in St Giles and Westminster. . . . representing, as it was said, the electors of Westminster, was certainly the lowest possible step of degradation.'[28]

Scenes like this drew Place back into active politics, and helped convert William Cobbett from a Tory to a radical propagandist. In a second Westminster election in 1806 the radical candidate, James Paull, came within 300 votes of victory. In 1807 Burdett stood for Westminster, and with the support of the veteran campaigners Horne Tooke and Major Cartwright, Cobbett's *Political Register*, Place's organizational brilliance, and a committee of local tradesmen (mostly ex-LCS members), the radicals easily won both seats. This group of 'common tailors and Barbers', 'as insignificant a set of persons as could well have been collected together', created a new type of electoral machine, based on care and commitment rather than money and deference, and demonstrated that meticulous canvassing and strong arguments could outdo beer and bullying in a popular constituency. Burdett was rather too aloof to be another Wilkes, but his brief imprisonment in 1810 confirmed his status as a popular hero. He held the seat for thirty years, and his Westminster Committee, led by Place, became the focus and inspiration for the revival of national radicalism in the decade ahead. They represented a brand of sober and respectable lower-middle-class radicalism, as hostile to popular rowdiness as it was to aristocratic privilege, which also characterized the Chartism of the London Working Men's Association (LWMA) in the late 1830s. The epitome of these attitudes, and the link between the Westminster Committee and the LWMA, was Francis Place.[29]

Place and the Westminster radicals saw cheap education as the way to break the pernicious interaction between aristocratic corruption and popular ignorance exemplified in the 1806 election. In association with dissenters (especially Quakers) and reformist philanthropists and philosophers (James Mill, Samuel Romilly, Josiah Wedgwood, Sir James Mackintosh, Henry Brougham), the Westminster radicals set up the West London Lancasterian Association in 1811, to bring the benefits of cheap 'monitorial' education (as developed by Joseph Lancaster) to the 356,000 people of Westminster. Since there was a fundamental disagreement between the freethinkers (Place, Mill, and Edward Wakefield) and the Quakers as to whether these benefits were to be secular or spiritual the association broke up within a few years. Its existence indicates, though, that London radicalism was now in the hands of men who were committed to the social and intellectual advancement of the lower class, rather than its political exploitation. Popular politics had travelled a long way since the days of Henry Sacheverell.[30]

PART FIVE

NINETEENTH-CENTURY
LONDON, 1815–1914

Chapter 15

Population, Health and
Local Government

LONDON'S POPULATION IN 1801, when the first national census was taken, was 958,863, not quite double its 1700 figure, and still (as it was in 1700) about a tenth of the total population of England and Wales. But by 1901 the population of Greater London (a much larger area, but still a single conurbation) had risen to 6,586,000, a fifth of the inhabitants of England and Wales. This was London's explosive century, in which its population grew by about a fifth in every decade until 1891. Even in the context of rapid urban growth all over England, and in much of Europe, London's expansion was spectacular. Its population in 1901 equalled that of the next eighteen largest cities in the British Isles, and was about the same as the combined populations of Europe's four greatest cities, Paris, Berlin, Vienna and St Petersburg. What would Defoe, who thought London was an overgrown monster in the 1720s, when it was a compact town stretching a mere 4 miles from east to west, have made of the London of 1900, almost 18 miles across, and covering nearly 70 square miles?

MIGRANTS

As in the sixteenth century, London's population explosion was a reflection of the national picture. The large gap between national birth rates and death rates that opened up in the period 1740–1820 caused the population of England and Wales to rise from about 6 million in 1741 to over 12 million in 1821, and to nearly 33 million by 1901. Much of this increase was generated in the countryside, but the inability of rural areas to employ or accommodate more than a fraction of the increase, along with the expansion of urban economies, improvements in communications, and the growing (and well-publicized) differential between rural and urban wages, ensured that there would be a heavy flow of migrants from agricultural areas to towns and cities. With the rise of industrial and commercial towns in the Midlands and the North, and the growing attractiveness of emigration to the USA, Canada and Australasia, the choice of destinations for young rural migrants was much wider than it had ever been before. Still, London's incomparable reputation with restless countryfolk, its vast and varied economy, and its nearness to the overpopulated agricultural counties of the South, the South-West and East Anglia (the regions with the biggest migrant outflow), ensured that the stream of recruits did not run dry. Especially before the coming of the railways in the 1830s and 1840s, most migration was over short distances and on foot, and youngsters unable to find work in the declining woollen counties of Norfolk, Wiltshire, Gloucestershire or Somerset were more likely to turn their faces, as their ancestors had so often done, towards London than to make the long trek overland to Bradford or Manchester.

From 1851 onwards birthplaces were recorded in the census, and a rough calculation of the origins of London's migrant population is possible. Migrants made up about 38 per cent of Londoners in 1851, diminishing slightly to about 34 per cent in 1891. Of these a steady 63 per cent (over 20 per cent of London's population) came from the southern, south-western and eastern counties, south of a line from the Wash to the Severn. Another 15 per cent were born abroad or in Ireland, and only about 22 per cent came from the Midlands, the North or Scotland, regions which had provided over half London's immigrant freemen in the 1550s. The number of migrants arriving in each decade from 1841 onwards has been estimated as follows:

	British	Irish	Foreign	Total
1841–51	256,000	46,000	26,000	328,000
1851–61	243,000	14,000	29,000	286,000
1861–71	288,000	7,000	36,000	331,000
1871–81	440,000	19,000	39,000	498,000
1881–91	334,000	20,000	48,000	402,000[1]

The inflow was higher in the 1840s because of the arrival of Irish refugees from the Famine, and in the 1870s because of the onset of a severe and prolonged agricultural depression, hitting the south particularly hard, in 1873. In the 1880s the rival attraction of the United States, where there was an economic boom, and the depletion of the rural population by earlier migration, may have diminished the flow of migrants to London, but the settlement of new migrants on the fringes of London, beyond its registration boundaries, may account for part of the apparent fall in numbers.[2]

For much of the century the largest and most conspicuous immigrant group in London was the Irish. The 1851 census counted 109,000 Irish-born Londoners (and missed many more), and although the decline of migration from Ireland after 1851 reduced the size of the Irish-born population of London to 66,000 by 1891, the broader Irish community (including those of recent Irish descent) certainly continued to grow. Lynn Hollen Lees calculated that Irish immigrants and the children living with them amounted to at least 156,000 people, 6.6 per cent of the population of London, in 1851. Irish Londoners did not (in spite of popular assumptions) have large families, and their death rates were high, since such a high proportion of them, compared to Londoners in general, lived in bad housing and earned low wages as unskilled workers. But strong cultural, political and religious bonds held the Irish community together, and it was replenished by a flow of new migrants.[3] It seems likely, then, that 5 or 6 per cent of Londoners saw themselves as Irish, by birth, descent or cultural affiliation, in the 1890s. Roman Catholic elementary schools, which drew their pupils mainly from Irish families, had 5 per cent of London's elementary school population in 1890, despite the fact that many Irish children went to non-denominational schools. Charles Booth's figure of 200,000 in 1900 was based on baptisms, and therefore did not count lapsed Catholics.[4]

By the 1890s, the anxiety and hostility that had characterized the attitudes of non-Irish Londoners towards the Irish had been transferred to a more 'alien' and less easily assimilated group, the Jews. London's Jewish population had risen slowly in the nineteenth century, from about 25,000 in 1815 to about 46,000 (75 per cent of the British total) in 1881. This was a fairly prosperous and well-established community, in which middle- or upper-class families were in a majority. There were Jews at the very pinnacle of the City's financial world, and many Jewish traders had moved out of the disreputable world of street-selling and second-hand dealing into more respectable manufacturing, wholesaling and retailing businesses. There were Jewish paupers, perhaps 11,000 in 1881, but wealthier Jews had established their own Jewish Board of Guardians to look after them in 1859. The image of a prosperous and largely British-born community changed rapidly after 1881, when Jewish refugees from Tsarist Russia and Poland, stripped of their wealth and status by persecution, began to arrive in British ports and industrial cities, particularly Leeds, Manchester and London, at the rate of between 2,000 and 7,000 a year. By 1905, when legislation reduced the flow of immigrants, London's Jewish population was about 140,000.

Most of the refugee ships docked in East London, and the majority of Jewish immigrants settled there, particularly in Stepney, which had the advantages of an existing Jewish community, plentiful unskilled work (mainly in the clothing industry) and cheap rooms. In 1901 there were 54,000 immigrants living in Stepney, making up about 18 per cent of its population. Polish and Russian Jews, with their distinctive clothing and speech, were a conspicuous and concentrated group, and since many more landed briefly in London on their way to the United States (their favourite destination) it was easy for the London public to develop exaggerated fears of an alien 'invasion' of the East End. There was no doubt that the streets of Spitalfields and Whitechapel, from Houndsditch in the west to Vallance Road in the east, were transformed almost into a foreign, Yiddish-speaking town in the space of fifteen or twenty years. Popular hostility almost exploded in 1888, when the 'Jack the Ripper' murders, right in the heart of the area of densest Jewish settlement, were widely rumoured to have been the work of a Jew. There were minor anti-Jewish disturbances, but a full-blown riot was avoided by the action of a policeman who rubbed out the murderer's chalked message implicating 'Jewes' in the fifth killing.[5] Anti-immigration campaigners, particularly the ultra-racist publicist Arnold White, inflated the number of arrivals to almost a million, and readily blamed Jews for the East End's chronic economic and social problems, unemployment, sweated labour, overcrowding, crime and disease. Concern over the social and economic impact of mass immigration was not confined to anti-semites: the Jewish Board of Guardians, fearing that the new arrivals would create hostility towards the anglicized Jewish community, organized the repatriation of 31,000 Jewish immigrants between 1881 and 1906.[6]

In the 1890s, and especially in the 'Khaki' election of 1900, Conservative politicians in East London tried to turn popular anti-alienism into votes. In 1901 one of the new East London Conservative MPs started the British Brothers League, which held a series of large rallies in Stepney and Bethnal Green. Balfour's Conservative government tried to satisfy this rather unwelcome agitation by setting up a Royal Commission on Alien Immigration, before which all the complaints against aliens – their willingness to work for starvation wages, their effect on rents, their noisy and 'disgusting' habits – could be paraded again. The Commission's report in 1903 offered the Conservatives a popular issue which could bind wealth and poverty together in a patriotic alliance, and enable them to retain the East End seats in the next election. The 1905 Aliens Act imposed immigration restrictions for the first time in eighty years, by allowing immigration officers to inspect immigrant ships and exclude aliens who appeared to be criminal, diseased, insane or destitute, unless they were genuine political or religious refugees. Aliens living in England as paupers or in 'unsanitary conditions' could be deported by the Home Secretary. After the 1906 election (in which the Conservatives lost all but one of their East London seats) the Liberal government enforced the Act without enthusiasm, excluding about 4,000 immigrants between 1906 and 1910. Anticipating their exclusion, Jews turned to friendlier havens, and numbers entering Britain fell from over 12,000 in 1906 to 4,223 in 1910.[7]

The motives of rural migrants were not very different from those of young men and women who came to London in earlier centuries. As well as jobs and better wages, London offered opportunities for self-advancement, a wider choice of marriage partners, greater personal freedom and more excitement. Countrymen, said the social investigator H. Llewellyn Smith in 1890, travelled 'in search of a known and real economic advantage', but they were also drawn by 'the contagion of numbers, the sense of something going on, the theatres and the music halls, the brightly lighted streets and the busy crowds – all, in short, that makes the difference between the Mile End Fair on a Saturday night, and a dark and muddy country lane, with no glimmer of gas and nothing to do'. It was true that there was a shortage of jobs and houses in London, exacerbated by the arrival of so many migrants, but the shortage was not as desperate as it was in many rural areas, where there was a glut of farm labour, and where craft industries were declining in the face of urban competition. London rents were high, but so were wages, and efficient wholesaling and retailing ensured that food was often cheaper in London than in the countryside. Railways, newspapers and the penny post brought news of London wages, London jobs, London girls and London sophistication to the remotest villages, and railways also enabled prospective migrants to take trips to the capital, and to revisit their families once they had taken the plunge and moved there for good. In any case, friends and relatives had often gone on ahead, and most new migrants had a network of fellow-villagers to help them when they arrived in town.[8]

For young women, the most mobile group of all, London's vast number of domestic service jobs, many of them advertised nationally, exerted a powerful pull, and for young men London's position as the world's largest centre of employment, both for labourers and for skilled men, was its main recommendation. It was not easy for migrants to break into the old-established skilled crafts (furniture-making, printing and coopering, for instance), but they found it easier to find work in breweries, gasworks, railways, building sites, omnibus companies and the police force. Many employers preferred country workers, with their reputation for strength, honesty, obedience and cheapness, to born Londoners, who were thought to be physically and morally degenerate, argumentative and expensive. London men, a brewer said in the 1860s, are 'shuffling, lazy and know too much'. These jobs were mostly in the newer suburban areas and the West End, and since most migrants settled there, away from the crowded inner industrial districts, they avoided the worst of the filth and disease that had always been the price people paid for living in London.[9]

MORTALITY

Although London probably attracted over 40 per cent of all rural migrants in the nineteenth century, it was not a migrant-dominated city. Only three of its thirty registration districts (Kensington, Paddington and St George's Hanover Square) had a migrant majority in 1881, and just over a half of its 3 million population growth between 1851 and 1891 came from natural increase, rather than migration. Victorian London was by no means a healthy town, as we shall see, but it no longer suffered the surplus of burials over births that had characterized the period from 1550 to 1800. There had been a marked improvement in health since the 1780s, in which smallpox vaccination (introduced by Edward Jenner in 1796), better maternity care, washable and lice-free cotton clothes, and the fall in bread prices after 1813 each played an important part. The London Bills of Mortality suggest that the death rate fell from 50 per 1,000 in the 1770s to 32 per 1,000 in the early 1830s, but accurate figures are only available from the 1840s, after the introduction of voluntary civil registration of births, marriages and deaths in 1837. Outbreaks of typhus, cholera, smallpox and influenza created fluctuations in mortality figures, but in general London's annual death rate was around 24 per 1,000 people between 1840 and 1870, one or two deaths per 1,000 above the national average, and below that of Manchester, Liverpool, Glasgow and most of the great European cities. Its birth rate was near the national average of 35 per 1,000, giving London a 'natural' growth rate of over 1 per cent a year. Between 1870 and 1901 London's mortality rate fell, in line with the national trend, to 17.1 per 1,000, only a fraction above the English average, but since its birth rate also fell to 29 per 1,000, its natural rate of growth remained almost unchanged.

The improvement in London's health was largely the result of the decline of seven infectious diseases: whooping cough and scarlet fever (specialist killers of young children), tuberculosis, typhoid, smallpox, typhus and cholera. The last three of these had almost disappeared by the start of the twentieth century. In the 1770s smallpox, a loathsome and dreaded disease, may have killed five of every 1,000 Londoners each year, accounting for one in ten of all deaths, but by 1831–5, thanks to mass inoculation and vaccination, it killed less than one in 1,000, about one death in every thirty-eight. Vaccination was made free in 1840, after an epidemic which killed 41,600 (6,400 in London), and compulsory in 1853, but many parents ignored the law, and most people did not have 'boosters' to maintain their immunity. The fact that until 1872 vaccinations were provided by the Poor Law authorities, sometimes in workhouses, may help to explain public resistance to compulsion. As a result, progress in eradicating smallpox was slow. Mortality fell in the 1840s and 1850s, but increased in the 1870s, when nearly one Londoner in every 2,000 died of smallpox each year, almost twice the national rate. Finally a more effective system of compulsory infant vaccination was introduced in 1872, after a great epidemic in 1871–2 which killed 42,000 people, a third of them in London. This epidemic, in the words of Anne Hardy, was 'a watershed in the history of smallpox in London', because it prompted the introduction of a 'stamping out' policy which all but eradicated the disease by 1898. New isolation hospitals were opened in the suburbs, to the consternation of local residents, who believed (perhaps rightly) that fever hospitals were sources of infection. In 1873, in a move which recalled the old struggle to exclude the plague, the government established port sanitary authorities, including one for the Port of London, to stop and inspect incoming shipping for smallpox, cholera and other infectious diseases. This combination of policies was effective, and though there were further epidemics in 1881, 1884–5 and 1893–4, smallpox deaths in London fell to an annual average of under fifty a year (ten in a million) in the late 1890s.[10]

The history of tuberculosis, one of the greatest of London's killer diseases, is harder to trace. Until the 1990s medical historians generally believed that tuberculosis mortality declined steadily throughout the nineteenth century, but now the predominant view is that the period of significant decline did not begin until the 1870s, and was less dramatic than was once thought.[11] For most of the century doctors misunderstood and mistreated the disease, hospitals turned its victims away, and politicians ignored suggestions that the sale of infected milk should be controlled. Probably because of better diet and accommodation, perhaps also through better hygiene, cleaner milk and the gradual penetration into the public mind of the sanitary gospel of fresh air, the annual rate of death from tuberculosis in London fell from about 3 per 1,000 in the 1850s and 1860s to about 2 per 1,000 in the 1890s. Improving medical knowledge, and the campaign of London's Medical Officers of Health against slums, common lodging-houses, unventilated workshops and other nests of infection also, in Anne Hardy's view, contributed signally to beating the disease. While tuberculosis declined, deaths from bronchitis and other respiratory complaints remained high, and whooping cough, though in retreat, was still common among children at the end of the century. One of the most familiar noises in this smoky and overcrowded city, especially in Southwark and the East End, was the sound of coughing.[12]

Although the defeat of cholera has generally attracted most attention, the decline of typhus had a greater demographic and social significance for London. The typhus-carrying louse was the constant companion of unwashed and overcrowded Londoners, and typhus epidemics did their greatest damage in the rookeries or 'fever-nests' of St Giles', Whitechapel and Southwark. Typhus thrived in hard winters, economic depressions, and times in which slum demolition disrupted patterns of working-class settlement. In the 1860s, when road and railway building kept the Inner London poor on the move, there was a ten-year epidemic. In the longer run, though, these demolitions may have helped to break the power of typhus in London. There were many hard years in the last decades of the century, but typhus did not return except in localized outbreaks, and in 1898 the Metropolitan Asylums Board, which had led the fight against fever, could boast that ordinary London doctors hardly ever saw the disease. Some credit for the elimination of typhus should go to the East London Water Company, which extended its piped supplies into the Whitechapel slums in the 1870s, and to the working-class mothers who waited at the stand-pipes, carried their heavy buckets into their houses, and introduced their families to the enormous advantages of cleanliness.[13]

Only one group failed to benefit from the sanitary and nutritional improvements of the later nineteenth century. The national and the metropolitan death rate for infants under a year old was still as high in the 1890s as it had been in the 1840s, when figures were first kept. Three of the diseases that most affected young children, infantile diarrhoea, measles and diphtheria, seemed to be far more resistant to environmental and medical improvements than other killers, and diphtheria in fact staged a remarkable recovery among London children in the early 1890s, before beginning its fifty-year retreat in 1893.[14] Infant mortality is a sensitive index of overcrowding, poverty, malnutrition, lack of hygiene, parental ignorance and neglect, and in London's poorest areas, where these conditions prevailed, infant death rates were appalling. In the 1890s, babies born in London's poorest neighbourhoods (Shoreditch, Limehouse and Southwark, for example), had one chance in five of dying before their first birthday, while those born in healthy Hampstead had a chance in ten. Statistics, if they had existed, would no doubt have shown an even worse state of affairs in the eighteenth century, but the lack of improvement in infant health since 1840 was a cause for concern in 1900, particularly in view of the rapidly falling birth rate.

Seen in the national context, London's record was not bad. Its infant mortality between 1851 and 1901 (about 157 per 1,000) was only fractionally above the national average of 150, and after 1900, when national infant mortality was falling fast, London's fell faster, to 90 per 1,000 by 1912. Only one of the twenty-nine London boroughs, Shoreditch, was among the fifty worst towns in 1901–10, and four London boroughs (as well as nine outer suburban districts) were in the list of twenty-five healthiest towns. Babies born in Lancashire towns were far less likely to survive than London babies, and even Shoreditch compared well with central Manchester, Birmingham and Liverpool. There were, though, pockets of extreme misery within many London boroughs: the 1911 infant mortality figures show that East Deptford's rate was 197 per 1,000 (compared with South Deptford's 68), Limehouse's rate was 189, and West Barking's 205 (compared to East Barking's 105).[15] The growth of health visiting, which began in Westminster and Battersea in 1904, the establishment of mothercraft centres, day nurseries and milk depots, and the government's imposition of higher standards on milk suppliers in 1901, all helped to bring infant mortality down with amazing speed between 1900 and 1914.[16]

THE SANITARY QUESTION

Rapid population growth placed enormous environmental, social and administrative pressures on London. The task of draining, cleaning, policing and housing such a vast city had never been faced before, and problems of water supply, traffic control, poor relief, Church provision and health care presented challenges which English governments initially lacked the experience, knowledge and unity of purpose to solve. The usual practice was to rely on business, charity and local activity to keep matters under control, with state or collective action only being accepted when others had manifestly and disastrously failed. Government intervention in such high-priority issues as fire and plague prevention had long been accepted, but state-controlled metropolitan policing had been decisively rejected in 1785, and was not fully accepted until 1829.

From around 1830, national politicians and civil servants began to accept a more direct role in a wider range of urban social issues, particularly in matters of public health, poor relief and factory conditions. The origins of this new spirit of interventionism have often been debated, with some historians arguing that it was a pragmatic reaction to the new problems created by industrialization and urban growth, and others emphasizing the impact of interventionist ideologies and pressure groups, among them Benthamism, humanitarian paternalism, the medical and engineering professions, the Press, the civil service and middle-class public opinion. Whatever its origins, interventionism usually met resistance from existing interest groups, in the shape of local ratepayers, factory, mine or water company owners, and local authorities. Nowhere was the task of imposing new structures of public administration more dogged by local resistance than in London, where the power and independence of the City Corporation was a rock that sunk many government initiatives.

Although public attitudes towards government intervention were slowly becoming more favourable, it usually took a well-publicized crisis or disaster to awaken aristocratic politicians to an awareness of their new social responsibilities. The arrival of cholera, a dramatic bacterial infection of the gut previously unknown in Europe, whose westward progress had been watched with dread since it appeared in India in 1818, was such a crisis. Cholera reached Sunderland in October 1831 and London in February 1832, and killed over 31,000 in Great Britain (5,000 in London) by a process of rapid and painful dehydration. Cholera fell far short of tuberculosis, typhus or influenza in the numbers it killed, and it hit the poor of Rotherhithe and Bermondsey much harder than the rich of the West End, but its newness, its dramatic impact on its victims, and fears that it might become the new plague forced politicians to act.

Sadly, ignorance of the causes of cholera meant that the response to it was often ineffective and sometimes harmful. Cholera was transmitted by the ingestion of the faeces of infected people, sometimes from contaminated food or clothing, but most often from sewage-polluted water. It thus entered London households in buckets and pipes. Six of London's eight piped-water companies took their supplies from the Thames, while two, the New River Company and the East London Company, got theirs wholly or mainly from the Lea. Piped water was dirty enough in the first place, but since supplies were intermittent and did not run on Sundays until

1872, most consumers stored water in cisterns or tubs, in which it became filthier still. Poorer families, who had to fetch water from street stand-pipes, often preferred to fill their buckets from the pump of a local well, or to dip them into the Thames, the Wandle, the Regent's Canal, or some other convenient and tasty source. The Thames, sadly for the millions of Londoners who drank from it, was as much liquid biology as it was 'liquid history'. As Sydney Smith, the witty canon of St Paul's, wrote to a friend in 1834, 'he who drinks a tumbler of London water has literally in his stomach more animated beings than there are men, Women and Children on the face of the Globe'.[17] At least 140 sewers discharged their contents (which contained an increasing proportion of household sewage) into the Thames in 1828, and the growing use of flush toilets in the 1830s and 1840s meant that the problem got much worse by the middle of the century. The Lea, which carried large quantities of industrial and household waste, was hardly any better.[18]

The deterioration of Thames water was clearly noticeable by the 1820s, and two reports (from a Royal Commission in 1827, and a Commons Select Committee in 1830) had suggested that London should find an unpolluted source, or that the water companies that drew their water from the Thames should use sand filters to purify their supplies. But the orthodox medical belief was that diseases were spread by contagion, and the newer view, which became official dogma under Edwin Chadwick and Dr Southwood-Smith (of the London Fever Hospital) in the 1830s and 1840s, asserted the infectious agency of bad air, or 'miasma', arising from animal or vegetable putrefaction. Government policy in 1832, reacting in panic to the arrival of cholera, combined the advice of both schools of thought, reviving the old plague quarantine measures, and also ordering makeshift local Boards of Health to flush sewers, empty cesspools, clear away piles of rubbish and dung, and cleanse slaughterhouses and infected homes. Meanwhile the true source of infection, the reeking Thames, was made filthier still by the efforts of the Boards.[19]

The 'sanitarian' interpretation of disease, which emphasized foul urban conditions and putrefying matter as the main removable cause of ill-health, began to dominate public medical policy after 1832. This had much to do with the rising influence of Edwin Chadwick, friend and follower of Jeremy Bentham, admirer of Dr Southwood-Smith, and England's most powerful and dynamic bureaucrat. Chadwick had largely created the New Poor Law of 1834, and control of its operations gave him a strong power base in the 1830s. The Poor Law grouped the old parishes into larger Unions, run by Boards of Guardians (elected by ratepayers), which had the duty of providing 'indoor' (workhouse) and limited 'outdoor' relief to paupers, under the general supervision of three Commissioners in Somerset House. As secretary to the Poor Law Commission, Chadwick became convinced that typhoid, influenza and typhus, which were epidemic in London between 1834 and 1838, were a major source of pauperism, and thus of high poor rates, and that their causes could be removed by sanitary reform. He persuaded the Commission to ask three like-minded doctors, Kay, Arnott and Southwood-Smith, to report on sanitary conditions in London, drawing attention to the removable causes of fever. The doctors' reports were published as appendices to the Poor Law Commissioners' Report of 1838, and by circulating 7,000 copies of the reports Chadwick began to turn the obscure and distasteful subject of the sanitary condition of working-class London into a major public issue. Those who were not horrified by the accounts of neighbourhoods plagued by stagnant and putrefying pools, open ditches filled with sewage and refuse, piggeries, piles of rotting refuse in close and unventilated alleys, and crowded cellars regularly flooded by foul water, might be moved instead by the argument that the fever generated in these miserable districts could spill into richer streets, and that the cost of cleaning up the worst areas would easily be met by the savings on poor relief which a healthier working class would bring.

The problem was not confined to a few unlucky districts: there were areas of permanent fever in Holborn, Clerkenwell, Covent Garden and Bloomsbury, as far west as Wandsworth, and from Lambeth in the south to Edmonton in the north. Southwood-Smith reported from Whitechapel and Bethnal Green, where conditions were among the worst. For a flavour of his report, here is his account of John's Passage and Granby Row, in Bethnal Green: 'In the middle of the street is a large gutter always full of filth, the overflowing of which sometimes renders the place impassable, and the noxious matter is with difficulty kept from flowing into the houses. The street, for the extent of three hundred or four hundred yards, consists of hovels of the last degree of wretchedness.'[20]

THE GENERAL BOARD OF HEALTH

Chadwick and his allies became more and more convinced that the real villains of the piece, as far as London was concerned, were the eight Commissions of Sewers, which had been responsible for building and maintaining London's drains since the reign of Henry VIII. At first, sewers carried only surface water, and households, forbidden to use the sewers, deposited their waste in cesspools. Population growth, the growing popularity of Joseph Bramah's water closet, and the tendency for houses to discharge their waste directly into the sewers (which they were allowed to do after 1815), put an increasing strain on an already inadequate system. Those Londoners who took their water from wells (an important source of supply until the 1870s) were hardly better off, since most of these had been corrupted by their proximity to cesspits. The safest method of solid waste disposal, the old night-soil system, was falling into disuse in the early nineteenth century.[21]

Chadwick's widely circulated and influential *Inquiry into the Sanitary Condition of the Labouring Population of Great Britain*, published in 1842, and the Royal Commission on the State of Large Towns and Populous Districts, reporting in 1844 and 1845, demonstrated with clarity and relish the inadequacy and incompetence of the Commissioners of Sewers. The Commissioners of Sewers did their work, when they did it at all, without regard for the operations of neighbouring Commissions, the needs of the city as a whole, or even the laws of gravity. Most of the Commissions, corrupt, lazy and incompetent in equal measure, were quite unready to cope with the greatly increased flow of sewage they had to deal with, and were unwilling to admit the consequences of their failure. Any sewage that managed to find its way to the end of the clogged, leaking and labyrinthine drainage system discharged from about sixty outlets into the Thames, from which most of London's water companies drew their largely unfiltered supplies. When Commissioners and their officials were asked why large parts of London were without main sewers, but relied on cesspools and open ditches to take their household waste, they generally claimed that their task was only to maintain existing sewers and drain off surface water. 'Do you consider it your duty to alter a sewer, or carry up a sewer, with reference to the health of the inhabitants? – Certainly not,' was a fairly typical exchange.[22]

These reports built up an unstoppable public demand for sanitary reform in London and other towns. The movement's central organization, the Health of Towns Association (formed in December 1844) brought together in Chadwick's support an enormous range of opinion, from the Tory Disraeli to the Whig Lords Normanby and Morpeth, from doctors and bishops to tailors and tradesmen, and two of the most powerful propagandists of the day, Lord Ashley (later Shaftesbury) and Charles Dickens. The Whig government dragged its feet, but eventually in 1847 it set up a Royal Commission, dominated by Chadwick, to examine London's drainage, paving, street-cleaning and water supply, all of which Chadwick wanted placed under a single new metropolitan authority to replace the Courts of Sewers, the improvement commissioners, the water companies and the dozens of other bodies which were to blame for the capital's filthy condition. The Metropolitan Sanitary Commission heard a comprehensive and well-informed denunciation of London's sewage system from the chief surveyor of the Westminster Court of Sewers, John Phillips, who argued, as others did, that squalor was a moral as well as a physical problem:

> I am of the opinion, that not one half of the entire filth produced in the metropolis finds its way into the sewers, but is retained in the cesspools and drains in and about the houses, where it lies decomposing, giving off noxious effluvia and poisonous sulphuretted hydrogen and other gases which constantly infect the atmosphere of such houses from bottom to top, and which, of course, the inhabitants are constantly breathing. . . . There are hundreds, I may say thousands, of houses in this metropolis which have no drainage whatever, and the greater part of them having stinking overflowing cesspools. And there are also hundreds of streets, courts, and alleys that have no sewers; and how the drainage and filth is conveyed away, and how the poor miserable inhabitants live in such places it is hard to tell. In pursuance of my duties, from time to time I have visited very many places where filth of all kinds was lying scattered about the rooms, vaults, cellars, areas, and yards, so thick, and so deep, that it was hardly possible to move for it. I have also seen in such places, human beings living and sleeping in sunk rooms, with filth from overflowing cesspools exuding through and running down the walls and over the floors. It is utterly hopeless to expect to meet with either civilization, benevolence, religion or virtue, in any shape, where so much filth and wretchedness abounds. . . . Morality, and the whole economy of domestic existence is outraged and deranged by so much suffering and misery.[23]

In 1848 Lord John Russell's Whig government, pushed by the Health of Towns campaign and the approach of cholera, but impeded by the opposition of ratepayers, local authorities, anti-centralists and vested interests, passed a Public Health Act which gave a General Board of Health limited powers over the health and sanitation of provincial towns, and encouraged (but did not compel) these towns to begin solving their own problems. For political reasons the act excluded London, which was, almost everyone agreed, the biggest sanitary problem of all. In London, the discredited Commissions of Sewers (except the City's) were abolished in December 1847, and replaced by a single crown-appointed Metropolitan

Commission dominated by Chadwick, who started work on an ordnance survey of London, as the essential prelude to the comprehensive replanning of metropolitan drainage. But the battle for control of London was far from won: paving and water supply were still outside the Commission's control, and so was the mighty City. The most that could be wrung from the City was that it would reform its own Commission of Sewers, and cooperate with the larger Metropolitan Commission on drainage questions.

THE FALL OF CHADWICK

In late 1848, cholera reached England again. Chadwick was sure that the disease spread through the gases rising from putrid matter, rather than contagion or infected water, and when his General Board of Health won control of anti-cholera measures in September 1848 he began pressing local Poor Law Guardians to empty cesspools, clear piles of refuse and night-soil and other nuisances, and visit infected homes, removing the healthy to safety. Most ignored him, and throughout the epidemic, which killed 14,000 Londoners between July and October 1849, the parish vestries showed a capacity for inaction, obstruction and selfishness which appalled *The Times*: 'The parochial officers did nothing – absolutely nothing. They left the graveyards festering – cesspools seething – the barrels of blood steaming in the underground shambles – the great mounds of scutch putrefying in the Bermondsey glue yards.' Decisive action came from the new Metropolitan Commission of Sewers, which began to investigate, under Chadwick's direction, the best long-term solution to the problem of London's sewage disposal. As a short-term measure, Chadwick organized the flushing of the public sewers into the Thames, which, as it turned out, made the epidemic much worse. By September 1849 the Commission had been fatally disrupted by the opposition of parochial and cost-conscious vestrymen (particularly John Leslie of St George's Hanover Square) to Chadwick, and by disputes between those who favoured huge brick tunnels to intercept the sewage alongside the Thames, and the Chadwick group, which advocated small glazed pipe sewers in which a rapid flow would constantly clear obstructions. Hounded also by *The Times*, Chadwick lost his place on the Metropolitan Commission in October 1849.

Between 1849 and 1852 Chadwick tried to use his position on the General Board of Health to regain his control over London's sanitary affairs. First he pressed for the replacement of the foul and overflowing parish graveyards, whose appalling state he had exposed in 1843, with a series of public cemeteries beyond the metropolitan boundary, under the Board's control. Lack of Parliamentary and Cabinet support for this ambitious and costly scheme brought it to nothing, and it was left to Lord Palmerston, when he became Home Secretary in 1852, to order all London's parish graveyards to be closed, forcing the vestries to find their own extramural cemeteries. At the same time, the General Board tried to seize control of London's water provision from the cartel of eight private companies which was responsible for the city's polluted and intermittent supply. Chadwick knew the value of clean and plentiful water, not only for individual health and hygiene, but to keep the sewers running fast and freely. In May 1850 the General Board issued a Report which argued that London's water should be brought from Farnham, Surrey, in a constant steam-pumped supply, and that the water companies should be amalgamated under the control of a public Board, which would also reconstruct the sewer system using the small egg-shaped pipes favoured by Chadwick. This was an impressive scheme, but it stirred up a formidable political opposition. About eighty MPs held water company shares, and the eight companies were rich enough to buy the support of newspapers and Parliamentary agents. Moreover, the Vestries and the London MPs opposed Chadwick's centralizing scheme, and the Farnham supply was unproven. The government feared a confrontation, and opted for a Metropolitan Water Act (1852) which allowed the companies to continue as before, so long as they took no water from downstream of Teddington Lock after 1855–6 (too late to prevent the 1854 cholera epidemic), covered their reservoirs and filtered their supplies. They were not obliged to provide a continuous supply unless 80 per cent of their consumers wanted and could receive it, and supplies remained intermittent in many areas until 1902, when the water companies were finally taken into public control.

Several factors prevented Chadwick and his allies (notably Lord Ashley and Dr Southwood-Smith) from achieving a comprehensive solution to London's sanitary problems in the atmosphere of public alarm created by the cholera epidemics of 1849 and 1854. Chadwick's unshakeable faith in his own solutions, and in his own right to carry them out, made it impossible for him to operate in a world of suspicious and parsimonious vestrymen, of lazy and self-important politicians, and sensitive and inflexible 'experts'. Even those who agreed with him that strong centralized action was needed could not agree on the practical measures that should be taken. Chadwick favoured a fast-flowing and self-cleaning drainage system based on constant household water supplies and the small and cheap egg-shaped stoneware sewer pipe invented by John Roe. He also believed, rather unrealistically, that London's sewage, converted into liquid form, could be piped on to farms and sold as manure. His successors on the Metropolitan Commission of Sewers in 1849, the engineers Robert Stephenson, Thomas Cubitt, Joseph Bazalgette and Thomas Hawkesley, favoured big (and expensive) brick tunnels which could be cleaned by hand. Since neither party had mastered the techniques of effective drainage, it was easy for each side to discredit the other by publicizing its failures. A typhus epidemic in Croydon in November 1852 was blamed on Chadwick's small-bore pipes, and Stephenson's costly brick tunnel under Victoria Street collapsed after a few months. Unlike his critics, Chadwick acted quickly in the face of urgent necessity, and sometimes, as in the flushing of the sewers in 1849, his mistakes exposed him to attack from doctors, engineers and vested interests. In the end, Chadwick's reputation as a bureaucratic tyrant, ready to trample local rights and democratic procedures in the pursuit of a sanitary dictatorship, enabled his self-interested opponents, particularly the London vestries and water companies and their allies in Press and Parliament, to drive him from the General Board of Health, and out of public office, in 1854. Lord Ashley, his ally on the Board of Health, went too.[24]

John Simon and the City

The anti-interventionist impulse that broke Chadwick did not always express itself in sterile inactivity. Most big cities forestalled Chadwick's interference by obtaining their own local Acts and undertaking their own programme of sanitary reform. Among these was the City of London itself, which had fought a tough battle to maintain its sanitary independence from the Metropolitan Commission of Sewers and the General Board of Health, but which saw that the best way to stop others interfering was to do the job itself. The Lord Mayor (who was also head of the City's Commission of Sewers) claimed that the City's sanitation was 'perfect' in 1847,[25] and it is true that the City, with 51 miles of paved road and 44 miles of man-sized brick sewers, had enjoyed better sanitary administration than the rest of London. But in the squalid courts and alleys of the poorer eastern and western districts, thousands of houses relied on a few filthy privies, emptying into around 5,000 cesspools, many of them overflowing. Rubbish piles, foul slaughterhouses, noxious workshops, overflowing grave-yards and standpipes running for only a few minutes a day were as common in the City as elsewhere in London, and City death rates were among London's highest. Most members of the City Corporation (a convenient designation for the Court of Aldermen and the Common Council) never visited the filthiest areas, and were unaware of the need for reform, while others resisted it for selfish or doctrinaire reasons.

The City Sewers Act of 1848, a rather poor copy of Liverpool's 1846 Act, gave the existing Commission of Sewers extensive powers over sewage, drainage, paving, rubbish removal and noxious trades, and the right to enter and deal with filthy and unsanitary private houses. Unlike the most advanced towns, the City left its water supply in private hands. These powers would have meant little if the Corporation had not unwittingly appointed as the City's first (and England's second) Medical Officer of Health a surgeon of determination and vigour, Dr John Simon. Simon used his limited powers and even more limited resources to initiate a public cleansing campaign on Chadwickian lines, flushing sewers, draining cess-pools, and removing 'nuisances', in a vain attempt to impede the spread of cholera in 1849. The cholera epidemic of 1849, which killed 854 City dwellers, enabled Simon to overcome the ingrained complacency and stinginess of the City fathers and Poor Law Guardians, and to build up a system of inspection and house-visiting by the City police and by poor law medical officers.

Simon's inspectors, visiting thousands of families, exposed the enor-mous scale of squalor and suffering in the City's poorer fringes. Using this information, Simon published a series of shocking weekly reports, partly suppressed by the Corporation, but fully publicized in *The Times*, which began to shake the City authorities out of their complacency. Simon's first annual Report, issued in October 1849, called for municipal action to eradicate slums, build model dwellings for the poor, provide public wash-houses, take control of water supply, suppress offensive trades, provide a municipal cemetery, complete the drainage system, and establish a perma-nent sanitary inspectorate. This was a new manifesto for urban sanitary reform, coming not from a Whitehall bureaucrat but from an officer of England's most powerful, and most anti-Chadwickian, local authority. Although the report won the fullest newspaper coverage and support, making Simon a national figure overnight, the Common Council rejected or shelved nearly all its more radical proposals. But under Simon's influence the Corporation acquired extensive new environmental powers, covering all major sanitary issues except water supply, in its 1851 City Sewers Act. In two respects, the power to order the demolition of unfit houses and to inspect and regulate low-rented tenement housing, this Act took the power of local government to new limits. The water supply of the powerful New

River Company, spasmodic and impure, 'the largest sanitary evil of the day', was the only blemish on the new regime. 'Authority so complete for this noble purpose has never been delegated to any municipal body in the country,' Simon said. Under Simon's skilful guidance, the parsimonious tradesmen of the Common Council had become the most unlikely sanitary pioneers.[26]

Simon at once instituted an efficient system of inspection and enforcement to take advantage of his new powers. Between 1851 and 1855 he demonstrated what could be achieved by a combination of sound legislation and determined execution. By 1854 the whole City was adequately drained, cesspools were a rarity, and every house had a water supply, albeit intermittent. Half of the City's 155 slaughterhouses were closed. The City had acquired the toughest industrial nuisance and smoke regulations and the best scavenging and rubbish removal system in London, and its controls on slaughterhouses, markets and unwholesome food were a model for the rest of the metropolis, and the whole country, to follow. The revolting problem of foul and overflowing City graveyards was solved in 1856, with the opening of the Corporation of London Cemetery in Manor Park, which is still the largest municipal cemetery in Europe. A few slum landlords were forced to demolish or repair their properties, but this was new territory, and the City entered it timidly.

One of the biggest environmental problems Simon had to deal with was the enormous growth of Smithfield Market, which covered over 6 acres on the north-western edge of the City, and handled (in 1846) 210,000 cattle and 1,518,000 sheep each year. This was the largest animal market in the world, and it is not surprising that the area around it was full of 'knackers' yards, tainted-sausage makers, slaughterhouses, tripe-dressers, cat's-meat boilers, catgut-spinners, bone-houses', paunch-cookers, bladder-blowers, and all the stench and brutality of backyard butchery. Only 200 yards from St Paul's Cathedral, the narrow lanes off Newgate Street were, in the literal meaning of the word, a shambles, with excrement and entrails piled by the roadside, and the gutters running with blood. The noise and filth in the market and the streets leading to it on a Sunday night, before the main Monday market, were unimaginable. In *Oliver Twist* Dickens described a scene which was increasingly incompatible with the growing wealth and dignity of the City:

> It was market morning. The ground was covered nearly ankle-deep with filth and mire; and a thick steam perpetually rising from the reeking bodies of the cattle, and mingling with the fog, which seemed

to rest upon the chimney tops, hung heavily above. . . . Countrymen, butchers, drovers, hawkers, boys, thieves, idlers, and vagabonds of every low grade, were mingled together in a dense mass: the whistling of drovers, the barking of dogs, the bellowing and plunging of beasts, the bleating of sheep, and the grunting and squeaking of pigs; the cries of hawkers, the shouts, oaths and quarrelling on all sides, the ringing of bells, and the roar of voices that issued from every public house; the crowding, pushing, driving, beating, whooping and yelling; the hideous and discordant din that resounded from every corner of the market; and the unwashed, unshaven, squalid, and dirty figures constantly running to and fro, and bursting in and out of the throng, rendered it a stunning and bewildering scene which quite confused the senses.

A Royal Commission recommended the closure of Smithfield in 1850, but the City Corporation, which owned the market, had a sentimental and financial attachment to it, and resisted its removal for some years. Finally, in 1855, Smithfield was closed, and the animal market was transferred to a 30-acre site in Copenhagen Fields, Islington, off the Caledonian Road. Smithfield reopened as a meat market in 1868, in a functional and handsome building of stone, brick and cast iron, served by underground sidings of the Metropolitan Railway. It remains in business today, the last survivor of central London's old wholesale markets.[27]

The proof of Simon's success came in 1854, when cholera returned to London. Of the 10,738 Londoners who died of cholera in 1854, only 211 lived in the City. This was largely due to the fact that the City's water did not come from the Thames, as most of London's did, but from the New River Company's newly covered reservoirs. But cholera could also be spread by filth, and Simon's systematic programme of inspection, cleansing, removal and repair probably saved many lives. It certainly seemed so to Simon's contemporaries, who now regarded him as the greatest exponent of practical sanitary reform, and as living proof that success could be achieved without the destruction of precious municipal rights. Within the City, Simon's achievement was to destroy the Common Council's tendency to put economy before cleanliness, and to establish a sanitary administration that would continue to expand, even under less inspired leadership. Nationally, Simon's medical officership set the standard others aspired to, and placed medicine and scientific research at the centre of the sanitary effort.

One important piece of research had direct relevance to Simon's work. In 1849 Drs William Budd and John Snow had suggested that cholera was spread by the swallowing of its living organism in drinking water. Comparison of death rates in 1848 in parts of South London served by two different water companies was used to support their argument. Most authorities, still wedded to contagionist or miasmatist theories, dismissed the idea, but in 1854 Snow proved his point by his study of the disastrous outbreak in Soho, between Regent Street, Wardour Street, Brewer Street and Great Marlborough Street. Snow was able to show that the bulk of the 500 people who died in this small district drew their water from a pump in Broad Street (now Broadwick Street), while users of local wells had escaped. Once the pump was sealed off, the outbreak subsided. A much larger study, covering 500,000 South Londoners, was published by Simon in 1856. This showed that customers of the Lambeth Water Company, whose water came from Ditton, had a death rate in 1854 of 37 per 10,000, compared with a rate of 130 per 10,000 for those who drank the Southwark and Vauxhall's filthy supplies from Battersea. In 1848–9, before the Lambeth Company moved its source upstream, there had been little disparity between the two rates. It took another ten years for the medical community to accept that cholera was water-borne.[28]

The Metropolitan Board of Works

As Simon was enjoying his great triumph over cholera, London was enjoying a triumph over Edwin Chadwick. When Chadwick was removed from the Board of Health in August 1854, Sir Benjamin Hall, the anti-centralist MP for Marylebone, and the chief spokesman of the do-nothing London vestries in the battle against Chadwick, took over as President of the Board. But the delight of the anti-sanitarians was brief, because Hall, taking office in the middle of a cholera epidemic, underwent an extraordinary conversion from non-interventionism to sanitary enthusiasm. Advised and encouraged by Simon, he determined to introduce a measure which would enable the parishes to emulate the City, and cleanse themselves without losing their independence. This, even the most conservative could see, called for a modicum of local government reform. A metropolis administered by about 300 different bodies, containing over 10,000 commissioners, and guided by around 250 local Acts of Parliament, could not possibly be governed effectively. A street which was in the hands of nine different paving boards (as the Strand was) was not likely to be well paved.

London had been left out of the great municipal government revolution of 1835, when the Municipal Corporations Act had created borough councils elected by all male householders with a three-year residence qualification in 178 English towns and cities. A further report of the Royal Commission on Municipal Corporations in 1837 had recommended that the whole of London should be given a single elected government, despite the practical and historical objections to such a change. The idea that the various parts of the town should be governed as 'independent and isolated communities', or that such duties as paving, sewage and lighting could be performed efficiently without metropolitan unification, was dismissed as an absurdity. But the report lacked the strength and clarity of that of 1835, and redrawing the constitution of London was such a massive and controversial project that it could not be expected to command the cross-party consensus that had smoothed the passage of the 1835 Bill through the Commons and Lords. Lord Melbourne, the Whig Prime Minister, favoured a quiet political life, and (like every other Prime Minister of the century) drew back from a confrontation with the City Corporation. Radical pressure for the democratization of local government, which had driven the reforms of 1835, had already been partially satisfied in London's case by the widespread implementation in London of Hobhouse's 1831 measure to democratize vestry elections. It was not easy to ridicule the City of London's ancient, dignified and generally effective government as others had been in the 1835 report. The City's dominant policy-making and executive body, the Court of Common Council, was elected by wards on a householder franchise, and although aldermen, the City magistrates, were still elected for life they had lost much of their political power. The City's claim to be a model of local democracy, rather than an archaic anachronism in need of immediate dissolution, still carried some conviction.[29]

In 1854 a Royal Commission on the London Corporation looked at the question of London's government once again. This time the Commissioners rejected the idea of creating a single municipal authority for the whole of London on the grounds that its 2.3 million people, spread over 78,000 acres, lacked the 'minute local knowledge and community of interests' upon which good municipal government had to be founded, and that the administration of such a large and diverse population would be 'a work of great difficulty'. Instead, in view of the failure of the parish vestries to provide efficient local government, they recommended their replacement by seven municipal councils, each covering one of London's seven parliamentary boroughs, and each sending representatives to a single Metropolitan Board of Works, which would have responsibility for public works of common interest. Sir Benjamin Hall accepted the Royal Commission's argument that London was too big to be governed by one authority, but he balked, unlike the Commission, at the prospect of interfering with the City's constitution, or abolishing the authority of all the parish vestries. His much less radical plan, which became the Metropolis Local Management Act of 1855, created a two-tiered system, which retained the twenty-three largest parishes, and grouped the fifty-five smaller ones into fifteen district boards, without destroying their individual identity.[30] By abolishing open vestries, and imposing on all vestries a common constitution based on a householder franchise, and by giving them sanitary powers and duties comparable to those acquired by the City (including the duty to appoint Medical Officers of Health), Hall rescued the parish system from disrepute and ensured its long-term survival. Metropolitan public works, especially a new intercepting sewer system, were to be in the hands of a Metropolitan Board of Works, whose forty-five members were to be drawn from the vestries (with one or two representatives each), the district boards and the City (with three representatives). This was not a formula designed to produce lavish or costly public projects. Vestrymen and their representatives on the Metropolitan Board of Works were likely to be drawn from the class of tradesmen and middling householders whose adherence to public economy, even at the price of public squalor, was legendary.[31]

THE NEW SEWERS

The Metropolitan Board of Works' borrowing powers were weak, its income from rates was always inadequate, and it lacked the authority and public support that it might have won if it had been directly elected. On top of these problems it was also dogged, as Chadwick's Commission of Sewers had been, by disagreement among engineers as to how London should be drained. Chadwick's small-pipe system was no longer considered, but the technical and financial problems of the intercepting tunnel system proposed by Joseph Bazalgette, the Board's engineer, were great enough to keep the Board and its political boss, Benjamin Hall, locked in fruitless argument until 1858. The contentious issue was the location of the outfalls, where the great northern and southern tunnels would discharge their cargo into the Thames as the high tide began to ebb. Bazalgette and the Board preferred Barking Creek and Plumstead Marshes, while Hall, fearing that the sewage might be swept back upriver, insisted on an extra mile of tunnels. Meanwhile, the stench rising from the Thames got worse each year, and in July 1858, the year of the 'Great Stink', parliamentary sittings became almost impossible. Whether one believed in the atmospheric or water-borne theory of infection, the situation was intolerable, and MPs became instant converts to the sanitary cause. They quickly decided to help the Metropolitan Board of Works out of its difficulties, giving it the power to raise a £3 million loan, and the right to spend it as it thought fit.

Bazalgette's sewer plan, which was adopted at once by the Board, involved the construction of five intercepting sewers, three north of the Thames and two to the south. In the north, a high-level sewer ran from Hampstead, and a mid-level one from Kensal Green, converging at Old Ford, on the river Lea, and flowing on together to the outfall at Barking Creek. At Abbey Mills Pumping Station, a mighty Gothic-Byzantine sanitary temple, these two were joined by the low-level sewer which had begun its journey in Chiswick. All three flowed by gravity, but the lower-level sewage had to be lifted twice by great steam pumps, once at Pimlico, and again at Abbey Mills, whose eight 142-horsepower beam engines could raise 15,000 cubic feet of sewage 36 feet in a minute. South of the Thames the high-level sewer from Balham joined the lower level one from Putney at Deptford, where the sewage was pumped up 18 feet to the outfall sewer, which then ran a further 8 miles to Crossness, on the Erith Marshes, about 1½ miles downstream of the northern outfall. On the way, the southern sewers picked up the contents of the Effra Ditch and a branch sewer from Rotherhithe and Bermondsey. The whole system, which was completed in 1868 at a total cost of £4.6 million (£1.6 million more than expected), was greeted as a triumph of modern engineering, which indeed it was. The five huge brick tunnels, 82 miles in length, deposited about 52 million gallons of rainwater and untreated sewage in the Thames each day, and were capable of handling 400 million gallons daily, should London's population growth make it necessary. In fact, London's population grew faster than Bazalgette had expected, and in 1887 it was decided, after growing public protests about the deterioration of the river near the outfalls, to separate solid from liquid sewage by chemical precipitation, and dump the solids out at sea. This was the policy pursued until the 1980s. It took a long time, of course, for poorer houses to get connected to this magnificent drainage system. Well into the next century, the bucket and the night-soil man played a greater part in sewage disposal than the flush toilet for a great many Londoners.

The new sewage system did not come soon enough to save London from the last English cholera epidemic of 1865–6. Despite the 1852 Metropolis Water Supply Act, and the well-known work of John Snow, the East London Water Company, 'with criminal indifference to the public safety', was still supplying its unlucky customers with unfiltered water from the Lea. Thus, when cholera reached the capital in July 1866 it was spread efficiently along the Company's pipes, and killed 4,276 East Londoners, while only 1,639 died in the rest of London. It was this disaster that prompted Simon to hope that 'for a population to be thus poisoned by its own excrement will some day be deemed ignominious and intolerable'.[32] In the longer run, the 1852 Act (which forced water companies to draw their Thames supplies from above Hampton Court) and the growing use of filtration greatly improved piped supplies, making them much safer than the well waters which many Londoners still seemed to prefer. Medical Officers closed most of London's public wells in the 1860s and 1870s, and only private ones remained by 1900. The famous and flavoursome waters of the Aldgate Pump came from the New River Company's pipes after 1876. The eight water companies made piped supplies generally available all over London by the 1860s, either in the street or the kitchen, and in the 1870s and 1880s several companies (especially the East London) started providing constant supplies to even the poorest districts. By 1900 the Lambeth Company was the only one still giving many of its customers an intermittent service. When the new Metropolitan Water Board took control of London's water supply in 1904 it took over a system which had become, after decades of error, evasion and delay, a generally modern and healthy one.[33]

THE MBW IN ACTION

The Metropolis Local Management Act established the shape of London's local government until 1888. It swept aside the jumble of paving and lighting commissions that had accumulated over the previous 100 years, and created the two-tier system of government, a compromise between unity and fragmentation, that London enjoyed, in one form or another, until the abolition of the Greater London Council in 1986. The area covered by the Metropolitan Board of Works (MBW), 117 square miles stretching from Putney to Plumstead, and Hampstead to Lewisham, was the one also allotted to the London County Council in 1888. London now had a central municipal authority, but one with very limited powers and responsibilities. The Board's initial powers were confined to the building of a main sewerage system, the building and improvement of main roads and bridges, the naming of streets, the numbering of houses, and the administration of the 1855 Building Act. Almost from the start, the Board had the power to acquire land for public parks, and by 1888 it had created two parks,

Finsbury Park and Southwark Park, both opened in 1869, and preserved and taken control of several large commons and heaths, including Blackheath, Hackney Downs, Tooting Bec Common, Clapham Common, Hampstead Heath and Parliament Hill.[34] When governments introduced legislation controlling metropolitan nuisances or services in the 1860s and 1870s, they usually turned to the Board as the most appropriate agency of administration and enforcement. Laws dealing with dairies, slaughterhouses and cattle diseases, the 1871 act against 'baby farming', the 1875 Cross Act on slum demolition, regulations governing petroleum and explosives, controls on water and gas companies, laws on the safety of theatres and music halls, the creation of the Metropolitan Fire Brigade in 1865, all added to the powers of the MBW, making it look increasingly like a full-blown municipal government.

One of the great tests of the ability of a local authority to serve and protect its citizens in the 1860s and 1870s was the extent to which it could win control of two of the key municipal commodities, gas and water. By the 1870s many of the vigorous and ambitious town councils of the Midlands and North had taken over local gas companies, or started their own, and several, notably Birmingham and Bradford, controlled their own water supplies. The Metropolitan Board was less assertive, and faced tougher resistance. In 1871 a Bill giving the MBW power to purchase London's eight highly profitable water companies was abandoned after strong opposition, and in 1878 a second Bill was rejected. Although there was general condemnation of London's costly, interrupted and sometimes impure water supply, Parliament's suspicion of the Board's ambitions and of its lack of democratic accountability, the lobbying power of the companies, and the unwillingness of many Board members to commit their vestry ratepayers to a heavy expense, repeatedly thwarted attempts to municipalize the service. In 1880 the Board had a chance to buy out the water companies for £33 million, a figure which future profits would have covered, but it hesitated, the government did not press the issue, and the opportunity was lost. Further Water Bills failed in the 1880s, and it was not until 1902 that the Metropolis Water Act created a new body, the Metropolitan Water Board, to buy out the eight companies for about £40 million.[35]

The MBW also failed to gain control of London's gas supply. About twenty competing gas companies supplied London with gas, mostly for lighting streets and public buildings, in the 1850s. The oldest and largest of these, the Gas Light and Coke Company, had been lighting streets and bridges in central London since 1812. In 1857 the companies abandoned competition, divided London into thirteen local monopolies, and proceeded to raise their prices and dividends. In the 1860s the City Corporation exerted its mighty lobbying power to gain control over the price and quality of the City's gas, and achieved this in the 1868 City of London Gas Act. In 1875, when some gas prices had risen by a third, the MBW tried to follow the City's example, but the companies' Parliamentary spokesmen blocked its efforts, and the Board had to be satisfied with powers over quality, but not prices.[36]

Perhaps, as John Davis has argued, the poor performance of London's government owes more to the unique size and diversity of London than to the personal failings of those who sat on the Board and the vestries. London had no 'natural' ruling élite ready to give the metropolis a lead. The titled aristocracy of the West End and the monied aristocracy of the City were not keen to take responsibilities outside their own districts, and London's small-scale economy had not produced a dominant group of big industrialists. Until the late 1880s there was no great battle between the political parties to generate public debate about the future of the metropolis, and vestry elections (when they took place at all) were controlled by avowedly non-political ratepayer associations which did as little as possible to arouse public interest in municipal issues. Vestries chose the oldest and least adventurous of their members to sit on the MBW, which was in turn controlled by an inner clique of senior members whose security of tenure insulated them from the pressures of public opinion. As the MBW's duties grew, so did the burden it imposed on the parish ratepayers, whose vestry representatives became increasingly unwilling to pay for civic improvements that did not bring benefits to their own districts. The MBW could also raise money through loans, but its power to do so was controlled by the Treasury to a greater degree than that of other civic governments.

The failings of the MBW were compounded by those of the vestries themselves. Victorian environmental legislation imposed growing duties on parish governments, especially in the fields of sanitary inspection and street-cleaning, paving and lighting, to be paid for from rates levied on the value of houses and business premises ('rateable values') within the parish. The system intensified the already great inequalities between different parts of London, forcing East End parishes with the worst environmental problems, the lowest property values and the fewest and poorest ratepayers to impose much higher rates in the pound than West End parishes, in return for inferior services. Although legislation to spread the cost of poor relief was passed in 1865, nothing was done to equalize the burden of vestry services between rich and poor parishes until 1894. It is not surprising that vestrymen in poorer parishes resisted the growing demands of the MBW, especially when they could see that most of the Board's projects seemed to favour its biggest paymasters, the West End parishes.[37]

Although the MBW performed its allotted tasks and handled a £3 million budget (in the 1880s) with a reasonable degree of competence it never won widespread public support, or succeeded in establishing itself as a champion of the interests of Londoners. Its difficulties were increased by the fact that it had no official spokesman in the House of Commons, and that many MPs regarded it as little more than an overgrown vestry, without direct responsibility to its ratepayers. Unlike the City Corporation it had no historic roots, no colourful and archaic ceremonies, nothing to stir the hearts of sentimental traditionalists. Nor did it satisfy the wishes of radical reformers, who objected to the lack of elections to the Board, and the fact that the local vestries, renowned for their tight-fisted conservatism, supplied nearly all its members. How could a Board composed of small-minded and secretive tradesmen, who quibbled over all expenditure which did not benefit their own parishes, bind together a city of such diverse interests, and inspire a sense of civic pride and identity to equal that of Birmingham or Leeds? The Board could never shake off the public accusations of corruption which had begun during the building of the main sewers in the 1860s. Public suspicion that the Board of Works was really (as *Punch* insisted) a 'Board of Perks' seemed to be confirmed in 1886, when the *Financial News* exposed corruption among some architects and surveyors in the Estates Department, involving land deals around Piccadilly Circus. Eventually, these accusations led to a Royal Commission on the MBW, whose report in 1889 confirmed that there was long-standing corruption in the Estates Office and on the part of two Board members, but found no evidence that the Board's members or officers were generally corrupt.[38]

THE CREATION OF LONDON COUNTY COUNCIL

Although the MBW was attacked almost from the moment of its creation, its critics were divided as to which system should replace it. Should London be governed by one elected metropolitan authority, taking over the powers of the Corporation, the vestries and the more specialized agencies, or should the capital's diversity be recognized by the establishment of stronger and more democratic local government bodies, perhaps based on the Parliamentary boroughs? John Stuart Mill, the radical and Utilitarian philosopher, swung from one view to the other in the space of six years. In

Representative Government, published in 1861, he argued that London needed a single municipal council to manage all its affairs, rather than 'a mere Board of Works'. Subdivision, either by district or function, as well as deterring the 'very best minds' from playing a part in local government, 'prevents the possibility of consecutive or well regulated co-operation for common objects, precludes any uniform principle for the discharge of local duties, compels the general government to take things upon itself which would be best left to local authorities. . . . ; and answers no purpose but to keep up the fantastical trappings of that union of modern jobbing and antiquated foppery, the Corporation of the City of London'.[39] But in 1866–8, as MP for Westminster and a member of the newly formed Metropolitan Municipalities Association, Mill argued for the creation of ten municipal authorities (including the City), and introduced unsuccessful Bills to that effect.

In the 1870s opinion began to swing in favour of a centralized system. Bills introduced by Charles Buxton in 1870 and Lord Elcho in 1875 proposed an expansion of the City Corporation to encompass the whole metropolis, and in 1878 the Commons passed a resolution calling for a directly elected government for London. The centralization movement was given new vigour in 1880 by the election to Parliament of J. F. B. Firth, whose book *Municipal London* had caused a stir in 1876. In 1881 Firth became Chairman of the new London Municipal Reform League, which won the support of leading Liberals, including Sir Charles Dilke, Sir Arthur Hobhouse and the Home Secretary, Sir William Harcourt. Harcourt won Gladstone's Cabinet over to reform, although there was disagreement over whether the new authority should control the Metropolitan Police. Most ministers did not regard municipal reform as an urgent or especially popular measure, and the introduction of a Bill was put off until April 1884. Harcourt's London Government Bill sought to transform the City Corporation into an elected central authority, absorbing the powers of the MBW, the vestries, the Middlesex magistrates and other administrative bodies, but not the police powers of the Home Office. Vestries, whose failure to deal with slum housing was widely publicized by Dilke and in Mearns's pamphlet, *The Bitter Cry of Outcast London*, were to be abolished, and the new elected district councils would only exercise powers delegated to them by the central council. Gladstone spoke for the Bill, but his interest in it was not very great, and most Liberal MPs, like their constituents, were indifferent to questions of metropolitan reform. The Bill was too centralizing to win much popular or political support in London, and only one London authority, Lewisham, supported it. The City Corporation, fearing that centuries of wealth, power and privilege were about to be destroyed, spent £14,000 in 1884 to stir up public hostility to reform, organizing mass petitions, publishing fifty pamphlets and manipulating the Press. Conservative MPs with City connections opposed the Bill, and so, inevitably, did the vestries. The *Quarterly Review* expressed their fears about a measure which would give the voters of London, 'the majority of them ignorant of public affairs, and many of them extremely poor', control over 'the richest and most important urban area in the world'. In the light of this opposition, and with an important franchise reform to enact, Gladstone dropped Harcourt's Bill in July 1884.[40]

The question of London's administration was not taken up again until 1886, when a new Conservative government under Lord Salisbury decided to deal with the reform of London as part of a broader scheme for a national system of elected county councils. The 1888 Local Government Act, which created a new county of London based on the MBW area, did enough to satisfy those who wanted a directly elected and efficient metropolitan authority to replace the discredited Metropolitan Board of Works, without antagonizing those who feared excessive centralization. The London County Council (LCC) took over the MBW's responsibilities for parks, drainage and constructing metropolitan transport routes, and the county justices' powers over bridges, asylums and entertainment licences, but it did not control education, housing, town planning, water supply, policing, the Port of London, the wholesale markets or poor relief, and the local powers of the vestries were untouched. The City remained a borough within a county (but not an independent county borough), retaining control of judicial matters in return for agreeing to make substantial contributions to the cost of metropolitan services. The almost universal condemnation of the MBW, among those who wanted a more energetic central authority as well as those who wanted a cheaper one, united Londoners, for a while at least, in their support for the new Council. Even Conservatives, no great lovers of the democratic principle, were reconciled to elections which (to judge from their sweeping victories in the 1886 general election) they had every prospect of winning.[41]

In the event, the Liberals (calling themselves 'Progressives') beat the Conservatives (the 'Moderates') in the January 1889 LCC election, and kept control of the Council until their defeat in 1907. Although in its structure and in the distribution of powers the new system was not very different from the old one, its spirit was altogether new. Party politics played a much greater role in London's government after 1888 than ever before, and the radical Liberals (along with a few socialists) who dominated the new LCC believed they had a mandate to bring to London the municipal revolution that other cities had enjoyed thirty or forty years earlier. The Progressives believed that they could use the power of centralized London government to solve the social problems which had been exposed in the 1880s: sweated labour, slum housing, extremes of poverty and privilege, inadequate public utilities. In fact, the LCC's initial powers in these areas were very small, and its efforts to extend its authority were often thwarted by Parliament and central government, which were in Conservative hands from 1886 to 1892 and 1895 to 1906. The LCC failed to gain control of water, gas and electricity (whose profits might have supported other municipal initiatives), and when the London water supply was finally taken into public ownership in 1904 it was not given to the Council, but to the Metropolitan Water Board, a body composed (like the old Metropolitan Board of Works) of local authority delegates. By the 1891 Public Health (London) Act the vestries and district boards became the local sanitary authorities, responsible for street cleaning, nuisance and refuse removal, and local drains, while the LCC gained a few miscellaneous duties.[42]

In spite of such disappointments, the LCC acquired, in its first twenty years, an important range of new powers. The 1890 Housing of the Working Classes Act allowed the Council to 'compulsorily purchase' slum land and to build new houses on it, initiating a programme of municipal estate building. The first of the new LCC developments was the Boundary Street Estate, which was built on the ruins of the notorious Bethnal Green slums known as the Nichol, or the Jago, in the 1890s. The London Building Act of 1894 codified and extended the LCC's control over building standards, and the 1906 London Squares Act enabled the Council to protect some squares from development. Legislation in 1889 and 1890 gave the LCC the power and the money (from a penny rate and a local tax on beer and spirits) to provide technical education and build polytechnics, and in 1904, when the London School Board was abolished, the LCC took charge of London's entire publicly funded education system. In addition, the Council used existing powers to take over London's horse-drawn tram companies between 1892 and 1903, and to unify and electrify the whole system. And it continued the MBW's work in creating new transport routes and buying or acquiring open spaces: Blackwall and Rotherhithe road tunnels, Greenwich and Woolwich foot tunnels, the new Battersea and Vauxhall Bridges and Kingsway were built between 1889 and 1914, and Lincoln's Inn Fields, Hackney Marsh, Hainault Forest and Waterlow Park were added to the stock of public parkland.[43]

THE LONDON BOROUGHS

Municipal revolutions, even small ones, are not cheap, and the restraints placed on the LCC's eighteen free-spending Standing Committees by the full Council were not very strong. In the LCC's first six years the cost to the London ratepayer of county services rose by 46 per cent.[44] These rate rises prompted the formation in 1894 of the London Municipal Society, a Conservative organization whose aim was to attack overspending and press for a return to a more decentralized London government. At the same time the vestries were awoken from their slumber by a new level of public interest in parish politics, and the triumph of radical Liberals in vestry elections. Social policies which had once been adopted grudgingly, if at all, were now pursued with gusto. Vestry sanitary powers, strengthened by the 1891 Public Health (London) Act, were wielded with new vigour, and parish sanitary inspectors and Medical Officers found a more cooperative spirit in local council chambers. Seventeen new town halls were built or planned in the last fifteen years of the century, and spending on public baths rose from under £6,000 in 1881–2 to £107,000 in 1899–1900. A few authorities even installed electric street-lighting. Most impressive of all, thirty-four vestries built libraries using the powers created by the Public Libraries Acts of 1850 and 1855, which only two districts had taken up before 1886. Library spending rose from £1,200 in 1881–2 to £70,000 in 1899. As a result of this late flowering of the civic spirit, vestry expenditure rose by a third (£620,000) between 1884 and 1894.[45] The impact of rising vestry and LCC spending (along with the heavy costs of the police and the London School Board) on the ratepayers of the poorer parishes created pressure for the introduction of a system which would increase the contribution of parishes with a high rateable value to London's common services, just as the establishment of a Common Poor Fund had spread the burden of poor relief in 1865. The Liberal government's Equalization of Rates Act (1894) was a victory for the working-class parishes of East and South London and for the principle of metropolitan integration, and a blow to West End and City ratepayers, who had to pay about £900,000 (35 per cent of total vestry spending) into an equalization fund in support of social policies which they did not need.[46]

Rate equalization encouraged two West End vestries, Westminster and Kensington, to petition for independent municipal status in 1897, but their devolution campaign was decisively rejected by the ratepayers of the poorer east and south London vestries in the LCC election of 1898. The advocates

of municipal decentralization now had the support of the Conservative
Prime Minister and creator of the LCC, Lord Salisbury, who announced his
conviction that London was not 'one great municipality, but ... an
aggregate of municipalities' in a speech in November 1897. Salisbury set
the First Lord of the Treasury, A. J. Balfour, to devise a Bill which would
create a set of London municipal authorities large enough to govern
themselves, and open the way for the wholesale transfer of powers from
the centre to the localities once the LCC fell under Conservative control.
In practice, parochial pride made it impossible to create the ten or twelve
very large units that the scheme required, and support for the LCC among
Local Government Board officials, vestries, ministers and MPs persuaded
Balfour to back down on the devolution of powers. What emerged from
the compromise and confusion in 1899 was a 'legislative mouse', the
London Government Act.[47]

The 1899 Act, which established the shape of London government for
the next sixty-five years, created twenty-eight Metropolitan Boroughs (plus
the unchanged City) to replace the thirty-eight vestries and district boards
(and at least 100 lesser bodies), but retained, with minor changes, the
existing distribution of powers between the centre and the localities, and
preserved rate equalization. Many of the new boroughs were simply the old
vestries decked out with mayors, aldermen and the trappings and ceremonial of municipal government. Others were amalgamations of vestries:
Wandsworth with Battersea, Woolwich with Plumstead, Rotherhithe with
Bermondsey, Holborn with St Giles'. Whitechapel, Mile End, Limehouse
and St George's were reunited as the Borough of Stepney, and St James's,
St Martin-in-the-Fields and the Strand were forced to join St George's
Hanover Square and St Margaret's in the new City of Westminster. The
LCC kept its London-wide powers, and, with the abolition of the London
School Board in 1904, increased them. Of the £24.7 million spent on
London's government in 1906–7, the LCC spent £9.5 million (mainly on
education and interest on its £50 million debt), the boroughs £5 million,
the City Corporation £1.3 million, and the Boards of Guardians, the
Metropolitan Police, the Water Board and the Asylums Board almost
£9 million.[48]

The Progressives did not enjoy their triumph over devolutionism for
long. In the election of 1907, following the embarrassing and costly failure
of the LCC's new steamboat service, and with the weight of the Conservative press behind them, the Moderates won a large majority on the LCC,
and for the next twenty-seven years wielded the powers that the Progressives had fought to preserve.[49]

Chapter 16

The Richest City in the World

MANUFACTURING IN LONDON

The skyline of nineteenth-century London was not dominated by smoking factory chimneys, and the city did not owe its existence, as Bradford or Oldham did, to the Industrial Revolution. So it was easy enough for contemporaries to assume, as the author of an 1851 guide-book put it, that London was 'a vast trading and commercial, rather than a manufacturing town'.[1] The statistics yielded by the census taken in that year show that the author was mistaken. In 1851 London had a working population of 1,115,000 men and women, 13.75 per cent of the working population of England and Wales. It is true that London's workforce included an especially high percentage of the country's workers in non-manufacturing occupations. About a quarter of England's wholesale and retail dealers, government employees, professionals and transport workers lived in London, as did 40 per cent of those in banking, insurance and the law, and 67 per cent of those in art, entertainment, literature and science. Over 22 per cent of working Londoners (and over half of London's working women) were domestic servants, making up over 22 per cent of the country's 1.1 million servants, and London had nearly 70,000 builders, a tenth of its male workforce and 16 per cent of the national total. But although observers might regard London as a city of clerks, porters, messengers, shopkeepers, sailors, cabmen, lawyers, carpenters, entertainers and housemaids, it also contained 373,000 manufacturing workers (more than the whole population of Manchester or Glasgow), who constituted a third of London's occupied population and 13.5 per cent of the national manufacturing workforce. This huge concentration made London, at the time of the Great Exhibition of 1851, by far the largest industrial city in the world.[2] The well-established contemporary and modern opinion that the South, and London in particular, was simply a centre of consumption, in which 'well-to-do and leisured families' lived, without conspicuous exertion, on the labours of the North, ignores so much of the reality of the London economy that (as an account of London, rather than a group of Londoners) it has to be dismissed.[3]

London's manufacturing strength was still, as it had been for centuries, in the finishing trades, in high-value goods for the affluent consumer, in industries in which the advantages of a huge local market, excellent national and international communications, a great port, ample skilled and unskilled labour and ready access to imported raw materials outweighed the disadvantages of high wages, rents and fuel prices. It had the distinctive characteristics, in short, of a truly metropolitan economy. Industries that involved making cheap basic goods using coal, steampower and heavy raw materials, such as iron, steel, and woollen or cotton textiles, were not well represented in inner London.[4] But over 80 per cent of England's manufacturers of jewellery and musical instruments, over 40 per cent of its printers, bookbinders, tailoresses and furniture-makers, and a quarter of its makers of carriages, clocks and bread, and workers in fur, leather and paper, were Londoners in 1851. Many of these industries gained social and economic benefits from their dense concentration in parts of London's inner industrial belt. This curved from Marylebone and Westminster, the production centres for good-quality furniture and clothing, south-east into Southwark, the centre of hatting, eastwards to the leather district of Bermondsey, then back across the river, thick with shipbuilding, woodwork and all the riverside trades, north into Stepney, the home of cheap furniture, clothing and sweated production of all kinds, north again to the silk-weaving district of Bethnal Green, and finally west into Shoreditch, another centre for cheap furniture, and Clerkenwell, the headquarters of watchmaking and the production of high-value metal goods.

London had no 'staple industry', but the clothing industry, which employed 28,000 men and 84,000 women in 1851, was the closest it came to it. Thirty per cent of London's manufacturing workers, and 63 per cent of its female manufacturing workers, were in the clothing trade, and another 38,000 (a tenth of its manufacturing workforce) were shoemakers. Apart from about 8,000 jobs in fur, hair, paper, furniture, jam and baking, 7,000 in boots and shoes, and 17,000 in the textile industries (mostly silk), there was very little manufacturing work for women in 1851 outside the clothing industry. It must be remembered, though, that many women who took in mending, laundry or needlework to supplement their family's income would not be recorded as workers in the census, and that the women listed as 'baker's wife' or 'shoemaker's wife' (12,616 of these in 1851) might have taken an active part in their husbands' work. Men had a wider choice of industrial jobs. To take only the largest categories, about

33,000 men worked in wood and furniture, 23,000 in the metal trades, almost 22,000 in textiles (mainly silk), 14,000 in printing and bookbinding, nearly 14,000 in baking and confectionery, over 10,000 in furs, leather, glue and tallow, over 9,000 in watch and instrument production, over 9,000 in carriages and harness, 9,000 in machinery and tools, over 7,000 in drink, nearly 6,000 in gold and jewellery, and 5,000 in shipbuilding, in 1851.[5]

London's manufacturing economy was based, in the main, on the home and the workshop, not the large factory. The 1851 census recorded only twelve London factories with over 300 employees, only two industries (tanning and silk) with more than 10 per cent of their workers in firms of over fifty, and three-quarters of London's manufacturing workers in firms of five or less. At the end of the century one of Charles Booth's assistants, Ernest Aves, noted that in the industrial suburbs the 'factory system' had largely displaced home and workshop production in chemicals, soap, dyes and engineering, and was spreading in the jam, candle, rubber, envelope, printing, bookbinding, watch, rope, can, sack and scientific instrument industries. But even in 1891 the average firm employed about thirteen people, only four industries (bookbinding, paper, printing and engineering) had an average workforce per firm of over twenty, and in several of the largest industries (clothing, shoes, watches, cabinet-making, musical instruments), self-employed craftsmen outnumbered employers. In an age of factory production, London was still 'the stronghold of small industries'.[6]

In recent years the familiar picture of London as a centre of small-scale and generally inefficient and outdated production has been modified in various ways. David Green has drawn attention to the incompleteness of the workforce figures in the 1851 census, including its omission of large firms that sub-contracted their work to dozens of small workshops. The clothing wholesaler Nicholls and Co. employed over 1,000 sweated workers in this way, but the scale of its operation (and that of other firms of a similar size) is obscured by the census. Non-census evidence, especially reports of strikes and lockouts, suggests that large enterprises, including breweries, shipbuilders, printing works, engineers and construction firms, were more common than the official figures suggest. As in other industrial towns, where economies of scale and the need for expensive machinery gave big enterprises a clear advantage over small ones, they tended to predominate.[7]

The Origins of the Sweated System

The fact that most London production remained small-scale and generally unmechanized did not mean that it was unchanging. Cheaper materials, rising population, growing overseas trade, lower transport costs and more commercial retailing and wholesaling created a rapidly expanding market for clothes, shoes, furniture, books, metalwares, watches and other consumer goods in the early nineteenth century. In this new world of mass consumption, London could not meet the challenge of northern and Midlands manufacturers by continuing to produce expensive high-quality goods in small workshops, employing skilled craftsmen and their apprentices in the traditional way. High rents and fuel prices, along with the nature of London's prevailing industries, inhibited the growth of steam-powered factory production, but there was another way to produce large quantities of cheap goods. This was to break down the apprenticeship rules and traditional wage rates of skilled artisans by dividing manufacturing processes into simple tasks which could be quickly learned by cheap semi-skilled labour, often women and children, working at home, or under the supervision of a 'sweater' or 'garret-master' in an attic or cellar. Industrialization is usually regarded as a process which removed production from the home or workshop to the factory, but in London it was more practical to move it from the workshop to the home.

The 'sweated system', which increasingly characterized the major London industries, especially clothing, footwear and furniture, took several forms. An expert witness to the House of Lords Select Committee on the Sweating System in 1888 defined the system as 'one under which sub-contractors undertake to do work in their own houses or small workshops, and employ others to do it, making a profit for themselves by the difference between the contract prices and the wages they pay their assistants'. Often, the 'sweater' or 'chamber-master' was not a middleman or sub-contractor, but a small manufacturer who suffered the hardships of the system alongside his assistants, probably his own family. In many cases, there was no 'contract' at all, just a hope that a wholesaler would be interested in the goods once they were made. Whether sweated workers worked under the supervision of a master, or independently for a wholesaler or retailer, they shared the same conditions: hours driven up and piece-rates driven down by labour surplus, and a working life in which craft customs, trade unions, factory legislation and sanitary inspectors had no influence.[8]

The degeneration of skilled luxury crafts into mass-production industries, with sweated labour playing the part played elsewhere by machinery, began in the later eighteenth century, when boot and shoe manufacturers started to employ cheap piece-workers, usually families working at home, as stitchers. In the tailoring trade a division developed between skilled tailors paid by the day, the 'flints', and a much smaller number of less skilled 'dungs', paid by the piece.[9] Skilled artisans were protected at first by the strength of their unions, based on the public houses, or 'houses of call', where they waited for work, and also by the fact that most eighteenth-century customers were well-off, and wanted high-quality goods made by skilled craftsmen. The mass market was for second-hand clothes, not new ones. This began to change during the wars of 1793–1815, when the male workforce was reduced by military recruitment and there were huge army and navy contracts for uniforms and boots. This encouraged manufacturers to use unskilled labour, often women and children, to produce cheap and inferior ready-to-wear goods, working at home or in 'slop-shops'. After the war London's growing population, and the rapid fall in the price of cloth (especially 'shoddy' cloth, made from recycled rags) ensured that the mass production of 'cheap and nasty' clothes and shoes continued to expand, whatever the skilled artisans tried to do about it.[10]

Although buoyant wartime demand helped to soften the impact of these changes, the dilution of skilled labour so worried London artisans that they formed a committee, representing seventy trades, to petition Parliament to strengthen the moribund apprenticeship regulations of the 1563 Statute of Artificers. The government's response was to abolish the rules altogether in 1814, leaving the skilled artisans to defend their position, if they could, by their own efforts. This was difficult in the depressed postwar decades, when a glut of labour in all the skilled crafts, exacerbated by mass demobilization and provincial competition, made it easy to replace workers on strike. The following thirty years saw a collapse in apprenticeship regulations and customary wage agreements in almost every skilled London craft. The shoemakers' strikes over cheap work and wage cuts were defeated in 1824 and 1826, as were those of the tailors, London's most strongly unionized workers, in 1827, 1830 and 1834. Carpenters, hatters, cabinet-makers, shipwrights, silk dyers, twine spinners and ropemakers all struck against cheap labour and wage cuts in the 1820s, but all were unable to preserve their old craft privileges.[11]

MAYHEW AND THE SWEATED TRADES

We can see the decline of an old craft, and its division into a small skilled sector and a much larger sweated or 'slop-work' sector, in the shoemaking industry. The main forces for change here were the rise of a mass market for cheap shoes, and the efforts of efficient Northampton producers, who opened a London warehouse in 1818, to satisfy it. London masters reacted by driving down prices by sending their cut leather to workmen who stitched and finished the shoes at home, perhaps using the labour of their families or unskilled assistants. From this developed the full-blown sweated system found by Henry Mayhew in 1850. In shoemaking, the system took several forms. In some cases, a shoemaker, unable to find well-paid work, would enlist the help of his family to earn what he once would have earned alone: 'The wife cuts out the work for the binders, the husband does the knife-work; the children sew with uncommon rapidity. The husband, when the work is finished at night, goes out with it' to sell it for whatever the shopkeeper or wholesaler will give. Such a family would be in competition with sweaters, or 'chamber-masters', who used the labour of parish apprentices, paid only with board and lodging, or children hired by the week in Bethnal Green market, or desperate men ready to work and sleep ten to a room for about 9s a week. 'The men feel they are in a state of slavery,' one of these sweated workers told Mayhew. 'My master has the false measurement in his size stick.... I feel degraded by the way I'm employed, and we all do, but how are we to get out of it? It's just degradation or starvation, and I'm not quite ready for starvation.' 'The object of each and all of these different practices,' Mayhew concluded, 'is to bring an inferior and consequently cheaper, labour into competition with that of the skilled artisan, and to be able to undersell others in the market.'[12]

Mayhew found the same division between a small 'honourable' trade of skilled and unionized craftsmen and a much larger 'dishonourable' trade of sweated workers in the various branches of the clothing industry. By 1850 the number of 'honourable' tailors, working for reputable West End employers, had been reduced to about 3,000, compared to about 18,000 'dishonourable' slop-workers, mostly working in the East End. Early in the century slop-workers had been used mainly for the production of cheaper garments, especially uniforms for prisoners, West Indies slaves, sailors, soldiers, railwaymen, postmen and policemen, but since the 1830s they had entered the quality market. This had forced skilled tailors into sweated work, and driven down the wages of those remaining in the 'honourable' trade. Typically, sweated tailors worked more than eighty hours a week in the sweater's crowded garret, and paid most of their wages to their employer in return for bread, butter and weak tea, and the right to sleep two or three to a bed in the work-room. Most were exhausted, mal-nourished and consumptive. Tailoring and the whole clothing trade was very vulnerable to sweating, because the market for cheap garments was enormous, the skills of the trade were easy to learn, and there were many thousands of women in London who needed work at any price. Mayhew calculated that of London's 33,500 seamstresses, shirtmakers, staymakers, embroiderers, bonnet-makers, dressmakers and milliners, over 28,000 were women under twenty, and that average earnings were under 5s a week. A high proportion of female sweated workers, Mayhew was told, sup-plemented their earnings by begging, prostitution and the pawnshop.[13]

Cabinet-making had gone the same way, with some large West End workshops around Tottenham Court Road and Euston Road producing high-quality furniture for sale in such fashionable shops as Maples (opened in 1841), and a new Shoreditch 'slop trade', based on cheap home workers, producing poorly made goods for the mass market. Buyers of cheap London furniture were warned in 1844 'never to sit upon the chairs, use the tables, or lie upon the beds'.[14] The wholesalers who controlled this trade had moved soon after 1800 from the City to Curtain Road, Shoreditch, which remained the centre of the cheap furniture business for the rest of the century. They were supplied by 'garret-masters', who worked (Mayhew was told) ninety hours a week in their own rooms in Stepney and Bethnal Green, often helped by their wives and children. Like all sweated workers, they were trapped in a circle of exploitation. Low piece-rates forced them to work long and fast, and by doing so they intensified the labour surplus which enabled the dealers to pay them so little. Or, as Mayhew put it, 'over-work means under-pay'. Yet new 'masters' were still attracted to the trade, because its skills were easy to learn and it required little capital, except about 10s for second-hand tools and money for the first week's supply of wood.[15]

Where the threat to skill and status did not come from sweating, it came from mechanization. Ropemakers were gradually displaced by machinery from the 1820s, and sawyers in the furniture and shipbuilding industries were displaced by steam-driven sawmills, of which there were sixty-eight in London by 1850. Newspaper pressmen were threatened by the steam cylinder-press, which was used for *The Times* from 1814, and which, by 1828, could print sixteen times as fast as a skilled hand-printer.

The eight-feed rotary press installed by *The Times* in 1848 produced 9,600 copies an hour, over thirty times as many as a hand-printer could do.[16] In the clothing and furniture industries mechanization had affected the making of the basic materials (textiles and planed planks), rather than the finished article. A greater threat to London craftsmen came from the enormous supply of unskilled labour which could enter an industry once its system of training and apprenticeship had broken down. Rural and Irish immigrants, unemployed workers in seasonal or declining trades, adolescents, demobilized servicemen, single women who would not, or could not, become domestic servants, and wives of unemployed men or casual workers, crowded into the sweated trades. And this surplus was made much greater by the decline of one of London's major employers, the silk industry.[17]

In 1824 the Spitalfields, Mile End and Bethnal Green silk industry employed 20,000 handlooms and perhaps 50,000 workers, many of them women and children working in 'sweated' conditions. Their survival depended upon protectionist legislation passed after riots in 1766. In 1826, in the spirit of free trade, French silk imports were allowed into England with a 30 per cent tariff. The impact on the industry was devastating. Employment and wage rates were halved, and the weavers began a frantic and doomed campaign of petitioning, rioting and radical politics to get their protection restored. Some even petitioned to be resettled in Australia. In the 1830s observers found the weavers ragged and underfed, and the 1840 Handloom Weavers' Commission reported that they were a 'Lilliputian' race, whose children were 'squalid, wretched and starved'. The Commission believed that only 11,000 weavers were left in London, living on earnings of 4s to 8s a week.[18] The duty on French silk was halved in 1846, and the weavers' sufferings intensified. When Henry Mayhew went in search of acute poverty for the readers of the *Morning Chronicle* in 1849 he turned first to Spitalfields, where he found weavers living in a state of gloomy destitution, sitting in their wretched rooms dreaming of the neat houses and roast beef of long ago. 'In all there was the same want of hope – the same doggedness and half-indifference as to their fate.' Mayhew was unsure about numbers, but the 1851 census shows about 10,000 men and 11,000 women left in the London silk industry.[19] Men, women and children who would once have made their livings in the silk industry were forced to join the overcrowded casual labour market, taking their chances as street-sellers, laundresses, dockers, or sweated workers in the clothing, shoe or furniture industries. In 1860 the tariff on French silk was abolished by the Cobden Treaty, and the remaining weavers were ruined. In 1888 Jesse

Argyle, working for Charles Booth, found only thirty-eight firms, 900 looms, and 1,674 workers, in the silk industry.[20]

LATER VICTORIAN SWEATING

The exploitation of sweated labour had disturbed some observers of the London economy even before Mayhew's comprehensive exposure of the system in December 1849. A new radical and satirical magazine, *Punch*, had published an article on seamstresses' wages in 1843, following it with Thomas Hood's poem, 'The Song of the Shirt', which is said to have tripled *Punch*'s circulation:

> Work – work – work
> Till the brain begins to swim;
> Work – work – work
> Till the eyes are heavy and dim!
> Seam, and gusset, and band,
> Band, and gusset, and seam,
> Till over the buttons I fall asleep,
> And sew them on in a dream![21]

Mayhew was one of the founders of *Punch*, and he might well have been led to his own work on sweating by the success of Hood's poem. Interest in sweating was increased by the resurgence of Chartism in 1848. The following year Lord Ashley (later Shaftesbury) organized an Association of Milliners and Dressmakers, and Charles Kingsley, a young Christian Socialist, started his novel *Alton Locke*, which explored the connection between the sweated system and Chartism. Kingsley denied the charge that he had been 'picking and stealing' from Mayhew's letters, but his 1850 pamphlet against sweating, *Cheap Clothes and Nasty*, quoted extensively from them, and *Alton Locke* was published a year after Mayhew's reports appeared.[22]

Between 1861 and 1891 the manufacturing workforce grew more slowly than the working population as a whole (by 37 per cent compared to 48 per cent) and newer industries outpaced the older ones. In the furniture industry the workforce grew by 16 per cent to over 52,000, and in clothing it grew by 21 per cent, from 138,000 to 167,000.[23] Employment doubled in scientific instruments, paper goods, printing, bookbinding, gas, rubber, engineering and chemicals, and declined in silk, shipbuilding (which collapsed dramatically in 1866–7), watches, hats (where machine-made felt hats replaced hand-made beaver and silk hats), brushes, footwear, sugar refining (hit by foreign imports) and cooperage (owing to a shift from wooden to metal casks). The footwear industry was affected by the growing use of sewing, cutting and riveting machines, but as long as workers in Northampton, Leicester, Norwich and other provincial cities resisted the introduction of a full-blown factory system, the London outwork industry declined only gradually, from a workforce of 43,000 in 1861 to 39,000 in 1891. But in 1895 the provincial shoemakers' unions were defeated by a national lock-out, and the factory system triumphed. Metropolitan producers could not easily follow suit, and London shoemaking, both in the East and West Ends, went into a sharp decline. By 1921 there were 26,000 shoemakers in London, under 1 per cent of the metropolitan workforce.[24]

In the clothing industry new technology encouraged the sweated system, rather than destroying it. The invention of the sewing machine in 1846, and the band-saw (which could cut many pieces of cloth simultaneously) in 1858, transformed production, but did not take it out of the home. Clothes were cut out with band-saws in the wholesaler's warehouse, but were then given out to home-workers or small sweated workshops in Whitechapel, St George's or Mile End New Town for stitching, button-holing, pleating and embroidering. Faster production lowered prices instead of increasing wages, and thus encouraged ordinary Londoners to switch from buying used to new clothes. As the market for ready-made clothes grew, wholesale clothiers began to open warehouses in Whitechapel and the eastern edge of the City, especially along Houndsditch, the old centre of second-hand clothes dealing. Elias Moses, who opened new premises on Aldgate and the Minories in 1846, was probably the first of these, but there were about fifty in all by 1860. By the 1880s, ready-made clothes had even invaded the quality West End market, threatening the livelihoods of the Court dressmakers who had traditionally satisfied the demands of upper-class ladies who were in London for the Season. To protect their position in the upper-class market the West End drapers opened large workshops near their Oxford Street and Regent Street stores. Their growing success, especially after the opening of the Central and Bakerloo Underground Lines in 1900 and 1907, began to challenge the Houndsditch wholesalers' control of the ready-made clothing industry.[25]

The pool of cheap labour which fed the sweated trades was enlarged by the collapse of the silk and shipbuilding industries, and constantly replenished by migrants who arrived from rural England, from Ireland and from overseas. After 1881 the problem of surplus labour was intensified by the arrival of Jewish immigrants, in flight from persecution and poverty in

Poland and Russia. As their critics claimed, Jewish immigrants were desperate for work, and moved into the East London sweated trades in large numbers. By 1901 almost 35 per cent of London's East European Jews were working in the clothing industry, and another 10 per cent in the footwear trade. The clothing trade was easy to enter and quick to learn, and many of the leading clothing wholesalers were Jews. The increasing identification of the sweated trades with Jewish immigration revived public and political interest in the sweated system in the 1880s. The *Lancet* published a report on 'the Polish Colony of Jew Tailors' in May 1884, and in 1887 the Board of Trade's Labour Correspondent, John Burnett, reported that 'the enormous influx of foreign paupers' had redoubled the hardships of native sweated workers. The outcome of this agitation was a House of Lords Select Committee, whose five reports, published between 1888 and 1890, were a comprehensive exposure of the exploitation of casual and unskilled labour in sweated industries and the London docks. Although the Committee was bombarded with evidence of Jewish involvement in the sweated trades, both as workers and as employers, it concluded that 'undue stress' had been laid on the impact of immigration on wages, and on the immorality of the Jews. 'On the contrary, they are represented on all hands as thrifty and industrious, and they seldom or never come on the rates, as the Jews support by voluntary contributions all their indigent members. What is shown is that the Jewish immigrants can live on what would be starvation wages to Englishmen, that they work for a number of hours almost incredible in length, and that until of late they have not easily lent themselves to trade combinations.'[26] By 1914, many Jewish tailors had overcome this last problem. Although only 30 per cent of the 65,000 London tailors were Jewish, they made up two-thirds of the trade's 8,000 union members.[27]

Although sweated labour was widely recognized as a metropolitan social problem in the 1890s, the solution to it was not easy to find. The Select Committee of 1888–90 had not suggested any practical remedy, and though a Royal Commission recommended in 1894 that stricter workplace regulations should be enforced, the scattered and small-scale nature of East London outwork made this hard to achieve. In poorly paid and unskilled industries, where new workers could easily be found to fill the places of those on strike, effective trade union action was almost impossible, and when unions campaigned against outwork, as the shoemakers did in the 1890s, they tended to drive their industry out of London altogether. There was a Parliamentary resolution against sweating in 1891, and a London County Council boycott of sweatshop goods in 1894, but it was not until

1909, following a vigorous campaign by the radical *Daily News* and the widely supported National Anti-Sweating League, that legislation was introduced to tackle the problem. The Liberal government's Trade Boards Act, which established boards to set minimum wages in four industries, including box-making and ready-made tailoring, was extended between 1913 and 1920 to cover forty-nine British industries, employing 3,500,000 low-paid workers. In conjunction with the impact of the Great War on the London labour market, and the rise of new service and manufacturing industries between the wars, the Trade Boards Act helped to diminish the destitution of London's sweated workers, but the clothing trade remained an important part of the London economy for much of the twentieth century, and sweated conditions did not disappear.[28]

The fact that the sweated system exploited its workforce did not mean, of course, that it was unproductive or economically 'backward'. Recently historians have questioned the assumption that efficiency and modernity are exclusively synonymous with the factory system of production. Many of the economies of scale that in some other towns were achieved by concentration of production under one roof were gained in London by the size and efficiency of the city itself, and by the development of specialized centres of production within it. Labour, capital and markets were all available on a vast scale in London, and London's excellent transport system and rapid transmission of information made it easy for London manufacturers, even small-scale ones, to respond flexibly and efficiently to market conditions.[29] Small workshops could be highly efficient means of production in the London context, and their levels of output and profit could stand comparison with the best in England. Even the clothing sweatshop, condemned by social critics and historians for the past 150 years, has found its defenders among economic historians. Andrew Godley's study of the clothing industry in the East End between 1881 and 1939 suggests that the small workshops of Stepney, Bethnal Green and Westminster beat the clothing factories of Leeds (easily the biggest provincial producer) in output and productivity, and that in the clothing industry in general small units of production outperformed large ones. The East London industry specialized in women's ready-to-wear outer garments, dresses, coats, suits, blouses, and so on. As the demand for these clothes expanded, especially with the development of department and chain stores from the 1870s onwards, the East End industry grew. The scale of manufacture in womenswear was different from that in menswear, because styles were more varied, and fashions changed more rapidly. Even big stores did not order very large numbers of the same garment, but wanted instead the greatest possible variety of patterns and styles. Since long production runs were not required, large factories did not have the advantage over workshops that they had in the menswear trade, and East End producers with skilled and flexible workers and without a costly management hierarchy could gain higher profits (and even pay higher wages) than Leeds factories. Decisive evidence of the superior profitability of the East London industry is not available until the 1935 census of production, but it seems fairly clear that small late-Victorian clothing firms, working closely with each other and keeping a keen eye on the metropolitan market, were by no means inefficient or outdated, although they do not conform to the conventional image of industrial development.[30]

INDUSTRY IN SOUTH LONDON

The sweated industries clung to inner London because closeness to the market and to each other gave them a vital advantage. But industries that were dependent upon water-borne raw materials, and these included furniture, paper, printing, baking, brewing, sugar refining, leather, gas, rubber, chemicals and coal-powered industries, might well prefer a riverside site to a location in the cramped inner industrial belt. In the riverside suburbs transport was convenient, land was cheaper, and London's various environmental regulations were even more feebly enforced than they were in the centre. To the west, there were the engineering works, distilleries, lead mills and oil mills of Hammersmith, and the 'gas works ... , soap works, colour, mineral oil, varnish and size factories, potteries, saw mills, malt houses' and brewery of Brentford, where the Thames, the Grand Junction Canal and the Great Western Railway met.[31] In South-West London, the suburb of Wandsworth, on the busy River Wandle, was surprisingly industrial. It had long been a centre of calico printing, flour- and snuff-milling and bleaching, and was known in the 1870s for its large Royal Paper Mill, and 'extensive corn mills, distilleries (Messrs Watney's), breweries, maltings, dye-works, chemical works, colour factories, cloth printing and bolting mills, match factories, artificial manure works, and so forth'. The Wandle, which was said to have provided power for forty industrial works in 1805, ran through the suburban village of Merton, which became, thanks to the river, a centre of bleaching, calico printing and flour-milling. Liberty's cloth was printed here, and William Morris's fabric printing works opened in Merton in 1881. By the end of the century,

Lower Merton and the neighbouring district of Mitcham had about twenty varnish factories, and also produced floor coverings, felt and leather.[32]

The inner South London area, from Battersea and Vauxhall through Lambeth, Southwark and Bermondsey to Rotherhithe and Deptford, was a vigorous and varied manufacturing district, producing some traditional South London products, including pottery, glass, soap, candles, hats, leather and beer, on a large scale. Since the seventeenth century Lambeth had been famous for its potteries. These included Coade's Artificial Stone Manufactory, which closed in 1840, taking the secret of its wonderful weatherproof Coade stone with it, and the Doulton company, which stayed in Lambeth until 1956. From the 1870s onwards, Doulton won prizes for its 'Crown Lambeth' and 'Lambeth Faience', but its prosperity was built on humbler and stronger foundations, making drainpipes and water closets for the Victorian sanitary revolution. In 1900 Doulton's factory on Lambeth High Street produced 13 miles of drainpipe a week, more than any other in the world. Another Lambeth pottery, Stiff and Sons, specialized in stoneware bottles and jars, and terracotta chimneys and architectural features.[33]

Bermondsey, the district to the east of London Bridge and Borough High Street, was the headquarters of the leather trade, one of London's (and England's) most important industries. Bermondsey was beyond the central district from which offensive trades had been excluded in the Middle Ages, and was ideally placed to benefit from the enormous supply of hides from London slaughterhouses, and the furs and skins that were landed at the docks. There was open land for tan yards and glue factories, a supply of oak bark for tanning, and an industrial water supply in ditches fed by the river Neckinger, which entered the Thames at St Saviour's Dock. It was estimated in 1850 that a third of the nation's leather-dressing and tanning was carried out on the Surrey side of London, and Mayhew, writing in the same year, described Bermondsey as a parish almost entirely devoted to leather and its by-products: 'On every side are seen announcements of the carrying on of the leather trade; the peculiar smell of raw hides and skins, and of tan pits, pervades the atmosphere; and the monotonous click of the steam engines used in grinding bark assails the ear.' Since the seventeenth century the centre of the industry had been Bermondsey Leather Market (rebuilt in 1832) on Weston Street, and the streets nearby (especially Long Lane) were lined with leather tanners, dressers, curriers, dealers, dyers, cutters and enamellers, as well as parchment-makers, glue-makers, fellmongers (wool-dealers), and makers of horn combs and knife-handles. By the end of the century there were signs that the leather industry was beginning to leave the area, but it still employed about 6,500 people in Bermondsey and Southwark in 1901. These two districts were also the centre of the manufacture of beaver or 'stuff' hats, which were made from horse hides and beaver and rabbit fur supplied by Bermondsey dealers. From the 1840s silk hats replaced beaver hats, and Mayhew found the industry moving west into Southwark. By the 1890s the silk hat industry was itself in decline, beaten by cheap machine-made rabbit fur or wool 'felt' hats from Lancashire and Cheshire. The rising London industry was the making of cloth caps, and this was a Whitechapel trade. In 1891 Booth found that there were only 5,500 London hatters, compared with 7,300 thirty years earlier.[34] The writer and critic V. S. Pritchett worked for an important Bermondsey leather factor as a young man, between 1916 and 1920, and gives an excellent account of the trade in his autobiography. Work in the office, among the clerks on their high stools, was long and tedious, but Pritchett found a strange pleasure in the leather trade:

> I liked its pungent smell. I liked watching the sickly green pelts come slopping out of the pits at the leather-dresser's down the street, I liked paddling among the rank and bloody hides of the market; I would cadge the job of cutting out the maggots of the warble fly out of a hide in our hide shed.... I spent days on the seven floors of the warehouse, turning over dozens of calf skins with the men, measuring sheepskins and skivers and choking myself with the (to me) aromatic shumac dust. At home my family edged away from me: I stank of the trade.[35]

London brewed its own beer, and there were large breweries in almost every section of the town. South of the Thames, there was Young's brewery in Wandsworth, Combs's in Clapham, Courage in Bermondsey, the Lion Brewery in Lambeth, and London's largest producer, the Anchor Brewery in Southwark, near Bankside, which had passed from the Thrales to Barclay, Perkins and Company in 1781. Brewing produced more great London fortunes than any other branch of manufacture: the London 'beerage' included such famous men as James Watney, Sir Henry Meux, Spencer Charrington, Robert Courage and Samuel Whitbread, each of them worth a million or close to it.[36] South London also had some large distillers (Watneys of Wandsworth, Hodgson's of Battersea, Burnett's of Vauxhall, Hodges of Lambeth), and four major vinegar companies which in 1850 produced almost half of all England's vinegar output. Later in the century, South London took part in the growth of mass-produced branded foods: England's leading maker of pickles, sauces and preserves, Crosse and

Blackwell, was a Southwark firm, and Peek Frean and Company, England's second-largest biscuit maker, which opened in Bermondsey (already a centre of flour-milling and ship's biscuit-making) in 1857, employed over 2,000 workers by 1900. Bermondsey was also a centre of jam-making, with Thomas Lipton's factory offering poorly paid work to a growing number of women, and drawing its raw materials from the fruit farms of Kent and the sugar refineries on the northern bank of the Thames. Visitors could find their way around Bermondsey in the 1890s by using their sense of smell: 'In one street strawberry jam is borne in on you in whiffs, hot and strong; in another, raw hides and tanning; in another, glue; while in some streets the nose encounters an unhappy combination of all three.'[37] V. S. Pritchett's memories of Bermondsey were dominated by a rather different set of smells:

> There was a daylight gloom in this district of London. One breathed the heavy, drugging, beer smell of hops and there was another smell of boots and dog dung: this came from the leather which had been steeped for a month in puer or dog dung before the process of tanning. There was also ... the stinging smell of vinegar from a pickle factory; and smoke blew down from an emery mill. Weston Street was a street of leather and hide merchants, leather dressers and fell-mongers. Out of each brass-plated doorway came either the oppressive odour of new boots; or, from the occasional little slum houses, the sharp stink of poverty.[38]

To add to the rich aromas of South London, there were numerous chemical works, producing starch, size, wood preservative, ink, dyes, paint, polishes, patent manure, dubbin, soap powder and sulphuric acid. Day and Martin's, one of the biggest firms, moved from Holborn to the Borough Road in 1889. There were chemical works of all types in all the South London riverside suburbs. Deptford Creek was a 'great stinking abomination', lined with glue works, dye and bleach factories, tar distilleries, breweries and manufacturers of asphalt and artificial manure, and East Greenwich, which began to develop as an industrial district in the 1860s, produced soap, cement, ammunition and gas.[39] Soap and candles, two of the most important household products, were made throughout the South London parishes. J. C. Field and Co. had candle factories in Bermondsey, Battersea and Lambeth until the 1890s, Wright's Coal Tar soap was made in Southwark, and Price's Patent Candle Company, pioneers of oil-based candle manufacture, employed over 2,000 workers in Battersea and Vauxhall.[40]

Candle manufacture prospered despite the growing popularity of gas lighting, which was used more for streets than for houses until the 1890s. The spread of gas street-lighting after its successful introduction on Westminster Bridge in 1816 led to the building of several gasworks in South London in the 1830s and 1840s. Later in the century most of these, including the works in Vauxhall, Old Kent Road, Bankside, Rotherhithe and Greenwich, fell under the control of the South Metropolitan Gas Company, but the Nine Elms works in Battersea, which opened in 1833, remained an outpost of the dominant North London producer, the Gas Light and Coke Company. Until the 1890s, when the pre-payment slot meter was introduced, the gas companies' main customers were commercial and municipal users. Until then, a gas company manager said, 'gas was practically unknown in the dwellings of the working classes. They would not incur the expense of putting in the gas fittings pipes, and the payment of a quarterly gas bill was also a difficulty.' But in the 1890s, when gas companies (sensing the coming challenge of electricity) invested many thousands installing meters, pipes and stoves in working-class homes, the use of gas for cooking and lighting increased enormously. By 1914 about 70 per cent of gas customers in London paid their bills in advance, a penny at a time.[41]

THE RISE AND FALL OF SHIPBUILDING

Until the 1860s London was Britain's leading shipbuilder. It had the advantages of a huge local market of merchants, shipowners, the East India Company and the Admiralty, a large pool of skilled craftsmen and 'amphibian' workers (plumbers, joiners and painters), a steady flow of repair work, and a reputation for building ships of the highest quality. The great shipyards of Blackwall, Poplar, Woolwich and Deptford were famous for their men-of-war, frigates and East-Indiamen. The shift from sail to steam-power and from wooden to iron hulls did not seem to threaten London's supremacy. No city in Britain except inland Birmingham could rival London's engineering expertise, and most of the early experimental work on steam-powered and iron vessels was done on the Thames. Even in the 1820s, when shipbuilding was in the doldrums following the boom years of the Napoleonic Wars, new marine engineering firms were established along the Thames: John Penn's of Greenwich and Deptford, Miller and Barnes of Ratcliff, and Seaward Brothers of Millwall. In addition to its many small engineering firms (400, it was estimated in 1825), London had some of England's outstanding engineering companies, many of them based in Lambeth and Southwark. Maudslay Sons and Field, of Westminster Bridge Road, Lambeth, built the engines for the Royal Navy's first steam-driven fighting ships, the *Comet* and the *Lightning*, which were launched at Deptford in 1822 and 1823. Until the 1860s Maudslay's were England's leading manufacturer of marine engines, leading the way in double-cylinder steam engines and screw propellers. Its Lambeth works, which employed 1,000 men in the 1850s, closed in 1900. The Rennies, South London's second great engineering family, were marine engineers too, and their works on Holland Street, near Blackfriars Bridge, produced cranes, winches, diving bells, coin dies and machines for almost everything from biscuit-making to dredging.[42]

From the 1830s to the 1850s shipping companies began to recognize the advantages of iron ships, and in the American Civil War (1861–5) the superiority of iron warships to wooden ones was dramatically demon-strated. The rise of iron steamships in the 1850s and 1860s gave Britain an enormous advantage over other shipbuilding nations (especially the USA), and allowed her to establish a world supremacy in shipbuilding which was not broken until after 1900. At first, when iron construction was experi-mental and quality took precedence over cost, the Thames yards were able to win a large share of this booming business. The quantity of iron used was still fairly small, and a high percentage of scrap iron could be used (until 1855, when Lloyd's, the insurers, insisted on a higher proportion of new iron), so the cost of transporting iron from northern suppliers was not a serious handicap. The navy's first ironclad, the *Warrior*, was built at Blackwall in 1860, and in 1854 Isambard Kingdom Brunel chose a London yard, Scott Russell of Millwall, to build a revolutionary iron steamer, the *Great Eastern*, supposedly capable of carrying enough coal for the round trip between London and Australia. At almost 19,000 tons, the *Great Eastern* was four times as big as any existing ship, and larger than any ship built in the next forty years. It took months to launch the huge vessel in 1857–8, and it was not a commercial success, but its construction was a triumph of scientific design, industrial standardization and London crafts-manship, and gave no hint that the Thames yards would not be able to survive in the new iron age.

In the 1850s and early 1860s, when Britain supplanted the United States as the world's leading shipbuilder and the Admiralty began replacing its wooden fleet with an iron one, the Thames shipyards were busier than ever before. In these circumstances, the introduction of general limited liability in 1856, which enabled owners of capital to invest in shipbuilding (or any other business) without risking more than their investment, created a speculative boom on the Thames. Three major new yards were opened in the later 1850s: Millwall Ironworks and Dudgeon's at Millwall, and Thames Ironworks at Canning Town. Rennie's and Maudslay, along with several others, opened new yards in Greenwich. The shipyard workforce rose from 6,000 in 1851 to 13,000 in 1861, and 27,000 at the height of the boom in 1865, when London yards were building nearly 29 per cent (by tonnage) of Britain's iron merchant ships. Within a year the bubble had burst, pricked by the fall of the great discount house of Overend and Gurney, which had invested heavily in shipbuilding. By the end of 1866 virtually the whole of London's 27,000 shipyard workers had lost their jobs, most of them for ever. The closure of the two Admiralty dockyards at Woolwich and Deptford in 1869, with the loss of about 3,000 jobs, completed the destruction of shipbuilding on the Thames. When the national industry revived in the 1870s it did so almost entirely on the Clyde, the Tyne, the Wear and the Tees, leaving the remaining Thames shipyards to scrape a living on repair work, river steamers, and a few Admiralty orders. Most of the important yards were gone by the 1880s, and only one, Thames Ironworks of Canning Town, lasted into the twentieth century. Its final commission, the dread-nought *Thunderer* (1912), was the last big ship launched in the Thames. Two successful yards established in the late 1860s, Thorneycroft's of Chiswick and Yarrow's of Poplar, built torpedo boats and destroyers for the navy until 1904 and 1906, when both moved away from London.

Why was London's decline so sudden, and so complete? High rents, high wages and a congested river all played a part in its downfall, but none of these factors was decisive. London seems to have suffered from two overwhelming disadvantages as a shipbuilder in an industrial age. First, and most important, it could not command cheap and reliable supplies of coal and iron plates and bars from nearby sources. London coal cost three or four times as much as coal on the Wear or Clyde in the 1860s, and London builders could not take direct control of their supplies, as northern builders could. Second, London labour was expensive, independent-minded and well organized. After 1824, when the Thames Shipwrights' Provident Union was formed, London shipyard workers were highly unionized, and operated a traditional contract system in which shipyard owners acted as middlemen between customers and workers, negotiating a total payment for a specified job with the leader of a group or 'gang' of workers, which the gang members would divide among themselves according to their own custom-ary rules. A strong sense of custom made it difficult for shipwrights to respond flexibly to new technology, and they allowed work on iron ships to fall into the hands of boiler-makers and engineers, another very well-organized group. A proud and skilful workforce had its advantages, but the great shipbuilding companies of the 1870s and afterwards wanted docile workers who were entirely dependent on the shipyard for their livelihoods, and therefore preferred company towns (Jarrow, Wallsend or Greenock) to cities which offered a wide diversity of employment. This may explain the decline of Liverpool, Dublin and Bristol as shipbuilding centres, along with London.[43]

The decline of shipbuilding, and especially the closure of the two Royal Dockyards in 1869, caused economic distress in Deptford and Woolwich. But Deptford still had the naval victualling yard, the new Foreign Cattle Market built on the Dockyard site, timber yards, flour mills, engineering and chemical works, and other typical riverside industries. Greenwich's popularity with London holidaymakers had faded in the 1850s, but it was an engineering centre too, and its industrial base was widened in the 1860s, when factories for cement, soap, chemicals, linoleum and ammunition were built on the East Greenwich marshes, near the new South Metropolitan Gasworks. The garrison town of Woolwich, which was the eastern outpost of late Victorian London, owed its importance almost entirely to the demands of warfare. The Royal Dockyard had been a major employer since the reign of Henry VIII, and even after its closure the site was used for War Office stores and wharves. The Woolwich Arsenal, which was founded in 1716, grew in the Napoleonic Wars into an enormous industrial enterprise, employing over 10,000 men in time of war, and 5–6,000 in peacetime. The Arsenal comprised three great factories, the Laboratory, the Royal Gun Factory and the Royal Carriage Department, which employed machinery of impressive power and precision to produce bullets, percussion caps, rockets, fuses and shells, guns, artillery, torpedoes, gun carriages, trucks and wagons for the British army and navy.[44]

THE LEA VALLEY

The most remarkable industrial concentration in suburban London was on the other side of the Thames, along the valley of the river Lea, which formed the eastern boundary of the County of London after 1888. The Lea, by far the largest tributary of the Thames in the London area, winds a meandering but navigable course across marshland and cattle pastures from Waltham Abbey, through Chingford, Stratford, Bow and West Ham, entering the Thames opposite Greenwich marshes. For about a mile, as it passes through Stratford, the Lea divides into five branches. Since the Middle Ages, the Lea had been a major route for the transport of corn, malt, hay and other produce into London. Water from the Lea, diverted into the New river, had been an important part of London's supply since 1618, and it still supplied a sixth of the city's water in the 1990s. In the 1720s Defoe found the villages along the Lea, especially Stratford, 'increased in buildings to a strange degree', as a result of settlement by rich or retired Londoners. A hundred years later, there were paper mills, silk- and calico-printing works and distilleries around Stratford, taking advantage of the water-power, wharfage and transport offered by the branches of the Lea. By the 1870s, these had been joined or replaced by engineering works, jute mills, and factories making soap, matches, ink, dyes, paraffin, patent manures, and other such products. In West Ham, a little to the south, there were forty-two firms in 1863, making rubber, manure, gas, creosote, vitriol, lampblack, varnish, tar and oil. The smell of boiling bones and putrid fish filled the air. The construction of the London to Colchester railway, passing through Stratford, in 1839, and the addition of a branch line to North Woolwich, on the northern bank of the Thames, in 1846, increased the attractions of the area as an industrial location, and helped create one of the district's greatest industrial enterprises, the Great Eastern Railway Company's works at Stratford.[45]

Between the 1850s and the 1880s the marshy riverside pastures between the Lea and Barking Creek, known as Plaistow and East Ham Levels, were transformed into the important industrial districts of Canning Town, Silvertown and Beckton. The prosperity of these towns rested on the opening of two modern deep-water docks, the Victoria Dock in 1855 and the Albert Dock in 1880. With the building of the Victoria Dock just west of the mouth of the Lea, the steam colliers which brought much of London's coal from the North-East were diverted from the Pool of London to the new docks, where modern unloading methods, using hydraulic cranes in place of men with baskets, saved money and time. Cheap coal helped Canning Town's Thames Ironworks and Shipbuilding Company to survive the crash of 1866, and struggle on to 1912. The most important result of this cheap coal supply was the opening of the Gas Light and Coke Company's huge Beckton gasworks just to the west of Barking Creek in 1870, as a replacement for the company's cramped and outdated Shoreditch works. The new works enabled the Gas Light and Coke to win control of almost all North London's gas supply during the 1870s, and to take over the other main companies, including its greatest rival, the Imperial.

Through their by-products, coal-tar and gas sulphur, the gasworks spawned and sustained several other East London industries. By 1876 the Silvertown and Millwall works of the tar distillers Burt, Boulton and Haywood were using 12 million gallons of gas tar to manufacture creosote, naphtha, pitch, anthracene, disinfectant, insecticide and aniline dyes. Gas sulphur was the raw material for the many local sulphuric acid (vitriol) factories, whose output, in turn, was used in large quanties by the soap, fertilizer, chemical and galvanized cable manufacturers of West Ham, Plaistow and Silvertown. Silvertown, the riverside area south of the Victoria Dock, took its name from the rubber and telegraph works of S. W. Silver and Co., and was also home to the Keiller marmalade works and the refineries of the Tate and Lyle sugar companies. By 1901 the borough of West Ham (which included Plaistow, Canning Town and Silvertown) had a population of 267,358, fourteen times greater than its population in 1851, and East Ham, which had been a large village of 4,334 people in 1871, had a population of 96,000.[46] Both districts were outside the County of London created in 1888. West Ham was given County Borough status in 1889, and returned two MPs after 1885.

It is impossible to conclude, after this tour through London's industrial quarters, that metropolitan manufacturing was in its dotage. Instead, we are bound to follow Ernest Aves, the author of much of Charles Booth's final volume on London industry, in emphasizing the variety, power and inventiveness of London's industrial producers:

> Ship-building may leave the Thames; silk-weaving decline in Spital-fields; chair-making desert Bethnal Green; books be printed in Edinburgh or Aberdeen; and sugar-refining be killed by foreign fiscal policy; but the industrial activity of London shows no abatement. Individuals and individual trades may suffer, but her vitality and productive energy, stimulated by a variety of resources probably unequalled in their number and extent by those of any other city either ancient or modern, remain unimpaired.[47]

THE WORLD'S GREATEST PORT

The prosperity of many London industries, especially those of the East End and the riverside, depended on the ample supplies of raw material they could draw from the docks and warehouses of the Thames. During the nineteenth century the value and volume of international trade grew rapidly, and Britain took an enormous, though declining, share of it.

Britain's trade, like that of the rest of industrialized Europe, mainly involved the export of manufactures in return for imported primary goods, particularly foodstuffs and industrial raw materials. London, the capital of the world's leading industrial exporter and greatest empire (and primary producer), was at the very centre of this system of international exchange, in terms of finance, organization and physical trade. Between 1876 and 1913, when good figures are available, primary products made up about 64 per cent of world trade, and of these a very high proportion went to Britain: 30 per cent in the late 1870s, falling to 25 per cent in 1896–1900, and 19 per cent in 1913. Britain also took about 9 per cent of the world's imported manufactures, and had a huge share in manufactured exports: 38 per cent in 1876–1880, 31.5 per cent in 1896–1900, and 25 per cent in 1913. The volume of British trade grew rapidly between 1816 and 1913: imports rose about seven-fold between 1816 and 1870, and tripled again by 1913. British exports rose more than thirty-fold between 1816 and 1913, and her re-export trade grew at about half that rate. The value of British trade was affected by falling prices after 1815 and in the last quarter of the century, but, in round figures, the total annual value of British imports, re-exports and exports was under £100 million in the 1820s, and about £1,200 million between 1908 and 1913.[48]

London's share of Britain's overseas trade had fallen since the decades of extraordinary dominance in the early eighteenth century. In 1790 London handled 63 per cent (by value) of England's imports and 52 per cent of exports, including the whole of the Pacific and Far Eastern trade, which was covered by the East India Company's monopoly until 1813. Measured in tonnage, London's share was less, and stood at 37 per cent of shipping entering and 27 per cent clearing (leaving) English ports in 1790. Its share of trade continued to fall, but more slowly, in the nineteenth century. London's share of foreign-going shipping tonnage entering United Kingdom ports fell from 35 per cent to 28 per cent between 1820 and 1850, and levelled out at around 20 per cent between 1870 and 1900. Its share of clearances fell from 30 per cent to 20 per cent by 1850, and steadied at 15 per cent from 1870 to 1913. London's decline in relation to other British ports was much slower in the second half of the century, and by 1913 it was still handling 30 per cent (by value) of Britain's foreign trade, compared to Liverpool's 27 per cent. London's dominance was greatest in imports (34 per cent) and re-exports (54 per cent), and less in exports (19 per cent, compared to Liverpool's 32 per cent). London's continuing position as the world's greatest entrepot, a warehousing, wholesale and distribution centre for foreign produce, a position it had held since the decline of Antwerp in the 1570s, was particularly important to its prosperity. Just over half of Britain's £100 million re-export trade (wool, tea, coffee, sugar, dyestuffs, rubber, silk, fur, metals, and so on) went through London in 1910–13, and of the £35 million-worth of raw wool imported into Britain annually in those years, £25 million came through London.[49] Alongside its international business, London was also the focal point of Britain's own coastal trade, handling about 15 per cent (by tonnage) of its coastal traffic in 1900. In 1835, three-quarters of the 3.7 million tons of shipping entering the port was coastal, and in 1899 coastal ships, especially colliers, made up almost 6 million of the 15 million tons entering the port of London.[50]

The decline in London's share of British trade was partly the result of the growing importance of the Lancashire and West Riding cotton and wool industries, whose most convenient port for raw cotton imports and manufactured exports was Liverpool, and the massive growth of coal exports in the later nineteenth century, in which London played no part. Better information and more sophisticated trading mechanisms made it possible to direct cargoes (especially cotton, wool, timber, wheat, metals and other bulky commodities) to regional ports, avoiding the delays and trans-shipment costs involved in sending them first to London. But producers who were unsure of the eventual destination of their goods still preferred London, where the largest concentration of buyers and dealers, the cheapest finance and the easiest trans-shipment was to be found. London remained or became the principal international market for an unrivalled variety of commodities: tea, rubber, wool, copper, tin, platinum, diamonds, drugs, spices, carpets, furs, feathers, ivory, silk, chinaware, and other oriental and colonial goods. Because of its huge local market and excellent distributive network, London's trade in grain, timber, coal, fish, meat, fruit and vegetables was enormous. Two-thirds of the meat imported into Britain in the 1880s came into the Port of London, and thence to Smithfield. London's unsurpassed skill and experience in handling, inspecting, storing and selling valuable or difficult commodities, its financial services and its incomparable network of European and imperial trading connections enabled it to stay ahead of Hamburg, Amsterdam, Liverpool and its other European rivals until well into the twentieth century.[51]

COMMODITY EXCHANGES

The control of London's import trade by a few chartered companies was all but over. The last of the old chartered companies, the Levant, South Sea and Muscovy Companies, lost their privileges very early in the century, and the great East India Company was stripped of its trading monopolies in 1813 and 1833. Only the Hudson's Bay Company kept its monopoly, and even after it was lost in 1859 the March fur sale at the Company's Lime Street warehouse remained the central event of the international fur trade.[52] The days of the Cornhill coffee houses as centres of commercial information and exchange, on the other hand, were numbered, but not yet gone. At least until the middle of the century, merchants and shippers in the Australian, Far Eastern and Indian trades met in the Jerusalem Coffee House to read newspapers and shipping lists and to transact their business, and the Jamaica, a few alleys away, was still the centre of the West Indies trade. Garraway's, the original home of tea-drinking in England, remained the centre for auctions of coffee, cocoa, ivory, bamboo, and imperial and tropical produce of all kinds, though by the time of its demolition in 1866 its place had been taken by the London Commercial Sale Rooms.

The coffee houses' competitors offered space and exclusivity, but not intimacy and comfort. The London Commercial Sale Rooms, which were built in Mincing Lane in 1815, took twenty years or more to become established as the leading centre for commodity auctions, and in 1843 the master of the Baltic Coffee House successfully repelled a challenge from the spacious and well-organized new Universal Hall of Commerce by promising to get rid of unpleasant smells 'by the removal of the kitchen and some additional care as respects the water closet'.[53] The merchants who met in the Baltic Coffee House traded in tallow, oils, hemp, grain and other Russian and north European imports. It was here that Richard Thornton, the greatest of the Baltic merchants, made a fortune by cornering the St Petersburg tallow supply in 1822. A year later the Baltic merchants set a limit of 300 members on the coffee house's subscribers' room, creating a members' market in which information would take the place of specu-lation. In 1857 the transition from coffee house to commercial exchange was completed by a move into South Sea House, the old home of the South Sea Company, which had ceased trading a year or two earlier. The rapid growth of the Baltic trade, and the large amount of tonnage that it required, gave the Baltic Exchange a large and eventually dominant role in organizing international merchant shipping. Its supremacy was confirmed in 1900 when it amalgamated with the new London Shipping Exchange, which specialized in liner shipping. Freight chartering became the main business of the Baltic Exchange. Even in the 1970s, when London's dominance in physical trade had long disappeared, two-thirds of the world's shipping freight was arranged at the Baltic Exchange.[54]

Merchants in corn, coal, wool, metals and hops had specialist exchanges, in which they or their agents could sample the commodities and bid for them in noisy open auctions. The Mark Lane Corn Exchange, which had been built by Thames Street corn merchants in 1749, was extended and rebuilt in 1850 and the 1880s, and a New Exchange was built next to it in 1828. Here London millers, granary-keepers, maltsters and mealmen inspected samples of wheat, barley, oats, seeds and beans displayed by Kentish or East Anglian dealers or shippers, and increasingly by foreign importers. The first wool auctions were held in Garraway's, but from 1875 almost all the Australian wool imported into England (as much for re-export as for English use) was sold at auction in the Wool Exchange in Coleman Street, where brokers made their bids on the strength of samples pulled from bales stored in dockside warehouses. Organized auctions of metals began in the Royal Exchange in 1862, and moved into the London Metal Exchange in Whittington Avenue about twenty years later. In this building a circle of forty merchants, shouting their bids for tin, zinc, lead, copper or silver, controlled the world market in metals. Other exchanges were of more local significance: the Shell Exchange at Queenhithe, the Hop Exchange in Southwark, the Home and Foreign Produce Exchange just across London Bridge, and the Fruit Sale Room in Monument Buildings.[55] The London exchanges were physical markets, in which merchants and shippers traded goods that could be seen in London warehouses, or which were at least cargoes in known vessels. Speculation in the future price of abstract goods as a hedge against price fluctuations was becoming common in New York, Chicago and Liverpool in the 1850s, but 'futures' trading, which in time became the main business of the London exchanges, was not usual in London until a futures market in grain was introduced in 1888. With most other commodities price depended on quality, and London traders wanted to see what they were getting.[56]

London's bulkiest import was coal, which arrived from the Tyne by its traditional coastal route, and also, from the 1840s, by railway. London consumed about 2 million tons a year in the 1820s, and 12 million in the 1880s. By 1870 'inland coal' (arriving by rail) had overtaken sea coal, but the coastal trade fought back, and by the 1890s screw-propelled steam colliers had regained the more than half of London's coal trade. Until 1831 the dealings of London coal merchants were regulated by an astonishingly complex and archaic set of regulations, which had been codified but not simplified in 1807. As well as paying Mayor's dues, market dues, factorage, stamp duty, insurance and the King's duty on the coal (which was already taxed on the Tyne), merchants had to employ, at regulated rates of pay, 'water meters' and their deputies, coal whippers, watermen and 'land meters', all at the expense of the coal-burning Londoner. When these rules and dues were abolished in 1831 London coal prices (which had fallen by a quarter in the 1820s) fell by 50 per cent. Between 1807 and 1831 all coal arriving in the Thames had to be sold at the London Coal Exchange, and even after 1831 this remained the centre of the business. The Exchange had been on Lower Thames Street since 1770, and was rebuilt there in 1847–9. This immensely detailed and impressive building, one of the first and best glass and cast-iron buildings in England and perhaps London's finest Victorian commercial building, was demolished, despite vigorous protests, in the early 1960s.[57]

The Docks

London's survival as a major port in a century of rapidly expanding trade and revolutionary changes in shipping depended on an intelligent and adventurous dock-building policy. Unlike most other ports, London had no overall administrative body to plan a coordinated programme, but relied instead on the efforts of a set of competing dock companies. The crisis of the 1790s, which involved problems of security as well as congestion, had been overcome by heavy investment between 1802 and 1812 in walled and policed wet docks, three on the north bank of the Thames (the West India, East India, and London Docks), and a set of interconnected docks in Rotherhithe, which were later known as the Surrey Commercial Docks. The Surrey docks specialized in timber and other Baltic supplies, and held this trade successfully throughout the century. The prosperity of the other docks was less assured, because they were built in ignorance of the imminent arrival of the steamship and the railway, and because they depended on temporary monopoly privileges. The London Dock had a twenty-one-year monopoly on cargoes of rice, wine, brandy and tobacco, and the East and West India Docks had twenty-one-year monopolies on trade with the East and West Indies. When these monopolies expired in the 1820s the docks were thrown into competition with each other, with the riverside wharves, and with any new docks that might be built. Even the opening in 1828 of the small St Katharine's Dock, whose design and location was even less suited to the age of steam transport than its competitors', forced the West India Company to halve its dividend.[58]

When the docks were created, many had predicted (or hoped for) the extinction of the lightermen, watermen and wharfingers who had handled goods in the port and on the quayside for 1,000 years, and cluttered the river with their craft. But although bridges and steamers took away most of their passenger trade, small boatmen did not disappear from the Thames during the nineteenth century, and riverside wharves survived the upheaval created by the first phase of dock building. Wharves continued to handle nearly all London's coastal trade, which was not covered by dock monopolies and did not need secure warehousing, and won a growing share of international trade, too. In this they were helped by the ending in 1853 of the dock companies' exclusive right to store dutiable goods in their bonded warehouses, and by the rapid decline, after 1842, in the number of goods on which customs duty was payable. The wharves also benefited from the long-standing 'free water clause', which allowed lighters and barges to enter docks free of charge. To avoid dock charges, ships moored in the security of the walled and policed docks and unloaded their cargoes on to lighters, which took the goods to conveniently placed wharves for warehousing, sale or trans-shipment. As trade grew and the dock monopolies expired, specialist wharves spread along the whole length of the Thames from London Bridge to Plumstead: the low-bulk wharves of Southwark, Bermondsey and the City, handling tea, coffee, sugar, spices, fruit and groceries, the grain wharves of Rotherhithe and Shadwell, the private industrial wharves of the Lea and Silvertown, serving the cement, gas, flour, sugar and paper industries, and the deep-water wharves of North-fleet and Greenhithe, for larger vessels. There were 116 wharves in 1866 and 320 in 1900, handling just over half the shipping tonnage entering London with 41 per cent of the port's workforce. This had a disastrous impact on the dock companies' income from warehousing, which was the cornerstone of their prosperity. To make things worse, the growing use of steamships, the railway and the electric telegraph later in the century enabled merchants to arrange for goods to arrive in London at the right time and in the right quantity, and to be sent on to their next destination quickly, rather than remaining expensively in warehouses, as they had in the days when trade had depended on guesswork and seasonal sailing fleets. The growth of the 'just in time' system (as it would be called today) left London with an over-abundance of warehousing, which benefited the trader but gravely weakened the finances of the dock companies and many of the wharves.[59]

By the 1840s it was already plain that city-centre docks, despite their advantages, would not be able to cope with the demands of the new steam age. None of them was served by railways, nor could railway lines easily reach them in future. They were too small and shallow for larger ships, their locks were too narrow, and navigating the last reaches of the Thames, which were cluttered with passenger steamers, lighters, barges and colliers, was increasingly difficult. In 1836 a Select Committee condemned the Corporation of London, the Admiralty and Trinity House for failing to keep the main channel clear, but nothing was done about it until 1857, when the Thames Conservancy was set up. What London needed, if it was to hold its own against other ports, was larger docks a mile or two downriver, served by an efficient railway system. The established companies had no interest in building a competitor to their existing docks, but the great railway contractors Samuel Peto and Thomas Brassey had no such inhibitions. In 1850 they bought a large stretch of low-lying marshy pastureland on the Plaistow Levels, east of the river Lea, and within five years their new 100-acre dock, the largest so far built, was open to shipping. The Victoria Dock had an entrance lock wide enough for ocean-going steamships, and the disadvantage of its distance from the City was overcome by its excellent railway and lighterage facilities, low charges and modern hydraulic cranes, which offered the rapid unloading and fast turn-round that steamship owners wanted. By 1860 the new dock was handling over 40 per cent of all the shipping tonnage entering the north Thames docks, and had cut so far into the profits of the upstream companies that two of them, the St Katharine and the London, were forced to amalgamate with the Victoria in 1864.[60]

Four years later, competition was increased again by the opening of the Millwall Dock on the Isle of Dogs. By offering modern facilities and a railway service, and charging unprofitably low rates, the Millwall Dock captured much of the Baltic grain trade, and tried (but failed) to win the timber trade from the Surrey Docks. In the 1870s the rise of larger steel steamships, and the further deterioration of the Thames channel, especially the Woolwich Reach, forced the dock companies downstream again. In 1880 the London and St Katharine Company built a huge new dock, the Albert Dock, which extended (with its lock and tidal basin) almost 2 miles eastwards from Victoria Dock into East Ham, allowing steamships to enter from Gallions Reach, avoiding Woolwich Reach. It was, at the time, the finest dock in the world, capable of accommodating any ships likely to appear in the Thames for the next twenty years. In 1886 the East and West India Company (an amalgamated company formed in 1838) responded to this challenge by building a new deep-water dock at Tilbury, 25 miles below London Bridge. This was a fine 74-acre dock, able to take the largest vessels, whatever the tide. But there was a trade depression in the 1880s, and even at the best of times London did not need so much dock and warehouse space. The Tilbury Dock attracted less shipping than expected, the London and St Katharine's Company (owners of the Victoria and Albert Docks) were forced to cut their rates and their dividends, and the East and West India Company was driven into receivership. In 1888 the companies, exhausted by years of mutually destructive rivalry, were forced into an alliance which led to full amalgamation in 1901. Seven years later, following a Royal Commission on the state of the port, all London's docks were placed under the control of a public body, the Port of London Authority (PLA), on which representatives of the users of the river and docks sat alongside those of the City Corporation, the Admiralty and the London County Council.[61] The PLA celebrated its new responsibilities by commissioning Sir Edwin Cooper to design its 'showy, happily vulgar, and extremely impressive' offices in Trinity Square, facing the Tower of London.[62]

The dock companies would look back on this century of free competition and falling profits without great pleasure, but their mistakes and misfortunes had not served London badly. Cheap rates, modern services and a set of finely engineered and well-located deep-water docks had enabled the old port to hold its own against fresher and better-placed rivals in an age of unprecedented commercial expansion and technological change. The swift decline in London's share of national trade was arrested between 1870 and 1913, and between those years the international tonnage entering and clearing London more than tripled, from under eight million to over 24 million tons. London entered the twentieth century, as it had entered the nineteenth, as the world's greatest port.

DOCKERS

More than 20,000 men made their livings in the wharves and docks of the Port of London, and many more worked in its warehouses. Most of these, apart from a small group of permanent dock employees, were casual workers who were taken on at a daily or half-daily rate when there was work to be done. But port workers were not an undifferentiated mass of unskilled men, and many of the jobs they had to do demanded distinctive skills and experience. In general, those who worked on board ship, the shipworkers, were more skilled and better-paid than those who worked on the quayside, and those involved in loading ships, especially ocean-going ones, were more skilled than those who unloaded them. Stevedores, who specialized in loading ships for export, were regarded as skilled craftsmen, and were able to form an effective trade union in 1870, nearly twenty years before other dock labourers. Those who worked with coastal ships or lighters, mainly in the wharves, usually enjoyed lower pay and status than those working with ocean-going ships, though the distinction was not always very clear. On the quayside, there were jobs that demanded special skill or endurance, especially handling and stacking heavy cargoes such as timber, grain, guano or coal, and men who had mastered this work, the timber-lumpers, deal-porters, corn-porters and coal-whippers, were reluctant to take less prestigious work, even when their specialism was not in demand. Among warehousemen, who were not skilled, specialists in tea and wool had higher status and (when work was available) more pay than the rest. At the other extreme, unloading lighters or receiving cargo on the quayside, and pushing it in hand-trucks to the shed or warehouse, was work that could be left to unskilled drifters, refugees from the East End's declining trades.[63]

Although port workers were divided by their skills and status, they shared the common predicament, except at times of exceptional activity, that there were too many of them, and that much of their work was open to all the unemployed and half-employed men in East London. From the 1830s, and perhaps before, the employers, trying to gain through cheap labour the profits that sensible planning and mutual cooperation might otherwise have given them, clung to a system of casual labour which involved thousands of men scrambling and fighting for work every day at the dock gates. Those who looked strong, or were known to be skilled, were chosen first, while the old and the malnourished would be ignored unless the dock was busy. Henry Mayhew's description of the scene outside the London Dock at half past seven on a morning around 1850, when the foremen started to call out the names of those who would work that day, captures the atmosphere of 'the Call':

> Then begins the scuffling and scrambling forth of countless hands high in the air, to catch the eye of him whose voice may give them work.... All are shouting. Some cry aloud his surname, some his christian name, others call out their own names, to remind him that they are there.... To look in the faces of that hungry crowd is to see a sight that must be ever remembered. Some are smiling at the foreman to coax him into remembrance of them; others, with their protruding eyes, eager to snatch at the hoped-for pass. For weeks they may have gone there, and gone through the same struggle – the same cries; and have gone away, after all, without the work they had screamed for.[64]

The nature of dockwork made it inevitable that employment would vary with the seasons, the weather and the trade cycle. The growth of steam shipping after about 1870 diminished seasonal variations, but replaced them with a new instability. The arrival of a large steamship created a short burst of frantic activity to achieve the fastest turn-round, but might be followed by days or weeks without work. Mayhew found that in the London Dock in May 1849 the number of men taken on in a day varied from 1189 to 3012, and he guessed that in all the London docks at that time there would be 7,000 more men employed on a busy day than on a slack one. In 1891–2 Charles Booth calculated that all the London docks (excluding Tilbury) at their busiest could employ 21,353 men, and at their slackest employed 9,829. The 11–12,000 men left idle on these slack days might find work by moving to docks or wharves which had work available, but the casual system, which gave an advantage to men who were known and trusted, discouraged such mobility, and created a separate labour reserve for each dock. In Booth's view the wharves and docks (excluding Tilbury) could keep about 15,000 men in fairly steady work, and offer a few weeks' or months' work, mainly in the winter, to another 3,000. The other 4,000 men who called themselves dockers would never be needed, and should look elsewhere for their livings.[65] In 1891, after the dockers' strike of 1889, the companies introduced a scheme that reflected Booth's analysis, creating three new classes of casual worker in addition to the small group of permanent workers they already employed. This system sheltered the regular dockers from competition from the lowest casuals (Booth's 'loafers'), but in other respects the casual system was preserved, and remained the basis of dock work until after the Second World War.[66]

THE CITY BANKS

Victorian London dealt in many things, but the commodity which brought it the greatest profits, and through which it achieved its position of unique international importance, was money. During the nineteenth century London became the world's greatest money market, the supreme international centre of banking, commercial credit, overseas loans, commodity transactions, share-dealing and insurance. In London the skill, experience, integrity, stability and wealth that made possible the growth of an international system of commerce and exchange based on credit and confidence reached their highest level of development. Some historians have argued that Paris was London's equal as a financial centre in the 1850s and 1860s, especially in her dealings with Italy and Russia, but Paris's worldwide role never matched London's, and its position was severely damaged by the siege and Commune of 1870–71. Between 1870 and 1914, the brief period in which almost the whole world was on the gold standard, London's position at the centre of the international economy was unchallenged.[67]

The part London played in the world economy did not depend upon the wealth generated in the capital itself, great as this was. Walter Bagehot, whose study of the London money market, *Lombard Street,* was first published in 1873, argued that the City's great contribution to the world economy was to draw private wealth into the banking system, and thus into profitable investment, to an extent that was unknown in other places or at other times. Thanks to Lombard Street, and the confidence it inspired in the holders of surplus capital, no promising enterprise need fail for lack of investment: 'English capital runs as surely and instantly where it is most wanted, and where there is most to be made of it, as water runs to find its level.'[68] Money flowed into London from prosperous rural England, from the growing provincial network of London-based joint-stock banks, from the great Scottish banks (and thus from rural Scotland), and increasingly from foreign banks and their depositors, because London offered the safest and highest returns for short-term deposits. Thanks to London merchant banks and discount houses, the savings which East Anglian farmers or Kentish shopkeepers thought were safe in a country bank might be helping to build a waterworks in Argentina, or a railway track in Canada, or keeping an Indian tea planter solvent while he waited for last year's crop to be sold.[69]

The foundation stone of London's pre-eminence was its banking system. The Bank of England, a privately managed joint-stock bank with no well-defined constitutional role, was alone among all the world's central banks in producing a paper currency with a fixed and guaranteed gold value. The supremacy of sterling originated in decisions taken soon after the ending of the French War in 1815. In 1797, as a wartime measure, the Bank of England had been allowed to suspend the convertibility of its notes into gold, and England entered an inflationary period of unconvertible paper money. After 1815 leading political figures, especially Robert Peel and William Huskisson, pressed for a return to a bullion-based currency, and in 1821 the Bank resumed cash payment (in gold) for its notes. In effect, Britain was on the gold standard, and remained on it until the First World War. Throughout this period sterling was never devalued, and gold sovereigns, worth £1 sterling, contained as much 22-carat gold in 1914 as they did in 1816, when they were first minted. When other major economies abandoned the silver or the bi-metallic (gold and silver) standard or unconvertible paper money and adopted the gold standard between 1870 (Germany) and 1897 (Russia, India and Japan), sterling notes and bills of exchange became the universally accepted international currency, as secure as gold, and more convenient to handle.[70]

Around the Bank of England gathered a banking community of unequalled wealth and reputation. In 1832 London had about sixty private banks, each owned by a maximum of six partners. About thirty of these, including Barclays, Glyns, Hanburys and Hoares, were general purpose 'clearing banks', whose clerks met twice a day in the Clearing House in Lombard Street to exchange bills and cheques, and calculate the balances each owed to each of the others. Others were merchant banks, which had progressed from trading on their own account to offering short-term finance to other merchants, and from there to handling overseas investment and government loans. Commercial banks owned by shareholders, known then as joint-stock banks, were not allowed in England until 1826, or in London until 1833, and the latter only on condition that they gave up issuing their own banknotes. After this, joint-stock banks, notably the London and Westminster, the London and County and the National Provincial, played an increasingly powerful part in the London banking world, overtaking the private banks in wealth and importance (if not self-importance) in the 1850s and 1860s. Joint-stock banks were allowed into the London Clearing House in 1854, and by the end of the century there was only one private bank left in the London clearing system. By 1906 the London Clearing House was handling £12 billion a year and was, according to Sir Robert Palgrave, Bagehot's successor as editor of the *Economist*, 'the most easily worked paper circulation and circulating medium in existence. Like the marvellous tent of the fairy Paribanou, it expands itself to meet every want and contracts again the moment the strain is passed.'[71]

London emerged as a centre of international merchant banking in the eighteenth century, when the Amsterdam finance houses set up London branches to take advantage of Britain's industrial expansion, and particularly during the American wars, when Amsterdam's concentration on transatlantic business increased the independence of London financiers. London's final victory was won during the French Wars of 1793–1815. Amsterdam, already in decline, was finally ruined by the French occupation in 1795, and much of its financial business migrated to London, one of the few major European cities which did not fall under Napoleon's control during the war. European banking and commercial families who wanted stability in a continent disrupted by war and revolution transferred some of their business to London, and remained there when peace returned, giving London the benefit of their experience, money and worldwide contacts. Sephardic Jews arrived from Amsterdam, and Jewish and gentile families came from Frankfurt, Hamburg, Bremen, Berlin and Leipzig. Nathan Rothschild, the son of a Frankfurt family which dealt in English textiles, was the most important of these new arrivals, but Schroders, E. H. Brandt, Frederick Huth, and Fruhling and Goschen were all significant City firms which began with migration from Germany under Napoleonic occupation. After the war Turkish persecution drove Greek financiers, notably the Ralli brothers, to settle in London. As London's predominance grew, it became common for European merchant banks to open offices there: Hambros arrived from Germany and Denmark in 1840, Kleinwort from Germany in 1855, Bischoffsheim and Goldschmidt from Frankfurt in 1846. George Peabody opened the first major American merchant bank in London in 1843, but the rush of American bankers came in the 1860s, when Seligman Brothers, Morton, Rose and Co., Speyers and J. S. Morgan all opened London offices. The trend continued: of the twenty-one leading London merchant banks in 1914, twelve were Anglo-German, three were American (Morgan Grenfell, Seligman, and Brown, Shipley and Company) and one (Lazard Brothers) French.[72]

Twenty years of European war created vast opportunities for profit for investors, loan contractors and financial fixers of every kind. The growth of the British National Debt, which rose between 1793 and 1818 from £243 million to £844 million, a figure not exceeded until 1915, created a new group of specialist financial contractors who could make huge gains (and sometimes disastrous losses) by undertaking to raise money on the government's behalf. Walter Boyd, a banker who had left Paris for London after the Revolution, handled the bulk of government loans until his bankruptcy in 1800, and he was followed by the Goldsmid brothers, who committed suicide after financial failures in 1808 and 1810. The Barings, Lutheran wool merchants who had moved from Bremen to Exeter in 1717 and from Exeter to London in 1763, were more successful. Between 1800 and 1815 they were the government's leading loan contractors, and established themselves as the most powerful financiers in the City. Their closest rivals, the Rothschilds, whose European connections were as extensive as the Barings', also made their fortune in the service of the government. Nathan Rothschild's involvement in raising government loans probably began in early 1814, when he used his family connections to collect nearly £1 million in French coin to pay for Wellington's advance into France. In the following year Rothschilds raised further loans to cover Wellington's expenses and British subsidies to Austria, Russia and Prussia.[73]

The success of the Rothschilds, the Barings and other London financiers in using their London and continental connections to raise wartime loans led European government to turn to them for money in the immediate postwar years. The Barings raised over £12 million for the French government in 1817, and in 1818 the Rothschilds raised £5 million for Prussia. In 1821–2 the Rothschilds organized large loans for Prussia, Russia and Naples, and City investors, awash with spare capital, rushed to subscribe to loans for Peru, Chile and other newly independent South American states. In 1823 the Stock Exchange, which until then had largely confined itself to British government stocks, opened a foreign securities dealing room to cope with the explosion of interest in overseas loans. Loans worth over £18 million were raised on the London money market for Mexico and South America between 1821 and 1825, and in the excitement generated by the prospect of easy profits unsound speculations of all kinds were undertaken. In December 1825 the inevitable crash came, and most of the Latin American loans were shown to be unsafe. This disaster, along with the failure of loans to the United States in the 1830s, put a damper on the City's enthusiasm for overseas speculations for a decade or two.[74]

THE STOCK EXCHANGE

Although many of the enterprises that raised capital in the City needed stable long-term finance, most of the investors who placed their money in London did so on the understanding that they could reclaim it at short notice. The City performed the trick of turning volatile money into stable long-term investment by means of the Stock Exchange, whose importance and range of activities expanded enormously in the nineteenth century. Until 1840 the Stock Exchange was concerned almost exclusively with government stocks. In 1840 securities with a nominal value of £1.3 billion were known to the London Stock Exchange, and of these 40 per cent were foreign government issues (many of them valueless New World stocks) and nearly 50 per cent were British government securities. Most of the remaining 11 per cent were shares in semi-official bodies such as the East India Company and the Bank of England.[75] What changed this was the arrival of the railway, which needed investment on a scale which was much greater than that required by earlier industrial enterprises, and which seemed to promise steady returns. By 1853 over 18 per cent of the value of securities quoted on the London Stock Exchange were railway stock, and this share rose to 32 per cent by 1873, and to a high point of almost 50 per cent by 1893. By this time, government issues represented only about 40 per cent of quoted securities, and industry, commerce, finance, mining and urban services the other 11 per cent.[76]

At the same time, the London Stock Exchange recovered its confidence in overseas lending. In 1853 the value of foreign securities, mostly government and railway issues, quoted in London was £101 million, under 10 per cent of the London total. But in the 1850s and 1860s opportunities for profitable and fairly safe investment in railway building and, to a lesser extent, mining, industry and public works, in America, India, Australia, Canada and New Zealand revived the City's interest, and by 1883 foreign securities on the London Stock Exchange stood at £1,814 million, almost half the total value of quoted securities. By 1913 the value of overseas securities quoted in London stood at over £5 billion, roughly half the total value of all the world's overseas investment. Of course, since London was the focal point of world investment, a large proportion of this money originated overseas, and much of the business was handled by the London offices of American and German finance houses.[77]

The internationalization of the City was partly the result of the introduction of the electric telegraph, which enabled deals between London and the other world financial centres to be done in minutes, rather than days or weeks. London was linked by submarine cable to Paris in 1851, to New York in 1866 and Melbourne in 1872. Competition cut the cost of a one-word coded transatlantic message from £20 in 1866 to 2s in 1906, and by 1913 about 5,000 telegrams were sent between the London and New York exchanges each day.[78] When rapid international communication allowed dealers to choose which market to buy or sell securities in, London was the favourite choice. Compared to its rivals, the London Stock Exchange was much more open to new members and to companies wishing to be quoted on it, and was freer from troublesome laws and regulations. In 1900, the New York Stock Exchange, which pursued a far more restrictive membership policy, had only 1,040 members to London's 5,500, and quoted 1,157 securities to London's 3,631, with a total value of £2.8 billion, to London's £8.8 billion. The London Stock Exchange had another advantage in its long-established fortnightly settlement system, which enabled dealers and speculators to buy and sell securities without ready cash. This created an active and stable securities market which attracted much business from New York, where dealers were obliged to settle their transactions on a daily basis, or incur interest charges. No doubt, as a Royal

Commission discovered in 1877–8, this freedom made the Stock Exchange rather a disreputable place, a world in which young gamblers, doing their business in shouts and whispers, speculated in stocks or foreign loans that (in many cases) had been 'puffed' by corrupt journalists and unscrupulous promoters. Jobbers had been speculating in the future value of shares, and buying and selling shares that they had no intention of ever owning or paying for, for 100 years or more, in spite of the law of 1733 (repealed in 1868) that forbade them to do so. Openness and lack of regulation also meant that it was easier to find a market for large amounts of stock in London than anywhere else in the world. So between 1850 and 1914 the London Stock Exchange was transformed from a largely domestic securities market into the world's most important international stock exchange. In 1913 one-third of all the securities quoted on world Stock Exchanges were quoted in London.[79]

So completely did the City of London overcome its uneasiness about overseas investments in the later nineteenth century that it has been accused of neglecting the needs of British industry in favour of foreign opportunities, and thus contributing to Britain's relative industrial decline. The City's great advantage over its main rivals was that it was a free market, and its investment decisions were motivated by expectations of profit and security, not patriotism or social conscience. In general, investment in railways, mines, docks, tramways and gasworks in the United States, Canada, India, South Africa, Australia and Argentina (the leading receivers of British investment in 1913), gave higher returns, for less risk, than investments in manufacturing, whether home or overseas. When domestic enterprises needed money on a large scale, and appeared to offer healthy returns, as was the case with railways fron the 1840s, and brewing, gas, telegraphs and telephones later in the century, they could find it in the City. But City investors were not tempted by small-scale manufacturing investments, and, as a rule, smaller industries did not need the City. Most British industries found all the capital they needed in provincial banks and stock exchanges and from their own profits.[80]

FINANCING WORLD TRADE

In one very important respect the City of London's money underpinned the success of British industry. British manufacturers did not generally rely upon the City for fixed capital (the money spent on factories, machinery, and so on), but they also needed working capital, to pay for raw materials and to cover the cost of finished goods in the period between their production and the receipt of payment, which could, in the case of exported goods, be up to twelve months. Nearly all English overseas trade, whether it was conducted by manufacturers, merchants or agents working on commission, was done on credit. Buyers paid for goods by signing a bill which promised payment in, say, three or six months, and they assured the seller of the reliability of the promise by having the bill guaranteed by a reputable London finance house. Houses specializing in guaranteeing, or 'accepting', these bills of exchange were (and are) known as acceptance houses, or merchant banks. The acceptance house would pay the appropriate sum (with a deduction representing interest on the sum for the time remaining on the bill) into the seller's account, and then either keep the bill until its maturity, when the buyer would pay the debt, or sell it on, at slightly less than its face value, to another finance house, which would then take over the risk, and await payment, or resell it. Institutions specializing in the purchase and resale of bills of exchange or promissory notes, as well as government bonds and securities, were (and are) known as discount houses, and those who negotiated the purchase and sale of bills were known as bill brokers.

Discount houses had some capital of their own, but in general they financed their purchases by borrowing money at very short term, generally on twenty-four-hour recall, from London and provincial banks. Their profits came from the difference between the interest rates they paid for this short-term money, and the rates they charged for taking on the bills. Borrowing short and lending long and holding little in reserve can be a dangerous business, as the greatest discount house, Overend, Gurney and Co, found in 1866, but in a crisis a reputable discount house could borrow money on the security of its bill portfolio from the Bank of England, the lender of last resort, to cover its immediate commitments. These activities may sound obscure, or even parasitic, but without short-term credit the vast expansion of British and world trade in the nineteenth century could not have taken place. It became increasingly rare, in the early nineteenth century, for Lancashire spinners or Midlands manufacturers to organize and finance their own exports, as they had done fifty years earlier. Commission agents handled most overseas trade, and they would have been unable to do so without the help of the London acceptance houses. It was not the London banknote (of which there were relatively few) but the London bill (or 'the bill drawn on London') that financed world trade.[81]

When commercial banks with a national network of branches linked to a London headquarters developed in the middle of the nineteenth century, cheques replaced bills of exchange in domestic trade, but the use of overseas bills continued to grow, and the strength of the City's reputation was such that foreign merchants, especially Germans and Americans, used its accepting and discounting services to an increasing extent, even when their trade was not with England. By 1913 two-thirds of the commercial bills drawn on London involved trade which neither began nor ended in Britain. London branches of foreign banks took a growing share of this business, but it was only their presence in London, the undisputed centre of international capital, that enabled them to do so. Although German and American exports started to outstrip Britain's at the end of the century London's importance was not dependent any longer on the growth of British trade alone, nor did its capacity to provide credit depend upon capital from British investors. By the 1870s, the City was banker to the world, outstripping its nearest rivals, New York and Paris, in every respect. In 1873 the published deposits in London banks amounted to £120 million, compared to £40 million in New York and only £13 million in Paris, whose business had been badly damaged in 1870–1. London also easily outdid its British rivals, Liverpool, Manchester and Glasgow. Probably 80 per cent of their transatlantic trade was financed through London bills, and at least fourteen provincial banking houses moved to London, or opened offices there, mostly in the 1860s and 1870s. A Canadian banker wrote in 1914–15, at the very moment when London's unique role was coming to an end:

> The bill on London is better currency than gold itself, more economical, more readily transmissible, more efficient ... by means of the bill on London not only the vast commerce of Britain herself, but also a substantial share of the purely foreign traffic of the world is financed and liquidated.[82]

The system of credit upon which all the City's transactions, and those of the international trading world, were based was, in the words of Walter Bagehot, 'a set of promises to pay'. Discount houses, acceptance houses and merchant banks promised to pay the value of the bills they issued or guaranteed, and the Bank of England promised to pay (as every banknote still reminds us) the value in gold of the paper currency that bore its name. If trust in London's bills of exchange, or in sterling itself, was broken, the whole system would be destroyed. At the heart of this system stood the Bank of England, a private institution run by a governor and directors who had to combine their obligations to their shareholders with an imprecise but important duty to the government, the banking system, and to the national economy. The way this was to be done was worked out slowly during the nineteenth century, often at times of panic or crisis. Two questions in particular needed to be answered: what rules, if any, should determine the amount of paper currency issued by the Bank, and to what extent was the Bank obliged to sustain other banks and finance houses from its own reserves when they were unable to meet their commitments? Was the Bank to be the lender of last resort, and how far should it go in saving fools or scoundrels from destruction?

From Crisis to Crisis

In 1824 and 1825 there was a period of speculative fever, fuelled by the growing interest in South American loans and a boom in joint-stock companies which were taking advantage of the repeal of the Bubble Act to raise money on the Stock Exchange. The boom was fuelled by banknotes issued by the country banks, and by bills of exchange. When share prices fell in November and December 1825 six London banks and many provincial ones stopped payment. Large and small investors, realizing that they were over-committed to speculative loans which might be unsound, turned to the Bank of England to discount their bills, and to provide cash to see them through the crisis. The Bank's first reaction was to protect its own reserves by refusing to discount, but when growing panic in the City persuaded it to reverse its policy early in December 1825 the demand for cash was so intense that the Bank's reserves of notes and bullion were almost exhausted within a fortnight. Only the opening of an emergency box of pound notes on 16 December, the arrival of a fresh supply of notes from the printers on 18 December, and a consignment of £400,000 in gold bullion from the Bank of France on the 19th (organized by Nathan Rothschild) enabled the Bank to meet the demand and stop the panic. By the time the crisis subsided in 1826 about sixty English banks, more than a tenth of the national total, had failed.[83]

After the 1825 crisis the government took steps to give the Bank of England greater control over the money supply, and to strengthen the national banking system by ending the prohibition on joint-stock banks. The 1826 Bank Act ended the issue of £1 banknotes (to encourage the greater use of the gold sovereign), and in 1833 Bank of England notes were made legal tender, acceptable instead of gold in all transactions anywhere in the country, except in the Bank itself. Following the crisis, London banks decided that they could not rely on the Bank of England to discount their bills (and provide liquid funds) in an emergency, and therefore began building up their own balances, and placing them on deposit with bill brokers or bill dealers of the highest reputation, who would in turn be able to rely upon the Bank of England to discount their bills as a lender of last resort. The four major bill brokers who were recognized by the Bank of England in the 1830s, Sandersons, Alexanders, James Bruce and Overend, Gurney and Co., became London's leading discount houses.[84]

Further crises led to the refinement of the system. In 1837 a downturn in the United States economy destroyed three of London's main Anglo-American finance houses, Wiggin and Co., Wildes and Co., and Wilson and Co., the 'three Ws', after the Bank of England had refused to rescue them. Two years later, the Bank itself needed to be rescued, when a drain on its gold reserves, mainly because of heavy grain imports, forced it to borrow £2 million in gold from the Bank of France. These two crises led to a long debate about the role of the Bank of England, especially the criteria that determined how much paper currency it should put into circulation. In Peel's Bank Charter Act of 1844 the views of the 'currency school', which blamed financial crises on excessive paper currency and held that note issue should be tied rigidly to gold reserves, triumphed over those of the 'banking school', which argued that the Bank should issue paper currency according to the needs of business. The 1844 Act separated the Banking Department of the Bank of England from the Issue Department, and limited the value of banknotes that it could issue or have in circulation to the value of its bullion reserves plus £14 million, the so-called fiduciary issue, which would be backed by its holdings of government securities. The value of gold was fixed at its eighteenth-century price of £3 17s 9d an ounce.[85]

The virtue of this rigid and inconvenient system was that it guaranteed 'sound money', free from government manipulation and certain to hold its value, but its disadvantage was that it tied the Bank of England's hands when City panics created heavy demands for sterling. Gradually, the Bank developed alternative ways of steadying the money market, chiefly by using changes in the Bank's interest rate to regulate the flow of gold in and out of its reserves, but it took over twenty years and three serious crises to make the new system effective. In 1846 and 1847 massive and costly corn imports drained the Bank's gold reserves, and in the summer of 1847 a good European harvest brought corn prices down, seriously exposing City grain dealers and finance houses which had speculated on the high price of corn. In August W. R. Robinson and Co., the Governor of the Bank of England's own firm, collapsed. Several East and West India merchant houses, hit by changes in sugar duty, went down in September, and in October a succession of stock-brokers, insurance-brokers and provincial bankers failed. One of the four major discount houses, Sandersons, suspended payments with liabilities of £2.6 million, and even the great Overend, Gurney and Co. was under pressure. At last, on 23 October, the government gave way to appeals from the City (not the Bank), and announced the temporary suspension of the Bank Charter Act, enabling the Bank to issue banknotes beyond its gold reserves, and offer help more freely than it had been able to do until then. This steadied the City's nerve, and made it unnecessary for the Bank to use its new freedom. In all, by February 1848, eighty City firms had failed, along with another 112 in Liverpool, Manchester and Glasgow.[86]

By 1857, when the next major crisis occurred, free trade, the reputation of sterling bills, and the growth of railway and telegraph communications had placed the London money market, and especially London bill brokers, at the centre of a rapidly expanding network of international trade and credit. 'A man in Boston cannot buy a cargo of tea in Canton without getting a credit from Messrs Matheson or Messrs Baring', a select committee was told in 1858.[87] But international involvement meant international vulnerability. When businesses were in trouble they turned to London bill brokers for the money they had deposited with them. Bill brokers did not hold large cash reserves, and when unexpected calls were made upon them they turned to the Bank of England to rediscount the bills they held, enabling them to meet their obligations. In the autumn of 1857 American banks and railway companies started to fail, bringing banks in Liverpool and Scotland down with them, and those committed to them turned to London bill brokers for cash. When one of the leading brokers, Sandersons, was unable to meet its obligations in November pressure on the others, including Alexanders and Overend, Gurney and Co., became intense. But the Bank's reserves were also running low, and to keep the bill brokers afloat the government had to suspend the 1844 Act again, as they had done in 1847. Sticking to the Bank Charter Act, as George Norman, a director of the Bank of England, wrote to the banker Lord Overstone, the architect of the Act, 'might have brought down the whole credit system of the Country – a vicious system beyond doubt, but which ought to owe its gradual reform to the action of the country's good sense. Its extinction by a Catastrophe would have been awful.'[88] But the Bank warned Overend and the other discount houses that they could not expect to be rescued again, and should keep money in reserve for future emergencies.

Overend, Gurney and Co.

Dealing in short-term credit was a precarious business, but some of the greatest City reputations rested upon it. Except for the Bank of England, and perhaps Rothschilds and Barings, no City financial institution was held in higher regard than the great discount house of Overend, Gurney and Co., the 'Corner House' at the junction of Lombard Street and Birchin Lane. In a dangerous world, the survival of discount houses depended on skilful and tireless management. When Samuel Gurney, who had dominated the firm since the 1830s, died in 1856, the business fell into the more ambitious but less capable hands of Henry Gurney and David Chapman. In the late 1850s, Chapman decided to move beyond the known world of bill discounting into the unknown one of shipping, shipbuilding, grain dealing, iron-making and railways. In short, they broke Samuel Gurney's golden rule of bill broking, that money should not be tied up in speculative, insecure or inaccessible investments.[89] In 1865, when the firm was already nearly (but secretly) bankrupt, Gurney tried to save it by floating it as a limited company. The boom conditions of 1865–6 hid the company's weaknesses, but well-informed men in the Bank of England and the *Economist* were not surprised when a few smaller business failures brought Overend, Gurney, and Co., Ltd. to bankruptcy on 10 May 1866, with debts of over £5 million, a sum almost equal to the Bank of England's reserves. The next day, Black Friday, there was 'panic and distress ... without parallel in the recollection of the oldest men in the City of London', banks were mobbed by terrified crowds, and City deputations persuaded Gladstone, Chancellor of the Exchequer, to suspend the Bank Charter Act again. The Bank of England, encouraged by the government, undertook to use its reserves to defend the national and international credit of the City, and issued loans worth over £4 million that day to London bankers, merchants and bill brokers. 'We have not refused any legitimate application for assistance,' the Governor wrote to Gladstone that night.[90] By this precedent, the *Economist* argued, the Bank and the government had accepted the duty of the Bank of England 'to support the banking community, to make the reserves of the Bank of England do for them as well as itself'.[91]

The reputation of the City was saved, but the consequences of Overend and Gurney's collapse were felt, as *The Times* put it, 'in the remotest corners of the kingdom'. To steady the economy and protect its own reserves the Bank of England increased the bank rate to 10 per cent (two or three times its normal rate), initiating a three-year period of industrial depression and unemployment. About 180 credit and finance companies went bankrupt in the three months after the crisis, including the Agra and Masterman's Bank, which held the savings of Indian Army officers and imperial civil servants. Shareholders suffered, too: in 1867, 1,600 people gave up their private carriages.[92] One of the greatest railway contractors, Peto and Betts, went down with debts of £4 million when Overend and Gurney fell, and men working on the District Line and the Victoria Embankment who had never heard of discount houses were thrown out of work. Corruption and mismanagement were exposed in many other railway companies in the enquiries following the 1866 crisis. The collapse of London shipbuilding in 1866, with the loss of 27,000 jobs, was no doubt inevitable sooner or later, but it owed its suddenness to the fall of Overend and Gurney.

There were no more 'Black Fridays' over the next half-century, and the Bank's discount rate was not raised again to the 'panic' level of 10 per cent that it had reached in 1857 and 1866. In the international crises of 1870 and 1873, and when the City of Glasgow Bank failed in 1878, the London money market held steady, redoubling its reputation for strength and reliability. The Bank of England and the major joint-stock banks, which grew rapidly in size and importance in the later nineteenth century, had learned how to prevent a misfortune from turning into a disaster. Their skills were needed, because the business of international lending was hazardous, and even the greatest family firms could falter when the second or third generation took over. In 1890 Lord Revelstoke, the head of Barings, the most trusted and reliable of City finance houses, took his firm to the very edge of bankruptcy by foolishly underwriting loans to Uruguay and the Argentine which the public (wisely) was unwilling to invest in. At the same time the Russian government declared its intention to withdraw most of the £2.4 million it had on deposit at Barings. By November, when Barings' inability to honour payments of around £9 million (equal to a third of all English banknotes in circulation that year) was about to be exposed, it was clear to Henry Lidderdale, at the Bank of England, and G. J. Goschen, at the Exchequer, that Barings' fall would endanger the whole delicate structure of London banking and credit. 'All houses would tumble one after the other. All credit gone,' Goschen wrote in his diary.[93] Finally, on 14 November, the Prime Minister, Lord Salisbury, reluctantly agreed that the government would share the cost of saving Barings with the Bank of England, and Lidderdale, the hero of the moment, took only twenty-four hours to assemble a consortium of London merchant and joint-stock banks which supported the Bank of England's rescue of Barings with a fund of £10 million. Panic was averted, London's good name was saved, and Barings, greatly diminished in wealth and reputation, survived as a limited company, having learned a lesson that it would take 100 years to forget.[94]

INSURANCE

Insurance, which had been the preserve of the unusually cautious and provident in the eighteenth century, became an everyday necessity in the nineteenth. The shipowner, the industrialist or the householder who did not insure his property was almost a rarity by the 1860s. The value of property insured against fire in England and Wales rose more than six-fold between 1800 and 1869, from about £200 million to £1,358 million, almost two-thirds of England's insurable property. At the same time a growing middle class steeped in the Victorian ethos of thrift and prudence, people with enough money to pay regular premiums, but not enough to put their families beyond the reach of misfortune, began to see life insurance as an important part of their financial planning. The value of life insurance cover bought in England rose from £11 million in 1800 to £290 million in 1870, making the English, per head, 100 times better insured than the French. This was not just a matter of foresight and family responsibility, but reflected also the growth of a society in which loans, partnerships and marriage settlements needed to be guaranteed against premature death.[95] Marine insurance boomed, too, especially during the wars of 1793–1815, which began to transform shipping insurance from an optional precaution into an act of common business routine, ignored only by the improvident few.

Thus, a business which had begun on a fairly small scale in eighteenth-century London became an industry of national and international importance. This was not entirely a metropolitan industry, but London kept the lion's share of the business. In the 1790s almost all English insurance was handled by eight London companies and, in the case of marine business, the individual underwriters of Lloyd's. During the wartime insurance boom several provincial companies were set up (including the future Norwich Union in 1797), but the bulk of new business went to the London companies, either the prewar ones (the Sun, the Royal Exchange, the London Assurance, the Phoenix, the Amicable, the Equitable and the Westminster) or those founded in the war years (the Pelican, the Globe, the Atlas, the Rock, the Eagle and several others). London companies covered about 90 per cent of English fire insurance in 1810, 75 per cent in the 1830s and 1840s, and 60 per cent in the late 1860s, when big Liverpool and Manchester companies were taking a substantial share.[96] The number of companies grew rapidly in the boom years of 1824–5 and 1844–56, and by the early 1850s there were about 200 fire or life companies in London. Competition forced the older offices to lower their premiums and introduce bonuses and with-profits life policies to protect their market share. New life tables had to be drawn up to reflect the increasing longevity of middle-class clients. Older companies pressed for protection against their new rivals, but the political climate favoured a free market, although freedom allowed a few rogues into the industry. The Independent West Middlesex (Thackeray's 'West Diddlesex'), which collected £200,000 before it was exposed in 1841, was immortalized as the Anglo-Bengalee Disinterested Loan and Life Assurance Company in *Martin Chuzzlewit* in 1843. It took a bigger scandal, the collapse of the Albert Life Assurance Society in 1870, to push Parliament into passing the Life Assurance Companies Act, which made it harder to start a new company on a shoestring.[97]

THE DANGER OF FIRE

Fire insurance companies cooperated with each other to protect their profits and reduce their losses in a competitive market. The older companies had run a joint fire-watching system in the 1790s but all had their separate and competing fire brigades. In 1832 nine major London fire offices agreed to cut their costs by combining their forces into a single London Fire Engine Establishment. This efficient but inadequate force, with nineteen engines and eighty men (rising to 127 by 1862), was central London's main defence against fire, though the police, Thames watermen, enthusiastic bystanders, a few parish brigades and a voluntary society which operated mobile fire-escapes, also played a part.

In its first decade the new brigade had some spectacular failures. On 16 October 1834, men burning cartloads of redundant Exchequer tally-sticks in the House of Lords stoves caused a fire which spread rapidly through both Houses of Parliament. The fire brigade, helped by soldiers and the police, saved Westminster Hall but not the main buildings of the Palace. Just over three years later, on a January night so cold that the fire plugs were frozen, the Royal Exchange, the home of London's insurance industry, burned down, destroying also the records of Lloyd's and the Royal Exchange Assurance. In 1841 fire destroyed Astley's Ampitheatre, at the foot of Westminster Bridge, and the Armoury of the Tower of London.

Theatres, shopping bazaars and department stores seemed to be especially vulnerable to fire. Whiteleys, the 'Universal Provider' of Bayswater, had six serious fires in the 1880s (arson was suspected), and the Queen's Bazaar of Oxford Street was destroyed when a diorama depicting 'the Destruction of York Minster by fire' became a little too realistic.

London's greatest fire since 1666 took place on 22 June 1861, when five wharves and twelve riverside warehouses along Tooley Street, just across the river from Pudding Lane (where the fire of 1666 started), were destroyed. £2 million-worth of property and goods (hemp, tallow, coffee, tea, paint, oil and foodstuffs) were lost, and the great James Braidwood, superintendent of the insurance companies' brigade since its foundation, was killed. Following this disaster a select committee recognized the inadequacy of the existing force and the absurdity of leaving fire-fighting in the hands of insurance companies. A plan to put fire-fighting under Metropolitan Police control foundered when the City police demanded a separate brigade, and in 1865 the Metropolitan Board of Works was given the job instead. The new Metropolitan Fire Brigade, funded by the government, the insurance companies and the ratepayers, was always short of money and often short of water, but it grew rapidly under the Board, and had 674 men (all ex-sailors), fifty-five main stations, and a large force of steam- and hand-powered engines by 1889, when the new LCC took control.[98]

In the light of their heavy losses in the Tooley Street disaster the main London insurance companies decided to quadruple their premiums for riverside warehouses. This led City merchants to form two new companies, the Commercial Union and the Mercantile Fire Insurance Company, both of which became extremely powerful over the next forty years. But from the 1870s onwards London insurance companies had more to worry about than fires on their doorstep, since their business, like that of other City financial services, was worldwide. By the 1890s the biggest companies were earning half or three-quarters of their premiums abroad, especially in the United States. The Hamburg fire of 1842 and the great fires in Chicago and Boston in 1871 and 1872 led to heavy claims on London, and the disastrous fire that followed the San Francisco earthquake of 1906 cost British companies (mostly in London and Liverpool) £10 million. Prompt payment of this enormous sum enhanced the reputation of London companies in the American market.[99]

THE PRUDENTIAL

Until the 1840s insurance companies covered three main risks: death, fire and losses at sea. From mid-century, new risks brought new business. Accident insurance, which began with the arrival of the railway in the 1840s, became big business after 1897 when the Workmen's Compensation Act forced employers to insure against workplace accidents. Motoring, travel and burglary insurance brought new customers around the end of the century, and endowment policies, which allowed investors to save money for dowries, school fees or old age, were almost as important as 'whole life' policies by 1913. One London company, the Prudential Mutual Assurance Association, extended the insurance habit to the working class. In the 1860s it began an advertising campaign to stimulate the growth of 'industrial insurance', low-value burial policies paid for on the doorstep at about 2d a week. This produced a spectacular expansion in the habit of life insurance, and created a new City giant. By 1912 the Prudential, in its palatial terracotta offices in Holborn, was running 12 million life policies, including 2.5 million on children under ten.[100] The rise of the Prudential reflected fundamental changes in the insurance business around the end of the century. The companies that prospered were those most attuned to the world of advertising and the mass market, and those that could offer cover against a multitude of risks, rather than a single one. Some of the older London companies, the Royal Exchange, the Sun, the Phoenix and the Atlas, thrived and grew in this more competitive climate, but others were swallowed by newer and bigger rivals. The mighty Commercial Union absorbed the Hand-in-Hand (founded in 1696) in 1905, and the Union (1714) in 1908, and the Alliance took over the Westminster (1717) in 1906.[101]

Big insurance companies were among the City's wealthiest institutions, and had under their control a substantial proportion of England's non-landed capital – around 5 per cent in 1913. Their wealth, and their need to invest it safely at a profit, made them important players in the London money market. Early in the nineteenth century most of their money went into government securities, with a little going into mortgages. The Royal Exchange, for instance, lent the government a fifth of the cost of building Regent Street in 1813.[102] In the 1830s and 1840s insurance companies began to invest more adventurously, in colonial loans, mortgages, annuities and urban development. The ability of London estate owners and speculative builders to develop large housing estates in the expectation that demand would follow supply rested heavily upon the willingness of London banks and insurance companies to advance them credit. The Royal Exchange advanced over £300,000 to developers in Denmark Hill, Bayswater, Belgravia and other smart neighbourhoods in the 1840s and 1850s, the Hand-in-Hand invested over £100,000 in Kensington and Paddington in the 1870s, and the London Assurance lent money to at least eighty London builders between 1839 and the 1880s. These were not the safest of investments, and insurance companies were more inclined to put their funds into railways, loans to poor law unions and local boards of health, and the wide range of British and foreign company stocks and shares that became available later in the century.[103]

MILLIONAIRES AND CLERKS

Within the square mile of the City there was a concentration of personal wealth without parallel in the world. The total income tax assessment on the City of London in 1879–80 was £41 million, more than half the combined assessment of Britain's twenty-eight major provincial cities. Of the forty richest men dying between 1809 and 1914 at least fourteen were City merchants, bankers or brokers.[104] We may remember the rich men brought low by misfortune or folly, as Henry Gurney and Lord Revelstoke were, or the corrupt or ruined financiers of Victorian fiction, Dickens's Mr Merdle, or Trollope's Lord Melmotte. But many more City financiers managed to reach the grave with their fortunes and reputations intact. The very richest men in early Victorian England were the noble owners of great landed estates, especially those with valuable London developments: the Dukes of Westminster, Bedford, Devonshire, Portland, and so on. But the greatest challenge to the landed aristocracy's position at the top of the pyramid of wealth came not (as one might expect in an industrializing society) from the manufacturers of Manchester and the Midlands, but from the bankers and merchants of London and other commercial centres. Work on the nineteenth-century probate calendars shows that the majority of non-landed millionaires and half-millionaires who died in the period 1820–1919 were financiers or merchants, rather than industrialists. Nearly a third of urban millionaires (sixty-three out of 198) and a quarter of urban half-millionaires (140 out of 574) dying in these years had made their fortunes in the City, nearly all of them as financiers or merchants. Many of these men won fame as well as fortune: Nathan Rothschild (died 1836), the wealthiest non-landlord of the century, whose financial genius dominated the City and established the richest and most enduring of the merchant banking dynasties; the Barings, who netted four peerages between them before the humiliation of 1890; Samuel Loyd, Lord Overstone, head of the London and Westminster Bank, whose ideas shaped the 1844 Bank Act and who, unusually for a City millionaire, used his fortune to buy a huge landed estate. Others achieved an uncanny obscurity: James Morrison (died 1857) made a fortune of about £4 million, second only to Rothschild's, as a London wholesale draper and merchant banker, and his son Charles (died 1909) almost tripled his inheritance. Sir John Ellerman (1862–1933), the immensely wealthy shipping magnate and City financier, was famously secretive about his private life, though his vast and mysterious investment empire included a controlling share of the *Illustrated London News*, the *Tatler*, and many other London publications. In the 1920s, and perhaps before, Ellerman owned hundreds of acres in Chelsea, South Kensington and around Oxford Street.[105] The creators of some of the greatest City fortunes were overlooked even by the meticulous editors of the *Dictionary of National Biography*: Richard Thornton (died 1857), who made £3 million from daring speculations in Baltic hemp and tallow, the merchants Hugh McCalmont and Giles Loder, also worth around £3 million each, and several millionaire merchant banking dynasties, the Sterns, the Raphaels and the Schroders.[106]

The City, of course, was not a community of millionaires. For every Ebenezer Scrooge, there were a dozen Bob Cratchits, for every Lord Overstone, 1,000 Charles Pooters. The City seemed to be, in the words of a guide-book of 1851, 'a very city of clerks': 'Clerks of all ages, clerks of all sizes, clerks from all quarters, walking slowly, walking fast, trotting, running, hurrying into the Bank from the very moment the clock strikes nine, till, at the latest, a quarter after.'[107] It is not possible to count these black-coated crowds with accuracy. In London as a whole there were 31,000 clerks in 1861 and 90,000 in 1891, but most of these worked outside the City. According to the City's own census, 9 per cent of the City's working population of 200,000 in 1871, and 364,000 in 1911, worked for banks and finance houses, and more than 40 per cent for merchants, commodity markets, lawyers, insurance companies, accountants, and so on, but many of these were not in 'white-collar' positions. Most financial institutions were small: according to the City census of 1911, the average bank or discount house employed forty-eight people, and a typical merchant bank or investment company around ten.[108] Some institutions were much bigger: large merchant banks (Brandts, Barings or Kleinworts) had sixty or seventy clerks in 1900, the Royal Exchange Assurance, one of the City's bigger insurance companies, had a head office staff of 76 in 1890 and 314 in 1913, and the Bank of England had about 1,000 employees in 1900.[109]

Clerks got their jobs by answering advertisements, or through family connections. Charles Booth, who knew the world of the late Victorian clerk very well, tells us that 'well-known commercial houses have waiting lists on which they enter the names of those recommended to them, and commonly give preference to sons of clerks already in their employ'. To get a job in the face of competition from efficient German clerks, and increasingly from young women, an aspiring clerk needed to make a good impression: 'A good appearance, unobtrusive dress, and neat handwriting, are the most essential qualifications for a clerk. Further, if he is to stand the constant strain of office life, a sound constitution is required.' Once in, a competent and well-behaved clerk could hold a job in the same firm for life, enjoying a rising salary as he grew in experience and seniority. An office boy starting at 5s a week might end his teens on 25s, and a valued and experienced clerk might, at the very top of his profession, earn £1,000 a year. Women, of whom nearly 9,000 were employed in 1891 as typists (or typewriters, as they were called), copyists and telephone operators, would never rise above £100 a year, and were lucky to get more than £50 or £60. Young clerks were more likely to dream of wealth than to achieve it: 'As in the legal profession, the eminence of a small minority dazzles the eyes of a large number whose talents might perhaps have been more profitably directed elsewhere.' And those who could not stand the tedium of office work, or who lost their footing on the career ladder, had poor prospects of re-employment: 'Those who drop out, drop under.'[110] Those who stuck with a good employer would eventually achieve a comfortable middle-class status. Two-thirds of Kleinwort's male staff earned enough (£160 or more) to pay income tax in 1910, and Booth believed, on the strength of accommodation occupied and servants employed, that 64 per cent of London's 108,000 clerks and commercial workers (including 20,000 'merchants and brokers') were 'of the central or upper classes'. This was a matter of attitudes and styles of living, as well as income:

> Financially the great mass of clerks are on a level with the great mass of artisans, £75 to £150 a year comparing with 30s, 40s, 50s, and 60s a week. But socially, and economically too, they are on an entirely different footing. From top to bottom clerks associate with clerks and artisans with artisans – but comparatively seldom with each other. A clerk lives an entirely different life from an artisan – marries a different

kind of wife – has different aims and different ideas, different possibilities and different limitations. . . . It is not by any means only a question of clothes, of the wearing or not wearing of a white shirt every day. . . . More undoubtedly is expected from the clerk than the artisan, but the clerk's money goes further – is on the whole much better spent.[111]

Chapter 17

Ragged London

NINETEENTH-CENTURY LONDON inspired amazement, pride, revulsion and fear in roughly equal measure. Conventionally, it was regarded as a place of contrasts: the unparallelled wealth of the West End and the City alongside the unspeakable poverty of the worst slum districts; the splendour of the Court, of Parliament and high society alongside the shame of overflowing cesspits, cholera epidemics, street prostitution and rampant criminality. The roots of this grotesque inequality were to be found, many Victorian observers thought, in the naked competition for wealth and power that characterized London life. Thomas Carlyle, the most influential of Victorian sages, lived in Chelsea from 1834 to 1881, but denounced the selfish competitiveness of his adopted city: 'It is a huge Aggregate of little systems, each of which is again a small Anarchy, the members of which do not work together, but scramble against each other.' Friedrich Engels, who visited London in 1842 when he was in his early twenties, made the same point. On the one hand, he was enormously impressed by London's commercial power, and by his first sight of the Thames, lined with wharves and crammed with countless ships. On the other, he saw that this 'colossal centralisation, this heaping together of two and a half millions of human beings', had exacted a heavy price from its citizens:

> Londoners have been forced to sacrifice the best qualities of their human nature, to bring to pass all the marvels of civilization which crowd their city; that a hundred powers which slumbered within them have remained inactive, have been suppressed in order that a few might be developed more fully and multiply through union with those of others. ... The brutal indifference, the unfeeling isolation of each in his private interest becomes the more repellent and offensive the more these individuals are crowded together, within a limited space. ... The dissolution of mankind into monads of which each one has a separate principle and a separate purpose, the world of atoms, is here carried to its utmost extreme.[1]

DISCOVERING THE POOR

There can hardly be an urban population whose poverty has been more fully described and analysed than that of Victorian London. Victorian novelists, from Charles Dickens, Charles Kingsley, George Gissing and George Moore to now forgotten writers such as Augustus Mayhew, Douglas Jerrold and Thomas Wright, often set their works in the poorer parts of town, and in the 1880s and 1890s the London slums, especially those in the East End, were discovered and rediscovered by one novelist after another. Of the factual accounts of the mid-Victorian London poor, Henry Mayhew's *London Labour and the London Poor*, published between 1851 and 1862, is the best-known and most important, but many others were produced, some cool and objective, others designed to send shivers down the spines of their comfortable suburban readers. How many people lived in conditions of squalor and malnutrition was not known, although some writers tried to quantify London poverty, on the basis of inadequate evidence. Mayhew produced many pages of statistics, but most of them referred to the 'street folk', beggars, hawkers, scavengers and entertainers, a tiny proportion of the London poor. John Hollingshead's *Ragged London in 1861*, an honest but hastily researched study based on house-to-house enquiries, concluded that at least a third of Londoners, a million people, lived in 'filthy, ill-constructed courts and alleys' or 'in unwholesome layers, one over the other, in old houses and confined rooms'.

Hollingshead's estimate was surprisingly close to the figure produced in the 1890s, when Charles Booth and his team of researchers calculated that, of London's population of just over 4 million, 8.4 per cent (354,444) lived in extreme poverty (classes A and B) and another 22.4 per cent (938,293) were poor (classes C and D). Booth's calculations depended upon subjective definitions of poverty, as such classifications always do, but they give us as good a picture of late Victorian poverty as we are likely to get. His classification, like that of most analysts of poverty, was based largely on visual impressions. If people *looked* poor (their clothes and houses, especially) then they *were* poor. Classes A and B, Booth said, 'are at all times more or less "in want." They are ill-nourished and poorly clad.... From day to day and from hand to mouth they get along; sometimes suffering, sometimes helped, but not always unfortunate, and very ready to enjoy any good luck that may come in their way.... Some may be semi-paupers, going into the "house" at certain seasons, and some few receive outdoor relief, but on the whole they manage to avoid the workhouse.' Classes C and D, the 'poor', were not, he said, 'in want'. 'They are neither ill-nourished nor ill-clad, according to any standard that can reasonably be used. Their lives are an unending struggle, and lack comfort, but I do not know that they lack happiness'. Most of Booth's poor were wage-earners, and real wages, and thus average living standards, had risen by about 40 per cent between 1850 and 1900, making the population studied by Booth a good deal more prosperous than that described by Dickens or Mayhew. Booth's impression, too, was that the conditions he found were better than those of a generation earlier.[2]

Although Booth shared some contemporary attitudes towards the very poor which do not strike us today as enlightened, his work was successful, as he hoped it would be, in tearing down the lurid fairground curtain that had till then separated the poor from those who wished to understand their plight. The causes and extent of poverty, the material conditions in which the poor lived, the working lives and cultural activities of the poor, were all illuminated by his seventeeen painstaking volumes. Booth also shed new light on where poverty was to be found. Until the 1860s those concerned with poverty had focused on the 'rookeries', pockets of crime and destitution hidden only a few houses away from London's finest shopping streets. Charles Dickens, the supreme connoisseur of London poverty, maintained that the back-streets of Westminster, around Holborn, Oxford Street and Covent Garden, were the poorest neighbourhoods. 'There is more filth and squalid misery near these great thoroughfares than in any part of this mighty city.'[3] Henry Mayhew, writing in 1849–50, regarded poverty as a general metropolitan condition, rather than a localized one, and the many writers who took their readers on a tour of London slums in the 1850s and 1860s accepted that this was so. Thomas Beames's *Rookeries of London* (1850) were to be found in every part of town, and in 1859 George Godwin, the well-informed editor of *The Builder*, described *Town Swamps* in Clerkenwell and Holborn, as well as Bermondsey and Spitalfields. Two years later John Hollingshead emphasized that *Ragged London* could be found in the centre of town and in every suburb:

> In the west there is Knightsbridge, rendered filthy and immoral by the presence of its large military barracks, with Chelsea and Brentford; in the south there are Lambeth, Walworth, embracing Lock's Fields, and the Borough, with its notorious Kent Street; in the north there is Agar Town, built on a swamp, and running down to the canal in every stage of dirt and decay, with Somers' Town, Kentish Town, and Camden Town, each contributing its share to the general mass of misery; and

in the east there are St George's, Whitechapel, Bethnal Green, and overgrown Shoreditch.[4]

When many of the worst central London rookeries were demolished in the 1840s, writers began to focus their attention on impoverished suburban areas, perhaps south of the river or east of the Tower, that their readers were unlikely ever to visit. To introduce the hero of *Alton Locke* to the lowest depths of urban squalor in 1850 Charles Kingsley sent him across Waterloo Bridge and along Tooley Street into Bermondsey, and in 1866, when James Greenwood wanted to shock the readers of the *Pall Mall Gazette* with an account of 'A Night in a Workhouse', he took a carriage across the river to Lambeth, a parish which, in 1869, had more paupers than any other in London.[5] Thomas Archer's study of *The Pauper, the Thief, and the Convict*, published in 1865, concentrated on the area of East London known as the Nichol, between Shoreditch High Street and Brick Lane. In the 1860s the French writer and statesman Hyppolite Taine lingered over the horrors of Shadwell, on the East London riverside, where 'harlots' fought in the filthy streets and barefooted children swarmed out of narrow courtyards. 'Nothing is more lugubrious than these white bodies, that pale flaxen hair, these flabby cheeks encrusted with old dirt.' But he saw destitution in central London too: 'I recall the alleys which run into Oxford Street, stifling lanes, encrusted with human exhalations; troops of pale children nestling on the muddy stairs; the seats of London Bridge, where families, huddled together with drooping heads, shiver through the night; particularly the Haymarket and the Strand in the evening.'[6] Even in the 1880s, there was never an exclusive focus on the poverty of the East End. George Gissing, who knew London poverty at first hand, set his grim and informative account of slum life, *The Nether World* (1899), in Clerkenwell, north-west of the City.

East London's reputation as a place of exceptional hardship and menace grew in the 1870s and 1880s. In part, this reflected real changes in the East End economy, especially the decline of silk-weaving and shipbuilding and the growth of sweated industry and casual dock labour. But Victorian fears were fed on fantasy, too. Stepney and Poplar had a small Chinese population, making its living by running lodging-houses, shops and laundries for Chinese sailors in Shadwell and Limehouse. In 1868 a magazine described opium smoking in a Chinese 'opium den' in Bluegate Fields, an alley in Shadwell, just off the once-notorious Ratcliff Highway, and in 1870 Charles Dickens made an opium den, reeking of evil and corruption, the centrepiece of his account of the East End in his unfinished novel, *The Mystery of Edwin Drood*. Two years later Gustave Doré's engraving of the same opium den in *London: A Pilgrimage* reinforced the belief that the East End was a place of racial, sexual and social danger. In the 1880s popular novelists began to propagate the idea that the East End was an unknown land of destitution, immorality and disease, a world to be 'explored' by intrepid social investigators or reclaimed for Christianity by missionaries, but avoided by those of a delicate disposition. Walter Besant's *All Sorts and Conditions of Men*, published in 1882, was the first of the genre, and others followed in the 1890s, notably Arthur Morrison's East End trilogy (*Tales of Mean Streets, A Child of the Jago* and *To London Town*) and Israel Zangwill's novels of the Jewish East End. The horrific Jack the Ripper killings in 1888, and the appearance of Booth's first volume, *East London*, in 1889, reinforced the general impression that the East End represented the deepest abyss (another much-used image at the end of the century) into which urban man could fall.

In beginning his researches in East London, Booth had accepted the new view, widely held in the 1880s and 1890s, that this was where the great bulk of poverty was concentrated, with only isolated pockets elsewhere. By 1891 he had changed his mind. His findings suggested that the worst concentrations of poverty were in the riverside parts of South London, rather than in the East End. Dividing London into fifty districts of roughly equal population, Booth found that the only two districts with over 50 per cent living in poverty (classes A to D) were Southwark and Bermondsey, south of the river, and that poverty levels in the districts immediately north of the City (Clerkenwell and Shoreditch), in North Camberwell and in riverside Westminster were as bad as those in Bethnal Green and in St George-in-the-East and Shadwell (the poorest eastern districts), and worse than those in Whitechapel, Poplar and Limehouse. The part of Southwark between the Borough High Street and Blackfriars Road was, in Booth's view, the worst in London: 'It contains a number of courts and small streets which for vice, poverty, and crowding, are unrivalled in London, and as an aggregate area of low life form perhaps the most serious blot to be found on the whole of our map.'[7] Overall, South London, which had large and affluent outer suburbs, had about 37 per cent of London's population, and over 38 per cent of its 'poor', while East London, with smaller and less wealthy outer suburbs, had 21 per cent of London's population and over 24 per cent of those in poverty. North London (which Booth defined as the area stretching, roughly, from Kingsland Road to York Way–Brecknock Road, and also including Somers Town), with under 14 per cent of London's population, had over 16 per cent of its poor, and West London had 27 per cent of Londoners, but only 21 per cent of the poor.[8] Infant mortality statistics for 1907–10 tell a similar story: Shoreditch, Bermondsey, Southwark and Bethnal Green (in that order) had the worst record, with Poplar, West Ham, Stepney, Hammersmith and Kensington some way behind.[9] So the best contemporary evidence suggests that poverty was spread thickly and fairly evenly all around the inner suburban districts of the north, east and south, rather than being concentrated in the East End, as the late Victorian public was usually led to believe.

THE CAUSES OF POVERTY

Booth was ready enough to describe individuals as drunken, idle or feckless, but his general impression, in contrast to many of those who came before him, was that over 80 per cent of poor Londoners were poor because of low or irregular wages, unemployment, illness, widowhood, old age, or having too many children, rather than 'habits of intemperance'. People living so close to the margins of survival, unable to put much money aside, were especially vulnerable to the personal and economic misfortunes that waited around every corner: illness, widowhood, new mouths to feed, cold winters, dismissal and eviction. As Booth wrote in the 1890s: 'One of the most stupendous facts of life is the uncertainty of the position of the vast majority of those, no matter what their status may be, who are dependent upon industry for their livelihood.'[10]

Although London was a high-wage city, it was also a city that relied on a large pool of surplus labour to meet its fluctuating industrial needs. Most London industries experienced peaks and troughs of production, related to the weather, the trade cycle, or variations in demand because of the London season. Some highly skilled craftsmen (jewellers, for instance) and workers in very steady industries such as railways and brewing had security of employment, but for most workers bouts of heavy work were interrupted by periods of short-time work or complete unemployment. Others, particularly in the docks, found work on a casual basis, and were lucky if they worked two or three days in a week. Many London trades and services had a brisk period during the fashionable season, roughly between February and mid-July, then a summer slump, followed by a pre-Christmas revival. This was the annual pattern for West End tailoring, shoemaking, dressmaking and millinery workers, pastry-cooks and confectioners, workers in the cab, coach and saddlery trades, barbers, waiters, upholsterers, printers, and all those who depended on the spending of the West End and Westminster élite. The more fashionable the work, the greater the fall when the rich left town. The number of Court dressmakers in work (to take an example from 1910) fell by about 64 per cent between June and August.[11] Since different trades had different slack seasons, it was possible for workers to transfer from one seasonal product or service to another: from summer jam to winter pickles and sweets, from houses to gas, from cabinets to pianos, from clocks to gasmeters, or boots to harnesses. In the winter pantomime season there were Covent Garden porters shifting the scenery, and flower-girls in the chorus. Laundry-work was a useful sideline for seamstresses and milliners, or the wives of unemployed building workers. But this 'dovetailing' was not a perfect solution, since it added labourers to already overcrowded trades, pushing the least skilful into street trading or pauperism.[12]

The weather was a great source of uncertainty. Undertakers, sweeps, furriers, gas workers and those connected with the coal trade had their slack season in the summer. But the most severe hardship came in bad winters, when fuel and food costs were high and up to a third of the male workforce, including dockers handling grain and timber, costermongers and workers in the building trades, was short of work. In February 1855 the freezing of the Thames closed the docks, and threw 50,000 out of work. There were bread riots in Whitechapel that winter, as there were again in January 1861, after a month of freezing weather. Numbers on poor relief in January 1861 rose from 96,752 to 135,389 in five weeks, and many thousands more were relieved by magistrates' courts or charities, without the normal records being kept. That winter, as thousands skated on the Serpentine in scenes reminiscent of the Thames ice fairs of two centuries before, John Hollingshead set off to discover the reality of *Ragged London*. There were more bread riots in early 1867, and gangs of unemployed workers toured London begging for money in January 1879, the first of a run of three very harsh winters. Acute distress in the bitter winter of early 1886 led to the most terrifying riots of the half-century on 8 February, when unemployed dock and building workers looted West End shops. It was just at this time that Charles Booth, deeply concerned about London poverty, but irritated by what he saw as the exaggerated accounts of sensationalists and socialists, decided to discover its true causes and extent by the application of 'scientific' methods.[13]

Workers in chronically overcrowded jobs, particularly dockers, water-men, coal porters, shipwrights (and most river trades), carters and other land transport workers, market porters, building labourers, painters, bakers, silk weavers, and workers in rubber and white lead factories, had to compete for work on a daily basis, often waiting hours for a call that never came. London's vast casual labour force, which probably involved over a tenth of the city's workers, was constantly being enlarged by young provincial or (to a lesser extent) overseas migrants, and by those who had lost their jobs in other trades. Workers might slip from skilled work into the casual labour market because of a seasonal or cyclical depression, or because their old trade was in long-term decline, which was the case with silk-weaving from the 1820s to the 1860s, and shipbuilding, disastrously, in the 1860s. Business failure, dismissal, or ageing could precipitate a decline into casual work. It was common for youngsters in their early teens to be employed as servants, messengers, barmen, printers, drapers or shop assistants, and then find themselves thrown out of work in their twenties. With luck, they might find work in the building or transport trades, but many would end up as dock casuals, or in one of London's street trades. A spell in the army might postpone the evil day, but not avert the final outcome.[14]

For the employer, this glut of labour made London a fine place to do business, but for the working man or woman without marketable skills it was a shifting and uncertain world, in which misfortune or misjudgement could lead to destitution, and in which new opportunities, although they existed, were not easy to find. Booth quoted the words of an operative brushmaker: 'The great curse of a journeyman's life is irregularity of employment. When I thought it likely that I should be thrown out of employment it seemed to paralyze me completely, and I used to sit at home brooding over it until the blow fell. . . . The fear of being turned off is the worst thing in a working-man's life.'[15] No doubt there was work to be found somewhere in the town, but late Victorian London was a big place for a man on foot, as Will Crooks, unemployed cooper and future Mayor of Poplar, found when he searched for work:

> I first went down to the riverside at Shadwell. No work to be had.
> Then I called at another place in Limehouse. No hands wanted. So I
> looked in at home and got two slices of bread in paper and walked
> eight miles to a cooper's yard in Tottenham. All in vain. I dragged
> myself back to Clerkenwell. Still no luck. Then I turned homewards in
> despair. By the time I reached Stepney I was dead beat.[16]

The unemployed worker might seek casual work, or try his (or her) hand at one of the multitude of street jobs described in such meticulous detail by Henry Mayhew in 1851–2. Many of Mayhew's street-sellers, crossing-sweepers and scavengers were not born into their work, but took it up as a last refuge from the workhouse. In Mayhew's volumes we find Irish labourers turned orange-sellers, destitute ex-mechanics and laundresses selling watercress, and desperate people, from children to the very old, scavenging in London's dirty streets for things to eat or sell. 'Many of the very old live on the hard dirty crusts they pick up out of the roads in the course of their rounds, washing them and steeping them in water before they eat them.' On every half-respectable street or square there were crossing-sweepers, ready to clear the road of mud or dust for a small tip. Stories were told of fortunes made in this way, but in Mayhew's view sweeping was another of London's last-ditch jobs, only a step away from begging:

> People take to crossing-sweeping either on account of bodily afflictions, depriving them of the power of performing ruder work, or because the occupation is the last resource left open to them of earning a living, and they considered even the scanty subsistence it yields preferable to that of the workhouse. . . . Among the bodily infirmities the chief are old age, asthma, and rheumatism; and the injuries mostly consist of loss of limbs. Many of the rheumatic sweepers have been bricklayers' labourers.[17]

In a poor community, every piece of rubbish had its value. Along the banks of the Thames there were mudlarks looking for pieces of coal, wood, bones and metal, from which they might earn around 3d a day. Some of these were children sent out by parents whose own incomes, perhaps from cleaning or casual labour, could not sustain their large families. Others were much older: 'Among the mud-larks may be seen many old women, and it is indeed pitiable to behold them, especially during the winter, bent nearly double with age and infirmity, paddling and groping among the wet mud for small pieces of coal, chips of wood, or any sort of refuse washed up by the tide.' Dog dung, or 'pure', could be sold for up to a shilling a bucket to the Bermondsey tanneries, where it was used to dress morocco and kid leather. Among the 250 or so men and women who made their livings as pure-finders, Mayhew met a well-educated woman of sixty, 'broken up with age, want, and infirmity', the widow of a Thames waterman. For fifteen years she had gathered 'pure', trudging from Aldgate to Bow with her covered pail, and crossing the river to sell its contents for 6d in Bermondsey. She spoke to Mayhew when she was ill in her dark and empty room, stretched out on some dirty straw. '"No, I have earned no money today. I have had a piece of dried bread that I steeped in water to eat. I haven't eat anything else today; but pray, sir, don't tell anybody of it.

I could never bear the thought of going into the 'great house'. I'm so used to the air, that I'd sooner die in the street, as many I know have done." [18]

THE POOR LAW

The alternative that the old pure-gatherer feared was the one offered by the Poor Law Guardians. Since 1834, when the Poor Law had been amended under the influence of the principles of Edwin Chadwick's Royal Commission report, poor relief in most of England had been administered by groups of parishes known as Poor Law Unions. In London, thirteen Unions were established, each run by Boards of Guardians elected by ratepayers and property owners. In addition, thirteen large parishes had their own Boards, and eleven parishes were able to claim independence from the new national system by virtue of existing local acts. The autonomy of these eleven parishes, among them St Marylebone and St Pancras, was often challenged by the central government's Poor Law Commission (the Poor Law Board after 1847), but was not finally broken until the Metropolitan Poor Law Amendment Act of 1867.

The Poor Law reforms introduced in 1834 were designed to deal with the problem of able-bodied paupers, especially men, who, it was believed, had been drawn into dependence on poor relief by the excessive generosity of the system of 'outdoor' (non-workhouse) relief that had become common in parts of England since the 1790s. The intention was that while the old, the sick, the feeble-minded, the widowed and the young should continue to receive indoor or outdoor relief, depending on their needs, able-bodied male paupers should be forced to prove their genuine need by submitting to the harsh discipline of the union workhouse. This 'workhouse test', or the 'less eligibility' principle, could not be rigorously enforced in London because here, as in other large towns, the number of able-bodied people needing relief fluctuated greatly from season to season, and year to year. Unions could not be expected to build enough spare workhouse capacity to cope with peaks of unemployment, nor (if decency and public order were to be maintained) could they refuse help to desperate people in times of acute hardship. Instead, most Unions continued some outdoor relief for the able-bodied and many, from the 1840s onwards, imposed a 'labour test' on the unemployed, forcing them to spend a day breaking rocks or chopping wood to earn a few shillings.

The driving away of the fit meant that most of London's forty union workhouses were filled with children, old people and invalids who had not been offered, or could not survive on, outdoor relief. A *Lancet* enquiry in 1865 found that 85 per cent of workhouse residents were 'unfit', and when Charles Dickens took a walk in one of the huge mixed workhouses, he found its 2,000 or so inmates to be a pitiful and defenceless crowd: 'Upon the whole, it was the dragon, Pauperism, in a very weak and impotent condition; toothless, fangless, drawing his breath heavily enough, and hardly worth chaining up.'[19]

From time to time the London unions tried to remove 'deserving' paupers from the unsatisfactory regime of the general workhouse, into more specialist institutions. Since Hanway's Acts of 1762 and 1767, London parishes had been obliged to maintain homes for pauper children in the suburbs, and after 1834 these Infant Establishments, generally run at a profit by private contractors, grew in size and importance. The greatest of the pauper schools was in Norwood, South London, where over 1,000 pupils lived and worked. Norwood's industrial system was much admired, but a cholera outbreak in 1849 forced the school to close, and an even worse outbreak at the Infant Pauper Asylum in Tooting, where 118 children died in two weeks, exposed the miserable conditions in which London orphans were kept. Thanks to the vigour of Thomas Wakley, the West Middlesex coroner, the culpability of the owner of the Tooting asylum, Bartholomew Drouet, was exposed, along with that of the guardians and inspectors who had supplied his victims. Drouet was acquitted of manslaughter, but his economical system of child care, as Dickens wrote in a famous series of articles, was 'effectually broken up' by the trial. A trade 'which derives its profits from the deliberate torture and neglect of a class the most innocent on earth, as well as the most wretched and defenceless, can never on any pretence be resumed'.[20] Following the Tooting scandal some of the London unions collaborated in establishing large District Schools, while others eventually set up smaller Union Schools. In the late 1880s there were over 11,000 children in pauper schools, many of them in large suburban 'barrack schools' with up to 2,000 pupils. The public exposure of the dangers these children faced, from disease (particularly conjunctivitis), cruelty and overcrowding, led some unions to move their children into 'Cottage Homes' and ordinary local schools in the 1890s.[21]

In the early years of the New Poor Law no special provision was made for the sick, and the guardians played little part in the fight against epidemic disease. In the 1860s the appalling quality of medical care in London workhouses was exposed by medical officers and publicists, particularly Dr Joseph Rogers, workhouse medical officer to the Strand Union, and the *Lancet*, which organized an influential 'commission of enquiry' into London's workhouse infirmaries in 1865. According to Dr Rogers, the nursery of the Strand workhouse was a 'wretchedly damp and miserable room, nearly always overcrowded with young mothers and their infant children.... Scores and scores of distinctly preventable deaths of both mothers and children took place during my continuance in office through their being located in this horrible den.' In Shoreditch Workhouse infirmary in 1866 600 patients were cared for by one part-time doctor, with no trained nurses.[22]

In the face of this pressure, the government decided to abandon the idea that the sick could be 'deterred' from their sickness by the 'less eligibility' principle, and introduced legislation that brought a touch of humanity to workhouse medical care. Under the 1867 Metropolitan Poor Law Act, or Metropolitan Asylums Act, a Metropolitan Asylums Board (MAB) was established, funded by a new Common Poor Fund to which all Unions subscribed, to build and run a network of hospitals for typhus, smallpox, scarlet fever and other 'fevers', and asylums for the insane. For other diseases, the London unions were grouped into 'asylum districts' large enough to run hospitals away from the main workhouse, and dispensaries for outpatients were to be set up. Conditions did not change quickly. Few dispensaries were opened, and workhouse infirmaries remained overcrowded and grossly understaffed. In the Bethnal Green infirmary in the 1890s there were 335 female patients in the care of one nurse, whose main function was to turn away 'sturdy beggars', and mortality among infants born in workhouse nurseries around 1900 was probably double the national average.[23] Still, London was far better served than other parts of the country, and by 1900 a true municipal hospital system, not confined to paupers, had taken shape. The MAB's budget for 1905 was £640,833, almost half the national Poor Law medical budget, and in 1929, when the London County Council (LCC) took over the Poor Law hospitals, the municipal network had 20,000 staff and 41,000 beds in seventy-four hospitals. Guy's, St Bartholomew's, and the rest of the independent voluntary hospitals, with another 14,000 beds, remained outside the state system until 1948. In the hands of the LCC, with the workhouse stigma at last removed, London's Poor Law hospital and ambulance system was regarded as perhaps the best municipal health service in the world.[24]

Outcast London

Tens of thousands of mid-Victorian Londoners scraped together a miserable living from a combination of casual work, charity and outdoor relief. Old people and fatherless families commonly received a few shillings a week from the Guardians, and they, along with the unemployed, could top up their income with money from the capital's innumerable charities. In the winter, when survival was most difficult, there were refuges for the homeless, stoneyards for the unemployed, and Christmas appeals through which the guilty, fearful, or even generous, wealthy of the West End paid their tribute to the East. In all, charitable spending in London in the late 1860s was thought to run at over £7 million a year, about three times the budget of the London Poor Law.[25]

Gareth Stedman Jones, in his influential study of *Outcast London*, drew attention to an important change of attitude towards the wisdom of charity and outdoor relief in the late 1860s and 1870s. This was triggered by a severe economic and social crisis in the East End between 1866 and 1869, brought about by industrial depression, the collapse of shipbuilding, hard winters, cholera and dear food. This crisis led, as others had done, to a rush of money and goods, not always carefully distributed, from the City and the West End, much of it channelled through the Lord Mayor's Mansion House Fund. Reflecting on this experience, many London clergymen and professionals revived the ideas of the 1834 Poor Law Commission, and argued that casual charity, distributed without careful investigation of the character and circumstances of the recipient, allowed 'clever paupers' to grow rich on hand-outs, attracted able-bodied 'loafers' to the most generous districts, and created a general culture of dependency and idleness among the poor. London's 'Pauper Frankenstein' was the creation, they said, not of real economic problems, but of indiscriminate charity and outdoor relief.[26]

The problem was tackled on two fronts. As the Webbs explained in 1929, there was a distinct change of policy on the part of the Local Government Board and its Metropolitan inspectors, Uvedale Corbett and Henry Longley, towards outdoor relief in the early 1870s. The inspectors urged London unions to 'offer the house' to applicants for relief, even the old, the widowed and the unfit, whose right to outdoor relief had been accepted in 1834. Encouraged by the offer of a daily subsidy for each workhouse inmate from the Common Fund, about twelve Unions, including Paddington, Kensington, St George's Hanover Square, Stepney,

Whitechapel and St George-in-the-East, adopted the new policy whole-heartedly. Outdoor relief was greatly restricted, and to ensure that the able-bodied did not benefit from the gentler workhouse regime needed by the old and unwell, a new type of workhouse, the 'able-bodied test workhouse', was introduced, in which a strict penal regime would drive the 'loafer' back into the labour market. One of these was established in Poplar in the 1871, and another in Kensington between 1882 and 1906. London unions were able to rid themselves of able-bodied applicants by giving them an 'order for Poplar', in the knowledge that most paupers would rather beg and sleep rough than submit to a regime of oakum-picking and prison discipline in a 'test workhouse'.[27] By these methods, the number receiving outdoor relief was driven down rapidly, from an average of 116,555 (36.2 people per 1,000) in 1871 to 48,755 (11.2 per 1,000) in 1890. Some of those refused outdoor relief found their own way of making a living, but others ended up in workhouses, which held about 14 per 1,000 Londoners in the 1890s (and about 17 per 1,000 from 1905 to 1912), compared to 10 per 1,000 in 1875.[28]

Many of the stricter Boards of Guardians were strongly influenced by the Charity Organization Society, whose members played a key role in Poor Law policy in the 1870s. The COS was founded in 1869, aiming to coordinate all London's charitable agencies and to act as a clearing house for all applicants for relief. By doing this, the COS hoped to end the exploitation of overlapping charities and outdoor relief by 'clever paupers', and to restore to charity the social purpose which urbanization, and particularly the separation of the classes in London, had destroyed. Without personal sympathy, guidance and control on the part of the giver, and respect, gratitude and self-improvement on the part of the receiver, charity could only demoralize and pauperize the working class, they believed. The leading members of the COS, who included Octavia Hill, J. R. Green, C. S. Loch, the Rev. Samuel Barnett and Sir Charles Trevelyan, were mostly people with a professional background, who believed that the methodical investigation and supervision of claimants would transform charity from a corrupting to a beneficent force in the lives of the poor. For the COS, the greatest enemy was not poverty but indiscriminate alms-giving, which destroyed the self-reliance of the poor, and taught them to prefer easy handouts to hard work. Throughout the 1870s the COS worked tirelessly to stop the flow of gifts and doles to the London poor. Worst of all, in the minds of the COS, were the emergency relief funds, such as the one raised and distributed by the Lord Mayor in the winter of 1866–7. Winters were mild in the 1870s, but when bad weather returned in January 1879, and again in the next two winters, the Society had to exert all its influence to stop the old habit from returning.[29]

The root of the problem, as the COS saw it, was the flight of the well-off from working-class London, especially East London, since 1815. In 1861, only 3.4 per cent of the adult male population of East London (not including Hackney) were upper or upper middle class (large employers, financiers, property owners, higher professionals), compared to 12.6 per cent in the north and west, and 7 per cent in the centre and south. By 1891, East London's social élite was a mere 2 per cent, too few (according to the COS) to ensure sound local government or to provide the personally supervised charity of the old, beneficial type.[30] Samuel Barnett, writing in 1886, blamed upper-class absenteeism for the plight of the East End: 'It is this practice of living in pleasant places which impoverishes the poor. It authorizes, as it were, a lower standard of life for the neighbourhoods in which the poor are left; . . . it leaves large quarters of the town without the light which comes from knowledge, and large masses of the people without the friendship of those better taught than themselves.'[31] One practical consequence of the separation of classes was that poorer Unions, which had the most applicants for poor relief, had few rich ratepayers, and were forced to set their rates high, and their levels of relief low. East London poor rates were sometimes six or seven times as high as those in West London, and paupers were given perhaps a third of what richer Unions could offer. This imbalance was only partly corrected by the Metropolitan Poor Act of 1867, which created a Common Poor Fund which covered almost half the cost of London's poor relief.[32]

From the 1860s to the end of the century, a succession of adventurous and well-meaning people tried to bridge the social and geographical gulf between rich and poor London by settling and working in the East End. The pioneer was Edward Denison, whose eight months in Whitechapel in 1867, followed by his death in 1870 and the publication of his letters two years later, inspired many others to explore or settle in the slums. The focus for much of this settlement work was Samuel Barnett, who became vicar of St Jude's, Whitechapel, in 1873. Among the many Oxford undergraduates who were drawn into social work in the East End by Barnett in the 1870s was the social philosopher Arnold Toynbee, whose early death in 1883 inspired the building of Toynbee Hall as the head-quarters of the University Settlement movement. From this bridgehead in Commercial Street Barnett and his followers, who later included William Beveridge, Clement Attlee and R. H. Tawney, went on to achieve an understanding of poverty and its remedies which went far beyond the 'new feudalism' of the COS. The Whitechapel Art Gallery (1899), the Workers' Educational Association and the modern Welfare State all owe a debt to the work of Samuel Barnett.[33]

The opening of Toynbee Hall in 1884 took place just as a new economic and social crisis, more severe than that of the 1860s, was developing. A serious cyclical depression between 1884 and 1887 brought unemployment in the building, engineering, shipbuilding, metal, textile, chemical and printing industries, and an agricultural depression damaged all the West End workers who relied on the spending of the landed classes. Workers in the declining leather, sugar and watch-making industries found it harder than ever to make a living. Alongside this, a new awareness of the depth of London's housing crisis, and the moral and social consequences of overcrowding, developed, stimulated especially by the publication of a sensational pamphlet, *The Bitter Cry of Outcast London*, in 1883. The enthusiastic reception given to the American socialist Henry George in 1882, and the growth of the Marxist Social Democratic Federation (SDF) in London after 1881 reminded the well-off that there might be something worse in prospect than an epidemic of scrounging and loafing. Then, on 8 February 1886, in the middle of the coldest winter for thirty years, about 20,000 unemployed dock and building workers poured out of a rally in Trafalgar Square into Mayfair and St James's, robbing and terrorizing the rich in their carriages and clubs, and looting the shops of Piccadilly and Oxford Street. Over the next two days uneasiness turned into full-blown panic, fuelled by rumours (some of them true) that crowds of 'roughs' were gathering all over London, from Deptford and Bermondsey to Bethnal Green and Kentish Town, ready for a fresh assault on the West End.[34]

The 8 February riots breached the dam which the Charity Organization Society had erected against the flow of emergency relief. In the rush to pour money into the Lord Mayor's relief fund, which reached £78,000 by the end of February, the COS's warnings about encouraging beggars and loafers were brushed aside. As the grip of the COS started to weaken, new ideas on poverty and its relief began to emerge, including state, or 'collectivist', systems which were anathema to the COS. In 1883 Barnett, who had been moving further and further away from the individualist principles of the COS, began to advocate non-contributory pensions for those who had reached old age without claiming poor relief, an idea which was endorsed by Charles Booth in 1891 and widely supported in the 1890s. Although Old Age Pensions were not introduced until 1908, there were many signs of a softening attitude towards the aged poor in the 1880s and 1890s. From about 1885 the Local Government Board began to suggest that the aged inmates of workhouses be given the right to sleep in separate rooms, make and receive occasional visits, read newspapers, wear their own clothes, and enjoy a small allowance of tobacco and tea. Following a Royal Commission in 1893–5 guardians were urged to give outdoor relief to the respectable aged poor, and in 1900 this became an instruction. Since the relief was usually only about 2s a week, destitution among the aged poor remained widespread.[35]

Attitudes towards the temporarily unemployed also softened. A month after the 1886 riot, Joseph Chamberlain, President of the Local Government Board, issued a minute urging local authorities to provide non-punitive public work for the unemployed in times of emergency. Several vestries responded by setting up registries which attempted to match unemployed men with empty jobs, and London became, in the words of William Beveridge, 'a pioneer in the movement for public labour exchanges'. More significantly, the 1894 Local Government Act abolished the rate-paying qualification for guardians (already reduced to £5 in 1892), and widened the franchise, making it much easier for women and working men to become guardians. This led to a minor revival in outdoor relief for unemployed or destitute men and women after 1900, when unemployment began to rise to depression levels (over 10 per cent in the building industry) after a decade of relatively high employment. In Poplar a strong labour contingent on the Board of Guardians introduced a policy of enlightened workhouse reform and liberal outdoor relief after 1893, and the Poplar Board, notorious for its severity in the 1870s, became a by-word for open-handedness in the winter of 1904–5, when a quarter of its workforce was unemployed.[36] These changes were reinforced by the publication in the early 1890s of Charles Booth's five volumes on the London poor, which began to sweep away some of the myths and misunderstandings that had bedevilled the debate on poverty over the previous thirty years.

Booth reinforced some myths, too. He shared with many late Victorian commentators, including Canon Barnett, the socialist H. M. Hyndman, the liberal economist Alfred Marshall and William Booth, founder of the Salvation Army, the belief that there was at the bottom of London's social structure a hopelessly degraded class of casual workers and semi-paupers, which they called the residuum, the submerged tenth or (in Charles Booth's case), classes A and B. They all agreed that the residuum tended to impoverish and corrupt respectable working people, and all proposed that its members should be removed from London and confined or retrained in rural labour colonies. There were even more extreme proposals. Some imperialists favoured enforced emigration to distant colonies, and eugenicists suggested compulsory sterilization. In the aftermath of the Boer War (1899–1902), in which Britain's narrow victory prompted a critical re-examination of the problem of poverty, schemes for the compulsory elimination of the 'idle and incompetent' (perhaps a tenth of London's population) were supported by Fabian socialists (including Bernard Shaw, Sidney Webb and H. G. Wells), Liberal economists, and imperialists. Through Beveridge and Winston Churchill, at the Board of Trade, these ideas came close to becoming government policy, and might have done so if the First World War had not eliminated the problem in a different way.[37]

THE FOOD OF THE POOR

The conditions of poverty in Victorian London were much the same as those in any other nineteenth-century city. So long as its head was not a drunkard, the poor family devoted the bulk of its income to the necessities of life, rent, food, fuel, soap and candles, with very little to spare for clothing, furniture, schooling, fares or entertainment. Later in the century provident working-class families would pay a weekly premium to a Friendly Society, a local burial club or an insurance company (usually the Pruden-tial) for burial insurance, a reasonable precaution in view of the very high infant and child death rates they suffered. Most of the published examples of lower-working-class London diets contain the same basic components: bread, potatoes, meat, fish, milk, tea, sugar, beer, butter and cheese. This sounds nutritious enough, but quantities were inadequate, and quality was extremely low. Poorer families bought the worst meat from stalls or street vendors, either cheap offal, or meat that was old or diseased. From 1860, the City's Medical Officer was active against sellers of bad meat, but the trade was not halted. Canned and frozen meat from America or Australia, which was available later in the century, was very poor stuff. Large pieces of meat were only eaten for Sunday dinner, but there might be cold leftovers, or some herring, bacon or stew, mainly for father, for dinner later in the week. Breakfast and tea generally consisted of bread, with a scraping of dripping, butter or (from the 1870s) margarine and some sweet tea. Add some potatoes, greens, pickles, suet pudding and the occasional scrap of meat or fish for dinner and you have the regular diet of the poorer working-class Londoner.[38]

The effects of poverty were compounded by dishonesty among London food manufacturers and retailers, some of whom seemed ready, until the enforcement of purity laws in the 1870s, to cheat and poison their customers at every opportunity. Bread, the basis of working-class survival, was the worst of all. Small London bakers used cheap sweated labourers who put no premium on hygiene, and had a high rate of tuberculosis. Loaves might contain potato or rice flour, bran or sawdust, whitened and bound together with alum, or be sold undercooked (and therefore unsafe) to retain excess water and keep up their weight. This was not a problem for the poor alone: a *Lancet* study in the early 1850s found that every loaf sampled in London contained alum. Later in the century more effective legislation and the rise of large-scale bakers, such as the Aerated Bread Company of Camden Town, improved the quality and cut the price of bread. Beer was commonly watered down, with sugar, salt and vitriol added to restore its flavour and 'strength'. In the 1840s a pound of cheap China tea cost about 3s, two-thirds of which was tax. Between 1853 and 1890 the tea tax fell from over 2s to 4d, and this, along with growing imports of cheaper, stronger tea from India and Ceylon from the 1870s, made tea into the universal drink of the poor. There was cheating here, too. Tea could be heavily adulterated, with sand, dirt, cheap leaves and dangerous colourings and flavourings, and milk was often watered, and might carry tuberculosis.[39]

There was great improvement later in the century. Thanks to cheaper transport (especially steamships and railways), rising food production in the United States, South America, Europe, India, Australia, and all parts of the Empire, and more efficient processing and retailing, food prices fell by an average of around 30 per cent between 1870 and 1900. The price of tea, coffee, cocoa and sugar almost halved between the early 1870s and the early 1890s, and the price of a 4-pound loaf fell from 8d or 9d in the 1850s and 1860s to 5d or 6d in the 1890s. A London loaf was cheaper in 1901 than it had been in any year since 1762, and working people were more likely to eat it with butter and jam than ever before. The rising demand for meat and bacon prevented their price falling much, and eggs, alone among foodstuffs, actually rose in price. The fall in the price of most basic foods, without a corresponding fall in wages, meant that the poverty discovered by Booth in the 1890s, bad as it seemed, was almost certainly less severe than that studied by Chadwick in the 1830s or by Mayhew in the 1850s. Despite this, malnutrition was commonplace among London children at the end of the century. Surveys in the early 1890s found about 50,000 malnourished schoolchildren, around 7.5 per cent of the total, and a government committee in 1904 found that a sixth of London schoolchildren were underfed. In 1890 Booth's researcher found these children 'sitting limp and chill on the school benches', 'puny, pale-faced, scantily clad and badly shod', and twenty years later Mrs Pember Reeves found the diet of poorer children in Lambeth, whose mothers had to feed them for about 1s 8d a day, to be 'insufficient, unscientific, and utterly unsatisfactory'.[40]

CLOTHING AND HYGIENE

It was common knowledge among well-off Victorians that the London poor were scruffy, smelly and immoral. In the lowest parts of town the inhabitants no doubt deserved the epithets 'ragged' and 'unwashed' that were so commonly applied to them. In the 1860s Hippolyte Taine found the women and children in the worst streets of Shadwell 'in filthy and unseemly tatters'. But these were the lowest of the low, sensationally described. Old photographs of London street-sellers, slum-dwellers, and working people (those taken by John Thomson in the 1870s, for instance) show clothes which are shabby and functional, rather than ragged or indecent. Excellent information on the clothes worn by the poor is provided by the diaries and photographic collection of Arthur Munby, a Victorian civil servant with an unorthodox interest in labouring women. His careful descriptions of London milkwomen, maidservants and labourers in their working dress tend to temper the impression left by more sensational accounts. Two diary entries for June 1861 are fairly typical. A Bermondsey sackmaker, carrying her load of sacks across London Bridge, 'wore an old gown of nameless material, sodden with laborious sweat ... a tattered blue and white apron hung from her wide waist, and her gown, gathered up under it, showed beneath a short and very ragged petticoat, below which were a pair of strong ankles and large feet, clad in dirty white stockings and muddy masculine boots, worn and shapeless. A coarse plaid shawl fell back from her square shoulders...'. A young milkwoman in Trafalgar Square 'wore the usual plain straw bonnet, woolen shawl, and clean cotton frock', and the following April a laundress on Westminster Bridge had 'a very shabby but once fashionable bonnet, a grey shawl stained and worn, a lilac cotton frock and apron, and stout laced boots'.[41]

Working people wore second-hand clothes and shoes, perhaps passed on by an older brother or sister, or bought in one of London's many clothes markets. All the poorer districts had second-hand clothes dealers, but the centre of the trade was in Petticoat Lane (or Middlesex Street) and its surrounding streets, which had begun to take over the second-hand market from Cornhill in the seventeenth century.[42] Even cast-offs were not cheap, and Maud Pember Reeves's interesting study of the lives of working-class families in Lambeth between 1909 and 1913, *Round about a Pound a Week*, tells us that clothing was bought at 'extraordinarily distant intervals', when extra money came to hand, or need was urgent. Boots, the most expensive item, were many times repaired, and women who did not go out to work might not have any at all. Some families paid sixpence or a shilling a week into a clothing or boot club run by a local tradesman, and many women made dresses and underwear from flannelette, a cheap cotton substitute for wool.[43] Clothes announced the social class of their wearer. Charles Booth, writing in 1897, described the poorest workers, on low and irregular earnings (class B), as wearing cast-off clothes that were warm, but 'disreputable in appearance, ill-fitting and unsuitable', often showing signs of faded smartness and outdated fashion. 'This class may almost be distinguished by its deplorable boots.' Classes C and D, whose wages put them on or just below the poverty line, wore a mixture of good second-hand and cheap new clothes, and looked 'creditably dressed'. The well-paid working class, Booth's Class E, wore new clothes that were warm and serviceable, and could dress smartly on Sundays and holidays.[44]

The shortage of clean water and spare clothes, and the high cost of soap, which carried a heavy excise duty until 1853, help to explain why the London poor were known as the 'Great Unwashed'. Throughout the century doctors commented on the stench of a surgery full of working-class patients, and smell created a potent barrier between the classes. Yet it seems that women did their best to keep their families clean, in spite of the practical difficulties. The General Board of Health, reporting in 1850, claimed that working-class Londoners' washing expenses amounted to half what they paid in rent, and that labouring women spent about two days on their weekly wash. When public health campaigners tried to transmit the new 'sanitary ideal' to the poor in the 1840s, they met with a fairly ready response. Legislation in 1846 and 1847 allowed local authorities to build public baths and wash-houses subsidized from the rates, and by 1865 eight large London parishes had public baths, charging about a penny for an hour in the laundry, and the same for a bath. Demand was high. Each week between 1846 and 1848 about 900 people did their laundry, and nearly 3,000 bathed, in the new St Pancras baths. Later in the century boroughs were obliged to build baths, and by 1910 (when there were fifty London wash-houses) over 60,000 Londoners took their weekly wash, or did their laundry, in municipal baths which, with their marble floors and ornate brickwork, were monuments to civic competitiveness. But this was only

1 per cent of the population. Most working-class people washed at the kitchen sink or in the yard, and the falling price of soap, and improved domestic water supplies, did much to create a cleaner, louse-free, working population.[45]

HOUSING

One of the greatest problems for members of London's constantly growing commercial and industrial workforce was the difficulty of finding decent accommodation at a rent they could afford. Land and property in central London were expensive, and those who needed to live there had to pay a high price for doing so. Middle-class Londoners, with shorter working hours and higher salaries, could commute from suburbs where rents were lower, but the poor were trapped in the centre of town, not only by the cost of transport, but also by the nature and location of their work. The 1885 Report of the Royal Commission on the Housing of the Working-Classes explained the problem clearly:

> for a large class of labourers it is necessary to live as nearly as possible to the middle of the town, because they then command the labour market of the whole metropolis from a convenient centre. Sometimes they hear of casual work to be had at a certain place provided they are there by 6 o'clock the next morning, so they must choose a central position from which no part of the town is inaccessible. The dock labourers are a class that must be on the spot, because they have always to wait for calls that may arise at any moment. . . . The only choice a costermonger seems to have in settling his residence is either to live near the locality where he obtains a market for his goods or else near the place where he lays in his stock; hence, on the latter account, their dwellings are also found in the crowded courts round about Drury Lane, within reach of Covent Garden. Nor are there wanting instances of skilled artizans who likewise must live close to their work: for instance, there are the watchmakers of Clerkenwell, because the apparatus required in their trade is so costly that no man can afford to have the whole of it; he therefore borrows from his friends, and may have to borrow three or four times in the course of the day. Then there are the women who must take their work home, such as those who work for the city tailors; and the girls who are employed in small factories, such as those for artificial flowers.

The list of trades whose livelihoods depended on their living within easy walking distance of markets, suppliers, employers or fellow-craftsmen also included tailors, shoemakers, furniture-makers, printers, leather-workers, lightermen, ropemakers, market porters, casual labourers, and sweated workers of all types. In the suburbs, moreover, it would be harder for wives and children to find work, and food would be more expensive. Finally, there was 'the natural reluctance that is found among the poor to leave their old neighbours and form new associations'. Working-class families moved, sometimes very often, but they usually did so within a well-defined radius, to preserve their social and employment connections.[46]

So, until the tram and the workmen's train began to disperse the working population of London into cheaper suburban homes in the 1880s, the poor were forced to stay in the central districts, where the building of roads, railways, warehouses, offices and public buildings steadily reduced the amount of land available for housing. This, combined with the rising population, made the problem of overcrowding worse with each decade. Measured by the number of people per house, overcrowding increased in most inner London districts between 1841 and 1881: in Holborn the average occupancy rose from 8.4 to 10 per house, in Shoreditch from 6.6 to 8.4, in Whitechapel from 8 to 9.5, in St Pancras from 8.8 to 9.6, in St George-in-the-East from 6.9 to 8.2, and so on. Only seven of London's twenty-nine registration districts experienced a decline in occupants per house between 1851 and 1881.[47] Averages are misleading, since they may reflect the size of houses and the proportion of middle-class residents in a district, but it was clear to the 1885 Royal Commission that overcrowding was worse, and rents were higher, than ever before. In 1850 a single room in central London might cost 2s a week, and a miserable two-roomed house in Bethnal Green could be had for 3s, but by the 1880s 4s a room was usual. The 1885 Commission found that 88 per cent of poorer Londoners spent over a fifth of their incomes on rent, usually for accommodation in which decent and healthy living was impossible.[48]

To rent a whole house in London was beyond the means of all but the best-paid artisans. Working-class families rented rooms: a single room for the lower-paid, and perhaps two, or even three, for better-paid workers with large families. Thousands of London families slept, ate and lived together in small single rooms, sharing a subdivided house, and whatever sanitary facilities it might have, with several other families. The 1884–5 Royal Commission concluded that the 'single room system' and thus the 'single bed system' (with all its dark moral consequences) was the usual one for working-class families. Cheap working-class houses took many forms, and London had many examples of all of them. There were damp and airless cellars, vulnerable to the overflowing of gutters and cesspools, cheap lodging-houses, in which families paid a nightly fee to sleep alongside tramps and prostitutes, and tenement houses, built for single family occupation but rented as individual rooms.

The demand for cheap housing was growing rapidly throughout the century, but most landlords and developers were not interested in satisfying it. The best profits were made from well-off tenants, and suburban houses were built for them in abundance. Middle-class developments which failed to attract the intended tenants, or houses in districts abandoned by the well-off, were let instead to poorer tenants, fell into disrepair, and often became the worst slums of all. Some of the worst housing examined by the 1884–5 Royal Commission was on the Clerkenwell Estate of the Marquess of Northampton. Here, under the control of leaseholders and middlemen ('house farmers'), houses originally intended for the well-off had been subdivided into working-class tenements and fallen into decay. Campbell Road, Upper Holloway, was built in the 1860s for clerks and craftsmen, but market conditions did not favour the developers, and the whole district became unfashionable among the middle classes in the 1870s. So some of the houses, decent enough in themselves, were subdivided and let to labouring families. Better-off families who had rented whole houses realized their mistake and moved on, and the street slid a little further downwards. In 1880 a well-known lodging-house keeper, John King, opened a lodging-house in Campbell Road, and by the 1890s there were six in the street, with 251 residents. The rest of the houses were mostly let as cheap and overcrowded furnished rooms. By this time almost every family that could afford to move had left the street and its reputation as Campbell Bunk, 'the worst street in North London', was well established and well deserved.[49]

Occasionally, houses were built intentionally for working-class occupancy. In Somers Town (the Euston and St Pancras area) and Portland Town, on the north-west corner of Regent's Park, for instance, builders took advantage of loosely drawn leases to create incongruous slum districts alongside affluent neighbourhoods. In the Sultan Street area of Camberwell, sandwiched between a railway line and a linoleum factory, developers in the 1860s built cheap and cramped six-roomed houses, which soon became Camberwell's worst slums. Working-class housing was built on a very large scale in the East End. Early in the century, when dock construction ensured that a growing workforce would be tied to the East End, speculative builders recognized the nature of their market, and built hundreds of terraces of cheap two-storey houses. Even these proved to be beyond the means of working-class families, and they were generally rented room by room. In Bethnal Green the two-roomed houses built in the 1820s for silk weavers had been subdivided by 1848 into single-room dwellings for labourers' and weavers' families, sleeping from four to nine in a room of about ten feet square.[50] Developers tried to establish middle-class districts in the East End, but these were almost certain to fall, sooner or later, into working-class multi-occupancy.

In theory, builders were bound by the 1774 London Building Act, which established structural requirements for four standard types of house, from the 'First Rate' to the 'Fourth Rate'. In 1844 the Metropolitan Building Act established standards for street and alley widths, room heights, back-yard dimensions, foundations and building materials, and the 1855 Metropolis Local Management Act added controls on drainage and other sanitary issues. Public health legislation from the 1840s onwards gave the City, the Metropolitan Board of Works and the parishes powers to inspect, control and even demolish houses that were 'unfit for human habitation'. But in most districts, for most of the century, enforcement was lax, and builders were driven by economic realities and the rents their tenants would be able to pay. The 1884–5 Royal Commission found that only Hackney and Chelsea vestries had taken their inspection and enforcement powers under the 1866 Sanitary Act seriously. In Clerkenwell, at the other extreme, committees were dominated by men with property interests who blocked the implementation of the Act. Typical working-class houses were squashed into the smallest possible plots, perhaps built back-to-back, with thin walls of cheap bricks and poor-quality mortar, floorboards or flag-stones laid on damp soil, badly made and leaky roofs, and small and ill-fitting windows. Old houses, often poorly built in the first place, had deteriorated through age and neglect, and most new ones (the 1884–5 Royal Commission said) were 'rotten from the first'. When developers built housing of a higher standard, as the charitable housing trusts and the London County Council did later in the century, they were forced to set rents which the poor could not afford to pay.[51]

In the early nineteenth century there were other British cities with housing conditions that were as bad as London's, but in nearly all of them there was improvement as the century went on, especially through building on the edge of town. London's high rents and intense competition for inner-city land, the vast extent of its slum areas, the remoteness of its undeveloped fringes, and the inability of its building industry to respond to rising demand, made its problem unique. In 1865 Dr Julian Hunter, who had been commissioned by John Simon to investigate housing conditions in over fifty British towns, found that parts of London, along with Bristol, Merthyr, Newcastle, Plymouth and Sunderland, had the worst slums in the country. 'There are about 20 large colonies in London, of about 10,000 persons each, whose miserable condition exceeds almost anything he had seen elsewhere in England,' he reported. The state of these slums was 'much worse than was the case twenty years ago'. Forty years later, an official enquiry found that over 22 per cent of Londoners lived in one or two rooms, compared with under 5 per cent in Manchester, Birmingham, Nottingham and Sheffield. Eighty per cent of the populations of Birmingham, Bristol, Leeds, Manchester, Nottingham and Sheffield lived in flats or houses of four rooms or more, compared with 61 per cent of Londoners. Only the north-eastern towns of Gateshead, Newcastle and Jarrow were in a worse state. In general it was London's housing problem that caused greatest concern, and which set the pace of national legislation from the 1860s onwards.[52]

THE FEAR OF ROOKERIES

Public interest in the housing problem generally related slums to the other prevailing concerns of the day. In the 1830s and 1840s slum areas were identified as the breeding-grounds of cholera and fever, and investigators concentrated on the state of their streets and drains. This was the focus of the studies of Chadwick and Drs Kay, Arnott and Southwood-Smith, and of Dr Hector Gavin's *Sanitary Ramblings* in Bethnal Green, which appeared in 1848. Dr Gavin rambled in a world of overflowing privies, stagnant pools, slimy mud, unburied corpses, pig sties, dung heaps and fever cases. His interest in overcrowding centred on the length of time the occupants of a room could sleep in it before being killed by their own 'poisonous exhalations'.[53] The earliest legislation to control overcrowded and unfit houses in London, the City Sewers Acts of 1848 and 1851, which gave the City the power to enforce the cleansing of foul houses and to demolish houses deemed dangerous or unfit for habitation, emerged from the public health movement. The emphasis on overcrowding as a source of disease also permeated the 1866 Sanitary Act and the Torrens Act of 1868, which extended these powers to all local authorities.[54]

The second evil that was traced back to the slums was the problem of crime. In the Victorian imagination, crime and the criminal class were always associated with rookeries, the dense slum areas in which criminals were said to live and breed, where every lounging man was a garotter waiting for nightfall, every shabby woman was an off-duty prostitute, every urchin was a pupil in a school for pickpockets. To most Victorian commentators, rookeries were the descendants of the medieval sanctuaries and eighteenth-century Alsatias, places where criminals sought refuge from the forces of order, found crude pleasure in the company of thieves and whores, and planned their forays into the respectable world around them. Rookeries gained their reputation not because of their known levels of criminality, but because they were concentrations of poverty, especially Irish poverty, and because their layout of courtyards, narrow alleys and culs-de-sac made them impenetrable and confusing to outsiders. The people within them appeared to be a race apart, living their lives, and making their livings, in ways that strangers, not understanding them, assumed to be criminal. The fact that the worst rookeries had attracted heavy Irish settlement intensified this sense of separation, and reinforced it with feelings of racial fear and contempt.

The most feared rookeries were those in the central parts of town, conveniently placed for raids on respectable districts. The most notorious of the central rookeries was St Giles', otherwise known as The Rookery. Its evil reputation was not new. In 1751, when it was said that over a quarter of its 2,000 houses were gin shops, and that its eighty-two lodging houses harboured prostitutes and receivers, Hogarth had depicted it as a place of sin and corruption in *Gin Lane, The First Stage of Cruelty, A Harlot's Progress* and *The Idle Apprentice*. It had a large and long-established Irish population, and its tangled network of streets and alleys was perfectly designed to mystify and intimidate the stranger. It was 'one dense mass of houses, through which curved narrow tortuous lanes, from which again diverged close courts – one great mass, as if the houses had originally been one block of stone, eaten by slugs into numberless small chambers and connecting passages'.[55] The district of St Giles' extended from Great Russell Street south to Long Acre, with Drury Lane and Crown Street (now replaced by Charing Cross Road) as its east and west boundaries. Within this area there were, in 1851, 54,000 people, about one-fifth of them Irish-born, living on average almost twelve to a house. The district had sixty-nine common lodging-houses, fifteen slaughterhouses, a workhouse, a police station, and 'upwards of seventy streets, courts, and alleys, in which there is no thoroughfare, or which are approached by passages under houses'. Its population density, birth, illegitimacy and death rates, were well above the London average.[56]

Impressions of the social and moral tone of St Giles' varied, depending on the prejudices of the observer, and the audience being addressed. To

Inspector Tetterton and Superintendent Grimwood of E Division, St Giles'
in 1836 was the home of a third of London's beggars, a centre for low
lodging-houses, brothels, receiving and petty theft. To the architect Sydney
Smirke, urging its demolition in 1834, it was 'the retreat of wretchedness,
the nest of disease, and at once the nursery and sanctuary of vice'. The
journalist William Weir, writing in 1841, saw a distinction between the
southern half of St Giles', around Seven Dials, and the poorer area north
of Broad Street (St Giles' High Street), the true Rookery. Monmouth Court,
off Seven Dials, was the headquarters of James Catnach, England's most
important publisher of broadsheets and popular literature until 1838, and
stationers' and booksellers' shops, along with flower-sellers and caged song-
birds, gave the nearby streets a lively and picturesque atmosphere. North
of St Giles' High Street, in contrast, there was a district of 'utter apathy and
moral deadness'. 'The men lean against the wall or lounge listlessly about,
sometimes with pipes in their mouths. In this region there are no birds or
flowers at window or on wall, the inmates can scarcely muster sufficient
liveliness to exchange words.... Shops are almost unknown – in the
interior of the district quite unknown.' If there were wild revels here at
night, the local residents did not join in them.[57]

The ambiguity of St Giles', its juxtaposition of desolate poverty and
human resilience, of idleness and vigorous activity, along with its labyrinthine street pattern, gave it a special fascination for the young Charles
Dickens. His friend and biographer, John Forster, recalled that Dickens
'had a profound attraction of repulsion to St Giles'. If he could only induce
whomsoever took him out to take him through Seven-dials, he was
supremely happy. "Good Heaven!" he would exclaim, "what wild visions of
prodigies of wickedness, want, and beggary, arose in my mind out of that
place!"'

> Wretched houses with broken windows patched with rags and paper;
> every room let out to a different family, and in many instances to two
> or even three – fruit and 'sweetstuff' manufacturers in the cellars,
> barbers and red-herring vendors in the front parlours, cobblers in the
> back; a bird-fancier in the first floor, three families on the second,
> starvation in the attics, Irishmen in the passage, a 'musician' in the
> front kitchen, a charwoman and five hungry children in the back one
> – filth everywhere – a gutter before the houses, and a drain behind –
> clothes drying, and slops emptying from the windows; ... men and
> women, in every variety of scanty and dirty apparel, lounging, scolding,
> drinking, smoking, squabbling, fighting, and swearing.[58]

Saffron Hill, a district of lodging-houses and blind alleys between Clerkenwell Green and Smithfield, ranked second to St Giles' in notoriety. An Italian colony developed here in the 1840s, but to readers of *Oliver Twist*, which appeared in monthly instalments in 1837, Saffron Hill was the home of Fagin and the Artful Dodger, a refuge of thieves, who were supposed to use trap-doors, interconnecting cellars and the Fleet Ditch to evade the police. *Oliver Twist*, in which the London locations are described with precision, also introduced its readers to the slums of Whitechapel and Bethnal Green, where the housebreaker Bill Sikes lived, and of Jacob's Island, the riverside district of Bermondsey, east of St Saviour's Dock, in which Sikes was cornered and died. This, Dickens told his readers, was 'the filthiest, the strangest, the most extraordinary of the many localities that are hidden in London, wholly unknown, even by name, to the great mass of its inhabitants'. It was an area of about 8 acres, surrounded by a foul ditch, a 'Venice of drains', where wooden houses were built on piles, ramshackle galleries overhung the Thames, and flimsy bridges connected one slum with another. Within the tottering houses were 'rooms so small, so filthy, so confined, that the air would seem too tainted even for the dirt and squalor which they shelter; wooden chambers thrusting themselves out above the mud, and threatening to fall into it – as some have done; dirt-besmeared walls and decaying foundations; every repulsive lineament of poverty, every loathsome indication of filth, rot, and garbage; – all these ornament the banks of Folly Ditch'.[59] The worst Southwark rookery, the old Mint, where thieves and debtors had taken refuge since the Middle Ages, had been tamed in the 1840s by intensive policing, so that Dickens found it in 1851 'infinitely quieter and more subdued' than it had been when he visited his father in the Marshalsea Debtors' Prison in the 1820s.[60]

Observers readily associated the rookeries with criminality, but it is doubtful whether these areas deserved their frightening reputations. In August 1840 Superintendent Maisey of the Metropolitan Police was asked to report on crime in the Saffron Hill liberty. In the previous seven months, he said, twenty-seven thefts had been reported, involving property worth £37. This amounts to one reported theft a week in one of London's poorest and most notorious rookeries. In May 1845 a similar report covered six months in the life of the area between Tooley Street and Bermondsey Street, a poor district only a stone's throw from Jacob's Island. Here, there had been twenty-two reported thefts, mostly of clothes and household objects, with a total value of about £50. Of course, true losses were much higher, but reported losses for the whole Metropolitan Police District of about £36,000 a year in the late 1840s, a third of the value of property reported lost through fire, hardly justified the high level of public anxiety over rookeries and the criminal classes.[61]

SLUM DEMOLITION

To nineteenth-century planners and politicians, by far the most effective way to deal with the rookeries was to demolish them and allow their diseased and criminal occupants to disperse harmlessly into the great metropolis. John Simon's proposed solution to the City's slum problem in the 1840s was large-scale clearance, and most of the legislation produced under his influence from the 1840s to the 1860s continued to promote demolition as the answer to bad housing. Providentially, London's urgent need for new roads, railways, docks and public and private buildings offered ample opportunities for putting this policy into practice. When select committees considered proposals for new roads in the 1830s and 1840s they placed almost as much emphasis on their impact on London's health and morals as they did on their value to the transport network. If Farringdon Road, New Oxford Street, Commercial Road, Victoria Street or Cannon Street would destroy 'congregations of vice and misery', all the more reason for going ahead with them. Most prospective developers found this argument convenient, even though their prime motives were more selfish. Slum land was cheaper, slum landlords were easy to deal with, and slum tenants could not effectively resist their eviction, although they sometimes tried to put up a struggle. Even when the Metropolitan Board of Works, which was responsible for major road building between 1855 and 1888, was given an obligation to rehouse the evicted in 1877 it was easy enough to avoid this duty by paying each tenant a pound or two to move out.[62]

The combined effect of all these building schemes on the inhabitants of central London was enormous. The clearance of just 23 acres of densely populated land east of the Tower for St Katharine's Dock in 1827 meant the eviction of 11,300 people, mostly without compensation. Railway building involved the demolition of 800 acres of central London, with destruction concentrated in heavily populated working-class districts such as Somers Town, Agar Town, Bermondsey, Lambeth, Shoreditch, Westminster and the City. The numbers evicted for railways were not recorded until 1853, but Kellett estimates that at least 120,000 lost their homes between 1840 and 1900, almost a third of them in the 1860s. By 1856, most of the older inner-London rookeries had been demolished or, as the

Victorians liked to say, 'opened up' by new roads. St Giles' was bisected by New Oxford Street in 1846–7, part of the Saffron Hill district had been cleared for the building of Farringdon Road on top of the Fleet Ditch in 1845–6, Victoria Street penetrated the Pye Street rookery, 100 yards from Westminster Abbey, in the 1850s, and Commercial Street cut a path through Whitechapel and Spitalfields. There was also extensive slum clearance in the City, much of it for street widening or new roads. The pace of road building increased later in the century, with Shaftesbury Avenue, Charing Cross Road, Queen Victoria Street, Clerkenwell Road and Holborn Viaduct doing the most damage to working-class housing. It has been estimated by Stedman Jones that new roads led to the eviction of almost 100,000 people between 1830 and 1880.[63]

In the course of the century, and especially after 1850, the City was transformed from a densely peopled district into a world of banks, insurance offices and warehouses. Its population of nearly 129,000 (193 per acre), almost a seventh of London's total, in 1801, remained almost static until 1851. Then, in successive decades, its population fell to 113,000, 75,000, and, in 1881, 51,000. By 1901 the City had only 27,000 night-time residents, and by 1911 the number had fallen below 20,000.[64] The inexorable rise of banking and insurance and the growing need for warehouses to service London's enormous trade drove up City land prices, and left no room for sentiment about the destruction of housing, pictur-esque frontages, or even of the finest and most historic buildings. It has been estimated that about 80 per cent of City buildings were demolished and rebuilt between 1855 and 1905, increasing office space from around 50 million to 75 million square feet.[65] It was not just housing that disappeared. Twenty-three City churches, eighteen of them by Wren, were demolished to make way for development between 1830 and 1901. The great City streets, Cheapside, Lombard Street, Cornhill, Fenchurch Street, lost their late Stuart and Georgian appearance, and were lined instead with new offices built in a variety of classical, Renaissance, Baroque and Gothic styles. The whole of central London seemed to going the same way. 'More real ruin has been done to old London within my own memory than in the two centuries which preceded it,' Frederic Harrison wrote in 1884.

> Bit by bit the old London sinks before our eyes into the gulf of modern improvement.... We who have lived to see the remnants of St Stephen's carted away, and a mammoth caravanserai take the place of Northumberland House ... we who have seen the tavern dear to Shakespeare and Ben Jonson disappear, and the houses of Milton go

and leave not a wrack behind; who have seen the 'Tabard' and the 'George' disappear, and the Savoy and the Watergate swallowed up in the torrent – we must brace ourselves up for the rest. Villas will soon cover the site of Holland House. The Temple will be wanted for a new restaurant.[66]

None of the other London registration districts lost its residents as rapidly as the City, but Finsbury, Holborn, Westminster and St Marylebone all experienced heavy population loss between 1861 and 1911, amounting, in these four boroughs, to 230,000 people, over a third of their population. Much of this loss was the result of demolition and eviction. In Holborn and the Strand, for instance, about 6,000 tenants from thirty filthy courts and alleys between Bell Yard and Clement's Lane were evicted in the late 1860s to make way for the Law Courts, and thousands more were cleared out for the construction of the Holborn Viaduct. Between 1861 and 1881 the Strand district lost 15,000 residents, nearly a third of its population. Population loss in Shoreditch was much slower, but most central boroughs (Islington, Lambeth, Bermondsey, Poplar, St Pancras, Stepney, Southwark) started losing their inhabitants quite quickly after 1891 or 1901. Much of this loss, though, was the result of transport improvements and the free decisions of many working-class families to seek better accommodation in the suburbs, rather than enforced migration.[67]

Where did those who had lived, or would have lived, in the demolished houses go? Merchants and professionals could move to places such as Bayswater and St John's Wood, and clerks could choose Kentish Town, Peckham, or any of the cheaper suburbs. But poor slum-dwellers, as many perceptive observers began to realize, could not go so far. The 1846 Royal Commission on Metropolis Railway Termini was strongly influenced by several witnesses who argued that displaced slum-dwellers simply crowded into neighbouring areas, making conditions there much worse. Charles Pearson, the City Solicitor, anticipated the findings of the 1885 Royal Commission: 'A poor man is chained to the spot; he has not the leisure to walk, and he has not the money to ride. They are crowded together still more ...' This view was supported by a report by a committee of the London Statistical Society in March 1848, which showed how Church Lane, one of the streets that survived the building of New Oxford Street through northern St Giles' in 1844–7, had been invaded by refugees from demolished slums. The committee found 463 people living in twelve houses, and it seemed that the total population of Church Lane's twenty-eight houses had risen from 655 to around 1095 between 1841 and 1847.[68] By the 1860s it was clear to many Medical Officers that slum demolition inevitably put pressure on surrounding neighbourhoods. Displaced families, the Strand's Medical Officer reported in 1865, 'merely migrate to the nearest courts and streets, and then provide themselves with homes, by converting the house, up to this time occupied by a single family, into one tenanted by nearly as many families as the rooms which it contains'.[69]

HOUSING THE POOR

Parish vestries could protect themselves against an invasion of displaced families, and reduce their own slum population, by using the powers against overcrowding contained in the 1855 Nuisances Removal Act and the 1866 Sanitary Act, but the London authorities did not gain clear demolition powers until the passing of the Artisans' and Labourers' Dwellings Act (the Torrens Act) in 1868. Medical Officers, who saw slums as repositories of disease, crime and immorality, were often keen to use these powers, but their masters in the vestries were not. Vestrymen were ratepayers, answerable to fellow-ratepayers, and economy almost always took precedence over other considerations. Only the City and Holborn used the Torrens Act to any extent, and most parishes virtually ignored it altogether.[70] The failure of the vestries led to pressure for responsibility to be transferred to a more active agency. In 1874 the Charity Organization Society, usually so hostile to state interference, petitioned for new housing powers to be given to the City and the Metropolitan Board of Works, and their call was supported by the Royal College of Physicians, the British Medical Association, and Sir Sydney Waterlow, chairman of the Improved Industrial Dwellings Company. These petitions helped to shape the bill introduced in 1875 by Disraeli's Home Secretary, Sir Richard Cross. Cross's Artisans' and Labourers' Dwellings Improvement Act did not sanction local authority house-building, other than in exceptional circumstances, but it did allow the City Commissioners of Sewers and the Metropolitan Board to demolish insanitary housing and sell the cleared land to societies or individuals (primarily the model dwellings companies) who had to provide accommodation for as many working people as had been evicted from the original houses.[71]

   This policy was made possible by the emergence after 1840 of a powerful group of housing charities in London, the so-called model dwellings companies. These companies raised money by appealing simultaneously to the charitable and business impulses of well-off Victorians by offering them a 5 per cent return on their investment in housing for the deserving poor. Of the thirty or more companies operating in London in the 1870s the oldest was the Metropolitan Association for Improving the Dwellings of the Industrious Classes, which was founded in 1841. By 1875, when its energies were flagging, the Metropolitan Association had tenement blocks in several of London's poorer districts, housing around 6,000 people at high but not unhealthy densities. It was easily outstripped by Sir Sydney Waterlow's Improved Industrial Dwellings Company (founded in 1863), which had spent over £1 million and housed 30,000 people by 1900, and the builder William Austin's Artisans', Labourers' and General Dwellings Company (founded in 1867), which had 6,400 flats and 42,000 residents at the end of the century. New trusts continued to be founded up to the First World War: the East End Dwellings Company (1884), Lord Rothschild's Four Per Cent Dwellings Company (1885) for Jewish artisans and labourers, the Guinness Trust (1889), the Lewis Trust (1906) and the Sutton Trust (1907). The famous Peabody Trust, founded in 1862, was a little different from the others, since most of its money came from an American banker, George Peabody, whose interest in the London poor had been aroused by Lord Shaftesbury. It was therefore free from the obligation of paying 5 per cent dividends, and was able to undercut the rents charged by the other companies by about a quarter. This, the secretary of the Metropolitan Association complained in 1881, allowed tenants to take advantage of a competitive market in model dwellings, and prevented other companies from making improvements and putting up their rents.[72]

Most model dwellings companies had rents and rules which excluded tenants on low or irregular wages, and people of immoral habits. The Metropolitan Association's supervisors were skilled in spotting 'drunkards, brawlers, prostitutes, receivers of stolen goods, and other bad characters'. The companies' aim was to rescue respectable working families, especially those of the artisan class, from harmful association with the lowest of the poor, and ' by lifting them up to leave more room for the second and third [class] who are below them'.[73] The Peabody Trust drew its tenants from further down the social scale, since its rents were lower and it had been instructed by its benefactor to spend his money on the poor of London 'in the ordinary sense of the word'. They took this to mean the employed, respectable and industrious poor, rather than the destitute: in 1891 more than a half of the Trust's 5,000 rent-payers were labourers, porters, needlewomen, charwomen, carmen, constables, warehousemen or printers. Its rules were strict and paternalistic, but perhaps necessary for harmonious tenement living: tenants had to be vaccinated against smallpox and take their turn in cleaning the passages and lavatories; they could not sublet, take in lodgers or run a shop; they could not keep dogs, throw refuse out of their windows, or let their children play on the stairs.[74]

The model dwellings companies built as cheaply and decently as they could, and although the grim ugliness of the model tenements was often criticized, the buildings were generally dry, clean and healthy, and offered working men a chance to live close to their work at a reasonable rent. Jerry White's study of Rothschild Buildings in Spitalfields, based on the recollections of sixteen people who lived in them in the early twentieth century, suggests that the strongest criticism of the blocks came from those who saw them from outside, rather than those who occupied them. These drab and functional blocks were built for Jewish immigrants by the Four Per Cent Dwellings Company in 1887 on land cleared by the demolition of part of the notorious Flower and Dean Street rookery. They housed over 200 families, about 1,000 people in all, in relatively healthy conditions, though there were bed bugs and the flats were overcrowded. Critics believed that family life, a spirit of community and a sense of individual worth could not flourish in these barrack-like blocks, but White's researches show that this was far from the truth. A strong sense of community and mutual support developed in Rothschild Buildings, and the tenement rules, which look so forbidding on paper, were generally enforced by the tenants themselves in the interests of safe and orderly communal living:

> After that first and crucial decision about who could have a flat and who could not, the people of Rothschild Buildings were largely on their own. The myth of an all-powerful rooting system of 'rebuke and repression' which kept the people orderly owed more to bourgeois prejudice than to reality ... the community life which centred on the landings of Rothschild Buildings was friendly and vibrant. 'At Rothschild, we were like one family' is a frequently heard description of the relationship between neighbours.[75]

White gives an excellent picture of tenement life from the inside (which is what really mattered), but he does not claim that his account is representative of life in all model dwellings. Rothschild Buildings were considered to be among the best of their kind, and the Jewish immigrants who lived in them probably had a closer communal bond than tenants in other blocks. George Arkell and Octavia Hill, writing in Booth's *Life and Labour of the People in London*, brought out the great variation between the best and worst blocks in their design, sanitation and social tone. Arkell doubted whether tenements built at a price that poorer working-class families could afford would ever achieve acceptable sanitary standards, and Hill (bringing her distinctive experience as an improver and manager of small-scale working-class housing to the discussion) argued that 'untrained' people of the lowest class could not meet the demanding standards of behaviour required by tenement living:

> For the strong and self-contained and self-reliant it may be all right, but the instinct of the others who cling on to smaller houses is right for them. . . . People become brutal in large numbers who are gentle when they are in smaller groups and know one another, and the life in a block only becomes possible when there is a deliberate isolation of the family, and a sense of duty with respect to all that is in common. The low-class people herd on the staircases and corrupt one another, where those a little higher would withdraw into their little sanctum. But in their own little house, or as lodgers in a small house, the lower class people get the individual feeling and notice which often trains them in humanity.[76]

The philanthropic housing companies learned by experience that it was not easy to make a success of tenements in the poorest parts of London, where poverty and housing need were greatest. The sites the housing companies wanted, whether from the Metropolitan Board of Works or such private benefactors as the Duke of Westminster, were in Finsbury and Westminster, where there were plenty of tenants able and willing to pay 6s or 7s a week, not in the East End, where flats remained empty and rents were often unpaid. Only 2 per cent of the population in Tower Hamlets, and 2.8 per cent in Southwark, lived in charity tenements in 1891, compared with 8 per cent in Westminster. Several slum clearance sites in Wapping, Shadwell, Limehouse and Deptford were rejected by housing charities in the 1870s and 1880s, and remained undeveloped until the LCC took them on. The LCC, which was looking for just the same tenants as the housing charities, found the same problems of rent arrears and unlet flats in its East End estates as the philanthropists had. Over 4 per cent of the County of London's population (189,000 people) lived in philanthropic housing blocks in 1891, and this clearly made a significant contribution to the housing of the artisan class. But the charities did not provide much housing for the mass of poorer Londoners, and the demolitions which they encouraged and depended upon probably intensified the housing problems of the really poor. The 1884–5 Royal Commission was convinced that the really poor, including those evicted in the demolition schemes undertaken to satisfy the Peabody Trust's need for land, did not find places in the Peabody Buildings, and that preference was given to respectable artisans and families with more than one income. Even Octavia Hill, whose efforts on behalf of poor slum-dwellers made her a Victorian heroine, only had about 3,000 people living under her care at the time of her death in 1912.[77]

The Metropolitan Board acted vigorously between 1875 and 1877, buying and demolishing some of London's most notorious slum property, including large sites in Whitechapel (Flower and Dean Street), St Luke's (Whitecross Street), Westminster (Old Pye Street and Great Peter Street) and St Giles' (Great Wild Street). In all, it bought sixteen slum sites, comprising 42 acres, mostly in Stepney, Finsbury and Islington, for £1,660,000, and sold most of them to housing charities (especially Peabody and the Improved Industrial Dwellings Company) for about £330,000. This left the Board with a much greater loss than it had expected, and because of this few new schemes were begun after 1877. The main beneficiaries from the Act were slum landlords like Thomas Flight, owner of 18,000 houses in St Giles', Leather Lane, Bermondsey and elsewhere. Such men were generously compensated at the ratepayers' expense, while their tenants were left homeless and destitute. Even if new housing was built at once, which was rarely the case, it was offered at rents which the displaced slum-dwellers were unable to afford, and with tenancy conditions they could not meet. Most of the 22,868 evicted from the sites seem to have been costermongers, laundresses, home-workers, prostitutes, casual labourers, dockers, paupers and hawkers, whose irregular incomes or home-based work made them ineligible for places in the new tenements. The new tenants, over 27,000 in all, were more likely to be artisans, porters, policemen or well-paid labourers. The housing charities which took over the cleared sites did not provide cheap one-roomed apartments, except for widows, and did not like their tenants keeping sewing machines, mangles, donkeys, barrows, or other tools of trade. The rent for a decent two-roomed flat, 6s or more, was beyond the reach of people who had lived until then in single rooms for around 3s a week.

The idea that evicted slum-dwellers would move to the suburbs, where houses stood empty, or take over the property left empty by the better-off when they moved into charity tenements (a process known as 'levelling up'), quickly proved to be unrealistic. Evicted tenants, tied by work, long hours and high fares, moved to the nearest cheap room they could find, not to the leafy suburbs. The experience of the old woman who spoke to the Royal Commission on the Housing of the Working Classes in 1885 was not unusual: 'I came to London twenty-five years ago, and I've never lived in any room for more than two years yet: they always say they want to pull down the house to build dwellings for poor people, but I've never got into one yet.'[78] The amendment of the Cross Act in 1882, following sustained pressure from the Metropolitan Board of Works, remedied its financial inadequacies but not its social ones. The new Artizans' Dwellings Act reduced compensation for slum landlords and halved the amount of new housing the Board was compelled to provide, allowing it to sell some of the cleared land for commercial use and to shift some of its rebuilding efforts to cheaper suburban sites.

THE HOUSING SCANDAL OF THE 1880S

In the 1880s public concern over London's poor housing transformed what had until then been a political side-issue into a question of national significance. The underlying reason for this was the clear failure of the Torrens and Cross Acts, and of the vestries, the Metropolitan Board and the housing charities, to cope with London's population growth, and to prevent overcrowding from getting steadily worse. Medical Officers, who had generally favoured demolition in the 1860s and 1870s, now argued increasingly that destroying slums without replacing them with affordable alternatives made the housing problem worse. In 1883 a succession of sensational pamphlets and newspaper articles on the London slums was published. George Sims started the bandwagon in June 1883 with a series of illustrated articles for the *Pictorial World*, entitled 'How the Poor Live'. Sims, a popular journalist and playwright with radical leanings, wrote as an explorer, taking his comfortable readers on a disturbing journey into 'a dark continent that is within easy walking distance of the General Post Office', and reminding them that 'wild races' at home needed their support just as much as 'savage tribes' overseas. Sims's aim was to bring knowledge of the evils of overcrowding 'to a world of readers outside the hitherto narrow circle of philanthropists', using a combination of wit, anecdote and descriptive power to maintain his audience's interest in what was in many ways a monotonous and miserable subject. To the usual accounts of physical squalor and suffering he added brief references to 'nameless abominations' fit only for the pages of the *Lancet*, and a warning that thoughtless slum clearance had forced the honest poor 'to come and herd with thieves and wantons, to bring up their children in the last Alsatias, where lawlessness still reigns supreme'. Sims's final message was that charity alone could not solve the problem, but that state action was needed. He called for the 'immediate erection on cleared spaces of tenements suitable to the classes dislodged', enforcement of decent standards of sanitation and spaciousness, cheap tram or rail fares to encourage decentralization, and sheds and stables for costermongers to store their goods and their donkeys. But although Sims wrote with wit and intelligence, and although his message was repeated in November to the wider readership of the *Daily News* in a series called 'Horrible London', his work seems to have had little impact.[79]

It was left to a lesser writer, and a more sensational and lurid pamphlet, to create the stir that Sims had hoped for. The influence of *The Bitter Cry of Outcast London*, a twenty-page penny pamphlet published in October 1883, and mostly written by the Reverend Andrew Mearns, Secretary of the London Congregational Union, was out of all proportion to the quality of its research or argument. What gave *The Bitter Cry* its impact was its powerful title, its brevity, its forceful language, its honest first-hand observation, its outspoken references to sex and crime, and the evangelical intensity of its call for action. Most important of all, perhaps, was the fact that the pamphlet was at once reprinted, without its more tedious religious passages, in the popular *Pall Mall Gazette*, whose editor, W. T. Stead, one of the greatest publicists of his day, gave much tighter definition to Mearns's vague call for legislation. Mearns described the stench and filth of courts and alleys, the determination of many slum-dwellers to earn a livelihood even when they were in the last stages of physical decline, and, in his most famous passage, the disastrous moral consequences of slum life:

> One of the saddest results of this overcrowding is the inevitable association of honest people with criminals. Often is the family of an honest working man compelled to take refuge in a thieves' kitchen ... Who can wonder that every evil flourishes in such hotbeds of vice and disease? ... Ask if the men and women living together in these rookeries are married, and your simplicity will cause a smile. Nobody knows. Nobody cares. ... Incest is common; and no form of vice or sensuality causes surprise or attracts attention. ... The low parts of London are the sink into which the filthy and abominable from all parts of the country seem to flow.[80]

The Bitter Cry of Outcast London started an avalanche of public comment, first in the correspondence columns of the *Pall Mall Gazette*, then in the *Daily News*, *Reynolds' Newspaper*, the *Daily Telegraph*, in pulpits, and in public meetings. There was talk of bad housing leading to popular unrest, or even the rise of socialism. In the winter of 1883–4, almost every serious periodical and review devoted articles to the London housing crisis, and influential figures, including Joseph Chamberlain and Lord Salisbury, both of whom saw political advantages in a housing campaign, debated the merits of private and state provision. Even the royal family took up the issue. The Prince of Wales visited St Pancras and Soho and spoke in the Lords, and the Queen urged a reluctant Gladstone to order an enquiry. In March 1884, after a powerful speech by the Conservative leader, Lord Salisbury, a Royal Commission on the Housing of the Working Classes was established. This was no time-wasting device, but one of the most powerful and effective commissions of the century. Its membership included Salisbury, the leading radical politician Sir Charles Dilke, the minister and financier George Goschen, the MP and trade unionist Henry Broadhurst, Torrens, Cross, and George Godwin of the *Builder*. The inclusion of two Churchmen, Cardinal Manning and the Bishop of Bedford, and the omission of doctors from the Commission, symbolized the fact that overcrowding was now seen as a moral rather than sanitary problem. The Commission's scope was national, but it concentrated heavily on the most overcrowded parts of London (Clerkenwell, St Luke's, Holborn, Bermondsey, Whitechapel, Southwark and Notting Hill), and questioned Mearns, Sims, Shaftesbury, civil servants, medical officers, vestry clerks, clergymen and school inspectors (over 100 witnesses in all) to find out why the problem had not yielded to the efforts of the housing charities and the demolition men. Slum-dwellers themselves were not asked for their views. It discovered what many already knew, that the problem of overcrowding and high rents was worse than ever in London, and that artisans and respectable working families, as well as the very poor, were exposed to the moral and physical corruptions of slum living. It established also that the policies and agencies relied upon hitherto were a failure: slum clearance under the Torrens and Cross Acts had intensified overcrowding, charity blocks did not make a significant contribution to the needs of the poorest classes, the London vestries (particularly the Clerkenwell vestry) were incapable of effective action, and suburban housing was not a practical alternative for a large section of London's workforce.[81]

MUNICIPAL HOUSING

Although some regarded the Commission's report in 1885, and the Housing of the Working Classes Act which quickly followed it, as dangerously socialistic, in reality the report covered familiar ground, and the 1885 Act took only the most timid of steps towards subsidized municipal housing. Powers given to local authorities by the ineffective 1851 Lodging Houses Act, which allowed them to borrow money from the Public Works Loan Commissioners to build houses, were revived, expanded and placed in the hands of the Metropolitan Board of Works. The process was made cheaper by a reduction in interest rates and compensation costs, and by the government's proposed sale to the Board of prison land at Millbank, Pentonville and Cold Bath Fields, but tenants would still be asked to pay rents which reflected the full cost of the building. The Act lacked the element of compulsion which public health legislation had acquired in 1866, and house-building remained a power, rather than a duty, for local authorities until 1919. The full impact of the Act was delayed, therefore, until 1889, when the Metropolitan Board, which had lost interest in housing schemes, was replaced as London's central government by the London County Council (LCC), whose Progressive (radical Liberal) majority was committed to a vigorous housing policy. The LCC's powers were broadened and clarified by a new Housing of the Working Classes Act in 1890, enabling it to buy and demolish insanitary housing and build new housing of its own, on condition that it rehoused those evicted nearby, and that its houses would be sold off (unless exception was granted) within ten years. London was thus given housing powers which Liverpool had enjoyed since 1869, and Glasgow since the 1880s.[82]

Between 1890 and 1914 the LCC completed six schemes inherited from the Metropolitan Board, and began its own clearance and rebuilding programme, involving the demolition of 58 acres of slums, and the construction of 12,444 rooms, mostly in two- or three-roomed flats in five-storey blocks, in central London. The LCC's building programme was not confined to replacing demolished slums. From 1900 it began to buy land and build upon it, both in the central area and in the suburbs, which the 1883 Cheap Trains Act and the growth of tram services had made more accessible to the working class. By 1914 there were large LCC estates in Tooting (4,496 rooms), Hammersmith (1,079 rooms), Croydon (1,790 rooms), White Hart Lane, Tottenham (3,444 rooms), and smaller estates in Brixton, Islington and Deptford. Most of these were pleasant 'cottage' estates, designed under the influence of William Morris, Norman Shaw and the Arts and Crafts Movement. In all, the LCC built about 30,000 rooms between 1890 and 1914, nearly a third of the number that had been built by the housing trusts and model dwellings companies since the 1840s.[83]

This was a triumph of municipal enterprise, and the beginning of a

new era in which working people could live in decent suburban accommodation without dependence on private charity. But the tenants evicted for
LCC schemes faced exactly the same predicament as before: decent housing
was not cheap to build, and since LCC buildings had higher standards of
design, materials and space than private or charitable housing, they cost
more to build, and more to rent. This placed them beyond the reach of the
lowest paid, and ensured that clerks, policemen, postmen, salesmen,
engineers and skilled craftsmen would rank high in the list of LCC tenants,
along with better-paid labourers, porters, carmen and cleaners, whilst the
poorest were harried from slum to slum.

One of the first and biggest prewar LCC estates, Boundary Street,
illustrates the difficulty of building decent homes for people on indecent
incomes. The estate occupies 13 acres in the space created by the meeting
of Hackney Road and Bethnal Green Road with Shoreditch High Street,
near enough to the City to attract tenants, but not in a district of very high
land values. This was the area known until its demolition as the Nichol, a
notorious rookery of delapidated and subdivided Georgian houses, whose
world of street gangs, petty crime and casual labour was captured by
Arthur Morrison in *A Child of the Jago* in 1896, at the very moment of its
destruction. Charles Booth described the district, giving it the pseudonym
of Summer Gardens, in one of his early volumes. It was an area of 'almost
solid poverty and low life', with women and children queuing in the cold
for soup from a mission house, and squalid rooms occupied by costermongers, sweated workers, washerwomen and casual labourers. The Nichol
was near the centre of the East London furniture industry, and all around
Booth saw carts piled with sawn boards and men carrying 'great bundles of
chair backs or legs'. When the old houses came down piecemeal in the
1890s 5,719 people were evicted, and housing for 5,500 was built. The LCC
did its best to provide workshops and places for costers' barrows in the
new estate, but 'the cost was too great, the rents too high, and, in addition,
the regulations to be observed under the new conditions, demanded more
orderliness of behaviour than suited the old residents'. Only eleven of the
old tenants were rehoused in the fine LCC blocks, radiating grandly from
the new Arnold Circus. Most of the rest moved to existing slums within a
quarter of a mile of the Nichol, with only about 5 per cent moving more
than a mile. 'Everywhere,' Booth wrote, 'these people were recognized as
coming from the "Nichol", and everywhere they have brought poverty, dirt
and disorder with them, and an increase of crowding, the rooms previously
occupied by one family having to serve for two.' The people who moved
into the new blocks were steady wage-earners, mostly from the nearby

streets, the respectable slum-dwellers whose moral welfare had so worried the Royal Commission of 1884–5. Providing decent housing for these families was valuable, but it did not, as Booth could see, solve the problem of the lowest classes.[84]

In the first years of the new century, the more radical of the twenty-eight local borough councils, which had replaced the parish vestries in 1899, became substantial house-builders in their own right. Bermondsey, St Pancras, Shoreditch and Stepney, along with the City, used powers granted by the 1890 Act to demolish slums and build twenty-seven new blocks, providing 2,089 rooms in all, and after 1900 twelve boroughs built council housing on land acquired without slum clearance. Four boroughs, Chelsea, Camberwell, Westminster and Battersea, built or renovated a total of 4,000 rooms by 1914. Chelsea, which built over 1,000 rooms on land acquired cheaply from local benefactors, provided cheaper flats with shared facilities for the low-paid, including single rooms at 3s a week, Camberwell provided 1,722 rooms in new blocks and renovated houses, and Battersea provided tenants on its two well-designed housing estates with electric lighting, kitchen ranges and larders. There were also new local council cottage estates beyond the LCC area, especially in Barking, Croydon, Ealing, East Ham, Hornsey, Richmond and West Ham. Between them the outer London boroughs provided 1,795 houses with 8,579 rooms, slightly more than those provided by the boroughs within the LCC area.

So by 1914 there were in London, including the City and the outer boroughs, over 46,000 rooms in local authority houses and blocks, about two-thirds of them built by the LCC. This was a small beginning, and still offered little to the really poor, but a standard of decent provision had been set, a system of design, construction and management had been established, which, with the help of a local subsidy or government grant, might offer a solution to the problem of working-class housing in the century ahead. The solution would be a suburban one. Within the County of London (or Inner London) demolition for public improvements, schools, streets, railways, businesses and working-class dwellings easily outran the provision of new accommodation. Between 1902 and 1910 over 50,000 rooms were lost in Inner London, while only about half that number were built by the LCC and the boroughs. The population of Inner London, which had been growing (with a few interruptions) since the Wars of the Roses, fell by 15,000 between 1901 and 1911.[85]

The movement of poorer Londoners into the LCC's cottage estates or private houses in the suburbs depended on the provision of cheap transport for the working-class commuter. In the 1880s only the Great Eastern Line, serving the increasingly overcrowded suburbs of Walthamstow, Tottenham and Edmonton, threw itself wholeheartedly into the running of workmen's trains, but cheap services on other lines had improved by the end of the century. In South London, where provision had been particularly bad, the major railway companies gradually yielded to local pressure groups, and began to run cheap trains from such places as Penge, South Croydon, Greenwich, Southfields, Plumstead, Norwood, Kennington and East Dulwich. By 1912 working men or women living within a line drawn through Clapham Junction, Herne Hill, South Bermondsey and the Surrey Docks could travel to the centre for 2d return, and those living as far out as Putney, Tooting, Crystal Palace, Catford and Greenwich could do the return journey for 4d, a sum which only the well-paid worker would wish to spend. In the hands of the LCC (as most of them were by 1900), tram services were an even more potent force for mass suburbanization. By the 1890s there were hundreds of workmen's trams offering early-morning penny fares, enabling men and women who worked in the middle of town to live in Battersea, Camberwell, Peckham, Stratford, Stoke Newington, Kentish Town, or any other cheap suburb within 5 or 6 miles of the centre. There were still plenty of workers who could not afford these fares, or who had other reasons for clinging to the centre of town, but there is no doubt that cheap fares had enormously extended the area of land available for working-class housing by 1914.

Chapter 18

Transport and Suburban Growth

TO OPERATE EFFICIENTLY, a city must have a transport system which allows the smooth and speedy passage of goods and people from one part of town to another. For London, the Thames had always provided an excellent east–west highway, interrupted only by the dangerous rapids under London Bridge. But as London spread away from the river the need for convenient road transport became more urgent, and London's old roads, narrow, twisting and ill-surfaced, became increasingly inadequate. The widening of most City roads to 14 feet or more after the Great Fire had helped accommodate the growing number of carriages and dray-carts, and the post-Fire planners had done something to create satisfactory routes through the City. But in the eighteenth century the traffic problem grew worse again, eased only a little by the laying out of the New Road in 1756–7 as a route into the City for carts, carriages and cattle. London's other east–west routes both had awkward bottlenecks. Traffic along the Oxford Street and High Holborn route had to thread its way through St Giles' High Street and Broad Street, and the Strand–Fleet Street route, which narrowed in several places, had to descend into the Fleet valley and skirt the great bulk of St Paul's before the two routes met in Cheapside. North–south routes were even worse. The New Road stopped at Finsbury Square, three-quarters of a mile from the Thames; the road north from London Bridge, Fish Street Hill, was narrow, and that north from Blackfriars Bridge was impeded by the Fleet Market. In the West End, there was no clear and wide north–south thoroughfare until the opening of Regent Street in 1823. The position south of the river was more satisfactory: Westminster and Blackfriars Bridges were served by good wide roads, although the Borough High Street, south of London Bridge, was narrow.[1]

REGENCY IMPROVEMENTS

In the absence of effective metropolitan government, many of the early nineteenth-century efforts to improve London's traffic flow came from private initiatives. Vauxhall, Waterloo and Southwark toll bridges were all projected, funded and constructed between 1809 and 1819 by commercial companies whose shareholders hoped to profit from toll-paying traffic from Lambeth, Camberwell and the rest of South London. Of the three, Vauxhall Bridge, with nine iron arches supported by ten stone piers, was the cheapest (at £300,000) and most commercially sound. It was completed in 1816 and replaced by the present bridge in 1906. John Rennie's Waterloo Bridge, whose massive and handsome granite arches and approach roads covered 800 yards at a cost of over £1 million, was never profitable, and was bought by the Metropolitan Board of Works for £475,000 in 1878. It was demolished, amidst controversy, in 1936. Southwark Bridge, also by Rennie, crossed the Thames in three iron spans, to avoid obstruction to river traffic. It was never a success, and was sold to the City Corporation for £218,000, a quarter of its original cost, in 1866. It was demolished in 1919, its centenary year. Toll bridges, even at a penny a crossing, could not prosper while three other bridges were free, and the tolls were abolished when the bridges came into public ownership. Meanwhile the ancient and increasingly unsteady London Bridge, which had been so intimately involved with London's history for over 600 years, was unsentimentally demolished and replaced in 1831–2. It had already lost its picturesque but inconvenient houses and shops between 1757 and 1762, and was regarded as an impediment to easy communications by land or water. The new five-arched bridge and its approach roads, designed by Rennie and built by his son, cost £2 million, mostly drawn from the City's Bridge House fund. It was replaced in its turn between 1968 and 1972.

The Regency years (1810–20), in which the three toll bridges and many of the docks were built, also saw the beginning of one of the greatest and most comprehensive pieces of town-planning London has ever experienced. This was the redesign of the West End by an ambitious and ageing architect, John Nash, in partnership with his patron, the Prince Regent, who hoped, like James I, to aggrandize himself by beautifying his capital. When the lease of Marylebone Park, 500 acres of farmland north of the New Road, reverted to the Crown in 1811, Nash proposed the creation of a new garden suburb there, whose beauty would draw aristocratic settlers into northern districts they had previously shunned. Nash planned a beautiful pleasure garden, with a 'Valhalla' to great Englishmen at its centre, and fifty-six noble villas scattered all around. In the end, Treasury and other pressures eliminated the monument, limited the villas to eight, and reduced the planned Circus on the New Road to a more modest semi-circle, Park Crescent. The remaining parts of the plan, including a large park (Regent's Park) surrounded by handsome (but rather hurriedly built) stucco terraces masquerading as palatial mansions, a working-class and market area east of the park, and a grand boulevard running south from Park Crescent to St James's, were completed by 1825. Nash's terraces were a sham, in which the individual houses were 'identical in their narrowness, their thin pretentiousness, their poverty of design' (Sir John Summerson), but the overall effect of the Regent's Park scheme was, and remains, impressive, standing comparison with any other urban landscape of Nash's day.[2]

Nash had a vision of royal splendour, but he was a pragmatist, too. To build Regent Street, the magnificent triumphal way from the Regent's palace on Pall Mall, Carlton House, to the new park, he had to take account of a variety of social, economic and aesthetic factors. First, Nash had to find a route which followed existing streets, ran through Crown land, or went through areas where land was cheap. Starting at Carlton House, Waterloo Place and Regent Street ran north through Crown land to Piccadilly, where an elegant Circus was formed. This lower section was of mixed use and appearance, to accommodate those businesses prepared to take sites on it. Then the street curved north-westwards through Crown land, to join and follow the narrow old road known as Swallow Street, whose southern tip survives. The curved section, the Quadrant, in which 'those who have nothing to do but walk about and amuse themselves' could do so under the shelter of a graceful colonnade, was the fashionable centrepiece of the street. Although its shape was imposed on Nash by economic necessity, he was able to use the curve to give charm and surprise to Regent Street, and these qualities have survived even the uninspired rebuilding of the 1920s and 1930s. Swallow Street marked the boundary between aristocratic estates to the west and poorer streets to the east. By following its route, Nash was able to buy cheap Soho land, avoiding costly Mayfair premises, and to establish Regent Street as 'a boundary and complete separation between the Streets and Squares occupied by the Nobility and Gentry, and the narrower Streets and meaner houses occupied by mechanics and the trading part of the community'. Regent Street acts as a frontier between these two socially contrasting districts even today. A little north of Oxford Street (where Nash created another circus) the new street swung west again, with the new church of All Souls Langham Place giving interest and harmony to the turn. Then it joined the Adam brothers' Portland Place (1774), one of London's widest and most beautiful streets, to run north to Park Crescent, Park Square and Regent's Park. The final result was, by general agreement, a work of genius, an 'amazingly successful blend of formality and picturesque opportunism' (Sir John Summerson). But today, little of Nash's design remains to the south of Park Crescent except the shape of the street. Portland Place was ruined by late-Victorian and twentieth-century commercial developers, and Regent Street, having lost its colonnade in 1848, was mostly rebuilt in the 1920s and 1930s.

While these great schemes were under construction, Nash and the Regent, who became George IV in 1820, pressed on with their transformation of the West End into a royal quarter worthy of the capital city of a triumphant empire. The new King decided to demolish Carlton House, on which a fortune had been lavished, and prevailed upon Parliament to pay for the conversion of the delapidated Buckingham House, which George III had bought in 1762, into a new and grander palace. Buckingham Palace was unfinished when George IV died in 1830, and the work, which had cost far more than expected, was taken from Nash and placed in less distinguished hands. Carlton House was replaced by Carlton House Terrace, part of Nash's aborted plan for the encirclement of St James's Park. At the same time (1827–8) Nash landscaped St James's Park, widening its canal into an ornamental lake, and making it, by general consent, central London's loveliest park.

In 1828 Nash was over seventy-five, and his career depended on the favour of an ailing monarch. His final task, before the King's death in 1830 ended his career, was to unite his new royal quarter with the political world of Westminster and the commercial world of the City. To achieve this, Nash extended Pall Mall eastwards to Charing Cross, demolished the King's Mews and the mean houses in front of St Martin-in-the-Fields, and created a huge square, Trafalgar Square, which acted (and still acts) as a fitting meeting place for Whitehall, Pall Mall and the Strand. Nash was forced into retirement in 1831, and the construction of the buildings around the square was left to others. The most important of these, the new National Gallery, was designed by William Wilkins, whose careful but humdrum effort failed to take advantage of the best site in London. Trafalgar Square itself was designed by Sir Charles Barry in 1840, and the addition of the Nelson Column in 1839–43 made the whole site a celebration of British naval power. Nash's plan for a great road running north from Trafalgar Square to Bloomsbury and Robert Smirke's new British Museum was abandoned.

New Roads

Nash's new streets and the four new bridges were the most striking improvements to London's road network before 1830, but not the only ones. The widening of the High Holborn and Fleet Street routes eased the way into the City, and the demolition of the Fleet Market in the late 1820s opened the road to Blackfriars Bridge. In a last flurry of activity before the coming of the railways, the turnpike companies opened up the outskirts of London with several new roads north of the New Road: New North Road (1812), Archway Road (1813), Caledonian Road (1826), Finchley Road (1826–35) and Albany Street–Camden Road–Seven Sisters Road (1825–34). South of the Thames, they added Waterloo Road (1823) and Southwark Bridge Road (1819) to the existing network of turnpike roads across St George's Fields. After 1826, when the London turnpike trusts north of the Thames were united under a single Metropolitan Turnpike Commission, most of their roads were cambered, drained and surfaced on principles developed by the Commission's surveyor-general, the great road-builder John McAdam. Most of London's major roads were macadamized by the 1830s, enabling them to withstand an increasingly heavy burden of cart, carriage and coach traffic. A further improvement came in 1830, when tolls and toll-gates were removed from many of London's main turnpike roads, including Oxford Street, Edgware Road, the New Road and Gray's Inn Road.[3]

The death of George IV removed the only powerful influence favouring high expenditure on fine new roads for London. Still, new roads were badly needed, especially to ease the congestion of Fleet Street and the Strand, and parliamentary select committees toyed with various proposals in the later 1830s. Four new streets were finally agreed upon, and opened in 1844–5: Cranbourn Street, extending the line of Piccadilly eastwards to Long Acre; Endell Street, joining Waterloo Bridge to Bloomsbury; New Oxford Street, ending the bottleneck on a major east–west route; and Commercial Street, which would eventually link Shoreditch High Street with Whitechapel Road and Commercial Road. None of these was a great success as a retailing street, and hopes that their cost (over £900,000) would be recovered from business rents and leases were over-optimistic. But Commercial Street and New Oxford Street became major thoroughfares, and both served the secondary purpose of cutting through and partly destroying two of London's most notorious slum districts. New Oxford Street, the 1839 Committee believed, would facilitate 'the removal of congregations of vice and misery, and the introduction of a better police' in St Giles', and Commercial Street, according to the local MP, was 'of the last moment to the happiness, comfort, health and morality' of the Wentworth Street area of Spitalfields.

The idea that problems of crime, disease, overcrowding and moral decay in London's worst rookeries could be solved by driving wide roads through them, thus opening them up to air, light, policing and public inspection, continued to influence road-building decisions, even when it was shown that the inhabitants of demolished rookeries simply moved to neighbouring slums, taking their vices and misfortunes with them. The line of Victoria Street, built in 1851, was diverted to cut through the notorious area south-west of Westminster Abbey, in the hope that the residents of Duck Lane, Tothill Street, Old Pye Street, Orchard Street and nearby alleys would disperse and bother respectable citizens no more. In the end it seems that these new roads did little to reduce crime and disease in the rookeries, and much to intensify overcrowding in the slums left standing.[4]

Traffic, as any user of the M25 knows, expands to fill the roads available for it. Rising population and the consequent growth in social, economic and administrative activity were bound to increase London's traffic flow, and congestion was intensified, in the words of Charles Pearson, by 'the vast increase in ... the migratory population, the population of the City who now oscillate between the country and the City'. Pouring into the City and West End every day came visitors, shoppers, and what we would call commuters, from London's newer suburbs and outlying villages: Lambeth, Camberwell, Clapham, Kentish Town, Belgravia, Chelsea, Islington, Hoxton, Hackney, Edmonton, Blackwall, Hammersmith and, above all, Paddington. In 1825 about 600 short-stage coaches made around 1,800 daily journeys into the City or West End, picking up their passengers at public houses along the way. They shared the roads with 1,265 licensed hackney coaches and cabriolets and, after 1829, fleets of omnibuses.

OMNIBUSES AND THE EARLY TRAINS

The omnibus, which was introduced by George Shillibeer in imitation of a successful Parisian innovation, was an elongated coach, usually seating around twenty passengers on a single covered deck, and pulled by three horses. By 1845 omnibuses had superseded short-stage coaches, which were slower, less reliable, harder to get on and off, and more expensive. Omnibuses were also competing effectively with hackney coaches, which had lost, in 1832, their treasured monopoly on plying for hire in central London. 'Buses quickly won control of the busy suburban routes from Paddington, Hammersmith, Kennington, Camberwell, Deptford and Blackwall, adding their share to the congestion of City and West End streets. By 1836, according to Dickens's *Sketches by Boz*, the technique of 'a second buss keeping constantly behind the first one' had been mastered, and an accomplished conductor, or 'cad', could '"chuck an old gen'l'm'n into the buss, shut him in, and rattle off, afore he knows where it's a-going to"'.[5] Perhaps, as *The Times* said in 1842, omnibuses were 'lumbering, clumsy conveyances in which the public were packed like coal sacks', but their value to the suburban middle classes, from clerks and shopkeepers to merchants and civil servants, was immense, and they remained profitable and popular throughout the century, surviving the challenge of railways and horse trams.[6]

Although railways were at their best over longer routes, virtually destroying long-distance stage coach companies in the 1830s, they also competed on some shorter urban routes. Two London stations, London Bridge and Fenchurch Street, handled quite heavy short-distance traffic in the 1840s. The first railway to be built in London was a suburban commuter line from Deptford to London Bridge, opened in 1836, and extended to Greenwich in 1838. The Croydon line, picking up passengers in Penge and Norwood, reached London Bridge in 1839, and lines from Brighton, Folkstone and Dover followed in 1841–4. Just across the river, Fenchurch Street Station, built in 1841, received passengers from Blackwall, Shadwell and Limehouse. But other suburban areas had to wait until the 1850s or 1860s for a train service to compete with the omnibus. The West London termini of the London and Birmingham and Great Western lines, Euston (1837) and Paddington (1838), handled longer-distance traffic, with their first stops respectively at Harrow and Ealing, in rural Middlesex. The same was true of King's Cross (1852), the terminus of the Great Northern Line, whose first stop was at Hornsey, 4 miles away. By 1854 only around 6,000 Londoners came to their jobs in the City by train. Rail commuters in 1854 included those using two new lines: the North London Line (1850–3), running through Kew, Acton, Camden Town, Islington and Hackney to Fenchurch Street, and the London and South Western's line from Twickenham and Richmond to Waterloo (1848).[7]

The development of London's railways in the 1840s and afterwards was not shaped by commercial interests alone. London was the imperial capital, and the permanent or seasonal residence of England's most powerful men. It is not surprising, then, that governments and Parliament, which largely ignored the effects of railways on provincial cities, spent many days examining their social and aesthetic impact on London. Given a free hand, the railway companies, it was said in 1846, would have taken 'a sponge and sponged out the whole of the City, leaving St Paul's standing in the midst'. That this did not happen is largely thanks to a succession of Royal Commissions and Parliamentary Select Committees from the 1840s to the 1860s. Every proposed new line and terminus needed a private Act of Parliament to give the company power to buy land by compulsory purchase. In 1846 nineteen railway proposals, including nine new termini in the area between the Bank and Lincoln's Inn, were considered by a Royal Commission. The Commissioners calculated, as well as they could, the impact of the proposals on local businesses, property values, traffic congestion and present and projected road communications. They even discussed the impact of wholesale demolition and eviction on slum-dwellers, who would clearly be driven into nearby houses, making conditions even worse. 'Under no circumstances,' the Commission concluded, 'should the thoroughfares of the metropolis and the property and comforts of its inhabitants be surrendered to separate schemes brought forward at different times and without reference to each other.' Only two proposals, including the extension of the Vauxhall line to Waterloo, were accepted.[8]

Meanwhile, London's traffic congestion went from bad to worse. Before long, it was claimed in 1853, wagons, omnibuses and other traffic would 'render London insupportable for purposes of business, recreation and all ordinary transit from place to place'.[9] Railways, which might have been expected to ease the congestion of the city's roads, did as much as anything else to make it worse. Trains enormously increased the flow of goods and passengers into London, but once they had arrived it was left to carters, cabmen and omnibuses to take them on to their final destinations. 'We thought when railways first came in that we should have nothing to do, but it has not turned out so,' said a London stable-keeper in 1873. 'The greater the increase of railways, the greater will be the use of the horse. . . . The horses have to work in connection with with the railways; for every new railway you want fresh horses.' There were horse-drawn wagons and carts by the thousand at Paddington, Euston, Nine Elms and other rail depots, some of them owned by independent firms such as Pickfords (which had 1,500 horses in London in 1873), and others belonging to the railway companies themselves. The number of four-wheeled and two-wheeled (hansom) cabs in London rose especially fast, from 2,500 in 1845 to 6,800 in 1863, and 11,000 in 1888. In 1897, according to Baedeker's

Guide, over half central London's omnibus routes began or ended at a main railway terminus.[10]

Omnibus numbers rose from 620 to 1,300 between 1839 and 1850, and in the 1840s their capacity was increased from fifteen to twenty-two by the introduction of the knifeboard seat, allowing nine passengers to ride on the roof. This, along with tax reductions, enabled some omnibus operators to cut their fares from 6d to 2d or even a penny on more competitive routes in the late 1840s. Cut-throat competition reduced the number of omnibuses to 810 by 1856. At this point the Compagnie Générale des Omnibuses, which had recently been given a monopoly of all Parisian omnibus services, tried to buy out all the London proprietors. By 1857 the company owned 600 omnibuses and 6,000 horses in London, and was the largest omnibus company in the world. In the early 1860s the company, now under English control and renamed the London General Omnibus Company, carried over 40 million passengers a year, although competition, low fares and expensive fodder kept its profits low.[11]

Underground and Suburban Railways

Two important measures were taken to remedy the traffic problem in the 1850s. In 1855 a new London-wide authority, the Metropolitan Board of Works, took over responsibility for strategic road-building in London from the Commissioners of Woods and Forests, and a period of vigorous road-building began. In the same year the Select Committee on Metropolitan Communications, influenced by Pearson, recommended that the main railway termini 'should be connected by railway with each other, with the docks, the river, and the Post-office' to take passengers and goods off the roads.[12] The best way to achieve this was to build a railway underground, an idea that Charles Pearson had been advocating since 1837. As it happened, there were two existing schemes which might be combined to produce a useful new line. One of these was Charles Pearson's plan for a new road to extend Farringdon Street (opened in 1830) north to the New Road, where the new King's Cross terminal was being built. An eight-track railway would run beneath the road to bring trains from King's Cross and perhaps the other north and west London termini into a new City terminus on Farringdon Street. A viaduct would carry the Holborn–Cheapside road across the new road and railway, and the Fleet River sewer would be completely enclosed. The second was a plan to link Paddington to King's

Cross by a railway buried under the New Road, thus avoiding the expense of buying and demolishing buildings, or the unknown hazards of tunnelling beneath them. In 1859 the Metropolitan Railway Company and the City Corporation, guided by Pearson, reached agreement on the two schemes, and later that year work began on the world's first underground railway.[13]

The Metropolitan Railway from Paddington to Farringdon Street, like all the underground lines until 1890, was built by the 'cut and cover' method, in which a huge trench, about 100 feet wide, was dug along the line of the road, then covered with a brick arched tunnel to carry the new road. Finding a way through the gas, water and sewer pipes was not easy, and in June 1862 the Fleet sewer burst into the workings near King's Cross. Despite this, the line was opened in January 1863 (four months after Pearson's death), and the public quickly decided that travelling in 'the Drain' was a safer and more comfortable experience than they had been led to expect. Trains were frequent (every ten minutes at peak times), the dark green carriages were spacious and well lit, electric telegraph signalling gave maximum safety, tickets were competitively priced at 3d, 4d or 6d (depending on class, not distance), and although the smell and the smoke were unpleasant they may not have been much worse than the air in the world above. The Metropolitan line was an instant success. In its first year it carried almost 10 million passengers, took over £100,000 in ticket sales (twenty times higher, per mile of track, than major trunk lines), and paid dividends of 5 per cent. An extension to Finsbury Circus (Moorgate) was opened in December 1865.[14]

The 1860s brought a new wave of railway proposals. Some of these were squashed in 1863 by the Select Committee on Metropolitan Communications, which considered thirteen applications which would between them have demolished a quarter of the City, and rejected ten of them. Only the Great Eastern was allowed to advance into the City, and its new station, Liverpool Street, was opened, after many delays, in 1874. Other plans in the early 1860s were less objectionable. The efforts of the various South London companies to divert traffic from London Bridge to other termini were generally welcome, especially when they did not involve cutting through central London. The London, Brighton and South Coast Railway's new terminus, Victoria Station, was opened in 1860, and the South Eastern Railway's two stations, Charing Cross and Cannon Street, were built in 1864 and 1866, the first displacing the Hungerford Market, and the second standing where the Roman Governor's palace and the Hanseatic Steelyard had once stood. By 1868 most residents of the South London suburbs could commute by rail to jobs in the City or West End, as long as they could afford the fare.

North of the Thames, the suburban commuter network took a little longer to complete. Shepherd's Bush and Hammersmith were linked to the Metropolitan railway in 1864, and in 1865 the busy North London line, passing through Kew, Acton, Willesden, Kentish Town and Islington, was extended to Broad Street, on the edge of the City. Between 1867 and 1872 the Great Northern constructed a suburban network linking Edgware, Finchley, High Barnet, Muswell Hill and Enfield to King's Cross and Farringdon Street, and in 1868 the Midland Railway began bringing passengers from Camden Road, Finchley Road and Hendon into St Pancras, its impressive new station on the New Road. Last of all, the Great Eastern ran lines from Edmonton, Walthamstow and Chingford into its extremely busy new terminus, Liverpool Street (1874).[15]

The outcome of thirty years of hectic planning and building was a railway system which delivered commuters and visitors to the edge of the central area of town, but did not make it easy for them to cross it. Out to the west, travellers could move quickly between north and south by passing through the great junctions at Willesden and Clapham, but only one company, the London, Chatham and Dover, managed to win permission to build a line that went right through central London's 'charmed circle'. Its line passed through two new stations, St Paul's (now called Blackfriars) and Ludgate Hill, and joined the Metropolitan line at Farringdon Street in 1866. Not a single railway line was allowed to spoil the fashionable beauty of the district bounded by the New Road, Edgware Road–Park Lane, the Strand and Farringdon Road, an area of over 3 square miles, until the building of the Central Line, about 100 feet underground, in 1900. In part, this was a matter of economics. Buying densely inhabited land in the centre of London cost so much that most companies were happy to settle for a less central terminus. 'The cost of carrying the works of a railway into London is such as to defy all previous calculation,' said the chairman of the Midland railway company, after the completion of St Pancras at a cost of £4 million. Charing Cross Station cost £3 million, three times the amount expected, and the Great Eastern company was almost ruined by the £2 million it had to spend on the last mile of its line into Liverpool Street. The last of the main termini, Marylebone, cost (with its approaches) more than £6 million, an investment which could never be recovered. Still, railway projectors often undertook uneconomic schemes, and it took the efforts of a determined government, and particularly the 1846 Royal Commission and the 1863 and 1864 Select Committees, to preserve London's uniquely railway-free centre.[16]

The success of the Metropolitan line persuaded Parliament in 1864 to accept plans for a complete underground circuit, extending the existing line to connect all the main London termini (except London Bridge and Waterloo) with each other, and thus reduce horse traffic on the roads. The District Company, which was to build the southern half of the circuit, had difficulty in attracting investors, and in 1866 Peto and Betts, its chief backers, were bankrupted by the collapse of the finance house Overend, Gurney and Co. Only parliamentary support enabled it to complete the stretch under the Metropolitan Board of Works' new Embankment between Westminster Bridge and Blackfriars. Its line from Paddington, through Kensington and Westminster to the Mansion House, which involved buying and demolishing very expensive property in Bayswater, Westminster, Blackfriars and the City, was completed in 1871. The Metropolitan line, dogged by corruption and mismanagement, did not reach Aldgate until 1876, and it took another eight years for the two companies to resolve their differences and turn their horseshoe into a Circle by building the short but costly line between Aldgate and Mansion House. It was hoped that the new line would pick up passengers coming into London on the East London underground line from New Cross, which crossed the Thames through the Wapping to Rotherhithe tunnel, the world's first underwater tunnel, built by Marc and Isambard Brunel between 1825 and 1843. Profits from this connection fell short of expectations, since South London commuters could already reach central destinations by surface train, without the bother of changing on to the slower underground. The Metropolitan and District companies, which ran their trains around the Circle line in unfriendly and unprofitable competition, concentrated in the 1870s and 1880s on extending their lines far into the London suburbs in search of new customers. The District's trains reached Richmond, Ealing and Putney between 1877 and 1880, and Wimbledon in 1889, and the Metropolitan, more hemmed in by main line competitors, drove a single line into the north-western countryside, through Hampstead (1879), Harrow (1880) and Pinner (1883) to Rickmansworth (1887) and Aylesbury (1892).[17]

The Metropolitan Board and the LCC
as Road Builders

The growth of the railway network was bad news for its competitors. Steamboat services above and below London Bridge began after 1815, and prospered at the expense of traditional watermen in the 1820s and 1830s. But the railway services from Greenwich, Woolwich and Blackwall, which were faster and safer than travelling on the river, damaged these steamboat routes in the 1840s, and longer-distance steamer services to Richmond and Gravesend were ruined by railway competition in the 1850s. The opening of the District line in 1871 was a further blow, and in 1876 the main steamboat companies merged to keep their regular Chelsea to Woolwich route running. The sinking of the paddle-steamer *Princess Alice* with the loss of 640 passengers (the highest loss of life in any disaster in the kingdom for almost a century) in September 1879 accelerated the decline of steamer services, and the unified company went down in 1886.[18]

Unlike steamers, omnibuses could change their routes, and this flexibility enabled them to survive. The LGOC struggled in the late 1860s, and only managed to keep its annual passenger total above 40 million by cutting fares and dividends. But with the exception of the longer suburban routes, where the railway's speed was a decisive advantage, omnibuses could still compete effectively with trains. Although they were no cheaper than third-class railway carriages, and much less comfortable than first-class ones, they had the advantage of convenience on shorter journeys in the suburbs, and were unchallenged along the thriving shopping streets of the rail-free West End. The abolition of most turnpike and bridge tolls in 1864, and of the government's mileage duty in 1870, together with the rapid fall in the price of horse feed from around the same time, put the LGOC on a very sound commercial footing for the rest of the century.[19]

The survival of the omnibus companies depended to a large extent on further improvements being made to London's archaic road network. This problem could be addressed more systematically after 1855, when the new Metropolitan Board of Works was given responsibility for the main streets of the town. The Board's greatest road-building task was the construction of the Thames Embankment between Westminster and Blackfriars bridges, from 1864 to 1870. The idea of reclaiming the stinking mudbanks of the Thames and creating a wide road to relieve the Strand–Fleet Street route was an old one, but opposition from wharf interests and landowners with river frontages held it up until 1862, when Parliament decided that the

Metropolitan Board of Works should undertake the enterprise at public expense, drawing its funds from duties on coal and wine. The fact that the new main sewer and the riverside underground railway could be included in the construction, avoiding the disruption of laying them under the Strand, added greatly to the appeal of the scheme. Under Bazalgette's supervision the work progressed well, despite the usual difficulties with faltering contractors (made worse by the Overend and Gurney collapse of 1866) and delays caused by the financial problems of the District Railway Company. Of the 37 acres reclaimed from the Thames, the roadway used 19, and 10 were made into public gardens. The Albert and Chelsea Embankments, further upstream, were completed at the same time, at a cost of £1,284,000.[20]

Oddly, the Victoria Embankment did not draw traffic away from the Strand and Fleet Street, as everyone had expected it would. In 1874, four years after its grand opening, the Embankment was described as 'a desert', used only by 'a few foreigners or country people, or Hansoms with uncommonly knowing drivers', while Fleet Street was 'gorged, crowded from end to end' with waggons, carts and omnibuses, mostly local traffic drawn by its shops and offices. Even at the end of the century the new road was under-used. Yet the Embankment did not lack access roads. Defying the opposition of the City Corporation, the Metropolitan Board of Works built Queen Victoria Street from Blackfriars to the Bank, with the District Line beneath it, at a cost of £1 million, between 1863 and 1871. To clear the way for this street 550 properties were bought and demolished, including the courts and offices of ecclesiastical law known as Doctors' Commons, that 'lazy old nook near St Paul's Churchyard' where young Charles Dickens had been a shorthand reporter, and in which his David Copperfield had worked for Spenlow and Jorkins. Work on the street made possible an early triumph of rescue archaeology, when John Price recorded a large and beautiful Roman mosaic floor, which was saved and transferred, amidst great public interest, to the Guildhall Museum. It can be seen today at the Museum of London. A sad loss was suffered during the construction in 1874 of Northumberland Avenue, which connected the Embankment with Charing Cross. The Metropolitan Board of Works paid £500,000 for Northumberland House, a fine Jacobean mansion and the last of the many noble palaces that used to line the Strand. The new road could easily have avoided the house, but the Board defied a strong public campaign and insisted on its demolition.[21]

The 3 miles of embankments, with their associated sewers, gas and water pipes and railways, were the Metropolitan Board of Works' proudest achievement, but its work did not end there. By 1888 the Board had undertaken over forty road construction or improvement schemes, some of which made a real difference to the shape and operation of the capital. Cutting its way through a jungle of property owners and compensation claims, the Board managed to open up London's east–west routes in several places. South of the Thames, the building of Southwark Street in 1864 and the widening of Tooley Street and Jamaica Road eased the way between Blackfriars, Southwark and Rotherhithe. To the north, the construction of Shaftesbury Avenue (1886) and Clerkenwell Road (1878) and the widening of Theobald's Road created a new route from Piccadilly Circus to Old Street and the north-eastern suburbs. In 1867 the important Holborn route was improved by the removal of Middle Row, an island of houses blocking the road near Staple Inn. North–south communications were eased by improvements to Park Lane in 1871, and the transformation in 1887 of two small roads, Castle Street and Crown Street, into Charing Cross Road, a new thoroughfare between Trafalgar Square and Oxford Street. The growing needs of the docks were served by the widening of Wapping High Street in 1879, the construction of Great Eastern Street (extending Commercial Street), and the building of Burdett Street in 1862 between Limehouse and Victoria Park. One of the most important improvements of all was not the work of the Board. This was the City Corporation's vast and expensive Holborn Viaduct, built between 1863 and 1869, which carried Holborn over Farringdon Street and the new north–south railway, and ended the difficult descent into the Fleet valley.

The London County Council, which took over responsibility for road-building in 1889, committed itself to two major schemes in the 1890s. The 1,490-yard Blackwall road tunnel was built between 1891 and 1897 to join Greenwich and Blackwall, at a cost of £1.38 million. Shortly afterwards the LCC undertook a massive redevelopment of the area to the north of Somerset House, to relieve congestion in the Strand and create a wide north–south route between the Strand and Holborn. The Strand was widened by the demolition of its north side, and between 1900 and 1905 28 acres of slum alleys and workshops were cleared to make way for the Aldwych, a great crescent curving north from the Strand, and Kingsway, a 100-feet wide highway with a tram tunnel beneath it. Londoners lost the Gaiety Theatre, famous for its 'Gaiety Girls', the Globe Theatre and the Opera Comique (the 'Rickety Twins'), Holywell Street, the centre of London's indecent book trade, and the Tudor houses of Wych Street. Over the next ten years the new district was gradually filled with monumental offices, theatres, hotels and imperial high commissions. The social and financial costs of building new inner-city streets was very great, and this was the last major road improvement in central London for fifty years.[22]

WORKMEN'S FARES

Historians have argued, as contemporaries did, about the comparative social costs and benefits of the road- and railway-building of the nineteenth century. On the positive side, as Donald Olsen points out, roads and railways created enormous amounts of work, both for the labourers who built them and the railwaymen, cabmen and omnibus drivers and conductors who worked on them when they were finished. In 1891 there were 28,300 railwaymen and 48,200 road transport workers (excluding carters) in London, making up about 6 per cent of the male workforce. Most of this work was steady and well paid, by the standards of the time. Improved transport enabled the whole London economy to operate more efficiently, allowing London-made goods to reach wider markets at lower cost, and delivering food to the capital more cheaply and quickly than ever before. Although their impact on food distribution was not immediate, railways brought animal carcasses to Smithfield, which reopened as a meat market in 1869, and helped end the unwholesome practice of slaughtering in the cellars and backyards of London butchers. The milk trade was resistant to milk brought by rail, which was not as fresh as that from urban dairies. But an outbreak of rinderpest in 1865–6 almost ruined urban dairying, and although local cow-keeping recovered, by 1900 most of London's supplies were coming by rail from as far afield as Somerset and Derbyshire.[23]

At first, the main beneficiaries of improved road and rail travel were the well-off, who could afford to spend 5–10s a week to commute between their work in central London and their homes in the spacious suburbs, and whose working hours were short enough for them to do so. In 1854, fewer than 10,000 commuters arrived in the City by train, around 15,000 by steamboat, and at most 20,000 by omnibus. The vast majority of City workers, about 200,000, came on foot.[24] By the 1860s omnibus fares on shorter suburban routes had fallen to 3d or 4d, suburban railway services were more widely available, and well-paid clerks and craftsmen, on weekly wages of around £2–3, might be tempted to ride to work in comfort from their terraced houses in Islington or Camberwell. But many still chose to save 10 per cent of their incomes by walking. Ordinary working men, earning perhaps £1 a week, had no choice to make. Since six return fares would have absorbed almost a sixth of their wages, they had to live within walking distance of their work.

The only way to spread the advantages of railway travel to working men, and thus ease the inner-city housing shortage which railway demolitions had exacerbated, was to lower the fares. It was not difficult for Parliament to force railway companies to run cheap and early workmen's trains as a condition of planning consent. In 1864 the London, Chatham and Dover Railway was forced to run a train for artisans and labourers from Victoria to Ludgate Hill, and another from Loughborough and Peckham Junctions to Ludgate Hill, at a penny a journey. There were fifty-nine workmen's trains running in South London by 1882. In 1864, the Great Eastern Company was given permission to build Liverpool Street Station only on condition that it ran cheap workmen's trains daily at convenient hours. Bound by this obligation, the Great Eastern eventually found itself carrying as many cheap ticket passengers, either clerks on half fares or workmen on penny fares, as full-fare passengers to its suburban stations in Walthamstow and Edmonton. By 1883, when the Cheap Trains Act imposed the duty to run early workmen's trains on all companies (if ordered to do so by the Board of Trade), there were already over 100 such trains, carrying over 25,000 passengers a day.

The response to the 1883 Act was patchy. The Great Western, the London and North Western and the Midland, serving the whole north-western quarter of the town, all refused to make any concessions, and the cheap trains of the Great Northern, serving Hornsey, Wood Green and Southgate, were for half-fare clerks, not workmen. There were over 200 cheap trains running from the southern suburbs, but most of these charged well over a penny a journey, and an LCC report in 1892 considered the services were too crowded, too dear and too early to encourage large-scale working-class commuting. There were working-class colonies along the cheapest routes in south London, but nothing to compare with the dense settlement in the parts of north London served by the Great Eastern Railway, which sold the vast majority of 2d return tickets for working men. When suburban railway journeys were surveyed for the 1903–5 Royal Commission on London Traffic, it was plain that the railway companies had effectively stifled the workmen's trains policy. Of around 250,000 daily railway commuters in 1901, only 27,569 were on 2d workmen's fares, and of these the Great Eastern Company was carrying nearly 20,000 (72 per cent). The other 100,000 passengers travelling on so-called 'workmen's' or cheap fares were clerks and artisans, paying up to 11d a day for their tickets. Only the outer suburbs served by the Great Eastern had acquired a working-class character, a distinction they retained well into this century.[25]

The effects of this policy on the Great Eastern and the suburbs it served reveal a great deal about the social divisions of late Victorian London. According to William Birt, general manager of the Great Eastern, working-class passengers had a way of 'taking a train over', and making life unpleasant for others using their stations. They spat, used foul language, bothered young women, smoked noisome pipes, cooked herrings in the waiting rooms, cut off the leather window straps, and tried to evade payment. 'They have a rough, boisterous way about them; it is difficult perhaps to say that it is wrong; it is natural with them, but it is still very annoying indeed to a very large section of our passengers.' Edmonton, Stratford and Walthamstow, Birt claimed, had been 'spoilt for ordinary residential purposes', with consequent losses for his shareholders. Birt urged that working-class commuters should be concentrated in one area, rather than dispersed throughout the suburbs: 'We ... are prepared to provide any number of trains that may be wanted for their accommodation, but we shall have to urge ... that other districts which are not spoilt should not be thrown open to the working classes.' There were practical arguments against running a peak hour commuter service, with very little off-peak traffic. Companies had to build large stations, which would be almost deserted outside of peak hours; trains had to run empty on their return journeys; it was practically impossible to prevent clerks, and even the well-off, from using workmen's trains, although this was illegal; and the creation of large working-class suburbs with few rate-payers gave railway companies a disproportionate share of the rate bill. No wonder that the other companies did their best to avoid the Great Eastern's predicament.[26]

TRAMS

It was not the high technology of the train, but the low technology of the tram, that did most to release working-class families from their inner-city slums in the last decades of the century. The horse-drawn tram, essentially an omnibus with iron wheels running on a grooved iron track, had been in use in New York since 1832, and in Paris since 1855. The idea failed in London in 1860–1, when its American promoter, George F. Train, foolishly tried to introduce his tracks into parts of the West End where even omnibus companies had not prospered. But trams succeeded in several European cities, and in 1869 Parliament approved three experimental lines, two in

South London and one along the Mile End Road. Trams proved to be popular with passengers, investors, the government, the Metropolitan Board of Works and most local authorities, and by 1870 promoters had won approval and raised capital for routes along most of the major suburban streets. But several West End parishes, especially St Marylebone and St George's Hanover Square, resisted the laying of tramlines in their streets, and in 1872 Parliament agreed to exclude trams from central London. By 1875 the three main companies had 348 trams and about 60 miles of suburban track, and carried as many passengers annually (49 million) as the main omnibus company, LGOC. But the omnibus still enjoyed its profitable monopoly between the Thames and the New Road, and the West End remained as free from tram tracks as it was from railway tracks.

Trams were no faster than omnibuses (about 6 miles an hour), and they did not push the limits of the suburban area outwards as railways had done. But they ran frequently (every three or four minutes), they started early in the morning, and they were cheap, since they were subject, as 'railways', to the terms of the 1883 Cheap Trains Act. The ease of drawing an iron-wheeled vehicle along smooth iron tracks meant that two horses could pull fifty passengers (twice as many as an omnibus carried), and the resulting saving in fodder, stabling and wages enabled tram companies to make reasonable profits on average fares of around 1½d or (in the 1890s) a penny. Trams were not shunned by middle-class travellers, but their main customers were the working class, who found themselves for the first time able to commute from suburbs not served by cheap workmen's trains. As the suburbs spread in the 1870s and 1880s, so did the network of tramlines. By the late 1880s there were lines out to Highgate, Wood Green, Ponders End (beyond Edmonton) and Leytonstone in the north, to Woolwich and Plumstead in the east, and Wandsworth, Brixton, Tulse Hill and Peckham in the south. But there were awkward gaps in the network. Only one of the South London lines, the route to Victoria, was allowed to cross the river. In the west there were routes to Richmond and Acton, but they came no nearer the centre than Shepherd's Bush and Hammersmith, because the local authorities in Westminster and Kensington, responding to middle-class pressure groups, would not allow them through.[27]

The Tramways Act of 1870 gave local authorities the right to buy the tram companies after twenty-one years, and in the 1890s the London County Council, which regarded trams as an excellent means of solving inner-city housing problems, bought 100 miles of track, the bulk of the London system. The northern routes were at first operated under lease by the two main northern companies, North Metropolitan Tramways and London Street Tramways, but the southern network, bought from London Tramways in 1899, was operated by the LCC itself. The tram network thus became the first part of London's transport system to be run as a municipal service.[28]

Omnibus companies withstood this competition with surprising ease. Omnibuses benefited from their access to central and west London, their freedom from tolls, taxes and regulations, the good quality of London's roads, and a steep decline in fodder prices after 1873. Unlike trams, they also gained from the five new bridges built or rebuilt in the later nineteenth century (Putney, 1886; Battersea, 1890; Albert, 1873; Lambeth, 1861; and Tower Bridge, 1894) and the removal of tolls from London's nine commercial bridges between 1877 and 1880. For middle-class passengers the omnibus, with its padded seats, large windows and respectable clientele, offered a cheap alternative to the cab, without the slight loss of status involved in travelling on a tram. The appearance of the London Road Car Company in 1881 as a competitor to the dominant London General Omnibus Company brought omnibus fares down, and passenger numbers increased, mostly at the expense of cabs and the underground, whose business expanded more slowly. The number of omnibuses entering the City doubled between 1881 and 1895 (from 6,176 to 12,236), and by the end of the century buses were passing the Bank or Piccadilly Circus, at peak hours, at the rate of over 600 an hour. All forms of transport benefited from the growth in London's fare-paying public, and especially the recruitment into it of working-class men and women. By 1896 there were around 300 million omnibus journeys a year, 280 million by tram, and about 400 million (usually longer and more expensive) by underground and surface trains. Tram and omnibus travel in London had risen by almost 400 per cent, and train travel by about 150 per cent, since 1875. In 1901 the average Londoner took about 177 journeys by tram, bus or train each year, almost three times the figure for 1875.[29]

THE ORIGINS OF THE ELECTRIC TUBE

In January 1900 the buses, trams and cabs that crowded the streets of central London were still horse-drawn, and nearly all of London's trains ran on steam. But within ten years new technology had revolutionized London's public transport system. The revolution began, as revolutions often do, underground. Modern tunnelling techniques, using a moving shield to hold up the earth around the excavation, protecting the excavators until walls were put into place, was pioneered by Marc Isambard Brunel in the construction of the Thames tunnel from Rotherhithe to Wapping between 1825 and 1843. Brunel's tunnel took eighteen years to build, and cost over £400 a foot. The shield system was improved by Peter Barlow in the building of his foot tunnel under the Thames near the Tower in 1868. The tunnel (which now carries water under the Thames) was lined with cast-iron rings bolted together to form a continuous tube, a method of construction which enabled Barlow to complete the work in five months at a cost (it was said) of under £7 a foot. Barlow's tunnel was not successful as a railway tunnel, and its life as a foot tunnel was ended when Tower Bridge opened in 1894, but it showed that deep tube railways under the river, and under parts of London where the cut and cover method could not be used, were technically and economically feasible, as long as a power source that did not poison or suffocate the passengers could be found.[30] The answer to this problem was the electric motor, which was demonstrated by Z. T. Gramme in Vienna in 1873. Edison's exhibition of the practical benefits of electric lighting at the Crystal Palace and in some houses around Holborn Viaduct in 1882 showed that electricity could light trains as well as move them.

The world's first electric trams ran in Ulster in 1883, and in Richmond, Virginia, in 1888. But the first electric underground railway was the City and South London Line, running 3 miles from King William Street via the Elephant and Castle to Stockwell, which opened in 1890. Its builders, led by James Greathead (Barlow's assistant on the Tower tunnel), used the latest tunnelling and electric technology, but it turned out that the tunnels were too narrow and the electric voltage too weak to allow the line to carry the volume of traffic it needed to compete profitably with the horse trams overhead. Those who followed the City and South London Line learned from its mistakes, and benefited also from the development of more powerful electric locomotives in the later 1890s. The Waterloo and City line ('The Drain'), which was built between 1894 and 1898, was an economic success, and the City and South London was extended (usefully, if not profitably) south to Clapham and north to Islington in 1900 and 1901, and reached Euston and King's Cross in 1907.

Powerful American, European and City financial interests saw the commercial possibilities of electric tube trains in the 1890s, and a lively demand for new parliamentary franchises developed. The most serious proposal was for a deep-level Central London Railway that would penetrate the hitherto train-free West End by following London's extremely busy east–west route, Cheapside, High Holborn, Oxford Street and Bayswater Road, from Bank to Shepherd's Bush. The Anglo-American syndicate behind this scheme was led by Ernest Cassel, a City financier and friend of the Prince of Wales. The proposal was approved, and the Central London Railway was opened in 1900, setting new standards in comfort and service. The trains were fast, frequent, smooth, smoke-free and well-lit, the stations were handsome, spacious, and served by electric lifts. By 1901 the Central Line was carrying 41 million passengers a year (112,000 a day) at 2d a journey, or a penny on workmen's trains. Profits were good, and investors received the high dividend of 4 per cent.[31]

CHARLES TYSON YERKES

The position of the older steam-powered underground companies, the Metropolitan and the District (who also jointly operated the Inner Circle), was gravely threatened by competition from the cleaner, faster and cheaper Central Line in west and central London. Both companies began to grapple with the difficult and expensive business of electrification in the 1890s, but the District Railway, in particular, was hamstrung by lack of capital. At this point Charles Tyson Yerkes, a smart but shady Philadelphia financier who had made a fortune in Chicago electric trams and trains, entered the London scene. By the time he died in 1905 Yerkes had transformed the London underground system and established the foundations of a company that would dominate London's public transport for thirty years. In 1900 Yerkes and his associates bought control of the Charing Cross, Euston and Hampstead Railway Company, which had permission to build a line from Charing Cross to Hampstead and Kentish Town. In June 1901 Yerkes and a group of Boston and New York financiers took control of the District (now renamed the Metropolitan District Electric Traction Company), with the aim of electrifying its lines and constructing the new deep-level Tube from South Kensington to Piccadilly or Russell Square, a proposal already being considered by Parliament. Before the year was out Yerkes had bought the Great Northern and Strand Company, which had parliamentary approval for a line from King's Cross to the Strand, and the Baker Street and Waterloo, whose line was left half finished when its backers went bankrupt. The new company that emerged from this whirlwind of takeovers and amalgamations, the Underground Electric Railways Company of London (UERL), was committed to building lines that would cost £16 million.[32]

The dividends that these new lines would earn were uncertain, and Yerkes was known to be untrustworthy, but the company was backed by Edgar Speyer, of the great international banking house of Speyer Brothers, and English and American investors readily invested the initial £5 million that UERL needed. Yerkes's growing control of the London underground system was not unchallenged. In 1902 the powerful New York banking house, J. S. Morgan, in alliance with London United Tramways, put before a parliamentary committee impressive proposals for an 18-mile line from Hammersmith through central London to Tottenham and Southgate. In a typical masterstroke, Yerkes and Edgar Speyer destroyed the scheme by buying a commanding stake in London United Tramways, thus driving a dangerous rival from the scene and depriving North London of a useful service.[33]

The spectacle of a conflict between two American-led financial syndicates deciding the shape of London's transport system prompted the government to establish a Royal Commission on London Traffic in 1903. This Commission concluded that slow, expensive and uncoordinated transport was damaging the efficiency of London workers of all classes, and preventing the alleviation of inner-city housing problems. Poorer Londoners with work in the centre were unable to take advantage of lower suburban rents, and were often forced to move house whenever they changed their jobs. Delays on central London's busiest streets could stop traffic for a total of up to four or five hours a day, and for forty-three minutes in a Piccadilly rush hour (a phrase first used in 1898). 'London must fall behind in competition with other cities and the life and growth of the Metropolis will be slowly, but not the less surely strangled by the choking of the great arteries of traffic.' The Commission offered various solutions to the problem. London's narrow streets could be widened to Parisian dimensions when opportunity arose, and the Board of Engineers' expensive plan for two great avenues crossing London from east to west and north to south, each 140 feet wide and over 4 miles long, should be part of a long-term plan. These wider roads would allow electric tram services to be extended across the whole of London, with sensible links and interchanges between the different systems. Trams and shallow suburban underground lines offered the best way forward, despite the fact that one day motor buses might supersede them. Finally, since the area administered by the LCC was too small for it to supervise the whole London transport system, the Commission urged the government to establish an independent Traffic Board, which would ensure that Londoners would not in future suffer from conflicting and uncoordinated transport development. Instead of doing this, the government created a largely powerless London Traffic Branch in the Board of Trade, leaving the prospects for a coordinated transport system in the hands of Yerkes and his growing Underground conglomerate. The creation of a unified London transport authority was delayed for another twenty-eight years.[34]

Perhaps this was for the best. Unlike the LCC, which had a misplaced faith in running electric tramways in shallow tunnels, Yerkes had confidence in the future of the deep-level Tube, and he was prepared to bet other people's money on it in very large amounts. With Edgar Speyer's support he moved quickly, ensuring that an extensive Tube network would be almost completed by 1905, the year in which it first became clear that motor buses could run at a profit. If Yerkes had delayed by even two or three years, it is likely that he would never have raised the £15 million he needed, and the Hampstead and Piccadilly lines would not have been built. By June 1903 experimental District Railway electric trains were running between Acton and Harrow, and in 1905 electric trains replaced steam over the entire District and Inner Circle network. The independent Metropolitan Railway, which had extended its lines out to Harrow, Ruislip and Uxbridge, had also electrified a little earlier in the same year. By 1906 or 1907 the UERL's three new Tubes, Edgware Road and Baker Street to Waterloo and Elephant and Castle (the 'Bakerloo'), Charing Cross to Hampstead and Golders Green, with a fork to Highgate (the Hampstead line), and Hammersmith to Finsbury Park (the 'Piccadilly'), were opened, complete with Otis lifts, distinctively tiled stations, well-designed interchanges, and the latest and most efficient automatic braking systems, allowing a very frequent service. The West End, which had no railway lines running through it in 1899, was now served by four.[35]

Only the profits were missing. UERL's shareholders, who had subscribed over £15 million to build about 25 miles of Tube line, expected some return on their investments but, as Yerkes used to say, 'it is the straphangers who pay the dividends'. The problem was that competition between Tube lines and with electric trams forced fares down, and the doubling of passenger numbers that Yerkes had predicted simply never happened. Like the Metropolitan line, the District found that the new services attracted few extra customers, and its ticket sales in 1906, at 55 million, were only 10 per cent up on 1904, and well short of the predicted 100 million. In their first full years the Bakerloo, Hampstead and Piccadilly lines carried a total of 61 million passengers, 84 million short of expectations. The imminent arrival of motor bus services meant that nothing better could be hoped for in the years ahead.[36] Yerkes died in debt in December

1905, leaving his shareholders angry and impoverished, and his company close to bankruptcy. But the London public, who gained a modern Tube network without paying extra rates or taxes, might regard Charles Yerkes (if they remember him at all) as their benefactor.

MOTOR BUSES AND ELECTRIC TRAMS

The new electric Tubes had powerful competitors on the streets. When the LCC took control of London Tramways in 1899 it began investigating the idea of electrification, but London United Tramways (LUT) got there first, with electric routes connecting the western suburbs of Southall, Ealing, Acton, Hounslow, Brentford and Kew with Chiswick, Hammersmith and Shepherd's Bush (the western terminus of the Central line) from 1901. As the well-off residents of Ealing had feared, the speed, comfort and capacity of the new sixty-nine-seater electric trams began to lower the social level of these attractive and hitherto remote suburbs. 'Such is the demand for house property,' the managing director of LUT wrote in 1904, 'that estates where one dwelling formerly stood on its own acreage now are being cut up into building plots for houses that average 20 or 30 to the acre.' Ealing's population rose by 85 per cent between 1901 and 1911, and Southall's doubled. Smaller suburban electric tramway systems opened in East Ham and Croydon in 1901, and the electrification of the LCC's South London system began in 1903. The LCC's routes north of the Thames, taken over from the North Metropolitan Company in 1906, were not electrified until 1906–7. In 1906 the LCC had at last persuaded Parliament to allow trams to run on Westminster Bridge and the Victoria Embankment, and in 1909 Blackfriars Bridge was opened to trams. Using the Kingsway tunnel, the LCC joined its southern and northern tram networks in 1908, making it possible to travel by LCC electric tram from West Norwood to Highgate Hill. But the boroughs of Westminster and Kensington still resisted the tram, and in the whole of West London from Kingsway to Hammersmith there was only one tram route, from Wembley into Paddington.[37]

All classes used the electric tram, but its social benefits to poorer commuters were widely recognized. The 1905 Royal Commission on London Traffic concluded that the electric tram was 'the most efficient and the cheapest means of street conveyance', and in Charles Masterman's opinion the spacious, fast and well-lit electric tram at last opened up the suburbs to the working class: 'Family after family are evacuating the blocks and crowded tenements for little four-roomed cottages, with little gardens, at Hither Green or Tooting.... The two greatest boons which have come to our working people are the gas stove and the electric tram.' The LCC's first suburban cottage estate, Totterdown Fields, in Tooting, owed much of its success to the fact that workmen living there could get into central London by electric tram in forty-five minutes, for 2d return. For the same fare, working men could commute from Streatham, West Norwood, Peckham, Lewisham, Clapham or Holloway by LCC electric tram, where the workmen's train or omnibus would have cost them two or three times as much. By 1910, workmen were rattling down Archway Road, Green Lanes and Brixton Hill at 8 miles an hour, from their homes in the once exclusive suburbs of Finchley, Wood Green and Streatham. The passenger statistics show how popular the electric tram was in the first decade of the century, before the motor bus began to steal its customers. Between 1901 and 1911 annual tram journeys increased from 340 million to 822 million, giving them almost as many passengers as local surface and underground railways (436 million) and buses (400 million) combined.[38]

The search for a horseless vehicle that would not need to run on electric rails had been going on for many years. Walter Hancock had run a few steam-powered omnibuses along the New Road in the 1830s, and there was a steam-driven tram service between Stamford Hill, Ponders End and Wood Green in the 1880s. There were some electric cabs and a few experimental electric buses on London streets in the 1890s, but their accumulators had to be recharged too often. Petrol engines offered better chances of success. Harry Lawson's Motor Traction Co. operated London's first motor bus service from Kennington to Victoria from October 1899 to December 1900, and by the end of 1902 there were motor bus services to Streatham, Lewisham, Putney and Cricklewood. These motor buses (which looked like horse buses) were too small to be profitable, but they attracted the attention of the big omnibus companies, whose profits were being squeezed by underground and tram competition. Experimental services run by the Road Car Co. and the dominant LGOC in the winter of 1904–5 were unsuccessful, but Tillings of Peckham operated a Daimler motor bus on its Oxford Circus route in 1904, and ordered a fleet of twenty-four in November. The economics of the motor bus were convincing: a motor bus cost about 25 per cent more than a horse bus and the ten horses needed for a fifteen-hour day, but it carried eight extra passengers, could cover 30 or 40 miles more each day, and did not need extensive stabling. In 1905 four new motor bus companies, with a total capital of over £1 million, were launched in London, two horse omnibus companies, Tillings and the Road Car Co., moved decisively from horses to petrol, and the LGOC, wary of mechanical problems, began ordering its first machines. In 1906 and 1907 the number of motor buses in service grew rapidly, from 241 to 1,205, while horse buses fell from 3,484 to 2,557. Over the next three years intense competition and falling profits, which forced several companies into closure or amalgamation, held the number of motor buses almost steady, although horse buses continued to disappear from the streets. There were only 1,771 at the end of 1909, and 786 two years later.[39] Between 1909 and 1911 the LGOC took control of its three main rivals, the Road Car Co., the Vanguard Co. (itself a merger of four companies), and the Great Eastern, and had regained its dominant position in London. Its mechanical breakthrough came in 1910, when engineers in the LGOC's Walthamstow works produced the B type, the first really reliable and efficient motor bus. The price of LGOC shares rose more than ten-fold between 1910 and the end of 1911. Over the next three years motor bus routes spread right across London, joining the most distant suburbs to the centre and to each other. Total bus journeys rose from 400 million in 1911 to 750 million in 1914, putting buses a little way behind trams (812 million), but ahead of local surface and underground trains (440 million). By the end of 1912 there were almost 3,000 motor buses and only 376 horse buses in London, and on 4 August 1914, London's one remaining regular horse bus, owned by Tillings, carried its last passengers from Peckham to Honor Oak. The occasion was overshadowed by other events that day.[40]

The men behind all these transport enterprises were interested, above all, in profits, and it was plain to them that more money would be made if trams, buses and Tubes worked in collaboration with each other, rather than in competition. In April 1912, after two years of courtship, the Underground Electric Railways Co. of London (Speyer's and Yerkes's company, UERL) took over the LGOC, and over the next year this great combine either absorbed its rival bus companies, or made anti-competitive alliances with them. UERL already had control of two major tram companies, and at the end of 1912 it added the City and South London and the Central London Tube companies to its empire. This left it in control of the bulk of London's public transport system. Only the surface railways, the LCC's trams, Tillings buses, and the Metropolitan, Waterloo and City, and Great Northern and City underground lines remained outside the combine.[41] The managing director of UERL, Albert Stanley, and its commercial manager, Frank Pick, shaped the development of London transport for the next thirty years. Edgar Speyer, the financial mastermind behind the growth of UERL, was not so lucky. In 1915 he was attacked on account of his German birth, and he was forced to quit London for New

York. In 1921, on the pretext of minor trading misdemeanours, he was stripped of his British citizenship.

The age of the horse was drawing to a close, and a fairly rapid one, as far as passengers were concerned. In 1900 there had been almost a quarter of a million horses in London: 80,000 pulling trams and omnibuses, 22,000 for its 11,000 four-wheelers and two-wheeled hansom cabs, about 110,000 cart and van horses, and an unknown number, perhaps 30,000, for private carriages. By 1913, according to a traffic census, only 6 per cent of London's passenger vehicles (but still 88 per cent of its goods vehicles) were horse-drawn.[42] Some regretted the passing of the hansom and the horse bus, but from an environmental point of view the decline of London's horse population brought significant advantages. Each horse produced between three and four tons of dung each year, helping to give London its characteristic smell and to sustain the swarms of flies that spread typhoid, diarrhoea and dysentery in the summer months. The dramatic fall in London typhoid cases between 1902 and 1904 (from 4,300 a year to 1,500) came too early to be credited to the introduction of the motor bus and the electric tram, but London without horses was a cleaner and less fly-infested city.[43] An old danger passed, and a new one took its place: between 1901 and 1911 the number of Londoners killed by horse vehicles fell from its peak of 175 to 116, while those killed by motor vehicles rose from 5 to 291. Road injuries, half of them caused by motor vehicles, doubled to 18,749 in the same decade.[44]

THE SUBURBAN IMPULSE

Nothing struck visitors to Victorian London more forcibly than the enormous extent of its suburbs. Other great European cities were different. Paris and Rome, for instance, remained compact, within fairly clear boundaries, while London spread like a huge stain over its rural hinterland, and surrounded itself, to use a different metaphor, with 'suburb clinging to suburb, like onions fifty on a rope'.[45] London's spreading habit, and the tendency of the City rich to take over and 'gentrify' accessible farmsteads, were among the most furious of William Cobbett's many charges against the 'Great Wen' in 1830. Whenever his *Rural Rides* took him across the countryside on the edge of London he broke into the same refrain: 'When you get to Beckenham, which is the last parish in Kent, the country begins to assume a cockney-like appearance; all is artificial and you no longer feel any interest in it.' 'Between Sutton and the Wen there is, in fact, little besides houses, gardens, grass plats and other matters to accommodate the Jews and jobbers and the mistresses and bastards that are put out a-keeping.' 'When the old farm houses are down (and down they must come in time) what a miserable thing the country will be!'[46]

The reasons for London's growth were not simple. Of course, population growth had a great deal to do with it, but London's area grew twice as fast as its population in the nineteenth century. Partly, it took place because London's middle-class population was growing so fast, and these people, unable to afford a second home in the country, but able to pay a daily bus or train fare into their City offices, were the ones most likely to choose a suburban existence. Later in the century rising real wages, shorter working hours and lower transport costs broadened the social range of the commuting classes to include lower-middle-class and even some working-class Londoners. Charles Booth's figures show that in 1891 over 80 per cent of commercial clerks, schoolteachers, lawyers, merchants and architects lived outside London's crowded inner circle, compared with 62 per cent of the population as a whole.[47] Transport improvements were an important facilitating factor: without stage coaches in the 1820s, omnibus services in the 1830s and 1840s, surface and underground trains from the 1850s, horse trams from the 1870s, and motor buses, electric trams and deep-level Tubes after 1900, the extent and population of the suburbs could not have grown as they did.

But why did well-off people want to move out to the suburbs, when for centuries they had clung to the city centre? Why did the image of suburban life undergo so radical a change? In the past, London's suburbs had been a refuge for non-citizens, unapprenticed labourers and undesirables, 'a nether world of dungheaps, stinking trades, bloodsports, gallows, low taverns, prostitutes, foreigners, thieves, the poor and the mob'.[48] Early seventeenth-century writers often used the word 'suburb' to suggest, in the words of the *Oxford English Dictionary*, 'a place of inferior, debased and especially licentious habits of life'. But the other meaning of the word, denoting a place of semi-rustic retreat from the stresses of city life, began to predominate in the eighteenth century, when well-off City families sometimes took suburban villas, and the proliferation of pleasure gardens introduced the delights of London's rustic fringe to a wider public. The new Horse Patrol, established in 1805, played its part by ridding suburban districts of highwaymen, although crime remained a problem until the extension of the Metropolitan Police District in 1839.

Although respectable suburban growth accelerated rapidly after 1815, the process was not entirely new. For many centuries London had been steadily encroaching in every direction on the open land on the fringes of the town. Further out, well-off London settlers and holidaymakers were changing London's outlying villages into satellite towns, and the roads joining these towns to the centre were themselves lined with villas and ribbon development. The most important of these residential towns in 1800 were Hampstead, Highgate, Islington, Stoke Newington and Hackney in the north, Bethnal Green, Stepney and Stratford-le-Bow in the east, and Clapham, Lambeth, Camberwell and Greenwich in the south. To the west there was a succession of riverside towns and villages which would sooner or later become a part of London's suburban empire: Chelsea, Wandsworth, Fulham, Putney, Hammersmith, Chiswick, Barnes, Mortlake, Brentford, Isleworth, Richmond, Twickenham and Kingston. Some suburban towns, particularly Islington, were so close to London that the spreading metropolis had reached them by 1815, while more distant or inaccessible places (Hampstead and Highgate, for instance) lost their separate identity much later in the century. In the long run, the same fate awaited them all. Gradually, the spreading centre moved closer to the expanding suburban towns and the villa-lined roads, until they met in a vast urban sprawl.

The resulting mixture of town and country, or *rus in urbe*, as Victorians (quoting Martial) liked to call it, had a particular appeal to middle-class Londoners. Perhaps this was because it enabled them to mimic, at modest expense, the country life of the aristocracy, or the garden suburb existence of the rich inhabitants of Nash's new Regent's Park development. Perhaps its appeal was strongest to the newly arrived migrants, who wanted to combine the economic benefits of the town with a few remnants of the country life they had abandoned. Country-dwellers, rather than refugees from central London, made up the majority of suburban migrants. Perhaps, as some historians argue, suburbs suited the new domestic ideology of the middle class, which emphasized family life, the separation of work and home, privacy, respectability, social segregation, and the domestication and isolation of women.

The choice for many middle-class Londoners, especially those with families, was very simple: central London offered cramped accommodation, filthy water and air, overcrowding, high death rates, and the company of criminals, beggars and prostitutes, while the better suburbs offered, for a lower rent, quiet, cleanliness, safety, green spaces, social and cultural segregation from the poor, and increasingly convenient public transport. What suburbians wanted, Henry James explained in 1877, was 'the mingling of density and rurality, the ivy-covered brick walls, the riverside holiday-making, the old royal seats at an easy drive, the little open-windowed inns, where the charm of rural seclusion seems to merge itself in that of proximity to the city market'.[49] No matter how strongly the suburbs were criticized by moralists and architects for their dull uniformity, their narrow-minded respectability, their failure to be either real town or real country, they were the places in which most middle-class, and many working-class, Londoners chose to live when improving wages, working hours and transport links made it possible. Suburban life, in their view, offered not the worst of both worlds, but the best.

THE SPREAD OF SUBURBS

Before 1851, population growth in suburbs more than 3 miles from the City was slow, and settlement consisted of large villas set in spacious gardens, or clusters of denser housing around railway stations, along main roads, or in villages such as Twickenham, Battersea or Bow, still separated from each other and the urban sprawl by farmland or market gardens. After 1851 the focus of population growth shifted outwards. The City, whose population had been static at about 125,000 since 1801, started to lose its inhabitants rapidly, and the inner areas, Holborn, Westminster, Strand, St Giles', St Marylebone, Whitechapel and Shoreditch, also declined, though more slowly, as housing gave way to roads, railways, offices, shops and public buildings. Established suburbs such as Kensington, Islington, Hackney, Poplar, Lambeth, Wandsworth and Camberwell continued to grow quickly, these seven registration districts gaining about a million people (half of London's population growth) between 1851 and 1881. From 1861 the outer suburbs, beyond the boundaries of the Metropolitan Board of Works or the London County Council, but within the reach of surface and underground trains and horse-drawn trams, began their spectacular growth. In 1861 the outer suburban ring had 400,000 inhabitants, only 12 per cent of London's population. By 1911 it had 2.7 million, which was 37 per cent of the metropolitan total. For many of these later arrivals, suburban settlement was not really a matter of choice. The population of London was growing rapidly (almost 100,000 a year in the 1870s), and land in the centre was increasingly used for non-residential purposes. Only the very poorest, whose long hours of work in the docks, markets, or sweated trades trapped them in the inner-city slums, or the very wealthy, who could afford a house in the West End or its nearby extensions, remained in the centre of London in large numbers.

The suburban urge, whatever its motives, completely changed the size and shape of London. In 1813 Ralph Horwood's map shows a built-up area of roughly 15 square miles, stretching about 6 miles from Paddington to Limehouse, and 3 miles from Islington to Walworth. Over the next century London's capacity to overtake and engulf once outlying villages amazed and often depressed Victorian observers. By the 1860s the rising suburban tide had advanced 3 or 4 miles to reach Clapham, Peckham, Blackheath, Stratford-le-Bow, Old Ford, Hackney, Stoke Newington, Upper Holloway, Notting Hill and Hammersmith. And the Ordnance Survey of 1901–3 shows the built-up area stretching from Acton and Brentford in the west to East Ham and the banks of Barking Creek in the east. In the north, London had reached Tottenham and Wood Green, and in the south, Penge, Streatham and even Croydon. In 1900, starting from any extremity of the town, a walker could go 14 miles before reaching the other side of London.

The growth of late-Victorian suburbs was fuelled by the arrival of the lower-middle-class commuter. By 1891 10 per cent of London's males (over ten years old) were white-collar workers, mostly clerks in commerce, banking or insurance, workers in local or central government, schoolteachers, railway officials or commercial travellers.[50] Along with shopkeepers and skilled artisans, most of these 150,000 white-collar workers were keen to take advantage of rising wages, shorter hours and cheap transport to settle in modest and accessible suburbs, such as Islington, Holloway, Hackney, Wood Green, Hornsey, Hendon, Willesden, Balham and Camberwell. Thanks to workmen's tickets on trains and trams, better-off working-class families were able to join them. The rapid growth of these outer London suburbs was an outstanding feature of England's population history after 1861. Of the sixty-seven substantial English towns or boroughs whose populations grew by over 30 per cent in any decade between 1861 and 1911, thirty were London suburbs, and in the 1880s the four fastest-growing English towns were all in outer London: Leyton (133 per cent), Willesden (122 per cent), Tottenham (95 per cent) and West Ham (59 per cent). In each decade, the centres of growth moved a little further out. In the 1890s, Acton, Edmonton, Ilford (278 per cent), East Ham (194 per cent) and Wimbledon made impressive progress, and in 1901–1911 electric trams and Tube extensions brought great population increases to Ealing, Southall, Wembley (137 per cent), Chingford, Coulsdon and Purley (128 per cent), and Merton and Morden (156 per cent).[51] Some of these suburban settlements were small places, but others were huge: in 1901 London's four most populous boroughs, Camberwell, Islington, Lambeth and Stepney, ranked among England's ten largest towns, ahead of such places as Hull, Newcastle and Nottingham.[52]

Each part of London's suburban growth followed its own particular pattern. London did not develop, as some urban models suggest, as a set of concentric circles, with the social level of each circle rising as distance from the centre and the cost of commuting increased. This model fits north and south London, where the inner suburbs were generally poorer than the outer ones, but not the west, where the social level tended to be higher nearer the centre, or the east, where poverty prevailed throughout. The poor were heavily concentrated in inner districts, but they were by no means confined to them. All suburbs generated local work, which poorer residents could do without commuting, and many, especially in the east, had important local industries. The idea that suburbs developed as a series of segments radiating from a central core, in which the outer part of each segment took on the social quality of the inner district of which it was an extension, has some value, but it cannot explain the complex pattern of London's growth. Local factors, including the quality of adjoining neighbourhoods, the nature of the terrain, the decisions of landowners and builders, the proximity of industrial employment, and the transport system, all played their part in determining the social level of new suburban developments. Parks and main roads attracted wealthier tenants, while areas near canals, railway sidings, gasworks or the Thames were almost always poor.[53]

SUBURBAN DEVELOPERS

In many respects the process of suburban development followed a pattern established in the previous century. Individual and corporate landlords, some of them with very large estates, seized the opportunity to profit from housing London's growing population, and either sold their land to builders or developers, or (more often) leased it to them for a period of years (usually between eighty and ninety-nine years in the late nineteenth century), receiving ground rent until the land and houses reverted to them at the end of the lease. Often, the leasehold agreement would oblige developers to build to a certain standard and density, to use materials of a good quality, perhaps to exclude taverns and offensive trades, in order to preserve the value and social tone of the neighbourhood.

Most suburban developers were small jobbing builders who contracted work out to independent craftsmen, and ran their businesses on a highly breakable shoestring. If, as often happened, the supply of houses ran ahead of demand, or the new neighbourhood failed to attract tenants of the expected quality, few builders had the capital reserves they needed to avoid bankruptcy. Many builders who started up in the boom years of 1817–25 went under in the severe slump of 1826–32, when the vacant houses built in the boom slowly found tenants, and London brick production fell to a sixth of its 1825 peak. When demand recovered in the later 1830s, reaching a peak in 1846–7, new businesses were formed to replace the failures. In 1851 there were 739 building firms in London, of which 682 employed under fifty men. Even in 1872 three-quarters of London building firms were working on under seven houses a year, and only two large firms built more than sixty houses a year. Thereafter, large firms, which were more able to ride out the regular building slumps, gradually became more dominant, and seventeen firms accounted for 30 per cent of London's 7,000 new houses in 1899.[54]

There were large building businesses in the early nineteenth century, but most of them concentrated on theatres, markets, public buildings, bridges, railway stations and other large-scale projects, leaving suburban work to the small fry. The great exception to this rule was Thomas Cubitt, nineteenth-century London's most successful and prolific builder and developer. Cubitt's independent career began in 1815, at a time when cheap capital, ample supplies of labour and the postwar housing shortage were about to create a ten-year building boom. In that year, Cubitt decided to abandon the sub-contracting system traditionally used by London builders, and opted instead to establish his own building workshop on Gray's Inn Road, employing all the labourers and craftsmen necessary to complete his contracts. By 1828, when Cubitt and his brother William divided their business, there were 700 men employed at the Gray's Inn Road works and 1,000 in Belgravia. By the time of his death in 1855 he had accumulated a fortune of around £1 million, and left his mark on the development of Belgravia, Pimlico, Camden Town, Islington (Barnsbury and Highbury), Stoke Newington, Bloomsbury, and Clapham Park, London's first garden suburb.[55]

Cubitt started with a few streets on the Calthorpe estate, east of Gray's Inn Road, and some high-quality residential building in Highbury and Stoke Newington in the early 1820s. From the 1820s to the 1850s he was engaged in building the area from Tavistock Square and Gordon Square to Euston Square, on the Duke of Bedford's huge estate in Bloomsbury. This, like his other ventures, was a speculation, based on the hope that the demand for houses would increase to match the supply. As it turned out, Cubitt's north Bloomsbury houses did not easily attract the wealthy residents they were designed for. 'The fact is,' Cubitt concluded in 1842, 'the place is become unfashionable. Everybody is running away to the west, and though my Houses may be classed with the best that have ever been built anywhere; and the situation is really good and airy, yet I cannot get rid of the Houses.'[56]

A New West End

The tenants Cubitt lost in Bloomsbury he gained in Belgravia. The Grosvenor estate owned 400 acres of undeveloped land between Buckingham House Gardens and Hans Town (the area round Sloane Street), from Knightsbridge to the Thames. In 1824, almost at the end of the postwar building boom, Lord Grosvenor began leasing plots to Cubitt and several other builders. Between 1826 and 1832 Belgrave Square took shape as the centrepiece of a fashionable new quarter between Sloane Street and Chelsea Road (now Buckingham Palace Road). Eaton Square, to the south, was not completed till the 1850s. Cubitt's business acumen, the quality of his buildings and services (streets, pavements, gardens, sewers and gas lighting), and the advantages of the location helped see the estate through the slump of the 1830s, and in the second half of the century Belgravia ranked alongside Tyburnia and Mayfair as 'one of the most fashionable quarters of the town'. Gates and bars protected parts of the exclusive neighbourhood from heavy traffic and undesirable outsiders.[57]

Cubitt's influence was even more strongly felt in the Grosvenor lands south of Chelsea Road and the Grosvenor Canal, a low-lying district of market gardens and osier beds (providing willows for basket-making) known then as the Neathouses and now as Pimlico. Cubitt took 124 acres in 1825, and leased most of the remaining land over the following decade. For the next twenty years work went on to raise the level of the land, and to construct a network of streets and sewers. In the 1840s, when the demand for housing revived, the whole district was covered with substantial stuccoed houses, taking London to the borders of the expanding riverside town of Chelsea.[58] Pimlico, in the words of Cubitt's biographer, 'is still the largest single area of London developed by one man'. Cubitt hoped that Pimlico would attract the business and professional families who could not afford the grandeur of Belgravia, but the district always had a certain social ambiguity, which was increased by the opening of Victoria Station (on the site of the Canal basin) in 1860, and of the vast Army Clothing Depot, employing over 1,000 seamstresses, in 1859. In 1902 Charles Booth regarded it as 'a depressing district, passing, as regards much of it, from the shabbiness of shabby gentility to.... gradual decay and grimy dilapidation'.[59]

Mercantile and professional men who could not afford a house in Belgravia might prefer to live north of Hyde Park, where the Bishop of London's estates were developed into the fine stucco terraces of Paddington ('one of the most elegant and recherché districts') in the 1830s, or in St John's Wood, where the large Eyre estate, west of Regent's Park, was covered with fine houses from the 1820s onwards. Even at the end of the century St John's Wood remained, for many, the ideal middle-class suburb, leafy, secluded, socially segregated, easily reached from central London, yet well removed from the centre's environmental and moral decay. Its distinctive contribution to the development of suburbia was the semi-detached house, which combined, for middle-class families, the status and privacy of a 'villa' with the cheapness of a terrace. A development of semi-detached houses was first proposed in plans for the Eyre estate produced in 1794, and the anonymous author of these plans is probably the 'inventor' of a style of housing that came to typify the Victorian suburb.[60]

The whole area to the north of Hyde Park and Kensington Gardens became a successful extension of the West End in the 1840s and 1850s. West of Paddington, or Tyburnia, there were the impressive Regency-style terraces of Bayswater, arranged around squares almost as grand as those of Mayfair. The opulence of the families who moved into this area is attested by the success of the shops, clubs and ladies' colleges along Westbourne Grove, where William Whiteley built up London's first department store in the 1860s. For the rest of the century, as Booth's 1902 'poverty' map shows, the district north of Hyde Park and Kensington Gardens remained wealthy or comfortable, only deteriorating north of the railway line and the canal.[61] Further west, Bayswater met the well-designed, but socially less successful, suburban town of Notting Hill, where there had been intermittent building work on the Ladbroke estates since the 1820s. By the 1870s, Notting Hill was a well-established middle-class suburb, and the frontiers of West London were marching on towards Kensal New Town, Willesden, Shepherd's Bush, Acton, and the growing suburban village of Ealing.[62]

South of Kensington Gardens the market gardens surrounding the village of Brompton began their transformation into the smart suburb of South Kensington in 1852, when the commissioners for the Great Exhibition bought 70 acres of land as a site for museums, colleges, and a great hall of arts and sciences. By the time the South Kensington Museum (the future Science and Victoria and Albert Museums) was opened in 1857 an

Italianate 'new town' was under construction between Cromwell Road and Kensington Gardens. In 1870, when the Metropolitan District Railway linked West Brompton and Kensington with Westminster, the whole area around the south and west of Kensington Gardens had already been developed, and lines of houses were stretching out south-westwards towards the hitherto separate settlements of Hammersmith, Fulham, Putney and Chiswick.

Suburban Poverty

Although the driving force behind the development of these West London suburbs was the demand of the capital's growing commercial and professional classes for respectable and convenient housing, they were not one-class neighbourhoods. As well as the servants and tradesmen who inevitably accompanied the well-off, almost every suburb had its working-class enclaves, perhaps in converted mews, in speculative developments that 'went wrong', or in areas close to railways, canals, brickfields, gasworks, or some other source of local employment. Some of the most notorious of these isolated slum districts were in the affluent parish of Kensington, which covered the 2½ miles from Brompton Road to the Harrow Road. West of Notting Hill, in the area around the present Avondale Park, there was a shanty town of brickmakers, labourers, pig-keepers and pigs known as the Potteries, a district of such poverty and squalor that life expectancy there in the 1840s was under twelve years, lower than almost anywhere else in England. Where the clay had been dug out for bricks and pots, there was a foul lake, 'the Ocean', contaminating the neighbourhood. In the 1860s and 1870s the number of brickmakers and pig-keepers declined, but builders and costermongers took their place, and in 1893 life in the Potteries was still, in the words of a *Daily News* reporter, 'more hopelessly degraded and abandoned' than anywhere else in London.[63] Charles Booth, writing in 1902, regarded the inhabitants of the Potteries as 'rather criminal than poor', and found more abject poverty in the five or six streets just to the south of the Potteries, known as Notting Dale. In 1898 infant mortality in these streets was 419 per 1,000, compared with a London average of about 160 per 1,000. In the north of the parish, in the angle between Harrow Road and Ladbroke Grove, was Kensal New Town, a rather better-off community of labourers, railwaymen and gas workers, the kind of industrial enclave that could be found in many parts of suburban London. In the south of the parish, in a set of back-streets off Kensington High

Street, almost opposite Kensington Palace, were the low wooden tenements known as Jennings Buildings. Over 1,000 people, mostly of Irish origin, lived here in conditions of the utmost squalor and overcrowding, until the slum was demolished in 1873. Most of the men in Jennings Buildings did casual labouring work in local building sites and market gardens, and the community had a bad reputation for drunkenness and crime. When their tenements were destroyed they moved on, as displaced slum-dwellers usually did, to other nearby slums, particularly Notting Dale.[64]

Working-class districts played a vital part in the suburban economy. Their men provided labour for the three main local industries, building, gas and brickmaking, and constructed and ran the new transport services, and their women took in the washing, starching and ironing of the richer families nearby. The rich needed cab drivers, omnibus conductors, laun-dresses, builders and craftsmen, and well-planned developments usually included pockets of cheaper housing for those providing these essential services. Suburbs were socially segregated, but the interdependence of rich and poor ensured that the distances dividing the two should not be great. In 1871 1,000 women, two-thirds of the female workforce in the four Kensington slum areas, were recorded as being laundry workers, and in Kensal New Town, or 'Soap-Suds Island', women had hardly any other paid work. Despite the assertions of hundreds of lurid contemporary and modern accounts, it is likely that laundry work easily surpassed prostitution or crime as a means by which money passed from rich to poor in Victorian London.

In 1902 Charles Booth, the social investigator, published a poverty map of London, in which streets occupied by the poor, very poor and 'semi-criminal' were marked respectively in blue, dark blue and black. Hardly any suburban areas, however exclusive, were without their pockets of poverty. In the west, the wealthy of Lansdowne Road and Holland Park (coloured gold) were only 300 or 400 yards from the destitution of Notting Dale, and the affluent residents of Cheyne Walk and Onslow Square were no more than a stone's throw from the miserable inhabitants of the back-alleys of Chelsea. In Paddington there were slums around the Grand Union Canal basin and the railway terminus, and in Hammersmith, according to James Thorne's *Handbook to the Environs of London* (1876), there was an area of squalid tenements between King Street and the Thames, the homes of workers in the local boatyards, engineering works, distilleries, oil mills, lead works and water-pumping station. In north London, the respectable clerks of Holloway shared their neighbourhoods with the slum-dwellers of Queensland Road, Hampden Road and Campbell Road, reputedly 'the worst street in North London, the resort of criminals and tramps'.[65] Even Hampstead, St John's Wood and Belsize Park, a vast district of middle- and upper-middle-class housing, had slum quarters in Hampstead Village, and in the area on the edge of Regent's Park, between Avenue Road and Wellington Road, known as Portland Town.

HAMPSTEAD AND FINCHLEY

The north-western sector of suburban London, between Regent's Park and Hampstead, began to grow in the 1840s and 1850s when, after many delays, Eton College's large Chalcots Estate, north of Primrose Hill, was developed as an area of villas and semi-detached houses for prosperous middle-class tenants. The district's success in establishing and maintaining its social level owed a great deal to its nearness to St John's Wood, Regent's Park and Primrose Hill, which was acquired and preserved by the government in 1842. Well-planned and well-built housing also had something to do with it, but in the 'wrong' area this would not have ensured success. This wedge of comfortable middle-class housing was extended northwards in the 1860s and 1870s by the development of the Belsize Park estate, part of the ancient lands of the Dean and Chapter of Westminster. In recognition of the changing realities of middle-class life, Belsize Park was built without stabling for private carriages. Its residents went to work, if they worked at all, by omnibus or cab.

West of Belsize, in the fields north of St John's Wood, there was a 416-acre estate owned by the Lord of the Manor of Hampstead, Sir Thomas Maryon Wilson, who also had the right to build on Hampstead Heath. For legal and personal reasons (fully explained in F. M. L. Thompson's *Hampstead. Building a Borough*) the estate was not developed in Sir Thomas's lifetime, but in the twenty years after his death in 1869 the spacious streets of South Hampstead were built, 'delicious Frognal' lost its woods and its mock Gothic Priory to make way for houses for wealthy professionals and businessmen, and Fitzjohn's Avenue (1878) became 'one of the most beautiful avenues in the suburbs of the metropolis'. This brought London to the hilltop town of Hampstead, whose springs, open land and fresh air had made it a centre for London day-trippers and a fashionable residential resort since the early eighteenth century. By the 1890s, in the words of Baedeker, Hampstead had 'been long since reached by the ever-advancing suburbs of London, from which it can now scarcely be distinguished'.

In the case of Hampstead, though, the countryside which had initially attracted settlers to it was not completely destroyed by the arrival of the suburbs. Intense and highly influential local pressure, assisted by parliamentary allies and the wider popularity of the Heath as recreational land, prevented Sir Thomas Maryon Wilson from selling building leases on the Heath, and a year after his death in 1869 the Metropolitan Board of Works bought 240 acres of heathland for £295,000. Further public pressure, involving the Duke of Westminster, Octavia Hill, and an impressive group of local worthies, forced the Metropolitan Board, in one of its last actions, to buy Parliament Hill and the eastern part of the Heath in 1889. For economy's sake, the Heath was allowed to develop naturally, with more gorse than dahlias, and so remains 'the most convincing illusion ever created of real country brought to the heart of a vast city'.[66]

To the north of the Heath, Finchley was 'a pleasant rural village' in the 1860s, served by stage coaches and a few omnibuses. But the arrival of the Great Northern Railway in 1867 began its conversion into a busy London suburb. 'Streets, terraces, villas and cottages are rising all around, and the outlying hamlets threaten soon to become good-sized villages.'[67] Its population increased from 2,200 to 22,000 between 1871 and 1901. From 1905 electric trams ran from Whetstone to Archway (along the old Great North Road), and Finchley's population increased to 40,000 by 1911. Golders Green retained its rusticity a little longer. It was only 'a little outlying cluster of cottages' in 1876, connected by pretty lanes and footpaths to the larger settlements of Hendon and Mill Hill, and ignored by steam trains and horse trams. Its transformation came in 1907, when Golders Green station was built as the terminus of the new Hampstead underground railway, and the village was suddenly only twenty-five minutes from Charing Cross. As soon as the line was approved, estate agents and builders moved in, and the peace of the district was broken by 'a continuous hammering'. By 1911 Golders Green had a population of about 20,000, and two years later the opening of a 3,500-seat Hippodrome theatre, cinema and music hall confirmed the district's new urban status.[68]

North London

In general, the western sector of London's suburbs, at least until they spread west of Kensington Gardens, took on the social character of the West End, catering for well-off professionals, businessmen and even aristocrats. In North London, east of Regent's Park and north of the New

Road, suburban development in the parishes of St Pancras and Islington followed a rather more complex social pattern. Two 'new towns', Somers Town and Pentonville, had been built on the northern side of the New Road in the last decades of the eighteenth century, and both continued to grow after 1815, attracting mostly lower-middle-class and working-class tenants. The social tone of this part of the parish of St Pancras was damaged in the 1840s when a notorious shanty district known as Agar Town sprang up between them. This, in the words of Charles Dickens, was 'an English suburban Connemara', a place of bogs, ash-heaps and hovels whose stench could 'knock down a bullock'. Agar Town was demolished in the early 1860s to make way for St Pancras Station and a huge area of railway sidings and goods yards, and its miserable population of navvies, refuse-collectors and casual workers moved elsewhere. Spreading northwards in the 1830s and 1840s, Somers Town and Agar Town met Camden Town, an unambitious 'new town' of the 1790s, and the whole area between Albany Street (the protective barrier between Regent's Park and its shabby neighbours) and Pancras Road was filled with mediocre housing for clerks, artisans and workmen.

Although there was work in local printing, engraving, furniture and clothing workshops, in railways and the ubiquitous laundries, the typical resident of these inner northern suburbs was the clerk, commuting on foot to his City office. Charles Dickens, who lived in Bayham Street, Camden Town, in 1822–4, as a child of eleven or twelve, must have walked alongside men of this type as he tramped daily to his work in a shoe-blacking factory on the Strand: 'The early clerk population of Somers and Camden Towns, Islington, and Pentonville are fast pouring into the City, or directing their steps towards Chancery Lane and the Inns of Court. Middle-aged men, whose salaries have by no means increased in the same proportion as their families, plod steadily along, apparently with no object in view but the counting-house.'[69]

The social tone of Somers Town and Camden Town seemed to infect the area further north. The road going north from Camden Town towards Highgate ran through the elongated and overgrown village of Kentish Town, which had developed as a gentlemen's health resort in the eighteenth century. Most of the land to the west of the village, part of the huge Southampton Estate, was leased to small builders in the 1840s and 1850s, and Kentish Town began to lose its separate village identity. Although its developers aspired to something better (as suburban developers usually did), Kentish Town attracted a mixed group of settlers, mostly clerical or working-class, with a sprinkling of well-off residents in the best streets, and patches of extreme poverty in the worst. Kentish Town is a long walk from the City, and many of its residents, unable to afford a daily omnibus fare, found work in local industries or services. The growth of these industries, particularly piano-making and railway work, further diminished the area's social status, and by the 1880s it could be described as 'one of those shabby, prosaic, monotonous residential quarters that could well be spared from the Metropolis'.[70]

Of all London's satellites, the modest roadside town of Islington was the most vulnerable to suburban encroachment. Between 1801 and 1831 Islington's population rose from 10,000 to 37,000, as small estates in Canonbury, Barnsbury and around Liverpool Road were covered with villas and terraces, many of which still survive, for the City's middle classes. The North London Railway, opened in 1850, roughly marks the northern limit of these districts at mid-century. The railway itself encouraged development north of the line. In 1855 a new Metropolitan Cattle Market (replacing Smithfield), with slaughterhouses and cheap housing around it, was built on Copenhagen Fields, between York Road and Caledonian Road, once a favourite meeting place of radicals and trade unionists. North of this, the Tufnell family's large estate was developed from the 1850s to the 1890s, and succeeded in attracting well-off tenants, despite the fact that the 10-acre City House of Correction (now Holloway Prison) was at its centre.

Holloway Road, running north-west from Islington to Highgate (along the eastern edge of Tufnell Park), already had hamlets along it, known as Upper and Lower Holloway, in the eighteenth century. In the 1850s and 1860s these settlements spread across the fields between Holloway Road and Stroud Green, reaching out to touch the hitherto secluded northern hamlets of Crouch End and Hornsey. Unlike Tufnell Park, Upper and Lower Holloway were not favoured by the well-to-do, and their shabby terraces were occupied by a mixed population of labourers, railwaymen, artisans, shopkeepers and clerks. Here and there, particularly in Lower Holloway and in Campbell Road (near Finsbury Park Station), there were centres of desperate poverty. Perhaps the rather seedy suburban world of Holloway is best represented in the fictional lives of Charles and Carrie Pooter, struggling to be 'respectable' on a senior clerk's salary. George and Weedon Grossmith's Diary of a Nobody, which introduced this likeable couple to the world in 1892, almost achieved the unlikely feat of making Upper Holloway famous. The Pooters were in a numerous, if not particularly fashionable, company in moving to Islington. No other parish (perhaps excepting Camberwell) experienced population growth as fast as

Islington's in the nineteenth century, and none passed the 300,000 mark before Islington did, in the mid-1880s.

The spread of suburban housing was not quite unstoppable. Part of Hornsey Woods was saved from development in 1869, when it was opened as a municipal park, named (for complicated reasons) Finsbury Park. A more ambitious rescue was attempted in 1851, when the fields of Highbury were threatened with development. In response to public agitation, a grand scheme was drawn up by James Pennethorne, Nash's protégé, for a 500-acre park, to be called Albert Park, stretching north from the North London Railway line to the New River Company's reservoirs, 1½ miles away. But Islington did not carry Hampstead's political weight, and the scheme came to nothing. Instead, between 1853 and the 1870s, part of the area was laid out as a spacious suburb called Highbury New Park. This attracted an affluent population of City businessmen, bankers, manufacturers and professionals, commuting by omnibus to the Bank, or by train to Fenchurch Street. Almost every house had servants, who made up 30 per cent of the inhabitants. In Charles Booth's 1902 map of income and social class Highbury New Park stands out as the only significant area of wealth in Islington, or in any part of North London east of Hampstead and Belsize Park.[71]

Between Islington and the river Lea there were the large parishes of Stoke Newington and Hackney. From 1801 to 1821, when the population of the two parishes doubled to about 26,000, the only significant development was along Stoke Newington High Street (the main road to Cambridge) and in the quiet villages of Clapton, Homerton, Dalston and Hackney. The fields between were occupied by market gardens, brickfields, pastures and watercress beds. London's northward spread from Shoreditch into south Hackney began in the 1830s, when the De Beauvoir family developed their estate north of the Regent's Canal into the well-planned suburb of De Beauvoir Town. There was easy access from Hackney to the City by omnibus or stage coach down Kingsland Road or Essex Road, and in 1850 the North London Railway gave Hackney an alternative route into the City. As middle-class demand for housing grew, Hackney landowners, of whom the largest was the Tyssen-Amherst family, gradually released plots of land to small speculative builders, who built detached and semi-detached villas for the professional and clerical classes. By 1862 most of the area up to the North London Railway was built up, and over the next fifteen years housing spread northwards to surround Hackney Downs and eastward along the northern edge of Victoria Park, towards Hackney Marshes. Hackney's population doubled between 1841 and 1861, and doubled again by 1881, when it was 163,000.[72]

By the late 1880s development had almost filled the area up to Seven Sisters Road and the river Lea, and middle-class Hackney was beginning its degeneration into working-class poverty, especially in its eastern and southern parts. This is how Charles Booth found Hackney in the 1890s. Around London Fields ('a rather dismal open space') 'a number of very rough poor people seem to have drifted from Bethnal Green across the canal at the Cat and Mutton Bridge, hangers-on to the skirts of the boot-finishers, who in the neighbourhood of London Fields have made a second centre for their trade'. And on the eastern edge of Hackney, in Hackney Wick and Homerton, 'it would ... seem as though the rejected from the centre had been flung completely over the heads of the rest of the population, to alight where no man has yet settled, occupying undesirable ill-built houses by the marshy land that is drained or flooded by the River Lea'. Even in the rest of the borough (as it became in 1900) large houses had been subdivided, replaced by smaller ones or turned into factories, and the well-off were moving out, leaving behind a residue of lower-middle-class families 'who are struggling to maintain a social position they cannot afford'.[73]

LAMBETH AND CAMBERWELL

There were well-established industrial districts south of the Thames before 1815: timber yards and potteries in north Lambeth, wharves and breweries in Southwark, tanneries and glue factories in Bermondsey. During the rest of the century this industrial belt thickened, and its social level deteriorated. For riverside villages caught up in this industrial growth, the demographic results could be spectacular. Battersea was a small town of about 3,000 people in 1801, and only 6,600 in 1841. By 1861 its population was 20,000, and by 1881 it had risen by nearly 450 per cent to 107,000, a population as large as Brighton's or Aberdeen's. By 1900 the riverside districts of North Battersea, North Lambeth, Southwark, Bermondsey and Rotherhithe, from Clapham Junction to the Surrey Commercial Docks, were as poor as any other part of London. On Booth's map half their streets are marked with the blue of poverty or the black of destitution, and the rest with the pink of the comfortable working class. Only the houses along the main roads attracted the well-to-do, and the rich had abandoned the districts near the southern banks of the Thames (except for Putney and the distant south-western suburbs) altogether.

Those in search of true suburban comfort south of the river had to

36. Lithograph of the West End in 1842 by Thomas Shotter Boys (1803–74). Regent Street from Piccadilly Circus, looking south towards the Duke of York's Column.

37. The last days of Vauxhall Gardens. A balloon ascent in 1849. Engraving from Thornbury and Walford, *Old and New London* (1883–5).

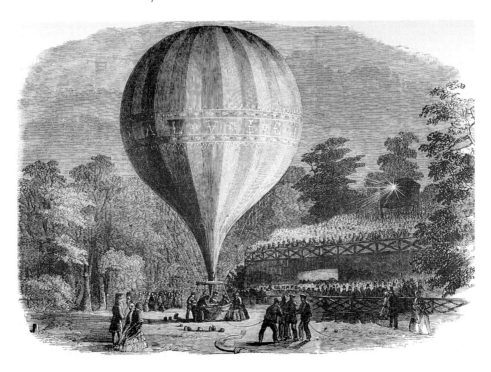

[" Pots to mend !"]

[" Old Shoes for some Brooms !"]

38. Despite the rise of fixed shops, there were still thousands of basket women and itinerant traders on London's streets in the 1840s and 1850s. The broom-seller and the pot-mender are from Charles Knight's *London* (1841–4), and the coffee-seller and the formidable costermonger are from Henry Mayhew's *London Labour and the London Poor* (1861).

39. The Thames Police Office and Wapping riverside in 1859. One of James McNeill Whistler's sixteen etchings of Thames life.

40. Building Holborn Viaduct across the Fleet Valley in the 1860s. The Viaduct provided a better route between the West End and the City, but caused the eviction of thousands of slum-dwellers living in its path. From the *Illustrated Times*, 18 September 1869.

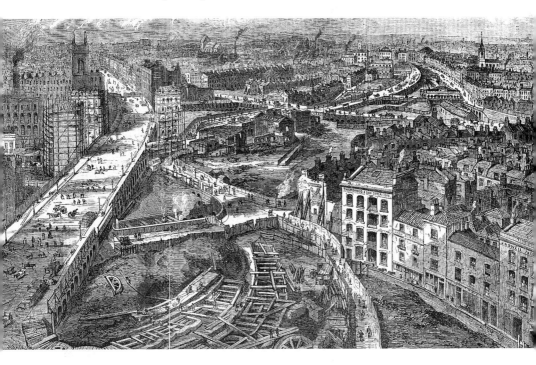

41. St Katherine's Docks and Thomas Telford's warehouses in the 1880s.
Engraving for *Old and New London*, 1883–5.

42. Sunday Crowds in the Petticoat Lane (Middlesex Street) Market,
London's leading market for second-hand clothes, in the 1880s.
Engraving for *Old and New London*, 1883–5.

43 & 44. G. R. Sims' 'How the Poor Live', published in *The Pictorial World* in 1883, achieved much of its impact through the engravings of Frederick Barnard (1846–96).
'A Critical Audience' (4 August, page 121) showed a music hall crowd on a Saturday night (see Mayhew's description on page 659), and 'All Sorts and Conditions of Men' (18 August, page 173) depicted the daily struggle for work at the dock gates.

45. Some of the residents of Moss Alley, Southwark, in 1896. Moss Alley disappeared under Bankside Power Station in 1963.

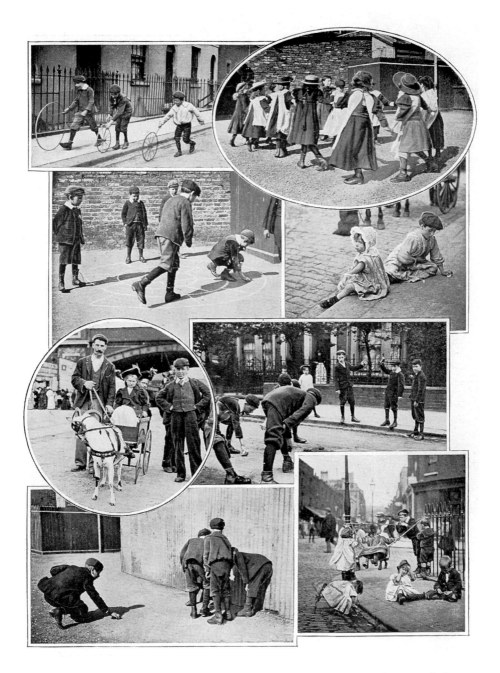

46. Children enjoying their traditional street games about 1900, a few years before the coming of the motor car. They are playing: wheels and hoop, kiss-in-the-ring, spider's web, five stones, goat-shay, gully, cherry-bobs and swinging.

47. Whiteley's of Westbourne Grove, the 'Universal Provider', in 1900
(see page 652).

48. Ratcliff Highway (St George Street), running from the Tower to Shadwell.
By 1900 this street, once notorious for the murders of 1811, was known for its
bird and animal sellers.

move out to villages along the main roads to the south and south-west, into the parishes of Wandsworth, Lambeth, Camberwell and Lewisham. From 1815 to 1820 the construction of three new bridges (Vauxhall, Waterloo and Southwark) and the roads leading from them made this much easier. Coach services between the City and the South London settlements proliferated, and within a few years of the introduction of omnibuses in 1829 there were around 100 services in south London, taking middle-class commuters to their new suburban homes in Clapham, Brixton, Herne Hill, Dulwich or Blackheath. Some of these were in well-established settlements. Samuel Pepys had retired to Clapham, where he was visited by his fellow-diarist, John Evelyn, in 1701. Clapham prospered in the eighteenth century, when its marshy Common was drained and beautified by local subscription, and from the 1790s it won fame as the home of the evangelical and reformist religious group known as the Clapham Sect. By the 1850s it had grown into a large but still pleasant suburban town, big enough to provide congregations for five churches (four Anglican, one Roman Catholic) and a Congregational chapel. In the 1870s Clapham, with a population of about 30,000, was 'daily becoming more a part of London'. East and south of the Common, about 250 acres had been leased by Thomas Cubitt in 1824, and his development of Clapham Park, a large 'garden suburb' stretching as far as Brixton Hill and Tooting Bec Common, was still incomplete when he died in 1855.

The study of suburban growth south of the Thames was pioneered by H. J. Dyos's work on Camberwell. The parish (later borough) of Camberwell was a long wedge of land running 4½ miles from Albany Road and Rolls Road in the north (where it met Southwark and Bermondsey) to Crystal Palace in the south. To its west was the even more elongated parish of Lambeth, and to its east, Deptford and Lewisham. Its 4,450 acres included the villages and hamlets of Camberwell, Peckham, Denmark Hill, Herne Hill, Goose Green and Dulwich. In 1815 it was still a parish of market gardens, meadows and scattered villas, with most of its 13,000 inhabitants concentrated along the main roads from London. But a patch of squalid development, mixing houses and shops with piggeries, cowsheds, workshops and a glue factory, the notorious Sultan Street estate, was already taking shape in the north-western corner of the parish (between Camberwell Road and Camberwell New Road), and urbanized Walworth and Kennington were less than half a mile to the north.[74]

Twenty landlords owned 84 per cent of Camberwell's undeveloped land in 1837, and their decisions largely determined the pace and nature of Camberwell's suburban development. Many leased their land to builders as soon as they sensed the prospect of increasing the rental income of their estates, while others, perhaps through lethargy, conservatism, or inability to attract a suitable builder, waited for twenty or thirty years before doing so. So suburban Camberwell developed like a jigsaw, spreading generally from north to south, but with patches left uncompleted when all the fields around had been built upon. In the 1830s and 1840s most of the landlords of North Camberwell, roughly between Albany Road and Peckham Road, began leasing their land to speculative builders, and streets of terraced and semi-detached houses started to spread from the main roads into the fields and market gardens behind them. But the last pockets of open space in North Camberwell were not built over until the 1870s, by which time the district had been colonized by working-class residents, many of whom were employed in the local gasworks or canalside industries.[75]

Away from the main roads, the area south of Peckham Road was still largely open land in 1870. But over the next twenty years the landowners of Nunhead and East Dulwich (the area east of Lordship Lane) seized the opportunities offered by the rising demand for lower-middle-class and working-class housing and the coming of the tram, and leased their fields to the builders of modest terraced houses. West of Lordship Lane the picture was completely different. Here a 1,500-acre estate stretching from Denmark Hill to the Crystal Palace, a third of the parish, was owned by Dulwich College, which had received the land in 1619 from Edward Alleyn, the Elizabethan actor and brothel-keeper.[76] The governors of the College began leasing small areas of the estate to builders from the 1850s, always insisting on low-density and high-value housing, but they were in no hurry to develop, and much of the estate retained (and still retains) its rural character. The wealthiest street in Camberwell, Denmark Hill, ran along the western edge of the Dulwich College estate, and was still surrounded by pastures and market gardens in 1900.[77]

Dulwich felt like the edge of the town, but it was not. Beyond it to the south was the Crystal Palace and its popular pleasure-ground, and the growing railway suburbs of Penge and Upper Norwood. Norwood's population grew from under 3,000 in 1841 to 19,000 in 1881. Beyond them still, but connected by several railway lines and an ever-thickening belt of housing, was the important market and commuter town of Croydon, with a population in 1901 of 134,000. It would be easy to see Croydon, and other north Surrey towns, such as Richmond and Kingston, as commuter suburbs that owed their growth entirely to their railway connections with London. Contemporary accounts of commuter trains crowded with portly City men add plausibility to this interpretation. Such men, as John Kellett has shown, made up a small proportion, probably less than a tenth, of the outer suburban population. The great majority stayed at home, as the wives, children or servants of the commuting class, or as workers in local service or manufacturing industries. These towns had a social and economic life of their own, which was only partly dependent on the wealth of the commuting minority.[78]

THE QUALITY OF SUBURBAN LIFE

Late Victorian commentators were divided as to whether suburban living represented a refinement in urban civilization, or its degradation. The advantages of suburban life were clear enough to Mrs Panton, whose book of domestic advice, *From Kitchen to Garrett*, appeared in 1888:

> To young people, like my couple, I would strongly recommend a house some little way out of London. Rents are less; smuts and blacks conspicuous by their absence; a small garden, or even a tiny conservatory ... is not an impossibility; and if Edwin has to pay for his season-ticket, that is nothing in comparison with his being able to sleep in fresh air, to have a game of tennis in summer, or a friendly evening of music, chess, or games in the winter, without expense.[79]

But as suburbs became more accessible, they began to suffer from the social and environmental disorders their inhabitants had hoped to escape. The narrow streets and tiny back-yards of lower-middle-class suburbs seemed to *The Architect* in 1873 to have nothing to recommend them: 'What can be the advantage in search of which poor clerks and shopmen bring themselves to travel backwards and forwards all the year round, by the first train in the morning and the last at night, ... it is not really easy to see.'[80] And in 1890 *Building News* complained (rather prematurely) that 'Putney, Fulham, Richmond, Kew, on the west; Hampstead, Highgate, Hornsey, Finsbury, on the north; Clapham, Brixton, Dulwich, and Norwood, on the south, are already being irretrievably spoiled by the reckless speculator. . . . The greedy landowner and the speculative builder are doing more to bring about an equality between the two classes than any other individuals, for they are rendering town and suburbs as much like one another as possible.'[81] In the opinion of Frederic Harrison, the eminent barrister and positivist philosopher, 'to bury Middlesex and Surrey under miles of flimsy houses' where 'millions of working people are forced to live in dreary, bleak suburbs miles and miles away from all the freshness of the country, and away miles and miles even from the life and intelligence of cities' was one of the nineteenth century's least admirable achievements.[82] To the prolific late-Victorian historian of London, Sir Walter Besant, the suburbs epitomized the narrow-mindedness, isolation and dull respectability of middle-class life. Women in particular, he believed, had 'lost all the London life – the shops, the animation of the streets, their old circle of friends; in its place they found all the exclusiveness and class feeling of London with none of the advantages of a country town ... there was no society, and so for fifty years the massive dullness of the London suburb continued'.[83] To put it another way (as William Morris did in 1884), London was 'a spreading sore ... swallowing up with its loathsomeness field and wood and heath without mercy and without hope'.[84] Many suburban Londoners, who had never been involved in the intellectual or social life of the West End, but who had discovered in Dulwich, Richmond or Upper Norwood domestic and environmental comforts which they could never have found in the inner city, would no doubt have been shocked to discover that they were participants in such a deplorable enterprise.

There were others who argued that suburbs were an inevitable part of urban growth, and that with care and planning they could be built as places of beauty and social variety. Jonathan Carr showed what could be done in the 1870s, when he employed Norman Shaw to build a modest residential estate on his 113 acres in Turnham Green, near the new District underground railway. The result, Bedford Park, was (in Pevsner's words) 'the earliest of planned garden suburbs'. Its curved streets, lined with old trees and picturesque gabled and tile-hung brick houses in the Dutch or 'Queen Anne' style, attracted actors and aesthetes, and even pleased William Morris. Bedford Park was one of the influences on a much grander project at the end of the century, Hampstead Garden Suburb. The intention of Henrietta Barnett and the other directors of the Trust she founded in 1905 was to create a suburb in which the worst evils of conventional suburbs, uniformity, social segregation and the destruction of countryside, would be avoided. The new suburb's low-density housing (eight houses to the acre) would harmonize with the landscape around it, and offer accommodation for the rich and poor of all ages. As the suburb grew before and after the First World War, it became obvious that while its aesthetic and environmental aspirations had been achieved, its social ones had not. 'The population is on the whole comfortably off and ranges from true sensibility to amateur arty-craftiness,' Nikolaus Pevsner wrote in 1951.[85]

London's two garden suburbs, along with Ebenezer Howard's new garden city at Letchworth, 30 miles north of London, had a powerful influence on the development of the idea of town planning in the years around 1900. Garden suburbs were seized upon by a variety of architects, politicians, and municipal administrators as the answer to the social and environmental problems of city growth. In these suburbs, the Liberal politician C. F. G. Masterman wrote in 1909, 'something of the larger sanities of rural existence could be mingled with the quickness and agility of the town', and life in them might be 'the healthiest and the most hopeful promise for the future of modern England'. These hopes inspired the Liberal Government's Town Planning Act of 1909, a weak and ineffective measure which aimed, in the words of John Burns, President of the Local Government Board, to achieve 'the home healthy, the house beautiful, the town pleasant, the city dignified and the suburb salubrious' by giving local authorities modest planning powers over new development land. In practice, the act left the suburban developers of the next thirty years free to consume London's countryside as fast as they wished, using the low-density, land-hungry style of suburban planning that they borrowed from the pioneers of Bedford Park and Hampstead Garden Suburb.[86]

Chapter 19

Keeping the Peace

THIEVES' KITCHEN?

In December 1811 two families, seven people in all, were brutally murdered in two houses along the Ratcliff Highway, the main road to Shadwell (now called the Highway). Over twenty years later, Thomas De Quincey recalled these murders as 'the sublimest and most entire in their excellence that were ever committed', but at the time they had all London in a panic.[1] All Shadwell's nightwatchmen were sacked and replaced by armed patrols, and an unprecedented £500 reward was offered for the capture of the culprit. When the probable killer, John Williams, hanged himself in his prison cell, the turmoil subsided, and many would have agreed with John William Ward (a future Foreign Secretary) that a few killings in the poorest parts of London were a fair price to pay to avoid the costly and authoritarian system of state policing the French had to endure: 'I had rather half a dozen people's throats should be cut in Ratcliff Highway every three or four years than be subject to domiciliary visits, spies, and all the rest of Fouché's contrivances.'[2]

This attitude, combining a defence of traditional 'liberty' against the threat of 'tyranny' with a dislike of centralized interference in local policing responsibilities, led a succession of five Parliamentary Select Committees to reject the idea of full-scale professional policing for London between 1812 and 1827. Instead, London had to make do with a modest extension of the Bow Street Horse and Foot Patrols, which had kept a nightly watch over the outer highways and the inner streets since 1805. In 1821 a new 100-man Dismounted Patrol was introduced to cover the nearer suburbs at night, and from 1822 a Day Patrol of twenty-seven men watched the central area by day. These new forces, along with the seven local forces established in 1792 and the Thames River Police set up in 1800, gave London a professional force of more than 400 men, under the control of magistrates who were paid and controlled by the Home Office. In addition to these, there were almost 4,000 parish constables and watchmen, of variable quality and commitment. St James's and Marylebone were efficiently policed, while Kensington, Fulham and Deptford, with over 55,000 inhabitants between them in 1821, had no nightwatch at all.[3]

Gradually, the balance of public and political opinion shifted away from allegiance to the traditional system of parochial and unpaid policing, and towards the idea that London needed a trained professional force under central control. Probably the most powerful pressure for change came from the growing public belief that London was a thieves' kitchen, a paradise for swindlers, robbers and prostitutes. The demobilization of thousands of soldiers and sailors at the end of the Napoleonic wars in 1815 brought the usual fears of a crime wave, and these fears seemed to be confirmed by the rapidly rising number of people committed for trial in England and Wales, a figure published annually from 1810. From 1811–13 to 1825–7 London and Middlesex committal figures rose 53 per cent faster than the population as a whole, and although these might have been inflated by more generous help for those bringing prosecutions, and the introduction of new police patrols, opinion generally blamed demobilization and the moral degeneration of urban life for rising crime.

For those who did not care for statistics, there were lively accounts of London low-life on sale in every bookshop, warning visitors (as John Lydgate, Robert Greene and Ned Ward had done in earlier centuries) to be on their guard against impostors, rogues and cut-throats. Readers of John Badcock's (alias John Bee's) *Living Picture of London for 1828, and Stranger's Guide through the Streets of the Metropolis* were warned that in a city where skilful 'sharps' preyed upon guileless 'flats' they should not behave like visitors, not trust coachmen, street-sellers, fainting women or running men, and avoid crowds, back-streets and slum areas. If John Bee was to be believed, the careless newcomer, having lost his luggage in the inn yard as he arrived in town, would be surrounded by shady characters, who would pass him bad coin or offer to take him to inns of doubtful reputation. Asking his way outside the coach yard the 'flat' would be directed into a dark alley, where he would be beaten and robbed, or relieved of his purse by a pickpocket, using one of many tricks familiar to that ancient craft. Trying to economize after his losses, the visitor might wander into a mock auction, where 'flat-catchers' would trick him out of his remaining funds. If he managed to hold on to a coin or two, he would be bamboozled by a 'ringdropper', whose craft involved dropping and finding a gold-covered brass ring, and selling it for a third of its apparent value to a country bumpkin under the pretence of sharing his good fortune with him. Perhaps such events rarely took place, but stories, often repeated, helped prepare public opinion for a new form of policing, and persuaded many people, then and since, that London in the 1820s was indeed a criminals' paradise.[4]

RADICAL DISORDERS

There was a second reason for believing that London was outgrowing its policing system. The apparent rise in crime was accompanied by a spate of radical disorders in the six years after Waterloo. In these postwar years, London played its traditional part as the focal point of popular politics for the last time, before the initiative slipped away to the growing industrial cities of the Midlands and the North. Despite determined repression since the 1790s, there was still a tradition of popular radicalism in London. It was kept alive by the leadership of Francis Place and Sir Francis Burdett, the writings of William Cobbett, the speeches of 'Orator' Henry Hunt and wheat prices which in 1800–1801 and 1810–13 reached levels far higher than any experienced before or since (until recent times). Wheat prices started to fall in 1814, but before they could return to their old level Parliament passed the Corn Laws, which prohibited wheat imports until domestic prices reached 80s a quarter, a level which had never been reached, as an annual average, before 1800. The Corn Laws were modified later, but until their repeal in 1846 they remained a powerful symbol of all that was most objectionable in the landed dominance of government and legislation.

During the third reading of the Bill, on 6 March 1815, there were crowd scenes outside Parliament which were reminiscent of the beginning of the Gordon Riots. For the first of many times in these difficult postwar years the Home Office had to call upon the army to restore order. There were several thousand regular troops in barracks in central and suburban London, as well as London's own well-trained militia and its volunteer mounted force, the yeomanry. Between them, these forces were adequate for any emergency, but they were unpopular, and their deployment tended to intensify radical opposition to the government. Seven regiments brought the riots of March 1815 to an end, but the Corn Law issue, along with the postwar depression and high unemployment, brought radical intellectuals and popular feeling together again, and helped make the following four years 'the heroic age of popular radicalism'.[5]

Several leading radicals, including Francis Place and Major Cartwright, wanted to pursue Parliamentary reform by petitioning and peaceful meetings, but another group, led by Arthur Thistlewood and Dr James Watson, wanted London to play the part Paris had played in leading a national revolution. These men were followers of Thomas Spence, an eccentric republican and land reformer, who had died in 1814. On 2 December 1816 the Spenceans held a rally in Spa Fields, the New River Company land on the northern edge of Clerkenwell. A crowd of around 200 marched into the City, and finding the Royal Exchange defended by the Lord Mayor and an impromptu force of constables, moved on to threaten the Tower with weapons seized from local gunshops. They dispersed when the cavalry arrived, but their action exposed the vulnerability of the Tower to a well-planned attack. Throughout these years the government was kept fully informed by spies and *agents provocateurs*, and it was able to manipulate the Spenceans into organizing their own destruction. In February 1820 Thistlewood and his friends, acting on false information fed to them by the government, and actively encouraged by a ministerial agent, George Edwards, got involved in a foolish plot to murder the whole Cabinet. When the plotters met in Cato Street on 22 February the trap was sprung, and Thistlewood and his friends were arrested, tried and executed.[6]

In contrast to the emerging mass radicalism of Birmingham and Manchester, these London incidents were reassuringly old-fashioned, and did not seriously threaten the government. On the contrary, they provided the pretext for repressive legislation against seditious meetings and radical propaganda, and temporarily discredited the reformist cause. The only London episode that really frightened the authorities in these years was the popular movement in support of Queen Caroline, the exiled wife of the highly unpopular George IV. When George III died in February 1820, radicals saw the possibility of using the wronged Queen as a focus for popular hostility to the new King and his ministers, and Alderman Wood, the radical City MP, persuaded her to sail for England. Arriving in London on 6 June, Caroline won enormous popular adulation, which was encouraged by William Cobbett and the radical press. The rallies and parades in support of Caroline in the summer and autumn of 1820 were among the biggest that London had ever seen, and in mid-June signs of a mutiny in a battalion of the Coldstream Guards made the situation seem particularly dangerous. When the Bill to divorce and depose the Queen was abandoned on 10 November, there were bonfires and illuminations all over London for three days, and a service of thanksgiving was held in St Paul's. The London artisans turned out in force: large and colourful processions of shipwrights, brassfounders, bakers, weavers, coopers, corset-makers, printers, bricklayers and many other trade societies paraded for Caroline in the autumn and winter, reasserting a right of assembly which the government had tried to stifle after Cato Street. Public support faded in the spring, but in August 1821 Caroline revived her popularity by dying. The government's intention was to send the Queen's body to Harwich by a route that avoided the City. The City authorities and the crowd had other ideas, and on 14 August the procession, protected by Life Guards and the Bow Street police, had to fight huge crowds all the way from Hammersmith to the New Road. The troops responded to the throwing of stones and mud by firing on the crowd, killing a carpenter and a bricklayer. Eventually, where the New Road met Tottenham Court Road, thick barricades forced the funeral procession to turn south towards Fleet Street, and to pass along Cheapside and Cornhill, as the crowd had demanded all along. This public humiliation ended the career of the Chief Magistrate of Bow Street, Sir Robert Baker, and several observers believed that the London mob, now that it had learnt its strength, would be irrepressible in future. Lord Liverpool, the Prime Minister, expressed his fears to Chateaubriand: 'What can be stable with these enormous towns? One serious insurrection in London and all is lost.'[7]

The Origins of the Metropolitan Police

Historians of the police generally argue that the fear of crowd disorder, especially in the wake of the Queen Caroline riots and the other events of 1815–21, precipitated the creation of the New Police in 1829. Political considerations, it is argued, rather than the problem of 'ordinary' crime, overcame the long-standing resistance to the idea of professional policing. Stanley Palmer speaks for almost all historians of the Metropolitan Police when he argues that 'the institution represents the authorities' response to the new challenge from below – political radicalism and protest', and that crime, since it had been a problem for so long, could not have played a crucial part in the decision taken in 1828. Wellington's letter to Lord Liverpool after the near-mutiny of June 1820 is often quoted: 'The Government ought, without the loss of a moment's time, to adopt measures to form either a police in London or a military corps, which should be of a different description from the regular military force, or both.'[8] And it is likely that Sir Robert Peel, who became Home Secretary a few months after the Queen Caroline riots, was motivated by the same fears when he set up another select committee on the policing of London in 1822. But the problem for Peel, as it had been for Pitt thirty-seven years before, was to persuade Parliamentary opinion that professional policing was necessary. Here the argument which focuses on disorder breaks down. The 1822 committee, sitting less than a year after the Queen Caroline riots and chaired by Peel, rejected professional policing with the often-repeated argument that the loss of liberty outweighed the advantages in terms of crime control, and in 1823 *The Times* was still sticking to the old line, that a centralized police force was 'an engine ... invented by despotism'. Whatever changed the minds of MPs and *The Times* by 1828 it was not a resurgence of political disorder in the capital, since there was none for the remainder of the 1820s. Nationally, in the words of E. P. Thompson, 'the decade of the 1820s seems strangely quiet – a mildly prosperous plateau of social peace'.[9] George Rudé's argument, that 'the decisive factor that tipped the balance in favour of the "proposers" [of the new police] was the alarm caused by the new wave of civil commotion starting about 1829' just will not do, since the key decisions were taken by the Select Committee and Parliament in 1828, and the Parliamentary reform agitation which Rudé is referring to did not begin until the economic slump of 1830. Rudé and some other police historians have confused the crime control purpose for which the Metropolitan Police was introduced in 1829 with the crowd control purpose for which it was almost immediately, but unexpectedly, used in 1830–32.[10]

During the 1820s Peel worked on parliamentary, press and public opinion to soften their resistance to a trained professional police force under Home Office control, using the growth of crime, rather than the spectre of political unrest, to drive his message home. As he explained to Wellington, who was by then Prime Minister, in 1829: 'I want to teach people that liberty does not consist in having your house robbed by organized gangs of thieves, and in leaving the principal streets of London in the nightly possession of drunken women and vagabonds.'[11] And when he moved successfully for a new Select Committee in February 1828 he used the criminal committal figures, still rising convincingly, to make his point. The Select Committee, which reported in July 1828, completely ignored the question of radicalism and popular unrest. Not a single member of the committee, and not a single witness, so much as mentioned the problem. Instead, the investigation concentrated exclusively on the adequacy of London's parochial policing, the effectiveness of the Bow Street patrols, and the level of everyday crime in the metropolis.

The magistrates, High Constables, clerks of the peace and parish officials who appeared as witnesses before the committee presented a picture of a city bothered but not endangered by petty crime. Many of them spoke about neglected or homeless children sleeping rough under stalls or in baskets in Covent Garden and other London markets, trained and corrupted by older criminals, and making a living by begging, pilfering and shoplifting. Others emphasized the saloons, coffee houses, oyster shops and pubs that acted as social centres, or flash-houses, for criminals, and the marine stores, old iron shops and pawnshops that received the goods they had stolen. Larcenies by servants and shopmen, thefts from over-enticing shop displays, and stolen goods carried by night in covered horse carts, were the matters of most concern. The story from the suburbs varied according to who was telling it. Magistrates and High Constables from Barking, Leytonstone, West Ham, Hackney, Barnet, Edgware, Acton, Pinner, Kingston and Croydon claimed that policing was adequate and crime levels low, but witnesses from Camberwell, Tottenham, Chelsea, Brixton and Brentford complained of burglaries, thefts from large suburban gardens and river crime, all thriving in a world of inactive constables, sleepy watchmen and fleeting visits from the Bow Street horse patrol. The Committee concluded that a patchy system of parochial policing, which enabled criminals to hide out in the worst parishes (Deptford, Edgware, Chelsea, Brentford, Kensington), needed to be replaced by a unified metropolitan force under Home Office control.[12]

The 1828 Committee's decision to recommend an entirely new force, replacing, rather than building upon, the Bow Street patrols and the executive authority of the London magistrates, was influenced by their discovery of scandalous corruption within the existing forces. They found an organized system, connived at by the magistrates, in which City and Bow Street officers helped banks recover stolen money from robbers, and shared large rewards with criminals and fences. The Committee knew of sixteen cases, involving over £200,000, but did not publish the details, which are now lost. It is certainly true that several Bow Street and City detectives retired with large and unexplained fortunes, and it is clear that the business of crime investigation, which was the Bow Street officer's special strength, involved corrupting contact with the criminal world. In the words of a later Select Committee, the Bow Street police were 'private speculators in crime, rather than efficient officers for the ends of justice'.[13] Joseph Thomas, a parish constable in Covent Garden, and later a Metropolitan Police superintendent, gave damaging evidence against the Bow Street officers. His efforts to clear the neighbourhood of vagrants, pickpockets and prostitutes were constantly impeded by Bow Street men, who socialized freely with offenders in the Brown Bear, Bow Street, and were only interested in arrests which carried rewards. The impression of collusion, corruption, and weak magisterial and parochial management, along with London's lack of unified local government, made it possible for

Peel to win over the New Police a degree of direct central control which later Home Secretaries were never able to achieve over provincial forces.[14]

THE POLICE AND CRIME

The Metropolitan Police Bill had an easy passage through Parliament, and in July 1829 Peel appointed two Commissioners, Colonel Charles Rowan and a barrister, Richard Mayne, to establish and command the new force. For their headquarters a building was rented in a turning off Whitehall, known as Great Scotland Yard. By 1830 they had recruited over 3,000 men, and organized them into seventeen divisions, each under a superintendent. Although about a seventh of the recruits, and all but one of the superintendents, were ex-soldiers, Peel did his best to establish the civilian nature of the force by dressing the men in top hats and blue swallow-tail coats, and arming them only with truncheons (and cutlasses on dangerous beats). Peel reduced the risk that policemen would become as corrupt as the Bow Street officers by emphasizing the preventive role of the Metropolitan Police rather than its detective one, and forbidding lower ranks to meet criminals and informers in public houses. Constables were to patrol openly in order to deter criminals, and to arrest as soon as a crime had been committed, rather than waiting for more serious offences to develop. Their aim should be to prevent crime, not to cultivate it in the hope of a bigger prize. Nor should the New Police act like government spies, however successful these had been in the past. When it was discovered that Sergeant Popay had infiltrated the National Political Union in 1832 there was an outcry and a select committee, and plain-clothes officers were rarely used thereafter.

From 1829 to 1839 the Metropolitan Police District covered an area of about 100 square miles, ending between 4 and 7 miles from Charing Cross, but excluding the City. This was the area covered by the three Bow Street foot patrols, which were at once disbanded, along with the local nightwatch and parish constabulary. Of the other older forces, the Horse Patrol and the Thames Police were absorbed into the Metropolitan Police in 1836 and 1839, and the small detective forces attached to London's nine Magistrates' Courts, or Police Offices, were disbanded in 1839, after ten years of uneasy coexistence with the New Police. To compensate for the loss of the Bow Street detectives the Commissioners reluctantly created the Metropolitan Police Force's own small Detective Department in 1842. The outer parochial forces were abolished in 1839, when the Metropolitan Police

District was extended to nearly 700 square miles, a radius of around 15 miles from Charing Cross, and the main force was increased to 4,300 men. This was an extremely generous definition of 'London', many times bigger than the area covered by the London County Council from 1888, and bigger even than that allocated to the Greater London Council in 1965. No administrative body of comparable importance controlled so large an area of London until the establishment of the London Passenger Transport Board in 1933. Only the City remained distinct. To the Select Committees of 1828, 1834 and 1838 the City's separate police force was a damaging and inefficient anachronism, an archaic reminder of the days when the City was London. But to the City it was a cornerstone of self-government, and every ounce of political influence was used to save it. The price of independence was reform, and in 1839 the City agreed to remodel its force along Metropolitan Police lines, rather than lose it altogether.[15]

No doubt many Londoners welcomed the new sense of order and security that regular police patrols brought to the capital, but reactions to the New Police were not always favourable. Relations with the stipendiary magistrates of the old police offices were very difficult for a few years, and the Chief Magistrate of Bow Street, Sir John Roe, found it hard to accept that he was no longer London's chief of police. Charles Reith has given us an indignant and minutely detailed account of the battle between Roe and the two commissioners, which culminated in the enforced dismissal of Inspector Wovenden and Superintendent Lazenby in 1834, over an allegation that Wovenden had raped a prostitute. This was Roe's last major victory over Scotland Yard. Select Committees in 1833 and 1838 praised the Metropolitan Police, and led the way to the final removal of the stipendiary magistrates' remaining policing powers in 1839. At the same time, the hostility of many parishes to a police force which they paid for but did not control was softened by the Treasury's decision in 1833 to pay a quarter of police costs. The Home Office could also keep costs down by paying low wages, but this meant taking recruits whose occasional drunkenness, indiscipline and insolence gave fresh ammunition to the opponents of the new system, and ensured an extraordinarily fast turnover of staff. Within two years of 1829 nearly 2,000 men had been dismissed for drunkenness and over 1,000 had resigned, unwilling to endure the discipline, danger and unpopularity of police duty in return for less than £1 a week.[16]

Ratepayers and property owners had much to gain from efficient policing, and after initial doubts they seem to have accepted the new system as an ingredient of civilized urban life. James Grant, whose *Sketches in London* appeared in 1838, probably expressed a widely held satisfaction with the impact of the New Police on crime: 'Person and property are now incomparably safer than they were under the old system. The new police are now the objects of universal approbation, and deservedly so. . . . Almost all the extensive confederations which then existed for the purpose of carrying on a regularly organized system of robbery . . . have been broken up and scattered in all directions. . . . With respect to crimes against the person, they are now comparatively rare.'[17] John Murray's *World of London*, published in 1843, was more critical of the police, but agreed that crime was well under control: 'When we reflect how much property is accumulated in every district within the Bills of Mortality, we are amazed at the comparative infrequency of outrage and plunder, and the comparative certainty with which attempts at either are detected and suppressed.' A lone policeman could even disperse a brawling mob. The authority of the police uniform was such, Murray said, that although its occupant was usually an 'ungainly lout' the mob 'slinks away at his approach: the combatants are effectively cowed'. And an essay by W. O'Brien in the *Edinburgh Review* of July 1852 was full of admiration for the policing of London: 'The arrangements are so good, the security so general, and the complex machinery works so quietly, that the real danger which must always exist where the wealth and luxury of a nation are brought into juxtaposition with its poverty and crime, is too much forgotten, and people begin to think it quite a matter of course . . . that they sleep and wake in safety in the midst of hordes of starving plunderers.' Credit for this was due, O'Brien wrote, to the beat system, the information network, the crowd control methods and the growing detective skills of the Metropolitan Police, and the uncanny moral authority the police had won over the criminal class. 'The habitual state of mind towards the police of those who live by crime is not so much dislike, as unmitigated, slavish terror . . . a ruffian will drop his usual tone of bullying audacity, and follow every look of the police officer like a beaten hound creeping to lick his master's feet.'[18]

Charles Dickens was a great admirer of the police, especially the Detective Branch, and he helped reinforce the reassuring impression that policemen wielded an almost magical authority over London's darkest rookeries and blackest villains. In 1851 he went 'On Duty with Inspector Field', head of the Detective Branch, to three of London's worst slum districts, St Giles', Whitechapel, and the Old Mint, alongside the Borough High Street. All fears of London's dark and unsavoury places (fears which

Dickens did his share to propagate) melted away when they were visited in the company of an experienced officer. When Inspector Field enters the Rat's Castle, a notorious thieves' cellar in St Giles':

> All watch him, all answer when addressed, all laugh at his jokes, all seek to propitiate him. The cellar company alone – to say nothing of the crowd surrounding the entrance from the street above, and making the steps shine with eyes – is strong enough to murder us all, and willing enough to do it; but, let Inspector Field have a mind to pick out one thief here, and take him; let him produce that ghostly truncheon from his pocket and say, with his businesslike air, 'My lad, I want you!' and all Rat's Castle shall be stricken with paralysis, and not a finger move against him, as he fits the handcuffs on!

Even the murky Thames held no mystery for Inspector Field: 'He does not trouble his head as I do, about the river at night. He does not care for its creeping, black and silent, on our right there, rushing through sluice gates, lapping at piles and posts and iron rings, hiding strange things in its mud, running away with suicides and accidentally drowned bodies. . . .'[19]

Ordinary constables did not command the respect accorded to Inspector Field and his party. There were 2–3,000 arrests each year in the 1840s for assaulting police officers, and around 300 for attempting to rescue a prisoner from police custody, a crime which demonstrated a degree of communal solidarity against the police.[20] Among young costermongers, Mayhew tells us, it was a matter of honour to pay back an interfering policeman with a brick or boot, and police efforts to control street trading were met with determined resistance.

THE POLICE AND POPULAR CULTURE

Historians sometimes claim that the power of the Metropolitan Police was so great that within a few decades London's rowdy and immoral working class was cowed into submission and relative respectability. Robert Storch credits the police with 'a successful seizure of control of all urban public spaces', and David Goodway argues that the police force was 'a far-reaching system of social control' which made 'significant incursions . . . into the city's easy-going ways'. 'A great mass of previously non-criminal activity became unlawful and was regulated, with amazing success, by the force.'[21]

The reality was more complex than this. The police were given extensive powers, especially in the very comprehensive Metropolitan Police Act of

1839, to bring decency and order to the streets of London. Under this Act, bowling hoops, making ice slides, knocking on doors, putting out lamps, lighting fireworks and begging, selling or entertaining with noisy instruments became arrestable offences, and the police gained new powers over fairs, public houses, gaming houses, unlicensed theatres, street musicians, and those who conducted noisy or dirty trades on the street. But the powers of the police over prostitutes, beggars and street entertainers and traders depended on public complaints and the cooperation of magistrates, and the 1839 Act did not give the police a right to enter London's several thousand brothels, coffee shops, 'cigar divans', dancing saloons and night houses, although these were the breeding grounds, so the police believed, of the city's immoral and criminal subculture. These places survived at least until the 1870s, when the police rather reluctantly used the 1869 Wine and Beerhouses Act to enter them and close them down.[22]

Even where they had the legal powers, the police had to tread a difficult path between laxity and tyranny, between the demands of the 'respectable' minority of clergymen, parish officials and solid citizens, and the practical necessity for good relations with the working-class majority. The police realized that prostitution, street selling, Sunday trading, noisy games and rowdy pubs were features of big-city life which no amount of repression could remove, and that if their constables made enemies of the whole working class by attacking their social and cultural institutions then they would never again be safe to walk their beats, alone and unarmed, on London's poorer streets. As the Royal Commission on the Police put it in 1839, 'if those for whose protection such an agency is devised feel that their social or political liberty is compromised ... the action of the police will be paralysed'. Time and again, in the Metropolitan Police and Home Office records, in evidence to Select Committees, and in answers to public complaints, we find the Commissioners and their superintendents resisting pressure to adopt a more interventionist form of moral policing. This was Commissioner Mayne's view on prostitution: 'There is perhaps no branch of the duty which calls for greater discretion in its execution by the Police, or in which any excess of authority would expose the Police to greater odium and public censure.' And on seizing the goods of Sunday street traders: 'It led to a breach of the peace; the women and children cry out, and make a disturbance it is so desirable to avoid ... it makes a greater brawl, and I think seizing things on the street on Sunday is very objectionable, and indeed on any day.' The police defied pressure to close down street markets in Leather Lane, Oxford Street and the New Cut, and supported the annual fairs in places such as Stepney, Croydon, Barnet and

Pinner against their critics. Beyond the closure of public houses between midnight on Saturday and 1 p.m. on Sunday, which was included in the 1839 Act, Mayne resisted evangelical demands for a Sunday without drinking, shopping or entertainment. In 1855 he strongly opposed Lord Grosvenor's Bill to abolish all Sunday trading in London, on the grounds that it would bring the law into dangerous and unnecessary confrontation with popular feeling. Events on 1 July 1855, when a crowd of about 150,000 gathered in Hyde Park and attacked the carriages of the well-off, proved Mayne's point, and the Bill was withdrawn. Karl Marx's announcement 'that yesterday in Hyde Park the English revolution began' turned out to be premature.[23]

Both sides, the police and the London poor, developed codes of conduct which enabled them to live in relative peace and harmony with each other. Beggars begged more discreetly, or pretended to sell matches; prostitutes solicited more quietly, and perhaps befriended the local constable; traders and entertainers chose their pitches more carefully, and moved on when they were told to do so; children moved their games from streets to pieces of waste ground; and publicans developed the defensive techniques later used by American speakeasies: peepholes, sentries, alarm signals and back-door escape routes. For their part the police decided to establish minimum standards of public order and decency, but not to provoke social conflict by striving for unattainable perfection, even when the local clergy pressed them to do so. Thus London in the 1850s still had thirty-seven Sunday markets, about 3,000 known brothels, and over 1,000 disreputable coffee houses. Prostitutes still lined the streets, especially in St James's, Marylebone, Covent Garden and Whitechapel, but only about thirty were arrested (usually for being drunk or disorderly) on a typical night. This infuriated anti-vice campaigners, but the Home Office viewed the problem with worldly pragmatism: 'The police seem to have done their duty, and the law is as stringent as it can well be,' the Home Secretary noted in 1857. 'An attempt to suppress these things in London by legislation would be quite absurd.'[24]

This compromise between the police and popular culture helps account for the picture of London life that emerges from the works of Mayhew and Charles Manby-Smith in the 1850s, and of Thomas Wright, James Greenwood and Gustave Doré in the 1860s and 1870s. Their London may have been less criminal than the London of the 1820s, but it was far from being a tamed and respectable city. There is no account of London in the wild pre-1829 days which gives as full or rich a picture of thriving street life as Mayhew's in the well-policed 1850s, and Mayhew's poor are still playing, singing, fighting, swindling, drinking, soliciting, trading and tramping as if the Metropolitan Police Act of 1839 had never been passed, and social control had never been thought of. If Mayhew's costermongers were at war with the police, they were not defeated by them, and Mayhew's street entertainers seemed to look upon the police as protectors, not persecutors. Guy Fawkes parades were more numerous, more elaborate, and more political in the 1850s than ever before, in spite of the fact that the Metropolitan Police (according to Storch) had tried to suppress them in the 1830s. Mayhew was told by a man who had organized the parades since 1844: '"It's very seldom that the police say anything to us, so long as we don't stop too long in the gangway to create any mob. They join in the fun and laugh like the rest. Wherever we go there is a great crowd from morning to night."'[25]

The history of London's fairs is a good illustration of police tolerance of popular culture. The strongest attack on inner London fairs came in the 1820s, when magistrates and the old police suppressed the Shoreditch, Hampstead, Bow, Brook Green, Tothill Fields, Edmonton and Peckham fairs. In the 1830s and 1840s the Metropolitan Police took a more indulgent view, and most of the remaining fairs survived until the 1850s, when the Bartholomew, Camberwell, Greenwich and Stepney fairs were closed, but not as a result of pressure from the police. For the rest of the century, the police generally defended fairs against their critics, and the fairs at Croydon, Barnet, Pinner, Edgware and Feltham survived thanks in part to police support. This is a typically realistic assessment of the Barnet Fair from a superintendent in the 1880s:

> The fair is almost the only source of amusement brought within reach
> of the poorer country people during the year, and it is much enjoyed
> by them, and in addition it is a means of assisting small and struggling
> tradesmen of the town, as well as private persons who let lodgings.[26]

CRIME IN VICTORIAN LONDON

Evidence from Metropolitan Police records goes some way to confirm that the early nineteenth-century 'crime wave' (if there had ever been one) was brought under control in the 1830s and 1840s. The force kept statistical records of the number of arrests and convictions, analysed by age group, trade and level of education, from 1831 onwards. Arrests and convictions are affected by many factors, including police efficiency and manpower, the instructions passed from Scotland Yard to local stations in the Commissioners' Daily Orders, changing legal definitions of crimes, and the policies pursued in magistrates' and higher courts. For what the figures are worth, they show that between 1834 and 1848 the Metropolitan Police arrested about 64,000 people a year, of whom around 47 per cent were convicted, mostly in magistrates' courts. The figures did not rise, despite the fact that the population covered by the Metropolitan Police rose from about 1.6 million to about 2.5 million over the period. Thus the arrest and conviction rate, per 1,000 of the population, fell from about 39 and 17.5 respectively in 1834 to 26 and 12.5 in 1848. Just under a quarter of these convictions, in a typical year, were for property offences.[27]

Most nineteenth-century experts on crime, certainly those who wrote after about 1850, believed the problem was concentrated in a specialized 'class' of criminals, people who were culturally and economically distinct from the working class as a whole. The prevalence of this concept has been well documented by J. J. Tobias, who argues that it was widespread from the mid-1830s. Henry Mayhew was a great believer in the criminal class, and through his work the idea was firmly implanted in public consciousness. Unlike Tobias, most historians now regard the emphasis on professional crime as misleading. Certainly, London had its professional burglars, pickpockets, housebreakers and prostitutes, but to focus exclusively upon them is to ignore the much larger (though unquantifiable) amount of workplace crime, and amateur crimes committed as a result of habit, impulse, temptation or desperation, rather than as planned professional acts.[28]

As in our own time, murders, bank robberies and burglaries shaped public perceptions of crime, without in themselves being particularly common. In an average year in the 1830s or 1840s, there were only ten convictions for murder or manslaughter in London, and only 130 for burglary, shopbreaking, housebreaking and robbery. Even in 1899, in a city of over 6 million people, there were only twenty-one reported murders (three of which were deaths after abortions), and seven burglaries or housebreakings involving violence to the person. The great majority of arrests and convictions were for common assault, assault on a police officer, various forms of non-violent larceny and other minor property crimes (illegal possession, loitering with intent to steal, wilful damage), and different types of immoral or disorderly behaviour. While newspapers were full of murderers, burglars and street robbers (or 'garotters'), police cells, magistrates' courts and even the Old Bailey itself were filled with petty thieves, 'suspected characters', 'reputed thieves', disorderly prostitutes, vagrants, disorderly characters and drunkards. These last four categories constituted over a half of all Metropolitan Police arrests in the 1830s and 1840s, an average of well over 30,000 people a year.[29]

Of course, the pattern of crime in Victorian London is not accurately reflected in the police arrest statistics. In 1837 three-quarters of reported property offences in London were listed as being 'unpreventable by police vigilance'. These included embezzlement, fraud, forgery, thefts by servants, lodgers or prostitutes, housebreaking through gardens not visible to the police, and theft of goods from unguarded shop displays, open houses, washing lines or drunkards. Sprawling suburban areas were especially difficult to protect by the beat system. Street criminals, especially those already known to the police, were sure to feel the constable's hand on their collar from time to time, but those who committed acts of theft or violence in the privacy of their homes and workplaces were fairly safe from arrest. Servants, laundresses, omnibus conductors, carters, building workers, dockers, lightermen, milkmen, deliverymen, railwaymen and shopworkers habitually supplemented their wages by pilfering or overcharging, and their employers kept their wages low because they knew it was happening. These cases rarely came to court, and when they did defendants usually claimed that they were following the common practice of their trade. Pawnbrokers and second-hand dealers were only too willing to buy stolen goods without asking questions, but they were hardly ever prosecuted for it.[30]

Domestic violence, especially wife- and child-beating, was almost certainly far more common than the police or court figures suggest. Nationally, infants under one year old made up around 60 per cent of known homicide victims between 1863 and 1887, and it is clear that most cases of infanticide went undiscovered among the mass of non-criminal infant deaths in nineteenth-century London. A half of London's working women were servants, who were vulnerable to sexual exploitation or misadventure, and certain to be dismissed without references if this resulted in pregnancy. A servant's chances of winning maintenance from the father by going to court were very slim, and many would have chosen to abandon or do away with their children rather than enter a workhouse or live in shame and poverty on outdoor relief. Their babies probably account for a good proportion of the 276 infant bodies found abandoned in London in 1876, floating in ponds, or left in dustholes, churches, cellars and cesspits. Others might have belonged to well-off women who had come to London to have their illegitimate children, leaving them to 'midwives' to dispose of.[31]

The identification of infanticide depended on the medical skills and social attitudes of coroners, none of whom were medically qualified until Dr Thomas Wakley was elected coroner for West Middlesex (covering all of North and West London except Westminster) in 1839. Wakley died in 1862, but his successor as coroner for the new district of Central Middlesex (including St Pancras, Paddington, St Marylebone, Islington and Clerkenwell) was Dr Edwin Lankester, who was even more determined to expose the difference between accidental death and murder. Between 1839 and 1874 these two men made infanticide into a national issue, with London as its focal point. In 1866–7, 75 of Lankester's 361 infant inquests led to murder verdicts, giving central Middlesex, with a third of London's population, half the national total of known infanticides. Such verdicts hardly ever led to arrests or convictions. In seventeen months in 1859–60 the Metropolitan Police knew of 464 infanticides, brought fourteen prosecutions, and won seven convictions.[32]

Public awareness of infanticide was heightened in the late 1860s and 1870s by publicity given to 'baby farmers', who took charge of unwanted infants for a single payment, and profited from the early death of their 'adopted' children. In 1870 there was a sensational case involving two sisters, Sarah Ellis and Margaret Waters, the 'Brixton Baby Farmers'. Following the finding of several dead babies on Lambeth streets, police entered Ellis's lodgings, where they found nine babies, five of them dying from malnutrition and opium poisoning. Waters, the less culpable of the sisters, was hanged, but Ellis, who was only charged with fraud, escaped with 18 months' hard labour. The police had little success against other South London 'baby farmers', and public and police interest soon waned. The Brixton case prompted the formation of the Infant Life Protection Society, and the passage (in 1872) of a weak and ineffective law to force baby farmers to register with their local authority.[33]

Murder in Whitechapel

As cheaper newspapers increased their readership after the abolition of stamp duty in 1855, public perceptions of crime relied increasingly on press campaigns and well-publicized cases. As well as the baby-farming scandals of the early 1870s, there were press-induced panics over violent attacks by street robbers, or 'garotters', in London in 1856 and 1862, over armed burglars in the 1880s, over child prostitution in 1885, and over the expected eruption of the East End following the Trafalgar Square riots of February 1886. The greatest panic of all occurred in the autumn of 1888, when lurid accounts of the Whitechapel Murders obsessed London newspapers and their readers. Between 6 August and 9 November, the mutilated bodies of six impoverished street prostitutes were found in squalid rooms and alleys within 500 yards of Whitechapel High Street, where the wealth of the City met the poverty and mystery of the East End. The brutality of the killings, the taunting letters of 'Jack the Ripper' to his baffled pursuers, the failure of the police to identify the murderer, the element of prostitution and sexual depravity, the excitement of waiting for the killer to strike again, the dark and sinister location, so close to 'respectable' London, made this the newspaper story of the century. Public suspicion fell on doctors, butchers, foreigners and Jews, and confidence in the detective powers of the police evaporated. In future, fictional detective heroes were more likely to be private operators than Scotland Yard men. Sherlock Holmes, whose first appearance was in *A Study in Scarlet* in 1887, was the epitome of the new breed. Real detectives did not have Holmes's mental powers, and the 'Ripper' was never caught. If, as many believe, the killer was Montague Druitt, a mentally unstable barrister with East End connections, then he escaped justice by drowning himself in the Thames in December 1888. If, on the other hand, it was the Polish immigrant George Chapman (originally Severin Klosowski), a Cable Street hairdresser, he was finally hanged for another murder in 1903.[34]

The police statistics, with all their faults, give us a more accurate picture of the real experience of late Victorian Londoners than newspaper accounts do. In the second half of the century recorded crime rates fell all over the country, thanks, it is generally believed, to improving education, rising real wages and more intensive policing. London shared in these trends, and by the late 1880s, when the 'Jack the Ripper' murders were creating a panic even greater than that induced by the Ratcliff Highway killings of 1811, Londoners were probably less likely to suffer from a crime, and certainly less likely to be arrested for one, than in any earlier decade in the century. In the 1880s the arrest rate (per 1,000 of the population) was about a quarter of the rate in the early 1850s, and London, according to the Director of Criminal Investigation, was 'the safest capital for life and property in the world'. The improvement continued until the end of the century. In the late 1860s, when London's population was about 3.5 million, over 21,000 felonies involving property were reported to the police each year. This figure fell to around 18,000 between 1870 and 1875, and returned to over 20,000 in the 1880s (24,754 in 1882), but it fell steadily in the 1890s, and by the end of the century it was just over 16,000, the lowest it had ever been. This meant that the rate of reported serious property crime in London, taking population growth into account, had fallen by 60 per cent in thirty years.[35]

Despite this spectacular fall in recorded crime, which was not reversed until after the Second World War, the old criminal crafts lived on, at least in the writings of those who made their livings by describing the tricks of the London underworld. Ernest Carr, writing in George R. Sims's *Living London,* described a world of skulduggery that Henry Mayhew, Patrick Colquhoun or Ned Ward (the 'London Spy') would have recognized fifty, 100 or 200 years earlier. Carr's London was still full of 'swell mobsmen', watch stealers ('buzzers'), begging-letter writers, cab thieves, pillar-box thieves, horse and dog stealers, pickpockets with dummy arms or false-bottomed handbags, coiners, forgers and confidence tricksters. Yet the crime statistics tell us that either these colourful rogues were much rarer than they once had been, or that their victims were too dazed, drugged or indifferent to report their losses to the police.[36]

Chapter 20

Popular Politics and
Trade Unionism

THE WORKING PEOPLE of nineteenth-century London were not a homogenous mass, and no one with any insight regarded them as such. They were distinguished from each other by income, education, religion, drinking habits, domestic arrangements, membership of clubs and societies, and the skills and status involved in their work. There were important distinctions between workers in traditional crafts and those in new mechanical industries, between people in trades which were threatened by economic growth and trades which prospered under it, and between industries in which skills and apprenticeship had been maintained and those in which they had broken down. Within particular industries there were distinctions between different levels of skill, experience and working conditions which meant a great deal to those involved in them, and defined their social status as accurately as conventional class labels do. Artisans who possessed scarce skills, which could not easily be replaced by machinery or casual labour, commanded high and regular wages, good conditions of work and better social status than the rest of the working class. Literacy, domestic comfort, respectability, membership of trade unions and friendly societies, independence from charity and poor relief, were characteristic of this group.

Although the term usually applied to the working-class élite, the 'aristocracy of labour', is generally used in relation to the period after about 1850, it is clear that the distinction between artisans and labourers was as important in London in the 1790s or 1820s as it was in the 1850s. Many of the labour struggles of the early decades of the century were concerned with maintaining this distinction by preventing the free entry of unskilled labour into skilled crafts.[1] In 1849 Henry Mayhew spoke of the moral and cultural gulf between the 'honourable' and 'dishonourable' ends of London trades as a division of long standing: 'The very dwellings of the people are sufficient to tell you the wide difference between the two classes. In the one you occasionally find small statues of Shakespeare beneath glass shades; in the other all is dirt and foetor. The honourable part of the trade are really intelligent artisans, while the slop-workers are generally almost brutified with their incessant toil, wretched pay, miserable food, and filthy homes.' Later he added: 'In passing from the skilled operative of the west-end to the unskilled workman of the eastern quarter of London, the moral and intellectual change is so great, that it seems as if we were in a new land, and among another race. The artisans are almost to a man red-hot politicians. They are sufficiently educated and thoughtful to have a sense of their importance in the State.'[2]

LONDON AS A POLITICAL CENTRE

Except at times of intense public excitement, the pursuit of working-class interests, especially in the fields of trade union rights and franchise reform, was in the hands of the well-paid, educated and organized élite, or 'aristocracy', of labour. Since before 1700, in London and other towns, men in skilled and better-paid crafts had defended their pay and conditions, maintained the exclusiveness of their trades, and supported each other through illness and unemployment, by forming local societies or combinations. Their aims had not been, as a rule, to win radical political reform, or to unite all working men in huge 'General Unions', but only to defend their own relatively privileged position in the workforce. Unskilled and poorly paid workers, in London and elsewhere, were rarely able to set up long-lived unions until the 1880s. Their wages were too low and irregular to form strike or welfare funds, or to survive a strike or lock-out, and their lack of organizational and craft skills made them easy to bully and replace, except at times of exceptional labour scarcity.[3]

Despite its enormous population, its closeness to the centre of government and journalism, and its long tradition of political activity, London did not lead the way in popular radicalism after 1830, as it had done until the 1820s. Manchester, Leeds, Nottingham, Birmingham, and other industrial cities of the Midlands and North, increasingly shared London's role as a source of ideas and organization for the Parliamentary Reform movement, and sometimes set an example of decisive radical leadership which the capital was unable to follow. London was no longer the only city with a large working population, or the only one with good sources of political information. London's vast size, and the diversity of economic and social interests it contained, made it more difficult for its working people to act with unity and speed, compared with the more compact and easily organized provincial cities. No leader, however charismatic, could hope to win the loyalty of the whole city, or hold his supporters together once they had been won. This is how J. C. Coombe, editor of the *London Democrat*, explained the capital's failure to mobilize in support of provincial Chartists in 1839: London was 'too huge a place to carry out the details of organization in a business-like or satisfactory manner; and besides, the people are not sufficiently known to, nor have they the necessary confidence in each other'.[4] In 1840 Francis Place, one of the most skilful organizers of London radicalism, wrote to Richard Cobden, leader of the Anti-Corn Law League, on the question of London's resistance to political organization:

> London differs very widely from Manchester, and, indeed, from every other place on the face of the earth. It has no local or particular interest as a town, not even as to politics. Its several boroughs in this respect are like so many populous places at a distance from one another, and the inhabitants of any one of them know nothing, or next to nothing, of the proceedings in any other, and not much indeed of those in their own. London in my time, and that is half a century, has never moved [politically].[5]

The radical statesman and journalist John Morley observed in 1878: 'In London there is no effective unity; interests are too varied and dispersive; zeal loses its directness and edge amid the distracting play of so many miscellaneous social and intellectual elements.'[6]

RADICALISM AND PARLIAMENTARY REFORM

London's failure to move as a united political force did not mean, of course, that its working people were inactive. In the 1820s, a decade which seems uneventful after the excitement of Spa Fields, Cato Street and the Queen Caroline riots, London craftsmen were in the forefront of a campaign to win legal recognition for trade unions, which triumphed in the repeal of the Combination Acts in 1824. The key figures in this campaign were Francis Place, the grand old man of respectable radicalism, and John Gast, leader of the Thames shipwrights in their long and unsuccessful strike in 1825.[7] In the later 1820s several important London trades, including the silk weavers, shoemakers, carpenters, hatters, tailors, silk dyers, printers, sawyers and ropemakers, saw their wages depressed by mechanization, cheap female and child labour, or provincial and foreign competition. A series of unsuccessful strikes in the mid-1820s showed how hard it was for individual trades to fight their battles alone, and Gast's great ambition was to unite London and provincial trades into a general union. Every attempt to achieve this, from Gast's 'Philanthropic Hercules', which lasted for a few months in 1818–19, to Owen's Grand National Consolidated Trades Union in 1834, ended in failure.

A powerful sense of morality and self-improvement motivated the respectable craftsmen who were the backbone of the London radical movement. To many of them, the key to political, moral and economic progress was the acquisition of knowledge. Enormous efforts were made in the 1820s to study, to read, to listen to radical speakers in coffee houses, pubs and lecture rooms, to establish institutions where intelligent working men could acquire 'useful knowledge', and to defy and destroy the newspaper taxes. William Lovett, one of the central figures in metropolitan radicalism from the 1820s to the 1840s, arrived in London in 1821, friendless and penniless, and joined a working men's literary and debating association in Soho. Through reading and discussing the books they shared, Lovett's political awareness was aroused: 'My mind seemed to be awakened to a new mental existence; new feelings, hopes and aspirations sprang up within me, and every spare moment was devoted to the acquisition of some kind of useful knowledge.'[8] Many more working men must have experienced a similar transformation, perhaps through reading William Cobbett's popular *Political Register*, Jonathan Wooler's *Black Dwarf*, Richard Carlile's *Republican*, Hetherington's *Poor Man's Guardian*, or another of the dozens of radical journals available in the streets, shops and coffee houses of early nineteenth-century London. A significant outcome of this thirst for knowledge was the establishment in 1823 of the London Mechanics' Institution. Francis Place was, once again, the organizing force behind this, but he received enthusiastic support from liberal-minded men, including Lord Brougham, Jeremy Bentham and Dr George Birkbeck, and from engineering employers who wanted a better-educated workforce. The London Mechanics' Institution inspired the founding of eight local Institutions in South and East London in 1825–6, but high subscriptions and long non-political lectures made them more attractive to clerks than to working men, and most radical artisans preferred to argue and learn in the more informal setting of the pub, coffee house or bookshop.[9]

There was an important parochial element in the London radicalism of the 1820s and 1830s. From about 1826 several select vestries, in which parish administration was in the hands of a rich minority, were challenged by local householders, who objected to paying rates to cover extravagant expenditure (much of it on churches) which they did not control. In April

1829, after sustained pressure from Francis Place and John Hobhouse, MP for Westminster, a select committee was set up, which reported in early 1830 in favour of elected vestries. Economy, rather than democracy, was the guiding principle of the parish radicals, but the struggle of ordinary householders against the corrupt authority of a privileged oligarchy seemed to be part of the larger battle against the power of the landed élite, and the Parliamentary and parish campaigns shared many of the same ideas and members. Hobhouse's success in October 1831, at the height of the parliamentary Reform crisis, in securing the passage of an Act allowing parishes to replace select vestries with vestries elected by ratepayers, if a majority of ratepayers favoured the change, was hailed as a great radical triumph. St George's Hanover Square, St John's Westminster, St James's Westminster, St Marylebone and St Pancras introduced elected vestries under Hobhouse's Act in 1832, and economy-minded radical regimes took power.

In 1829 the passing of the Catholic Relief Act split the ruling Tory Party, cracking the conservative consensus that had dominated the parliamentary world since the beginning of the century. At the same time an economic slump revived metropolitan and national interest in electoral reform and universal manhood suffrage. London had many (perhaps too many) experienced and charismatic radical leaders ready to take advantage of a change in the popular mood. Among the established leaders, 'Orator' Henry Hunt, the hero of Peterloo, William Cobbett, the great radical publicist, and Richard Carlile, the London tinsmith, republican and publisher of Thomas Paine, were outstanding for their popular influence and their mutual hostility. Then there were the three radical London MPs, Sir Francis Burdett and John Cam Hobhouse (Westminster), and Joseph Hume (Middlesex), who were more at ease in the drawing rooms of reformist Whig politicians than in the company of working-class radicals. By far the most influential of these 'respectable' radicals was Francis Place, the radical tailor, who acted as an intermediary between reformists in the political establishment and popular movements in London and the provinces. On the other extreme there were men such as William Benbow, the shoemaker and agitator, who was in the thick of almost every radical movement from 1815 to the 1840s.

In the excitement of 1829–32 new leaders emerged, who would take the radical movement into its Chartist phase in the later 1830s. The outstanding figures here were William Lovett, the moderate and thoughtful cabinet-maker, and Henry Hetherington, a compositor, who in 1830 took on the task of printing and publishing a succession of radical penny weeklies, generally known as the *Poor Man's Guardian*, in defiance of the government's 4d stamp duty. Their editor was another newcomer to the London radical scene, the Irish nationalist James Bronterre O'Brien. The struggle of radical street-sellers and publishers to keep the unstamped press alive in the face of arrest and imprisonment became a radical *cause célèbre* in the 1830s, until the government reduced the tax to a penny in 1836. Sales of unstamped papers quickly outstripped those of the legitimate press, and in radical pubs and coffee houses all over London 'the great unstamped' introduced working men to a rich variety of radical, reformist and revolutionary ideas in the 1830s.

In July 1829 Lovett, Hetherington, James Watson and other London radicals formed the Radical Reform Association (RRA), with the aim of campaigning for civil and religious liberty, universal manhood suffrage, and economic reform on the lines suggested by the cooperative socialism of Robert Owen. When a radical Birmingham banker, Thomas Attwood, set the Parliamentary Reform campaign alight in January 1830 by uniting Birmingham's middle-class and working-class Parliamentary Reformers into one effective pressure group, the Birmingham Political Union, London radicals tried to follow his lead. In March 1830 the RRA called a public meeting at the Eagle Tavern, City Road, to form a Metropolitan Political Union (MPU) on the Birmingham model, under the leadership of the popular but untrustworthy 'Orator' Hunt. This organization attempted to unite Lovett, Hetherington, Hume, and almost all London's radical leaders, along with the Irish nationalists, Bronterre O'Brien and Daniel O'Connell (the 'Liberator'), behind a programme of universal suffrage. Predictably, the MPU suffered from insuperable personal and political divisions, and disappeared in August 1830, after an argument over the desirability of revolution. Reformist agitation did not die with the MPU. Richard Carlile owned the lease of an old museum and concert house in Blackfriars known as the Rotunda, which held far larger audiences than the coffee shops, assembly rooms and public houses in which radicals usually met. Between 1830 and 1833 the Rotunda was the focal point of London radicalism, and the venue for huge rallies addressed by Cobbett, Carlile, Hunt and other popular orators.[10]

Political excitement reached a peak in November 1830, in the last days of Wellington's administration. On 9 November, Lord Mayor's Day, several thousand weavers and labourers from South and East London, motivated as much by economic distress and a fierce hostility towards the New Police as by desire for reform, marched into central London, where they attacked the Covent Garden police station, smashed the windows of Wellington's home, Apsley House, and fought with the police, before gathering, perhaps 6–7,000 strong, to hear Carlile speak at the Rotunda. A government informer reported that there was a crowd of 8,000 in and around the Rotunda that night: 'I never before saw so many persons of all classes so thickly crowded.'[11]

During the winter the new Whig ministry worked on a modest Reform Bill, which would enfranchise the middle classes and thus forge a new propertied alliance against universal suffrage. In early April 1831 the Reform Bill was passed in the Commons by one vote, and Earl Grey called a general election to strengthen the majority for reform. In London, radicals were divided in their attitudes to the Bill. Lovett, Hetherington, Carlile, Benbow and the more extreme radicals, who formed the National Union of the Working Classes (NUWC) in April 1831, regarded the Bill as inadequate and dishonest, and only rallied to its support when opposition in the House of Lords threatened to destroy it in October. The NUWC did not achieve a mass membership (a maximum of about 2,000 attended the weekly meetings of its twenty-five local classes), but it reached a wide working-class audience through the unstamped press, and at times of high tension it could bring crowds of 25,000 or thereabouts on to the streets.[12] Place and 'moderate' radicals, whose support for the Reform Bill was wholehearted, formed a separate London organization, the National Political Union, in October 1831.

In his letters to Hobhouse, Melbourne and other leading Whigs, Place made much of the fact that England faced revolution if the Bill was not passed. Many historians have accepted that these predictions were accurate, but it now seems that Place was skilfully exploiting 'the language of menace' to frighten politicians into making concessions they would not otherwise have made. If Place was bluffing, it was a bluff that the government, with no effective police forces outside London, only 11,000 regular soldiers, and little knowledge of public feeling, was afraid to call. Events in London and elsewhere certainly lent plausibility to Place's warnings, helping to create a feeling that reform was inevitable. When the House of Lords rejected the Second Reform Bill on 8 October 1831, there were severe riots in Nottingham, Derby and (a little later) Bristol. In London radical opinion was more controlled and less violent. Place helped to organize a huge procession to St James's Palace on 12 October, which the police were powerless to stop. The peacefulness of the vast crowd (apart from some scattered stone-throwing) seemed to create a greater sense of menace than the rougher behaviour of traditional mobs. Plans for another rally on 7 November, this time armed with sticks and staves, were dropped after a government ban. The fact that Melbourne, the Home Secretary, had over 10,000 soldiers, policemen and special constables ready to deal with the rally shows how seriously he took the threat of unrest. The second moment of apparent danger came in May 1832, 'the Days of May', when middle-class and working-class radicals mobilized their supporters to prevent the return of a Tory government, after the King had refused to create enough new Whig peers to force the Bill through the House of Lords. Meetings of the NUWC grew larger and more violent in tone, and radical strategists, especially Place, tried to bring pressure on the government by mobilizing the economic power of the people, either in a tax strike or a run on gold. Following the appearance of placards announcing that the best way to 'Stop the Duke' was to 'Go for Gold!', there was a mass withdrawal of gold from the Bank of England, which reduced its reserves by almost a half. In the event, Wellington was unable to form a government, Grey returned, and the Bill went through the House of Lords in June 1832. Talk of revolution faded away, and the potentially dangerous alliance between middle-class and working-class reformers was dissolved.

Nowhere in England had more need of the 1832 Reform Act than London. Although historians have generally emphasized the under-representation of the newer industrial areas of the Midlands and the North, they did not suffer greater unfairness than the capital. Until 1832 ten members, four from the City and two each for Southwark, Westminster and the County of Middlesex, sat for London constituencies. With 13.6 per cent of the population of England and Wales in 1831, and a far higher proportion of the national wealth, London might have expected about seventy MPs (out of 513 English and Welsh members) in a fair distribution of seats. The six counties of South-West England (Cornwall, Devon, Dorset, Somerset, Wiltshire and Hampshire), had as many inhabitants as London (1.9 million) in 1831, but returned 168 MPs. The 1832 Act created five new London constituencies, each with two MPs (Finsbury, Marylebone, Lambeth, Tower Hamlets and Greenwich), and also gave two MPs to the urban part of Surrey. This gave London's 1.9 million inhabitants 22 MPs, compared to Yorkshire's 37 members for 1.4 million people, and Lancashire's 26 members for 1.3 million people. Cornwall, with 300,000 inhabitants in 1831, which had 44 members before 1832, still had 18 after the Reform Act. The Second Reform Act in 1867, which created the two-member constituencies of Hackney and Chelsea, and gave two more seats to urban Surrey and one to London University, did little to redress the balance. It was not until the 1885 Redistribution of Seats Act, which created a total of 73 metropolitan MPs, that London was given an appropriate allocation of seats.

The 1832 Act enfranchised all male ratepayers who owned or rented shops or houses 'of the clear yearly value of not less than ten pounds'. In most of England the £10 qualification excluded working-class householders from the electorate, but property values and rents in London were high, and a large proportion of tenants and freeholders got the vote in 1832. In 1866 the London electorate was 179,607, out of a male adult (over twenty-one) population of about 800,000.[13] Still, to most working men the 1832 Act was a betrayal of the radical efforts of the previous three years, and the early legislation of the reformed Parliament reinforced this feeling.

CHARTISM IN LONDON

Working-class activity continued after 1832, especially in the craft unions, which were struggling to get their pay and hours of work restored to traditional levels, and to win recognition from their employers, in the more prosperous circumstances of the mid-1830s. In 1833 and 1834 there were unsuccessful strikes of tailors, plasterers, coopers, hatters, carpenters, bricklayers and sawyers, and union activity among bakers, gas workers, laundresses and women in the garment trades. Often, these ended with workers being forced to sign the 'Document', renouncing union member-ship. The high point of this wave of activity was the formation in February 1834 of the famous Grand National Consolidated Trades Union (GNCTU), which attempted for a few months to establish a system of mutual support for striking workers. Sidney and Beatrice Webb, whose *History of Trade Unionism*, published in 1894, dominated trade union history for over sixty years, grossly exaggerated the importance and membership of the GNCTU, and their belief that it had half a million members led them to regard the history of unionism later in the century as a story of contraction and anti-climax. In fact the GNCTU was mainly a metropolitan organization, with London tailors, shoemakers and silk weavers making up the majority of its 16,000 paying members. Its most important industrial action was a strike of the London tailors in April and May 1834 against the spread of homework, piecework and cuts in the daily rate. The striking tailors were short of funds, their masters had plenty of non-union men to call upon, and the strike was easily defeated. With its defeat, the GNCTU effectively came to an end. A four-month lock-out in the building industry, which ended in November 1834 in victory for the employers, made it clear that all Robert Owen's grand talk of cooperation and mutual support had not altered the realities of power in London's industrial world. During the long depression of 1836–42 trade unions were generally inactive, although there were strikes by the ropemakers, engineers and goldbeaters in the late 1830s. In periods of depression political pressure seemed to offer more hope of success than industrial action, and radicalism replaced unionism at the centre of the stage.[14]

The main vehicle for London radicalism, the National Union of the Working Classes, remained active after 1832. Its popular support was sustained by disappointment with the Reform Act, the continuing battle for the unstamped press, hostility to the Metropolitan Police, and anger at political repression in Ireland, exemplified by the Irish Coercion Act of 1833. The NUWC's leaders wanted to call a national convention, and held a mass meeting in Cold Bath Fields, Clerkenwell, on 13 May 1833, in pursuit of this aim. The meeting degenerated into an armed battle with the Metropolitan Police, and ended in the fatal stabbing of a police constable, Robert Culley. The NUWC gained some satisfaction from the widespread condemnation of the brutal police baton charge that broke up the rally, and the coroner's jury's verdict that the killing of Culley had been 'justifiable homicide', but its membership fell steadily, and it disappeared altogether in 1835.[15]

In June 1836 a group of ex-members of the defunct NUWC, including Lovett, Hetherington, Gast and John Cleave, encouraged by Place and a Kentuckian, Dr Black, formed a new organization, the London Working Men's Association (LWMA), to work for a free press, social reform and the vote. The influence of the LWMA in the creation of the Chartist movement, whose strongest roots were in Birmingham and the industrial North, was for many years exaggerated by historians, who were misled by the claims of Lovett and other LWMA members, and by the fact that the Charter which gave the movement its name and democratic programme was produced (in May 1838) by Lovett and Place. The LWMA was a union of respectable craftsmen, whose aim was to unite 'the honest, sober, moral, and thinking portion' of their class in pursuit of gradual social and political improvement 'without violence or commotion'.[16] Not surprisingly, the LWMA did not attract (or want) a mass membership. In its three-year existence (1836–9) it admitted 291 members, almost half of whom were shoemakers, tailors, carpenters, cabinet-makers or compositors. Lovett and his friends played an important part in stimulating provincial Chartism through their lecture tours in 1838, but they did very little to arouse opinion within the capital, and their failure to do so helps explain London's weak contribution to national Chartism in 1838–9.

Although the LWMA got the lion's share of London's representation in the General Chartist Convention, which met in London between February and May 1839, it did not represent the majority of metropolitan Chartists. In many parishes, including St Pancras, Marylebone, Bethnal Green, Hammersmith and Lambeth, local Chartist organizations grew out of existing parochial radical groups. In January 1837 a group of radical followers of the ideas of Tom Paine, led by George Harney, formed the East London Democratic Association (ELDA), which recalled the more violent traditions of the Cato Street conspiracy, and echoed the tone and policies of the northern 'physical force' Chartism of Feargus O'Connor. By 1839 the ELDA (now renamed the London Democratic Association) and its ally, the West London Democratic Association, had branches in most parts of London, and offered a popular alternative to the non-violent gradualism of the fastidious LWMA. In the spring and summer of 1839 the LDA did its best to arouse mass enthusiasm for the Charter in London, but the level of support they won was deeply disappointing. While Chartist meetings in Manchester and the West Riding attracted perhaps 250,000, the largest London crowds in 1839 were only 10,000 or 12,000. Only one in 100 (19,000) Londoners signed the Chartist petition in March 1839, compared with Birmingham's 94,000, over half its population. In the spring, summer and autumn of 1839, when the government's forces were challenged by violence or the threat of violence in many parts of England and Wales, police informers reported that Chartist meetings in London were peaceful, apathetic and poorly attended. Commissioner Mayne concluded in August 1839: 'The general impression of the Superintendents is that the number of Chartists in their relative Divisions is inconsiderable, that they have not funds, nor are they organised so as to act together throughout the whole Metropolis.'[17]

The lack of mass support in the capital was disastrous to Chartism in 1839–40, when the movement's strength elsewhere was at its greatest. Most Chartists blamed London's apathy on the fact that its working men were too well paid. A Dundee delegate to the 1839 Convention thought that as long as Londoners 'could procure beef and porter, and enjoy their comforts' they would ignore the sufferings of those in the North. More to the point, London did not suffer a depression in jobs or wages in 1839, and its workers were not likely to listen to the LDA's frantic encouragement to 'ARM! ARM! ARM!' when their economic conditions were no worse than usual. The more moderate Chartist case, thanks to the aloofness of the LWMA, was not put. Finally, while northern Chartism could gain its early momentum from existing mass campaigns for factory reform and against the Poor Law, in London these issues had not prepared the ground for Chartism.[18]

In the autumn of 1840 and the winter and spring of 1841 London workers at last began to show an interest in the Chartist cause. This was partly because a new group of O'Connorite leaders emerged, taking the place of those arrested in the repression that followed the Newport Rising in November 1839. Such men as Edmund Stallwood and Philip M'Grath led the efforts of the new National Charter Association (formed in July 1840) to establish Chartist 'localities', of which there were about forty in 1842. In reality, it was the severity of the economic depression of 1841–2 which turned thousands of London craftsmen, particularly stonemasons, tailors, printers, shoemakers, silk weavers, hatters and carpenters, into active Chartists. By May 1842, when a crowd of at least 100,000 Londoners marched to Parliament with the second Chartist petition, the old apathy had vanished. Instead, London had become a centre of massive Chartist militancy. Between 15 and 19 August 1842, when news of widespread strikes and Chartist riots elsewhere in the country caused growing excitement in London, a series of large meetings were held on Clerkenwell, Stepney and Islington Greens, some of them ending in violent clashes with the police. The climax came on 22 August when about 40,000 Chartists, defying a ban on evening rallies, met on Kennington Common. The police, using horses, sabres and truncheons, captured the Common without much difficulty, but found it harder to clear the surrounding streets, or smaller gatherings at Paddington and Clerkenwell. The success of the Metropolitan Police in maintaining order in the capital in August 1842 without calling upon the army showed what advances had been made in the techniques of urban control since the 1820s. The popular triumphs of 1780, 1820 and 1832 would not be so easily repeated in the future.[19]

1848

In the economic recovery of the next four years Chartism lost its mass support. But over the same period London's Irish population grew rapidly, and so did the movement for the repeal of the Act of Union with Ireland. There was a long-standing affinity between radicalism and Irish nationalism, and in 1848 Chartist leaders made an alliance with the Irish Repealers. This, along with the news of the French Revolution of February 1848, and the severe economic depression of 1847–8, brought popular support for the Charter to a level not reached even in 1842. Between March and June 1848 there was a succession of large Chartist meetings, many of which ended in violent confrontation with the police. On 6 March an unruly crowd of about 10,000 men, apparently protesting against income tax as well as supporting the Charter, took possession of Trafalgar Square, which they held, defying police efforts to dislodge them, for two days. Meanwhile, groups of young men rioted and looted around Whitehall and St James's, and marched along Fleet Street and Ludgate Hill, smashing shop windows and street lamps. There was looting and violence on a smaller scale in Camberwell on 13 March, after another meeting on Kennington Common. These unfortunate incidents, together with unease at the Irish connection, helped to turn clerks and shopkeepers, whom O'Connor had wooed for Chartism, into supporters of the government in 1848.[20]

Meanwhile, in Paris, Berlin, Vienna, Milan and other European cities popular insurrections were bringing conservative governments down. Not surprisingly, a climate of panic began to develop within political and propertied circles when it was learned that the Chartist Convention, then meeting in London, was planning a great rally on Kennington Common on 10 April, followed by a march on Parliament with a monster petition. The Chartists wanted to demonstrate irresistible public support for reform, rather than start a revolution, but nervous shopkeepers could not see the difference. In the weeks before the meeting, the government was able to organize a display of mass opposition to Chartism, by enlisting over 80,000 special constables, mostly propertied men, students, or employees who would have been unwise to refuse, but also over 1,000 Wapping coal-whippers. 'Every gentleman in London is become a constable, and there is an organization of some sort in every district,' Charles Greville, clerk to the Privy Council, recorded on 9 April. Victoria and her Court were sent to Osborne House, putting the Solent between her and the feared revolution, and tough legislation against seditious speeches was rushed through Parliament.

Faced with the government's extensive preparations, some Chartist leaders wanted to call the meeting off, but O'Connor was determined to assert the right of peaceful assembly and demonstrate popular support for the Charter. On the dreaded day London was defended by 4,000 policemen, almost 8,000 soldiers and over 1,000 pensioned-off servicemen. All but 3,000 of the 80,000 special constables were confined to local duties. The General Post Office, the British Museum, Somerset House, the Guildhall, the prisons, the Bank of England and other major buildings were sand-bagged, and their employees were issued with muskets and cutlasses. The

Police Commissioners and the Prime Minister had agreed that all the Thames bridges would be held by the police and pensioners, confining the Chartists to the Surrey side. Wellington's troops and artillery were to remain in barracks and hiding places around London, but control of the West End parks, together with Whitehall and the river, would give them free access to all important parts of the town if they were needed.[21]

The enormous preparations for the Kennington Common rally, and the atmosphere of fear and expectation that pervaded London that day, made the event itself, which was never intended to be the start of a violent insurrection, look like a damp squib. Contemporaries and historians disagree about the size of the crowd that assembled that morning on Kennington Common, with press estimates as low as 10,000, and Chartist claims as high as 250,000. A famous contemporary photograph, perhaps taken before the meeting was at its height, shows a huge crowd apparently half-filling the Common. Since the Common, like the present Kennington Park, which occupies the site today, was about 18 acres in area, large enough to hold a crowd of 200,000, it is possible that more than 100,000 Chartists were gathered there that morning. Perhaps there were enough Chartists to take on the police and the specials, but professional soldiers were another matter, and O'Connor, motivated by timidity or realism, decided to avoid bloodshed and abandon his planned march on Westminster. After 1 o'clock the crowd left the Common, and the crisis, real or imagined, was over.[22]

It is an injustice to London Chartism to depict the events of 10 April as a fiasco, an insurrection which fizzled out. It was the government that had expected a revolution, and mounted preparations which the actual intentions of the Chartists did not justify. Nevertheless, there was a general feeling among respectable Londoners that the Chartists' bluff had been called, that they did not have the power or courage to challenge the army and the police, and that even in terms of popular support, the constitution had beaten the Charter. But this was by no means the end of Chartism in London. Throughout April and May 1848 there were weekly open-air meetings in Bethnal Green, Somers Town and Paddington, and new leaders organized Chartist clubs and classes in dozens of neighbourhoods. News that John Mitchel, editor of the *United Irishman*, had been sentenced in Dublin to fourteen years' transportation, brought feelings to a head on 29 May. That evening a huge Irish and Chartist crowd, perhaps 60,000 strong, marched from Clerkenwell and Stepney, through the City and the West End to Trafalgar Square, taking the authorities by surprise and sending new waves of anxiety through respectable London. There were demonstrations and battles with the police on Clerkenwell Green on 31 May and 1 June, and on Sunday, 4 June, an afternoon meeting on Bonner's Fields, Bethnal Green, one of several rallies that day, was violently broken up by the police. Faced with the threat of an even larger meeting on April 12, the government adopted more repressive tactics. Five Chartist leaders, including Ernest Jones, were arrested for seditious speeches, and over 1,000 policemen occupied Bonner's Fields, forcing the abandonment of the 12 April rally. The destruction of most of the remaining Chartist leadership was made easier by their decision to join Irish nationalists in planning an armed uprising, to take place on 16 August 1848. The conspirators met secretly in radical coffee houses and beershops, but their discussions were reported to the government by informers, and on the day of the intended uprising police arrested twenty-seven Chartists, most of them at the Orange Tree, Red Lion Square, and the Angel, Southwark. The subsequent transportation for life of six Chartist leaders, and the imprisonment of another fifteen, brought Chartism to an end as an effective mass movement in London.[23]

The failure of Chartism in 1848 no doubt convinced many that the Charter was unattainable for the time being, and that more might be achieved in more narrowly focused movements, such as trade unions, friendly societies and campaigns for educational or temperance reform. Chartist ideas continued to be propagated and discussed in London clubs and coffee houses during the 1850s, and such leaders as Julian Harney, Bronterre O'Brien and Ernest Jones struggled on in the hope that popular support would make the movement powerful in the capital again. When the reform movement eventually revived in the 1860s it did not do so under the name of Chartism, but it drew upon a tradition of popular radicalism which the Chartist leaders of the 1850s had helped to keep alive.

TRADE UNIONISM

The relative prosperity of the 1850s dampened down political radicalism, but stimulated trade unionism. As a general rule (to which there are several exceptions), unions were more confident and assertive in times of economic boom, and quiescent in depressions, when the demand for their skills was less. Radical political activity, on the other hand, was greater in depressions, when hardship made working people desperate for change, and when industrial action was ineffective. Thus, London trade unions were relatively unsuccessful in the depressed years of 1837–42, but revived in the mid-1840s. For the most part, the unions of the 1840s and 1850s were small, localized, politically unambitious and confined to skilled workers, just as they had been in the 1820s and 1830s. There were new developments, especially among the engineers, towards amalgamation of smaller local unions into larger national ones, but such tendencies were not typical of the union movement as a whole.[24]

The most important of the new amalgamated unions was the Amalgamated Society of Engineers (ASE), which was created in 1851, after seven years of careful negotiation, by the absorption of several small London and Lancashire engineers' societies into a large established union, the Journeymen Steam-Engine and Machine Makers. The ASE was bigger and richer than other unions, and its London headquarters, elaborate constitution and paid general secretary made it a model for the future. In other respects it was fairly traditional, with its high weekly fee (a shilling), exclusively skilled membership, friendly society benefits (covering accidents, unemployment, sickness, old age, funeral costs and travelling money), and limited industrial aims. But the size and organization of the ASE enabled it to survive defeats which would have crushed a smaller union. From January to March 1852 there was a lock-out in London and Lancashire engineering works on the issue of overtime and piecework. The ASE was defeated after spending £43,000 in strike pay, but it remained solvent and over the next few years it regained and greatly increased its membership.[25]

The question of the role of trade unions in London industry was brought to a head in 1859 by a dispute in the building trade. Throughout the 1850s the carpenters and stonemasons had been demanding a nine-hour working day, which the employers had consistently refused. The concern was intensified in May 1859, when eight builders, working forced overtime on the Westminster Palace Hotel, were killed in a fall from an overloaded scaffold. In July 1859 a unionist was dismissed for joining in a deputation for the nine-hour day. When the joiners, plasterers, bricklayers and labourers struck against his firm, Trollope's of Pimlico, the employers responded with a general London lock-out, involving 225 firms and 24,000 men. The aim of the Association of Master Builders was to exclude trade unionists from the building trade, and force their workers to sign the anti-union Document. The builders' struggle became a *cause célèbre*, and other unions formed a strike committee (which became the London Trades Council) which raised a total of £23,000 for the strike fund (including £3,000 from the ASE), enabling the builders to stay out until February 1860, when the Document was withdrawn. As a result of the builders' lock-out, the various local societies of carpenters saw the advantages of amalgamation, and transformed themselves into the Amalgamated Society of Carpenters and Joiners, modelling their constitution on the ASE.[26]

The men who dominated London trade unionism and the London Trades Council in the 1860s, William Allan of the Engineers, Robert Applegarth of the Carpenters, George Odger of the Ladies' Shoemakers, Daniel Guile of the Ironfounders, and Edward Coulson of the London Bricklayers, were cautious and respectable men, who regarded strikes as a regrettable last resort, and who worked, with much success, to make trade unions an accepted part of the industrial and political world.[27] The spokesman for more militant unionism in London was George Potter, a carpenter who had been the most charismatic leader in the builders' strike of 1859–60. Potter broke with the Trades Council in 1865, and started a rival organization, the London Working Men's Association. It was Potter, not the Trades Council, who represented London unionists at the first meeting of the Trades Union Congress in Manchester in June 1868, and it was Potter who founded, managed and later edited London's best and most popular union newspaper in the 1860s, *The Beehive*.[28]

THE 1867 REFORM ACT

Although the main aim of Applegarth and his colleagues was to advance the interests of union members, they also campaigned with confidence and growing authority on the major political issues of the 1860s. Encouraged by their contacts with Christian Socialists and with scientific rationalists, or Positivists, such as Edward Beesly and Frederic Harrison, they supported the northern cause in the American Civil War, welcomed Garibaldi, the hero of Italian unification, to London in 1864, and took up once again the Chartist campaign for franchise reform.[29] In February 1865, in the radical atmosphere that followed Garibaldi's visit, a group of working-class leaders, including Applegarth and George Howell, a bricklayer who had been prominent in the 1859–60 strike, joined a radical barrister, Edmond Beales, to found the Reform League and revive the manhood suffrage campaign. In the 1865 General Election unionists worked for radical candidates, helping Thomas Hughes to win in Lambeth and John Stuart Mill in Westminster. There were echoes of 1832 in the events of 1866: harvest failure and high bread prices, a cholera epidemic and bread riots in the East End, a commercial crisis and high unemployment following the collapse of the Overend and Gurney finance house, public anger in London following the defeat of Gladstone's Reform Bill, and Applegarth and the Reform League taking Francis Place's role by offering to restore order on the tacit understanding that in return their views would be taken seriously.[30]

Russell's reformist government fell in May 1866, following the defeat of its Reform Bill, and was replaced by Lord Derby's Conservative ministry. On 2 July the Reform League held a rally in Trafalgar Square, which drew a peaceful crowd of 80,000. A larger rally in Hyde Park was planned for 23 July, but Lord Derby ordered the park to be locked, and banned the meeting. That evening the League marched to the park in protest, and the pressure of the crowd, now between 100,000 and 200,000 strong, was so great that the railings gave way, and the reformers swarmed over them, brushing aside the 1,600 policemen who stood in their path. Mayne, the ageing Police Commissioner, called upon the support of five Guards' battalions, and the crowd, which seemed to regard the troops as their protectors against the police, gradually drifted away as darkness fell. There was disorder in and around the park the next day, this time involving rougher elements, and the leaders of the League met the Home Secretary, Spencer Walpole, to offer help in controlling the crowd in return for permission to hold future meetings. The outcome of these discussions was confused, but the general impression was created that the League represented a powerful and decent body of men, who had pushed the railings down, but not picked them up as weapons, and that the government did not have the forces to keep order in London if a measure of reform was not granted.[31]

In May 1867 the Reform League announced another great rally in Hyde Park, and Spencer Walpole prohibited it once again. The central issue now was how much force each side was prepared to use to get its way. Would the Reform League use violence, or endure the violence of the army or police, to assert its right to rally in Hyde Park, and would the government call upon the army to defend the constitution, as it had with such success in 1848? In the event, the League decided to test the government's resolve (as O'Connor had failed to do in 1848), and on 6 May a crowd of about 100,000 or more met in Hyde Park. The government had about 10,000 police and troops ready, but Walpole did not use them, and the rally went ahead in peace. This time, in contrast to 1848, the League emerged with prestige and the appearance of power, while the Prime Minister, admitting that his government had 'suffered some slight humiliation in the public mind', accepted the resignation of his Home Secretary.[32]

Some historians have argued that what MPs decided behind the closed doors of the Houses of Parliament owed hardly anything to the tumultuous events that took place in London in 1866 and 1867.[33] It is no doubt the case that many of the details of the 1867 Reform Act were shaped by complex party tactics and parliamentary manoeuvres, but it is difficult to believe that the conservative consensus that had dominated the previous fifteen years would have been broken, or that politicians who were not innately reformist would have been driven to the belief that some form of constitutional reform was unavoidable, if a powerful popular movement for reform had not developed in London and northern England in the mid-1860s. The decisive reformist argument that a substantial section of the working class was more dangerous outside the political system than it would be within it, that the essentials of the constitution would be better preserved by change than by resistance to change, drew upon many examples from all over England, but none illustrated the case more strongly than the events in Hyde Park in 1866 and 1867.[34]

The next few years were important ones for the trade union movement. In 1866 there were some violent incidents between union and non-union labour in the Sheffield cutlery industry (the 'Sheffield outrages'), which led to the setting up of a Royal Commission on Trade Unions in 1867. Applegarth, Allan, Coulson and the other silk-hatted London union leaders managed to convince the Commission (of which Frederic Harrison was an influential member) that unions were respectable and beneficial institutions which deserved a more favoured position in the civil and criminal law. Despite the Commission's favourable reports, and the increased electoral power won by the working class in the 1867 Reform Act, reforms which placed trade unions on a modern legal footing were fairly slow in coming, and it was not until 1875 that two key measures, legalizing peaceful picketing and removing the threat of criminal prosecution for conspiracy or breach of contract from strikers, were passed.[35]

In the 1860s the somewhat parochial leaders of London radicalism rubbed shoulders with a man of much greater international importance. When Karl Marx arrived in London in 1849, after the collapse of the European revolutions of 1848, he joined about 1,000 continental radicals, revolutionaries and socialists, mostly refugees from Germany, Poland and Russia, who had come to London to find a freedom of expression and association that they could not be sure of elsewhere in Europe. In the 1850s Marx lived an impoverished and rather isolated life, first in Soho (two grubby rooms in Dean Street) and later in Kentish Town, seeing a few German friends and working on *Das Kapital* in the library of the British Museum, whose magnificent new Reading Room was opened in 1857. But in 1864, when the English working class seemed to be waking up after fifteen years of political slumber, Marx emerged from obscurity when he was invited to the first meeting of the new International Working Men's Association in St Martin's Hall, Covent Garden. The International was founded by English and French trade unionists, partly in order to reduce the flow of foreign blackleg workers during strikes, but Marx quickly took control of it, and wrote its inaugural address. For a few years Marx worked well enough with Beesly, Applegarth, Odger and other distinctly unrevolutionary leaders of London radicalism, and even hoped that they would be brought round to his belief in revolutionary class struggle. Their failure to support the Paris Commune in 1871 disillusioned him, and in the bitter arguments following its fall the working agreement between revolutionists, anarchists and pragmatic trade unionists broke down. Marx moved the headquarters of the International from London to New York, where it faded away after a few years. By 1872 Marx's brief period of activity in the London labour movement was over, and he spent the last ten years of his life isolated from London working-class politics. He died in his house in Kentish Town in 1883, and although he had spent over half of his life in London his death was largely unnoticed. The impressive monument that now covers his grave in Highgate Cemetery was not erected until 1956.[36]

The 1867 Reform Act removed from the centre of the stage the 'big issue' which had united and motivated the politically active working class in London for 100 years, but it cannot be said to have made London a democratic city. The 1867 Act which gave the vote (subject to a one-year residence qualification) to male householders and lodgers in rooms worth at least £10 a year, increased London's registered electorate by 41 per cent, from about 180,000 in 1866 to 304,400 in 1868, when many lodgers had still to be registered. But the new electoral system was still heavily weighted against the poor. Not only were men who occupied the cheapest lodgings (worth under £10 a year unfurnished) excluded from the franchise, but so were those on poor relief and those who had moved house in the year preceding the compilation of the register, as many poorer families did. Lodgers were enfranchised in 1867, but unlike those owning or renting whole houses they were not automatically registered, but had to re-register each year, with the chance that their registration would be challenged. Registration of poorer voters became a vital part of party activity until 1900, when the new boroughs took on the job. As a result, the total lodger vote in the County of London in 1914 was only 108,000, and probably only about a quarter of lower-working-class men were registered to vote, compared with about two-thirds of better-off working-class and three-quarters of middle-class men. Furthermore, plural voting by men with property in more than one borough gave the well-off an extra advantage in the outer suburbs and the city centre, and the closure of polling stations at 8 p.m. made it hard for some working men to vote.[37]

LIBERALS AND CONSERVATIVES

The increasing number of Parliamentary seats allotted to London made it a vital target for the Liberal and Conservative parties in the later nineteenth century. The importance of victory in London was especially great after the Redistribution of Seats Act of 1885, which gave London seventy-three seats (fifty-nine within the County and fourteen in the outer suburbs, including Croydon), over 10 per cent of the House of Commons. Up to the 1860s London had consistently supported the Whig or Liberal Party, and Liberals might have expected that their position in the capital would be strengthened by the extension of the franchise. This is not how things turned out. There had been no Tory or Conservative MPs among London's eighteen members in the 1859 and 1865 general elections, and a total of only seven in all the elections since 1832, but they won three seats (out of twenty-two) in 1868, ten in 1874 and eight in 1880, and in the next five general elections (1885, 1886, 1892, 1895 and 1900) Conservatives won a clear majority of London seats. In 1886, 1895 and 1900 the Liberals, who had once dominated London politics, were reduced to a rump of about ten seats (out of seventy-three), all in working-class districts. The Liberals recovered in the national landslide of 1906, when they took forty-six London seats, and they held twenty-nine and thirty seats in the two elections of 1910.[38]

The development which did most damage to Liberalism in London was the rise of suburban conservatism among the villa-dwellers, shopkeepers, professionals, clerks and businessmen whose votes dominated a majority of London constituencies after 1867. These people would once have been natural Whig–Liberal supporters, but after the death of Palmerston in 1865 the Liberal Party under Gladstone became increasingly radical, and the Conservative Party of Disraeli and Lord Salisbury was able to present itself as the guardian of property, the status quo and safe government against radical Liberalism and the rising working class. The Conservative Party was well funded, and was able to promote this message in large urban constituencies by using professional agents, paid canvassers and local political clubs, as well as old-fashioned corruption. The victory of W. H. Smith over John Stuart Mill in Westminster in 1868 was a harbinger of things to come. Smith was a moderate Conservative who had been a follower of Palmerston, and he had the money to offer voters 'treats' and transport, and to employ an agent, while Mill was an unconventional radical who refused to canvass or spend money to win support. Middlesex, another famous radical constituency, fell to the Conservatives in the same election, and both seats remained firmly Conservative thereafter. After the 1874 election, in which the Conservatives won ten of London's twenty-two seats, Frederic Harrison drew the lesson that the middle classes, those 'sleek citizens, who pour forth daily from thousands and thousands of smug villas round London, Manchester and Liverpool, read their *Standard* and believe the country will do very well as it is' had 'gone over to the enemy bag and baggage'. 'The Conservative Party has become as much the middle-class party as the Liberal used to be, as much and more.'[39] By the 1880s, the conversion of middle-class London was complete. In every general election between 1885 and 1910, except the Liberal landslide of 1906, the Conservatives had a clean sweep in the eighteen richest constituencies in the County of London, and in six of the seven Middlesex seats. Even in socially mixed constituencies, in such districts as Islington, St Pancras, Hammersmith, Greenwich and Fulham, Conservatives nearly always won, until the Liberal revival of 1906.[40]

As might be expected, Liberals were more successful in working-class constituencies, where their traditional association with radicalism and trade unionism, and their growing interest in social reform and the attack on privilege, won them support. Even in the poorest inner-city constituencies, though, the Conservatives' richer and more professional party organization, and their strong appeal to the deferential, patriotic and xenophobic feelings of poorer voters, gave them an average of between 40 and 50 per cent of votes between 1885 and 1910. Several of London's poorest constituencies, including Stepney, Limehouse, Mile End, Rotherhithe and Bermondsey, repeatedly returned Conservative MPs between 1885 and 1906.[41]

In London, as in other parts of England, the Liberal Party countered the Conservative challenge by building upon its trade union connection. In the 1886 general election, in which the Liberals held only ten London seats, three were taken by working men with Liberal endorsement, known as Lib–Labs: George Howell (North-east Bethnal Green, 1885–95), Randal Cremer (Shoreditch, 1885–95 and 1905–8) and James Rowlands (East Finsbury, 1886–95). Lib–Lab cooperation also helped secure the election of Keir Hardie of the Independent Labour Party, who held West Ham South from 1892 to 1895, and of John Burns, hero of the 1889 Dock Strike, who held Battersea for the Liberals from 1892 to 1918. Most of all it helped the Liberals win their last great victory in London in 1906, when an electoral pact with the new Labour Party gave the Liberals a free run against the Conservatives in many seats which Labour might have won, in return for Liberal support for two Labour candidates, Will Thorne in West Ham South and Will Crooks in Woolwich. In 1910 this arrangement was repeated, again bringing more advantages to the Liberals than to Labour. In the 1920s and 1930s Labour took from the Liberals all the constituencies which the Conservatives had not already taken from them, destroying the Liberal Party as a force in London. But there were few signs of this before 1914. Liberals dominated most of London's poorer constituencies in 1906 and 1910, and Labour won an average of only two seats in the three general elections of those years.[42]

SOCIALISM

Conservatism and Liberalism were not the only political ideologies competing for popular support in the later nineteenth century. In 1882 an American land and tax reformer, Henry George, popularized vaguely socialistic concepts in a London lecture tour, and in the following year London's first socialist party was created when a radical Liberal organization, the Democratic Federation, adopted a socialist programme and renamed itself the Social Democratic Federation (SDF). Its leader, H. M. Hyndman, was a well-off journalist with many conservative views, who had been converted to socialism by reading *Das Kapital* in French. He was a volatile and tyrannical personality, who alienated followers almost as quickly as he attracted them, but there is no doubt that the SDF was the dominant socialist organization in London, where the bulk of its membership was to be found. The SDF has often been depicted as an alien and doctrinaire organization without roots in London society, but nearly all of the important London socialist leaders were members of the SDF, including William Morris (until 1884), H. H. Champion, John Burns, Tom Mann, Annie Besant, Will Thorne, George Lansbury, Ben Tillett and Eleanor Marx. Alone of the socialist organizations in London in the 1880s and 1890s, the SDF built up a substantial working-class membership, and made converts among the unskilled and unemployed.[43]

There were three other socialist organizations in late nineteenth-century London. The Fabian Society, which was founded in 1884, was a network of middle-class discussion groups, whose members had little faith in the political instincts of the working class, and preferred to influence events by working through the Liberal Party. Fabian membership was tiny in the

1880s, but rose to around 400 in the 1890s, and reached a peak of over 1,300 in the wake of Labour's success in the 1906 general election. The strength of Fabianism amongst journalists and academics, and particularly the writings of Bernard Shaw and Sidney and Beatrice Webb, have left the impression that the Fabians were a much more important force in London socialism than was really the case.[44] The SDF's other rival in the 1880s was the Socialist League, which was founded in 1884 as a breakaway from the SDF by William Morris, the poet, designer and successful industrialist, and Eleanor Marx, Karl Marx's daughter. The League soon broke up into separate socialist societies in Hammersmith, Bloomsbury and Woolwich. The Bloomsbury branch, led by Eleanor Marx, played an important part in the 1889 gas strike. The Independent Labour Party, which was strong in the industrial North, established branches in London in the early 1890s, but it did not manage to unite labour and socialism factions as it had hoped, and it did not win great popular support in London. The victory of Keir Hardie in West Ham South in 1892 owed more to Liberal support than to his association with the ILP, and when he fought the seat as leader of the ILP in 1895 he lost it to the Conservatives. By 1900 it was clear that the ILP had failed to establish itself as London's main Labour Party, and its leaders decided to join with the Fabians, the SDF and some of the unions to form a new labour (rather than exclusively socialist) grouping, the Labour Representation Committee, which became the Labour Party in 1906.[45]

The failure of other labour groups to thrive in London owed much to the solid strength of the SDF. The SDF's street-corner speakers took the message of socialism to the most impoverished areas of London, and the SDF's local branches managed to draw workmen of the poorest groups into the political and social culture of socialism. It was the SDF that turned the unemployed rally in Trafalgar Square into the riotous crowd that terrified the West End in February 1886, and organized the unemployed occupation of the Square in October and November 1887. Hyndman's pamphlet, *A Commune for London*, was the first programme for municipal socialism, and the SDF's success in local elections in the 1890s enabled it to put some of its ideas into practice. SDF members won seats on local Boards of Guardians in the 1890s, and used their position to improve the workhouse regime, especially for children and the old, and to increase outdoor relief. This process went furthest in Poplar, where George Lansbury's achievements established a tradition of local socialism which continued beyond the First World War. The socialists' most important local government success was in West Ham, where Will Thorne, of the SDF, could call upon the support of the gas workers he had led in 1889. During the 1890s the SDF worked with the trade unions, the ILP and sympathetic middle-class councillors to build up a Labour Party on West Ham Council. Between 1898 and 1900 the party used its majority, the first on any town council, to show what future Labour local authorities might do: tighter sanitary controls on slum housing, work schemes for the unemployed, an eight-hour day, 30s minimum wage and paid holidays for Council employees, new baths and wash-houses, scholarships to Technical Institutes, and concerts in the park. In 1900, when a ratepayers' alliance ended Labour control, there were plans for council houses, workmen's lodgings, council laundries and dispensaries, a new hospital, and the municipalization of gas, water and the trams.[46]

New Unionism

The success of socialists and Lib–Labs in the elections of the early 1890s was heavily dependent upon the emergence of a new kind of mass trade unionism in London between 1889 and 1891. Until that time, trade unions were small, exclusive and Liberal-inclined. Membership figures are not known, but by the early 1880s only two unions, the compositors and engineers, had 6,000 members in London, and of the other major unions the tailors, bricklayers and carpenters had about 2,000 each, and the stonemasons, boiler-makers, railway servants and bootmakers had around 1,000. Thus in these relatively well-unionized industries, which had a total London workforce of about 200,000 men, around 11 per cent were union members. Although several national trade unions had their headquarters in the capital, London was not a great union stronghold. The lack of great factories, and the preponderance of sweated and casual work and small workshops, hindered the growth of London unionism, and many of the largest groups of London workers, including railwaymen, dockers, gas workers, road transport workers, shopworkers, servants, clerks, bakers and warehousemen, were not unionized. By 1914 all this had changed, thanks to two periods of economic prosperity and rapid union growth amongst unskilled workers, in 1889–91 and 1909–13.[47]

In a time of economic boom and labour scarcity, unskilled and casual workers had a temporary bargaining power which they could use to win higher wages, shorter hours and other improvements which in normal times would be beyond their reach. The problem, of course, was to hang on to these gains when the boom ended and normal conditions returned.

In the boom of 1872 previously unorganized groups, including gas workers, building labourers, railwaymen and dockers, had struck for better pay and conditions, but without long-term success. The gas workers' strike ended when its leaders were given a year's imprisonment for conspiracy. A new factor in 1889–91 was the involvement of socialists, who were able to provide unskilled unions with publicity, organization and leadership of a high order. The first success of this powerful combination came in July 1888, when 672 Bryant and May matchgirls, fired by articles written by Annie Besant, a member of the Fabians and the SDF, came out on strike. Besant aroused public support, and the employers were forced to make concessions.[48] In the spring of 1889 the London gas workers formed the National Union of Gas Workers and General Labour to press for the reduction of shifts from twelve to eight hours, a demand which was being made right across the country. Within two weeks the union had 3,000 members (about half the workforce), and by June it had branches from Beckton and Nine Elms to Brentford. Gas stokers were not highly skilled, but nor could they be instantly replaced, and since the gas industry was facing the threat of competition from electricity for the first time a breakdown in supply might have been disastrous. So the eight-hour day was won without a strike, and Will Thorne, the young Beckton gas worker and SDF member who had organized the union (with some help from Eleanor Marx), became an instant hero. He went on to become a West Ham town councillor (1891–46) and Labour MP for West Ham South (1906–45).[49]

Unlike the craft unions, the Gas Workers' union was a general one, open to all workers. Brick-makers, munitions workers, carmen, railwaymen, rubber workers, women workers, and anyone else able to pay the weekly fee of 2d, were recruited into the union. One of the main reasons for this was the vulnerability of gas workers, and all unskilled workers, to the use of blackleg labour in times of strike. The way to prevent this was to unionize all those who might take their jobs, including farm workers, casual workers, and so on.[50]

The London dockworkers, a desperate and under-employed mass of labourers who had never been successfully unionized, except for a few months in 1872, were one of the likeliest sources of blackleg labour. In normal conditions the labour surplus on the docks made dockworkers powerless to improve their pay or conditions. Most of them lacked the skills, income or continuity of work to form a permanent trade union, and there were always casual workers waiting to take their jobs if they went on strike. Even when a trade boom enabled port workers to strike and win an increase in hourly rates from 4d to 5d in 1872, the employers were able to undo the concession by imposing a stricter system of hourly payment once the boom was over. Only the stevedores managed to keep their union alive in the depression of the rest of the decade. In the 1880s, when the dock companies were squeezed by an oversupply of docks and warehousing and a depression in trade, port workers suffered a cut in the bonuses they received for completing a job quickly (the 'plus' payment), and an intensification of the very unpopular contract system, which made dockers the hourly paid employees of small sub-contractors. The exploitation of the contract, bonus and hourly-pay systems brought dockwork within the scope of the House of Lords Committee on Sweating in 1888.[51]

In 1887 and 1888 Ben Tillett, secretary of a small union of tea warehousemen in the East India warehouses, and Tom McCarthy of the Amalgamated Stevedores' Union, had been trying to recruit members throughout the Port of London, with little success. The situation was changed on 12 August 1889 when Will Thorne, fresh from his amazing victory over the gas companies, addressed dockers in the South Dock (part of the West India Dock system) and brought them out on strike. Thorne then withdrew, leaving it to Tillett, who had called in Tom Mann of the SDF, to broaden the strike. Over the following week the strike was joined by stevedores, lightermen, dockers, sailors, firemen, wharf and warehouse workers, and by 22 August the Port was at a standstill from Tilbury to St Katharine's and Rotherhithe. Pickets were set up, and the stevedores, with their experience of union administration, organized a system of food tickets, which kept workers loyal to the strike and increased union membership to about 20,000. This system, without which the strike would have failed, was kept going by an enormous flood of public donations, about £20,000 from London and £30,000 from Australia, where there was sympathetic press coverage and a strong labour movement. The dockers' cause had already been publicized by Charles Booth and the House of Lords Committee, but its appeal was greatly increased by the 'respectable' and eloquent leadership of Tillett and Tom Mann, who became secretary and president of the new union. John Burns, who was, like Mann, an engineer and a member of the SDF, became a well-known figure, leading the dockers' daily marches through the City in his large straw hat. The sight of thousands of orderly dockers marching through the City 'without a pocket being picked or a window broken' presented middle-class Londoners with an image of decency and self-help which contrasted reassuringly with the frightening Trafalgar Square riots (in which Burns had also been involved) of three years before. They were right not to fear

Burns, who went on to become Liberal MP for Battersea (1892–1918) and an unadventurous Liberal minister.[52]

The dockers' victory in mid-September ended the contract and plus systems, and increased the hourly rate from 5d to 6d, or, as Burns famously described it, 'the full round orb of the dockers' tanner'. The employers also introduced a system which divided dockers into four categories, the permanent men and three casual grades: 'A' men, who would be chosen for work first, 'B' men, who would be hired next, and 'C' men, who would only get work when there was more than the 'A' and 'B' men could manage. This system protected regular dockworkers from competition from the lowest-quality casuals, but it did not end the casual system or the 'call', and it did not give Tillett and Mann what they wanted most, which was the exclusion of non-union labour from the port. The employers believed that the union closed shop deprived them of control over discipline and the pace of work, and thus reduced productivity. When the boom faded in 1890 and 1891 the employers reasserted their right to employ non-union men, and the dockers' resistance was easily broken by the importation of blackleg, or 'free', labour. Even the new system of labour grades worked to the employers' advantage, since they could use it to penalize unionists and promote 'free' workers.[53]

UNIONS IN THE 1890s

In the bleak years for unskilled (or 'new') unionism between 1891 and 1910, the Dockers' Union suffered most of all. In the Shipping Federation (formed in September 1890) it faced a relentless and unscrupulous opponent, which was always ready to use the police or one of London's many 'free labour' organizations to break a strike, and to bring workers to the docks by sea from other English or European ports. The Sailors' Union was destroyed, and the Dockers' Union, which had well over 20,000 members during the strike, was down to about 1,000 in 1900. The brief burst of sentimental sympathy for the striking dockers among journalists and propertied Londoners in 1889 did not last beyond the strike, and the dockers, like other unskilled workers, had to wait until 1911 for the breakthrough that would at last establish their union on a permanent footing.[54]

Although the Dockers' Union collapsed after 1891, the years 1889–92 can still be seen as a turning-point for the London (and British) labour movement. In the wake of the dockers' success, many workers who had not previously unionized formed or joined unions, notably the bargebuilders, shop assistants, clerks, vestry employees, postmen, building labourers, coach-builders, coal porters, carmen and busmen. Less skilled tailors, shoemakers and railwaymen entered unions which had previously excluded them, and traditional craft unions such as the Compositors widened their membership. The anti-socialist London Trades Council, which had refused to help the dockers' strike, found itself invaded by socialists and new unionists when its affiliated membership tripled to 67,000. Men and women who could not sustain a permanent union had felt the power that organization could bring, and were ready to use it again when conditions were favourable.[55]

Although many of the new unions faded when the boom ended, total union membership in London was much higher (perhaps more than twice as high) in the mid-1890s than it had been in 1888. According to Edward Aves (one of Booth's researchers) total union membership in the County of London in 1895 was about 177,000, or 17 per cent of the manufacturing and transport workforce, which stood at just over a million in 1891. Compared to mining and industrial counties, London unionism was not especially strong. The Webbs calculated that in Greater London (including Croydon, Kingston, West Ham and Middlesex) in 1892 3.5 per cent of the population were trade unionists (194,000 in a population of 5.5 million), compared with a British figure of 4.4 per cent.[56] Printers, lightermen, building craftsmen, engineers, stevedores, and shoemakers were strongly unionized (with between a third and two-thirds of their men in unions), and some groups of unskilled labourers, especially dockers, gasworkers and coal porters, had quite high rates of membership, but unionism was weak or non-existent among the 880,000 Londoners engaged in retail, commerce, the professions, or public or domestic service. Unions were larger than they had been in the late 1880s (twenty-six had over 2,000 members, compared with three in 1888), but small local unions still predominated, and several trades had not seen the advantages of amalgamation. There were over 240 unions in all, including sixteen unions of printers, five of brushmakers, sixteen of non-ferrous metal-workers, sixteen of leather-dressers, twenty-three of cabinet-makers, fourteen of painters and glazers, and eight of carpenters. Unionism was weakest in clerical work, in clothing and other sweated trades, and in occupations where employer–employee relationships were personal, as in domestic service and shopwork. Women workers found it hard to unionize: 95,000 milliners, machinists and shirtmakers and 300,000 servants had no trade organization. But men had their problems, too: 100,000 commercial clerks, 62,000 warehousemen and messengers, and 40,000 grocers, butchers and fishmongers could hardly muster a trade unionist between them.[57]

London unions were on the defensive between 1892 and 1910, although there were some surprising areas of growth, especially among shopworkers, postmen and railway servants, who had 13,000, 8,000 and 6,000 members respectively in 1910. Most unions were cautious and uncombative, and when there were strikes they generally failed. But more than ten years of rising prices and falling real wages created an underlying mood of resentment, and when the economy expanded in 1911 union membership and militancy revived, particularly in the transport unions, which were united in the Transport Workers' Federation. In 1910 there were disputes in the railway, cotton and coal industries in other parts of England, and in June 1911 there was a successful national seamen's strike. This gave courage to other workers, and in August 1911 London dockers and carters won 8d an hour after a brief strike, and 15,000 women from the Bermondsey sweated trades came out on strike. At the same time a national railway stoppage began, and troops were camped in the London parks to discourage unrest. Nothing happened in London to compare with the riots and shootings in Liverpool in August 1911, but there was an atmosphere of tension and impending violence in the capital, which was heightened by the unusual heat of the summer, the hottest since 1868, and by the return of Tom Mann from his foreign travels, full of the new syndicalist idea that strikes could be used to win the class struggle. The euphoria did not last. In May 1912 100,000 London dockers struck over the implementation of the 1911 agreement, and they returned to work in July, beaten by Lord Devonport, the new Port of London Authority and 13,000 blackleg labourers. The expected national dock strike did not materialize. In 1913 there was a successful strike by London cabmen between January and March, and a series of about fifty strikes in the booming construction industry, mostly over the use of non-union labour, culminating in a lock-out which began in January 1914 and ended when war broke out in August.

In all, the London strikes of 1911–14 involved the loss of over 6 million working days, and although there were failures as well as successes, the London union movement in 1914 was stronger than it had ever been. On Paul Thompson's figures, London District membership of unions with over 1,000 members was 217,000 in 1914, compared with 125,000 in 1910 and 137,000 in 1900. Some previously weak industries were now well unionized. There were 30,000 Londoners in the new National Union of Railwaymen, and union membership among gas workers and shop assistants had risen to 25,000 (from 4,000) and 20,000 respectively.[58] As far as London was concerned, the events of 1911–14 were not as dramatic or dangerous as they are sometimes claimed to have been, and socialism and trade unionism, despite their recent growth, were not a great power in the capital. But they stood, in August 1914, on the brink of a great transformation.

Chapter 21

Passing the Time

IF LONDON WAS a working town that outstripped Manchester or Birmingham, it was also a leisure town that dwarfed Brighton and Bath. Nor were the delights available in London restricted to people of one social class, as those of its seaside and spa rivals usually were. London was the indispensable social rendezvous of the leisured aristocratic élite, the centre of entertainment and self-improvement for the respectable middle classes, and the first and greatest market for those who made their fortunes by selling cheap entertainment to the labouring poor. Leisure reflected London's class divisions, but also the imprecision of social boundaries, and changes in the distribution of economic and social power in the course of the century. Although some leisure activities were the exclusive preserve of one social group, many of the most important ones were not: theatres, pleasure gardens, parks, museums, tea shops, music halls, horse races, exhibitions and newspapers were within the reach and taste of Londoners of all classes. Even the exclusive world of the club, the Court and the season was invaded by middle-class Londoners later in the century, and it was middle-class spending power that created the new world of department stores, restaurants, hotels and smart West End theatres that transformed late Victorian London.

THE SEASON

At the apex of London's social pyramid there were men and women of the aristocracy and wealthy gentry, families with incomes of £10,000 a year or more, who occupied spacious and well-staffed West End houses for three or four months each year, during the London season. The duration of the season was not precisely defined, and it tended to lengthen later in the century, as well-off London-based professional and business families were drawn into it. Roughly speaking, it ran from March (the end of the fox-hunting season) or April to July, when Parliament was in session, glittering receptions were held at Court, the great mansions in Mayfair and along Park Lane were occupied, the best international artists performed at the Haymarket or Covent Garden Opera Houses, and a series of fashionable cultural and sporting events took place. The private view at the start of the Royal Academy's summer exhibition at the beginning of May was one of the early highlights, but the calendar of events was much fuller in June, the most important month of the season. There was Eton College speech day on the fourth, followed by the Epsom Summer Meeting (at which the Derby and the Oaks were run), Ascot week in the middle of the month, and the Eton and Harrow cricket match at Lord's. The Henley Regatta was in late June or early July, then a last rush of garden parties, boat trips, balls and proposals of marriage brought the season to its end. In July and August the London weather became more oppressive, theatres closed down, the private art collections were packed away, and the 'best' people moved on to Cowes for the yachting, or back to their country estates to hunt and shoot, leaving the town 'empty', as far as the fashionable world was concerned. 'London is very deserted,' Lady Holland wrote in September 1817. 'Only a few stragglers, and those not likely to encrease; as September is invariably the most empty month. Lawyers and sportsmen are always absent, and they are a numerous part of the community.'[1]

The Court, which had once been the real centre of aristocratic London, still retained an important part in the ritual of the season. For a young woman, presentation by a well-placed sponsor to the monarch at an afternoon *levée* (known as a Drawing Room) in St James's or Buckingham Palace, marked her entry into adult society, and the beginning of her participation in the London marriage market. Invitation to a royal *levée* (an evening gathering for men) or Drawing Room was a sign of social acceptance, but Court rituals no longer played a central part in the social pleasures of the season. The unsuitability of the first three Georges for leadership of London society had, Walter Bagehot argued in 1867, long ago forced London's 'upper ten thousand' to develop an oligarchic social world which revolved around the club and the mansion rather than the Court. 'The Court is a separate part, which stands aloof from the rest of the London world, and which has but slender relations with the more amusing part of it. . . . Careful observers have long perceived this, but it was made palpable to everyone by the death of the Prince Consort. Since then the Court has always been in a state of suspended animation, and for a time it was quite annihilated. But everything went on as usual. . . . The queen bee was taken away, but the hive went on.'[2]

The steady growth in the numbers involved in London 'society', and the declining control exercised over it by the landed class as their economic power waned in the last quarter of the century, has been traced through the lists of those invited to Queen Victoria's Drawing Rooms. In a typical year in the 1840s, the Queen would receive about 300 debutantes and married women, of whom over 60 per cent were from aristocratic families. By the 1890s the number presented at Court in a season had tripled, and the proportion of titled women had fallen to a quarter. The wives and daughters of professional men, financiers and merchants, only 10 per cent of the 1841 group, were in a slight majority in 1891, confirming the widely held opinion that the old aristocratic season had been diluted (some said ruined) by the intrusion of metropolitan wealth into London high society. Beatrice Potter (later the socialist historian Beatrice Webb), a debutante and society hostess in the 1870s and 1880s, was an observer and beneficiary of this process. She described London society as 'a shifting mass of miscellaneous and uncertain membership' representing 'certain dominant forces within the British governing class' and revolving around four interconnected centres of wealth and power, the Cabinet, the Court, the racing set and 'a mysterious group of millionaire financiers'.[3]

The public face of the London season was displayed at Ascot and Henley, in the crowded royal Drawing Rooms, and at great balls and receptions. A little more privately, there was Almack's Assembly Rooms, in St James's, where seven aristocratic ladies ruthlessly excluded the self-made, the over-ambitious, and anyone else they disliked. Almack's lost its fashionable appeal in the 1830s, but it did not finally close until 1893. The increasing openness of these events to a much wider circle of aspiring Londoners diminished their attractiveness to those of the highest social rank, and the really important business of the London season went on in gentlemen's clubs, where membership was by nomination and election, and private dinner parties and balls, where entry was by invitation rather than payment. The daily routine followed by William Lamb (the future Lord Melbourne) at the beginning of the century would still have been familiar to men of his class fifty or sixty years later:

> He rose late in the morning, breakfasted largely, strolled up St James' Street, to loiter for an hour or two in the window of his Club, hearing the news, surveying the world. Later might come a ride in the Park or an afternoon call; the evening was time for dinner-parties followed by the opera, the theatre, or a ball; then back to the Club for supper till four or five struck, and it was time to go to bed.[4]

The town houses and mansions of the landed and monied aristocracy were the command centres of the London season. To possess a good house, not necessarily a mansion, in London was almost obligatory for the English social élite, and in 1880 all but one of England's richest families and at least three-quarters of the landed aristocracy had London houses for occupation during the season. A minority of these houses, perhaps forty or fifty, were true aristocratic mansions, bearing a family name rather than just a number. Most, about 350, were large town houses on the better streets or squares in Mayfair, St James's or Belgravia, within easy reach of the main social events of the season. Most of the greatest London mansions had been built in the eighteenth century, and of the handful of new ones built after 1830 several were paid for with 'new' money. Dorchester House, in Park Lane, was financed by a fishmonger's fortune; Brook House, also in Park Lane, was built for a member of the Coutts banking family, and Aldford House, South Street, was built for Sir Alfred Beit, one of the South Africa millionaires ('randlords') whose money made such an impact on London society in the 1890s. And some of the finest mansions, including Bedford and Northumberland Houses, were demolished or converted to other uses. But 'old' money was still plentiful, and some of the greatest London houses were expensively remodelled and extended in the nineteenth century, even after 1900: Stratford House, Bute House and Bourdon House were all enlarged a few years before the outbreak of the Great War.[5]

The possession or enlargement of a great house was not simply a matter of ostentation. Landed families came to London to find suitable (and suitably rich) husbands for their daughters, and (as F. M. L. Thompson pointed out in an interesting article in the *London Journal* in 1995) this meant arranging balls from which unsuitable men could be excluded, and in which a degree of supervised intimacy (in the more innocent sense of the word) could take place through the agency of the waltz and the polka. These great dances were nothing more than mating rituals. 'The dance floor and more particularly the sitting out spaces round the ballroom were the heart of the marriage market, the place where the possibilities of attachments and mergers were rumoured, mooted, tried out, accepted, and rejected.' So central was the part played by the marriage market in the London season, Thompson suggests, that fundamental changes in courtship procedures after 1914 dealt a fatal blow to the life of the great London mansions. What was the point of maintaining an expensive house or building a new ballroom, if the young men who would have been invited to the balls were dead, if one's daughters were choosing their own husbands, and if their choice was so limited that they snapped up almost anyone they could find?[6]

In Victorian London, young women looking for a husband, and men in search of political or professional advancement, had to win favour with the powerful hostesses who controlled entry to the great houses. The social and political importance of these women was especially striking in the first half of the century, when it was still possible to accommodate a substantial proportion of London society under one roof. The letters of the young Thomas Macaulay, after his speech in favour of Parliamentary Reform in March 1831 made him 'a sort of lion' in London society, give a flavour of the pleasures of being welcomed into London's finest houses. On 26 May he attended a midday concert at Lansdowne House, where he was introduced to Lady Holland and was invited to join her glittering circle. 'As to the company,' he wrote to his sister, 'there was just everybody in London (except that little million and a half that you wot of,) – the Chancellor, and the First Lord of the Admiralty, and Sydney Smith, and Lord Mansfield, and all the Barings and Fitzclarences.' The following night, 'more gaieties and music-parties' in William Marshall's mansion in Hill Street, with 'singing by all the first singers in England'. On 29 May he made his début at Holland House, where the food, the conversation and the aristocratic company met all his expectations, and he was there again two days later, this time breakfasting with the Hollands and being shown around the house. Over the following weeks, Macaulay met the finest wits, the most beautiful and influential women, the richest aristocrats and the most powerful Whig Cabinet ministers as he made his way from one dining room or club to another, polishing his conversational skills as he went.[7] Three years later the young Benjamin Disraeli, who had been blackballed at the Athenaeum, rejected by the voters of High Wycombe and mocked as a Jew, a dandy and a philanderer, won acceptance in London's political and social world. 'In a single week in June he went on Monday to the Duchess of St Albans's, on Tuesday to the opera with Lady Essex, on Wednesday to the Duchess of Hamilton's. A month later he made his début at Almack's. He dined regularly with Lady Blessington at Gore House. . . . At Lady Cork's he meets the Duke of Wellington, at Lady Blessington's Lord Durham, at Mrs Norton's Lord Melbourne.'[8]

Gore House, where Lady Blessington and her lover, the Count d'Orsay (who was also her son-in-law), entertained people of wealth, power and fashion until their bankruptcy in 1849, was more than matched on the Whig side by Holland House, Lord and Lady Holland's magnificent

Jacobean mansion in Kensington. Grey, Melbourne, Brougham, Macaulay, Sydney Smith, Thomas Creevey and Thomas Moore, the Irish poet, dined or breakfasted at Holland House, which could boast (in Macaulay's words) 'a greater number of inmates distinguished in political and literary history than any other private dwelling in England'.[9] The house declined in importance after Lord Holland's death in 1840, and for the next twenty years Lady Palmerston, who had been one of the seven guardians of Almack's, took over as London's leading Whig hostess. Her famous Saturday dinner parties in Carlton Gardens and in Cambridge House, Piccadilly, are said to have contributed significantly to her husband's political success.[10] Lady Waldegrave kept the tradition of the Whig and Liberal salon going from the 1850s to the 1870s at Strawberry Hill, where Joseph Chamberlain met the Prince of Wales and the young Charles Dilke was introduced to London society. Other political salons flourished from time to time, mostly on the Whig side: Stafford House (now Lancaster House, next to St James's Palace), owned by the immensely wealthy Duke of Sutherland; Lansdowne House, where Grey, Brougham, Russell and the Whig Cabinet met in the 1830s, and Argyll House, where the Earl of Aberdeen formed his coalition government in 1852. Lord Derby's house on St James's Square (now Chatham House) and Londonderry House did similar service for the Tories in the 1850s.

Political salons were less successful later in the century, perhaps because the political world had grown too big to fit round a dinner table. To organize the larger and more socially diverse political élite of the later nineteenth century, the parties needed to develop some of the techniques of modern party organization.[11] Landed politicians still met in Lansdowne and Grosvenor Houses, but they no longer held a monopoly on political power, and their social and economic influence was on the wane, too. Some aristocratic families used their matchmaking skills to replenish their family fortunes with new wealth from America, South Africa or the City. In Thompson's words, 'in late Victorian and Edwardian London the marriage market hummed with activity as never before, and it was in Devonshire House, Londonderry House, Berwick House, Wimborne House, and Crewe House that the plans were made and executed which saw to the digestion of American brides and heiresses and other exotics into the social system.'[12] But by 1914 the social and political functions of the aristocratic season had almost disappeared, leaving empty rituals which cost more than most landed families, in a world of death duties and falling rent rolls, could afford. In David Cannadine's view, 'As one of the most important institutions through which the traditional élite had exercised power as a class, London society was effectively dead by 1914, and the First World War merely accelerated its terminal decline.'[13]

GENTLEMEN'S CLUBS

Those who could not gain access to the best dining rooms could enjoy many of the pleasures of London society (the exclusively masculine pleasures, at any event) by becoming a member of one of the West End clubs, which enjoyed their golden age of power and prosperity in the nineteenth century. There had been temporary clubs in Restoration London, meeting informally in a favourite tavern or coffee house. In the eighteenth century a few coffee or chocolate houses, especially in St James's, were taken over by groups of gentlemen who paid membership fees to a proprietor in return for dinner, newspapers, accommodation, perhaps gaming facilities, and the exclusion of undesirables. William Almack, whose club in Pall Mall (Almack's) split into Brooks's and Boodle's in 1764, was the most successful of these proprietors, but Robert Arthur, who transformed White's Chocolate House into White's Club in the mid-eighteenth century, ran him close. Each of these clubs attracted men of a particular character or taste: Tories at White's, Whigs at Brooks's, country gentlemen and hunters at Boodle's. In the 1820s and 1830s, when tax cuts made coffee a working man's drink, clubs replaced coffee houses as the rendezvous for well-off men of shared interests and background, and over the century their number increased from half a dozen to over 100. Wits and scholars who in the 1720s would have made a coffee house their special meeting place were more likely in the 1820s to form a club. In February 1824 Walter Scott, Humphrey Davy, Michael Faraday, the artist Sir Thomas Lawrence and about ten others, led by Thomas Wilson Croker, decided to establish a club, to be known as the Athenaeum, as a rendezvous for artists, writers, scientists, ecclesiastics and aristocratic patrons. For a man of political or intellectual ambition, membership of the Athenaeum became the supreme symbol of success, and to be black-balled the greatest mortification. On the other hand, the one Victorian Prime Minister who did not join the Athenaeum was Gladstone, the most successful and distinguished of them all.

Clubs were exclusive, but not especially expensive. By building and running their clubs as collective enterprises, members could enjoy food, service and palatial accommodation which none but the very richest could have afforded individually. For an initial 30 guineas and 6 guineas a year a member of the Athenaeum had the use of a fine library, the free run of a magnificent mansion, and the company of men of distinction in science, the arts, politics or the church. 'Every member is master, without the trouble of a master: he can come when he pleases and stay away when he pleases, without anything going wrong; he has the command of regular servants, without having to pay or manage them; he can have whatever meal or refreshment he wants, at all hours, and served up as in his own house.' Clubs were free of the stifling 'etiquette' of balls and dinner parties, and offered excellent value: 'The wine and viands, which are sold at little more than cost price, often attain a pitch of excellence unequalled by the most elaborate and expensive restaurants.'[14] The ready availability of such comforts made it easier for well-off bachelors to remain unmarried well into their thirties, as most of them did.

The finest and most fashionable architects were employed to build the clubs' premises in Pall Mall, Piccadilly, and the streets nearby. Robert Smirke designed the United Services Club (for Army and Militia officers) in 1816–17, and the Union Club (open to a wide range of gentlemen) in 1824, before moving on with his brother to the British Museum and the Oxford and Cambridge Club. In 1827–8 John Nash designed the United Services Club's new premises on one side of Waterloo Place, while his protégé, Decimus Burton, outdid him with the Athenaeum's grand head-quarters on the other. William Wilkins, the architect of University College and the National Gallery, designed the University Club in 1826, and Benjamin Wyatt, who redesigned Apsley House and Lancaster House, was responsible for Crockford's (for gamblers) and the Oriental Club (for East India Company servants and those who had lived or travelled in the East) in 1825–6. Charles Barry, who rebuilt the Houses of Parliament in the 1840s and 1850s, made his name with the Travellers' Club (for travellers and Europhiles) in 1829, and the Reform Club (for Liberals and Parliamentary Reformers) in 1838. The Tories' answer to the Reform Club was the Carlton Club, which moved from building to building as its membership and influence grew in the 1830s and 1840s, until it came to rest in a sumptuous Italianate mansion in Pall Mall designed by the Smirke brothers. The Reform and the Carlton Clubs, both of which were founded during the reform crisis of 1832, functioned as the headquarters of their political parties until 1867. Later in the century, especially after 1867, growing interest in party politics among City men, professionals and provincial visitors led to the creation of less exclusive partisan clubs: the Junior Carlton, the City Carlton, the Conservative, the Junior Conservative, the

Constitutional and the Junior Constitutional on one side, the National Liberal, the City Liberal and the Devonshire on the other. Some of these clubs had 5–6,000 members, but none of them gained the influence of the Carlton or the Reform.[15]

The more prestigious clubs often had long waiting lists, but the system was infinitely expandable. Groups without club membership could form a new club of their own, or perhaps a 'Junior' or 'City' version of an existing club. Actors, writers and 'men of refinement' who were excluded from the Athenaeum, or felt inhibited by the bishops and Cabinet ministers who were so well represented among its members, could try the Windham Club in St James's Square (1828), the Garrick in Covent Garden (1831), the Savage (1857) or the Arts Club (1863). There were clubs for journalists, authors, photographers, lawyers, civil servants, diplomats, fly-fishers and sports enthusiasts of all kinds. By 1900 London had around 100 clubs, including at least eight for army and naval officers, five for university graduates and nine for women. City merchants and bankers of differing degrees of distinction might belong to the City of London Club (1833), the Gresham Club (1843), the City Athenaeum or the City Carlton.

RESTAURANTS AND HOTELS

The success of clubs in providing economical board and lodging for better-off men helps to explain the relatively slow development of fashionable hotels and restaurants in early Victorian London. In the early nineteenth century there were several fine West End 'hotels', but these were usually hired as a whole house, rather than room by room. In 1814 Tsar Alexander I of Russia and his sister, Grand Duchess Catherine, stayed in the Pulteney Hotel, and Louis XVIII lodged in Grillon's Hotel, both near Piccadilly. The Prince Regent used Mivart's, which later became Claridge's, in Brook Street. Lesser visitors usually stayed in inns or lodgings, as they would have done in Boswell's day, but there were a few genuine hotels, especially in New Bond Street, which had Long's, which was used by Byron and Walter Scott, Steven's, popular with army officers and men about town, and the Clarendon, which claimed to have London's only French chef. Naval men preferred Fladong's in Oxford Street, and the racing set met in Limmer's in Hanover Square. Yet by the middle of the century it was said that London was less well supplied with good hotels than New York, Paris or any European capital city.[16]

By 1850 the expanding wealth and numbers of professional, financial and commercial families either resident in London or visiting it promised tempting profits to those offering them respectable food, accommodation and entertainment at a fair price. The railway companies were first in the field. The London and Birmingham line began modestly with two hotels at Euston in 1839, but in the 1850s and 1860s hotels on a much grander scale, and in the most elaborate Gothic and French Renaissance styles, were built alongside the main termini. The Great Western at Paddington and the Great Northern at King's Cross both opened in 1854, followed by the Grosvenor at Victoria (1861), the London Bridge (1861), the Charing Cross (1864), the City Terminus at Cannon Street (1867), and George Gilbert Scott's stupendous Midland Grand at St Pancras (1868–72). The success of the first railway hotels drew others into the business, especially after the easing of the law on limited liability company formation in 1862. The Westminster Palace in Victoria Street (1860) had 300 bedrooms, fourteen bathrooms and London's first lifts, and the Langham, in Portland Place (1865), had ten floors, 600 rooms, an excellent restaurant and its own artesian well. In the late 1870s Frederick Gordon, the biggest of the Victorian hotel entrepreneurs, built three huge hotels (the Grand, the Metropole and the Victoria) on the new Northumberland Avenue, making Trafalgar Square the hub of London's hotel industry.[17] In the late 1880s Richard d'Oyly Carte, who had made a fortune producing Gilbert and Sullivan operas, brought American standards of comfort to London with the Savoy, which had eighty bathrooms, six lifts, electric lighting, César Ritz as manager and Auguste Escoffier, the world's greatest chef, in charge of the kitchens. The Hotel Cecil, the biggest in the world, was built on the Strand, next to the Savoy, in 1890, and César Ritz's Carlton (on Haymarket), the Imperial and the Russell (both on Russell Square) and the Grand Central (opposite Marylebone Station) followed in the 1890s. In the few years after 1900 there came the Ritz (in Piccadilly), the Piccadilly and the Waldorf (in the Aldwych). Finally, between 1912 and 1915, a 2-acre site near Piccadilly Circus was cleared for the 1,000-room Regent Palace Hotel, which became a favourite retreat for officers during the First World War. These colossal constructions finally put an end to London's shortage of luxury hotels, replacing it, except during the season, with an unprofitable surplus. Edwardian London's twelve biggest hotels could accommodate about 12,000 people, and its smaller hotels and boarding-houses could hold another 50,000 or more.[18]

The history of the London restaurant parallels that of the hotel. For most of the nineteenth century London gentlemen away from their home or club were most likely to eat, as Boswell had done, in a chop-house, a coffee house or a tavern. Such places were plentiful: London directories listed 345 dining rooms in 1848, and 700 in 1878.[19] Respectable London women ate in private houses, where, in general, the best dinners were served. There were fine chefs in London, but they worked in private clubs, not public restaurants: Louis Ude at Crockford's, Alexis Soyer at the Reform and Charles Francatelli at both of these. A few small hotels offered excellent food to private groups, but not to the public at large. In 1857 the *Building News* called for someone to build large and comfortable dining halls in London, which 'could almost serve as clubs for the middle classes', but nobody rushed to take up the challenge. Over the next twenty years there was some improvement, especially in restaurants associated with railway stations and theatres. The Café Royal opened off Regent Street in 1865, and the Gaiety Theatre on the Strand, which opened in December 1868, had a café, a luncheon bar and two dining rooms. Another theatre, the Criterion, which opened in Piccadilly Circus in 1874, had a restaurant attached to it which fed about 2,000 people a day. There were two chains of economical restaurants: Spiers and Pond, who ran the Criterion and refreshment rooms in some of the London stations, and the Gatti brothers, whose business included two music halls, the Adelphi Theatre and restaurant, and a restaurant in the Adelaide Gallery in the Strand. There were also some good French and Italian restaurants in Soho, but this district was too cosmopolitan to appeal to most London diners, and only became fashionable towards the end of the century.[20]

By the 1890s restaurants were beating West End clubs in the contest for high-spending diners. Not only was restaurant food generally better than club food, but men could eat it in the company of women. The presence of women, Walter Besant thought, had 'made a great alteration: there is always an atmosphere of cheerfulness, if not of exhilaration; one is always welcome; the waiters are all obliging'.[21] Baedeker's 1898 *Guide* listed about sixty good restaurants in the West End, including those in the Savoy, the Cecil, the Métropole, and the other big hotels. Most of the best restaurants in 1900 were less than ten years old: Simpson's and Romano's in the Strand, the Trocadero, Prince's and Scott's near Piccadilly, Frascati's in Oxford Street, the Holborn (with fifteen dining rooms) in High Holborn. Down the social scale, traditional chop-houses and taverns were challenged by new catering chains, which appealed especially to shoppers, clerks, commuters and women office workers: Slater's luncheon and tea rooms, British Tea Table (BTT) tea shops, Express Dairy 'milk and bun' shops, and Spiers and Pond station buffets. The Aerated Bread Company (ABC) pioneered the tea shop, opening its first one near London Bridge in 1880. But it was overtaken in the 1890s by Joseph Lyons and Montagu Gluckstein, whose company, Lyons and Co., opened its first London tea shop in Piccadilly in 1894, its first high-class restaurant (the Trocadero) in 1896, and the first of its four Corner Houses (each with seating for 3,000) in 1909. By this time Lyons had nearly 100 London tea shops, and was on its way to becoming the biggest catering business in the world.[22]

DEPARTMENT STORES

London's backwardness in the development of hotels and restaurants was matched by its slowness to introduce department stores. Since the late 1830s there had been embryonic department stores in Newcastle and Manchester, offering a variety of keenly priced goods (mostly clothes) with marked prices, and expecting cash payment from their customers. The full-blown department store emerged first in Paris, where Aristide Boucicaut, apparently inspired by the displays of the 1855 Paris Exposition, built the Bon Marché on the Left Bank in the 1860s. In the Bon Marché well-off Parisian women could wander for hours, choosing from several floors of beautifully displayed and clearly priced goods, struggling (as Zola put it) 'between their passion for clothes and the thrift of their husbands'.[23]

London in the 1860s was a city of small specialist shops, and all it could offer to compare with Bon Marché were its arcades and bazaars, in which customers could visit a succession of small shops or stalls under one roof. London's first bazaar, according to John Timbs, was the Soho Bazaar in Soho Square, which was set up by an army contractor, John Trotter, in 1816 to give war widows a way of making an honest living through trade. It thrived until the 1880s, when its buildings were taken over by a publisher. The Soho Bazaar's success inspired many imitators in the West End, including one created in 1834 by Sydney Smirke inside the Oxford Street Pantheon, which had once been London Society's 'winter Ranelagh'. This lasted until 1867, when it was converted into a wine warehouse. A Marks and Spencer store now occupies the site. Other ventures included the Lowther Bazaar in the Strand, for fancy goods, and the Baker Street Bazaar, for carriages, glass and furniture. Arcades, covered precincts in which the goods were displayed in fixed shops rather than stalls, were almost as numerous, and rather more enduring. At least four survive in the West End, two from the Regency, the Burlington and Royal Opera Arcades, one opened in 1879, the Royal Arcade, and the Piccadilly Arcade of 1910. The Lowther Arcade, off the Strand, which specialized in toyshops, was demolished in 1904.[24]

London's growing population of middle-class consumers, of well-off suburban wives with time to shop and money (but not unlimited money) to spend made it virtually certain that Boucicaut's strategy would be imitated in London before long. There were plenty of prosperous West End drapers who might have followed the Bon Marché path, but the first London retailer to do so was William Whiteley, the owner (since 1863) of a small fancy drapery shop in an unpromising location in Westbourne Grove, in the suburb of Bayswater. The completion of the Metropolitan Underground Railway line between Paddington and Hammersmith in 1864 increased Bayswater's fashionable appeal, and as the area's population and social tone rose, so did Whiteley's profits. By 1878 he had taken over fifteen shops in Westbourne Grove, and expanded his range of goods to include food, drink and furniture. He advertised himself as the 'Universal Provider', able to supply anything from a pin to an elephant, and paid special attention to window displays and mail order business. Non-retailing services were added from the 1870s onwards: estate agency, banking, dry cleaning and theatre tickets in the 1870s, railway tickets and ceremonial catering in the 1880s. Whiteley's combination of quality, fashion, variety and value had a very wide appeal, and by 1900 the store's turnover was more than £1 million a year. Whiteley, a notorious womanizer, was shot dead in his office in 1907 by a man claiming to be his illegitimate son.[25] Fortunately, one of his store's 159 departments was an undertaker's.

Just as Whiteley's rose (and eventually fell) with Bayswater, so Harrods, on the other side of the park, rose (and kept on rising) with Knightsbridge. Harrods started as a grocer and tea merchant in Stepney, and moved to the Brompton Road, Knightsbridge, in 1853, just after the Great Exhibition of 1851 had elevated the tone of the area. Like Whiteley, Charles Digby Harrod used his growing profits to buy neighbouring shops, with the aim of eventually gaining control of a complete 'island site'. The store was rebuilt on a larger scale after a disastrous fire in 1883, and prospered in the 1890s under the management of Richard Burbidge, who had previously managed Whiteley's. The store was rebuilt in its present grandiose form, a vast terracotta monument to the wealth and commercial power of Edwardian London, in 1901–5.

In the 1880s and 1890s other London drapers followed Whiteley's lead. Dickins and Jones, Marshall and Snelgrove, Swan and Edgar and Debenham and Freebody, all well-established drapers in the Regent Street, Piccadilly and Oxford Street area, expanded their premises and their range of goods to capture the mass middle-class market. Arthur Liberty (whose retailing style had been inspired by the International Exhibition of 1862) began taking over shops in Regent Street for the sale of East India goods and oriental finery in the 1880s. These individual entrepreneurs faced competition from two large cooperative stores (supposedly for members only), the Civil Service Supply Association on the Strand (founded by Post Office clerks in 1868), and the Army and Navy Stores in Victoria Street (opened by officers in 1872). At the same time department stores on almost as grand a scale developed in the smarter suburbs, where local demand was strong: John Barnes in Finchley Road, Jones Brothers in Holloway, Pratts in Streatham, Arding and Hobbs in Clapham, Chiesmans in Lewisham, Peter Jones in Sloane Square. Most of these, like Whiteley's, Harrods, the John Lewis store in Oxford Street and Arthur Gamage's 'People's Popular Emporium' in Holborn, were accumulations of small shops. The first purpose-built department store in London was Bon Marché in Brixton, which was built in 1877 by a Tooting printer and racehorse owner, James Smith, with prize-money won at Newmarket races.[26]

Grander purpose-built stores followed around the end of the century. Whiteley's was rebuilt in Queensway in 1908–11, Debenham's in Wigmore Street (near Oxford Street) in 1909, Burberrys in the Haymarket in 1911–12, Waring and Gillow (for furniture) in Oxford Street in 1901–6. The greatest and most distinguished of the furniture specialists, John Maple and Co., was in Tottenham Court Road, the centre of high-quality furniture-making. Maple's small shop was rebuilt on a larger scale in 1851, and more grandly still in 1896, next to Shoolbred's, another of London's big department stores.[27] Big stores needed new technology. Gas lighting added to the high risk of fire in department stores (Whiteley's had six serious fires in the 1880s), and in the 1880s and 1890s the more advanced shops installed electricity. Pneumatic tubes to carry cash and orders between sales floors and cashiers were introduced at about the same time. Some shops installed Otis lifts in the 1880s, and from 1898 Harrods, alone among London stores, had an escalator. Harrods led the way, too, in becoming a public company. Its flotation took place in 1889, two years before Maples and ten years ahead of Whiteley's. The most important innovation of all, Santa's Christmas Grotto, came first to Roberts store, Stratford, in 1888. Other stores copied the idea in 1889.[28]

In 1906 the profitable and conservative world of London department stores was shaken by the arrival of Gordon Selfridge, the world's most famous and successful retailer, who had lately retired from America's leading store, Marshall Field's of Chicago. The opening of Selfridge's vast new Oxford Street store in 1909 brought new American methods to London: well-designed and spacious window and floor displays replaced the crowding and floor-to-ceiling clutter of English stores, information desks replaced floorwalkers, and the hounding and ejection of 'tabbies', women who wanted attention but had no intention of buying, was gradually dropped. By copying some of these methods Harrods managed to keep abreast of its rival, and the two giants, having successfully weathered the First World War, entered the 1920s strong enough to take over many of their West End and suburban competitors.[29]

A trade journal in 1910 depicted the department store as an almost entirely female world: 'Buying and selling, serving and being served – women. . . . Simply a moving, seeking, hurrying mass of femininity, in the midst of which the occasional man shopper, man clerk, and man supervisor, looks lost and out of place.' This was not entirely true. Nearly 9,000 (63 per cent) of the 14,000 workers in London general and multiple shops in 1891 were men, and over 10,000 (58 per cent) of the 18,000 in 1911. It was only between 1911 and 1921, with the influence of the First World War, that women took over the majority (55 per cent) of department store jobs.[30] Big stores employed young men and women on an almost industrial scale. In 1886 Shoolbred's, Marshall and Snelgrove, Barkers and Debenhams had over 2,000 assistants between them. The biggest stores had even more employees. The Army and Navy Stores had 5,000 staff in 1887, but most of these were in its workshops or its mail order department. Shop assistants were often bullied by floorwalkers and fined for petty misdemeanours (especially in Whiteley's), but there was a paternalistic tradition in the drapery trade, too. Most big retailers provided dormitory accommodation for their staff (a practice rejected by Selfridge), and many offered their workers sports and social clubs, musical societies and recreation rooms. Paternalism reached its apotheosis in the John Lewis chain when John Spedan Lewis made it into a profit-sharing partnership in the 1920s. Department stores also had to respond to pressure from concerned shoppers, who did not enjoy the idea that their pleasures depended on the hardships of others. Most later Victorian department stores closed at 6 p.m. (perhaps at 7 in the summer) and, thanks to the Early Closing Movement, at 2 p.m. on Saturdays. But about 90 per cent of retailing staff worked in smaller shops, and many of these, especially those that relied on working-class evening and weekend customers, kept much longer hours.[31]

Pubs and Eating Houses

Leisure was not confined to the 'leisured' classes. The old assumption that the early nineteenth-century working class suffered a 'bleak age', in which a combination of industrial discipline, urbanization and resurgent puritanism robbed them of almost all forms of recreation except the public house, does not ring true for London. Certainly, the well-off viewed popular recreations with distaste (as they had in the previous century), and their disapproval, in alliance with effective professional policing, inflicted some serious losses on the London poor. In the 1820s and 1830s urban animal sports were driven underground, street games were curtailed, several fairs were closed down and public houses were shut on Sunday mornings. But the limitations on the power of nineteenth-century morality movements are illustrated by the survival and prosperity of the public house. However much temperance campaigners and politicians hated or feared pubs as the source of vice, crime and poverty, their social and commercial importance made an assault upon them, except in the limited field of Sunday opening, unthinkable. London had fewer pubs per 1,000 inhabitants than other English cities (2.5 in the 1890s, compared to Manchester's 6 or Birmingham's 4.5), but in the West End, the City and the poorer suburbs there were drinking places on almost every street corner. A man walking for a mile along the Whitechapel Road in the 1890s, or for less than a mile along the Strand, could take a drink in more than forty-five different pubs or beerhouses, and dozens of other East and West End streets were almost as welcoming. In richer residential districts, where householders used off-licences and drank at home, there were pubs for tradesmen and servants, and only one neighbourhood, the Duke of Bedford's Bloomsbury estate, was entirely 'dry'. A writer in 1854 calculated that London's drinksellers outnumbered all its butchers, bakers, fishmongers, cheesemongers, greengrocers, grocers and dairy-keepers together.[32]

So long as public houses survived, the recreations and the vices of the London working class had a degree of protection from the hostile attentions of Victorian morality-mongers. Boxing, prostitution, community singing, gambling and animal sports were all promoted and protected by publicans. In the 1850s Henry Mayhew interviewed Jimmy Shaw, the landlord of a London public house well known for its rat fights, who claimed to buy around 26,000 rats a year, at 3d each, from farm labourers in Essex and Enfield, to be killed by dogs 100 at a time.[33] Those of more refined tastes would have preferred the Eagle Tavern and tea garden, just off the City

Road in Islington, which had its own music hall (built in 1825), which was in turn converted into a popular theatre, the Grecian, in 1832. As Brian Harrison has explained, public houses served as meeting places for those in search of newspapers, transport, companionship, work, bargains, credit, medical advice, warmth, comfort, gossip or political debate, as well as refreshment and entertainment. Trade unions, political groups, friendly societies, savings clubs and even coroners' juries met in pubs, and the beer they drank no doubt added cheerfulness and vigour, if not clarity, to their discussions. The miserable condition of most working-class homes, and the shortage of alternative public meeting places (other than churches) made it difficult for working men to avoid meeting in public houses, even if they had been inclined to do so.[34]

Temperance and Sunday observance campaigners made serious inroads into the drinking time of the London working class. London public houses were allowed to open at all hours (except during Sunday morning church services) until 1839, when the Metropolitan Police Act, reflecting concern over Saturday-night disorder, forced them to close from midnight on Saturday to 1 p.m. on Sunday. The workman's dinner time was protected, but Sunday afternoon closure (from 3 p.m. to 5 p.m.) followed in 1855. A further measure in 1864 forced London public houses to close between 1 a.m. and 4 a.m., a rule that would have bothered prostitutes and their clients in the notorious Haymarket drinking saloons more than ordinary working men. Finally, national licensing acts in 1872 and 1874 imposed night-time closure (12.30 a.m. to 5 a.m. in London's case) throughout the week, and brought Sunday night closure forward to 11 p.m.[35]

By the 1870s, although public houses retained their central place in working-class life, the growing availability of other places of entertainment and refreshment made their services a little less important than they had been earlier in the century. Parks and music halls offered alternative attractions, and there were more cheap places to eat and drink. At the start of the century, when water and milk were dirty, coffee and tea were heavily taxed, and cordials and ginger beer were not available, London porter, strong, cheap and healthy, was the almost universal drink. Fifty or sixty years later, much had changed. Victorian Londoners never became milk drinkers, but clean water was easier to find by the 1870s, thanks to the Metropolitan Free Drinking Fountain Association and its 300 fountains. Tea and coffee were much cheaper in the 1840s, and by 1841 London had over 1,600 coffee shops, selling cheap snacks and coffee at 1d or 2d a cup. The age of the fashionable coffee house was over, but far more coffee was drunk in Dickens's London than in Dr Johnson's.[36] Henry Mayhew describes (with echoes of *London Lickpenny*) the enormous range of drink and cooked food the Londoner could buy in the 1850s, from between 3,000 and 5,000 street-sellers, without entering a pub:

> Men and women, and most especially boys, purchase their meals day after day in the streets. The coffee-stall supplies a warm breakfast; shell-fish of many kinds tempt to a luncheon; hot-eels or pea-soup, flanked by a potato 'all hot', serve for a dinner; and cakes and tarts, or nuts and oranges, with many varieties of pastry, confectionery, and fruit, woo to indulgence in a dessert; while for supper there is a sandwich, a meat pudding, or a "trotter"....
>
> The solids then, according to street estimation, consist of hot-eels, pickled whelks, oysters, sheep's trotters, pea-soup, fried fish, ham-sandwiches, hot green peas, beef, mutton, kidney, and eel pies, and baked potatoes. In each of these provisions the street poor find a mid-day or midnight meal.
>
> The pastry and confectionery which tempt the street eaters are tarts of rhubarb, currant, gooseberry, cherry, apple, damson, cranberry, and (so-called) mince-pies; plum dough and plum-cake; lard, currant, almond, and many other varieties of cakes, as well as of tarts; gingerbread-nuts and heart-cakes; Chelsea buns; muffins and crumpets; "sweet stuff" includes the several kinds of rocks, sticks, lozenges, candies, and hard-bakes; the medicinal confectionery of cough-drops and horehound; and, lastly, the more novel and aristocratic luxury of street-ices; and strawberry-cream, at 1d a glass, (in Greenwich Park).
>
> The drinkables are tea, coffee, and cocoa; ginger-beer, lemonade, Persian sherbet, and some highly-coloured beverages which have no specific name, but are introduced to the public as "cooling" drinks; hot elder cordial or wine; peppermint water; curds and whey; water (as at Hampstead); rice milk; and milk in the parks.'[37]

For those who wanted to sit down to eat, cheap restaurants were common later in the century. In the 1890s there were fifty Lockhart's coffee rooms, selling pork pies, sausages and sandwiches, and twenty Pearce and Plenty dining rooms, where a clerk or working man could get a breakfast, tea or supper for 2d, and a midday dinner of steak pudding and potatoes for 5d.[38]

THE THEATRE

London's rising population sustained an enormous number of providers of cheap and lively entertainment. Pleasure gardens were past their fashionable prime, but many of them continued as places of popular entertainment until mid-century or beyond, using fireworks, circus acts, balloon ascents, races, plays and concerts to draw in the crowds. Some older gardens declined and made way for suburban development: Islington Spa in 1840, Bagnigge Wells in 1841, White Conduit House in 1849, and Vauxhall in 1859. Highbury Barn, Islington, once an eighteenth-century tea room and bowling green, attracted large crowds when its owners built a huge open-air dance floor, the 'Leviathan', in 1858. It lost its licence and closed after a riot in 1869.[39] Some new gardens opened, and did well for a few decades. The most successful of these was Cremorne, on Chelsea riverbank (west of Battersea Bridge), which had an American bowling saloon and a theatre as well as the usual balloonists, ropewalkers, grottoes and fireworks. The familiar charges of vice and disorder forced it to close in 1877.[40] Beulah Spa, in Upper Norwood, which had a maze, an orchestra and local gipsy fortune-tellers, was a fashionable success in the 1830s and 1840s. One of the largest recreational spaces in South London, the Surrey Zoological Gardens (opened in 1831), had a 3-acre lake, around which were created vast and spectacular moving picture-models, usually representing an erupting volcano or the city of Rome. The park and its zoo were closed in 1856, when the huge Surrey Music Hall, which was said to hold over 10,000 people, was built on the site. The decline of the Beulah and Surrey gardens was accelerated by the removal in 1854 of the great glass exhibition building known as the Crystal Palace from Hyde Park to a 200-acre pleasure garden in Sydenham, where it became a vast concert and recreation hall, offering for a shilling all the indoor and outdoor entertainments that a decent Victorian could desire. Until the Crystal Palace was destroyed by fire in 1936, the spirit of the pleasure garden was not quite dead.

Henry Mayhew's study of London costermongers around 1850 offers some useful insights into the recreations of working-class Londoners, although costers were not typical London workmen. Their leisure time, he tells us, were spent in the beershop, the dancing room and the theatre. In beershops they played cards, skittles and shove-halfpenny, sometimes for money or beer, and watched boxing contests between fellow-costers. At their 'twopenny hops' they danced jigs and hornpipes, 'vigorous, laborious capering', to the music of a fiddle and perhaps a harp. They were devoted to betting, and their gambling rings gathered every Sunday to toss coins for money while boys kept watch for the police. Their favourite sports, like those of the country gentry, took advantage of the local wildlife: rat-killing, dog-fighting and pigeon-shooting were always in season. Mayhew went to a 'penny gaff', an improvised theatre in which children and adolescents of both sexes greeted songs, plays and dances of the most crude and suggestive type with noisy delight. When costers had the money, one told him, they preferred to go to a play or musical show at the Surrey, the Victoria, the Bower Saloon, or one of the other cheap South London theatres: 'Love and murder suits us best, sir.' Mayhew describes the huge crowd of young costermen and women pushing their way into the threepenny gallery of the Victoria (the 'Vic'), scrambling for the best seats, buying porter and pigs' trotters, drowning the sound of the orchestra with their shouts and laughter, whistling and cheering the actors in a succession of dramatic sketches, and joining lustily, 1,800-strong, in the choruses of popular songs.[41]

Mayhew's account of an evening at what became the Old Vic is a reminder that the theatre in nineteenth-century London was not an élite entertainment, but one of the chief pleasures, in one form or another, of every social class. In 1815 London was in the middle of a period of impressive growth in popular theatre. In addition to its two large 'patent theatres', the Theatres Royal in Drury Lane and Covent Garden, and a smaller patent theatre, the Haymarket, with a licence to perform full-length plays in the summer season, London had ten 'minor theatres', including three on the Strand (the Sans Souci or Adelphi, the Olympic and the Lyceum), Sadler's Wells near the Pentonville Road (the oldest of the 'minors'), two converted circuses, Astley's and the Surrey, several fairground and pleasure-garden theatres, and innumerable public-house concert rooms and 'saloon theatres'.

None of these places was allowed, by the terms of Walpole's 1737 Licensing Act, to perform full-length dramas, so instead they offered a diet of circus acts, spectacles, pantomimes and dramatic presentations known as burlettas, which used verse recitative with musical accompaniment instead of dialogue. Although burletta was devised initially to meet legal requirements, it turned out to be enormously popular among middle- and working-class theatregoers, drawing them away from the two big patent theatres into new suburban ones. The very large Coburg Theatre (later the Victoria) was opened in 1818, after which there was a ten-year lull, followed by a period of intensive building between 1828 and 1842, in which the number of theatres and saloon theatres (based on public houses) in London was doubled to about twenty-six. These included four in the East End (the Garrick, the City of London, the Effingham and the Pavilion) and four (the Standard Theatre, and the Britannia, Grecian and Royal Albert Saloons) in the increasingly shabby and crowded suburbs of Hoxton and Shoreditch, where London's first theatres had been built in the 1570s. This was roughly how things stood until the late 1860s, when seven new West End theatres were built on or near the Strand.[42]

The seat prices of the minor theatres suggest that they appealed to a cross-section of society. Tickets to see an equestrian extravaganza at Astley's Royal Ampitheatre in 1842 cost 5s in the stalls, 2s in the pit, and 6d (two-thirds of the price of a 4-pound loaf) in the upper gallery. For about the same price North Londoners could go to Sadler's Wells to see one of its famous nautical shows or the great clown Joseph Grimaldi, who gave his farewell performance in 1828. In 1850 the cheapest gallery seats in the Britannia (Hoxton) and the Victoria (Lambeth) were only 3d, and in the Bower Saloon (Lambeth) they were 2d.[43]

Most descriptions of early nineteenth-century audiences concentrate on their moral tone, rather than their social class. Playgoers were riotous, noisy and abusive, they drank beer, threw fruit, blew catcalls and set off crackers. Sadler's Wells in the early 1840s 'was a bear-garden, resounding with foul language, oaths, catcall shrieks, yells, blasphemy, obscenity – a truly diabolical clamour'.[44] The open presence of prostitutes, even in the major theatres, intensified the disreputable atmosphere, and helps explain why respectable and fashionable families had largely deserted drama for the opera. Class-mixing through leisure was often recommended in theory, but in practice it was generally unwelcome. 'People will not go, sir, where sweeps are,' a well-off customer wrote to the manager of the Surrey Theatre in 1827. When observers note the social composition of audiences, they usually describe them as lower-middle or working class. Charles Dickens knew the theatre well, from both sides of the curtain. Each of the suburban theatres, he wrote in 1836, constituted 'the centre of a little stage-struck neighbourhood. Each of them has an audience exclusively its own.' Their principal customers, he believed, were 'dirty boys, low copying clerks in attorneys' offices, capacious-headed youths from City counting-houses, ... shopboys ... and a choice miscellany of vagabonds'. At the Britannia in Hoxton in the 1850s he found 'mechanics, dock-labourers, costermongers, petty tradesmen, small clerks, milliners, stay-makers, shoe-binders, slop workers', much the same social groups as those found by Mayhew in the gallery of the Victoria at the same time.[45]

The two major 'legitimate' theatres were beset with troubles. Both of them had burned down in 1808–9, and since neither was adequately insured, the cost of rebuilding left them deep in debt. John Kemble, the manager of the Covent Garden Theatre, had tried to attract a more élite audience in 1809, when the rebuilt theatre was reopened with exclusive facilities for the well-off, increased ticket prices, more private boxes and fewer cheap gallery seats. But sixty-seven nights of protest (the 'Old Price riots') forced him to revert to the old system, with plenty of cheap seats in the pit and gallery. Perhaps this was the best policy, because fashionable interest in the theatre declined over the next two or three decades, as a result (contemporaries believed) of a lack of royal patronage, a shift in the smart dinner hour from 3 o'clock to 8 o'clock, and a falling off in the quality of new drama. Both theatres had 2,500 seats to fill if they were to make a profit, but competition from the opera and from the 'minor' theatres in the West End, especially the Adelphi and the Olympic, made this hard to do, despite the popularity of such great stars as Edmund Kean and William Charles Macready. Their best results came when they imitated their suburban rivals in staging crowd-pleasing patriotic spectacles, animal shows and pantomimes, or when they presented melodrama, which, in its early form, combined sensational Gothic dramas with vigorous musical accompaniment.

When the 1843 Theatres Act ended the old duopoly and introduced a free market in drama, the two patent theatres abandoned plays altogether. The Covent Garden became an opera house in 1847 and the Drury Lane turned to concerts, pantomimes and circus acts until its revival as a 'straight' theatre under Augustus Harris in the 1880s. Contrary to expectations, no significant new theatres were built in London between 1843 and 1866, and the existing minor theatres did not rush to abandon burletta and spectacle for serious drama. For the rest of the century most theatres, especially those in the poorer districts, concentrated on melodrama, in which virtue triumphed over vice and bombast vanquished dramatic subtlety. Writers produced their plays in bulk. Dion Boucicault, the most prolific and popular Victorian playwright, wrote or adapted almost 200 plays between 1840 and 1880. Melodrama offered very little of lasting literary value, but like television soap operas it provided lively entertainment, engaged the emotions of its audience, and often addressed moral and social issues which were relevant to the lives of Londoners.[46]

Fashionable interest in drama gradually revived, encouraged by Queen Victoria's patronage in the 1840s and 1850s, and fostered by the efforts of a few managers, notably Samuel Phelps, who rescued Sadler's Wells from notoriety between 1844 and 1862, and Charles Kean (Edmund's son), whose Shakespearean revivals drew large and respectable audiences to the Princess's Theatre in the 1850s. Between 1865 and 1879 Marie Wilton and her husband, Squire Bancroft, transformed the Queen's Theatre, in Tottenham Court Road, from a 'dust hole' specializing in low melodrama into a highly fashionable and profitable theatre, the Prince of Wales's. The Bancrofts introduced half-guinea (10s 6d) stalls instead of the cheaper pit, initiating a practice which other West End managers copied. By the 1890s twenty-four West End theatres (all except the Princess's) charged 10s 6d for stalls and a shilling for gallery seats. The fourteen new London theatres of the 1880s and 1890s were richly furnished and decorated, and provided their customers with buffets, smoking rooms and saloons.

Economic and demographic conditions favoured this new policy. The growing size and affluence of the upper middle class (men in business, finance, the civil service and the professions), and improved omnibus, railway and underground transport from the suburbs and beyond the metropolitan area, increased the potential audience and made it possible for managers to run the same play for months (even years) on end, rather than relying on constant changes of programme to keep the seats full. Longer runs, larger and richer audiences, and the replacement of payment by the night with a more generous royalties system, eventually drew more skilful writers into the theatre, but the change was not fast. The new playgoers were well-off, respectful and undemanding, and the productions they paid so handsomely to see were generally Shakespearean revivals or poor adaptations of French plays. In the words of the contemporary critic, William Archer:

> For twenty-five years, from 1865 to 1890, the English stage was overrun with French operettas of the school of Offenbach. Hastily adapted by slovenly hacks, their librettos (often witty in the original) became incredible farragos of metreless doggrel and punning ineptitude. The majority of them are now so utterly forgotten that it is hard to realise how, in their heyday, they swarmed on every hand in London and the provinces.[47]

In the 1880s and 1890s the names of W. S. Gilbert, Arthur Pinero, Oscar Wilde and Henrik Ibsen began to replace those of Boucicault, Tom Taylor, T. W. Robertson and H. J. Byron on West End playbills, with J. M. Barrie and George Bernard Shaw joining them after 1900. The commercial success of the late Victorian and Edwardian stage probably owed more, though, to the great actor-managers who dominated the major West End theatres between about 1880 and 1914: Henry Irving at the Lyceum,

Beerbohm Tree at the Haymarket and Her Majesty's, Charles Wyndham at the Criterion, and George Alexander at the St James's. Irving's twenty-five-year partnership with Ellen Terry ended in 1902, and the deaths of the other three in 1917–19 brought an outstanding period in London's theatrical history to an end.[48]

MUSIC HALLS

West End theatre was entertainment for the well-to-do. Those with only 3d or 4d to spend went instead to the big inner suburban theatres (the Pavilion in Whitechapel, the Britannia in Hoxton, the Surrey in Lambeth, the Royal Standard in Shoreditch) or to the music halls, which had developed rapidly since about 1850. The history of music halls has been obscured by nostalgia and sentiment, but in essence they simply continued the traditions established by variety theatres at the beginning of the century. The mixture of songs, sketches and circus acts that they offered would have been familiar to a visitor to any of the early nineteenth-century minor or saloon theatres, fairground booths or pleasure gardens. There was not much to choose between seeing selections from *King John*, Mr Mullings as 'Billy Vhite (in Character)', and Master Luce performing a sailor's hornpipe and a 'negro song' at Bagnigge Wells in the 1830s and watching Mrs Rust ('the pleasing serio-comic'), Mr W. Cubitt ('skate dancer'), Paddy Tyrell ('Irish Comic'), Billy Gibbons ('The Broth of a Boy') and scenes from *Othello* at Miller's Grand Music Hall, Hoxton, in the 1860s.[49]

Music halls also drew on the musical entertainment offered in taverns, public houses and West End song and supper rooms, large licensed dining rooms in which well-off men could sing, eat and drink in convivial surroundings. There were several song and supper rooms in Covent Garden in the 1840s. W. H. Evans's music and supper room (known as Evans' Late Joys, because Joy was the previous owner) at 43 King Street, Thackeray's favourite, was rebuilt as a music hall in 1855, and the Cyder Cellars, in Maiden Lane, was converted into a simple music hall in the late 1840s. Public houses had attracted customers by offering music, or opportunities for communal singing, for centuries. Some had simple 'sing-songs' in the bar, while others provided club rooms or cellars in which local 'harmonic clubs' could meet and sing. The publican and his staff made sure that the singers' glasses were always full, but would generally leave the entertainment to the customers themselves. Many pubs stayed like this, but some enterprising publicans built large concert rooms, with a raised stage, a balcony and a ticket office, alongside or behind their pubs, and employed professional singers, comics and acrobats to draw in larger crowds.

The 1843 Theatres Act gave the bigger tavern saloons the chance to become licensed theatres, and some did so: the Britannia, Effingham, Grecian, Albert and Bower Saloons all opted for licensed legitimacy. Others decided that a drinking licence was more profitable than a theatre licence, and carried on offering a mixture of songs, variety acts and short sketches to customers who drank, smoked, talked and perhaps walked around while the show went on. Places licensed for drinking were not allowed to show full-length plays, and the argument over the distinction between a 'sketch' and a play continued as before, with the legitimized 'minor' theatres now putting the case that had once been put against them by the monopoly theatres.[50] In the 1850s a very large number of London public houses applied for music licences, and became, by the broadest definition, music halls. The Middlesex magistrates issued only sixty-seven music and dancing licences in 1847, but 255 for music only in 1855, and 291 in 1865.[51]

Many public houses disappeared from the licensing records after three or four years, and most of the rest were content to remain as nothing more than pubs with music. But a few ambitious publicans grasped the opportunity offered by growing popular demand for cheap and lively entertainment, and raised the capital to build new music halls on a grand scale. The halls were as large and ornate as theatres, differing from them only in that the customers sat around tables, and that there was a large promenade area for those without seats. The best of these new music halls, the Canterbury, was built by Charles Morton in 1851 (and enlarged in 1854), at the back of the Canterbury Arms in Upper Marsh (now Westminster Bridge Road), Lambeth, next door to the Bower Saloon. Others quickly followed Morton's lead: Evans' in Covent Garden (1855), Weston's in Holborn (1857), Wilton's in Stepney (1858), the South London Palace in St George's Fields (1860), Deacon's in Clerkenwell (1861). Three big West End halls were opened in 1861: the Alhambra, occupying a huge domed building in the Moorish style in Leicester Square, which had been built in 1854 as a Royal Panopticon of Science and Art, the London Pavilion, Piccadilly Circus (previously the Black Horse Inn), and Charles Morton's Oxford Music Hall, on the site of an inn and coach yard in Oxford Street. By 1866 there were over thirty large London halls, generally holding between 1,000 and 2,000 customers each, as well as over 200 smaller halls or 'sing-song' saloons.[52]

Over the next thirty years music halls grew in size, rather than number. Many smaller halls were forced to close by the introduction of stricter fire regulations in the Metropolis Management and Building Act of 1878, and more disappeared when the London County Council took over as the licensing authority in 1889. In its first three years the LCC demanded alterations to 167 music halls and dance halls, and over the same period the number of music and dancing licence applications it received fell from 348 to 215. Moral crusaders, who were always suspicious of entertainments that attracted the working class, made life difficult for less well-run houses, where drunkenness and prostitution were conspicuous or the songs were indecent. LCC inspectors patrolled the halls in the 1890s, reporting cases of indecorum to the licensing committee. Temperance and sexual purity campaigners on the committee (including the redoubtable Mrs Ormiston Chant) used their power to deprive poorer halls of their licences, and to force richer ones to police themselves more rigorously and remove their promenades. In spite of these pressures music hall thrived in the last two decades of the century, and its greatest stars – Dan Leno, Albert Chevalier, Gus Elen, Marie Lloyd, George Robey, Little Tich, Vesta Tilley – won a degree of fame that earlier variety stars (except the great Grimaldi) had never achieved. By 1900 there were 328 places with music licences in the County of London, as well as an unknown number of unlicensed halls.[53]

The bigger halls began to look more like conventional theatres, with rows of tip-up stalls in place of tables and promenade space, an enclosed bar, and separate staircases for different classes of customer. Many of them charged a shilling for their cheapest seats, as much as a West End theatre, and four times the price of a gallery seat in the Britannia or the Whitechapel Pavilion. From the 1890s several London halls, especially in the suburbs, were opened or taken over by national syndicates, notably those led by Oswald Stoll and Edward Moss, whose grandiose ambitions were expressed in the huge West End music halls they commissioned from the theatre architect Frank Matcham. Moss's London Hippodrome (1900) had a circus ring which could be converted into a 100,000-gallon tank, recalling Astley's and the old Sadler's Wells, and Stoll's London Coliseum (1904), later the home of the English National Opera, had a 75-foot revolving stage, and seating for over 3,000. There was grandeur in the suburbs, too. Stoll's fourth suburban music hall, the Hackney Empire (built by Matcham in 1901) was as splendid as any West End theatre.[54] These great palaces, which represented the final stage in the development of music halls before the cinema brought about their decline during and after the First World War, were a strange hybrid, combining the architectural and social pretensions of the West End theatre with the comical and musical 'turns' who had made their names in Victorian halls. This uneasy alliance was seen at its most extreme in the Royal Variety Performance, which has been delighting or depressing London audiences since 1912.

PARKS

The cultural amenities of Victorian London served several purposes. At the same time they could bring civilization and comfort to the poor, pleasure to the well-off, and grandeur to the imperial capital. Nineteenth-century politicians and moralists generally held the view that the moral tone of the working class could be shaped for good or ill by the cultural influences to which it was exposed. Londoners whose lives revolved around the public house, the gin palace, the boxing ring, the 'penny gaff' and the brothel would tend to fight, steal and fornicate, while those who came under the influence of the church, the school, the park, the library, the museum and the cocoa room would not. The motives of Victorian reformers were thus a complex mixture of altruism and self interest, of conflicting desires to involve the poor in middle-class culture and exclude them from it, and it would be crude and misleading to argue that those who advocated the provision of parks, churches and schools did so only from a desire to exert moral or social control over the poor. The simple desire of middle-class Londoners to use their rates and taxes to provide themselves with the pleasures and comforts appropriate to modern city life was an important and sometimes forgotten factor. Nevertheless, concerns for morality and order were never far from the surface, and they helped to shape nineteenth-century London in some fundamental ways.[55]

It was widely understood that the replacement of undesirable recreations with beneficial, or 'rational', ones was a wiser policy than their outright suppression. In 1833 the Select Committee on Public Walks argued that an increase in the number of open spaces for poorer Londoners 'would assist to wean them from low and debasing pleasures. Great complaint is made of drinking houses, dog fights, and boxing matches, yet unless some opportunity for other recreation is afforded to workmen they are driven to such pursuits.' Recreation, the report went on, was a 'spring to industry', a route to health and respectability.[56] The committee was already too late to save most of the open fields that Londoners had played on since Fitz-stephen's day. In the north, Moorfields, Lamb's Conduit Fields, White Conduit Fields and Finsbury Fields were all gone, or disappearing fast; in the east Bethnal Green and Stepney Green had been built over; and across the river the new Bethlehem Hospital occupied the last remnant of St

George's Fields. In the whole of the built-up area of North London there was only Regent's Park, which was still partly closed to the public, and a few endangered remnants of common land. In South London there was only one large open space with free public access, Kennington Common, although there were open fields just beyond the built-up area. In other words, beyond the West End, with its four royal parks, nearly 2 million Londoners had little more than 20 acres of public parkland to play in. Moreover, riverside walks were obstructed by wharves and timber yards, and the police had driven children from their familiar and safe bathing places on the Thames and the Lea.[57]

The idea that public money rather than private initiative might be used to alleviate urban problems was in its infancy in the 1830s, but pressure from radical MPs and 30,000 petitioners from Tower Hamlets, and the realization that profits might be made by enhancing the value of development land around a new park in East London, prompted the government to act. In 1841 the Commissioners of Woods and Forests were authorized to spend £115,000 raised by the sale of Stafford House (now York House) to the Duke of Sutherland to buy 290 acres of land just beyond Bethnal Green, stretching from the Regent's Canal almost to the river Lea. The new Victoria Park, which was opened to the public in 1845, was a poor imitation of Regent's Park. Its designer, James Pennethorne, was no John Nash, and the predictable failure of the plan to build fashionable housing around the park left the scheme short of money. Still, the *Gardener's Chronicle's* judgement that 'an image of deformity has been set up there to which, we suspect, there is no parallel in Europe' seems a little strong. Over time the park was embellished with fountains, follies and flowerbeds, and attracted 30,000 visitors a day. The failure of the park to stimulate the growth of a middle-class community in the neighbourhood at least meant that the people who enjoyed the park, playing cricket on its lawns and swimming or sailing model yachts in its lake, were those who needed it most.[58] Whether the park had the calming moral influence that its originators had anticipated is another matter. Chartists demonstrated in Victoria Park, 'controversialists' and secularists preached there until 1856, and in the 1890s Charles Booth noted that 'Victoria Park is the arena for every kind of religious, political or social discussion, and, with the exception of Peckham Rye in South London, it is unlikely that any other open space in the world could compete with it in this respect.'[59]

In 1843 the builder Thomas Cubitt drew the attention of the Royal Commission on Metropolitan Improvements to Battersea Fields, 300 acres of marsh and scrubland on the southern bank of the Thames, which was occupied by gipsies and vagabonds, a wild and disreputable Sunday fair, and the old Red House tavern, a centre of pigeon shooting. Following the Commission's recommendation, the government authorized the purchase of the land for £200,000, in the hope that the combination of a new royal park, a new Thames embankment and a new suspension bridge from Chelsea (completed in 1858) would bring health and respectability to a squalid neighbourhood, and yield profits from housing development. Under Pennethorne's direction, barges brought thousands of tons of spoil from the newly excavated London Docks to raise the level of the marshy land, and shrubs and palms from Kew to stock the sub-tropical garden. The transformation in working-class leisure achieved by the opening of Battersea Park in 1858 realized all the aspirations of London's cultural and environmental reformers. Land that had once been the scene each Sunday of 'horses and donkeys racing, foot-racing, walking matches, flying boats, flying horses, roundabouts, theatres, comic actors, shameless dancers, conjurers, fortune-tellers, gamblers of every description, drinking-booths, stalls, hawkers and vendors of all kinds of articles' was now given over to cricket, football, trap-ball, rounders, boating and the enjoyment of plants.[60]

By the time the Metropolitan Board of Works took responsibility for open spaces in 1856 it was too late to make new parks within the central and inner suburban districts. In 1864 the Board managed to buy 63 acres in Rotherhithe to create Southwark Park for the growing dockland population of Bermondsey, but in the 4 miles between Rotherhithe and Battersea there was still only one small park, in Kennington. Across the river, there was (and still is) a huge area, stretching from Canning Town in the east to King's Cross in the west, and northwards through Tufnell Park and Upper Holloway, whose inhabitants were more than three-quarters of a mile from a park. Victoria Park, Hackney Downs and Highbury Fields were too far away to be of much use to the crowded populations of Holborn, Finsbury, Islington, Shoreditch and Whitechapel, who still had almost nowhere to play.

The Board's finest and most enduring achievements were in the better-off outer suburbs, where huge tracts of heath and common land were threatened by urban development in the 1860s and 1870s. The Metropolitan Board of Works and its parochial paymasters showed little enthusiasm for the costly business of rescuing the commons from those who claimed manorial rights over them, but pressure from local residents and the Commons Preservation Society was irresistible, and between 1866 and 1888 the Board gained control of Blackheath, Hackney Downs, Tooting Bec Common, Clapham Common, Hampstead Heath (including Parliament

Hill and Kenwood), and several smaller pieces of land. The Board was generally flat-footed and unadventurous in its acquisition of commons, and it was beaten in its attempt to win one of the greatest prizes, the remaining 6,000 acres of Epping Forest, by the intervention of the City Corporation in 1871.[61] After 1888 the London County Council added to the growing stock of outer suburban parkland in Brixton, Dulwich, Hackney and Streatham, but for most inner London children their playground was still the street. The popular music-hall song of the 1890s, in which Gus Elen, the coster comedian, sang 'Wiv a ladder and some glasses you could see to 'Ackney Marshes, if it wasn't for the 'ouses in between', was more than a joke.

EXHIBITIONS AND MUSEUMS

Pleasure alone was not enough for the Victorians. The ideal recreation was intended to educate and elevate, as well as amuse. A walk around Crystal Palace Park, where bronze iguanodons and palaeotheriums still lurk in the shrubbery, or the Natural History Museum in South Kensington, in which visitors could absorb (for no charge) the latest theories of Darwinian biologists, illustrates the point. As it happens, both the Crystal Palace Park and the South Kensington museums owed their existence, in part, to the most spectacular and successful of all these didactic entertainments, the Great Exhibition of the Works of Industry of all Nations in 1851. The idea of an exhibition of industrial achievements was borrowed from France, and put into effect by Prince Albert, Henry Cole and the Royal Society of Arts. Cole, a man of many parts (public record keeper, publisher, crockery designer, editor, administrator), played an important role in the development of Victorian Kensington. After his work on the Great Exhibition he was the guiding force behind the creation of the Victoria and Albert Museum, the Albert Hall and the Royal College of Music. The Great Exhibition was a triumph from beginning to end. Joseph Paxton's revolutionary pre-fabricated exhibition building, 19 acres of glass and iron, married beauty and strength in a way that captured the public imagination and epitomized the spirit of the exhibition. The exhibition itself, which involved 100,000 exhibits and nearly 14,000 exhibitors (half British, the rest imperial or foreign) was like an enormous international bazaar, magical to some, bewildering to others. Over 6 million people visited the exhibition, three-quarters of them on the crowded 'shilling' days, and many on cheap railway excursions from the provinces. The orderly and sober behaviour of these huge crowds, only three years after the last outburst of London Chartism, reinforced the mood of confidence which characterized the 1850s. Inside the Crystal Palace (a nickname invented by *Punch*) visitors admired the achievements of the great British engineers (Nasmyth's steam hammer, Whitworth's precision gauges and machine tools, Brunel's hydraulic press), and the inventions (often American) that would soon change the way they lived: the sewing machine, the Colt revolver, the mechanical reaper, the electric telegraph, the daguerrotype. What seemed to excite them most, though, were old ideas in new materials: a 4-ton glass fountain, a zinc Amazon on horseback, a garden bench carved from coal, Pugin's medieval ironware, Elkington's electro-plated coffee-pots.[62]

Although the Great Exhibition was mounted without government funding, and the organizers denied themselves the money that might have been made from Sunday opening and selling drink, it made a profit of £186,000. The Commissioners spent some of this money on an 87-acre estate in South Kensington (mostly between Cromwell Road and Kensington Road), on which they would continue to pursue the ideas that inspired the original exhibition, the unions of manufacturing, science and art, and of exhibition, education and entertainment. A second exhibition, in a massive brick building (topped by the two largest domes ever built) was held in 1862, but it was only a modest success, and the hall was demolished. The spirit of 1851 was more successfully recaptured in the South Kensington Museum of manufactures and fine art, which spread into a ramshackle collection of galleries between 1857 and 1899, when its rebuilding as the Victoria and Albert and the Science Museum began. The Royal Albert Hall of Arts and Sciences was opened (on the site of Mrs Blessington's Gore House) in 1870, and a collection of Colleges of Science, Mines, Engineering, Art, Music and Needlework moved into the gardens south of the Albert Hall between the 1850s and the 1880s. The Natural History Museum, which was built to display the British Museum's zoological and fossil collections, was opened on the Cromwell Road end of the site in 1881. Alfred Waterhouse's magnificent Romanesque structure, richly carved terracotta cladding on an iron frame, expressed in its plan and its decorative detail the principles of evolution and classification that the scientific establishment wished to transmit to the wider public. By 1910, when Imperial College and the Victoria and Albert Museum (both by Aston Webb) were complete, the Commissioners' 87 acres contained a collection of cultural institutions which was, in Pevsner's judgement, 'probably unparalleled anywhere, and certainly ... unparalleled when the buildings were first planned'.[63]

South Kensington's rival as London's cultural centre was Bloomsbury, where the British Museum had been growing in size and importance since it was first opened to a carefully vetted public in 1759. One fabulous collection after another was crammed into Montagu House: Towneley's classical sculptures in 1807, Lord Elgin's marbles in 1816, George III's library in 1823, Richard Knight's bronzes and coins in 1824, Sir Joseph Banks's botanical specimens in 1827. The Museum's old home was replaced in the 1820s and 1830s by a much larger museum designed in the prevailing Grecian style by Robert Smirke, the architect most favoured by Robert Peel and the Tory patrons. At the same time the Museum began to relax its very restrictive rules for visitors, and started opening on public holidays (but not Sundays) to give 'the vulgar class' a chance to see the collections. The consequences of this policy were not as disastrous as many had feared: 30,000 people visited the British Museum on 2 January 1843, without 'one single instance of drunkenness or indecorum'.[64] Five years later, Charles Kingsley praised the Museum as almost the only place 'where the poor and the rich may meet together ... a truly equalizing place'.[65] The holiday crowds would have been less welcome, of course, in the vast and beautiful Reading Room, which was built in the Museum courtyard by Sydney Smirke (Robert's brother) in the 1850s, during the tyrannical but brilliant administration of Anthony Panizzi, 'the Napoleon of librarians'. Under Smirke's cast-iron dome, bigger in diameter than St Paul's or St Peter's, there was a collection of books and readers that rapidly outstripped all its European rivals.[66]

The experience of the British Museum strengthened the arguments of radicals who argued that the achievements of art and intellect should be freely available to poorer Londoners. They had notable successes in the 1850s, when entrance charges for Westminster Abbey and St Paul's Cathedral were abolished.[67] A common compromise was to reserve one or two weekdays for those who were prepared to pay 6d to avoid the crowd. This was the practice at the National Gallery, the South Kensington Museum, the Bethnal Green Museum, and the Tate Gallery later in the century.

LONDON UNIVERSITY

Bloomsbury's second claim to intellectual pre-eminence was the building there of London's first university college in 1826–8. The idea of a university 'for the youth of our middling rich people' and open (unlike Oxford and

Cambridge) to non-Anglicans was proposed by a Scottish poet, Thomas Campbell, in a letter to *The Times* in February 1825, and was at once taken up by the radical politician Henry Brougham. Brougham gathered a group of radicals and utilitarians (including Joseph Hume, James Mill and Zachary Macaulay), Dissenters, Jews and Catholics, to plan and finance a new university for London. The group formed a limited company to raise money by selling shares in the enterprise, and in October 1828 the university's building in Gower Street, on the northern edge of Bloomsbury, was ready for its first students. The Tory and Anglican response to the opening of the 'Cockney College' was to found a rival Church of England institution, King's College, which opened in 1831, next to Somerset House on the Strand. In 1836 Lord Melbourne's Whig government chartered an examining body, the University of London, with the power to award degrees to candidates from the two new colleges or other affiliated institutions. A Senate of thirty-eight distinguished men, mainly doctors, lawyers and fellows of the Royal Society, was appointed by the government to conduct the examinations and determine the syllabus of the new university. By the 1850s London University was conducting examinations for over 100 schools and colleges all over Britain, including the medical schools of nine London hospitals and the colleges and future universities of some of the great industrial cities.

In these years the University and its affiliated colleges were at the forefront of major advances in English higher education: the extension of university education to women (who got their first colleges, Queen's and Bedford, in 1848–9, and their first degrees in 1880), the provision of evening classes for clerks and working men (at King's from the 1850s), and the recognition of science, as distinct from medicine, as an important and independent branch of knowledge. A separate Faculty of Science was created in 1858, and the first BSc degree was awarded in 1860. The main focus of non-medical scientific teaching in London was in South Kensington, where the School of Mines, the School of Science and the Central Technical College stood adjacent but independent until they were united to form Imperial College in 1907. The introduction of degrees for women led to the creation of three women's colleges in the 1870s and 1880s: the London College of Medicine for Women (1874), Westfield College (1882) and the magnificent Royal Holloway College in Egham, built with the profits of Holloway's Famous Pills. Women were also a substantial minority in the older colleges. About a third of University College students were women in the 1880s, and 45 per cent in the 1890s. The University of London itself remained a purely examining body, without classes or teachers, until the 1890s when, following a report by a Royal Commission (the Gresham Commission, 1892–3), the University was reconstituted to combine the Senate with twenty-four affiliated teaching colleges in and around London. The Liberal MP Richard Haldane and Sidney Webb, creator (with his wife Beatrice) of the new London School of Economics, were largely responsible for the compromise scheme that Parliament eventually accepted in 1898.[68] The following year, the University decided that its headquarters in Burlington Gardens, in Mayfair (later the Museum of Mankind), did not match the needs of Britain's biggest university, and moved to the grand but impractical buildings of the Imperial Institute in South Kensington. They remained there in splendid discomfort until 1936, when the new Senate House was opened in Bloomsbury, behind the British Museum.

Gentlemen and scholars without university membership were well supplied with libraries in nineteenth-century London. Several West End clubs had excellent libraries, and so had the Inns of Court and the many scholarly and professional associations with London headquarters. Of the older associations, the Royal College of Physicians (1525), the Royal Society (1667) and the Linnaean Society (1788) had good libraries, and of the newer ones the London Institution (1806), the Zoological Society (1829), the Royal Geographical Society (1830) and the Royal Colonial Institute (1868) were all well stocked. In 1840 London's lack of a scholarly lending library prompted Thomas Carlyle and a few friends (including Gladstone and John Stuart Mill) to establish a new subscription library, for 'all followers of literature and science who cannot study with comfort and advantage in a public room'. The London Library, which opened in Pall Mall in 1841 and moved to St James's Square in 1844, had accumulated 167,000 books by 1893, paid for by the £2 annual subscriptions of its several thousand members. Less demanding readers could borrow books for a fee from a commercial circulating library, an eighteenth-century innovation which achieved great influence over publishers and the reading public in the nineteenth century. The leading company from the 1850s was Mudie's, on the corner of Museum Street and New Oxford Street, whose stock approached a million volumes by the end of the century. Mudie's biggest competitor was W. H. Smith, who had a large lending library in the Strand, as well as London's biggest newspaper wholesale business and a chain of station bookstalls. Competition from free municipal libraries was much slower to develop. Local authorities (including London parishes) were given the power to fund public libraries from a halfpenny in the pound levy on ratepayers in 1850 (raised to a penny in 1855), if two-thirds of ratepayers agreed. But ratepayers, who could afford to subscribe to commercial libraries, were not convinced that the poor should be 'civilized' at their expense, and only one London parish, St Margaret and St John's, Westminster, opened a free public library in the 1850s. Ratepayer resistance declined in the 1880s, when several parishes opened municipal libraries (some of them to celebrate Victoria's golden jubilee in 1887), and in 1899 the new London boroughs were relieved of the obligation to consult their ratepayers. Only two boroughs, Marylebone and Bethnal Green, had no free public library in 1910.[69]

LATE NINETEENTH-CENTURY LEISURE

In London, as in the other big English cities, the pattern of leisure changed in the second half of the nineteenth century as disposable income, mobility, spare time and literacy grew, and as technology, cheap transport, local government and commerce expanded the available range of activities. The spread of the Saturday half-holiday among clerks and working men from the 1870s (though many still preferred to take Monday off), along with the provision of parks and playing fields, encouraged the more organized playing and watching of football, a game whose traditional roughness had been reduced by the imposition of Football Association rules in the 1860s. Teams were organized from public houses, schools, churches, workplaces and cricket clubs, and the best of them began competing in local or national championships. Eight London clubs took part in the first FA Cup in 1871–2, and twenty-one in 1883–4, when working-class professional teams were just starting to dominate the game. Five London clubs joined the professional Football League, which was initiated and dominated by northern teams, between 1893 and 1908: Arsenal (the first and most successful professional club in London), Leyton Orient, Chelsea, Fulham and Tottenham Hotspur. Popular professional matches drew crowds of over 10,000 on Saturday afternoons in the 1890s, and the crowds at Cup Finals, which moved from the Kennington Oval to Crystal Palace in 1895, exceeded 50,000 by 1900.[70] No other sport attracted such crowds. Middle-class Londoners who wanted physical recreation without social mixing were safe on the golf courses and tennis courts which were becoming increasingly common in the late Victorian suburbs.

Londoners could no longer walk out of town, but the steamer, the train, the horse-coach and (from the 1880s) the bicycle meant that it was still possible to escape from London for the day, either to one of the traditional suburban resorts (Richmond, Blackheath, Hampstead or Epping) or, for those who could afford it, to the seaside. Margate, Ramsgate and Gravesend were popular with London steamboat excursionists from the 1840s, and pioneered the techniques of mass tourism. The smarter resorts on the south coast, especially Brighton, began to lose their aristocratic tone in the 1840s and 1850s, when they were discovered by middle-class Londoners, and in the 1880s and 1890s two Essex coastal villages, Clacton and Southend, were rescued from sleepy obscurity by the arrival of East Enders on holiday for the day or even the week. Towards the end of the century Charles Booth found a growing number of Londoners, especially clerks, policemen, shopworkers and local government employees, who had a week's or even a fortnight's paid holiday, and were thus able to join in London's colonization of the Sussex, Kent and Essex coast.[71]

In the conflict between respectable and popular culture Sunday, the day of worship and the day of play, was the main battleground. In the 1890s, Charles Booth asked clergymen to describe the ways in which the London poor spent their Sundays. The answers he received suggested a secular but not uncivilized culture, in which time was divided between traditional pleasures, mainly drinking and sleeping, and newer commercial and municipal recreations: 'In the homes the men lie abed all the morning, mend rabbit hutches and pigeon lofts in the afternoon, and go for a walk in the evening.' 'Up at twelve to be ready for the "pubs.", which open at one; dinner any time between two and four, then sleep, then off with wife and children to hear the band on the Common.' 'As he passes to his chapel he sees them sitting at breakfast half-dressed or lounging in the window reading *Lloyd's Weekly Newspaper*.' In better neighbourhoods 'Sunday is spent in lounging about or gardening, and in the evening you hear the tinkle of the piano and the mandoline'. Of the changes in leisure that had taken place in the past few decades Booth singled out a growth in betting, the wide circulation of the horse-racing press, the rising importance of the music hall, and the habit of taking coach outings, especially on Bank Holidays.[72]

SCHOOLS AND CHURCHES

Booth devoted seven of his seventeen volumes to the religious life of London, and the conclusion he drew was that although working-class Londoners were attached to Christian moral values and would have called themselves Christians, 'the great masses of the people remain apart from all forms of religious communion, apparently untouched by the Gospel'. Those who believed that the Saturday half-holiday would encourage working people to devote their Sundays to God had been wrong: 'The maw of pleasure is not easy to fill. The appetite grows, Sunday is increasingly regarded as a day of mere recreation.'[73]

For those interested in such things, the decline of working-class churchgoing in London and other urban areas, and the growing influence of non-Christian (and non-Anglican) attitudes, had been evident for 100 years or more. In 1786 the moral reformer and Sunday school pioneer Sarah Trimmer blamed overgrown parishes and the lack of free (as opposed to rented) pews for 'the great estrangement that has taken place between the lower orders of people and their parochial ministers' in London.[74] Some of the worst problems were in the suburbs, and it was in the suburbs, too, that the struggle to re-establish Christian belief and observance was most strongly fought. In the 1790s the centre of Anglican resistance to the combined dangers of radicalism, secularism, Methodism and apathy was the wealthy suburban village of Clapham, where the Rector, John Venn, led an evangelical revivalist movement which aimed to reawaken the spirit of true Christianity in all social classes. The influence of the 'Clapham Sect' spread far beyond London. Wilberforce's campaign against the slave trade had its headquarters there, and both the Church Missionary Society and the British and Foreign Bible Society originated in Venn's congregation.

At around the time of Venn's death in 1813 Churchmen in Hackney, on the other side of London, took up the good fight. The 'Hackney Phalanx', led by Joshua Watson, a City wine merchant, identified state-subsidized church-building and the provision of cheap education as the two policies most likely to save Christianity in London. In 1811 they formed the National Society for Promoting the Education of the Poor in the Principles of the Established Church, to encourage the building of schools run on Andrew Bell's so-called Madras system, in which one skilled teacher (with one book) could teach as many as 1,000 children, using older pupils ('monitors') to pass on simple and rigidly planned lessons to younger ones. Its first school was opened in Baldwin's Gardens, off the Gray's Inn Road. A similar system had also been pioneered in the Borough Road, Southwark, since the 1790s by a Quaker, Joseph Lancaster, whose work was taken up by the mainly Nonconformist British and Foreign School Society in 1814. These two Church societies, drawing their income from fees, contributions and (after 1833) increasingly generous state subsidies, dominated the education of poorer children in London up to (and beyond) the introduction of local authority schools in the 1870s. In 1816 a Select Committee chaired by Henry Brougham, the educational and legal reformer, exposed the great extent of the work to be done. Witnesses from London's poorer districts, Spitalfields, St Giles', Shadwell, Southwark and Bethnal Green, reported that more than half the children had no schooling, and lived in 'a very depraved state'. Of those receiving schooling, about half seemed to rely upon Sunday schools, and the rest were divided between private commercial schools and schools run by churches and charities.[75]

Seeds sown in the childish mind had to be nurtured in the adult one. London suffered from an acute shortage of church accommodation, brought about by rapid population increase and a failure to build new churches. Between the 1730s, when the last of the Queen Anne churches were completed, and 1815 hardly a dozen churches had been built in London. Richard Horwood's map of London in 1813 shows about 110 Anglican churches (mostly in the City), serving a population of almost 1.4 million people. Between 1815 and 1837 the Church of England, helped by two large Parliamentary grants for a national programme of church-building (£1 million in 1818, and £500,000 in 1824), added another fifty. The £1 million granted in 1818, of which just over a third went to London, helped to build thirty-three churches in the capital, with seating for over 56,000 worshippers. Some of these so-called Waterloo churches were buildings of distinction (Nash's All Souls Langham Place, the Inwoods' St Pancras Church on the Euston Road), but most were spacious and functional, giving a certain Grecian or Gothic dignity to new suburban centres: Brixton, Kennington, West Norwood, Hammersmith, Bermondsey, Camden Town, Poplar, Hackney, Islington and Stoke Newington.[76] The Church Building Commissioners, who administered the Parliamentary grant, contributed towards the building of ninety-four new London churches, nearly all in the fashionable Gothic style, between 1824 and 1856. There were no new state subsidies after 1824, but London's bishop from 1828 to 1856 was the able and energetic Charles Blomfield, who believed fervently in the moral and social benefits of slum churches. Blomfield established a Metropolitan Churches Fund, raising money by imposing savings on cathedrals, and from appeals to private donors and businesses. William Cotton, a banker whose fortune had come from a Limehouse rope factory, was especially generous. Blomfield's suggestion that new churches should be financed by a coal tax, as they had been in 1670 and 1711, was not taken up. Blomfield's churches, unlike those of the 1820s, were concentrated in working-class districts. Bethnal Green, whose 70,000 people had only two churches and a chapel in 1839, gained ten new churches in the 1840s, with enough seats for 28.5 per cent of its population.[77]

THE DISCOVERY OF HEATHENISM

In 1854 the report on the 1851 Census of Religious Worship, based on questions to all ministers of religion included in the decennial census, was published. The results confirmed what many already knew, that all the efforts of the previous thirty years had failed to Christianize the metropolis. The census showed that the position of the Church was weak in nearly all the big cities, but weakest of all in working-class London. London's 1,097 churches, chapels and synagogues had room for only 29.6 per cent of the population, and of the twenty districts in England with the most inadequate church provision, nineteen were in London. Shoreditch, St George-in-the-East, Newington, St Saviour (Southwark), Clerkenwell, Lambeth and Whitechapel could all accommodate only a quarter or less of their population, and Marylebone, Poplar, Stepney, Bermondsey and Kensington were hardly any better. The really bad news was that these churches, inadequate as they were, were scarcely ever full. Attendances were hard to calculate because it was not known how many evening worshippers (who were almost as numerous as morning ones) were morning worshippers on a second visit ('Twicers', as Gladstone called them), and some ministers had not completed their returns, but it was plain, in the words of the census report, that the poor, even those who had been to Church schools, were 'as utter strangers to religious ordinances as the people of a heathen country'. On the weekend of the census, under 20 per cent of Londoners went to a morning service, and only 13 per cent to an evening one. Among 460,000 morning worshippers, there were 261,000 Anglicans, over 100,000 Congregationalists and Baptists (old Dissent was still strong in London), and surprisingly few Methodists (35,000), Catholics (36,000), and Jews (1,500). In a few richer areas churchgoing was high, but far from universal: nearly 34 per cent of people in Wandsworth went to morning service, and 39 per cent in Hampstead. But in the East End parishes the average morning attendance was only 15 per cent, in Bermondsey it was 14 per cent and in Shoreditch it was just over 9 per cent.[78]

Horace Mann, the author of the census report, argued (as others argued earlier and later in the century) that working-class non-attendance did not reflect a conscious rejection of Christian doctrine, but resulted from the unwillingness of the poor to go to churches which were dominated by middle-class worshippers, and in which the rented pew system reinforced their sense of social inferiority. The poor, Mann argued, misunderstood the motives of the clergy and were prevented by the poverty and squalor of their daily lives from turning their minds to spiritual matters. He might have added that slum-dwellers, living entirely among people of their own class, were freed from the social pressures (from employer, landlord or clergyman) which made absenteeism difficult in the countryside, and that social conformity, always a powerful force, led Londoners to the public house, not the church. The attempt to introduce a law to close shops and markets on Sundays in 1855 provoked a response among the working classes that no religious occasion could ever have inspired. The social and moral message of Christianity (which in any case was delivered in language which those on the free benches would not understand) had little apparent relevance to the poor, except in its hostility to their domestic and recreational habits. The poor felt (rightly) that they were not especially welcome in church, and it is not surprising that they generally spent their one free day in playing, lounging, drinking or shopping. There is very little in the case of London to support the argument that the poor and desperate were especially vulnerable to religious persuasion, or that 'men and women felt themselves to have some place in an otherwise hostile world when within the Church'. The Church was a part of the hostile world, not a refuge from it.[79]

Evidence on what working-class Londoners actually believed is too anecdotal to form the basis for trustworthy generalization. Henry Mayhew questioned many street people about their religion, but his interviewees cannot be taken as representative of the London poor in general. A particularly ignorant costermonger, who hardly knew that St Paul's Cathedral was a church, told him that if Christ was the Redeemer, he might help him redeem his clothes from the pawnshop. 'Religion is a regular puzzle to the costers,' an ex-coster told Mayhew. '. . . the costers somehow mix up being religious with being respectable, and so they have a queer sort of feeling about it.'[80] Mayhew also discussed religion with women street-sellers. The Irish women, he believed, were regular Catholic church-goers, but the English sellers claimed to be too tired, too busy, or too ragged to go to church. Many felt uneasy or despised in church. A scavenger told him:

> I never goes to any church or chapel. Sometimes I hasn't clothes as is fit, and I s'pose I couldn't be admitted into sich fine places in my

working dress. I was once in a church, but felt queer, as one does in them strange places, and never went again. They're fittest for rich people. Yes, I've heered about religion and about God Almighty.... I'm satisfied with what I knows and feels about it, and that's enough about it.[81]

Evidence later in the century supported the idea that the working-class objection to churchgoing was social, rather than doctrinal. A meeting of working men in a London coffee house in 1867 gave these reasons for not going to church: obscure and tedious sermons, the social and practical gulf between the clergy and the poor, and the importance of Sunday as a day of recreation. Thomas Wright, 'the Journeyman Engineer', repeated these points, adding the problem of unsuitable clothing and unwelcoming congregations, in 1873.[82]

THE MISSION TO DARKEST LONDON

The idea that Christians could respond to the unwillingness of the poor to enter churches by taking religion on to the streets, into working-class homes, and even into pubs and music halls, was not new. Methodists had used open-air preaching in the eighteenth century, and Bishop Blomfield had urged his clergy to 'hunt out the poor at their own homes' in the 1830s. The inter-donominational London City Mission, founded in 1835, already had its missionaries on the streets, spreading the word among carmen, canal boatmen, dockers, or some other target group. By the 1860s or 1870s most denominations had accepted the need for such policies in the London slums. Bishop Tait decided to send Anglican mission clergy into poorer parishes in 1863, and in the 1880s, when Walsham How was suffragan Bishop of Bedford (and effectively East London) most slum parishes had evangelical mission churches, sometimes drawing larger congregations than the parish church. The Church also began to overcome the problem of finding clergymen of high calibre who were prepared to live and work in slum parishes, sacrificing the social and economic advantages most young graduates expected to enjoy once they were ordained. Canon Samuel Barnett, the highly influential rector of St Jude's, Whitechapel (1873–1894), is the best known of these slum clergymen, but others deserve to be remembered, too: William Champneys, vicar of St Mary's, Whitechapel from 1837 to 1868, who established the first ragged school in London, formed a bootblacks' brigade, and supported the dockers against the casual labour system; Brooke Lambert, vicar of St Mark's, Whitechapel (1866–70) and of Greenwich (1880–1901), who played a central part in drawing Oxford undergraduates into the Whitechapel settlement movement; J. R. Green, the Christian Socialist and popular historian, who died at forty-six from tuberculosis probably contracted when he was vicar of St Philip's, Stepney, in the 1860s; Stewart Headlam, curate of St Matthew's, Bethnal Green, an outspoken defender of social reform and working-class culture, who led the revival of Christian Socialism in the 1870s and stood bail for Oscar Wilde in 1895. On the opposite wing of the Church of England there were clergymen who believed that a return to incense, candles, vestments and other elements of Catholic ritual would reconvert the working man: Alexander Mackonochie, whose High Church services in St Alban's, Holborn filled his church (with mostly middle-class worshippers), but infuriated Low Church Anglicans so much that they took him to court; and 'Father' Charles Lowder, vicar of St Peter's, London Docks, in the 1860s and 1870s, another ritualist with a popular following, whose High Church services caused riots in St George's-in-the-East in 1859.[83]

In some ways, the Church of England was in a better position to meet the challenge of the slums than the Nonconformists were. Its popular strategies could embrace near-Catholic ritual at one extreme and socialism at the other, and it had the central funds, in the hands of such men as Bishops Blomfield, Tait and Temple, to support East End missions which could not be self-funding. Anglicans were first to introduce churches without rented pews, starting with St Barnabas, Pimlico, in 1850, and St Philip's, Stepney, in 1859. The Nonconformists were more dependent on the support of middle-class congregations, and their unbending opposition to drinking and Sunday recreations made it hard for them to bridge the cultural gulf with the poor. Congregationalists were stimulated into vigorous missionary work among the poor by the publication of *The Bitter Cry of Outcast London* by the London Congregational Union in 1883, but their lack of central organization and funding made it particularly difficult for them to support chapels in areas without a strong middle class. 'Where these classes prevail,' Charles Booth concluded, 'Congregationalists are to be found in force; where not, their churches lead a struggling existence.'[84] Wesleyans, who had once been so effective in conquering new territories, were handicapped now by their circuit system, which moved their ministers around and prevented them from building up the large personal followings that gathered round some Anglican and Baptist ministers in London. The Wesleyan Conference suspended the system for poorer parts of London in 1885, and authorized the new London Wesleyan Mission, with a fund of

£50,000, to carry the gospel to the degraded inner districts of the city. Despite the energy of Hugh Price Hughes and the Wesleyan Forward Movement, progress was disappointing, and after thirteen years the Mission had won only 7,000 new members (although it claimed that another 20,000 attended its services).[85]

While some Christians put their faith in mission chapels and house-to-house visitation, others believed that first-rate hell and damnation sermons, accompanied by tuneful and popular hymns, would revive working-class Christianity. The great success of the American evangelist Dwight Moody, who came to London on a revivalist mission in 1874–5, along with the hymn-singer Ira Sankey, showed what direct and homely preaching could achieve. Moody and Sankey drew crowds of 20,000 to the Islington Agricultural Hall, and it was claimed that over a million Londoners attended their services.[86] Later Victorian London's most powerful popular preachers were generally Baptists. The working-class and lower-middle-class worshippers who went to the Baptist Tabernacles in Shoreditch and Mile End in the 1890s were, Charles Booth believed, 'the largest popular congregations in London', and the greatest preacher of the age was the Baptist Charles Spurgeon (1834–92), a clear and powerful puritan in the tradition of John Bunyan and George Whitefield. Spurgeon drew such large crowds when he started preaching in the 1850s that he was forced to move from his chapel in Southwark to Exeter Hall (which held about 4,000) and then to the Surrey Music Hall, which was more than twice as big. His service in the Crystal Palace at the time of the Indian Mutiny in 1857 is said to have drawn a congregation of 24,000. In 1861 he built the Metropolitan Tabernacle in Newington Causeway, Elephant and Castle, whose 6,000 seats were filled every Sunday and Thursday by large and generous congregations which were (in Booth's view) largely middle-class.[87]

SALVATIONISTS AND CATHOLICS

William and Catherine Booth, who first pitched their tent in a Quaker burial ground in Whitechapel in 1865, tried to combine the popular appeal of lively music and simple salvationist preaching with the local work of the slum mission. The Booths had abandoned Methodism (much as Wesley had drawn away from Anglicanism) because they were sure that its middle-class tone and its chapel-based system could never win back the working classes. The poor would only be converted, Catherine Booth said, 'by people of their own class, who would go after them in their own resorts, who would speak to them in a language they understood, and reach them by means suited to their own tastes'.[88] The Booths were powerful and courageous street-corner evangelists, and in ten years they had gained more than 2,000 converts and several dozen active missionaries, a group large enough to need a formal organization. In 1877 William Booth imposed a constitution which placed all power in his hands, and over the next five years the Salvation Army (a title first used in 1878) adopted the uniforms, military ranks, brass bands and popular tunes that are familiar today. The Army's music-hall showmanship drew disapproval, and its militant tee-totalism encouraged publicans to organize thuggish 'Skeleton armies' to break up its meetings, but Booth's apparent success in reaching social groups no other evangelists had reached won him admiration and imitation. The Anglicans even formed their own Church Army (beginning in Walworth in 1882), copying the uniforms, brass bands and open-air preaching of the Salvation Army.

By the mid-1880s, the Salvation Army seemed to have passed its peak in London. When the *British Weekly* published a census of worship in London that showed that only 53,591 people (a tenth of the 'submerged tenth') attended Army services on a typical Sunday in 1887, it reported the figure with 'amazement and keen disappointment'. William Booth's conversion to the cause of social reform, first expressed in the opening of night shelters in 1888, and then in the publication in 1890 of *In Darkest England and the Way Out*, publicized and partly written by the popular journalist W. T. Stead, did not increase the Army's mass appeal to the extent that Booth had hoped. When Charles Booth (the social investigator) reported on London's spiritual condition in 1902–3, he was sure that despite the honesty, courage and joyfulness of the Army's message, its amazing international growth, and the true value of its social work, its crusade in London had failed, especially amongst the very poor: 'It remains encamped in what must still be regarded as the enemy's country, and the increase in its militant strength has not by any means kept pace with the increase in the territory it seeks to cover.' As for their street-corner services, people watched them out of curiosity, and then moved on.

> Never have I seen the slightest sign of interest beyond such as could find full expression by the addition of a penny or so to the collection gathered in. . . . If anything attracts it is the music. Some of the corps have excellent bands of instrumentalists, the singing is hearty, and sometimes solos are very well given. A crowd will then gather, especially if the pitch be in some popular resort or busy thoroughfare.

But for the Gospel nothing visible is done. Those present are invited to come to the barracks, and thither the Salvationists march, singing as they go. But the crowd, if there has been one, disperses and goes its way, and only a ragged tail of children accompanies the march.[89]

The *Daily News* survey of 1903 justified Charles Booth's doubts. The Salvation Army's attendances seemed to have collapsed from 53,000 to 22,000 in seventeen years, and in its East London heartland it could muster only 6,373 worshippers, 'a wretchedly inadequate total for a population of nearly a million after all these years of unremitting work'.[90]

Only one major religious group, the Catholics, enjoyed substantial growth in the second half of the nineteenth century, thanks mainly to London's large Irish population (nearly all from the Catholic southern provinces), with a little help from Italian immigrants and English converts. There were at least 109,000 Irish-born Londoners in 1851, and although only 60,000 Irish migrants came to London between 1851 and 1891, natural growth within the migrant population must have created a community of over 250,000 people with an Irish Catholic background by the end of the century. At the time of the 1851 census, when only about 43,000 Catholics attended worship (making some allowance for those attending more than one service a day), the Catholic hierarchy in England had only just been restored, and in London an inadequate number of priests were over- whelmed by the arrival of 76,000 Irish migrants. Over the next fifty years the Catholic Church, led by three active and resourceful Archbishops of Westminster (Wiseman from 1850 to 1865, Manning from 1865 to 1892, and Vaughan thereafter), struggled to maintain or restore the habit of worship among Irish immigrants and their children, and to save the Church from what they called 'leakage'. Within ten years of his appointment, Wiseman had established thirty-four religious orders in London, and between 1851 and 1900 the number of Catholic churches was increased from thirty-five to ninety-three. Catholics also placed great emphasis on the power of education, and by 1900 there were 102 Catholic elementary schools, a tenth of the London total.[91] The Catholic Church was always short of money, and Cardinal Manning regarded the ministry to the poor as more important than prestigious projects. Brompton Oratory was built in his time (it opened in 1884), but the construction of Westminster Cathedral was delayed until after his death in 1892. Manning had a real concern for the London poor, and his support for the striking dockers (many of whom were Irish) in 1889 may well have done more to increase popular support for Catholicism than all the tracts scattered by the Catholic

Truth Society. The results of all these labours were revealed in 1902, when the *Daily News* survey counted 96,281 Catholic worshippers in Greater London. This was a disappointing figure, in view of the size of the Irish community, but it was much better than the frighteningly low number counted in 1886 (54,315), and compared well with the stagnation of Anglican congregations since 1886.[92] Apparently Irish loyalty, combined with the efforts of the Catholic Church, had slowed down, but not halted, the process of secularization which was the experience of all denominations in Victorian London.

'IT IS HEATHEN LONDON STILL'

By the end of the century the Churches' previous neglect of working-class London had been well and truly undone. In the twenty-nine County of London boroughs there were 2,688 churches, chapels, missions and synagogues, a more than twenty-fold increase over the century, with another 1,338 in outer London.[93] There was hardly a corner without a Hallelujah band, hardly a street without a mission hut, hardly a day without the knock of a Christian hand on the door. Every slum suburb had its 'settlement' of Catholic, Anglican, Wesleyan or Congregationalist university graduates, perhaps campaigning for social reforms, running adult classes or getting involved in local government, but more often concentrating on propagating the gospel.[94] The response of the poor to this overwhelming effort was, on the whole, disappointing. Doorstep evangelists were generally greeted with the enthusiasm reserved in later generations for brush salesmen and double-glazing specialists. The novelty that once gave slum missions a brief illusion of success had long ago faded. 'Brass bands and negro evangelists are played out, the extraordinary has become the ordinary, and no longer attracts,' Charles Booth was told. Slum services which did not offer food, money, or some other inducement were thinly attended, and the few successful ministers appeared to attract worshippers from nearby churches, rather than from the heathen mass. Smaller missions, where breezy hymns played on cheap harmoniums could not counteract the dispiriting effects of shabby buildings and uninspired preaching, had tiny congregations. 'One may perhaps rejoice,' C. F. G. Masterman wrote in 1903, 'at the complete failure of this fundamentally vicious system.'[95] It was no doubt true that doctrines hostile to Christianity had not taken root in working-class London, and that most poor Londoners treated Church workers with a friendly tolerance. What these missionaries encountered was not atheism or feeble-mindedness, but a robust indifference to religion, which was strong enough to withstand the unprecedented Christian onslaught of the 1880s and 1890s. No wonder that many of the clergymen Charles Booth spoke to were 'almost despairing as to [the] results' of their labours, and told him, 'It is heathen London still.'[96]

These general impressions were confirmed by two Nonconformist statistical surveys, one organized by the *British Weekly* in 1886, the other by Richard Mudie-Smith and the *Daily News* in 1903. The 1903 survey, which involved 400 well-supervised enumerators over eleven months, was more accurate than those of 1851 and 1886, and gives a convincing picture of London worship at the end of the century. According to Mudie-Smith, Greater London, with a population of 6,240,336, had 1,514,055 church attendances, and (allowing for 39 per cent of these being 'Twicers') 1,252,433 worshippers, about a fifth of its population. Of these 538,477 were Anglican, 545,317 Nonconformist, and 96,281 Roman Catholic. Comparisons with the 1886 survey, which covered a smaller area and used different methods, may be misleading, but it appeared that in seventeen years the churches in the County of London (with a population rising from about 4,000,000 to 4,560,000) had lost about 160,000 worshippers, most of them Anglicans. The general rule that 'the poorer the district the less inclination is there to attend a place of worship' was largely borne out by comparisons between the London boroughs, with the comfortable middle-class boroughs of Barnet, St Marylebone, Lewisham and Westminster at the top of the attendance league, and some of the poorest ones, Shoreditch, Battersea, Bethnal Green, Tottenham and Poplar, at the bottom. Differences in social class do not explain why the middle- and working-class inhabitants of Stoke Newington and Woolwich were among London's best churchgoers, and those of Hammersmith and Fulham were among its worst, but the overall picture, with attendance rates (including 'Twicers') in West London (35 per cent) so much higher than those in the east (19 per cent) and the south (22.5 per cent), is clear enough.[97]

THE MORAL TONE OF LATE VICTORIAN LONDON

Since many Victorians believed that religion was the essential basis of good moral conduct, they would have been puzzled by Charles Booth's conclusion, after twenty years of careful observation, that London was a heathen city, but not a sinful one. Legal marriage was the general rule among the working class, although young men often married only when their girlfriends were pregnant. There was perhaps more drinking than before (mainly because women were drinking more) but there was less drunken rowdiness, and pubs and publicans were more respectable than in the past. 'Go and look at Hampstead Heath on Bank Holiday and compare it with what it was twenty years ago, or walk in the streets on Saturday night,' a policeman of thirty-three years' experience told him. Metropolitan Police arrest figures confirm this personal impression. There were some worrying fluctuations, but in general the proportion of Londoners taken into custody for assault, larceny and other serious crimes had fallen dramatically since the 1850s, and was still falling at the end of the century. Arrests for disorderly prostitution rose sharply in the mid-1880s, reflecting changes in the rules of evidence rather than an increase in the crime, and arrests for drunkenness (the most common cause of arrest in London) declined after an 'epidemic' in the 1870s. In both cases, the numbers taken into custody (as a percentage of the population) were much lower than they had been in the 1830s and 1840s. 'Such scenes of open depravity as occurred in years gone by do not happen now,' Booth believed. 'There is greater intelligence, even though it be largely devoted to betting, and wider interests prevail, even if they be too much absorbed in pleasure seeking.' 'Men, women and children, all or nearly all, are keenly pursuing some aim, so much so, that the few of whom this is not true attract attention and become objects of suspicion.'[98]

The apparent improvement in London's moral tone in the later nineteenth century may, of course, be an illusion created by changing police arrest practices and the reports of more sympathetic observers, including slum vicars, mission workers, settlement undergraduates, and Charles Booth himself. Many earlier fears had been based on ignorance and misunderstanding, and when working-class Londoners had been expected to misbehave (at the Chartist rally of 1848 or the Great Exhibition of 1851, for instance) they had usually failed to live up to their reputation. A new and kinder picture of the East Ender, as unrealistic in its way as the old one, may have been created by the dignified parades of the striking dockers in 1889, the growing involvement of the working classes in orderly political and trade union organization, and the demolition of the fearful rookeries. In a few slum stories and poems of the 1890s, especially Henry Nevinson's *Neighbours of Ours* (1895) and Rudyard Kipling's *Barrack Room Ballads* (1892) the 'cockney' Londoner appears as a figure of wit and resilience, recalling the qualities that had made Dickens's Sam Weller so popular in the 1830s. Thanks to Kipling, Tommy Atkins, the cockney private soldier, came to represent the sturdy virtues of the British imperial army from Mandalay to the Sudan:

> They sent me to the gallery or round the music-'alls,
> But when it comes to fightin', Lord! they'll shove me in the stalls!
> For it's Tommy this, an' Tommy that, an' 'Tommy, wait outside',
> But it's 'Special trains for Atkins' when the trooper's on the tide.[99]

The new cockney was just as much a fiction as the violent and morally debased character readers had grown used to since the appearance of Bill Sikes in 1837, but a much more likeable one. Kipling was influenced by the new image of the loveable cockney being presented in the music-hall songs of the 1880s and 1890s. Peter Keating, in his study of Victorian fiction, credits the music-hall singers of these decades, Jenny Hill, Charles Coborn, Gus Elen, Marie Lloyd, and especially Albert Chevalier, with implanting in middle-class minds an indulgent and sentimental attitude towards the working-class Londoner which has survived to this day. Gareth Stedman Jones focuses on one night, in February 1891, when Albert Chevalier, 'a puny, crouching, angular figure' in a peaked cap, a check jacket, a ragged scarf and trumpet-shaped trousers, made his first appearance at the London Pavilion. Chevalier was a middle-class writer and actor playing the cockney, but his performance was taken for the genuine article, and the songs he sang that night, 'Knocked 'em in the Old Kent Road', 'My Old Dutch' and 'The Coster's Serenade', were regarded as insights into the life of the costermonger. Chevalier was lionized as 'the coster laureate', and the path was cleared for a new representation of the cockney spirit: Shaw's Eliza Doolittle, the British Tommy on the Western Front, Pearly kings and queens (a music-hall invention of the 1880s), the Lambeth Walk, and the East Enders cheerful and determined as German bombers destroyed their homes.[100]

MUNICIPAL EDUCATION

London's improved 'moral tone', if it were more than an illusion, might have been connected with the more favourable economic and environmental conditions enjoyed by the late Victorian working class: cheaper food, better sanitation, subsidized transport and (on a small scale) municipal and charity housing. The shift in drinking habits from beer and spirits to coffee, cordials and especially tea would have played its part, too. And the moral influence of the churches was not lost. Although a declining proportion of Londoners went to church, a growing number sent their children to school, where many of the same moral and spiritual lessons were taught. With the help of a state subsidy the British and National societies, linked respectively to the Nonconformist and Anglican churches, expanded their elementary school provision steadily between the 1810s, when both societies were founded, and 1870, when local authority schools were first introduced. When the London School Board tried to count the number of children in school in 1870 it found that of the 681,000 three- to thirteen-year-olds living in the Metropolitan Board of Works area, one in seven (97,307) were better-off children being educated at home or in schools with a weekly fee of over 9d, and 9,100 were in workhouses, orphanages or other institutions. Over a quarter (176,014) were not at school, mostly as a result of parental neglect, but some because they were unfit (17,500), or out at work or helping at home (38,193). Of the almost 400,000 children enrolled in a cheap or subsidized day school, the majority (about 250,000) were at National or British Society 'voluntary schools', and the rest were at cheap private schools, dame schools (run by an unqualified but not always incompetent individual teacher) or ragged schools.[101] Ragged schools were schools for homeless, neglected or 'derelict' children, which had been set up by philanthropic working-class or middle-class individuals or agencies (especially the London City Mission) since the early decades of the century. After 1844 most of these schools were managed by the Ragged School Union, of which the tireless Lord Ashley (Shaftesbury) was the president.

The 1870 Education Act established local school boards, elected by ratepayers, to provide elementary schools where existing provision was not adequate. Parents sending their children to Board schools paid fees of around 2d or 3d a week until free schooling was introduced in 1891, and until 1876 the question of compulsory attendance was left to individual Boards to decide. Thanks to an amendment to the 1870 Act proposed by William Torrens, MP for Finsbury, London was given a single School Board, covering the 117 square miles and 3,261,000 people administered by the Metropolitan Board of Works. Voting for the London School Board, the first directly elected London-wide body, took place on 29 November 1870. In several ways, the election broke new ground. Voting was secret, and women with the right property qualification could not only vote but stand for election. Dr Elizabeth Garrett, England's first female doctor, won more votes than any other candidate. In another respect the election was oddly old-fashioned. Most campaigning concentrated on religious issues, and the controversial 'cumulative' voting system, in which voters in

London's ten electoral divisions had as many votes as there were seats in their division (usually four or five), and could, if they chose, cast all their votes for one candidate, ensured that religious denominations would be heavily represented on the Board. On the first Board the great scientist T. H. Huxley, W. H. Smith (whose company's sales of books and newspapers would gain enormously from the success of the Board schools) and Lord Lawrence of the Punjab sat alongside two future bishops and a collection of Anglican and Nonconformist clergymen, whose chief concern was to ensure that the efforts of the Board did not undermine or outpace the voluntary schools.[102]

Like most local government bodies, the London School Board was divided between those who put performance before economy, and those who wished to fight extravagance and protect the ratepayer. Though most Church representatives and Conservatives voted with the parsimonious 'Moderates', the more free-spending 'Progressive' group were dominant until 1885 and most subsequent years, and established the active and reformist spirit which characterized the work of the Board. Within twelve years the number of places in the new Board schools had overtaken those in the voluntary schools, and by 1904, when the London County Council took over the Board's work, there were 554,198 Board school places, and 217,088 in voluntary schools. The London School Board had 469 schools, and its red-brick three-storey Queen Anne-style buildings, standing in their walled ashphalt playgrounds, were almost as common, and surely as influential, as churches.

The schools may not have conquered ignorance, Charles Booth thought, but 'obedience to discipline and rules of proper behaviour have been inculcated; habits of order and cleanliness have been acquired; and from these habits self-respect arises'.[103] The effect was not universal. From the early 1870s the London School Board had compulsory attendance by-laws for five- to nine-year-olds, and a body of visitors (whose local knowledge proved so useful to Charles Booth in the 1880s) to enforce them. Still, there were children in the rookeries and under the railway arches who escaped registration, and only 80 per cent of those enrolled in Board or voluntary schools were at their desks on an average day in 1900. A survey of 112 Board schools in 1899 found that over 2,000 pupils worked for nineteen or more hours a week, generally earning about 3s for thirty hours in a shop or factory, delivering newspapers, selling milk, or in domestic service. Officers who tried to force these children into school, Charles Booth's researcher (Mary Tabor) said, met 'a front of sturdy defiance, ... masterly inactivity or infinite evasiveness'.[104]

At the same time, the rest of London's secondary education system was going through a period of rapid change. The Schools Enquiry Commission (or Taunton Commission) of 1864–8 had exposed general corruption and decadence among schools based on old (often Tudor) charitable endowments, of which London had well over 100. In the following decades the Charity Commissioners imposed drastic reorganization schemes on most of these schools, giving London an impressive collection of efficient schools for the children of middle-class parents who could pay around £8 a year, but not the £25 or £30 demanded by the great London public schools, Westminster and St Paul's. While middle-class boys went to Merchant Taylors', Dulwich College or the City of London School, their sisters, who once would have been taught at home, could go to one of the twelve high schools established between 1873 and 1887 by the Girls' Public Day School Company. There were also many small private schools for middle-class boys and girls, but these were finding life difficult in the more competitive atmosphere of the later nineteenth century. In 1908 the LCC counted 468 boys' and girls' private schools in the County, but of their 27,000 pupils the majority (perhaps 60 per cent) seem to have been under twelve.[105]

Secondary education was not entirely confined to the private sector. Like some other Boards, the London School Board gradually strayed beyond the field of 'elementary' education for which it had been established. Lower-middle-class children were drawn into Board schools, and brighter children stayed on in their teens to study arts and science subjects that took them well beyond the '3 Rs'. Many of these older children were accommodated in 'higher grade' schools, of which there were seventy-nine in the London School Board area in 1900. In addition, the London Board ran evening classes which, it claimed, took pupils to university entrance level. These activities aroused the opposition of the LCC, which had been recognized in 1897 as the authority with responsibility for science and art in London, of the government's education spokesman, Sir John Gorst, and of an extremely dynamic civil servant in the Education Department, Robert Morant. Gorst crushed the Board's higher-grade schools by issuing a minute in 1900 which set conditions which hardly any of them could meet, and successfully challenged their right to finance evening classes through local rates in the Cockerton case of 1899–1901.

The 1902 Education Act transferred responsibility for education from School Boards to local authorities, and gave the LCC, along with other counties, the duty to provide appropriate elementary and secondary education in their area, paid for from a 2d rate. The LCC used its money to send a small number of able local children to secondary schools, to support approved secondary schools which were prepared to submit to Council inspection, and to set up secondary schools of its own where there was a need for them. In 1910 this huge educational enterprise helped to support over 100 private or endowed schools, maintained twenty of its own secondary schools, and paid scholarships to over 7,000 pupils, more than a third of all London secondary schoolchildren. In addition, the LCC funded 550 council and 380 Church elementary schools, with almost 18,000 teachers and a total of 730,000 children on their rolls.[106]

Opportunities for poorer Londoners who wanted to continue their education beyond the age of fifteen or sixteen were much greater in 1914 than they had been fifty years earlier, partly because of the development of a new type of further education college, the polytechnic, in the closing decades of the century. The first true polytechnic began as a private charitable venture. In 1880 Quintin Hogg, a philanthropic London sugar merchant with evangelical inclinations, took over a failed educational institute in Regent Street, 'the Polytechnic', and reopened it as a college in which young Londoners (artisans, shop assistants, and the like) could study in the evening to develop, as he put it, the 'athletic, intellectual, spiritual or social' aspects of their personalities. Hogg struck a rich vein. Nearly 7,000 students joined in the first year of the new Polytechnic, and the number doubled by 1900. London's dependence on the commercial and technical skills of its workforce was increasingly recognized by the government, the City and the LCC. In the early 1880s the City of London guilds were persuaded (especially by T. H. Huxley) to spend some of their wealth on technical training for London artisans, and founded the City and Guilds of London Institute and Finsbury Technical College. And in 1888 the Drapers' Company took over the funding and control of the People's Palace in the Mile End Road, a grandiose project which had been initiated in the wake of Walter Besant's slum novel, *All Sorts and Conditions of Men* (1882), as a means of bringing laughter and learning to the East End. Under the Drapers' control Besant's dream of a 'Palace of Delights' became the rather duller reality of East London Technical College, offering evening classes to working men and women.[107]

Concern over Britain's comparative weakness in technical education (stimulated by a Royal Commission in 1882–5) led to legislation in 1889 and 1891 which allowed local authorities to use income from a penny rate and from spirit duties ('whisky money') to finance technical colleges. At the same time, the Charity Commissioners recommended that some of the great and underused wealth in City parish charities should be diverted from defunct causes to the construction and support of polytechnics, on the lines already established in Regent Street and the Mile End Road. In 1891 the LCC and the City Corporation agreed to use their joint resources to support eight polytechnics and other similar trade colleges, to bring recreational and vocational education to the working classes. The Goldsmiths' Company undertook to found and maintain a separate college at New Cross, primarily for teacher training, which became part of London University in 1904. Much of the work of welding London's various colleges into a coherent system of technical instruction was done in the 1890s by the LCC's Technical Education Board, of which Sidney Webb was the tireless chairman. By 1906 (by which time the LCC Education Committee had superseded the Board) London had eleven polytechnics (or similar institutions), funded jointly by the LCC and the City, with about 40,000 students. In addition the LCC controlled and maintained seventeen technical institutes and schools of art, and twenty teacher-training colleges.[108]

London could no longer thrive as a city of labourers and dockers, servants and seamstresses. In 1914, all over London, in Battersea, Finsbury, Chelsea, Woolwich, Hammersmith, Southwark, Islington, Marylebone, Holloway, Clerkenwell and the City, young men and women were learning to be engineers, electricians, printers, photographers, clerks, designers and bookbinders, preparing themselves for the scientific and high-technology industries that would ensure London's prosperity in the decades ahead.

PART SIX

LONDON, 1914–1997

Chapter 22

The Great War

On 3 August 1914, the last full day of peace before the Great War, the Prime Minister, Herbert Asquith, described the scene in central London to his confidante, Venetia Stanley:

> There were large crowds perambulating the streets and cheering the King at Buckingham Palace, and one could hear this distant roaring as late as 1 or 1.30 in the morning. War or anything that seems likely to lead to war is always popular with the London mob. You remember Sir R. Walpole's remark: 'Now they are ringing their bells; in a few weeks they'll be wringing their hands.' How one loathes such levity.[1]

This is a well-known account, and a true one. But a city of 7 million people does not have a collective 'mood', and Llewellyn Woodward, a young scholar who later became a distinguished historian, saw a different side of London's response to the news of war:

> I find that my recollections differ from a good many accounts written about half a century later by people who were not there at the time – accounts of excited crowds, bellicose enthusiasm, and demonstrations around the central areas of Westminster. Such demonstrations did take place and some demonstrators were excited, but the vast majority of Londoners did not stand or move around Buckingham Palace, Downing Street, or the precincts of Parliament. They went back to their homes in the suburbs at the usual times, by their usual trains, trams or buses; they were neither elated nor frightened, only bewildered by news of which they could not guess the consequences. There had been many more signs of hysterical excitement over a single and comparatively simple event such as the news of the relief of Mafeking more than a dozen years earlier.[2]

THE ECONOMY AT WAR

In an influential book, *The Great Illusion*, first published in 1908, Norman Angell had predicted an international economic disaster if a European war broke out. In England the predicted and widely expected economic collapse did not happen, and London's economic life thrived in the war. In August 1914 London experienced a temporary economic crisis, but it was modest compared with those experienced in Berlin and especially Paris, which was almost a city under siege. Local Government Board figures show that London industrial employment had fallen by 13 per cent by mid-September, compared with about 25 per cent in Berlin and perhaps 70 per cent in Paris. Peacetime industries such as paper, printing, furniture, laundry and house-building contracted, and clothing and leather workers turned from civilian to military markets. The decline in manufacturing was not caused at first by mass mobilization, as it was in the continental capitals, but by the loss of European markets, the closure of the Baltic ports, raw material shortages, transport problems and (for small firms) lack of credit. In the autumn of 1914 London's economy began to adapt itself to wartime conditions, and male unemployment among insured workers, which reached a peak of 10 per cent in September, returned to its prewar level of about 6 per cent in December, and fell to 1.8 per cent in April 1915. Thereafter London's economy was running on full power, with all its available men and a growing proportion of its women involved in the war effort.[3]

The main reason for full employment was military recruitment, which had taken over 20 per cent of London's prewar male workforce by July 1915, before the introduction of the semi-compulsion of the 'Derby scheme' in October. The steady removal of men from the workforce, first by voluntary enlistment, and after January 1916 by conscription, created a shortage of labour which was met by the recruitment of women into parts of the economy they had not occupied before. The main London tram, underground and bus companies released a total of 17,669 men, 45 per cent of their prewar workforce, for war service by 1918, and replaced them by employing women as conductors and station staff. Many of these women moved from non-essential work (43 per cent of the London General Omnibus Company's early recruits came from domestic service), but others were entering work for the first time. The movement of middle-class and educated women into clerical, commercial and administrative work, which had begun in the late nineteenth century, went ahead rapidly in the war, and the great growth in the civil service (with ten new Ministries) relied heavily upon London women. Unlike the wartime jobs in transport and engineering, most of which were strictly 'for the duration', these jobs in banking, commerce and government were a permanent addition to the work available to women.[4]

In the munitions crisis of spring 1915 the government realized that the army's unprecedented demand for shells, guns and high explosives could not be met by private industry and existing royal ordnance factories. The more vigorous and interventionist policy of the new Ministry of Munitions led to the rapid expansion of the munitions industry in London and elsewhere, and drew women into jobs in engineering and heavy industry from which they had previously always been excluded. At Woolwich Arsenal, the centre of the London arms industry, the workforce grew from 10,900 to 65,000 in the war, with the number of women increasing from 125 to 28,000. Beyond Woolwich, there were about 50,000 workers in Ministry of Munitions factories in London by 1918, with major concentrations in the Lea Valley, where there were 15,200 men and women working in the small-arms factory at Enfield and the Waltham Abbey gunpowder factory, and in Erith and Crayford, where Vickers factories produced machine-guns. In West London there were munitions factories in Cricklewood, Hayes and Park Royal (west of Willesden Junction), an abandoned agricultural showground that was to become postwar Europe's largest industrial estate.[5] Park Royal's excellent rail connections with Birmingham and the Channel ports, and its ability to draw on the skilled workforce in the established engineering districts of Acton, Hammersmith and Willesden, made it a perfect centre for the inspection, storage and manufacture of ammunition. By mid-1917 Park Royal's National Filling Factory was filling 1.8 million fuses, gaines, detonators and primers a week. This and other works and depots in Park Royal employed about 9,000 workers, many of whom were women recruited from outside London. They were housed in a hostel which had once been the Willesden workhouse.[6] The dangers faced by munitions workers were dramatically illustrated in January 1917, when an explosion in the Brunner Mond TNT factory in West Silvertown killed sixty-nine people, and demolished much of the surrounding area.

The war's most severe impact on London, as on the rest of the kingdom, was the slaughter of its young men. About 124,000 Londoners (over 10 per cent of men in their twenties and thirties) were killed in combat, and the family that did not lose a father, brother, husband or son was very lucky indeed.[7] For Londoners who did not answer Kitchener's call to arms, the experience of war was one of petty inconveniences and occasional shortages, a few moments of localized danger and destruction, readily available work and a clear rise in living standards. London streets were dimly lit, buses and cabs were scarcer and more crowded, and private cars were discouraged. Several big hotels and clubs were commandeered as hospitals or for military use, and parks were cluttered with temporary government buildings or allotments. The British Museum and the Tate Gallery were closed for the duration, many sports events (including League football matches, the Oxford and Cambridge Boat Race and most horse racing) were suspended, and the closure of public houses at 10 p.m. (from October 1914) brought an unusual quiet to London streets. On the other hand, theatres, music halls, dance halls and cinemas did excellent business, and French and Italian restaurants in Soho enjoyed a sudden popularity.[8]

The availability of well-paid work for men and women, plentiful overtime, the virtual disappearance of unemployment and casual work, and the government's freezing of house rents (a policy hastily introduced in November 1915) created a sense of economic well-being in wartime London, despite the high cost of food and the loss of many male bread-winners. German submarine warfare created severe shortages of certain foods in later 1917, and there were long queues for margarine, sugar, tea and meat, but in general nutritional standards did not fall, and poorer Londoners, especially children, were healthier after the war than before it. C. F. G Masterman revisited South and East London after the war, and found the houses neglected, but their inhabitants in surprisingly good shape:

> The children were well fed, well dressed, well shod. . . . That swamp of forlorn humanity round Dockland, Bermondsey, Wapping, South-West Ham, found itself for the first time well fed, and with good feeding came health and a new chance for the coming generations. Except for anxiety for those at the Front, many would have wished these conditions to continue for ever.[9]

Food shortages only undermined morale when it was suspected that profiteers were manipulating supplies for their own gain, or that champagne drinkers in the West End hotels were not sharing the common sacrifice. The introduction of rationing at the beginning of 1918 ensured that Londoners entered the last phase of the war with their patriotic harmony almost intact.[10]

In the Front Line

The contrast between the suffering of those at the Front and the ease and prosperity of those who watched the war from a safe distance was nowhere more apparent than in the West End of London, where Siegfried Sassoon fed his resentment of armchair patriots by watching 'society' at dinner in the Strand in 1917: 'Evidence of civilian callousness and complacency were plentiful, for the thriftless licence of war-time behaviour was an unavoidable spectacle, especially in the Savoy Hotel Grill Room which I visited more than once in my anxiety to reassure myself of the existence of bloated profiteers and uniformed jacks in office.'[11]

To be fair to these 'guzzlers at the Savoy' (some of whom were officers on leave), London was no longer safe from the dangers of warfare. Bombing raids by Zeppelin airships, which had been feared since the outbreak of war, began on 31 May 1915, when Captain Linnartz flew the Zeppelin airship LZ38 over the docks and the East End in full moonlight, dropping 120 high-explosive bombs and incendiaries on Stoke Newington, Dalston, Hoxton, Whitechapel and Stepney, and killing seven people. There were ten airship raids (all by night) on London in 1915 and 1916, and a final one in October 1917. A raid on the City on 8 September 1915 did about £500,000 worth of damage, and seventy-one people were killed in Woolwich a month later. There was widespread anger at the inability of London's air defences (searchlights, artillery and aircraft under various commands) to stop the Zeppelins, and in January 1916 an advocate of better air defence, Pemberton Billing, almost won a by-election in Mile End.

Greater defensive successes in 1916, especially the killing of the most successful German commander, Heinrich Mathy, in October, persuaded the German high command to switch from airships to daytime aeroplane raids. There had already been some experiments. A single plane attacked the East End on 6 May 1916, and another dropped six small bombs near Victoria Station on 28 November. By May 1917 a powerful squadron of Gotha biplanes, the 3rd Bombing Squadron, was assembled on airfields around Ghent, in Belgium. Two raids in late May and early June lost their way in Essex, but on 13 June fourteen Gothas, flying in formation, bombed the Royal Albert Docks, Liverpool Street Station (destroying the front carriages of the Cambridge express), and Poplar, where seventeen children were killed in the cellar of an elementary school. In all, 160 people were killed and 424 injured in the raid, easily the most destructive of the war. On 7 July, twenty-two Gothas hit Shoreditch, St Pancras and the City, where the young V. S. Pritchett, working in the Bermondsey leather trade, saw the after-effects. 'Over London Bridge I went down the steps by St Magnus the Martyr into Billingsgate and saw the street walls of several houses and wharves had been stripped off, carts were overturned and horses lay dead among the crowds. The pubs in Bermondsey had filled with women pouring drink into themselves and their babies as I left.'[12] These two daylight raids, which produced 832 casualties at the rate of 121 casualties per ton of bombs dropped, strongly influenced expert predictions about the likely effects of future raids on London in the 1920s and 1930s.[13]

The two raids proved the ineffectiveness and incoherence of London's defences, and forced the Prime Minister, Lloyd George, to announce their thorough review in a secret session of Parliament. General Smuts was given the task of reorganizing London's defence, and placed the whole system under one commander, General Ashmore. Ashmore established a line of anti-aircraft guns 20 miles east of London, and had his pilots trained to fly patrols in formation, and to coordinate their efforts with those of the big guns, rather than get in their way. In September the Germans turned to moonlight attacks, approaching London from the north or south to avoid the anti-aircraft barrage sent up by the eastern guns. There was a succession of raids on Paddington, Stratford, Hornsey, Holloway, Highbury, Camberwell, Bermondsey and Westminster, and a bomb in Hyde Park killed the fish in the Serpentine. In December 1917 the destructive power of German raids was increased by the introduction of the four-engined Giant, the largest plane used against England in either war, which was capable of carrying 300-kilogram bombs. One of these killed thirty-eight people sheltering in the Odhams printing works in Long Acre on 28 January 1918, and another made a huge crater near Eaton Square. At the same time, London's defenders were beginning to match the skills of their attackers, using better searchlight control, dense barrages of anti-aircraft fire and more experienced pilots to turn back or destroy German bombers. On 19 May 1918 over eighty English planes and 30,000 anti-aircraft rounds brought down six German planes, and the raids were called off. So the new ground-to-air wireless that was ready by August was never used in the defence of London. In all, nearly 100 tons of incendiary or high explosive bombs were dropped on London, killing 670 people and injuring 1,960. Property damage was estimated at £2 million.[14] But as if to prove that bacteria were still more powerful than bombers, the world influenza pandemic arrived in London a month after the Gothas left it, causing incomparably greater loss of life. In the autumn and winter of 1918–19

18,000 Londoners died of the disease, with an especially high death rate among young men and women.[15]

If Germany's intention was to damage the morale of Londoners, then its air raids were fairly effective. In his memoirs, Lloyd George claimed that 'there was grave and growing panic' in the East End, especially after the raid of 7 July 1917, in which the German pilots showed much greater flying skills than their opponents. 'At the slightest rumour of approaching aeroplanes, tubes and tunnels were packed with panic-stricken men, women and children. Every clear night the commons around London were black with refugees from the threatened metropolis.' But the soldier Siegfried Sassoon, who saw the mayhem in Liverpool Street Station during the heavy raid of 13 June 1917, regarded the mixture of alarm and stoicism he saw there as entirely reasonable:

> This sort of danger seemed to demand a quality of courage dissimilar to front-line fortitude. In a trench one was acclimatized to the notion of being exterminated and there was a sense of organized retaliation. But here one was helpless; an invisible enemy sent destruction spinning down from a fine weather sky; poor old men bought a railway ticket and were trundled away again dead on a barrow; wounded women lay about in the station groaning.[16]

East Londoners, vulnerable in their crowded and flimsy slums, found a new use for the underground railway system. At the height of the German attacks, in September and October 1917, over 250,000 people took shelter in Tube stations and the tunnels under the Thames. Some deserted London for safer districts. East London clothing firms, the Cabinet was told in October 1917, had lost many of their machinists, and a visitor to Brighton found it packed with Londoners taking refuge 'till the end of the Harvest Moon'.[17] Beatrice Webb, like many others, found that she could get used to dangers that once would have terrified her. This is her diary for 5 October 1917, after the first moonlit aeroplane raids on north and central London:

> Six successive air raids have wrecked the nerves of Londoners, with the result of a good deal of panic even among the well-to-do and the educated. The first two nights I felt myself under the sway of foolish fear. My feet were cold and my heart pattered its protest against physical danger. But the fear wore off, and by Monday night's raid, I had recovered self-possession and read through the noise of the barrage with the help of an additional cigarette.[18]

The naturalist W. N. P. Barbellion (Bruce Cummings), not the hardiest of men, showed less fortitude. His first raid, on 8 September 1915, left him with 'a fit of uncontrollable trembling', and his next, a month later, brought on a heart attack. In November (after another raid and another heart attack) he fled the town in terror, and settled in the country.[19] For more resilient Londoners it was the sense of defencelessness, as much as the danger and loss of life, that undermined morale. Ashmore concluded that 'the moral effect of raiding is found to depend not so much on actual damage as on the success or ill-success of defensive measures'. Barrage fire was costly and searchlights were as much help to the bombers as to the defenders, but at least they gave Londoners a feeling that they were fighting back.[20]

Air raids and other examples of German 'frightfulness' intensified an ugly anti-alien mood among some Londoners. On 12 May 1915, after the news of the sinking of the *Lusitania*, there were riots against Germans and others with Central European names in the East End and Kentish Town, in which over 250 people were injured and many shops (especially German bakers' shops) looted and destroyed.[21] East Enders rioted again after the first Zeppelin raid (of 31 May 1915), and although the internment or deportation of many enemy aliens removed the most provocative targets, anti-alien feeling remained strong throughout the war, incited by the right-wing Press. There was a huge anti-alien demonstration in Trafalgar Square on 13 July 1918, and the following month a large crowd gathered in Hyde Park to carry a petition against aliens to Downing Street.[22]

11 November 1918

The ending of the war on 11 November 1918, was marked, as great national triumphs had been for centuries, with wild celebrations in central London. When the maroons fired at 11 o'clock that Monday morning work stopped all over the city, and people poured into the streets. The young C. H. Rolph, who was working in the City textile warehouse of Spreckley, White and Lewis in Cannon Street, was one of the 100,000 people who crowded round the Mansion House:

> Hundreds of sellers of small flags appeared from nowhere. . . . Huge military lorries came from nowhere crammed with standing and cheering civilians. Then down came the rain, and no-one cared a damn. Piano-organs appeared and people danced in the roads – the

only adequate way, it seemed, to express excited joy and otherwise inexpressible relief. Those who couldn't dance rang handbells, banged trays, adding to the din of the Klaxons, the screaming whistles, anything and everything that could bellow, echo, vibrate, or shrill ... when [the Lord Mayor] began singing the Old Hundredth, it was gradually taken up by the thousands of rain-soaked revellers in the mightiest quasi-musical roar I have ever heard; and I was astounded that everyone near me seemed to know the words ... it was a colossal sound, frightening, isolating; it was as though the God of Thunder himself had taken possession of that mysterious entity by which any crowd exceeds the sum of its constituent members. The very road and buildings seemed to shake with it.... Then I noticed for the first time that everyone was either crying or mopping up.

Rolph made his way to St Paul's Churchyard, where the Saxon folkmoot had met 1,000 years before, and into the crowded Cathedral. 'The silence in this vast and lofty auditorium, where thousands of people stood motionless, was as shattering as the uproar still going on outside.' The following day, according to Rolph, it was all quiet again. Stories (repeated in Taylor's *English History, 1914–1945*) of three days of increasingly wild celebrations, and strangers copulating on the pavements, were based on gross newspaper exaggerations. 'I believe I should have noticed some of this, especially what was happening on wet London pavements. I was there.'[23] Across the river in Bermondsey celebrations were more muted. Young V. S. Pritchett was let out of work an hour early: 'There was a bonfire in the yard at Guy's Hospital and a fireman's helmet was stuck on top of the statue there.'[24]

THE IMPACT OF WAR

The Great War was without doubt a cataclysmic event in the lives of Londoners, as it was in the lives of most Europeans, but its impact on their social and economic life was limited. It introduced them to air raids, food queues and the eight-hour working day, and speeded the arrival of the wireless, but it was not the gateway through which Londoners entered the modern world. Many of the most striking characteristics of a 'modern' society were already well established in prewar London. Electricity was widely used in transport and lighting, motor buses had replaced horse buses, the motor car industry was thriving, cinemas were popular, cheap newspapers had mass circulations, the foundations of the welfare state (old age pensions and selective insurance against sickness and unemployment) were laid, birth control was widely practised, the 'new woman' had become a topic of conversation, and women ('new' or otherwise) had made substantial gains in white-collar work, retailing and the lower-paid professions.

The war did not increase the number of women in London's permanent labour force. The female workforce grew three times more quickly between 1891 and 1911, when it rose from 736,000 to 912,000, than it did between 1911 and 1921, when it rose by 34,000. The striking change was not in the total number of women in work, but in the rise of clerical, administrative and retailing work at the expense of more traditional jobs. In 1921, when women had left their much-publicized jobs as munitions workers and bus conductors, there were still 128,000 women working in national and local government in London and the Home Counties, compared with 21,000 in 1911. In banking and insurance the increase was from 3,000 to 31,000, and in retailing and commerce, from 47,000 to 93,000. On the other hand, there was a dramatic movement away from the two dominant Victorian employments, dressmaking (down from 133,000 to 74,000 between 1911 and 1921), and domestic service (down from 416,000 to 324,000). Within the County of London, indoor domestic service employed 242,500 women, a third of all those in work, in 1901, and 220,500 (29 per cent) in 1911, but only 157,000 (20 per cent) in 1921. The door through which women passed, a little faster thanks to the First World War, led them from the scullery and the sweatshop into the office, the shop and the world of white-collar work.[25]

The effects of the war on the City and the complex financial world of which London was the centre were bound to be dramatic. There was panic selling of securities in New York and European capitals in July 1914, and by the end of the month it looked as if the inability of foreign debtors to pay money owing to London would bring down the City accepting houses that had guaranteed their bills of exchange. This would in turn endanger the banks and discount houses that held bills drawn on the accepting houses. Anticipating the crisis, the powerful joint-stock banks began calling in their loans from discount houses, and withdrawing gold from the Bank of England. 'Financiers in a fright do not make an heroic picture,' Lloyd George wrote later. 'One must make allowances, however, for men who were millionaires with an assured credit which seemed as firm as the globe it girdled, and who suddenly found their fortunes scattered by a bomb hurled at random from a reckless hand.' To rescue the situation and to get the discount market going again, Lloyd George, the Chancellor of the

Exchequer, gave the accepting houses a month's moratorium on their debts, and announced (on 12 August) that the Bank of England, backed by government guarantees, would discount all outstanding bills. By taking responsibility for about £500 million in foreign (including German) debts to London the government averted a crisis, and ensured that the City's major financial institutions would survive.[26]

Lloyd George's efforts were rewarded when the City's money-raising powers were diverted from financing international trade to funding the government's enormous wartime expenditure. Almost the whole of the National Debt, which rose from £700 million to £7.5 billion in the war, was raised in or through the City (much of it borrowed abroad), and government stocks, which had fallen to about 5 per cent of Stock Exchange securities in 1914, rose to around a third over the next ten years. Like railway stock in the 1830s and 1840s, government war securities mobilized previously inactive middle-class savings, making the City a conduit for the investments of millions of patriotic shareholders. By 1925, privately held government securities represented 'a quarter of all private property'.[27] Insurance companies, whose fire and marine business naturally boomed in the war, invested heavily in government stock too, selling off their overseas investments. Other factors shifted the focus of City interest from the international to the domestic scene. Wartime nationalism, and the inevitable closure of German banks and the expulsion of German traders and brokers destroyed (for the time being) the important Anglo-German relationship. London's overseas commodity trade (which often brought financial business with it) declined, thanks partly to the decision of many traders, especially American ones, to avoid dangerous European waters. The total tonnage of shipping involved in overseas trade entering and clearing the Port of London in 1917–18 was under 9 million tons, compared to 21 million tons in 1913–14. It had only recovered to 15 million tons in 1919–20. Foreign bankers and traders learned to do without the City's once indispensable services, and it was far from certain that London would recover its position at the centre of the international economy when the world was at peace again.[28]

Chapter 23

Between the Wars, 1918–1939

DESPITE THE LOSS OF 124,000 of its young men, and of all the children they would have fathered if they had lived, London remained the world's greatest city in the 1920s, larger by far than any of its European rivals, and just ahead of New York, the biggest non-European city. The growth of London's population in these years took place entirely beyond the County boundary. The population within the County fell by about half a million (from 4,540,062 to 4,062,800) between the wars, largely because of migration to the outer suburbs. At the same time, the population inside the Metropolitan Police District increased from 7,488,382 to about 8,655,000, and that of the much wider metropolitan area encompassed by Professor Abercrombie's 1944 *Greater London Plan* (which reached out about 30 miles to Luton and Sevenoaks) rose from 8,611,314 to 10,324,002, a growth which represented over a third of British population increase between the wars. Almost 2 million migrants (a third from Inner London, the rest from elsewhere in Great Britain) settled in suburban London in the interwar years.[1]

THE REJECTION OF LOCAL GOVERNMENT REFORM

The growing size and population of Outer London made the position of the London County Council, which even at the moment of its creation in 1888 had not been given control of the whole urban area, increasingly anomalous. The Progressive Party, the Liberal and radical alliance that controlled the LCC until 1907 and formed the main opposition group until 1925, had long argued for the creation of a single Greater London authority. After the war the Conservative leadership of the LCC (calling themselves Moderates or Municipal Reformers) joined the Progressives in pressing Lloyd George's Coalition government for an enquiry into the question of London's fragmented administration, and in 1921 a Royal Commission on London Government was appointed, under the chairmanship of Lord

Ullswater. In the event, the Commission was a disaster for the advocates of London unification. The Conservative leadership faced a revolt from its own councillors and supporters in the London Municipal Society, and R. C. Norman, the Conservative leader and main LCC witness for unification, found himself opposed before the Commission not only by the spokesmen of the suburban boroughs and counties, but by leading figures in his own party. Witnesses for the LCC were unable to convince the Commission of the disadvantages of London's existing system, and failed to present a considered proposal for regional government for the whole of Greater London. Labour's spokesman, Herbert Morrison, argued vigorously for a unified authority, but the support he received from the Labour-controlled London boroughs was half-hearted. Only two members of the Commission were convinced of the need for a new authority to govern London as 'one great civic and urban community', and a third who might have favoured unification, Neville Chamberlain, left the Commission before it reported. The majority was not persuaded that outer London was badly administered (a case which the LCC had been reluctant to put), and took the view that any advantages that might come from administrative unity would not justify the curtailment of the powers of the surrounding councils, or compensate for the friction between old and new authorities that would inevitably occur.[2]

The fact that the LCC had no authority beyond the County boundary meant that it could not play the part of a true regional authority, even if its Conservative masters wanted it to. Two key regional services, water supply and the management of the Thames, had already been given to *ad hoc* boards, answerable to central government (the Metropolitan Water Board in 1904 and the Port of London Authority in 1908), and two more, transport and electricity, were dealt with in the same way after 1922: the Central Electricity Board in 1926 and the London Passenger Transport Board in 1933. Unlike any other great English city, London did not even control its own police force. Between the wars, the LCC's policy of resettling inner-city slum-dwellers in outer London estates was impaired by its lack of control over Outer London's public services, and it could only take the lead in regional planning, as it did when it initiated the buying of green belt land in the 1930s, if it could persuade the Outer London boroughs to cooperate with it. In the early 1920s the Labour Party had advocated municipal control of public services under the slogan 'Home Rule for London', but when it eventually achieved power in London in 1934 this battle was lost, and most of the key regional services were in other hands.[3]

THE AGE OF THE BUS

The reshaping of interwar London was largely the work of transport enterprises and private builders, combined with the individual decisions of thousands of mainly middle-class families who wanted a suburban life and could afford a mortgage. As in the nineteenth century, the relationship between suburban house-building and the development of transport was close and complex. It would be too simple to say that the two went hand in hand. In some places (as with the huge LCC estate at Becontree) housing ran ahead of adequate transport, and in others, such as those served by the north-western branches of the Metropolitan Railway, transport improvements were slow to attract housing development. In general, though, London's suburban explosion would have been impossible without the enormous changes in urban transport that began at the start of the century, and continued, rather less dramatically, between the wars. The spread of underground lines and arterial roads into the outer suburbs and London's rural hinterland, the rapid growth of motor-bus services and the electrification of Southern Railways, between them made possible the urban sprawl of the interwar years.

The motor bus, which had replaced horse buses on London's streets in the decade before the First World War, was the most widely used form of transport between the wars. The main bus company, the London General Omnibus Company (LGOC), or 'General', had lost more than a third of its 3,000 buses to the War Office in the war, and because of vehicle production difficulties it took until 1921 to restore the fleet to its prewar capacity. In 1922 and 1923 small independent operators, taking advantage of the restoration of peacetime production in the vehicle industry, started to challenge the General's monopoly. Most of the roughly 250 independent companies that went into bus transport in the 1920s ran only one or two buses, but others (Bennett, Birch Brothers, Cambrian, City and Redburn's) were substantial concerns, with fleets of thirty or forty. Passengers may have welcomed the competition (which was more a matter of speed and frequency than price), but the problem of buses racing at high speed to pick up customers, and clogging the roads on popular routes, created pressure from police and public for a degree of regulation. The 1924 London Traffic Act did not end competition, but it regulated routes and the number of buses allowed to use them, and thus gave the General an incentive to buy out its rivals, which it did greedily over the next eight years. In 1931 there were only 213 independent buses (owned by fifty-five companies) operating in London, compared with about 550 in 1925.[4]

In the later 1920s London motor buses began to lose the features they had inherited from their horse-drawn ancestors, and took on the appearance of the familiar modern double-decker. In 1926 the police grudgingly allowed the experimental use of pneumatic tyres instead of solid ones, and of covered upper decks, which made it possible to install upholstered upstairs seating. The speed limit for vehicles with pneumatic tyres was raised from 12 to 20 miles an hour in 1928, and drivers' windscreens and four-wheel brakes were introduced at around the same time. Early motor buses had only carried about thirty-four passengers, but most models of the later twenties were designed to take about sixty people, though some huge seventy-seaters were found to be too cumbersome on corners and narrow roads, and too much for a single conductor to manage. In the 1930s the fifty-six-seat bus, running (after 1933) on diesel rather than petrol, became the accepted standard, and in the later thirties passengers were asked to wait for buses at fixed stops, as they did for trams, rather than hailing them like cabs.[5]

These technical improvements helped motor buses capture a growing share of the travelling public from their rivals, the tram and the train. In 1920 buses carried 930 million passengers a year, rather less than trams or trains, which each carried over 1,000 million. But the growth in total passenger numbers in the 1920s, from 3,000 million to 4,000 million a year, was due entirely to the fact that the number of bus travellers doubled to 2,000 million. The position stabilized in the 1930s. Although the population of the London Transport area rose from 8 million to almost 10 million, rising car ownership reduced the number of public transport journeys per head, leaving the total annual number of passengers at a little over 4,000 million in 1938. A quarter of these journeys were by train, a quarter by tram or trolleybus, and the rest by motor bus.[6] In the suburbs, buses carried commuters to their nearest underground or main line station, and served the many workers whose journeys were between one suburb and another. Shopping, school and social trips were also likely to be by bus, except for the small but growing section of the middle-class population that could afford a car.

Electric trams, which many had seen as the rapid transit system of the future at the beginning of the century, could not match motor buses for economy or convenience. LCC protection and subsidies saved trams from decline in the 1920s, but they increased road congestion without attracting extra passengers, and a Royal Commission on Transport in 1931 declared that they were 'in a state of obsolescence'. From 1931 trams were gradually replaced by electric trolleybuses, especially in North London. Trolleybuses were powered by overhead wires and ran without tracks, which made them safer and more mobile than trams, and less likely to cause traffic jams or kill cyclists.[7]

ARTERIAL ROADS AND RIBBON DEVELOPMENT

The inability of London's narrow streets to cope with the increasing volume of tram and bus traffic had already been discussed at length by a Royal Commission in 1905. Between 1913 and 1916 the Greater London Arterial Roads Conferences had proposed to relieve the growing congestion in the suburban stretches of the old high roads leading out of London (Brentford High Road, Uxbridge Road, Edgware Road, Kingsland Road, Romford Road, Kingston Road, Barking Road, Shooters Hill, the Great North Road, and so on) by constructing a network of by-passes and arterial roads. Work was delayed by the war, but when the postwar slump began in 1920 the government seized upon road-building as a way of easing mass unemployment. The 1920 Unemployment (Relief Works) Act made it possible to acquire the land for new roads without delay, and work began at once. Within a few years the Great West Road, Eastern Avenue and the Great Cambridge Road were finished, providing new routes to the west, east and north, and a succession of by-passes relieved the crowded centres of Watford, Kingston, Richmond, Barnet, Sutton, Croydon, East Ham, Sidcup, Orpington, Bexleyheath and Barking. Work also began on Western Avenue, relieving the old London to Oxford Road, and the North Circular, linking the western, northern and eastern suburbs, but these were not finished until the 1930s. The South Circular Road, which was intended to form the southern section of the circle around London, was never completed.[8]

The efficiency of these new arterial roads as through routes was undermined by the phenomenon known (since 1928 or 1929) as 'ribbon development'. Most highway authorities failed to buy the land fronting their new roads, and there was a predictable tendency for houses, factories and shops to congregate along them, cluttering them with local traffic. Developers saved money by building along main roads, and house buyers still regarded a main road location as an advantage rather than a drawback. Industrial sites along arterial roads offered easy transport and free publicity, and they were especially popular with American companies. The factories built along the Great West Road read like a roll-call of the new industries that helped London to thrive in the Slump. The motor industry was represented by three American car companies, Packard, Hudson Essex and Lincoln, and by Firestone Tyres, Trico windscreen wipers, Tecalenit lubrication systems and Henleys showrooms and service stations. For food and pharmaceuticals, there were Smiths Crisps, Macfarlane Lang's Imperial Biscuits, Coty's perfume and make-up, and Maclean's toothpaste and medicines. There was room between these for Gillette razors, Pullin projectors and camera motors, Pyrene fire extinguishers, Simmonds Aerocessories, Curry's electrical goods warehouse and Sperry's compasses and gyroscopes.[9]

The Great West Road was the outstanding example of industrial ribbon development, but most of the new roads attracted factory builders. In 1936 it was said to be 'practically impossible to obtain a site of any size on the Great West Road, Kingston By-Pass Road or the Western Avenue'. In 1935 the Restriction of Ribbon Development Act gave local authorities some powers to protect the frontages of arterial roads, but the Act, Abercrombie reported in 1944, was 'a superficial remedy for a deep-seated disease' which 'did little good and chiefly served to confuse the administration of planning'. 'Though it is still preferable to motor along the Great West Road than across Hounslow Heath or along the New Cambridge Road than through the old Lee Valley with its almost continuous shopping street, the new roads are nevertheless a compromise and have already lost much of the through-traffic efficiency for which they were designed.'[10]

Many of the new arterial roads built in the 1920s had to be widened in the 1930s, when large numbers of private cars joined the buses, trams, lorries and horse carts that already used them. Car ownership, a rich man's indulgence before 1914, became fairly common among middle-class Londoners in the 1930s. Mass production and the design of smaller vehicles reduced the price of the average car from £684 in 1920 to £279 in 1928 and £210 in 1938, and running a car got cheaper, too. In 1933 the number of private cars in London and Middlesex reached 170,000, about six times the figure for 1920, and ownership in the larger London Transport area increased from 292,000 to 475,000 between 1933 and 1938. London was slow to introduce parking restrictions, and narrow streets were made narrower still by cars and vans parked along their kerbsides. The congestion caused by private cars, trams, buses and taxis was exacerbated by the growing number of vans and lorries, stopping and unloading where they chose, and by the continuing presence of heavy horse-drawn vehicles on the roads. There were still 20,000 horses in London in 1935, and about

5 per cent of the vehicles passing London's busiest points in 1928 were horse-drawn. In central London, where the road network was almost unchanged (except for the introduction of one-way streets) since the opening of Kingsway and the Aldwych in 1905, traffic moved more slowly in 1938 than it had done in 1908, and the commercial cost of road congestion was estimated in 1935 at around £25 million a year. The problem was not seriously addressed until London's retiring chief road engineer, Sir Charles Bressey, was commissioned, along with the architect Sir Edwin Lutyens, to conduct a Highway Development Survey of Greater London in 1935. Their report, completed in 1937, included proposals for orbital roads, new Thames tunnels, radial motorways, and the segregation of fast and slow traffic which were repeated in all the plans published during and after the Second World War.[11]

A UNIFIED TRANSPORT SYSTEM

The underground railway companies, which had hitherto linked well-established suburbs with the City and West End, decided that the way to fill more trains and cut their operating losses was to extend their reach into the outer suburbs and to the very fringes of the built-up area. The Bakerloo Line was extended to Watford in 1917, the Central Line to Ealing (1920), the Northern Line (an amalgamation of the City and South London and the Hampstead Lines) to Edgware and Morden (1922–4), and the Piccadilly Line to Cockfosters, Uxbridge and Hounslow (1932–3). The Underground group (UERL), which owned the whole underground network except the Metropolitan Line, also controlled two-thirds of London buses and many of its trams, and was able to manipulate their routes and fares to draw commuters on to its railways from an even wider catchment area. At the same time Frank Pick, the group's very able managing director, employed modern artists and architects to give UERL stations, signs and posters a distinctive and appealing image. Charles Holden's Piccadilly Line stations at Arnos Grove, Southgate, Park Royal, Sudbury Town and elsewhere, all built in the early thirties, are regarded as the best examples of the new approach to station design. 'Modest, functional, yet not without elegance ... the right mixture of standardization and variation', was Nikolaus Pevsner's verdict on Holden's work.[12]

The best response of the surface railway to the underground challenge was electrification, but in North London the major companies could not afford it. In South London, where only one underground railway (the Northern Line to Morden) penetrated the suburbs and one amalgamated railway company, the Southern, controlled the surface network, there was a huge electrification scheme between 1925 and 1930. Eight hundred miles of track (293 route miles) were electrified, cutting journey times by 20 or 30 per cent and more than doubling the frequency of commuter trains. Southern opened only one new line (Wimbledon to Sutton) between the wars, but over a third of the seventy new stations built in these years were on its routes. The impact of Southern's electrification extended to the south coast, and began to establish a pattern of long-distance commuting that became normal in the 1950s. In 1936 10,000 people commuted daily to London from Brighton on the Southern's fast new electric service.[13]

By the late 1920s it was obvious to the Ministry of Transport, most politicians and the heads of the Underground group, A. H. Stanley (Lord Ashfield from 1920) and Frank Pick, that competition had done as much as it could do to improve London's transport system. To avoid congestion of the popular routes, neglect of the less profitable ones, and a ruinous driving down of profits, the system needed unified management. The LCC, whose tramways nearly always ran at a loss, was keen to talk to the Underground group, but a Bill to coordinate their management fell when a new Labour government came to power in 1929, with Herbert Morrison, an implacable opponent of the proposed private monopoly, at the Ministry of Transport. Finally, after three years of negotiations between the government, the LCC, the Underground group, the Metropolitan Railway, the four surface railway companies, Green Line Coaches, and the smaller bus and tram companies, the London Passenger Transport Act of March 1933 created the London Passenger Transport Board, the world's largest transport organization. This was not a private company but a public corporation, rather like the BBC or the Metropolitan Water Board. As such, it won the approval of Herbert Morrison, who was soon to become the leader of the LCC. The surface railways were not managed by the LPTB, but they had an arrangement to pool and share receipts with the Board, and to coordinate their investment and development with it. The Board's task for the next fourteen years (when the system was nationalized) was to manage London's entire local public transport system within a 2,000-square-mile area stretching from Crawley to Hitchin, and Slough to Gravesend. This task was performed, it was generally recognized, with an impressive combination of entrepreneurial flair and public spiritedness, satisfying the expectations of stockholders and the needs of passengers. The underground network was turned into a single coordinated system, rolling stock was standardized and modernized, and extensions were made in the late 1930s, with the help of cheap government loans, to Mill Hill and High Barnet.[14]

An Explosion of Suburbs

It was regarded as certain, and it was nearly always the case, that good transport facilities on the outskirts of London would quickly attract suburban settlement. This was the assumption, based on many decades of experience, that persuaded the heads of the Underground group, Southern Railways and the Metropolitan Company to drive their electric lines into the countryside, and the calculation that encouraged landowners and developers to subsidize the building of new stations in their districts. To some extent, the railway companies built new lines to serve the people who had already gone to the suburbs, but they were also a prime mover in the process of suburbanization, and had to stimulate new settlement on the edges of London to fill their carriages. One company, the Metropolitan, was a house-builder as well as a transport provider. Between 1920 and 1932 Metropolitan's property subsidiaries built ten estates (or 'Garden Villages') along its lines to Uxbridge and Amersham, from Neasden and Wembley Park to Harrow, Pinner, Ruislip and Rickmansworth. Other companies were unable to share directly in the rising property values which their lines always produced, and had to console themselves with growing ticket sales. These increases could be considerable. The number of passengers using Rayner's Lane grew from 22,000 a year in 1930 to 4 million in 1937.[15]

Between 1921 and 1939 the pace of growth in many of the suburbs served by new underground or Southern electric trains was spectacular. In suburban Essex, growth was particularly fast in Ilford (96 per cent), Barking (116 per cent), Romford (163 per cent), Billericay (179 per cent), Chingford (295 per cent), Hornchurch (335 per cent) and Dagenham (1,076 per cent). In Hertfordshire, the districts of Rickmansworth, Elstree and East Barnet doubled in population, and in Kent there was similar growth in Crayford, Beckenham, Orpington, Chislehurst and Sidcup, and Bexley (264 per cent). Surrey had six boroughs or urban districts that at least doubled in population (Banstead, Coulsdon and Purley, Surbiton, Sutton and Cheam, Egham and Malden) and two that quadrupled (Merton and Morden, and Carshalton). Middlesex, which covered the whole northern and north-western section of London (beyond the LCC boundary) from Enfield and Edmonton to Uxbridge, Staines and Twickenham, became an almost entirely suburban and industrial county, with a population of over 2 million in 1938. Within it, the populations of Uxbridge, Heston, Hendon and Feltham more than doubled, and five centres grew much faster: Potters Bar (273 per cent), Harrow (275 per cent), Ruislip-Northwood (348 per cent), Hayes and Harlington (386 per cent) and Wembley (552 per cent). Harrow, with 184,000 people in 1938, had a bigger population than Southampton or Swansea.[16]

COTTAGE ESTATES

In the first three years of peace, when high wages and material costs discouraged private builders, most suburban house-building was the work of the LCC and other local councils. The LCC had been building suburban 'cottage estates' on the fringes of London since 1900, when a new Housing of the Working Classes Act gave it powers to buy cheaper housing land outside the County boundary. By 1914 there were LCC estates in Totter-down Fields (just inside the County's southern boundary at Tooting), Norbury (between Streatham and Croydon) and Tottenham, and another under construction at Old Oak, on the western edge of Wormwood Scrubs. The working occupants of these little houses generally travelled to their jobs in central London by electric tram or workman's train, at a cost of between 1s and 4s a week.[17]

The First World War interrupted most house-building, except in districts where there was an influx of war workers. The Well Hall Estate in Eltham, with over 1,000 houses for Woolwich munitions workers, was the largest wartime housing scheme. At the end of the war the main feature of the Coalition government's reconstruction plan was a new housing policy that would make Britain, in Lloyd George's much misquoted phrase, 'a country fit for heroes to live in'. The LCC, with its experience of large-scale rehousing schemes, was regarded (by itself and the Local Government Board) as the body that was best equipped to keep this promise in the Greater London region, and it had been involved in discussions with the Board since 1917.[18] Addison's Housing Act of 1919 compelled local authorities to survey and satisfy their district's housing needs, with the encouragement of an extremely generous state subsidy to enable councils to let the houses they built at low rents. Private house-builders were also subsidized if their houses were of an appropriate type. The LCC had plans to house 145,000 Londoners in suburban estates, but building costs were so high after the war that the Addison scheme had to be abandoned in 1921, with only about a third of its national target achieved. In London, the Act enabled the LCC and the London borough councils to build 27,441 new houses for rent (a third of them LCC), and private builders another 6,889.[19]

After 1922 housing policy oscillated between subsidizing private and municipal house-building, depending on the complexion of the government. The Conservative Housing Act of 1923 subsidized private houses for middle-class buyers with building society mortgages, and helped to fund the construction of 28,000 private houses and about 18,000 municipal ones in London. The 1924 Labour government's Wheatley Act restored the advantage to council housing, and subsidized the building of 64,000 LCC and borough council houses, but only 2,000 private ones, over the next nine years. Subsidies for suburban houses were finally removed in 1933, after which government policy concentrated on encouraging inner-city slum clearance. Private house-builders, helped by low interest rates and the rise of the building society movement, built the great majority of London houses.[20] Local authorities continued to build in the thirties, but they concentrated on blocks of flats on cleared slum land, and eventually abandoned the cottage-building that had characterized the 1920s. After 1922 private builders always constructed more houses than municipal ones, and from the late twenties, and especially between 1934 and 1938, there was a spectacular boom in private house-building in the outer suburbs. The height of the boom was in 1934, when nearly 73,000 private houses were completed in London, and 287,500 in England and Wales. In all, private firms built 80 per cent of the 771,759 houses and flats built in Greater London between the two world wars, with the rest shared almost equally between the LCC and the borough councils.[21]

By the late 1930s there were eight large LCC estates, and several smaller ones, in the London suburbs, with a total population of around 250,000. By far the biggest of these was Becontree in Essex, between Ilford and Dagenham, which had 116,000 tenants (more than the population of Ipswich or Halifax) by 1939. Becontree was begun in a hurry under the Addison scheme, and its early residents suffered from a lack of schools, jobs, public houses, shops and transport. But by the late thirties it was the world's biggest municipal estate, with 25,769 dwellings, 400 shops, thirty schools, twenty-seven churches, nine public houses and four cinemas. Although the LCC remained committed to the policy of dispersing London's slum population until the early thirties, estate building on the scale of Becontree was not repeated elsewhere in the London suburbs. There was a cluster of four LCC estates with a joint population of about

50,000 (Downham, Bellingham, Whitefoot Lane and Mottingham) near the LCC border between Lewisham and Kent, and the only big LCC estate in Surrey, St Helier, had a population of about 40,000 when it was completed in 1934. The biggest North London LCC estate, Watling (near Burnt Oak underground station) had just under 20,000 tenants, but the other LCC suburban estates (Castlenau, Roehampton, Hanwell and Kenton) were all much smaller.[22]

The building of cottage estates taught the LCC some lessons in town planning. The tenants on these new estates (mostly better-off working people) enjoyed standards of domestic space and comfort which were almost unprecedented in working-class housing. Their council houses had indoor toilets, hot and cold water, upstairs bathrooms, three bedrooms, separate living rooms and sculleries (and sometimes a parlour), and side passageways leading to large back-gardens. These were the 'Tudor Walters' standards, named after the chairman of the Local Government Board Committee that recommended them in 1918. This was a far cry from the grim Victorian world of Guinness and Peabody.[23] But the new estates did not seem to grow into communities which were cherished, or even recognized, by their inhabitants. Becontree was an artificial community, without administrative, economic or social cohesion. Until 1931, when Ford's opened its Dagenham factory, it suffered from a severe shortage of local jobs. As an observer wrote in 1938, 'to build 22,000 houses and to assemble 22,000 families does not in itself create a town; it creates a wilderness of puzzled and discontented persons'.[24] Watling, which was studied by Ruth Durant (later Ruth Glass) in the late 1930s, seemed to suffer from the same lack of civic and social spirit, though it may well be that its problems were no worse than those of the privately built estates in the same area.[25]

A SEMI-DETACHED WORLD

Cheap materials, cheap labour and a steady supply of customers made the 1930s a golden decade for London building firms, and several leading modern companies, including Costain, Laing, Taylor Woodrow, Wates, Wimpey and New Ideal Homesteads, made their fortunes in suburban estate development in these years. Semi-detached houses in a variety of 'styles' (Tudor, Queen Anne, 'cottage') were their standard product, but builders also offered bungalows, 'maisonettes', 'chalets' (bungalows with an extra bedroom in the roof space), and flats to suit almost every taste and pocket. Michael Robbins, the historian of Middlesex, describes the typical interwar semi-detached:

> The building itself is of brick, of two stories, with bow windows on ground and upper floors on one side, surmounted by a gable. The roof, of fairly steep pitch, is tiled, not slated. The gable is finished with plaster or rough-cast, with three or five vertical planks painted black affixed to the front. (These planks may seem a quaint conventional survival of half-timbering ... but they have in fact a purpose, to inform the observer that the house was not built by the council.) There may be a porch with a decorative pattern of brick or tile; the casement windows probably have metal frames and leaded panes, and one window at least, perhaps the one in the door, varies the monotony by displaying some coloured glass in a design of uncertain inspiration. The front elevation asserts its individuality by picturesque variations in details, though the house is in fact exactly the same in height and plan as all its neighbours.[26]

The Modern Movement did not have much influence over these commercial builders, but there was a brief attempt to sell flat-roofed 'houses of tomorrow' to suburban buyers in the early thirties, when the architects Walter Gropius and Berthold Lubetkin arrived in London as refugees from Nazism. The ideals of the new architecture were better suited to blocks of flats: the Isokon flats in Lawn Road (Belsize Park, 1933), and Lubetkin's Highpoint One and Two (Highgate, 1936–8) are the best-known examples. Perhaps the most famous residents of a Lubetkin building were the penguins and gorillas of London Zoo, which were rehoused in the Modern style in the early 1930s. House-buyers in Purley, Croydon, Wembley, Hendon and Ilford met the modern world in the shape of electric power points, vacuum cleaners, gas cookers or rings (in 81 per cent of London houses by 1942) and steel windows, rather than the ideas of Le Corbusier or the Bauhaus.[27]

The number of Londoners who could afford a modest suburban semi-detached house increased steadily in the interwar years. Not only was London's population rising, but the trend towards smaller families meant that the number of separate households was rising faster still, and economic changes produced an even greater growth in the number of skilled and professional families, who were most likely to buy their own homes. In addition, the economics of house-ownership were unusually favourable for people of modest incomes. Plentiful labour and falling building costs reduced the price of a cheap suburban semi-detached house from about £600 in the 1920s to £400 in the mid-1930s, and a four-bedroomed one from £1,200 to about £900. Lower interest rates and changes in building society rules meant that houses could be bought on easier weekly terms by families without the capital for a deposit. In the 1930s bigger building firms and the building societies stimulated the housing market by using an arrangement known as the Pool Deposit system, which reduced the deposit on a cheaper house from 20 or 25 per cent to 5 per cent or even less. With mortgage rates at 5 or 4.5 per cent in the 1930s, a clerk, foreman, teacher or well-paid skilled worker would be able to buy a £650 house for 18s a week (plus local rates of about 5s), only 2s or 3s more than the rent on a council house of similar size. Those who dithered between buying and renting might be persuaded by a visit to the Ideal Home Exhibition (a regular London event since 1908), or by the Metropolitan Railway's offer of a free first-class ticket to Metroland. Whether paying a mortgage really amounted to 'buying' a house was another matter. George Bowling, the narrator of George Orwell's novel of suburban frustration just before the Second World War, *Coming up for Air*, thought not:

> Of course, the basic trouble with people like us, I said to myself, is that we all imagine we've got something to lose. To begin with, nine-tenths of the people in Ellesmere Road are under the impression that they own their houses. Ellesmere Road, and the whole quarter surrounding it, until you get to the High Street, is part of a huge racket called the Hespirides Estate, the property of the Cheerful Credit Building Society. Building societies are probably the cleverest racket of modern times. My own line, insurance, is a swindle, I admit, but it's an open swindle with the cards on the table. But the beauty of the building society swindles is that your victims think you're doing them a kindness. You wallop them, and they lick your hand. . . . Every one of those poor downtrodden bastards, sweating his guts out to pay twice the proper price for a brick doll's house that's called Bell Vue because there's no view and the bell doesn't ring – every one of those poor suckers would die on the field of battle to save his country from Bolshevism.[28]

'In every one of those little stucco boxes', Orwell said, 'there's some poor bastard who's *never* free except when he's fast asleep and dreaming he's got the boss down the bottom of a well and is bunging lumps of coal at him.'

THE LOSS OF COUNTRYSIDE

The town-planning ideas that had developed in the late nineteenth century under the influence of Ebenezer Howard, and which still prevailed in the 1920s, regarded low-density expansion into the fields around London (on the 'garden suburb' principle) as the best solution to urban overcrowding, so long as there were good transport links to the working centre of the town. The bigger the gardens, the more space between the houses, the more admiration a new development attracted. The Town Planning Act of 1909 was revised in 1919, but there was no suggestion that local authorities should use their planning powers to slow down the disappearance of the London countryside or halt the policy of 'dispersal'. Instead, by building cottage estates on green field sites, they joined in the process. In their posters and leaflets, suburban developers boasted that their new estates were built in the countryside, and offered their customers moss-grown churchyards, the song of nightingales, and 'the lazy delights of the country house'.[29]

The consequences of this unrestrained development were staggering. By 1939 the area occupied by the London conurbation was more than twice as great as that occupied in 1914, and about six times that of 1880.[30] Most of the London we know today only became part of the conurbation in the interwar years, and well over half the rest is late Victorian or Edwardian. Much of the newly developed land was fertile agricultural land of the very highest quality, upon which London's manure and organic refuse had been deposited, its cattle grazed, and its fruit and vegetables grown for centuries. In the words of the distinguished geographer Dudley Stamp, 'The market gardens and orchards of south Middlesex and the similar market gardening land of south Essex became some of the most highly farmed and productive lands in the world, from which four and even five crops a year could be taken.' Of all the surrounding counties, Middlesex suffered most severely from London's expansion. In 1885 the County had a seventh of England's acreage of market gardens and about 118,000 acres of crops and grass, but by 1940 this had been reduced to about 32,000 acres.[31] In a poem published in 1954, John Betjeman, the poet laureate of the London suburbs, lamented the Middlesex countryside that had been all but destroyed by the spread of Metroland:

> Gentle Brent I used to know you
> Wandering Wembley-wards at will,

Now what change your waters show you
In the meadowland you fill!
Recollect the elm-trees misty
And the footpaths climbing twisty
Under cedar-shaded palings,
Low laburnum-leaned-on railings,
Out of Northolt on and upward to the heights of Harrow hill.

Parish of enormous hayfields
Perivale stood all alone,
And from Greenford scent of mayfields
Most enticingly was blown
Over market gardens tidy,
Taverns for the *bona fide*,
Cockney anglers, cockney shooters,
Murray Poshes, Lupin Pooters,
Long in Kensal Green and Highgate silent under soot and stone.

The favourite device of those who were concerned about the preservation of recreational or agricultural land on London's fringes was the creation of a 'Green Girdle' or 'Green Belt' of undeveloped land around the built-up area. Lord Meath, chairman of the LCC Parks Committee, had promoted the idea in 1890, and many progressive and socialist councillors had been attracted by it. The pursuit of this or any other regional objective was made difficult by the fact that Greater London had no single planning authority. Discussion of the broader problems of London's development was therefore entrusted to a cumbersome advisory body, the Greater London Regional Planning Committee, set up by the Minister of Health, Neville Chamberlain, in 1927. The Committee's financial support from the LCC and other local authorities was inadequate, and it disappeared in 1936. Its main contribution to the planning debate was the publication of two reports in 1929 and 1933 in which its technical adviser, Raymond Unwin (one of the architects before the First World War of Letchworth and Hampstead Garden Suburb), advocated the preservation of a Green Belt of recreational land around London. Herbert Morrison, the leader of the London Labour Party, had been a supporter of the planned dispersal of population and industry into garden cities, and the preservation of a Green Belt, since the First World War, when he had lived in Letchworth and met his wife there. When Labour won control of London in 1934 it became LCC policy to subsidize local councils in buying open land. Between 1935 and 1944 the LCC spent about £1,820,000, and local councils about three times that much, in buying around 72,000 acres of green land and preserving it for recreational or agricultural use. Although the 1938 Green Belt (London and Home Counties) Act confirmed that the land bought in this way would be preserved, the Act did not provide extra resources, or prevent landlords from selling their land at its full development value. A few important spaces were saved in the late 1930s (Nonsuch Park and Enfield Chase, for instance), but London's Green Girdle would have been a moth-eaten and insubstantial garment if the Second World War had not brought suburban expansion to a standstill in 1940. When building began again in the postwar years, developers found that London's countryside was protected by much stronger rules.[32]

MANUFACTURING PROSPERITY

London kept on growing, both in area and population, because its economy was so prosperous. While most other parts of the country stagnated in the 1920s and sank into a deep depression in the early 1930s, London's economy flourished. In part, this was because of the nature of London's main industries. Only 1 per cent of London's manual workers worked in the five most rapidly declining industries (coal, shipbuilding, cotton, wool, and iron and steel), which employed 23 per cent of the national industrial workforce, and whose problems were at the root of Britain's depression in the 1920s and 1930s. On the other hand, London was much more heavily involved than any other industrial region in industries and services that were aimed at the domestic market, which was stimulated by falling food prices and rising real wages until 1933, and protected by tariffs from 1932. The Ministry of Labour identified twenty-three industries with an above-average growth rate between 1923 and 1937, including building, laundry, tram and omnibus work, distributive, hotel and catering trades, electrical engineering, food processing, paper and printing and the production of motor vehicles, cycles, aircraft, artificial silk, furniture, electrical cables, lamps and electrical appliances. Throughout the interwar period a third of the national workforce in those industries was in London and the Home Counties, and in 1923 55.5 per cent of the London region's insured workers (not including most of its commercial and professional employees) worked in them, more than double the proportion in Lancashire and the West Riding of Yorkshire. The London building boom sustained an insured workforce of over 200,000 (nearly 8 per cent of London's insured workers) in the late 1930s, and commerce and finance, which employed over 21 per cent of working Londoners, had a lower unemployment rate than any other significant sector in the 1930s.[33]

Although London's prosperity sprang partly from the nature of the industries in which it specialized, it also enjoyed other advantages as a business and industrial location, which attracted new employers towards it. It was, as it had been for two centuries, Europe's largest and richest consumer market, including a huge middle class whose jobs in the civil service, the professions, commerce and finance were generally secure even in a depression, and a growing working-class population whose wages were above the national average. As its economy prospered, so the size and wealth of its market grew. Closeness to the market was especially important for the consumer goods industries that grew fastest between the wars. 'The customer expects free service, and if this is to be properly met it means a factory, or assembly plant, or at least a service depot, near the main market.' London had unrivalled transport connections with the Midlands, the North-West and the rest of the world, giving it ready access to national and international markets, and to the steel, textiles, wood, leather and foodstuffs which were the raw materials of its main industries. The Port of London handled imports and exports worth £510 million in 1936, about 70 per cent more than its only major British rival, Liverpool. As a centre of financial, warehousing, marketing and distributive services, a wholesale market, a provider of public utilities and as a pool of labour with every degree of skill, London could not be beaten. It also shared with Birmingham the advantage of being able to adapt its buildings, machinery and workforce to meet the changing needs of industry. Unlike a coal mine, an iron works or a shipyard, London's light industrial buildings were fit for a wide range of manufacturing uses. Factories for rent were available all over London, especially in Park Royal and other 'trading estates', for those who wanted to take their chance in a new business.[34] Manufacturers liked London because it enabled them to be near to other related industries, especially those that supplied their materials or components, bought their half-finished goods, or packed their finished product. Central London had always had this advantage, but a successful suburban trading estate could offer it, too. As a witness to the 1937–9 Barlow Commission put it: 'On a Trading Estate it is usual to find "on the spot" the services of Wood-workers, Packing Case Makers, Carton and Box Manufacturers, Printers, Foundries, Press Metal Workers, Electrical and other Engineers and Pattern Makers.'[35]

London's old industrial weakness, a shortage of cheap power, was alleviated by the rise of electricity as a source of industrial power in the

1920s. Even before the creation of a national electrical grid (beginning in 1927) London's own electrical power stations ensured its supply. As the Barlow Commission concluded in 1940: 'Some of the industries that are highly concentrated in Greater London – manufactured stationery; musical instruments; scientific instruments; leather goods; fancy articles; fur – would have been in that area even without the development of electricity, but in other cases – such as vacuum cleaners, wireless apparatus, and light engineering generally – the use of electricity is an important cause of their growth there.' The other London drawback, the high cost of land, declined when better transport enabled industrialists to move to cheaper suburban sites. There was a psychological attraction, too: producers were drawn by 'the sight of numerous flourishing factories and the general air of prosperity associated with Greater London, which is, in itself, a big inducement to other industrialists to seek success in an area where the chances of failure must seem remote'.[36] Three-quarters of all foreign firms that opened in England between 1931 and 1935 came to London. To be near the London market, the Barlow Report argued, gave a producer advantages which were not simply a matter of numbers or convenience:

> It has those advantages that are associated with a capital city – probably in greater measure than any other capital city. For some new industries London is the first market in point of time; it provides a sort of initial goodwill and is the first which an industrialist seeks to capture. It contains a large body of wealthy potential customers and attracts many others from the provinces: these constitute the first approach to the national market. Further, many industrialists wish to be near the pooling centre of experience and initiative and the centre of discussion and communication.[37]

The ability of interwar London to attract new jobs and new factories when other cities were losing them was impressive. In 1923 Greater London had 1,950,000 insured workers (those covered by the Unemployment Insurance Acts), making up 18 per cent of Great Britain's 10,826,000 insured workers, and by 1937 its share had increased to 20 per cent (2,653,610 of 13,244,000).[38] If the figure for employed, rather than insured, workers, is taken, London's record is even more impressive. While national employment rose by 24.4 per cent between 1923 and 1937, London and the Home Counties' rose by 49 per cent, and the Midlands, London's nearest rival, by 36 per cent.[39] In general, London attracted workers rather than industry from the depressed areas. A Ministry of Labour survey in 1938 found that nearly 9 per cent of the insured workers of London and the

South-East between the ages of twenty-one and sixty-four (about 280,000 of 3,163,300 men and women) had begun their working lives in another part of Great Britain.[40] Only a handful of firms (fifteen between 1935 and 1938) moved into London from elsewhere in England, and the Ford Motor Company's move from Manchester to Dagenham was exceptional.

London was by far the most popular choice for firms opening new factories. Board of Trade figures show that 3,635 new factories with over twenty-four employees opened in Great Britain between 1932 and 1938, of which 1,573 were in the Greater London region. Of the 2,994 that closed in the same years, only 1,055 were in Greater London. Thus, of Great Britain's net gain of 641 factories in the period of recovery from the Depression, London gained 518, or over 80 per cent. London's new factories were on average smaller than provincial ones, and when the gain is measured in jobs rather than the number of factories, London's share was 97,700, or 40 per cent of the national gain. This was only about a third of the growth in London's insured workforce in these years. The rest came, in roughly equal shares, from the expansion of existing firms and from growth in the non-manufacturing sectors covered by unemployment insurance, mainly building, distribution, catering, road transport and clerical work. The result of all this was that London's share of Great Britain's industrial output rose from 17.1 per cent in 1924 to 24.8 per cent in 1935.[41]

Before 1914 unemployment was at least as high in London, to judge from the levels reported by various trade unions, as it was in other parts of industrial England. Between the wars, though, a gulf began to open between London's experience of unemployment and that of most other manufacturing regions. There was a period of severe industrial contraction in the postwar slump of 1921–2, in which the level of unemployment among manual workers in London (about 14 per cent) was only 1 or 2 per cent below the national average. But in the 1920s, when national unemployment among insured workers remained at over 10 per cent, London's declined to 5 or 6 per cent, and in 1929, when the national rate was almost 10 per cent, the rate within the LCC district was under 2 per cent. In 1932, the worst year of the world depression, Greater London's rate was 13.7 per cent, compared with the Midlands' 20 per cent, the North's 27 per cent, Scotland's 28 per cent, and a national average of 22 per cent. By 1936 unemployment in London had fallen to 6.5 per cent, about half the national rate, while Scotland, Wales and the North were all at 16 per cent or more. In reality London's advantage over the rest of England was even greater than this, since the figures exclude work not covered by unemployment insurance, including commerce, finance and the professions, in which unemployment was low, and which were especially strong in London. In addition, because London had so few workers in industries that were suffering permanent decline (shipbuilding, mining, textiles, iron) and because its economy was so varied, it had a much lower percentage of long-term unemployed, people with little chance of finding work even when the world depression ended. Nationally, 24 per cent of the unemployed in 1936 had been out of work for over a year, but in London and the South-East only 9 per cent were in this position. Most of London's unemployment was cyclical and short-term, rather than structural and long-term.[42] All this does not mean, of course, that unemployment was not a serious problem in London. In 1932, out of 2,745,000 registered unemployed in Great Britain, almost one-eighth, 322,000, were in Greater London.[43]

OLD INDUSTRIES

Because accounts of London's economic success between the wars usually concentrate on the new industries of the Outer London suburbs, it is sometimes forgotten that London's industrial heartland was still in its centre. In 1938, in spite of half a century of industrial decentralization, the LCC district still had 36,911 factories or workshops employing a total of 743,473 workers, half of Greater London's manufacturing workforce. The growth in its insured workforce between 1923 and 1937 (23.7 per cent) was faster than the national rate, and faster than that of any county outside the South-East, though it could not compare with the unrivalled growth of Outer London (81.4 per cent).[44] There was still intense industrial concentration in the central boroughs. In Finsbury, London's second smallest borough, there were over 66,000 manufacturing workers in 587 acres in 1938, as many as there were in the 20,000 acres of Wandsworth, Lewisham and Greenwich combined, and over three times as many as there were in the booming Middlesex industrial estate, Park Royal. There were still clothing workshops by the thousand in Finsbury, Hackney, St Marylebone, Stepney and Westminster, printers in Westminster, Finsbury and South-wark, engineers in Finsbury, Woolwich, Greenwich, Lambeth, Islington, St Pancras, Battersea and Southwark, tanners and brewers in Bermondsey and Stepney, and furniture-makers in Shoreditch, St Pancras, Hackney and Bethnal Green. Businesses that did not need large premises or heavy machinery, and in which proximity to the market and to other industrial services and suppliers was paramount, clung to central London despite its inconveniences. Most of the central London manufacturers were long-established consumer industries, especially clothing, furniture, food and drink, printing, chemicals and engineering (an industry which encompassed new and traditional products), and they were not in decline. New suburban homes needed furniture, wallpaper, electric lamps, irons and wiring, radios, gramophones, telephones and gas stoves, and their affluent inhabitants wanted (and could afford) smart clothes, processed food, beer, cigarettes, books, newspapers, stationery, toys, records and cameras. London's manufacturers could supply them all.[45]

The assumption that 'new' industries were expanding and 'old' ones contracting between the wars does not match London's experience. New factories did not necessarily mean new industries. Of the 929 new factories opened in Greater London between 1933 and 1936, 253 produced clothing, 138 timber and wooden goods, 87 paper, printed goods and stationery, and 53 food, drink and tobacco.[46] Even in Park Royal, the very model of a modern industrial estate, a clear majority of the 325 firms that located there between the wars, including the four biggest employers, were making traditional London goods: clothes, food, drink, furniture, paper products and machinery.[47] Some traditional industries were certainly fading, but even in leather, where shoemaking and tanning were in decline, the rising demand for leatherwares in sport, motoring and furniture increased the London workforce by 18 per cent. The number of workers employed in London's enormous clothing industry continued to grow, despite the decline of the sweated system and the rise of mass production methods. The number of insured clothing workers in Greater London increased by about 20 per cent (from 130,530 to 155,680) between 1925 and 1937, and the full workforce (including people beyond the sixteen to sixty-four age range covered by the state insurance scheme) was probably about 50,000 more than that. Electrification and the simplification of women's dress styles, along with the enforcement of a minimum wage by the Trade Boards established after 1909, encouraged the growth of factory production, but there were still many homeworkers and small workshops in the clothing industry, especially in tailoring and the higher-class West End trade. In 1938 there were over 14,000 premises in which clothing was manufactured within the County, with the greatest concentration (3,261) in Westminster.[48] With all its appearance of Victorian backwardness, the London clothing industry outproduced the more 'modern' industry of Leeds and West Yorkshire in the 1930s, both in its total production and in the output of each worker. According to the 1935 census of production, nearly a half of the United Kingdom's clothing was London-made, and London productivity per worker was over 40 per cent higher than the West Riding's.[49]

The most successful of London's old industries was furniture-making, which reversed its prewar decline and grew at a pace and level that almost matched that of the vehicle industry. Suburban house-building and the rise of hire purchase created as large a mass market for cheap furniture as it did for cheap cars. The insured labour force in the furniture industry, which stood at 35,600 in 1925, rose by nearly 75 per cent to over 62,000 in 1937. An increasing number of these workers were employed in factories in Hackney or Tottenham, but the small workshop industry of Bethnal Green and Shoreditch was still thriving, too.[50] Other traditional London industries grew more modestly. London's huge food, drink and tobacco industry, which had an insured workforce of 118,500 in 1925, grew by 8 per cent (to 128,500) over the next twelve years. Luxury and processed foods, which formed a rising percentage of the metropolitan diet, were a London speciality: it led the country in the production of sweets, biscuits, jam, pickles, distilled spirits, bottled beer, refined sugar, bacon and ice-cream. Ice-cream, the *New Survey of London Life and Labour* reported in 1933, 'has very largely superseded aerated waters as a commodity upon which the street urchin spends his casual penny, and its use as part of the domestic menu has also increased.... To supply this growing demand from all sections of the community, there has arisen a wide variety of ice-cream manufacturers.' London also remained the centre of book, newspaper and magazine production and of legal and commercial publishing, with over 45 per cent of the English workforce. There were 100,000 London printers and bookbinders in 1925 and 107,000 in 1937, most of them working in central London.[51]

NEW AREAS OF GROWTH

The most spectacular growth took place in industries connected with the commercial application of new technology. From the beginnings of electrical telegraphy and submarine electrical cables in the mid-nineteenth century, London's port and railway termini had made it a leading centre of the electricity industry. Several of London's theatres and public buildings (including the Mansion House, the British Museum and the House of Commons) invested in electric incandescent lighting in the early 1880s, and some London suburbs were early investors in municipal electrical enterprise. After 1900 several big firms, especially those involved in heavy electrical engineering (Siemens, Ferranti, General Electric), moved from London to the Midlands or the North, but Woolwich remained an important centre for electric cable production. The growing domestic uses of electricity after 1918, for cooking, lighting, heating, cleaning and refrigeration, reasserted the advantages of London as an industrial location, especially in the lighter branches of the trade. Between 1925 and 1937 London's insured workforce in the production of electrical cables, lamps, flex, telegraph and telephone apparatus, stoves, irons, kettles, wirelesses, motors, switchgear, batteries, meters and similar goods rose by 138 per cent, from 47,580 to 113,480, and London's share of the national workforce rose from 41 per cent to 45 per cent.[52] The production of cars, buses, trams, charabancs (coaches), cycles and aircraft employed 33,840 insured Londoners in 1925 and 64,410 in 1937, a rise of 90 per cent. Many of the skills needed in these industries were familiar to London workers, because they were the same as those in the cabinet-making, upholstery and carriage industries. Engineering and metalware was another success story of the interwar years. In the 1890s, according to Charles Booth, high land and labour costs were driving metal work out of London, which was becoming 'more and more exclusively a repairing shop'. But in the following thirty years provincial manufacturing costs rose, and the open spaces of Outer London became available to industry. The insured London workforce in general engineering, watches, stoves, tools, metalwares and constructional engineering rose by 41 per cent, from 135,000 to 191,000, between 1925 and 1937. There was also strong growth in several smaller industries that benefited from the rise of a modern consumer society: cardboard boxes, paper bags, wallpaper, artificial silk, toys and sports equipment, cameras and glass.[53]

Although the manufacturing strength of the County of London was beyond compare, the main centres of industrial growth between the wars were in Outer London, especially in the 'new' industries, electrical and general engineering and vehicle production. About a third of the industrial growth of Outer London in the 1920s and 1930s resulted from the migration of production, mainly furniture, clothing and light engineering factories, from Inner London. Between 1934 and 1938 203 factories (with twenty-five employees or more) moved from Inner to Outer London, mostly from the crowded central boroughs (Shoreditch, St Pancras, Finsbury, Hackney and Islington) to the open spaces of the northern and western suburbs, where convenient buildings along railway lines or new arterial roads were easy to find. Between 1934 and 1938 Outer London made a net gain of 429 new factories, while the County of London suffered a net loss of 191, and Great Britain as a whole gained 369.[54]

Industries were attracted to Outer London by the availability of cheap land and buildings, sometimes by the supply of labour on new housing estates, by good transport and the proximity of the London market. Export industries, and those that needed heavy imported raw materials, were drawn to the well-established concentration of industry around the docks of the lower Thames, stretching 30 miles from Limehouse and Bermondsey to Tilbury and Gravesend. This riverside belt contained large-scale industries of almost every kind: oil refineries, cement, chemical and asbestos works, paper mills, gasworks, electricity generators, sugar refineries, timber yards, factories making chains, steel ropes, boilers, electric cables, margarine, flour, soap, cars, locomotives, marine engines, munitions, shoes and plasterboard. Ford Motor Company's move to Dagenham Dock in 1931 brought much-needed work to the tenants of the Becontree estate and stimulated other industries in the area. By 1951 (the first census since 1931) 12 per cent of London's manufacturing workforce (180,000 people) worked in this riverside belt, as far downstream as Dagenham.[55]

The second major industrial zone in Outer East London was the Lea valley, between Waltham Abbey and Walthamstow, including Enfield, Edmonton and Tottenham. Many East End clothing, furniture and engineering firms in need of cheaper or larger premises within easy reach of the London market moved into the Lea valley in the early twentieth century. Between 1900 and 1933 the number of firms in the area had increased from twenty to 120, at least thirty of them having moved from the East End. Between 1935 and 1938 another sixty-eight new factories opened, of which about half were new, and a third migrants from the East End. The Lea valley also diversified into office equipment, chemicals and electrical engineering, especially the production of radios, light bulbs and other small electrical goods for the London market. In 1951 8 per cent of London's 1.5 million industrial workers worked in the district.[56]

The greatest of the new industrial zones was in north-west London, with major centres in Park Royal, Hayes, Wembley, Southall and Acton. This industrial district also spread along the North Circular Road and the Edgware Road to Cricklewood, Hendon and Colindale, where there were important aircraft and munitions factories, and along the Great Western Railway and Western Avenue to Perivale, Greenford and Northolt. North-west London had the advantage of easy communications with the shops of the West End, and also with Birmingham and the Midlands, a major market and a supplier of components and raw materials. At the centre of this huge industrial district was the Park Royal estate. This was an area of about 330 acres, bounded and served by the Grand Junction Canal, Western Avenue, the Great Western Railway, the North Circular Road and the railways of the established industrial suburb of Willesden. In 1924 a catering company, Allnatt's of Reading, converted derelict First World War munitions factories into accommodation for children who were visiting the British Empire Exhibition at Wembley. When the exhibition closed Major Allnatt cleared the site and erected factory buildings to rent, lease or sell to industrial enterprises. Smaller landowners in the neighbourhood followed suit, and by 1939 there were 250 firms in Park Royal, employing about 20,000 people. Between 1928 and 1935, when industry was collapsing in other parts of England, new factories or workshops were built and occupied in Park Royal at the rate of one a fortnight. Some, like McVitie and Price biscuits and Cerebos salt, moved to London from elsewhere in Britain (these two from Edinburgh and Newcastle respectively), and others escaped from cramped premises in Inner London. Harold Wesley (stationery) and Gevaert (photographical supplies) came from Finsbury, Crypto Electrical from Bermondsey, and so on. Although about 36 per cent of the firms in Park Royal made 'new' products (motor vehicles and their components, cosmetics or electrical goods), about a third of the workers on the estate in the late 1930s worked for four fairly traditional businesses, McVitie's, Heinz, Harold Wesley, and Guinness, whose brewery opened in 1935. What the firms had in common was not their 'newness', but their need for cheap and spacious premises and easy access to the London market.[57] Park Royal was unique, but not alone. In Wembley, about a mile to its north, buildings left empty after the British Empire Exhibition of 1924–5 were converted to industrial use. And to the west, large-scale industry developed in Southall and Hayes, where the main products were food (jam, cocoa, groceries, tinned food), heavy vehicles, cycles, aircraft engines, gas and gramophones.[58]

THE BARLOW COMMISSION

Just as London's commercial success had been identified as the reason for the stagnation of provincial ports in earlier centuries, so in the 1930s London's industrial prosperity began to be seen as a cause of the problems of the depressed areas. The idea that stopping the growth of industry in London might open the way to recovery for northern England and South Wales was given official support by Sir Malcolm Stewart, the Commissioner for Special Areas, in 1936, and exhaustively investigated between 1937 and 1939 by a Royal Commission on the Distribution of the Industrial Population, chaired by Sir Montague Barlow. The Barlow Commission learned from expert witnesses and government departments the extent to which London's industrial growth had outpaced the rest of the country, and why industry, left to its own devices, would usually choose London in preference to other industrial locations. It heard arguments from the Port of London Authority and the London Passenger Transport Board that London's growth was not achieved at the expense of other areas, and could not realistically be stopped:

> Recent developments are justified as naturally and economically sound. To stay what is being done is difficult, to undo it absurd. Neither industry nor the state could afford the cost of such a transformation. . . .
>
> The country can only be saved at the price of concentrating industry and population in large aggregates. . . . The saving of the country depends upon the industrialization of the towns. . . .
>
> A living organism cannot be static and survive. . . . A metropolis in decay must be one of the greatest evils that can befall a country.[59]

The evidence presented by the LCC showed that the environmental and medical consequences of London's growth had not been as severe as those of the previous century. Although London's death rates from some urban diseases (infantile diarrhoea, bronchial pneumonia, tuberculosis) were still above the national average, overall death rates (12.1 per 1,000 in 1931–5) were only fractionally above the English average of 12 per 1,000. London infant mortality, which was always taken as a sensitive index of economic and environmental conditions, had not only fallen (in line with national trends) by over 40 per cent since the Great War, but had actually been lower than the national average (64 per 1,000 compared with 68 per 1,000) in the later 1920s. Middlesex County Council's submission showed that in Outer London, the focus of the Commission's concern, death rates, both general and infant, were almost 20 per cent below the national average in 1936. On the other side, they heard from Sir Charles Bressey, the engineer in charge of London's highway development, that London's uncontrolled growth was undermining the value of its new arterial roads, and from Sir Raymond Unwin, the great town planner, that London's roads could never be adequate, because they simply created 'opportunities for more traffic to rush in; so that saturation point is again soon reached'.[60]

Sir Ernest Simon, one of the business and political leaders of Manchester, argued that London's attractiveness was impoverishing the public life of the provincial cities: 'The best people in every walk of life almost inevitably gravitate to London; the high salaries and profits are in London;

power is in London.'[61] The most emphatic denunciation of London's growth came from William Robson, of the London School of Economics, whose book on the history of London's government appeared in 1939. Robson argued that London had grown too big to be well governed, or to command the loyalty and interest of its citizens. 'There is virtually no recognition of the metropolis as a whole. Most people have come to think mainly of their own district.' Only by controlling the location of industry, Robson argued, could London's growth be stopped. Robson's most compelling argument, and one which carried great weight in the Commission's final report, was a strategic one: 'Great Britain is clearly running enormous risks in having so great a proportion of her population, wealth and manufacturing resources concentrated in one area situated within a few minutes' flying distance of the coast.'[62]

The Commission's final report, which had a powerful influence on the planning of London during and after the Second World War, emphasized (as its terms of reference had invited it to do) the 'social, economic, and stategical disadvantages' of the growing concentration of industry in London. Although the Commission was forced to concede that Londoners no longer suffered disproportionately from the old social evils of disease and high mortality, and that their medical, educational and cultural facilities were unrivalled, it identified the problems of traffic congestion, long and costly journeys between home and work, unplanned suburban sprawl and the remoteness of the countryside, as the new social evils from which Londoners needed to be released. On the strength of Simon's evidence, the Report claimed that 'the attraction to the Metropolis of the best industrial, financial, commercial, and general ability' represented 'a serious drain on the rest of the country', though it was unable to offer evidence that London's industry had grown at the expense of other regions. More convincingly, the Report (which was completed in December 1939) emphasized London's vulnerability to air attack. The Commission recommended the creation of a National Industrial Board with powers to prevent the location of new industry in London and the Home Counties, and with a duty to encourage the dispersal of industry from London in order to achieve 'a reasonable balance of industrial development' throughout the country. The members of the Commission disagreed about London's responsibility for the plight of the depressed areas. A minority argued that London's growth was 'little more than the normal expansion of a prosperous area able to feed its prosperity by drawing human resources from other places', and that the depressed areas lost population because of their own industrial decline, not because of London's magnetic attraction: 'The solution to the problem of unemployment in the Depressed Areas is also the solution of the problem presented by the rapid growth and further excessive industrialization of London and the Home Counties.'[63]

THE CITY

If the Barlow Commission had looked beyond manufacturing industry, into the worlds of commerce, finance, retailing, entertainment, catering, building or government, it would have exposed an even greater degree of metropolitan prosperity and dominance. In 1937 over 47 per cent of London's insured workers (about 1.25 million people) worked in the service industries (building, distribution, local government, public works, road transport, hotels, entertainment, sport, professional services and laundry), constituting roughly a quarter of all England's insured service workers. The number of London office workers is not easy to calculate. The City had a working population of just over 500,000 in 1939, but probably only about 300,000 of these were office workers. If the amount of office space is any guide, there were slightly more office workers in the rest of central London. This would give a figure close to the one calculated for central London by D. F. Stevens for 1948: 615,000.[64]

In many respects, the City remained very prosperous for much of the interwar period. Its banks and insurance companies built impressive new offices, its workforce rose by over 40 per cent between 1911 and 1938, and its importance in the national economy was as great as ever. The postwar world economy was unstable and fragmented, but the City's financiers had the skill and flexibility to take advantage of the new opportunities this instability offered. In the early 1920s the City became the world's main centre for dealing in foreign exchange, until the return of the gold standard and fixed exchange rates spoiled the business in 1925. The rise of motoring and air travel, and the growing fear of burglary and kidnap, created new markets for the insurance industry, making up for the decline in shipping business in the 1930s. Life insurance funds and Lloyd's membership both tripled between the wars, and several important northern insurance companies moved their headquarters to London in order to manage their investments more easily. London accountancy firms, especially those concerned with insolvency, also did particularly well in the 1930s.[65]

But underlying trends were not so promising. By the end of the war the City's uniquely important place in the international financial system had been seriously damaged, and the system itself had been undermined by the suspension of the gold standard, the disruption of exchange rates, the decline of free trade, and great changes in the pattern of international commerce. The City's ability before the war to regulate the international economy rested on the fact that the Bank of England could adjust the bank rate to draw short-term funds into London (mainly from Europe) and redirect them (at a price) to countries that needed them. London's strong creditor status and the power of the British economy enabled the Bank to make interest-rate decisions in the light of the international situation, without worrying unduly about their effects on foreign confidence in sterling or their impact on domestic industry. After 1918 all this had changed. Britain's falling economic competitiveness, the enormous industrial and commercial prosperity of the United States (two trends which the war accelerated, but did not create), and the United States' emergence after the war as the world's leading creditor and overseas investor, undermined the economic foundations of the City's supremacy. The weakness of the British economy prevented the City from recovering its position as the dominant international investor, and wartime inflation and the growing strength of the dollar meant that sterling was no longer the unrivalled world currency, as trusted as gold itself. The City was more involved in British government and industrial finance, and interest-rate decisions had to be made in the light of their domestic effects as much as their international ones. Moreover, London's heavy short-term debts (the result of massive wartime borrowing) meant that financial decisions, especially on interest rates, had to take into account the reactions of foreign holders of sterling securities. 'The possible liquidation of these securities at times of general financial difficulty meant that London could no longer regulate the flow of sterling to the rest of the world on its own terms.'[66] The gold standard, which had given Victorian London its pivotal position, was only restored imperfectly for a few years in the late 1920s, and then it lacked the foundations of confidence, economic harmony and a single undisputed focal point that had stabilized it in the past. When London tried to operate in the world economic crisis of 1929–31 as she had done in earlier crises, acting as a lender of last resort to shore up struggling economies in Europe, South America and the Commonwealth, the Bank of England was unwilling to raise interest rates sufficiently to draw in the necessary short-term funds, and foreign confidence in sterling was so weak that funds flowed out of London rather than into it. The two other great financial centres, Paris and New York, were unwilling or unable to shoulder the burden that was proving too heavy for London to carry alone, and the system collapsed.[67]

The London banking system, unlike those of Germany and the United

States, proved strong enough to withstand the crisis of 1931, but the rise of economic protectionism and the collapse of the network of international trade and credit in the 1930s robbed the City of some of its most important functions. National policies of currency devaluation, import tariffs and exchange controls prevented the recovery of world trade in the 1930s, and greatly reduced the demand for trading or investment finance, which the City had always specialized in providing. Plenty of money flowed into London in the 1930s, but most of it was invested in Treasury bills and government stock, an activity which hardly tested the skills and experience of London bill brokers. 'Between 1914 and 1938, the London money market had been transformed from an international centre for the collection and use of funds into an increasingly domestic institution channelling British savings into the finance of the National Debt.'[68] The National Debt, which had risen ten-fold in the First World War, assumed an importance in the City's affairs that it had not had since the early nineteenth century, before the coming of the railways. Foreign securities, which had made up 60 per cent of all securities listed on the Stock Exchange in 1910, were only 30 per cent in 1938, while the proportion of government stocks had risen to 43 per cent. The Stock Exchange's declining international importance led to a fall in the number of jobbers, from 2,500 to 1,500, over the same period. But the domestication of the City also involved a greater willingness on the part of its financial institutions to direct their investors' money into the more profitable parts of British industry. Promising new enterprises such as Pye Radio and Hepworth's tailoring got finance from specialist City investment trusts in the 1930s.[69]

THE OFFICE WORLD

The growth of London's office workforce reflected the continuing expansion of traditional office employers, banking, insurance, trading houses and government, and also a tendency for manufacturing firms to build large and heavily staffed administrative headquarters in central London. By 1939 about a half of Britain's major companies had a London head office, compared with about a fifth in 1914.[70] There was evidence of the growth of London's office economy in almost every part of central London north of the Thames. The City still led the way in office building, although its network of narrow courts and alleys remained largely unchanged. Two big clearing banks, the Westminster and the National Provincial, built new City headquarters between the wars, but the Midland outdid them by employing

Sir Edwin Lutyens, the architect of New Delhi, the Trafalgar Square fountains and the Cenotaph, to design its magnificent head office in Poultry. The Bank of England solved its shortage of space by gutting Sir John Soane's beautiful and interesting single-storey bank, and replacing it with a vast and pretentious building by Herbert Baker, Lutyens's collaborator in New Delhi. This, in Pevsner's opinion, was 'the worst individual loss suffered by London architecture in the first half of the twentieth century'.[71] Trading and shipping companies built themselves new City offices in the 1920s: Cunard and Lloyd's underwriters in Leadenhall, the Hudson's Bay Company in Bishopsgate. Other office blocks, such as Adelaide House, near London Bridge, were built with no particular client in mind. On the northern edge of the City the building of River Plate House (for the Buenos Aires and Great Southern Railway) and Britannic House (for the Anglo-Persian Oil Company) completed the transformation of Finsbury Circus and Moorgate into an entirely commercial quarter in the 1920s. Finsbury Square, in which the Maypole Dairy built its new headquarters in the 1920s, was going the same way. These new buildings, along with the increasing employment of women inside them, were beginning to give the City a more modern atmosphere, although the conditions of work in many City offices would not have seemed strange to Paul Dombey or Charles Pooter.[72]

The westward expansion of office-building continued between the wars. On the western edge of the City, the vast Unilever House was built next to Blackfriars Bridge, on the site of Henry VIII's Bridewell Palace (demolished in 1863), in 1931. Between 1928 and 1935 the building of new offices for the *Daily Telegraph*, *Daily Express* and Reuter's began to give Fleet Street a distinctively modern appearance, and beyond it the Aldwych–Kingsway development of 1900–1905 was given over almost entirely to offices. Between 1906 and 1930 a succession of imposing government and commercial buildings filled the two streets: Australia House, India House, Africa House, Bush House (the headquarters of the BBC), Kingsway House (the Public Trustee Office), the Air Ministry and the offices of Marconi, Kodak, the *Morning Post*, W. H. Smith, Waterman's Pens, General Electric, Shell and General Assurance. In the West End, the huge Hotel Cecil in the Strand was rebuilt in 1931 to become Shell-Mex House (with London's largest clock), and two of Frederick Gordon's vast hotels in Northumberland Avenue, the Metropole and the Grand, were taken over as offices. Nearby, the Adam brothers' beautiful 1770s riverside terrace, the Adelphi, was destroyed to make room for a large office block, also called the Adelphi, in 1936.

The great public corporations that were established between the wars generally built their headquarters in the West End. The BBC moved to Broadcasting House, its massive new office in Portland Place, in 1931, and the London Passenger Transport Board took over the Underground group's new Broadway House (designed, like their stations, by Charles Holden) in Victoria. Only the LCC chose a South London site, building its impressive County Hall on the riverside near Waterloo Station between 1911 and 1933. The transformation of Bloomsbury by the expansion of London University accelerated in the 1930s, when Senate House, a massive administrative and library centre for the university, was built (to Holden's designs) on a site created by the clearance of 11 acres behind the British Museum. Government offices began to overflow from Whitehall into Millbank, where the Board of Trade occupied a vast new office building known as Thames House, at the end of Lambeth Bridge. Next door to it one of the biggest of the new industrial conglomerates, ICI, occupied its imposing new offices, Imperial Chemical House, in 1928.

Smaller businesses were also on the move. A study of business locations between 1918 and 1966 shows that the drift away from traditional concentrations, especially in the City, Fleet Street and Covent Garden areas, was already taking place between the wars. Publishers were still clustered around St Paul's and Covent Garden, but new companies were opening in Bloomsbury, especially near the British Museum. Advertising agencies moved into Soho (to be near the Wardour Street film business) and the West End, reducing the proportion of agencies in Fleet Street, their traditional location, from 31 to 23 per cent between 1918 and 1938. At the same time the concentration of constructional engineering firms around Victoria Street increased, while the number of such firms in the City apparently declined.[73] The shift from residential to business use often took place without rebuilding. A study of Fitzroy Square, on the northern border of the West End, found that half the houses were predominantly residential in 1886, and that the rest contained about forty clubs, hotels, and professional or financial offices. Between 1920 and 1940, the number of businesses in Fitzroy Square rose from forty to seventy, with professions, dealers and manufacturers making up a growing proportion of them, leaving only one or two houses in private hands. The effect of this process, repeated in hundreds of streets and squares in Westminster and St Marylebone, was to reduce the residential population of these two boroughs from 316,000 in 1901 to 246,000 in 1921 and 215,000 in 1938.[74]

Shopping Centres

The growth in the mass market for new clothes, furniture and other consumer goods continued to have an impressive impact on the economy and appearance of London. According to the 1921 census, 540,000 people in Greater London worked in wholesale or retail distribution. About 369,000 of these worked in retailing, and 128,000 were shop assistants. By 1938, to judge from the statistics for insured workers, these numbers had risen by about 40 per cent. Although the striking development in retailing since the 1870s had been the rise of the cooperative store, the department store and the multiple or 'chain' store (such companies as Lipton's, Maypole Dairies, Boots, W. H. Smith and Woolworth's), most London shops were still small independent businesses. A typical suburban Broadway surveyed in the 1920s had 130 small shops, forty-four multiples, two cooperatives, and eleven local department stores.[75] These small businesses faced growing competition, in the suburbs as well as the West End, from chains such as Woolworth's, which opened about sixty new stores in the County of London between 1912 and 1930, and Marks and Spencer, which added thirty-two new stores to its fourteen older ones in the same period.[76] About half the shop assistants in these stores were women, generally unmarried and under thirty-five. But the total retailing workforce included a majority who did not serve behind counters: clerks, porters, packers, lift attendants, window-dressers, cashiers, errand boys and van boys (typical first jobs for London school leavers), warehousemen and managers.

London's main shopping centre seemed to be moving west again, just as it had moved from Ludgate Hill and St Paul's Churchyard to Oxford Street and Regent Street in the first half of the nineteenth century. The two greatest Edwardian stores, Selfridge's and Harrods, were on the western edge of the established shopping centre, and between the wars High Street Kensington, which had been a busy street of small shops before 1914, gained three big department stores, Derry and Toms, Pontings and Barker's.[77] Barker's owned all three of these by 1920. Rising to the challenge, Oxford Street, 'the greatest shopping thoroughfare in the British Empire', added to its collection of large stores: Peter Robinson (1924), Bourne and Hollingsworth (1924), Marks and Spencer (1930) and C & A (1933), joined Marshall and Snelgrove (1870), John Lewis (1890s, rebuilt 1939), Waring and Gillow (1906), D. H. Evans (1908, rebuilt 1937) and Selfridge's (1908).[78] Many of the new stores were built with steel frames, a method of construction whose advantages became clear during the Blitz.

During and after the First World War the richest stores took control of their weaker rivals. Debenhams gained control of Marshall and Snelgrove and Harvey Nichols; Harrods, which already owned Dickins and Jones, took over Swan and Edgar, D. H. Evans and Shoolbred's (which it closed); and Selfridge's bought several big suburban stores and (in 1927) Whiteley's. The decline of Whiteley's undermined the new group's financial position, and in 1940 Selfridge was forced to sell his stores in Brixton, Hampstead, Streatham and Holloway to the expanding John Lewis Partnership.[79]

The most dramatic concession to the demands of modern retailing was the demolition and rebuilding of the whole of John Nash's Regent Street. Discussions began before the First World War, when the original leases were about to end, and when it was generally agreed that the street's small shops (many of which had already been converted and expanded to the limits of safety) could no longer compete with rival West End streets in the growing market for clothes and other consumer goods. Disagreements between planners and shopkeepers delayed the redevelopment until after the war, but in the 1920s the rebuilding of the whole street went ahead at full speed. The most striking features of the new Regent Street, which was virtually completed by 1926, were Norman Shaw's large baroque Piccadilly Hotel (1905–8), Blomfield's new Swan and Edgar store and County Fire Office, Tanner's Oxford Circus, and the new Liberty's department store, which combined a fairly conventional colonnaded building on Regent Street with an extraordinary half-timbered Tudor one, made from the timbers of two Victorian warships, on Great Marlborough Street. The new street was generally compared unfavourably with Nash's masterpiece, but at least, as the *Daily News* said, its 'vitality and brilliance and audacity' represented the spirit of the age. 'It is more suited to the flashing bus and the rapid streams of polished motorcars than to the old-fashioned coach-and-four. It is a part of changing London and changing England.'[80]

THE DECLINE OF HIGH SOCIETY

Tourism, business and shopping rescued the West End when a traditional source of its prosperity, the expenditure of a few hundred landed families, was in decline. Lady Kitty Vincent, writing in 1926, spoke of the London season as a rather faded version of what it had once been: 'The days of the magnificent functions are over.... Before the war very few of the young men and practically no women worked.... Nowadays the majority of the men work in the City, and the women who do not earn their living by running a hat shop or a decorating business are employed in assisting various charitable associations.'[81] This was not a matter of hardship, but of the growing sense of independence among upper-class young women which made the parentally supervised marriage market (and thus the London season) an anachronism.[82]

The landed aristocracy between the wars were in the last stages of a long process of economic decline. The position of landowners had been undermined since the mid-1870s by cheap imports and falling grain prices, which meant struggling tenants, falling rent incomes and declining land values. The impact of the agricultural depression of 1873–96 varied according to the crops grown, but in the arable South-East, which was likely to produce more West End gentry than the pastoral North-West, rental incomes fell by about 41 per cent between 1874 and 1898. This meant that by the 1890s fewer southern landlords were enjoying the income levels needed to own or rent a second home in London. The introduction of death duties in Lloyd George's 1909 budget made the position of landowners even worse. There were heavy land sales just before the First World War, and a great rush of selling between 1918 and 1921, a period of booming crop prices (but controlled rents) in which up to a quarter of English land changed hands. The position of those who did not sell deteriorated sharply between the wars. The average price of a quarter of wheat, which had been about 55s in the 1860s and about 25s in the 1890s, fell after its wartime recovery to about 11s in the later 1920s and 5s or 6s between 1931 and 1935. This spectacular fall did not bring great benefits to the consumer of the London loaf, which cost more in the 1930s than it had in the 1870s and 1880s, but it certainly transformed the position of landowners, whose rents fell in the 1930s to their lowest point since 1870.[83]

With falling rents, land prices at a third of their mid-Victorian levels, and mortgages and rising taxes to pay, landlords had to cut their costs or find better investments than property. Shortening their annual visit to London or selling their London house was a policy that many families adopted. The disposal of the great aristocratic estates had started around 1890, when Lord Salisbury sold his property in the Strand and Lord Calthorpe sold his houses in the City Road. Lord Kensington sold London property worth £865,000 in 1902–3, and the Duke of Bedford sold Covent Garden, which had been in his family since the Reformation, for £2 million in 1913. During the First World War the Duke of Sutherland sold his magnificent Stafford House (now Lancaster House) to William Lever, the millionaire soapmaker (a transaction that symbolized the shifting balance of power and wealth), and in 1919 Lord Salisbury's mansion in Arlington

Street, Lord Dartmouth's in Mayfair and the Duke of Devonshire's in Park Lane were all sold off. Over the next few years the 20-acre Berkeley Square estate was sold for £2 million, the Duke of Bedford raised £2 million by selling land in Bloomsbury, and Lords Portman, Southampton and Camden sold property in St Marylebone, Euston and Camden Town. Towards the end of the 1920s Lord Howard de Walden sold 40 acres around Great Portland Street and the Duke of Westminster sold the Millbank estate. One by one, the aristocratic estates that had been accumulated and developed in the eighteenth century were falling apart.[84]

The triumph of commerce over aristocracy is best represented by what happened to Park Lane and Berkeley Square. In Park Lane Lutyens's large Grosvenor House Hotel was built on the site of the Duke of Westminster's Grosvenor House in 1926–8, and the Dorchester Hotel replaced the demolished Dorchester House in 1929. In Berkeley Square, one of the centrepieces of aristocratic Mayfair, Lansdowne House, which had been one of London's greatest political mansions ever since Lord Shelburne moved into it in 1768, was demolished in 1936 and replaced by the huge office block, also called Lansdowne House, which filled the south side of the Square. A year later, more modest houses on the east side were cleared to make room for an even bigger block, Berkeley House.

Sales such as this knocked the heart out of the old aristocratic season. Of the great houses that the Duke of Portland remembered as providing the best hospitality in London before the First World War, Hertford, Grosvenor, Dorchester, Montagu, Lansdowne, Devonshire, Spencer, Chesterfield, Stafford, Bridgewater, Apsley, Londonderry and Holland Houses, only the last four remained as private mansions in 1937.[85] Of the other nine, five were demolished to make way for offices or hotels, one (Montagu House) was taken over in 1916 by the Ministry of Labour, one (Spencer House) became a club, and two (Hertford and Stafford Houses) were converted into museums. By 1939 only eight London mansions remained of the twenty-five or so that there had been in 1914. Even those aristocrats who retained their London mansions generally withdrew from social leadership between the wars, leaving London 'society' in the hands of upstarts and American heiresses whose moral and political weaknesses were exposed at the time of Edward VIII's abdication in 1936. The old exclusiveness and extravagance that had characterized prewar London 'society' seemed outdated and inappropriate in the 1930s, and leading Conservative politicians (unlike Labour's Ramsay Macdonald) generally kept away from it. 'Society as such now means nothing, and it represents nothing except wealth and advertisement', Lady Londonderry wrote in 1938. '. . . England has become Americanized.'[86]

Lady Londonderry kept up the tradition of grand entertaining at Londonderry House into the 1960s, but she was alone in doing so. The Second World War virtually brought the last days of aristocratic entertaining to an end. There were no more balls after 1939 in Stratford House (or Derby House), which became a publisher's office and then the Oriental Club after 1945. Holland House was ruined by bombing in 1941, and Bridgewater House, also damaged in the Blitz, was sold by the Earl of Ellesmere to the Legal and General Assurance Society after the war. So the second Great War finished off the job which the first one had begun.[87]

'GENUINELY SEEKING WORK'

The money troubles of West End aristocrats, distressing as they must have been, were not the worst of London's economic problems. There was a dark side to London life between the wars, which historians sometimes ignore in their anxiety to demolish the myth of the 'hungry thirties'. Registered unemployment (counting only those in insured industries) in London in the interwar years averaged 200,000. In bad years (1921–2, 1931, 1933–4 and 1938) it was around 250,000, and in 1932 it was over 320,000. There were heavy concentrations of unemployment in London's own depressed areas, the riverside districts of Bermondsey, Poplar, Stepney and especially West Ham, where unemployment was about 27 per cent, 4 or 5 per cent above the national average, in 1931 and 1932. London offered so many opportunities to find work that most of its unemployed were only out of work for two or three months at a time, but this meant that a far higher percentage of Londoners suffered a spell of unemployment in a typical year than the 8 or 9 per cent registered as out of work. The Ministry of Labour put the figure in an average year at around 25 per cent, or 500,000 people.[88]

In London the phrase 'genuinely seeking work' carried a meaning that it could not carry in Durham or South Wales. The vigour and variety of the London economy meant that Londoners had within an hour's journey jobs that a Welshman or Liverpudlian would have to travel hundreds of miles to find. But, as Hubert Llewellyn Smith explained in the *New Survey of London Life and Labour*, finding work in a depression was not easy, especially for the unskilled:

Labourers are still to a large extent dependent on walking, and their morning tramps in search of work are often more or less random wanderings, only preferable to mere loafing as a means of killing time. As days and weeks pass without success the very aimlessness of the tramp and the absence of the stimulus of hope conduce to physical fatigue and exhaustion ... thanks to unemployment benefit the tramping has not to be done on an empty stomach nor under the harassing anxiety lest wife and children should starve.

Skilled workers were more discriminating in their search for jobs:

The search is usually confined within the limits of wage-earning occupations, and skilled men cling tenaciously to their trade before they will bring themselves to accept unskilled work. There is little inclination among the unemployed to attempt to strike out an independent line by taking up such occupations as street selling, window cleaning or wood chopping.... the unemployed tend to cling to the relative certainty of insurance benefit rather than to take unknown risks.[89]

There was still plenty of casual and short-term work in London. The building industry, which employed roughly one insured Londoner in thirteen, was based almost entirely on casual labour. A building employer would tender for one job after another, and (as the *New Survey* put it) 'even if he secures a succession of jobs he will not normally engage his men for more than one at a time. Although one can find cases of labourers, as well as skilled craftsmen, remaining in the employ of one firm for many years, the essence of building employment is that when a job is finished it is for the worker to find another.' Most builders were on one or two days' notice, and a spell of bad weather could throw them out of work without any warning.[90]

The casual system also survived in the docks, although Lord Shaw's Court of Inquiry in 1920 had declared that it should be 'torn up by the roots'. A registration scheme agreed after the First World War gradually reduced the dock labour pool from 60,000 to 36,000 men in the 1920s, making it much harder for the London unemployed to take refuge in casual dock work, and changes in the pattern of world trade reduced some of the wild fluctuations in the demand for labour that had plagued the Victorian docks. At the same time, the greater use of cranes, electrical trucks and grain conveyors, the spread of piecework, and the tendency of traders to remove goods without using the docks' warehouses, cut the number of men given work on an average day from about 34,000 in 1921 to 26,000 in

1931. As a result, most registered dockers could only expect about three days' work a week, and much of their time was wasted in fruitless journeys, waiting for the call to work, and loitering in the hope that work would turn up later in the day. On the other hand, dockers' interests were protected by a large and powerful union, the Transport and General Workers' (created by amalgamation in 1922), and their daily rate of pay in the 1920s was about 150 per cent more than the prewar rate, giving them a real increase of roughly 60 per cent. Furthermore, a change in unemployment insurance rules in 1924 enabled dockers to draw benefit for their non-working days. There were still great disparities between the best- and worst-placed dockers, but as a group, the *New Survey* concluded, their position had been transformed since 1918 by registration, unionization and unemployment insurance. 'The docker is no longer a social pariah and his trade is becoming one to which fathers are glad to bring their sons.'[91]

LEVELS OF POVERTY

Two things made the impact of unemployment less savage than it had been in the nineteenth century: employment exchanges made the search for jobs a less hit and miss affair, and unemployment benefit, however meagre and hedged around with conditions, saved the unemployed and their families from destitution and the workhouse. Unemployment insurance, which had been introduced for a narrow range of industries (employing under a quarter of the male workforce) in 1911, was extended in 1920 to most industrial workers, and many others earning under £250 a year. As mass unemployment and social unrest developed in the early 1920s the pretence that this was a self-funding insurance scheme, rather than a Treasury-funded substitute for Poor Law outdoor relief, was abandoned. Insured workers who were unemployed for longer than the period covered by their insurance contributions could draw 'extended benefit' (which was also called 'transitional' or 'uncovenanted' benefit, or the 'dole'), at a level which was determined, in the depression years of 1931–4, by a searching 'means test' of a family's resources and income. The amount generally given in benefit (29s a week for a family of five in the early 1930s) ensured survival, but it did not buy enough food to keep a family in health, and it was only three-quarters of the income needed to reach the poverty line, as defined by the *New Survey*. It was certainly not enough to keep a lazy man in comfort. Llewellyn Smith rejected the common view that the 'dole' discouraged its recipients from seeking work: 'The unemployed now have greater powers of waiting, which is equivalent to greater bargaining power with regard to the terms of their future employment. But the abuse of this waiting power is exceptional, and the bulk of the unemployed earnestly desire and actively seek re-employment.... Wherever work is to be had there is no lack of eager applicants.' The men seen 'loafing' on the streets or in libraries, E. W. Bakke observed, were nearly all youngsters, old age pensioners, or men demoralized by their repeated failure to find work.[92]

The *New Survey of London Life and Labour*, which attempted to measure poverty in the London of the later 1920s in order to compare it with the levels found by Charles Booth in the 1890s, is by far the fullest and most thorough contemporary account of working-class life and living standards in interwar London. Its investigations, which cover the years 1928–31, were carried out and written up by a London School of Economics team which included Sir William Beveridge, Director of the LSE, Sir Hubert Llewellyn Smith, the government's chief economic adviser until 1927, and Professor A. L. Bowley, a pioneer in social statistics and sampling techniques. The results of their survey were marred (as Booth's had been) by the difficulty of defining poverty. The writers of the *New Survey* claimed to be using the same poverty yardstick as the one used by Booth, but in fact the income level they chose as marking the poverty borderline, 40s a week, was based on the average spending (adjusted for inflation) of Booth's classes C, D and E. Since class E was above Booth's poverty threshhold, and represented 42 per cent of the population of East London in Booth's day, the *New Survey* in fact measured a much more broadly defined group than Booth's poor. Therefore their finding, that 8.7 per cent of Londoners (10.6 per cent, or 260,000, in East London and 7.2 per cent, or 230,000, in West London) lived in poverty in 1929 cannot be compared with Booth's famous 30.7 per cent.[93] Colin and Christine Linsley, who have reworked the *New Survey* figures, calculate that the percentage of Londoners 'in poverty' in 1929, according to Booth's 1890 yardstick, was around 5 per cent. But accepted minimum standards of diet, accommodation and clothing had changed greatly between 1890 and 1930, and if the basic household budget described in Rowntree's *The Human Needs of Labour* (1937) is applied to the findings of the *New Survey*, it appears that 21 per cent of London households lived in poverty in 1929.[94] In any case, poverty was not something that would stay still long enough for Llewellyn Smith and his colleagues to measure it. Even in 1929, a year when unemployment levels were low, the *New Survey* found that 48 per cent of poverty was the result of unemployment, with 8.5 per cent due to old age, 24.5 per cent to the lack of a male earner, and the rest to low wages and large families. The number in poverty must have risen significantly – probably doubled – when unemployment rose by 160 per cent between 1929 and 1932.[95]

THE POSTWAR CRISIS

The development of unemployment benefit and poor relief policy in the interwar years took place in an entirely different political and economic atmosphere from the one that had prevailed before 1914. In a period of mass unemployment, in which working people had been radicalized by the experience of war, postwar disappointment and the international growth of socialism, universal benefit was a public order necessity, not a temporary gesture of sympathy or a modest extension of the insurance principle. In the months following the armistice of November 1918 there was a keen sense of anxiety in government circles (stimulated by graphic and well-informed reports from Scotland Yard's Director of Intelligence, Sir Basil Thomson) over the possibility of revolutionary violence in London, Glasgow, Liverpool and other cities. The fact that most of the Metropolitan Police had gone on strike over pay and union recognition for a week in August–September 1918 created lingering doubts over their reliability in an emergency. High prices, food and fuel shortages, rapid demobilization, unemployment, the influence of the Russian Revolution, and exaggerated expectations of postwar social and economic reform (especially among ex-soldiers), all contributed towards the tension of 1919–21. London's part in creating this dangerous atmosphere cannot be disentangled from that of other cities, but it certainly played an important role. The powerful combination of industrial militancy and socialist sympathies was symbolized by the *Jolly George* incident of 10 May 1920, when workers in the East India Docks refused to allow a ship laden with munitions to sail for Poland, which was at war with Soviet Russia. To ease the national crisis, the government extended the 1911 unemployment insurance scheme to cover 11 million urban manual workers, first with a temporary 'out of work donation' in late 1918, and then in the 1920 Unemployment Insurance Act.[96] This was a vital concession. In 1937 George Orwell suggested, in *The Road to Wigan Pier*, that 'fish-and-chips, art-silk stockings, tinned salmon, cut-price chocolate ... the movies, the radio, strong tea, and the Football Pools have between them averted revolution'. Perhaps. But without unemployment benefit, who could have afforded them?

The new Act came just in time. In the winter of 1920–21 the postwar boom ended, and unemployment rose to 2 million (including 300,000 ex-servicemen) in England, and about 250,000 in London. 'It must be remembered', Sir Basil Thomson reported to the Cabinet, 'that in the event of rioting, for the first time in history, the rioters will be better trained than the troops.'[97] On 18 October 1920 a large demonstration of unemployed Londoners, led by George Lansbury, 'the John Bull of Poplar', was violently broken up by police in Whitehall. During the winter Wal Hannington and other members of the new Communist Party organized unemployed marches on Poor Law offices all over London, demanding outdoor relief. In Islington, the unemployed occupied the public library for three weeks, and there were fierce battles in Upper Street after the police dislodged them. Unemployed agitation, much of it organized by the Communist London District Council of the Unemployed, remained high throughout 1921, with large marches, battles with the police, and raids on factories which were using overtime working. The government's response to the nationwide crisis was to pass legislation in 1921 which cut the link between contributions and benefit and established the principle that the level of relief should reflect family size and the cost of living. The first of the hunger marches, which have done so much to shape our memory of the interwar years, took place in this postwar slump. In June 1921 200 unemployed Londoners marched to the Labour Party conference in Brighton, and on 15 November 1922 a march made up of contingents of men from every part of Britain began arriving in London. They spent the winter in London, sleeping in workhouses, local authority buildings and Salvation Army hostels, and demonstrating in Trafalgar Square and Whitehall, before returning home in February.[98]

POPLARISM AND THE POOR LAW

Workers who did not qualify for unemployment benefit, and those whose poverty was not the result of unemployment, had to rely on the Poor Law for help. There were still 41,737 adults (35 per cent of them over sixty-five) in London Poor Law institutions in 1929. A government committee had recommended the dismantling of the Poor Law in 1917, but the system survived throughout the interwar decades, and enjoyed a resurgence in its importance in the lives of working people in the 1920s, especially in London. This was partly the result of higher unemployment, and partly due to the political rise of Labour in London. Socialist parties had not been very successful in prewar London, but during the war Herbert Morrison

built the London Labour Party (LLP) into an efficient electoral organization, able to take advantage of the greatly extended electorate introduced
in 1918. In the borough elections of 1919 (in which paupers could vote for
the first time) Labour won 39 per cent of the votes, and took control of
half of the twenty-eight borough councils and many Boards of Guardians,
especially in the East End. It did well in the LCC elections, too, but here its
35 per cent of the votes only won it fifteen of the 123 elected council seats.

Control of councils and Boards of Guardians in poorer boroughs
placed socialists in a powerful but difficult position when mass unemployment began at the start of 1921. Since the Rate Equalization Act of 1893,
workhouse relief was largely financed from a common fund, supported by
the contributions of all London boroughs. But outdoor relief (which
Labour boroughs preferred to give) was paid for by individual boroughs,
and the poorest boroughs, with the lowest property values and rate income,
had the heaviest relief costs. This was especially so in Poplar, George
Lansbury's borough, which had paid generous outdoor relief to all who
asked for it since the beginning of the century. In the 1921 slump this
open-handed policy became disastrously expensive. By December Poplar's
able-bodied unemployed on outdoor relief made up almost a tenth of its
total population, four times the London average and five times the national
average. In protest at the fact that other boroughs did not contribute
towards this expense, the Council refused to levy rates to pay its contribution towards the LCC, the Metropolitan Police and the Metropolitan
Asylums Board. In July 1921 the Conservative LCC took thirty Poplar
councillors to court. The thirty refused to reverse their policy, and in
September they cheerfully went off to Brixton and Holloway Prisons. Fear
of public anger in the East End forced the government to release them after
six weeks, and to introduce legislation to transfer most of the cost of
outdoor relief to the Ministry of Health. The effect of this was to increase
Poplar's annual external funding from £50,000 to over £300,000, allowing
it and other Labour East End boroughs to pay outdoor poor relief for the
rest of the decade at levels which were over twice as high as those set for
unemployment benefit. Thus Poplar and the boroughs that followed it
(including Clement Attlee's Stepney) managed to make outdoor poor relief,
which had once been a last resort, more popular than unemployment
benefit. The number receiving 'domiciliary' (outdoor) relief, including
dependants, in the County of London and West Ham had generally been
around 60,000 between 1888 and 1908, but on 1 January 1923, not a time
of unusual distress, it was 276,000. As a result of 'Poplarism', the *New*

Survey of London said in 1929, 'recourse is now had to Poor Law relief just as to other forms of social assistance, and ... a person no longer feels that in applying to the relieving officer he is crossing the Rubicon'.[99]

The support of Labour's East End councils for workers' rights and, as Lansbury put it, 'the transformation of Capitalist Society into Socialism' extended beyond the Poor Law. Ten Labour councils (according to a government survey in 1926) insisted that municipal workers, and those with local government contracts, should be trade union members, and four councils (Bethnal Green, Shoreditch, Poplar and Stepney) introduced a £4 minimum wage for their male employees. Several councils (Stepney, Shoreditch, Bethnal Green) used large-scale public relief works (road mending, housing repairs, and so on) to alleviate winter unemployment and hardship during strikes, especially among dockers and other casual workers. There was potential for corruption and 'jobs for the boys' in these practices, and in some councils, especially Stepney and Bethnal Green, this potential was fulfilled. To Herbert Morrison and the London Labour Party, who were working all through the 1920s to establish Labour's reputation among middle-class voters as a party of responsible government and sound finance, high-spending and over-politicized East London councils which relied too heavily on the support of the unemployed were the Conservatives' best allies. The loss of all Labour seats on Bethnal Green Council in 1928 illustrated Morrison's point.[100]

STRIKERS AND HUNGER MARCHERS

The tide began to turn against militant labour in 1926, the year of the General Strike. Although the coal dispute had nothing directly to do with Londoners, who benefited from falling coal prices, workers in the 'front line' industries in London (transport, docks, printing, power, chemicals and metal trades) responded well to the TUC's call to action on 3 May. Public transport was almost completely suspended at the start of the strike, although volunteer drivers had 500 buses, 100 trams and over 100 underground trains running by 11 May, the day before the strike was called off. About half of London's sixty-one electric power stations (including the ones needed to supply the underground system) were kept going by volunteers and sailors, and by supplies of coal that the government, which was much better prepared than the unions, had previously stockpiled. London provided far more volunteer strike-breakers than were needed: 114,000 had come forward by 11 May. Of these 51,800 were enlisted as special constables, and many were used to drive lorries, distributing milk around the town or carrying flour and sugar from the docks to the government's huge food depot in Hyde Park. About 1,000 volunteers (including Covent Garden porters as well as Cambridge undergraduates) worked in the Victoria Docks. The government placed great emphasis on maintaining food and fuel supplies to London, and made its greatest display of military and police strength there. Twenty armoured cars and 105 lorries full of Grenadier Guards escorted a convoy of lorries from the docks to Hyde Park on 8 May, and on the following day, thanks to Churchill's bellicose influence, lorry-loads of soldiers were deployed all over central London. The violence that Churchill anticipated (and perhaps hoped to provoke) did not occur, but neither was the strike in London the good-natured affair of popular memory. Crowds stoned and destroyed strike-breaking buses and lorries, and there were battles between the police and strikers in Poplar, Deptford, New Cross, and a dozen other places.[101] After 1926, strikes were not very common in interwar London (or in the rest of Britain), not because the workers had 'learned their lesson' in the General Strike, but because depression and labour surplus makes it hard for workers to win industrial disputes. In all, there were 181 large strikes in London between 1921 and 1936, a fifth of the national total.[102]

After the collapse of the General Strike the Minister of Health, Neville Chamberlain, brought the East End Boards of Guardians to heel by tightening the Inspectors' control over relief scales and introducing two important pieces of legislation. The 1926 Board of Guardians (Default) Act allowed the Minister of Health to replace bankrupt Boards with commissioners of his own choice, a power he exercised in 1927 in West Ham, where the Board was over £2 million in debt. The 1928 Emergency Provisions Act undid the concessions made to the East End boroughs in 1921, by giving the Metropolitan Asylums Board (which was dominated by West End boroughs and government appointees) control over the Common Poor Fund and its subsidies to poorer boroughs. This was the end of 'Poplarism'. In West Ham the number of unemployed drawing outdoor poor relief fell from 15,325 to 1,046 between 1926 and 1929, and in Poplar, Bermondsey and Bethnal Green the number fell from 9,785 in 1927 to 2,727 in 1929. In 1929 the Local Government Act transferred control over poor relief from local Guardians to county councils.[103] In the County of London, the LCC took over the work of twenty-five Boards of Guardians and the Metropolitan Asylums Board (MAB), including the running of twenty-eight general hospitals and twelve 'mixed' Poor Law institutions, twenty-six MAB hospitals for fever, smallpox, tuberculosis and VD, six children's hospitals and two epileptic colonies, containing over 40,000 beds and 20,000 staff in all. During the 1930s the LCC's new Central Public Health Committee improved and rationalized its hospital system at a cost of £3 million, and removed the pauper stigma from its medical services. By 1939, with nearly 60 per cent of all English municipal hospital beds under its control, the LCC was the 'greatest Local Health Authority in the Empire'.[104]

The 250,000 or more Londoners unemployed in 1930–33 could not look to sympathetic Labour councils to sustain them as they had ten years before. The LCC and its new Public Assistance Committee were dominated by Conservatives (Municipal Reformers) until 1934, and in the elections of 1931 Labour lost thirty-one of its thirty-six MPs and 200 of its 459 borough councillors. At least, with the many opportunities offered by London's complex and relatively buoyant economy, the London unemployed were better off than the marchers from depressed industrial areas (organized by the Communist-led National Unemployed Workers Movement) who arrived in London in October 1932. The atmosphere in London grew increasingly tense as workers and police waited for the 2,000 marchers to arrive. On 18 October there were battles between several thousand unemployed Londoners and mounted police outside County Hall and at St George's Circus (which now occupied the fields where the supporters of Wilkes and Gordon had once gathered), and when the march reached Hyde Park on 27 October it was met by about 100,000 Londoners (if we can believe Wal Hannington's figure) and 2,600 police. There was fierce but indecisive fighting between the crowd and the police all afternoon, and again three days later, when an even larger crowd gathered in Trafalgar Square. It was generally agreed that the police 'specials', inexperienced and inclined to panic, were the main cause of the breakdown of order. There was further violence between the unemployed and over 3,000 police on the night of Wal Hannington's arrest, 1 November, as a huge crowd tried to hand a petition in to Parliament. Fighting lasted until after midnight, and spread from Whitehall into Trafalgar Square, Piccadilly and Westminster Bridge. The police followed their forty-two arrests by rounding up three leaders of the NUWM, including Tom Mann, the veteran of the 1889 dockers' strike. Most of the marchers left London on 5 November, having been told by the LCC that they could only stay on in their workhouses as casual paupers.

This was the most violent episode in London during the Depression. The next NUWM march, which arrived in London in February 1934 and left in March, was large but well disciplined, and the Metropolitan Police, having learned their lessons in 1932, handled it with much greater skill and restraint. Their moderation was probably encouraged by the fact that several well-known London intellectuals and members of the newly founded National Council for Civil Liberties, including H. G. Wells, Julian Huxley, Harold Laski and Vera Brittain, were waiting in Hyde Park to observe the police handling of the march. The so-called Jarrow Crusade of October and November 1936 was a peaceful and rather tepid affair, which hardly deserves its present renown. None of these events, despite their fame, seem to have influenced government policy as the 1919–21 unrest did, but they may have helped to create a more sympathetic attitude towards unemployment in the minds of the London middle classes.[105]

THE FAILURE OF FASCISM

The unemployed were not the only marchers on the London streets in the 1930s. In October 1932 Sir Oswald Mosley's British Union of Fascists (BUF) held its first rally in Trafalgar Square, and its first Blackshirted parade. By the spring of 1934, it had about forty-two branches in London and a national headquarters, Black House, in Chelsea. For a few months at this time Lord Rothermere, owner of four national newspapers (including the *Daily Mail*), supported the BUF, but he distanced himself from them, as did many other Conservative sympathizers, in June 1934, when hecklers at the great Fascist rally at Olympia brought out the ugly brutality of the movement. Thereafter, the Fascists were only able to make an impact in London because of the size and passion of the opposition they provoked. Kingsley Martin, the editor of the *New Statesman*, went to a Fascist rally in Hyde Park in September 1934, in which 2,500 Blackshirts were heavily outnumbered by a counter-demonstration, and their speakers inaudible and invisible behind a tight police cordon. As the BUF became more openly anti-semitic in 1934–5, it was able to draw upon some support in parts of London which had large or growing Jewish populations. There were successful branches in Hackney and Stoke Newington, fairly prosperous boroughs into which East End Jews had recently been moving. Shopkeepers, who resented the competition of Jewish shops with long opening hours, were active in the Hackney branch of the BUF. In 1936 Mosley tried to revive public interest in his party by organizing a series of rallies and marches in East London districts with high Jewish populations. A rally in Victoria Park in June 1936 ended in fighting between Blackshirts and anti-Fascists, and on 4 October a proposed Fascist march through the East End was opposed by the Communist Party, the ILP, the NUWM and the Jewish organizations. Up to 100,000 anti-Fascist demonstrators gathered along the intended route through Stepney, but the 3,000 Blackshirts who had assembled near the Tower followed police advice and marched off to the west and away from trouble. The so-called 'Battle of Cable Street' was mainly a clash between anti-Fascists, who had blockaded Cable Street against the march, and the police, who used baton charges to disperse them. The Fascist supporters who were injured were, in Kingsley Martin's view, 'silly youths of from fifteen to eighteen years of age who ... have no political opinions, but are merely budding Jew-baiters'. The Metropolitan Police Commissioner, Sir Philip Game, was sure that if the Fascist march had gone ahead 'serious rioting and bloodshed would have occurred'.[106]

In October and November 1936 there were marches and counter-marches in the East End, with attacks on Jews and their shops, and London Labour MPs, councillors and local parties, led by Herbert Morrison, organized a campaign for new anti-Fascist legislation. The outcome was the Public Order Act of December 1936, which banned the wearing of uniforms for political ends, prohibited paramilitary organizations, and gave the police greater powers to prevent provocative processions which might cause disorder. This deprived the Fascists of the psychological advantage of the uniform, and forced them to route their future marches through working-class districts outside the East End, especially Bermondsey. Large meetings also became more difficult when the LCC banned the use of loudspeakers in its parks, and the owners of most large halls refused to rent them to the BUF. Still, the police had to attend over 7,000 Fascist or anti-Fascist meetings in 1937, and even more in 1938, and Jews (including thousands of recent refugees from Nazi Germany) continued to be insulted and attacked in East London. In July 1939, only two months before the war, the BUF held its biggest indoor meeting, with an audience estimated at 20,000, at Earl's Court. After the outbreak of war the police, who had in the past shown more sympathy for the disciplined and ostentatiously patriotic BUF than for its unruly opponents, came down heavily on the Fascists, and in 1940 the movement was broken up and its leaders imprisoned.[107]

Allegiance to the Labour and Conservative Parties was very strong in London (as it was in the rest of England), and extremism of the right and left could never convert its noisy street presence into substantial electoral support. In 1937 the BUF contested Bethnal Green, Limehouse and Shoreditch, Labour strongholds with large Jewish populations, committing money and their best speakers to the campaign, but ended up with 7,700 votes, about 16 per cent of those cast in the three seats. In the borough elections of the same year, forty BUF candidates in the same three boroughs were all badly defeated. The Communists did a little better. In 1924 the Communist Parliamentary candidate, Shapurji Saklatvala, won North Battersea, but this was a seat he had previously held for Labour. In the borough and LCC elections of 1925–37 under 1 per cent of voters (about 5,000) voted Communist. Their best showing, 11,600 votes, was in the LCC election of 1928. The weakness of the Communist Party contributed, it was generally believed, to the failure of Fascism to win significant support in London, since the latter's greatest attraction, for those who did not care for its anti-semitism or its advocacy of the corporate state, was its promise of strong-arm opposition to communism.[108]

HERBERT MORRISON AT COUNTY HALL

The strongest political force in London in the 1930s was the London Labour Party, which won a surprising victory in the LCC elections of 1934, taking 51 per cent of the vote and sixty-nine of the 124 elected seats. The Municipal Reformers (Conservatives) went into permanent opposition, the Progressives (Liberals), who had done poorly in the previous three elections, lost their remaining six seats, and London became a Labour-run county for the next thirty-one years. Beatrice Webb was sure that this was a victory for the dogged efficiency of Herbert Morrison: 'He is a Fabian of Fabians; a direct disciple of Sidney Webb's ... the very quintessence of Fabianism in policy and outlook.' Morrison's policy of wooing well-off voters with municipal efficiency and political moderation had clearly won some converts, but 'Poplarism' was a powerful memory, and the middle-class suburbs were still strongly Conservative. In comfortable East Lewisham it was solid Labour organization in the new LCC estates, along with a low turnout in richer wards, that won the council seat for Labour in 1934. In Parliamentary elections, when participation was higher, Labour did poorly in middle-class suburbs until 1945. What solidified Labour's hold on the LCC was not the conversion of middle-class voters, but their migration to houses beyond the county boundary.[109]

Morrison was an urban administrator of exceptional energy and ability, and his six years as leader of the LCC gave Londoners a much stronger sense of the existence and purpose of their county government than they had gained under the Municipal Reformers. A good deal of this was a matter of public relations. Morrison recruited advertising men and created an LCC publicity department to help him win support and attention in the Press, and to create for himself and the LCC a public image as strong as that of 'Mr Therm' or the 'Ovaltineys'. The floodlighting of County Hall, the building of which had been initiated by the Progressives in 1905 and completed by the Municipal Reformers in the 1920s, and the commissioning of a two-volume *History of the London County Council*, both helped to raise the LCC's public profile. The sight of Morrison, surrounded by Press reporters, pulling the first slab of granite from the Rennie's old and unsafe Waterloo Bridge in June 1934, putting an end to over ten years of debate and delay over its demolition and replacement, epitomized the workmanlike and 'no-nonsense' impression he created in the public mind. Morrison's critics, both contemporary and recent, claim that there was little substance behind the 'Labour gets things done' image promoted by his publicity machine. But the abolition of the ban on married women teachers in July 1935 was more than a gesture, and so was the introduction of a Green Belt policy, by which the LCC subsidized Outer London boroughs in buying and preserving open spaces. Young and Garside argue that this policy postponed the implementation of a coordinated regional strategy, and that Labour's success in sidestepping the problems of London's divided administration, by enhancing the standing of the LCC and 'the whole existing structure of London government', simply helped to preserve an unsatisfactory state of affairs.[110] Perhaps, but it seems unreasonable to expect the LCC to have postponed measures of practical improvement while it waited for administrative reforms which, as the Ullswater Commission had shown, were not in its power to achieve.

Council Housing

The greatest challenge faced by all LCC administrations between the wars was the problem of bad housing. An official survey of overcrowding published in 1936 found that years of municipal effort had not managed to lift London from the bottom of the national housing league. Using a low standard of two people per room (with under-ten-year-olds counted as halves) the survey found that the County of London had almost twice the national level of overcrowding, and that East London and the North-East coast were the most overcrowded parts of England. After Sunderland (20.6 per cent of families overcrowded), the three London boroughs of Shoreditch (17.2 per cent), Stepney (15.4 per cent) and Finsbury (15.2 per cent) were the most overcrowded in the country, and no great city except

Liverpool had anything near London's 7 per cent overcrowding. Measured in numbers, rather than percentages, London's problem was in a class of its own. The County had 70,676 overcrowded families, more than twice the total number in the six biggest English provincial cities. A larger, if less acute, problem was brought out in the 1931 census: 459,402 London families, 63 per cent of all families in the LCC area, shared their dwelling with another family. This sharing was not always unwilling, but the fact that multi-occupancy was so much more common in London than in any other city (it was under 18 per cent in Liverpool, and about 6 per cent in other conurbations) indicated the extent of London's housing shortage.[111]

The way to tackle the problem of overcrowding, it was increasingly believed in the 1930s, was to concentrate on clearing slums and rehousing their occupants in tenement estates which were not too far away from their jobs and their familiar communities. Labour's shift from suburban cottage estates to inner-London flats was a continuation of a change that began around 1930, and had as much to do with the difficulty of finding suitable green field sites as with a change of political control. The Labour LCC kept up the search for suburban sites, while in their public statements they criticized the policy of dispersal, and continued to build about 2,000 cottages a year, mostly on existing suburban estates, until 1938, when the policy was dropped.[112] The difference was that Morrison embraced with enthusiasm a slum clearance and inner-city rebuilding policy which the Municipal Reformers had accepted with regret. Helped by the economic revival, and by the 1935 Housing Act, which gave local authorities the power to designate inner-city 'redevelopment areas' (in which a third or more of the houses were unfit or overcrowded) for demolition and subsidized flat-building, the Labour LCC made much faster progress in slum clearance and rehousing than its predecessors had done. In its first three-year term, the Labour council displaced and rehoused 34,036 people, compared with the 12,055 and 6,823 achieved in the previous two terms (1928–31 and 1931–4) and by 1937–8 its capital spending on housing was three times its level in 1933–4. In 1936–9 it built an annual average of over 4,000 flats a year, more than four times as many as were built annually between 1930 and 1933.[113]

As it had done with cottage estates, the LCC built its new inner-city estates wherever it could. Some boroughs resisted almost all council building (Paddington, Kensington, Chelsea, Hampstead and Battersea), while others preferred to carry out their own building programmes (Bermondsey, Woolwich and Westminster). Four boroughs, Lambeth, Lewisham, Camberwell and Wandsworth, provided sites for half of the

LCC's dwellings in the 1930s, and Hackney, Poplar, Greenwich, Islington, Southwark and Stepney were not far behind. The LCC's policy involved redistribution of population as well as rehousing. Nearly 20,000 families, 35 per cent of those rehoused between 1934 and 1939, came from Inner East London (Finsbury, Shoreditch, Stepney, Bethnal Green, Poplar, Bermondsey and Southwark), but only 4,500 new LCC dwellings were built there. In general, displaced East Enders found themselves in quite well-equipped five-storeyed blocks of flats on large LCC estates in South-East London. Ideally, Mass Observation found in 1938, most of the tenants of these LCC flats would have preferred a house, but they liked their modern facilities and their new neighbourhoods. On an estate in Camberwell, Deptford or the White City (on the Empire Exhibition site) they did not suffer the sense of uprootedness and distance from work and London life that had depressed the residents of the LCC cottage estates.[114]

In the field of education, Labour's achievement fell short of what many had expected, despite such well-publicized initiatives as the ending of military training in council schools and the replacement of Empire Day with Commonwealth Day. Progress in achieving H. A. L. Fisher's vision (enacted in the 1918 Education Act) of elementary schooling until 14, compulsory continuation classes for fourteen- to sixteen-year-olds, and the growth of nursery provision, had been blighted in the 1920s by government 'economies', especially the infamous 'Geddes Axe' of 1922. The Conservative-led LCC reduced its education budget by introducing a range of economies, including a bar on married women teachers, the ending of compulsory continuation classes, and the appointment of untrained infant teachers. The growth of free secondary education, as advocated in the 1926 Hadow Report, was painfully slow. In the 1920s the LCC aimed to provide ten secondary school places per 1,000 of its population, but fell far short of its target, especially in the poorest inner-city boroughs, where the proportion was less than 3 per 1,000. The majority of these places were filled by fee-paying children, whose simple entrance test was much easier than the demanding examination by which the LCC's 2,000 'scholarship' children were selected. Another 5,000 children were sent to LCC Central Schools, which gave them a more commercial and industrial education to the age of fifteen. The rest, about 80 per cent of schoolchildren, remained in elementary schools until they went to work at fourteen. In the more prosperous years between 1925 and 1930 the LCC built twenty-five primary and twelve secondary schools, but these advances were halted by a new package of cuts introduced in the crisis of 1931–2. Labour, coming to power in a period of recovery, and with a long-standing commitment to the principle of equal opportunities in education, might have achieved great things. But in the event the continuing influence of the LCC's anti-egalitarian Education Officer, E. M. Rich, and Morrison's own financial caution, delayed the implementation of radical reforms until the end of the Second World War.[115]

PRIESTLEY'S LONDON

When J. B. Priestley arrived in London at the end of his *English Journey* in 1933, driving south along the Great North Road, he was convinced that he had entered a third England, a new world which was unlike the two Englands of cathedrals and manor houses, and of coal mines and cotton mills, that he had just visited:

> This third England, I concluded, was the new post-war England, belonging far more to the age itself than to this particular island. America, I supposed, was its real birthplace. This is the England of arterial and by-pass roads, of filling stations and factories that look like exhibition buildings, of giant cinemas and dance halls and cafés, bungalows with tiny garages, cocktail bars, Woolworths, motor-coaches, wireless, hiking, factory girls looking like actresses, greyhound racing and dirt tracks, swimming pools, and everything given away for cigarette coupons. If the fog had lifted I knew that I should have seen this England all round me at that northern entrance to London, where the smooth wide road passes between miles of semi-detached bunga-lows, all with their little garages, their wireless sets, their periodicals about film stars, their swimming costumes and tennis rackets and dancing shoes.[116]

If Priestley had arrived in London along Romford Road, or by steamer at the docks, or got off a train at Waterloo or Liverpool Street, his first impressions would have been very different. Laurie Lee, who walked from Stroud to London in the year of Priestley's journey, arrived in Paddington: 'There was a smell of rank oil, rotting fish and vegetables, hot pavements and trodden tar; and a sense of surging pressure, the heavy used-up air of the cheek-by-jowl life around me.' Ian Niall, who arrived in Brixton by bus in the 1920s, saw only 'an endless Glasgow only with bigger slums and longer streets. They had acres upon acres of sooty brickwork through which colourful, open-topped buses hurried, overtaking horse-drawn brewers' drays, coalcarts and rubbish carts filled to overflowing with litter that blew away in the wind.'[117] But there was truth in Priestley's description. London was the driving force behind the modernization of England, the home of its film, recording, advertising and broadcasting industries, the route by which new dance and musical fashions entered the country, the bridgehead, some would say, for America's cultural and industrial invasion of Europe.

The creation in October 1922 of a national broadcasting monopoly based in London meant that the enormous influence of radio would be used to transmit London voices, entertainments, events and ideas to the whole nation. The building of a set of relay stations all over Great Britain in 1923–4, and the opening of the powerful long-wave station at Daventry, the world's biggest broadcasting station, in July 1925, made it possible for London programmes to reach the whole country, and stifled the development of independent regional broadcasting. London dance bands, orchestral concerts (especially the Promenade Concerts from the Queen's Hall), theatres, sporting events and church services became nationally famous through the BBC, and the BBC's studios, until 1932 at Savoy Hill (off the Strand) and then in Broadcasting House, Portland Place, came to represent the voice of England wherever their broadcasts were heard. In general, listeners without their own regional station preferred London programmes to those from a region other than their own. On the other hand, the BBC knew that it was a national, rather than a metropolitan, institution. It had eight regional stations broadcasting regional programmes, and many of the broadcasters who became national figures through the BBC were non-Londoners: the Northern comedians Tommy Handley and John Henry, the Scottish singer Sir Harry Lauder, the Yorkshire novelist J. B. Priestley, and so on. The public school English employed by the BBC sounded as foreign to a cockney as it did to a Lancastrian, and the traditional Christian morality promoted by its Scots Calvinist Director General, Sir John Reith, had probably been more completely abandoned in London than anywhere else in the country.[118]

HOLLYWOOD ON THAMES

London was also the centre of the British film industry, and, in the 1930s, one of Europe's major centres of film production. In the 1920s British filmmakers were almost overwhelmed by the power of the American industry, which supplied over three-quarters of all the films shown in English cinemas. There were several struggling British production companies, mostly making uninteresting and unsuccessful low-budget films in studios dotted all around the northern and western London suburbs. In the early 1920s there were large studios in Twickenham, Walthamstow and Harlesden, and smaller ones in Catford, Ealing, Kew Bridge, Isleworth, Croydon, Wembley Park, Surbiton, Teddington, Islington and Elstree. Gainsborough Pictures, which Michael Balcon started in Islington in 1924, was one of London's more successful silent film companies. Ivor Novello and Betty Balfour, the two top British silent stars, worked for Gainsborough, and so did the young Alfred Hitchcock, whose first important film, *The Lodger*, was shot in Islington in 1926. Hitchcock's *Blackmail* (1929), the first English sound film, was made for the biggest English company of the 1920s, British International Pictures (BIP), whose large and well-equipped studios gave Elstree, on the Hertfordshire fringes of London, the notion that it was the 'British Hollywood'.[119]

The introduction of a quota system in 1927 gave British films some protection from American imports, and stimulated a great revival, in quantity if not quality, of film production in London. The industry centred on five major companies, all with studios in or near London. In Elstree, in the countryside just west of Barnet, BIP was busy in the 1930s making about 200 feature films for the domestic market, mostly unambitious music-hall comedies, operettas and stage plays. Its neighbour in Elstree, Herbert Wilcox's British and Dominion Film Corporation, specialized in costume dramas and light musical comedies, and had big stars in Jack Buchanan and Anna Neagle. There were important studios in Islington and Shepherd's Bush, where Michael Balcon, of Gainsborough and Gaumont-British, assembled an impressive collection of talent, including Alfred Hitchcock, Jessie Matthews and Will Hay. Hitchcock's best 1930s films were made at Shepherd's Bush (*The Man Who Knew Too Much*, *Sabotage*, *The Secret Agent*, *The Thirty-Nine Steps*) or Islington (*The Lady Vanishes*). In 1932 Basil Dean moved his production company, Associated Talking Pictures, from Beaconsfield to Ealing, where the first English studio designed especially for talkies had been built. Here he developed the talents of Carol Reed and David Lean, and made a succession of cheerful musicals starring Gracie Fields, one of the biggest British stars of the thirties, and light comedies featuring George Formby. London film-makers found many of their stars (as well as their writers and directors) in the West End theatre: Vivien Leigh, Gordon Harker, Margaret Lockwood, John Gielgud, Ralph Richardson, Robert Donat, Laurence Olivier and Noël Coward all shared their time between stage and screen in the 1930s. London studios also preserved on film the music-hall culture whose death they were helping to bring about. George Formby, Stanley Lupino, the Crazy Gang, Tommy

Trinder, Stanley Holloway, Will Hay and Arthur Lucan (Old Mother Riley) won a popularity, through their appearances in London-made films, which the great Victorian music-hall stars could never have imagined.[120]

The only London film-maker whose films matched those of Hollywood in scale and quality was the Hungarian Alexander Korda, whose company, London Film Productions, generally used Wilcox's studios at Elstree. The enormous success of Korda's *The Private Life of Henry VIII*, which made stars of Charles Laughton, Robert Donat and Merle Oberon, created a fashion for lavish historical dramas. In 1936 Korda moved to Denham, on the fringes of West London, where he had built the biggest and most modern studios in England. *Rembrandt*, again with Charles Laughton, was made there that year. Two years later, in a general slump in the British film industry, Korda lost control of his Denham studio to his main creditor, the Prudential, and to J. Arthur Rank. Rank, a millionaire flour miller, was poised to take control of the British film industry as the decade ended. He had a big studio at Pinewood, near Denham (between Uxbridge and Ruislip), another in Elstree, and part-ownership of Denham and the growing Odeon chain.[121]

As it had in other cities, cinema largely replaced the music hall and the popular theatre as the favourite place of entertainment for ordinary Londoners, particularly the young and the less well-off. The cinema had become an established part of popular entertainment at the beginning of the century, when exciting narrative films such as *Rescued by Rover* (1905) were produced. By 1911 there were ninety-four cinemas in the County of London, with seating for 55,000 people. Some of these were little more than sheds or halls with wooden benches, but others were converted theatres or music halls, and some were purpose-built cinemas, such as the Bishopsgate Daily Bioscope, which opened in 1906. In the Great War the cinema audience grew rapidly, especially among women, and several theatres and music halls were converted into picture houses, including the Scala (near Fitzroy Square), and the London Opera House, Kingsway, which became the Stoll Picture Theatre. There were 266 cinemas in the County by 1921, compared with under 100 theatres and music halls. In the 1920s the smaller independent and makeshift cinemas gave way to larger 'super' cinemas in the West End and in the suburbs, often under the ownership of syndicates, or 'circuits', the largest of which were Associated British Cinemas (ABC) and Gaumont-British. The County of London had 258 cinemas in 1931–2, with 344,000 seats, or one for every thirteen Londoners. This seems a very ample provision, but it was much lower than that in Lancashire, Yorkshire, Scotland and South Wales, where there was one seat to every nine or ten people. Middlesex, with 138 cinemas and 190,000 seats for a population of 2 million in 1938, was a little closer to the northern average. Cinema building continued rapidly in the 1930s, particularly in the new suburbs. Oscar Deutsch, a newcomer to London in 1933, built nineteen suburban Odeons in 1934–5, and by 1939 there was hardly a London suburb without its lavish 1,500-seat supercinema.[122]

Some of the new London cinemas were even bigger than the great monopoly theatres of Regency London. The Tooting Granada (much admired for its Moorish interior), the Finsbury Park Astoria, the Hammersmith Gaumont Palace, the Whitechapel Rivoli and the Croydon Davis Theatre all held about 4,000 people, and when it was built in 1937 the Elephant and Castle Trocadero, with 5,000 seats, was the largest cinema in the world. The interiors of the new cinemas of the 1920s and 1930s, even those in the grimmest working-class districts and the dullest suburbs, were built in the most ornate and exotic of styles, creating in plasterwork, tiles and coloured lights scenes as fantastic as those their audiences would see upon the screen. The aim of these vast caricatures of Moorish palaces, Italian Renaissance courtyards and Egyptian temples was apparently to fill the audience with 'an atmosphere of hope and cheer'. It is not clear whether they had the desired effect. At least the new cinemas were cheap, convenient, comfortable and dark. Most young Londoners did not have much money to spend, but in the cinema they could buy a full afternoon's or evening's entertainment for 6d, the same price as a cheap music hall, and a quarter of the cost of the theatre. For their ticket they would enjoy two films, a cartoon, a newsreel, probably an organ recital, and perhaps some live variety acts on stage. The social atmosphere was respectable enough for girls or women to go alone, but not so stuffy that young working couples felt out of place, as they might in a theatre. The English or American 'stars' who could be seen (and clearly seen) on films would never have appeared in local theatres or halls. For those who wanted to go twice a week (as most filmgoers did), most local cinemas still changed their programmes every three days.[123]

Although the cinema eclipsed London's theatres and music halls, it did not kill them. In 1931 there were still ninety-two theatres and music-halls in the LCC district, with as many seats (142,000) as there had been in 1911. In the view of the *New Survey of London*, cinema had 'created and supplied an entirely new demand', filling hours that had previously been spent at work, in the public house or on street corners. Two of the greatest Edwardian music-hall stars, Albert Chevalier and Marie Lloyd, died in the early 1920s, and a third, Vesta Tilley, retired, but new 'turns' took their place in the suburban or West End halls: George Formby, Sid Field, Tommy Trinder and Max Miller. But tastes had changed (perhaps through the influence of cinema), and between about 1906 and 1920 most of the major halls abandoned traditional music hall, with its individual 'turns' and audience participation, and went over to musicals and revues, which offered more polished and structured entertainment (often with American music) to more 'sophisticated' audiences. The Middlesex, the Empire, the Alhambra, the New Oxford and the Hippodrome all moved in this direction before 1918. A key figure in the transition was the great showman C. B. Cochran, who had gone in and out of bankruptcy before the war by promoting boxing and wrestling matches, circuses, roller skating shows, and the Great Houdini. During the First World War, Cochran staged successful West End musicals and farces, and after it he converted the New Oxford and the London Pavilion for musical revues. Cochran's plays and revues, especially those written by Noël Coward and A. P. Herbert, were a notable feature of West End entertainment in the 1920s and early thirties. The Victoria Palace in the 1920s and the London Palladium in the 1930s offered a modified form of music-hall variety, and the Holborn Empire kept the tradition alive until it was destroyed in the Blitz. Otherwise, the London music hall survived longest in the suburbs, where it had begun: in the Chiswick, Shepherd's Bush and Hackney Empires, Wilton's, Collins', the South London Palace, the Canterbury.[124] By the 1930s music hall was regarded with nostalgia as 'old-time' entertainment, kept alive by radio, cinema, and Royal Variety performances.

NEW PLEASURES AND OLD

Most young Londoners did not want the comical words of music-hall songs (which in any case they could hear on the radio), but the danceable rhythms of American jazz and swing. Ragtime came to London two or three years before the First World War, when the American Ragtime Octette performed at the Hippodrome, and enterprising couples started dancing the Bunny-Hug, the Turkey Trot, and other short-lived dancing crazes. Its popularity increased during the war, when there were American soldiers in London and Irving Berlin musicals on the West End stage. In 1919 the first of the great London dance halls, the Hammersmith Palais de Danse, opened, and by the end of the 1920s there were about twenty-five such places, all with well-sprung floors, and good dance bands that played waltzes, fox-trots and one-steps in the American style. There had been dance halls in London for centuries, and solitary Victorians had been able to hire dancing partners at the Cremorne and the Argyle Rooms just as they now could at the Hammersmith Palais. But there was a new informality about ballroom dancing now, and an easier relationship between the sexes. The best exponents of the new dances were not the wealthy and well-connected, but delivery boys, typists and shop-assistants. 'The best amateur dancers today', the *New Survey* thought, 'come from Jewish families in Whitechapel.' As well as the big dance halls, there were about 500 places licensed for dancing, including swimming pools, town halls, schools, churches, clubs and restaurants, in the LCC area in the early 1930s.[125]

American music did not have everything its own way. At the end of 1937 an English musical about a South London cockney who inherited an earldom, *Me and My Girl*, started a long run at the Victoria Palace. Its big song, 'Doing the Lambeth Walk', which Lupino Lane performed with a jaunty swaggering 'cockney' walk, was transformed into an easy dance routine by Adele England, the chief instructress of the Streatham Locarno, South London's biggest dance hall. Mainly as a result of repeated playing on the radio, the Lambeth Walk became a national and international craze: 'It's cocky. Everyone can do it, they don't have to learn it. There's never been an English dance success like it before,' Miss England told an interviewer from Mass Observation, the pioneering anthropological organization, in 1938. The dance, which always ended with a shouted 'Oi!', seemed to represent the uninhibited cockney spirit ('Everything free and easy, do as you darn well pleasey') which appeared to have stood out, almost alone, against the Americanization of London life. Its success in 'Mayfair ballrooms, suburban dance halls, cockney parties and village hops' suggests that the nostalgic fiction of the cheerful, resilient, easy-going cockney had taken root not only in fashionable circles (where knowledge of the London poor had always been second-hand at best) but in working-class London itself.[126]

Things changed, but they also stayed the same. New recreations did not destroy simpler and more traditional pastimes. Children still played with windmills, conkers, marbles, balls and cigarette cards, and enjoyed their bafflingly complicated skipping-rope games. Despite the increased availability of LCC play centres, and of paddling pools and sandpits in local parks, and the growing danger from traffic, the side streets were still their regular playgrounds. Adults, too, enjoyed life on the streets. The pleasures of a stroll along a busy borough high street were captured by the *New Survey* in 1935:

The shops in many cases remain lighted up until midnight. The cafés, sweet shops and fish-and-chip shops remain open till ten o'clock or later. The cinemas, the fun fairs and the theatres are brilliantly lighted. The main roads are full of people, some shopping (the shops do not close until eight), some shop-gazing, some going to places of amusement, some to the cafés, others to the public houses. Older women, sometimes with a small child and a large basket, are chiefly engaged in buying, while the younger ones, usually in couples, appear to be mostly interested in the shop windows, or in the young men, when they are not queuing up for the cinemas. Young couples sit in the cafés, usually drinking coffee or eating ices and smoking cigarettes. Young men in threes and fours walk along the streets whistling at the girls, or gather in the amusement arcades and cinemas, and sometimes outside the public houses. The older men are not seen about so much, except for little groups outside the public houses, near the tobacconists and wireless shops, and in the amusement arcades. There is usually a wireless shop that broadcasts music on to the streets, in competition with the noise of the traffic, the shouting of the costers and the newsboys. Gradually after nine o'clock the noise diminishes, the cinema and café doors swing open less often. The shoppers drift home, the public houses close; about eleven o'clock the cinemas and music halls empty, the dances finish and the crowds go home.[127]

As for sports, Londoners still played cricket and football on municipal pitches or in the street, and they went swimming in larger numbers than before. Nearly 7 million bathers used municipal swimming pools in the LCC area in 1932–3, compared with under 4 million in 1910–11. Cycling was not the fashionable pursuit it had been in the 1890s, but it was more popular than ever among poorer Londoners, who found it the easiest and cheapest way to reach the ever-receding countryside. Football was by far the most popular spectator sport. Saturday afternoon Cup Ties involving the best of London's eleven professional league teams often drew crowds of 50,000, and Cup Final crowds were almost twice as big. The North London club Arsenal, managed by the great Herbert Chapman, was England's best team in the 1930s, winning the League five times and the FA Cup twice. From 1923 the Cup Final was played in Wembley Stadium, which was built as the centrepiece for the British Empire Exhibition of 1924–5. The first Cup Final there drew a crowd of 200,000, far more than the stadium could hold. Wembley became London's main sporting centre, and provided tracks for two popular new spectator sports, motor cycle speedway (introduced in 1928) and greyhound racing, which began in London just after the First World War. There were seventeen greyhound tracks in Greater London in 1939, but the appeal of the sport, like that of horse racing, lay as much in the opportunities it offered for gambling as in the excitement of the race itself. Street betting, according to the *New Survey*, had become far more common in London since the war, in spite of the Street Betting Act of 1906. In the eyes of moralists, gambling had taken the place of drinking as the most serious working-class vice, but to others the street-corner bookie's tout, 'engaged in a perpetual and stimulating warfare with authority', had become 'indisputably one of the most popular figures in poorer London'.[128]

'The Worst Street'

The enduring memory of interwar London is of a safe and generally peaceful city, in which crime rates were low, and the streets were secure by day and night. There were no echoes here of Al Capone's Chicago or Damon Runyon's New York, and only a remnant of the 'submerged tenth' that had so unnerved the later Victorians. The outcasts described in George Orwell's *Down and Out in Paris and London* were a malnourished and harmless crowd of tramps and beggars, easily controlled by the police and by the keepers of the casual wards, hostels and lodging-houses in which, if they were lucky, they spent their nights. 'Indeed, when one sees how tramps let themselves be bullied by the workhouse officials, it is obvious that they are the most docile, broken-spirited creatures imaginable.'[129]

The rookeries and criminal quarters that had haunted the Victorians had mostly disappeared, and the old middle-class fear of the London underclass had largely given way to an indulgent affection for an equally fanciful cockney 'Knees up, Mother Brown' culture. But every working-class district still had its streets which parents warned their children to avoid, and down which policemen and strangers did not walk alone. Of these disreputable streets, nearly all of which were destroyed in the Second World War or in postwar slum clearance, the one we know best, thanks to Jerry White, is Campbell Road, Upper Holloway, 'the worst street in North London'. Campbell Road (or 'the Bunk', as locals called it) was an 1860s terraced street near Finsbury Park, most of whose 100 houses had been converted into lodging-houses and cheap furnished rooms in the 1880s and 1890s. Its reputation as a centre of overcrowding, disease, casual labour, street gambling and immorality was firmly established by the end of the century. 'This road is the king of all roads,' the local sanitary inspector wrote in 1908–9.

> I have been in practically all the slums in London; Notting Hill, Chelsea, Battersea, Fulham, Nine Elms, and also the East End, but there is nothing so lively as this road. Thieves, Prostitutes, cripples, Blind People, Hawkers of all sorts of wares from boot laces to watches and chains are to be found in this road, Pugilists, Card Sharpers, Counter Jumpers, Purse Snatchers, street singers, and Gamblers of all kinds, and things they call men who live on the earnings of women. . . . Of course, there are a few who perhaps get an honest living, but they want a lot of picking out.[130]

In the 1920s, Campbell Road was still a street that Henry Mayhew would have felt at home in. The poorest families still slept together in one bed, still relied on their children's earnings, and still sent them to school in clothes that bore no relation to their size, age or sex. Almost 40 per cent of the residents who earned a living were costermongers, street-sellers, dealers or entertainers, and most of the rest were charwomen or casual labourers in the building and haulage industries, or people whose livings came from begging, crime or prostitution.[131] Over 30 per cent of households were overcrowded (four times the Islington average), and as a result most activities took place out in the street: fighting, quarrelling, playing, gambling, celebrating or just passing the time. This street had not yet been conquered by the motor vehicle, and anyone rash enough to park a car in Campbell Bunk was likely to find, on their return, that its removable parts had entered London's black economy. Theft and violence, often committed against other members of the street community, were commonplace, and this, along with open defiance of the law on street gambling, attracted the cautious but persistent attention of the police. Local newspapers reported 400 court cases involving street residents between 1919 and 1939, and in a typical year perhaps a dozen local men would be sent to prison. The community had not forgotten how to fight back against the police, and the traditional crime of rescue was still alive and (literally) kicking in Campbell Bunk, as it was, to a lesser degree, in other poor parts of London in the 1920s. It is realistic to see some of the crime of streets like this as a protest against inequalities of wealth and power, but not all of it. Thieves were as ready to steal from neighbours' rooms and washing lines as they were to raid local shops and employers, and the victims of assault were probably more likely to be an assailant's wife or children than rent collectors and policemen.[132]

Campbell Road and the many streets like it seem to have been part of a timeless world, but in fact they were being dragged along by wider economic and social changes, especially in the 1930s. Poverty and irregular work had kept the road as it was, but as real wages rose in the 1930s, and steady work replaced unemployment and casual jobs, the nature of the community altered. Families with rising incomes did not want Campbell Road's cheap and crowded furnished rooms, and many moved on to council estates, or into houses left empty by the drift to the suburbs. Islington's population fell by a tenth in the 1930s, and Campbell Road lost 30 per cent of its registered voters. Policing and moving out eroded the old culture, and schooling, the cinema, the radio and new jobs helped to create a new one. A community in which people proved their worth by fighting, gambling and drinking began to lose its appeal, and youngsters, especially young women, wanted to join the consumer culture that others of their age were enjoying. There was an extremely buoyant demand for juvenile labour in London after 1933, and teenagers with jobs did not need the communal support that Campbell Road offered them, any more than they needed its rats, bed bugs, oil lamps and shared outside toilets. To judge from the local press, theft, assault and street gambling in Campbell Road and its neighbourhood fell substantially between the 1920s and 1930s, and a more 'respectable' pattern of life began to prevail even in these mean streets.[133]

The Criminal Underworld

Gambling and prostitution were cottage industries in Campbell Bunk, but big business in the West End. The gambling boom of the 1920s attracted criminal gangs to the racecourses and illicit West End gambling clubs, whose profits could be milked by extortion and protection rackets. The leaders in this business were the Sabini brothers, Anglo-Italians from Saffron Hill, who had arrived in London around 1910, and wrested control of the major racetracks from Billy Kimber's 'Birmingham mob' before 1914. The Sabinis, according to the recollections of Arthur Harding, 'got in with the race-course police, the special police, and so they had the police on their side, protecting them.... They used to import young gangsters from Sicily, give them a couple of knives.' Knives were the weapon of choice for those London gangsters who preferred to go armed in these decades. Guns were not often used in London crime until the 1940s. The Sabinis were involved in protection rackets, gambling, and feuds within the Italian community throughout the interwar years, but they did not suffer from the level of police attention that ordinary pavement gamblers attracted. Their reign only came to an end in 1940, when they were interned as enemy aliens.[134]

Mrs Rolfe, the *New Survey of London Life and Labour*'s specialist in 'sex delinquency', claimed that there were only about 3,000 professional prostitutes in London in the early 1930s, but she based her calculations on the number of London prosecutions for soliciting in 1931, when the figure was exceptionally low. Arrests fell from about 3,700 in 1911 and 2,500 in 1921 to 940 in 1931, but they were back at around 3,000 between 1935 and 1938. These variations plainly reflect changes in police activity rather than sexual activity. In some ways, the business of prostitution remained much as it had been a century before. There were cheap prostitutes in the East End and around the docks and railway stations, and others who met and satisfied their clients, Boswell-style, in Hyde Park and other dark open spaces. Cinemas, dance-halls, night clubs, restaurants and hotel lounges now took the place of theatres as rendezvous, and some dance-hall proprietors, according to the *New Survey*, had taken over the functions of brothel-keepers. There was still open soliciting on West End streets, though not on its old scale, and more successful women operated from apartments or hotel rooms, especially around Soho, Shaftesbury Avenue, Russell Square and the main railway stations. 'Motoring has introduced a new factor, and both men and women solicit from cars in the West End and the suburbs.'[135]

Respectable writing about prostitution was still of the 'road to ruin' variety, emphasizing destitution, exploitation and the white slave traffic, and ignoring the prosperous and relatively easy lives many London prostitutes appear to have led. They had to share their earnings, though, with a variety of protectors, pimps, ponces and (perhaps) policemen. In 1929 Sergeant Goddard, of the Metropolitan Police, was convicted of taking bribes from brothels and night clubs, but it is possible that his activities were exceptional. About three years later an Italian family, the Messina brothers, began to build a vice and gambling empire in Soho, which was becoming the centre of London's sex industries. The Messinas imported Belgian, French, Italian and Spanish girls into London, set them up in West End flats, and took a large share (80 per cent, it was said) of their income. Their business flourished during the Second World War, when demand was very high, and prospered, despite the occasional conviction, for decades afterwards.[136] Soho was also becoming a centre of the illegal cocaine trade between the wars. A series of well-publicized deaths from cocaine misuse between 1918 and 1922, the subsequent trial and deportation of a dealer, Brilliant 'Billy' Chang, and the Fu-Manchu novels of Sax Rohmer (Arthur

Ward), revived an old stereotype and drew public attention to the drug connection between the Chinese community in Limehouse and the West End party and night club world. The problem, if it had ever been severe, seemed to become less so in the 1930s.[137]

Although, as we have seen, the relations between police, strikers and the unemployed were less genial than some accounts suggest, the image of London as a relatively safe and law-abiding city is probably fairly accurate. The official statistics, despite their inadequacies, give the impression that London was a city in which crime was commonplace but not dangerous. Recorded indictable crime rose fairly quickly (about 5 or 6 per cent a year in the later 1930s), but most of these were thefts from cars and shops, bicycle-stealing and other simple larcenies. In an average year, there were only 100 reported robberies with violence in London, and about a dozen murders (other than infanticide). As far as crime was concerned, Londoners were rightly confident of the safety of their streets. The real danger came from another quarter. By 1937 there were well over 2 million cars, buses, vans and lorries on the streets of Greater London, and many of them were driven without care, skill or sobriety. Deaths on London's roads averaged about 1,000 a year in the 1920s, and almost 1,400 a year (four times the level of the 1990s) from 1929 to 1934, before falling to a little over 1,000 for the rest of the decade. Over 80 per cent of those killed were pedestrians and cyclists.[138] This was a shameful carnage, but in 1938 and 1939 Londoners were troubled by the prospect of incomparably greater dangers.

Chapter 24

Under Fire, 1939–1945

A SITTING TARGET

When the Prime Minister, Neville Chamberlain, tried to justify his Munich agreement with Hitler in September 1938 that Germany should be allowed to take western Czechoslovakia, he used this argument to a sceptical Cabinet:

> That morning he had flown up the river over London. He had imagined a German bomber flying the same course. He had asked himself what degree of protection they could afford for the thousands of homes which he had seen stretched out below him, and he felt that we were in no position to justify waging a war today, in order to prevent a war hereafter.[1]

This was a persuasive and familiar argument, which had been used by politicians who favoured rearmament, as well as the advocates of appeasement, ever since the early 1930s. Stanley Baldwin warned the Commons in 1932 that 'the bomber will always get through', and by 1934, with Hitler in power in Germany, the growing strength of the German Air Force, and the need to defend London and other cities against it by developing the power to retaliate, was one of Winston Churchill's regular themes. London was 'the greatest target in the world ... a kind of tremendous, fat, valuable cow, tied up to attract the beasts of prey'.[2] In a week or ten days' intensive bombing of London, Churchill declared, at least '30,000 or 40,000 people would be killed or maimed', and 3 or 4 million panicking Londoners would be 'driven out into the open country'. 'The flying peril is not one from which we can fly. It is necessary to face it where we stand. We cannot possibly retreat. We cannot move London. We cannot move the vast population that is dependent on the estuary of the Thames.'[3]

Inside the government, plans for coping with a future air attack on London had been discussed since 1924, when the Home Office set up an Air Raid Precautions (ARP) sub-committee. The committee, which sat in one form or another until 1936, took as its starting-point the Air Staff's calculation, based on the experience of the two great daylight attacks of summer 1917 and sixteen night raids on London in 1917–18, that each ton of bombs dropped would produce fifty casualties, including seventy dead. Over time the fifty casualty multiplier gained unquestioning acceptance, although the figures and calculations on which it was based were faulty in several respects. The 1917 casualty figures used by the Air Staff included the unusual Odhams Printing House disaster in Long Acre, in which a single bomb killed thirty-eight and injured eighty-five, and 130 casualties produced by anti-aircraft shells, as well as 100 injuries added in error. Expert predictions of the tonnage of bombs that would be dropped, and of the accuracy of German bomb aimers, grew more gloomy as time went on. In 1924 the Air Staff predicted about 4,000 dead in London in the first forty-eight hours of war, with another 850 dead and 1,650 wounded in every subsequent twenty-four hours. By 1935, when the ARP Committee issued its first circular to local authorities, the Air Staff thought that German bombers would drop 150 tons of bombs on Britain (mostly on London) each day, and in 1937 the powerful Warren Fisher Committee was told to expect 600 tons of bombs a day, and 66,000 deaths in the first week of war. Bodies on such a scale could not be buried in the normal way. Mass graves and lime pits were made ready, and in April 1939 local authorities were issued with a million burial forms.[4]

The events of the later 1930s, as well as making war with Germany seem ever more likely, also confirmed the terrible effects of the bombing of undefended urban targets. Those who did not remember the Zeppelin and Gotha raids on London in 1915–18 had seen newsreels of the Japanese bombing of Shanghai and other Chinese cities in 1937–8, the German raids on the Basque market town of Guernica in 1937, or the Italian poison-gas attacks in Abyssinia in 1935–6, and knew what was in store for London if war broke out. The Italian raids on the Spanish port of Barcelona in March 1938, in which 44 tons of bombs were said to have killed about 1,000 people and injured another 2,000, gave further support to the Air Ministry experts and their fifty casualty rule, although the figures for a longer period of bombing in Barcelona were only around seventeen casualties for each ton of bombs.[5]

DEFENSIVE MEASURES

By 1939 it was the received wisdom that in wartime, in spite of Britain's fighter and bomber building programme, and the secret development from 1935 of radar, London's 9 million citizens would be subjected to heavy and accurate day and night raids, in which up to 3,500 tons of bombs would be dropped in the first twenty-four hours, and 700 tons on each day thereafter. About half of these bombs, it was predicted, would be high explosives, with the rest divided equally between incendiaries and poison gas. The least feared (but in many ways the most fearsome) of these weapons was fire, London's oldest enemy. There were rather half-hearted efforts to arm civilians with stirrup pumps against smaller fires, but by the spring of 1940 local authorities had only been issued with 86,000 of these. In 1937 the LCC and the London boroughs, along with other urban authorities, were required to prepare fire precautions schemes, and the government began to organize the production or import of huge quantities of hosepipe, couplings, nozzles, ladders, axes, buckets, trailer pumps, water tanks and canvas dams.

The thousands of auxiliary firemen recruited by the LCC, and their growing, but inadequate, stocks of equipment, would mean nothing without a sufficient supply of water. It was estimated, with some accuracy, that a big incendiary raid might start 1,500 fires in the County of London, and that fighting these fires would use 80,000 to 100,000 gallons of water a minute (enough to control about twenty large fires) in the City alone. Work on laying three emergency 24-inch mains and 8-inch pipelines from the Serpentine and the Kensington Gardens Round Pond, placing hydrants on existing trunk mains, constructing water tanks underground and in London squares, and providing new fire boats and riverside pumping stations began in 1938, but progress was modest. By September 1939 London's sixty-seven fire brigades (the LCC, and sixty-six in Outer London) were quite well organized and had reasonable supplies of men and equipment, but, as the events of December 1940 were to show, they did not have enough water to cope with a sustained incendiary attack when part of the mains system had been damaged.[6]

Gas and high explosives created more anxiety and thus stimulated more defensive activity than incendiaries. The mass production of gas masks began in 1936, and went ahead so successfully that it was possible to issue one to every adult in the country during the Czechoslovakian crisis of September 1938. No aspect of air-raid preparation was more thoroughly

49. London's smartest traffic jam, about 1900. Every early evening during the 'season' the Drive in Hyde Park was filled with the carriages of the rich and fashionable. Horse-riders used Rotten Row, to the right.

50. At the other end of the social scale, seats for the pantomime in the Standard Theatre, Shoreditch High Street, only cost fourpence in 1900.

51. Tunnelling for the new deep-level underground, the 'Tube', in 1900. Excavators worked inside a moving 'shield' (see pages 560–61).

52. Patriotic Londoners take to the streets: crowds celebrate the Relief of Mafeking in front of the Royal Exchange on 18 May 1900.

53. Destitute men enjoying a sermon in a Field Lane Refuge in Vine Street, Clerkenwell, *c.* 1900.

54. 'They come to scoff and stay to pray'. A Salvation Army band gathers a crowd for a street-corner service in the East End, *c.* 1900.

55 & 56. Street musicians for the modern age: a street gramophone man, replacing the Victorian barrel-organist, and a band of unemployed men (perhaps ex-soldiers) taking the place of the German bands that disappeared in 1914.

57. Soldiers and armoured vehicles protecting food convoys between the docks and the Hyde Park food dump during the General Strike, May 1926.

58. In the 1920s motor buses became London's most popular form of transport, though most (like this number 15) were open-topped, and until 1928 their speed limit was 12 mph (see pages 710–11).

59. A foggy night in London Town: lighting the gloom of a 'pea-souper' with an acetylene flare.

60. The City in ruins. Paternoster Square after the Blitz, seen from the Stone Gallery of St Paul's Cathedral.

61. Bombed-out Londoners on the move during the Blitz.

62. The Barbican Estate, built by Chamberlin, Powell and Bon on blitzed land in Cripplegate in the 1960s and 1970s. When they were built, these were the tallest residential blocks in Europe.

63. The new face of the East End: A point block, a slab block and low-rise flats on the Bigland Estate, Shadwell.

64 & 65. High Finance: Seifert's National Westminster Tower (600 feet, 1981), on the left, was supplanted in 1992 as London's (and Britain's) tallest office block by 1 Canada Square, Canary Wharf, which is 800 feet tall.

66. The view from Hungerford Bridge in March 1998.

achieved than this, and none, as it turned out, was so unnecessary. It is possible, of course, that the fact that British preparations were so much more thorough than Germany's was a factor in discouraging Hitler from using gas against London.[7] The best practical defence against high explosives, it was believed, would be the provision of splinter-proof (but not bomb-proof) domestic shelters for use in the house or garden, along with fortified trenches, shelters in factories and the basements of large buildings (especially those with steel frames), and some public shelters for flat-dwellers and those caught away from home at the time of a raid. Communists and others on the left (including Herbert Morrison) campaigned for deep shelters, but the official view was that these would be too expensive in labour, materials and money, that they would only protect the small proportion of the population that happened to live near them, and that they would engender a 'shelter mentality' which would create a permanent underground population and damage war production. If a deep shelter failed, it was argued, the mass casualties would be more damaging to morale than the scattered casualties produced by a more dispersed system of small shelters. It was not intended that the Tube stations would be used as shelters (although the public was not told this until the start of the war), but floodgates were constructed to protect the underground system from inundation during a raid, so the way was left open for a change of policy once bombing began.[8]

The provision of public shelters began in earnest during the Munich crisis of September 1938, when trenches were dug in the royal parks and other open spaces, and retained once the emergency had passed. A few months later Sir John Anderson, the new and extremely effective minister in charge of air-raid precautions, strengthened and popularized the policy of dispersed sheltering by announcing the introduction of sectional steel shelters (known as Anderson shelters) for use in the home. Anderson shelters, which were mass-produced at a cost to the Exchequer of £5 each, were issued free to 1,500,000 families by September 1939, and to over 2 million by April 1940, when steel shortages ended their production. Tests showed that the four or five people in the shelter, which could be erected inside a house or covered with earth in a garden, would be protected against the blast and debris of a 500-pound high-explosive bomb about 40 feet away. With the addition of strengthened cellars and of brick and concrete surface shelters (which were sometimes poorly constructed with lime mortar), the basis of an effective and trusted home-sheltering policy was established before the outbreak of war.[9]

FALSE EXPECTATIONS

Drawing upon the limited experience of 1917–18, the known behaviour of crowds in natural disasters, and studies of shell-shock among First World War soldiers, the government expected outbreaks of panic and mass disorder on a dangerous scale once the bombing of London had begun. India Office experts in crowd control were consulted, and thousands of regular troops stood ready to restore order at food depots and railway stations if panic broke out. Leading psychiatrists and medical authorities wrote papers and books by the dozen claiming that urban bombing would produce 'a mass outbreak of hysterical neurosis among the civilian population', although information from Barcelona in May 1939 suggested that this was unlikely.[10]

It was the expectation of 'a disorderly general flight' from London and other bombed cities, creating chaos and disruption of transport, that led the government to develop in the early 1930s an outline policy for the orderly evacuation of 3,500,000 people from Inner London in the event of war. In May 1938, under pressure from the LCC and the Commons, the government set up a committee under Sir John Anderson to examine the question of evacuation and related issues of education, transport, food and war production, and to produce guidelines for a detailed policy. The scheme, it was decided, should be voluntary (though billeting would be compulsory in receiving areas), the government should meet its initial costs, and schoolchildren could be evacuated with their teachers, rather than their parents. Nobody who wished to leave would be prevented from doing so, but every effort would be made to maintain war production. The development of a practical evacuation plan seemed to be beyond the ability of the Home Office, and in the crisis of September 1938 it was the LCC's plan, involving the removal of 637,000 children, that was about to be implemented when Neville Chamberlain returned from Berchtesgaden bearing 'peace with honour'. The experience of September 1938 indicated that over 80 per cent of the parents of London schoolchildren wanted them to be evacuated, and that even if official evacuation was restricted to schoolchildren, younger children and their mothers, pregnant women and the disabled, the government and the LCC would have to deal with 4 million evacuees, including 1.4 million Londoners. Through the summer of 1939 LCC and borough education officers worked out the details of collecting, registering, transporting, feeding and billeting a huge but un-known number of children, teachers and mothers at a time, they expected, of panic and devastation.[11]

When the realities of war replaced speculation and prediction, it became clear that some problems had been exaggerated, while others had been overlooked. The gas masks produced and issued in such vast numbers were never needed, and Londoners soon stopped carrying them. The empty hospital beds and the mass graves were not filled, because the London civilian casualties for the whole war (29,890 killed and about 50,000 badly injured) were fewer than the number that just a few days of bombing had been expected to produce. There was no mass hysteria or general loss of nerve, and the troops standing by to control the panicking crowds were moved to other duties. There was no wild flight from London, evacuees turned up in smaller numbers than expected, and most of them did not stay away from London for long. On the other hand, the problem of fire was much greater than the government had anticipated, and the serious disruption caused to traffic, business and housing by unexploded and delayed action bombs had not been foreseen. Because Londoners did not die or flee in the numbers anticipated, the number of people without homes or furniture was much greater than the government had foreseen. Homelessness had not been a great issue in prewar planning. Some warnings in a report on high-explosive damage to buildings in 1936, and evidence from the war in Spain, had been ignored. The Ministry of Health, which took over responsibility for the homeless in October 1938, set up a Relief in Kind Committee which hurriedly put together plans for feeding stations and temporary shelters, but officials generally assumed that those who had been bombed out would find shelter with friends or in the country. The LCC and some other authorities moved quickly in 1939 to plan their own feeding centres for the homeless, but their efforts were hindered by the Treasury's insistence that it would only pay for the care of people who had arrived from other local authorities. The LCC, it insisted, should use its own public assistance funds to feed and shelter its own destitute residents, and should do so on terms that would not encourage undue dependence on public relief. Even on the brink of war the old poor law spirit of 'less eligibility' was still living, although there were strong hopes that it would soon become a casualty of war.[12]

THE FIRST DAYS OF WAR

In the last days of peace, between the announcement of the Nazi-Soviet pact on 21 August and the German invasion of Poland on 1 September, the plans for defending London against a massive air attack were put into effect, under the vigorous and efficient direction of the Regional Commissioner for the London district, Sir Harold Scott. Babies' gas masks were distributed, barrage balloons, searchlights, anti-aircraft guns and fighter squadrons were deployed, extra trenches were dug, suitable buildings were marked as 'Public Shelters', public buildings were sandbagged, and the air-raid warning system was made ready. Sites all around London were excavated for sand, and huge craters were dug in Hyde Park and Hampstead Heath. Citizens were told to buy supplies of paint, curtains and blinds for the coming black-out, to erect and equip their Anderson shelters, prepare their hoses and fire buckets, and learn the air-raid warning signals and ARP drill. In the opening days of September hospital wards were emptied, vehicles were requisitioned as ambulances, and emergency mortuaries were opened, complete with papier maché coffins. At sunset on 1 September black-out regulations were brought into effect.[13]

Just after 11 a.m. on 1 September, two days before the declaration of war, the LCC was ordered to begin its well-rehearsed evacuation of London's priority groups. Within two or three days, 393,700 schoolchildren, about half of London's school population, along with about 50,000 teachers and 257,000 mothers and young children, were moved by railway into safer reception districts. Although 700,000 Londoners were evacuated, out of a national total of 1,473,000, about half the parents of London schoolchildren, a much larger proportion than expected, and 65 per cent of mothers with young children, decided to keep their families together in London, many preferring the horrors of bombardment to the pain of separation. It is likely that some of these families left London privately, to spend the war in country houses or hotels. How many Londoners did this is unknown, but it appears that the unofficial exodus from London between late August and early September 1939 was roughly 1,200,000 people, or 13 per cent of the population of Greater London, and that about 900,000 of these were still away at the end of September.[14] These figures exclude the many thousands who moved from Inner London to safer homes in Outer London. Most of London's remaining aristocratic mansions were closed, and there was a rush to sell houses in the great West End squares. Robbed of its best customers, the Covent Garden Opera

House closed its doors, to reopen later as a dance hall. About 25,000 civil servants were moved to spas and seaside resorts, and the Bank of England, parts of the BBC and several private firms moved out of London. Not all the evacuees were human. London Zoo's mating elephants were evacuated to Whipsnade (presumably not while they were mating), but some others were less fortunate: the dangerous snakes were chloroformed, the aquarium was emptied and the manatees were shot.[15]

EVACUEES

Evacuated children, who were drawn largely from poorer families, carried with them all the ills of inner-city life, amplified by hurried departures, the anxiety of separation, long train journeys and longer delays in reception centres, waiting to be selected by their new hosts. Within days newspapers and MPs' postbags were full of complaints about the condition of some of the young evacuees and their mothers. A minority (but the repetition of stories made it seem like a majority) arrived in plimsolls and thin and dirty clothes, and were unwashed, verminous, undisciplined, and ignorant of the most basic rules of sanitation. These children wore no knickers or pyjamas and did not use toilet paper, they wet their beds and (in the worst cases) defecated on the floor. Rather less shocking to modern parents is the news that 'they would not eat wholesome food, but clamoured for fish and chips, sweets and biscuits', and that 'they would not go to bed at reasonable hours'.[16] The frequency of bed-wetting, which might have been foreseen in a population of distressed and anxious children, was a troublesome and unexpected problem for many host families, many of whom seem to have drawn from it general conclusions about the inadequacy of urban parents and the sanitary ignorance of the London poor.

The sense of social and cultural conflict was not all on one side. Moving in with richer families embarrassed and humiliated poorer children, and seemed to challenge their allegiance to their own parents and their old way of life. As Richard Titmuss put it, in his honest and humane study of wartime social policy: 'Conflicting loyalties touched and troubled the child in many situations when these differences were sharply marked. To be expected to use strange things like forks at meal-times and pyjamas at bed-times seemed, to some children, to represent a betrayal of their parents. There were children who refused new clothes and who fought and clung desperately to old and dirty things.' According to Titmuss, the instinctive desire of working-class families to cling together through thick and thin, and especially the inability of mothers to accept the diminished role implied by the loss of their children, or by evacuation alongside them to a house run in an unfamiliar way by another woman, created a powerful resistance to long-term evacuation:

> The stubbornness of family life against which evacuation continually surged and broke during six years of war rested, almost alone, on the maternal personality. . . .
>
> A longing for home, worries about husbands and older children, and social and temperamental incompatibilities were the chief forces which impelled so many evacuated mothers to return. The isolation and strange quiet of the country – "they call this spring, mum, and they have one down here every year" – boredom, uncomprehended ways of life; these were the things which sometimes led to bad manners, ingratitude and irresponsibility. For that is how many people in the country read such behaviour; they knew little about the liveliness of crowded city life and the friendliness of the slums. But they did know what it had cost them to be tolerant of the intrusion into their homes of another woman dyed to the colour of a different environment.
>
> The life of the working-class mother begins, ends, and has its being in the setting of husband, children, home. The small, dark, unorganized workplace in which the mother spends most of her day, the neighbours, the shops, the gossipy streets; they are all an integral part of the daily round. Life had meaning for these women in the environment they knew so well. In a billet in the country it lost its meaning. They understood Mr Churchill and the *Luftwaffe* among their own people, and in their own homes, not in somebody else's. And so they went home.[17]

In the autumn of 1939, when the long-predicted air raids did not take place, there was a steady drift back to London. By January 1940 34 per cent of London's evacuated schoolchildren, and almost 90 per cent of its evacuated mothers and younger children, had returned to their homes in the 'target area', and an even higher percentage of evacuees from other cities had done the same. Mothers from East London, the bull's-eye of the target, were keenest of all to get back home.[18] The return surprised the government, which had been preparing to deal with an urge to flee, not a desire to stay put. When children returned to London they found that their schools, nurseries, clinics and medical services had been closed down. Schools were not reopened in large numbers until the spring term of 1940, and attendance was not made compulsory until after Easter. In the meantime many children were left to run wild in London, and vandalism in open but as yet unused air-raid shelters became a problem.

Most returnees had learned their lesson from the mass evacuation of September 1939. When the government tried to persuade parents to register their children for future evacuation in April 1940, less than a tenth of London families were ready to sign, and when the fall of France and the invasion of England seemed imminent in June 1940, the government could only persuade the parents of 100,000 schoolchildren to send them away from London. Efforts to encourage mothers and younger children to leave London, except by assisting their private arrangements, were half-hearted. During July and August 1940, when the danger of invasion was growing by the day, more children returned to London than left it, and in September 1940, when air raids began, there were 520,000 schoolchildren living in the target area.[19]

THE TWILIGHT WAR

During the early months of the war, between the German attack on Poland in September 1939 and the invasion of Norway, France and the Low Countries in April and May 1940, Londoners experienced a mixture of relief and anticlimax. Cinemas and theatres, which had been closed when war was declared, quickly reopened, and although several important sports grounds (Twickenham, Wimbledon and the Oval) had been taken over for military or agricultural use, football and greyhound racing restarted on a modest scale in the autumn. When dance halls and West End cinemas and theatres were allowed to stay open until 11 p.m. in December, and museums and galleries reopened (without some of their best exhibits) in January, life had almost returned to normal. Some of the controls and regulations introduced in the expectation of immediate air raids, and enforced by an army of officious air raid wardens, began to seem burdensome and unnecessary in this twilight or 'phoney' war. Such feelings applied most of all to the nightly black-out, which made work and shopping difficult, spoiled the pleasures of home and street life, and made walking in London extremely hazardous. Over 400 pedestrians were killed on London streets, mostly at night, in the last four months of 1939, more than twice as many as in the same period in 1938. Things improved a little in October and November, when dimmed torches and masked headlights were permitted, and around Christmas, when shops and restaurants were allowed to show dim lights, and 'glimmer' street lamps began to be introduced.[20] The black-out also seemed to encourage crime, once wrongdoers had adjusted to the new conditions. Recorded indictable crime was higher in December 1939 than it had been for the previous seven years. But the Metropolitan Police Commissioner denied newspaper stories of a boom in gambling, vice and racketeering under the cover of black-out darkness. 'There was no noticeable increase in any of the activities mentioned and, in some respects, the position was unusually good.'[21]

A war which had seemed distant and unreal early in 1940 drew disturbingly closer in May and early June, with the bombing of Rotterdam, the fall of Holland and France, and the escape of British troops from Dunkirk. Londoners learned now what the German *Blitzkrieg* (lightning war) technique could achieve, and readily adopted the first half of the word, Blitz, as an appropriate description for the air raids they were waiting for. The removal of street names and road signs, the construction of pill-boxes on the approaches to London, the formation of the London Home Guard and the internment of British Fascists and enemy aliens in May 1940 all announced that the phoney war was over, and that the real one was about to begin. The warlike oratory of Winston Churchill, who replaced Chamberlain as Prime Minister on 10 May, and J. B. Priestley's influential radio talks, stimulated an appropriately determined spirit as the British faced their greatest challenge. Air-raid and invasion precautions took on a fresh significance, and Londoners joined with enthusiasm in the hunt for spies and fifth columnists.

THE FIRST RAIDS ON LONDON

After the French surrender was signed on 22 June the German plan, which was never carefully worked out, was that the *Luftwaffe* should destroy the RAF and then use its superiority to protect a seaborne invasion of southern Britain from the power of the Royal Navy. This was an amateurish strategy, based on Goering's false assumptions about the power of the *Luftwaffe* and the weakness of the RAF. Germany's light bombers had been designed to give tactical support to ground forces, not for strategic bombing, and they lacked long-range fighter protection against the RAF's highly effective Hurricanes and Spitfires. The air battle began on 10 July, when naval convoys were attacked in the Straits of Dover, and developed in August into an attack on British Fighter Command's airfields and control centres. Between 24 August and 5 September the RAF lost fighters and pilots at a rate it could not sustain, and the highly effective attacks on Biggin Hill and other south-eastern sector stations left London dangerously exposed. Throughout these weeks the *Luftwaffe* also bombed important industrial and strategic targets, including Croydon's aerodrome and aircraft factories (where sixty-two died on 18 August), but they had been ordered not to attack central London and other civilian centres. The great attack on London was intended to take place only at the start of the invasion, to create a flood of refugees to block the roads around the city.[22]

The first raid on central London happened by mistake. On the night of 24 August, some German pilots with orders to attack aeroplane factories and oil refineries in South London and the Home Counties lost their bearings, and dropped incendiaries and high explosives on the City, the East End and the inner suburbs. Bomber Command responded with an eighty-plane raid on Berlin on the following night and several subsequent nights, and this prompted Hitler, who had assured Berliners that such a raid could never happen, to order retaliatory raids against London. These incidents do not in themselves explain the German decision to shift the weight of their attack from the RAF and key industrial installations to civilian targets. Perhaps, as Calvocoressi and Wint argue, Hitler thought the battle against the RAF was almost won, and he hoped (as Angus Calder believes) to lure it to its final destruction in a battle over London. Gordon Craig's argument that Goering's strategic thinking was amateurish and unintelligent, and that the ill-conceived attack on London was characteristic of the whole invasion plan, has much to recommend it. Or it may be, as Alan Bullock suggests, that Hitler hoped to avoid the losses and delay involved in wearing down Fighter Command by striking instead at the heart of Britain. He certainly had no moral objections to doing so, and he had every reason to believe (as many people in Britain believed) that a full-scale attack on London would force the British to acknowledge defeat. Night raids on Liverpool and Birkenhead between 28 and 31 August, which were believed to have caused more damage than they actually did, confirmed that this was a cheap and effective way to strike at the enemy. Hitler had previously avoided British civil targets through fear of reprisals and the impact these might have on public opinion in Germany. But once the RAF had raided Berlin, the need to sustain German morale pushed him towards reprisal instead of restraint. In retrospect the decision is regarded as a cardinal error, which saved Fighter Command from destruction and made a German seaborne invasion, which had always been an unlikely proposition, impossible. But the resilience of civilians, whether British, German or Japanese, in the face of terrifying bombardment was not understood until the events of 1940–45 demonstrated it, and the ability of a great city to soak up punishment and keep on working, or (in the patriotic expression of the day) to 'take it', came as a surprise to all sides.[23]

The great attack on London was signalled by Hitler in a public speech in Berlin on 4 September, and orders for its execution were issued the next day. German bombers dropped flares on London on the night of the 4th, and on the next night Rotherhithe was raided. These were warnings of what was to come, but the switch from attacking sector stations to bombing civilian targets was so unexpected, and so illogical, that it took Fighter Command and the British Chiefs of Staff completely by surprise. When a huge force of 320 bombers, accompanied by more than 600 fighters, flew along the Thames at about 5 o'clock on the evening of Saturday, 7 September, it was at first virtually unopposed, except by anti-aircraft fire. London's most important industrial and commercial districts were hit that afternoon: the Woolwich Arsenal, Beckton Gas Works, West Ham Power Station, the vast network of docks from Silvertown and Poplar to Rother-hithe and Wapping, and with them the crowded and vulnerable East End slums. The bombers moved on to the City, Westminster and Kensington, under attack now from RAF fighter squadrons. At 8 o'clock that night, guided by the huge fires that lit up the eastern skies over London like a bright orange sunrise, a force of 250 bombers returned to continue the attack. Their task was easy. Many of the anti-aircraft guns allocated to London at the start of the war had been moved to other targets, and ninety-two guns defending the inner zone blasted away from 9 p.m. to 3 a.m. to no effect. The bombers just went round them. The single-seater fighters available for London's defence were virtually useless at night and were not sent up, and two squadrons of Blenheims equipped for night fighting could not take off from Hornchurch aerodrome because of thick smoke. A few Blenheims flew over north-east London, but in effect the seven-hour German raid was unopposed, except by balloons.[24]

By the morning, over 1,000 fires were burning, some of them out of control, three main railway termini were closed, 430 Londoners were dead, and 1,600 badly injured. Battersea and West Ham power stations were closed, and there was extensive damage all along the Thames, from Silvertown to Putney Bridge. Another night raid on 8 September, again guided by the fires started by previous raids, killed another 412 and seriously injured 747. Fires in the docks, more immense and dangerous than anything seen in London since 1666, released the pungent smells of London's imperial trade:

There were pepper fires, loading the surrounding air heavily with stinging particles, so that when the firemen took a deep breath it felt like burning fire itself. There were rum fires, with torrents of blazing liquid pouring from the warehouse doors and barrels exploding like bombs themselves. There was a paint fire, another cascade of white-hot flame, coating the pumps with varnish that could not be cleaned for weeks. A rubber fire gave forth black clouds of smoke so asphyxiating that it could only be fought from a distance. . . . Sugar, it seems, burns well in liquid form as it floats on the water in dockland basins. Tea makes a blaze that is 'sweet, sickly and very intense'.[25]

This was a disaster for the East End, but it fell far short of the holocaust that politicians had predicted. There had been no poison gas, the tonnage of high explosives had been much less than expected, and deaths and serious injuries per ton had been six, not fifty. Only the power of incendiaries and the destruction of property had outrun expectations. Even on this, one of the worst of all nights, the mass hysteria and cowardly flight that many had foreseen did not take place. Londoners, Home Intelligence reported, had adjusted to the late-August raids with determination and neighbourliness, and on 9 September there was 'little sign of panic and none of defeatism' in the East End. When Churchill toured the devastated dockland districts on 8 September he found people in good spirits, and Mass Observation reporters (who were now collecting information on public attitudes for the Ministry of Information) found the understandable panic and horror induced by the first raid was already tempered by the somewhat self-conscious mood of bravado and humorous resilience that very soon became the characteristic 'spirit' of bombed Londoners. It was not long before nervousness or hysteria, which until 1940 were regarded as normal civilian behaviour under air attack, were being regarded as signs of unusual mental weakness.[26]

THE AUTUMN RAIDS

This first phase of the Blitz, with its concentration on industrial and riverside targets in the East End in a combination of day and night raids, lasted until 18 September, when major daylight raids on London were abandoned, and 'Operation Sealion', the plan to invade Britain, was indefinitely postponed. The German aim in the first ten days of heavy bombing was to destroy the East End and the London docks ('Target Area

A'), and to defeat the RAF by drawing it into battle for the defence of London. As it turned out, the *Luftwaffe* lost rather more planes than the RAF in the six daylight raids of 7–18 September, especially in the great raid of 15 September, in which sixty out of 900 German planes were brought down. Losses on this scale forced Goering to suspend daylight raids on 18 September. Night raids were a much safer proposition. German bombers, usually between 100 and 200 in a raid, were able to spend a leisurely seven or eight hours unloading their 150 or 200 tons of high-explosive bombs and 200 or 300 incendiaries. London's defences were almost entirely ineffective. Anti-aircraft guns were fairly inactive during the first three night raids, and only four out of 600 bombers were brought down. From 10 September General Pile, the head of A.A. Command, decided to send up an indiscriminate barrage, which frightened the bombers and reassured their potential victims, but actually killed more Londoners (through falling shrapnel) than Germans. In addition, the anti-aircraft searchlights provided a useful locational guide for German pilots who were disoriented by the effectiveness of the black-out. In the last three months of 1940 only fifty-seven German planes were brought down by anti-aircraft fire. Night fighters were even less successful. Only the Blenheims, of which there were two squadrons near London, were at all useful at night, but they were too slow to do much damage to German bombers. Faster Beaufighters began coming into service in the autumn, but they had many technical problems. The answer was the development of a coordinated system of ground and airborne radar, but this only worked if the fighter could get within about 3 miles of the bomber, and if it was then fast enough to catch it. Until the spring of 1941, British night pilots were unable to find German bombers or to get into positions from which to attack them. Shooting down a bomber in the dark was never easy, but techniques gradually improved, and in the big raids of April and May 1941 radar-equipped Hurricanes and Defiants could at last claim some worthwhile successes.[27]

The second phase of the German attack, from mid-September until 14 November, no longer concentrated on the East End and the docks, but spread its destruction over the rest of London, 'Target Area B'. Except for the night of 3 November, when weather conditions prevented an attack, there were raids every night in the autumn of 1940, involving an average of 160 planes, 200 tons of high explosives and 180 incendiary canisters in each raid. This westward shift, of which the heavily publicized bombing of Buckingham Palace on 13 September was an early sign, helped to diminish the worrying mood of resentment that had begun to build up in Stepney, West Ham and other East End boroughs during the previous week, and which had culminated in an attempt by East Enders to occupy the Savoy during the raid of 15 September. A sense of shared suffering, of bombs falling on palaces (and palaces whose inhabitants had not scuttled off to the country) as well as slums, was a vital ingredient of the Blitz spirit. The diversification of targets also meant that no single district of London was brought to physical or mental breaking point, as the East End might have been if the raids had not moved elsewhere. Although London was hit almost every night for over two months, no individual or borough had to endure such a long period of unbroken attack. Most raids, for most Londoners, were only the noise or sight of distant explosions, and stories in the morning paper.[28]

The great raid of 7 September was by no means the biggest raid of the autumn. On the night of 18 September, by the bright light of a bomber's moon, 300 planes dropped 350 tons of high explosive (more than the total dropped on London in the First World War) and over 600 incendiaries. The newly famous Lambeth Walk was destroyed that night, along with John Lewis's big Oxford Street store. Among the bombs dropped were huge naval mines, each weighing around a ton, which floated down silently on parachutes, and exploded with an overwhelming blast and a noise which was described as 'something like a colossal growl'. These mines (which Londoners called land mines) were bigger than any bomb dropped from the air before, and when they failed to explode (which often happened) the disruption they caused to transport and to the life and work of the town was immense.[29]

Great disruption was caused, too, when raids damaged sewers, broke water and gas mains, or cut electricity supplies and telephone services. Early in October London's main sewage outfall was broken, releasing raw sewage into the Thames, and in the heaviest raid of the autumn, on the moonlit night of 15 October, when 400 bombers killed 430 people and disabled five main railway termini and the District Line, the City's water supply was cut and the Fleet sewer was broken open, releasing smells Londoners had not smelt (from this source, at least) for 200 years. The repair of these services was regarded as urgent business, since without them the town could not function and morale and fire-fighting would suffer. It is a measure of the government's success in this that there was not a single recorded case of water-borne typhoid in wartime London, and that breakdowns in essential services were only local and temporary.[30] London's ability to recover from severe air-raid damage was impressive. Roads and railway lines were quite quickly repaired, and the docks, despite repeated heavy raids, continued to cope with the flow of imports and exports that kept the capital and its economy going. After two months of intense attack damage to the docks was reported to be 'serious, but not crippling'. German expectations that the commercial and industrial life of London could be gravely damaged by air raids proved to be over-optimistic.[31]

'TAKING IT'

The attitudes and behaviour of Londoners during their long ordeal were recorded, reported and analysed in unprecedented and honest detail by Mass Observation and the Home Intelligence division of the Ministry of Information in 1940, and they have been mythologized, romanticized and analysed ever since.[32] Angus Calder, in his study of *The Myth of the Blitz*, found that, allowing for simplification and patriotic exaggeration, most Londoners *did* cope with the Blitz with stoicism and determination, and that the 'Myth' was not a myth, in the *Oxford English Dictionary* definition of the word (a 'fictitious narrative'), after all. Secret and well-researched Home Intelligence reports, produced daily from 18 May 1940 and weekly from 30 September, presented a clear picture of steadiness and pragmatism in the period of heaviest raids, at a time when the government was on the alert for signs of panic. Calder recognizes that Mary Adams, the director of Home Intelligence, and her assistants 'were not complacent, or easily fooled', and that they had enough information 'to distinguish temporary and local crises from general and repeated patterns'. Although he talks of 'paradigms' being established and claims that 'the basic story' of London's courage under fire was 'scripted' for public consumption, he recognizes that some stories, even those upon which patriotic 'myths' are based, are true. The argument promised on the dust jacket of Calder's book, that 'people performed, by and large, as their own "myth" told them they should', proved impossible to sustain in the text itself. The myth, the pre-written story, was a tale of cowardice and catastrophe. Londoners had heard this story often enough in the 1930s, but for their own reasons they behaved altogether differently, and the story had to be changed in recognition of this surprising fact. The tale of popular fortitude in the face of nightly hardships and dangers, of 'London can take it' and 'Cockney cheerfulness', was polished and promoted in films and newspaper articles to win American support, and perhaps to induce people in other cities to live up to London's reputation, but it was not, in its essentials, based on falsehood. The extent of pacifism and Communist anti-war feeling were played down, Calder argues, but 'no one has detected evidence of any large-scale "cover-up" concerning events in 1940'.[33]

In retrospect, the resilience of Londoners in 1940–41 was not unbelievable, and it was certainly not unique. Later in the Second World War the citizens of Berlin, Hamburg, Tokyo, and even Nagasaki showed similar endurance in the face of much greater devastation. Londoners were simply the first to demonstrate the error of the prewar belief that only soldiers (and only men) could accustom themselves to danger and death, and that women, children, old people, shop assistants and bank clerks were generally incapable of sustained courage. Perhaps, as Constantine FitzGibbon argued, Londoners 'had set a sort of precedent' which fortified other cities when their turn came, but it is unlikely that the 'myth of the Blitz' meant much in Tokyo in 1945 or Hanoi in the 1960s.[34]

Londoners' adjustment to bombing was helped by the brief apprenticeship of 24 August–6 September, and by the fact that, after the initial concentration on the East End, different districts were bombed on different nights. The first panic of 7 September was soon gone, partly because the most timid fled from the target area, and in its place an oddly humdrum attitude to danger developed. Risks and privations which once would have seemed intolerable were soon being treated with the irritation or glum resignation induced in normal times by a cancelled train or a broken tooth. The diary kept by Vere Hodgson, who lived and worked as a social worker in Holland Park throughout the war, conveys the mixture of weariness, anger, fear, interest, sadness and resignation that seems to have been common among Londoners in the autumn of 1940:

> September 16, 1940: 'Not such a good night. In fact – awful. I was in the basement with my neighbour, and we thought every moment would be our last. I kept saying: "This is ours!" as Swish down it came. I slept about an hour, and crept upstairs with the All Clear. I looked out, and expected to see London in ruins; but strangely enough the landscape looked the same.'

> September 23, 1940: 'Blitzkrieg on as I write ... it is 10.45 p.m. It would be lovely to be somewhere else, and able to sleep in peace. But it's no good – it has to be faced. And so to bed.'

> October 3, 1940: 'Three ghastly swishings. They were in Kensington, because this house shook to its foundations. It brought back all the old sick feeling again. One sort of wishes for the Final Bomb to end it all, then one can investigate the never-never land in peace!'

October 5, 1940: 'I am getting so accustomed to the blitz that I shall sleep through the bomb that gets us, I think, and arrive peacefully on the other side, without knowing it! I had no idea the body could get used to sleeping through such a din. But I shall make a soldier yet!'[35]

The records kept by Mass Observation diarists suggest that while the constant repetition of bombing and sleepless nights wore some Londoners down, many found an unforgettable excitement in air raids and being in the 'front line', and discovered in themselves surprising reserves of courage. This is a woman in her thirties, who had fled to Scotland before the war, and had only returned because the Blitz seemed to be 'off':

Sweated with fear at the mere idea of being woken in the night by sirens, let alone at that of bombs and shells; was constantly imagining car and other noises were sirens or guns. Convinced of being most utter and complete coward – very ashamed. Sure I was bound to panic and lose control if things got hot.... Now I find myself almost completely proof against fear and jumpiness ... am the most fearless among my own circle of friends ...[36]

And here a young woman explains how she felt after a narrow escape in Hampstead, on 9 September:

'Are you all right?' ... people kept asking; and it was only then – silly though it sounds – that it occurred to me that I *might* have been hurt! That I had been in *actual danger*, really! Somehow, right up to that minute I had taken everything for granted, in a queer, brainless way, as if it was all perfectly ordinary. I never even *thought* about injury or death, for any of us....
    ... I lay there feeling indescribably happy and triumphant. 'I've been *bombed*!' I kept on saying to myself, over and over again – trying the phrase on, like a new dress, to see how it fitted. 'I've been *bombed*!' ... '*I've* been bombed – *me*!'
    It seems a terrible thing to say, when many people were killed and injured last night; but never in my whole life have I ever experienced such *pure and flawless happiness*.

This was not a passing nervous reaction. Over thirty years later she still remembered the incident as a 'peak experience', a 'gigantic personal achievement'.[37] The many thousands of men and women who served as ARP wardens or special constables, or in the Rescue or Auxiliary Fire Services, were exhilarated (at least in the early weeks) by the work they did.

A Mass Observer recorded a conversation between men who had helped deal with Mill Hill's first big raid in late September 1940:

> It was an awful night, I expect you heard about it; it was in the news. I was up half the night with incendiaries – the A.R.P. couldn't cope, and we all turned out to help.... we got a packet our way.... I thought I'd feel like death this morning – but I don't. I feel marvellous – on top of the world.[38]

This sense of usefulness, of playing an important part in the national struggle, was a significant element in civilian morale. As Richard Titmuss explained in 1950:

> What this period of the war meant to a great many people was less social disparagement. There was nothing to be ashamed of in being 'bombed out' by the enemy. Public sympathy with, and approval of, families who suffered in the raids was in sharp contrast to the low social evaluation accorded to those who lost in material standards through being unemployed during the nineteen-thirties. The civilian war of 1939–45, with its many opportunities for service in civil defence and other schemes, also helped to satisfy an often inarticulate need; the need to be a wanted member of society. Circumstances were thus favourable to fuller self-expression, for there was plenty of scope for relieving a sense of inferiority and failure.[39]

Individuals reacted to danger in different ways, but the general picture, as recorded in Ministry of Information Home Intelligence summaries, or in the words of doctors still waiting for the flood of nervous breakdowns they had been told to expect, was the same. The mental wards did not fill, and prewar expectations were confounded again.[40]

Keeping Spirits Up

In some ways, Titmuss argued, civilians had an advantage over soldiers in coping with bombs. If they felt afraid, they were free to show it, and to do what they could to avoid the danger. Those who trekked out to Epping Forest or into the underground system for a safe night's sleep were not condemned as shirkers or shot as deserters, and the government, which had feared the shelter mentality, quickly realized that it was better to leave people to protect themselves as they chose. Evacuation was another important safety valve, even for those who never used it. They knew that when the strain got too great, or when circumstances changed (with the birth of a baby, for instance) they would be free to go. Those who stayed in London, like those who left, did so through their own free choice. Another great advantage enjoyed by civilians, in contrast to soldiers, was that they could share their fears and hardships with their families. 'Staying at home, keeping the family together, and pursuing many of the ordinary activities of life made adjustment easier.'[41] First World War soldiers, it is true, formed friendships in the trenches, but death often broke them again. The number of British soldiers killed on a single day in July 1916 was as great as the number of Londoners killed in eight months of the Blitz.

It was not so difficult to keep cheerful in wartime London, despite the fact that there was hardly a scrap of good news from Europe between the fall of France in June 1940 and the invasion of the USSR a year later. Londoners did not turn to the churches for comfort or reassurance. Mass Observation looked for signs of a spiritual revival, but could find nothing but a continuing decline in religious observance, despite the great personal popularity of William Temple, Archbishop of Canterbury from 1942 to 1944. Instead, Londoners did what they had done for the past thirty years, and went to the 'pictures'. Cinema-going boomed in wartime, and reached its all-time peak in 1946. A Mass Observation report on older London teenagers in January 1941 found that only one in 100 went to church at the weekend, but 34 per cent went to the cinema.[42] Cinemas were not especially safe places, and sixty were destroyed in London during the war, sometimes (but not often) with substantial casualties. Attendances fell in the early raids, but audiences soon got used to sitting through films while the sounds of bombs and guns outside in the streets rivalled the noises coming from the screen. For a while, some Granada cinemas kept up all-night performances during long raids, helping their audiences to adjust to a frightening new experience in the company of others. A Granada manager recalled that 'the atmosphere of these long nights was one of terrific tension, but there was something companionable about it; a sense of comradeship, what might be described as a *clubby* feeling. . . . It is untrue to suggest that people were not as frightened in cinemas as anywhere else, but their fear was mingled with a determination not to show it and with curiosity.' The great hit of the war was *Gone With the Wind*, which played in the West End from April 1940 to the spring of 1944. The long queues for the film, as fires blazed in Leicester Square, seemed to epitomize Londoners' increasingly phlegmatic attitude to the dangers of the Blitz.[43] None of the other successful Hollywood productions – *The Wizard of Oz*, *Destry Rides Again*, *Rebecca*, *The Grapes of Wrath*, *Random Harvest*, *Casablanca*, *Going My Way*

– could match this popularity. There was still a strong taste for London-made films, especially Gainsborough melodramas, Ealing comedies, the slapstick of George Formby and Will Hay, and well-made war films which did not patronize audiences with over-optimistic propaganda. The most successful of these was Noël Coward's *In Which We Serve*, but *The 49th Parallel, One of Our Aircraft Is Missing* and *The First of the Few* also drew large audiences.

Home Intelligence believed that several factors helped to maintain London's high morale. First, the much lower than expected number of dead and injured. People were upset by the loss of friends and relatives, and 'temporary entombment ... has a definite "unnerving effect"'. It was important also that Londoners were well fed, and that they believed that hardships (including food shortages) were fairly distributed. Gradual 'conditioning' by a steady build-up of raids, rather than the sudden onslaught experienced by other British cities, worked to London's advantage, but a long run of broken nights undermined efficiency and spirit. Sleeplessness was a problem for Londoners, but Mass Observation surveys found that the percentage of people sleeping for more than four hours a night rose from about 30 per cent in mid-September to about 90 per cent in late October. This was partly because they were getting used to the raids, and partly because they had made better sleeping arrangements, generally by bringing their beds downstairs. Finally, Home Intelligence believed that Londoners stood up to continuous raids well because they felt 'that there is a safe refuge *somewhere*'. In smaller towns, 'not only does the proportion of homeless following a series of severe blitzes exceed the capacity of the rest of the town, but the homeless themselves often do not regard the rest of the town as a "secure base"'.[44] The vastness of London, which prewar experts had believed would intensify the effects of air raids, in fact ameliorated them. London could be wounded, but it was too big to be obliterated. Even its docks, battered as they were, kept on going. Although the cumulative destruction in London was great, Londoners never felt that they were living in a devastated or defeated city. They woke up each morning to fresh losses and strange new vistas, but they did not feel, as the population of Coventry, Plymouth or Portsmouth did, that their town had been destroyed. To be in such a place at such a time, a great city in its finest and most desperate hour, kept many Londoners going. A man of fifty was offered evacuation after being bombed out twice: 'What, and miss all this?' he exclaimed, '[not] for all the gold in China! There's never been nothing like it! Never! And never will be again.'[45]

Taking Shelter

But thousands of Londoners left the city at the start of the Blitz, with or without government assistance. About 40,000 schoolchildren and over 100,000 mothers with their younger children accepted assisted evacuation between September and November 1940, and many thousands of 'unauthorized evacuees' arrived in Oxford, Windsor and other nearby towns. In September 1940 about 5,000 East Enders went off to camp in Epping Forest, but the practice of 'trekking' out to the city periphery each night was far more common in provincial cities (where the periphery was easier to find) than it was in London. Many Londoners, either those who had lost their homes or those who did not find the government leaflet *Your Home as an Air Raid Shelter* a convincing read, simply moved from one part of the city to another. Some moved out to the suburbs, helping to reduce the population of the County of London from 4,062,800 (its 1938 figure) to 3,204,000 by November 1940.[46] Perhaps the most famous of these suburban 'treks' was to Chislehurst Caves, on the Kentish fringe of London, where 12–15,000 people slept in gradually improving conditions in autumn 1940.

Others moved down, rather than out. Tube stations, which had been used in the First World War, were a convenient and obvious place of refuge, and the government's ban on their use as shelters was immediately brushed aside by East Enders when the heavy raids started. Many bombed and homeless citizens were strongly attracted towards the deep, quiet and apparently safe shelter of the Tube, and they were ready to queue for hours to claim their places on the platforms and corridors. The crowds they found there gave them a sense of safety in numbers, a reassurance that they had made the right choice. In late September 1940, at the time of their greatest use, about 177,000 people slept in the underground system, either in one of the seventy-nine available stations, or in the disused Aldwych and Liverpool Street extensions. Tube sheltering was conspicuous, visible of course to every evening or early-morning underground traveller, and it soon became a part of the 'myth' of the Blitz. In reality London did not become a city of troglodytes. Only one Inner Londoner in eighteen slept in the Tube system on its busiest night, and in mid-November, when a rough census of shelterers was conducted, only 4 per cent of Londoners slept in the Tube, while 9 per cent slept in other public or communal shelters (trenches, basements, railway arches, large buildings, and so on), 27 per cent used domestic Anderson or brick shelters (blast proof, but not bomb proof), and 60 per cent stayed in their own beds. In this respect, the 'real' Londoner was more stoical than the 'mythical' one, and the myth is a myth of timidity.[47]

Understandably, the public's choice of shelters was often irrational and badly informed. Deep underground stations were very safe, but some shallower ones proved vulnerable to direct hits, often with terrible results from blast or flooding. Twenty were killed at Marble Arch on 17 September 1940, nineteen at Bounds Green on 12 October, sixty-four at Balham three nights later, and 117 at Bank on 11 January 1941. The worst incident of all, when 178 people were crushed and suffocated on the stairs at Bethnal Green station on 3 March 1943, happened on a night without a raid.[48] Railway arches, a popular choice, were often much more dangerous than they appeared to be, and many shelterers were convinced that large buildings, especially large basements, were safer than small ones, even when their walls and roofs were unsound. In Whitechapel, about 10,000 people occupied a huge railway warehouse known as the Tilbury shelter, which had also been used in the First World War. The building was not as safe as it looked, and conditions inside the shelter quickly became unspeakable, but Londoners chose it in preference to smaller and sturdier buildings. There was more comfort and safety to be found by trekking to the West End, where the basements (and even the higher floors) of the steel-framed shops and offices built between the wars made excellent shelters. The 700 lucky enough to find places in Dickins and Jones's basement got coffee and cake, a clean floor and a safe night.[49]

HOMELESSNESS AND HARDSHIP

Many of those who spent their nights in public shelters were homeless. In the first six weeks of the Blitz about 16,000 houses were destroyed, and another 60,000 seriously (but not irreparably) damaged. Many more houses had to be abandoned because of unexploded bombs, of which around 3,000 were awaiting disposal at the end of November 1940. A quarter of a million Londoners were left without furniture, possessions or shelter by mid-October, and the number was growing week by week. By June 1941 about one Londoner in six had endured a period of homelessness, with a much higher proportion in some central boroughs. The government, which had made such extensive plans for corpses and refugees, had not anticipated this. They had expected the majority of homeless people to make their own arrangements, with a fairly small remnant being left to the care of the LCC and the metropolitan boroughs. The system did not work. By the end of September there were 25,000 homeless people in local authority rest centres (usually schools), living in squalid conditions. A social worker remembered

> dim figures in dejected heaps on unwashed floors in total darkness: harassed, bustling, but determinedly cheerful helpers distributing eternal corned-beef sandwiches and tea – the London County Council panacea for hunger, shock, loss, misery and illness.... Dishevelled, half-dressed people wandering between the bombed house and the rest centre salvaging bits and pieces, or trying to keep in touch with the scattered family.[50]

The position was made worse by the fact that the rest centres were run by local poor law officials, who often treated the homeless as if they were the undeserving poor. Voluntary social workers and supplies sent by the Canadian Red Cross helped ease the position, and early concessions by the Ministry of Health and the Treasury produced 'substantial' improvements in LCC rest centres by the end of September, and 'enormous' ones by the end of October. Gradually old assumptions were abandoned, a new government-funded social policy was developed, and supplies of hostels, blankets, mattresses, camp beds, first-aid kits and furniture began to catch up with the need for them. Over the winter the LCC and the Women's Voluntary Service (WVS) organized a system of mobile canteens and school-based feeding centres, the Londoners' Meals Service, to bring hot food to those who had lost their homes or their gas and water supplies, and the rest centres were supplied with sanitary and medical services. By the end of 1941, too late for the victims of the early raids, 'the transformation was complete. The bleak, inhospitable poor law standards of the centres in September 1940 had given way to good and kindly board and lodging, available without charge to the homeless victims of air attack'.[51] The Beveridge Report and the new welfare state had not yet been born, but perhaps in these hurried and humane changes we can feel them kicking.

The LCC's rest centres were meant to be places of temporary refuge. Their reform could only be effective if the boroughs developed a rehousing programme that would make room in the rest centres for each week's new wave of homeless. But by mid-October, when there were about 250,000 homeless Londoners, including 25,000 in 129 LCC rest centres, London's ninety-six housing authorities had only rehoused 7,000 people. The maze of local and central authorities with responsibility for some aspect of the London housing problem was too complex for many local officials to understand, and baffling for dazed and bombed-out families, trudging from one office to another. Some local authorities did not know what their billeting and repair duties were, others did not realize the extent of their power to requisition empty properties, of which London had very many, and some could not shed the parochial and punctilious habits that had served them well enough in peacetime. Some, like Shoreditch, showed intelligence and foresight, and others, notably Stepney, were overwhelmed by the size of their tasks. Even those ready to move quickly were hindered by severe shortages of skilled builders (except in the army), materials, furniture and transport. Most bombed-out Londoners, as we have seen, would not leave the city, and the early expedient of moving East Londoners to the West End, away from their work, their markets and their friends, was not pursued for long.[52]

IMPROVISED POLICIES

At the end of September the Ministry of Health, which knew through Home Intelligence of the growing discontent in the rest centres, appointed a Special Commissioner for the London homeless, H. U. Willink, to bring order to the chaos of London's many housing authorities. Willink, the Conservative MP for North Croydon, clarified the division of duties between the LCC and the boroughs, leaving the latter in charge of billeting, requisitioning, furniture supply, and welfare work for the homeless. Willink employed a staff of trained social workers (a group in which governments had taken little interest in the past), who began treating the homeless as individuals, each with unique welfare needs. To give the homeless the information they needed to help themselves, the Ministry of Health started poster and leaflet campaigns in bombed areas, and stimulated the establishment of around eighty information centres, many of which were staffed by volunteers from the Charity Organization Society and the London Council of Social Service. In the chaos of war information was vital if people were to get help and housing quickly, to reassemble their scattered families and get back to work.[53]

In the autumn of 1940 the weight and continuity of raids, the unexpected disruption caused by unexploded bombs, and the shortage of labour and money defeated the efforts of even the better local authorities to maintain their stocks of habitable houses. Only after the London raids subsided in early December, when the War Office agreed to give up some of its trained builders and the Ministry of Works introduced its mobile repair squads, did the boroughs and the LCC get to grips with the task of repairing damaged houses. By August 1941 over 1,100,000 houses had been patched up to a low but habitable standard, and the LCC's 291 rest centres, which could now take 33,000 people, were never half full, even in the huge raids of spring 1941. That same spring the War Damage Act relaxed the rules governing the allocation of compensation for lost furniture and clothing, enabling those who were rehoused to bring some comfort to their new homes. Generosity replaced the poor law spirit, and the roughly 1,300,000 Londoners who were given payments by the Assistance Board in the war were no longer made to feel like paupers. There had been several weeks of incompetence and avoidable hardship at the start of the Blitz, but by its end London had a new system of post-raid services which would cope easily when heavy raids began again in 1944.[54]

The government's handling of public shelters also went through a period of rapid improvisation in response to public discontent, and the Communist Party's campaign for more deep shelters, in the autumn of 1940. On 14 September, only a week after the start of the Blitz, the Horder Committee began investigating conditions in the shelters, especially the overcrowded public dormitories that had developed as a result of all-night raids. Horder reported within a few days, recommending that big shelters should have bunks, toilets, first-aid boxes, sick bays, paid marshals, lights, heaters, medical inspections and regular cleaning, all at government expense. The LCC, unlike most local authorities, moved fairly quickly to implement these recommendations. In October it introduced a ticket system to prevent overcrowding, installed chemical toilets and started to appoint shelter wardens. In November and December there were bunks, refreshments and special underground food trains, and in January, when a full-time Regional Welfare Adviser was appointed for London, medical posts, libraries, classes and entertainments. In Chislehurst Caves, where the shelterers had developed their own rules and services, bunks and medicines were provided at public expense.[55] The government still maintained that dispersed home sheltering was the best policy, and in December it introduced a new indoor shelter, the Morrison, a steel-topped wire cage for three or four which could double, its users were told, as a table. But for the minority of Londoners who preferred to shelter deep, work was begun on ten new Tube tunnels, each with room for 8,000 people. By 1942, when some of these very expensive tunnels were finished, shelterers did not need them, and they were used instead by British and American troops. The numbers sleeping in public shelters fell after the end of the Blitz in May 1941, and in 1942 many stations were closed at night. The Tubes and public shelters filled up again two years later, first in the 'Little Blitz' of January–March 1944, and then during the V-bomb raids of June 1944–March 1945.[56]

The Great Raids of November 1940–May 1941

The night of 14/15 November 1940, when London was left in peace while the centre of Coventry was destroyed, marked the start of a new German policy, and a recognition that the intensive bombing of London could not have the decisive effects that had been expected in September. On the following night, a full moon, there was a heavy and unusually widespread raid on London, in which every metropolitan borough but one was hit. A gigantic 1,800-kilogram delayed-action bomb, with the name of 'Satan', landed on the main Post Office sorting office at Mount Pleasant, and there was damage to Westminster Abbey, Euston Station and the National Portrait Gallery. Bombs fell on London for the next two nights, but between 18 November and 19 January London had only six big raids, and the *Luftwaffe* divided its efforts between the capital and other important industrial towns. Of the 19,000 tons of high explosive dropped on London between September 1940 and May 1941, 14,000 tons had already been dropped by 14 November. But some of the worst and most destructive nights of the Blitz were still to come. Late November and early December were quiet, but on 8/9 December there was a 400-bomber raid, which killed 250 and injured 630. Over 3,000 incendiary canisters, nearly three times as many as in any previous raid, were dropped, and 1,700 fires were started. There was damage to Westminster Abbey, Broadcasting House, the Royal Naval College and the Port of London Authority building that night. London was hit again on 27/28 December, and again on the night of 29 December, with appalling consequences.

The raid of Sunday, 29 December was not unusually big: only 136 bombers came over, and far fewer incendiaries were dropped than on 15 November or 8 December. But it was a windy night, and the raid's concentration in the small area of the City, when warehouses, churches and offices were locked, deserted and unwatched, made it dangerous. Incendiary canisters which might have been smothered if they had been seen quickly were left to burn, and by about 9 p.m., when the raid stopped, there were over 1,400 fires in the City, including twenty-eight 'major' fires and six 'conflagrations'. The biggest of these covered half a square mile. Once these great fires had taken hold, the London Fire Brigade did not have the trained officers, the equipment or the water to contain them. The inadequacy of the water supply was intensified by the fact that the Thames was very low, making it difficult to use fire boats and riverside pumps, and because at least twelve large water mains were broken, including the new emergency main between the Thames and the Grand Union Canal. In large parts of the City, especially the area north and east of St Paul's, enormous fires were burning out of control. The death toll in this largely uninhabited area was fairly small (about 163 died that night, including sixteen firemen) but the loss of buildings in the historic City was shocking. The Guildhall was burned out (though its walls survived, as they had in 1666), Paternoster Row was destroyed along with millions of books, Christ Church Newgate, St Lawrence Jewry, St Bride's, and five other Wren churches were ruined, along with All Hallows-by-the-Tower and many livery company halls. Nine hospitals, five main line termini and sixteen underground stations were damaged in the raid, the Central Telegraph Office was destroyed, and the important Wood Street telephone exchange was burnt out and abandoned. St Paul's, which had already been damaged on 10 October, was hit by twenty-eight incendiaries, but it was saved by skilled and devoted fire watching. Its dome was famously photographed that night, rising defiantly from the smoke of the burning City, by Herbert Mason on the *Daily Mail* roof.[57]

It was common knowledge the next day that the City's disaster was partly the fault of inadequate fire-watching. 'All through neglect!' Vere Hodgson wrote on 31 December. '... Common sense should tell us that it is madness to leave buildings to one caretaker, or to no one at all, in times like these.'[58] Among the several fire-fighting reforms prompted by the 29 December disaster the most important were the laying of new emergency mains in 6-inch steel piping, which (unlike the existing cast-iron mains) would not be broken by high explosives, and the introduction of compulsory fire-watching. The weak and loosely drafted Fire Watchers Order of September 1940, which had left business districts largely unguarded, was replaced in January with new regulations which introduced compulsory fire watching for men living in business districts or working in the City. These new regulations did not cover empty houses or the Palace of Westminster, which remained poorly guarded.[59]

For the next five months London was raided intermittently, as part of a wider bombing campaign against British ports. There were five raids on London in January, one of which caused the Bank Station disaster, in which many shelterers were blown into the path of a train. February was quiet, but on the 13th a giant 2,500-kilogram bomb fell on Hendon High Street, ruining about 360 houses, damaging another 400, and killing seventy-five people. Another on Harrow the next night did less damage. Between 19 February and 12 May there were sixty-one raids involving fifty or more bombers, and of these seven were on London. Three great attacks stand out from the rest. On 19/20 March there was a raid on the docks and the East End, bigger than the raids that had begun the Blitz. Five hundred bombers came over, causing 1,880 fires, 750 deaths and 1,200 serious injuries, mostly in West Ham, Stepney and Poplar. In April there were two massive raids, each of them much heavier and more costly in human life than anything that had gone before. On the night of Wednesday, 16 April 685 bombers dropped 890 tons of high explosives and 4,200 incendiaries, which started 2,250 fires, mostly in central and South London, and killed 1,180 people. St Paul's, which seems to have been deliberately targeted, sustained its worst damage that night, and its east end would have been destroyed if a parachute mine that landed there had gone off. Wren's church of St Andrew Holborn was ruined, and most of Chelsea Old Church, where St Thomas More had preached and worshipped, was destroyed. Wallis's, one of the two big Holborn department stores, was gutted. There was another raid of even greater destructive force three nights later, this time concentrated on the docks and the East End. More tons of high explosives and more incendiaries were dropped on 19 April than on any other night of the war.[60] In these two great raids, the 'Wednesday' and the 'Saturday', a total of 2,380 people, more than a tenth of all Londoners who died in the 1940–1 Blitz, were killed, and 148,000 houses were destroyed or damaged. Bombs were getting more powerful and bombers more accurate, and although civil defence and night fighters were improving too, the impact of these raids was getting closer to the predictions of the 1930s. By now, though, Londoners had learned to live with the Blitz, and earlier reforms in shelter conditions and the treatment of the homeless prevented the growth of social unrest.[61]

Before the end of 1940, Hitler had decided to go to war against the Soviet Union without waiting for victory in the battle with England. Although Londoners did not know it, the Blitz was becoming a sideshow, a diversion of men and material from Germany's coming conflict in the east. There was time for one last enormous attack on London, the biggest of them all, before German bombers were withdrawn for other duties. Between 11 p.m. and 4 a.m. on the night of 10–11 May, a bomber's moon again, 550 planes dropped over 700 tons of high explosive and thousands of incendiaries on seventy-five London boroughs, paying special attention to central, eastern and south-eastern areas. The damage from fires (of which over 2,000 were started) and explosions was worse than it had been on any other night, and so was the human cost – 1,436 killed and 1,800 seriously injured. Fire-watching was much better now, but the Thames was low again, 605 water mains, including ninety-eight large ones, had been ruptured, and the London Fire Brigade had a desperate struggle to keep the bigger fires under control. Some of them were still burning ten days later. The docks were alight again, and there was heavy damage in Poplar, Bermondsey and Westminster. The most famous casualty that night was the Chamber of the House of Commons, which was destroyed by incendiaries and an oil bomb. Westminster Hall, the House of Lords, Victoria Tower, Westminster Abbey, St James's Palace and Lambeth Palace were damaged, and the Queen's Hall, the home of the Proms, was destroyed. Almost every main-line terminus was blocked, fourteen hospitals were hit, five City livery company halls were destroyed, and there was damage to the Tower, the British Museum, the Old Bailey and the Mansion House. This was the night that the early medieval Temple Church, St Clement Danes, St Mary-le-Bow and St Olave Hart Street, the church which Samuel Pepys had saved from the Great Fire, were reduced to ruins.[62]

FLYING BOMBS

Although Londoners were left in relative peace between May 1941 and January 1944, they did not believe that their ordeal was over. There were still occasional raids on London and many attacks on other towns and cities. A sixty-plane raid on 27 July 1941 killed ninety people and damaged many houses in the East End, and two raids on 17 and 20 January 1943 killed 107, including forty girls in a school in Lewisham. Total London air-raid deaths, which had fallen to twenty-seven in 1942, rose to 542 in 1943.[63] There was a period of more persistent attacks, the 'Little Blitz', between 21 January and 18 April 1944, when about 2,000 tons of explosives and an almost equal weight of incendiaries were dropped on London in thirteen raids. Five raids between 18 and 24 February inflicted heavy damage on houses in Battersea and West London, and large fires burned in Islington and the southern suburbs on 19 and 24 March. But despite some refinements in radar techniques and the design of bombs, these raids were only rather feeble replays of those of 1940–1, and did not present a serious challenge to the civil defence, sheltering and rehousing systems that had been developed in the Blitz.[64]

Something much worse was to follow. In October 1942 German army scientists at Peenemunde (on an island off the Baltic coast) had carried out successful tests on a 46-foot rocket, the A4 or V2, which was capable of carrying a one-ton warhead for 220 miles at 3,600 m.p.h. This was the culmination of work on liquid fuels and gyroscopic stabilization that had been going on all through the 1930s. At the same time the *Luftwaffe* developed a rival weapon, the FZG.76 or V1, a pilotless jet aircraft which could carry a 1-ton warhead about 250 miles at 470 m.p.h. The V stood for *Vergeltung* (vengeance), and it was this, rather than victory, that the new bombs were intended to deliver. The V1 was an inferior weapon, but since forty-eight of them could be produced for the cost of one £6,000 V2 both systems had their advocates. Rivalry between the army and the *Luftwaffe*, along with technical problems and a successful British bombing raid on Peenemunde, delayed the final introduction of the V1 until June 1944 and the V2 until September 1944, when Allied forces were already in France, and perhaps within a few months' advance of the firing sites near Dunkirk.[65] Thanks to information from agents or German anti-Nazis, and the decipherment of the German Enigma codes, the British government knew about the development of V-bombs in 1943, though there was disagreement about their range and power, and confusion about which of the two weapons to expect. Lord Cherwell, Churchill's obstinate and idiosyncratic scientific adviser, thought rockets were a hoax. As in the 1930s, the British government reached unduly pessimistic conclusions about the likely effects of the new weapons. They exaggerated the number of V-weapons that would be produced and the destructive power of each weapon, and suggested that rockets, arriving in London at a rate of one an hour, could kill up to 10,000 people a day. On the strength of such predictions the government began preparing new plans to evacuate 100,000 people from London, and initiated the production of 100,000 Morrison shelters. Heavy bombing raids on V-weapon production sites were launched, delaying their deployment for several crucial months. Armed with fuller information on V1s (flying bombs) in February and March 1944, the Air Ministry predicted raids of between 80 and 160 tons every two or three days for a month, diminishing thereafter. At the same time the Ministry planned three defensive belts around London: the flying bombs would have to get past a ring of fighters, another of guns, and a third of barrage balloons to reach their target.[66]

On 12 June 1944, six days after the Allied landings in France, ten V1s were launched, of which six crashed and only one managed to reach London. It killed six people in Bethnal Green. Three days later heavier raids began, with V1s crossing the Channel at the rate of about 100 a day.

Although fighters and guns stopped about 40 per cent of these, the rest hit Greater London, and since many fell during the day, when people were in the open and exposed to blast, casualties were very high. In two weeks about 1,600 Londoners were killed and 4,500 badly injured, many of them by flying glass. The ratio of serious casualties to deaths was nearly twice as high as it had been in the piloted attacks of 1940–3.[67] The V1s, variously known as buzz bombs or doodlebugs, spluttered and growled across the sky like a cheap car, which is what the word doodlebug originally meant. When the fuel supply ran out and the engine stopped, those below it dived for cover. It was a type of attack which caused nervous strain, extensive property damage and glass injuries, but little damage to gas or water mains, and few fires. Damage was scattered, but the South London districts of Lewisham, Camberwell, Wandsworth, Woolwich, Greenwich, Lambeth and especially Croydon were worst hit. This was partly the result of efforts by British intelligence to persuade the Germans (using reports sent by captured German agents) that they were overshooting their target, central London, and should therefore shorten their range.[68] In the worst single incident, 119 people, mostly army officers, were killed when the Guards Chapel, near St James's Park, took a direct hit. Over 20,000 houses were damaged each day in July, and after three weeks of the attack there were nearly 200,000 houses awaiting repair. A huge repair force, numbering 129,000 at its peak, was organized to patch up these damaged houses over the autumn and winter.[69]

Vere Hodgson described the experience of V1 raids in early July:

The papers call it the baby blitz. It is annoying to have it all the time. You just dodge out for a few minutes to shop. People are amazingly unconcerned – except the old. All the men think about is to get into the open and see one! . . .

. . . One listens fascinated to the Doodle Bugs passing over, holding one's breath, praying they will travel on, but feeling a wretched cad, because you know that means they will explode on someone else. . . .

. . . The atmosphere in London has changed. Back into the Big Blitz. Apprehension is in the air. Buses half empty in the evening. Marked absence of people on the streets. Thousands have left, and many go early to the shelters. Children have been going in their hundreds. . . .

. . . Perhaps it is not so bad as the Big Blitz, though it is nerve-racking to have it all day. But then the nights were wild with gunfire, and the great bombs came tearing and whistling down the sky, driving deep into the earth. These beastly things are only unpleasant if they explode near you. In the distance they don't sound much.[70]

There was a rapid but short-lived exodus from London in July and early August. Since many of those who left went privately, rather than as part of the government's scheme for evacuation of mothers and their children, the full number is unknown, but it was probably over a million.[71] Dr Johnson's aphorism could now be stood on its head, a wit remarked: only those who were tired of life still lived in London. By the end of August the worst of the V1 raids were over, and the evacuees were drifting back. The V1 launching sites were gradually coming under Allied control, and a very high percentage of the bombs still being launched were stopped by fighters and radar-guided guns. When all the launching sites were lost, V1s continued to be launched from planes and from Holland, but most were brought down, and only seventy-nine reached London between mid-September 1944 and March 1945.[72]

ROCKET ATTACKS

The return of evacuees in August 1944 was not welcomed by the government, which anticipated the early arrival of rocket bombs that would be more terrible than V1s, and feared a stampede of refugees. Instead, Churchill urged in the Commons on 2 August, those outside London should stay away, and those with no war duties should depart 'in a timely, orderly and gradual manner'. A few weeks later the capture of the V1 bases, and the discovery that the new rockets carried a warhead of 1-ton rather than the predicted 7 tons, changed the government's mind, and on 7 September, Duncan Sandys, who had been head of the government's committee on rocket attacks since 1943, declared that 'except possibly for a few last shots, the Battle of London is over'. He spoke too soon. The following day V2 rockets landed in Chiswick and Epping, and London became the first city in the world to come under sustained long-distance rocket attack. This was a truth too terrible to tell. For the next two months the government maintained that the enormous explosions that Londoners heard every day were caused by gas, but no one was fooled. 'It was the great topic of conversation as soon as people meet,' Vere Hodgson wrote on 13 September. 'But neither radio nor newspapers speak. . . . It is all hush-hush. They seem to be rockets which drop from the stratosphere. You may be out peaceably walking and one drops. Nice prospect!'[73]

The destructive power of the V2s was no greater than that of flying bombs, and the speed at which they hit the ground meant that much of their energy was absorbed by the huge craters that they made. But V2s could not be tracked by radar or stopped by any known means of defence, no warnings could be given and civilians could not take shelter from them, except by abandoning the city. London's first line of defence now was in the Low Countries, where the Allied advance was pushing the mobile V2 bases back out of range. The loss of bases interrupted the rocket attacks on London after 17 September, but on 3 October they began again from new bases, rising in number from two to six a day by late November. In January 1945 the raids intensified (thirteen fell on 26 January), but they slackened in February and March, and finally ended on 27 March, when the last launchers had been captured. The end might have come sooner, but the Chiefs of Staff were insistent that their forces should not be diverted from more important objectives (Dresden, for instance), and that London (and Antwerp, which was hit even harder) could 'take it' for few months more.[74]

Over 1,000 rockets were fired at London between September 1944 and March 1945, and 518 reached it. These were light raids in comparison with those of 1940–1, but the concentrated power of V2s led to some appalling disasters, including the deaths of 160 people in Woolworth's store in New Cross on 25 November, 110 people near Holborn Circus and Smithfield Market on 8 March and 134 in Hughes Mansions in Stepney, where the intensive bombing of London began and ended, at 7.20 in the morning of 27 March. This was almost the last raid of the war. As they had with V1s, British intelligence tried to deceive the Germans into aiming short, by feeding them false information about the timing and location of their hits in the centre. 'In this way over a period of some eight months we contrived to encourage the enemy steadily to diminish his range,' a participant in the deception recorded. 'Thus in the four weeks from 20 January to 17 February 1945 the real MPI [mean point of impact] moved eastward about two miles a week and ended well outside the boundary of the London region.'[75] Perhaps as a result of this ruse 378 of the 1,054 V2s launched landed in Essex, and most of those that hit London fell in its eastern suburbs. No doubt the people of Ilford, West Ham, Barking, Dagenham and Walthamstow, who were already angry, demoralized and frightened by the ferocity of these attacks when victory had seemed so near, would not have been pleased to find out that central Londoners were being saved at their expense. In all, V2s killed 2,511 Londoners and seriously injured nearly 6,000, bringing the total killed in 1944 and 1945, by rockets, flying bombs and the 'Little Blitz', to 9,238, almost half the number killed in the 'Great Blitz' of 1940–1. Thanks to the high level of injuries caused by flying bombs, serious injuries in 1944 outnumbered those suffered in 1940.[76]

London's Losses

So London's long ordeal came to an end. The suffering had been drawn out, as well as intense. Londoners had been at war, experiencing or expecting raids, for almost five years. Bomb alerts had sounded 1,224 times, roughly once every thirty-six hours, and there had been a total of 354 raids by piloted aircraft, and 2,937 by pilotless bombs. The weight and destructiveness of the attack had been much lighter, in the event, than everyone had feared, and much lighter, too, than in the Allied attacks on German cities in the last years of the war. More civilians died in Hamburg in July 1943, and in Dresden in February 1945, than in London during the whole war. In comparison with other parts of Britain, London suffered badly. A total of 29,890 Londoners were killed, with another 50,000 badly injured, out of national totals of 60,595 and 86,182.[77] The number of Londoners who died early because of the strains and hardships of the war is hard to calculate, but it is striking that a rise in deaths from heart disease, bronchitis and strokes increased the death rate in the County of London from its normal 12 per 1,000 to 18.8 per 1,000 in 1940–1, 15 per 1,000 in 1942 and 16.8 in 1944. Part of this increase was no doubt due to the fact that many young and healthy Londoners were away from the capital on war service or as evacuees.[78] The physical devastation, both in dwellings and public buildings, was also severe, though less so than had been feared. Greater London lost 116,000 houses (50,000 within the County), and had another 288,000 in need of major repairs. Another million, over half the remaining stock, needed smaller repairs of some sort.[79]

Many of London's great landmarks were destroyed, or ruined (so it seemed) beyond repair. In the City, where 164 of 460 acres of buildings were devastated, there were grievous losses. Eighteen City churches (fourteen by Wren) were ruined, seventeen Company halls (including the medieval Merchant Tailors' Hall) were virtually destroyed, and six badly damaged. Only three (Apothecaries, Ironmongers and Vintners) were undamaged. The Staple Inn Hall was destroyed (but not the houses in front of it), and the Inns of Court were badly hit. The halls and libraries of Gray's Inn and the Inner Temple were destroyed, but the Elizabethan Middle Temple Hall was not damaged beyond repair. The British Museum lost ten upper galleries, 150,000 books and (at Colindale) 30,000 volumes of newspapers. Holland House, the Jacobean mansion in which Macaulay had first tasted social success, and Chelsea Old Church were West London's worst losses.[80]

The most severe losses were in the City, where there was complete devastation around St Paul's, and in a wide band running from the river northwards to Cripplegate and what is now the Barbican, between Moorgate and Aldersgate Streets. There was heavy damage near Ludgate Circus, all along the riverside, and in the area round the Tower, which was itself hit many times. The north-eastern quarter of the City, bounded by Moorgate, Cornhill and Aldgate High Street, escaped the worst of the damage, just as it had in the Great Fire. Outside the City, the three East End boroughs, Stepney, Poplar and Bethnal Green, and the three boroughs north of the City (Holborn, Finsbury and Shoreditch) suffered the heaviest losses, about 19 per cent of their built-up area. The inner boroughs to the south of the river, Bermondsey and Southwark, lost about 15 per cent of their built-up area, and the larger eastern and south-eastern suburban boroughs, Greenwich, Lambeth, Camberwell, Deptford, Hackney, Woolwich and Lewisham, lost about 10 per cent. The boroughs with the lightest damage were in West London: in Chelsea, Westminster, Fulham, Kensington and Paddington only 5 per cent of the developed land was devastated.[81]

For around ten years after the end of the war, there were large areas of bombed land all over London, which were quickly colonized by wild flowers and taken over as playgrounds by local children. The land under London is very fertile, and the bomb-sites were soon full of weeds and flowers, many of which had previously been rare in London. Among the 126 species identified in London bomb-sites, the most common were groundsel, coltsfoot, Oxford ragwort, Canadian fleabane, chickweed, and the once rare but now ubiquitous rose-bay willow herb, which became central London's most familiar flower. London rocket (*Sisymbrium irio*), which had flourished in the ruins of 1666, did not reappear in 1940.[82] The rebuilding of these wild and fascinating playgrounds as housing estates and office blocks in the 1950s left London children (of whom I was one) with a sense of bafflement and loss.

Bombing destroyed workplaces as well as homes. The destruction of shops, factories, docks and offices accelerated the prewar movement of jobs from Inner to Outer London, and did permanent damage to the economies of some central boroughs. Finsbury's huge prewar industrial workforce never recovered from the bombing of its factories and workshops. Its factory workforce fell from 66,556 in 1938 to 36,229 in 1947, and more slowly to 29,660 in 1962. The City, which lost over half its industrial and warehouse property between 1938 and 1949, also lost 40 per cent (14,300) of its industrial workers between 1938 and 1947. In St Marylebone and Westminster, where bombing had been much less severe, the war did not precipitate such a sharp and rapid fall, although the trend was the same and the long-term decline was almost as great. The factory workforce in these two boroughs fell from 76,311 in 1938 to 60,599 in 1947 and 41,256 in 1962. The factors producing decentralization of work from Inner to Outer London had been operating for many years before the war, and would continue to do so after it. But where bombing was most intense, as it was in Stepney, Finsbury and the City, economic changes which might have taken decades were crowded into a few years. On the other hand, where bombing interrupted a process of growth, as in the rise of the City and West End office economy, wartime damage was eventually made good, and prewar trends re-established themselves. Central London office space was reduced from 87 to 77.5 million square feet during the war, but recovered to its prewar level by about 1954, and increased by a further third between 1954 and 1962. Similarly, the destruction of shops might be permanent in fading retail districts, but not elsewhere. Wallis's, in the already declining shopping district of Holborn, was never reopened, but John Lewis, in thriving Oxford Street, was rebuilt in the 1950s on a grander scale.[83]

THE IMPACT OF WAR

Some of the most serious effects of the war could not be so easily seen or measured. Clearly, the war had a very harmful effect on the quality, continuity and availability of schooling in London. As the LCC's Chief Inspector of Education reported in 1943: 'The shock of war and evacuation has been heavy on London schools. . . . Schools were broken up and rapidly lost their identity. . . . For long periods many children were out of school; many others were only part-time and attendance was not enforced because of accommodation rectrictions.' In an average term, about a third of London children missed a quarter or more of their classes, either through illness, work or family duties, or because parental control had weakened. Not surprisingly, when the reading and arithmetic of London children of thirteen to fourteen was tested in 1943, their performance was significantly worse than that of children twenty years earlier. Even more harmful than disrupted schooling, in the view of Richard Titmuss, was the dislocation of family and neighbourhood brought about by the war. Fathers were away, mothers went to work, friends and grandparents were scattered, and 'the old routine of life with its accepted and regular cycle of discipline was knocked awry. . . . Generosity with time is essential to the good discipline and the consistent handling of children, and time spent with parents and teachers was just what children lost in great measure during the war.' Titmuss suggests that as a result of this London children developed a spirit of self-reliance which seemed out of place when peace returned. 'When they were sheltering from the bombs, roaming adventurously through the littered streets, or travelling to the country as evacuees, they were regarded as important and honourable young citizens. But as they grew up during the early postwar years these formative influences were often forgotten by older people, and the ugly epithet, "spiv", was thrust into prominence and indiscriminately bandied about.'[84] It is impossible, though, to measure the influence of six years of disrupted home and school life, or to separate it from the many other forces that shaped the postwar world.

The population loss that the County of London had experienced in every decade since 1901 was greatly accelerated by the disruptive effects of the war. Between 1931 and 1938 the County's population fell by under 8 per cent, from 4,408,000 to 4,063,000, but between 1938 and 1947 (when most of those who were going to return had done so) it fell by 20 per cent, to 3,245,000. In the most damaged boroughs, population dispersal that would have taken a generation was accomplished in a few years. Bermondsey, Finsbury and Southwark each lost 38 per cent of their population (comparing 1938 with 1947), Poplar, Shoreditch and the City lost about 45 per cent, and Stepney lost over half. And yet, as the researches of Young and Wilmott in Bethnal Green in the early 1950s showed, the sense of shared history that bound what remained of these impoverished communities together had not been destroyed, and had perhaps been strengthened, by the war. And now, after enduring high explosives, incendiaries, the doodlebug and the V2, they faced the most relentless enemy of all, the municipal bulldozer.[85]

Looking at their damaged and depopulated city in 1945, with several years of austerity and food shortages still ahead of them, Londoners could nevertheless feel an honest pride in the part they and it had played in the war. Perhaps London did not deserve the heroic reputation that films such as Humphrey Jennings's propaganda masterpiece, *London Can Take It*, sent across the Atlantic in the darkest days of the Blitz, but there was no denying that in the face of an unprecedented technological onslaught it had set an example of civilian courage which would not be forgotten. The image of London's dogged defiance is captured and recalled in countless sounds and images: the dome of St Paul's surrounded by the smoke and flames of the burning City, Henry Moore's sleeping figures huddled on underground platforms, the labelled children waiting for their evacuation trains, barrage balloons, searchlights scanning the night sky for enemy bombers, the Windmill Theatre that 'never closed'; the words that began the BBC's broadcasts to occupied Europe ('This is London'), and the morse code rhythm of the Victory sign; the voice of Churchill, the music of Henry Hall, the sound of the all-clear. Noël Coward, whose play *Blithe Spirit* ran in the West End for nearly 2,000 performances from 1941 to the end of the war, seems to have captured the spirit of Londoners (or London theatregoers) in his song of that year: 'London pride has been handed down to us, London pride is a flower that's free'. At last Londoners had something to be proud of, beyond the mere size and productive power of their city. As Titmuss put it: 'London, that is, the people of London, symbolized to many onlookers the spirit and strength of resistance. It may not have merited greatness, it may not have borne its trials with greater fortitude than other bombed cities of Western civilization, but greatness, an uncomfortable greatness, was thrust upon it during the winter of 1940–1.'[86]

Chapter 25

Postwar London, 1945–1965

LONG BEFORE THE WAR was over, and even before victory was assured, it was understood by politicians of all parties that the British people would not be satisfied with a return to the world they had known before 1939. Even Churchill, who was cautious about raising hopes that could not be fulfilled, promised on 8 October 1940 that London and other bombed cities would 'rise from their ruins, more healthy and, I hope, more beautiful'. The blueprint for a new world, in which the techniques of economic planning and social intervention that had proved so valuable in the struggle against Nazism would be deployed in peacetime against the Five Giants of Want, Ignorance, Disease, Squalor and Idleness, was the Beveridge Report, published to enormous public acclaim in December 1942. London had its fair share of these problems, and would benefit along with the rest of the country from the Welfare State legislation of the Labour government of 1945–51. But London also had some special problems of its own, many of which had been identified by the Barlow Commission's report in 1940, and the spirit of renewal created by the war, along with the large extent of bomb damage, offered a unique opportunity to solve them at a speed which would have seemed impossible before the Blitz.

ABERCROMBIE'S PLAN

The Barlow Report established the fundamental principles that would guide the planning of London in the 1940s and 1950s. Industry and population were too heavily concentrated in the London area, and the country needed a national planning agency with powers to control the location of new industry, to prevent the establishment of new factories in London, and to encourage the dispersal of industries and their workers from London. When the creation of a new Ministry of Works, with the dynamic Lord Reith, creator of the BBC, at its head, was debated in the Commons in October 1940, 'discussion returned again and again to post-war planning and reconstruction'.[1] Reith seized his opportunity, and during his seventeen months in the Ministry initiated a series of enquiries which helped to pursue the implications of the Barlow report and map out the shape of postwar Britain. Two of these enquiries had a bearing on the possible growth of London beyond its existing boundaries. The Scott Report on Land Utilization in Rural Areas (1942) recommended an embargo, except in special circumstances, on the urban development of agricultural land, and endorsed the concept of the Green Belt. The Uthwatt Report on Compensation and Betterment (1942) argued for the introduction of a system of state control over land prices that would make it simpler and cheaper for bombed cities to buy new land for postwar reconstruction, and prevent speculators from making excess profits from the nation's need for land.[2]

In 1941, prompted by a request from Reith, the LCC appointed Sir Patrick Abercrombie and the Council's own architect, J. H. Forshaw, to prepare 'a plan for the reconstruction of the County of London'. Worried by some of the radical anti-metropolitan schemes that were being promoted at the time, the LCC instructed Abercrombie to pay full regard to London 'as the seat of government, as the capital of Empire, an ancient city with established character and tradition, as well as a great industrial and commercial location', and its leader, Lord Latham, emphasized that Londoners 'were not machine tools to be taken up and moved about at will'.[3] But Abercrombie was a leading advocate of decentralization and planned population dispersal in the tradition of Ebenezer Howard and Raymond Unwin, and the *County of London Plan* that he produced in May 1943 persuasively promoted these ideas. Following the conclusions of the Barlow Commission (of which he had been a member), Abercrombie argued that the remedy for London's four great problems, traffic congestion, depressed housing, inadequate open spaces and indiscriminately mixed industrial and residential development, was the planned removal of about 600,000 people from the County, along with the gradual decentralization of an equivalent number of jobs. Although this was only about a seventh of the 1938 population of the County, it involved 39 per cent of the population of the most crowded boroughs, and half the population of Stepney, Shoreditch, Southwark and Bethnal Green. The removal of so many people would be made much easier, Abercrombie argued, by the fact that many houses in the most overcrowded boroughs had already been destroyed in the Blitz, and that population and jobs had dispersed for the duration of the war. The County's population in mid-1943, when the plan was completed, was only 2,482,000, and the job of those who planned and rebuilt the blitzed areas would be to make sure that many of the missing people did not return to their old districts when the war ended.[4]

Abercrombie's approach was to retain and clarify the existing structure of London, and 'make it workable under modern conditions'. 'To ignore London as it exists and treat it as one vast area for experiment would lead to incalculable and unnecessary disturbance to people's lives and, moreover, would be the least economical method of procedure.' Drawing his ideas from the work of the New York regional plan of the 1920s, and from his survey of London as it stood, Abercrombie saw the city as 'a collection of units or communities, fused together', and commanding their own local loyalties. 'Though their boundaries may have been lost', he argued, 'their centres are often clearly marked, having descended from ancient villages;.... It should be one of the first objectives of the planner to disengage these communities, to mark more clearly their identities, to preserve them from disturbing intrusions such as streams of through traffic and generally to reconstruct them where reconstruction is necessary.'[5] Within each community there would be smaller units, perhaps traffic-free precincts, each centred on a local primary school, and self-sufficient in basic local amenities. The location of new roads and open spaces should, where possible, be used to emphasize the boundaries between existing communities.

Abercrombie argued that housing densities should not be left to chance, or allowed to simply duplicate what had gone before. He proposed three housing density zones, with height limits on residential buildings of 80, 60 and 40 feet respectively: a high-rise West End zone, where an upper limit of 200 people per acre would allow a large number of residents to enjoy a central location and the Royal Parks; a mixed 'sub-central' zone, including the East End and the South London riverside boroughs, with a maximum of 136 an acre; and the suburban parts of the County, with 100 people an acre. Beyond the County boundary, housing densities would be lower still, falling to fifty an acre in the suburbs and about twenty an acre in Green Belt developments.[6] Abercrombie paid special attention to the second of these zones, the derelict and badly blitzed boroughs of the East End and Inner South London. In preparing detailed plans for the reconstruction of this area he tried to combine several desirable but conflicting features: individual houses for the many families that wanted them, new open spaces at the rate of 4 acres per 1,000 people, homes for a large (though reduced) population and industries to provide local employment. 'In other words a balance has to be struck between the number of people to be rehoused, the type and size of the dwellings, the amount of open space to be provided for recreation and amenity, and the degree of decentralization.' Abercrombie's solution was a mixed development of terraced houses for families, low-rise flats, and a few blocks of higher flats for the single and childless.[7] He also suggested that much of the industry that occupied the banks of the Thames, especially where it no longer used the river, should be swept away (a process which the *Luftwaffe* had already begun) and replaced with riverside open space for public use. The derelict and gloomy south bank of the Thames, between County Hall and Southwark Cathedral, Abercrombie said, should be tied to Westminster by two new road bridges, and transformed into a great cultural centre with a modern theatre, a large concert hall, and government and commercial offices.[8]

The preservation of local communities was linked to Abercrombie's solution for London's traffic and open space problems. To separate through traffic from local vehicles and from pedestrians in residential and shopping districts, Abercrombie drew upon the 1937 Bressey Report, and suggested the construction of two ring roads inside the existing North and South Circulars, one a local (sub-arterial) road circling the City, Southwark and the West End, and the other a faster arterial route enclosing a larger central area, from Notting Hill, Islington and Stepney to Clapham, Peckham and Rotherhithe. There would be a network of fast radial routes linking to existing trunk roads, most stopping at the outer ring, but two crossing the centre, mainly in tunnels. The building of these new roads, like the creation of the new open spaces that inner Londoners so badly needed, would be made much easier by the extent of bomb damage, and the location of both would be used to re-establish the boundaries, and the sense of separateness, of London's individual communities.[9]

DISPERSING THE POPULATION

Abercrombie said little about the destination of the dispersed 600,000 in the County of London Plan, except to suggest that the area immediately west and north-west of the West End could absorb about 150,000 people of modest incomes – clerks, shop assistants and East End workers – in blocks of flats and converted houses. But along with most planners and politicians, he was very hostile to the resumption of the suburban sprawl which had resulted from the unplanned dispersal of inner Londoners between the wars. He addressed the problem of encouraging dispersal without creating sprawl in a larger and more ambitious study covering about 2,600 square miles, which Reith initiated, after discussions with Home Counties local authorities, in January 1942.[10] This study, which was published in 1945 as *The Greater London Plan, 1944,* set out to show how the aims of the Barlow Report could be achieved in the special circumstances created by the Second World War, and with new planning powers that were strong enough to prevent the growth of industry or population in London.

Abercrombie identified four 'rings' in the London region. The first, which needed to lose over a million people, was the Inner Urban Ring, which included the County and the overcrowded boroughs just beyond its boundary, especially East and West Ham, Leyton, Walthamstow, Tottenham, Willesden and Croydon. The next, the Suburban Ring, including the rest of the built-up area, had room for about 90,000 through the development of small vacant plots, but was not to be treated as a reception area for the Inner Ring's overspill. Beyond that was a Green Belt Ring, forming a circular belt about 10 miles thick, with its outer limits about 20 miles from Charing Cross. This area would be saved from suburban sprawl and ribbon development by strict planning controls, though a few of its existing towns would receive London overspill. Beyond the Green Belt was the Outer Country Ring, stretching, at its widest, 70 miles from Royston in the north to Horley and Haslemere in the south. Some of the million people to be removed from the crowded boroughs would be rehoused in existing urban areas: 125,000 in urgent postwar housing programmes in the Suburban Ring and the Green Belt, 260,000 in suitable towns in the Outer Country Ring (such places as Slough, Guildford, Reigate, Gravesend, Brentwood, Welwyn Garden City, St Albans, Luton, Letchworth and High Wycombe), 164,000 in more distant towns within about 50 miles of London, including Basingstoke, Didcot, Aylesbury, Bletchley and Braintree, and 100,000 'wholly outside the Metropolitan influence'.[11] The largest group of dispersed Londoners, about 380,000, would go to a number of new satellite towns, all in or near the Outer Country Ring, and each with a projected population of around 60,000. Abercrombie proposed ten sites, three each in Essex and Hertfordshire, two in Surrey, and one each in Kent and Berkshire, all near enough to 'retain an intimate link with London', especially for amusements and cultural events, but far enough from London's influence to develop an economic life and communal spirit of their own. These were to be living and working communities in the spirit of Ebenezer Howard and the Garden City movement, not dormitory towns inhabited by commuting 'strap-hangers'.[12]

Abercrombie's plans had enormous influence over the postwar development of London, and created the ideal against which the efforts of postwar planners and politicians would be judged. Four of his aims guided the government's planning for London for at least the next twenty-five years: the decentralization of London's population and employment; the protection of the Green Belt; the control of housing densities by zoning; and the relocation of London jobs and people into satellite towns beyond the Green Belt. But a plan is just a plan, and predictions are only as good as the assumptions upon which they are based. Abercrombie drew upon expert opinion as it stood in the late 1930s, and as a result made several assumptions which turned out to be incorrect. He followed the best demographers of the day in assuming (with some hesitation) that the demographic stagnation of the interwar years would persist, giving Greater London and Great Britain no significant natural population growth over the next thirty years.[13] But birth rates are notoriously unpredictable, and in fact the population of England and Wales rose by 7.2 million (17 per cent) between 1939 and 1971, and the expected stagnation did not take place until the 1970s and 1980s (by which time it was no longer expected). Greater London had a natural population growth of about 600,000 between 1951 and 1966, and a natural growth of 460,000 in the Outer Metropolitan Area (which extended a little beyond Abercrombie's Green Belt and Outer Country Ring) meant that the 'reception areas' which Abercrombie expected to fill with migrating Londoners also had to find room for a growing number of local people.[14] Abercrombie assumed, following the Barlow Report, that the decentralization of manufacturing employment would solve the problem of London's excessive share of the national workforce, and failed to plan for the office boom which would replace London's lost factory jobs and reinvigorate the London economy. Abercrombie had not the slightest idea that the trade of most of the docks, one of the mainstays of London's industrial and commercial prosperity, would fade almost to nothing in the 1960s and 1970s, or that dockland would eventually become part of London's office economy. And if he had known that Londoners would soon be spending most of their leisure time in front of televisions, would he have insisted on 4 acres of open space for every 1,000 citizens?

THE TOWN AND COUNTRY PLANNING ACTS

Abercrombie's main principles appealed to the leaders of the wartime Coalition and the new Labour government, and between 1944 and 1947 they created the legislative framework which could put them into effect. The Coalition created the Ministry of Town and Country Planning in 1943, and introduced the 1944 Town and Country Planning Act, which gave local authorities powers of compulsory purchase over blitzed and derelict sites at 1939 prices (Uthwatt's 1942 recommendation), and to designate them Reconstruction Areas. It was under this Act that the LCC began its comprehensive redevelopment of Stepney, Poplar and Bermondsey in 1947. The 1945 Distribution of Industry Act enabled the Board of Trade to refuse planning permission for new factories or large factory extensions, and thus steer industry away from London and towards depressed areas. As it turned out, this Act, even when it was strengthened in 1947, did not decentralize employment as effectively as Barlow had expected, partly because firms could still grow by piecemeal extensions or buying vacant factories, and mainly because the Act ignored the fact, as Barlow and Abercrombie had, that office work and the service industries, rather than manufacturing, would be the growth sectors in the postwar economy.[15]

The system of planning that had been introduced piecemeal since 1944 was extended and codified by the massive and complex Town and Country Planning Act of 1947. The number of planning authorities was cut from 1,440 to 145, and their decisions were to be made in accordance with government-approved local development plans. Planning in the London region, which had been the responsibility of 136 authorities, was now in the hands of the LCC, the six surrounding counties (Essex, Middlesex, Hertfordshire, Kent, Surrey and Buckinghamshire) and the County Boroughs of Croydon, East Ham and West Ham. The City, whose own *City of London Plan* had just been completed, lost its planning powers to the LCC, which now had planning responsibility for the whole County. The Act made all development and change of land use subject to local authority planning permission, and affirmed the government's commitment to the Green Belt. In future, this could be achieved by planning controls, not, as in the LCC's 1930s scheme, by purchase. In an important endorsement of the Uthwatt report, the Act established that landlords owned only the existing rights and values of their land, not its future development value. Development rights were, in effect, nationalized, and the full enhancement of an estate's value created by planning permission or compulsory purchase was to be repaid to the State, as a 'development charge' or 'betterment levy'. The development charge created some practical difficulties and was said to discourage the development of land, and in 1954 the Conservative government (with its friendlier attitude to landlords and private profit) abolished it, restoring landowners' right to profit fully from the public or private development of their land. This hasty change in the law opened the way for the 1950s property boom, and made millionaires out of farmers in new town or overspill areas, and of the owners of inner-city redevelopment land.[16]

The ten London planning authorities created by the 1947 Act all produced Development Plans which followed the outlines established by Forshaw and Abercrombie. The LCC's own plan, published in 1951, explained in detail how it would achieve Abercrombie's aims, deviating from them only by reducing his yardstick of 4 acres of open space per 1,000 people to 2.5 acres, and replacing his ring roads with cheaper and less ambitious 'cross routes', mostly based on existing roads. The London Development Plan identified nine districts in the County (amounting to 4,000 acres) which were designated Areas of Comprehensive Development, either because they had been heavily bombed, or simply because they were considered, in the language of the Plan, 'obsolete', 'muddled' or 'congested'. These included 244 acres of the City, especially the wide swath of blitzed land running between St Paul's and the Guildhall from the Thames to the Barbican; Bunhill Fields, a 43-acre northern extension to the City's main blitzed area; a 1,300-acre wedge of land in Stepney and Poplar, which was to be rebuilt as a 'new town' for 100,000 people, half its prewar population; the South Bank, which was to be developed, in line with Abercrombie's plan, as a cultural and office centre; 120 acres of the Bermondsey riverside, a badly blitzed area of outworn housing and warehouses; and 30 acres at the Elephant and Castle, whose commercial redevelopment would (it was hoped) revitalize Southwark and North Lambeth.[17] Other areas were added in the 1950s, including 150 acres of west Bethnal Green, between Hackney Road and Shoreditch Station, a district of 'narrow and confined streets lined with outworn and sub-standard buildings', and Lambeth Walk, 50 acres of 'closely packed and obsolete dwellings' which had suffered heavy bomb damage. The pace of redevelopment in these areas was uneven. By 1960 about a third of the City development area had been rebuilt, and about a half of the new housing in the Stepney–Poplar new town was built or in progress. North Bermondsey's transformation into a district of low-rise flats was expected to be complete by 1970, and Erno Goldfinger's dramatic reconstruction of the Elephant and Castle was accomplished in the early 1960s. Bethnal Green still retained much of its old 'muddled and congested' way of life in 1953–5, when Young and Wilmott did their research for *Family and Kinship in East London*, but lost it over the next ten years, when this lucky district became a laboratory for 'virtually every English experiment in public housing'.[18]

PARKS AND A FESTIVAL

One of the intended compensations of moving from houses to flats was the gaining of new areas of parkland and open space. In Abercrombie's Plan, the people of the County of London, especially those in the inner boroughs which had always been short of parks, were to be given an extra 5,428 acres of public land, the equivalent of fifteen Hyde Parks. By 1960 the LCC had managed to find 521 acres, including the 50-acre gardens of the bombed Holland House and the South Bank promenade. There were some useful but modest additions to the green spaces of some very poorly provided districts, especially Stepney, Shoreditch, Bethnal Green, Bermondsey and North Camberwell. The LCC's efforts in the 1950s produced Hammersmith Park, New River Gardens, King George's Fields, Haggerston Park and Hague Street Open Space, but the bigger parks proposed by Abercrombie and promised in the LCC's 1960 Review of the County of London Plan were forgotten, and the inhabitants of King's Cross, Islington, Shoreditch, Spitalfields, Stepney, Walworth, Stockwell, Brixton, north Peckham and New Cross remained (and in most cases remain) sadly short of local playgrounds.[19] Since 1965 there have been two impressive additions to Inner London's parkland. In Tower Hamlets, Mile End Park follows the Grand Union Canal for almost a mile from Victoria Park to King George's Fields, and in Walworth what began as the 15-acre North Camberwell Open Space had been increased, by a painstaking process of piecemeal acquisition, into the 135-acre Burgess Park, with London's biggest postwar lake. Smaller, but useful, parks have been created in Islington since the 1960s: Barnard Park, Paradise Park, and Caledonian Park, on the site of the old cattle market.[20]

The earliest and most dramatic achievement of the comprehensive development programme was the complete replanning of the blitzed and decayed South Bank, between Waterloo Bridge and County Hall. This had been bogged down for lack of funds until the government announced, in February 1949, that the area was to be the site of the 1951 Festival of Britain. The Festival had been intended as an international trade exhibition, like the 1851 Great Exhibition that it commemorated, but the need for economy forced the government to reduce it to a simple British trade fair, with an emphasis on education, patriotism and enjoyment. Herbert Morrison, who had ministerial responsibility for organizing the Festival, saw it as a chance for a great celebration after eleven years of war and austerity: 'I want everyone in Britain to see it, to take part in it, to enjoy it. I want to see the people happy. I want to hear the people sing.' The Festival had its serious side. Twenty-seven pavilions told the story of Britain, and more recent achievements were displayed in the the Design Review Pavilion and the huge Dome of Discovery, where radar and the jet engine stood under the same vast metal roof as penicillin and a model nuclear power station. The whole Festival was a glittering display of the styles, materials and technologies that would help to reshape postwar London: buildings in aluminium, plastics, concrete and glass, furniture in the 'Contemporary' Scandinavian style, continental outdoor restaurants with striped umbrellas, the slim and graceful Skylon obelisk, the 100-seater Brabazon airliner flying overhead, and the marvellous modern architecture of the Festival's only permanent monument, the impressive, beautiful and functional Royal Festival Hall.

No doubt its well-meaning organizers were too keen, like the Victorians, to educate the working classes, but at least they offered them some fun, too. In Battersea Park Osbert Lancaster and John Piper designed a fantastic fairground, the Festival Pleasure Gardens, in which, along with the latest funfair rides, visitors could enjoy firework displays, a tree walk, the Guinness Clock and a crazy railway designed by Emmett, a *Punch* cartoonist, and then dance in a circular dance hall supported by the world's biggest tent pole. Even in a world made blasé by theme parks, these wonders still linger in the mind. They did not linger on the ground, however. The new Conservative government, which made no secret of its hostility to the Festival idea, demolished the South Bank pavilions, the Dome and the Skylon (but not, of course, the Festival Hall) at the end of the Festival in October 1951, making way for the enormous new Shell building. The Battersea funfair remained until the mid-1970s, when its popularity declined and it was removed.[21]

TACKLING THE HOUSING SHORTAGE

The Council's most urgent problem in 1945, and one which hardly allowed them the luxury of long-term planning, was to provide houses for London's rapidly returning population. The Second World War had destroyed 50,000 houses in the County and 66,000 in the rest of Greater London, and left another 1.3 million in need of major or minor repairs. Private building, which had provided the bulk of housing before the war, was virtually at a standstill in the later 1940s, thanks to labour and building material shortages and tight government controls. But the servicemen, evacuees and war workers who were flooding back to London needed homes, and bombed-out Londoners and the many new families created by the postwar baby boom were tired of living with their relatives. The population of the LCC area rose by 800,000 between 1945 and 1950. A brief Communist-organized occupation of empty Kensington flats in September 1946 showed that the housing shortage could not be safely ignored. The LCC and the metropolitan boroughs responded with an emergency repair programme which made 103,000 damaged dwellings fit for habitation by 1947. They also used wartime powers to requisition over 60,000 houses, and although these powers were withdrawn in 1948, London councils still held some of the properties as late as 1960. The local authorities also took over army camps, and erected about 15,000 temporary bungalows or 'hutments' on bombed or open land. The popularity of these aluminium-framed 'prefabs', which were produced in their tens of thousands by redundant aircraft factories at the end of the war, was one of the surprises of the postwar years. All but 500 of them were still in use in 1955.[22]

After these immediate measures, the London authorities were still left with a serious housing deficiency, largely inherited from the 1930s. In 1951 Greater London contained 2,631,000 households (including single adults) but only 2,152,000 dwellings, giving it a 'crude net deficiency' of 479,000 dwellings. Over 60 per cent of this deficiency (300,000 dwellings) was within the County. This meant that roughly 600,000 households in the County of London, and nearly a million in Greater London, had to share their dwelling with another household, some willingly, others not. The houses they shared often reflected the standards of working-class comfort and hygiene that had prevailed before the First World War, when over 70 per cent of houses within the County had been built. In 1951 only a third of the County of London's 1,121,000 households had exclusive use of a fitted bath, lavatory, kitchen sink and cooker. Nearly 490,000 (44 per cent) had no fitted bath at all, and another 200,000 (18 per cent) had to share one with another family. Almost 390,000 households (35 per cent of the County's families) had to share a lavatory, and 16 per cent shared a kitchen sink.[23] When we look upon the gaunt but relatively well-equipped tower blocks of the 1950s and 1960s, and regret the passing of the Victorian slums that they replaced, we should remember these figures.

In 1948 the LCC and the Inner and Outer London borough councils set to work to remedy some of these deficiencies. Each year for the next fifteen years the LCC and the Inner London boroughs between them built around 10,000 new dwellings in the County, and in addition between 1946 and 1955 the LCC built another 38,000 houses and flats outside the County, mostly on Green Belt sites it had acquired during or before the war. By 1949 there were nearly 32,000 new LCC dwellings on the Green Belt fringes of London, and by 1965 the number of LCC houses and flats in its out-county estates had risen to almost 45,000. The biggest of these were Britwell and Langley in Buckinghamshire, Aveley, Debden, Hainault and Harold Hill in Essex, Borehamwood and Oxhey in Hertfordshire, and St Paul's Cray in Kent.[24] Suburban private builders recovered after 1954, when licensing restrictions were lifted, and built 93,000 new dwellings between 1951 and 1961, mostly in the Outer London suburbs, where suburban local authorities were also active. Over this period conversions of larger proper-ties into smaller units seem to have added another 76,000 dwellings, giving Greater London a total net gain between 1951 and 1961, after subtracting the 65,000 houses lost in slum clearance programmes (mainly after 1955) and other demolitions, of 283,600 dwellings.[25] Over the same period the number of separate households in London had increased by about 40,000 (though its population had declined), and Greater London's 'crude net deficiency' of dwellings had fallen to about 250,000. Of course, some multi-occupied houses were adequate (those shared by several single people, or where solitary grandparents lived with their children, for instance), and many single-occupied ones, especially the 340,000 without a fitted bath, were not. The Milner Holland Committee, which weighed evidence from the LCC, the government, and various academic contributors in 1963–5, tentatively concluded that in 1961 there were 190,090 Greater London households in urgent need of new dwellings, and a larger number (between 366,000 and 532,000) that needed new or improved housing because they had no bath. Another indication of housing need was the fact that there were 180,000 households on council waiting lists in Greater London in 1962.[26] Almost the whole burden of providing homes for these people, who were of very little interest to private builders, fell on the local authorities.

THE VOGUE FOR TALL FLATS

For more than twenty years after the Second World War, there was a widespread belief among architects, planners and politicians in local and central government that the best way to cope with the proliferation of small households, at the same time achieving the population densities envisaged by Abercrombie and creating inner-city open space, was to house a proportion of the urban working classes in blocks of flats. High-rise flats were not cheap to build, and local authorities would not have turned to them so enthusiastically had it not been for the decisive influence of the policy adopted by the Macmillan government in 1956. In the belief that only high flats would enable cities to meet its ambitious housing targets, the government introduced a scale of subsidies in which high-rise flats attracted three times as much government support as houses. The premium on tall flats was reduced in 1965, but as long as tall flats were favourably subsidized, councils continued to build them. The cheaper alternative policy of repairing old houses and providing them with modern heating and plumbing, which was often preferred by the tenants themselves, did not attract significant government support, and did not seem to local authorities to offer the mass housing they had in mind. So it was only when the extra high-rise subsidy was removed in 1968 that tall blocks went out of favour.[27]

London already had a tradition of flat-building, and many of its prewar flats had shown that high densities were compatible with good standards of design and comfort. The successful 1930s Dolphin Square estate had a density of 415 people per acre, twice the maximum set by Abercrombie, and Lubetkin's luxurious Highpoint apartment blocks seemed to show that a happy marriage between garden-city ideals and Le Corbusier's high-rise technology was possible. Influential European architects, especially Walter Gropius and Le Corbusier, and their English disciples, emphasized the positive virtues of high-rise living: ample light, fresh air, fine views, open space, community (a favourite word of 1940s planners) and the convenience of a home in the city centre. The attractions of using the science of planning and design, and the new technology of tower cranes, high-speed lifts, reinforced concrete and prefabricated panels, to solve the problem of inner-city overcrowding were immense. To the architects and planners of the Modern Movement, tower blocks were not a cheap alternative to houses, but an improvement upon them. On a practical level, flats would solve the modern problem of small households (single people and childless couples) who would otherwise wastefully occupy three-bedroomed family houses. By exploiting the 'free ... aesthetic of height', modern architects would create 'fine sheer towns that will make their inhabitants proud to live in them'. High buildings, like 'sculpture in the sky', would give 'scale and interest' to otherwise drab landscapes, they would 'stir men's blood' and intensify their experience of urban living. As to the fear that tower blocks would undermine the spirit of neighbourliness, nothing could be further from the truth: 'On a sunny evening or at the week-end each balcony has its tenants leaning elbows on the rail, smoking, gossiping, happy, like a group of cottagers perched above each other on a steep cliff.'[28] It was understood that perhaps only 30 or 40 per cent of people would want to live in high blocks, but cottage estates and mixed developments would cater for all tastes and household types. Only around a quarter of public housing built in Greater London between 1945 and 1975 was in multi-storey flats.[29]

FROM BETHNAL GREEN TO WOODFORD

The advocates of comprehensive redevelopment would have been wise to have set aside a few hours to read *Family and Kinship in East London*, a book by Michael Young and Peter Wilmott that first appeared in 1957. Young and Wilmott described the complex pattern of kinship and friendship ties (and especially the bonds between mothers and daughters) that bound together the population of Bethnal Green, one of those districts of 'obsolete' and insanitary housing that would be largely flattened and rebuilt in the postwar decades. For all its squalor and overcrowding, Bethnal Green was loved and valued by its inhabitants, because within it the 'community' that tower block builders talked so confidently of creating really did exist.

> In Bethnal Green the person who says he 'knows everyone' is, of course, exaggerating, but pardonably so. He does, with varying degrees of intimacy, know many people outside (but often through) his family, and it is this which makes it, in the view of many informants, a 'friendly place'. Bethnal Green, or at any rate the precinct, is, it appears, a community which has some sense of being one. There is a sense of community, that is a feeling of solidarity between people who occupy the common territory, which springs from the fact that people and their families have lived there a long time. We cannot do better than put it in our informants' own words.
>
> 'Well, you're born into it, aren't you? You grow up here. I don't think I'd like to live anywhere else. Both my husband and me were born here and we have lived here all our lives.'
>
> 'You asking me what I think of Bethnal Green is like asking a countryman what he thinks of the country. You understand what I mean? Well, I've always lived here, I'm contented. I suppose when you've always lived here you like it.'
>
> ... For many people, familiarity breeds content. Bethnal Greeners are not lonely people: whenever they go for a walk in the street, for a drink in the pub, or for a row on the lake in Victoria Park, they know the faces in the crowd.[30]

The crowd was getting thinner by the year. The population of Bethnal Green had fallen from 108,000 to 90,000 in the 1930s, collapsed to 47,000 in 1941, and recovered to 60,000 by 1948. By 1955 the population was down again, to under 54,000. Between 1931 and 1955 40,000 Bethnal Greeners had moved, willingly or otherwise, to LCC estates. Young and Wilmott followed some of them to Woodford (they called it 'Greenleigh'), a new LCC cottage estate in the Essex Green Belt:

> Instead of the shops of Bethnal Green there is the shopping centre at the Parade; instead of the streetbarrows piled high with fruit, fish and dresses, instead of the cries of the costermongers from Spitalfields and Old Ford, there are orderly self-service stores in the marble halls of the great combines. In place of the gaunt buildings rising above narrow streets of narrow houses, there are up-to-date semi-detached residences.... Instead of the hundred fussy, fading little pubs of the borough, there are just the neon lights and armchairs of the Merchant Venturer and the Yeoman's Arms. Instead of the barrel organ in Bethnal Green Road there is an electrically amplified musical box in a mechanical ice-cream van. In place of tiny workshops squeezed into a thousand backyards rise the first few glass and concrete factories which will soon give work to Greenleigh's children. Instead of the sociable squash of people and houses, workshops and lorries, there are the drawn-out roads and spacious open ground of the usual low-density estate.[31]

By moving, Bethnal Greeners made enormous material gains. 'Who can wonder that people crowded into one or two poky rooms, carrying water up three flights of stairs, sharing a w.c. with other families, fighting against damp and grime and poor sanitation, should feel their hearts lift at the thought of a sparkling new house and garden?' Especially for mothers who had been evacuated in the war, Bethnal Green now seemed a grim and dirty place, and the fresh air and open spaces of the new estate seemed much better for their children. For adults, there were losses to balance the gains. The higher cost of rents and fares (for the many men who still worked in Bethnal Green) meant less money to spend in the pub, and a more home-based social life. The separation from friends and family led in the same direction: 'You seem to centre yourself more on the home. Everybody lives in a little world of their own.' Neighbours seemed more unfriendly and competitive, and relatives were 20 miles away in Bethnal Green, or in other suburban estates (Oxhey, Debden, Harold Hill, Becontree) which were not linked by bus routes. 'They all keep themselves to themselves. They all come from the East End but they all seem to change when they come down here.' Pubs and shops were too large to be friendly, and estates were too strung out – 'low density does not encourage sociability'. Perhaps community spirit would grow again when the children of the migrants grew up in 'Greenleigh', and regarded it as their home. 'After all, Bethnal Green was once a Greenleigh.' But LCC housing allocation policies made it unlikely that kinship networks would grow as they had done in Bethnal Green.[32] The conclusion that Young and Wilmott reached was that planners should think carefully before breaking up London's old working-class districts and moving their populations to estates on the edge of the town, or new towns beyond it. 'The purpose of rehousing is to meet human needs, not as they are judged by others but as people themselves assess their own.' Most East Londoners wanted to stay in the East End, and they valued their local network of relatives and friends as highly as material comforts. Rehousing, Young and Wilmott argued, should take place within the town, not beyond it, even if that meant giving up some of the parks and open spaces that Abercrombie had proposed. Ideally, old houses should be brought up to modern standards by installing new bathrooms, lavatories and kitchens, and new houses should be in the same district as the ones they replaced. Breaking up the three-generation community and severing the bond of interdependence between mothers and their married daughters might have social consequences which the planners did not anticipate:

> Even when the town planners have set themselves to create communities anew as well as houses, they have still put their faith in buildings, sometimes speaking as though all that was necessary for neighbourliness was a neighbourhood unit, for community spirit a community centre. If this were so, there would be no harm in shifting people about the country, for what is lost could soon be regained by skilful architecture and design. But there is surely more to a community than that. The sense of loyalty to each other amongst the inhabitants of a place like Bethnal Green is not due to buildings. It is due far more to ties of kinship and friendship which connect the *people* of one household to the *people* of another. In such a district community spirit does not have to be fostered, it is already there. If the authorities regard that spirit as a social asset worth preserving, they will not uproot more people, but build new houses around the social groups to which they already belong.[33]

By the time politicians and planners realised the wisdom of this advice, it was too late to follow it.

HIGH-RISE ESTATES

The LCC's first important venture in postwar redevelopment, the Lansbury estate in the Stepney–Poplar Reconstruction Area, was a modest mixed estate which was hurriedly completed as the Council's contribution to the 'Live Architecture' exhibition of the Festival of Britain, following the suggestions in the *County of London Plan*. Its houses and gardens were pleasant and popular, but they were dull stuff from the modern architect's point of view. The exciting architecture was being produced in Finsbury (Lubetkin's Spa Green and Priory Green) and Westminster (Powell and Moya's Churchill Gardens in Pimlico), not in County Hall. This changed in 1950, when planners with garden-city leanings were ousted from control of the LCC's Housing Department, and innovative young architects who had been brought up on Corbusierite principles rushed to join the re-vitalized department. During the 1950s the LCC achieved an unrivalled reputation for the quality and innovation of its housing design. Its policy, unlike those of some other city councils, was to build with care and imagin-ation, rather than to yield to government pressure and put high output and low cost before everything else.[34] The LCC's first and finest attempt to achieve Le Corbusier's ideal of high blocks in open parkland was the Roehampton Estate (Alton East and Alton West), on the western edge of Wandsworth, the only West London borough that welcomed large LCC developments. The Roehampton Estate, built in the 1950s in the grounds of several old houses alongside Richmond Park, was a mixed development of houses and little bungalows for families and the old, and high-rise flats and 'maisonettes'. These were either in 'slabs' (as recommended by Gropius and Le Corbusier) or in slimmer 'point blocks', which had been pioneered in Stockholm and tried out by the LCC in Oatlands Court, Wimbledon (1953). By the time it was completed at the end of the 1950s the estate housed almost 10,000 people. Its undoubted social and aesthetic success, which owed much to its unique site and the exceptional ability of its architects, inspired lesser architects to imitate its achievements, and especially its point blocks.[35] Point blocks obscured less light and view than slabs, gave greater privacy by removing the need for balcony access, allowed for an efficient internal service shaft, and were visually more impressive. LCC architects built more than 100 of them by 1965, gradually increasing their height from the modest eleven storeys of Roehampton to the eighteen of the Brandon estate in Southwark (1955) and the twenty-one of Warwick Crescent in Paddington (1961).[36] The four- and five-storey estates that the

LCC was still building in the 1950s (Highbury Quadrant was a good example) now seemed friendly and old-fashioned by comparison.

The LCC was not alone in seeing high-rise estates as the answer to its housing problems. Some London boroughs (Southwark, Stepney, Camberwell) left the majority of house-building to the LCC, and Conservative-controlled West London boroughs generally resisted LCC developments and were also inactive on their own behalf. But several boroughs competed vigorously with the LCC for good blocks of development land, and took a pride in outdoing the LCC in the quantity or quality of housing they produced. The most enthusiastic tower block builders were Bethnal Green, Bermondsey, Finsbury, Stoke Newington, Woolwich, Hackney, St Pancras, Lambeth, Islington and especially Shoreditch, which built twice as many dwellings in relation to its population as any other borough between 1945 and 1964. There was less activity in Outer London, but there was energetic development in a few County boroughs and districts, including Croydon, East Ham, West Ham, Willesden, Barking, Leyton and Tottenham.[37] Often the LCC acted as a brake on the boroughs, using its great planning powers to stop developments which breached its planned density levels. Paddington's Paddington Green proposal (320 people per acre) was stopped in 1954, and Chelsea's World's End estate (338 people per acre in a 136-per-acre zone) was delayed until after the abolition of the LCC in 1965.

The City Corporation, which had responsibility for a 244-acre comprehensive development area, was one of the most daring and successful high-rise developers. Holford's St Paul's precinct was pedestrian in both senses of the word, but the Chamberlin, Powell and Bon estate at Golden Lane (1954–9), the first in London to rise above fifteen storeys, managed to combine modernity with humanity. 'Every trick in the book is brought in, and not for cleverness's sake, but to create a real place out of statistical units of accommodation,' Ian Nairn wrote in 1966. '. . . This is no ivory tower, and these places are meant for rude human beings playing rough games.'[38] The same firm of architects were involved in the creation of the City's great showpiece, the Barbican, which was built on 35 acres of blitzed land in Cripplegate, north of London Wall, in the 1960s. Unlike the other high-rise estates of the postwar decades, the Barbican was built for well-off residents, rather than people on council waiting lists and those evicted by slum clearance schemes. Here, the combination of immensely high apartment blocks (at forty-three storeys, they were the tallest in Europe) and enjoyable and usable open space really seemed to work. The public spaces and linking walkways were well maintained, the local entertainment was provided (from the 1980s) by the Royal Shakespeare Company and the

London Symphony Orchestra, and the well-heeled residents were there because they wanted to be, not because there was nowhere else to put them. It was an estate, in short, on which even architects and town planners would have been prepared to live. The commercial part of the Barbican development, along London Wall, was less well received.

RACHMANISM

Those who might have doubted the importance of council renting were reminded of the disadvantages of the working-class alternative, private renting, in 1963. In the summer of that year the Profumo scandal (about the involvement of the Minister for War with a prostitute with Soviet connections) threw up the story of Perec (or Peter) Rachman, a slum landlord whose name gave a new word, Rachmanism, to the English language. According to the 1961 census about 40 per cent of London households (1,125,000 households) rented their homes from private landlords. The proportion had fallen steeply since the First World War and was still falling fast, because easier mortgages and prosperity were encouraging middle-class Londoners to buy their homes, and fifty years of rent controls had made it difficult for honest landlords to earn a living from private renting. Concern over the growing shortage of private rented accommodation in London, together with reports of bullying and intimidation by unscrupulous landlords, led to the setting up of the independent Milner Holland Committee in 1963. Rachman, who featured in many of these stories, was a Pole who had arrived in London in 1946. Between 1954 and his death in 1962 he built up a chain of small property companies, owning at least 145 large and dilapidated multi-occupied houses in Shepherd's Bush, Notting Hill, Paddington and Earl's Court. Rachman paid his statutory tenants (those with controlled rents) to leave, and turned their flats into furnished rooms, which were not rent-controlled. The 1957 Rent Act removed rent controls on many tenancies, and on all new lettings, furnished or not. This encouraged Rachman to use a variety of techniques to bully his statutory tenants into giving up their rooms, so that he could replace them with prostitutes and other good payers.[39]

Rachman was probably the biggest operator of this type, but he was not a typical 'Rachmanite'. The practices he used (assault, eviction, threats, persistent annoyance, interference with rooms, cutting off essential services, introducing intolerable neighbours, withholding rent books, imposing illegal rent increases, and so on) were much more common among small landlords, especially those who lived in the same house as their tenants, than they were among company landlords. Families with children and tenants living in single furnished rooms in decayed multi-occupied houses were the usual victims. These abuses were probably not very common, and a survey of 1,000 tenants in 1963–4 showed that only 8 per cent and 4 per cent of tenants were 'rather' or 'completely' dissatisfied with their landlords' treatment of them.[40] The bigger problem was that the decontrolling of rents, which was necessary to stop the decline of private renting, made it increasingly difficult for families and poorer tenants to find homes at rents they could afford. The Committee concluded that the solution to London's housing problem depended on a coordinated effort on the part of public and private providers. It recommended the development of a tax and rent control policy which would give landlords the chance of a fair income from their property, alongside a system of tenant security and rent review which would protect private tenants from the worst abuses exposed in the report. For those who could not afford economic private rents or find a council tenancy, a 'very great addition to the stock of assisted housing', provided by housing associations and local authorities, was needed.[41]

THE GREEN BELT

Except in the early postwar years, the obvious solution to London's land and housing shortage, the resumption of its prewar sprawl, was ruled out by the sanctification of the Green Belt. The idea of a Green Belt around London won almost universal support among politicians and planners in the postwar years, even though they disagreed about what purpose it should serve. Unwin's 'Green Girdle' of the 1920s and 1930s had been intended for recreational use, and many of the open spaces bought with the help of LCC money in the 1930s (Ockham Common, for instance) were (and still are) used in this way. Abercrombie's Green Belt was meant to have a dual purpose, to control London's sprawl and to give its citizens some space to play. It was here, he said, that much of London's fresh food would be grown, and here that Londoners would breathe pure country air: 'Organized large-scale games can be played, wide areas of park and woodlands enjoyed and footpaths used through the farmland.'[42] But the government's first explicit endorsement of the Green Belt policy, Duncan Sandys' circular of 1955, saw it only as a barrier to London's growth, with no particular recreational purpose. In 1961 Sandys' successor at the Ministry of Housing and Local Government, Henry Brooke, made it clear that what had begun as London's sports jacket was now its straitjacket: 'the very essence of a Green Belt is that it is a stopper. It may not all be very beautiful and it may not all be very green, but without it the town would never stop, and that is the case for preserving the circles of land around the town.'[43]

The counties around London shared the government's understanding of the function of the Green Belt, and therefore had no difficulty in expressing their proposals for huge extensions to it in accordance with the Sandys criteria. Between 1956 and 1961 six major proposals for extensions to the Metropolitan Green Belt, increasing it from about 800 to 2,000 square miles, were put forward by County Councils whose motivation, plainly, was a desire to keep Londoners out, not to give them somewhere to play 'organized games'.[44] This was the 'nimby' ('not in my back yard') philosophy put into practice on a grand scale. So well did the Green Belt suit their interests that in 1958 Home Counties councils formed the Metropolitan Green Belt Council to defend their *cordon sanitaire* against those who might encroach upon it. They were supported by the Council for the Preservation of Rural England (a body co-founded and for many years led by Abercrombie), the Countryside Commission, the Town and Country Planning Association and the growing environmental lobby, although the land preserved by the Green Belt was of no greater natural importance than that sacrificed to new towns. Working-class Londoners gained few benefits from the Green Belt, since it added to the shortage of building land and thus to the high cost of property in London without offering them accessible recreational amenities, and it was not as easy for them to move to pleasant towns beyond the Green Belt as it was for well-off Londoners. By confining Londoners to the land they had occupied by about 1950, the Green Belt made it impossible for the LCC to pursue Abercrombie's ambitious plans for doubling Inner London's open spaces and building low-density housing, two aims which never achieved the sacred cow status of the Green Belt. Children playing on London's increasingly busy streets, and without most of the new local parks that Abercrombie had promised, could console themselves with the thought that 10 or 15 miles away there was a belt of agricultural land that they would never be allowed to spoil. Vacant land within the city, which Abercrombie would have turned into playgrounds, was seen instead as 'brown land' which should be redeveloped before a brick was laid on the protected 'green land' of the Green Belt. A survey by the Countryside Commission in the early 1980s showed that the great majority of those who used Green Belt land lived near it, and only 5 per cent came from the inner cities. Yet Londoners were attached to the idea and the name of the Green Belt, and did not add their political weight to the builders, politicians and civil servants who argued that the policy penalized London for the benefit of the Home Counties.[45]

EIGHT NEW TOWNS

In Abercrombie's Plan, Londoners were to be rescued from the Green Belt trap by the development of new and expanded satellite towns in or beyond the Outer Country Ring. Although the concept of the new town had been well known since 1902, when Ebenezer Howard founded Letchworth Garden City, the policy was unpopular with landlords, industrialists and urban and rural local authorities (one unwilling to lose ratepayers, the other unhappy to gain slum-dwellers). The idea was not pursued by the wartime coalition, or mentioned in election manifestos in 1945. But the new Labour Town and Country Planning minister, Lewis Silkin (previously chair of the LCC's Housing and Planning committees), favoured new towns, and in October 1945 he established an Advisory Committee under Lord Reith to look at the practicalities of building and running them. Within nine months Reith's committee issued three reports outlining the principles and practice of new-town planning, and recommending that new towns should be run by government-appointed development corporations. Silkin had already declared the government's support for the Greater London Plan, and on the very day that the New Towns Act, embodying Reith's recommendations, received royal assent (11 November 1946) the first new town, Stevenage, was designated. The establishment of new towns and the preservation of the Green Belt went hand in hand. Silkin and Aneurin Bevan (the Minister of Health) only turned down the LCC's proposed 800-acre cottage estate for 20,000 people on Green Belt land at Chessington in 1946 on condition that Dalton, the Chancellor of the Exchequer, agreed to the designation of Crawley as the second new town.[46]

Eight new-town sites were chosen in the London area (and six in other regions) between 1946 and 1950, although only two of these, Stevenage and Harlow, were on Abercrombie's suggested sites. The new Stevenage survived a legal challenge from the outraged residents of the existing town, and work on it and the other seven sites (Hemel Hempstead, Hatfield and Welwyn in Hertfordshire, Harlow and Basildon in Essex, Crawley in Surrey and Bracknell in Berkshire) went ahead. But building a new town from scratch was a slow process, made slower still in the austere postwar years by the unwillingness of the Treasury to provide adequate funding for land purchase or builders' wages. So by 1951 only 1,000 houses had been built in the new towns in the London region, and many of these were occupied by building workers employed by the new-town corporations. In some new towns, especially Stevenage, progress was painfully slow.[47]

No new towns were designated in the London area between 1950 and 1967, but the existing ones at last started to grow: 37,000 houses were built in them between 1951 and 1954, and by 1961 the total population of the eight towns was 329,000, of which recent London migrants made up about half.[48] Some new-town residents commuted to London, but most found work locally: in 1961 there were 73,000 factory jobs and about 35,000 service jobs in the eight towns. The LCC's attempt to start its own new town at Hook in Hampshire was blocked by the government and local landlords in 1959, but the 1952 Town Development Act already offered a more promising way forward, by allowing the LCC to negotiate for permission to build estates in established towns in the South-Eastern region. By a combination of subsidy and skilful negotiation, the LCC had persuaded seventeen towns, including Basingstoke, Swindon, Thetford, Ashford, Bury St Edmunds, Canvey Island and Banbury, to accept London overspill estates by 1961, and about 28,000 ex-Londoners were already living in them, with many more to follow.[49]

The value of the new towns was not universally accepted. It was pointed out by Labour and Conservative economic ministers that the creation of new towns did nothing to achieve Barlow's chief aim, the redistribution of industrial employment from the London region to the depressed areas. On the contrary, Douglas Jay (Financial Secretary to the Treasury) predicted in 1946 that the new towns would draw industry from the rest of England, just as Slough had done in the 1930s, unless rules were made to force them to take only factories transferring from London. Similar disputes took place between Macmillan (Ministry of Housing) and Peter Thorneycroft (Board of Trade) in the Conservative governments of the 1950s, and between Jay (Board of Trade) and Richard Crossman (Ministry of Housing) in the new Labour government of 1964. Not only were the new towns increasing the attractiveness of the London region at the expense of Scotland and the economically depressed parts of England, Jay argued, but they favoured London's skilled workers, not those in real poverty and housing need. 'I think it is not realized in Whitehall how virtually impossible it is for the worst-housed families in central London to get a house in a new town. In the hundreds of cases I have handled over fifteen years I can hardly recall a single one where the new towns were a real help to the housing problem.'[50] And this charge, that new towns were skimming off the most successful and mobile Londoners and leaving the rest worse off than before, became a common complaint against the new towns policy in the later 1960s, even though the great majority of those leaving London each year in the 1960s (60,000 out of 85,000) moved privately to houses in the outer metropolitan area, not to planned 'overspill' towns.[51]

LONDON REFUSES TO SHRINK

The census of 1961 showed that Barlow's dream of a shrunken London, diminished in population and economic weight for the benefit of the poorer regions of Britain, was almost as far from realization as it had been in the 1930s. Although the population of Inner London (the LCC area) had fallen to 3.2 million (800,000 down on its 1938 population), many Londoners had simply moved into the suburbs, the Green Belt or the Outer Country Ring. The population of Greater London as a whole was still almost 8 million in 1961 (compared with 8.1 million in 1931 and 8.6 million in 1939), well above Abercrombie's target, and the number of people living in the wider metropolitan region (including the Green Belt and the Outer Country Ring) had risen to 10.6 million, instead of falling to 10 million as Abercrombie had expected.[52] All that had been achieved by fifteen years of planned and unplanned dispersal was a new and more extensive sprawl, in which Londoners had moved, mostly without official encouragement, to growth points 30 or more miles from the centre of the town, and had in many cases retained their economic links with the centre. 'This is the contemporary Greater London', the Ministry of Housing's Senior Research Officer (A. G. Powell) wrote in 1960. 'Hemel Hempstead, Romford, Watford and Slough – even Luton, Reading, Gillingham and Southend are closely inter-linked by a daily interchange of workers and are increasingly tied to central London by the ebb and flow of a great tide of commuters.' Electric and diesel railways, especially on the Essex and East Kent routes, along with a much larger number of cars to get commuters to their stations, had enabled people to live beyond the Green Belt and still work in London's apparently irrepressible industrial and service economies, creating 'an embryonic conurbation 100 miles wide. This must inevitably consolidate still further.' In Powell's view the attempt to reduce London's economic power was bound to fail:

The further expansion of industrial and allied employment in and around London is inevitable. The national interest and economic forces at work are too strong to be reversed. The brakes can be applied as hard as possible, new controls can be devised, ... but the continued economic expansion of South-East England as a whole is a basic economic fact which must underlie all realistic economic planning for the future. Plans cannot be negative in this respect; they must provide for expansion – controlled as tightly as possible, but expansion nevertheless – of general economic activity within easy reach of London's geographical advantages.[53]

London's resilience had several roots. One of them was that Londoners were having more babies than had been anticipated. After the national 'baby boom' of 1945–9, in which the birth rate in South-East England briefly exceeded 20 births per 1,000 people, a level not seen in England since the early 1920s, the rate reverted, as Abercrombie expected, to its 1930s level of about 14.5 births per 1,000. But in 1956 the birth rate in South-East England (and in the rest of the country) began to rise again. By 1961 the rate was almost 17 per 1,000, and it remained at around this level, with a peak of 18 per 1,000 in 1964–5, for the rest of the 1960s.[54]

London's high fertility was no longer counteracted by its high mortality. By 1948 London's death rate had fallen to 11 per 1,000, a little below its prewar level, and it generally remained slightly below the national average. There were, though, a few reminders of London's dirty past. In December 1952 one of London's old scourges, the smoke-laden fog which had been known since 1905 as smog, returned with a vengeance. At the beginning of the month a period of high humidity and a stationary anti-cyclone (producing very still air) encouraged the heavy accumulation of domestic coal smoke in London. By 5 December smoke and sulphur dioxide levels were about ten times higher than normal, and the fog was denser than any since 1873. The Great Smog lasted less than a week, but it resulted in at least 1,600 (perhaps 4,000) excess deaths in London, mainly from bronchitis, pneumonia and coronary disease among infants and the old. The weakness of existing pollution controls was exposed, and the report of the Beaver Committee in 1954 led to a new Clean Air Act in 1956, which allowed (but did not compel) local authorities to establish 'smoke control areas' in which smoky fuel would be forbidden. This legislation did not quite put an end to the 'pea-souper' or (as it was no longer called) the 'London Particular'. In the seven years it took for the Act to take full effect there were several dense smogs in London, including one in December

1957 which killed about 1,000 Londoners and caused the Lewisham railway disaster, in which eighty-seven people died, and another in December 1962, which killed 750. In the longer run, though, this legislation (helped by the rise of electricity and domestic central heating) was effective. Vehicle emissions (lead, carbon monoxide, nitrous oxide, ozone, diesel particles, and so on) have taken the place of coal smoke in London air and Londoners' lungs, but never again will cab drivers lose their cabs, washing turn black on the line, schoolboys see their schools suddenly appear before them a few yards away, or American tourists thrill at London's murkily 'Dickensian' atmosphere.[55]

The rise in fertility in the late 1950s, temporary and insignificant as it may seem now, forced politicians and planners to think again about the problem of London's population. A government White Paper published in February 1963 summarized the position as it appeared at the time. Although about half a million people had left Greater London between 1951 and 1961, natural growth had ensured that its population had only fallen from 8.2 million to 8 million. Further population growth, and the trend towards smaller households, meant that London would need 200,000 extra homes by 1971, in addition to the 150,000 needed to meet the existing shortage and about 150,000 to replace slums and houses lost through road building and other developments. About 200,000 of these, the White Paper argued, would have to be built in the outer metropolitan area, on land which might otherwise have been part of the Green Belt. The same assumptions guided the *South East Study*, an official analysis of the housing and land use problems of the whole South-Eastern region published in March 1964, and the 1965 report of the Milner Holland committee, *Housing in Greater London*. The central problem for the South-East, according to the *South-East Study*'s accompanying White Paper, was 'the disproportionate growth of population and employment in and around London'. London, it said, 'was in danger of choking'. To hold London's population at 8 million until 1981, the study argued, plans had to be made for 'a second generation of new and expanded towns planned on a large scale, to accommodate 1–1.25 million people, well away from London'. Existing Green Belt would not be violated, but local authorities in the region should think again about new Green Belt proposals, and 'consider the possibilities offered by such land as there is in the Green Belt which in itself contributes little of value to the purpose of the belt'. By one means or another, the study warned, the South-East would have to find room by 1981 for another 3.5 million people.[56] Both parties accepted these predictions, and in 1964 the new Labour government promised a vigorous programme of house-building in

London, a major expansion of three cities about 60 miles from London (Ipswich, Peterborough and Northampton), and the creation of a new town in north Buckinghamshire, the future Milton Keynes.[57]

INDUSTRIAL AND DOCKSIDE RECOVERY

Not only was London's population unexpectedly buoyant in the early 1960s, but its economy showed few signs of shrinking in the way the town planners wanted it to. London's share of the total employed workforce of England and Wales was higher in 1951 than it had been in 1921 (21.5 per cent, compared to 18.7 per cent), and only fell by 0.5 per cent in the 1950s, despite the use of development certificates to control the establishment of new factories. In the 1951–61 census period, when Greater London's population fell by 200,000, employment in the conurbation rose by 400,000. Only about a fifth of these new jobs were in manufacturing, but London was still (in 1961) an immense manufacturing centre, with over 1.6 million workers, nearly a fifth of the total for England and Wales.[58] Many of its main industries, as in the 1930s, were ones with excellent prospects of future growth, including electrical engineering, television and electronics, aeroplanes, cars and buses, chemicals, food and drink, paper, printing and clothes. In the newer industrial areas in suburban Middlesex (Park Royal, Wembley, the Great North and Great West Roads, the Lea valley) factory growth continued in the 1950s. The expansion of Heathrow Airport, which employed 26,000 people by 1958, created London's fastest-growing industrial district in the 1950s, and there was also industrial growth in the new Green Belt settlements, Cheshunt, Debden, Hainault, Ruislip, Chertsey, St Mary Cray, and so on. The new towns had 40,000 manufacturing jobs by 1958, and nearly all the towns in the northern half of the Greater London region had fast industrial growth: Watford, St Albans, Romford, Hornchurch, King's Langley and Luton.

A second component of London's postwar economic success was the rapid revival of the trade of the Port of London, which even the most ardent decentralizers were reluctant to discourage. Despite the savage battering the Port sustained in the Second World War, by 1961 its share of British trade (by tonnage) was as great as it had been in 1900 (about 19 per cent), and in terms of value its share in 1958–60 (36.3 per cent) was greater than the 30 per cent it had handled in 1901. The 94 million net registered tonnage of shipping entering the Port in 1962–3 was about 50 per cent greater than the figure for 1938, and nearly three times as great as the tonnage in 1901 or 1946. The increase in oil imports played a major part in this growth. London's share of total UK tonnage was higher in 1964 (19.6 per cent) than it had been in 1948 (16.7 per cent) or 1910 (13 per cent). The weight of goods handled rose more slowly, but still impressively: 45 million tons in 1938, 36 million tons in 1948, and 59 million tons in 1961. The West India Docks were still the centre of the sugar, fruit and hardwood trades, and the Surrey Commercial Docks still managed, despite a shortage of cranes and lighters, to cope with the vast bulk of London's timber imports. Two-thirds of the Port's tonnage was handled on the river itself, rather than in the five dock systems, and oil refineries, power stations, sugar refineries, cold stores and industrial enterprises (including Ford's Dagenham wharf, one of the biggest on the Thames) lined its banks for more than 30 miles downstream from London Bridge. A fleet of 6,300 barges took cargoes directly from ships to quays or warehouses, and the four inner dock systems (excluding Tilbury) were served on an average day by 11,000 lorries and vans.[59]

Despite this recovery, there were doubts about the long-term future of the London docks. The inner docks, especially the London and St Katharine Docks, were already becoming uneconomic, and the 1947 agreement with trade unions known as the National Dock Labour Scheme had made it difficult for the dock system as a whole to introduce more competitive mechanical methods of handling goods. This gave an advantage to English ports outside the scheme, especially Felixstowe, and to the great Belgian and Dutch ports, Antwerp, Zeebrugge and Rotterdam, which could (and did) act as entrepots for British imports. London's own entrepot trade was undermined by the growing tendency of producers to ship their commodities directly to world markets. This was encouraged by the Second World War and improvements in world transport, and reinforced by Britain's loss of imperial control over many of the most important primary producers. In the case of wool and tea, postwar London did not regain the central role it had played in the interwar years, and in rubber, where London recovered and improved upon its old position in the 1950s, there was a sharp decline in the 1960s. Malaysia and Ceylon stopped using London as an entrepot, and London's imports fell, between 1959 and 1968, from 82,000 to 9,000 tons. Except in a few high-value commodities, such as gold, diamonds, oriental carpets, works of art and fur, London was quickly losing its position at the centre of the world's physical trade.[60]

Property Developers

The most powerful contributor to London's economic prosperity, and one that Abercrombie and his fellow planners had not foreseen, was the growth of the office economy. During the Second World War, office floor space in the 11 square miles of central London had fallen from 87 million to 77.5 million square feet, and between 1945 and 1951 shortages and the strict licensing system of the 1947 Town and Country Planning Act limited rebuilding to about 2.5 million square feet, mostly of government offices. In 1951 the new Conservative government was determined to increase the pace of building in London, and its Town and Country Planning Acts of 1953 and 1954 abolished Labour's 100 per cent betterment levy, although it retained planning controls and the public authorities' right of compulsory purchase at 1947 values. In November 1954 the Minister of Works announced the abolition of building licences, and a further Act of 1959, which Labour did not oppose, established that compulsorily purchased land should be bought at current market rates. This restored a 'free market in land', and gave the extra value created by the granting of planning permission to the owner of the land. The predictable result of these measures, after fifteen years of tight control, was a spectacular property boom. The LCC made some effort to slow the boom down, but its powers were not strong enough. Under the Third Schedule of the 1947 Town and Country Planning Act property owners were allowed to add 10 per cent to the *volume* of their buildings when they redeveloped. With lower ceilings, this allowed a 40 per cent increase in floor space when prewar or Victorian offices were rebuilt. But if the LCC refused permission for this it was liable to pay heavy compensation, which it could not afford to do. Under the 1954 Act, even newly erected buildings could be enlarged by 10 per cent in volume, and even more in floor space, after construction had begun. In 1961–2 Charles Clore claimed the right to add three floors to his unfinished twenty-four-storey Hilton Hotel in Park Lane, and in 1957 BEA gained two extra floors for their West London Air Terminal by insisting on their Third Schedule rights.[61]

About 24 million square feet of new office space were built in central London in the 1950s, and by mid-1962 there were 114 million square feet of offices, an increase of 50 per cent on the 1938 figure. Many of these offices were constructed with care and style by firms or institutions building for their own use, but it was increasingly common for large and nondescript offices to be built by professional property developers, who made their fortunes by assembling sites, finding financial backers, employing competent architects, and renting or leasing the finished building to an appropriate tenant. The architects they used tended to be drawn from a narrow group of firms, membership of which owed more to an understanding of the intricacies of the planning system and an ability to squeeze a large amount of floor space onto a given site than to architectural brilliance.[62] Harry Hyams' favourite architect, Richard Seifert, was the most resourceful of these men. In the 1960s and 1970s Seifert's practice designed Centre Point, Space House, Drapers Gardens, the Inland Revenue building in Carey Street, Telstar House, the Penta, Park Tower, Royal Garden, Metropole and Britannia Hotels, Dunlop House, St Botolph's House, Beagle House, Univac House, the National Westminster Tower and dozens of others, perhaps justifying Christopher Booker's claim that Seifert 'had more influence on the London skyline than anyone since Wren'.[63] The financiers who supplied most of the capital for these developments were generally banks, pension funds or insurance companies, who increasingly saw London property as a safe and profitable investment for their vast wealth. By a process of steady accumulation insurance companies and pension funds had acquired about half of central London (by value) by the mid-1980s, and one company, the Prudential, owned London property worth over £1,500 million, including Burlington Arcade, the Adelphi, the whole north side of Holborn, and large office blocks all over the City and West End. The Legal and General, which financed the Bucklersbury House development in the City, and provided backing for Jack Cotton and Charles Clore, was another important player, and so was the Norwich Union, which was a development partner with Max Rayne's London Merchant Securities.[64]

The speculative property developers whose names and faces were most associated with the office boom of the 1950s and 1960s had often started as estate agents, using their knowledge of the property market to buy up potentially valuable land during or soon after the war, when prices were low. Harold Samuel, head of the world's biggest public property company, Land Securities Investment Trust, started in this way, and so did Joe Levy of Stock Conversion, Harry Hyams of Oldham Estates, and Jack Cotton of City Centre Properties. These men made fortunes that were out of all proportion to their skills and work, but it must be acknowledged that they knew London well, they had an instinctive grasp of the potential value of unpromising sites, and they were ready to stake their wealth on the future prosperity of London. The profits they made should in justice have gone to the town whose vigour gave their land its value, and to provide the transport and cultural amenities for which money could never be found. But did they deserve their fortunes less than their predecessors as landlords to London, the aristocratic families whose West End estates were theirs by accident of birth, and who were losing them in the 1940s and 1950s (thanks to estate duties) by accident of death? Joe Levy's painstaking and secret purchase of over 300 little properties in the late 1950s to assemble a 13-acre site for his immense (and immensely profitable) Euston Centre was a harder road to a property fortune than the one taken nearly 300 years earlier by Sir Thomas Grosvenor, whose child bride brought Mayfair as her inheritance. Perhaps the difference between the two groups of men is not moral, but aesthetic. Eighteenth-century landlords built functional and (to our eyes) handsome buildings, and are regarded as the creators and custodians of the beauty of the West End. Samuel, Cotton, Hyams, Clore, Rayne and the rest built highly functional but (to many eyes) ugly buildings, which have spoiled London's intimacy and human scale, and made walking along some of its bigger streets (Victoria Street, Baker Street and Euston Road, for instance) a grim and uninteresting experience. Yet even here the passage of time can bring out a beauty that was not perceived at first. Some of the early 1960s towers that were criticized for their ugliness when they were built – Centre Point, Millbank Tower, New Zealand House – are now listed and preserved. The developers' defence would be that modern commerce must have modern buildings, and that London's prosperity in the middle of the twentieth century could not have been achieved in offices designed for Sir Nathan Rothschild or Bob Cratchit. It is an inescapable fact that a modern commercial city will lack the architectural charm of an eighteenth-century aristocratic quarter, and that cities that have lost their economic purpose will find it easier to preserve their old buildings than ones which are still earning a good living.[65]

THE OFFICE BOOM

In 1956 the government suspended the 1888 London Building Act, which restricted the height of buildings to 100 feet (as high as a fireman's ladder could reach), and over the next few years Londoners got their first taste of the glass and concrete office blocks and 'skyscrapers' that were to dominate large parts of the postwar city. The early blocks were fairly modest: Fountain House, in Fenchurch Street (twelve storeys on a two-storey podium) was completed in 1957, and Publishing House, in Holborn, was finished two years later. But on the South Bank, the LCC gave approval for one of Europe's biggest office blocks, the 7-acre Shell Centre (350 feet and 26 storeys high), which was inspired by the New York Rockefeller Center. It was opened in 1962, at around the same time as Bucklersbury House, 325,000 square feet of nondescript glass offices, which was built next to the Mansion House (in the City) by the developer Sir Aynsley Bridgland with financial backing from Legal and General. This block attracted public interest because of Professor Grimes's discovery of the Roman Temple of Mithras on the site, which was on the ancient river Walbrook. The building was delayed, and the Temple was excavated, moved, and reassembled in the forecourt of the development, where it still stands, lifeless, crazy-paved and unconvincing.

Local authorities seemed to be as keen on office developments as private developers: the six almost identical eighteen-storey blocks built in the 1960s by the City of London on London Wall, as the 'commercial zone' of its ambitious Barbican scheme, are particularly uninspired and depressing examples, despite the breezy elevated walkways that link their matching podiums. And the LCC's redevelopment of 30 acres at the centre of the Elephant and Castle, which the planners promised would transform a lively but scruffy district into 'the Piccadilly Circus of South London', was an utter failure from almost every point of view. The shopping centre was not a success, the pedestrian subways seemed dangerous and uninviting, local people regarded their new town centre without affection, and even the new roundabouts and eight-lane highway, the LCC's reason for the whole development, proved unable to cope with the flow of traffic from the six major roads that fed them.[66]

Thanks to the legislation of the 1950s, the LCC was hemmed in by the very high price of acquiring central London land for road widening or other public uses, and the prohibitive cost of compensating private landowners to whom they refused planning permission. To have refused permission to the Westminster Trust when they decided in 1960 to demolish four old offices in Victoria Street and replace them with a 400,000-square-foot office block (twice the size allowed by the LCC's zoning rules, but permitted under the 1954 Act) would have cost the Council £7.5 million, the developer's expected profit. The offices were built and rented to the Metropolitan Police, as New Scotland Yard.[67] Instead the LCC, whose young architects and planners were in any case attracted to the high-rise solution to London's business and housing problems, entered into collaborative deals with speculative property developers in the 1950s and 1960s, trading planning permission for land for roads or public amenities. Jack Cotton's two huge blocks at Notting Hill Gate (1958–61),

Harold Samuel's 320,000-square-foot Bowater House (1958–60) in Knightsbridge, and the giant office blocks in Stag Place (1962), on the site of the Stag Brewery, between Victoria Street and Buckingham Palace, were all the result of deals with the LCC. The most impressive of all these cooperative ventures was the Euston Centre, a 'miniature new town' of offices, shops, showrooms, underground car parks and pedestrian walkways built between 1964 and 1970 at the western end of the Euston Road. Joe Levy's Stock Conversion and the building contractors Wimpey shared a profit of around £22 million on the development, a return of 130 per cent on their investment. Londoners lost a scruffy but interesting neighbourhood, and gained the Euston Road underpass.[68]

THE DEFENCE OF OLD LONDON

There was no formal provision for public participation in the planning process, and public objections could not be considered after planning permission had been given. The secrecy of the planning system usually ensured that major schemes were half completed before Londoners knew what they would look like. But one of the biggest of these deals, which involved the replanning of Piccadilly Circus, the West End's garish but much-loved focal point, was halted by a combination of public and architectural protest when its details were carelessly revealed. Jack Cotton bought Café Monico from the Express Dairy for about £500,000 in 1954, and by 1959 he and his partner, the Legal and General, had reached an agreement with the LCC that an office block, no uglier than these things usually were, should be built on the site, giving the developers a £2 million profit and the LCC a better traffic flow round the Circus. Delighted with his project, Cotton called a press conference, in which his crude sketches were exposed to public contempt. In the resulting public enquiry in 1960 conservationist and political opinion united in rejecting the plan, and the Circus, with its garish but popular illuminated advertisements for Bovril and Wrigley's gum, was preserved.[69]

Until about 1957 95 per cent of new offices were built on bombed land, where the appearance of modern blocks was not in itself enough to arouse public anger.[70] But when, from 1958 onwards, developers began making room for their towers by knocking down streets and buildings that the *Luftwaffe* had missed, indifference changed to disquiet. Public resistance to the destruction of London's varied and distinctive neighbourhoods by developers who were plainly inspired by the expectation of immense profits and architects and planners who were infatuated with American and Continental ideas of civic design, gradually became more organized and aggressive. Recognizing that the Royal Fine Arts Commission and the LCC were ineffective as defenders of London's traditional landscape, opponents of unbridled redevelopment formed the Civic Trust in 1957, to act as a national focus for local amenity groups. The number of London groups affiliated to the Civic Trust grew from thirty in 1960 to ninety in 1974. In 1958 the Victorian Society was formed, with such influential figures as Sir Nikolaus Pevsner and John Betjeman in its lists, to defend what was left of old London from the hitherto triumphant march of functionalism, modernism and big business. In 1961, having tasted blood for the first time in the Piccadilly Circus enquiry, preservationists united to oppose the gratuitous demolition of Philip Hardwick's monumental Euston Station portico (built in 1838) as part of British Railways' rebuilding of the station in a style more in tune with its modern 'British Rail' image. The campaign failed, and in 1963 the Euston Arch came down, along with the station's hotel, screen and Great Hall.

Perhaps an even greater stimulus to the public rejection of office blocks was the fate of St Giles' Circus, where Oxford Street meets Charing Cross Road. In 1956 the LCC decided to create a roundabout at this busy junction, but found its way blocked by Beatrice Pearlberg of the Ve-ri-best Manufacturing Company, who had bought property on the Circus in 1949. In 1959 Harry Hyams presented himself as the LCC's ally, and began buying the properties belonging to Pearlberg and others around the Circus on the LCC's behalf, on the understanding that he would be given permission to build a 380-foot skyscraper (higher than St Paul's Cathedral) on the site. In return the LCC would get a fixed annual rent of £18,500, and the land it needed for its roundabout. Having learnt its lesson from the Café Monico fiasco, the LCC decided not to risk public discussion by submitting the scheme to the Royal Fine Art Commission, and the building of Centre Point in 1963–4 took the public by surprise.[71] Over the next few years Centre Point came to represent in the public mind the ugliness and injustice of the property boom, not because of its height or its design, which was no worse than that of many other blocks, but because it was pointless. The justification for other eyesores, that they were needed and that they worked, could not be advanced for Centre Point, which remained useless and empty for over a decade, yet still yielded enormous profits to Hyams and Oldham estates. The roundabout was never built, and the Centre Point piazza, typical of those little gifts with which developers tried to win public gratitude, did not become a popular meeting place. Unjustly,

Centre Point made Seifert's name notorious, while the chairman of the LCC Town Planning Committee, Richard Edmonds, and the Conservative minister whose 1954 legislation had given property owners an armlock on LCC planners, Harold Macmillan, escaped without blame.[72]

Important as conservationist pressure groups could be, the key determinants of the pace of office development were commercial demand and government policy. In 1962, when the boom was already slowing down, the government began to worry about the effects on the London labour market and transport system of the rapid increase in central London office space. According to a government working party report on 'Offices in London', published in February 1962, and a White Paper on 'Employment, Housing, Land', published a year later, 150,000 of the 200,000 new jobs created in central London between 1951 and 1961 were office jobs, and it was likely that another 125,000 or 150,000 would be added in the next ten years, 'unless something unexpected happens'. This growth in banking, business and commerce was economically desirable, the reports argued, but its social costs were too high. The growth of employment in central London created demands for more housing in London, threatening the government's decentralization and Green Belt objectives. Even more pressing was the effect of the growth of office work on London's transport system. Because office workers generally commuted from the suburbs or the wider metropolitan area, London's overloaded roads and railways had to carry about 1,250,000 peak-hour commuters, and the congestion was expected to increase steadily during the 1960s. To slow down the growth of the central London office economy by a combination of planning controls, persuasion and the creation of alternative commercial centres, without depriving those who really needed a central location of the right to find one, was identified as one of the main tasks facing politicians and planners in the 1960s.[73]

As it happened, the assumption that office jobs in central London had been growing in the 1950s by 15,000 a year, which was drawn from Board of Trade estimates and repeated in the LCC's Review of its Development Plan in 1960, the 1962 Report, the 1963 White Paper and the 1964 South-East Study, was quite wrong. Detailed results of the 1961 census, which were only published in 1965, showed that the actual growth in the 1950s had been 56,000 (almost all in the City), and further evidence demonstrated a 5,000 fall in central London office employment between 1961 and 1966. Many of the huge new offices, it appeared, had been giving previously overcrowded clerks, typists and businessmen more space, rather than making room for a vast new white-collar army. Between 1960 and 1980 the floor space occupied by the average London office worker doubled. Thus the government's office decentralization drive in the 1960s was based on a complete misunderstanding of past and future employment trends.[74]

The new anti-office policy began in 1963, and was pursued vigorously after the Labour election victory of October 1964. Acting on the official report of 1962 and the White Paper of 1963, the Conservative government changed the notorious Third Schedule in 1963 so that the 10 per cent addition it allowed referred to floor area, not volume. It also set up a Location of Offices Bureau (LOB), which would inform businesses of the advantages of moving their headquarters to suburban London, a new town, or beyond the metropolitan region. It was claimed that LOB propaganda persuaded firms to move 10,000 jobs a year out of central London in the later 1960s, but it is hard to know how many of these would have left without the Bureau's efforts. Many firms had already seen the value of building or renting their offices in the Greater London suburbs, where rents were much lower, road and railway links were good, the environment was more wholesome, and local white-collar workers (especially women who wanted to work near their homes) were plentiful. From 1957 to 1960 Middlesex gave permission for about 9,000,000 square feet of offices, over half the central London figure for the same period. By the early 1960s there were concentrations of office blocks in Edgware, Wembley and Ealing, and along the Great West Road from Hammersmith to Hounslow and Heathrow Airport. In Surrey, there were office concentrations in Putney and Kingston, but none of these matched the startling transformation of Croydon, in which about 5 million square feet of new offices were built between 1957 and the mid-1960s. Croydon Airport, which had been London's main airport between the wars, was closed in 1959, in recognition of the growth of Heathrow (which had its first flight in May 1946) and Gatwick, which was opened in 1958. But Croydon was a major population centre with excellent railway services, plenty of blitzed land, excellent cultural and shopping facilities, and a dynamic planning committee chairman, Sir James Marshall, who used special local compulsory purchase powers to clear the way for developers and turn his town into one of England's biggest office centres outside central London.[75]

When Labour came to power in 1964 it imposed an almost complete ban on new office building in London, beginning at midnight on 4 November. The following year the Control of Office Employment Act introduced Office Development Permits (ODPs), to control offices as factories were already controlled, and in 1967 the government introduced capital gains tax (to tax the developers' profits at last) and established a Land Commission which would restore at a reduced rate the betterment levy which had existed from 1947 to 1954. By the time these draconian measures took effect the rate of office building in central London was already in decline. The annual rate of growth in central London office space reached a peak of 4.8 million square feet in 1954–5, levelled off at about 4.3 million square feet in the late 1950s, and fell to 2.5 million square feet between 1962 and 1964. By 1966–7 it was down to 1.5 million square feet, despite the completion of several important projects which had been granted planning permission before the ban: Centre Point in 1965, Drapers Gardens and the Swiss Centre in 1967, Euston Centre and the Commercial Union tower in 1968.[76] Since the market was almost saturated with office space, the 1964 Brown ban (named after the Minister of Economic Affairs, George Brown) and the ODP system were unintended gifts to those who had offices empty or under construction, ensuring that rents would remain high. Central London office rents, which rose from about 15s per square foot in 1952 to over 30s in 1960, had increased to between £14 and £27 (City of London figures) in 1970. This made City of London rents about three times as high as those of central Paris, and nearly fifteen times as high as those in Frankfurt or Brussels. This in turn helped to encourage firms to move to cheaper premises in the wider London region, thus achieving the aim of the ban. After 1970, although the Conservative government revoked Labour's more radical controls (including the Brown ban and the Land Commission), central and local government continued to influence the location of new offices in central London, favouring sites near railway termini, or places where a 'planning gain' (usually road or railway improvement) could be achieved.

Making Way for the Motor Car

A fundamental issue in the debate over office building was the question of how many commuters the central London road and rail system could cope with. Even in the 1950s it was plain that private car ownership was growing rapidly, and that the unrestricted use of cars in central London would soon overwhelm London's existing roads. Between 1949 and 1958 traffic flow within the County of London increased over 40 per cent and vehicle licences by 88 per cent. The LCC's solution to this problem, following the thinking of Abercrombie, was to separate local from through traffic by building new primary roads, and to widen and improve the whole network to enable the growing volume of traffic to flow freely on it. Even when on-street yellow line parking controls and parking meters were first introduced in the West End in 1958 (and elsewhere in central London soon afterwards) the aim was to widen the roads and increase traffic flow, not to discourage motorists from driving into London. In 1959, when there were about 50,000 cars parked on central London streets, the Committee on London Roads argued that the 'broad effect of clearing all parked vehicles off the streets, except at parking meters, might be to increase their traffic capacity by 15 per cent to 20 per cent'. Lack of government finance made Abercrombie's orbital and radial road network impossible in the 1950s, but the LCC's road improvements at Euston, the Elephant and Castle, Cromwell Road, Park Lane, St Giles' Circus, Blackwall Tunnel and elsewhere were all intended, in the words of the 1960 County Plan, 'to improve traffic flow and conditions, to increase capacity and to reduce delays and accidents'. 'Although many cars are brought into central London unnecessarily', the Plan added, 'artificial restriction would be difficult to impose, would inconvenience many road users and might have harmful effects on the life of the community, including the depression of values in the Central Area'.[77]

The belief that central London should be altered to accommodate unrestrained motor car use was the dominant view in the LCC, the GLC and the Ministry of Transport throughout the 1960s, and gained powerful expert support from Sir Colin Buchanan's influential 1963 report, *Traffic in Towns*. This argued that cars could be given a free run in cities, but that traffic and pedestrians could be separated from each other by the construction of a new 'building deck' above ground and road level on which (as the report put it) 'it would be possible to create, in an even better form, the things that have delighted man for generations in towns – the snug, close, varied atmosphere, the narrow alleys, the contrasting open squares, the effects of light and shade, and the fountains and the sculpture'. The 1965 plan to reconstruct Piccadilly Circus with its traffic capacity increased by 50 per cent, and the 1968 proposal to redevelop Covent Garden with new modern roads to replace its 'obsolete' pattern of streets and buildings, emerged in this road-obsessed Buchanan era.[78] Its climax, as far as London was concerned, came with the Greater London Development Plan of 1969, which revived, in an extraordinarily expensive, destructive and unpopular form, the ring-road proposals of the Abercrombie Plan.

The general belief among politicians and planners that a combination of traffic management and road building would enable London to cope with an uncontrolled expansion in car use tended to dampen their interest in the alternative public transport strategies. Increased car use damaged the efficiency of bus services in two ways: by clogging up main roads they lengthened journey times and increased unreliability, and by reducing the number of passengers (especially at off-peak times) they increased running costs and fares. Between 1950 and 1970 the number of people using London buses fell by 40 per cent, and the number of buses in service fell slightly faster. Off-peak passenger numbers fell twice as quickly as peak-hour numbers. One way of redressing the balance of advantage between buses and cars was to introduce bus lanes to cut journey times on busy roads. Bus lanes were introduced in Paris and Milan in the 1960s, but in Britain the idea was not seriously considered in the Ministry of Transport until 1965, and the first schemes (in Park Lane, Vauxhall Bridge and Brixton Road) were not started until 1968–9. The first contra-flow bus lane, which eliminated the problem of encroachment by private cars, was introduced in Tottenham High Road in 1970, five years after it had first been proposed.[79] As for the underground, there was a brief period of activity in the late 1940s, when the Central Line was extended to West Ruislip and Leytonstone, but then almost complete inactivity until 1960, when most of the Metropolitan Line was electrified. The proposal for a new north–south Tube line (from Finsbury Park to Croydon) put forward by the Inglis Committee in 1946 attracted little interest in the 1950s, and it was not until 1962 that the government authorized the building of the Victoria Line. Work began at Oxford Circus in August, and the Walthamstow–Victoria part of the line was finally opened in 1968–9. The southern extension to Brixton was not ready until 1972. The new line brought economic and social benefits (and higher property prices) to Tottenham, Walthamstow, Stockwell and Brixton, but it was far more effective in drawing passengers from buses and British Railways than in persuading drivers to leave their cars at home.[80]

European Migrants

Although London was a net loser from migration in the postwar decades, it still attracted migrants in huge numbers, as it had always done. Between 1961 and 1966, for instance, Greater London had a net loss of 406,000 migrants. But in fact a total of 1,067,000 people moved out of Greater London in those five years (about 409,000 to the Outer Metropolitan Area and the rest further afield), and 658,000 moved in. Of these incomers, 354,000 came from mainland Britain, and 304,000 came from Ireland or further afield.[81] The biggest and most familiar group of overseas migrants in London was Irish-born. The introduction of quota systems and immigration restrictions by the United States in the 1920s and 1930s encouraged Irish men and women in search of work and good wages to come to England, and in the Second World War, although restrictions on migration from the Republic of Ireland were imposed for the first time, about 100,000 Irish workers were recruited by the Ministry of Labour. By 1951 there were 111,671 Irish-born people in the County of London (3.3 per cent of the population), and 90,967 (1.1 per cent) in the rest of Greater London, almost twice as many as there had been in 1851. By 1991 the number had increased to 256,276, or 4 per cent of the population of Greater London. The inclusion of those born of Irish parents gives a higher figure. In 1981 it was estimated that 5.3 per cent of Greater London's population, or 350,000 people, were first- or second-generation Irish, including about 46,000 from Northern Ireland. The postwar building boom and the expansion of the National Health Service relied heavily on Irish workers, but Irish Londoners were also important in catering, shop work, office work and the professions. Irish settlers generally favoured the western quarter of London, stretching out from Paddington to Kilburn, Willesden and Cricklewood, and it was in these areas that a distinctive Irish culture of dance halls, pubs, clubs, churches, festivals and county associations was strongest.[82]

There were other foreign migrant groups in postwar London, but their numbers were not so large. The biggest was the Polish community, which was mainly composed of servicemen who had fled with General Sikorski to London on the fall of France, and members of General Anders's Polish Second Corps who had arrived in England through Palestine and Italy in 1946, along with others who had been in Germany as prisoners or conscripts, and Polish Volunteer Workers from European refugee camps. Of the 140,000 Poles trapped in England by the Communist takeover of Poland, about 33,000 were living in the County of London in 1951, but these included some Polish-born Jews, who did not generally see themselves as part of the Polish community. The number was virtually unchanged in 1961. Poles settled wherever they could find cheap housing, including Clapham, Lewisham, Islington, Croydon, Willesden, Ealing, and especially Earl's Court Road, the 'Polish Corridor'. They were a community of exiles, rather segregated from the host population by a common desire to return to their homeland, and by their strong attachment to their own political, religious, cultural and ex-combatant organizations in London. But the great majority of London Poles were men, and intermarriage with English women, and the rise of a new generation of children without their parents' passionate sense of 'Polishness', slowly eroded their isolation in the 1950s and 1960s.[83]

Greek Cypriots started arriving in London in the 1920s, mostly settling in Soho and Camden Town. There were around 8,000 in London in 1951, and about 4,000 came to London each year in the 1950s and 1960s, with a rush of around 25,000 in 1960–61, between Cypriot independence and the 1962 Immigration Act. Cypriots settled in Islington, Hackney and Camden, and made Camden Town their social and cultural headquarters. In the 1960s the community spread outwards from their early settlements into Enfield, Barnet, Brent and especially Haringey, moving from cheap rented accommodation to owner-occupation on the strength of business success in clothing, catering, hairdressing or retailing. In 1991 Greater London had about 50,000 Cyprus-born citizens, and another 100,000 or so from Cypriot families, giving London a Cypriot population almost as large as Nicosia's, and equal to 22 per cent of the population of Cyprus.[84]

CARIBBEAN SETTLERS

Although there had been a scattering of black Africans and West Indians in London for many years, their numbers do not seem to have grown since the eighteenth century. A few black sailors, students, writers, politicians and entertainers lived in London in the 1920s and 1930s, but there was no substantial settlement until the Second World War. West Indians migrated for work, but their preferred destinations were Panama (especially during the building of the Canal), Costa Rica, Cuba and the United States. This pattern began to change in 1924, when the United States introduced immigration restrictions, and during the Second World War, when 8,000 West Indians served in the RAF in Britain, and others came as war workers. About a third of these did not return home, and others took their free passage to the West Indies, carrying to their islands information on economic and social opportunities in Britain. The 1948 British Nationality Act, passed to standardize Commonwealth citizenship laws, confirmed that all citizens of the British Commonwealth and British colonies had the right to settle in Britain. After the war the West Indies suffered from high unemployment, low wages and very rapid population growth. Jamaica's population rose by 2 per cent a year in the 1950s, and Barbados had a population density almost twice as high as England's. But migrants were seeking work, not just escaping poverty. They knew the state of the labour market in Britain, and moved there in much larger numbers when its economy was buoyant and unemployment low. Some were recruited on their own islands by labour-hungry British employers. The London Transport Executive sent an interviewer to Barbados in 1956 to begin recruiting conductors and stationmen, and by the end of 1961 over 2,000 Barbadians had been employed. Other employers, including British Railways, pursued the same policy on a smaller scale.[85]

Jamaicans began arriving in England soon after the war in small numbers, as stowaways or paying passengers. The really important day was 22 June 1948, when the SS *Empire Windrush* docked at Tilbury, bringing the first large group of West Indian migrants, 492 in all, mostly young skilled or semi-skilled workmen from Jamaica. The imminent arrival of the *Empire Windrush* threw the Colonial Office into a panic: 'This unorganized rush is a disaster,' their spokesman said. 'We knew nothing about it.' They were persuaded by a community worker, Baron Baker, to open the Clapham Common deep air raid shelter, which had also been used to house prisoners of war, as a temporary refuge for those Jamaicans without addresses to go to. About 230 of the new arrivals spent their first nights in the shelter, and found their first jobs through the local Labour Exchange in Coldharbour Lane, Brixton.[86] Later migrants were given the same accommodation, or were lodged in the LCC reception centre in Peckham. Brixton was ideal migrant territory. It was within easy reach of the centre and several areas offering manufacturing work. It had a cheap market, good shops, tolerant immigrant communities (Polish, Cypriot, Irish) and theatrical landladies with cheap rooms to rent. Property there was cheap, dilapidated, roomy and unwanted. Ruth Glass, in a study published in 1960, explained the special attractions of London's 'zones of transition' for migrants and outsiders:

> West Indians find rooms in streets where the tall houses, covered with grime and peeling plaster, display their decay. The streets have been by-passed because their location – near a railway, a noisy market, on a main traffic route, in areas of mixed land use – has become an unfavourable one. And the four- and five-storey houses, usually with dark basements, which were built mainly in the late nineteenth century for the large households of the middle-middle classes, have been left to deteriorate because they are so clumsy and ugly.... Gradually these houses have been sub-divided, though not adapted to multiple occupation.... Each of the rooms, once scrubbed by servants, is now often occupied by a separate group of people – by a family; the remnants of a family; by one lodger, or by several who pay their rent jointly....
>
> The arrival of the new migrant group has occurred at a period when the zones of transition are hemmed in on all sides – by the

continued expansion of London's commercial centre; by the consolidation of socially homogenous districts; by physical reconstruction; by the middle class invasion of the little streets which are adaptable to contemporary residential use; and also by the hopeless slums, which have apparently long been forgotten.[87]

Other blighted areas whose mean streets offered poor and generally unwelcome newcomers cheap rooms to rent included Notting Dale (the old 'Potteries') and Kensal New Town in North Kensington.

News of the warm welcome given to the *Empire Windrush* pioneers by the mayor and citizens of Lambeth, and of the ease with which they found work in London's booming economy, did not precipitate a rush of migrants from Jamaica to Britain. About 1,200 West Indians arrived in England in 1948, 1,000 in 1949, 1,400 in 1950, 1,000 in 1951, and 2,200 in 1952 and 2,300 in 1953. In 1953 only three ships, making a total of five sailings a year, were involved in carrying West Indian migrants to Britain. By the time of the 1951 census there were only 15,000 people of West Indian birth in the UK, and of these only 4,200 lived in London. Ministers were alarmed by even these small numbers, and in 1950 they secretly discussed the possibility of revoking the settlement rights granted in 1948. Commonwealth reaction, they decided, ruled this decision out.[88] The position changed in 1952, when the McCarran-Walter Act closed the United States to West Indian migrants, forcing them to turn to the United Kingdom for work. Several Italian ships joined the migrant fleet, and the number of sailings rose to seventeen in 1954 and forty in 1955. Over 9,000 West Indians arrived in Britain in 1954, 24,400 in 1955 and 26,400 in 1956. Numbers fell to an average of under 20,000 a year in 1957–9, perhaps because of rising unemployment, but rose again to nearly 52,700 in 1960 and 61,600 in 1961. This rise was partly the result of a snowball effect, in which friends, relatives and dependants come to join those already settled in a new country, and also reflected the fall in British unemployment in 1960–1. The high 1961 figure also represented a last-minute rush precipitated by the expectation that immigration controls would soon be imposed, as indeed they were on 1 July 1962.[89]

By early 1961, when the census was taken, there were 172,379 people of West Indian birth in the UK, and 98,811 in Greater London. Of the London West Indians, about 55 per cent were Jamaicans, with the rest coming mainly from Barbados, Trinidad and British Guiana. These island differences meant little to most Londoners, but a great deal to the earlier West Indian settlers, as Sheila Patterson explained in 1963:

Only now are migrants from British Guiana, Trinidad, the Windward and Leeward Islands, Barbados, and Jamaica beginning to mingle in the markets and streets of Brixton. As yet, most know little more of each other than a few common notions or stereotypes. For instance, Trinidadians are considered to be gay, Jamaicans touchy and flamboyant, Barbadians ('Bajans') dull and hard-working. Migrants from the smaller islands hold aloof from the more sophisticated 'Big Island people' of Jamaica and Trinidad. Nor do all West Indians even speak the same language. Working-class migrants from such islands as St Lucia and Dominica speak not English but a French 'Creole' patois as their first language.[90]

Compared to the West Indian population in general, migrants were well educated and well qualified. Only 2 per cent were unable to sign their names, and about 70 per cent had been in white-collar or skilled manual work in the West Indies. Predictably enough, most migrants experienced a drop in status when they found work in London. Very few West Indians with managerial or white-collar backgrounds got similar jobs in London in the 1950s, and many skilled workers took unskilled jobs, which they could get without competing with white applicants. To some extent this was the result of difficulties in transferring skills from one economy to another, but the more important factor (as it appeared to migrants and those researching their experiences) was prejudice among employers and their assumption, justified or otherwise, that their white workers would not take orders from a black superior.[91] West Indians also faced widespread discrimination in their search for housing. Although under 10 per cent of advertisements for furnished rooms in the *Kensington Post* from November 1958 to January 1959 were discriminatory ('No coloureds') only 15 per cent of landlords and estate agents, when approached directly, would consider taking black tenants. 'We personally don't mind, but the other people in the house do' was a common explanation.[92]

Painful experiences with discriminatory landlords no doubt reinforced the tendency of new migrants to seek accommodation through (and often with) friends and relatives, and to settle in streets or neighbourhoods where West Indians were already established. Very few West Indians settled in East London, and only about 15 per cent lived in the outer suburbs, beyond the County boundary. The heaviest concentrations were in West London, from Paddington, North Kensington and Notting Hill to Shepherd's Bush and Hammersmith, and in South London, in Stockwell, Camberwell and Brixton, especially in the streets south of Coldharbour Lane. But only about 35 per cent lived in these two districts, and most West Indians were scattered around the poorer inner suburbs of London. Migrants from particular islands went where their friends and fellow-villagers had already gone: in the 1960s about 2,500 of the 3,000 migrants from the little island of Montserrat who were resident in London lived in close-knit communities in Stoke Newington, Hackney and Finsbury Park, well away from the Grenadians of Hammersmith and Ealing, the Antiguans of Hackney and Newham, and the Jamaicans of South London.[93]

RIOTS IN NOTTING HILL

Racial prejudice in 1950s London was ubiquitous but camouflaged. Those who campaigned to 'Keep Britain White', or joined the White Defence League or Oswald Mosley's revived Fascist Party (now called the Union Movement) were greatly outnumbered by those who regarded West Indians as exotic inferiors, and treated them with friendly condescension. Events in North Kensington in the summer of 1958 forced some of these people to reconsider their attitudes. Racial conflicts were not unknown in London. There had been white riots against small groups of blacks in Stepney in 1919, Deptford Broadway in 1949, and Camden Town in August 1954, but these ugly incidents did not compare with the so-called 'Notting Hill' riots of August 1958. The trouble began with a series of attacks by gangs of 'Teddy boys' on black-owned cafés and houses. Mosleyite slogans and leaflets began to appear in North Kensington, and there were several cases of drivers trying to run down black pedestrians. At closing time on Saturday, 23 August there were attacks on black people and their houses, and a gang of nine youths from Shepherd's Bush went, as they put it, 'nigger hunting', wounding at least five solitary black men. The next Saturday and Sunday trouble broke out again, mainly in Bramley Road and other streets near Latimer Road Underground Station. For four days white crowds of up to 700 people attacked houses occupied by black families, and individual blacks who were caught on the streets had to run for their lives. Mosley's Union Movement agitators set up stands on street corners, and gangs armed with milk bottles, iron bars, bicycle chains, knives and petrol bombs roamed the streets. About 140 arrests were made between 30 August and 4 September, mostly of white teenagers from white streets in Notting Dale. One of the cult novels of the period, Colin MacInnes' *Absolute Beginners* (published in 1959), was set in Notting Hill before and during the riots. MacInnes describes the riots as vicious but directionless, more a series of 'incidents' than a full-blown riot: 'People were telling about what had happened here, or there, or in some other place, and they all seemed disappointed nothing was happening for them then and there.... It all popped up here, and subsided, then popped up there, then somewhere else, so that you never knew what streets were frantic, and what streets peaceful.' The riots might have taken a different turn if the Brixton West Indians had sent help to the besieged blacks of Notting Hill, or if the rioters had moved on Brixton. A West Indian told Sheila Patterson:

> The boys in Somerleyton Road was all for marching over there in a gang to help. Then we heard that the Teds were moving in on the Brixton area and we got ready. But nothing happen. The police here don't want that sort of trouble. They meet the Teds on the outskirts and move them away so we never get to put a finger on them. The boys here are really sorry. They organizing in strength, not like the Notting Hill men, who scattered all over.[94]

On 15 September, when tension was gradually easing, Mr Justice Salmon gave a warning to future rioters by passing four-year prison sentences on the nine 23 August 'nigger hunters'. His verdict echoed Lord Mansfield's judgement of nearly 200 years earlier: 'Everyone, irrespective of the colour of their skin, is entitled to walk through our streets in peace, with their heads erect, and free from fear. That is a right which these courts will always unfailingly uphold.'[95] But this assurance did not save Kelso Cochrane, a young West Indian carpenter, who was knifed and killed by a white gang in Golborne Road, a few streets away from the centre of the riots, in May 1959.

A PASSAGE FROM INDIA

Migration to Britain from India and Pakistan developed more slowly than West Indian migration. South Asians did not have the West Indians' strong sense of cultural affinity with Britain, and they were not well informed of the economic opportunities presented by Britain's postwar boom. Hardly more than 5,000 had arrived in Britain by 1954, and the 10,000 or so who arrived each year in the later 1950s contained a high percentage of English-speaking professionals with British connections. A relaxation of Indian and Pakistani emigration restrictions in 1960, combined with anticipation of the 1962 Immigration Act, created a rush of 92,000 migrants, many of whom were poorer and could not speak English, in 1961–2. Most came from Bengal and the Punjab, the two provinces of British India whose populations had been the most severely uprooted by the India–Pakistan partition of 1947. Asian migrants were less inclined to settle in London than West Indians. They were not so interested in the excitement of metropolitan culture, and Pakistanis in particular were attracted by the industrial work and low cost of living of the Midlands and the North. Nevertheless, the 1966 census showed that over 30 per cent of Indian and Pakistani-born British residents (about 95,000 out of 306,000) lived in Greater London, and by 1991 633,000 of Britain's 1,693,000 ethnic South Asians were Londoners.[96]

In the early years Asian migrants did not seek, as West Indians did, to share the lives and culture of white Londoners, and they were therefore less likely to feel the sting of racism and the 'colour bar', unless they tried to use their teaching or medical qualifications to get professional positions. They tended to form self-contained communities with their own cinemas, shops, restaurants and places of worship, generally in districts where work was available and where previous settlers offered help and hospitality. Only the Bengalis chose to remain in Inner London. In Spitalfields and White-chapel they moved into the streets left empty as prosperous Jews moved out to North London in the 1950s and 1960s. The new migrants took over the cheap clothing businesses in the houses around Commercial Street and Brick Lane that had once been run by East End Jews. The old Huguenot chapel in Fournier Street, which became in turn a synagogue and a mosque, perfectly symbolizes the part these streets have played in sheltering one group of newcomers after another. In Southall, on the western edge of the borough of Ealing, there was an even bigger Asian community, mainly Punjabi and Sikh. They were attracted by the ample work opportunities in West London industries and Heathrow, and many found work in Woolfe's rubber factory, where recruitment was in the hands of an Englishman who had once been a police officer in the Punjab.[97]

A third centre of South Asian settlement developed in north-west London (mainly Harrow) in the late 1960s and the 1970s, when East African Asians came to England as refugees from the process of 'African-ization' in Kenya and Uganda. Many of these refugees were from business and professional families which had moved from Gujarat and the Punjab to East Africa earlier in the century, and were now forced to move on again by those jealous of their commercial success. Some of those who came to London settled in Southall, where travel agencies, financial institutions, shops and other businesses proliferated as a result of their commercial skills. Others preferred to avoid the dilapidated industrial districts which had been chosen by poorer settlers, and moved to outer suburbs that were more in keeping with their social and economic status. In Harrow, the share of the population living in households headed by people born in the New (non-white) Commonwealth rose from 6 per cent to 15 per cent in the 1970s as a result of East African settlement.[98] By the 1980s London's 90,000 first generation East African Asians were dispersed across the whole of Greater London, invigorating its business life with their enterprise and hard work. One of the most visible and welcome results of this dispersal was the proliferation of Asian-owned grocers and newsagents, whose survival until then had been threatened by the rise of supermarkets and chain stores.

'Teddy Boys' and the Crime Wave

The Notting Hill riots, as well as being a landmark in the development of London's race relations, were also an incident in the history of its youth culture. Teddy boys, who were generally blamed for the riots, were the first of London's postwar youth cults. They came to public notice in the early 1950s, when boys from Southwark and Lambeth adopted the exaggerated 'Edwardian' style of dress that had been promoted by Mayfair tailors in 1948–9. The sight of gangs of teenagers on the street corners of Vauxhall and the Elephant and Castle dressed like caricatures of Edwardian dandies, with very long velvet-collared jackets, bootlace ties, tapered trousers, suede shoes with thick crêpe soles, and elaborate Brylcreemed quiffs, instead of the cloth caps and second-hand clothes they would have worn a few years earlier, was comical and slightly menacing. But the fact that boys from the lower end of the working class, just out of school and into their first unskilled jobs as labourers or van boys, could now afford to spend £20 on smart suits and fancy hair-styles was a clear sign that postwar austerity was over, and that the prosperity that kept Conservative governments in power for thirteen years had begun. Most Teddy boys came from the London slums, or from the high-rise estates that had replaced them, and from the secondary modern schools that educated '11-plus' examination failures in the post-1944 education system. Their wages were about 50 per cent higher in real terms than they would have been in 1938, and they spent a high proportion of their earnings on clothes and entertainment. They passed their evenings in the 'pictures', hanging around in cafés, coffee bars, dance halls and youth clubs, listening to American 'Top Twenty' hits on jukeboxes, playing on pin-tables, and in the nightly quest for willing women. The café, not the public house, was the favourite haunt of these youngsters. 'The price of the coffee is cheap, there may be music, and above all the ordinary café is a small enough place for a group of young people to be able to regard it as "theirs". "When a bloke goes to the same café every night, well, I mean he's known – he's somebody." '[99]

Many Teddy boys came from London's more lawless areas, and press and public opinion generally regarded them as criminal delinquents, the hooligans who were responsible for the rapid increase in London's crime rate in the 1950s. As their reputation spread, Teddy boys were moved on by the police, refused entry to dance halls and cinemas, analysed in print by psychologists, doctors and clergymen, and blamed by the press for every nasty incident. One well-informed contemporary analyst, T. R. Fyvel, emphasized the 'peculiar, nasty viciousness in Teddy-boy assaults', and the involvement of Teddy boys in gang fights, vandalism and group attacks on individual victims. A few notorious incidents fixed this impression of Teddy boy violence in the public mind: the 'battle' of St Mary Cray in April 1954; the destructive riot in the Elephant and Castle Trocadero in 1956, during the showing of Bill Haley's *Rock Around the Clock*, which was followed by imitative riots in other cinemas; the killing of a youth on Clapham Common in 1954 by a gang with flick-knives; the Notting Hill race riots; and two dance-hall brawls in 1958 in which a young man and a police officer were stabbed to death.[100] Leaving the worst of these crimes aside, much of this hooliganism can be seen as a rebellion of teenagers, with their new sense of economic and cultural power, against parental authority and middle-aged standards. Ray Gosling, who was in the Trocadero during the 1955 riot, remembered the sense of freedom and power it gave him:

> At the end of the Old Kent Road, all the fire engines were there, and they got their hoses all ready, and it was a big thing, terrible big thing. You felt you were it. Not only just because you were young, but you felt the rest of your lives would be, well, ordered by you and not ordered by other people. We thought we could do what we bloody well wanted – we thought we could do anything at all – nothing could stop you. You were the guv'ner – you were the king. The world was free – the world was open.[101]

The Cambridge criminologist F. H. McClintock, in his meticulous study of crimes of violence in London, did not find evidence of a violent teenage 'crime wave' in the 1950s. It is true that the rate of indictable (serious) crimes of violence in London for which youths of fourteen to twenty-one were found guilty increased by 170 per cent between 1950 and 1960, but McClintock argued that possibly half the increase could be attributed to 'a greater readiness on the part of the public to report aggressive behaviour by "teenagers"', and that the total number of convictions was small. 'There were 624 persons under the age of 21 found guilty of indictable crimes of violence in the London area, which represents less than two convictions a day in a total population of more than eight million.' And violent crimes which might be called 'hooliganism' (unprovoked assaults, attacks on strangers, pitched battles and rowdyism) were rarer still. In 1957 only 286 cases (indictable and otherwise) were successfully prosecuted in London, at a time when there were perhaps 30,000 Teddy boys in the city. But McClintock acknowledged that 'a general attitude of hostility, verbal aggressiveness and wanton destruction of property by the younger members of the community can contribute to a general uneasiness among the adult population'.[102] Teenage gangs and the publicity they received in the Press and television helped to revive in the 1950s some of the old Victorian fears of London's unsafe areas and dangerous classes. But what was feared in the 1950s was not a class, but an age group.

Perhaps public attention focused too exclusively on conspicuous youth cultures, but there was little doubt by 1960 that the problem of crime in London had become much more serious than it had been in the 1930s, or even during the last years of the Second World War. Reported indictable crimes, which had been about 95,000 a year before the war, rose to nearly 130,000 a year in the unsettled postwar years (1945–8), before falling back to 95,000 in 1953–5. Then, in the twelve years between 1955 and 1967, the number of reported indictable offences in Greater London tripled to 295,000. In an age of increasing affluence, this unprecedented crime wave defied conventional explanations. At first, some criminologists suggested that the generation whose schooling and family life had been disturbed by the war, who reached their late teens towards 1960, might be responsible for it. This hypothesis lost its force when reported crime continued at a high and rising level in the 1960s and 1970s, when most of the culprits were born after 1945. Popular culture (especially cinema and television) and a failed educational system were, once again, among the usual suspects in the search for a social explanation for rising crime, but it was hard to see why these should have done more damage in the 1950s than they had in the 1930s. It would have been more convincing to blame the decline of 'community' in bombed, cleared and rebuilt areas, and the consequent weakening of the informal and three-generational controls exerted over youngsters in a settled and familiar neighbourhood. Children on the new estates still had their parents, but where were their grandparents? The favourite explanation among sociologists in the 1960s was that many teenage boys felt a sense of failure in a meritocratic and materialistic society which prized educational and career success and the accumulation of goods. Theft and hooliganism was their way of gaining desirable possessions, or of showing that they rejected a society in which they had failed. Peter Wilmott put these ideas to the test in his research among adolescent boys in Bethnal Green between 1959 and 1964, and found them to be, as far as he could tell, broadly accurate.[103]

Crime was getting easier. Supermarkets were easier to steal from than small shops, housing estates offered more opportunities for vandalism than traditional terraces, scooters and bicycles were simple to steal. A breakdown of the figures shows that a large part of the increase in crime was connected with the greater availability of certain kinds of property. Theft from vehicles, one indictable crime in twelve in 1955, made up a sixth of the total in 1964. Reported theft from telephone boxes and meters rose fivefold over the same period. Housebreaking and stealing from houses, which rose from 13,000 to 43,000 reported offences, were easier and more profitable in an affluent society in which household possessions were more valuable, and where homes were less often guarded by housewives and grandmas. Increasing levels of household and car insurance, more telephones, and perhaps a growing intolerance of violence and rowdiness, made it more likely that crimes would be reported and recorded. Commentators and journalists tended to reject these mundane explanations in favour of laments over falling moral and religious standards, youthful hedonism, and a decline in respect for age and authority. It is possible, of course, that they were right.[104]

THE RISE AND FALL OF 'SWINGING LONDON'

These were prosperous times for independent young wage-earners, especially if they lived at home and had no bills to pay. Real earnings rose by about 70 per cent between 1950 and 1970, and in London unemployment rates were nearly always under 1 per cent in the 1950s and early 1960s, and only about 1.4 per cent in the later 1960s.[105] The growing spending power of young working-class and middle-class consumers had a powerful impact on parts of London's economy and culture, especially its clothing and entertainment industries. Each new generation of teenagers adopted a new style of dress. Teddy boy styles looked dated by 1960, when well-tailored Italian-style suits, perhaps bought at Cecil Gee in the Charing Cross Road, or in one of the John Michael shops, came into fashion. This was the 'Mod' style, which spread far more widely among young men in the 1960s than the Teddy boy look had done. Designers and retailers who anticipated these changes of style and managed to capture the affluent teenage market, could make a fortune in the 1960s. In men's clothing, John Stephen opened a shop in Carnaby Street, an unpromising little road behind Regent Street that became the centre of Mod fashions. By the early 1960s Stephen had several shops in Carnaby Street, which was on its way to becoming one of London's most popular tourist attractions. Young women preferred the King's Road in Chelsea, where Mary Quant's shop, Bazaar, became enormously popular in the early 1960s. In the words of George Melly, Mary Quant 'changed the whole approach of the British to fashion. Up until then "fashion" was French and for the rich and frivolous. English upper-class girls were expected to dress like their mothers.... Quant changed all this. She chucked lady-like accessories into the dustbin, recognized the irrelevancy of looking like a virgin.'[106] Alexandra Pringle, as a Chelsea schoolgirl, remembered the change that overtook the King's Road in the sixties, thanks to Bazaar and its many imitators:

> From Bazaar, remarkable at first for the simplicity of its lines, came the mini-skirt. This smallest of shops reached fame through the very *smallness* of its garments. Local residents stared and pointed as young women catwalked up and down the King's Road.... They wore big floppy hats, skinny ribbed sweaters, key-hole dresses, wide hipster belts and, I believed, paper knickers. They had white-lipsticked lips and thick black eyeliner, hair cut at alarming angles, op-art earrings and ankle-length white boots. They wore citron-coloured trouser suits and skirts that seemed daily shorter. They rode on miniature motorbikes. They had confidence and, it seemed, no parents.[107]

The new styles were promoted by new women's magazines, glossy Sunday supplements, photographers such as Anthony Armstrong-Jones and David Bailey, and the women they photographed, Jean Shrimpton, 'Twiggy', and the rest. By 1967 there were about 2,000 boutiques (as these little shops called themselves) in London, and the fashion centre had spread from Chelsea to Kensington High Street. Alexandra Pringle recalled a new shop opening in Abingdon Road, off the High Street:

> It was black and gold, it had brothel-like interiors of palms, ostrich feathers and glittering sequins. It was Biba's.... As it moved from a backstreet to the main thoroughfares of Kensington, a sort of volup-tuousness crept in. Crowded into dimly lit communal dressing rooms ... I tried on clothes for the sinful and the *louche*; slithery gowns in

glowing satins, hats with black veils, shoes stacked for sirens. . . . And for real life there were raincoats to sweep the London pavements, tee-shirts the colour of old maids' hats, dusky suede boots with long zippers.

Towards the end of the 1960s 'psychedelic' influences, a mixture of San Francisco 'flower power' and vague impressions of eastern mysticism, gave London fashions another twist:

Psychedelia vibrated from Sloane Square to the World's End. . . . Men with long curling hair showed off their Mr Freedom velvets. Brightly buttoned into military jackets, . . . tall in platform boots, necks hung with Indian scarves and beads, the men were now the peacocks, the strutting confident creatures of the King's Road.[108]

For local people, the rise of this new fashion quarter had its drawbacks:

One could not even buy the ordinary stuff of life in the King's Road. There was no grocer any more, no fishmonger or butcher. Dozens of new clothes boutiques stretched down the street. Shops came and went so fast you never remembered their names. Even Bazaar disappeared. There was no glamour now, only tat. The old residents of Chelsea were squeezed out, including us.[109]

You could, though, buy well-designed furniture and household goods to match your Mary Quant clothes and Vidal Sassoon haircut. Terence Conran, another London art college product, opened the first branch of Habitat in the Fulham Road in 1964.

Each new phase of this youth culture was accompanied by its own type of music, much of which, in the sixties, was produced in London. In 1956 two music promoters, Larry Parnes and John Kennedy, had 'discovered' Tommy Hicks, a young Presley imitator, singing in a Soho coffee bar, the 'Two Is' in Old Compton Street. They changed his name to Tommy Steele, and turned him into England's first rock star. Others followed in the later fifties: Marty Wilde, Billy Fury, Terry Dene, Adam Faith, Cliff Richard, and many less well-remembered names. These were not international stars, but in the sixties, when Bazaar and Carnaby Street were providing the costumes, London became (along with Liverpool) the temporary capital of the musical world. In April 1963 Mick Jagger was signed up by agents (Andrew Oldham and Brian Easton) who heard him singing in the Crawdaddy Club in the Railway Hotel, Richmond, and the Rolling Stones made the break into stardom. In 1964 the Beatles left Liverpool for London (just as they did in their film of the same year, *A Hard Day's Night*), and the Who were formed by an Ealing art college student, Pete Townshend. Other successful bands started, or came to London, at around the same time: the Animals, the Kinks, Manfred Mann, Georgie Fame and the Blue Flames, the Yardbirds and the Small Faces, the archetypal Mod band. Broadcasting added to the new music's commercial success: Independent television's *Ready, Steady, Go* started in 1963, and in spring 1964 Radio Caroline and Radio London, the first of the floating pirate radio stations, were (literally) launched. London clubs and discotheques rode to prosperity on the wave of popular interest in London music. Ordinary fans made do with cheap clubs in Streatham or Hammersmith, but for those with youth, style and plenty of new or old money, the West End clubs, the Ad Lib, the Scotch of St James and the Cromwellian were the places to be seen.[110] Jonathan Miller described the new élite, drawn from the linked worlds of music, photography and fashion, admiring itself at the Whitechapel Art Gallery in 1964:

> There is now a curious cultural community, breathlessly *à la Mod*, where Lord Snowdon and the other desperadoes of grainy blow-ups and bled-off layout jostle with commercial art-school Mersey stars, window dressers and Carnaby pants-peddlers. Style is the thing here – Taste 64 – a cool line and the witty insolence of youth. Tradition has little bearing on any of these individual talents and age can go stuff itself.[111]

This, in short, was the 'Swinging London' which a group of American journalists revealed to the world through the pages of *Time* magazine on 15 April 1966, just as its brief moment was passing. The article gave American readers and potential tourists a fairly superficial guide to the clubs, boutiques, restaurants and discotheques that epitomized London's youth culture, and fed them some lazy clichés about 'a city steeped in tradition, seized by change, liberated by affluence'. 'In a decade dominated by youth, London has burst into bloom. It swings; it is the scene.'[112] Weak as its analysis was, the article did something to displace the foggy Dickensian image which had previously dominated international impressions of London, and its emphasis on London's cultural and social vigour was not entirely misplaced. English and American film-makers cheerfully exploited and perpetuated the 'Swinging London' myth for the rest of the decade, with films that seemed daring or significant at the time: *Alfie, Darling, Georgy Girl, The Knack* and *Blow-Up* were typical cinematic depictions of the swinging city. In March 1968 *Time*'s rival, *Life*, announced that '"swinging London" is dead', but it is unlikely that many Londoners noticed the difference.

Chapter 26

A Divided City, 1965–1997

THE HERBERT COMMISSION

In 1965, after years of argument and enquiry, London was finally given a local authority, the Greater London Council (GLC), that could oversee the strategic development of the whole of the city within the Green Belt. The benefits of having a single authority for Greater London, especially for transport planning and control, had been recognized in the interwar years, but the local authorities that would have lost their powers to the new Council were opposed to the change, and interwar governments saw no advantage in promoting unification in the face of their combined opposition.[1] In 1945, when the appetite for reform engendered by the war and the Abercrombie Plans might have opened the way for radical reconstruction, the Churchill Coalition issued a White Paper denying that it intended to 'disrupt the existing structure'. Instead it established a Local Government Boundary Commission which was forbidden to consider the government boundaries of London. It was also told to avoid discussion of the problems of Middlesex, which was threatened with disintegration by the ambitions of nine of its most populated districts, Ealing, Hendon, Wembley, Willesden, Twickenham, Tottenham, Harrow, Enfield and Heston-Isleworth, to achieve County Borough status. In 1949 the committee set up by the Labour government to examine ways of implementing the Greater London Plan (chaired by Clement Davies) recommended the establishment of a local government commission to report on London government reform, and in the meantime the implementation of the Abercrombie Plan was left to the central government, in consultation with the LCC and the counties and county boroughs given planning powers by the 1947 Act. There was general support among civil servants in the Ministry of Housing and Local Government for 'tidying up' the government of London, but they lacked strong ministerial encouragement until the appointment of Duncan Sandys in 1954. Sandys initiated the production of three White Papers on local government areas, functions and finance, and when Henry Brooke replaced

Sandys in 1957 he announced the establishment of a Royal Commission on the government of Greater London. Young and Garside argue that Brooke acted because his civil servants persuaded him to do so, but Brooke's own long-standing interest in London government, as a borough and County councillor and leader of the Conservative opposition on the LCC, probably led him in the same direction.[2]

The outcome of some Royal Commissions is determined by the careful selection of their members, but in the case of the Herbert Commission on Greater London government, which sat from 1957 to 1960, the issues were examined by seven people without London interests or preconceived ideas on how the city should be governed. Their terms of reference were neutral and fairly wide, but they were not asked to look at two services which were presently run by independent London-wide bodies, police and water supply, and public transport was also outside their remit. In its open-minded search for understanding, the Herbert Commission cast its net wide, inviting evidence from over 200 institutions and every British university, as well as the 117 local authorities in the area and the relevant government departments. Most of the local authorities argued vigorously and at length for their own survival, preferably with enhanced powers, and the leaders of the LCC stuck firmly to the *status quo*, which ensured them (though they did not say so) a permanent Labour majority.[3] As for the government departments, three (Health, Education, and the Home Office) told the Commission that the present arrangement worked 'tolerably well', since the services with which they were concerned could be performed as efficiently by large authorities (with populations of 200,000 or so) as by huge ones. Even Dame Evelyn Sharp, Permanent Secretary at the Ministry of Housing, was equivocal in her criticisms of the way the existing system dealt with planning, transport and 'the really big problems of the region', and cautious about suggesting what might replace it: 'Well, it is so much too difficult for us that we thought it needed a Royal Commission!' Only the Ministry of Transport dared to submit an uninhibited denunciation of the existing system and its component councils: the 'multiplicity of authorities ... makes it impossible to deal efficiently with present-day problems, ... even the simplest measure takes an inordinate time to put into effect'. Two London University academic groups offered the Commission conflicting advice on how London's problems might be solved. The LSE's Greater London Group, led by William Robson, the veteran campaigner for a unified London, argued for a Greater London Council to take charge of planning and various regional issues, with other functions left to a second tier of large local authorities. Opposing this, the Centre for Urban

Studies, based in University College, argued that the County of London, with its distinctive social identity, should be preserved as an administrative unit, with government regional committees to handle those issues which needed a wider metropolitan approach.[4]

By early 1960 the seven commissioners were convinced that London needed an elected metropolitan authority to develop its overall strategic plan, to bring order to the chaos of London's system of major through-roads, to deal with large redevelopment projects and overspill housing, and to make broad educational policy for its 8.5 million people. To abdicate these matters to central government would be to surrender London's control of its own local government. But they believed that many other administrative functions could be efficiently performed at a more local level, and that it was at this level that the spirit and vitality of urban democracy was most likely to thrive: 'It is best to give as much power and responsibility as possible to those who are in the closest touch with the people for whose benefit local government services are provided.' So in its Report, published in October 1960, the Herbert Commission recommended the division of Greater London government into two tiers, with fifty-two large and powerful Metropolitan Boroughs taking responsibility for the bulk of local government functions, and a Greater London Council to carry out the tasks 'which can only be or can better be performed over a wider area'.[5] One ancient administrative entity, the City of London, survived with the powers and independence of a borough in this plan and its subsequent amendments, but another, the County of Middlesex, disappeared for ever.

THE GLC AND THE BOROUGHS

The Commission's case was well argued, although the division it suggested between regional and local educational and housing matters was a little obscure. The Press welcomed the plan, and there was support, though not enthusiasm, for it from about half the Greater London local authorities, especially the Conservative Metropolitan Boroughs and many of the authorities beyond the LCC boundary. But the most important supporters of the proposed reforms were the Macmillan government and Conservative Central Office, which had been arguing since 1938 for a redefinition of London to include more middle-class (and Conservative-voting) areas, and had long favoured the strengthened borough governments advocated by the Commission. As Young and Garside argue, 'the Cabinet were resolutely committed to metropolitan government for London ... in large part for those reasons of party advantage that Conservatives often identify with the public interest'.[6] In the year between the Commission's report and the government's White Paper, the Central Office, led by the Party chairman, Rab Butler, and his deputy, Sir Toby Low, mobilized Conservative support for the plan, and identified the fears of the Outer London authorities. The White Paper and its associated circular made two important changes to the Herbert proposals. It suggested thirty-four Metropolitan Boroughs with populations of between 200,000 and a little over 300,000, instead of Herbert's fifty-two, in the belief that bigger boroughs would attract better councillors, and have the specialist staff and resources to run their services more efficiently. And it replaced Herbert's difficult division of education between the GLC and the boroughs with a system in which Outer London boroughs ran their own education, but the education of a large area of Inner London (perhaps 2 million people) would be run by a special single authority. This was a concession to the Minister of Education, Sir David Eccles, who preferred big education authorities, and wanted to retain the unity of an area which had been a single authority since the introduction of state education in 1870.[7]

The London Government Bill, which was brought before the House of Commons by Dr Charles Hill, Brooke's replacement at the Ministry of Housing, in November 1962, embodied two important concessions to the opponents of the White Paper. The first was the enlargement of the Inner Education Authority to include the whole of the existing County of London, the future Inner London Education Authority (ILEA) area. The second was the exclusion from the new Greater London of seven South-Eastern areas, Staines and Sunbury in Middlesex, and Esher, Walton, Banstead, Epsom and Caterham in Surrey. In yielding to the pressure of these authorities and some influential Surrey MPs the government threw away the great advantage they had anticipated from the reform, a guaranteed Conservative majority on the Greater London Council. Labour won the first GLC election in 1964, and in the Council's twenty-one years political control was divided roughly evenly between the two parties.

How valuable a prize control of the GLC would be was another matter. The London Government Act, which became law in July 1963, created a regional authority that was bigger but weaker than the LCC had been. Unlike the LCC, the GLC had no control over children's services or personal health and welfare services, and it had no direct control of education, though Inner London GLC councillors were a majority on the ILEA. The GLC was the planning authority for the whole area, but its powers to implement its development plans were weak, and its grand schemes could generally be thwarted by borough opposition. The boroughs issued planning permissions in their own districts (except for developments of major strategic importance), and the GLC could not build houses in Greater London without the consent of the relevant borough or the Minister of Housing. The GLC retained the right to build houses in overspill towns (under the 1952 Town Development Act), but the housing stock and the demolition powers it inherited from the LCC would pass in time to the boroughs. The GLC took over responsibility for public transport when the London Transport Executive was abolished in 1970, and it had limited traffic management powers, but its control over London's roads was restricted to 550 miles of 'metropolitan' roads, as opposed to 150 miles of trunk roads, the Ministry's responsibility, and 7,000 miles of local roads, which were left to the boroughs. Dr Hill's brief effort in 1962 to abolish the Metropolitan Water Board came to nothing, and the GLC had no control over London's water supply, though it had responsibility for land drainage, main sewers and Thames flood prevention.[8] The vast Thames Barrier at Silvertown, built between 1975 and 1982 to make London safe from disastrous floods, is one of the GLC's most impressive and valuable monuments. The GLC shared a role in arts and recreational support, park management, building control, home defence, refuse disposal and the care of historic buildings with the metropolitan boroughs, and was London's ambulance, fire-fighting, intelligence-gathering and betting track licensing authority.[9] These were important duties, but they did not make the GLC London's government, and they were not enough to save it from destruction on its twenty-first birthday.

The boroughs, in contrast, were bigger and more powerful than before. They had complete responsibility for housing, personal and environmental health, consumer protection, libraries, local roads and parks, and local planning matters, and the twenty Outer London boroughs were also education authorities. With populations of between 145,000 (Kingston) and 329,000 (Croydon and Lambeth) they were roughly as big as all but five of England's provincial cities. Except in the case of Harrow, their size was achieved by amalgamating two or more existing boroughs (or parts of boroughs) into artificial and unfamiliar entities which had great difficulty in achieving local loyalty or recognition. The new boroughs of Brent (Wembley and Willesden), Newham (East and West Ham), Bromley (Bromley, Penge, Beckenham and Orpington), Haringey (Hornsey, Tottenham and Wood Green), Havering (Romford and Hornchurch) and Hillingdon (Hayes, Harlington, Uxbridge and Ruislip) seem to have been particularly unloved, and there was much regret at the loss of historic names and identities. Finsbury, Shoreditch, Holborn, St Marylebone, Hampstead, Bethnal Green, Stepney, Poplar, Deptford, Bermondsey, Battersea and Camberwell had no place on the new administrative map, though their names still mean more to most Londoners (and to most house buyers) than those of Brent, Havering or Redbridge.[10]

Over the next twenty years many of the new boroughs used their control of traffic, retail development and the location of council offices to reshape their multi-centred territories into districts with a single dominant civic centre. The chosen town hall would be enlarged or rebuilt, while its rivals were sold off or converted to minor uses, and preferential planning permission encouraged office, hotel and retail developments in the favoured town centre at the expense of secondary centres on the edge of the borough, which were more likely to get 'do-it yourself' warehouses and retail parks. A few boroughs resisted these centralizing tendencies (Richmond, Barking, Newham, Tower Hamlets, Brent, Barnet and Hackney), but elsewhere they have helped to create some of modern London's main civic and economic growth points: Kingston, Ealing, Bromley, Croydon, Wood Green, Hammersmith, Ilford and Uxbridge.[11]

THE RINGWAY PLAN

The growth of independent planning in the Metropolitan Boroughs between 1965 and 1975 was encouraged by the fact that the final version of the overall strategic plan which the GLC was meant to devise to coordinate and guide the efforts of individual boroughs took ten painful years to produce. Between 1965 and 1969 the planners and engineers in County Hall worked on a 'structure plan' which was intended, according to the terms of the 1968 Town and Country Planning Act, to indicate 'the general principles upon which development in the area will be promoted and controlled', rather than a detailed land use plan such as those produced by the LCC and other counties under the 1947 Act. Their first effort was submitted by the Minister of Housing (Anthony Crosland) to a Panel of Enquiry chaired by Frank Layfield, QC, which sat from May 1970 to December 1972. In the course of this very long and controversial enquiry the Greater London Development Plan (GLDP) was loudly condemned, both by the public and the panel. Layfield rejected the GLDP's assumption that the GLC could influence trends in London's population and employment, and was extremely critical of the weakness of the Plan's policies on issues over which the GLC did not have direct control, but still had a duty to plan, especially housing and public transport. 'Our basic criticism of the Plan', Layfield's report concluded, 'is that there are, too often, either no links between its aims and its policies, or no policy at all to support a wholly desirable aim.'[12]

The one policy which the GLDP expounded at length, its proposal for an extremely ambitious and expensive network of urban motorways, turned out to be almost universally unpopular. But the scheme reflected the popularity of motorway solutions to urban traffic problems among planners in the 1960s, especially in the wake of Professor Colin Buchanan's 1963 study, *Traffic in Towns*, and it was also one of the few policies in the Plan which the GLC could implement itself, without persuading the boroughs to dance to its tune.[13] The GLC's policy was based on the London Transportation Survey of the early 1960s, which showed a strong growth in non-work car journeys in the suburbs, and indicated that such journeys would roughly double between 1962 and 1981. This growth could not be stopped, but it could be diverted away from smaller streets and the city centre by a series of three orbital Ringways, each of which would link London's existing and proposed radial roads to each other. One ringway, the so-called Motorway Box, would be about 3 miles from the centre of London, running through Hackney, Camden, Hampstead, Shepherd's Bush, Fulham, Battersea, Lewisham and Greenwich. The eastern and western sections of the box were eventually built, as the West Cross Route from Shepherd's Bush to Westway, and the East Cross Route and the northern and southern approaches to the Blackwall Tunnel. Ringway Two, about 7 miles from the centre, involved a widening of the North Circular Road and the construction of its southern equivalent from Barnes to Thames-mead, through Streatham, Norwood and south Lewisham. The third would be in the Green Belt, just beyond the built-up area, and a fourth road, to be built by the Department of Transport, was what we now know as the M25. The Ringway roads and the dozen radial roads that would link them amounted to about 400 miles of motorway, costing £2 billion (nearly 5 per cent of Britain's Gross Domestic Product in 1970), and would involve evicting 100,000 people and making life unbearable for many more.

When a similar network of pleasantly named expressways and parkways had been advocated by Patrick Abercrombie in 1944 it had been greeted with equanimity, but in 1969–70 hostility to the proposal united Londoners as no other GLC action (except its last-ditch resistance to its own dissolution) ever did. The London Motorway Action Group, led by the Labour ex-minister, Douglas Jay, campaigned strongly against the scheme.

Three-quarters of the 28,000 objections to the GLDP were against the road plans, and 130 of the Layfield Panel's 237 days of public hearings were devoted to them.[14] Layfield castigated the GLC for failing to consider the contribution improved public transport could make to London's traffic problems, and pointed out that new motorways would generate new and unnecessary journeys, but still endorsed the Motorway Box and the future M25, while rejecting most of Ringways Two and Three. The Labour Party, which had originally proposed the Motorway Box, won the 1973 GLC elections by opposing it. It was left to the Environment Secretary (Crosland again) to delete Ringway One and shift the emphasis of the GLDP to traffic restraint and improved public transport when the Plan was at last approved and published in 1976.[15]

LONDON'S TRANSPORT PROBLEM

The abandonment of the Ringways was greeted with general relief, but the question of what was to be done about London's growing transport congestion still needed to be answered. A way had to be found of preserving the attractiveness of London as a place to visit, live and work in, while at the same time ensuring that London's economy could still function efficiently in the age of mass car ownership. These were not alternative paths, each of which might be chosen at the expense of the other. The happiness of Londoners depended not only on safe and quiet streets and clean air, but also on their ability to move freely around their city, and on the prosperity of the commercial and manufacturing economy that gave them their livelihoods. Many London employers, including most of the biggest ones, had a choice about where their businesses should be located, and a transport system that allowed insufficient room for cars and lorries would encourage them to move elsewhere. By the 1970s the flight of manufacturing industry from London was becoming a serious issue for those concerned about the future of the city. On the other hand, the environmental and social degradation that would result from unrestricted road building would not only harm its population, but also, in the end, damage its economy by accelerating the dispersal of its more mobile citizens and driving away those activities, especially tourism and international business, which were attracted by the quality of London life. Furthermore, it was recognized by this time (and had even been noticed in the 1930s) that building more and better roads would encourage more people to use their cars instead of public transport, until the new roads were as congested, on a grander and dirtier scale, as the old ones. London policy-makers have faced a similar choice between economic prosperity and environmental protection many times since 1945, over airport extensions, office develop-ment and factory building, as well as transport investment. In most cases, though, a clear victory for one side over the other was not a victory for London. London's economic prosperity and its quality of life are dependent on each other: if one is damaged, the other will suffer too.

As well as balancing economic and environmental interests, London's planners had to match the transport needs of the inner city, where space was so scarce and commuting was on so enormous a scale that public transport was bound to be dominant, with the outer city, where private car ownership and use was certain to increase and could reasonably do so. To link these two cities by building radial motorways, such as Westway (1970), which enticed Outer London car owners to drive into central London, would create intolerable congestion in the relatively narrow streets of the centre. The only practical way to deliver over a million workers into central London every morning was to provide and maintain an efficient and well-funded railway system. Transport planning also involved balancing individ-ual freedom with the wider public interest, and the interests of car owners with those of people who were unable to drive. For many individuals, the private car would be the preferred mode of travel, for speed, comfort and convenience, but for the community as a whole, including car drivers, the effect of millions of such individual decisions was plainly harmful, in pollution, traffic congestion, accidents and the loss of freedom for children to play and walk outside. Road congestion itself is one of the most effective deterrents to the use of the car, but in the process the environment is damaged and all road users, including buses, deliveries and essential services, are impeded too. Bus services, which had been enormously important for short and suburban journeys, were made slower and more unattractive by traffic congestion, and this pushed an even greater number of people into using their cars. One way to break this spiral was to introduce direct controls on car use, such as limits on access to the centre, or road pricing to reflect the environmental costs of driving, but these did not appeal to politicians who had elections to win. Only on-street parking restrictions, which were introduced in the centre in 1958–9, have limited the motorists' freedom to drive into central London. It was easier to pursue a compromise policy, in which buses were given priority over cars in selected streets and at some junctions, or allowed to run in roads from which cars were excluded. About 150 bus lanes were introduced in the 1970s (each one saving about two minutes on a peak-hour journey), but the GLC was reluctant to implement the comprehensive bus route system advocated by Camden Council in 1972 because, they said, of its disadvantages to other road users.[16]

Until 1970 London had no single body to coordinate its transport policy. But in 1969 the Transport (London) Act replaced the London Transport Board, which ran the underground and red London buses under the control of the Ministry of Transport, with the London Transport Executive, under the control of the GLC. It was considered impractical to separate London suburban rail services from the rest of the national network, but under the Act British Railways had to plan its London commuter services and fares in consultation with the GLC. The GLC was to be London's overall transport planning authority, and to have responsibility for an extra 325 miles of borough main roads, to add to its existing 550 miles of metropolitan roads.[17] Its control of London Transport gave the GLC an alternative way forward when its motorway plans were rejected by the electorate in 1973, and placed it in a position to tackle one of London's most serious and intractable problems by revitalizing its public transport system. The victorious Labour Party had campaigned on the promise that London Transport fares would be cut and eventually reduced to a low flat rate or abolished altogether, with the help of a GLC subsidy. The GLC pursued this policy in 1973–4 by holding fares steady in a period of rapid inflation, and London Transport's consequent losses (38 per cent of its operating costs) were covered by interest-free GLC grants. The results of this policy were disappointing. London Transport, which had made a small profit in 1972, made a loss of £50 million in 1974 and over £100 million a year for the next three years, with only a modest increase in the number of passengers it carried. There was a slight rise (of about 4 per cent) in the number of bus passengers, which had been declining steadily since the 1950s, and a reduction of about 2 per cent in the amount of traffic on London's main roads during the low fares period. But most of those who used their cars instead of public transport did so because car travel was faster, more reliable or more convenient, not because it was cheaper, and the temporary transfer of travellers from cars to buses was not much to show for an outlay of over £100 million a year. The GLC policy subsidized passengers, many of whom (especially those on railways and the Tube) were in no need of such help, rather than the transport system itself.[18] The policy was abandoned towards the end of 1974, when the Labour leadership of the GLC, under pressure from its own officials and from the Labour government, and resisted by a small group of young radicals led by Ken Livingstone and Tony Banks, decided that fare increases would cause less political damage than increasing the GLC rate (on houses and businesses) by 137 per cent. Fares rose by over 60 per cent in 1975, and there were further steep rises in 1976, signalling the complete abandonment of the transport policy on which Labour had won the 1973 GLC election. These cuts, along with an equally severe reduction in the Council's housing programme, did not save the Labour Party from a comprehensive defeat in the 1977 GLC election, but they did have the effect of persuading Ken Livingstone to work towards unseating Sir Reg Goodwin as leader of the Labour group on the GLC.[19]

HOUSE-BUILDING IN THE 1960s

The replacement of the LCC by the GLC in 1965 broke County Hall's power over the borough housing departments, and allowed the new boroughs to develop distinctive and independent construction policies of their own. Where once the LCC had delayed and vetoed borough housing proposals and taken the best sites for itself, now the GLC found its own developments blocked by the enlarged and much more powerful metropolitan boroughs, and had to take the sites nobody else wanted. The biggest of these unwanted sites was 1,600 acres of unpromisingly boggy land on the Erith and Plumstead Marshes, on the south bank of the Thames opposite Barking and Dagenham, which had previously been occupied by a sewage works and an explosives testing range. In 1966 the GLC published its plan for Thamesmead, a new town for 60,000 people, complete with employment, transport, schools, entertainment, and private as well as public housing. Work began in the early 1970s, and by 1985 there were 20,000 residents, predictably without the town centre, Jubilee Line Tube extension, river crossing and extensive social facilities which they had been promised. This was the GLC's last major housing project. When the Council was wound up in 1986 control of Thamesmead passed to a trust rather like those that had run the new towns.[20]

In its first ten years the GLC managed to match the rate of building set by the LCC in its last decade (about 5,000 dwellings a year), but the boroughs increased their completions by nearly 50 per cent, from 10,000 to 16,000 a year.[21] Some boroughs (Westminster, Camden, Lambeth) emulated the LCC's emphasis on careful design, while others, notably Enfield, Croydon, Waltham Forest, Southwark and Newham, went all out for quantity. They were attracted by system-building techniques, using standardized designs, factory-made prefabricated components and a variety of new insulated claddings, offered by the big contractors, Wates, Laing, Taylor Woodrow-Anglian, Costain and Concrete Ltd, whose popular Bison Wall-Frame system could make a complete two-bedroom flat from only twenty-one precast components. By buying these packages local authorities lost much of their control over the design of their estates, but they were attractive because they were fast, cheap, and did not demand much skilled labour.[22] The architects' love affair with tower blocks was ending in the 1960s, but high flats still served the needs of local authorities with long waiting lists and not much land or money, and some huge estates were built in these years, including Haringey's Broadwater Farm (1063 housing units), Greenwich's Ferrier estate (1,898 units) and Southwark's North Peckham and Aylesbury estates (1,400 and 2,127 units).

Until the late 1960s, local authority estate builders were encouraged and subsidized by Conservative and Labour central governments, who boasted at each election of the number of housing units they had completed, or would complete in their next term of office. The subsidy system pushed local authorities towards standard designs and costings, and made it difficult to pursue an independent housing policy. Council decisions to bulldoze large areas of substandard houses which could easily have been rehabilitated (Camden's 'comprehensive redevelopment' of Gospel Oak in the 1960s is a notorious example) was not the result of collective megalomania in their planning departments, but of a government subsidy system which rewarded rebuilding but not (until 1969) improvement. Central government, which had retained power without responsibility in the field of local housing, was the driving force behind the redevelopment policies of London and other councils in the 1950s and 1960s. Although there had been warnings of the undesirable social effects of tower block estates since the 1950s, these seemed insignificant compared with the problem of homelessness and multi-occupation they were helping to diminish. The major public enquiry into London housing in the 1960s, the 1965 Milner Holland Report, did not question the slum clearance and estate building policy, but concentrated on the shortage of public and private housing, the poor quality of old stock, and the insecurity of tenure suffered by the tenants of some private landlords. The fact that about 200,000 London families had no decent home of their own, and were compelled to share a bathless house with other households and an assortment of vermin, seemed to the committee to be more significant than questions of modern housing design, and the good quality of new council flats seemed to be more important than their distance from the ground. The problem with London's local authority housing was simply that there was not enough of it, and that its rate of production was not fast enough to eradicate slums and multi-occupation in the near future. The policy of high-density redevelopment was endorsed, too, by the first report of the South East Planning Council, *A Strategy for the South East*, in 1967. The high birth rate of the 1960s, which was expected to create increasing population pressures for decades to come, made the abandonment of high-rise development hard to contemplate.

SECOND THOUGHTS ABOUT TOWER BLOCKS

In retrospect, the wholesale demolition of working-class neighbourhoods from the 1950s to the 1970s was a terrible mistake. Very many of the houses destroyed could easily and cheaply have been brought up to modern standards. In a survey conducted in 1967 the Greater London Council found that 69 per cent of the houses it was knocking down were structurally sound, and between 1967 and 1971 London lost 54,000 sound houses through 'slum clearance' schemes. Many of these were condemned because they stood in the way of the creation of a well-shaped building estate, or because their gardens were too big. Slum clearance was a slow and piecemeal process, which sometimes blighted districts for many years. This pushed people on to council housing lists (thus justifying the building of more estates), and made it impossible to rehouse whole communities together. To do so, in the oddly Victorian opinion of the Housing Ministry's Chief Planner in the early 1960s, was in any case undesirable: 'The task is surely to break up such groupings, even though the people seem to be satisfied with their miserable environment and seem to enjoy an extrovert social life within their own locality.' So the resentful inhabitants of Inner London terraces were forced out of their homes and communities, and into blocks of flats in uncongenial estates, far away from old and familiar faces and places. Once in their flats and in front of their televisions, they could watch the inhabitants of *Coronation Street* and *East Enders* leading lives rather like the ones they had been forced to give up.[23]

The political mood changed in the later 1960s, when a growing public resentment of tower block estates was stimulated by the partial collapse of Ronan Point, a twenty-three-storey point block in the Clever Road development in Canning Town, Newham. In May 1968 all twenty-three rooms in one corner of Ronan Point collapsed as a result of a gas explosion, killing five people. The effects of the explosion were no more disastrous than gas explosions in traditional houses had often been, and did not demonstrate the structural unsoundness of system-built tower blocks, which have in recent years often proved to be extremely hard to demolish. But it crystallized and confirmed a long-lasting public distrust of system-built blocks, giving them a reputation almost as bad, and perhaps as undeserved, as the old working-class terraces had been given by Le Corbusier and the tower block propagandists. The significance of the Ronan Point disaster as a turning point should not be exaggerated. Many boroughs were already turning away from tower blocks in the early 1960s, when Westminster's red brick Lillington Gardens and Camden's unnecessary redevelopment of the pleasant Victorian streets of Gospel Oak created a new fashion for high-density low-rise estates. Others continued to build high flats: Erno Goldfinger's Trellick Tower, near Westbourne Park, the tallest and most impressive of London's blocks of council flats, was built between 1968 and 1973, and so were most of the Broadwater Farm estate in Haringey, Stockwell Park in Lambeth and the Ferrier estate in Greenwich. But Ronan Point changed the political climate, and this, in conjunction with the economic crisis of the late 1960s, persuaded the Labour government to move towards a cheaper and more popular policy of rehabilitating older homes, rather than bulldozing them for new estates. Its 1968 White Paper, *Old Houses into New Homes*, promoted the idea of rehabilitation, and the 1969 Housing Act increased improvement grants and introduced General Improvement Areas.[24]

'GENTRIFICATION'

One of the effects of the improvement grant policy in the 1970s was to accelerate the existing process of 'gentrification', by which working-class properties in poor condition were bought and improved, often with public financial help, by entrepreneurs or middle-class owners. This increased the problems of poorer Londoners, who now had to compete for inner-city housing against middle-class buyers with easy access to mortgages and enough money to tempt private landlords into selling up. The competition grew stronger in the 1960s and 1970s, when some middle-class households began to look for houses and flats in inner-city neighbourhoods, instead of moving to the suburbs, as earlier generations of well-off Londoners had done. This made nonsense of the common idea that Inner London would become increasingly impoverished and neglected, a prediction based on the experience of some American cities. As early as 1963, Ruth Glass described the process of 'gentrification', in which shabby cottages were transformed into elegant middle-class homes, and large Victorian houses which had been in working-class multi-occupation for decades were converted into expensive flats for well-off occupants:

> Once this process of 'gentrification' starts in a district, it goes on rapidly until all or most of the original working-class occupiers are displaced, and the whole social character of the district is changed. There is very little left of the poorer enclaves of Hampstead and Chelsea: in those boroughs, the upper-middle class take-over was consolidated some time ago. The invasion has since spread to Islington, Paddington, North Kensington – even to the 'shady' parts of Notting Hill – to Battersea, and to several other districts, north and south of the river. (The East End has so far been exempt.)[25]

The typical 'gentrifiers' were professional people, often working in education or the arts, who were looking for decent but neglected houses in working-class districts that seemed to be on the way up, especially those near a high-status neighbourhood. Usually with the help of council improvement grants, they stamped their new houses with their increasingly familiar hallmarks: stripped pine doors, sanded floors, 'knocked through' downstairs rooms, Habitat furniture, Laura Ashley wallpaper, fitted kitchens and gas-fired central heating. This transformation was taking place all over the Inner London boroughs in the 1960s and 1970s, but perhaps the Islington district of Barnsbury, which moved rapidly from working-class private rental to middle-class owner-occupation between 1965 and 1975, was the outstanding example of the process.[26]

Gentrification was blamed, not altogether unfairly, for displacing working-class families from their traditional neighbourhoods, and turning the improvement grant system against the people it was meant to help. But it also helped to save some parts of London from decay and demolition, at a time when borough councils were driven by an almost unstoppable urge to knock down and redevelop perfectly decent working-class neighbourhoods. In Hackney, the Council planned to demolish de Beauvoir Town, a fine Victorian planned suburb, in the 1960s. In 1967 professionals who had just begun to 'gentrify' the neighbourhood formed an association to resist the Council's plans, to preserve and improve the area, and to ensure that poorer tenants were not 'winkled out' by unscrupulous landlords. Acting alongside their working-class neighbours, middle-class residents used their contacts in the press, the GLC, the Victorian Society and the newly formed Hackney Society to mobilize public support, and went on to defeat the Council's proposals in a local enquiry. A similar defence was mounted in

Mapledene, a socially mixed Victorian suburb just east of de Beauvoir Town, when the Council decided to demolish it in 1972, in order to extend its unsuccessful Holly Street tower block estate. The residents' victory over the Council in the public enquiry was yet another sign of the rising power of conservationism, and the decline of 'comprehensive redevelopment'.[27]

CONSERVATION AND COVENT GARDEN

The conservationist movement, which had begun to take shape with the creation of the Civic Trust and the Victorian Society in the late 1950s, during the first postwar office-building boom, enjoyed some of its greatest triumphs in the years around 1970. Many of the conservationists' early battles (against the Euston redevelopment and Centre Point, for instance) were unsuccessful, but in the later 1960s the public and political mood seemed to turn against the insensitive redevelopment of what was left of historic London. The work of the GLC's Historic Buildings Board, which guarded London's 20,000 listed buildings, was strengthened by the 1968 Town and Country Planning Act, which increased penalties for neglecting or destroying protected buildings, and gave the Council new compulsory purchase powers. Even more important was the introduction of Conservation Areas by the 1967 Civic Amenities Act, a private measure proposed by Duncan Sandys, president of the Civic Trust, and supported by the Labour Local Government minister, Richard Crossman. Within seven years there were over 250 conservation areas in London, encompassing, among other places, a third of Westminster, half of Kensington and Chelsea, and the whole of Belgravia. The effect of these changes was to bring the era of secret deals and *faits accomplis* to an end, and to force public or private developers to expose their plans to the often painful experience of public discussion and enquiry.[28]

An early victim of the new mood of public openness was the GLC's Comprehensive Development Plan for Covent Garden (the whole of the area bounded by Charing Cross Road, the Strand, High Holborn and Kingsway), published in 1968. The Plan proposed the demolition of nearly two-thirds of the area, replacing a neighbourhood of old-fashioned small-scale housing and manufacture, and the fruit and vegetable market (which was due to move to Nine Elms, Vauxhall, in 1974) with an up-to-date business district, complete with major highways, sunken roads, high-rise housing, office blocks, open spaces and the inevitable conference centre. The scheme, which was hardly more extreme than others that had been introduced without publicity a few years before, provoked a public reaction that was overwhelmingly hostile. After a long campaign, led by the Covent Garden Community Association, the Environment Minister, Geoffrey Rippon, announced the listing of about 200 buildings in the area in 1973, and this, along with the Labour victory in the 1973 GLC election, put an end to the plan. As it turned out, the local people who had fought to save Covent Garden did not enjoy the fruits of their victory. As Ian Nairn had predicted, the disappearance of the market ended the creative tension between cockney and concertgoer that gave the neighbourhood its unique quality: 'When the market goes, as it will some time in the next ten years, ballerina is likely to meet office clerk: one kind of unreality meeting another.' The refurbishment of the abandoned market as a craft, retail and restaurant centre was a great commercial success, and the whole area was transformed in the 1970s by the spending power of office workers, theatre-goers and tourists. There was soon no room for the cheap housing and low-profit businesses that the Association had fought to protect, and they fell victim to a form of commercial gentrification.[29]

Nevertheless the Covent Garden victory, together with the campaign against the Motorway Box, which was fought over the same years with the same result, marked an important shift in the balance of power between developers and local communities. The success of the Covent Garden Community Association inspired the residents of Tolmers Square (Euston), Coin Street (Waterloo), Peckham, Spitalfields and various parts of Dock-lands to organize and campaign when their own neighbourhoods came under threat in the 1970s and 1980s. The success of these local campaigns usually depended on winning the support of a powerful ally, especially the GLC. A change of party in County Hall snuffed out the Motorway Box and the Covent Garden scheme, and it was the GLC, in its final days, that handed over the valuable Coin Street site to the local community for cooperative housing, instead of offices.

THE MISMANAGEMENT OF HOUSING ESTATES

It became as fashionable in the 1970s to denounce high-rise housing estates as it had been to advocate them fifteen years earlier. Responsibility for rising crime, depression, moral decay, the decline of family and community values, were laid at their door. It is not easy to disentangle the effects of tower-block estates on London's working-class community life from that of other changes that were taking place at the same time: rising working-class affluence, the increased emphasis on privacy, domestic comfort and home-based leisure activities (especially television), the growth of the West Indian and Asian population, the decline of the extended family and the rise of the smaller household unit (including the one-parent family), the growth of recorded crime, the collapse of manufacturing and the emergence of mass unemployment since the 1970s, the squeeze on local authority spending, and the uprooting of established neighbourhoods by slum clearance and economic change. Big London housing estates often seemed to represent a distillation of many of these changes, but it is too facile to blame the social ills that some of these estates suffered on the layout and architecture of their buildings alone, rather than on more complex underlying forces. Huge estates, with their extensive communal facilities and shared corridors, balconies and open spaces, demanded a special kind of management and a new form of community cooperation. Like Highpoint and other prewar luxury blocks they needed on-site managers and janitors to settle disputes, discourage vandalism, repair lifts and rubbish chutes, maintain common corridors and gardens, and stimulate the growth of community organizations. Some estates were harder to look after than others, but it was widely agreed, as an official survey of housing in Lambeth was told in 1977, that 'the quality of the environment seems to depend more on the way the estate is maintained and cared for than on the standard of design'.[30] Estates which had been built cheaply could not be maintained cheaply.

This was the argument of *Faith in the City*, the report of the Archbishop of Canterbury's Commission on urban priority areas published in 1985. The social problems of the new estates, it said, sprang from several causes. Local authorities had failed to provide their 'streets in the sky' with the shops, public houses, launderettes and community facilities that would have made them into real communities. They had filled them with low-income and unemployed families, or the occupants of low-grade slums, thus creating 'unbalanced communities' which were unattractive to prospective or existing tenants who had a choice about where to live.

> Maintenance has been skimped from the beginning, resulting in an atmosphere of neglect. Governments, both national and local, have seen more votes to be won in meeting new construction targets than in cyclical painting.... The maintenance service is seen as very unresponsive. At many public meetings we have attended the poor delivery of repairs has featured high on the list of complaints....

Tenants have, almost without exception, never been involved at any stage. Tenant opinion for example has always been against the building of high-rise estates. Pre- and post-war surveys show that the overwhelming majority of people who were rehoused in such estates would have preferred a house with a plot of garden.[31]

Inner London, which had 8 per cent of England's council housing in 1983, had 28 per cent of its 'difficult-to-let' council properties. In general, these unpopular estates were very large, but they were not always modern. Meanly constructed four-storey estates built in the 1930s and 1950s to rehouse displaced slum-dwellers were often hated as much as new high-rise developments. In 1982 a Department of the Environment study of a selection of twenty of England's worst estates (eleven of which were in London) demonstrated that the most disastrous features of these estates stemmed from well-intentioned but misconceived efforts on the part of architects and planners to turn them into 'communities'. Tower blocks without walkways or balconies, despite their poor reputation, created fewer problems than blocks that were linked by walkways, decks and balconies, turning them, as one manager put it, into 'giant climbing frames'. Those on estates without communal facilities (drying rooms, meeting halls, play areas) complained about the deficiency, but in bad estates communal facilities were part of the nightmare. Drying rooms were smashed and defaced, unused plots of land were turned into scrapyards or meeting places for drug-takers and glue-sniffers, and communal areas, which were meant to compensate tenants for the high densities in which they lived, were colonized and fouled by dogs (kept against the rules by lonely or insecure tenants), and did not provide the safe playgrounds so badly needed by high-rise children. Underground car parks, empty garages, rubbish stores, walkways, bridges, decks and corridors, created crime, noise, vandalism and fear. 'Often a communalistic design fantasy turned into an ugly and abused eyesore.' The effect of walkways and decks, the architects' beloved 'streets in the sky', was 'to break down even further any sense of neighbourliness or identity within a block', and 'to provide a strangulating line of access and escape for strangers'. The locks, lights, hinges and doors that made communal areas usable were too vulnerable to destruction, and lifts, the essential link between high-rise tenants and the outside world, presented a simple challenge to destructive young fingers. 'The ease with which they could be damaged made residents feel vulnerable and therefore incited bullying behaviour as weak spots always do.'[32] The tragedy of these unpopular estates was intensified by the fact that their tenants, the most desperate and ill-favoured people on the councils' waiting lists, were generally unable to escape from them.

> The poorest estates often seemed to residents more like a collection of failures from somewhere else than a community of interest. Their size and separation helped set in train a circular decline, as their unpopularity invited low-income, vulnerable residents who also disliked the estate for the same reasons and who found it hard to identify with their neighbours because of the overpowering anonymity. Their failure to identify with their community in turn enhanced the estate's problems. People with intense social and economic problems often did not want to identify with others in the same boat.[33]

One of the eleven London estates included in the 1982 study was Broadwater Farm, in Tottenham. Three years afterwards, in October 1985, the estate was the scene of one of the worst of the London riots of the 1980s. The independent enquiry into this riot, in which a community police officer, PC Keith Blakelock, was murdered, analysed the reasons for the estate's decline in the 1970s. The estate was built between 1967 and 1973 by Taylor Woodrow, using the Swedish Larsen-Neilson system-building method. Broadwater Farm's tenants found their quiet, spacious, clean and very warm new flats a great improvement on their old slums, but the height and design of the flats created some problems, especially from damp penetration and from cockroaches, which found life easy between the cladding slabs. But the true cause of the decline of this estate (and of many others like it) was the unwillingness of the local council to spend money on its upkeep and repair, to provide on-site management and maintenance and to pay for the well-kept social and cultural facilities needed by a community of over 1,000 households. There was no doctor's surgery, public house, launderette, community centre or bus service, and Haringey Council was very slow to deal with problems of damp, faulty lifts, graffiti, broken doors and windows, rotting woodwork and accumulated rubbish. Tenants who were able to find better accommodation left the estate, and the council found that it could only let its vacant flats to families who were homeless, unemployed or desperate. Local newspapers depicted the estate as a concentration of crime and unmarried motherhood, and this gave another twist to the spiral of social and economic decline. In 1986, when London's unemployment rate was about 9 per cent, only 31 per cent of adults on Broadwater Farm were in work, and 54 per cent of households on the estate had no working adults in them. The recovery of social life on Broadwater Farm before and after the 1985 riots shows that the estate was not incapable of generating an active community spirit, that it was neglect, rather than the structure of the estate in itself, which had dragged the neighbourhood down. In the early 1980s, after intense pressure from revitalized tenants' organizations, the council launched a repair programme which rectified minor design flaws that had caused social problems: doors and locks were strengthened, dark areas at the bottom of blocks which had hidden thieves and drug dealers were opened up, and entryphones were installed on the bigger blocks to increase their security and privacy. In 1983 Haringey Council established a neighbourhood office on the estate to handle repairs, management and housing benefits, and to plan the improve-ment of the estate, and the disastrous period of neglect came to an end. The riots had more to do with the breakdown in relations between the local police and young black men on the estate than with conditions on the estate itself.[34]

'BUILDING STABLE COMMUNITIES'

Disillusionment with tower blocks and comprehensive redevelopment in the early 1970s did not have immediate effects on London house-building, because it was widely recognized that its shortage of decent accommodation was still very severe. The Milner Holland Report, the London Housing Survey (published in 1970) and the Report of the Layfield panel of enquiry into the Greater London Development Plan (1973) all argued that the housing problems of the Inner London boroughs could not be solved without continued large-scale public building. Public housing completions in London reached a peak of over 27,000 in 1970, and in 1980 there were still over 16,000 completions, only slightly fewer than the average for the 1960s. What finally ended the great age of municipal house-building was the Conservative victory in the 1979 General Election, which brought to power, for the first time since 1918, a government which doubted the value of public housing, and which was prepared to exploit the worst examples of poor design and bad management to discredit it. The government's arm was strengthened by the results of the 1981 census, which seemed to show that Greater London had more dwellings (2.75 million) than it had households (2.51 million), and that the remaining housing problem was one of allocation, not construction. This ignored the fact that many London dwellings belonged to non-Londoners, that over 100,000 dwellings (mostly privately owned ones) were empty, and that almost a quarter of London dwellings (according to the 1979 Greater London House Condition Survey) were unsatisfactory, or needed extensive repairs. It also disregarded the existence of 'concealed households' (single mothers living with their parents, for instance), the occupation of large houses by small households (and vice versa), and the geographical and economic mismatch between empty properties (mostly expensive and suburban) and those in need of homes (mostly poor and inner-city). The withdrawal of the GLC from most of its housing functions in 1981, and its abolition five years later, ended its role in matching tenants to dwellings across the whole of London and beyond, leaving the process of redistribution to the free market. Because of Department of the Environment restrictions on the boroughs' borrowing powers, Greater London local authority house completions fell by more than 68 per cent (from 16,249 to 5,149) between 1980 and 1983, and by 1991, when rate-capping (a government limit on the amount councils could raise on their local rates) had closed off the boroughs' other route to new money, there were only 123 borough housing starts. Local authority building, which had represented 75 per cent of all London house building in 1970 and 72 per cent in 1980, represented under 11 per cent in 1990, and 1.5 per cent in 1991.[35]

The boroughs were still London's most important landlords, but even here their position was eroded by the privatization, or 'right to buy', legislation introduced in 1980. Some authorities began the process of selling off their housing stock even before 1980. In 1977 the new Conservative administration on the GLC decided to sell its recently completed Brentford Dock estate, and entered agreements that bound its successor, Ken Livingstone's Labour administration, to sell GLC houses that were nearing completion.[36] During the 1980s London boroughs sold off more than 177,000 dwellings, a fifth of their stock, either to tenants or to private landlords. Tenants were encouraged to buy by generous discounts, the prospect of a large capital gain, and the doubling of real rent levels in the 1980s. The movement towards 'market rents' for council houses was accelerated by the 1989 Housing and Local Government Act, which was intended to squeeze the remaining element of public subsidy out of the system. Between 1991 and 1994 council rents rose by 31 per cent, over four times as fast as private rents. Sales brought the councils' share of London's total housing stock down from a third to 22 per cent (in 1994), leaving them with the properties that were the least desirable and hardest to sell.[37] A small proportion of the money raised from these sales could be used to build new homes, but the suburban councils whose properties were easiest to sell were least likely to embark on new housing programmes, and the inner-city boroughs that needed new homes could not sell their old ones.

Tenants in the older and least popular estates, who were most likely (thanks to council allocation policies) to be black or previously homeless, were unable and unwilling to buy their flats. But they saw the better council properties, their hope of an eventual transfer, being snapped up at bargain prices, leaving them at the bottom of a ladder that had no top.[38]

The tendency of council tenants to vote Labour and home owners to vote Conservative did not escape those who framed the 'right to buy' policy in central government, or those who implemented it in the boroughs. Wandsworth was probably in the best position to sell and rebuild, but its council was committed to reducing its public housing stock as fast as possible, and, in the words of the chairman of its property sales committee, to 'make Battersea a Conservative constituency'. This policy of politically motivated gentrification was taken to its extreme in Westminster, where it was the Conservative Council's policy between 1986 and 1988, according to the housing chairman of the time, to use 'designated sales' of council property to 'to increase the number of upwardly mobile Conservative-type voters in specific key areas to ensure the vote went up'. Those in need of homes, who once would have been housed in such properties, were moved out of the borough or left in hostels or on the street. The exposure of this programme, known by its inventors as 'Building Stable Communities', by the BBC's *Panorama* in 1989 and in a district auditor's report led to the Council leader, Dame Shirley Porter, one of the most prominent figures in London local government, being surcharged £27 million for wasting ratepayers' money.[39] This was not the first time, of course, that council housing allocation had been used to serve the political interests of a governing party, but the somewhat seedy nature of the exercise, and the suggestion that some of the families Westminster had a duty to house were knowingly placed in asbestos-ridden flats in Labour wards, made this scandal particularly embarrassing.

HOMELESSNESS

The decline of municipal housing left the private sector to cope with the housing needs of Londoners of all classes, as well as absorbing the 200,000 new households London gained in the 1980s. Non-municipal renting did not seem to be the answer. The share of London's stock owned by housing associations, which the government wished to promote to the forefront of public rented housing provision, only rose from 4 per cent to 7 per cent between 1984 and 1994, and the share of the private rented sector, which had fallen from 42 per cent in 1961 to 22.5 per cent in 1976 and 14 per cent in 1981, fell again (to 12 per cent) in the 1980s.[40] The share of London housing in owner-occupation rose in the 1980s from 49 to 57 per cent, but private building did not rise fast enough in the 1980s to compensate for the collapse of public building, and there was no question of private builders being able to meet the needs of poorer Londoners, something which they had not managed to do for the past two centuries. The private sector's greatest contribution to London's housing stock from the 1970s to the early 1990s, especially in the Inner London boroughs of Camden, Westminster and Kensington, came from the conversion of private houses into flats for sale or rent. This process, which was far more common in Inner London than in the rest of England, was especially important in providing affordable and convenient accommodation for small middle-class households, but it helped to push house prices beyond the reach of the less well-off. The doubling of London house prices between 1985 and 1989 placed even a modest terraced house beyond the reach of working-class families without property to sell, and most of those who had traditionally relied on the public rented sector for their accommodation continued to do so. Many of those who managed in the 1980s to buy a house or flat by taking out a large mortgage, in the hope that inflation and rising property prices would justify their investment, found themselves trapped and impoverished by the property price slump of the late 1980s and early 1990s. An obscure economic phrase, 'negative equity', entered the language of newspaper headlines and dinner-table conversation.[41]

The waiting list for council properties remained at about 240,000 in the 1980s and early 1990s, while the number of council houses becoming available for rent fell steeply, and the few that became empty were ear-marked for the homeless and other priority cases. In 1989–90 only 6,000 of these households (2.5 per cent) were offered secure accommodation. By the early 1990s the number of homeless households that the London boroughs were compelled by law to house was far greater than the number of council properties available for them. Of the 39,726 households recognized as homeless in 1991–2, almost half (18,320) were placed in accommodation leased from the private sector, and 10,700 were in bed-and-breakfast rooms or hostels, a situation that was not compatible with the happy family life that was given such high priority in contemporary political rhetoric.[42]

In addition to the 'official' homeless, there were in London, according to studies conducted in 1989–90, about 70,000 single homeless people sleeping rough, squatting, or in temporary accommodation, and about 250,000 forced to stay with family or friends because they could not afford a room of their own.[43] A small segment of this hidden mass of homelessness became highly visible in the late 1980s, when a combination of government policies, including the ending of state benefits for sixteen- to seventeen-year-olds who had left home, the general reduction in social security payments and the closure of psychiatric hospitals, drove several thousand homeless people to make their homes in shop doorways, under railway arches, and in the 'cardboard cities' that sprang up in Lincoln's Inn Fields, the South Bank and other parts of central London. A high proportion of those sleeping rough were youngsters who had recently left children's homes. Thus homelessness became once again an aesthetic problem, on a level with street litter and dogs' mess, a discouragement to tourists, an embarrassment to theatre-goers, a worry to the users of underpasses and walkways. Even if this problem were to be solved (which at the time of writing it had not) the underlying and much greater problem of the shortage of affordable and decent accommodation for the lower paid in a free and unsubsidized London property market would still remain. In 1996 London Pride, an association of London local government and business organizations, reported that it was looking for ways of providing London with '100,000 affordable new homes'. But the revival of local authority housing departments, which often exceeded this five-yearly total between 1950 and 1975, was apparently not on their agenda.[44]

THE REJECTION OF ABERCROMBIE

A notable difference between the 1969 Greater London Development Plan (GLDP) and earlier plans was that it hinted for the first time that it might be time to abandon the Abercrombie–Barlow dogma, that people and jobs should be moved out of London as fast as places could be found for them to go. The GLDP still paid lip-service to the Green Belt and to the idea of dispersal, but its emphasis was on the need to slow down London's rate of population loss, and to 'foster the commercial and industrial prosperity of London' by providing local housing for the workers London's industries still needed. During the course of the Layfield Inquiry the GLC became more confident of this position, and argued that its aim should be to reduce rather than encourage the outflow of jobs.[45] Contrast this with the South-East Planning Council's first report in 1967, which repeated the old policy aims: 'major and sustained efforts to move out manufacturing industry ... continued control of office development and every possible encouragement of moves to office centres away from London ... there is a national interest in moving out manufacturing from London ... we urge the Government to make a major contribution to the buying up of vacated premises'.[46] In 1971 the South-East Joint Planning Team's important *Strategic Plan for the South-East* took a more cautious line, but still proposed the development of five major urban growth areas (Swindon, Ashford, Ipswich, South Hampshire and Milton Keynes) to syphon jobs and population away from London.[47] But by 1976, when this Strategic Plan was reviewed, the tone was entirely different. The Review's section on London amounted to a renunciation of the Abercrombie–Barlow principles that had guided the planning system for the previous thirty years. What seemed to have happened, the Review argued, was that London's population and employment had fallen, especially since the mid-1960s, without producing the gains in housing, transport and open space that the 1943–4 plans had expected. 'The present problem of London is basically one of population and employment decline coupled with declining resources and sustained pressures to provide, for example, additional housing and to cater for the rapid movement of vast daily flows of the people, goods and services essential to a major world capital.' The fall in the birth rate from 1966 meant that London's net annual loss through migration of about 100,000 people was no longer partly offset by natural growth. In fact, it seemed that in 1974–5 there would be more deaths than births in London.

Employment was falling, too, though not as fast as population. The fall in manufacturing jobs had accelerated so much (27 per cent were lost, 1966–74) that the growth in the service sector (itself slower than it once had been) did not compensate for it. In any case, many of those who had lost unskilled manufacturing jobs were not in a position to take office work, and pockets of high unemployment (especially among transport, dock and construction workers) had developed. Despite the falling population and the efforts of local councils the housing problem remained severe, in terms of cost, quality, density and homelessness. Environmental problems, especially poor housing, but also dirt, noise, vandalism and traffic congestion, encouraged better-off families to find better and cheaper homes outside London, and this trend added to London's transport congestion by increasing the flow of commuters from the Outer London region into the centre. Having identified the nature and causes of the problem, the 1976 Review tentatively proposed some solutions. The aim of public policy should be 'to slow things down in order to ease problems which arise through an excessive rate of change', to reduce the rate of outward migration by improving environmental and housing conditions, and discourage manufacturing closures (or encourage new industry) by providing sites and better transport and environmental services. In short, the Review turned Abercrombie inside out. Abercrombie had asked the government to reduce London's population and jobs in order to improve its quality of life but the 1976 Review argued that 'the prime public policy objective' should be 'an overall improvement in the quality of life for Londoners – the success of which will improve employment and slow the decline in London's population'.[48]

What had happened to bring about such a dramatic reversal? Essentially, as the Review explained, there had been two developments which neither Abercrombie nor the planners of the 1960s had anticipated. One was the fall in the birth rate, from almost 20 births per 1,000 people in 1962–4 to 15 per 1,000 in 1971 (and 13.6 in 1981). London's birth rate fell more slowly than England's as a whole, but the consequences for London were more severe, because of heavy outward migration. So Greater London's population, which had stayed obstinately high in the 1950s and early 1960s, thanks to its high birth rate and Commonwealth immigration, started to tumble in the later 1960s and in the 1970s. Between 1961 and 1981 Greater London lost 1,186,000 people, or 15 per cent of its population. The decline continued until 1984, but then, confounding all expectations, the trend reversed again. In Outer London the population stabilized, and in Inner London, after more than seventy years of decline, it began to grow. Population rose fastest in Tower Hamlets, where the recently arrived Bangladeshi community had a high birth rate, and where there were new middle-class settlers in Docklands. By 1993 the population of Inner London was 2.63 million, 100,000 (4 per cent) higher than its 1981 figure, and in the mid-1990s that of Greater London had recovered to almost 7 million.[49] The Greater London figures were these:

1939	8,615,000
1951	8,197,000
1961	7,992,000
1971	7,452,000
1981	6,806,000
1991	6,890,000
1993	6,933,000[50]

There was little the planners could do about all this, but the fluctuating figures, and the projections they made from them, help to explain London's changing image in their plans: at one moment, a lusty brute to be tranquillized or bled, the next a failing invalid in need of transfusions and a pacemaker.

THE COLLAPSE OF MANUFACTURING

The decline of London's manufacturing economy happened with dramatic suddenness. Between 1961, when Greater London had a manufacturing workforce of 1.6 million, and 1974, when it had declined to 900,000, London lost more than 50,000 manufacturing jobs a year. This was the state of affairs that worried the authors of the 1976 Greater London Development Plan and the 1976 Review of the South-East Strategic Plan. But worse was to follow. Figures from the Department of Trade and Industry's Business Statistics Office show that the number of Greater London factories employing over twenty people fell by 60 per cent, and their workforce by 40 per cent, between 1975 and 1982, when national manufacturing employment fell almost as fast. And in the national recovery of 1985–8, London kept on falling: employment in all London manufacturing units registered for VAT fell by 10 per cent (50,000 people) in three years. By 1993, according to the London Research Group, the number of manufacturing workers in Greater London was 328,000, about a half of the number in 1981, and hardly a fifth of the number in 1961. There is no strong reason to believe that London's long-term decline as a manufacturing centre has ended, but since manufacturing industry's share of London's output and workforce in the 1990s is much smaller than it was in the 1960s the economic and social impact of its further decline will not be as great as it was in earlier decades.[51] The decline of the manufacturing workforce did not imply a fall in output. Between 1982 and 1993 increased productivity increased the value of London's manfactured output by almost 1 per cent a year. London's economy as a whole grew faster, and therefore manufacturing's share of Greater London's Gross Domestic Product (GDP) fell from 18 per cent in 1984 to 13.3 per cent in 1993. This was less than the share of distribution, hotels and catering (14.2 per cent), and under half the contribution made by the financial and business sector (31.2 per cent).[52]

To some extent London's decline was a reflection of the decline of manufacturing in Britain as a whole after 1960. But London's manufacturing workforce fell more than twice as quickly as that of the UK, and its share of the national manufacturing workforce fell from over 18 per cent in 1961 to under 8 per cent in 1992.[53] A part of London's decline resulted from the failure of weak or poorly organized manufacturers, especially Inner London clothing firms, to match the quality or cost of imported goods, but in general London did not decline because most of its industries were, on the national or international scale, 'declining' industries. London in the 1960s had a small share of archaic or fading industries (textiles and shipbuilding, for instance) and a large share of modern and expanding ones, such as engineering, electronics, vehicles, aircraft, printing, food and pharmaceuticals.[54] It was the flight of these modern and competitive industries that posed the greatest threat to London's economy. The metal goods, vehicles, and engineering industries, the foundation of London's industrial prosperity before and after the Second World War, still employed 582,500 people in 1968. By 1992 they employed 137,000, less than a quarter of their 1968 workforce.[55]

THE 'LONDON FACTOR'

The main problem for most employers was London itself: the urban environment which favoured London's industrial growth in the 1920s and 1930s was favourable no longer. A study of firms that moved or closed down between 1966 and 1974 established that about 16 per cent of manufacturing job losses in those years resulted from government-promoted moves to overspill towns or assisted (depressed) areas, and another 11 per cent came from independent decisions to move. But about 285,000 of the 390,000 job losses resulted simply from the closure or shrinkage of London factories, and especially from the decisions of large multiplant companies to close their London factories and move their production to others in better locations. When they were asked why they moved out of London, most employers replied that their London factories were outdated, congested or badly arranged, and inadequate to cope with expanding production. Almost every employer mentioned the high cost of renting adequate new premises in London, and about 40 per cent listed labour shortages and 20 per cent transport difficulties as important factors, but the refusal of government development permits was not generally important.[56] There was, employers said, a 'London factor' which prevented successful firms from growing, and discouraged new ones from opening, in London. This climate of discouragement was created by central and local government controls and planning regulations, which trapped growing firms in old and inconvenient buildings that offered poor working conditions and impeded the free movement of vehicles and goods. Unlike Liverpool, Birmingham or Leeds, London (and especially East and South-East London) had no urban motorway network, and its industrial vehicles had to use congested by-roads, wasting time and money. Industry suffered from a high labour turnover, a permanent shortage of skilled labour and good middle managers, and a dearth of less skilled labour when business was buoyant:

> These problems are seen to arise from the discontent of skilled labour with the decaying environment of much of London's residential area; from a desire for their own homes rather than council tenancies . . .; from the cost to middle management of homes in the better suburbs which involve them in expensive and physically wearing journeys to work; from an erratic, expensive and often inconvenient public transport system to which workers are captive in the absence of adequate facilities for private car movement; from the irritations of living and working in London, compared with development areas, and New Towns in particular, which induce lively young and intelligent workers . . . to get up and go, thereby losing to London those that it most needs to keep.

The combination of these factors, the 1976 Review said, meant that 'each upward movement of the economic cycle causes extreme pressures on labour, preventing firms from reaping the full benefits of buoyancy and each depression creates lower troughs than the last with increasing contraction, redundancy and insolvency. . . . The resulting atmosphere is one of despair for industrialists wishing to stay, employees wishing to work and school-leavers who opt for service employment in consequence.'[57] Twenty years later, the same factors were still listed when manufacturers met Tim Eggar, the minister in charge of the government's latest industrial initiative: 'the availability of suitable, affordable land for expansion, poor access, difficulties recruiting people to work in London and problems with training existing workers'.[58]

Modern firms using assembly-line technology needed large one-storey premises, and found it difficult to find sites for these in London, except at prohibitive costs. The growth of bigger multiplant firms, especially as a result of mergers and acquisitions, made it much easier for businesses to move their centres of production to take advantage of cheap land or labour, easier transport or regional subsidies.[59] The government itself had spent several years explaining the social and economic advantages of moving out of London, and it was no wonder that multiplant firms, or companies going through merger or rationalization, should eventually follow their advice, perhaps keeping a London head office for those activities that needed a metropolitan location. In 1989 merger and ration-alization sealed the fate of one of London's biggest biscuit factories, Peek Frean's of Bermondsey, when it was sold by its American owners to a

French company, BSN, which decided to concentrate its production in France. London's interwar and 1950s prosperity had rested heavily on American and other international companies, many of which had chosen a London location. In 1953, 129 of the 306 US firms in Britain were in or near London, and US-owned London factories employed 115,700 people. In the 1970s and 1980s these companies needed to modernize their production and plant to take advantage of new technology and to meet European and Japanese competition, and to achieve this they usually chose cheaper, more spacious, more convenient and perhaps subsidized sites elsewhere in Britain or Europe. Hoover, Xerox, Motorola, IBM and Electrolux were among the big American firms moving out of London in the 1970s and 1980s, and Ford, one of London's most important manufacturing employers, gradually moved its steel-making and car manufacture out of the capital, reducing Dagenham to the status of an assembly plant for its cheaper models.

When big companies moved out, many smaller companies went with them, or disappeared altogether. The multiplier effect, which had worked in London's favour for so long, could work in the other direction, too. One of the main reasons for staying in London, especially for engineering firms, but also clothing, furniture, food and packaging companies, had been the advantage of being near other businesses with whom useful linkages could be made. Small companies that might not have survived alone prospered because they were part of a cluster of similar or related firms, using the same facilities, passing on business, supplying materials, offering finishing or packaging services, sharing solutions to production or marketing problems. East End clothing, central London printing, Park Royal engineering, Clerkenwell clock-, watch- and jewellery-making, South London food-manufacturing, Shoreditch and Tottenham Court Road furniture production all benefited from the mutual support of being part of a cluster. But once the cluster started to break up, perhaps because of the local authorities' 'comprehensive redevelopment' of an area, the individual weakness of each small and outdated business was exposed. How could London clothing, furniture, food or electrical manufacturers, with their high land and labour costs, hope to produce goods at the prices demanded by the new dictators of the London market, Marks and Spencer, British Home Stores, MFI, Tesco, Sainsbury or Dixon's? London lost its big clothing factories in the 1960s and 1970s, and instead work was subcontracted to much cheaper Far Eastern producers. Only a revival of casual or sweated production, generally using part-timers and low-paid female Bangladeshi, Pakistani or Cypriot home-workers, preserved a remnant of the East End and North London clothing industry in the 1970s and 1980s. Much the same happened to London's lampshade, electrical goods, toy and zip industries. In an increasingly competitive and standardized international market, in which products and tastes could cross the globe so much faster than ever before, local advantage did not count as it once had done. In just six years, from 1975 to 1981, London lost a quarter of its workers in food and drink, a third of those in the furniture and timber trades, and 45 per cent of those in the clothing and footwear industries.[60] The pace of decline was hardly any slower in the 1980s. Between 1981 and 1991 employment in most of London's major industries (food and drink, furniture, footwear and clothing, vehicles, chemicals, metal goods, mechanical engineering) was halved. The two most important manufacturing industries followed different paths. Employment in paper and printing, London's biggest manufacturing employer, only declined by 22 per cent, but in electrical engineering, the second biggest, it fell dramatically, by 60 per cent. So by the early 1990s almost a quarter of London's manufacturing workers were in the printing and publishing industry, which contributed a third of the value of London's manufacturing output.[61]

The collapse of manufacturing in London's central industrial districts might have been seen as a continuation of the suburbanization of industry between the wars. But the almost equally dramatic decline of the newer industrial areas that had grown and prospered in the interwar years (Ealing, Hounslow, Brent, Hillingdon, Croydon) showed that something more serious than relocation within the town was going on. Employment in metal goods and engineering in Outer London fell by 55 per cent between 1981 and 1987.[62] The West London industrial area, whose growth had been such an important part of London's interwar prosperity, continued to grow in the 1950s, and held its own in the 1960s, but between 1971 and 1981 40 per cent of its manufacturing jobs disappeared, and the decline continued through the 1980s. The decline of Park Royal and the Great West Road, two outstanding examples of London's interwar prosperity, symbolize the collapse of West London's manufacturing sector. On the Great West Road, Firestone, the American tyre manufacturer, closed down in the 1970s, and its magnificent listed factory building was demolished in 1980. Other American firms, including Trico and Hoover, moved to South Wales, and the United Biscuits factory in Osterley closed down. Park Royal and Southall lost their British Leyland bus and truck works, and the concentration of smaller firms that had made Park Royal so vibrant in the 1930s was depleted by merger and relocation. For example, Acton Bolt and Fine Threads Ltd was closed in 1976, after it had been taken over by GKN, and the British Indestructo Glass Company, having been absorbed by Triplex (part of the Pilkington empire), was closed in 1971. Many of the buildings abandoned by manufacturers are occupied now by repair shops and warehouses. On the other hand, Heinz and Guinness, two of the major contributors to Park Royal's interwar growth, are still thriving on the industrial estate, and the decline in their workforce is a reflection of improved production methods rather than falling output.[63]

To some extent, Greater London's loss of manufacturing jobs reflected a continuing process of decentralization, with the Outer Metropolitan Area (OMA) and the Outer South-East playing the part played by Middlesex between the wars. Greater London's 106,300 lost jobs in electrical, mechanical and instrument engineering between 1966 and 1981 were matched by gains in the OMA and the South-East over the same period, and in chemicals, vehicles and metal goods there was some compensation for London's loss of 58,000 jobs (1966–81) in the rest of the South-East's gain of 38,000. But only about 27,000 of London's 125,000 lost jobs in printing, paper, food, drink, clothing and furniture seem to have found their way into the wider South-Eastern region. Overall, between 1971 and 1989, when Greater London lost 600,000 of its 1,049,000 manufacturing jobs, the OMA lost another 220,000. There was some growth in the rest of the South-East, but new manufacturing jobs in the more distant parts of the region, which stretches to the borders of Dorset, were not much help to the unemployed worker in Greenwich or Southwark.[64]

THE END OF THE PORT

One supreme advantage for many London manufacturers, the mighty trading power of the Port of London, disappeared in the 1960s and 1970s. What killed the docks was not the decline of trade, but its expansion. Almost from the moment they were built, the upstream docks had struggled to cope with the growing size of cargo ships, and had lost business to the bigger docks in the wider stretches of the Thames. In the 1950s London's docks adapted well enough to the new methods of rapid cargo handling (especially mobile cranes, pallets and forklift trucks) that had been popularized during the Second World War. But containerization was an altogether more dangerous challenge to the smaller docks. London Dock was adapted in 1959 to handle 550-gallon tanks of wine, but its 800,000-gallon storage capacity was soon inadequate, and the bulk wine trade was lost to the India and Millwall docks. When a Committee of Enquiry examined the docks in 1961 it had found them in a busy and prosperous condition, but it concluded that future development in the Port should take place away from the centre of London, and especially at Tilbury, which could be improved using money raised by draining and redeveloping the London and St Katharine's Docks.[65] In the 1960s goods started arriving in London in containers 8 feet high, 8 feet wide, and up to 40 feet long. The ships that carried them needed berths of up to 25 acres, and the goods inside them needed no warehouses or porters, just a juggernaut. Tilbury, adapted in the late 1960s for £30 million, could turn an ocean-going container ship round in thirty-six hours (instead of the ten days a ship of this size would have taken before containerization), and soon became master of the container trade. Tilbury dockers fought to protect their jobs against the threat of containerization, but in four years (between 1969 and 1973) the number of registered dockers had fallen from 23,000 to 12,000, and the Port of London Authority's office staff had been cut from 800 to 100, and moved from the grand PLA building on Trinity Square to more modest offices in the new World Trade Centre at St Katharine's Dock.

In the PLA's drive for profit and survival in a containerized world, the loss-making upstream docks had to go. The East India Dock, opened in 1806 to handle the East India Company's 750-ton sailing ships, could play no part in the container trade, and was closed in 1967. The closure of London Dock and St Katharine's Dock, which were losing the PLA over a million pounds a year in the 1960s, followed in 1969. St Katharine's Dock was sold to the GLC for the bargain price of £1.5 million, £200,000 less than it had cost to build in the first place. The GLC in turn leased the dock to Taylor Woodrow, who demolished many of the fine warehouses and constructed the huge Tower Hotel and the World Trade Centre. The docks were converted into a yacht marina and a (now closed) museum of old ships. This was the future for all the smaller docks. Local people, represented by the East End Dockland Action Group, saw which way the wind was blowing, but spat into it all the same: 'We will not commute to work outside London while office blocks are built in our backyard for other people to work here. . . . We want play space for our kids, better schools, better shopping centres, decent public transport and community facilities for the people of the East End. We want the riverside to be enjoyed by all the people – not to be parcelled off for sale to the rich. We have no use for safari parks, yachting marinas and luxury hotels.'[66] This complaint, which neatly summarized two visions of the future of docklands, would be heard many times over the next twenty years, as local people and City invaders struggled for control of the East End.

The rest of the dock system (apart from Tilbury) followed St Katharine's and the East India Docks into retirement over the next few years. The Surrey Commercial Docks, having lost their timber trade to Tilbury's more efficient bulk handling system, stopped working in 1970, and the Rotherhithe peninsula, which had been almost completely occupied by docks and warehousing for the previous 160 years, was restored to dry land when all but the Greenland and South Docks (and parts of the Canada Dock and Surrey Basin) were filled in to make land for housing, business and parks. The West India and Millwall Docks were closed in 1980, and the huge Royal Docks (the Royal Albert, the Royal Victoria and the King George V), which were big enough to handle the largest interwar liners, lasted until 1981. This left only about 4,000 dockers of the 25,500 there had been in 1965, and only one major London dock, at Tilbury, which was 26 miles down river from the Tower, but now only a few miles beyond the eastern edge of Greater London. The importance of Tilbury meant that London remained a significant seaport, but its share of UK trade (by value), which had been over 35 per cent in 1966, had fallen to 13 per cent by 1978, and the weight of goods it handled each year fell from about 60 million tons in the 1960s (the figure scarcely changed over the decade) to a little over 30 million in the early 1990s.[67] Much of London's trade had moved to bigger and more efficient ports, especially Dover and Felixstowe. The effects of the closure of the inner docks on the economy of the East End were serious. The loss of manufacturing jobs through factory closures was severe in most parts of London between 1966 and 1974, but of the four boroughs which suffered a decline of over 30 per cent three were riverside boroughs whose industries had traditionally depended on goods and raw materials unloaded on the Thames: Newham (30 per cent), Southwark (38 per cent) and Greenwich (43 per cent).[68]

TOURISM AND THE SERVICE ECONOMY

The loss of more than a million manufacturing jobs in the space of twenty-five years would have destroyed many cities, but London's great strength had always been the diversity of its economic activities and its ability to compensate for decline in one area by achieving growth in another. While manufacturing declined, the service industries, the mainstay of London employment since the nineteenth century, grew steadily, employing just short of 3 million people in 1989, compared with under 2 million in 1964. Thanks to the rise of services, total employment in Greater London only fell by about 1 per cent a year between 1971 and 1984, and actually rose a little in the later 1980s. Within the service sector, which includes transport, distribution, catering, the professions, health, education and public administration, the area of outstanding growth was banking, insurance and finance, in which employment more than tripled (from 270,000 to 847,000) between 1964 and 1989. In other words, in 1989 there were nearly twice as many financial and insurance workers in London as there were manufacturing workers.[69] This great structural change did not do much for the prospects or the self-esteem of dockers, tailors or engineers, who did not have the training or inclination to find themselves new jobs as computer operators or shop assistants. To see ordinary streets in run-down parts of London taken over by office workers and professionals ('yuppies' was their popular nickname) whose spending power inflated the price of modest houses beyond all reason was the bitter experience of many working-class Londoners in the 1970s and 1980s. But it was office work, and service industries in general, that maintained London's enormous earning power into the 1990s, and offered the chance of a job to the sons and especially the daughters of ex-manufacturing workers, if not to the workers themselves.

An important source of new jobs in the 1960s and 1970s was the tourist industry. In the 1960s London gained an international reputation as a 'swinging' city, and however shallow and inaccurate this image was it certainly made London a more appealing holiday destination than a city known for its slums, banks and bomb-sites would have been. To take advantage of the rapid growth in international tourism that took place from the later 1950s onwards, London needed hotels. There had been no great increase in London's hotel accommodation between the wars, although new hotels had replaced older ones, and during the Second World War many hotels were destroyed or requisitioned. The 1951 Festival of Britain and the Coronation of Elizabeth II in 1953 drew large crowds to London, but only two large new hotels (and a total of 1,650 additional beds) were added in the 1950s, giving the County of London a total of about 50,000 hotel beds for visitors (as opposed to permanent residents) in 1960. The number of overseas visitors to London probably doubled (from 500,000 to a million) in the 1950s, but in the 1960s cheaper air travel, the revival of European prosperity and the 1967 devaluation of sterling (a more important factor than whether London was 'swinging' or not) produced a tourist boom. Foreign visitors, hoping to see what was left of old London, or to spend their money in the 'new' London of Carnaby Street and the King's Road, arrived in rapidly increasing numbers. Between 1960 and 1965 the number of foreign visitors to London tripled to about 3 million, then continued to rise a little more slowly to 5.6 million in 1972. In 1969 the dollar-hungry Wilson government introduced a £1,000-per-room subsidy for new hotels in London, but it was the prospect of growing business, rather than the subsidy, that created the hotel building boom of the next few years. The construction of new 'international' hotels, especially around Hyde Park and Kensington Gardens, and near Heathrow, increased the number of tourist bedrooms in the central area from 44,000 (in 1964) to 83,500 in 1970 and nearly 100,000 in 1974.[70] By the time the subsidy ended in 1974 London had about 1,400 hotels with 130,000 beds, about half of which were left empty when the fuel crisis, the world economic recession and a series of Irish terrorist bombings burst the tourist bubble in 1973–4. Tourism recovered to a new peak of 8.4 million foreign visitors (or 94.8 million foreign and domestic visitor nights) by 1978, and remained high for most of the next ten years, before falling back in the late 1980s and 1990s.[71]

Foreign tourists came to England for 'heritage', ceremony, culture and entertainment, and despite the efforts of various tourist boards to divert them to regional centres and the countryside they concentrated heavily in London. Some critics of the tourist boom argued that the concentration of millions of visitors in one place intensified the shortage of housing for Londoners, exacerbated traffic problems and made a growing proportion of Londoners dependent on seasonal, low-paid and unreliable jobs in the catering and hotel industries. The GLC expressed some of these concerns in a paper, *Tourism and Hotels in London*, in 1971. The Layfield Inquiry into the Greater London Plan, which took a consistently hostile view of the GLC's attempts to influence London's social and economic development, reprimanded the Council for adopting 'this merely suspicious and somewhat hostile view', and argued (rightly, as it turned out) that tourism would not continue to grow at its 1969–72 pace.[72] Although the Layfield Report brushed the issue aside, tourism did create problems for central London, and led to the conversion of housing in central districts (Bayswater, Bloomsbury, Kensington, St Marylebone) into makeshift hotels. On the other hand, when office employment was in decline and manufacturing in free fall in the 1960s and 1970s, tourism was one of London's few major growth industries. By the early 1980s London tourism employed over 300,000 people, in restaurants, shops, hotels, theatres, or one of the major museums, galleries or 'attractions' that tourists visited in their millions.

Many of these (20 per cent, it was estimated in the 1980s) were casual or temporary workers, with low pay and poor working conditions.[73] In 1994 more than half of all tourist expenditure in Britain was spent in London. London's 19 million foreign and domestic tourists were responsible for 8 per cent of London's Gross Domestic Product, and helped to maintain the rich diversity of its retailing and entertainment economy. Many of the workers in central London's fifty theatres and countless shops, and the 70,000 employees of London's two major airports, owe their jobs to the vast seasonal flow of tourists. The meagre wages of the 350,000 workers in Greater London's 1,500 hotels and more than 5,000 cafés and restaurants are paid, to a great extent, from German, American and Japanese pockets.[74] Whether tourism is a 'blessing or blight' (to use Sir George Young's phrase) depends whether you work in the duty free shop or live under the flight path.

The rise of the office economy was not welcomed from the start as the saviour of London's economy. When George Brown announced his ban on new office building in November 1964 the policy was a great popular success, a sign that Wilson's new government meant business. It turned out a few years later that the rising tide of office workers that Brown and Wilson had decided to resist was not flowing as strongly as everyone had assumed. Office employment in central London, which had risen to 754,000 by 1961, fell slowly but steadily to 680,000 between 1961 and 1981, though growth in other parts of Greater London compensated for this fall. The central government promoted decentralization through its Office Development Permits, the work of the Location of Offices Bureau (LOB) and by moving its own civil servants to provincial cities. By the late 1970s it seemed that this policy had gone too far. Office automation and decentralization appeared to point towards a further decline in Central London office employment, and the government abandoned its anti-office programme and closed down the LOB in 1979. In 1985 one of the editors of an authoritative work on modern London warned that London could not safely rely on the growth of office work in the future:

> there is considerable evidence that business office employment is moving away from the city, in search of lower rents, more pleasant environments, an accessible labour force, and new buildings that can accommodate automated working techniques, linked if necessary to the City of London by modern telecommunications. . . . Although London remains predominant, therefore, considerable uncertainty hangs over the future of employment in private-sector 'office' functions. . . . A combination of the relative decentralization of virtually all activities,

including those most associated with London's special economic role, technological change, especially in telecommunications and office management, and cuts in government employment, point to a declining level of service employment in the 1980s.[75]

In the event, the next few years saw a spectacular growth in the office economy following the City deregulation known as the 'Big Bang', but in the longer run it is not certain that service employment will continue to grow. Between 1989 and 1992 there was a 10 per cent fall in service jobs, caused by a decline in transport and retail work, cuts in public services, a severe economic recession and the impact of new technology on the office economy.

THE STRENGTH OF THE CITY

The main reason for the strength of London's service economy (apart from the everyday needs of 7 million Londoners) was the survival, against the odds, of the City of London as one of the world's three main centres of international finance. The City of London had achieved its international status in the nineteenth century because of the power of the British economy and the wealth of its citizens, and it might have been expected to lose it again when Britain's industrial and trading power faded and the importance of sterling as an international trading currency declined. In some respects, this is what happened. As a handler of the world's physical trade, and as an organizer of international trade, the City lost its previous importance. As a relatively small producer and consumer, London could no longer dominate world markets in wool, tea, sugar, cocoa, cotton or metals, though it could hold its own against foreign centres in the competition to dominate the futures markets in those or other commodities. By the late 1980s the New York and Tokyo Stock Exchanges had turnovers ten and eight times as high as the London Stock Exchange, because of the much greater size of their domestic business. In financing industrial or public enterprises, in providing shipping or insurance services, London could not be the supreme power it had once been. A recent history of the City explained the position well: 'Put into the context of the world economy the City of London has fared almost as badly as the rest of Britain since 1945, even if certain components, like reinsurance and the money markets, have managed to preserve for themselves a continued importance out of line with the domestic economy.'[76]

The City, nevertheless, was a huge and long-established centre of financial services, skills, contacts and institutions, and it still offered investors an unrivalled range of opportunities for using their money profitably. This was London's greatest single advantage. There were more banks concentrated in the City's square mile than anywhere else on earth, as well as an enormous number of other financial institutions offering profitable and tax-efficient investments of every conceivable description. The huge scale of London's operations attracted business to it, thus increasing its scale and attractiveness still more. London's size and reputation, along with the skills and resourcefulness of its financial operators, enabled it to beat or equal Tokyo, New York and its European rivals (Paris, Frankfurt and Zurich) in the struggle for supremacy in a range of specialized (and often obscure) international markets and services. After the abolition of foreign exchange controls in 1958 London captured much of the foreign exchange market from Zurich and New York, handling about 30 per cent of transactions in the 1980s. The market in Eurobonds (fixed interest securities) which developed in the 1960s was largely London-based, and by 1989 nearly a quarter of international bond dealers, and 70 per cent of the most active ones, were in London. Currency and interest rate swaps, financial futures (at Liffe, the London International Financial Futures Exchange), metals and freight futures (at the London Metal Exchange and the Baltic Exchange), and reinsurance were all London specialities.[77]

London was especially attractive to foreign banks and financial institutions that wanted to operate in a market that was relatively free of controls, restrictions and taxes. It prospered, to some degree, because the British government made fewer regulatory mistakes than its competitors' governments. The imposition of strict controls on banking and investment in the USA from the early 1960s until 1974 created a huge and growing market in dollars outside America, and this market (the so-called Eurodollar market) rapidly found its way to the City, where dealings in currencies other than sterling were remarkably free of regulation. American, Japanese and Arab bankers wanting to borrow or invest on the best terms, in a market where intervention and taxation were low and opportunities were high, chose London. The fact that London was in a time zone midway between Tokyo and New York (enabling it to trade with both on the same day), and that its business was conducted in English, were additional advantages. In the 1970s more American banks were represented in the City of London than in New York, and between 1957 and 1989 the number of foreign banks in London rose from about eighty to 521, more than twice as many as the number in any other centre. London was a convenient conduit for other countries' money: in 1979 about 75 per cent of the money passing through British banks was foreign in origin and destination. Like Switzerland, London offered foreign investors, especially those with volatile short-term funds, an attractive combination of freedom and security. Oil-rich states wishing to find a safe and profitable home for their vast profits after the price rises of the early 1970s invested their 'petrodollars' in the City, and communist or oil-based countries that feared that the US government could seize their American-based assets had no such fears about their City funds.[78] By 1989 London turnover in foreign (mainly European) equities amounted to £40 billion a year, nearly half of the world market. The continuing internationalization of world financial activity, the tendency for investors to look for opportunities worldwide, rather than in their own country, offer good prospects for London's future growth as a financial centre.[79]

The 'Big Bang' and the Global City

While the City flourished in the 1960s and 1970s as a base for foreign financial operations, its own institutions, especially the Stock Exchange, were sidelined. The Stock Exchange prospered because of its near-monopoly of the British share market and government securities, its high fixed commissions, and the system of sterling exchange controls which made it difficult for foreign dealers to trade in sterling securities. But for many of the same reasons dealing in Eurobonds and other foreign securities generally by-passed the Stock Exchange. When the Thatcher government suddenly abolished exchange controls in 1979 the protective barrier between the domestic and international sectors of the City economy was pulled down, and the Stock Exchange started to lose its business to outsiders and foreign exchanges. There was a dramatic illustration of the weakness of the Stock Exchange between 1979 and 1984, when foreign firms handled about 95 per cent of the £12 billion new overseas investments of insurance companies and pension funds generated by the North Sea oil boom. Both the government and the Stock Exchange realized that something had to be done, and the outcome of their negotiations was a bonfire of restrictive practices, the so-called 'Big Bang', on 27 October 1986, which abolished fixed commissions, opened the renamed International Stock Exchange to foreign companies, allowed the formation of large merchant banking and brokerage houses and introduced electronic dealing and market-making. The Big Bang enabled foreign firms to take over existing broking and jobbing houses to create highly competitive multi-purpose financial conglomerates. Electronic dealing quickly brought the noisy scrummage on the Stock Market trading floor to an end, and old stockbroking companies and merchant banks began to disappear into the pockets of big American, English and European banking houses: Kitcat and Aitken, Philips and Drew, Scrimgeour Kemp Gee, Vickers da Costa, and Lang and Cruikshank were swallowed up along with many others. By 1990 154 of the 408 Stock Exchange member firms were foreign, mostly American, Japanese, French and Swiss, and in 1995, a year of many takeovers, four of London's most distinguished merchant banks, Barings, S. G. Warburg, Kleinwort Benson and Smith New Court, were absorbed by Dutch, Swiss, German and American banks.[80]

The International Stock Exchange was a new and powerful player in the very competitive and overcrowded European market, and by 1996 nearly half the trade in big French and Italian shares, and perhaps 90 per cent of all European cross-border share trading, took place in London. Despite a succession of scandals and embarrassments in the 1990s (the BCCI collapse, the Maxwell pension fund fraud, the failure of Barings, the insurance crisis at Lloyd's, the failure of Taurus, the Stock Exchange's computerized trading system), London remained far ahead of its European rivals in almost every international field, including bank lending, fund management and foreign exchange trading. In 1994 London processed $300 billion of foreign exchange each day, as much as New York and Tokyo together, and five times as much as Germany. Half of world shipbroking, and half the world's mergers and acquisitions business, was done in London. Seventeen per cent of cross-border lending was handled in London, more than in any other centre. London, according to the *Economist*, had the world's biggest concentration of international economic analysts, and was the source of more international telephone calls than anywhere else on earth.[81]

In short, as Saskia Sassen argued in 1991, London had secured its place (along with Tokyo and New York) as one of the world's three 'Global Cities'. The worldwide dispersal of industrial production, of which London's own manufacturing sector had been a major victim, demanded the growth of regional command centres, or 'centralized service nodes for the management and regulation of the new space economy'. Finance and management were the driving force in the globalized economy, and only a few cities had the concentration of skills, institutions and contacts to handle massive and rapid financial flows, and to provide the specialized 'producer services' (legal and management advice, accountancy, public relations, information, communications) required by international corporations. The three cities, Sassen argues, 'function as one transterritorial marketplace', each playing its specialized part. Briefly, in the 1980s Tokyo emerged as the main centre for the export of capital; London as the main centre for the processing of capital, largely through its vast international banking network linking London to most countries in the world and through the Euromarkets; and New York City as the main receiver of capital, the centre of investment decisions and for the production of innovations that can maximize profitability.[82]

London's global role explains why its population rose in the 1980s, reversing its own long-term pattern and defying general European and American trends. It also helps explain London's striking social and economic polarization, with a large and prosperous business and professional population, the inhabitants of the 'global city', at one extreme, and a huge number of unemployed, deprived and struggling families, many of them from ethnic minorities, the occupants of the declining manufacturing city, at the other.[83]

Financial activity is mobile, and London's future as a financial centre is still uncertain. Other European centres have had their own 'Big Bangs', and Frankfurt, London's most serious rival, has the power of the German economy and government behind it. But the development of the massive telecommunications systems needed by global cities makes it very difficult for new cities to compete against the established centres. Security is another problem. The IRA's change of tactics in the early 1990s, in which bomb attacks on barracks, shops and stations were replaced by extraordinarily effective attacks on office buildings, cast a shadow over the City's future, but Paris, New York and Tokyo had their problems with terrorism, too. The bombing of the Baltic Exchange and its surrounding streets in April 1992, and of the Hong Kong and Shanghai Bank, the Natwest Tower and 25 nearby office buildings a year later, together cost the City and its insurers close to £1 billion. The utter destruction of the little late medieval church of St Ethelburga Bishopsgate ('one of the sweetest things in the City'), in the second explosion, and the severe damage to Great St Helen's, 'the Westminster Abbey of the City' and the burial place of Sir John Crosby and Sir Thomas Gresham, seemed unimportant in comparison with the threat to the City's international position.[84] This threat was countered by the imposition of a security cordon (the 'ring of steel') around the financial district, and the negotiation of an ultimately unsuccessful ceasefire with the IRA. The ending of this ceasefire, in February 1996, was announced by another costly attack on London office property, this time in the new financial district, Canary Wharf.

The impact of the introduction of European Monetary Union on the contest between London and other cities is unclear, but many informed observers in the early 1990s believed that the City had the strength and advantages to retain its position as Europe's leading financial centre. A study published in 1989, but largely based on pre-1982 data, predicted that London would be overtaken by Paris and Frankfurt, but two newer studies of international business opinion by Coopers Lybrand Deloitte and Weatherall Green and Smith concluded that London would still be Europe's leading financial centre at the end of the century. Perhaps the biggest threat to London comes not from its European rivals but from the growth of new telecommunications technology, which could make the expensive physical closeness offered by global cities redundant, and lead to a dispersal of their financial and managerial functions.[85]

THE CITY BURSTS ITS BANKS

Such speculations did not seem to worry developers or politicians in the mid-1980s. Financial deregulation and its consequences, along with the computer revolution, the laissez-faire policies of the Thatcher government and the removal of London's planning authority, the GLC, sparked off an office-building boom comparable to that of the 1950s. Victorian and interwar offices, and even those built in the postwar boom, did not have the air conditioning, cabling space and large open-plan dealing rooms which (it was predicted) modern financial conglomerates would need, and London's growth as an international financial centre was believed to depend upon their replacement. In 1987 the City of London relaxed its planning guidelines, removing conservation status from some areas and greatly increasing the permitted density of development. Office buildings rose almost six-fold, from 1.2 million square feet (the 1977–85 average) to 6.8 million square feet in 1987. New offices spilled out of their traditional centres, the City and West End, into declining industrial or warehousing districts on the edge of the central area, sometimes bringing developers into conflict with the local communities they intended to evict. In Spitalfields there was an unequal (and as yet unresolved) struggle for land between local residents, many of whom were Bengali settlers, and property developers with City backing. Development was easier on the south bank of the Thames, between London Bridge and Tower Bridge, where the Kuwaiti royal family planned a development containing 2.2 million square feet of offices, as well as shops and a private hospital. Its first stage, London

Bridge City, was finished in 1986. Railway land offered some of the best opportunities. The vast and impressive Broadgate development, over a million square feet of lavish offices, complete with an open air ice rink, on the site of the demolished Broad Street Station, showed how far office developers (and office workers) had come since the days of the dismal Elephant and Castle scheme and the windswept London Wall slabs of the 1960s. Discussions between British Railways and the two Broadgate developers (Rosehaugh and Stanhope) over the future of an even bigger railway site, 134 acres of sidings, trainsheds, warehouses, gasholders and workshops north of King's Cross and St Pancras, began in 1987. The development group, renamed the London Regeneration Consortium, put forward attractive plans which included a 30-acre park as well as 700,000 square metres of offices, but an effective campaign by local community groups delayed the scheme until 1989, when the collapse of the office boom led to its postponement. The world economic depression that began at the end of the decade exposed the errors of those who had expected deregulation to generate exponential growth in the financial sector. Many of the new offices found no tenants, and the City (along with other financial centres) experienced a halving of rents and a slump in property values that did not start to lift until 1993.[86]

As the office world expanded, London's old trading and manufacturing world withdrew from the City and its hinterland. The Billingsgate Market, which had been a centre of London's grain or fish trade since 1016 or before, moved to a new site on the Isle of Dogs in January 1982, making way for offices for the London and Edinburgh Investment Trust. The smell of fish was gradually replaced by the smell of money. The newspaper industry, perhaps drawn by the natural affinity between the two commodities, followed the fish into Docklands. By the end of the 1980s Fleet Street, which had been at the heart of the newspaper industry since the eighteenth century, and of printing for much longer, had lost most of its publishing enterprises. Rupert Murdoch began the stampede, when he abruptly moved his News International empire, which included the *Sun*, *The Times*, the *Sunday Times* and the *News of the World*, to a walled and guarded enclave in Wapping (a little east of the Tower) in 1985. By using the latest computerized typesetting technology Murdoch broke the stranglehold of the print unions on newspaper production, and reduced the production staff (excluding journalists) on his titles to under 1,000. Other proprietors, more timid than Murdoch but just as keen on a healthy profit, moved even further east into Docklands over the next few years. The *Daily* and *Sunday Telegraph*, the

Guardian and the *Observer* joined the Billingsgate porters on the Isle of Dogs, and the Mirror Group followed them there from Holborn a few years later. Rothermere's Associated Newspapers (the *Daily Mail* and *Evening Standard*) moved across the Thames to the Surrey Docks, and the *Financial Times* moved its editorial department from its fine City offices to Southwark, and its printing works to the East India Docks. Express Newspapers, abandoning their famous black-tiled offices in Fleet Street, travelled in the opposite direction, and found new premises across Black-friars Bridge. This was not quite the end of the 'street of ink', since the two main news agencies (Reuters and UPI), the Press Association and the Press Complaints Authority stayed in or near Fleet Street in the 1990s.[87]

DOCKLANDS

An important factor in the overheated office boom of 1986–7 was the government's decision to promote the redevelopment of Docklands as a new centre of business and industry, in the hope that this would stimulate economic growth in the so-called East Thames Corridor, the huge expanse of land, much of it undeveloped or derelict, between Tower Bridge and Sheerness and Southend. The development of the Docklands area had been under discussion since the property boom of 1970–3, when Peter Walker (at the Department of the Environment) commissioned a redevelopment study from the civil engineers Travers Morgan. The study's insensitive suggestion that Docklands might be replanned as 'Europa', 'Fun City' or 'Waterside' alerted local people to the danger that their communities might be 'gentrified' out of existence. During the 1970s planning by a new Docklands Joint Committee got bogged down in complex negotiations between the GLC, the riverside boroughs and the local communities. The Labour government of 1974–9, which gave a higher priority to development in the north, did little to push the planning forward or to give the Docklands Joint Committee the funds it needed, and by 1979 little seemed to have been achieved. The new Conservative government, with Michael Heseltine at the Department of the Environment, decided to abandon normal planning procedures and hand the area over to an Urban Develop-ment Corporation, which would organize a market-led scheme on the lines of those in Boston and Baltimore. The London Docklands Development Corporation (LDDC) was eventually created in July 1981, uniting the talents of Nigel Broakes, of the property developers Trafalgar House, Bob

Mellish, ex-MP for Bermondsey, the leaders of three dockside boroughs, and a generous (and generously rewarded) selection of legal, financial and management consultants.[88]

Over the next ten years the 6,500-acre site controlled by the LDDC was treated as a showpiece of Thatcherite urban regeneration, a testing ground for the enterprise culture, and a demonstration that private developers did not need the guidance of local authority planners. Development was meant to be market-driven, but the free market pump was lavishly primed with public funds. Grants-in-aid of £1,098 million, over 59 per cent of the money allocated to all eleven Urban Development Corporations, went to the LDDC between 1981 and 1990. Resources and planning powers were transferred from the local boroughs (Tower Hamlets, Newham and South-wark) to the LDDC, which was thus enabled to develop Docklands without the inconvenience of democratic accountability and to pursue private investment instead of responding to local social needs. The two conflicting approaches collided in the enquiry into the development of Greenland Dock in 1984, in which Southwark Council's emphasis on public-sector housing and industrial units was opposed by the LDDC's proposal for a neighbourhood of water sports and high-cost private housing.[89]

The LDDC's task of making derelict and fairly inaccessible land attractive to commercial developers was eased by the approach of the 'Big Bang' in 1985. Their great breakthrough came, though, through the vision of a banker, Michael von Clemm, chairman of Credit Suisse First Boston, and the ambition of a Manhattan property consultant, G. Ware Travelstead. In February 1985 Clemm saw the possibility of building his bank's new head office, with the large open-plan dealing floors the new financial environment would demand, on a derelict 71-acre site in Canary Wharf, three miles from the City. The wharf, which was named after a warehouse used to store Canary Islands tomatoes, was part of the West India Docks, at the northern end of the Isle of Dogs and a few hundred yards south of the postwar model suburb of Lansbury. Clemm put the idea to Travelstead, who realized the advantages of developing a new financial district in an enterprise zone, free of planning controls and rates, in which building costs could be offset against tax, and rents set well below City and West End levels. He had some plans drawn up in New York, and in the summer of 1985 the LDDC announced his grandiose proposal for a new commercial district with nearly 9 million square feet of offices and three 800-foot towers, easily the tallest in England. The government was enthusiastic about the scheme, and the local borough, Tower Hamlets, was won over by the promise of new jobs and other community gains. After initial delays caused by the withdrawal of Travelstead, who could not raise the capital to match his ambitions, the building of Canary Wharf began in earnest in 1988, under the direction of a huge Toronto property company, Olympia and York. The prospect of a growing demand for commercial property lured the owners of Olympia and York, the Reichmann brothers, into investing their fortune in the construction of 10 million square feet of offices, including Europe's tallest office block, at a cost of £3 billion. In 1992, with a third of Canary Wharf and one 800-foot steel tower completed but largely unoccupied, a slump in the market for offices brought Olympia and York down with debts of £10 billion. The banks that had financed the development took it over in 1993, and in 1995 Paul Reichmann, at the head of an international consortium, bought it back again. By this time the prospects for Canary Wharf seemed surprisingly bright. Three-quarters of its 4.5 million square feet of offices were let, at rates that undercut those of the City or West End, and another 8 million square feet were planned. Prestigious tenants, including Barclays Bank's investment arm, BZW, had been attracted by the availability of high-quality offices at half City rents, and the Wharf had proved that it was not a wild speculation, but a response to a real, if unpredictable, demand.[90]

One of the main ingredients in the recovery of Canary Wharf was the improvement in its transport links with the City and the rest of London. In its early years the development relied on the highly congested Commercial Road (the A13) and the Docklands Light Railway (DLR), a driverless, computer-driven and unreliable elevated line which had a bright modern image but an inadequate capacity. Thatcher's fixed hostility to public transport, and her unwarranted confidence in the ability of the private sector to finance its own transport infrastructure, made it difficult to persuade her government to pay for an adequate railway system, but after the 1987 general election she agreed to the construction of a very expensive dual carriageway, the Docklands Highway, between Tower Hill and Beckton. The real solution to Canary Wharf's transport problems, the eastward extension of the Jubilee underground line from Waterloo and London Bridge to Bermondsey, Canary Wharf, Greenwich and Stratford, was delayed for several years by wrangling over Olympia and York's share of its cost, and only received outline approval in 1991, when Canary Wharf was already on the verge of financial disaster. The decision to build the Jubilee Line (almost entirely with money diverted from other parts of the transport network), with a completion date of 1998, and the great improvement in the Docklands Light Railway, revived the fortunes of the whole Docklands area in the mid-1990s. In 1995 the LDDC had impressive plans for an exhibition centre, a university, a business park and an 'urban village' in West Silvertown, near the Royal Victoria Dock, and there were proposals for a large retail park and leisure development in Rotherhithe, near the Jubilee Line station. Terence Conran's Butler's Wharf development (near Tower Bridge), suspended in the late 1980s, was also revived. Urban villages, theme parks and leisure complexes seemed a poor replacement for the vanished industrial and commercial greatness of the Port of London, but they offered, at least, the prospect of new life and money for the riverside boroughs, and perhaps some new jobs to replace those that had disappeared when the docks and factories closed down. East Londoners, though, could not live on promises. During the 1980s, Docklands lost over 20,000 jobs (mostly through industrial decline), the LDDC created fewer than 17,000 new local jobs, and unemployment in the Docklands wards in 1992 was over 17 per cent, 2.5 times the average for Greater London. The government's initial expectation that the LDDC would bring industry, as well as commerce, to Docklands proved to be almost entirely false.[91]

According to a survey of rental and property tax levels in 1990, office space in the City cost almost twice as much as in central Paris, and three times as much as in the financial districts of Frankfurt or New York. Only Tokyo was more expensive. The eventual success of Canary Wharf and the rest of Docklands in the 1990s, along with developments in other peripheral districts (King's Cross, Paddington, Bermondsey), helped to prevent London rent levels rising to such a degree that its attractiveness as a financial centre would be undermined.[92] The supply of office space was further increased by the City Corporation's decision to respond to the growth of Canary Wharf by giving developers a much freer hand in or near the Square Mile. Huge office buildings arched over Upper Thames Street and London Wall in the early 1990s, and in 1995 there was planning permission for another 16 million square feet of offices on over 100 sites in the City, and for new developments (each nearly a million square feet) on the sites of Spitalfields Market and the Mirror Group headquarters in Holborn, and in London Bridge City, south of the Thames. Low City rents (thanks in part to competition from Canary Wharf) delayed many of these developments, but in 1996 the next round of development seemed to be about to begin. The outstanding new proposal of that year, at least in terms of its height and bulk, was Sir Norman Foster's ambitious plan for a 1,265-foot glass tower, Europe's highest office block, on the site of the Baltic Exchange, which had been bombed by the IRA in 1992.

A CRISIS OF UNEMPLOYMENT

In Docklands, Spitalfields, Bermondsey and King's Cross a new commercial world was being built on the graveyard of an old industrial one. It was a world that called for different skills, a different kind of workforce, and in which under-educated young men had poor prospects of finding a job. About three-quarters of London's lost jobs in manufacturing, building and transport had been the preserve of male workers, and a quarter of them demanded no formal qualifications. But the new jobs in business, finance, public service, retailing and other services that were replacing them in Greater London were more likely to employ women than men, and tended to demand some proof of success at school. To some extent the growth in the percentage of qualified school leavers reduced the problem, but many of the rest could look forward to a future in low-paid service work or without a job at all, especially in the recurrent recessions that dogged the British economy in the 1980s and 1990s.

For almost thirty years after 1945, London unemployment was at 1 per cent or less, and never rose higher than the number of jobs on offer in employment exchanges in the capital. The rate started rising in 1974–5, and between 1976 and early 1980 it was steady at about 4 per cent, with registered unemployed outnumbering registered vacancies for the first time in postwar history. Then, between 1980 and 1984, and in spite of new calculation methods which hid a tenth of the previous figure, unemployment rose to over 10 per cent, and stayed at that level until early 1987. This meant that between 350,000 and 400,000 Londoners (excluding men over sixty and people on 'training schemes') were out of work during the early and mid-1980s, when job centre vacancies stood at about 30,000. Even in the so-called recovery of 1988–90 unemployment only fell to 200,000 (5 per cent), and in the recession of 1992–4 it was over 11 per cent, around 500,000 people. Between 1989 and 1994, total employment in Greater London fell by 380,000 (11 per cent), while its population rose by about 80,000. According to the International Labour Organization, London's true unemployment rate in 1993–4 was over 13 per cent (about 600,000), which was higher than any other region in the UK, including Northern Ireland. Job centre vacancies at that time were under 8,000, and there was little hope of work for an unskilled man. Measured in terms of the number of people looking for work, the position was much worse in 1982–7 and 1991–5 than it had been in 1932.[93]

These dry statistics, collected by the London Research Centre, were at the root of the 'crisis of London' which was so often talked about in the early 1990s. Unemployment was not distributed evenly across the capital, or between age, gender and racial groups. It was heavily concentrated in the Inner London boroughs, where unemployment was over 23 per cent in 1992 and 16.5 per cent (double the national average) in 1995. Seven Inner London boroughs, Hackney, Tower Hamlets, Newham, Southwark, Haringey, Lambeth and Islington, were at the top of the list of English districts with the highest unemployment levels in February 1995.[94] Male unemployment among twenty to thirty-four-year-olds in Inner London was over 30 per cent in 1992, and nearly 40 per cent in Hackney and Haringey. Among young black men, who were more likely to have been working in Inner London manufacturing jobs than the population as a whole, the rate was highest of all.[95] The Thatcherite 'enterprise culture', which was expected to create new jobs for people like these, seems to have had little impact on the Inner London employment problem. The main developers of London's Docklands, the enterprise economy's flagship, committed themselves in 1988 to 'reviving the economy of an area of London with a vibrant community life', and talked loosely of creating 200,000 new jobs. But in Tower Hamlets and Newham, which might have expected the greatest benefits from these commitments, unemployment among twenty to twenty-four-year-old men was over 35 per cent in 1992. In the words of a recent study, the London Docklands Development Corporation 'is not regenerating an old economy; it is creating a new and quite different one – one from which local residents are less likely to benefit'. No doubt some of the new wealth brought into East London by the redevelopment of Docklands (including well over £1 billion of public money) 'trickled down' into the local economy, but very little seems to have trickled into the pockets of young men who had the misfortune to be unskilled, unqualified or black.[96]

RIOT

In 1981 there were 945,000 Londoners of Afro-Caribbean or Asian descent, constituting 14.6 per cent of the population of Greater London and almost 20 per cent of that of Inner London. Asians, like whites, had tended to move to the suburbs (especially the West London boroughs of Ealing, Brent and Hounslow) and thus avoid some of the worst of Inner London's social and economic problems. Afro-Caribbeans, on the other hand, were much more likely to remain near the centre, especially in Hackney, Haringey, Lambeth and Lewisham, where they bore the brunt of mass unemployment, substandard housing and environmental decline. Afro-Caribbeans were heavily over-represented in the semi-skilled and unskilled sections of the workforce, especially in manufacturing and declining public services, and for this and other reasons they suffered much higher unemployment than whites and South Asians. In 1981, when unemployment was about 18 per cent among sixteen to nineteen-year-old whites and 20 per cent among young Indians it was over 35 per cent among young Afro-Caribbeans.[97]

The rise of mass unemployment among young blacks added an explosive new ingredient to the tensions that had developed between the police and various black communities since the 1960s. Despite the routine denials of government ministers (who often confused explanation with justification), there is little doubt that the sense of frustration, boredom and injustice generated by localized mass unemployment, especially among young black men, contributed significantly to the waves of street violence that London experienced in the 1980s. In April 1981, after a year in which London unemployment had almost doubled and was rapidly approaching 300,000, there was a violent riot in Brixton, an area with a large black population and high levels of social and economic deprivation. Unemployment in Brixton in early 1981 was 13 per cent, but among blacks it was 25 per cent, and among black men under nineteen it was 55 per cent. A year later, it was said that over three-quarters of sixteen to nineteen-year-old black men in Brixton were out of work. In addition, Brixton had very high levels of overcrowding, bad housing and homelessness. The immediate cause of the riot was an intensive five-day police operation against crime on Brixton's back streets ('Operation Swamp 81'), in which 943 people, mostly young blacks, were stopped and searched. Without 'saturation' policing on this scale the riot would not have happened, but Lord Scarman (whose official report on the riot was widely praised) and other impartial analysts were clear that intense economic deprivation was a major factor in creating the petty crime that led to the police operation and in generating the frustrations that disposed Brixton youngsters to violent protest. With miserable and overcrowded homes and no money in their pockets, Scarman argued, 'the street corners become the social centres of people, young and old, good and bad, with time on their hands and a continuing opportunity, which, doubtless, they use, to engage in endless discussion of their grievances. . . . And living much of their lives on the streets, they are brought into contact with the police who appear to them as the visible symbols of authority of a society which has failed to bring them its benefits or do them justice.'[98]

The extent and seriousness of the Brixton riots of 10–12 April were exaggerated in contemporary press accounts, and even in Lord Scarman's measured and sympathetic report, which spoke of a 'total collapse in law and order', damage reminiscent of 'the aftermath of an air raid', and a threat to the stability of London as a whole. In reality, the riots were confined to a few streets (especially Railton Road), and at their worst point, Saturday evening, involved about 500 rioters. About 170 shops were looted or destroyed by fire, but human injuries were not very serious, and no one was killed. There is no evidence that the rioters intended anything more than an attack on the police in their own back streets, or that some wider revolutionary action was planned. On the other hand, the use of petrol bombs for the first time in an English riot indicated that rioters, as well as policemen, were importing their tactics from Northern Ireland. To judge from the arrest statistics, the rioters were predominantly black, local, and over twenty-one, though those arrested for looting (a separate activity) included a higher proportion of whites, teenagers, and people from other neighbourhoods. It seems, therefore, that the riots reflected genuine local frustrations, but that those who took the opportunity to loot from shops were more likely to be opportunists and outsiders.[99]

Prophets of imminent race war were given more material to work on on 9–11 July 1981, when there were riots, or (more commonly) minor local disturbances which could be represented as riots, in about twenty-five London suburbs, including such unlikely places as Golders Green, Chiswick, Sutton and Penge. There was clearly an element of contagion (or 'copycat' behaviour) in many of these incidents, especially on the part of journalists, police officers and frightened shopkeepers. But in Brixton, Southall and Hackney there were serious disturbances, involving petrol bombs, looting and street battles. In Hackney, as in Brixton, the riots were a culmination of an extended period of hostility between the police and local black communities stemming (depending on the observer's standpoint) from police efforts to reduce persistent street robbery and drug dealing, an incompatibility of cultures, or ingrained police racism.

In the 1970s Hackney's Sandringham Road had become a 'Front Line' street in the struggle between the police and young blacks, with the conflict revolving around a few clubs and cafés that were reputedly centres for dealing in cannabis and stolen property. To make matters worse, the deaths in police custody of Asetta Sims (1970) and Michael Fereira (1978) had given the local Stoke Newington police station an appalling reputation for racism and violence. In Notting Hill, the scene of the most serious white attacks on blacks in the late 1950s, police–black relations deteriorated in the 1960s, and most young black men had been arrested at one time or another for loitering, obstruction, or similar offences. Here the 'front line' street was All Saints Road, and the focal point of the conflict was the often-raided Mangrove Restaurant. The annual Notting Hill Carnival, which had gradually grown in scale and importance since its introduction in 1966, turned into a test of strength between the police and the increasingly assertive black population, and a very heavy police presence produced violent and luridly reported clashes in 1975 and 1976. In July 1981, by contrast, more sensitive and low-key policing prevented a tense situation from turning into the riot that almost everyone expected.[100]

In areas with large South Asian populations it was ineffective, rather than over-zealous, policing that was seen as the problem. During the 1970s and 1980s Indian and Bengali districts became the target for racist propaganda and attacks. 'Paki-bashing', an ugly new name for an ugly old crime, received wide press coverage in early 1970, as a result of a succession of brutal attacks on South Asians in Southall and the East End, the murder of an East Pakistani and a 'skinhead' attack on the shops of Brick Lane. Attacks were continuous, but seemed to reach occasional peaks, especially when neo-fascist organizations, the National Front, the British Movement and the British National Party, were active in the East End or Southall. These attacks, and especially the murder of a young Sikh by a white gang in Southall in June 1976, and a Bangladeshi clothing worker in Whitechapel in May 1978, prompted previously apolitical young Asians to form anti-racist Action Committees and vigilante patrols. In alliance with the largely white Anti-Nazi League, Asians confronted the Whitechapel National Front in the summer of 1978, and forced them into a temporary retreat. This conflict reached an unfortunate climax in Southall in April 1979, when the Southall Youth Movement, the Indian Workers' Association and the Anti-Nazi League demonstrated against a National Front meeting in Southall, and a white teacher, Blair Peach, was killed by a powerful blow to the head, perhaps from the truncheon of a member of the new police rapid reaction force, the Special Patrol Group. Two years later, on 3 July 1981, young Asians attacked and fire-bombed a Southall public house, the Hamborough Tavern, which was sheltering 'skinheads' who had been smashing Asian shops. Once again, the incident turned into a conflict between Asians and the Metropolitan Police, who were perceived as being more zealous in their protection of provocative racist marches than they were in the defence of Asian shops and lives.

POLICING AND RACE RELATIONS

There had been many violent crowd disorders in London since the Second World War. A few, like the Notting Hill riots of 1958, had been predominantly racial, and others had resulted from radical protests over defence or foreign policy. In 1968, at the height of the protest against the Vietnam War, there were large and occasionally violent demonstrations outside the American Embassy in Grosvenor Square, and in 1974 a young man was killed in a demonstration against the National Front in Red Lion Square, Holborn. The long-running and bitter labour dispute at the Grunwick photographic processing works between 1976 and 1978 cast the police as protectors of strike-breaking workers against the poorly paid Asian women who had organized the strike. But the riots of 1981, and the even more serious outbreak on Broadwater Farm, Tottenham, in October 1985, broke new ground in crowd violence and riot control methods, and in the deterioration in relations between the police and black communities in London, as well as in Birmingham, Liverpool, Manchester and other cities. The Metropolitan Police learnt lessons from these riots, and there was a new emphasis, expressed in the 1990 Plus Programme, on the virtues of community policing, and on the need to temper law enforcement with common sense and judgement: 'We must be compassionate, courteous and patient, acting without fear or favour or prejudice to the rights of others.' It was easier to enunciate these admirable principles than it was to transmit them to the young men who were attracted to police work, and who themselves felt harassed and afraid when they patrolled black neighbourhoods.[101]

An important insight into the culture of the Metropolitan Police at the time of the Brixton and Southall riots was provided by a full study conducted by the Policy Studies Institute between 1980 and 1982. The researchers found that racist language ('coons', 'niggers', 'spades', and so on), arguments and jokes were used frequently and without reproach among policemen, even some senior officers, and that racist attitudes were engendered by the pervasive culture of the force. The study found that racist talk and attitudes did not generally translate into unreasonable behaviour towards black people, though they sometimes did. The police were more likely to stop black people than whites or Asians, and they made 'a crude equation between crime and black people', assuming that blacks were criminals and criminals were black.

> Our more general impression is, very strongly, that police officers rarely behave badly in such a way as to make it obvious that a person's ethnic group is the reason for their bad behaviour. It is still possible that police officers behave differently and more badly towards black people (and maybe Asians) without making it plain that they are motivated by a racial prejudice.... However, although the thing cannot definitely be proved, we are fairly confident that there is no widespread tendency for black or Asian people to be given greatly inferior treatment by the police.

Hostility towards black people became more intense at times of conflict between the police and the black community, especially during the investigation of a disastrous fire in Deptford in January 1981, in which thirteen black youngsters were killed and thirty injured. Black people in the area (along with many whites) were sure that the fire was the result of an arson attack by a racist group, the culmination, as they saw it, of years of discrimination and abuse. The police discarded this interpretation, and questioned black youths who were in the house when the fire broke out. Early in March, about 12,000 people demonstrated against the police approach to the case. The cause of the fire was never established, but the incident created an atmosphere of suspicion and hostility which was still strong at the time of the Brixton riot in April 1981.[102]

To tell the story of race relations in London through accounts of riots and police misconduct, important as these things are, is to give only half the picture. According to the 1991 census London's non-white population amounted to about 1.3 million people (over half a million of whom were born in Britain), nearly 20 per cent of the population of Greater London. London, with under 13 per cent of the population of Great Britain, had nearly 45 per cent of its non-white population. Over a quarter of the population of Inner London in 1991 was non-white, and in several boroughs the proportion was a third or more: Newham, Tower Hamlets and Hackney in Inner London, Brent and Ealing in the suburbs. But in general, in spite of the tensions created by mass unemployment, heavy and repeated reductions in social spending, and racial prejudice inside and outside the police force, the apocalyptic predictions of anti-immigrationists have not come true. Thanks in part to the Race Relations Acts of 1965,

1968 and 1976, open discrimination, which was so widespread in the 1950s and 1960s, now seems to be the preserve of an obstinate and often shamefaced minority. Even among private landlords racial prejudice appears to have declined. In 1990 the Commission for Racial Equality's survey of 144 private landlords and landladies found only four who showed evidence of discrimination, although the record of accommodation agencies (ten discriminated out of forty-seven) was much poorer.[103] The increasing acceptance of the Notting Hill Carnival, a racial flashpoint in the 1960s and 1970s, as one of London's favourite public celebrations, symbolized the general recognition of the fact that London was a truly multiracial city. Although economic circumstances seemed to favour it, mass support for racist political parties did not develop in London as it did in France, and the brief victory of a single British National Party candidate in a local council by-election in Millwall in 1993, in odd local circumstances, caused widespread shock and was quickly reversed. Not many would now predict, as Enoch Powell did in 1968, that the Thames (or the Tiber, as he liked to call it) would soon be foaming with blood.

'FARES FAIR'

The government was always happier to devote money to strengthening the police force than to dealing with the underlying economic and social problems that (in the judgement of most analysts) promoted the growth of lawlessness. A succession of brightly named government 'initiatives' (Inner City Partnerships, Action for Cities, City Challenge) could not disguise the damage done to London's poorer boroughs by the progressive tightening of local authority housing, education and social service budgets in the 1980s and 1990s. In general the government's policy was one of encouragement, freedom and substantial public support for private enterprise, alongside the curtailment, impoverishment and even abolition of local government and the services it provided. Probably the most important sufferers from this policy in the 1980s and 1990s were the metropolitan boroughs, whose social, educational and environmental services were so vital to the lives of most Londoners, but the most famous victim was the Greater London Council itself. In 1986, when City businessmen were beginning to settle into their handsome new offices in Broadgate or London Bridge City, GLC staff and councillors were clearing their desks and leaving County Hall for the last time. It was a conjunction of events that symbolized the impact of Thatcherism on the development of London.

The GLC's destruction began in the local election of May 1981, in which Sir Horace Cutler's Conservative administration was narrowly beaten, giving the Labour Party control of County Hall. As soon as it was in office the Labour group replaced its ineffective leader with a dynamic left-winger, Ken Livingstone, whom the press soon made a national hate figure with the predictable nickname of 'Red Ken'. Livingstone's plans to restore the recent cuts in GLC transport, housing and community services spending were impeded by the Thatcher government's 1980 Local Government Act, which drove down local authority spending by cutting the central government's contribution to local government budgets (the rate support grant), and linking the payment of the full grant to the ability of local councils to reduce their spending to meet tight new budgets. In effect this Act gave the central government control over local authority spending and revenue, and those Labour councils (notably Camden and Lambeth) that defied the government in 1980 and 1981 were forced to submit by the threat of crippling individual surcharges on councillors. Livingstone's intention was to exceed the government's budget limit, sacrifice the GLC's rate support grant, and rally public support by explaining the resulting sharp rate increases as the result of Conservative policies and London's urgent need for new investment.[104]

Livingstone overplayed a very weak hand. His majority on the GLC was small enough to give the more cautious Labour councillors a veto over his more radical proposals (such as the removal of obstructive and conservative-minded GLC officials), and the press campaign against him, especially on the issue of his sympathy for the IRA, robbed him of public support. Many of the issues Livingstone stood for, including Irish unity, gay rights and resistance to council house sales, were unpopular, and it was not difficult for the Conservative press to attach the 'Loony Left' label to the GLC and its leader. Moreover, the Thatcher government's policies on controlling council spending had already limited the GLC's room for manoeuvre, and would bind it still more tightly in the years ahead.

The one issue on which the Labour group stood a chance of rallying public support was its decision to revive the cheap public transport strategy abandoned in 1975, now renamed the 'Fares Fair' policy. In October 1981 the GLC reduced London Transport fares by a third, increasing its GLC subsidy from 29 per cent to 56 per cent. The £100 million cost of this policy was more than doubled by the loss of government rate support grant, and the GLC was prevented (by the Minister of Transport, Norman Fowler) from financing a similar cut in British Rail's South London services. As a result Bromley's Conservative council, whose voters would have the rate increases without the fares cuts, challenged the legality of the GLC's fares reduction policy in the High Court. Bromley lost its case in the High Court in October 1981, but won it on appeal (before Lord Denning) and again before the Law Lords, who declared that London Transport should break even, as far as possible, without a subsidy (a principle foreign to the 1969 Act and the practice of the previous twelve years), and disinterred the old principle that a council's primary duty was to safeguard its ratepayers' money. This judgement, which came from men who were perfectly ignorant of London's transport problems, implied that LT fares should be doubled or even tripled, and that the highly popular pensioners' travel pass, introduced in 1981, was illegal. Fares were doubled, with more increases to follow, in January 1982. Public hostility to the judgement, especially from London's million pensioners, persuaded the government to introduce a bill protecting travel passes and to announce that a doubling of fares would be enough even if it left LT in need of a subsidy. The GLC had a court victory in January 1983 which enabled it to reduce fares by 25 per cent in May, but its days as a transport authority were almost over. An all-party House of Commons report in 1982 recommended the creation of a separate agency to run London Transport, and in 1984 the London Regional Transport Authority, a body controlled by the Ministry of Transport, took responsibility for London's buses and underground trains.[105]

In the twelve years following the failure of 'Fares Fair' there was no slump in bus usage. In fact passenger miles rose by 8 per cent between 1981 and 1986, thanks in part to the introduction of the single-payment travelcard, before falling by 10 per cent between 1987 and 1994. Commuting into central London continued to be dominated by underground and surface railways, while road commuting, by bus, car or bicycle, continued to fall between 1983 and 1993. The growth of traffic congestion and consequent air pollution had more to do with the increased use of cars (including the ubiquitous 'company car') for social and leisure purposes (shopping, entertainment, and the 'school run') than with journeys to work. The underground, despite its many faults, remained essential to the free flow of Londoners, especially into the centre. Underground passenger miles rose by over 50 per cent between 1981 and 1988, before falling back slightly in the economic slump of the early 1990s, when commuting in general fell by more than 10 per cent.[106]

Goodbye GLC

Although the GLC was defeated and increasingly impotent, it was still spoiling the Thatcherite party, and during her first term of office (1979–83) the Prime Minister became more and more determined to put an end to it. Thatcher's motives for adopting this policy, which was inserted into the 1983 Conservative election manifesto on her personal insistence, were rooted in her strong dislike of Livingstone and the anti-Thatcherite principles that his administration had so defiantly proclaimed from its County Hall redoubt.[107] But Thatcher was also a convert to monetarist ideas, and regarded the GLC as a source of inflationary and unnecessary public spending. There was Treasury pressure to reduce the cost of local government, and the GLC, with its radical leadership, its large bureaucracy, and its shifting and sometimes unclear range of responsibilities, was an obvious candidate for closure. In fact the government's control over GLC and other local authority spending was already tight, and became still more so with the introduction of rate-capping (fixing an upper limit on local rates) in the 1984 Rates Limitation Act. It was far from clear that the high costs of disbanding the GLC would be offset by the annual savings its abolition might produce. The 1983 White Paper, *Streamlining the Cities*, argued that the GLC was an expensive and unnecessary layer of government, all of whose functions could be performed more cheaply and efficiently by the boroughs, central government, or specialized London-wide agencies. These arguments were unresearched and, in the words of an authoritative judge, 'ludicrously thin'.[108] But it was true that the GLC's performance as a strategic planner for Greater London, the function which above all others justified its creation in the 1960s, had not been very impressive. Partly because the aims of its own planners did not match the aspirations of Londoners (especially articulate middle-class Londoners), partly because the central government was not willing to yield its control of major planning issues to an elected local body, and partly because the GLC lacked the powers and resources to impose its will on the boroughs, the GLC's Development Plans had failed to provide the strategic guidance that they had been expected to give. Planning, which inspired such high hopes in the 1940s, had turned out to be more difficult than its early advocates had realized. Fundamental demographic and economic trends changed more quickly and unpredictably than planners could foresee, and most plans, with their long gestation period, were out of date before they were printed.[109]

If London did not need a strategic planning authority, it would plainly be possible to dismantle the GLC. Indeed, the devolution of the GLC's powers to other bodies was already happening in the early 1980s: sewerage, ambulances and motor licensing were transferred before 1980, responsibility for the development of Docklands was given to the London Docklands Development Corporation in 1981, and much of the GLC's housing stock had been privatized or taken over by the boroughs. Housing and transport represented over 60 per cent of the GLC's budget in 1984, and with those removed, the fire service (which could easily go to a separate agency) would be its most expensive activity.[110] Of course, the fact that the removal of the GLC's powers was possible did not demonstrate that it was desirable. In 1978 the Conservative leaders of the GLC had established a committee under an experienced and independent chairman, Sir Frank Marshall (the ex-leader of Leeds City Council), to examine the future role of the GLC. Instead of declaring (as some Conservative councillors had hoped it would) that the GLC was redundant, the Marshall Report asserted that 'the existence of a metropolitan authority is necessary to enable London Government to function properly', and called for the GLC to be given new powers over trunk roads, public transport, Docklands development, industrial growth, the Metropolitan Police, and London's health services.[111]

The GLC was squeezed between the central government, which had a strong tendency (especially in the Thatcher years) to reclaim powers for itself, and the boroughs, which had taken advantage of the GLC's weakness to increase their own autonomy. Conservative suburban boroughs, which feared the GLC's inclination to redistribute wealth from richer to poorer parts of London, and which had challenged the Fares Fair policy in the courts, supported the abolition campaign, and even in Labour boroughs many professional engineers and planners looked forward to freedom from County Hall intervention. 'The GLC was thus politically vulnerable, the weakest tier in London government, attacked by suburban Conservatives, suspected by business, and exposed as harbouring the "enemy within" to the government at the moment of its populist triumph (victory over Argentina).' The ministers who piloted the Abolition Bill through Parliament (Kenneth Baker, Patrick Jenkin and Lord Whitelaw) seem to have acted out of obedience rather than conviction, but there was strong support for abolition from other ministers, especially Michael Heseltine and Norman Tebbit. Several Conservative boroughs called for abolition in 1982–3, and ideologists of the 'New Right' gave the abolitionist campaign outspoken support, though they do not appear to have initiated it. Roger Scruton, a philosopher and polemicist, called for the abolition of local elections and even local government itself, and such right-wing organizations as Aims of Industry and the Adam Smith Institute saw abolition as an opportunity to move important and potentially profitable GLC services (transport, housing, waste disposal, and so on) into the hands of specialist agencies which might in time become part of the private sector.[112]

As it turned out, the abolition of the GLC was a tiresome and lengthy process for the government, which had to fight to get its Bill through the Commons and especially the Lords in the spring and early summer of 1985. Ken Livingstone and his administration conducted a spirited and expensive campaign in their own defence that won for the dying GLC a degree of public support that it had never enjoyed when it was in good health. London church leaders, several suburban Conservative MPs, and over 60 per cent of London voters opposed abolition, and the usually huge government majority in the Commons (over 150) was reduced at one point to twenty-three. It became clear during the battle for the Bill that the GLC was not the overblown bureaucracy that its opponents claimed it was, and that much of its work for voluntary organizations, small businesses and metropolitan services gave good value to London. Its largest group of employees (7,000 out of 22,000) were fire-fighters, and only 8 per cent of its workforce were managerial and administrative staff. This cast doubt on the government's promises of substantial savings when the GLC's essential duties were reallocated to other bodies. A report commissioned by the GLC from the accountants Coopers and Lybrand found that savings would be small, and the *Financial Times* argued that after abolition 'a lot of luck and improved efficiency might be needed just to keep the overall costs of "running" London at the same real level as under the GLC'.[113] Where there were savings, they would accrue to the business ratepayers of Westminster and the City, whose rates were redistributed under the GLC's rate equalization fund to meet the needs of poorer boroughs. Mrs Thatcher's determination that the new London-wide bodies that took over many GLC duties should be appointed rather than elected left the impression that she could not tolerate democratic institutions which would not bow to her will.

Inevitably, the bill to abolish the GLC and the other six metropolitan authorities passed all its stages, and the GLC came to an end on 1 April 1986. The Inner London Education Authority, which Mrs Thatcher probably disliked even more than the GLC, survived until 1990, when its duties were divided among the Inner London boroughs. The GLC's strategic planning and trunk road management duties went to Whitehall, the South Bank arts complex was handed over to the unelected South Bank Board, and London's health, public transport, the police and the Port of London continued to be controlled by bodies composed of government appointees. Many of the GLC's responsibilities were transferred to individual boroughs, and others (reverting to the principles of the Metropolitan Board of Works) were allocated to thirty-five London-wide authorities or committees with borough representation. London services which have been run by the boroughs on a cooperative basis since 1986 include the ambulance and fire services, concessionary fares, road safety, tourism, waste disposal, canals, planning and research. Whatever was left over after the division of spoils was given to the London Residuary Body, a self-liquidating agency which took temporary charge of the GLC's debt, rate equalization, and the GLC-run parks. Complexity, confusion and duplication, three of the charges laid against the 1965–86 system, were certainly not eradicated by the abolition of the GLC.[114] On the other hand, to argue that its abolition robbed London of a unified urban administration, a firm hand on the metropolitan tiller, or the ability to speak with a clear and authoritative voice, is to ignore the drift, indecision and weakness that characterized London's central government for much of the previous twenty years. The GLC was never powerful enough to drive through its most ambitious schemes, the Ringways and the cheap public transport system, against the opposition of Whitehall or the boroughs. It is reasonable to argue, as many have done in recent years, that London needs a strong central government, but not that Thatcher destroyed one.

GOVERNING LONDON AFTER 1986

The GLC's role as a strategic planner was taken by a committee made up of representatives of the City and the thirty-two boroughs, the London Planning Advisory Committee (LPAC). Since the government had little faith in strategic planning, and did not want to recreate an authority with the power or scope of the GLC, the LPAC was given a small staff, an office on the fringes of London, an awkward constitution (spending decisions needed a two-thirds majority) and fragmented responsibilities. However, this rather unpromising body produced a widely praised planning document in 1988, advocating the development of the East Thames corridor, investment in public transport, coordinated business development and the regeneration of fading town centres. The government ignored most of this, and issued its own planning guidance which emphasized free commercial development, private initiative, road-building and the rejection of strategic master plans.[115] This was the planning context in which the uncontrolled commercial development of Docklands took place in the late 1980s.

The idea of a strategic authority, or at least a single 'voice' for London, crept back into fashion in the 1990s, when it was generally acknowledged that the abolition of London's strategic planning authority had been an ill-judged and petulant act. Businessmen who felt that the abolition of the GLC left London's economy and vital services drifting without strategic guidance came together in 1990 to form London First, with the aim of stimulating investment, civic pride and better public services in London. Many of those who had celebrated Livingstone's fall now called for the introduction of an elected mayor for London, to mimic the apparent success of Chirac in Paris and Koch in New York. Others suggested that there should be a Minister for London, a title which was in fact added to John Gummer's official Department of the Environment notepaper when he became head of the new Government Office for London in April 1994. Gummer, catching the new enthusiasm for imaginative and long-term civic planning (especially in the light of London's claim to be a 'world city'), established a Joint London Advisory Panel to guide the government on strategic issues. This was composed of government ministers and the London Pride Partnership, a coalition of the London local authorities, the Confederation of British Industry, the London Chamber of Commerce and Industry, London First, the LPAC, and various other bodies.

In May 1996 the government's Office for London published its planning guidance for the next ten or fifteen years. At last the dead weight of the Thatcherite anti-planning philosophy seemed to have lifted, and the new guidelines reflected the ideas which the LPAC had been advocating since the late 1980s. The guidelines, which were meant to influence the boroughs' Unitary Development Plans, emphasized the need to use planning to make people less dependent on their cars, especially by preserving the vigour of town centres and discouraging out-of-town shopping developments. They argued that London's environment should be preserved and enhanced (especially along the Thames), to encourage tourism and new investment, and that its unique variety of local 'villages' should be protected. The document encouraged the commercial and industrial regeneration of key economic zones, Docklands, the Lea valley, Stratford, Park Royal, the Thames Gateway and the West London corridor, and urged local authorities to work with business and the government to stimulate growth in London's strongest sectors, new technology, entertainment, finance and tourism. Boroughs should also plan to build at least 234,000 new dwellings by 2006, to meet the needs of new households without invading the Green Belt. Gummer (along with all his Conservative colleagues) lost his job on 1 May 1997, and Londoners will never know whether he was London's new Abercrombie, or merely a politician getting ready for a general election.[116]

The landslide that deposited Gummer on the opposition benches brought to power a Labour government which was committed to recreating a central strategic authority for London and correcting the capital's 'democratic deficit'. The new government published a consultation paper in July 1997, *New Leadership for London*, which was intended to promote public debate in preparation for a referendum on London's government in May 1998. The paper promoted the fashionable idea that London, like Paris and New York, should have a full-time elected mayor, who would act as a 'voice' for London's interests (especially in defending its 'global city' status) and share responsibility with a directly elected Greater London Authority (GLA) for many of the London-wide matters that had once been managed by the GLC. The government was keen to avoid the conflict and overlap between the central authority and the boroughs that had dogged the LCC and the GLC, and insisted that the new 'streamlined' GLA should avoid interference in local matters. Nevertheless, it proposed that the GLA should take back the GLC's strategic planning duties from the Government Office for London and LPAC, to provide a framework within which the boroughs would make their local decisions. The GLA's strategic vision would also coordinate and guide the efforts of the boroughs, businesses and various sub-metropolitan partnerships to stimulate London's economic regeneration and bring new jobs to the capital. The economic strategy formulated by the GLA would then be put into operation, the paper suggested, by another new body, the London Development Agency. The GLA would resume the GLC's responsibility for fire-fighting, and take a leading part in guiding and expanding London's cultural and tourist industries. In one respect, the GLA's proposed powers went beyond those of any of its predecessors: for the first time, London would have a police authority (with at least half its members drawn from the GLA), and the Metropolitan Police force, like the rest of England's police, would submit to a degree of local supervision. The most important and concrete proposal in *New Leadership for London* was that control of the whole of London's transport system, including buses, tubes and strategic roads (but not the now privately owned surface railways, the Port of London or the airports) should be vested in a new London Transport Authority, appointed by and accountable to the mayor and the GLA. With transport under its control, the GLA's role in the key areas of environmental protection, economic development and strategic planning was bound to be strong.[117]

At the time of writing, it was not known whether Londoners would accept these proposals, or what their impact would be on the future development of London. The respective powers of the mayor, the GLA and the boroughs were not yet established, and it was not clear that London's new constitution would avoid the delays and ambiguities that had undermined the effectiveness of the GLC. Certainly, it would be foolish to rest too many hopes on the election of a charismatic mayor who would 'speak up for London and Londoners',[118] when it is clear that the interests of Londoners are immensely diverse and very often conflicting, and that London's problems are complex and intractable. There is wide agreement that London needs a stategic planning and transport authority, but it is a mistake to blame the problems of London government in the 1980s and 1990s only on the abolition of the GLC, or to expect the restoration of central guidance to remedy what has gone wrong. The good government of London depends, and has depended since 1965, on the effectiveness of the thirty-two borough councils, on their income being sufficient to meet their communities' needs, and on their ability to work together. To some extent the abolition of the GLC made cooperation between boroughs easier than it had been. In the words of a recent essay, 'individual boroughs have found it easier to coordinate since acquiring unitary status, because they can "deliver" without intervention by a higher authority. . . . The traditional free-riders in the metropolitan system, Conservative-controlled suburban councils, . . . have taken a much more active interest in capital affairs since becoming unitary London Boroughs instead of reluctant victims of annexation within a two-tier "Greater London".'[119] But in other respects, as any user of London's social services, schools, libraries and other borough services knows, local authorities were under severe and increasing pressure in the 1980s and 1990s.

The problem for the London boroughs was not a lack of civic pride or strategic guidance, but a shortage of cash. The growing inadequacy of council income was a direct result of government policy, which drove down borough revenues at a time of great social need, in which the GLC's duties were being added to those already performed at borough level. It was a notable achievement of central government in these decades to diminish the willingness of rate- and taxpayers to contribute towards costly public services, and to foster the growing belief that taxation was a form of theft and that social problems could be solved without 'throwing money' at them. There was a vigorous government campaign against extravagant (or 'loony') local authorities, whose budgets, it was argued, were running free of democratic control, since most voters were not local ratepayers and the bulk of local rates were paid by non-voting businesses. The first stage of the attack, in the early 1980s, involved penalizing high-spending councils by cutting their central government grant. This was followed in 1985–6 by rate-capping, the imposition of upper limits on the rates which selected local authorities (especially Labour boroughs) could raise. In 1990 the government abolished local rates altogether, replacing them with a poll tax which would fall on all local voters. At the same time it introduced a system which gave it much tighter control over councils' capital spending, a successful move which attracted little publicity.

The introduction of the poll tax, on the other hand, was a case study in political ineptitude. The effect of this new tax was to shift the burden of local taxation from richer to poorer households, and to increase the revenue of commercially prosperous boroughs at the expense of poorer ones. Westminster, the City and Kensington and Chelsea made substantial gains in revenue, while struggling Greenwich, Tower Hamlets, Southwark and Lewisham were England's four worst-hit boroughs. The poll tax led to violent riots in Whitehall in March 1990, a sharp decline in the government's popularity and (indirectly) the fall of Mrs Thatcher, who went down with her 'flagship'. It was abandoned in 1991, and replaced with a property-based council tax which was rather like the old rates. Councils emerged from these changes far more dependent than before on direct government grants, and with their local revenues stringently 'capped' by central government.[120] Patrick Wright's rambling but interesting book, *A Journey Through Ruins: the Last Days of London,* conveys a sense of the squalor and neglect that has resulted from a decade of cuts in Hackney, London's most deprived borough. Wright's message for Londoners, as the title of his book suggests, is bleak. The dereliction and neglect of Dalston Lane, he warns, was a 'pilot project' for the city as a whole. 'London has become Dalston Lane writ large. The congested traffic and the crammed and inadequate public transport are already everywhere. The litter gusts over the whole city.'[121]

THE PROSPECT FOR LONDON

As the end of the millennium approached, many of the problems that London and its governors had been grappling with since 1945 seemed to be as severe as they had ever been. In spite of the enormous efforts of local and central government between the 1940s and 1980s homelessness had not been eradicated. It was estimated by the London Research Centre in 1995 that 230,000 London dwellings were 'unfit for habitation', and that there would be a shortage of nearly 100,000 dwellings (for new and homeless households) by 1998. Moreover, the way the old slum problem had been tackled had created new problems of dereliction, danger and despair on many of London's huge and under-managed housing estates. In 1997 nearly two-thirds of England's worst public housing was in London.[122] Inequalities between London's poorest and richest boroughs, according to an official index of local conditions, were reminiscent of those identified by Charles Booth 100 years ago. Although average earnings in London in the early 1990s were about 30 per cent above the national average (and 80 per cent higher in the City), seven of England's ten most deprived local government districts were London boroughs. Material from the 1991 census was used to calculate which English local government areas contained the highest proportion of very deprived enumeration districts (neighbourhoods of about 400 people). In this table of social and economic disadvantage, London boroughs (including Westminster, Kensington and Lewisham) took the first thirteen places, and sixteen of the top eighteen. And the consequences of this deprivation expressed themselves not merely in boredom, crime or discomfort, but in the most fundamental of ways: the standardized death rate (adjusted for age differences) in the poorest boroughs, Newham, Southwark, Hackney, Islington and Tower Hamlets, was about 25 per cent greater than that in the richest ones, Harrow, Bromley, Bexley and Sutton.[123] Politicians liked to talk of the 'north–south divide', and travelled (as they always say) 'up and down the country' to see it. But in the 1990s they could find England's most extreme social and economic contrasts within 5 miles of Parliament Square.

In the hands of politicians who either feared the motoring voter or positively welcomed the increase in car ownership and use, the amount of traffic on London's roads grew by around 10 per cent in the 1980s, and the 'rush hour' gave way to almost full-time congestion in the centre. Air pollution, generated now by vehicle exhausts rather than domestic or industrial smoke, made London's air dangerous to breathe on an increasing number of days. Politicians talked airily of the virtues of cycling and walking, but the real answers to the problem, well-funded public transport and restrictions on private car use, were not promoted. In the government's November 1996 budget, London Transport's funding for the rest of the decade was halved, and most of the money it received was earmarked for completing the Jubilee Line extension to Docklands. Pressing work on station and escalator modernization, and on the renovation of the decaying and inadequate Northern Line, was postponed. There was no Treasury support here for the shift from private to public transport announced by the 'Minister for London' only six months earlier. The fragmentation and privatization of London's bus and railway services made a coordinated and well-funded public transport system a more distant prospect than ever, though London had so far been spared the wholesale deregulation of bus services imposed on other British cities. The only bright spot, as cars and lorries choked London's roads and Londoners' lungs, was the very sharp decline in the number of people killed in traffic accidents: from 873 in 1965 and 703 in 1976 to 368 in 1991. There were advantages, then, in the fact that central London's daytime traffic moved at only 10 miles an hour.[124]

Many of London's problems could be solved by a government which gave adequate legislative and financial support to policies such as those advocated in Mr Gummer's 1996 planning guidelines or in the 1997 Green Paper, *New Leadership for London*. Dirty streets and overcrowded classrooms are not incurable disorders, but symptoms of misgovernment and underfunding. A government that was as ready to spend money on unglamorous local services as it was to allocate lottery money to ostentatious and socially valueless constructions to celebrate the millennium would be able to remedy them. Employment trends are a different matter. The rapid decline in its manufacturing sector, an experience shared with many great cities, has left London with an unemployment problem which remains massive even in periods of economic revival. No amount of economic planning or inducement is likely to make London a great manufacturing city again, or to create hundreds of thousands of new jobs for London's unskilled and poorly educated workers. The worst of this manufacturing decline is over, but its results, in the shape of unemployment, poverty, demoralization and crime, are still evident.

Yet London, unlike most other great cities that are losing their manufacturing base, has hopes of a prosperous economic future because of the growth of its financial sector, and all the professions and services sustained by the global economy. It is true that financial employment is volatile, and that many of London's financiers might decamp to Paris or Frankfurt, but predictions in the early 1990s that this was about to happen have not been borne out by events. In any case, the collapse of London manufacturing in recent decades, like the decline of silk weaving and shipbuilding in the nineteenth century, showed that manufacturing could be volatile too. London's immense capacity for generating wealth by one means or another has not deserted it yet. In 1993 London's Gross Domestic Product (calculated by place of work, rather than residence) was about $180 billion, around 18 per cent of the national GDP. This was almost twice the GDP of Saudi Arabia, bigger than that of Turkey or Russia, the equal of Austria's, two-thirds that of India. London's annual output was greater, in fact, than the national output of all but the world's twenty richest countries.[125] A city with the capacity to generate wealth on such a scale does not need to endure overfilled railway carriages, understocked classrooms, decaying social services, underfunded libraries, neglected housing estates or families living in fire-trap bed-and-breakfast accommodation. These things are a matter of choice, not necessity.

London is, as it always was, a city of spectacular contrasts. It is the richest and poorest city in the country. It is a town with innumerable entertainments and pleasures, a vast capacity for creating and spending wealth, and a rich variety of skills, cultures and intellects. These things inspire admiration and amazement, as they always did. But it also suffers from the prevailing social, economic and environmental maladies of its age on a colossal scale. Whether the ailments of today's London (unemployment, crime, family breakdown, traffic congestion, air pollution, homelessness, neglected public services, and the rest) are more disastrous than those of the past (epidemic disease, polluted drinking water, racial and religious bigotry, child and infant mortality, prostitution, rookeries, chronic unemployment, 'the frequency of fires and the immoderate drinking of fools') I leave the reader to decide. The challenge now, as ever, is to apply a share of London's vast economic and intellectual resources to solving its enormous social and environmental problems. The words used by William Fitzstephen in the first medieval account of London are as true today as they were in 1173: 'The city is delightful indeed, when it has a good governor'.

Maps

NOTES ON THE MAPS

1. ROMAN LONDON

This map shows the main features of Roman London that are mentioned in the text. At high tide the Thames, marked here in its modern and ancient dimensions, reached the Roman quay, and flooded into the Southwark marshes. (*Drawn by John Williamson*)

2. MEDIEVAL LONDON, c. 1400

The map shows the City wards as they were after the division of Farringdon Ward in 1394, and the main religious communities as they were after the founding of the Charterhouse in 1371. Three wards (Aldersgate, Cripplegate and Bishopsgate) straddle the City wall. (*Drawn by John Williamson*)

3. THE 'AGAS' MAP, 1560s

The 'Agas' map, showing London and Westminster in the 1560s. The map is named after an Elizabethan surveyor, Ralph Agas (1545–1621), but it was not drawn by him. It is a woodcut based on the slightly earlier and larger 'Copperplate' map (1557–9), of which only three sections (of about 15) are now known to exist. From W. Besant, *London in the Time of the Tudors* (1904).

4. FRANZ HOGENBERG, 1572

Franz Hogenberg's map of London, published in *Civitates orbis terrarum* (*Cities of the World*) in 1572, and probably based on a survey of about 1550. The hill on which the group of citizens stands is imaginary. (*Guildhall Library, Corporation of London*)

5. FREDERICK DE WIT, 1666

Frederick de Wit's map of London at the time of the Great Fire of 1666. The weeping boatman, the City gentleman paying a carter to rescue his belongings, and the picture of London on fire (Hollar's 1647 panorama with added flames) gave the map a dramatic impact. (*Guildhall Library, Corporation of London*)

6A. JOHN ROCQUE: THE WEST END IN 1769

Rocque's map was based on his meticulous survey carried out between 1737 and 1746. This version incorporates Rocque's later revisions, and was published in 1769. The map shows the older West End of Lincoln's Inn Fields and Covent Garden, the newer developments in St James', Soho, Mayfair, Bloomsbury and Marylebone, and the fields of Lamb's Conduit and Tottenham Court still waiting their turn (*Guildhall Library, Corporation of London*)

6B. JOHN ROCQUE: THE CITY AND SUBURBS IN 1769

The City, part of South London (Lambeth, Southwark, Bermondsey and Rotherhithe) and the East End (Spitalfields, Whitechapel and Wapping), from the 1769 edition of Rocque's map.(*Guildhall Library, Corporation of London*)

7. JOHN TALLIS, 1851

A souvenir map of London prepared by John Tallis for the Great Exhibition of 1851. The map shows recent dock, bridge and railway development, and the spread of suburban London beyond a 3-mile radius (marked by a circle) into Chelsea, Paddington and Stockwell. The pictures, by H. Lacey, display London's attractions for the tourist and the sightseer: the great public buildings of the City and Westminster along the top of the map and around its lower right-hand corner, and 14 theatres, two pleasure gardens and several exhibition halls down the sides and in the lower left-hand corner. (*Guildhall Library, Corporation of London*)

8. LONDON'S RAILWAYS AND TRAMWAYS, 1897

London's surface and underground railways and tramways in 1897, just before the construction of the deep-level Tube network and the building of Kingsway and the Aldwych. From J. G. Bartholomew's *Royal Atlas of England and Wales*, c. 1900.

9. LONDON'S GROWTH, 1840–1929

The growth of London's built-up area between 1840 and 1929. The inner circle indicates a 3-mile radius from Charing Cross.

10. LONDON, 1919–1939

This map shows major industrial areas, districts of rapid suburban growth, and the development of a new road network. (*Drawn by John Williamson*)

11. LONDON'S ADMINISTRATIVE DISTRICTS SINCE 1899

The districts are shown before and after the creation of the Greater London Council in 1965. The larger map shows the boundaries of the present Greater London boroughs, and the inset shows borough boundaries before 1965. The map also indicates the growth of London's built-up area, and the mismatch between its administrative and actual dimensions. (*Drawn by John Williamson*)

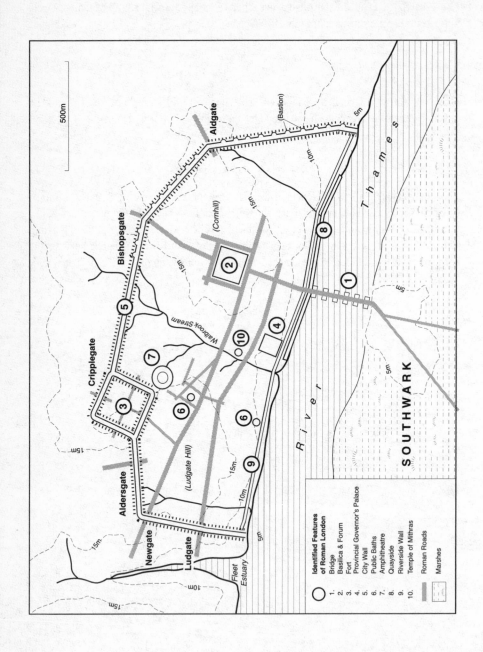

Identified Features of Roman London

1. Bridge
2. Basilica & Forum
3. Fort
4. Provincial Governor's Palace
5. City Wall
6. Public Baths
7. Amphitheatre
8. Quayside
9. Riverside Wall
10. Temple of Mithras

▬▬ Roman Roads

▨▨ Marshes

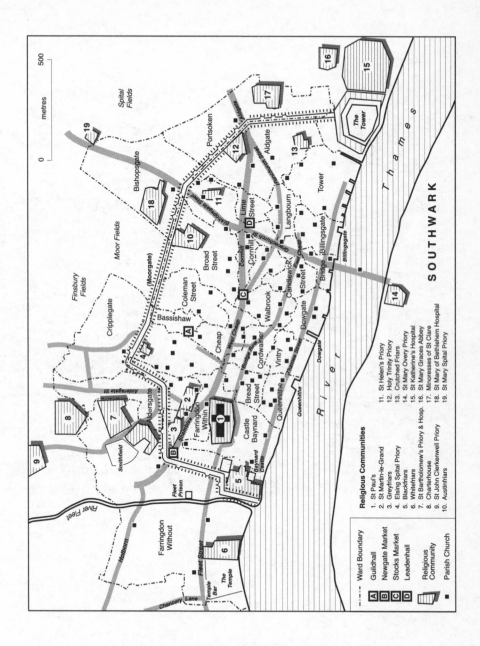

Religious Communities

1. St Paul's
2. St Martin-le-Grand
3. Greyfriars
4. Elsing Spital Priory
5. Blackfriars
6. Whitefriars
7. St Bartholomew's Priory & Hosp.
8. Charterhouse
9. St John Clerkenwell Priory
10. Austinfriars

11. St Helen's Priory
12. Holy Trinity Priory
13. Crutched Friars
14. St Mary Overy Priory
15. St Katherine's Hospital
16. St Mary Graces Abbey
17. Minoresses of St Clare
18. St Mary of Bethlehem Hospital
19. St Mary Spital Priory

----- Ward Boundary

[A] Guildhall
[B] Newgate Market
[C] Stocks Market
[D] Leadenhall

▦ Religious Community

■ Parish Church

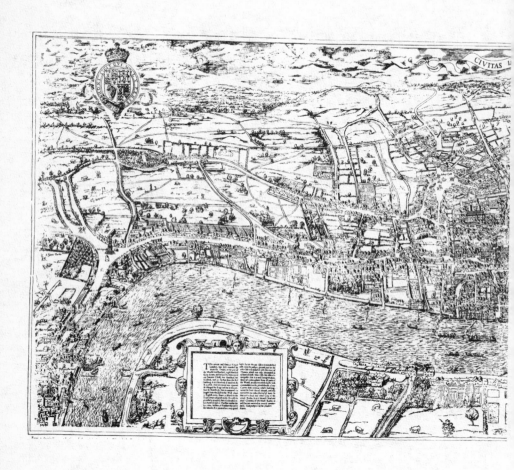

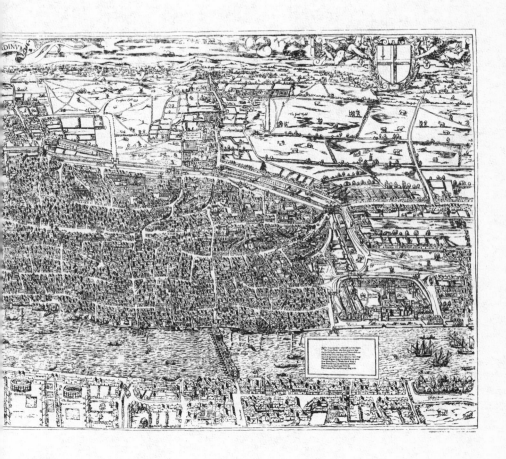

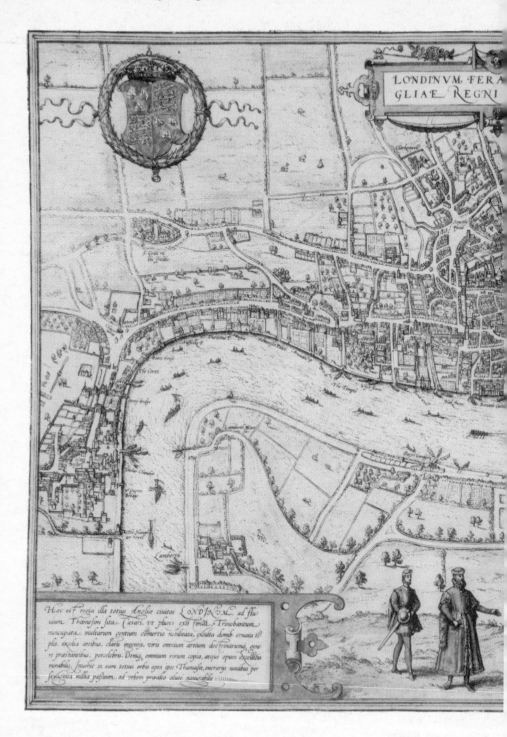

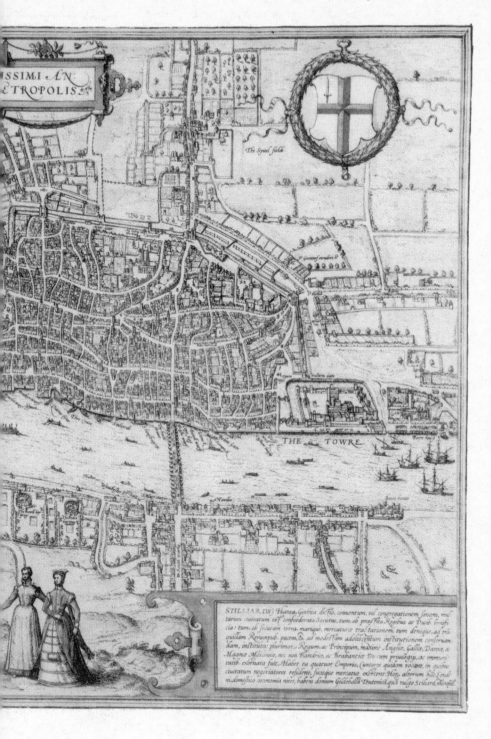

PLATTE GRONDT DER STADT LONDON MET NIE

Aenwysinge der Parochie Kercken
en Straten

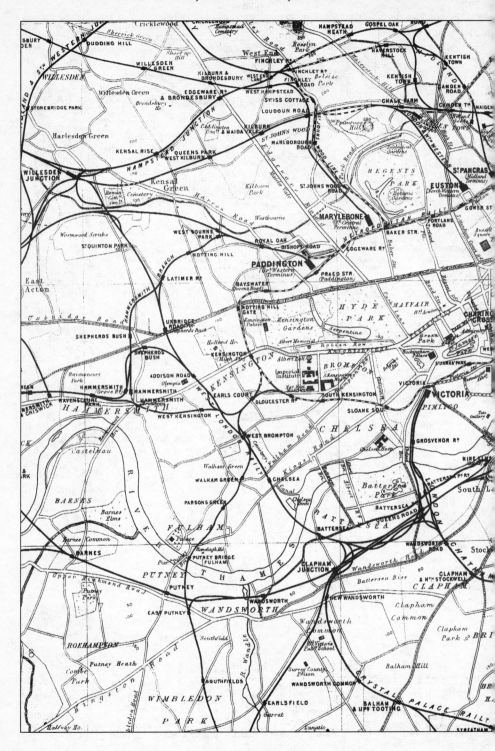

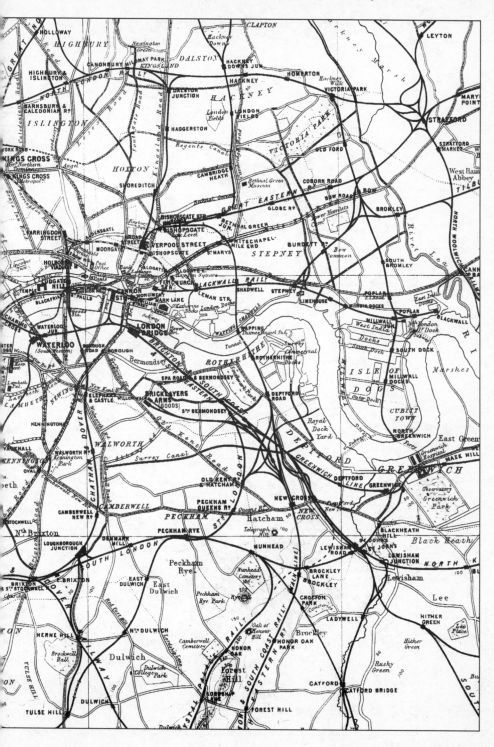

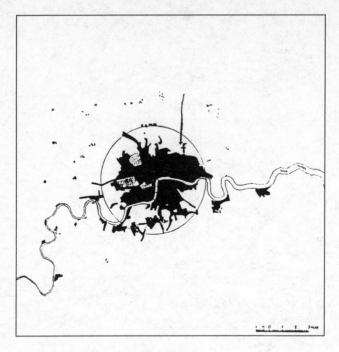

1840

1880

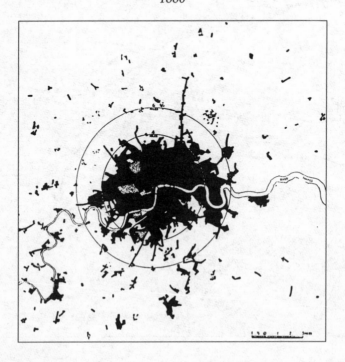

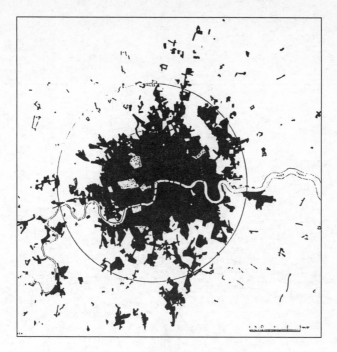

1900

1929

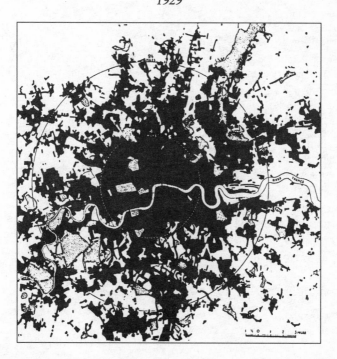

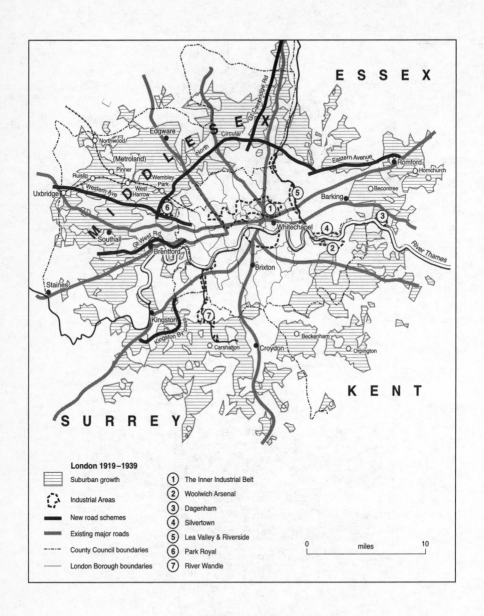

London 1919–1939

Suburban growth

Industrial Areas

New road schemes

Existing major roads

County Council boundaries

London Borough boundaries

① The Inner Industrial Belt
② Woolwich Arsenal
③ Dagenham
④ Silvertown
⑤ Lea Valley & Riverside
⑥ Park Royal
⑦ River Wandle

0   miles   10

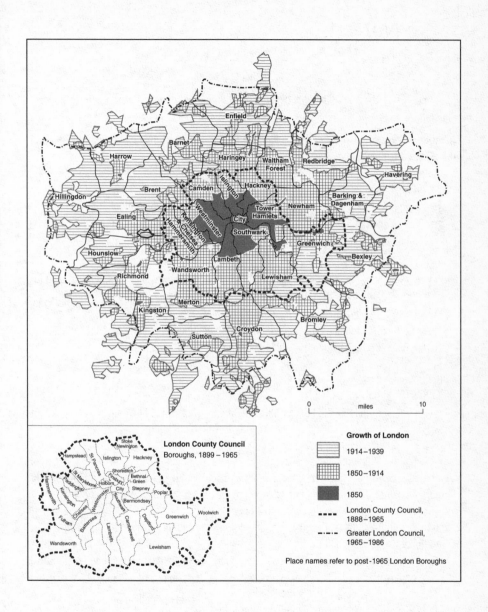

Enfield

Barnet

Harrow

Haringey

Waltham
Forest

Redbridge

Havering

Brent

Camden

Islington

Hackney

Hillingdon

Ealing

Westminster

Kensington
& Chelsea

Hammersmith

City

Tower
Hamlets

Newham

Barking &
Dagenham

Southwark

Greenwich

Bexley

Hounslow

Richmond

Wandsworth

Lambeth

Lewisham

Merton

Kingston

Bromley

Croydon

Sutton

0   miles   10

London County Council
Boroughs, 1899 – 1965

Stoke
Newington

Hampstead

St Pancras

Islington

Hackney

Shoreditch

Bethnal
Green

St Marylebone

Finsbury

Holborn

City

Stepney

Poplar

Paddington

Westminster

Bermondsey

Kensington

Chelsea

Battersea

Lambeth

Camberwell

Deptford

Greenwich

Woolwich

Fulham

Hammersmith

Wandsworth

Lewisham

Growth of London

1914 – 1939

1850 – 1914

1850

- - - London County Council,
1888 – 1965

-·-·- Greater London Council,
1965 – 1986

Place names refer to post-1965 London Boroughs

Notes

Number in square brackets indicate the place of first citation here, by chapter and note number.

INTRODUCTION

1 C. H. Lee, 'Regional growth and structural change in Victorian Britain', *Economic History Review*, 34 (1981), 438–52.
2 H. J. Dyos, 'Greater and Greater London', in *Exploring the Urban Past* (1982) (eds. D. Cannadine, D. Reeder), 40.
3 J. Boswell, *The Life of Samuel Johnson* (1906 edn), vol. 2, 454.
4 *The Letters of Charles Lamb* (2 vols, ed. W. C. Hazlitt, 1886), vol. 1, 292, Lamb to Wordsworth, 30 January 1801.

THE FIRST THOUSAND YEARS, AD 43–1066

1. LONDINIUM

1 Royal Commission on Historical Monuments (England), *An Inventory of the Historical Monuments in London*, vol. 3, *Roman London*. Mortimer Wheeler's introduction, pp. 1–7, gives the full texts.
2 M. Biddle, D. M. Hudson, C. M. Heighway, *The Future of London's Past* (Worcester, 1973), 3–4.
3 Geoffrey of Monmouth, *The History of the Kings of Britain* (1966), trans. and ed. L. Thorpe, 72–4; J. Stow, *A Survey of London*, vol. 1 (1908, reprinted 1971).
4 R. Merrifield, *London, City of the Romans* (1983), pp. 9–10; N. Merriman, 'A Prehistory for Central London?', *London Archaeologist*, vol. 5, no. 12 (1987); R. Merrifield, 'The contribution of archaeology to our understanding of pre-Norman London, 1973–88', in L. Grant (ed.), *Medieval Art, Architecture and Archaeology in London* (1978), 1–15.

5 Merrifield [1, 4], 9; Merriman [1, 4], 321, 324; D. Perring, *Roman London* (1991), 1–3.

6 Royal Commission on Historical Monuments (England) [1, 1], vol. 3, 19–20; E. Ekwall, *The Concise Oxford Dictionary of English Place Names* (4th edn, Oxford, 1960. 1st published 1936), 303.

7 J. Morris, *Londinium: London in the Roman Empire* (1982), 10–14, 30.

8 Morris [1, 7], 54–8; Royal Commission on Historical Monuments (England), [1, 1], vol. 3, 2.

9 Morris [1, 7], 78–84; P. Marsden, *Roman London* (1983), 11–29.

10 Perring [1, 5], vii.

11 According to D. Perring [1, 5], 6, coin evidence suggests a date between AD 50 and 55.

12 Merrifield [1, 4], 41–52; Morris [1, 7], 87–100; Marsden [1, 9], 30–34; Perring [1, 5], 8–16.

13 Tacitus, *Annals of Imperial Rome*, trans. M. Grant (Harmondsworth, 1956), 319.

14 Tacitus, *On Britain and Germany*, trans. H. Mattingly (Harmondsworth, 1970), 72.

15 Royal Commission on Historical Monuments (England) [1, 1], vol. 3, 36–44.

16 Perring [1, 5], 57–8; Merrifield [1, 4], 63–9.

17 Morris [1, 7], 150; P. Salway, *Roman Britain* (1981), 575–80.

18 W. F. Grimes, *The Excavation of Roman and Medieval London* (1968), ch. 2.

19 Perring [1, 5], 33–5: Perring suggests that the palace might have been on the site of Winchester Palace, in Southwark, where impressive remains have been found; P. Marsden [1, 9], 87–94.

20 Morris [1, 7], 180–81.

21 Perring [1, 5], 67–70.

22 Perring [1, 5], 61–3.

23 Merrifield [1, 4], 154–64.

24 Merrifield [1, 4], 100–106; Perring [1, 5], 50–51.

25 Merrifield [1, 4], 90; Marsden [1, 9], 68; B. Hobley, *Roman and Saxon London: A Reappraisal* (1986), 6; G. Milne, *The Port of Roman London* (1985), chs. 5, 9, 10, 12.

26 Milne [1, 25], 96–102, 142–50; Merrifield, [1, 4], 6–7, puts the case for reserving judgement.

27 Merrifield [1, 4], ch. 6.

28 Morris [1, 7], 291, 300, 305, 311–15; Marsden [1, 9], chs. 7–9; Merrifield [1, 4], chs. 7–9.

29 Perring [1, 5], 78, 84–9.

30 Merrifield [1, 4], chs. 7, 8; Marsden, [1, 9], chs. 8, 9; Perring [1, 5], 98–9.

31 Salway [1, 17], ch. 21; Morris [1, 7], ch. 11; Royal Commission on Historical Monuments (England) [1, 1], vol. 3, 4–5.

32 Eumenius' panegyrical account of Constantius' great victory, reproduced in Royal Commission on Historical Monuments (England), [1, 1] vol. 3, 4.

33 Salway [1, 17], 372.
34 Ammianus Marcellinus' account of these events is reprinted in [1, 1], vol. 3, 5–7.
35 Salway [1, 17], 434.
36 Milne [1, 25], 140–41.

2. ANGLO-SAXON LONDON

1 M. Carlin, *Medieval Southwark* (1996), 6–7.
2 Salway [1, 17], ch. 16; J. N. L. Myres, *The English Settlements* (Oxford, 1989), ch. 1.
3 Grimes [1, 18], 154; Merrifield, [1, 4], 11.
4 Bede, *Ecclesiastical History of the English People* (Harmondsworth, 1990), 102.
5 A. Vince, *Saxon London* (1990), ch. 2; M. Biddle, 'London on the Strand', *Popular Archaeology*, July 1984, 23–7; D. Whipp, 'Thoughts on Saxon London', *The London Archaeologist*, vol. 5 no. 6 (Spring 1986), 148–50; L. Blackmore, '"Des. Res." (Close City and Thames)', *The London Archaeologist*, vol. 5 no. 8 (Autumn 1986), 207–16.
6 Grimes [1, 18], 182–97; Vince [2, 5], ch. 6; C. Brooke, G. Keir, *London 800–1216: The Shaping of a City* (1975), 139–40.
7 S. Reynolds, *An Introduction to the History of English Medieval Towns* (Oxford, 1977), 19, 24–7.
8 Vince [2, 5], 54, 104–5; Brooke and Keir [2, 6], 367; D. Whitelock (ed.), *English Historical Documents, c. 500–1042* (1955), 440–41, 451–3.
9 Vince [2, 5], 111–14.
10 Carlin [2, 1], 10–12; A. P. Smyth, *King Alfred the Great* (Oxford, 1995), 45–50.
11 Asser's *Life of Alfred*, quoted in Sir F. Stenton, *Anglo-Saxon England, c. 550–1087* (Oxford, 1981), 256; *Anglo-Saxon Chronicle*, ed. G. N. Garmonsway, 81.
12 Smyth [2, 10], 519; Brooke and Keir [2, 6], 19–20.
13 Carlin [2, 1], 9.
14 Vince [2, 5], 20–21, 85–6; D. M. Wilson, *The Archaeology of Anglo-Saxon England* (1976), 124–34.
15 Vince [2, 5], 124–9; T. Dyson, 'King Alfred and the Restoration of London', *London Journal*, 15 ii (1990), 99–110; T. Tatton-Brown, 'The Topography of Anglo-Saxon London', *Antiquity* LX (1986).
16 Vince [2, 5], 20–22, 33–5; T. Dyson, J. Schofield, *The Archaeology of the City of London* (1980), 34–41; T. Dyson, J. Schofield, 'Saxon London', in J. Haslam, *Anglo-Saxon Towns* (Chichester, 1984), 296–7, 302, 308–9.
17 Vince [2, 5], 35–6, 94–103, 124–9; Dyson and Schofield, 'Saxon London', 299–305.
18 P. Nightingale, *A Medieval Mercantile Community: The Grocers' Company and the Politics and Trade of London, 1000–1485* (Yale, 1995), 12–14.

19 H. R. Loyn, *Anglo-Saxon England* (1962), 93–4; T. H. Lloyd, *The English Wool Trade in the Middle Ages* (1977), 2.

20 M. B. Honeybourne, 'The Pre-Norman Bridge of London', in A. E. J. Hollaender and W. Kellaway (eds.), *Studies in London History*, 17–39. There is a possibility that the bridge referred to in the charter was not in London.

21 Whitelock [2, 8], 423–7; G. Unwin, *The Guilds and Companies of London* (1963), ch. 2.

22 P. Nightingale, 'The origin of the Court of Husting and Danish influence on London's development into a capital city', *English Historical Review* CCCIV (July 1987), 559–78.

23 Brooke and Keir [2, 6], 191–4, for the mysterious origins of the London sheriff.

24 G. Williams, *Medieval London. From Commune to Capital* (1963), 81; Sir F. M. Stenton, *Norman London*, 14–15; Stenton, [2, 11], 522, 532; Brooke and Keir [2, 6], 149–57.

25 D. C. Douglas and G. W. Greenaway (eds.), *English Historical Documents, 1042–1189*, 1015–21; Unwin [2, 18], 23–7; Brooke and Keir [2, 6], 149–57; Stow [1, 3], vol. 1, 21; vol. 2, 202–3.

26 Stenton [2, 24], 376–87.

27 Whitelock [2, 8], 420; Brooke and Keir [2, 6], 378–80.

28 Nightingale [2, 22]; M. McKisack, 'London and the Succession to the Crown during the Middle Ages', in R. W. Hunt, W. A. Pantin, R. W. Southern (eds.), *Studies in Medieval History Presented to F. M. Powicke*, 76–8; F. Barlow, *Edward the Confessor* (1970), 56, 120–26.

29 Reynolds [2, 7], 37.

30 Nightingale [2, 22], 568–9, 572–4.

31 Nightingale [2, 18], 18–20.

32 Vince [2, 5], 61–76; Brooke and Keir [2, 6], 136–43.

33 Nightingale [2, 22], 567–8; Brooke and Keir [2, 6], 138–42; Vince [2, 5], 72.

34 Douglas and Greenaway [2, 25], 1021–4; Brooke and Keir [2, 6], 122–48.

35 Nightingale [2, 22], 568.

36 P. Hunting, *Royal Westminster* (1981), 21.

37 R. H. C. Davis, 'The College of St Martin-le-Grand and the Anarchy, 1135–54', *London Topographical Record*, vol. 23 (1974), 24.

38 Hunting [2, 36], 21–6.

MEDIEVAL LONDON, 1066–1520

3. POWER AND CONFLICT

1 Brooke and Keir [2, 6], 27.

2 Douglas and Greenaway [2, 25], 148–9, 227–8, 230, 245.

3 Douglas and Greenaway [2, 25], 1012, 246, quoting William of Poitiers, *Gesta Willelmi*.

4 Nightingale [2, 22], 562–3; Brooke and Keir [2, 6], 155, 162–70.

5 Reynolds [2, 7], 43; C. Stephenson, *Borough and Town* (Cambridge, Mass., 1933) and J. Tait, *The Medieval English Borough* (Manchester, 1936), put the cases respectively for and against the Norman Conquest as a turning-point in urban development.

6 C. M. Barron, 'Centres of conspicuous consumption: the aristocratic town house in London, 1200–1550', *London Journal* 20 (1995), 1–16: this point is made on p. 4.

7 Brooke and Keir [2, 6], 185–221; S. Reynolds, 'The rulers of London in the twelfth century', *History*, 57 (1972).

8 Nightingale [2, 18], 50–51.

9 R. H. C. Davis, *King Stephen* (1967), 61–2; Brooke and Keir [2, 6], 38, quoting *Gesta Stephani*.

10 C. Brooke, G. Keir, S. Reynolds, 'Henry I's Charter for the City of London', *Journal of the Society of Archivists*, 4 (1973), 558–78; Brooke and Keir [2, 6], 207–9; Reynolds [3, 7], 104–5.

11 Douglas and Greenaway [2, 25], 1012–13, has the text of Henry I's charter; Brooke and Keir [2, 6], 207–9; Tait [3, 5], 154–61.

12 Douglas and Greenaway [2, 25], 1013–14, has the text of Henry II's charter of 1155; A. L. Poole, *Domesday Book to Magna Carta, 1087–1215* (Oxford, 1955), 68–9.

13 H. Rothwell (ed.), *English Historical Documents, 1189–1327* (1975), 57–9. The Chronicle of Richard of Devizes; Poole [3, 12], 70–71, 357–8; Brooke and Keir [2, 6], 45–7.

14 Poole [3, 12], 471–5; Rothwell [3, 13] gives the 1215, 1216 and 1217 versions of Magna Carta.

15 Brooke and Keir [2, 6], 248–51; Williams [2, 24], 28–9, 80–84.

16 Examples of these decrees are in R. R. Sharpe (ed.), *Calendar of Letter-Books preserved among the archives of the City of London, 1275–1498* (1899–1912), *Letter-Book F*, 304–5, *Letter-Book H*, 241–2, and *Letter-Book K*, 55–6, 274–5, 288; Williams [2, 21], 41–3; S. L. Thrupp, *The Merchant Class of Medieval London* (Chicago, 1948), 60–73; C. M. Barron, 'London and the Crown, 1451–61', in J. R. L. Highfield, R. Jeffs (eds.), *The Crown and Local Communities in England and France in the Fifteenth Century* (Gloucester, 1981), 88–109, places greater emphasis on the part played by the whole body of freemen in electing the mayor.

17 Thrupp [3, 16], 65–9; Sharpe [3, 16], *Letter-Book F*, 162, 237–8.

18 C. M. Barron, *The Medieval Guildhall of London* (1974), 15, 44; Nightingale [2, 22], 46.

19 Barron [3, 18], 25–7; Brooke and Keir [2, 6], 280–81; T. Baker, *Medieval London* (1970), 182–3.

20 Stow [1, 3], vol. 1, 310–11.

21 Williams [2, 24], 30–35, 80; Reynolds [2, 7], 78, 174.
22 Williams [2, 24], 52–72, 320.
23 Rothwell [3, 13], 320–21. The 1216 and 1217 versions of Magna Carta confirmed the clause; Williams [2, 24], 62–75, 109–48, 309–11; T. H. Lloyd, *Alien Merchants in England in the High Middle Ages* (Brighton, 1983), 9–10; Nightingale [2, 18], passim.
24 Nightingale [2, 18], 77–9.
25 H. T. Riley (trans. and ed.), *Chronicles of the Mayors and Sheriffs of London* (1863), 59. This is also in Rothwell [3, 13], 159–97.
26 Williams [2, 21], 223–7.
27 Williams [2, 24], 232–6; F. M. Powicke, *King Henry and the Lord Edward* (Oxford, 1947), 446–7; Riley [3, 25], 66; Unwin [2, 21], 63–5.
28 F. M. Powicke, *The Thirteenth Century* (Oxford, 1953), ch. 8; Williams [2, 24], 251–6; Barron [3, 6], 3–4.
29 Williams [2, 24], 254–6; M. Prestwich, *Edward I* (1988), 264–5.
30 Williams [2, 24], 36–8, 243–63; Powicke [3, 28], 625–31.
31 Williams [2, 24], 258–63.
32 Nightingale [2, 18], 43–8.
33 Nightingale [2, 18], 62–8.
34 Lloyd [2, 19], 63–4, 80, 123.
35 Nightingale [2, 18], 82–7, 96–100, 103–7.
36 Nightingale [2, 18], 111–12; E. M. Veale, 'The "Great Twelve". Mistery and fraternity in thirteenth-century London', *Historical Research* 64 (1991), 237–63.
37 E. M. Carus-Wilson, 'Trends in the export of English woollens in the fourteenth century', *Medieval Merchant Venturers* (1954), 239–64; Lloyd [2, 19], 60–98, 312–17; M. M. Postan, *The Medieval Economy and Society. An Economic History of Britain, 1100–1500* (1972), 214–18.
38 Nightingale [2, 18], 562; Lloyd [2, 19], 101–8; Lloyd [3, 23], 31–2.
39 Nightingale [2, 18], 206–16; Lloyd [2, 19], 101–16.
40 Stow [1, 3], vol. 1, 278–81; F. D. Logan, 'Thirteen London Jews and conversion to Christianity: problems of apostasy in the 1280s', *Bulletin of Historical Research* 65 (1972), 214–29; R. C. Stacey, '1240–60: a watershed in Anglo-Jewish relations?', *Bulletin of Historical Research* 61 (1988), 135–50.
41 Powicke [3, 28], 625–31; Williams [2, 24], 255–6; Rothwell [3, 13], 515–18; Lloyd [3, 23], 21–9.
42 Nightingale [2, 18], 207–8; Lloyd [3, 23], 52–3.
43 Nightingale [2, 18], 123–44.
44 Williams [2, 24], 282; Nightingale [2, 18], 144.
45 Riley [3, 25], 253; Williams [2, 24], 282–4; Unwin [2, 21], 67–71; Thrupp [3, 16], 66–71.
46 McKisack [2, 28], 81–3; Williams [2, 24], 285–98; McKisack, *The Fourteenth Century, 1307–1399* (Oxford, 1959), 83–94; Nightingale [2, 18], 144–57.

47 Nightingale [2, 18], 201–27; Carus-Wilson [3, 37], ch. 6; McKisack [3, 46], 350–56.

48 Powicke [3, 27], 306–10.

49 Barron [3, 16], 101–4; W. M. Ormrod, *The Reign of Edward III* (1990), 172–5.

50 P. Nightingale, 'Capitalists, crafts, and constitutional change in the late fourteenth century', *Past and Present* 124 (1989), 16–20; *Liber Albus, or the White Book of the City of London*, compiled in 1419 by John Carpenter, and translated and edited in 1861 by H. T. Riley, 37.

51 Nightingale [2, 18], 256–65.

52 A. Prescott, 'London in the Peasants' Revolt: a portrait gallery', *London Journal*, 7 (1981), 131–8; A. R. Myers (ed.), *English Historical Documents, 1327–1485* (1969), 127–43, *The Anonimalle Chronicle*; Nightingale [2, 18], 263–8.

53 Nightingale [3, 50]; Nightingale [2, 18], 270–91.

54 R. Bird, *The Turbulent London of Richard II* (1949), 30–43; Tait [3, 5], 310–16; Reynolds [2, 7], 173–5; Thrupp [3, 16], 75–85.

55 C. L. Kingsford, *Prejudice and Promise in Fifteenth-Century England* (Oxford, 1925), 107–8.

56 Nightingale [2, 18], 303–17; McKisack [3, 46], 450–58.

57 Nightingale [2, 18], 321–43.

58 C. M. Barron, 'The Quarrel of Richard II with London', in C. M. Barron, F. R. H. Du Boulay (eds.), *The Reign of Richard II* (1970), 173–201; Myers [3, 52], 165–7, the account of the Monk of Westminster; Nightingale [2, 18], 331–45.

59 McKisack [2, 25].

60 Nightingale [2, 18], 360–62.

61 C. M. Barron, 'Richard Whittington: the man behind the myth', in Hollaender and Kellaway [2, 20].

62 Nightingale [2, 18], 373–4.

63 Myers [3, 52], 215–18, *Henrici Quinta Gesti*.

64 H. T. Riley (ed.), *Memorials of London and London Life in the 13th, 14th and 15th Centuries* (1868), 603–5, 619–20, 628–9, 664–5.

65 Barron [3, 16], 101–4.

66 Barron [3, 16], 91–104; R. A. Griffiths, *The Reign of King Henry VI* (1981), 119, 393.

67 C. M. Barron, 'Ralph Holland and the London Radicals, 1438–1444', in R. Holt, G. Rosser (eds.), *The Medieval Town: A Reader in English Urban History, 1200–1540* (1990), 160–83.

68 Myers [3, 52], 264–6, *An English Chronicle*; Griffiths [3, 66], 611–41.

69 Griffiths [3, 66], 646–9, 678–84; Myers [3, 52], 267–8, Robert Bale's *Chronicle*.

70 Myers [3, 52], 279–81, R. Fabyan's *Chronicle*.

71 Griffiths [3, 66], 857–63; Barron [3, 16], 94–8.

72 Griffiths [3, 66], 804–8, 860–74; Barron [3, 16], 89.

73 Myers [3, 52], 315–16, Journal 8, f.7 of the City of London.

74 E. F. Jacob, *The Fifteenth Century, 1399–1485* (Oxford, 1961), 569.

75 McKisack [2, 28]; R. R. Sharpe, *London and the Kingdom* (1894–5), vol. 1, ch. 12; S. B. Chrimes, *Henry VII* (1972), 52; Myers [3, 52], 334–5, *The Great Chronicle of London.*

76 G. Rosser, *Medieval Westminster, 1200–1540* (1989), 167–76.

77 Rosser [3, 76], 97–114.

78 Rosser, 'London and Westminster: The suburb in the urban economy in the late Middle Ages', in J. A. F. Thompson (ed.), *Towns and Townspeople in the Fifteenth Century* (1988), 45–61.

79 T. F. Tout, 'The Beginnings of a Modern Capital: London and Westminster in the fourteenth century', *Proceedings of the British Academy* XI (1923), 4–10; H. G. Richardson, G. O. Sayles, *The Governance of Medieval England* (1963), 235–7.

80 Hunting [2, 36], 26–37; N. Saul, 'Richard II and Westminster Abbey', in J. Blair and B. Golding (eds.), *The Cloister and the World* (Oxford, 1996), 196–218; Sir N. Pevsner, *The Buildings of England: London*, vol. 1 (1957), 337–49.

81 Rosser [3, 76], 18–22.

82 W. L. Warren, *Henry II* (1977), 296–8, 330–32.

83 Tout [3, 79], 9–10; Rosser [3, 76], 26–30; Warren [3, 82], 330–32; Prestwich [3, 29], 442–4; Ormrod [3, 49], 60–68.

84 Ormrod [3, 49], 71.

85 A. Harding, *A Social History of the English Law* (1966), 130.

86 Myers [3, 52], 369–72; Stow [1, 3], vol. 2, 116–8; G. W. Thornbury, E. Walford, *Old and New London* (6 vols, 1883–5), vol. 3, 542–54, 560–63.

87 Ormrod [3, 49], 70–71; J. R. Lander, *Politics and Power in England, 1450–1509* (1976), 13.

88 Prestwich [3, 29], 134–69.

89 Ormrod [3, 49], 50–54, 74–7.

90 G. Mathew, *The Court of Richard II* (1968), ch. 2, 6, 8.

91 Griffiths [3, 66], ch. 13; D. Starkey (ed.), *The English Court from the Wars of the Roses to the Civil War* (1987), 41, 48.

92 Barron [3, 6], 1–4.

93 Barron [3, 6], 12.

94 Barron [3, 6], 4–11; D. Keene, 'Medieval London and its Region', *London Journal*, 14 (1989), 102.

4. Economy and Society

1 Keene [3, 94], 100–105; Williams [2, 24], 161–2; M. Postan, E. E. Rich (eds), *Cambridge Economic History of Europe*, vol. 2, *Trade and Industry in the Middle Ages* (Cambridge, 1952), 119–23.

2 M. K. James, 'Fluctuations in the Anglo-Gascon wine trade in the fourteenth century', *Economic History Review* 2nd series, 4 (1951), 170–96.

3 E. M. Veale, *The English Fur Trade in the Late Middle Ages* (Oxford, 1966), ch. 1 and pp. 69, 134; Barron, [3, 61]; M. K. James, *Studies in the Medieval Wine Trade* (1971), ch. 7.

4 Veale [4, 3], 4–5; Riley [3, 64], 267.

5 Lloyd [2, 19], 6.

6 Lloyd [2, 19], 50–59.

7 Lloyd [2, 19], 123, 131–3; Postan and Rich (eds) [4, 1], vol. 2, ch. 4; Carus-Wilson [3, 37], 239–64; Williams [2, 24], 111–15, 149–51.

8 C. G. A. Clay, *Economic Expansion and Social Change: England, 1500–1700* (Cambridge, 1984), vol. 3, 103–12; Postan and Rich (eds) [4, 1], vol. 2, 413–21; H. S. Cobb, 'Cloth export from London and Southampton in the later fifteenth and early sixteenth centuries: a revision', *Economic History Review* 31 (1978), 601–9; E. M. Carus-Wilson and O. Coleman, *England's Export Trade, 1275–1547* (1963), 111–13.

9 Carus-Wilson [3, 37], 143–82.

10 Keene [3, 94], 99.

11 R. S. Schofield, 'The geographical distribution of wealth in England, 1334–1649', *Economic History Review*, 2nd series, 18 (1965), 504; A. R. H. Barker, 'Changes in the later Middle Ages', in H. C. Darby (ed.), *A New Historical Geography of England* (Cambridge, 1973), 245–6; A. Dyer, *Decline and Growth in English Towns, 1400–1640* (1991).

12 Dyer [4, 11], 25–32.

13 James [4, 3], ch. 7.

14 M. Carlin [2,1], 149–62; S. Thrupp, 'Aliens in and around London in the Fifteenth Century', in Hollaender and Kellaway [2, 20], 251–72.

15 Lloyd [3, 23], 127–42; Carlin [4, 14], 161.

16 L. W. Cowie, 'The Steelyard of London', *History Today*, XXV, Dec 1975, 178–9, 308–10; Nightingale [2, 18], 484. There is a full account of the Hanseatic League in England in T. H. Lloyd, *England and the German Hanse, 1157–1611* (Cambridge, 1991).

17 Lloyd [3, 23], 166–7.

18 Jacob [3, 74], 348.

19 Nightingale [2, 18], 391–2.

20 C. H. Williams (ed.), *English Historical Documents, 1485–1558* (1967), 187–92.

21 J. L. Bolton, 'The City and the Crown, 1456–61', *London Journal* 12 (1986), 11–24; J. L. Bolton, *The Medieval English Economy, 1150–1500* (1980), 306–15; Griffiths [3, 66], 790–95.

22 Riley [3, 64], 144.

23 Unwin [2, 21], 36, 42–3, 47–50; Brooke and Keir [2, 6], 278–81.

24 Veale [4, 3], 237–63.

25 Williams [2, 24], 264–84, 319–20; Unwin [2, 21], chs. 5, 7.

26 J. Schofield, 'Medieval and Tudor domestic buildings in the City of London', in L. Grant (ed.), *Medieval Art, Architecture and Archaeology in London* (1990), 16–28.

27 Riley [3, 64]; Unwin [2, 21], ch. 7.

28 Riley [3, 64], 156–62, 280–81, 330–31, 348–9, 364–5.

29 Riley [3, 64], 330.

30 Douglas and Greenaway [2, 25], 1026.

31 E. Ekwall, *Two Early London Subsidy Rolls* (Lund, 1951), 82–7.

32 E. Ekwall, *Street-Names of the City of London* (Oxford, 1954).

33 I. W. Archer (ed.), *Hugh Alley's Caveat. The Markets of London in 1598* (1988), 1–11.

34 Riley [3, 64], 221–3; M. D. Lobel (ed.), *The British Atlas of Historic Towns*, vol. 3, *The City of London from Prehistoric Times* (1989), 55; Archer [4, 33], 3–5.

35 Riley [3, 64], 228.

36 D. Keene, 'Shops and shopping in medieval London', in Grant [4, 26], 29–46.

37 D. Keene, *Cheapside before the Great Fire* (1985), 16–18.

38 Stow [1, 3], vol. 1, 81–2.

39 E. M. Veale, 'Craftsmen and the economy of London in the fourteenth century', in Hollaender and Kellaway [2, 20], 138–41; Unwin [2, 21], 167, 370–71.

40 Ekwall [4, 31], 71–80; Williams [2, 24], 315–17; Keene [3, 94], 107.

41 Ekwall [4, 31], 70–71.

42 J. Stow [1, 3], vol. 2, p. 81; Myers [3, 52], 782–4, Sir Walter Manny's foundation charter for the London Charterhouse, 1371; J. Hatcher, *Plague, Population, and the English Economy, 1348–1530* (1970); M. Keen, *English Society in the Later Middle Ages, 1348–1500* (1990), 27–33; Nightingale [2, 18], 194–7.

43 W. Langland, *Piers Plowman*, passus XX.

44 Thrupp [3, 16], 41–52; Williams [2, 24], 315–17.

45 Keene [3, 94]; D. Keene, 'A new study of London before the Great Fire', *Urban History Yearbook* (1984), 11–21; Keene [4, 37]; B. M. S. Campbell, J. A. Galloway, D. Keene, M. Murphy, *A Medieval Capital and its Grain Supply: Agrarian Production and Distribution in the London Region, c. 1300* (1993), 9–11, 172–3.

46 M. Honeybourne, 'The Leper hospitals of the London area', *Transactions of the Middlesex Archaeological Society*, 21, part 1 (1967).

47 Veale [4, 3], 92–100.

48 Clay [4, 8], vol. 2, 10.

49 Riley [3, 64], 56, 82, 245–7.

50 J. E. Thorold Rogers, *Six Centuries of Work and Wages* (1903), 326–7; Hatcher [4, 42], 47–52; Thrupp [3, 16], 112–14; C. Dyer, *Standards of Living in the Later Middle Ages* (Cambridge, 1989), 210, 229–33.

51 Riley [3, 64], 247–8, 306, 495, 542–3, 609–12; J. Burnett, *History of the Cost of Living* (Harmondsworth, 1969), 21–4; Thrupp [3, 16], 112–15.

52 Riley [3, 64], 86–90; A. H. Thomas, P. E. Jones (eds.), *Calendar of Plea and Memoranda Rolls of the City of London, 1323–64, 1364–81* (1924–61), vol. 1, xi.

53 Riley [3, 64], 3–19; R. R. Sharpe (ed.), *Calendar of Coroners' Rolls, 1300–1378*, xxi–xxiv. A gisarm was a six-foot staff with a long hooked blade for pulling mounted men to the ground.

54 Stow [1, 3], vol. 1, 99–100; Riley [3, 64], 21, 172–4; A. R. Myers, *London in the Age of Chaucer* (Norman, Oklahoma, 1972), 70–72.

55 G. Rosser, 'Sanctuary and social negotiation in medieval England', in Blair and Golding [3, 80]; Rosser [3, 76], 155–8, 218–19; M. Weinbaum (ed.), *The London Eyre of 1276* (1976), London Record Society, xv–xvi; anonymous article on 'Sanctuary' in *Encyclopaedia Britannica*, 11th edn (1910–11), vol. 24, 129–31.

56 Weinbaum [4, 55]; W. Kellaway, 'The Coroner in Medieval London', in Hollaender and Kellaway [2, 20], 75–91; Riley [3, 64], 3–17; Sharpe [4, 53], vii–xxv.

57 Stow [1, 3] vol. 1, 24; Baker [3, 19], 29.

58 Riley [3, 25], 184–5.

59 Riley [3, 25], 179–87.

60 H. M. Chew, W. Kellaway (eds.), *The London Assize of Nuisance, 1301–1431* (1973), documents 325, 326, 617.

61 Weinbaum [4, 55], 91–7.

62 Riley [3, 64], 33, 141–2, 166–7, 221, 228, 405–6, 532–3.

63 Thrupp [3, 16], 92–7; Myers [4, 54], 91–7; Bird [3, 54], ch. 5; Riley [3, 64], 268, 467, 481.

64 Keene [3, 94], 104; Riley [3, 64], 312–14; Archer [4, 33], 5–6; Sharpe [3, 16], *Letter-Book H*, 242–4 (ff. 178–178b).

65 Stow [1, 3], vol. 1, 11–19.

66 M. Honeybourne, 'The Fleet and its neighbourhood in early and medieval times', *London Topographical Record* 19 (1947), 13–67; Stow [1, 3], vol. 1, 12–14; Myers [4, 54], 59–65.

67 W. R. Prest, *The Inns of Court under Elizabeth and the Early Stuarts, 1590–1640* (1972), 1–18; Lobel [4, 34], vol. 3, 52.

68 K. McDonnell, *Medieval London Suburbs* (1978), 61, 77–83, 95–103.

69 Stow [1, 3], vol. 1, 127.

70 Carlin [2, 1], 19–22, 106–7.

71 Carlin [2, 1], 209–29; Stow [1, 3], vol. 2, 54–5, E. J. Burford, *The Orrible Synne* (1973), 51–6; Ekwall [4, 32], 122, 164–6.

72 D. J. Johnson, *Southwark and the City* (Oxford, 1969), chs. 3, 4; Carlin [2, 1], 119–27.

73 Douglas and Greenaway [2, 25], 1028–30, quoting W. Fitzstephen, *Life of Thomas Becket*.

74 Carlin [2, 1], 191–200; Veale [3, 36], 237–63; Thrupp [3, 16], 42.

75 G. Chaucer, *Canterbury Tales* (Oxford, 1988), General Prologue, lines 753–6; Carlin [2, 1], 193.

76 W. Langland, *Piers the Plowman*, B-Text, ed. A. V. C. Schmidt, 53–4; Stow [1, 3], vol. 1, 83.

77 Thrupp [3, 16], 169.
78 Chaucer [4, 75], lines 4375–84.
79 Myers [3, 52], 1067, London fire and watch regulations, 1385, 1410.
80 Myers [3, 52], 165–6, *The Monk of Westminster's Chronicle*.
81 W. Kent (ed.), *An Encyclopaedia of London* (1987), 534; M. Berlin, 'Civic ceremony in early modern London', *Urban History Yearbook* (1986), 18–20.
82 Stow [1, 3], vol. 1, 104, 93–5.
83 Thrupp [3, 16], 131–6, 139–42; J. Schofield, *The Building of London from the Conquest to the Great Fire* (1984), 86–95; J. Schofield, 'Medieval and Tudor buildings in the City of London', in Grant [4, 26], 16–28.
84 Thrupp [3, 16], 157.
85 Riley [3, 64], 557–8.
86 Myers [3, 52], 835; C. M. Barron, 'The expansion of education in fifteenth-century London', in Blair and Golding [3, 80], 239–45.
87 Barron [4, 86], in Blair and Golding [3, 80], 241–3.
88 S. Brigden, *London and the Reformation* (Oxford, 1988), 87.
89 Barron [4, 86], in Blair and Golding [3, 80], 219–45. The quotation is on p. 230.
90 Stow [1, 3], vol. 1, 73–5; Barron [4, 86], in Blair and Golding [3, 80], 220–24; M. E. Bryant, *The London Experience of Secondary Education* (1986), 1–11; R. W. Chambers, *Thomas More* (1967. 1st published 1935), 51–4.
91 J. A. F. Thompson, 'The clergy and laity in London, 1376–1531' (1960), 192; Stow [1, 3], vol. 2, 143–5; M. Carlin, 'Medieval English Hospitals', in L. Granshaw, R. Porter (eds.), *The Hospital in History* (1989), 21–39.
92 Stow [1, 3], vol. 1, 105–12; Thompson [4, 91], 147–93; Thrupp [3, 16], 177–80.
93 Thompson [4, 91], 13, 207–30; S. Brigden [4, 88], 47; C. Burgess, 'Shaping the parish: St Mary at Hill, London, in the fifteenth century', in Blair and Golding [3, 80], 246–86.
94 C. M. Barron, 'The parish fraternities of medieval London', in C. M. Barron, C. Harper-Bill (eds.), *The Church in Pre-Reformation Society* (Woodbridge, 1985), 13–37.
95 Brooke and Keir [2, 6], 338–59; Myers [4, 54], 80–84, 136–43; Chaucer [4, 75], General Prologue, lines 505–15.
96 Davis [2, 37], xxxiii, 9–26; Brooke and Keir [2, 6], 310–12; M. Honeybourne, 'The extent and value of the property in London and Southwark occupied by the Religious Houses, the inns of the bishops and abbots and the churches and churchyards before the Dissolution of the Monasteries', 54–6 (London University MA thesis, 1929).
97 Honeybourne [4, 96]; Brooke and Keir [2, 6], 293–337; Carlin [2, 1], 67–85; Douglas and Greenaway [2, 25], 1016–21, Henry I's charter for Holy Trinity, Aldgate, and the foundation narrative of Holy Trinity, Aldgate.
98 Thompson [4, 91], 197–205; Honeybourne [4, 96], passim; Stow [1, 3], vol. 1, 147–9, 361–2.

99 Brigden [4, 88], 73.
100 Riley [3, 64], 98; Honeybourne [4, 96], 8–9; Keene [4, 37], 6–7.
101 Honeybourne [4, 96], 9.
102 Thomas More, *Dialogue of Heresies*, quoted in Thompson [4, 91], 268; Thrupp [3, 16], 186; Brigden [4, 88], ch. 1.
103 Myers [3, 52], 693, 706–7, 718–21. The quote is from 'Gregory's Chronicle'; Thompson [4, 91], ch. 4.
104 W. Page (ed.), *Victoria History of London* (1909), vol. 1, 211–15; Myers [3, 52], 698–9, quoting T. Walsingham, *Historia Anglicana*.
105 K. B. McFarlane, *The Origins of Religious Dissent in England* (also published as *John Wycliffe and the Beginnings of English Nonconformity*) (1952), 148–50, 171–95.
106 Brigden [4, 88], 162–3.

LONDON FROM THE REFORMATION TO THE GREAT PLAGUE, 1520–1665

5. REFORMATION, POPULATION AND THE PLAGUE

1 A. G. Dickens, *The English Reformation* (1964), 49, 132–7; J. Ridley, *Henry VIII* (1984), 102–4.
2 Williams [4, 20], 652–60, 660–69.
3 Dickens [5, 1], 131–47; Brigden [4, 88], 98–103, 179–84.
4 Brigden [4, 88], 208–15.
5 Brigden [4, 88], 380–86; Thompson [4, 91], 14–15.
6 Dom D. Knowles, *The Religious Orders in England* (3 vols., 1948, 1955, 1959), vol. 3, ch. 19, 230–36.
7 Brigden [4, 88], 240–41, 268–71.
8 Brigden [4, 88], 315–77; Williams [4, 20], 837–8.
9 Brigden [4, 88], 398–422.
10 Brigden [4, 88], 426–69.
11 Stow [1, 3] for these changes.
12 E. J. Davis, 'The transformation of London' (1924), in R. W. Seton-Watson (ed.), *Tudor Studies Presented to A. F. Pollard*.
13 Davis [5, 12], 298–303; C. Rose, 'Politics and the London Royal Hospitals, 1683–92', in Granshaw and Porter [4, 91], 123–48.
14 I. Sutherland, 'When was the Great Plague? Mortality in London, 1563–1665', in D. V. Glass, R. Revelle (eds.), *Population and Social Change* (1972), 290.
15 V. Harding, 'The population of London, 1550–1700: A review of the published evidence', *London Journal* 15 (1990), 111–28.
16 A. L. Beier, R. Finlay (eds.), *London, 1500–1700* (Harlow, 1986), 37–59; J. Boulton, *Neighbourhood and Society: A London Suburb in the Seventeenth*

Century (Cambridge, 1987), 14–40, for a full discussion of Southwark's population growth.

17 Clay [4, 8], vol. 1, 2–4; Beier and Finlay [5, 16], 39.

18 E. A. Wrigley, R. S. Schofield, *The Population History of England, 1541–1871: a Reconstruction* (1989), 166–9.

19 Beier and Finlay [5, 16], 224.

20 Wrigley and Schofield [5, 18], 166–9.

21 R. Finlay, *Population and Metropolis. The Demography of London, 1580–1640* (Cambridge, 1981), 67–9.

22 P. Clark, P. Slack, *English Towns in Transition* (Oxford, 1976), 92–4; S. L. Rappaport, *Worlds within Worlds. Structures of Life in Sixteenth-Century London* (Cambridge, 1981), 76–81; G. D. Ramsay, 'The recruitment and fortunes of some London Freemen in the mid-sixteenth century', *Economic History Review* 31 (1978), 528–9; D. V. Glass, 'Socio-economic Status and Occupations in the City of London at the end of the Seventeenth Century', in Beier and Finlay [5, 16], 243.

23 R. H. Tawney, E. Power, *Tudor Economic Documents* (3 vols, 1924), vol. 3, 431, 438.

24 T. R. Forbes, 'By what disease or casualty: the changing face of death in London', in C. Webster (ed.), *Health, Medicine and Mortality in the Sixteenth Century* (1979), 121.

25 G. Salgado (ed.), *Cony-Catchers and Bawdy Baskets* (1972), 159.

26 Tawney and Power [5, 23], vol. 2, 337–9; A. L. Beier, *Masterless Men* (1985), ch. 8; P. Slack, 'Vagrants and vagrancy in England, 1598–1664', *Economic History Review*, XXVII (1974); A. L. Beier, 'Vagrants and the Social Order in Elizabethan England', *Past and Present*, 64 (1974); I. W. Archer, *The Pursuit of Stability: Social Relations in Elizabethan London* (Cambridge, 1991), 204–11.

27 Tawney and Power [5, 23], vol. 3, 416–18.

28 Tawney and Power [5, 23], vol. 2, 308.

29 A. L. Beier, 'Social Problems in Elizabethan London', in J. Barry (ed.), *The Tudor and Stuart Town, 1530–1688* (1990), 121–38; Beier [5, 26], 164–8; Archer [5, 26], 238–41.

30 Archer [5, 26], 165–79.

31 Archer [5, 26], 181–6; V. Pearl, 'Puritans and Poor Relief', in K. Thomas, D. H. Pennington, *Puritans and Revolutionaries* (1978), 207–8.

32 M. J. Power, 'East and west in early-modern London', in W. W. Ives, R. J. Knecht, J. J. Scarisbrick (eds.), *Wealth and Power in Tudor England* (1978), 180–81; Boulton [5, 16], 81–96; Archer [5, 26], 182–97.

33 Tawney and Power [5, 23], vol. 3, 430.

34 Pearl [5, 31], 206–32.

35 Beier and Finlay [5, 16], 95–105; Archer [5, 26], 211–15.

36 Sutherland [5, 14], 287–320.

37 P. Slack, *The Impact of Plague in Tudor and Stuart England* (1985), 151–69; Beier and Finlay [5, 16], 62–4.

38 Slack [5, 37], 199–216, 276–82, 304–6; Overall, W. H., Overall, H. C. (eds), *Analytical Index to the Series of Records known as the Remembrancia, 1579–1664*, 330–48.
39 Slack [5, 37], 217–19.
40 Slack [5, 37], 299; Beier and Finlay [5, 16], 60–81; Overall and Overall [5, 38], 330–49.
41 Entries in S. Pepys' *Diary*, May 1665–January 1666.
42 A. Appleby, 'The Disappearance of Plague: A Continuing Puzzle', *Economic History Review* 33 (1980), 161–75.
43 Overall and Overall [5, 38], 330, 349.
44 P. Slack [5, 37], 313–26; P. Slack, 'The Disappearance of Plague: An Alternative View', *Economic History Review* 34 (1981), 469–76.

6. STABILITY, PROSPERITY AND GROWTH

1 Tawney and Power [5, 23], vol. 3, 82–90; Brigden [4, 88], 130–32; S. Brigden, 'Youth and the English Reformation', in P. Slack, *Rebellion, Popular Protest and the Social Order in Early Modern England* (1984), 77–107; Rappaport [5, 22], 6–17; Archer [5, 26], 3–5.
2 Brigden [4, 88], 534–45.
3 Archer [5, 26], 33–44; J. E. Neale, *Queen Elizabeth I* (1960), 376–9.
4 Archer [5, 26]; Rappaport [5, 22]; V. Pearl, 'Change and stability in seventeenth-century London', *London Journal* 5 (1979), 3–34; F. F. Foster, *The Politics of Stability: A portrait of the Rulers in Elizabethan London* (1977); Boulton [5, 16].
5 Archer [5, 26], 45–52.
6 E. H. Phelps Brown, S. V. Hopkins, 'Seven Centuries of the Prices of Consumables', in E. M. Carus-Wilson, *Essays in Economic History* (1962), vol. 2, 194–5; Rappaport [5, 22], 123–53; S. Rappaport, 'Social structure and mobility in sixteenth-century London', *London Journal* 9 (1983), 125–9.
7 F. J. Fisher, 'The Development of the London Food Market, 1540–1640', in Carus-Wilson [6, 6], vol. 1, 135–51.
8 Fisher [6, 7]; J. Thirsk (ed.), *The Agrarian History of England and Wales* (Cambridge, 1967), vol. 4, 507–17; Beier and Finlay [5, 16], ch. 6; Archer [4, 33], 1–20.
9 M. J. Power, 'A "Crisis" reconsidered: social and economic dislocation in London in the 1590s', *London Journal* 12 (1986), 134–45.
10 Archer [4, 33], 11.
11 M. J. Power, 'London and the control of the "crisis" of the 1590s', *History* 70 (1985), 371–85.
12 Archer [5, 26], 1–6, 198–203; Overall and Overall [5, 38], 372–91.
13 Rappaport [6, 6], 109–14; Rappaport [5, 22], 49–53; Pearl [6, 4], 13–14; Boulton [5, 16], 151.
14 V. Pearl, *London and the Outbreak of the Puritan Revolution* (Oxford, 1961), ch. 2; Foster [6, 4], ch. 2.

15 Rappaport [6, 6]; Rappaport [5, 22], ch. 6; Pearl [6, 4], part two; Archer [5, 26], 63–8.

16 Archer [5, 26], 68–74, 83–9.

17 S. Rappaport, 'Social Structure and Mobility', *London Journal* 10 (1984); Rappaport [5, 22], ch. 8.

18 Archer [5, 26], ch. 4.

19 Veale [4, 3], 186–90.

20 Rappaport [5, 22], 110–17; G. D. Ramsay, *The City of London in International Politics at the Accession of Elizabeth Tudor* (Manchester, 1975), 41–4.

21 T. F. Reddaway, 'The Livery Companies of Tudor London', *History* 51 (1966), 287–99; Unwin [2, 21], chs. 13–15.

22 Tawney and Power [5, 23], vol. 1, 378–83; Rappaport [5, 22], 110–17.

23 Finlay [5, 21], 66–7.

24 Beier and Finlay [5, 16], ch. 5; Rappaport [5, 22], 92–4.

25 Stow [1, 3], vol. 2, 71–2; McDonnell [4, 68], ch. 5; Power [5, 32]; East London History Group, 'The population of Stepney in the early seventeenth century', in M. Drake (ed.), *Population Studies from Parish Registers* (1982); M. J. Power, 'East London housing in the seventeenth century', in P. Clark, P. Slack (eds.), *Crisis and Order in English Towns, 1500–1700* (1972), 237–62.

26 Power [6, 25].

27 Johnson [4, 72], ch. 8.

28 Boulton [5, 16], ch. 8.

29 Boulton [5, 16], ch. 5 and 247–61.

30 Boulton [5, 16], chs. 4, 6; Rappaport [5, 22], 162–71.

31 Boulton [5, 16], 263.

32 M. J. Power, 'Shadwell: The development of a London suburban community in the seventeenth century', *London Journal* 4 (1978).

33 Johnson [4, 72], part 4.

34 Boulton [5, 16], ch. 10.

35 Boulton [5, 16], 275–88.

36 Pearl [6, 14], 29–34; N. G. Brett-James, *The Growth of Stuart London* (1935), 226; R. Ashton, *The City and the Court, 1603–43* (Cambridge, 1979), 163–5.

37 Pearl [6, 14], 33–7; Brett-James [6, 36], 228–38; Ashton [6, 36], 165–7.

38 Brett-James [6, 36], 69.

39 Brett-James [6, 36], 77.

40 E. Thomson (ed.), *The Chamberlain Letters* (1966), 31 (27 June 1602).

41 Brett-James [6, 36], ch. 5; Power [5, 32].

42 Brett-James [6, 36], 89–90.

43 Brett-James [6, 36], 116; Pearl [6, 14], 13; P. Youngblood, 'Royal Favouritism in London Building', *History Today*, August 1981.

44 J. Summerson, *Georgian London* (1962), 28.

45 Dyer [4, 11], 32; P. Corfield, 'Urban development in England and Wales in the sixteenth and seventeenth centuries', in D. C. Coleman, A. H. John (eds.),

Trade, Government and Economy in Pre-Industrial England. Essays Presented to F. J. Fisher (1976), 224–7, 245.

46 Ramsay [6, 20], 44–5.

47 Ramsay [6, 20], 40–41; Tawney and Power [5, 23], vol. 1, 184–5.

48 Tawney and Power [5, 23], vol. 2, 49–50.

49 Ramsay [6, 20], 48–50, 61–7.

50 G. D. Ramsay, 'The undoing of the Italian merchant community in sixteenth-century London', in N. B. Harte, K. G. Ponting (eds.), *Textile History and Economic History* (1973), 23–39.

51 Ramsay [6, 20], 51–3

52 F. Braudel, *The Wheels of Commerce* (1982), 98–100; Sir W. Besant, *London in the Time of the Tudors* (1904), 220–22.

53 C. Hill, *The Intellectual Origins of the English Revolution* (1972), 34–67; C. Webster, *The Great Instauration* (1975), 51–7.

54 Ashton [6, 36], 83–98; F. J. Fisher, 'London's export trade in the early seventeenth century', *Economic History Review*, 2nd series, 3 (1950), 65.

55 Tawney and Power [5, 23], vol. 2, 88–9.

56 Clay [4, 8], vol. 2, ch. 9; B. Dietz, 'Overseas Trade and Metropolitan Growth', in Beier and Finlay [5, 16], 121–9.

57 F. J. Fisher, 'London as an "engine of economic growth"', in P. Clark (ed.), *The Early Modern Town. A Reader* (1976), 210–11.

58 R. Davis, *The Rise of the English Shipping Industry in the Seventeenth and Eighteenth Centuries* (1962), 259–62; B. Dietz [6, 56], 127–9.

59 B. Supple, *Commercial Crisis and Change in England, 1600–42: a Study in the Instability of a Merchant Community* (Cambridge, 1959), 52–61; Fisher [6, 54].

60 Supple [6, 59], ch. 2.

61 Supple [6, 59], 64–72, 240–42; R. Brenner, 'The Civil War politics of London's merchant community', *Past and Present* 58 (1973), 54–5, 64.

7. THE PLEASURES OF LONDON

1 J. D. Wilson, *Life in Shakespeare's England* (1944), 125–6.

2 M. Warner (ed.), *The Image of London. Views by Travellers and Emigrés, 1550–1920* (1987), 102–10; F. Barker, P. Jackson, *London. 2,000 Years of a City and its People* (1974, 1983) reproduces Wynegaerde's panorama with an explanation of what it shows.

3 F. Barker, P. Jackson, *The History of London in Maps* (1990), 12–19; A. Prockter, R. Taylor, *The A to Z of Elizabethan London* (Lympne Castle, Kent, 1979), v–vii: this book reproduces all three maps and explains the relationships between them; J. L. Howgego, *Printed Maps of London, circa 1553–1850* (Folkestone, 1979), i–xv: catalogues and describes every known map.

4 C. M. Barron, C. Coleman, C. Gobbi (eds.), 'The London Journal of Alessandro Magno, 1562', *London Journal* 9, ii (1983), 137–52.

5 F. J. Fisher, 'The development of London as a centre of conspicuous

consumption', in Carus-Wilson [6, 6], 202–4; L. Stone, *The Crisis of the Aristocracy, 1558–1641*, abridged edn. (Oxford, 1967), 189; S. R. Gardiner, *History of England, 1603–1642* (1883), vol. 7, 240.

6 W. Prest, 'The legal education of the gentry at the Inns of Court, 1560–1640', *Past and Present* 38 (1967), 20–39.

7 L. Stone, 'The residential development of the West End of London in the seventeenth century', in B. C. Malament, *After the Reformation* (Philadelphia, 1980), 177–84; H. J. Dyos, D. H. Aldcroft, *British Transport* (1974), 31–7.

8 Keith Thomas, *Religion and the Decline of Magic* (1971), 362–82.

9 Stone [7, 5], 257–8; Dover Wilson [7, 1], 161–5.

10 D. Davis, *A History of Shopping* (1966), 55.

11 Stow [1, 3], vol. 2, 210.

12 A. Gurr, *Playgoing in Shakespeare's London* (Cambridge, 1987), 115.

13 A. Harbage, *Shakespeare's Audience* (New York, 1941); A. J. Cook, *The Privileged Playgoers of Shakespeare's London, 1576–1642* (Princeton, 1981); Gurr [7, 12]; A. Gurr, *The Shakespearean Stage, 1574–1642* (Cambridge, 1992).

14 Cook [7, 13], 273; Tawney and Power [5, 23], vol. 1, 115–17.

15 Wilson [7, 1], 226–7.

16 Gurr [7, 12], 218, 227, 235.

17 Wilson [7, 1], 212.

18 Gurr [7, 12], 215.

19 Wilson [7, 1], 211.

20 Gurr [7, 12], 230.

21 R. Latham (ed.), *The Shorter Pepys* (1986), 723.

22 Stone [7, 5], 183–91; D. Loades, *The Tudor Court* (1986), chs. 3, 5; P. Zagorin, *The Court and the Country* (1969), 45.

23 Stone [7, 5], ch. 8.

8. LONDON AND THE CIVIL WAR

1 Lord Clarendon, *History of the Rebellion* (1839 ed.), 85.

2 Gardiner [7, 5], vol. 6, 319.

3 Foster [6, 4], ch. 8; Pearl [6, 14], 69–71

4 Pearl [6, 14], ch. 3.

5 P. Burke, 'Popular culture in seventeenth-century London', *London Journal* 3 (1977), 149.

6 Brenner [6, 61], 72–85; Ashton [6, 36], ch. 4.

7 P. S. Seaver, *Wallington's World: A Puritan Artisan in Seventeenth-Century London* (1985), 158, 166; C. Russell (ed.), *The Origins of the English Civil War* (1973), ch. 5; B. Manning, *The English People and the English Revolution, 1640–49* (1976), ch. 2.

8 Clarendon [8, 1], 61.

9 H. Trevor Roper, *Archbishop Laud* (1963), 388–9; Pearl [6, 14], 107–8.

10 Clarendon [8, 1], 72.

11 D. Cressy, *Literacy and the Social Order* (1980), 73, 121–3, 128–9, 144–7; Burke [8, 5], 154.

12 Manning [8, 7], 104–6, 80.

13 S. R. Smith, 'The London apprentices as seventeenth-century adolescents', *Past and Present* 61 (1973), 154–61; Burke [8, 5], 156–9.

14 Clarendon [8, 1], 87; for the petition, see S. R. Gardiner (ed.), *Constitutional Documents of the Puritan Revolution* (Oxford, 1906), 137–44.

15 Gardiner [8, 14], 109–10.

16 Manning [8, 7], 57.

17 Pearl [6, 14], 122–30; Gardiner [7, 5], vol. 10, 80–86.

18 Gardiner [7, 5], vol. 10, 118.

19 Manning [8, 7], 111; J. Bowle, *Charles the First* (1975), 213; Pearl [6, 14], 142.

20 Manning [8, 7], 112.

21 Bowle [8, 19], 214; Zagorin [7, 22], 294–5; C. Russell, *Crisis of Parliaments* (Oxford, 1971), 339.

22 Manning [8, 7], 215–16.

23 V. Pearl, 'London's Counter-Revolution', in G. E. Aylmer (ed.), *The Interregnum* (1972), 38–40.

24 C. H. Firth, *Cromwell's Army* (4th edn, 1962. 1st published 1902), 10–11, 17.

25 Pearl [6, 14], 262–5; Manning [8, 7], 216–18; Brett-James [6, 36], 268–95.

26 Manning [8, 7], 216; Clarendon [8, 1], 458; S. R. Gardiner, *History of the Great Civil War 1642–1649* (4 vols, 1893), vol. 1, 202–18.

27 Gardiner [8, 26], vol. 2, 5–6.

28 Pearl [8, 23], 29–56.

29 C. Hill, *The World Turned Upside Down* (1975), 73–4, 112; B. Capp, *The 5th Monarchy Men* (1972), 76, 271–4.

30 A. L. Morton, *Freedom in Arms. A Selection of Leveller Writings* (1975), 50–51, 350.

31 D. Underdown, *Pride's Purge* (Oxford, 1971), 94–102.

32 Underdown [8, 31], 106–80; J. E. Farnell, 'The Usurpation of Honest London Householders: Barebones Parliament', *English Historical Review* 82 (1967), 24–46.

33 Bowle [8, 19], 335.

34 Farnell [8, 32]; Underdown [8, 31], 304, 325–7, 340.

35 P. Scholes (ed.), *Oxford Companion to Music* (Oxford, 1938), 177, 579, 637, 739, 762, 766, 1007.

36 W. Bray (ed.), *The Diary and Correspondence of John Evelyn* (1818), entries for 10 May 1654, 15 September 1657, and 20 May 1658; C. Hibbert, B. Weinreb (eds.), *The London Encyclopaedia* (1983), 809; K. Thomas, 'The Puritans and adultery', in D. H. Pennington, K. Thomas (eds.), *Puritans and Revolutionaries*, 257–82; Pearl [6, 4], 26.

37 T. Liu, *Puritan London: a Study of Religion and Society in the City Parishes* (Newark, Delaware, 1986).

38 A. Woolrych, 'Last Quests for a Settlement, 1657–60', in Aylmer [8, 23], 201.
39 T. Harris, *London Crowds in the Reign of Charles II: Politics and Propaganda from the Restoration until the Exclusion Crisis* (Cambridge, 1987), ch. 3.

LONDON, 1660–1815

9. FIRE, REBUILDING AND SUBURBAN GROWTH

1   Thomas [7, 8], 17–20; P. Brimblecombe, *The Big Smoke* (1987), 29–36; C. Davidson, *A Woman's Work is Never Done* (1982), chs. 3–5.
2   G. Milne, *The Great Fire of London* (1986), 29.
3   Latham [7, 21], 660–62; G. Huehns (ed.), *Selections from Clarendon* (Oxford, 1955), 423.
4   H. and P. Massingham (eds.), *The London Anthology* (n.d.), 165–6: from *Memoirs of the Verney Family*.
5   Milne [9, 2], 43.
6   Bray [8, 36], 284–9.
7   Huehns [9, 3], 419; T. F. Reddaway, *The Rebuilding of London after the Great Fire* (1940), 66, 245.
8   Reddaway [9, 7], 68–70, 171–81.
9   P. Borsay, 'The London connection: cultural diffusion and the eighteenth-century provincial town', *London Journal* 19 (1994), 21–35; Reddaway [9, 7], 68–82.
10 Reddaway [9, 7], 72–7, 91–102, 144–51.
11 Reddaway [9, 7], 181–9.
12 Summerson [6, 44], 59.
13 Reddaway [9, 7], ch. 8.
14 Summerson [6, 44], ch. 4.
15 Reddaway [9, 7], 107, 282, 296–8; Archer [4, 33].
16 Reddaway [9, 7], 300–308.
17 D. Defoe, *A Tour through England and Wales* (2 vols, 1928 edn, introduced by G. D. H. Cole), vol. 1, 336.
18 J. Swift, *Journal to Stella* (ed. H. Williams, 1948), vol. 1, 48; L. Stone, J. C. F. Stone, *An Open Elite? England 1540–1880* (1984), 252–4.
19 Stone [7, 7], 174–5, 180, 194–5; M. H. Port, 'West End Palaces: the aristocratic town house in London, 1730–1830', *London Journal*, 20 (1995), 18–43, discusses the aristocrat's choice of a London house.
20 Summerson [6, 44], 39–41.
21 Summerson [6, 44], ch. 3; Brett-James [6, 36], ch. 15.
22 Brett-James [6, 36], 339–40.
23 Summerson [6, 44], ch. 5.

24 Figures from London County Council, *London Statistics* (1925–6), 24–5, based on 1900 borough boundaries.

25 H. J. Dyos, *Victorian Suburb: a Study of the Growth of Camberwell* (Leicester, 1961), ch. 2; London Topographical Society: *The A to Z of Regency London* (1985) (Richard Horwood's map).

26 F. Sheppard (ed.), *The Survey of London* (1977), vol. 39, 6–33.

27 E. B. Chancellor, *The History of the Squares of London* (1907), 43; Summerson [6, 44], 105–11.

28 Summerson [6, 44], ch. 11; J. Landers, *Death and the Metropolis: Studies in the Demographic History of London, 1670–1830* (Cambridge, 1993), 53–9, discusses the validity of Summerson's argument that 'waves' of building in London generally occurred in peacetime.

29 Summerson [6, 44], 125–46.

30 Summerson [6, 44], 138–40; Pevsner [3, 80], 293–6.

31 *Spectator*, no. 43, 12 June 1712.

32 G. Rudé, *Hanoverian London* (1971), 25–6, 87.

33 P. Corfield, *The Impact of English Towns* (Oxford, 1982), 78; Summerson [6, 44], 167–8.

34 Port [9, 19], 19–20.

35 Chancellor [9, 27], 40, 64; Sheppard [9, 26] 86–7.

36 Sheppard [9, 26], 83–6; L. D. Schwarz, 'Social class and social geography: the middle classes in London at the end of the eighteenth century', in *Social History* 7 (1982).

37 P. Earle, *The Making of the English Middle Class: Business, Society and Family Life in London, 1660–1730* (1989), 80–81; Rudé [9, 32], 57–8; L. D. Schwarz, 'Income distribution and social structure in London in the late eighteenth century', *Economic History Review* 32 (1979).

38 Earle [9, 37], 60–75, 354; G. Holmes, *Augustan England: Professions, State and Society, 1680–1730* (1982), ch. 5.

39 Holmes [9, 38], ch. 6; R. Porter, *Disease, Medicine and Society in England, 1550–1860* (1987), chs. 1–4; Hill [6, 53], 74–84.

40 J. Boswell, *London Journal* (1950), 162–250, passim. Stone's *Family, Sex and Marriage* (1977) has a long account of Boswell's sex life.

41 Holmes [9, 38], 218–23; Chancellor [9, 27], 55, 164, 202, 214.

42 H. Walpole, *Selected Letters* (ed. W. Hadley, 1926), 513–14.

10. Population and Health

1 J. Boswell, *The Life of Samuel Johnson* (Everyman edn, 2 vols, 1906), vol. 1, 261.

2 King's work is published in J. Thirsk, J. P. Cooper (eds.), *17th Century Economic Documents* (Oxford, 1972), 770–90: his methods are discussed by D. V. Glass, 'Two papers on Gregory King', in D. V. Glass, D. E. C. Eversley, *Population in History* (1965), 159–220; P. E. Jones and A. V. Judges, 'London

population in the late seventeenth century', *Economic History Review* 6 (1935), 45–63; V. Harding, 'The population of London, 1550–1700', *London Journal* 15 (1990), 111–28.

3 E. A. Wrigley, 'A simple model of London's importance in changing English society and economy, 1650–1750', *Past and Present* 37 (1967), 44.

4 Wrigley and Schofield [5, 18], 79.

5 J. Krause, 'The changing adequacy of English registration, 1690–1837', in Glass and Eversley [10, 2], 385.

6 M. D. George, *London Life in the Eighteenth Century* (1925), introduction, ch. 1 and p. 397.

7 Wrigley and Schofield [5, 18], 166–70; L. D. Schwarz, *London in the Age of Industrialisation: Entrepreneurs, Labour Force and Living Conditions* (Cambridge, 1992), 128–31.

8 Landers [9, 28], 194–5.

9 Wrigley and Schofield [5, 18], 77–83, 166–70.

10 Wrigley [10, 3], 46–9.

11 P. Earle, *A City Full of People: Men and Women of London, 1650–1750* (1994), 45–9.

12 George [10, 6], 118.

13 Landers [9, 28], 46–9.

14 Earle [10, 11], 50–51.

15 George [10, 6], 157.

16 C. Wilson, *England's Apprenticeship, 1603–1763* (1965), 195–6; N. Merriman (ed.), *The Peopling of London* (1993), 43–6.

17 Merriman [10, 16], 138–40; George [10, 6], 131–8.

18 F. Shyllon, *Black People in Britain, 1555–1833* (1977).

19 Shyllon [10, 18], 102; Peter Fryer, *Staying Power: The History of Black People in Britain* (1984), chs. 1–8, is my main source for these paragraphs.

20 J. Landers, 'Mortality and Metropolis: the case of London, 1675–1825', *Population Studies* 41 (1987), 63.

21 George [10, 6], 41.

22 P. Clark, 'The "Mother Gin" Controversy', *Transactions of the Royal Historical Society* 38 (1988), 63–84.

23 George [10, 6], 41–55; T. S. Ashton, *An Economic History of England: The Eighteenth Century* (1955), 6; P. Deane, W. A. Cole, *British Economic Growth 1688–1959* (1962), 127; Rudé [9, 32], 6; Clark [10, 22].

24 Landers [10, 20], 64; Landers [9, 28], 131–61.

25 Landers [9, 28], 152–9.

26 Landers [10, 20]; J. Landers, 'Mortality, weather and prices in London, 1675–1825: a study of short-term fluctuations', *Journal of Historical Geography* 41 (1986), 347–64; J. Landers, A. Mouzas, 'Burial seasonality and the causes of death in London, 1670–1819', *Population Studies* 42 (1988), 59–83; G. M. Howe, *Man, Environment and Disease in Britain* (1976), 157–65; Landers [9, 28], 94–102, 266–84.

27 C. Creighton, *A History of Epidemics in Britain* (2 vols, 1965. 1st published Cambridge, 1891), vol. 2, 756.

28 Weinreb and Hibbert [8, 36], articles on water supply and individual companies.

29 S. Webb and B. Webb, *English Local Government, IV: Statutory Authorities for Special Purposes* (1922), 68–93.

30 J. Swift, 'A Description of a City Shower', published in *The Tatler*, October 1710.

31 J. Swift [9, 18], vol. 2, 539–40; Weinreb and Hibbert [8, 36], 929; C. de Saussure, *A Foreign View of England in the Reigns of George I and George II* (1902), 155–8.

32 T. Smollett, *Humphrey Clinker* (Everyman edn, 1943), 114.

33 George [10, 6], 95–6.

34 George [10, 6], 71–2.

35 B. R. Mitchell, P. Deane, *An Abstract of British Historical Statistics* (Cambridge, 1962), 486–8, 497–8; L. D. Schwarz, 'The standard of living in the long run: London, 1700–1860', *Economic History Review* 38 (1985); Schwarz [10, 7], 144–55; Landers [9, 28], 64–8.

36 Creighton [10, 27], ch. 4; P. E. Razzell, 'Population change in eighteenth-century England', in M. Drake [6, 25], 128–56; F. F. Cartwright, *A Social History of Medicine* (1977), 80–89.

37 George [10, 6], 62–4, 326–7; Cartwright [10, 36], 46–7; F. B. Smith, *The People's Health* (1979), 31–2.

38 D. T. Andrew, *Philanthropy and Police: London Charity in the Eighteenth Century* (Princeton, 1989), 53–69, 98–133.

39 B. Mandeville, *An Enquiry into the Origin of Moral Virtue* in P. Harth (ed.), *The Fable of the Bees* (Harmondsworth, 1989), 108–9.

40 George [10, 6], 221–39, 423–4.

41 Andrew [10, 38], 58–65, 98–102, 156–8, 181; George [10, 6], 55–8.

42 Andrew [10, 38], 75–6, 109–33, 161–2, 197–202; George [10, 6], 143, 236–40.

11. AN URBAN CULTURE

1 The Tate Gallery, *Manners and Morals: Hogarth and British Painting, 1700–1760* (1987), 11–22.

2 Boswell [10, 1], vol. 1, 156.

3 Davis [7, 10], 171–2.

4 T. Belanger, 'Publishers and writers in eighteenth-century England', in I. Rivers (ed.), *Books and their Readers in Eighteenth-Century England* (Leicester, 1982).

5 Belanger [11, 4], 47–68.

6 Ian Watt, *The Rise of the Novel* (1963).

7 *Dictionary of National Biography*, vol. 5, 180–84.

8 Borsay [9, 9], 21–35.

9 M. Byrd, *London Transformed. Images of the City in the Eighteenth Century* (New Haven, Connecticut), 111–12.

10 Boswell [10, 1], vol. 2, 579–80.

11 Earle [9, 37], 241–2.

12 *A London Omnibus* (no author, 1927), 3–6.

13 Boswell [10, 1], vol. 1, 261, 541

14 Boswell, [9, 40], 13 January, 19 January, 19 March 1763.

15 P. Borsay (ed.), *The Eighteenth-Century English Town, 1688–1820* (1990), ch. 5.

16 J. M. Crook, *The British Museum* (1972), ch. 2.

17 F. Henriques, *Prostitution and Society* (1966), vol. 2, ch. 5; John Cleland, *Memoirs of a Woman of Pleasure* (1748–9), and *Memoirs of a Coxcomb* (1751).

18 Cecil Price, *Theatre in the Age of Garrick* (Oxford, 1973), 85; J. Donohue, *Theatre in the Age of Kean* (Oxford, 1975), 17–18.

19 D. Arundell, *The Story of Sadler's Wells, 1683–1977* (Newton Abbot, 1978), 1–38.

20 Donohue [11, 18], 1–56.

21 P. Rogers, *Literature and Popular Culture in 18th-Century England* (1985), ch. 3; N. Ward, *The London Spy* (1927 edition), 177–200.

22 *Spectator*, no. 113, 5 April 1711.

23 K. Richards, P. Thomson (eds.) *The Eighteenth-Century English Stage* (1972), ch. 5; Rogers [11, 21], 43–54, 102–13; Price [11, 18], ch. 6.

24 *Dictionary of National Biography*, vol. 6, 361.

25 Scoles [8, 35], 206–8; Holmes [9, 38], 28–31; Borsay [9, 9], 28.

26 W. Wordsworth, *The Prelude* (1850 edn), book VII, 'Residence in London'.

27 Defoe [9, 17], vol. 1, 97.

28 J. Strutt, *The Sports and Pastimes of the People of England* (1875 edn), xxxvi; Byrd [11, 9], 89.

29 Thornbury and Walford [3, 86], vol. 4, 14–16; W. B. Boulton, *Amusements of Old London* (1901), vol. 1, ch. 5.

30 George [10, 6], 137–8; Thornbury and Walford [3, 86], vol. 2, 302; Boulton [11, 29], vol. 2, ch. 9; Saussure [10, 32], 180–81; *Dictionary of National Biography*, vol. 37, 250.

31 Sir L. Radzinowicz, *A History of English Criminal Law* (vols. 1–3, 1948, 1956), vol. 1: *The Movement for Reform*, ch. 6; P. Linebaugh, 'The Tyburn riot against the surgeons', in D. Hay, P. Linebaugh, E. P. Thompson (eds.), *Albion's Fatal Tree* (1975); J. M. Beattie, *Crime and the Courts in England, 1660–1800* (Oxford, 1986), 613–16.

32 J. A. Chartres, 'The Capital's provincial eyes: London's inns in the early eighteenth century', *London Journal* 3 (1977), 24–39.

33 S. Mennell, *All Manners of Food* (Oxford, 1985), 140–41.

34 Ward [11, 21], 257; P. Clark, *The English Alehouse. A Social History, 1200–1850* (1983), chs. 8–10.

35 Boswell [9, 40], 15 December 1762, 112.

36 Saussure [10, 32], 164–5.

37 Boswell [9, 40], 11 December 1762, 100–102; B. Lillywhite, *London Coffee-Houses* (1963), 17–27.

38 A. Ellis, *The Penny Universities* (1956), gives the fullest account of coffee houses.

39 Rogers [11, 21], 54–64; E. B. Chancellor, *The XVIIIth Century in London: An Account of its Social Life and Arts* (1920), 110–19; Thornbury and Walford [3, 86], vol. 4, 196–200.

40 Boswell [10, 1], vol. 2, 220.

41 E. B. Chancellor, *The Pleasure Haunts of Old London During Four Centuries* (1925), chs. 14–15; Weinreb and Hibbert [8, 36]; Thornbury and Walford [3, 86]; Boulton [11, 29], vol. 1, ch. 2; George [10, 6], 105–6.

42 Baedeker's *London and its Environs* (1898 edn), 323–4; Saussure [10, 32], 48, 138; D. Marshall, *Dr Johnson's London* (New York, 1968), 150–54.

12. Making a Living

1 W. E. Minchinton (ed.), *The Growth of English Overseas Trade in the Seventeenth and Eighteenth Centuries* (1969), 35. According to Schumpeter's figures, London handled about 80 per cent of imports, 69 per cent of home-produced exports, and 86 per cent of re-exported colonial goods. Ralph Davis's figures, also in Minchinton, pp. 96–7, are 80, 62, 84 respectively, giving London 74 per cent of English overseas trade.

2 Minchinton [12, 1], 35. In 1770 London handled 73 per cent of English imports, 63 per cent of exports, and 69 per cent of re-exports. The percentages calculated by C. J. French, in '"Crowded with traders and a great commerce": London's domination of English overseas trade, 1700–1775', *London Journal* 17 (1992), 27–35, are almost exactly the same as these, but his sterling values are different; Corfield [9, 33], 72.

3 French [12, 2], 31–2.

4 R. Davis, 'England's foreign trade, 1660–1700', in Minchinton [12, 1], 96–7.

5 Davis [12, 4], 96–7. The comparison is between the average for 1663 and 1669, and 1699–1701.

6 R. Davis, *Aleppo and Devonshire Square: English Traders in the Levant in the Eighteenth Century* (1967), chs. 1, 3.

7 L. Sutherland, *The East India Company in Eighteenth-Century Politics* (Oxford, 1952), ch. 1; Davis [6, 58], ch. 12.

8 L. M. Penson, 'The London West Indian interest in the eighteenth century', *English Historical Review* 36 (1926).

9 Earle [9, 37], 32, 36.

10 Davis [6, 58], ch. 9 and p. 390; Mitchell and Deane [10, 35], 112.

11 R. J. Jarvis, 'The Metamorphosis of the Port of London', *London Journal* 3 (1977), 55–71; J. Pudney, *London's Docks* (1975), 22–57.

12 Pudney [12, 11], chs. 3–7; A. Palmer, *The East End: Four Centuries of London*

Life (1989), 36–44; Jarvis [12, 11], 60–66; O. Spate, 'The Growth of London', in H. C. Darby (ed.), *A Historical Geography of England* 543–7; Dyos and Aldcroft [7, 7], 59–62.

13 R. Pares, 'The London sugar market, 1740–69', *Economic History Review* 9 (1956–7), 254–7.

14 Davis [12, 6], 75–89, 107–14; Defoe [9, 17], vol. 2, 207.

15 W. Stern, 'Where are the Cheesemongers of London?', *London Journal* 5 (1979), 228–48.

16 See especially N. McKendrick, J. Brewer, J. H. Plumb, *The Birth of a Consumer Society: the Commercialization of Eighteenth-Century England* (1982).

17 Keene [4, 37].

18 R. B. Walker, 'Advertising in London Newspapers, 1650–1750', *Business History* 15 (1973), 114–30; McKendrick, Brewer, and Plumb [12, 16], 183–91; H. Phillips' *Mid-Georgian London: a Social Survey of Central and Western London about 1750* (1964) has good accounts of London's shopping areas, and pictures of shops and trade cards.

19 Davis [7, 10], 193.

20 Davis [7, 10], 192, 195.

21 Boswell [10, 1], vol. 1, 457–8; P. J. Grosley, *A Tour to London* (2 vols, 1772 edn), vol. 1, 35–6.

22 McKendrick, Brewer, and Plumb [12, 16], 70–77.

23 H. Perkin, *The Origins of Modern English Society* (1969), 91–5; M. J. Daunton, 'Towns and economic growth in eighteenth-century England', in P. Abrams, E. A. Wrigley (eds), *Towns in Societies* (1978), 253–4.

24 McKendrick, Brewer and Plumb [12, 16], 74. This argument is the theme of much of McKendrick's work. His ideas have been questioned, however, by B. Fine and E. Leopold, 'Consumerism and the Industrial Revolution', in *Social History* 15 (1990), 151–79.

25 G. Unwin, *Samuel Oldknow and the Arkwrights. The Industrial Revolution in Stockport and Marple* (2nd edn, 1968, Manchester).

26 M. J. Daunton, 'The City and industry: the nature of British capitalism, 1750–1914', in G. Alderman, C. Holmes (eds.), *Outsiders and Outcasts: Essays in Honour of William J. Fishman* (1993), 190–91.

27 L. A. Landa (ed.), *Essays in Eighteenth-Century English Literature* (Princeton, 1980), 226–7.

28 F. Braudel, *Capitalism and Material Life* (Fontana edn, 1974), 436–40.

29 Wrigley [10, 3], 44–70; Daunton [10, 23], 245–77.

30 S. D. Chapman, *The Cotton Industry in the Industrial Revolution* (2nd edn, 1987), 12; P. L. Cottrell, *Industrial Finance, 1830–1914* (1980), 22.

31 Daunton [12, 26], 191–2.

32 R. Samuel, 'The workshop of the world: steam power and hand technology in mid-Victorian Britain', *History Workshop Journal* 3 (1977), 6–72; M. Berg, P. Hudson, 'Rehabilitating the industrial revolution', *Economic History Review* 45

(1992), 31–2, 43–4; F. Sheppard, *London, 1808–1870. The Infernal Wen* (1971), 158–9.

33 Earle [9, 37], 18–34, 341–7.

34 Earle [9, 37], 20; Corfield [9, 33], 74, suggests only 10–12,000 adult weavers in the 1740s.

35 George [10, 6], 178–96; Earle [9, 37], 19–21; G. S. Jones, *Outcast London: a Study in the Relationship Between Classes in Victorian London* (Oxford, 1971), 101; M. Berg, *The Age of Manufactures, 1700–1820* (1985), 213–15.

36 R. Campbell, *The London Tradesman* (1747; repr. Newton Abbot, 1969), 193, 206–9, 228; Earle [10, 11], 116, 139–43; Earle [9, 37], 21–2; P. Earle, 'The female labour market in London in the late seventeenth and early eighteenth centuries', *Economic History Review* 42 (1989).

37 George [10, 6], 199, 368; Campbell [12, 36], 219.

38 George [10, 6], 198.

39 J. Rule, *The Experience of Labour* (1981), 111.

40 D. S. Landes, *Revolution in Time* (Cambridge, Mass., 1983), ch. 14.

41 *Dictionary of National Biography*, vol. 27, 283–7

42 L. C. T. Rolt, *Victorian Engineering* (1970), 128–32; T. K. Derry, T. I. Williams, *A Short History of Technology* (Oxford, 1970), 350–55; Sheppard [12, 32], 174–7.

43 G. Beard, C. Gilbert (eds.), *Dictionary of English Furniture Makers, 1660–1840* (1986), 793–6.

44 Campbell [12, 36], 230.

45 Defoe [9, 17], vol. 1, 348; Davis [6, 58], 70.

46 J. Burnett, *Plenty and Want* (1966), 100–104; J. C. Drummond, A. Wilbraham, *The Englishman's Food* (1957), 187–90.

47 S. Pollard, *The Genesis of Modern Management* (1965), 120; W. H. G. Armytage, *A Social History of Engineering* (1869), 90–92.

48 P. Mathias, *The Transformation of England* (1979), chs. 11, 12.

49 Earle [10, 11], 113–23; Earle [12, 36]; George [10, 6], 425–8.

50 D. A. Kent, 'Ubiquitous but invisible: female domestic servants in mid-eighteenth-century London', *History Workshop Journal* 28 (1989), 118; Earle [9, 37], 218–29, 357; Earle [10, 11], 113–16, 123–30.

51 Kent [12, 50]; C. Fox, *Londoners* (1987), ch. 5; P. Linebaugh, *The London Hanged: Crime and Civil Society in the Eighteenth Century* (1991), 248–55.

52 M. G. Davies, 'Country gentry and payments to London, 1650–1714', *Economic History Review* 24 (1971).

53 Davies [12, 52]; D. M. Joslin, 'London private bankers, 1720–85', *Economic History Review* 7 (1954); Earle [9, 37], 48–9.

54 Huehns [9, 3], 451–3; Wilson [10, 16], 212–15; Clay [4, 8], vol. 2, 269–80.

55 P. G. M. Dickson, *The Financial Revolution in England: a Study in the Development of Public Credit, 1699–1756* (1967), 253–60.

56 I. Kramnick, *Bolingbroke and his Circle: the Politics of Nostalgia in the Age of Walpole* (Cambridge, Mass., 1968), 39–55; Dickson [12, 55], 253–303; L.

Sutherland, 'The City of London in Eighteenth-Century Politics', in R. Pares and A. J. P. Taylor, *Essays Presented to Sir Lewis Namier* (1956).

57 J. H. Clapham, *An Economic History of Modern Britain* (3 vols, Cambridge, 1930–38), vol. 1, 103; J. H. Plumb, *Sir Robert Walpole* (2 vols, 1956), vol. 1, ch. 8; C. Wilson [10, 16], 316–17, 328–9.

58 C. H. Wilson, 'The Economic Decline of the Netherlands', in Carus-Wilson [6, 6], vol. 1, 254–69; F. Braudel, *The Perspective of the World* (1984), 268–73; Sutherland [12, 7], ch. 8; J. Clapham, *The Bank of England, A History* (2 vols, Cambridge, 1944), vol. 1, ch. 7.

59 Clapham [12, 58], vol. 1, 131–41, 217–221; L. Sutherland, *A London Merchant, 1695–1774* (Oxford, 1952), 19–23.

60 Clapham [12, 58], vol. 1, 205–12.

61 Joslin [12, 53].

62 Sutherland [12, 56], 23–6; L. B. Namier, *The Structure of Politics at the Accession of George III* (1965), 53–6.

63 Sutherland [12, 56], chs. 4–9.

64 E. V. Morgan, W. A. Thomas, *The Stock Exchange. Its History and Functions* (1962), 20.

65 Dickson [12, 55], ch. 20; Morgan and Thomas [12, 64], chs. 3, 4; Wilson [10, 16], 324–8.

66 P. G. M. Dickson, *The Sun Insurance Office, 1710–1960* (Oxford, 1960), chs. 4, 5.

67 B. Supple, *The Royal Exchange Assurance: a History of British Insurance* (1970), 52–3, 186–93; Sutherland [12, 59], ch. 3; Davis [6, 58], 87–8, 318–20, 376–7.

68 Stone and Stone [9, 18], 402–3.

69 Stone and Stone [9, 18], 221–5, 247–51.

70 R. G. Lang, 'Social origins and social aspirations of Jacobean London merchants', *Economic History Review* 27 (1974), 28–47.

71 H. Horwitz, '"The Mess of the Middle Class" revisited', *Continuity and Change* 2 (1987), 263–96; N. Rogers, 'Money, land and lineage: the big bourgeoisie of Hanoverian London', *Social History* 4 (1979).

72 Earle [9, 37], 143–57.

73 Defoe [9, 17], vol. 1, 15, 157–61, 168; Stone and Stone [9, 18], 17–27, 217–21.

13. THE ART OF GOVERNMENT

1 Brett-James [6, 36], 130–36; Rudé [9, 32], 127–8.

2 Webb and Webb [10, 29].

3 F. H. W. Sheppard, *Local Government in St Marylebone, 1688–1835* (1958), 245–53.

4 S. Webb and B. Webb, *English Local Government, I: The Parish and the County* (1906), 76–90, 207–11, 227–43.

5 Webb and Webb [13, 4], 173–207; Sheppard [13, 3], 102–22.

6 Sheppard [13, 3], ch. 16; Webb and Webb [13, 4], 233–75.

7 Webb and Webb [13, 4], 123–60; Sheppard [13, 3], 78–80.

8 M. Falkus, E. L. Jones, 'Urban improvement and the English economy', in Borsay [11, 15]; Webb and Webb [10, 29], 321–2.

9 M. E. Falkus, 'Lighting in the Dark Ages', in Coleman and John [6, 45].

10 Falkus [13, 9]; George [10, 6], 109–11; Boswell [9, 40], 10 May 1763; D. Cruikshank, N. Burton, *Life in the Georgian City* (1990), 5–10.

11 Webb and Webb [10, 29], 276–82.

12 Falkus [13, 8], 135–41; Webb and Webb [10, 29], 276–97.

13 Webb and Webb [10, 29], 323–4.

14 Webb and Webb [10, 29], 316–44.

15 D. Hay, 'War, dearth and theft in the eighteenth century', *Past and Present* 95 (1982).

16 Beattie [11, 31], 213–33, 500–504, 516–31, 598–604, 624–32; A. Aspinall, E. A. Smith (eds.), *English Historical Documents, 1783–1832* (1959), 394–9.

17 W. Maitland, *History of London from its Foundation* (2 vols, 1739), 1775 edn, vol. 1, 510.

18 Boswell [9, 40], 1762–3, 15 December 1762; Walpole [9, 42], 504; Saussure [10, 31], 129–30.

19 Grosley [12, 21], vol. 1, 49–50, 62–3.

20 V. A. C. Gatrell, *The Hanging Tree* (Oxford, 1994), 6–9, 616.

21 Boswell [9, 40], 5 December 1762, 95.

22 Beattie [11, 31], 184–90.

23 Beattie [11, 31], 149–58; J. J. Tobias, *Crime and the Police in England* (Dublin, 1979), 16–20.

24 G. Howson, *Thief-Taker General. The Rise and Fall of Jonathan Wild* (1970), 171–86, 312–14.

25 Howson [13, 24], passim.

26 C. Emsley, *Crime and Society* (1987), 170–75; Beattie [11, 31], 67–72.

27 Webb and Webb [10, 29], 321–37.

28 A. Babington, *A House in Bow Street: Crime and the Magistracy, London, 1740–1881* (1969), passim; T. A. Critchley, *A History of the Police in England and Wales* (1978), 32–4; Beattie [11, 31], 65–6, 278–81; J. Styles, 'Sir John Fielding and the problem of criminal investigation in eighteenth-century England', *Transactions of the Royal Historical Society*, 33 (1983).

29 D. Philips, '"A new engine of power and authority": the institutionalisation of law enforcement in England, 1780–1830', in V. A. C. Gatrell, B. Lenman, G. Parker (eds.), *Crime and the Law: a Social History of Crime in Western Europe since 1500* (1982), 165–8.

30 C. Emsley, *The English Police* (Hemel Hempstead, 1991), 20; Radzinowicz [11, 31].

31 P. Colquhoun, *A Treatise on the Police of the Metropolis* (1796), 45–53.

14. POLITICS AND PUBLIC ORDER

1 Harris [8, 39], 9–10

2 Harris [8, 39], ch. 4; Pepys, *Diary*, 24–6 March 1668.

3 J. R. Jones *The First Whigs* (Oxford, 1961).

4 Harris [8, 39], 164–72.

5 Harris [8, 39], 223–7; Jones [14, 3], ch. 7; J. Miller, 'The Crown and the Borough Charters', *English Historical Review*, January 1985, 74–5; J. R. Western, *Monarchy and Revolution* (1972), 69–75.

6 G. S. de Krey, 'Popular radicalism in London after the Glorious Revolution', *Journal of Modern History*, 55 (1983).

7 N. Rogers, 'The City Elections Act (1725) reconsidered', *English Historical Review* (1985).

8 G. Holmes, 'The Sacheverell Riots: The crowd and the church in early eighteenth-century London', *Past and Present* 72 (1976).

9 N. Rogers, 'Popular protest in early Hanoverian London', *Past and Present* 79 (1978).

10 N. Rogers, 'Popular disaffection in London during the Forty-Five', *London Journal* 1 (1975).

11 Saussure [10, 31], 162; G. Boyce, J. Curran, P. Wingate (eds.), *Newspaper History* (1978), ch. 4, 82–97; McKendrick, Brewer and Plumb [12, 16], 268–70.

12 Plumb [12, 57], vol. 2, 107–12; Rogers [14, 7]; N. Rogers, 'Resistance to oligarchy', in J. Stevenson (ed.), *London in the Age of Reform* (Oxford, 1977); for the opposite view, I. G. Doolittle, 'Walpole's City Elections Act', *English Historical Review* 97 (1982).

13 Plumb [12, 57], vol. 2, 246–70, 314–15; Boyce, Curran, and Wingate [14, 11], 95–6.

14 Rogers [14, 12], 13–22.

15 N. Rogers, 'Aristocratic clientage, trade and independency: popular politics in pre-radical Westminster', *Past and Present* 61 (1973).

16 R. B. Shoemaker, 'The London "mob" in the eighteenth century', in Borsay [11, 15].

17 A. E. Bland, P. A. Brown, R. H. Tawney, *English Economic History* (1914), 619–24; Rule [12, 39], ch. 6.

18 J. Stevenson, *Popular Disturbances in England, 1700–1870* (1979), 120; G. Rudé, *Paris and London in the Eighteenth Century* (1970), 201–21.

19 Rudé [9, 32], 185–7; Shoemaker [14, 16], 209, 212; George [10, 6], 178–96.

20 W. J. Shelton, *English Hunger and Industrial Disorders* (1973), 165–84; Stevenson [14, 18], 68–70; Rudé [9, 32], 196–7.

21 J. Brewer, *Party Ideology and Popular Politics at the Accession of George III* (Cambridge, 1976), ch. 9.

22 Rudé [14, 18], 247–8; Brewer [14, 21], ch. 8.

23 L. Sutherland, *The City of London and the Opposition to Government, 1768–74: a Study in the Rise of Metropolitan Radicalism* (1970), 21–3.

24 Sutherland [14, 23], 26–33.

25 P. Langford, 'London and the American Revolution', in Stevenson [14, 12].

26 Stevenson [14, 18], 76–90; Rudé [14, 18], 268–92; Linebaugh [12, 51], 333–70.

27 This account of the LCS draws on E. P. Thompson's *Making of the English Working-Class* (1968), chs. 1 and 5; J. Walvin and E. Royle, *English Radicals and Reformers* (Brighton, 1982), ch. 4; H. Collins, 'The London Corresponding Society' in J. Saville (ed.), *Democracy and the Labour Movement* (1955).

28 G. D. H. Cole, A. W. Filson (eds.), *British Working Class Movements: Select Documents, 1789–1875* (1951), 79.

29 J. A. Hone, 'Radicalism in London, 1796–1802', in Stevenson [14, 12]; Thompson [14, 27], ch. 14; Walvin and Royle [14, 27], 93–7.

30 A. Prochaska, 'The practice of radicalism', in Stevenson [14, 12], 102–16.

NINETEENTH-CENTURY LONDON, 1815–1914

15. POPULATION, HEALTH AND LOCAL GOVERNMENT

1 H. A. Shannon, 'Migration and the Growth of London, 1841–91', *Economic History Review* (1935), 1st series, 5.

2 G. S. Jones [12, 35], 147.

3 L. H. Lees, *Exiles of Erin. Irish Migrants in Victorian London* (Manchester, 1979), 42–8, 97–106, 135–9.

4 C. Booth, *Life and Labour of the People in London* (third edn, 17 vols, 1902–3). First Series: *Poverty*, vols 1–4 (1902). Second Series: *Industry*, vols 1–5 (1903). Third Series: *Religious Influences*, vols 1–7 (1902–3). *Final Volume: Notes on Social Influences and Conclusion* (1903). *Poverty* Series, vol. 3, 202–4, 218; Booth [15, 4], *Religious Influences* Series, vol. 7, 250.

5 W. J. Fishman, *East End 1888* (1988), 217–19.

6 D. Feldman, 'The importance of being English', in D. Feldman, G. S. Jones (eds.), *Metropolis London: Histories and Representations since 1800* (1989), 63; D. Feldman, 'Jews in London, 1880–1914', in R. Samuel (ed.), *Patriotism. The Making and unmaking of British National Identity* (1989), vol. 2, 207–29.

7 Feldman and Jones [15, 6], 76.

8 W. A. Armstrong, 'The flight from the land', in G. E. Mingay (ed.), *The Victorian Countryside* (1981), vol. 1, 118–35; Booth [15, 4], *Poverty* Series, vol. 3, chs. 2, 3, written by H. Llewellyn Smith.

9 Jones [12, 35], ch. 6.

10 A. Hardy, 'Smallpox in London: factors in the decline of the disease in the nineteenth century', *Medical History* 27 (1983), 111–38; A. Hardy, *The*

Epidemic Streets. Infectious Disease and the Rise of Preventive Medicine, 1856–1900 (Oxford, 1993), 110–50.

11 T. McKeown, *The Modern Rise of Population* (1976); Hardy [*The Epidemic Streets* 15, 10], 211–19.

12 Hardy [15, 10], 211–66.

13 Hardy [15, 10], 191–210.

14 Hardy [15, 10], 104–5.

15 42nd Annual Report of the Local Government Board, supplement: Report by the Board's Medical Officer on Infant and Child Mortality. PP1913, xxxii.

16 Smith [10, 37], ch. 2; A Wohl, *Endangered Lives: Public Health in Victorian Britain* (1983), ch. 2; H. Jephson, *The Sanitary Evolution of London* (1907), 121, 393.

17 N. C. Smith (ed.), *The Selected Letters of Sydney Smith* (Oxford, 1981), 150. The phrase 'liquid history' was coined by the labour leader John Burns.

18 A. Hardy, 'Parish pump to private pipes: London's water supply in the nineteenth century', in W. F. Bynum, R. Porter (eds.), *Living and Dying in London* (1991), 77–83.

19 M. Pelling, *Cholera, Fever and English Medicine, 1825–1865* (Oxford, 1978), ch. 1; Sheppard [12, 32], 247–9.

20 4th Annual Report of Poor Law Commissioners, appendix A, supplements 1 and 2. PP1837–8, xlv, House of Lords.

21 Hardy [15, 10], 157–9.

22 E. Chadwick, *Report on the Sanitary Condition of the Labouring Population of Great Britain* (ed. M. W. Flinn, Edinburgh, 1965), 370.

23 Royal Commission on Metropolitan Sanitation, Minutes of Evidence, 63–4. PP1847–8, viii.

24 For the paragraphs on Chadwick, my main sources were S. E. Finer, *The Life and Times of Sir Edwin Chadwick* (1952), books 5 and 7–10, and R. A. Lewis, *Edwin Chadwick and the Public Health Movement* (1952).

25 R. Lambert, *Sir John Simon and English Social Administration, 1816–1904* (1963), 69.

26 Lambert [15, 25], chs. 6–8.

27 J. Timbs, *Curiosities of London* (1885 edn. 1st published 1855), 560–61; Lambert [15, 25], 85–6, 184–217.

28 Pelling [15, 19], ch. 6; Lambert [15, 25], 247–9.

29 G. M. Young, W. D. Handcock, *English Historical Documents, 1833–1874* (1956), 639–41; J. Davis, *Reforming London: the London Government Problem, 1855–1900* (Oxford, 1988), 51–3.

30 Davis [15, 29], 11–16.

31 Sheppard [12, 32], 278–80; D. Owen, *The Government of Victorian London* (1982), ch. 2.

32 Jephson [15, 16], 192; Lambert [15, 25], 380.

33 Hardy [15, 18].

34 Owen [15, 31], 147–53.
35 Owen [15, 31], 134–40.
36 Owen [15, 31], 140–45.
37 Davis [15, 29], 16–50.
38 Davis [15, 29], ch. 8.
39 J. S. Mill, *Three Essays* (Oxford, 1975), 368–90.
40 A. Briggs, *Victorian Cities* (1963), 331–2; Owen [15, 31], 199–204; Davis [15, 29], 77–95; K. Young, P. Garside, *Metropolitan London: Politics and Urban Change, 1837–1981* (1982), 39–54; W. A. Robson, *The Government and Misgovernment of London* (1948), 73–9; I. Doolittle, ' "Obsolete Appendix?" The City of London's struggle for survival', *History Today*, May 1983, 10–14.
41 Davis [15, 29], 96–114.
42 Davis [15, 29], 133.
43 W. E. Jackson, *Achievement. A Short History of the London County Council* (1965), 12–29.
44 Davis [15, 29], 154.
45 Davis [15, 29], 158–67 and appendix 3.
46 Davis [15, 29], appendix 3.
47 Robson [15, 40], 93–9; Davis [15, 29], 223–47; Young and Garside [15, 40], 75–101; P. Garside, 'London and the Home Counties', in F. M. L. Thompson (ed.), *The Cambridge Social History of Britain, 1750–1950* (1990), vol. 1, 513–14.
48 *Encyclopaedia Britannica* (11th edn), vol. 16, 953.
49 B. Webb, *Our Partnership* (1948), 372–3.

16. The Richest City in the World

1 P. G. Hall, *The Industries of London since 1861* (1962), 9.
2 Schwarz [10, 7], appendix 3, 255–63.
3 M. Daunton [12, 26], 186–7, quoting J. A. Hobson.
4 Though, as Martin Daunton points out, many of these firms, including several of the biggest Welsh and Scottish iron works, were managed from London.
5 Daunton [12, 26], appendix 3, 255–8. Schwarz uses W. A. Armstrong's system of occupational classification, which allows him to make national comparisons. A different system of classification is used in Sheppard [12, 32], 388–9, and in Jones [12, 35], appendices 1 and 2, 350–59.
6 Booth [15, 4], *Industry* Series, vol. 5, 54–8, 104–5; Jones [12, 35], 27–30.
7 D. R. Green, 'The nineteenth-century metropolitan economy: a revisionist interpretation', *London Journal* 21 (1996), 9–26.
8 Booth [15, 4], *Poverty* Series, vol. 4, ch. 9; R. Pike, *Human Documents of the Age of the Forsytes* (1969), 206.
9 George [10, 6], 174–202; Schwarz [10, 7], ch. 7; D. Goodway, *London Chartism, 1838–48* (Cambridge, 1982), 153–4.
10 Schwarz [10, 7], chs. 8, 9.

11 I. Prothero, *Artisans and Politics in Early Victorian London. John Gast and His Times* (Folkestone, 1979), chs. 2, 3, 11.

12 E. P. Thompson, E. Yeo (eds.), *The Unknown Mayhew* (1971), 309–27; D. Bythell, *The Sweated Trades* (1978), 106–9.

13 Thompson and Yeo [16, 12], 137–273.

14 Hall [16, 1], 86.

15 Thompson and Yeo [16, 12], 432–82; Hall [16, 1], 71–95.

16 Derry and Williams, [12, 42] 645–6.

17 Jones [12, 35], 67–87.

18 Prothero [16, 11], 210–12; Goodway [16, 9], 185–9; Schwarz [10, 7], 35–8, 201–7.

19 Thompson and Yeo [16, 12], 122–36; Schwarz [10, 7], 35–8.

20 Booth [15, 4], *Poverty* Series, vol. 4, 239–55.

21 S. Briggs and A. Briggs, *Cap and Bell* (1972), 78.

22 *Alton Locke* (Macmillan edn, 1887), contains relevant correspondence and *Cheap Clothes and Nasty*.

23 Booth [15, 4], *Industry* Series, vol. 5, 60; Jones [12, 35], 358–9.

24 Bythell [16, 12], 110–14; P. G. Hall, 'The East London footwear industry. An industrial quarter in decline', *East London Papers* (April 1962), vol. 5i, 3–21.

25 Hall [16, 1], 52–9.

26 Fifth Report of Select Committee on Sweating, PP1890, xliii.

27 A. J. Kershen, 'Trade unionism amongst the Jewish tailoring workers of London and Leeds, 1872–1915', in D. Ceserani (ed.), *The Making of Modern Anglo-Jewry* (Oxford, 1990), 36.

28 Bythell [16, 12], 148, 232–47; S. Webb and B. Webb, *History of Trade Unionism* (1920. 1st published 1894), 494–5; Hall [16, 1], 39.

29 P. Johnson, 'Economic development and industrial dynamism in Victorian London', in *London Journal* 21 (1996), 27–37; M. J. Daunton, 'Industry in London: revisions and reflections', *London Journal* 21 (1996), 1–8.

30 A. Godley, 'Immigrant entrepreneurs and the emergence of London's East End as an industrial district', *London Journal* 21 (1996).

31 J. Thorne, *Handbook to the Environs of London* (1876), 273, 58.

32 Thorne [16, 31], 664; Sheppard [12, 32], 161–2; H. E. Malden (ed.), *Victoria County History of Surrey* (1905), vol. 2, 376.

33 Malden [16, 32], 286–92, 304, 395–400, 404–9.

34 Thompson and Yeo [16, 12], 533–54; Booth [15, 4], *Industry* Series, vol. 2, 125–40, vol. 3, 25–38, and vol. 5, 60; Thornbury and Walford [3, 86], vol. 6, 123–4; Malden [16, 32], vol. 2, 337–9.

35 V. S. Pritchett, *A Cab at the Door. An Autobiography: Early Years* (1968), 166.

36 W. D. Rubinstein, *Men of Property* (1981), 86–8.

37 Booth [15, 4], *Religious* Series, vol. 4, 121–2; W. H. Fraser, *The Coming of the Mass Market, 1850–1914* (1981), 167–70; Malden [16, 32], 260, 376–400.

38 Pritchett [16, 35], 152.

39 G. Crossick, *An Artisan Elite in Victorian London: Kentish London, 1840–1880* (1978), 46.

40 Malden [16, 32], vol. 2, 404–10.

41 M. J. Daunton, *House and Home in the Victorian City: Working-Class Housing, 1850–1914* (1983), 238–9.

42 Malden [16, 32], vol. 2, 416–17; S. Pollard, P. Robertson, *The British Shipbuilding Industry, 1870–1914* (Cambridge, Mass., 1979), 51–7, 132–3; K. T. Rowland, *Steam at Sea* (1970), 62–5.

43 S. Pollard, 'The decline of shipbuilding on the Thames', *Economic History Review*, 2nd series, 3 (1950–51), 72–89; Pollard and Robertson [16, 42], ch. 3, 49–65; Jones [12, 35], 102–3; Rowland [16, 42].

44 Crossick [16, 39], 45–53; Thorne [16, 31], 742–52.

45 J. Marriott, '"West Ham: London's industrial centre and gateway to the world" 1. Industrialisation, 1840–1910', *London Journal* 13 (1988), 123–42.

46 Marriott [16, 45], 123–42; *Encyclopaedia Britannica*, 11th edn (1910–11), vol. 26, 65–9, 'Sulphuric Acid'.

47 Booth [15, 4], *Industry* Series, vol. 5, 84, quoted in Daunton [12, 26], 194.

48 A. G. Kenwood, A. L. Lougheed, *The Growth of the International Economy, 1820–1960* (1971), 90–104; Mitchell and Deane [10, 35], 282–4, 328–9.

49 G. Jackson, 'The ports', in M. J. Freeman, D. H. Aldcroft (eds.), *Transport in Victorian Britain* (Manchester, 1988), 218–52; Sir J. G. Broodbank, *History of the Port of London* (2 vols, 1921), vol. 1, 3; *Encyclopaedia Britannica*, 11th edn, vol. 16, 950; R. C. Michie, *The City of London: Continuity and Change, 1850–1990* (Basingstoke, 1992), 34.

50 Freeman and Aldcroft [16, 49], Table 20, 248–9; J. Lovell, *Stevedores and Dockers* (1969), 14, 19.

51 Michie [16, 49], 30–65; Broodbank [16, 49], vol. 2, 487–8.

52 Clapham [12, 57], vol. 1, 251–4.

53 D. Kynaston, *The City of London, 1. A World of its Own, 1815–1890* (1994), 99–100, 112; Timbs [15, 27], 265–6.

54 Timbs [15, 27], vol. 2, 299–300; H. Barty-King, *The Baltic Exchange* (1977).

55 G. R. Sims (ed.), *Living London* (3 vols., 1902–3), vol. 3 (section 2), 286–92; Timbs [15, 27], 322–33.

56 Clapham [12, 57], vol. 2, 318–22.

57 Sheppard [12, 32], 192–5; Clapham [12, 57], vol. 1, 234–5, 303–6; vol. 2, 301–2; Mitchell and Deane [10, 35], 113, 482.

58 Broodbank [16, 49], vol. 1, 96, 114, 123, 161–2.

59 Lovell [16, 50], 14–20; Broodbank [16, 49], vol. 2, 390–95, 411–15; Jones [12, 35], 114–17.

60 Broodbank [16, 49], vol. 1, chs. 16, 18, 19; Freeman and Aldcroft [16, 49], 222–8.

61 Lovell [16, 50], 11–24; Broodbank [16, 49], vol. 1, chs. 18, 23, 24, 25; vol. 2, chs. 27, 28, 30; Freeman and Aldcroft [16, 49], ch. 6; Jones [12, 35], 117–18.

62 Pevsner [3, 80], 250.

63 Lovell [16, 50], ch. 2; Jones [12, 35], 111–24; Booth [15, 4], *Industry* Series, vol. 3, 399–432; H. Mayhew, *London Labour and the London Poor* (4 vols, reprinted 1968. 1st published 1861–2), vol. 3, 233–312.

64 Mayhew [16, 63], vol. 3, 304.

65 Booth [15, 4], *Industry* Series, vol. 3, 409–11, 419–21.

66 Lovell [16, 50], chs. 4, 5; Jones [12, 35], ch. 17.

67 C. P. Kindleberger, *Manias, Panics and Crashes* (1981), 182–92; Kenwood and Lougheed [16, 48], 116–24.

68 S. D. Chapman, *The Rise of Merchant Banking* (1984), 1–15, 173–4; W. Bagehot, *Lombard Street* (1888 edn. 1st published 1873), 10–15.

69 Clapham [12, 57], vol. 2, 353.

70 Kenwood and Lougheed [16, 48], 116–27.

71 *Encyclopaedia Britannica*, 11th edn (1911), vol. 3, 339.

72 S. D. Chapman, 'The international houses: the continental contribution to British commerce, 1800–1860', *Journal of European Economic History* 6, Spring 1977; Chapman [16, 68], 1–11, 45–55.

73 Kynaston [16, 53], vol. 1, 24–5; P. Ziegler *The Sixth Great Power, The Barings, 1762–1929* (1988), 56–8; R. Davis, *The English Rothschilds* (1983), 29–44; Sheppard [12, 32], 54–6.

74 Kynaston [16, 53], 45–52; Sheppard [12, 32], 56–9.

75 R. C. Michie, *The London and New York Stock Exchanges, 1850–1914* (1987), 4, 36.

76 Michie [16, 75], 52.

77 Kenwood and Lougheed [16, 48], 38–47; W. Ashworth, *The International Economy since 1850*, 195–8; Kynaston [16, 53], 172–5; Michie [16, 75], 109–12.

78 Michie [16, 75], 42–8.

79 Michie [16, 75], 249–76; Kynaston [16, 53], 269–85, 316–26.

80 D. Landes, *The Unbound Prometheus* (Cambridge, 1972), 348–52; Cottrell [12, 30], 141–54; R. Floud, D. McCloskey, *The Economic History of Britain since 1700* (2 vols, Cambridge, 1981), vol. 2, 75–87; Clapham [12, 57], vol. 2, 355–61.

81 Chapman [16, 68].

82 Chapman [16, 68], 137–40, 205; Michie [16, 49], 73.

83 Kynaston [16, 53], 63–71; Clapham [12, 57], vol. 2, 98–103.

84 Kynaston [16, 53], 87–8; Clapham [12, 57], vol. 2, 103–7, 126–30.

85 Clapham [12, 57], vol. 2, 177–85; Kynaston [16, 53], 126–30; Kenwood and Lougheed [16, 48], 116–27.

86 Clapham [12, 57], vol. 2, 195–214; Kynaston [16, 53], 151–62; C. N. Ward-Perkins, 'The commercial crisis of 1847', in Carus-Wilson [6, 6], vol. 3, 263–79.

87 Kynaston [16, 53], 167.

88 Clapham [12, 57], vol. 2, 226–33; Kynaston [16, 53], 192–7.

89 Clapham [12, 57], vol. 2, 261–2; Kynaston [16, 53], 89.

90 Young and Handcock [15, 29], 310; Kynaston [16, 53], 235–43.

91 Bagehot [16, 68], 166.
92 Clapham [12, 57], vol. 2, 263–70; S. G. Checkland, *The Rise of Industrial Society in England* (1971), 45.
93 Kynaston [16, 53], 430.
94 Ziegler [16, 73], 236–66; Clapham [12, 57], vol. 2, 326–39; Kynaston [16, 53], 422–37.
95 Supple [12, 67], 106–17.
96 Supple [12, 67], 121–4.
97 Supple [12, 67], 130–39.
98 Owen [15, 31], 127–34; Supple [12, 67], 163–6, 215–16.
99 Supple [12, 67], 246–51.
100 Supple [12, 67], 218–37; Sheppard [12, 32], 201.
101 Supple [12, 67], 296–9.
102 Supple [12, 67], 309–13.
103 Supple [12, 67], 309–48; H. J. Dyos, *Exploring the Urban Past: Essays in Urban History*, eds. D. Cannadine and D. Reeder (Cambridge, 1982), 169.
104 Rubinstein [16, 36], 109–10; W. D. Rubinstein, 'The Victorian middle classes: wealth, occupation and geography', *Economic History Review*, 2nd series, 30 (1977), 602–23.
105 *Dictionary of National Biography*, article on Ellerman.
106 Rubinstein [16, 36], 56–116; Barty-King [16, 54], 57–60.
107 Kynaston [16, 53], 149.
108 Michie [16, 49], 17.
109 Supple [12, 67], 376; Baedeker's *London and its Environs* (1898 edn), 136.
110 Booth [15, 4], *Industry* Series, vol. 3, 273–9.
111 Booth [15, 4], *Industry* Series, vol. 3, 277–8; Kynaston [16, 53], 248.

17. Ragged London

1 F. Engels, *The Condition of the Working Class in England* (1845), ed. E. J. Hobsbawm (1969), 58.
2 Booth [15, 4], *Poverty* Series, vol. 1, 131.
3 P. Keating, 'Fact and fiction in the East End', in H. J. Dyos, M. Wolff (eds.), *The Victorian City* (1973), vol. 2, 586–7.
4 J. Hollingshead, *Ragged London in 1861* (repr. 1986), 7–8.
5 J. Greenwood, *The Seven Curses of London* (1869), 270; C. Kingsley, *Alton Locke, Tailor and Poet* (1850), ch. 35, 'The lowest deep'.
6 H. Taine, *Notes on England* (1873 edn. 1st published 1872), 33–6.
7 Booth [15, 4], *Religious Influences* Series, vol. 4, 8.
8 Booth [15, 4], *Final Volume*, 1–19; *Poverty* Series, vol. 2, 23–39.
9 PP1913, xxxii, Supplement to the 42nd Annual Report of Local Government Board, 1913.
10 Booth [15, 4], *Industry* Series, vol. 5, 231.
11 Mayhew [16, 63], vol. 2, 299; Jones [12, 35], 34–5, 376–83.

12 Jones [12, 35], 39–41.

13 Jones [12, 35], ch. 2, 241–50, 291–5; Mayhew [16, 63], vol. 2, 298–9; Young and Handcock [15, 29], XII (1), 736–42; T. S. Simey and M. B. Simey, *Charles Booth* (1960), 65–70.

14 Simey and Simey [17, 13], ch. 4; Booth [15, 4], *Industry* Series, vol. 5, 43–50, ch. 9.

15 Booth [15, 4], *Industry* Series, vol. 5, 231–2.

16 Will Crooks, *From Workhouse to Westminster*, quoted in H. Llewellyn Smith (ed.), *The New Survey of London Life and Labour* (9 vols, 1934–5), vol. 3, 172.

17 Mayhew [16, 63], vol. 1, 105, 149; vol. 2, 465.

18 Mayhew [16, 63], vol. 2, 144–5, 155.

19 C. Dickens, 'A Walk in a Workhouse', *Reprinted Pieces* (1858).

20 C. Dickens, 'The verdict for Drouet' (21 April 1849), *Miscellaneous Papers* (ed. B. W. Matz, n.d.).

21 S. Webb and B. Webb, *English Poor Law History*, part 2 *The Last Hundred Years*, vol. 1, 259–92; D. Fraser (ed.), *The New Poor Law in the Nineteenth Century* (1976), ch. 3.

22 Fraser [17, 21], 57; Smith [10, 37], 386.

23 Smith [10, 37], 387; Webb and Webb [17, 21], part 2, vol. 1, 310.

24 J. Sheldrake, 'The LCC hospital service', in A. Saint (ed.), *Politics and the People of London: The London County Council, 1889–1965* (1989).

25 Jones [12, 35], 244, 264.

26 Jones [12, 35], ch. 13.

27 Webb and Webb [17, 21], part 2, vol. 1, 334–6, 352–4, 376–95, 435–54; Jones [12, 35], 254–5.

28 Llewellyn Smith [17, 16], vol. 1, 364, 386–7; figures refer to the County of London.

29 Jones [12, 35], chs. 13, 14.

30 Jones [12, 35], 350–57, 388–93.

31 S. Barnett, 'Distress in East London', *The Nineteenth Century*, November 1886.

32 Sheppard [12, 32], 382.

33 K. S. Inglis, *Churches and the Working Classes in Victorian England* (1963), 143–74.

34 Jones [12, 35], 281–96; D. C. Richter, *Riotous Victorians* (Ohio, 1981), ch. 8.

35 Webb and Webb [17, 21], part 2, vol. 1, 352–63.

36 Webb and Webb [17, 21], part 2, vol. 1, 395–400.

37 Jones [12, 35], 300–36.

38 Burnett [12, 46], ch. 8; M. Pember Reeves, *Round About a Pound a Week* (1913; 1979 edn with introduction by S. Alexander), chs. 7–9; Booth [15, 4], *Industry* Series, vol. 5, 325–7; Wohl [15, 16], 50–60.

39 Burnett [12, 46], 240–48; Drummond and Wilbraham [12, 46], ch. 17.

40 Smith [10, 37], 175–84; Wohl [15, 16], 51; Pember Reeves [17, 38], 145.

41 D. Hudson, *Munby. Man of Two Worlds* (1972), 99; M. Hiley, *Victorian Working Women: Portraits from Life* (1979), 11–15, 113; G. Winter, *A Cockney*

Camera: London's Social History recorded in Photographs (1975); R. White-house, *A London Album: Early Photographs recording the History of the City and its People from 1840 to 1915* (1980); B. Pullen, *London Street People* (Oxford, 1989); J. Thomson, A. Smith, *Street Life in London* (1877–8).

42 Mayhew [16, 63], vol. 2, 25–9; K. Perlmutter, *London Street Markets* (1983).

43 Pember Reeves [17, 38], 61–5.

44 Booth [15, 4], *Industry* Series, vol. 5, 327–330.

45 Wohl [15, 16], 64–77; Smith [10, 37], 218–19; Davidson [9, 1], ch. 7; Booth [15, 4], *Industry* Series, vol. 5, 330; London County Council, *London Statistics, 1911–12*, vol. 22, 182–3.

46 *Report of the Royal Commission on the Housing of the Working Classes*, PP1884–5, XXX, 18–19.

47 R. Price-Williams, 'The Population of London, 1801–1881', *Journal of the Royal Statistical Society*, September 1885, Table D, 405–29; Jones [12, 35], 175–6; A. S. Wohl, *The Eternal Slum: Housing and Social Policy in Victorian London* (1977), 23.

48 *Report of the Royal Commission* [17, 46], PP1884–5, xxx, 17.

49 J. White, *The Worst Street in North London. A Social History of Campbell Bunk, Islington, Between the Wars* (1986), 11–23.

50 H. Gavin, *Sanitary Ramblings* (1848), 34.

51 A. S. Wohl, 'Unfit for human habitation', in Dyos and Wolff [17, 3], vol. 2, 610–16; J. Burnett, *A Social History of Housing, 1815–1970* (Newton Abbot, 1978), 85–7; *Report of the Royal Commission* [17, 46], PP1884–5, xxx, 12, 22–3.

52 Lambert [15, 25], 348–9; Jones [12, 35], 174; Burnett [17, 51], 152–3.

53 Gavin [17, 50].

54 Wohl [17, 47], 80–93; Lambert [15, 25], 384–6.

55 Timbs [15, 27], 327–8.

56 George Buchanan, *St Giles's in 1857* (1858).

57 PRO Mepol 3/1, Thieves and their Habits, 1836; C. Knight, 'Suburban Milestones', in C. Knight (ed), *London* (6 vols, 1841), vol. 1, 254, and W. Weir, 'St Giles Past and Present', vol. 3, ch. 67, 257–72.

58 P. Collins, 'Dickens and London', in Dyos and Wolff [17, 3], vol. 2, 537–8; C. Dickens, *Sketches by Boz* (1836), Scenes, XXII, 207–8.

59 C. Dickens, *Oliver Twist*, 442–3 (Penguin edn, 1966, ed. P. Fairclough).

60 C. Dickens, 'On Duty with Inspector Field', *Reprinted Pieces* (1858), 340.

61 PRO, HO45/104, Supt. Maisie's Report to Col. Rowan, 7 August 1840; HO45/1091, Inspector John Yates's report on Bermondsey Street and Tooley Street, 13 May 1845.

62 Jones [12, 35], 181–2; Dyos [16, 103], ch. 5, 81–6: 'The objects of street improvement in Regency and Early Victorian London'; J. R. Kellett, *Railways and Victorian Cities* (1969), 332–6.

63 Jones, [12, 35], 161–9; Kellett [17, 62], 324–36.

64 London County Council [17, 45], vol. 22, 30, 34.

65 P. Cowan, *The Office. A Facet of Urban Growth* (1969), 157.
66 F. Harrison, *The Choice of Books and other Literary Pieces* (1886), 234, 255.
67 Price-Williams [17, 47]; London County Council [17, 45], vol. 22, 29–31; J. A. Yelling, *Slums and Slum Clearance in Victorian London* (1986), 149.
68 Kellett [17, 62], 35–8; *Journal of the Statistical Society of London* 9, March 1848, 1–18.
69 Jones [12, 35], 170.
70 Wohl [17, 47], 121–30.
71 Wohl [17, 47], ch. 5.
72 Wohl [17, 47], 157–8.
73 Wohl [17, 47], 150.
74 Wohl [17, 47], 154–60.
75 J. White, *Rothschild Buildings: Life in an East End Tenement Block, 1887–1920* (1980), 53–60 (quote on p. 60).
76 Booth [15, 4], *Poverty* Series, vol. 3, 34–5.
77 Booth [15, 4], *Poverty* Series, vol. 3, 5–13; R. Dennis, '"Hard to Let" in Edwardian London', *Urban Studies*, 26 (1989), 77–89; Wohl [17, 47], 170–74, 180; *Report of the Royal Commission on the Housing of the Working Classes*, PP1884–5, xxx, 54–5.
78 Wohl [17, 47], ch. 5; Jones [12, 35], ch. 10; Yelling [17, 67], passim.
79 G. Sims, *How the Poor Live* (1889 edn), in P. Keating, *Into Unknown England 1866–1913* (1976), 65–90; Wohl [17, 47], 201–5; Jones [12, 35], 223.
80 *The Bitter Cry of Outcast London* is reprinted in full in Keating [17, 79], 91–111.
81 *Report of the Royal Commission on the Housing of the Working Classes*, PP1884–5, xxx; Wohl [17, 47], ch. 9.
82 Wohl [17, 47], 248–53, 282.
83 Wohl [17, 47], ch. 10.
84 Booth [15, 4], *Poverty* Series, vol. 2, 94–101; *Religious Influences* Series, vol. 2, 67–72; Jones [12, 35], 230; Yelling [17, 67], 145–8.
85 London County Council [17, 45], vol. 22, 29, 161–74.

18. Transport and Suburban Growth

1 T. C. Barker, M. Robbins, *History of London Transport* (2 vols, 1963, 1974), vol. 1, 10–12.
2 Summerson [6, 44], ch. 13; Summerson, Sir J., *John Nash* (1980).
3 Barker and Robbins [18, 1], vol. 1, 10–14; Sheppard [12, 32], 108–9; Dyos and Aldcroft [7, 7], 82–4.
4 G. Tyack, 'James Pennethorne and London street improvements, 1838–55', *London Journal* 15 (1990); Dyos [16, 103], 81–6.
5 Dickens [17, 58], chs. 16–17.
6 Barker and Robbins [18, 1], vol. 1, chs. 1–2.
7 Barker and Robbins [18, 1], vol. 1, 44–58.

8 Kellett [17, 62], 35–43.

9 Barker and Robbins [18, 1], vol. 1, 106.

10 Kellett [17, 62], 311–14; F. M. L. Thompson, 'Nineteenth-century horse sense', *Economic History Review*, second series, 29 (1976).

11 Barker and Robbins [18, 1], vol. 1, ch. 3.

12 Sheppard [12, 32], 139.

13 Barker and Robbins [18, 1], vol. 1, 99–114.

14 Barker and Robbins [18, 1], vol. 1, 113–26.

15 Barker and Robbins [18, 1], vol. 1, 126–45.

16 Kellett [17, 62], ch. 9.

17 Barker and Robbins [18, 1], vol. 1, 208–40.

18 G. Thurston, *The Great Thames Disaster* (1965); Barker and Robbins [18, 1], vol. 1, 40–3, 165–6.

19 Barker and Robbins [18, 1], vol. 1, 166–77.

20 P. J. Edwards, *The History of London Street Improvements, 1855–97* (1898), 125–9.

21 Owen [15, 31], ch. 4; Edwards [18, 20], 33, 57, 125–9.

22 H. Clunn, *London Rebuilt, 1897–1927* (1927), 51–68; Barker and Jackson [7, 3], 146–7.

23 E. H. Whetham, 'The London milk trade, 1860–1900', *Economic History Review*, second series, 17 (1964), 369–80.

24 Barker and Robbins [18, 1], vol. 1, 58.

25 Kellett [17, 62], 376–82; *Report of the Royal Commission on the Housing of the Working Classes*, PP1884–5, xxx, 49–50.

26 Kellett [17, 62], 90–99, 365–90; Dyos, 'Workmen's fares in South London, 1860–1914', in Dyos [16, 103], 87–100.

27 H. Pollins, 'Transport lines and social divisions', Centre for Urban Studies, *London. Aspects of Change*, 44; Barker and Robbins [18, 1], vol. 1, ch. 6.

28 Barker and Robbins [18, 1], vol. 1, 268–70; vol. 2, 22–8.

29 Barker and Robbins [18, 1], vol. 1, ch. 8; vol. 2, 12, 15.

30 Barker and Robbins [18, 1], vol. 1, 300–303. *Encyclopaedia Britannica*, 11th edn, vol. 27, 400–401.

31 Barker and Robbins [18, 1], vol. 2, 35–47.

32 Barker and Robbins [18, 1], vol. 2, 54–70.

33 Barker and Robbins [18, 1], vol. 2, 77–84.

34 *Report of Royal Commission on London Traffic*, PP1905, xxx. The quotation is from p. 16; T. C. Barker, M. Robbins, *A History of London Transport, 2: The Twentieth Century, to 1970* (1974), vol. 2, 86–9; Robson [15, 40], 145–8.

35 J. T. Coppock, H. C. Prince (eds.), *Greater London* (1964), 68–70; Barker and Robbins [18, 34], vol. 2, 104–13.

36 Barker and Robbins [18, 34], vol. 2, 113–18.

37 Barker and Robbins [18, 34], vol. 2, 26–34, 91–101.

38 D. L. Munby, *Inland Transport Statistics, Great Britain. 1900–1970* (Oxford

1978), vol. 1, 537; A. A. Jackson, *Semi-Detached London: Suburban Development, Life and Transport, 1900–39* (1973), 54–6.

39 Llewellyn Smith [17, 16], vol. 1, 180.

40 Barker and Robbins [18, 34], vol. 2, 118–36, 164–70; Munby [18, 38], vol. 1, 537.

41 Barker and Robbins [18, 34], vol. 2, 170–83.

42 Barker and Robbins [18, 34], vol. 2, 190.

43 Thompson [18, 10], 60–81; Hardy [15, 10], 184–6.

44 Llewellyn Smith [17, 16], vol. 1, 314.

45 J. F. Murray, *The World of London*, 1843, quoted in D. A. Reeder, 'A theatre of suburbs', in H. J. Dyos (ed.), *The Study of Urban History* (1968), 251.

46 W. Cobbett, *Rural Rides* (1967 edn, ed. G. Woodcock), 165, 216, 229.

47 Booth [15, 4], *Industry* Series, vol. 5, 28–34.

48 Dyos [16, 103], 28.

49 H. J. Dyos, D. Reeder, 'Slums and suburbs', in Dyos and Wolff [17, 3], vol. 1, 370.

50 G. Crossick (ed.), *The Lower Middle Class in Britain 1870–1914* (1976), 19.

51 W. Ashworth, *The Genesis of Modern British Town Planning* (1954), 11–13; Jackson [18, 38], 36–41.

52 Mitchell and Deane [10, 35], 24–7.

53 Charles Booth's 'Poverty Maps', printed in his *Life and Labour of the People in London* [15, 4] or published separately by the London Topographical Society (1984), show this distribution of wealth and poverty clearly.

54 Dyos [16, 103], ch. 10; A. K. Cairncross, B. Weber, 'Fluctuations in building in Great Britain, 1785–1849', in Carus-Wilson [6, 6], vol. 3, 318–33.

55 H. Hobhouse, *Thomas Cubitt, Master Builder* (1971); Summerson [6, 44], 191–6; Sheppard [12, 32], 97–101.

56 Hobhouse [18, 55], 81.

57 Baedeker [11, 42], 357; Hobhouse [18, 55], 115, 127.

58 Summerson [6, 44], chs. 14, 21.

59 Booth [15, 4], *Religious Influences* Series, vol. 3, 87–9.

60 Summerson [6, 44], 175–6.

61 Booth [5, 4], *Religious Influences* Series, vol. 3, map 2.

62 D. J. Olsen, *The Growth of Victorian London* (1983), ch. 4; Reeder [18, 45].

63 G. Evans, *Kensington* (1975), 131.

64 P. E. Malcolmson, 'Getting a living in the slums of Victorian Kensington', *London Journal* 1 (May 1975), 28–55; J. Davis, 'From rookeries to communities: race, poverty and policing in London, 1850–1985', *History Workshop Journal* 27 (1989), 66–73.

65 Booth [15, 4], *Religious Influences* Series, vol. 1, 138–49.

66 F. M. L. Thompson, *Hampstead: Building a Borough, 1650–1964* (1974), chs. 1–8; D. Olsen, 'House upon House', in Dyos and Wolff [17, 3], vol. 1, ch. 14; Olsen [18, 62], 244–64; Coppock and Prince [18, 35], 129–31.

67 Thorne [16, 31], 216–17.

68 Thorne [16, 31], 233; Jackson [18, 38], 70–89.
69 Dickens [17, 58], 'The Streets – Morning', 64–5.
70 G. Tindall, *The Fields Beneath: the History of One London Village* (1977), 186, quoting the *London Argus*.
71 T. Hinchcliffe, 'Highbury New Park: a nineteenth-century middle-class suburb', *London Journal* 7, 27–44.
72 M. Hunter, *The Victorian Villas of Hackney*, 8–33 (The Hackney Society, 1981).
73 Booth [15, 4], *Religious Influences* Series, vol. 1, 73–9.
74 Dyos [9, 25], 109–13.
75 Dyos [9, 25], 39–49, 85–113.
76 Alleyn's career is described in Burford [4, 71], 182–8.
77 Dyos [9, 25], 99–100.
78 Kellett [17, 62], 367–71.
79 D. Read, *England 1868–1914* (1979), 259.
80 Olsen [18, 62], 240–41.
81 Olsen [18, 62], 242.
82 F. Harrison [17, 66], 438–40.
83 Sir W. Besant, *London in the Nineteenth Century* (1909), quoted in Olsen [18, 62], 210–11.
84 Ashworth [18, 51], 171.
85 Ashworth [18, 51], 158–63; Pevsner [3, 80], *Middlesex*, 59–64.
86 Ashworth [18, 51], 182–90.

19. KEEPING THE PEACE

1 T. de Quincey, 'On murder considered as one of the fine arts'; P. D. James, T. A. Critchley, *The Maul and the Pear Tree: the Ratcliffe Highway Murders 1811* (1971).
2 Gatrell, Lenman and Parker [13, 29], 174.
3 Radzinowicz [11, 31], vol. 4, 158; C. Emsley [13 30], ch. 1; D. Philips, 'A New Engine of Power and Authority', in Gatrell, Lenman and Parker [13, 29].
4 John Badcock, *John Bee's Living Picture of London for 1828, and Strangers' Guide through the Streets of the Metropolis* (1828); D. A. Low, *Thieves' Kitchen* (Gloucester, 1982).
5 Thompson [14, 27], 660.
6 Stevenson [14, 18], 193–8; Thompson [14, 27], 769–75.
7 E. Halevy, *A History of the English People in the Nineteenth Century*, vol. 2, *The Liberal Awakening*, 80–106 (quote, 103); Philips [19, 3], 183; Prothero [16, 11], 132–55; J. Stevenson, 'The Queen Caroline affair', in Stevenson [14, 12], 117–48.
8 L. Radzinowicz [11, 31] vol. 4, 156; Philips [19, 3], 183; S. Palmer, *Police and Protest in England and Ireland 1789–1850* (Cambridge, 1988), 288; Emsley [19, 2], 23.
9 Thompson [14, 27], 781.

10 G. Rudé, *Protest and Punishment* (Oxford, 1978), 63; Palmer [19, 8], 8–11, 286–94.

11 J. J. Tobias [13, 23], 77.

12 *Report of the Select Committee on Police of the Metropolis*, passim, PP1828, vi.

13 J. F. Moylan, *Scotland Yard and the Metropolitan Police* (1934), 178.

14 *Select Committee on Police* [19, 12], 1828, 9–13.

15 For the origins and early years of the Metropolitan Police, see: Emsley [13, 30], ch. 2; Radzinowicz [11, 31], vol. 4, ch. 5; Tobias [13, 23], ch. 4; C. Reith, *The British Police and the Democratic Ideal* (Oxford, 1943); C. Reith, *The Police Idea* (Oxford, 1938); D. V. Jones, 'The New Police, Crime and People in England and Wales, 1829–88', *Transactions of the Royal Historical Society*, fifth series, 33, 1983, 151–67.

16 Radzinowicz [11, 31], vol. 4, ch. 5; P. T. Smith, *Policing Victorian London* (Westport, Connecticut, 1985), chs. 1, 2; Jones [19, 15].

17 J. Grant, *Sketches in London* (1838), 391–9.

18 W. O'Brien, *Edinburgh Review* 96 (July 1852), 1–33.

19 Dickens [17, 60], 'On Duty with Inspector Field'.

20 Metropolitan Police Criminal Returns, Scotland Yard.

21 R. D. Storch, *Popular Culture and Custom in Nineteenth-Century England* (1982), introduction; R. D. Storch, 'Police control of street prostitution in mid-Victorian London', in D. H. Bayley (ed.), *Police and Society* (1972), 49–72; Goodway [16, 9], 3, 104–5.

22 Storch, 'Police control of street prostitution', in Bayley [19, 21], 56–9.

23 S. Inwood, 'Policing London's morals. The Metropolitan Police and popular culture, 1829–1850', *London Journal* 15 (1990), 131–5; J. Benyon (ed.), *Scarman and After* (1984), 51; W. R. Miller, 'Never on Sunday', in Bayley [19, 21], 128–42; H. Cunningham, 'The Metropolitan fairs: a case study in the social control of leisure', in A. P. Donajgrodzki, *Social Control in Nineteenth-Century Britain* (1977).

24 Home Office papers, Public Record Office, HO 45/6628. Note by Sir George Grey on a letter dated 25 February 1857.

25 Storch, *Popular Culture and Custom* [19, 21], 79–80; Mayhew [16, 63], vol. 3, 64–72; Inwood [19, 23], 131.

26 Cunningham [19, 23], 177.

27 Metropolitan Police Criminal Returns, Scotland Yard; D. V. Jones, *Crime, Protest, Community and Police in Nineteenth-Century Britain* (1982), 119–20.

28 J. J. Tobias, *Crime and Industrial Society in the Nineteenth Century* (Harmondsworth, 1972. 1st published 1967), ch. 4; Radzinowicz [11, 31], vol. 5, *The Emergence of Penal Policy*, 73–84; J. Davis, 'Law-breaking and law enforcement: the making of a criminal class in mid-Victorian London' (unpublished Ph.D. thesis, Boston College, 1985), chs. 1–4; Mayhew [16, 63], vol. 4; V. A. C. Gatrell, 'The decline of theft and violence in Victorian and Edwardian England', in Gatrell, Lenman and Parker [13, 29], especially 261–6.

29 *Report of the Commissioner of the Metropolitan Police*, 1899.

30 Davis [19, 28], chs. 2–3; Metropolitan Police Criminal Returns, 1841–50.
31 L. Rose, *Massacre of the Innocents: Infanticide in Britain, 1800–1939* (1986), chs. 3–5
32 Rose [19, 31], chs. 7–8.
33 Rose [19, 31], chs. 11–12.
34 Fishman [15, 5], 209–29; J. R. Walkowitz, *City of Dreadful Delight: Narratives of Sexual Danger in Late Victorian London* (1992), ch. 7.
35 *Report of the Commissioner of the Metropolitan Police*, 1899, Appendix 31, 72.
36 Sims [16, 55], vol. 3, 15–21.

20. POPULAR POLITICS AND TRADE UNIONISM

1 Thompson [14, 27], 266, 277, 284.
2 Thompson and Yeo [16, 12], 236; Mayhew [16, 63], vol. 3, 233. For the aristocracy of labour, see Hobsbawm's articles in *Labouring Men* (1964) and *Worlds of Labour* (1984); A. E. Musson, *British Trade Unions, 1800–1875* (1972), 15–21; R. Gray, *The Aristocracy of Labour in Nineteenth-Century Britain* (1981); Thompson [14, 27], ch. 8; Crossick [16, 39], passim.
3 On early trade unions, see Musson [20, 2]; E. H. Hunt, *British Labour History, 1815–1914* (1981), 192–206; Prothero [16, 11]; H. Pelling, *A History of British Trade Unionism* (1976), chs. 1–3; Webb and Webb [16, 28], chs. 1–3; Rule [12, 39].
4 D. Thompson, *The Chartists* (Aldershot, 1984), 106.
5 Sheppard [12, 32], 319.
6 J. Morley, *Life of Richard Cobden* (1903 edn), 144.
7 Prothero [16, 11], 159–82; G. Wallas, *The Life of Francis Place 1771–1854* (1898), 197–240.
8 D. Vincent, *Bread, Knowledge and Freedom* (1982), 134–5.
9 Prothero [16, 11], 191–203.
10 Prothero [16, 11], 272–81.
11 D. Large, 'William Lovett', in P. Hollis (ed.), *Pressure from Without in Early Victorian England* (1974), 122.
12 Large [20, 11], 121–3.
13 Sheppard [12, 32], 343; Jones [12, 35], 362.
14 Prothero [16, 11], ch. 15; Musson [20, 2], 32–4.
15 Prothero [16, 11], 293–6; G. Thurston, *The Clerkenwell Riot* (1967), passim.
16 J. T. Ward, *Chartism* (1973), 72–5.
17 HO 45/OS102, Mayne's memo, 5 August 1839; MEPO 2/59, informers' reports, 1839.
18 I. Prothero, 'Chartism in London', *Past and Present*, 44 (1969), 101; Jennifer Bennett, 'The London Democratic Association, 1837–41: A Study in London Radicalism', in J. Epstein, D. Thompson (eds.), *The Chartist Experience: Studies in Working-Class Radicalism and Culture, 1830–1860* (1882), 87–119; Goodway [16, 9], 24–37.

19 Goodway [16, 9], 38–53, 106–11, 123–6.

20 J. Belchem, '1848: Feargus O'Connor and the collapse of the mass platform', in Epstein and Thompson [20, 18], 278.

21 Goodway [16, 9], 68–77, 131–9.

22 Goodway [16, 9], 136–42; D. Large, 'London in the year of Revolutions', in J. Stevenson [14, 12], 192.

23 Goodway [16, 9], 111–22.

24 Musson [20, 2], 49–52; G. D. H. Cole, 'Some notes on British trade unionism in the third quarter of the nineteenth century', in Carus-Wilson [6, 6], vol. 3.

25 Webb and Webb [16, 28], 210–24; Pelling [20, 3], 49–51.

26 Webb and Webb [16, 28], 228–32; R. Harrison, *Before the Socialists: Studies in Labour and Politics, 1861–1881* (1965), 3.

27 Webb and Webb [16, 28], 233–41.

28 S. Coltham, 'The Bee-Hive Newspaper: its origin and early struggles', in J. Saville, A. Briggs (eds), *Essays in Labour History in Memory of G. D. H. Cole* (1967), 174–204.

29 R. Harrison, 'Professor Beesley and the working-class movement', in Saville and Briggs [20, 28].

30 A. Briggs, *Victorian People* (Pelican edn, 1965. 1st published 1954), 201–2.

31 Smith [19, 16], 162–72; Harrison [20, 26], 80–85.

32 Harrison [20, 26], 85–108.

33 M. Cowling, *1867: Disraeli, Gladstone and Revolution* (Cambridge, 1967).

34 Harrison [20, 26], 129–36; F. B. Smith, *The Making of the Second Reform Bill* (Cambridge, 1966); Briggs [20, 30], 199–204; R. Blake, *Disraeli* (1966), ch. 21.

35 Pelling [20, 3], 64–76; Webb and Webb [16, 28], 249–95.

36 I. Berlin, *Karl Marx* (Oxford, 1978), chs. 9–11; A. Briggs, *Marx in London* (1982); Henry Collins, 'The English branches of the First International', in Saville and Briggs [20, 28], 242–75.

37 P. Thompson, *Socialists, Liberals and Labour: the Struggle for London, 1885–1914* (1967), 70–74; H. Pelling, *Social Geography of British Elections, 1885–1910* (1967), 6–8.

38 Pelling [20, 37], ch. 2; Thompson [20, 37], 68–90; M. Pugh, *The Making of Modern British Politics* (1982), 81–7.

39 P. Adelman, *Gladstone, Disraeli and Later Victorian Politics* (1970), 86–7, quoting Harrison, *Fortnightly Review* 15 (1874).

40 Pelling [20, 37], 27–42, 60–67; H. J. Hanham, *Elections and Party Management* (Hassocks, 1978), 225–7; E. J. Feuchtwanger, *Disraeli, Democracy and the Tory Party* (Oxford, 1968), 95–8; R. Blake, *The Conservative Party from Peel to Churchill* (1970), 111–12.

41 Pelling [20, 37], 36–59.

42 Thompson [20, 37], ch. 8; Pelling [20, 37], ch. 2; Pugh [20, 38], 72–81, 120–29.

43 Thompson [20, 37], ch. 6.

44 E. J. Hobsbawm, *Labouring Men* [20, 2], 250–71, 'The Fabians reconsidered'; Thompson [20, 37], 137–49.

45 Thompson [20, 37], 149–65; B. Donoughue, G. W. Jones, *Herbert Morrison. Portrait of a Politician* (1973), 15–35, is a good account of Labour politics in London just before the First World War.

46 Thompson [20, 37], ch. 6.

47 Thompson [20, 37], 39–43.

48 Webb and Webb [16, 28], 402.

49 Hobsbawm, *Labouring Men* [20, 2], 158–78, 'British Gas Workers, 1873–1914'; Thompson [20, 37], 45–8.

50 Hobsbawm, *Labouring Men* [20, 2], 'General labour unions in Britain, 1889–1914', 181.

51 Lovell [16, 50], ch. 3, 59–91.

52 Lovell [16, 50], 92–112; Jones [12, 35], 315–17; Webb and Webb [16, 28], 403–5; Thompson [20, 37], 48–52.

53 Jones [12, 35], 318–21.

54 Lovell [16, 50], ch. 5; Jones [12, 35], ch. 17; J. Saville, 'Trade unions and free labour: the background to the Taff Vale decision', in Saville and Briggs [20, 28], 316–50.

55 Thompson [20, 37], 53–8; Pelling [20, 3], 102–6.

56 Booth [15, 4], *Industry* Series, vol. 5, 143–6; Webb and Webb [16, 28], 741–3.

57 Booth [15, 4], *Industry* Series, vol. 5, 136–51, 173–80.

58 H. A. Clegg, *A History of British Trade Unions Since 1889*, vol. 2, 24–74; Webb and Webb [16, 28], 482–509; Thompson [20, 37], 58–67; R. C. K. Ensor, *England, 1870–1914* (Oxford, 1936), 438–44; Lovell [16, 50], chs. 6–7; F. Owen, *Tempestuous Journey* (1954), 213–16.

21. PASSING THE TIME

1 J. Gore (ed.), *The Creevy Papers* (1963), 150, Lady Holland to Mrs Creevy, September 1817.

2 W. Bagehot, *The English Constitution* (New Thinker's Library edn, 1964), 94–5.

3 L. Davidoff, *The Best Circles* (1973), 63.

4 Lord David Cecil, *The Young Melbourne* (1948 Pan edn. 1st published 1939), 63.

5 F. M. L. Thompson, 'Moving frontiers and the fortunes of the aristocratic town house, 1830–1930', *London Journal* 20 (1995), 67–78.

6 Thompson [21, 5], 67–78.

7 G. O. Trevelyan (ed.), *The Life and Letters of Lord Macaulay* (2 vols, Oxford, 1932), vol. 1, 189–220.

8 Blake [20, 34], 113–14.

9 Timbs [15, 27], 433; Trevelyan [21, 7], vol. 1, 192–4.

10 J. Ridley, *Lord Palmerston*, 385–6, 702–3.

11 A. Kinnear, 'The Ways of the World', *Pall Mall Magazine*, May 1901, 133–9.

12 Thompson [21, 5], 75.

13 D. Cannadine, *The Decline and Fall of the British Aristocracy* (New Haven, 1990), 350–51.

14 Timbs [15, 27], 241–2; Baedeker [16, 109], 101; Kent [4, 81], 371–80.

15 Timbs [15, 27], 239–61; Hanham [20, 40], 99–101; Summerson [6, 44], 242–9.

16 Thornbury and Walford [3, 86], vol. 4, 295–6, 302–3; D. Taylor, D. Bush, *The Golden Age of British Hotels* (1974), 4–5.

17 Taylor and Bush [21, 16], 83–90.

18 A. Service, *London 1900* (1979), 146–50; Sims [16, 55], vol. 2, 236–42.

19 D. J. Oddy, D. S. Miller (eds.), *The Making of the Modern British Diet* (1976), 162.

20 Olsen [18, 62], 102–9; Kent [4, 81], 463–7.

21 Olsen [18, 62], 110.

22 Oddy and Miller [21, 19], 162–8; Sims [16, 55], vol. 1, 297–303; Kent [4, 81], 463–7; Baedeker [11, 42], 13–19.

23 B. Lancaster, *The Department Store: a Social History* (1995), 16–20.

24 Timbs [15, 27], 19–20, 40–42; G. Shaw, 'The role of retailing in the urban economy', in J. H. Johnston, C. G. Pooley (eds.), *The Structure of Nineteenth-Century Cities* (1982), 186.

25 Lancaster [21, 23], 20–23. *Dictionary of National Biography*, entry on William Whiteley; Olsen [18, 62], 123–7.

26 Hibbert and Weinreb [8, 36], entries on various stores; Lancaster [21, 23], 16–25, 112.

27 Service [21, 18], 110–17.

28 Lancaster [21, 23], 23–4, 48–51; Davis [7, 10], 288–93.

29 Lancaster [21, 23], 60–81, 90–91.

30 Lancaster [21, 23], 171; Llewellyn Smith [17, 16], vol. 1, 418; vol. 5, 195.

31 Lancaster [21, 23], 125–42.

32 B. Harrison, 'Pubs', in Dyos and Wolff [17, 3], vol. 1, 162–8; Booth [15, 4], *Final Volume*, map showing public houses, schools and places of worship in London, 1899–1900; B. Harrison, *Drink and the Victorians: the Temperance Question in England, 1861–1881* (1965), 58.

33 Mayhew [16, 63], vol. 3, 9–10; Harrison [21, 32], 48–50.

34 Harrison [21, 32], 46–8, 50–57.

35 Harrison [21, 32], 327–9.

36 Harrison [21, 32], 37–9, 298–34.

37 Mayhew [16, 63], vol. 1, 158–9. Pages 158–212 deal with street-sellers of food and drink.

38 Sims [16, 55], vol. 1, 297–9; Oddy and Miller [21, 22], 162–8.

39 Hibbert and Weinreb [8, 36], 378.

40 Hibbert and Weinreb [8, 36], 208.

41 Mayhew [16, 63], vol. 1, 11–19, 40–42.

42 M. R. Booth, R. Southern, F. Marker, L. Marker, R. Davies, *The Revels History of Drama in English*, vol. 6, 1750–1880 (1975), l–lxii.

43 L. James, *Print and the People* (1976), 82, 85; Booth, Southern, Marker, Marker, Davies [21, 42], 10; Arundell [11, 19], 107, 118–19.

44 Arundell [11, 19], 134; Charles Dickens, in *Household Words*.

45 Dickens [17, 58], 'Private Theatres', 138; Booth, Southern, Marker, Marker, Davies [21, 42], 12, 26–7; Donohue [11, 18], 156–9.

46 M. R. Booth, 'The metropolis on stage', in Dyos and Wolf [17, 3], vol. 1, 211–24; James [21, 43], 83–7.

47 *Encyclopaedia Britannica*, 11th edn (1911) vol. 8, 533.

48 G. Rowell, *Theatre in the Age of Irving* (Oxford, 1981), passim; H. Hunt, K. Richards, J. R. Taylor, *The Revels History of Drama*, vol. 7, *1880s to the Present Day*, 3–10, 74–104.

49 Playbills in D. F. Cheshire, *Music Hall in Britain* (Newton Abbot, 1974), 13, and D. Howard, *London Theatres and Music Halls, 1850–1950* (1970), 153.

50 See the Select Committee on Dramatic Literature of 1832 and the Select Committee on Theatre Licensing of 1892.

51 H. Cunningham, *Leisure and the Industrial Revolution c. 1780–1880* (1980), 165–9.

52 Howard [21, 49] gives details of 876 theatres, music halls and musical pubs licensed between 1850 and 1914; P. Bailey (ed.), *Music Hall. The Business of Pleasure* (Milton Keynes, 1986), x; Cunningham [21, 51], 169–70.

53 Saint [17, 24], 58–62; Cunningham [21, 51], 169.

54 Service [21, 18], 119–29; J. Earl, 'Building the halls', in Bailey [21, 52], 27–31.

55 Cunningham [21, 51], ch. 4; P. Bailey, *Leisure and Class in Victorian England* (1978), ch. 2.

56 Select Committee on Public Walks, PP1833, vol. 15, 5–9; Cunningham [21, 51], 92–3; G. F. Chadwick, *The Park and the Town* (1966), 50–51.

57 Chadwick [21, 56], 13–29.

58 Chadwick [21, 56], 111–23; B. Elliott, 'Victorian Parks', in M. Galinou (ed.), *London's Pride*, 152; Thornbury and Walford [3, 86], vol. 5, 508–9.

59 Booth [15, 4], *Religious Influences* Series, vol. 1, 65; Timbs [15, 27], 655.

60 Chadwick [21, 56], 125–31; Timbs [15, 27], 642–3.

61 Owen [15, 31], 147–53.

62 A. Briggs, *Victorian Things* (1990), 52–88; Rolt [12, 42], 148–77; C. H. Gibbs-Smith, *The Great Exhibition of 1851* (1981).

63 Pevsner [3, 80], *London*, vol. 2, 252–9.

64 The *Athenaeum*, quoted in Crook [11, 16], 196; Cunningham [21, 51], 104–5.

65 Cunningham [21, 51], 106; Crook [11, 16], 65–6, 73–82.

66 Crook [11, 16], 155–63.

67 Cunningham [21, 51], 104–5.

68 N. Harte, *The University of London 1836–1986. An Illustrated History* (1986), 61–76, 147–60.

69 R. Irwin, R. Staveley (eds.), *The Libraries of London* (1961), 109; Cunningham [21, 51], 105–6.

70 T. Mason, *Association Football and English Society, 1863–1915* (Brighton, 1980), 29, 141–3.

71 J. A. R. Pimlott, *The Englishman's Holiday* (1947), 118–26, 153–6, 160–66, 178–9.

72 Booth [15, 4], *Final Volume,* 47–57.

73 Booth [15, 4], *Religious Influences* Series, vol. 7, 422–6.

74 Aspinall and Smith [13, 16], 645–6.

75 Select Committee on Education in the Metropolis, PP1816, vol. 4, passim.

76 Summerson [6, 44], 212–29; Sheppard [12, 32], 211–16.

77 O. Chadwick, *The Victorian Church* (2 vols, 1970), vol. 1, 130–35, 325–37; Sheppard [12, 32], 227–8; A. Smith, *The Established Church and Popular Religion, 1750–1850* (1971), 109.

78 *Report on the Religious Census of 1851,* PP1852–3, lxxxix, 184, 296, and Detailed Tables, 3–9.

79 Young and Handcock [15, 29], 389–93; Thompson [14, 27], 417.

80 Mayhew [16, 63], vol. 1, 21–2.

81 Mayhew [16, 63], vol. 1, 459–61; vol. 2, 225.

82 T. Wright, *Our New Masters* (1873), 86–92; Chadwick [21, 77], vol. 2, 266–7; G. Parsons, 'A question of meaning: religion and working-class life', in G. Parsons (ed.), *Religion in Victorian Britain* (4 vols, Manchester, 1988), vol. 2, 63–87.

83 Sheppard [12, 32], 242–3; Chadwick [21, 77], 308–12.

84 Booth [15, 4], *Religious Influences* Series, vol. 7, 112.

85 Inglis [17, 33], 85–100; Booth [15, 4], *Religious Influences* Series, vol. 7, 129–38.

86 Parsons, *Religion in Victorian Britain* [21, 82], vol. 1, 218–23, 230–33.

87 Parsons [21, 82], 121–8.

88 Inglis [17, 33], 175–8.

89 Booth [15, 4], *Religious Influences* Series, vol. 7, 326–8; A. Fried, R. Elman (eds), *Charles Booth's London* (1969), 245–7, 325–7, 339–52.

90 R. Mudie-Smith, *The Religious Life of London* (1904), 25.

91 Booth [15, 4], *Final Volume,* 220–23; K. G. T. McDonnell, 'Roman Catholics in London', in Hollaender and Kellaway [2, 20], 429–43.

92 Chadwick [21, 77], 235; Inglis [17, 33], 119–42, 309–19; Lees [15, 3], 172–84.

93 Mudie-Smith [21, 90], 15–17; Booth [15, 4], *Final Volume,* 220.

94 Inglis [17, 33], 143–74.

95 Mudie-Smith [21, 90], 202.

96 Booth [15, 4], *Religious Influences* Series, vol. 7, 291–4, 416, 422–8; G. S. Jones, 'Working-class culture and working-class politics in London, 1870–1900', in G. S. Jones, *Languages of Class* (Cambridge, 1983), 192–8.

97 Mudie-Smith [21, 90], 15–18, 38, 87.

98 Jones [19, 27], 117–43; Booth [15, 4], *Final Volume*, 69, 200–201; *Industry Series*, vol. 5, 338.

99 R. Kipling, 'Tommy', *Barrack-Room Ballads* (1982).

100 P. Keating, *The Working Classes in Victorian Fiction* (1971), 152–66; G. S. Jones, 'The "cockney" and the nation', in Feldman and Jones [15, 6], 272–324.

101 S. Maclure, *A History of Education in London, 1870–1990* (1990), 24–9; J. Burnett, *Destiny Obscure: Autobiographies of Childhood, Education and Family from the 1820s to the 1920s*, has excellent first-hand accounts of London schooling in the nineteenth century.

102 Maclure [21, 101], 17–20.

103 Booth [15, 4], *Poverty* Series, vol. 3, 202.

104 Maclure [21, 101], 34–40; Booth [15, 4], *Poverty* Series, vol. 3, 219.

105 Booth [15, 4], *Poverty* Series, vol. 3, 290–3; London County Council (1911–12) [17, 45], vol. 22, 363.

106 London County Council (1911–12) [17, 45], vol. 22, 308–10, 363–70.

107 D. E. B. Weiner, 'The People's Palace. An image for East London in the 1880s', in Feldman and Jones [15, 6], 40–55.

108 London County Council (1911–12) [17, 45], vol. 22, 371–82; *Encyclopaedia Britannica*, 11th edn (1910–11), articles on Technical Education (Philip Magnus) and Polytechnics (William Garnett); Webb [15, 49], 76–82. The eleven Polytechnics and similar colleges supported by the LCC and the City were the Battersea, Borough Road, Northern, Regent Street, South-Western and Woolwich Polytechnics, Birkbeck, East London and City of London Colleges, Sir John Cass's Institute and Northampton Institute (Finsbury).

MODERN LONDON, 1914–1997

22. THE FIRST WORLD WAR

1 H. H. Asquith, *Letters to Venetia Stanley* (ed. M. Brock and E. Brock, Oxford, 1985), 148.

2 L. Woodward, 'The study of contemporary history', *Journal of Contemporary History* 1 (1966), 6–7.

3 J. Lawrence, M. Dean, J. L. Robert, 'The outbreak of war and the urban economy: Paris, Berlin, and London in 1914', in *Economic History Review* 45 (1992), 564–93.

4 E. Roberts, *Women's Work, 1840–1940* (1988), 63–8.

5 Barker and Robbins [18, 34], vol. 2, 194–5; Coppock and Prince [18, 35], 238–9.

6 J. E. Martin, *Greater London, an Industrial Geography* (1966), 30–1; Information drawn from records of the Ministry of Munitions (especially MUN5/365/1122/35), kindly supplied by Professor John Armstrong.

7 HLG 27/35, 4: LCC evidence to the Royal Commission on the Distribution of the Industrial Population, 1938.

8 A. Marwick, *The Deluge* (1965), 152–4.

9 T. Wilson, *The Myriad Faces of War* (Oxford, 1986), 765, quoting from C. F. G. Masterman, *England After War*.

10 Wilson [22, 9], 514–19, 648–50.

11 S. Sassoon, *Memoirs of an Infantry Officer* (1965 edn. 1st published 1930), 205–6.

12 Pritchett [16, 35], 172.

13 T. H. O'Brien, *The Official History of the Second World War: Civil Defence* (1955), 15–16.

14 *Encyclopaedia Britannica*, 12th edn, vol. 30, 95–100, E. B. Ashmore, 'Air Raids'; O'Brien [22, 13], 11; Palmer [12, 12], 117–23; D. Lloyd George, *War Memoirs* (1938 Odhams edn), vol. 2, 1097–1108.

15 Wilson [22, 9], 650.

16 Sassoon [22, 11], 207–8.

17 Wilson [22, 9], 509.

18 Wilson [22, 9], 1105; B. Webb, *Diary* (4 vols, 1982–5, N. and J. Mackenzie, eds), vol. 3.

19 W. N. P. Barbellion, *The Journal of a Disappointed Man* (1919), 252–61.

20 *Encyclopaedia Britannica*, 12th edn, vol. 30, 100.

21 *Daily News*, 13 and 18 May 1915.

22 Wilson [22, 9], 160, 645.

23 C. H. Rolph (C. R. Hewitt), *London Particulars* (Oxford, 1980), 197–201. The Old Hundredth is the hymn that begins 'All people that on earth do dwell'.

24 Pritchett [16, 35], 176.

25 Llewellyn Smith [17, 16], vol. 1, 335. The Home Counties figures refer to London, Essex, Herts., Middlesex and Kent.

26 D. Lloyd George [22, 14], vol. 1, 61–70; Kynaston [16, 53], vol. 2 *Golden Years, 1890–1914*, 600–611; S. Pollard, *The Development of the British Economy 1914–1980* (3rd edn, 1983), 35–6.

27 Morgan and Thomas [12, 64], 189–90.

28 Michie [16, 49], 79–80, 104–6, 116–17, 135; *Encyclopaedia Britannica*, 12th edn, vol. 32, 795.

23. BETWEEN THE WARS, 1918–1939

1 P. Abercrombie, *Greater London Plan, 1944* (1945), 27–8, 188. The estimated figure of war dead is taken from the LCC's evidence to the Barlow Commission, HLG 27/35, 4.

2 Robson [15, 40], 294–314; Young and Garside [15, 40], 128–39; Saint [17, 24], 109–11.

3 J. Gillespie, 'Municipalism, monopoly and management', in Saint [17, 24], 107–12.

4 Barker and Robbins [18, 34], vol. 2, 215–32.

5 Barker and Robbins [18, 34], 216–21, 295–9.

6 Munby [18, 38], 537–41.

7 Barker and Robbins [18, 34], vol. 2, 233–41, 299–303.

8 Jackson [18, 38], vol. 2, 112–14.

9 J. Marshall, *The History of the Great West Road: its social and economic influence on the surrounding area* (Hounslow Leisure Services, 1995), 58–69.

10 Abercrombie [23, 1], 64; Martin [22, 6], 32–5.

11 Llewellyn Smith [17, 16], vol. 1, 197; R. Sinclair, *Metropolitan Man. The Future of the English* (1937), 282–94; Dyos and Aldcroft [7, 7], 397; J. H. Forshaw, P. Abercrombie, *County of London Plan, 1943* (1943), 3–4, 48.

12 E. Jones, C. Woodward, *A Guide to the Architecture of London* (1983), 343, 359; Pevsner [3, 80], *Middlesex*, 26 (1951).

13 Coppock and Prince [18, 35], 71–5; Jackson [18, 38], 233–5; Barker and Robbins [18, 34], vol. 2, 242–60.

14 Barker and Robbins [18, 34], vol. 2, 202–14, 270–82; Donoughue and Jones [20, 45], 140–50, 187–8.

15 Jackson [18, 38], 241–2.

16 Abercrombie [23, 1], Appendix 2, 188–9; M. Robbins, *Middlesex* (1953), chs. 5, 7, 14.

17 Jackson [18, 38], 52–8.

18 Young and Garside [15, 40], 143–53.

19 Jackson [18, 38], 93.

20 Jackson [18, 38], 93–8; C. L. Mowat, *Britain Between the Wars, 1918–1940* (1955), 43–4, 164–5, 458–61; J. A. Yelling, *Slums and Redevelopment. Policy and Practice in England, 1918–1945* (1992), 87–107.

21 Jackson [18, 38], 157.

22 Jackson [18, 38], 299–311.

23 Jackson [18, 38], 291–9; Burnett [17, 51], 218–26.

24 Robson [15, 40], 435, quoting H. A. Mess.

25 Saint [17, 24], 224.

26 Robbins [23, 16], 183.

27 Robbins [23, 16], 103–11, 133–44; Davidson [9, 1], 68.

28 G. Orwell, *Coming up for Air* (Penguin edn, 1962), 14–17.

29 Jackson [18, 38], 205.

30 Abercrombie [23, 1], plan between pp. 30 and 31.

31 Robbins [23, 16], 41; Abercrombie [23, 1], 87–8.

32 A. Saint, '"Spread the people": the LCC's dispersal policy, 1889–1965', in Saint [17, 24], 215–35; Jackson [18, 38], 315–18; Coppock and Prince [18, 35], 292–5.

33 *Report of the Royal Commission on Industrial Location* (Barlow Report) (1940), 38–40; G. D. H. Cole and M. I. Cole, *The Condition of Britain* (1937), 221; D. H. Aldcroft, *The Interwar Economy: Britain, 1919–1939* (1970), 88–9.

34 Abercrombie [23, 1], 40–41.

35 Hall [16, 1], 168.

36 Forshaw and Abercrombie [23, 11], 91.

37 Barlow Report [23, 33], 48.

38 Insured workers, the group on whom the fullest statistics are available, included most workers between the ages of sixteen and sixty-four in manufacturing, building and the distributive trades, but excluded managers, domestic servants, the self-employed, established civil servants, teachers, nurses, policemen, people working for local government, public utilities, railways and the armed services, and non-manual workers earning over £250 a year.

39 Barlow Report [23, 33], 24, 37–8; Public Record Office, HLG 27/30 Ministry of Labour evidence to the Barlow Commission, 1938, Appendix 1, Table I.

40 HLG 27/30, Appendix 2, Table 1.

41 Abercrombie [23, 1], 39; Barlow Report [23, 33], 165–7; Aldcroft [23, 33], 82; Public Record Office, HLG 27/30 [23, 39], Appendix 1, Table 4.

42 Cole and Cole [23, 33], 224; Llewellyn Smith [17, 16], vol. 1, 354–6; Aldcroft [23, 33], 78–96; Mitchell and Deane [10, 35], 64–7; HLG 27/30 [23, 39], Ministry of Labour evidence to the Barlow Commission, Appendix 1.

43 J. Marriott, *The Culture of Labourism: the East End Between the Wars* (Edinburgh, 1991), 128.

44 Public Record Office, HLG 27/30, supplementary evidence of the Ministry of Labour to the Barlow Commission (paper 30A), 14–16.

45 Forshaw and Abercrombie [23, 11], 84–90.

46 Public Record Office, HLG 27/19, Board of Trade evidence to the Barlow Commission, Annexe V, Table 3.

47 J. Armstrong, 'The development of the Park Royal industrial estate in the interwar period: a re-examination of the Aldcroft-Richardson thesis', *London Journal* 21 (1996), 64–79.

48 Forshaw and Abercrombie [23, 11], 88–9.

49 A. Godley, 'Immigrant Entrepreneurs and the Emergence of London's East End as an Industrial District', *London Journal* 21 (1996), 41.

50 Public Record Office, HLG 27/30 [23, 39]. Ministry of Labour Memorandum of Evidence to the Barlow Commission, January 1938, Appendix 1, Table I. This seems to be the best summary of the insured workforce of the London Division (roughly equivalent to Greater London). The *County of London Plan* [23, 11], 88–9, has statistics which include uninsured workers, especially those outside the sixteen to sixty-four age group, but only for the County of London.

51 Public Record Office, HLG 27/30 [23, 39], Appendix 1, Table I; Llewellyn Smith [17, 16], vol. 2, chs. 5 and 6; vol. 5, chs. 2, 6 and 7. The quote is from vol. 5, 77; Hall [16, 1], chs. 3–7, and appendix.

52 Public Record Office, HLG 27/30 [23, 39], Appendix 1, Table I; Public Record Office, HLG 27/81, evidence of the Electrical Manufacturing Industry to the Barlow Commission.

53 Public Record Office, HLG 27/30 [23, 39]. Ministry of Labour Memorandum of Evidence to the Barlow Commission, January 1938, 7, Table X.

54 Forshaw and Abercrombie [23, 11], 158.
55 Abercrombie [23, 1], 42, 132–3; Coppock and Prince [18, 35], 235–7.
56 Hall [16, 1], 122–5.
57 Armstrong [23, 47].
58 Abercrombie [23, 1], 42–4; Hall [16, 1], 125–39.
59 Public Record Office, HLG 27/34, 4–10. Written evidence of the LPTB to the Barlow Commission.
60 Public Record Office, HLG 27/69, 5. Evidence of Sir Raymond Unwin.
61 Public Record Office, HLG 27/73, 3.
62 Public Record Office, HLG 27/68, 9, 14, 20.
63 Report of the Barlow Commission, 200–206, 212–14.
64 D. F. Stevens, 'The central area', in Coppock and Prince [18, 35], 181–3, 197–8; Michie [16, 49], 16–19.
65 Michie [16, 49], 83–4, 160–63, 178.
66 D. Williams, 'London and the 1931 financial crisis', *Economic History Review* 15 (1962–3), 520.
67 Williams [23, 66], 522–7; G. Hardach, *The First World War, 1914–1918* (1987), 290; Michie [16, 49], 36–8, 63–5, 79–80; D. H. Aldcroft, *From Versailles to Wall Street* (1977), 165–86.
68 Michie [16, 49], 79–83.
69 Michie [16, 49], 135–6, 121–2.
70 G. Weightman, S. Humphries, *The Making of Modern London, 1914–1939* (1984), 40.
71 Pevsner [3, 80], *London*, vol. 1, 164.
72 Clunn [18, 22], 16–21; D. Kynaston, 'A changing workscape: the City of London since the 1840s', *London Journal* 13 (1987–8), 99–105.
73 J. Goddard, 'Changing office location patterns within Central London', *Urban Studies*, 4iii (1967), 276–85.
74 Cowan [17, 65], 89–92; Forshaw and Abercrombie [23, 11], 32–3.
75 Llewellyn Smith [17, 16], vol. 5, 137–8, 163.
76 H. Clout (ed.), *The Times London History Atlas* (1991), 106–7.
77 Clunn [18, 22], 256–60.
78 Clunn [18, 22], 182–92.
79 Lancaster [21, 23], 90–92.
80 H. Hobhouse, *A History of Regent Street* (1975), 135.
81 St J. Adcock (ed.), *Wonderful London* (3 vols, *c.* 1924), 430–36.
82 Thompson [21, 5], 76–7.
83 Mitchell and Deane [10, 35], 488–9; P. Mathias, *The First Industrial Nation* (1969 edn), 474–5.
84 Cannadine [21, 13], 116–18, 122–3; F. M. L. Thompson, *English Landed Society in the Nineteenth Century* (1963), 322–37.
85 Thompson [23, 84], 339–40.
86 Cannadine [21, 13], 350–55; Davidoff [21, 3], 68–70.
87 Thompson [21, 5].

88 J. White, '"Penniless and without food": Unemployment in London between the wars', in Alderman and Holmes [12, 26], 118–35, 120; Llewellyn Smith [17, 16], vol 3, 160.

89 Llewellyn Smith [17, 16], vol. 3, 175–6.

90 Llewellyn Smith [17, 16], vol. 2, 46–7.

91 Llewellyn Smith [17, 16], vol. 2, 411–20.

92 Llewellyn Smith [17, 16], vol. 3, 173–81; Cole and Cole [23, 33], 111–40.

93 Llewellyn Smith [17, 16], vol. 6, 3–4.

94 C. A. Linsley, C. L. Linsley, 'Booth, Rowntree, and Llewellyn Smith: a reassessment of interwar poverty', *Economic History Review* 46 (February 1993), 88–104.

95 Llewellyn Smith [17, 16], vol. 6, 108.

96 B. B. Gilbert, *British Social Policy, 1914–1939* (1970), 16–32, 54–74; C. Andrew, *Secret Service: The Making of the British Intelligence Community* (1985), 325–53.

97 Gilbert [23, 96], 75.

98 P. Kingsford, *The Hunger Marches in Britain, 1920–1940* (1982), 13–71; W. Hannington, *Unemployed Struggles, 1919–36* (1973), 16–64.

99 Gilbert [23, 96], 214–19; Llewellyn Smith [17, 16], vol. 1, 361–88; Palmer [12, 12], 124–7; Marriott [23, 43], 144.

100 J. Gillespie, 'Poplarism and proletarianism', in Feldman and Jones [15, 6], 163–88; Donoughue and Jones [20, 45], 46–9, 102–3.

101 Mowat [23, 20], 310–17; P. Renshaw, *The General Strike* (1975), 17–19, 174–88.

102 D. R. Green, 'The metropolitan economy, 1800–1939', in K. Hoggart, D. R. Green (eds.), *London: A New Metropolitan Geography* (1991), 31.

103 Gilbert [23, 96], 219–32; Llewellyn Smith [17, 16], vol. 1, 375–6; J. Gillespie, 'Poplarism and proletarianism', in Feldman and Jones [15, 6], 181–2.

104 J. Sheldrake, 'The LCC hospital service', in Saint [17, 24], 187–97.

105 Kingsford [23, 98], 148–221; Hannington [23, 98], 246–67; K. Martin, *Editor: a Second Volume of Autobiography* (1969), 165–6.

106 R. Benewick, *The Fascist Movement in Britain* (1972), 217–34. A. Saint, G. Darley (eds.), *The Chronicles of London* (1994), 269–70.

107 Benewick [23, 106], 235–95; T. P. Linehan, 'The British Union of Fascists in Hackney and Stoke Newington, 1933–1940', in Alderman and Holmes [12, 26], 136–66.

108 Benewick [23, 106], 279–84; Donoughue and Jones [20, 45], 654–5.

109 Donoughue and Jones [20, 45], 190–91; Tom Jeffery, 'The Suburban nation', in Feldman and Jones [15, 6], 189–216.

110 Young and Garside [15, 40], 209–16.

111 Yelling [23, 20], 122–4; Cole and Cole [23, 33], 157–66.

112 Young and Garside [15, 40], 173–88; Yelling [17, 67], 169.

113 Yelling [23, 20], 102–6, 116–22, 166–9.

114 Yelling [23, 20], 164–70; Young and Garside [15, 40], 188–98; Donoughue and Jones [20, 45], 657; Burnett [17, 51], 242.

115 M. Richardson, 'Education and politics: the London Labour Party and schooling between the wars', in Saint [17, 24], 147–65.

116 J. B. Priestley, *English Journey* (1934), 401.

117 L. Lee, *As I Walked Out One Midsummer Morning* (Penguin edn, 1971), 25; I. Niall, *A London Boyhood* (1974), 22.

118 A. Briggs, *The History of Broadcasting in the United Kingdom* (Oxford, 1961 and 1965), vols. 1 and 2; P. Scannell, D. Cardiff, *A Social History of British Broadcasting* (Oxford, 1991), vol. 1, 304–7.

119 R. Low, *The History of the British Film, 1918–1929* (1971).

120 D. Robinson, *World Cinema* (1974), 148–9, 195–200; Low [23, 119], 218–27.

121 R. Low, *Film Making in 1930s Britain* (1985), chs. 8–9.

122 Llewellyn Smith [17, 16], vol. 1, 290–95; vol. 9, 43–5; D. Fowler, *The First Teenagers. The Lifestyle of Young Wage-earners in Interwar Britain* (1995), 118; Jackson [18, 38], 176.

123 Jackson [18, 38], 176–80; R. Low [23, 121], 51–2; Kent [4, 81], 89–92.

124 R. Mander, J. Mitchenson, *British Music Hall* (1965), 35–40.

125 Llewellyn Smith [17, 16], vol. 9, 64–5.

126 C. Madge, Tom Harrisson (eds.), *Britain by Mass Observation* (1938), 139–84; G. S. Jones, 'The "cockney" and the nation, 1780–1988'; Feldman and Jones [15, 6], 312–13.

127 Llewellyn Smith [17, 16], vol. 9, 51–2.

128 Llewellyn Smith [17, 16], vol. 9, 275.

129 G. Orwell, *Down and Out in Paris and London* (1933), chs. 26–7, 203–14.

130 White [17, 49], 24–5.

131 White [17, 49], 40–44, 71, 248.

132 White [17, 49], 4, 50, 85–8, 99–100, 114–30, 139–44.

133 White [17, 49], 219–26, 251–5.

134 E. Smithies, *Crime in Wartime* (1982), 111–24; R. Samuel, *East End Underworld. Chapters in the Life of Arthur Harding* (1981), 182–6, 328–9; P. Jenkins, G. W. Potter, 'Before the Krays: organised crime in London, 1920–1960', *Criminal Justice History* (1988), 9, 209–30.

135 Llewellyn Smith [17, 16], vol. 9, 296–300, 341; C. H. Rolph (ed.) *Women of the Streets* (British Social Biology Council, 1955), 204–5.

136 Smithies [23, 134], 130–41; Jenkins and Potter [23, 134], 209–30.

137 C. Holmes, 'The Chinese connection', in Alderman and Holmes [12, 26], 78–83.

138 *Reports of the Metropolitan Police Commissioner*, 1937 and 1938.

24. UNDER FIRE, 1939–1945

1 K. Middlemas, *Diplomacy of Illusion* (1972), 376.

2 T. Harrisson, *Living Through the Blitz* (1976), 24.

3 M. Gilbert, *Winston S. Churchill 1922–39* (1976), 573.

4 T. H. O'Brien, *Civil Defence*, 15–16, 95–6, 142–4; R. M. Titmuss, *History of the Second World War: Problems of Social Policy* (1950), 3–14, 21.

5 O'Brien [24, 4], 172; Titmuss [24, 4], 14.

6 O'Brien [24, 4], 238–77.

7 O'Brien [24, 4], 77–9, 160.

8 O'Brien [24, 4], 186–93, 199.

9 O'Brien [24, 4], 161–2, 170–71, 187–99.

10 Titmuss [24, 4], 18–22, 337–40.

11 Titmuss [24, 4], 23–44.

12 Titmuss [24, 4], 45–53.

13 O'Brien [24, 4], 286–94; P. Hennessey, *Never Again. Britain, 1945–51* (1992), 15–16.

14 Titmuss [24, 4], 543–9, for the calculations on which this estimate is based.

15 P. Ziegler, *London at War, 1939–1945* (1995), 57, 42–4.

16 *Our Towns. A Close Up* (a Study made in 1939–42 by the Hygiene Committee of the Women's Group on Public Welfare), 1943, 1–6; Titmuss [24, 4], 114–36.

17 Titmuss [24, 4], 181–2.

18 Titmuss [24, 4], 171–4.

19 Titmuss [24, 4], 176, 242–50.

20 O'Brien [24, 4], 321–4.

21 *Report of the Commissioner of the Metropolitan Police*, 1939, PP1939–40, V.

22 C. Fitzgibbon, *The Blitz* (1957), 37–42.

23 P. Calvocoressi, G. Wint, J. Pritchard, *Total War* (1989), vol. 1, 156; A. Calder, *The People's War: Britain in 1939–45* (1969), 154; G. Craig, *Germany, 1866–1945* (Oxford, 1978), 721–4; A. Bullock, *Hitler. A Study in Tyranny* (1962), 595–7; Fitzgibbon [24, 22], 40–42

24 B. Collier, *History of the Second World War: The Defence of the United Kingdom*, 238–40.

25 Fitzgibbon [24, 22], 49–50, quoting the Ministry of Information's *Front Line*.

26 Harrisson [24, 2], 61–7; A. Calder, *The Myth of the Blitz* (1991), 126; I. McLaine, *Ministry of Morale. Home Front Morale and the Ministry of Information in World War II* (1979), 108–14.

27 Fitzgibbon [24, 22], 98–105, 217–20; O'Brien [24, 4], 388–9; Collier [24, 24], 252–6, 270–9.

28 Fitzgibbon [24, 22], 96–8, 108–11.

29 Fitzgibbon [24, 22], 182–9.

30 Titmuss [24, 4], 534; O'Brien [24, 4], 399–401.

31 Collier [24, 24], 257–8.

32 Harrisson [24, 2]; Calder [24, 23]; Calder [24, 26]; McLaine [24, 26].

33 Calder [24, 26], 45–8, 119–31.

34 Fitzgibbon [24, 22], 177–8.

35 V. Hodgson, *Few Eggs and No Oranges* (1976), 55–66.

36 Harrisson [24, 2], 96–7.

37 Harrisson [24, 2], 82, 322.

38 Harrisson [24, 2], 85.

39 Titmuss [24, 4], 347.

40 McLaine [24, 26], 108–14.

41 Titmuss [24, 4], 341–50.

42 Harrisson [24, 2], 307–8; Calder [24, 23], 478–81, 486.

43 G. Morgan, *Red Roses Every Night. An Account of London Cinemas Under Fire* (1948), 74–5. I am grateful to Dr Nicholas Reeves for this reference.

44 McLaine [24, 26], 113; Harrisson [24, 2], 105–6.

45 Harrisson [24, 2], 126–7.

46 Titmuss [24, 4], 343.

47 O'Brien [24, 4], 392.

48 O'Brien [24, 4], 544–5; Fitzgibbon [24, 22], 158–61.

49 Fitzgibbon [24, 22], 144–51; Harrisson [24, 2], 65–6, 116–18.

50 Titmuss [24, 4], 259–61.

51 Titmuss [24, 4], 263–8; J. Mack, S. Humphries, *London at War* (1985), 75–9.

52 Titmuss [24, 4], 273–86, 295, 299.

53 Titmuss [24, 4], 286–93.

54 Titmuss [24, 4], 282–3, 294–300, 330–31.

55 O'Brien [24, 4], 512–22; Fitzgibbon [24, 22], 161–4.

56 O'Brien [24, 4], 527–47.

57 Fitzgibbon [24, 22], 204–15; O'Brien [24, 4], 408–9.

58 Hodgson [24, 35], 96.

59 O'Brien [24, 4], 457, 465–8, 592–5.

60 Collier [24, 24], 494–5, 503–5.

61 Calder [24, 23], 210–11; Titmuss [24, 4], 271.

62 O'Brien [24, 4], 419.

63 Titmuss [24, 4], 560.

64 O'Brien [24, 4], 427–44.

65 Collier [24, 24], 331–421, has a very full account of the development and impact of the V1 and V2.

66 O'Brien [24, 4], 645–52; Calvocoressi, Wint and Pritchard [24, 23], vol. 1, 556–8.

67 Titmuss [24, 4], 558.

68 J. C. Masterman, *The Double Cross System* (1973), 179–82.

69 C. M. Kohan, *History of the Second World War: Works and Buildings*, 225.

70 Hodgson [24, 35], 391–7.

71 O'Brien [24, 4], 655; Titmuss [24, 4], 427.

72 O'Brien [24, 4], 655–60.

73 O'Brien [24, 4], 660–66; Hodgson [24, 35], 425.

74 O'Brien [24, 4], 666–8.

75 Masterman [24, 68], 181.

76 O'Brien [24, 4], 677–8; Titmuss [24, 4], 557–9; Mack and Humphries [24, 51], 128–53.

77 O'Brien [24, 4], 677–84; Titmuss [24, 4], 324–5.

78 London County Council [17, 45], New Series (1957), vol. 1, 1945–54, 44.

79 *Report of the Committee on Housing in Greater London*, March 1965, 11 (the Milner Holland Report).

80 W. Kent, *The Lost Treasures of London* (1947).

81 Young and Garside [15, 40].

82 R. S. R. Fitter, *London's Natural History* (1945), 228–36, 265–8.

83 Coppock and Prince [18, 35], 183–7, 191.

84 Titmuss [24, 4], 408–20.

85 London County Council [17, 45], New series, vol. 1, 32; M. Young, P. Wilmott, *Family and Kinship in East London* (1957).

86 Titmuss [24, 4], 268.

25. POSTWAR LONDON, 1945–65

1 Kohan [24, 69], 78.

2 P. Hall, *Urban and Regional Planning* (1992), 100–103.

3 Young and Garside [15, 40], 233.

4 J. J. B. Cullingworth, *Environmental Planning, 1939–1969*. Vol. 3, *New Towns Policy* (1979); Forshaw and Abercrombie [23, 11], 30–5, 135–6.

5 Forshaw and Abercrombie [23, 11], 2–3, 21.

6 Forshaw and Abercrombie [23, 11], 114–20.

7 Forshaw and Abercrombie [23, 11], 77–8.

8 Forshaw and Abercrombie [23, 11], 126–35.

9 Forshaw and Abercrombie [23, 11], 13–14, 49–63.

10 Cullingworth [25, 4], vol. 3: *New Towns Policy*, 3–5.

11 Abercrombie [23, 1], 30–38.

12 Abercrombie [23, 1], 160–63; Hall [25, 2], 103–6.

13 Abercrombie [23, 1], 28–9, 190–91.

14 *Strategic Plan for the South East. Studies 1, Population and Employment* (1971), 18–19.

15 Hall [25, 2], 108–10.

16 Hall [25, 2], 114–19; F. Schaffer, *The New Town Story* (1970), 82–99.

17 *Administrative County of London Development Plan 1951. Analysis* (1951).

18 *Administrative County of London Development Plan, First Review* (1960), 157–209.

19 Jones and Woodward [23, 12], 374.

20 *Administrative County of London Development Plan, First Review* (1960), 115–21.

21 A. Forshaw, T. Bergstrom, *The Open Spaces of London* (1986), 93–6.

22 P. Addison, *Now the War is Over* (1985), 206–10; Hennessy [24, 13], 425–8; H. Hopkins, *The New Look* (1964), 269–78.

23 London County Council [17, 45], new series, vol. 1, 1945–54, 107–8; Milner Holland Report [24, 79], 1965, 11–12.

24 London County Council [17, 45], new series, vol. 1, 104–5; Milner Holland Report [24, 79], 1965, 12–16, 65–9, 108–110.

25 A. Saint, '"Spread the People": The LCC's dispersal Policy, 1889–1965', in Saint [17, 24], 230–31; London County Council [17, 45], New Series, vol. 7, 1955–64, 102.

26 Milner Holland Report [24, 79], 66–8.

27 Milner Holland Report [24, 79], 95–104, 127.

28 A. Power, *Property before People: the Management of Twentieth-Century Council Housing* (1987), 42–7.

29 M. Glendinning, S. Muthesius, *Tower Block* (London and New Haven, 1994), 35–42, 53–4, 112–13.

30 Glendinning and Muthesius [25, 29], 4.

31 Young and Wilmott [24, 85], 112–13.

32 Young and Wilmott [24, 85], 121–2.

33 Young and Wilmott [24, 85], 121–30, 164–8.

34 Young and Wilmott [24, 85], 197–9.

35 Glendinning and Muthesius [25, 29], 104, 265–6.

36 E. Harwood, A. Saint, *Exploring London's Heritage* (1991), 123–4.

37 Glendinning and Muthesius [25, 29], 55–62.

38 Glendinning and Muthesius [25, 29], 267, 271, 335, 346–50; *Administrative County of London Development Plan*, First Review (1960), 87.

39 I. Nairn, *Nairn's London* (1966), 40.

40 Milner Holland Report [24, 79], 251–2.

41 Milner Holland Report [24, 79], 340.

42 Milner Holland Report [24, 79], 228–9.

43 Abercrombie [23, 1], 8, 24–6.

44 R. Munton, *London's Green Belt: Containment in Practice* (1983), 20; M. J. Elsom, *Green Belts: Conflict Mediation in the Urban Fringe* (1986), 11–14; D. Thomas, 'The Green Belt', in Coppock and Prince [18, 35], 296–300.

45 Elsom [25, 44], 18–19, 26–7.

46 Elsom [25, 44], 26–7, 38–48; D. White, 'What Green Belts are for', *New Society*, 17 January 1985, 85–8.

47 Cullingworth [25, 4], 42–3.

48 Schaffer [25, 16], 29–38, 102–3.

49 Coppock and Prince [18, 35], 319, 365.

50 A. Saint, '"Spread the People": The LCC's dispersal policy, 1889–1965', in Saint [17, 24], 233–5; Coppock and Prince [18, 35], 365, 373–5.

51 Cullingworth [25, 4], 40–41, 139–40, 214–16.

52 Cullingworth [25, 4], 276, 532–3.

53 J. H. Westergaard, 'The Structure of Greater London', in Centre for Urban Studies, *London, Aspects of Change*, 93–9.

54 A. G. Powell, 'The recent development of Greater London', in *The Advancement of Science*, vol. 17, May 1960, 76–86.

55 *Strategic Plan for the South East. Studies 1, Population and Employment*, 29–30.

56 Brimblecombe [9, 1], 161–77; T. McKeown, C. R. Lowe, *An Introduction to Social Medicine* (Oxford, 1974), 163–70; Hibbert and Weinreb [8, 36], 288.

57 *South East England*, printed as an Appendix to J. B. Cullingworth, *Environmental Planning, 1939–1961: Land Values, Compensation and Betterment*, 544–50.

58 Cullingworth, [25, 4], 209–14.

59 P. Wood, 'Industrial changes in Inner London', in H. Clout (ed.), *Changing London* (1978), 38; Hall [16, 1], 172–85.

60 J. Bird, 'The growth of the Port of London', in Coppock and Prince [18, 35], 212–22; London County Council [17, 45], new series, vol. 1, 1945–54, 169; vol. 7, 1955–64, 167; *Report of the Committee of Enquiry into the Major Ports of Great Britain*, 1962.

61 Michie [16, 49], 35–8.

62 Cullingworth [25, 57], 222, 227.

63 O. Marriott, *The Property Boom* (1967, 1989), 27–37, 44–50.

64 C. Booker, C. Lycett Green, *Goodbye London* (1973), 154–5.

65 S. Green, *Who Owns London?* (1986), 148–74.

66 S. Jenkins, *Landlords to London: the story of a Capital and its Growth*, 209–27.

67 Marriott [25, 63], 70–77, 214–22.

68 Marriott [25, 63], 171–2.

69 Marriott [25, 63], 157–67.

70 Marriott [25, 63], 141–4.

71 Marriott [25, 63], 170.

72 Marriott [25, 63], 109–17.

73 Jenkins [25, 66], 250.

74 1963 White Paper, *London. Employment: Housing: Land*, and 1962 Report of Official Working Party on Offices in London, both printed in Cullingworth [25, 57], 512–42.

75 P. Cowan, 'Employment and offices', in J. Hillman (ed.), *Planning for London* (1971), 65–7; G. Manners, 'Central London', in H. Clout, P. Wood, *London: Problems of Change* (1986), 114; Coppock and Prince [18, 35] also uses the mistaken figures. See pp. 185 and 198.

76 Marriott [25, 63], 185–91.

77 *Strategic Plan for the South East. Studies 1, Population and Employment*, 228–9.

78 *Administrative County of London Development Plan*, 1960, 66–74.

79 S. Plowden, *Towns against Traffic* (1972), 79–107.

80 M. F. Collins, T. M. Pharoah, *Transport Organisation in a Great City: the Case of London* (1974), 40, 536, 414–35.

81 Collins and Pharoah [25, 80], 186–206.

82 *Strategic Plan for the South East. Studies 1, Population and Employment*, 18–21.

83 J. A. Jackson, 'The Irish', Centre for Urban Studies, *London. Aspects of Change*, 293–308; S. Hutton, 'The Irish in London', in Merriman [10, 16].

84 S. Patterson, 'Polish London', Centre for Urban Studies [25, 83], 309–43; K. Sword, 'The Poles in London', in Merriman [10, 16], 154–62; S. Patterson, 'The Poles: An exile community in Britain', in J. L. Watson (ed.), *Between Two Cultures. Migrants and Minorities in Britain*, 214–41.

85 S. Kyriacou, Z. Theodorou, 'Greek Cypriots', in Merriman [10, 16], 98–105.

86 A. H. Halsey, *Trends in British Society since 1900*, 2nd edn (1986), 576–8.

87 Hennessy [24, 13], 439–42.

88 R. Glass, *Newcomers: the West Indians in London* (1960), 49; S. Patterson, *Dark Strangers* (1963), 54–6.

89 Patterson [25, 88], 46–7; Hennessy [24, 13], 442–3.

90 Patterson [25, 88], 47–51, 359.

91 Patterson [25, 88], 318.

92 Glass [25, 88], 21–32, 66–75.

93 Glass [25, 88], 58–62.

94 Glass [25, 88], 32–43; S. B. Philpott, 'The Montserratians', in Watson [25, 84], 107–8.

95 C. MacInnes, *Absolute Beginners* (1957), 200–207; Patterson [25, 88], 324–5.

96 Glass [25, 88], 128–9, 133–42.

97 T. Travers, M. Minors (eds.), *London 95* (1996), 50–51; D. Hiro, *Black British, White British* (1991), 117–21, 331; Halsey [25, 86] (1972 edn), 497; R. Visram, 'South Asians in London', in Merriman [10, 16], 169–78.

98 S. Humphries, J. Taylor, *The Making of Modern London, 1945–1985* (1986), 113.

99 R. Dennis, 'Suburban London', in Clout and Wood [25, 75], 122–3.

100 T. R. Fyvel, *The Insecure Offenders: Rebellious Youth in the Welfare State* (1963), 69.

101 Fyvel [25, 100], 47–64; J. Springhall, *Coming of Age. Adolescence in Britain, 1860–1960* (Dublin, 1986), 199–215.

102 Quoted in T. Barker (ed.), *The Long March of Everyman 1750–1960* (1978), 287.

103 F. H. McClintock, *Crimes of Violence* (1963), 241–7.

104 P. Wilmott, *Adolescent Boys of East London* (1969), 142–67, 184–6.

105 T. Morris, *Crime and Criminal Justice Since 1945* (Oxford, 1989), 89–106; Greater London Council, *Annual Abstract of Greater London Statistics*, vol. 5, 266; London County Council [17, 45], new series, vol. 1, 130; vol. 7, 119. Vols 1–16 (1968–84) of the *Annual Abstract of Greater London Statistics* were compiled by the Greater London Council Intelligence Unit. Vols 17–24 (1985–92) were compiled by the London Research Centre.

106 London County Council [17, 45], new series, vol. 7, 1955–64, 43; *Annual Abstract of Greater London Statistics* [25, 105], vol. 5, 1970, 48.

107 G. Melly, *Revolt into Style: the Popular Arts in Britain* (1970), 147–51.

108 S. Maitland, *Very Heaven. Looking Back at the 1960s* (1988), 37–8.

109 Maitland [25, 108], 39–40.
110 Melly [25, 107], 90–100.
111 R. Hewison, *Too Much. Art and Society in the Sixties* (1986), 71.
112 Hewison [25, 111], 77–8.

26. A DIVIDED CITY, 1965–1997

1 G. Rhodes, *The Government of London: the Struggle for Reform* (1970), 4–10.
2 Young and Garside [15, 40], 301–2; Rhodes [26, 1], 10–19.
3 Rhodes [26, 1], 19–38.
4 Rhodes [26, 1], 39–62.
5 Rhodes [26, 1], 63–85.
6 Young and Garside [15, 40], 307–17. The quote is from p. 316.
7 Rhodes [26, 1], 106–10.
8 Rhodes [26, 1], 171–96.
9 Rhodes [26, 1], 247–51.
10 M. Hebbert, 'The Borough effect in London's Geography', in Hoggart and Green [23, 102], 191–5.
11 Hebbert [26, 10], 191–206.
12 *Report of the Panel of Inquiry on the Greater London Development Plan* (Layfield Report, 1973), vol. 1, 24–8, 657.
13 Layfield Report, vol. 1, 276.
14 Layfield Report, vol. 1, 275; J. M. Thomas, 'Transport: the motorway proposals', in Hillman [25, 75].
15 *Greater London Development Plan*. Notice of Approval, Written Statement, and ministerial amendments, 1976, 4–5, 36–42.
16 Collins and Pharoah [25, 80], 414–35, 537–52; T. Pharoah, 'Transport: how much can London take?', in Hoggart and Green [23, 102], ch. 8.
17 D. L. Foley, *Governing the London Region: Reorganisation and Planning in the 1960s* (1972), 64–7; Collins and Pharoah [25, 80], 51–61, 618–24.
18 M. Buchanan, N. Bursey, K. Lewis, P. Mullen, *Transport Planning for Greater London* (Farnborough, 1980), 206–25; *Annual Abstract of Greater London Statistics* [25, 105], vol. 24, 1991–2, 112; *London Transport Annual Report*, 1977.
19 K. Livingstone, *If Voting Changed Anything, They'd Abolish It* (1987), 58–82.
20 H. Clout, 'Thamesmead', in Clout [25, 59], 70–6; B. Lenon, *London* (1988), 26–7.
21 Glendinning and Muthesius [25, 29], 331–2.
22 Glendinning and Muthesius [25, 29], 82–8, 208–17; *The Broadwater Farm Inquiry* (1986), 14–15.
23 Power [25, 28], 49–54.
24 J. B. Cullingworth, V. Nadin, *Town and Country Planning in Britain* (11th edn, 1994), 196–7. There is a good discussion of the rebuilding of post-war

London in *A Broken Wave: The Rebuilding of Britain, 1940–1980* (1983), by Lord Esher, an architect involved in the process.

25 *London, Aspects of Change*, Centre for Urban Studies, R. Glass, 'Introduction', xviii–xix.

26 C. Hamnett, P. Williams, 'Social change in London: a study of gentrification', *London Journal* 6 (1980).

27 P. Wright, *A Journey Through Ruins. The Last Days of London* (1991), 83–9.

28 Jenkins [25, 66], 248–55; Cullingworth and Nadin [26, 24], 160–61.

29 Nairn [25, 39], 86; Booker and Green [25, 64], 87–99; Jenkins [25, 66], 256–7.

30 Power [25, 28], 89.

31 Archbishop of Canterbury's commission on Urban Priority Areas, *Faith in the City* (1985), 246–7.

32 Power [25, 28], 125–48.

33 Power [25, 28], 135–6.

34 *The Broadwater Farm Inquiry* [26, 22], 14–33.

35 S. Merrett, 'Housing', in J. Simmie (ed.), *Planning London* (1994), 42–9; *Annual Abstract of Greater London Statistics* [25, 105], vol. 5, 1970, 209; vol. 24, 1991–2, 223–7.

36 Livingstone [26, 19], 186–9.

37 Merrett [26, 35], 42–9; *Annual Abstract of Greater London Statistics* [25, 105], vol. 5, 1970, 209; vol. 24, 1991–2, 227; Travers and Minors [25, 97], 9, 94–6.

38 Power [25, 28], 102–15.

39 N. Cohen, 'Dumping the Poor', *Independent on Sunday*, 16 January 1994, 17.

40 Merrett [26, 35], 42–9; Milner Holland Report [24, 79], 208; M. Harloe, P. Marcuse, N. Smith, 'Housing for people, housing for profits', in S. Fainstein, I. Gordon, M. Harloe (eds.), *Divided Cities*, 183.

41 Harloe, Marcuse and Smith [26, 40], 185–6.

42 *Annual Abstract of Greater London Statistics* [25, 105], vol. 24, 1991–2, 222–38.

43 S. Brownill, C. Sharp, 'London's housing crisis', in A. Thornley (ed.), *The Crisis of London* (1992), 10–11.

44 Department of the Environment press release on the first meeting of the Joint London Advisory Panel, 7 February 1996.

45 M. Collins, 'Land-use planning since 1947', in Simmie [26, 35], 110; Layfield Report [26, 12], vol. 1, 629.

46 *A Strategy for the South-East*, a first report by the South-East Planning Council, 1967, 47–51.

47 Simmie [26, 35], 95–6.

48 *Strategy for the South-East: 1976 Review*, Ch. 4, especially pp. 36–40.

49 *Annual Abstract of Greater London Statistics* [25, 105], vol. 24, 1991–2, 28, 64; Travers and Minors [25, 97], 42–3; Department of the Environment, *Urban Trends in England: Latest Evidence from the 1991 Census* (1996), 21.

50 Travers and Minors [25, 97], 129. Estimates of London's recent population, including that at the time of the 1991 census, vary. These figures follow the

census for 1951–71, National Registration for 1939, and Office of Population Censuses and Surveys mid-year estimates for 1981, 1991 and 1993.

51 *Annual Abstract of Greater London Statistics* [25, 105], vol. 24, 1991–2, 84; Travers and Minors [25, 97], 27–9; P. Wood, 'Industrial changes in Inner London', in Clout [25, 59], 38–9; F. E. I. Hamilton, 'A new geography of London's manufacturing', in Hoggart and Green [23, 102], 61–3; *Financial Times*, 4 July 1996.

52 Travers and Minors [25, 97], 21.

53 *Annual Abstract of Greater London Statistics* [25, 105], vol. 24, 1991–2, 84; B. R. Mitchell, H. G. Jones, *Second Abstract of British Historical Statistics* (1971), 36–7.

54 N. Buck, I. Gordon, K. Young, *The London Employment Problem* (Oxford, 1986), 62.

55 *Annual Abstract of Greater London Statistics* [25, 105], vol. 5, 1970, Table 3.01, and vol. 24, 1991–2, 84; G. Manners, D. Keeble, B. Rodgers, K. Warren, *Regional Development in Britain* (Chichester, 1978), 123–54, summarizes London's industrial and demographic decline to 1978.

56 R. Dennis, 'The decline of manufacturing employment in Greater London, 1966–74', in A. Evans, D. Eversley, *The Inner City: Employment and Industry* (1980).

57 *Strategy for the South-East*, 1976 Review, 37.

58 Department of Trade and Industry press release, 21 February 1996.

59 Buck, Gordon and Young [26, 54], 86–8.

60 Hamilton [26, 51], 51–78; S. Sassen, *The Global City: New York, London and Tokyo* (1991), 294–7; Clout and Wood [25, 75], 63.

61 Travers and Minors [25, 97], 27–8.

62 Hoggart and Green [23, 102], 41.

63 Information supplied by Professor John Armstrong, Thames Valley University.

64 Buck, Gordon and Young [26, 54], 76–8; N. Buck, M. Drennan, K. Newton, 'Dynamics of the metropolitan economy', in Fainstein, Gordon and Harloe [26, 40], 82–4.

65 *Report of the Committee of Enquiry into the Major Ports of Great Britain* (1962), 178.

66 Pudney [12, 11], 173–82. The quotation is from p. 182.

67 *Annual Abstract of Greater London Statistics* [25, 105], vol. 5 (1970), 67; vol. 24, 1991–2, 93.

68 P. Gripaios, 'Economic decline in South London', 74–5, and R. Dennis, 'The decline of manufacturing employment in Greater London, 1966–74', in Evans and Eversley [26, 56], 58.

69 London County Council [17, 45], new series, vol. 7 (1955–64), 40, table 34; *Annual Abstract of Greater London Statistics* [25, 105], vol. 5 (1970), Table 3.01; and vol. 24 (1991–2), 84.

70 *Administrative County of London Development Plan*, First Review (1960),

150–51; D. Eversley, 'The Ganglion of Tourism', *London Journal* 3 (1977), 188–90; Manners [25, 75], 115.

71 *Annual Abstract of Greater London Statistics* [25, 105], vol. 24, 1991–2; (1993), 101.

72 Eversley [26, 70], 202–7; Layfield Report [26, 12], vol. 1, 528–30.

73 G. Manners [26, 70], 115–16; Sassen [26, 60], 294.

74 *Annual Abstract of Greater London Statistics* [25, 105], vol. 24 (1991–2), 84, 268; Travers and Minors [25, 97], 30; *Economist*, 20 August 1994, 'London: Yet it Moves'.

75 P. Wood, 'Economic change', in Clout and Wood [25, 75], 67. Also Manners [25, 75], 113–15.

76 Michie [16, 49], 23–8.

77 Michie [16, 49], 138–9; J. Plender, P. Wallace, *The Square Mile: a Guide to the City Revolution* (1985), 31.

78 Michie [16, 49], 88–97; Plender and Wallace [26, 77], 12–37.

79 Michie [16, 49], 140–41, 145.

80 Michie [16, 49], 142–3; *Guardian*, 3 October 1996, 20; *Economist*, 11 July 1992, 'London's Financial Future'.

81 H. Kates, *The London Factor* (1994), vol. 1, 12; *Economist*, 20 August 1994.

82 Sassen [26, 60], 327.

83 Department of the Environment, *Urban Trends in England: Latest Evidence from the 1991 Census* (1996), 6–7.

84 The description of St Ethelburga is Ian Nairn's, in *Nairn's London* [23, 59].

85 'Survey of Financial Centres', *Economist*, 27 June 1992; H. Kates [26, 81], vol. 1, 16–17; G. M. Lomas, *London in Prospect* (1991), 13–15; Sassen [26, 60], 323–31.

86 M. Edwards, 'A Microcosm: redevelopment proposals at King's Cross', in Thornley [26, 43], 163–84; R. Rodgers, M. Fisher, *A New London* (1992), 145–7.

87 C. Wintour, *The Rise and Fall of Fleet Street* (1989), 215–20, 248–9.

88 M. Hebbert, 'One "planning disaster" after another: London Docklands, 1970–1992', *London Journal*, 17 (1992), 115–25.

89 A. Thornley, *Urban Planning Under Thatcher* (1991), 165–79; N. Deakin, J. Edwards, *The Enterprise Culture and the Inner City* (1993), 95–103.

90 *Financial Times*, 3 September 1996 and 9 September 1995.

91 Deakin and Edwards [26, 89], 95–129; 'Report on London business property', *Financial Times*, 27 October 1995.

92 D. R. Diamond, 'The City, the "Big Bang" and office development', in Hoggart and Green [23, 102], 91.

93 *Annual Abstract of Greater London Statistics* [25, 105], vol. 24, 1991–2, 82–3; *Regional Trends*, vol. 31, 1996, tables 5, 18–19; Halsey [25, 86], 173–7.

94 Travers and Minors [25, 97], 36–7.

95 M. Cross, R. Waldinger, 'The ethnic division of labour', in Fainstein, Gordon and Harloe [26, 40], 151–74.

96 S. Brownill, *Developing London's Docklands* (1990), 98–100; Deakin and Edwards [26, 89], 205–16, 225.

97 M. Cross, 'Race and ethnicity', in Thornley [26, 43], 103–18; Sassen [26, 60], 302–7.

98 Lord Scarman, *The Brixton Disorders, 10–12 April 1981: Report of an Inquiry by the Right Hon. the Lord Scarman OBE* (1981), paras 2. 11–23, 6. 26–29; Benyon [19, 23], 164–6, 181–2.

99 Benyon [19, 23], 46–53; J. Clare, 'Eyewitness in Brixton', in Benyon [19, 23]; M. Keith, *Race, Riots and Policing: Lore and Disorder in a Multi-racist Society* (1993), 101–6.

100 Keith [26, 99], 22–48, 122–46.

101 Emsley [19, 3], 176–7; T. Parker, *The People of Providence* (1983), 139–44 (1992 edn), gives a constable's account of policing a big South London estate.

102 D. J. Smith, J. Gray, *Police and People in London* (Aldershot, 1985), 388–434, quotation from p. 404.

103 Commission for Racial Equality, *Sorry, it's Gone* (1990), 24–5.

104 Livingstone [26, 19], 120–43, 347–52.

105 Livingstone [26, 19], 189–223.

106 Travers and Minors [25, 97], 83–7.

107 I. Gilmour, *Dancing With Dogma* (1992), 222.

108 Cullingworth and Nadin [26, 24], 29.

109 D. Eversley, 'London after the GLC: does London need strategic planning?', *London Journal*, 10 (1984), 13–45.

110 B. O'Leary, 'Why was the GLC abolished?', *International Journal of Urban and Regional Research*, 11 (2), (1987), 195–6.

111 R. Freeman, 'The Marshall Plan for London's Government', *London Journal*, 5 (1979), 160–75.

112 O'Leary [26, 110], 204–5.

113 R. Pauley, *Financial Times*, 26 February 1985.

114 *Annual Abstract of Greater London Statistics* [25, 105], vol. 24 (1991–2), 2–3; M. Hebbert, 'Governing the Capital', in Thornley [26, 43], 140.

115 S. Faintein, K. Young, 'Politics in economic restructuring', in Fainstein, Gordon and Harloe [26, 40], 214–27.

116 Department of the Environment press release, 23 May 1996.

117 *New Leadership for London: The Government's Proposals for a new Greater London Authority* (1997).

118 *New Leadership for London. A Summary* (1997).

119 Hebbert [26, 114], 141–2.

120 T. Travers, 'Finance', in J. Stewart, G. Stoker (eds.), *Local Government in the 1990s* (1995), 9–27.

121 Wright [26, 27], 29.

122 Travers and Minors [25, 97], 9, 98–9; Brownill and Sharp [26, 43]; *New Leadership for London* [26, 117], 25.

123 Travers and Minors [25, 97], 46, 128.

124 *Annual Abstract of Greater London Statistics* [25, 105], vol. 24 (1991–2), 109–16.

125 Travers and Minors [25, 97], 20–21; United Nations, Department for Economic and Social Information and Policy Analysis, *Statistical Yearbook, 1993*, 153–69; London's GDP based on the incomes of those living in Greater London is about 16 per cent smaller than its GDP based on the incomes of those working in Greater London. The latter is a more realistic measure, because it includes commuters from the wider metropolitan area.

Bibliography

References to most of the works I have used are included in the endnotes, which also indicate the works that relate to specific topics. A slightly briefer list of useful books and articles (including a few which are not cited in the notes of this book) is given below. The place of publication is London, unless another location is stated.

GENERAL

BIBLIOGRAPHIES

Creaton, H. (ed.), *Bibliography of Printed Works on London History to 1939* (1994).

Dolphin, P., Grant, E., Lewis, E., *The London Region. An Annotated Geographical Bibliography* (1981).

Fulford, M., Keene, D., Barron, C. M., Harding, V., Schwarz, L., Davis, J., Hebbert, M., 'Twenty years of writing on London history', *London Journal*, 20 (ii) (1995), pp. 1–101.

Veale, E. M., *Teaching the History of London* (1981).

Urban History Yearbook (renamed *Urban History* in 1992) has annual bibliographies which include works on London, and the *London Journal* has frequent bibliographical surveys.

Perhaps the best place of all to look for works on London is the Catalogue of the Guildhall Library, the specialist library on London.

ANTHOLOGIES, SOURCES, WORKS OF REFERENCE AND GENERAL BOOKS

Adcock, St J. (ed.), *Wonderful London* (3 vols, c. 1924).

Aspinall, A., Smith, E. A. (eds.): *English Historical Documents, 1783–1832* (1959).

Barker, F., Jackson, P., *The History of London in Maps* (1990).

Bell, W. G., *Unknown London* (1919).

Bell, W. G., *More About Unknown London* (1921).

Bird, J., Chapman, H., Clark, J. (eds.): *Collectanea Londiniensia: Studies in London Archaeology and History Presented to Ralph Merrifield* (1978).

Brett-James, N. G., *A London Anthology* (1928).

Brimblecombe, P., *The Big Smoke* (1987).

Bryant, M. E., *The London Experience of Secondary Education* (1986).

Church, J., Holding, A., *Focus on London 97* (1996).

Clapham, J. H., *An Economic History of Modern Britain*, 3 vols (Cambridge, 1930–38).

Clout, H., *The Times London History Atlas* (1991).

Darby, H. C. (ed.), *An Historical Geography of England before A.D. 1800* (Cambridge, 1936).

Darby, H. C. (ed.), *A New Historical Geography of England* (Cambridge, 1973).

Davis, D., *A History of Shopping* (1966).

Douglas, D. C., Greenaway, G. W. (eds.): *English Historical Documents, 1042–1189* (1981).

Ekwall, E., *Street-names of the City of London* (Oxford, 1954).

Encyclopedia Britannica (11th edition, 1910–11).

Fairfield, S., *The Streets of London* (1983).

Forshaw, A., Bergstrom, T., *The Markets of London* (1983, 1989).

Fox, C., *Londoners* (1987).

Gibson, P., *The Capital Companion* (Exeter, 1985).

Greater London Council, *Annual Abstract of Greater London Statistics*, vols 1–15 (1968–84).

Harben, H. A., *A Dictionary of London* (1918).

Hartnoll, P. (ed.), *Oxford Companion to the Theatre* (Oxford, 1951).

Harwood, E., Saint, A., *Exploring London's Heritage* (1991).

Hibbert, C., Weinreb, B. (eds.): *The London Encyclopaedia* (1983).

Howgego, J., *Printed Maps of London, circa 1553–1850* (Folkestone, 1979).

Hyde, R., *Printed Maps of Victorian London, 1851–1900* (Folkestone, 1975).

Jones, E., Woodward, C., *A Guide to the Architecture of London* (1983).

Jackson, P., *George Scharf's London: Sketches and Watercolours of a Changing City, 1820–50* (1987).

Jackson, P., *Walks in Old London* (1993).

Kent, W., *An Encyclopaedia of London* (1937).

Lobel, M. D. (ed.), *The British Atlas of Historic Towns 3: The City of London from Prehistoric Times* (1989).

London County Council, *London Statistics* (1891–1939, 1957–68).

London Research Centre, *Annual Abstract of Greater London Statistics*, vols 16–24 (1985–92).

Malden, H. E. (ed.), see under *Victoria County History*.

Massingham, H., Massingham, P., *The London Anthology* (n.d.).

Merriman, N., *The Peopling of London* (1993).

Mitchell, B. R., Deane, P., *An Abstract of British Historical Statistics* (Cambridge, 1962).

Mitchell, B. R., Jones, H. G., *Second Abstract of British Historical Statistics* (Cambridge, 1971).

Muirhead, F. (ed.), *London and its Environs* (1918).

Myers, A. R. (ed.), *English Historical Documents, 1327–1485* (1969).

Pevsner, Sir N., *London*, vols 1 and 2, in the Penguin *Buildings of England* series (1952, 1957).

Pritchett, V. S., *London Perceived* (1962, 1986).

Pullen, B., *London Street People* (Oxford, 1989).

Robbins, M., *Middlesex* (1953).

Rothwell, H. (ed.), *English Historical Documents, 1189–1327* (1975).

Saint, A., Darley, G., *The Chronicles of London* (1994).

Saunders, A., *The Art and Architecture of London* (1988).

Stevenson, J., *Popular Disturbances in England, 1700–1870* (1979).

Survey of London, The, An enormous topographical work, begun in 1894, and now including more than forty volumes.

Tallis, J., *London Street Views, 1838–40* (1969).

Thorne, J., *Handbook to the Environs of London* (1876).

Timbs, J., *Curiosities of London* (1885. 1st published 1855).

Victoria County History, The, The volumes on Surrey (ed. H. E. Malden, 1902–12), Essex (1903–7, 1963–78), and Middlesex (1911, 1962–76) are useful. Only one volume was published (in 1909) on London, edited by W. Page, covering Roman, Anglo-Saxon and ecclesiastical London.

Warner, M. (ed.), *The Image of London. Views by Travellers and Emigrés, 1550–1920* (1987).

Whitelock, D. (ed.), *English Historical Documents, c. 500–1042* (1955).

Williams, C. H. (ed.), *English Historical Documents, 1485–1558* (1967).

Young, G. M., Handcock, W. D. (eds), *English Historical Documents, 1833–1874* (1956).

EARLIER GENERAL HISTORIES

Besant, Sir W., *London* (1892).

Burke, T., *The Streets of London through the Centuries* (1940).

Gomme, Sir G. L., *London* (1914).

Maitland, W., *The History of London from its Foundation* (1739).

Rasmussen, S. E., *London, the Unique City* (1934).

Stow, J., *A Survey of London*. (C. L. Kingsford's 1908 edn, 2 vols, reprinted in 1971, Oxford).

Thornbury, W., Walford, E., *Old and New London* (6 vols, 1883–5).

RECENT GENERAL HISTORIES

Barker, F., Jackson, P., *London: 2000 Years of a City and its People* (1974, 1983).

Dalzell, W. R., *The History of London* (1981).

Gray, R., *A History of London* (1978).
Hibbert, C., *London, the Biography of a City* (1969, 1977).
Hunting, P., *Royal Westminster* (1981).
Mitchell, R. J., Leys, M. D. R., *A History of London Life* (1958).
Palmer, A. W., *The East End: Four Centuries of London Life* (1989).
Porter, R., *London. A Social History* (1994).
Richardson, J., *London and its People* (1995).
Rose, M., *The East End of London* (Bath, 1951).

ROMAN LONDON

Biddle, M., Hudson, D. M., Heighway, C. M., *The Future of London's Past* (Worcester, 1973).
Frere, S. S., *Britannia* (1974).
Grimes, W. F., *The Excavation of Roman and Medieval London* (1968).
Marsden, P., *Roman London* (1983).
Merrifield, R., *The Roman City of London* (1965).
Merrifield, R., *London, City of the Romans* (1983).
Merrifield, R., 'The contribution of archaeology to our understanding of pre-Norman London, 1973–88', in L. Grant, *Medieval Art, Architecture and Archaeology in London* (1990).
Milne, G., *The Port of Roman London* (1985).
Milne, G., *Roman London* (1995).
Morris, J., *Londinium: London in the Roman Empire* (1982).
Perring, D., *Roman London* (1991).
Royal Commission on Historical Monuments (England). An Inventory of the Historical Monuments in London, vol. 3, *Roman London* (1928).
Salway, P., *Roman Britain* (1981).

ANGLO–SAXON LONDON

Barlow, F., *Edward the Confessor* (1970).
Biddle, M., 'London on the Strand', *Popular Archaeology*, July 1984.
Brooke, C., Keir, G., *London 800–1216: The Shaping of a City* (1975).
Dyson, T., 'King Alfred and the restoration of London', *London Journal*, 15 (1990).
Dyson, T., Schofield, J., *The Archaeology of the City of London* (1980).
Haslam, J., *Anglo-Saxon Towns* (1984, Chichester): Dyson, T., Schofield, J., 'Saxon London'.
Myers, J. N. L., *The English Settlements* (Oxford, 1980).
Nightingale, P., 'The origin of the Court of Husting and Danish influence on

London's development into a capital city', *English Historical Review*, 102 (1987).

Smyth, A. P., *King Alfred the Great* (Oxford, 1995).

Stenton, F., *Anglo-Saxon England, c. 550–1087* (Oxford, 1971).

Tatton-Brown, T., 'The topography of Anglo-Saxon London', *Antiquity*, 60 (1986).

Vince, A., *Saxon London* (1990).

Wilson, D. M. (ed.), *The Archaeology of Anglo-Saxon England* (1976).

MEDIEVAL LONDON

Baker, T., *Medieval London* (1970).

Barron, C. M., *The Medieval Guildhall of London* (1974).

Barron, C. M., 'The parish fraternities of medieval London', in C. M. Barron, C. Harper-Bill (eds.), *The Church in Pre-Reformation Society* (Woodbridge, 1985).

Barron, C. M., 'Ralph Holland and the London radicals, 1438–1444', in Holt, R., Rosser, G. (eds.), *The Medieval Town, 1200–1540* (1990).

Barron, C. M., 'Centres of conspicuous consumption: the aristocratic town house in London, 1200–1550', *London Journal*, 20 (1995).

Barron, C. M., 'The expansion of education in fifteenth-century London', in J. Blair, B. Golding (eds.), *The Cloister and the World* (Oxford, 1996).

Barron, C. M., Du Boulay, F. R. H. (eds.), *The Reign of Richard II* (1970).

Bird, R., *The Turbulent London of Richard II* (1949).

Blair, J., Golding, B. (eds.), *The Cloister and the World* (Oxford, 1996).

Bolton, J. L., *The Medieval English Economy* (1980).

Bolton, J. L., 'The City and the Crown, 1456–61', *London Journal*, 12 (1986).

Brooke, C., Keir, G., Reynolds, S., 'Henry I's Charter for the City of London', *Journal of the Society of Archivists* 4 (1973), pp. 558–78.

Campbell, B. M. S., Galloway, J. A., Keene, D., Murphy, M., *A Medieval Capital and its Grain Supply: Agrarian Production and Distribution in the London Region, c. 1300* (1993).

Carlin, M., *Medieval Southwark* (1996).

Carus-Wilson, E. M., *Medieval Merchant Venturers* (1954).

Carus-Wilson, E. M., Coleman, O., *England's Export Trade, 1275–1547* (1963).

Chew, H. M., Kellaway, W. (eds.): *The London Assize of Nuisance, 1301–1431* (1973).

Davis, R. H. C., 'The College of St Martin-le-Grand and the Anarchy, 1135–54', *London Topographical Record* 23 (1972).

Dyer, A., *Decline and Growth in English Towns, 1400–1640* (1991).

Dyer, C., *Standards of Living in the Later Middle Ages* (Cambridge, 1989).

Ekwall, E., *Two Early London Subsidy Rolls* (Lund, 1951).

Ekwall, E., *Studies in the Population of Medieval London* (1956).

Galloway, J. A., Murphy, M., 'Feeding the city: Medieval London and its agrarian hinterland', *London Journal*, 16 (1991).

Grant, L., *Medieval Art, Architecture and Archaeology in London* (1990).

Griffiths, R. A., *The Reign of King Henry VI* (1981).

Hanawault, B., *Growing Up in Medieval London* (1993).

Harding, V., 'Reconstructing London before the Great Fire', *London Topographical Record*, 25 (1985).

Hatcher, J., *Plague, Population and the English Economy, 1348–1530* (1977).

Hollaender, A. E. J., Kellaway, W. (eds.), *Studies in London History presented to P. E. Jones* (1969).

Holt, R., Rosser, G. (eds.), *The Medieval Town: A Reader in English Urban History, 1200–1540* (1990).

Honeybourne, M., 'The Fleet and its neighbourhood in early and medieval times', *London Topographical Record* 19 (1947).

Jacob, E. F., *The Fifteenth Century, 1399–1485* (Oxford, 1961).

James, M. K., *Studies in the Medieval Wine Trade* (1971).

Johnson, D. J., *Southwark and the City* (Oxford, 1969).

Keen, M., *English Society in the Later Middle Ages, 1348–1500* (1990).

Keene, D., 'A new study of London before the Great Fire', *Urban History Yearbook*, 1984.

Keene, D., *Cheapside before the Great Fire* (1985).

Keene, D., 'Medieval London and its region', *London Journal*, 14 (1989).

Kingsford, C. L., *Prejudice and Promise in Fifteenth-Century England* (Oxford, 1925).

Lloyd, T. H., *The English Wool Trade in the Middle Ages* (1977).

Lloyd, T. H., *Alien Merchants in England in the High Middle Ages* (Brighton, 1983).

Lloyd, T. H., *England and the German Hanse, 1157–1611* (Cambridge, 1991).

McDonnell, K., *Medieval London Suburbs* (1978).

McKisack, M., *The Fourteenth Century, 1307–1399* (Oxford, 1959).

McKisack, M., 'London and the succession to the Crown during the Middle Ages', in Hunt, R. W., Pantin, W. A., Southern, R. W. (eds.), *Studies in Medieval History Presented to F. M. Powicke* (Oxford, 1948).

Myers, A. R., *London in the Age of Chaucer* (Norman, Oklahoma, 1972).

Nightingale, P., 'Capitalists, crafts, and constitutional change in the late fourteenth Century', *Past and Present*, 124 (1989).

Nightingale, P., *A Medieval Mercantile Community: The Grocers' Company and the Politics and Trade of London, 1000–1485* (Yale, 1995).

Ormrod, W. M., *The Reign of Edward III* (1990).

Platt, C., *The English Medieval Town* (1975).

Poole, A. L., *Domesday Book to Magna Carta, 1087–1215* (Oxford, 1955).

Postan, M. M., *The Medieval Economy and Society. An Economic History of Britain, 1100–1500* (1972).

Powicke, F. M., *The Thirteenth Century* (Oxford, 1953).

Prescott, A., 'London in the Peasants' Revolt: a portrait gallery', *London Journal*, 7 (1981).

Prestwich, M., *Edward I* (1988).

Reynolds, S., *An Introduction to the History of English Medieval Towns* (Oxford, 1977).

Reynolds, S., 'The Rulers of London in the twelfth century', *History* 57 (1972).

Riley, H. T. (ed.), *Liber Albus* (1861).

Riley, H. T. (ed.), *Chronicles of Old London* (1863).

Riley, H. T. (ed.), *Memorials of London and London Life in the 13th, 14th and 15th Centuries* (1868).

Rosser, G., 'The essence of medieval urban communities: the vill of Westminster, 1200–1540', *Transactions of the Royal Historical Society* (1984).

Rosser, G., *Medieval Westminster, 1200–1540* (1989).

Schofield, J., *The Building of London from the Conquest to the Great Fire* (1984).

Sharpe, R. R., *London and the Kingdom*, 3 vols (1894–5).

Sharpe, R. R. (ed.), *Calendar of Letter-Books preserved among the archives of the City of London, 1275–1498* (11 vols, 1899–1912).

Starkey, D. (ed.), *The English Court from the Wars of the Roses to the Civil War* (1987).

Stenton, Sir F. M., *Norman London* (1934).

Thomas, A. H., *Calendar of Early Mayor's Court Rolls, 1298–1307* (Cambridge, 1924).

Thomas, A. H., Jones, P. E. (eds.), *Calendar of Plea and Memoranda Rolls of the City of London, 1323–64, 1364–81*, 6 vols (1924–61).

Thompson, J. A. F. (ed.), *Towns and Townspeople in the Fifteenth Century* (1988).

Thrupp, S. L., *The Merchant Class of Medieval London* (Chicago, 1948).

Tout, T. F., 'The beginnings of a modern capital: London and Westminster in the fourteenth century', *Proceedings of the British Academy*, 11 (1923).

Unwin, G., *The Guilds and Companies of London* (new edn., 1963).

Veale, E. M., *The English Fur Trade in the Late Middle Ages* (Oxford, 1966).

Veale, E. M., 'The "Great Twelve": mistery and fraternity in thirteenth-century London', *Historical Research*, 64 (1991), 237–63.

Warren, W. L., *Henry II* (1977).

Weinbaum, M. (ed.), *The London Eyre of 1276* (1976).

Williams, G., *Medieval London. From Commune to Capital* (1963).

TUDOR AND EARLY STUART LONDON (1500–1660)

Appleby, A., 'The disappearance of Plague: a continuing puzzle', *Economic History Review*, 33 (1980).

Archer, I. W., *The Pursuit of Stability: Social Relations in Elizabethan London* (Cambridge, 1991).

Archer, I. W. (ed.), *Hugh Alley's Caveat. The Markets of London in 1598* (1988).

Archer, I. W., 'The London lobbies in the later sixteenth century', *Historical Journal*, 31 (1988).

Ashton, R., *The City and the Court, 1603–43* (Cambridge, 1979).

Aylmer, G. E. (ed.), *The Interregnum* (1972).

Barron, C., Coleman, C., Gobbi, C. (eds.), 'The London Journal of Alessandro Magno, 1562', *London Journal*, 9 (1983).

Barry, J. (ed.), *The Tudor and Stuart Town, 1530–1688* (1990).

Beier, A. L., 'Social problems in Elizabethan London', *Journal of Interdisciplinary History*, 9 (1978).

Beier, A. L., *Masterless Men* (1985).

Beier, A. L., Finlay R. (eds.), *London, 1500–1700, The Making of the Metropolis* (Harlow, 1986).

Berlin. M., 'Civic ceremony in early modern London', *Urban History Yearbook*, 1986.

Besant, Sir W., *London in the Time of the Tudors* (1904).

Boulton, J., *Neighbourhood and Society: A London Suburb in the Seventeenth Century* (Cambridge, 1987).

Brenner, R., 'The Civil War politics of London's merchant community', *Past and Present* 58 (1973).

Brett-James, N. G., *The Growth of Stuart London* (1935).

Brigden, S., 'Religion and social obligation in early sixteenth-century London', *Past and Present* 103 (1984).

Brigden, S., *London and the Reformation* (Oxford, 1989).

Burke, P., 'Popular culture in seventeenth-century London', *London Journal*, 3 (1977).

Clark, P. (ed.), *The Early Modern Town. A Reader* (1976).

Clark, P., Slack, P. (eds.), *Crisis and Order in English Towns, 1500–1700* (1972).

Clark, P., Slack, P., *English Towns in Transition* (Oxford, 1976).

Clay, C. G. A., *Economic Expansion and Social Change: England, 1500–1700*, 2 vols (Cambridge, 1984).

Coleman, D. C., John, A. H. (eds.), *Trade, Government and Economy in Pre-Industrial England. Essays Presented to F. J. Fisher* (1976).

Cook, A. J., *The Privileged Playgoers of Shakespeare's London, 1576–1642* (Princeton, 1981).

Davis, E. J., 'The transformation of London', in Seton-Watson, R. W. (ed.), *Tudor Studies Presented to A. F. Pollard* (1924).

Dietz, B., 'Antwerp and London', in Ives, E. W., Knecht, R. J., Scarisbrick, J. J. (eds.), *Wealth and Power in Tudor England* (1978).

Dietz, B. (ed.), *The Port and Trade of Early Elizabethan London* (1972).

Finlay, R., *Population and Metropolis. The Demography of London, 1580–1640* (Cambridge, 1981).

Fisher, F. J., 'London's export trade in the early seventeenth century', *Economic History Review*, 2nd series, 3 (1950).

Fisher, F. J., 'The development of the London food market, 1540–1640', in Carus-Wilson, E. M. (ed.), *Essays in Economic History*, I (1954).

Fisher, F. J., 'The development of London as a centre of conspicuous consumption', in Carus-Wilson, E. M. (ed.), *Essays in Economic History*, II (1962).

Fisher, F. J., *London and the English Economy, 1500–1700* (1990).

Foster, F. F., *The Politics of Stability: A Portrait of the Rulers in Elizabethan London* (1977).

Gentles, I., 'The struggle for London in the Second Civil War', *Historical Journal*, 26 (1983).

Gurr, A., *Playgoing in Shakespeare's London* (Cambridge, 1987).

Gurr, A., *The Shakespearean Stage, 1574–1642* (Cambridge, 1992).

Harding, V., 'The population of London, 1550–1700: a review of the published evidence', *London Journal*, 15 (1990).

Lindley, J., 'Riot prevention and control in early Stuart London', *Transactions of the Royal Historical Society*, 33 (1983).

Liu, T., *Puritan London: a Study of Religion and Society in the City Parishes* (Newark, Delaware, 1986).

Loach, J. (ed.), *The Mid-Tudor Polity, c. 1540–1560* (1980).

Manley, L. (ed.), *London in the Age of Shakespeare: an Anthology* (1986).

Manning, B., *The English People and the English Revolution, 1640–49* (1976).

Overall, W. H., Overall, H. C. (eds.), *Analytical Index to the Series of Records Known as the Remembrancia, 1579–1664* (1870).

Patten, J., *English Towns, 1500–1700* (Folkestone, 1978).

Pearl, V., 'Change and stability in seventeenth-century London', *London Journal*, 5 (1979).

Pearl, V., *London and the Outbreak of the Puritan Revolution: City Government and National Politics, 1625–43* (Oxford, 1961).

Power, M. J., 'East London housing in the seventeenth century', in Clark, P., Slack, P. (eds.), *Crisis and Order in English Towns, 1500–1700* (1972).

Power, M. J., 'East and west in early-modern London', in Ives, E. W., Knecht, R. J., Scarisbrick, J. J. (eds.), *Wealth and Power in Tudor England* (1978).

Power, M. J., 'Shadwell: The development of a London suburban community in the seventeenth century', *London Journal*, 4 (1978).

Power, M. J., 'London and the control of the "crisis" of the 1590s', *History*, 70 (1985).

Power, M. J., 'A "Crisis" reconsidered: social and economic dislocation in London in the 1590s', *London Journal*, 12 (1986).

Prest, W., 'The legal education of the gentry at the Inns of Court, 1560–1640', *Past and Present* 38 (1967).

Prockter, A., Taylor, R. (eds), *The A–Z of Elizabethan London* (London Topographical Society, 1979).

Ramsay, G. D., 'The undoing of the Italian merchant community in sixteenth-century London', in Harte, N. B., Ponting, K. G. (eds.), *Textile History and Economic History* (1973).

Ramsay, G. D., *The City of London in International Politics at the Accession of Elizabeth Tudor* (Manchester, 1975).

Ramsay, G. D., 'The recruitment and fortunes of some London freemen in the mid-sixteenth century', *Economic History Review*, 31 (1978).

Rappaport, S., 'Social structure and mobility in sixteenth-century London', *London Journal*, 9 (1983) and 10 (1984).

Rappaport, S. L., *Worlds within Worlds. Structures of Life in Sixteenth-Century London* (Cambridge, 1989).

Reddaway, T. F., 'The livery companies of Tudor London', *History*, 51 (1966).

Salgado, G. (ed.), *Cony Catchers and Bawdy Baskets* (1972).

Schofield, J. (ed.), *The London Surveys of Ralph Tresswell* (1987).

Seaver, P., *Wallington's World: A Puritan Artisan in Seventeenth-Century London* (1985).

Slack, P., 'The disappearance of plague: an alternative view', *Economic History Review*, 34 (1981).

Slack, P., *Rebellion, Popular Protest and the Social Order in Early Modern England* (1984).

Slack, P., *The Impact of Plague in Tudor and Stuart England* (1985).

Smith, D. L., Strier, R., Bevington, D. (eds.), *The Theatrical City: Culture, Theatre, and Politics in London, 1576–1649* (Cambridge, 1995).

Smith, S. R., 'The London apprentices as seventeenth-century adolescents', *Past and Present*, 61 (1973).

Stone, L., 'The residential development of the West End of London in the seventeenth century', in Malament, B. C., *After the Reformation* (Philadelphia, 1980).

Stone, L., Stone, J. C. F., *An Open Elite? England, 1540–1880* (1984).

Supple, B., *Commercial Crisis and Change in England, 1600–42: a Study in the Instability of a Mercantile Community* (Cambridge, 1959).

Sutherland, I., 'When was the Great Plague? Mortality in London, 1563–1665', in Glass, D. V., Revelle, R. (eds.), *Population and Social Change* (1972).

Tawney, R. H., Power, E. (eds.), *Tudor Economic Documents* (3 vols, 1924).

Thompson, J. A. F., 'Clergy and Laity in London, 1376–1531' (Oxford University D.Phil. thesis, 1960).

Wilson, J. D., *Life in Shakespeare's England* (Harmondsworth, 1944. 1st published 1911).

Youings, J., *Sixteenth-century England* (1984).

LATER STUART AND HANOVERIAN LONDON (1660–1815)

Abrams, P., Wrigley, E. A. (eds.), *Towns in Societies: Essays in Economic History and Historical Sociology* (1978).

Alexander, J., 'The economic structure of the City of London at the end of the seventeenth century', *Urban History Yearbook* (1989).

Altick, R. D., *The Shows of London: a Panoramic History of Exhibitions, 1600–1862* (Cambridge, Mass., 1978).

Andrew, D. T., 'Aldermen and big bourgeoisie of London reconsidered', *Social History*, 6 (1981).

Andrew, D. T., *Philanthropy and Police: London Charity in the Eighteenth Century* (Princeton, 1989).

Arundell, D., *The Story of Sadler's Wells, 1683–1977* (Newton Abbot, 1978).

Babington, A., *A House in Bow Street: Crime and the Magistracy, London, 1740–1881* (1969).

Barker, T. C., 'Business as usual? London and the Industrial Revolution', *History Today*, 39 (1989).

Beattie, J. M., *Crime and the Courts in England, 1660–1800* (Oxford, 1986).

Bell, W. G., *The Great Fire of London in 1666* (1920).

Berg, M., *The Age of Manufactures, 1700–1820* (1985).

Borsay, P., 'The London connection: cultural diffusion and the eighteenth-century provincial town', *London Journal*, 19 (1994).

Borsay, P. (ed.), *The Eighteenth Century English Town, 1688–1820* (1990).

Boswell, J., *London Journal* (ed. F. A. Pottle, 1950).

Boswell, J., *The Life of Samuel Johnson* (Everyman edn, 2 vols, 1906).

Boulton, W. B., *The Amusements of Old London* (1901).

Bray, W. (ed.), *The Diary and Correspondence of John Evelyn* (1818).

Byrd, M., *London Transformed. Images of the City in the Eighteenth Century* (New Haven, Connecticut, 1973).

Campbell, R., *The London Tradesman* (1747; reprinted Newton Abbot, 1969).

Chancellor, E. B., *The History of the Squares of London* (1907).

Chancellor, E. B., *the XVIIIth Century in London. An Account of its Social Life and Arts* (1920).

Chancellor, E. B., *The Pleasure Haunts of Old London During Four Centuries* (1925).

Chartres, J. A., 'The Capital's provincial eyes: London's inns in the early eighteenth century', *London Journal*, 3 (1977).

Clapham, Sir J., *The Bank of England, A History* (Cambridge, 1944).

Clark, P., 'The "Mother Gin" controversy', *Transactions of the Royal Historical Society*, 38 (1988).

Clark, P., *The English Alehouse. A Social History, 1200–1850* (1983).

Cole, G. D. H., Filson, A. W. (eds.), *British Working Class Movements: Select Documents, 1789–1875* (1951).

Colquhoun, P., *A Treatise on the Police of the Metropolis* (1st edn, 1796).

Corfield, P., *The Impact of English Towns* (Oxford, 1982).

Cruikshank, D., Burton, N., *Life in the Georgian City* (1990).

D'Sena, P., 'Perquisites and casual labour on the London wharfside in the eighteenth century', *London Journal*, 14 (1989).

Davies, M. G., 'Country gentry and payments to London, 1650–1714', *Economic History Review*, 24 (1971).

Davis, R., *The Rise of the English Shipping Industry in the Seventeenth and Eighteenth Centuries* (1962).

Davis, R., *Aleppo and Devonshire Square: English Traders in the Levant in the Eighteenth Century* (1967).

de Krey, G. S., 'Popular radicalism in London after the Glorious Revolution', *Journal of Modern History*, 55 (1983).

de Krey, G. S., *A Fractured Society: the Politics of London in the First Age of Party, 1688–1715* (Oxford, 1985).

Defoe, D., *A Tour through England and Wales* (2 vols, 1928 edn, introduction by G. D. H. Cole).

Dickson, P. G. M., *The Sun Insurance Office, 1710–1960* (Oxford, 1960).

Dickson, P. G. M., *The Financial Revolution in England: a Study in the Development of Public Credit, 1688–1756* (1967).

Doolittle, I. G., 'Walpole's City Elections Act', *English Historical Review*, 97 (1982).

Dyos, H. J., 'The growth of a pre-Victorian suburb, South London, 1580–1836', *Town Planning Review*, 25 (1954).

Earle, P., 'The female labour market in London in the late seventeenth and early eighteenth centuries', *Economic History Review*, 42 (1989).

Earle, P., *The Making of the English Middle Class: Business, Society and Family Life in London, 1660–1730* (1989).

Earle, P., *A City Full of People: Men and Women of London, 1650–1750* (1994).

Ellis, A., *The Penny Universities* (1956).

French, C. J., '"Crowded with traders and a great commerce": London's domination of English overseas trade, 1700–1775', *London Journal*, 17 (1992).

Gatrell, V. A. C., *The Hanging Tree* (Oxford, 1994).

George, M. D., *London Life in the Eighteenth Century* (1925).

Gerhold, D., 'The growth of the London carrying trade, 1681–1838', *Economic History Review*, 41 (1988).

Glass, D. V., Eversley, D. E. C., *Population in History* (1965).

Goodwin, A., *The Friends of Liberty: the English Democratic Movement in the Age of the French Revolution* (1979).

Grosley, P. J., *A Tour to London* (2 vols, 1772 edn).

Harris, T., *London Crowds in the Reign of Charles II: Politics and Propaganda from the Restoration until the Exclusion Crisis* (Cambridge, 1987).

Hay, D., Linebaugh, P., Thompson, E. P. (eds.), *Albion's Fatal Tree* (1975).

Holmes, G., 'The Sacheverell Riots: the crowd and the church in early eighteenth-century London', *Past and Present*, 72 (1976).

Holmes, G., *Augustan England. Professions, State and Society, 1680–1730* (1982).

Hone, A., *For the Cause of Truth. Radicalism in London, 1796–1821* (Oxford, 1982).

Horwitz, H., '"The Mess of the Middle Class" revisited', *Continuity and Change*, 2 (1987).

Howson, G., *Thief-Taker General. The Rise and Fall of Jonathan Wild* (1970).

Hyde, R., Fisher J., Cline, R., *The A–Z of Restoration London* (London Topographical Society, 1992. Ogilby and Morgan's map).

Hyde, R., *The A–Z of Georgian London* (London Topographical Society, 1982. John Rocque's map).

Jarvis, R. C., 'The metamorphosis of the Port of London', *London Journal*, 3 (1977).

Jones, P. E., Judges, A. V., 'London population in the late seventeenth century', *Economic History Review*, 6 (1935).

Joslin, D. M., 'London private bankers, 1720–85', *Economic History Review*, 7 (1954).

Kellett, J. R., 'The breakdown of guild and corporation control over the handicraft and retail trade in London', *Economic History Review*, 10 (1957–8).

Kent, D. A., 'Ubiquitous but invisible: female domestic servants in mid-eighteenth-century London', *History Workshop Journal*, 28 (1989).

Kramnick, I., *Bolingbroke and his Circle: the Politics of Nostalgia in the Age of Walpole* (Cambridge, Mass., 1968).

Landers, J., 'Mortality and Metropolis: the case of London, 1675–1825', *Population Studies*, 41 (1987).

Landers, J., 'Mortality, weather and prices in London, 1675–1825: a study of short-term fluctuations', *Journal of Historical Geography*, 41 (1986).

Landers, J., *Death and the Metropolis: Studies in the Demographic History of London, 1670–1830* (Cambridge, 1993).

Landers, J., Mouzas, A., 'Burial seasonality and the causes of death in London, 1670–1819', *Population Studies*, 42 (1988).

Landes, D. S., *Revolution in Time* (Cambridge, Mass., 1983).

Lang, R. G., 'Social origins and social aspirations of Jacobean London merchants', *Economic History Review*, 27 (1974).

Langford, P., *A Polite and Commercial People* (Oxford, 1989).

Latham, R. C., Matthews, W. (eds.), *The Diary of Samuel Pepys, 1660–1669* (11 vols, 1970–83).

Latham, R. C. (ed.), *The Shorter Pepys* (1986).

Laxton, P., Wisdom, J., *The A–Z of Regency London* (London Topographical Society, 1985. Richard Horwood's map).

Lillywhite, B., *London Coffee Houses* (1963).

Linebaugh. P., *The London Hanged: Crime and Civil Society in the Eighteenth Century* (1991).

Marshall, D., *Dr Johnson's London* (New York, 1968).

Mathias, P., *The Transformation of England* (1979).

McKendrick, N., Brewer, J., Plumb, J. H., *The Birth of a Consumer Society: the Commercialization of Eighteenth-Century England* (1982).

Milne, G., *The Great Fire of London* (1986).

Minchinton W. E. (ed.), *The Growth of English Overseas Trade in the Seventeenth and Eighteenth Centuries* (1969).

Mingay, G. E., *Georgian London* (1975).

Olsen, D. J., *Town Planning in London: The Eighteenth and Nineteenth Centuries* (New Haven, 1964).

Pares, R., 'The London sugar market, 1740–69', *Economic History Review*, 9 (1956–7).

Pelzer, J., Pelzer, L., 'The coffee houses of Augustan London', *History Today*, October 1982.

Penson, L. M., 'The London West Indian interest in the eighteenth century', *English Historical Review*, 36 (1926).

Phillips, H., *Mid-Georgian London: a Social Survey of Central and Western London about 1750* (1964).

Port, M. H., 'West End Palaces: the aristocratic town house in London, 1730–1830', *London Journal*, 20 (1995).

Price, C., *Theatre in the Age of Garrick* (Oxford, 1973).

Pudney, J., *London's Docks* (1975).

Radzinowicz, Sir L., *A History of the English Criminal Law*, vols 1–3 (1948, 1956).

Reddaway, T. F., *The Rebuilding of London after the Great Fire* (1940).

Richards, K., Thomson, P. (eds.), *The Eighteenth-century English Stage* (1972).

Rivers, I. (ed.), *Books and their Readers in Eighteenth-century England* (Leicester, 1982).

Rogers, N., 'Aristocratic clientage, trade and independency: popular politics in pre-radical Westminster', *Past and Present*, 61 (1973).

Rogers, N., 'Money, land and lineage: the big bourgeoisie of Hanoverian London', *Social History*, 4 (1979).

Rogers, N., 'Popular disaffection in London during the Forty-Five', *London Journal*, 1 (1975).

Rogers, N., 'Popular protest in early Hanoverian London', *Past and Present* 79 (1978).

Rogers, N., 'The City Elections Act (1725) reconsidered', *English Historical Review*, 101 (1985).

Rogers, P., *Grub Street. Studies in a Subculture* (1972).

Rogers, P., *Literature and Popular Culture in 18th Century England* (1985).

Rose, C., 'Evangelical philanthropy and Anglican revival: the charity schools of Augustan London, 1698–1740', *London Journal*, 16 (1991).

Rudé, G., *Wilkes and Liberty* (Oxford, 1962).

Rudé, G., *Paris and London in the Eighteenth Century* (1970).

Rudé, G., *Hanoverian London* (1971).

Saussure, C. de: *A Foreign View of England in the Reigns of George I and George II* (1902).

Schwarz, L. D., 'Income distribution and social structure in London in the late eighteenth century', *Economic History Review*, 32 (1979).

Schwarz, L. D., 'Social class and social geography: the middle classes in London at the end of the eighteenth century', *Social History*, 7 (1982).

Schwarz, L. D., 'The standard of living in the long run: London, 1700–1860', *Economic History Review*, 38 (1985).

Schwarz, L. D., *London in the Age of Industrialisation: Entrepreneurs, Labour Force and Living Conditions* (Cambridge, 1992).

Schwarz, R. B., *Daily Life in Johnson's London* (Madison, 1983).

Shelton, W. J., *English Hunger and Industrial Disorders* (1973).

Sheppard, F. H. W., *Local Government in St Marylebone, 1688–1835* (1958).

Shoemaker, R. B., *Prosecution and Punishment: Petty Crime and the Law in London and Rural Middlesex, c. 1660–1725* (Cambridge, 1991).

Stern, W., 'Where are the Cheesemongers of London?', *London Journal*, 5 (1979).

Stevenson, J. (ed.), *London in the Age of Reform* (Oxford, 1977).

Strutt, J., *The Sports and Pastimes of the People of England* (1875 edn).

Styles, J., 'Sir John Fielding and the problem of criminal investigation in eighteenth-century England', *Transactions of the Royal Historical Society*, 33 (1983).

Summerson, J., *Georgian London* (1962).

Supple, B., *The Royal Exchange Assurance: a History of British Insurance* (1970).

Sutherland, L., *The East India Company in Eighteenth-century Politics* (Oxford, 1952).

Sutherland, L., 'The City of London in eighteenth-century politics', in Pares, R., Taylor, A. J. P., *Essays Presented to Sir Lewis Namier* (1956).

Sutherland L., *The City of London and the Opposition to Government, 1768–74: a Study in the Rise of Metropolitan Radicalism* (1970).

Sutherland, L., *A London Merchant, 1695–1774* (Oxford, 1973).

Tate Gallery, *Manners and Morals: Hogarth and British Painting, 1700–1760* (1987).

Thirsk, J., Cooper, J. P. (eds), *Seventeenth-century Economic Documents* (Oxford, 1972).

Thompson, E. P., *The Making of the English Working Class* (1968).

Walker, R. B., 'Advertising in London newspapers, 1650–1750', *Business History*, 15 (1973).

Walpole, H., *Selected Letters* (ed. W. Hadley, 1926).

Ward, N., *The London Spy* (1927 edition).

Webb, S., Webb, B., *English Local Government, I: The Parish and the County* (1906).

Webb, S., Webb, B., *English Local Government, II: The Manor and the Borough* (1908).

Webb, S., Webb, B., *English Local Government, IV: Statutory Authorities for Special Purposes* (1922).

Wrigley, E. A., 'A simple model of London's importance in changing English society and economy, 1650–1750', *Past and Present* 37 (1967).

Wrigley, E. A., Schofield, J. S., *The Population History of England, 1541–1871: a Reconstruction* (1989).

Wroth, W. W., *The London Pleasure Gardens of the Eighteenth Century* (1896).

LONDON, 1815–1914

Alexander, S., *Women's Work in Nineteenth-century London: a Study of the Years 1820–50* (1983).

Ashworth, W., *The Genesis of Modern British Town Planning* (1954).

Atkins, P. J., 'The spatial configuration of class solidarity in London's West End, 1792–1939', *Urban History Yearbook*, 17 (1990).

Badcock, J., *John Bee's Living Picture of London for 1828, and Strangers' Guide through the Streets of the Metropolis* (1828).

Baedeker's *London and its Environs* (1898).

Bagehot, W., *Lombard Street* (1888. 1st published 1873).

Bailey, P. (ed.), *Music Hall. The Business of Pleasure* (Milton Keynes, 1986).

Barker, T. C., Robbins, M., *History of London Transport* (2 vols, 1963, 1974).

Barty-King, H. D., *The Baltic Exchange* (1977).

Bayley, D. H. (ed.), *Police and Society* (1977).

Beames, T., *The Rookeries of London: Past, Present and Prospective* (1850).

Bermont, C., *Point of Arrival: a Study of London's East End* (1975).

Berridge, V., 'East End opium dens and narcotic use in Britain', *London Journal*, 4 (1978).

Besant, Sir W., *London in the Nineteenth Century* (1909).

Booth, C., *Life and Labour of the People in London* (third edn, 1902–3), 17 vols. First Series: *Poverty*, vols 1–4 (1902). Second Series: *Industry*, vols 1–5 (1903). Third Series: *Religious Influences*, vols 1–7 (1903). *Final volume: Notes on Social Influences and Conclusion* (1903).

Briggs, A., *Victorian Cities* (1963).

Briggs, A., *Marx in London* (1982).

Broodbank, Sir J. G., *History of the Port of London* (2 vols, 1921).

Burnett, J., *A Social History of Housing, 1815–1970* (Newton Abbot, 1978).

Burnett, J., *Destiny Obscure: Autobiographies of Childhood, Education and Family from the 1820s to the 1920s* (1982).

Bynum, W. F., Porter, R. (eds.), *Living and Dying in London* (1991).

Bythell, D., *The Sweated Trades* (1978).

Cannadine, D., Reeder, D., *Exploring the Urban Past: Essays in Urban History by H. J. Dyos* (Cambridge, 1982).

Centre for Urban Studies, *London. Aspects of Change* (1964).

Ceserani, D. (ed.), *The Making of Modern Anglo-Jewry* (Oxford, 1990).

Chadwick, E., *Report on the Sanitary Condition of the Labouring Population of Great Britain*, ed. M. W. Flinn (Edinburgh, 1965. 1st published 1842).

Chadwick, O., *The Victorian Church* (2 vols, 1970).

Chapman, S. D., 'The international houses: the continental contribution to British commerce, 1800–1860', *Journal of European Economic History*, 6 (1977).

Chapman, S. D., *The Rise of Merchant Banking* (1984).

Chesney, K., *The Victorian Underworld* (1979).

Clarke, L., *Building Capitalism. Historical Change and the Labour Process in the Production of the Built Environment* (1991).

Clunn, H., *London Rebuilt, 1897–1927* (1927).

Coppock, J. T., Prince, H. C. (eds.), *Greater London* (1964).

Crook, J. M., *The British Museum* (1972).

Crossick, G., *An Artisan Elite in Victorian London: Kentish London, 1840–1880* (1978).

Crossick, G. (ed.), *The Lower Middle Class in Britain, 1870–1914* (1976).

Cullwick, H., *The Diary of Hannah Cullwick* (1984, ed. L. Stan).

Cunningham, H., *Leisure and the Industrial Revolution, c. 1780–1880* (1980).

Daunton, M. J., 'Industry in London: revisions and reflections', *London Journal*, 21 (1996).

Daunton, M. J., *House and Home in the Victorian City: Working-Class Housing, 1850–1914* (1983).

Davidoff, L., *The Best Circles* (1973).

Davis, J., 'Law-breaking and law enforcement: the making of a criminal class in mid-Victorian London' (Ph.D. thesis, Boston College, 1985).

Davis, J., 'From rookeries to communities: race, poverty and policing in London, 1850–1985', *History Workshop Journal*, 27 (1989).

Davis, J., *Reforming London: the London Government Problem, 1855–1900* (Oxford, 1988).

Davis, R., *The English Rothschilds* (1983).

Dennis, R., 'Hard to let in Edwardian London', *Urban Studies*, 26 (1989).

Dickens, C., *Miscellaneous Papers* (ed. B. W. Matz, n.d.)

Dickens, C., *Sketches by Boz* (1836).

Dickens, C., *Reprinted Pieces* (1858).

Donajgrodzki, A. P. (ed.), *Social Control in Nineteenth-century Britain* (1977).

Donohue, J., *Theatre in the Age of Kean* (Oxford, 1975).

Doolittle, I., '"Obsolete Appendix?" The City of London's struggle for survival', *History Today*, May 1983.

Doré, G., Jerrold, B., *London: A Pilgrimage* (repr. New York, 1970).

Dyos, H. J., *Victorian Suburb: a Study of the Growth of Camberwell* (Leicester, 1961).

Dyos, H. J. (ed.), *The Study of Urban History* (1968).

Dyos, H. J., Wolff, M. (eds.), *The Victorian City: Images and Realities* (2 vols, 1973).

Edwards, P. J., *The History of London Street Improvements* (1898).

Emsley, C., *The English Police* (Hemel Hempstead, 1991).

Englander, D., O'Day, R. (eds.), *Retrieved Riches: Social Investigation in British History, 1840–1914* (Aldershot, 1995).

Epstein, J., Thompson, D. (eds.), *The Chartist Experience: Studies in Working-Class Radicalism and Culture, 1830–1860* (1982).

Feldman, D., Jones, G. S. (eds.), *Metropolis London: Histories and Representations since 1800* (1989).

Finer, S. E., *The Life and Times of Sir Edwin Chadwick* (1952).

Fishman, W., *East End 1888* (1988).

Fishman, W., *The Streets of East London* (1979).

Floud, R., McCloskey, D., *The Economic History of Britain since 1700* (2 vols, Cambridge, 1981).

Fox, C. (ed.), *London – World City, 1800–40* (1992).

Fraser, D., Sutcliffe, A. (eds.), *The Pursuit of Urban History* (1983).

Fraser, W. H., *The Coming of the Mass Market, 1850–1914* (1981).

Freeman, M. J., Aldcroft, D. H., *Transport in Victorian Britain* (Manchester, 1988).

Fried, A., Elman, R. (eds.), *Charles Booth's London* (1969).

Galinou, M. (ed.), *London's Pride: the Glorious History of the Capital's Gardens* (1990).

Garside, P. L., 'London and the Home Counties', in F. M. L. Thompson (ed.), *The Cambridge Social History of Britain*, 1 (3 vols, Cambridge, 1990).

Gatrell, V. A. C., Lenman, B., Parker, G. (eds.), *Crime and the Law: a Social History of Crime in Western Europe since 1500* (1982).

Gavin, H., *Sanitary Ramblings* (1848).

Godley, A., 'Immigrant entrepreneurs and the emergence of London's East End as an industrial district', *London Journal*, 21 (1996).

Goodway, D., *London Chartism, 1838–48* (Cambridge, 1982).

Goodwin, G., *Town Swamps and Social Bridges* (1859; repr. Leicester, 1972).

Grant, J., *Sketches in London* (1838).

Green, D. R., *From Artisans to Paupers. Economic Change and Poverty in London, 1790–1870* (Leicester, 1995).

Green, D. R., 'The nineteenth-century metropolitan economy: a revisionist interpretation', *London Journal*, 21 (1996).

Greenwood, J., *The Seven Curses of London* (1869).

Hall, P. G., *The Industries of London since 1861* (1962).

Hardy, A., 'Smallpox in London: factors in the decline of the disease in the nineteenth century', *Medical History* 27, 1983.

Hardy, A., *The Epidemic Streets. Infectious Disease and the Rise of Preventive Medicine, 1856–1900* (Oxford, 1993).

Harrison, B., *Drink and the Victorians: the Temperance Question in England, 1815–72* (1971).

Harrison, F., *The Choice of Books, and other Literary Pieces* (1886).

Harrison, R., *Before the Socialists: Studies in Labour and Politics, 1861–1881* (1965).

Harte, N., *The University of London, 1836–1986. An Illustrated History* (1986).

Hiley, M., *Victorian Working Women: Portraits from Life* (1979).

Hinchcliffe, T., 'Highbury New Park: a nineteenth-century middle-class suburb', *London Journal*, 7 (1981).

Hobhouse, H., *Thomas Cubitt, Master Builder* (1971).

Hobsbawm, E. J., *Labouring Men: Studies in the History of Labour* (1964).

Hobsbawm, E. J., *Worlds of Labour* (1984).

Hollingshead, J., *Ragged London in 1861* (repr. 1986).

Howard, D., *London Theatres and Music Halls, 1850–1950* (1970).

Hoyle, S. R., 'The first battle for London: the Royal Commission on Metropolitan Termini, 1846', *London Journal*, 8 (1982).

Hudson, D., *Munby. Man of Two Worlds* (1972).

Hunt, E. H., *British Labour History, 1815–1914* (1981).

Inglis, K. S., *Churches and the Working Classes in Victorian England* (1963).

Inwood, S., 'Policing London's morals. The Metropolitan Police and popular culture, 1829–1850', *London Journal*, 15 (1990).

James, L., *Print and the People* (1976).

James, P. D., Critchley, T. A., *The Maul and the Pear Tree: the Ratcliffe Highway Murders, 1811* (1971).

Jephson, H., *The Sanitary Evolution of London* (1907).

John, A. (ed.), *Unequal Opportunities* (Oxford, 1986).

Johnson, P., 'Economic development and industrial dynamism in Victorian London', *London Journal*, 21 (1996).

Johnston J. H., Pooley, C. G. (eds.), *The Structure of Nineteenth Century Cities* (1982).

Jones, D. V., 'The New Police, crime and people in England and Wales, 1829–88', *Transactions of the Royal Historical Society*, 5th series, 33, 1983.

Jones, D. V., *Crime, Protest, Community and Police in Nineteenth-century Britain* (1982).

Jones, G. S., *Outcast London: a Study in the Relationship Between Classes in Victorian London* (Oxford, 1971).

Jones, G. S., *Languages of Class* (Cambridge, 1983).

Keating, P., *The Working Classes in Victorian Fiction* (1971).

Keating, P., *Into Unknown England, 1866–1913* (1976).

Kellett, J. R., *Railways and Victorian Cities* (1969).

Knight, C. (ed.), *London* (6 vols, 1841).

Kynaston, D., *The City of London, 1. A World of its Own, 1815–1890* (1994).

Kynaston, D., *The City of London, 2. Golden Years, 1890–1914* (1995).

Lambert, R., *Sir John Simon and English Social Administration, 1816–1904* (1963).

Lancaster, B., *The Department Store: a Social History* (1995).

Lees, L. H., *Exiles of Erin. Irish Migrants in Victorian London* (Manchester, 1979).

Lewis, R. A., *Edwin Chadwick and the Public Health Movement* (1952).

Lovell, J., *Stevedores and Dockers* (1969).

Low, D. A., *Thieves' Kitchen* (Gloucester, 1982).

McCalman, I., *Radical Underworld: Prophets, Revolutionaries and Pornographers in London, 1795–1840* (New York, 1988).

Maclure, S., *A History of Education in London, 1870–1990* (1990).

Malcolmson, P. E., 'Getting a living in the slums of Victorian Kensington', *London Journal*, 1 (1975).

Manby-Smith, C., *Curiosities of London Life* (1853).

Marriott, J., '"West Ham: London's industrial centre and gateway to the world" 1. Industrialisation, 1840–1910', *London Journal*, 13 (1988).

Mayhew, H., *London Labour and the London Poor* (4 vols, reprinted 1968. 1st published 1861–2).

Metcalf, P., *Victorian London* (1972).

Michie, R. C., *The London and New York Stock Exchanges, 1850–1914* (1987).

Michie, R. C., *The City of London: Continuity and Change, 1850–1990* (Basingstoke, 1992).

Miller, W. R., *Cops and Bobbies: Police Authority in New York and London, 1830–1870* (Chicago, 1977).

Morgan, E. V., Thomas, W. A., *The Stock Exchange, its History and Functions* (1969).

Morris, R. J., Rodger, R. (eds.), *The Victorian City: A Reader in British Urban History, 1820–1914* (1993).

Moylan, J. F., *Scotland Yard and the Metropolitan Police* (1934).

Mudie-Smith, R., *The Religious Life of London* (1904).

Owen, D., *The Government of Victorian London, 1855–1889* (1982).

Olsen, D., *The Growth of Victorian London* (1983).

Palmer, S., *Police and Protest in England and Ireland, 1789–1850* (Cambridge, 1988).

Parsons, G. (ed.), *Religion in Victorian Britain* (vols 1, 2, 4, Manchester, 1988).

Pelling, H., *Social Geography of British Elections, 1885–1910* (1967).

Pelling, M., *Cholera, Fever and English Medicine, 1825–1865* (Oxford, 1978).

Pember Reeves, M., *Round About a Pound a Week* (1913).

Pictorial London: Views of the Streets, Public Buildings, Parks and Scenery of the Metropolis (1906).

Pollard, S., 'The decline of shipbuilding on the Thames', *Economic History Review*, 2nd series, 3 (1950–51).

Pollard, S., Robertson, P., *The British Shipbuilding Industry, 1870–1914* (Cambridge, Mass., 1979).

Potts, A., 'Picturing the modern metropolis: images of London in the nineteenth century', *History Workshop Journal*, 26 (1988).

Price-Williams, R., 'The Population of London, 1801–1881', *Journal of the Royal Statistical Society*, September 1885.

Pritchett, V. S., *A Cab at the Door. An Autobiography: Early Years* (1968).

Prothero, I. J., 'Chartism in London', *Past and Present* 44 (1969).

Prothero, I. J., *Artisans and Politics in Early Victorian London. John Gast and His Times* (Folkestone, 1979).

Reith, C., *British Police and the Democratic Ideal* (Oxford, 1943).

Richter, D. C., *Riotous Victorians* (Ohio, 1981).

Rook, C., *The Hooligan Nights* (1899; repr. 1979).

Rose, L., *The Massacre of the Innocents: Infanticide in Britain, 1800–1939* (1986).

Ross, E., *Love and Toil: Motherhood in Outcast London, 1870–1918* (Oxford, 1993).

Rowe, D. J. (ed.), *London Radicalism, 1830–1843: a Selection from the Papers of Francis Place* (1970).

Rowell, G., *Theatre in the Age of Irving* (Oxford, 1981).

Rubinstein, W. D., 'The Victorian middle classes: wealth, occupation and geography', *Economic History Review*, 2nd series, 30 (1977).

Rubinstein, W. D., *Men of Property* (1981).

Saint, A. (ed.), *Politics and the People of London. The London County Council, 1889–1965* (1989).

Saville, J., Briggs, A. (eds), *Essays in Labour History in Memory of G. D. H. Cole* (1967).

Schmiechen, J. A., *Sweated Industries and Sweated Labour: the London Clothing Trades, 1860–1914* (1984).

Service, A., *London 1900* (1979).

Shannon, H. A., 'Migration and the growth of London, 1841–91', *Economic History Review*, 1st series, 5 (1935).

Sheppard, F., 'London and the nation in the nineteenth century', *Transactions of the Royal Historical Society*, 5th series, 35, (1985).

Sheppard, F., *London, 1808–1870. The Infernal Wen* (1971).

Sims, G. R. (ed.), *Living London* (3 vols, 1902–3).

Sindall, R., *Street Violence in the Nineteenth Century: Media Panic or Real Danger?* (Leicester, 1990).

Smith, P. T., *Policing Victorian London* (Westport, Conn., 1985).

Storch, R. D., *Popular Culture and Custom in Nineteenth-Century England* (1982).

Summerson, Sir J., *The London Building World of the 1860s* (1973).

Summerson, Sir J., The Victorian rebuilding of the City of London', *London Journal*, 3 (1977).

Summerson, Sir J., *John Nash* (1980).

Sutcliffe, A., *London and Paris: Capitals of the Nineteenth Century* (Leicester, 1983).

Sutcliffe, A. (ed.), *Metropolis, 1890–1940* (1984).

Taine, H., *Notes on England* (1873 edn).

Taylor, D., Bush, D., *The Golden Age of British Hotels* (1974).

Thompson, E. P., Yeo E. (eds.), *The Unknown Mayhew* (1971).

Thompson, F. M. L., *Hampstead: Building a Borough, 1650–1964* (1974).

Thompson, F. M. L., 'Nineteenth-century horse sense', *Economic History Review*, 2nd series, 29 (1976).

Thompson, F. M. L. (ed.), *The Rise of Suburbia* (Leicester, 1982).

Thompson, F. M. L. (ed.), *The Cambridge Social History of Britain, 1750–1950* (3 vols, Cambridge, 1990).

Thompson, F. M. L., 'Moving frontiers and the fortunes of the aristocratic town house 1830–1930', *London Journal*, 20 (1995).

Thompson, P., *Socialists, Liberals and Labour: the Struggle for London, 1885–1914* (1967).

Tindall, G., *The Fields Beneath: the History of One London Village* (1977).

Tyack, G., 'James Pennethorne and London street improvements, 1838–55', *London Journal*, 15 (1990).

The Village London Atlas: the Changing Face of Greater London (1822–1903) (1986).

Walkowitz, J. R., *City of Dreadful Delight: Narratives of Sexual Danger in Late Victorian London* (1992).

Wallas, G., *The Life of Francis Place, 1771–1854* (1898).

Waller, P. J., *Town, City and Nation. England, 1850–1914* (Oxford, 1983).

Webb, B., *Our Partnership* (1948).

Webb, S., Webb, B., *A History of Trade Unionism* (1920 edn).

Webb, S., Webb, B., *English Poor Law History: Part I: The Old Poor Law* (1927. 2nd edn, 1963).

Webb, S., Webb, B., *English Poor Law History: Part II: The Last Hundred Years* (2 vols, 1929. 2nd edn, 1963).

Weightman, G., Humphries, S., *The Making of Modern London, 1815–1914* (1983).

Whetham, E. H., 'The London milk trade, 1860–1900', *Economic History Review*, 2nd series, 17 (1964).

White, J., *Rothschild Buildings: Life in an East End Tenement Block, 1887–1920* (1980).

Whitehouse, R., *A London Album: Early Photographs Recording the History of the City and its People from 1840 to 1915* (1980).

Williams, R., *The Country and the City* (1973).

Winter, G., *A Cockney Camera: London's Social History Recorded in Photographs* (1975).

Winter, J., 'The "Agitator of the Metropolis": Charles Cochrane and early Victorian street reform', *London Journal*, 14 (1989).

Winter, J., *London's Teeming Streets, 1830–1914* (1994).

Wohl, A. S., *The Eternal Slum: Housing and Social Policy in Victorian London* (1977).

Wohl, A. S., *Endangered Lives: Public Health in Victorian Britain* (1983).

Woods, R., Woodward, J. (eds.), *Urban Disease and Mortality in Nineteenth-Century England* (1984).

Wright, T., *The Great Unwashed* (1868).

Yelling, A., *Slums and Slum Clearance in Victorian London* (1986).

Young, K., Garside, P., *Metropolitan London: Politics and Urban Change, 1837–1981* (1982).

Ziegler, P. S., *The Sixth Great Power. Barings, 1762–1929* (1988).

TWENTIETH-CENTURY LONDON, 1914–1997

Abercrombie, P., *Greater London Plan, 1944* (1945).

Addison, P., *Now the War is Over* (1985).

Administrative County of London Development Plan: Analysis (1951).

Administrative County of London Development Plan: First Review (1960).

Alderman, G., Holmes, C. (eds.), *Outsiders and Outcasts: Essays in Honour of William J. Fishman* (1993).

Archbishop of Canterbury's Commission on Urban Priority Areas, *Faith in the City* (1985).

Armstrong, J. A., 'The development of the Park Royal industrial estate in the interwar period: a re-examination of the Aldcroft–Richardson thesis', *London Journal*, 21 (1996).

Barker, T. C., Robbins, M., *A History of London Transport, 2: The Twentieth Century, to 1970* (1974).

Benyon, J. (ed.), *Scarman and After* (1984).

Booker, C., Lycett Green, C., *Goodbye London* (1973).

Brownill, S., *Developing London's Docklands* (1990).

Buchanan, M., Bursey, N., Lewis, K., Mullen, P., *Transport Planning for Greater London* (Farnborough, 1980).

Buck, N., Gordon, I., Young, K., *The London Employment Problem* (Oxford, 1986).

Burke, T., *Son of London* (1947).

Calder, A., *The People's War: Britain, 1939–45* (1969).

Calder, A., *The Myth of the Blitz* (1991).

Cannadine, D., *The Decline and Fall of the British Aristocracy* (New Haven, 1990).

Centre for Urban Studies, *London, Aspects of Change* (1964).

Cheshire, P., 'The outlook for development in London', *Land Development Studies*, 7 (1990).

Clout, H. (ed.), *Changing London* (1978).

Clout, H., Wood, P., *London: Problems of Change* (1986).

Clunn, H., *The Face of London* (1970).

Cole, G. D. H., Cole, M. I., *The Condition of Britain* (1937).

Collier, B., *History of the Second World War: The Defence of the Kingdom* (1957).

Collins, M. F., Pharoah, T. M., *Transport Organisation in a Great City: the Case of London* (1974).

Coppock, J. T., Prince, H. C. (eds.), *Greater London* (1964).

Cowan, P., *The Office, A Facet of Urban Growth* (1969).

Cullingworth, J. B., *Environmental Planning, 1939–1969: New Towns Policy* (1979).

Cullingworth, J. B., *Environmental Planning, 1939–1969: Land Values, Compensation and Betterment* (1980).

Damesick, P., 'The inner city economy in industrial and post-industrial London', *London Journal*, 7 (1981).

Deakin, N., Edwards, J., *The Enterprise Culture and the Inner City* (1993).

Department of the Environment, *Urban Trends in England: Latest Evidence from the 1991 Census* (1996).

Donnison, D., Eversley, D. E. C. (eds.), *London: Urban Patterns, Problems and Policies* (1973).

Donoughue, B., Jones, G. W, *Herbert Morrison. Portrait of a Politician* (1973).

Elsom, M. J., *Green Belts: Conflict Mediation in the Urban Fringe* (1986).

Esher, L., *A Broken Wave: the Rebuilding of Britain, 1940–1980* (1983).

Evans, A., Eversley, D. (eds.), *The Inner City: Employment and Industry* (1980).

Eversley, D., 'London after the GLC: does London need strategic planning?', *London Journal*, 10 (1984).

Eversley, D., 'The Ganglion of Tourism', *London Journal*, 3 (1977).

Fainstein, S., Gordon, I., Harloe M. (eds.), *Divided Cities. New York and London in the Contemporary World* (Oxford, 1992).

Feldman, D., Jones, G. S. (eds.), *Metropolis London: Histories and Representations since 1800* (1989).

Ferris, P., *The City* (1965).

Fitzgibbon, C., *The Blitz* (1957).

Foley, D. L., *Controlling London's Growth: Planning the Great Wen, 1940–1960* (Berkeley, 1963).

Foley, D. L., *Governing the London Region: Reorganisation and Planning in the 1960s* (1972).

Forshaw, A., Bergstrom, T., *The Open Spaces of London* (1986).

Forshaw, J. H., Abercrombie, P., *County of London Plan, 1943* (1943).

Freeman, R., 'The Marshall Plan for London's Government', *London Journal*, 5 (1979).

Frost, M. E., Spence, N. A., 'Employment changes in Central London in the 1980s', *Geographical Journal*, 157 (parts 1 and 2, 1991).

Fyvel, T. R., *The Insecure Offenders: Rebellious Youth in the Welfare State* (1963).

Gilbert, B. B., *British Social Policy, 1914–1939* (1970).

Glass, R., *Newcomers: the West Indians in London* (1960).

Glendinning, M., Muthesius, S., *Tower Block* (London and New Haven, 1994).

Goddard, J., 'Changing office location patterns within Central London', *Urban Studies*, 4 (1967).

Greater London Development Plan: Report of the Panel of Inquiry (Layfield Report) (1973).

Green, S., *Who Owns London?* (1986).

Hall, J. M., 'A mighty maze but not without a plan', *London Journal*, 2 (1976).

Hall, P. G., *The Industries of London since 1861* (1962).

Hall, P. G., *London 2000* (1963).

Hall, P., *London 2001* (1989).

Hall, P., *Urban and Regional Planning* (1992).

Hall, P., Thomas, R., Gracey, H., Drewett, R., *The Containment of Urban England* (2 vols, 1973).

Halsey, A. H., *Trends in British Society since 1900* (1986 edn).

Hamnett, C., Williams, P., 'Social change in London: a study of gentrification', *London Journal*, 6 (1990).

Hannington, W., *Unemployed Struggles, 1919–36* (repr. 1973).

Harrisson, T., *Living Through the Blitz* (1976).

Hebbert, M., 'One "planning disaster" after another: London Docklands, 1970–1992', *London Journal*, 17 (1992).

Hennessey, P., *Never Again. Britain, 1945–51* (1992).

Heren, L. P., *Growing Up Poor in London* (1973).

Hewison, R., *Too Much. Art and Society in the Sixties* (1986).

Hillman, J. (ed.), *Planning for London* (1971).

Hiro, D., *Black British, White British* (1991).

Hodgson, V., *Few Eggs and No Oranges* (1976).

Hoggart, K., Green, D. R. (eds.), *London: A New Metropolitan Geography* (1991).

Humphries, S., Taylor, J., *The Making of Modern London, 1945–1985* (1986).

Jackson, A. A., *Semi-Detached London: Suburban Development, Life and Transport, 1900–39* (1973).

Jackson, W. E., *Achievement. A Short History of the London County Council* (1965).

Jenkins, P., Potter, G. W., 'Before the Krays: organised crime in London, 1920–1960', *Criminal Justice History*, 9 (1988).

Jenkins, S., *Landlords to London: the Story of a Capital and its Growth* (1975).

Kates, H., *The London Factor* (1994).

Keith, M., *Race, Riots and Policing: Lore and Disorder in a Multi-racist Society* (1993).

Kent, W., *The Lost Treasures of London* (1947).

Kingsford, P., *The Hunger Marches in Britain, 1920–1940* (1982).

Kohan, C. M., *History of the Second World War: Works and Buildings* (1952).

Kynaston, D., 'A changing workscape: the City of London since the 1840s', *London Journal*, 13 (1987–8).

Lawrence, J., Dean, M., Robert, J. L., 'The outbreak of war and the urban economy: Paris, Berlin, and London in 1914', *Economic History Review*, 45 (1992).

Lenon, B., *London* (1988).

Livingstone, K., *If Voting Changed Anything, They'd Abolish It* (1987).

Llewellyn Smith, H. (ed.), *The New Survey of London Life and Labour* (9 vols, 1934–5).

Lomas, G. M., *London in Prospect* (1991).

MacGregor, S., Pimlott, B. (eds.), *Tackling the Inner Cities: the 1980s Reviewed, Prospects for the 1990s* (Oxford, 1991).

Mack, J., Humphries, S., *London at War* (1985).

Madge, C., Harrisson, T. (eds.), *Britain, by Mass Observation* (1938).

Maitland, S. (ed.), *Very Heaven. Looking Back at the 1960s* (1988).

Manners, G., Keeble, D., Rodgers, B., Warren, K., *Regional Development in Britain* (2nd edn, Chichester, 1978).

Marriott, J., *The Culture of Labourism: the East End Between the Wars* (Edinburgh, 1991).

Marriott, J., '"West Ham: London's Industrial Centre and Gateway to the World". II: Stabilisation and decline, 1910–1939', *London Journal*, 14, 1989.

Marriott, O., *The Property Boom* (1967, 1989).

Martin, J. E., *Greater London, an Industrial Geography* (1966).

McClintock, F. H., *Crimes of Violence* (1963).

McRae, H., Cairncross, F., *Capital City: London as a Financial Centre* (new ed. 1985).

Melly, G., *Revolt into Style: the Popular Arts in Britain* (1970).

Middleton, M., *Cities in Transition* (1991).

Morgan, G., *Red Roses Every Night. An Account of London Cinemas Under Fire* (1948).

Morris, T., *Crime and Criminal Justice Since 1945* (Oxford, 1989).

Munby, D. L., *Inland Transport Statistics, Great Britain, 1900–70* (Oxford, 1978).

Munton, R., *London's Green Belt: Containment in Practice* (1983).

Nairn, I., *Nairn's London* (1966).

New Leadership for London: the Government's Proposals for a New Greater London Authority (1997).

Newman, A. (ed.), *The Jewish East End, 1840–1939* (1981).

Niall, I., *A London Boyhood* (1974).

O'Brien, T. H., *The History of the Second World War: Civil Defence* (1955).

O'Leary, B., 'Why was the GLC abolished?', *International Journal of Urban and Regional Research*, 11 (1987).

Orwell, G., *Down and Out in Paris and London* (1933).

Parker, T., *The People of Providence* (1983).

Patterson, S., *Dark Strangers* (1963).

Plender, J., Wallace, P., *The Square Mile: a Guide to the City Revolution* (1985).

Plowden, S., *Towns against Traffic* (1972).

Powell, A. G., 'The recent development of Greater London', *The Advancement of Science*, 17 (May 1960).

Power, A., *Property before People: the Management of Twentieth-Century Council Housing* (1987).

Report of the Committee of Enquiry into the Major Ports of Great Britain (1962).

Report of the Committee on Housing in Greater London (the Milner Holland Report) (1965).

Report of the Royal Commission on Industrial Location (the Barlow Report) (1940).

Report of the Royal Commission on Local Government in Greater London (the Herbert Commission) (1960).

Rhodes, G., *The Government of London: the Struggle for Reform* (1970).

Robson, W. A., *The Government and Misgovernment of London* (1948).

Rodgers, R., Fisher, M., *A New London* (1992).

Rolph, C. H. (C. R. Hewitt), *Living Twice* (1974).

Rolph, C. H. (C. R. Hewitt), *London Particulars* (Oxford, 1980).

Samuel, R., *East End Underworld. Chapters in the Life of Arthur Harding* (1981).

Sansom, W., *The Blitz. Westminster at War* (Oxford, 1947; new edn, 1990).

Sassen, S., *The Global City: New York, London and Tokyo* (1991).

Scarman, Lord, *The Brixton Disorders, 10–12 April 1981: Report of an Inquiry by the Right Hon. the Lord Scarman OBE* (1981).

Schaffer, F., *The New Town Story* (1970).

Sedjic, D., *The 100 Mile City* (1992).

Simmie, J. (ed.), *Planning London* (1994).

Sinclair, R., *Metropolitan Man. The Future of the English* (1937).

Smith, D. H., *The Industries of Greater London* (1933).

Smith, D. J., Gray, J., *Police and People in London* (Aldershot, 1985).

Smithies, E., *Crime in Wartime* (1982).

Strategic Plan for the South East. Studies 1: Population and Employment (1971).

Strategy for the South-East: 1976 Review (1976).

Thornley, A., *Urban Planning Under Thatcher* (1991).

Thornley, A. (ed.), *The Crisis of London* (1992).

Titmuss, R. M., *History of the Second World War: Problems of Social Policy* (1950).

Townsend, P., *The Family Life of Old People* (1963).

Travers T., Minors M. (eds.), *London 95* (1996).

Weightman, G., Humphries, S., *The Making of Modern London, 1914–1939* (1984).

Wheen, F., *The Battle for London* (1985).

White, J., 'Police and people in London in the 1930s', *Oral History*, 11 (1983).

White, J., *The Worst Street in North London. A Social History of Campbell Bunk, Islington, Between the Wars* (1986).

Williams, D., 'London and the 1931 financial crisis', *Economic History Review*, 15 (1962–3).

Wilmott, P., *Adolescent Boys of East London* (1969).

Wilson, T., *The Myriad Faces of War* (Oxford, 1986).

Women's Group on Public Welfare, *Our Towns. A Close Up* (Oxford, 1943).

Wright, P., *A Journey Through Ruins. The Last Days of London* (1991).

Yelling, J. A., *Slums and Redevelopment. Policy and Practice in England, 1918–1945* (1992).

Young, K., Garside, P., *Metropolitan London: Politics and Urban Change, 1837–1981* (1982).

Young, M., Wilmott, P., *Family and Kinship in East London* (1957).

Ziegler, P., *London at War, 1939–1945* (1995).

Index